DEDICATION

For lifelong explorers Liam, Tim, and Christopher Davis —C.T.

To Emma, with thanks and appreciation —N.E.

EXPLORE WITH US!

We have been fine-tuning *Maine: An Explorer's Guide* for more than 30 years, a period in which lodging, dining, and shopping opportunities have more than quadrupled in the state. As we have expanded our guide, we have also been increasingly selective, making recommendations based on years of conscientious research and personal experience. We describe the state by locally defined regions, giving you Maine's communities, not simply her most popular destinations. With this guide you'll feel confident to venture beyond the tourist towns, along roads less traveled, to places of special hospitality and charm.

WHAT'S WHERE

In the beginning of the book you'll find an alphabetical listing of special highlights and important information that you may want to reference quickly. You'll find advice on everything from where to buy the best local lobster to where to write or call for camping reservations and park information.

LODGING

We've selected lodging places for mention in this book based on their merit alone; we do not charge innkeepers to be listed. The authors always check every bed & breakfast, farm, sporting lodge, and inn in Maine personally.

PRICES

Please don't hold us or the respective innkeepers responsible for the rates listed as of press time in 2012. Some changes are inevitable. **The 7 percent state rooms and meals tax should be added to all prices unless we specifically state that it's included in a price.** We've tried to note when a gratuity is added, as it often is in high-end accommodations, but it's always wise to check before booking.

SMOKING

Maine B&Bs, inns, and restaurants are now generally smoke-free, but many lodging places still reserve some rooms for smokers, and some restaurants still offer a smoking area in their outdoor seating. If this is important to you, be sure to ask when making reservations.

RESTAURANTS

In most sections please note a distinction between *Dining Out* and *Eating Out*. By their nature, restaurants included in the *Eating Out* group are generally inexpensive.

KEY TO SYMBOLS

- ✪ **Authors' Favorites**. These are the places we think have the best to offer in each region, whether that means great food, outstanding rooms, beautiful scenery, or overall appeal.
- ⚭ **Weddings**. The wedding-ring symbol appears next to lodging venues that specialize in weddings.

- ✿ **Special value**. The blue-ribbon symbol appears next to selected lodging and restaurants that combine quality and moderate prices.
- 🐾 **Pets**. The dog-paw symbol appears next to venues that accept pets.
- ✐ **Child-friendly**. The crayon symbol appears next to lodging, restaurants, activities, and shops of special interest or appeal to youngsters.
- ♿ **Handicapped access**. The wheelchair symbol appears next to lodging, restaurants, and attractions that are partially or completely handicapped accessible.
- ((ஒ)) **Wireless Internet**. The wireless symbol appears next to public spaces, restaurants, and attractions that offer wireless Internet access.

We would appreciate any comments or corrections. Please write to:

Explorer's Guide Editor
The Countryman Press
P.O. Box 748
Woodstock, VT 05091

For more info, go to: http://maineguidebook.com/

You can also email
info@maineguidebook.com or ctree@traveltree.net

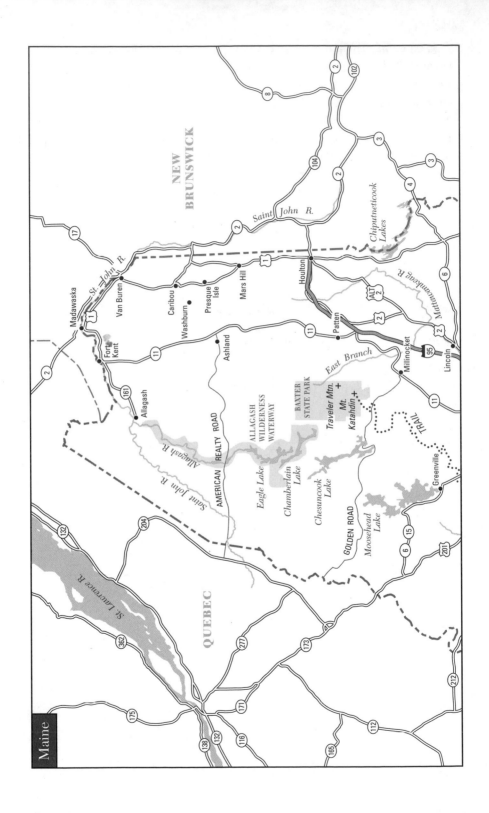

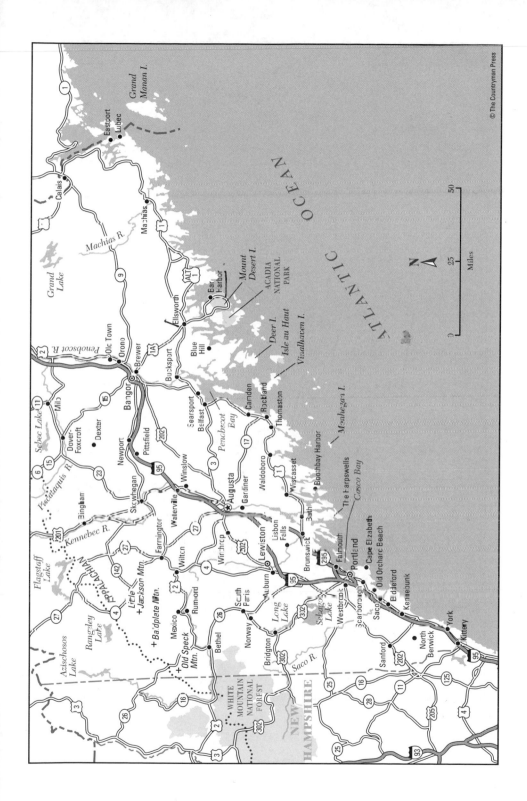

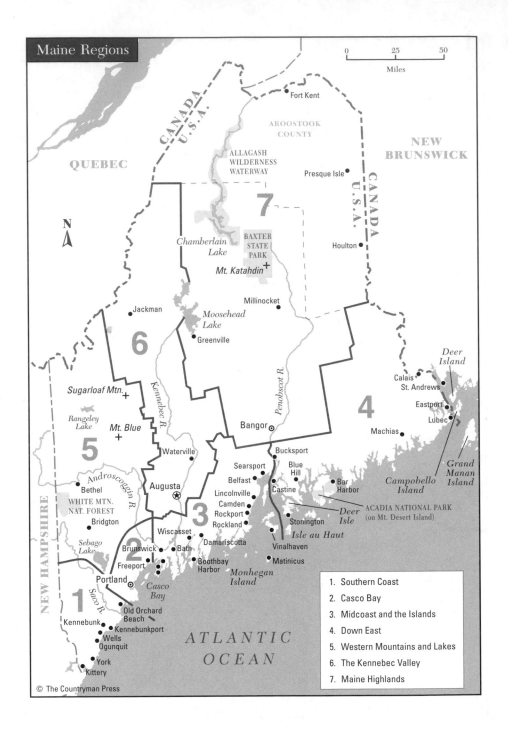

Maine Regions

0   25   50
Miles

CANADA
U.S.A.

QUEBEC

NEW
BRUNSWICK

Fort Kent

AROOSTOOK
COUNTY

ALLAGASH
WILDERNESS
WATERWAY

Presque Isle

CANADA
U.S.A.

N

7

*Chamberlain
Lake*

BAXTER
STATE
PARK

Houlton

Mt. Katahdin +

Millinocket

Jackman

*Moosehead
Lake*

6

Greenville

*Deer
Island*

Kennebec R.

Calais
St. Andrews

Sugarloaf Mtn. +

Eastport
Lubec

*Rangeley
Lake*

Mt. Blue +

5

Waterville

Bangor

Penobscot R.

Machias

4

*Grand
Manan
Island*

Bucksport

Androscoggin R.

Bethel

WHITE MTN.
NAT. FOREST

Bridgton

Augusta

Searsport
Belfast
Lincolnville
Camden
Rockport
Rockland

Blue
Hill

Castine

Bar
Harbor

*Campobello
Island*

*Deer
Isle*

ACADIA NATIONAL PARK
(on Mt. Desert Island)

Wiscasset

Damariscotta

Stonington

Isle au Haut

Vinalhaven

*Sebago
Lake*

Brunswick
Freeport

2

Bath

Boothbay
Harbor

Matinicus

Portland

*Casco
Bay*

*Monhegan
Island*

1. Southern Coast

NEW HAMPSHIRE

Saco R.

1

Old Orchard
Beach

Kennebunk
Kennebunkport
Wells
Ogunquit

2. Casco Bay

3. Midcoast and the Islands

4. Down East

5. Western Mountains and Lakes

ATLANTIC
OCEAN

6. The Kennebec Valley

York
Kittery

7. Maine Highlands

© The Countryman Press

CONTENTS

MAPS

INTRODUCTION

He who rides and keeps the beaten track studies the fences chiefly.
—Henry David Thoreau, *The Maine Woods*, 1853

Over the past 31 years *Maine: An Explorer's Guide* has introduced hundreds of thousands of people to many Maines.

When this book first appeared in 1982, it was the first 20th-century guidebook to describe New England's largest state region by region, rather than to focus only on the most touristed communities, listed alphabetically. From the start, we critiqued places to stay and to eat as well as everything to see and to do—based on merit rather than money.

The big news, however, isn't that *Maine: An Explorer's Guide* was first but that readers constantly tell us that it remains the best Maine guidebook—that despite current competition, this "Maine Bible" gets better with each edition.

We like to think of this book as the ultimate Maine search engine. Our own website—maineguidebook.com—doesn't put our entire book online, but we have adapted our format to the web and look forward to incorporating readers' comments on dining, lodging, and things to see and do. Please contact us at info@maineguidebook.com.

With each new edition we build on what we know, spending months on the road, checking every lodging we include, making sure it's a place we would personally like to stay.

Back in 1981, this didn't seem like a tall order. Chris's three sons—ages 3, 6, and 8—helped her research reasonably priced rental cottages, ice cream stands, and beaches. The guide, however, quickly grew as inns, B&Bs, and other lodging options proliferated, as did things to do and see, dining venues, and shopping options. The book also soon included all the parts of Maine in which a visitor can find commercial lodging, from Kittery to Caribou and from the White Mountains to

EAGLE LAKE, ACADIA NATIONAL PARK
Nancy English

SUMMER SEASON GARDEN PARTY IN YORK
BY FREDERICK QUIMBY, C. 1884

the island of Monhegan, not to mention all of Rt. 1 from Kittery to Fort Kent. After the first couple of editions it became obvious that no one person could explore this immense and richly textured state during one season.

We now describe more than 500 places to stay, ranging from campgrounds to grand old resorts and including farms as well as B&Bs, inns, and sporting camps—in all corners of the state and in all price ranges. We have also checked out a similar number of places to dine and to eat (we make a distinction between dining and eating), and, since shopping is an important part of everyone's travels, we include special stores we've encountered. We have opinions about everything we've found, and we don't hesitate to share them. In every category we record exactly what we see.

While the number of Maine guidebooks has multiplied, we remain proud of the depth and scope of this one. With each edition we strive not only to update details but also to simplify the format and to sharpen the word pictures that describe each area.

This book's introductory section, "What's Where in Maine," is a quick-reference directory to a vast array of information about the state. The remainder of the book describes Maine region by region.

Note that "off-season" prices are often substantially lower than those in July and August—except in ski centers, when winter is high season. September is dependably sparkling and frequently warm. Early October in Maine is just as spectacular as it is in New Hampshire and Vermont, with magnificent mountains rising from inland lakes as well as the golds and reds set against coastal blue. Be aware that the inland ski resorts of Sunday River near Bethel and the Sugarloaf area are "off-season" all summer as well as fall.

Maine is almost as big as the other five New England states combined, but her residents add up to less than half the population of Greater Boston. That means there is plenty of room for all who look to her for renewal—both residents and out-of-staters.

It's our hope that, although this book should help visitors and Maine residents alike enjoy the state's resort towns, it will be particularly useful for those who explore off the beaten track.

THE AUTHORS

Chris was born in Hawaii and bred in Manhattan, came to New England to attend Mount Holyoke College, and has been living in Massachusetts since she began to work for the *Boston Globe* in 1968. She is addicted to many Maines. As a toddler she learned to swim in the Ogunquit River and later watched her sons do the same in Monhegan's icy waters—and then learn to sail at summer camp in Raymond and paddle canoes on the Saco River and down the St. John. Her number two son was

TOURISM IN MAINE

We are fascinated by Maine's history in general and her tourism history in particular. It seems ironic that back in the 1920s "motor touring" was hailed as a big improvement over train and steamer travel because it meant you no longer had to go where everyone else did—over routes prescribed by railroad tracks and steamboat schedules. In Maine cars seem, however, to have had precisely the opposite effect. Now 90 percent of the state's visitors follow the coastal tourist route faithfully, as though their wheels were grooved to Rt. 1.

STATE OF MAINE STEAMER

Maine Maritime Museum

Worse still, it's as though many tourists are on a train making only express stops—at rush hour. At least half of those who follow Rt. 1 stop, stay, and eat in all the same places—Kennebunkport, Boothbay or Camden, and Bar Harbor, for example—in August.

Tourism has always been driven by images. In the 1840s Thomas Cole, Frederic Church (both of whom sketched and painted scenes of Mount Desert), and lesser-known artists began projecting Maine as a romantic, remote destination in the many papers, magazines, and children's books of the decade. While Henry David Thoreau's *The Maine Woods* was not published until 1864, many of its chapters appeared as magazine articles years earlier (Thoreau first climbed Katahdin in 1846), and in 1853 *Atlantic Monthly* editor James Russell Lowell visited and wrote about Moosehead Lake.

After the Civil War, Maine tourism boomed. Via railroad and steamboat, residents of cities throughout the East and Midwest streamed into the Pine Tree State, most toting guidebooks, many published by rail and steamboat lines to boost business. "Sports" in search of big game and big fish patronized "sporting camps" throughout the North Woods. Thanks to the rise in popularity of fly-fishing and easily maneuverable canoes, women were able to share in North Woods soft adventure. Splendid lakeside hotels were built on the Rangeleys and Moosehead, and farms took in boarders throughout the Western Lakes region. Along the coast and on dozens of islands, hotels of every size were built, most by Maine natives. Blue-collar workers came by trolley to religious camp meetings, and the wealthy built themselves elaborate summer "cottages" on islands and around Bar Harbor, Camden, and Boothbay Harbor. Developments and sophisticated landscaping transformed much of the previously ignored sandy Southern Coast.

Although it's difficult to document, it's safe to say that Maine attracted the same number of visitors in the summer of 1900 that it did in 2000. This picture altered little for another decade. Then came World War I, coinciding with the proliferation of the Model A.

The 1922 founding of the Maine Publicity Bureau (the present Maine Tourism Association), we suspect, reflects the panic of hoteliers (founder Hiram Ricker himself owned three of the state's grandest hotels: the Mount Kineo House, the Poland Spring House, and the Samoset). Over the next few years these hotels went the way of passenger service, and "motorists" stuck to motor courts and motels along Rt. 1 and a limited number of inland roads.

By the late 1960s, when Chris began writing about Maine, much of the state had all but dropped off the tourist map; in the decades since, she has chronicled the reawakening of most of the old resort areas. Whale-watching and whitewater rafting, skiing and snowmobiling, windjamming and kayaking, outlet shopping, and the renewed popularity of country inns and B&Bs have all contributed to this reawakening. Maine is, after all, magnificent. It was just a matter of time.

Recently the extent of waterside (both coastal and inland) walks open to the public has dramatically increased. It's interesting to note that this phenomenon of preserving and maintaining outstanding landscapes—from Ogunquit's Marginal Way to the core of what's now Acadia National Park—was also an offshoot of Maine's first tourism boom. In this 16th edition we note the dramatic growth of coastal trails way Down East in Washington County and the ever-increasing ways of exploring the North Woods.

A proliferation of fabulous restaurants, too, can be found in the Portland chapter and beyond, with an ever-increasing use of things locally grown.

THE CLAREMONT HOTEL, SOUTHWEST HARBOR, IN AN 1885 PAINTING BY XANTHUS SMITH
Courtesy of the Claremont Hotel

married on Little Cranberry Island off Mount Desert. She has skied Sugarloaf and Sunday River and dogsledded and cross-country skied between North Woods sporting camps, llama trekked and camped in Evans Notch, and sea kayaked off points from Portland to Pembroke as well as sailed whenever possible on Penobscot Bay. She values her Boston vantage point, far enough away to give her the perspective on what it means to be a visitor, yet near enough to comfortably and continually explore Maine.

Born in New York City and raised in northeastern Vermont, Nancy has spent most of her adult life in Portland, Maine. She has heard the cry of a bobcat at night in Vermont, listened to the calls of loons on Maine lakes, and watched a red-tailed hawk pluck a pigeon for dinner her Portland backyard. She was the restaurant reviewer for the *Maine Sunday Telegram* for more than six years. Her travel writing started in the 1970s while still an undergraduate at Vassar College, with articles in *Vermont Life* magazine. She wrote the first and now the recent second edition of *Chow Maine*, a guide to the best restaurants, cafés, lobster shacks, and markets on the Maine coast. Working on this edition of *Maine: An Explorer's Guide* took her inland, to great restaurants far from the summer crowds—although some of them are the favorites of year-round tourists, like the Oxford House Inn in Fryeburg. Traveling in Maine is a pastime she shares with many other Mainers, who have their own seasonal traditions, from eating a lobster roll at Harraseeket Lunch every summer to fly-fishing in the North Maine Woods every fall.

We would like to thank Lisa Sacks for her production help and Laura Jorstad for her careful copyediting of this edition. We would both also like to thank Nancy Marshall and Charlene Williams of Nancy Marshall Assoc. and Meg Maiden of the Maine Windjammer Association for their unfailing responses to all cries for help with gathering information whenever called for, and Elizabeth Roundy Richards and K. W. Oxnard for their contributions to previous editions.

Chris owes thanks to many more people than those listed here. As always, thanks to Virginia Fieldman in Jonesboro, also to Linda and Robert Godfry in Eastport, Joyce Owen and Janice Meiners of Campobello, and Heather MacDonald-Bossé of New Brunswick Tourism. Moving down the coast, thank you to Jackie Major of Cherryfield, Kurt Stoll of Blue Hill, Jack Burke and JulieVandergraff of Castine, Gina Bushong of Orland, and Tina and Tony Lawless of Deer Isle. In Midcoast and the Islands many thanks to Shari Closter, Edwin and Joan Hantz of Rockland, our peerless photographer Carol Latta of Rockport, Phil Crossman on Vinalhaven, and Krista Lisajus of Monhegan's Island Inn. In the Damariscotta area heartfelt thanks to Bobby and Sherry Weare; in Boothbay to Catherine Wygant and to Mark Osborn of Linekin Bay; in the Bath area, many thanks to Elizabeth Knowlton, Carolyn and Tom Church, and Ona Barnet; in Brunswick to Phyllis Truesdell; and in York, to Sue Antal and Elaine Burnham.

Turning inland, first and foremost thanks to East Vassalboro's Elizabeth David-son, to Scott Cowgar of Hallowell, and to Peg Churchill for finally setting me straight about the Belgrade Lakes; for help with the Upper Kennebec Valley, thanks to Brad and Andrea Holden of Jackman. In Rockwood many thanks to John Willard; in Greenville, to Dan and Ruth McLaughlin and Bob Hamer; in Millinocket, to Matt Polstein and Katie Mackin. Also thanks to Jean Hoekwater of Baxter State Park, Al Cowperthwaite of North Maine Woods, and Rob Burbank of the AMC. Finally, thanks are due the world's most helpful, talented, and long-suffering husband, former *Boston Globe* travel editor William A. Davis, who drove thousands of miles through Maine with me, and to son Liam for his company in the North Woods as well as tech help.

Nancy wishes to thank all the many people willing to speak to her when she called their businesses and nonprofits by telephone. Thanks for extensive assis-tance from Jessica Donahue, director of marketing and promotions at the Greater Bangor Convention & Visitors Bureau, who polished the Bangor chapter like a gem. Karen Arel of the Ogunquit Chamber of Commerce, Jennifer Tomlinson of the Greater Portland Convention and Visitors Bureau, and Jim Fitzgerald of the Kennebunks Chamber of Commerce were also generous with advice. Myra Hop-kins of Freeport USA offered many needed suggestions. Kate McCartney of Old Iron Inn and Leslie Jackson of Aroostook County Tourism in Aroostook County were invaluable assistants with details about the County. For help in Rangeley, Gail Spaulding and the staff at the Rangeley Chamber of Commerce deserve many thanks. In western regions, Nancy thanks Rick Whelchel and Brian Anderson, area innkeepers with a fine talent for hospitality. Thanks go to Bethel chamber director Robin Zinchuk. Along the coast the help has been generous. Thanks go to Mary Bennoch at the Bar Harbor Chamber of Commerce and Caroline Sulzer and David Walker of Surry, Dan Bookham and the rest of the staff of the Camden chamber, Debbie Reynolds at the Belfast chamber, and all the friendly people in Downeast Maine who took time from their busy schedule to answer questions. Thanks to Carrabasset Valley Town Clerk Wendy Russell, who found a moment after the election to update me on the population and other important changes in her old town. Thanks to volunteers everywhere, who answer so many questions so patiently! And all the chambers of commerce of Maine are staffed with courteous and generous people who have contributed many details to this book.

Kate O'Halloran deserves a special bow for enabling the comparison of Word documents. Thanks also are due to Emma English, Nancy's daughter, who has pro-vided details of meals and perceptions about inns that make descriptions come alive, while clocking many miles on travels through Maine.

WHAT'S WHERE IN MAINE

AREA CODE The area code throughout Maine is **207**.

ABENAKI See *Wabanaki*.

ACADIANS trace their lineage to French settlers who came to Nova Scotia in the early 1600s and who, in 1755, were forcibly deported by an English governor. This "Great Disturbance" dispersed a population of some 10,000 Acadians and brutally divided families. In a meadow overlooking the St. John River at Madawaska's **Tante Blanche Museum**, a large marble cross marks the spot on which several hundred displaced Acadians landed in 1787. **Village Acadien**, a dozen buildings forming a mini museum village just west of Van Buren, only begins to tell the story. While the sizable Franco-American communities in Biddeford, Lewiston, and Brunswick have a different history (their forebears were recruited from Quebec to work in 19th-century mills), they, too, have experienced a long repression of their culture and recent resurgence of pride in a shared French heritage. Exhibits at the **Museum Lewiston-Auburn** have focused on that history in Lewiston, where the **Festival de Joie** is held in August. **La Kermesse**, held in late June in Biddeford, is another major Franco-American festival. Con-

tact the **Maine Acadian Heritage Council** (207-728-6826) for more information.

In 2014 the St. John River Valley with Quebec and New Brunswick on the Canadian side will host the World Acadian Congress, with sporting events, family reunions (perhaps as many as 120), and other events. Maine is contributing $1 million to the event; past congresses have drawn 50,000 visitors. You may want to make a reservation early.

AGRICULTURAL FAIRS The season opens in late June and runs through the first week of October, culminating with the large, colorful, immensely popular **Fryeburg Fair**. Among the best traditional fairs are the **Union Fair** (late August) and the **Blue Hill Fair** (Labor Day weekend). **The Common Ground Country Fair** (third weekend in September, at the fairgrounds in Unity), sponsored by the Maine Organic Farmers and Gardeners Association (mofga.org), features organic Maine-grown food, farming techniques, dancing, and music and draws city folk and organic gardeners from all corners of the state. For details about fairs see the **Maine Department of Agriculture** site: getrealmaine.com. A vibrant tradition of harness racing at Maine fairs has been reinvigorated with a small percentage of revenues earned by Hollywood Slots, a racino in Bangor.

AIRPORTS AND AIRLINES
Portland International Jetport (207-774-7301), with connections to most large American and Canadian cities, is served by several carriers: Air-Tran (1-800-247-8726; airtran.com), Continental Airlines (1-800-523-3273; continental.com), Delta Air Lines (1-800-221-1212; delta.com), United (1-800-864-8331; united.com), U.S. Airways (1-800-428-4322; usair.com), and JetBlue (1-800-538-2583; jetblue .com). **Bangor International Airport** (207-947-0384; flybangor.com), serving northern and Downeast Maine, also offers connections to all parts of the United States via Allegiant Air (702-505-8888; allegiantair.com), Delta (1-800-221-1212; delta.com), and U.S. Airways (1-800-428-4322). Colgan Air operates U.S. Airways flights (1-800-428-4322; colganair.com) to **Hancock County Regional Airport** (Trenton/ Bar Harbor), and **Northern Maine Regional Airport** (Presque Isle). Cape Air (1-800-352-0714; flycapeair .com) flies to **Knox County Regional Airport** (207-594-4131) in Owls Head, south of Rockland, and between Augusta and Boston. **Manchester, NH**, and Boston's **Logan International Airport** are both popular gateways for Maine travelers; both are served by Mermaid Transportation (gomermaid.com) to Portland. Concord Coach Lines (see *Bus Service*) offers express service from Logan to Portland.

AIR SERVICES Also called flying services, these are useful links to wilderness camps and coastal islands. Greenville, prime jumping-off point for the North Maine Woods, claims to be New England's largest seaplane

base. In this book flying services are also listed under *Getting There* or *Getting Around* in "Rangeley Lakes Region," "Moosehead Lake Area," "Katahdin Region," and "Washington County." Check *Getting There* in "Rockland/Thomaston Area" for air taxis to several islands, including Vinalhaven, North Haven, and Matinicus.

AMTRAK Maine passenger service is not just back but moving more and more passengers every year! Amtrak's **Downeaster** (thedowneaster.com) offers five roundtrips per day between Boston's North Station and the Portland rail-bus station just off I-95. It's two and a half hours each way, with comfortable seats, friendly service, and a view of the shoreline you otherwise never see. Northbound from Boston you cross the wide Merrimac River into Haverhill (Massachusetts) and stop in the middle of the University of New Hampshire campus in Durham. In Maine the first stop is Wells at a regional transportation center, served by taxis and a seasonal trolley to the beach. In Saco the station is just beyond the mighty falls (taxi service and shuttle bus). In Old Orchard the stop is near the beach and Palace Playland, the amusement park (seasonal only). The Portland station doubles as

DOWNEASTER

a stop for Concord Coach Lines. The 9:05 AM from Boston arrives in Portland at 11:30; there's a southbound 7:55 PM train with a same-day roundtrip fare of $39, when booked three days in advance. The line will extend to Brunswick if all goes according to schedule by the end of 2012, stopping in Freeport on route.

AMUSEMENT AND HIGH ROPES PARKS **Funtown/Splashtown USA** in Saco is Maine's biggest, with rides, waterslides, and pools. **Aquaboggan** (pools and slides) is also on Rt. 1 in Saco. **Palace Playland** in Old Orchard Beach is a classic, with a carousel, Ferris wheel, rides, and a 60-foot waterslide. **York's Wild Kingdom** at York Beach has a zoo and amusement area. **Seacoast Fun Park** in Windham and **Wild Acadia Fun Park** in Trenton have a waterslide or tubing slide, mini golf, and rock climbing wall. **Monkey Trunks** in Saco and **Monkey C Monkey Do** in Wiscasset add ziplines and the challenge of maneuvering with ropes to the mix.

ANTIQUARIAN BOOKS Maine is well known among book buffs as a browsing mecca. **Maine Antiquarian Booksellers** posts a directory of 50 members at mainebooksellers.org.

ANTIQUES A member directory listing hundreds of dealers is produced by the **Maine Antiques Dealers' Association**. The association's active website lists members as well as auctions at maineantiques.org. The 60-plus-page *Antique Dealer Directory* can be ordered online.

APPALACHIAN TRAIL (appalachiantrail.org). The 267-mile Maine section of this 2,175-mile Georgia-to-Maine footpath enters the state in the Mahoosuc Range—accessible there

Bill Davis

ANTIQUES IN WINTER HARBOR

from Grafton Notch State Park (the Mahoosuc Notch section is extremely difficult)—and continues north into the Rangeley and Sugarloaf areas, on up through the Upper Kennebec Valley to Monson. West of Moosehead Lake it runs through Gulf Hagas and on around Nahmakanta Lake, through Abol Bridge to Baxter State Park, end-

AMC LITTLE LYFORD LODGE AND CABINS

Bill Davis

Nancy English

PRESSING APPLE CIDER

ing at the summit of 5,267-foot Mount Katahdin. Hikes along the trail are noted within specific chapters; lodging places catering to AT through-hikers include **Northern Outdoors** in The Forks, and **Little Lyford Pond Camps** near Gulf Hagas. July, August, and September are the best months to hike this stretch. The **Maine Appalachian Trail Club** (matc.org) helps with maintenance and in other ways; it publishes a trail guide that can be ordered online or by writing to Maine Appalachian Trail Club, P.O. Box 283, Augusta, ME 04332-0283. For a list of national publications, write to Appalachian Trail Conservancy, Dept. SD, P.O. Box 807, Harpers Ferry, WV 25425-0807.

APPALACHIAN MOUNTAIN CLUB (outdoors.org). In recent years the Boston-based AMC, the country's oldest nonprofit outdoor recreation/ conservation group, has acquired 66,500 acres in the North Woods (see "Moosehead Lake Area"), along with three historic sporting camps, and is working to maintain an extensive trail system geared to nonmotorized recreational use. The AMC has long offered seasonal "family camp" programs for adults and families seeking an organ-

ized outdoor-geared vacation at **Echo Lake** (amcecholakecamp.org) on Mount Desert, at **Cold River Camp** (amccoldrivercamp.org) in Evans Notch (within the White Mountain National Forest), and most recently at **Medawisla Wilderness Lodge** near Greenville, surrounded by 29,500 acres of AMC conservation land. Also see *Hiking* and *Cross-Country Skiing*.

APPLES Fall brings plenty of pick-your-own opportunities across the state, and many orchards also sell apples and cider. For a map/guide to PYO orchards, see maineapples.org or the Department of Agriculture's website: getrealmaine.com. And check out the Cornish Apple Festival and Apple Acres Bluegrass Festival, both held in Cornish in late September; Maine Apple Day in Unity; and Heirloom Apple Week at the Colonel Black Mansion in Ellsworth.

AQUARIUMS The **Marine Resources Aquarium** in Boothbay

MAINE STATE AQUARIUM, BOOTHBAY HARBOR

Christina Tree

Harbor displays regional fish and sea creatures, many of them surprisingly colorful. The stars of the show are the sharks and skates in a large touch tank. The **Mount Desert Oceanarium** is a commercial attraction with several locations in the Bar Harbor area.

ARTISTS, ART PROGRAMS, AND ART GALLERIES Maine's landscape has drawn major artists since the mid-19th century. The **Maine Arts Commission** (mainearts.com) offers a searchable database of artists, arts organizations, and events. Within each chapter we describe commercial galleries, which seem to have clustered in Portland, Boothbay Harbor, Rockland, Rockport, Stonington, Blue Hill, Northeast Harbor, and Eastport. A number of books profile the work of current Maine artists; a standout is *Art of the Maine Islands* by Carl Little and Arnold Skolnick (Down East Books). Artist-owned galleries, which have become destinations in their own right, are found in Sullivan and Stonington and on the islands of Monhegan, North Haven, Vinalhaven, and Little Cranberry. Summer arts workshops are offered in Stonington and at Rock Gardens Inn (rockgardensinn.com), as well as by the Maine College of Art (meca .org) in Portland. The most prestigious summer arts workshop in Maine is the **Skowhegan School of Painting and Sculpture** (207-474-9345 or 212-529-0505; skowheganart.org).

ART MUSEUMS Seven of the state's museums have formed a partnership and created the **Maine Art Museum Trail** (maineartmuseums.org). The **Portland Museum of Art** (portland museum.org) is known for its strong collection of works by impressionist and post-impressionist masters as well as Winslow Homer. **The Farnsworth Art Museum** with its **Center for the**

Wyeth Family in Maine in Rockland (farnsworthmuseum.org) has a stellar collection of Maine art, as well as frequent special exhibits. The seasonal **Ogunquit Museum of American Art** (ogunquitmuseum.org) and the newly expanded **Colby College Museum of Art** (colby.edu/museum) in Waterville are also well worth detours for art lovers. The **Bates College Museum of Art** (abacus.bates .edu/acad/museum) and **Bowdoin College Museum of Art** (bowdoin .edu/artmuseum) are also excellent and described within their respective chapters. The **University of Maine Museum of Art** in Bangor (umma .umaine.edu) is another worth exploring.

ATVS Alliance Trail Vehicles of Maine (atvmaine.org) offers information about the state's all-terrain vehicle clubs and riding opportunities.

BALLOONING Hot-air balloon rides are available from **Hot Fun** (hotfun balloons.com) in South Portland, **Sails Aloft** (207-623-1136; sailsaloft.com) in Augusta, **Rainbow's End** (207-782-1622) in Auburn, and **Dream Song Ballooning** (dreamsongballooning .org) and **Androscoggin Balloon Adventures** (207-783-4574) in Lewiston.

BEACHES Given the rising summer temperature of the Atlantic Ocean—62 degrees in Portland and 63 degrees at Bar Harbor, both in 2011—swimming has become more enjoyable, but it still isn't the primary reason most folks come to the Maine coast. Still, Maine beaches (for instance at York, Wells, the Kennebunks, Portland, Popham, and Pemaquid) can be splendid walking, sunning, and kite-flying places. At **Ogunquit** and in **Reid State Park** in Georgetown, there are also warmer

Nancy English

LONG SANDS BEACH, YORK HARBOR

BEER For information on Maine's ever-evolving breweries and micro-breweries, check out mainebrewers guild.org/BeerTrailWeb. The **Maine Brewer's Festival** (learnyourbeer .com) in Portland is held the first weekend of November and often sells out.

BICYCLING Mountain biking is particularly popular on the carriage roads in **Acadia National Park** and after a Chondola ride at **Sunday River**. Biking is also popular on Swan's Island off Acadia and on islands in Casco Bay. Route 1 is heavily traveled, and should be avoided. Dedicated recreation paths are beginning to appear, notably in Portland, South Portland, and Brunswick/Bath, along the Kennebec between Augusta and Gardiner, and farther north between Solon and Bingham. Bicycling also makes sense in heavily touristed resort areas in which a car can be a nuisance; rentals are available in Ogunquit, Kennebunkport, Portland, Camden, Southwest Harbor, and Bar Harbor. For good biking maps of various regions, **Map Adventures** (1-800-891-1534; mapadventures.com) makes very readable small maps of bike routes, stocked at most bike shops and bookstores. The *Explore Maine by Bike* book is available free of charge and can be ordered online at https://www.visit maine.com/guidebook.

Check out the excellent Maine DOT site, **exploremaine.org/bike**, for tours ranging from 20 to 100 miles. The **Bicycle Coalition of Maine** (207-623-4511; bikemaine.org) serves as a conduit for information about both off- and on-road bicycling throughout the state and maintains a calendar of bicycling events. Guided multiday tours are offered by **Summer Feet Cycling** (summerfeet.net) and by **Bike Vermont** (bikevermont.com);

backwater areas in which small children can paddle. Other outstanding beaches include 7-mile-long **Old Orchard Beach** and, nearby, state-maintained **Crescent Beach** on Cape Elizabeth, **Scarborough Beach** in Scarborough, **Ferry Beach** in Saco, and **Sand Beach** in Acadia National Park. The state-maintained freshwater beaches are on **Lakes Damariscotta**, **St. George**, **Sebec**, **Rangeley**, **Sebago**, and **Moosehead**; also on **Pleasant Pond** in Richmond. All state beaches include changing facilities, restrooms, and showers; many have snack bars. The town of **Bridgton** has several fine little lakeside beaches, while **Lake George Regional Park** (between Skowhegan and Canaan) offers sandy beaches and facilities on two shores.

BED & BREAKFASTS We have visited many B&Bs in Maine. They range from elegant town houses and country mansions to farms and fishermen's homes. Prices vary in-season from $70 to more than $860 (on the coast in August) for a double and average $110–150 in high season on the coast. With few exceptions, they offer a friendly entrée to their communities.

two-day camping tours are offered by L.L. Bean (llbean.com).

BIRDING An abridged map/guide version of *The Official Guide to the Maine Birding Trail* by Bob Duchesne (Down East Books) can be downloaded or ordered from the Maine Office of Tourism (visitmaine.com) or picked up at a state visitors center. The book itself details 260 places to watch and hear birds across the state. Four birding festivals are held every summer. The first is **Wings, Waves and Woods** in Deer Isle and Stonington in May. Next, Memorial Day weekend brings the **Downeast Spring Birding Festival** (downeastbirdfest.org) in Cobscook Bay. The **Acadia Birding Festival** on Mount Desert Island and **Aroostook State Park Birding Festival**, between Houlton and Presque Isle, are both held in June. **Maine Audubon** (207-781-2330; maineaudubon.org), based at Gilsland Farm Audubon Center in Falmouth, maintains a number of birding sites and sponsors nature programs and field trips year-round, including naturalist-led van tours and boat cruises to see birds and other wildlife statewide. Adirondack-style lodges alongside Sunset Pond at 1,600-acre Borestone Mountain Audubon Sanctuary are available for group rental. **Laudholm Farm** in Wells, **Biddeford Pool**, **Scarborough Marsh**, **Merrymeeting Bay**, and **Mount Desert** are also popular birding sites. **Monhegan** is the island to visit in May and September. **Aroostook National Wildlife Refuge** in Limestone is a great place for migrations. The **Moosehorn National Wildlife Refuge** (207-454-3521) in Washington County represents the northeastern terminus of the East Coast chain of wildlife refuges and is particularly rich in bird life. We recommend *Birder's Guide to Maine* by Elizabeth Cary Pierson, Jan Erik Pierson, and Peter D. Vickery (Down East Books). Also see *Puffin-Watching* and *Nature Preserves, Coastal* and *Inland*. The site **mainebirding.net** has checklists, events, and detailed descriptions.

BLUEBERRYING Maine grows 98 percent of US lowbush blueberries. More than 80 million pounds are harvested annually from an estimated 25,000 acres. Few growers allow U-pick, at least not until the commercial harvest is over. (One exception is **Staples Homestead Blueberries** in Stockton Springs.) Then the public can to go "stumping" for leftovers (except where posted)—but the berries might not be in the best shape. On the other hand, berrying along roads and hiking paths is a rite of summer. The **blueberry barrens**— thousands of blueberry-covered acres—spread across Cherryfield, Columbia, and Machias (site of the state's most colorful blueberry festival in August) in Washington and Union Counties. For more about Maine's famous fruit, click on **wildblueberries.com** and **wildblueberries.maine.edu**.

BOATBUILDING WoodenBoat School (207-359-4651; thewoodenboatschool.com) in Brooklin (see "Blue Hill Area") offers a plethora of courses, including more than 100 on various aspects of boatbuilding. The **Maine Maritime Museum** (mainemaritimemuseum.org) in Bath offers some classes in boatbuilding; Atlantic Challenge's program, the **Apprenticeshop** (207-594-1800; atlanticchallenge.com), in Rockland offers two-year apprentice programs and six-week (or longer) internships; and **The Boat School** at **Washington County Community College Marine Technology Center** in Eastport attracts many out-of-staters.

BOAT EXCURSIONS You really won't know what Maine is about until you stand off at sea to appreciate the beauty of the cliffs and island-dotted bays. For the greatest concentrations of boat excursions, see "Boothbay Harbor Region," "Rockland/Thomaston Area," and "Bar Harbor and Ellsworth"; there are also excursions from Ogunquit, Kennebunkport, Portland, Belfast, Camden, Castine, Stonington, Jonesport, Machias, Lubec, and Eastport. (Also see *Coastal Cruises; Ferries, in Maine* and *to Canada; Sailing;* and *Windjammers.* See "Sebago and Long Lakes Region" and "Moosehead Lake Area" for lake excursions.)

BOOKS Anyone who seriously sets out to explore Maine should read the following mix of Maine classics and guidebooks: *The Maine Woods* by **Henry David Thoreau**, first published posthumously in 1864, remains very readable and gives an excellent description of Maine's mountains. For those inspired to trace Thoreau's route there's *The Wildest Country: Exploring Thoreau's Maine* by Parker Huber (AMC Books), complete with maps and color photographs of local flora and fauna. Our favorite relatively recent Maine author is **Ruth Moore**,

GARY LAWLESS OF GULF OF MAINE BOOKS, BRUNSWICK, SPECIALIZES IN MAINE AUHTHORS

Christina Tree

who writes about Maine islands in *The Weir, Spoonhandle*, and *Speak to the Wind* (originally published in the 1940s and reissued by Blackberry Books, Nobleboro). The 1940s classic *We Took to the Woods* by **Louise Dickinson Rich** is now published by Down East Books in Camden. **Sarah Orne Jewett**'s classic *The Country of the Pointed Firs and Other Stories* (W. W. Norton), first published in 1896, is set on the coast around Tenants Harbor and still an excellent read. For historical fiction, try any one of Pulitzer Prize winner **Kenneth Roberts**'s novels about Maine during the Revolutionary War. **John Gould**, an essayist who wrote a regular column for the *Christian Science Monitor* for more than 50 years, published several books, including *Dispatches from Maine*, a collection of those columns, and *Maine Lingo* (with **Lillian Ross**), a humorous look at Maine phrases and expressions. For an overview of Maine-related poetry and prose we highly recommend *The Maine Reader: The Down East Experience from 1614 to the Present* (David R. Godine).

Maine has been home to the authors of many of our most beloved children's classics. **Robert McCloskey**, author of *Blueberries for Sal, Time of Wonder*, and *One Morning in Maine*, resided on an island off the Blue Hill Peninsula, also summer home to **E. B. White**, known for wonderful essay collections and his ever-popular children's novels *Charlotte's Web* and *Stuart Little*. Damariscotta-based **Barbara Cooney** wrote and illustrated some 200 books, among them *Miss Rumphius, Island Boy*, and *Hattie and the Wild Waves*.

Recent classics set in Maine include **Carolyn Chute**'s *The Beans of Egypt, Maine* (1985), *Letourneau's Used Auto Parts* (1988), *Merry Men* (1994), and *The School of Heart's Content Road*

(2008); and **Cathie Pelletier's** *The Funeral Makers* (1987) and *The Weight of Winter* (1991). *Maine Speaks*, an anthology of Maine literature published by the **Maine Writers and Publishers Alliance** (maine writers.org), contains all the obvious poems and essays and many pleasant surprises. **Linda Greenlaw's** *The Lobster Chronicles* (2002) describes the island of Isle au Haut. It's a good read with insights into life on all Maine's surviving island communities. *Where Cool Waters Flow: Four Seasons with a Maine Master Guide*, by **Randy Spencer**, describes the guiding culture at East Grand Lake and its traditions.

Guides to exploring Maine include the indispensable *Maine Atlas and Gazetteer* (DeLorme) and, from Down East Books, *Walking the Maine Coast* by John Gibson; and *Islands in Time: A Natural and Cultural History of the Islands of the Gulf of Maine* by Philip W. Conkling. From AMC Books comes the serious hiker's *AMC Maine Mountain Guide*; for a selection of hiking, paddling, sea kayaking, and biking trips there's *Discover Maine* by Ty Wivell. Also check out *50 Hikes in the Maine Mountains* by Cloe Chunn and *50 Hikes in Coastal and Inland Maine* by John Gibson (both Countryman Press).

Island Port Press (islandportpress .com) publishes books about Maine; *Tales from Misery Ridge* by registered Maine Guide Paul J. Fournier describes his adventures in the Maine wilderness and waterways.

Also worth noting: *Maine*, by Charles C. Calhoun (Compass American Guides), complements this guide with its superb illustrations and well-written background text.

BUS SERVICE Concord Coach Lines (1-800-639-3317; concordcoach lines.com) serves Portland, Brunswick, Bath, Wiscasset, Damariscotta, Wal- doboro, Rockland, Camden, Belfast, Searsport, Bangor, and the University of Maine at Orono (when school is in session). Its Boston/Portland/Bangor Express is the fastest service to eastern Maine. **Greyhound Bus Lines/ Vermont Transit** (1-800-231-2222 or 1-800-451-3292; vermonttransit.com) serves Augusta, Lewiston, Waterville, Portland, Bangor, and (seasonally but crucially) Bar Harbor. See explore maine.org for details about public transit buses. **West's Coastal Connection** (westbusservice.com) offers daily service year-round from Bangor Airport (stopping at both bus terminals) to Calais, with stops in Machias and Perry, along with many flag-down stops (call ahead) in between. **Cyr Bus Line** (207-827-2335 or 1-800-244-2335) offers bus daily service as far as Fort Kent from Bangor.

CAMPING See "North Maine Woods" for details about camping within these vast fiefdoms, and also for camping in **Baxter State Park** (see "Katahdin Region") and along the **Allagash Wilderness Waterway** (see *Canoeing* in "Aroostook County"). For camping within **Acadia National Park**, see "Acadia National Park." For the same within the **White Mountain National Forest**, see "Bethel Area." For private campgrounds, the booklet *Maine Camping Guide*, published by the Maine Campground Owners Association (207-782-5874; campmaine.com), lists most privately operated camping and tenting areas. Reservations are advised for the state's 13 parks that offer camping (campwithme.com; also see *Parks, State*). We have attempted to describe the state parks in detail wherever they appear in this book (see Damariscotta, Camden, Cobscook Bay, Sebago, Rangeley, and Greenville). Note that state campsites can accommodate average-sized campers and trailers, but only Sebago and Camden Hills offer (up to 40-foot) trailer electric and water hookups. **Warren Island** (just off Islesboro) and **Swan Island** (just off Richmond) offer organized camping, and primitive camping is permitted on a number of islands through the **Maine Island Trail Association** (MITA; see *Islands*). Within this book we occasionally describe outstanding private campgrounds.

CAMPS AND LEARNING PROGRAMS FOR ADULTS

Outward Bound (1-866-846-7745; outwardboundwilderness.org) offers a variety of adult-geared outdoor adventures in Maine as well as throughout the country. **L.L. Bean** (llbean.com) offers introductions to a variety of sports with programs lasting from a couple of hours to multiday family adventures and **Outdoor Discovery Schools**. The **Hog Island Audubon Center** on Hog Island off Bremen offers programs sponsored by Audubon's Project Puffin (see "Damariscotta/ Newcastle"). The **AMC** (see *Appalachian Mountain Club*) also offers weeklong "Family Camp" programs at several Maine venues. Photographers should check out the **Maine Media Workshops** (theworkshops.com) in Rockport. Also see *Boatbuilding* (**WoodenBoat** offers much more than boatbuilding). **Road Scholar**, formerly Elderhostel (roadscholar.org), offers a variety of programs throughout Maine for everyone over age 50. Check out **Haystack Mountain School** under *Crafts* and arts workshops under *Artists, Art Programs, and Art Galleries*. Entries under *Music Schools* and *Sailing* also have workshop information. Potters should check out the **Watershed Center for Ceramic Arts** (watershedceramics .org) in Newcastle.

CAMPS, FOR CHILDREN More than 200 summer camps are listed in the exceptional booklet published annually by the Maine Youth Camping Association (1-800-536-7712; mainecamps.org). Also check out Maine Camp Experience (mainecamp experience.com).

CANOEING, GUIDED TRIPS

Developed by the Wabanaki and still proudly manufactured in Old Town (see "Bangor Area"), the canoe remains popular on Maine rivers. Novices might begin with the slow-moving, shallow **Saco River**, which offers a number of well-maintained camping sites. Several outfitters in the Fryeburg area (see *To Do* in "Sebago and Long Lakes Region") offer rentals and shuttle service, and **Saco Bound**, just over the New Hampshire line, offers guided tours. The **Moose River** near Jackman (see *To Do* in "Upper Kennebec Valley") offers a similar camping/canoeing trip, and **Sunrise International**, based in Bangor (see *To Do* in "Bangor" and "Washington County and the Quoddy Loop"), offers staging for trips down the Grand Lake chain of lakes and the St. Croix River. Also see **northernforestcanoetrail .org** for the 348-mile portion of the Maine stretch. Within each chapter canoe rentals and guided trips are described under *To Do*.

CANOEING THE ALLAGASH The

ultimate canoe trip in Maine (and on the entire East Coast) is the 7 to 10-day expedition up the **Allagash Wilderness Waterway**, a 92-mile ribbon of lakes, ponds, rivers, and streams in the heart of northern Maine's vast commercial forests. We advise using a shuttle service. The general information number for the Allagash Wilderness Waterway is 207-941-4014; ask for the free map that pinpoints the 65 authorized campsites within the zone (and details other crucial information). A detailed topographic map, backed with historical and a variety of other handy information, is DeLorme's *Map and Guide to the Allagash and St. John*. The **North Maine Woods** offers its own information about campsites and a publication with a map (north mainewoods.org). Be aware of blackflies in June and no-see-ums when warm weather finally comes. For further information, see *Camping* and *Guide Services*, and check out maineoutdoors .com. Also see *To Do—Canoeing* in "Aroostook County." A map tracing Henry David Thoreau's three canoe/ hiking journeys described in *The Maine Woods* has been produced by Maine Woods Forever (thoreauwabanaki trail.org). Also see *Books*.

CHEESE Maine's 31 cheesemakers claim to create more than 150 artisan cheeses, but with the exception of Seal Cove Farm in Lamoine (producing goat cheese since 1980), many are available only locally. Check out **maine cheeseguild.org** for more information about where to find these wonderful cheeses, and learn about **Open Creamery Day** in early October.

CHILDREN, ESPECIALLY FOR Throughout this book, restaurants, lodgings, and attractions that are of special interest to families with children are indicated by the crayon symbol ✒.

CHRISTMAS TREES AND WREATHS Maine is a prime source of Christmas trees for the Northeast. The Maine Department of Agriculture maintains a detailed "Choose and Cut" list at **getrealmaine.com**.

CLAMMING Maine state law permits shellfish harvesting for personal use

Bill Davis

SIGN AT TREVETT COUNTRY STORE, BOOTHBAY

only, unless you have a commercial license. But rules vary with each town, so check with the town clerk (source of licenses) before you dig, and make sure there's no red tide. Some towns do prohibit clamming, and in certain places there is a temporary stay on harvesting while the beds are being seeded.

COASTAL CRUISES *Cruise* is a much-used (and -abused) term along the Maine coast, chiefly intended to mean a boat ride. Within each chapter we describe what's currently available, from ferries to multiday sails. (Also see *Windjammers*.)

COTTAGE RENTALS Cottage rentals are a reasonably priced way for families to stay in one Maine spot for a week or more. Request the booklet *Maine Guide to Inns and Bed & Breakfasts and Camps & Cottages* from the Maine Tourism Association (mainetourism.com). Many local chambers of commerce also keep a list of available rentals, and we list cottage rental websites in most chapters.

COVERED BRIDGES Of the 120 covered bridges that once spanned Maine rivers, just 9 survive. The most famous, and certainly picturesque, is the **Artists' Covered Bridge** (1872) over the Sunday River in Newry, northwest of Bethel. The others are **Porter Bridge** (1876), over the Ossipee River, 0.5 mile south of Porter; **Babb's Bridge**, rebuilt after burning in 1973, over the Presumpscot River between Gorham and Windham; **Hemlock Bridge** (1857), 3 miles northwest of East Fryeburg; **Lovejoy Bridge** (1883), over the Ellis River in South Andover; **Bennett Bridge** (1901), over the Magalloway River, 1.5 miles south of the Wilson's Mills post office; **Robyville Bridge** (1876), Maine's only completely shingled covered bridge, in the town of Corinth; the **Watson Settlement Bridge** (1911), between Woodstock and Littleton; and **Low's Bridge**, carefully reconstructed in 1990 after a flood took the 1857 structure, across the Piscataquis River between Guilford and Sangerville.

CRAFTS *Maine Guide to Crafts and Culture*, available free from the **Maine Crafts Association** (mainecrafts.org), is a geographic listing of studios, galleries, and museums throughout Maine. **United Maine Craftsmen, Inc.** (207-621-2818; unitedmaine craftsmen.com), also sponsors six large shows each year. **Haystack Mountain School of Crafts** (haystack-mtn.org; see "Deer Isle, Stonington") is a summer school nationally respected in a variety of crafts with three-week courses mid-June through mid-September. The surrounding area (Blue Hill to Stonington) contains the largest concentration of Maine craftspeople, many with open studios. There are 134 fiber studios, fiber farms, and galleries listed at **mainefiberarts.org**; a printed or online tour map is also available. Maine Fiberarts headquarters, at 13 Main St. in Topsham, is open weekdays. Also check out the **Center for Maine Craft** (207-588-0021) at the Gardiner rest area off I-95.

DOGSLEDDING Although racing is a long-established winter spectator sport, riding on a dogsled is an activity growing in popularity. **Telemark Inn** (telemarkinn.com) in West Bethel offers dogsledding. In the Moosehead Lake region, Stephen Medera's **Song in the Woods** (songinthewoods.com) offers a choice of trips. Don and Angel Hibbs have traveled more than 40,000 miles by dog team. Their **Nahmakanta Lake Camps** (nahmakanta .com) in Rainbow Township serve as a base for driving teams (guests can ride or drive) on trails in a 27,000-acre preserve that's Maine's largest roadless preserve outside Katahdin—which is clearly visible from the trail system. Guests ski in 10 miles from the Golden Road. The Northeast Dogsled Championships are held in Jackman in March.

EVENTS We have listed outstanding annual events within each chapter of this book; also see event listings on

A POTTER AT GEORGETOWN POTTERY

Christina Tree

visitmaine.com and **mainetourism .com**. A community calendar is posted at **mainepublicradio.org**.

FACTORY OUTLETS

We note individual outlet stores in their respective chapters throughout; we also describe the state's two major outlet clusters: in **Freeport** (freeportusa.com) and **Kittery** (thekitteryoutlets.com). L.L. Bean (llbean.com), Freeport's anchor store, is open 24 hours and is the single most spectacular store in northern New England. New Balance also makes sneakers and maintains major sports clothing outlets in Norway and Skowhegan.

FALL FOLIAGE

Autumn days tend to be clear, and the changing leaves against the blue sea and lakes can be spectacular. Off-season prices sometimes prevail, in contrast with the rest of New England at this time of year. Check the Maine Department of Conservation website, **mainefoliage.com**, for a map reporting leaf colors and places to visit.

FARM B&BS

The **Maine Farm Vacation B&B Association** (maine farmvacation.com) describes its 18 members in its brochure and at maine farmvacation.com. This is a promotional association, not an official approval and inspection group. Properties vary widely. Some offer plenty of space, animals, big breakfasts, and friendly informal atmosphere, but others are not working farms.

FARM STANDS, FARMS, AND FARMER'S MARKETS

The **Maine Department of Agriculture** (getreal maine.com) publishes *Finding Maine Food and Farms*, a thick, free pamphlet guide listing markets and contact information in the back.

FERRIES

The Maine Department of Transportation maintains a brilliant website (exploremaine.org) with schedules for **Maine State Ferry Service** (1-800-491-4883) from Rockland to Vinalhaven, North Haven, and Matinicus, from Lincolnville to Islesboro, and from Bass Harbor to Swans Island and Frenchboro. They also list services to Monhegan Island, Isle au Haut, and the Cranberry Islands. Casco Bay islands are served by **Casco Bay Lines** (cascobaylines.com) from Portland. **Quoddy Loop Ferries** (quoddy loop.com) travel from Eastport and Campobello Island to the New Brunswick mainland via Deer Island, and from Black Harbor to Grand Manan.

FILM

Northeast Historic Film (1-800-639-1636; oldfilm.org) is based at "The Alamo," a vintage-1916 movie house in Bucksport. This admirable group has created a regional moving-image archive of films based on or made in New England that were shown in every small town during the first part of the 20th century. Request the catalog *Videos of Life in New England*. The **International Film & Television Workshops** in Rockport offer

NORTH HAVEN FERRY

Christina Tree

NORTHEAST HISTORIC FILM LOGO

a variety of weeklong courses in various aspects of film. The **Maine International Film Festival** is a 10-day event, with more than 60 films shown in Waterville (miff.org). Portland hosts the **Maine Jewish Film Festival** (mjff.org) in mid-March. There are still five functioning **drive-ins** in Maine, in Saco, Bridgton, Skowhegan, Westbrook, and Madawaska.

FIRE PERMITS Maine law dictates that no person shall kindle or use outdoor fires without a permit, except at authorized campsites or picnic grounds. Fire permits in the organized townships are obtained from the local town warden; in the unorganized townships, from the nearest forest ranger. Portable stoves fueled by propane gas, gasoline, or Sterno are exempt from the rule.

FISHING Maine **sporting camps** (mainesportingcamps.com) catering to fishermen can be found in "Western Mountains and Lakes Region," "North Maine Woods," and "Upper Kennebec Valley." The **Maine Department of**

Marine Resources (207-633-9500) furnishes species information and launch sites at maine.gov/dmr/index .htm (look for RECREATIONAL FISHING on the left). **The Maine Department of Inland Fisheries and Wildlife** (207-287-8000) publishes a weekly fishing report at mefishwildlife.com. **Registered Maine Guides** (maine guides.org) know where and how to fish, and offer frequent courses. One-day fishing licenses are available at general stores and from outfitters throughout the state and come with a regulations book. Also check out FISH-ING at **visitmaine.com**.

FORTS Maine's 20 forts are actually a fascinating lot, monuments to the state's largely forgotten history. **Fort Knox** (see "Bucksport") is the state's grandest fort and offers a lively seasonal schedule of events. **Fort William Henry** at Pemaquid (see "Damariscotta/Newcastle") is genuinely fascinating, while **Fort**

LIBBY CAMPS, ASHLAND

Nancy English

Edgecomb off Rt. 1 in Edgecomb, just east of Wiscasset, is an easy hit. Also check out **Fort George** in Castine, **Fort McClary** in Kittery, **Fort Popham** near Bath, **Fort Pownall** at Stockton Springs, **Fort O'Brien** in Machiasport, and, at the northern end of Rt. 1, **Fort Kent** in Fort Kent.

GOLDEN ROAD This legendary 96-mile road is the privately owned high road of the North Maine Woods, linking Millinocket's paper mills on the east with commercial woodlands that extend to the Quebec border. Its name derives from its multimillion-dollar cost in 1975, but its value has proven great to visitors heading up from Moosehead Lake, as well as from Millinocket to Baxter State Park. It's also used by the whitewater rafting companies on the Penobscot River and the Allagash Wilderness Waterway, and for remote lakes like Chesuncook. Expect to pull to the side to permit lumber trucks to pass. Much of the

THE GOLDEN ROAD

Liam Davis

road is now paved and well maintained, even (especially) in winter. Be sure to bring along your Maine atlas or another detailed map. The **Silas Hill Road** linking Kokadjo and the Golden Road is free but fairly rough.

GOLF The **Golf Maine Association** website (golfme.com) offers information and links to its member courses. Also check out the **Maine Golf Trail** at visitmaine.com and the Maine State Golf Association (mesga.org). Within the book we list golf courses within each chapter. The major resorts catering to golfers are the **Samoset** in Rockport, the **Bethel Inn** in Bethel, **Sebasco Harbor Resort** near Bath, the **Country Club Inn** in Rangeley, **Sugarloaf** in the Carrabassett Valley (where you should also inquire about **Moose Meadows**), and **Sunday River golf Club** in Newry.

GORGES Maine has the lion's share of the Northeast's gorges. There are four biggies. The widest is the **Upper Seboeis River Gorge** north of Patten, and the most dramatic, "Maine's Miniature Grand Canyon," is **Gulf Hagas** near the Katahdin Iron Works (see "Katahdin Region"). Both **Kennebec Gorge** and **Ripogenus Gorge** are now popular whitewater rafting routes.

GUIDE SERVICES In 1897 the Maine legislature passed a bill requiring hunting guides to register with the state; the first to do so was Cornelia Thurza Crosby (better known as "Fly Rod" Crosby), whose syndicated column appeared in New York, Boston, and Chicago newspapers at the turn of the 20th century. Becoming a **Registered Maine Guide** entails passing tests in one of several categories, including hunting, fishing, whitewater rafting, canoeing, or sea kayaking—

administered by the Maine Department of Inland Fisheries and Wildlife. There are currently several thousand Registered Maine Guides, but just a few hundred are full-time professional guides. The website of Maine Professional Guides Association, maineguides.org, can give you contact information.

HANDICAPPED ACCESS Within this book, handicapped-accessible lodging, restaurants, and attractions are marked with a wheelchair symbol &. Maine, by the way, offers an outstanding handicapped snow sports program, including cross-country and alpine skiing, snowshoeing, and snowboarding (1-800-639-7770; skimhs.org). Summer programs offer paddling, golf, and cycling.

HIKING For organized trips, see Appalachian Mountain Club. Also see the exciting new Maine Huts and Trails System. While we list hikes we like within most chapters, we strongly suggest acquiring detailed trail guides. In addition to the *AMC Maine Mountain Guide* and the AMC map/guide to trails on Mount Desert, we recommend investing in *50 Hikes in Coastal and Inland Maine* by John Gibson and *50 Hikes in the Maine Mountains* by Cloe Chunn (both from Countryman Press), which offer clear, inviting treks up hills of every size throughout the state. The *Maine Atlas and Gazetteer* (DeLorme) also outlines a number of rewarding hikes. **Map Adventures** (1-800-891-1534; mapadventures.com) makes very readable small maps of bike routes. While hiking is generally associated with inland Maine and with Acadia, in recent years tens of thousands of acres of dramatic shore property have been preserved, much of this traversed by coastal trails detailed in Cobscook Trails, available from the Quoddy Regional Land Trust (qrlt

.org). Also see *Appalachian Trail*; Baxter State Park in "Katahdin Region"; and "Acadia National Park."

HISTORY We tell Maine's rich history through the places that still recall or dramatize it. See *Wabanaki* for sites that tell of the long precolonial history. For traces of early-17th-century settlement, see our descriptions of **Phippsburg**, **Pemaquid**, and **Augusta**. The French and Indian Wars (1675–1760), in which Maine was more involved than most of New England, are recalled in the reconstructed English **Fort William Henry** at Pemaquid and in historical markers scattered around **Castine** (Baron de Saint Castine, a young French nobleman married to a Penobscot Indian princess, controlled the coastal area we now call Down East). A striking house built in 1760 on **Kittery Point** (see "Kittery and the Yorks") evokes Sir William Pepperrell, credited with having captured the fortress at Louisburg from the French. The nonprofit **Museums of York** in **York Village** (oldyork.org) evokes Maine's brief, peaceful colonial period.

In the **Burnham Tavern** at Machias you learn that townspeople captured a British man-of-war on June 1, 1775, the first naval engagement of the Revolution. Other reminders of the Revolution are less triumphant: At the Cathedral Pines in **Eustis** and spotted along Rt. 202 in the **Upper Kennebec Valley**, historical markers tell the poignant saga of Colonel Benedict Arnold's ill-fated 1775 attempt to capture Quebec. Worse: Markers at **Fort George** in Castine detail the ways in which a substantial patriot fleet utterly disgraced itself there. Maine's brush with the British didn't end with the Revolution: The **Barracks Museum** in Eastport tells of British occupation again in 1814.

Climb the 103 steps of the **Portland Observatory** (built in 1807) and hear how Portland ranked second among New England ports, its tonnage based on lumber, the resource that fueled fortunes like those evidenced by the amazingly opulent **Colonel Black Mansion** in Ellsworth and the elegant **Ruggles House** way Down East in Columbia Falls. In 1820 Maine finally became a state (the 23rd), but, as we note in our introduction to "The North Maine Woods," not without a price. The mother state (Massachusetts), her coffers at their usual low, stipulated an even division of all previously undeeded wilderness, and some 10.5 million acres were quickly sold off, vast privately owned tracts that survive today as the unorganized townships.

Plagued in 1839 by boundary disputes with Canada that were ignored in Washington, the new, timber-rich state built its own northern forts (the **Fort Kent Blockhouse** survives). This "Aroostook War" was terminated by the Webster-Ashburton Treaty of 1842. In 1844 the state built massive **Fort Knox** at the mouth of the Penobscot River (see "Bucksport"), just in case. Never entirely completed, it makes an interesting state park. This era was, however, one of great prosperity and expansion within the new state.

As we note in the introduction to "Brunswick and the Harpswells," it can be argued that the Civil War began and ended there. Unfortunately the state suffered heavy losses: Some 18,000 young soldiers from Maine died, as Civil War monuments remind us. The end of the war, however, ushered in a boom decade. Outstanding displays in the **Vinalhaven Historical Society Museum** (see "The Fox Islands") and in the **Deer Isle Granite Museum** in Stonington (see "Deer Isle, Stonington") present the ways that Maine granite fed the demand for monumental public buildings throughout the country, and both schooners and Down Easters (graceful square-rigged vessels) were in great demand (see the **Penobscot Marine Museum** in "Belfast, Searsport" and the **Maine Maritime Museum** in "Bath Area").

In the late 19th century many Maine industries boomed, tourism included. We describe Maine's tourism history in our introduction because it is so colorful, little recognized, and so much a part of what you see in Maine today.

Maine, the Pine Tree State from Prehistory to the Present by Richard Judd, Edwin Churchill, and Joel Eastman (University of Maine Press) is a good, readable history (paperback).

HORSEBACK RIDING Northern Maine Riding Adventures (see "Katahdin Region") offers entire days and overnights as well as shorter stints in the saddle, and special-needs riders are welcomed. We describe other riding options throughout the book.

HORSE RACING Harness racing, in a renaissance since gambling with slots machines has been allowed in Bangor—the earnings subsidize the "purses" or winnings at Maine's two harness racing tracks—can be found at **Scarborough Downs** (207-883-4331), Rt. 1 (exit 6 off the Maine Turnpike), April through November. The **Bangor Raceway** is open late May through late July. Both allow betting on races. Bangor offers slot machines and table games in a casino called **Hollywood Slots Hotel & Raceway**. Many of the agricultural fairs also feature harness racing. Contact the Maine Harness Racing Commission (207-287-3221) for more information, or check the website of the Maine Harness Racing Promotions Board at maineharness racing.com for schedules.

HUNTING Hunters should obtain a summary of Maine hunting and trapping laws from the **Maine Department of Inland Fisheries and Wildlife** (207-287-3371; mefishand wildlife.com). Also see *Guide Services*. Within the book check out "Moosehead Lake Area," "Katahdin Region," "Upper Kennebec," and "Calais." Also see HUNTING at visitmaine.com.

ICE CREAM Here's the scoop on our favorite ice cream sources. **John's Homemade Ice Cream**, Rt. 3, Liberty, puts local berries into its homemade fruit purees. There's also **Scoop Deck**, Rt. 1 in Wells (40 flavors for 27 years); **Round Top** ice cream, Business Rt. 1 in Damariscotta (in business 85 years); **Dorman's Dairy Dream** (closed Sunday; ginger is best), Rt. 1 in Thomaston; **Mount Desert Island Ice Cream**, two shops in Bar Harbor; **Morton's Ice Cream** in Ellsworth. Inland, check out **Shaner's Family**

ICE CREAM BREAK IN RICHMOND

Christina Tree

Dining in South Paris and **Smedberg's Crystal Spring Farm** in Oxford. **Gifford's** (giffordsicecream .com) is a Skowhegan-based creamery that's been in the same family for a century, with a long list of flavors and the coveted "World's Best Vanilla" award. Gelato is now served, to Mainers' delight, at **Gelato Fiasco** in Brunswick and Portland and **Gorgeous Gelato** in Portland.

INNS Each edition of this book has become more selective as the number of places to stay increases. For each edition we personally inspect hundreds of inns and B&Bs. Our choices reflect both what we have seen and the feedback we receive from others; they are not paid listings. The **Maine Innkeepers Association** maintains a website of their members at maineinns .com. Also check listings at visitmaine .com and mainetourism.com.

ISLANDS Most of Maine's 3,250 offshore islands are uninhabited. We describe those that offer overnight lodging—**Chebeague** and **Peaks Islands** in Casco Bay; **Monhegan**, **Vinalhaven**, **North Haven**, **Islesboro**, and **Matinicus** along the Midcoast; and **Isle au Haut**, **Swans Island**, **Campobello**, and **Grand Manan** (New Brunswick) in the Down East section—in varying detail. In Casco Bay the ferry also serves **Cliff Island** (summer rentals are available); **Eagle Island**, former home of Admiral Peary, is served by daily excursion boats from Portland and South Freeport. For information on public and private islands on which low-impact visitors are welcome, contact the **Maine Island Trail Association** (207-596-6456; mita.org). MITA maintains 80 islands and charges $45 for membership, which brings with it a detailed guidebook and the right to land on these islands. **The Island Institute** (207-594-9209; island institute.org) serves as an umbrella organization for the island communities; with the $50 membership come its publications: *Island Journal* and *Working Waterfront*.

KAYAKING Outfitters who offer guided half-day and full-day trips, also overnight and multiday expeditions with camping on Maine islands, are too numerous to be listed here but are described within each relevant chapter. The leading outfitters are **Maine Island Kayak Company** (maine islandkayak.com) on Peaks Island off Portland, **Maine Sport Outfitters** (207-236-7120) in Rockport, **H2Outfitters** (207-833-5257) on Orrs Island, **Old Quarry Ocean Adventures, Inc.** (oldquarry.com) in Deer Isle, **Tidal Transit** (207-633-7140) in Boothbay Harbor, and **Castine Kayak Adventures** (castinekayak.com) in Machias. **L.L. Bean** offers instruction in kayaking at its **Outdoor Discovery Schools** (1-888-552-3261; llbean.com), Rt. 1, Freeport. Their mid-June **Paddle Sport Weekend** offers lectures, demonstrations, classes, and sea tours, when you can try out all the different

KAYAKS AT H2OUTFITTERS, ORRS ISLAND
Christina Tree

boats sold. Also see **maineseakayak guides.com** for a listing of members of the Maine Association of Sea Kayaking Guides & Instructors. *Sea Kayaking Along the New England Coast* by Tamsin Venn (AMC Books) includes detailed kayaking routes from Portland to Cobscook Bay as well as an overall introduction to the sport. Dorcas Miller's comprehensive *Kayaking the Maine Coast: A Paddler's Guide to Day Trips from Kittery to Cobscook* (Countryman Press) is an excellent resource for kayak owners and competent kayakers.

LAKES Maine boasts some 6,000 lakes and ponds, and every natural body of water of more than 10 acres is theoretically available to the public for "fishing and fowling." Access is, however, limited by the property owners. Because paper companies and other land management concerns permit public use (see *Camping*), there is ample opportunity to canoe or fish in solitary waters. **Powerboat owners** should note that most states have reciprocal license privileges with Maine; the big exception is New Hampshire. A milfoil sticker is required by law of all motorized boats using Maine rivers, lakes, ponds, and streams (maine.gov/ifw). For more about the most popular resort lakes in the state, see the Bridgton, Rangeley, Moosehead, and Belgrade Lakes chapters. **State parks on lakes** include **Aroostook** (camping, fishing, swimming; Rt. 1 south of Presque Isle), **Damariscotta Lake State Park** (Rt. 32, Jefferson), **Lake St. George State Park** (swimming, picnicking, fishing; Rt. 3 in Liberty), **Lily Bay State Park** (8 miles north of Greenville), **Peacock Beach State Park** (swimming, picnicking; Richmond), **Peaks-Kenny State Park** (Sebec Lake in Dover-Foxcroft), **Rangeley Lake State Park**

(swimming, camping; Rangeley), **Range Pond State Park** (Poland), **Sebago Lake State Park** (swimming, picnicking, camping; near Bridgton), **Mount Blue State Park** (Weld), and **Swan Lake State Park** (Swanville). Families with small children should note the coastal area lakes surrounded by rental cottages (see *Cottage Rentals*). *Quiet Water Maine Canoe and Kayak Guide* (AMC) suggests tours on 100 ponds and lakes.

LIGHTHOUSES Maine takes pride in its 68 lighthouses. **Portland Head Light** on Cape Elizabeth, completed in 1790, automated in 1990, is now a delightful museum featuring the history of lighthouses. Other lights that feature museums are the **Marshall Point Light** at Port Clyde, **Pemaquid Point** (the lighthouse itself is now open seasonally), **Monhegan Light** on Monhegan Island, **Grindle Point** on

Islesboro, and **West Quoddy Head** Light in Lubec, now part of a state park with a stunning shore path. **Wood Island Lighthouse** off Biddeford Pool is accessible during tours given in summer. At **Burnt Island Light Station** in Boothbay Harbor guides dress as lighthouse keepers from the 1950s and show visitors how life was lived on an isolated island. As lighthouses have become automated, many have been adopted by "Friends," volunteers dedicated to restoring them. The **American Lighthouse Foundation** (ALF) serves as umbrella for the organizations supporting 12 Maine lighthouses; their website (lighthousefoundation .org) is a place to check the current schedule of open house days at Rockland's two distinctive lights—**Owls Head** (1825) and the **Rockland Breakwater Light** (1827), both accessible by land. The site also includes details about **Little River Light**,

---

INFORMATION (OFFICIAL) ABOUT MAINE

The **Maine Office of Tourism** maintains **visitmaine.com** and a 24-hour information line (1-888-624-6345) that connects with a live call center or with a fulfillment clerk who will send you the thick, helpful, four-season guide *Maine Invites You* (accompanied by a Maine highway map). Other useful state publications available on request at this writing include: *The Maine Art Museum Trail*, *Explore Maine by Bike*, and *Maine Performs!* (a guide to performing arts). The *Guide to Inns and Bed & Breakfasts and Camps and Cottages*, a lodging guide, and *Maine Invites You* are published by the **Maine Tourism Association** (207-623-0363; **mainetourism.com**), a member-supported group that maintains well-stocked and -staffed welcome centers at its southern gateway at **Kittery** (207-439-1319) on I-95 northbound (also accessible from Rt. 1); in **Yarmouth** just off Rt. 1 and I-95 (207-846-0833); at the new **West Gardiner Service Plaza**, I-95 exit 102/103 and I-295 exit 51 (207-582-0160); **Hampden** near Bangor on I-95 both northbound and southbound (207-862-6628 or 207-862-6638); in **Calais** (207-454-2211); and in **Houlton** (207-532-6346). There's also an information center near the New Hampshire line on Rt. 302 in **Fryeburg** (207-935-3639). In each chapter we describe the local information sources under *Guidance*.

located on an island at the head of Cutler Harbor, open to the public both for overnights. See the Rockland chapter for details about these and Goose Rocks Lighthouse (beaconpreservation .org), a freestanding "spark-plug-style" light in the Fox Islands Thorofare between Vinalhaven and North Haven; "keeper stays" are available with a donation. **Fort Point Light** at Stockton Springs and **Bass Harbor Head Light** at Bass Harbor are easily accessible by land. Other popular lights include the vintage 1795 **Seguin Island Light Station** (seguinilsand .org) at the mouth of the Kennebec River, accessed by excursion boats (see "Bath Area"); the **Neddick (Nubble) Light** just off Sohier Park in York is within camera range. True lighthouse buffs also make the pilgrimage to **Burnt Harbor Light** on Swan's Island and to **Matinicus Rock**, the setting for several children's books. **Head of Harbor Lighthouse** on the island of Campobello, accessible at low tide, is the ultimate adventure; it is also a prime whale-watching post. Descriptions of all these lights are detailed in their respective chapters. Rockland's

MONHEGAN LIGHTHOUSE

Christina Tree

Gateway Visitor Center is home to the **Maine Lighthouse Museum** (maine lighthousemuseum.com). The ALF also now maintains an **interpretive center** at 464 Main St., Rockland. Check visitmaine.com for more lighthouse information and for open houses, which may include lighthouses in New Brunswick as well as Maine.

LITTER Littering in Maine is punishable by a $100 fine; this applies to dumping from boats as well as other vehicles. Most cans and bottles are redeemable.

LLAMA TREKKING The principle is appealingly simple: The llama carries your gear; you lead the llama. From the **Telemark Inn** (telemarkinn.com), surrounded by semi-wilderness west of Bethel, Steve Crone offers single- and multiday treks. At **Pleasant Bay Bed & Breakfast** (pleasantbay.com) in Addison you can walk the property's waterside trails with the llamas.

L.L. BEAN (llbean.com) was founded in 1912 by Leon Leonwood Bean. The company began as a one-room operation selling a single product, the Maine Hunting Shoe. Ninety out of the first 100 boots Bean sold that year fell apart. He refunded the purchasers' money, establishing a company tradition of guaranteed customer satisfaction still honored today, in Freeport and in stores throughout the United States, Japan, and China. This Maine icon's 200,000-square-foot flagship store in Freeport is open 24 hours a day, 365 days a year. Outdoor clothing and equipment remain the company's mainstay, and they can now also be found in the Hunting and Fishing Store, the Bike, Boat & Ski Store, and the Home Store. **Outdoor Discovery Schools** and **Walk-On Adventures**, ranging from kayaking to fly-fishing, get customers into action year-round. See the Freeport chapter for details.

LOBSTERS It's no secret that Maine's clean, cold waters produce some of the world's tastiest lobster. This hard-shelled crustacean has a long body and five sets of legs, including two large front claws, one large, flat, and heavy and the other smaller, thinner. They don't like light, hiding by day and emerging at night to eat mussels, sea urchins, and crabs. Most are at least seven years old by the time they are caught, because Maine regulates the minimum (also maximum) size of what can sold. The state also prohibits catching pregnant females, and imposes trap limits and license controls. In the 1880s most lobster was canned. Currently 90 percent of what's caught by Maine's 7,500 lobstermen is shipped live out of state. Maine lobster harvests have actually tripled since the early 1990s. Prices also climbed until 2007 but have taken a dramatic dip since then for a variety of reasons. Chief among these, lobstermen will tell you, has been distribution through Canadian processors to large chain restaurants and cruise lines rather than more local and targeted marketing. See lobsterfrommaine.com.

LOBSTERS, EATING Lobster is just another item on the menu elsewhere in the world, but in Maine it's an experience. While elsewhere its appeal may be the fanciful ways it's prepared, in Maine it's the opposite. The shorter the time between a lobster's last crawl—not in a restaurant tank but in its home waters—and your plate, the better. The preferred cooking method: 10 to 15 minutes in boiling seawater for an average-sized (1- to 1½-pound) lobster. Selecting the lobster is a bit more complicated. Choices may include a "cull" (a lobster with one claw), a "chicken" (a female, usually 1 pound, and considered to have the most delicate meat), and "hard shell" or "soft shell." Lobsters molt, usually shedding their shells in summer. The soft shell fills with seawater, which is replaced by new meat as the animal grows and the shell hardens. Which is better depends on whom you talk to. Many prefer "shedders" because the shells are easy to crack and the meat is sweet. These actually don't transport as well as the full and firmly meated "hard shells," so chances are you won't have a chance to sample one outside Maine. How to eat a lobster is a no-holds-barred experience best embarked upon (and always explained) at lobster pounds (read on).

LOBSTER POUNDS AND SHACKS Technically *lobster pounds* refers to the saltwater holding areas in which lobsters are literally impounded, but in tourist talk a lobster pound is a no-frills seaside restaurant serving lobsters and clams steamed in seawater and consumed outside, with a nearby sink for washing off. Short of a lobster bake or boil on a beach, this is *the* way to eat lobster in Maine. We have grouped lobster pounds and shacks, describing them in detail

A LOBSTER ROLL AT QUODDY BAY LOBSTER, EASTPORT

Christina Tree

within each relevant chapter, but here's a quick overview of our favorites. The Pemaquid Peninsula (see "Damariscotta/Newcastle") is especially blessed: Check out **Shaw's** in New Harbor; the nearby Harbor View Restaurant at the **Pemaquid Fisherman's Co-op**; and, in Round Pond, **Muscongus Bay Lobster**, the **Round Pond Lobster Co-op**, and **Broad Cove Marine** in Bremen. Near Rockland look for **Cod End** in Tenants Harbor. **Miller's Lobster Company** on Spruce Head and **Waterman's Beach Lobsters** in South Thomaston are both good. At the tip of the Georgetown Peninsula near Bath, **Five Islands Lobster and Grill** is an all-outdoors classic, and on the Phippsburg Peninsula our pick is the informal **Anna's Water's Edge**. In the Harpswells south of Brunswick the standout is **Allen's Seafood** (just a few waterside picnic tables). Other lobster-eating landmarks include **Robinson's Wharf** at Townsend Gut near Booth-bay, the **Lobster Shack** in Cape Elizabeth near Portland, **Young's Lobster Pound** in East Belfast, the **Lobster Pound** in Lincolnville Beach, and **Union River Lobster Pot** in Ellsworth. At the entrance to Mount Desert Island, the **Trenton Bridge Lobster Pound** has been in George Gascon's family a long time, and the view is great. On Mount Desert, **Beal's** is in Southwest Harbor, and **Thurston's**, which we prefer, is in Bernard. Another great spot worth finding is **Perry's Lobster Shack** on Newbury Neck in Surry, overlooking Acadia. Minutes from Freeport's outlets, the **Harraseeket Lunch & Lobster Company** in South Freeport is a find. On the Southern Coast the **Ogunquit Lobster Pound** on Rt. 1 in Ogunquit is now a full-service restaurant, but waterside **Chauncey Creek** in Kittery is still no-frills (BYO every-thing from salad to wine) and a good value. **Nunan's Lobster Hut** in Cape Porpoise and Fisherman's Catch in Wells Harbor are also the real thing. **Quoddy Bay Lobster Co.** in Eastport gets our vote this time around for the best lobster roll and prices. Owner Sarah Griffin's family operates four fishing boats, and both the quality and prices reflect a lack of middlemen. It's worth noting that in 2011 restaurant prices for a lobster dinner varied wildly, from $8.50 to more than $34.

LOBSTER-BOAT RACES The season's races (**lobsterboatracing.com**) represent one of the best spectator events along the Maine coast. Races begin mid-June in Boothbay Harbor, and the "World's Fastest Lobster Boat Races" are always held on Moosabec Reach between Jonesport and Beals Island on July 4. Other venues are Rockland, Stonington, Harpswell, Friendship, Winter Harbor, and Pemaquid. Participants accumulate points as they go along, and there's an awards ceremony and pig roast in late September.

MAINE GROWN Locally produced items include venison and beeswax as

LOBSTER-BOAT RACING

AmazingMaine.com

well as blueberries, Christmas wreaths, smoked seafood, teas, beer, wine, maple syrup, and lobster stew, to name just a few. The Maine Department of Agriculture (**getrealmaine.com**) publishes several helpful guides. The website lists farmer's markets, orchards, farm stores, and much more.

MAINE HUTS AND TRAILS Check **mainehuts.org** for updates and details on this ambitious Kingfield-based, hut-to-hut trail system that is planned to eventually run from the Mahoosuc Mountains to Moosehead Lake. The first three huts have opened, at Poplar Stream Falls and Flagstaff Lake in the Sugarloaf area; and at Grand Falls,14.2 miles west of the West Forks. These "huts" are fully staffed, offering three meals in a main building, bunkhouses with private and semi-private rooms, and a wood-fired sauna. The connecting trails are 8 feet wide and maintained for nonmotorized use (hiking, mountain biking, and cross-country skiing).

MAINE MADE Maine craftspeople and entrepreneurs produce an ever-increasing variety of specialty foods, handcrafted furniture and furnishings, apparel, toys, and much more (**maine made.com**).

MAINE MAPS Free state maps are available from the **Maine Tourism Association** welcome center, but we are sad to see the way these have deteriorated in recent years. The **AAA map** to Northern New England states is a step up, and within this book we have done our best to detail obvious destinations. Sooner or later, however, serious Maine explorers have to invest in *DeLorme's Maine Atlas and Gazetteer* (delorme.com). See **visit maine.com** for printable maps to specialized trails and http://iceagetrail.un

maine.edu for a glacial geology guide to the *Maine Ice Age Trail Down East.* The Bureau of Parks and Lands (maine.gov/ifw) publishes "Outdoors in Maine," a map worth securing in its glossy, hard-copy form. It lists, locates, and describes state parks and public reserved lands and indicates abandoned railroad corridor trails.

MAINE PUBLIC BROADCASTING Public broadcasting (mpbn.net) offers statewide television and radio. **Maine Public Television** stations are **Channel 10** in Augusta and Presque Isle, **Channel 12** in Orono, **Channel 13** in Calais, and **Channel 26** in Biddeford. Local programming includes *Maine Watch*, highlighting important issues in Maine each week. **Maine's seven public radio stations** can be found on the dial at 90.1 in Portland, 90.9 in Bangor, 91.3 in Waterville, 90.5 in Camden, 89.7 in Calais, 106.1 in Presque Isle, and 106.5 in Fort Kent. Local programming includes *Maine Watch* and *Maine Things Considered*, highlighting state news.

MAINE TURNPIKE For travel conditions and construction updates, phone 1-800-675-PIKE, or check maineturnpike.com. The 100 mile toll highway (I-95) begins in Kittery. Exit numbers will throw you if your map predates 2004. Rather than sequential numbering, they now represent the number of miles from the New Hampshire line. Tolls are a flat rate paid when getting on and sometimes off—the turnpike. Heading north, the first booth is in York. If you remain on the turnpike all the way to Augusta, you will pass through two more booths requiring a toll (New Gloucester and Gardiner). Unless you need to exit at Gray or Lewiston/Auburn, it's cheaper and quicker to follow I-295 rather than the Maine

Turnpike (I-95) north to Augusta. From there on north it's free.

MAPLE SUGARING Maine produces roughly 8,000 gallons of syrup a year, and the **Maine Maple Producers Association** (mainemapleproducers .com) publishes a list of producers who welcome visitors on **Maine Maple Sunday** (also known as Sap Sunday), always the fourth Sunday in March.

MARITIME MUSEUMS Maine Maritime Museum (mainemaritime museum.org) in Bath stands in a class by itself and should not be missed. The **Penobscot Marine Museum** (penobscotmarinemuseum.org) in Searsport is smaller but still substantial, focusing on the merchant captains and their experiences in far corners of the world, featuring yearlong special exhibits.

MOOSE The moose, Maine's state animal, has made a comeback from near extinction in the 1930s and now numbers more than 30,000 in the North Maine Woods alone. Moose are the largest animal found in the wilds of New England. They grow to be 10 feet tall and average 1,000 pounds. The largest member of the deer family, they have a large, protruding upper lip and a distinctive "bell" or "dewlap" dangling from their muzzle.

"Bull" (male) moose have long been prized for their antlers, which grow to a span of up to 6 feet. They are shed in January and grow again. Female moose ("cows") do not grow antlers, and their heads are lighter in color than the bull's. All moose, however, are darker in spring than summer, grayer in winter.

Front hooves are longer than the rear, as are the legs, the better to cope with deep snow and water. In summer they favor wetlands and can usually be found near ponds or watery bogs. They

Lori Duff

MOOSE

also like salt and so tend to create and frequent "wallows," wet areas handy to road salt (the attraction of paved roads).

Moose are vegetarians, daily consuming more than 50 pounds of leaves, grass, and other greenery when they can find it. In winter their diet consists largely of bark and twigs. Mating season is in mid-September until late October. Calves are born in early spring and weigh in at 30 pounds. They grow quickly but keep close to their mothers for an entire year. At best moose live 12 years.

Your chances of spotting one are greatest in early morning or at dusk on a wooded pond or lake or along logging roads. If you are driving through moose country at night, go slowly, because moose typically freeze rather than retreat from oncoming headlights. For details about commercial moose-watching expeditions, check "Rangeley Lakes Region," "Moosehead Lake Area," and the "Katahdin Region." The Moosehead Lake Region Chamber of Commerce sponsors **Moosemainea** mid-May through mid-June, with special events and a huge moose locator map. Suspicious that this promotion coincided with Moosehead's low tourist season, we queried the state's moose expert, who assures us that moose are indeed most visible in late spring. *Warning:* The state records hundreds of often deadly collisions between moose and cars or trucks. The common road sign and bumper sticker reading BRAKE FOR MOOSE means just that. Be extremely wary at dusk when vision is difficult and moose are active. There are about 700 collisions each year that result in four or five deaths.

MUSEUMS Also see *Art Museums*, *Museum Villages*, *Maritime Museums*, and *Wabanaki*. Easily the most undervisited museum in the state, the **Maine State Museum** (mainestatemuseum .org) in Augusta has outstanding displays on the varied Maine landscape and offers historical exhibits ranging from traces of the area's earliest people to exhibits on fishing, agriculture, lumbering, quarrying, and shipbuilding. It's a great place for families. The **Seashore Trolley Museum** (trolley museum.org) in Kennebunkport and the **Owls Head Transportation Museum** (obtm.org) near Rockland are also family finds (inquire about special events at both). Our favorites also include the **Peary-MacMillan Arctic Museum** at Bowdoin College in Brunswick, the **Wilson Museum** (wilsonmuseum.org) in Castine, and the **L. C. Bates Museum** (gwh.org) in Hinckley, a true "cabinet of curiosities" filled with stuffed animals and Indian artifacts and surpassingly lively. The **Lumbermen's Museum in Patten** (lumbermensmuseum.org) and the **Rangeley Lakes Region Logging Museum** are both glimpses of a recently vanished way of life in the North Maine Woods. The **Rangeley Outdoor Sporting Heritage Museum** (rangeleyoutdoormuseum .org) in Oquossoc focuses on the colorful history of fly-fishing in this area. The museum at the **Colonial Pemaquid Restoration in Pemaquid**, pre-

senting archaeological finds from the adjacent early-17th-century settlement, is also unexpectedly fascinating.

MUSIC CONCERT SERIES Bowdoin International Music Festival (bowdoinfestival.org) in Brunswick is the state's most prestigious and varied chamber music series, and the **Kneisel Hall Chamber Music Festival** (kneisel.org) in Blue Hill is its oldest chamber music festival, also still outstanding. The **Mount Desert Festival of Chamber Music** (mtdesertfestival .org), the **Bar Harbor Festival** (bar harbormusicfestival.org), and the **Arcady Music Festival** (arcady.org) are all highlights of the season on Mount Desert. The **Sebago/Long Lakes Region Chamber Music Festival** (207-583-6747) at the **Deertrees Theatre and Cultural Center** in Harrison is noteworthy, and **Bay Chamber Concerts** (baychamber concerts.org) present a summer series in Rockport and Rockland. The **Machias Bay Chamber Concerts** are held in the Machias Congregational church. There is, of course, the **Portland Symphony Orchestra** (portlandsymphony.org), which has a summertime pops series, and the

VINALHAVEN HISTORICAL SOCIETY

Christina Tree

Bangor Symphony Orchestra (bangorsymphony.com). Music lovers should also take note of the **American Folk Festival** (americanfolkfestival .com) the last weekend in August in Bangor, the **Lincoln Arts Festival** (lincolnartsfestival.org) of classical and choral music held throughout the Boothbay Harbor region in summer months, and the **Bluegrass Festival at Thomas Point Beach** in August. **SummerKeys** (summerkeys.com) offers a series of summer Wednesday-evening concerts in Lubec. Also see maineperforms.com.

MUSIC SCHOOLS Outstanding summer programs include the Bowdoin International Festival (summermusic .org); **Kneisel Hall in Blue Hill** (kneisel.org); Monteux School of Conducting in Hancock (monteuxschool .org); **New England Music Camp** in Oakland (nemusiccamp.com); and **Maine Jazz Camp** (mainejazzcamp .com) at the University of Maine, Farmington. **SummerKeys** (summer keys.com) in Lubec specializes in piano but welcomes students of all levels in a variety of instruments.

NATURE PRESERVES, COASTAL Within each chapter we describe these under *Green Space* or *To Do—Hiking*. On the Southern Coast the **Wells National Estuarine Research Reserve** at Laudholm Farm (wells reserve.org) includes two barrier beaches. On Casco Bay the Maine Audubon (maineaudubon.org) headquarters at **Gilsland Farm Audubon Center in Falmouth** offer 65 acres crossed by nature trails; Maine Audubon also offers canoe and kayak rentals, guided tours, and many summer programs at **Scarborough Marsh Audubon Center** as well as trails; it also maintains picnic sites at Mast Landing Audubon Sanctuary in

Freeport. In Midcoast **the Boothbay Region Land Trust** (bbrlt.org) and the **Damariscotta River Association** (draclt.org) maintain some exceptional preserves, and Camden Hills State Park includes miles of little-used trails with magnificent views. Down East in the Blue Hill area, the 1,350-acre **Holbrook Island Sanctuary** in West Brooksville is a beauty, and on Deer Island the **Island Heritage Trust** (islandheritagetrust.org) maintains a number of exceptional waterside properties. In Ellsworth 40-acre **Birdsacre** (birdsacre.com) includes nature trails and a museum honoring ornithologist Cordelia Stanwood. **Acadia National Park** (nps.gov/acad), the state's busiest preserve, offers 120 miles of hiking paths on Mount Desert, also trails on **Isle au Haut** and at **Schoodic Point**. Schoodic Mountain north of Sullivan is one of the area's most spectacular hikes. Right across the line in Washington County, Steuben's **Maine Coastal Islands National Wildlife Refuge** (fws.gov/northeast/maine coastal) is an 8,100-acre preserve with 49 offshore islands. Near Jonesport, **Great Wass Island** (accessible by road from Jonesport), maintained by the Maine Chapter of The Nature Conservancy, is a beautiful preserve with a 2-mile shore trail. **Western Head**, near Machias, is now maintained by Maine Coast Heritage Trust; Maine's Bureau of Parks and Lands maintains a 5.5-mile **Bold Coast Trail** along the high bluffs west of Cutler; **West Quoddy Light State Park** includes a splendid 2-mile shore trail. Roosevelt Campobello International Park also includes many miles of shore paths, and **Cobscook Bay State Park** (see "Eastport and Cobscook Bay") and **Moosehorn National Wildlife Refuge** (see "Calais and the St. Croix Valley") also offer hiking trails. The Nature Conservancy has protected more than a million acres in Maine; see the Maine chapter's site for details (nature.org/maine). The **Maine Coast Heritage Trust** (mcht.org) also publishes useful brochures about its holdings.

NATURE PRESERVES, INLAND

In the Rangeley area the **Rangeley Lakes Heritage Trust** (rlht.org) has preserved more than 12,300 acres, including 45 miles of lake and river frontage and 10 islands. In the Sugarloaf area the **Maine Bureau of Parks and Lands** now offers detailed maps to trails within the 35,000-acre **Bigelow Preserve**. Within each chapter we describe nature preserves along with state parks under *Green Space* or *To Do—Hiking*. Among our favorites are trails to the top of **Mount Kineo** overlooking Moosehead Lake, and **Gulf Hagas**, a remote part of the Appalachian Trail corridor, jointly owned and managed by the AT Conference and the National Park Service. In recent years the **Appalachian Mountain Club** (outdoors.org) has acquired 66,500 acres in the **Moosehead Area** and partners with state agencies and other nonprofits to maintain recreational trails and campsites within a 63-mile corridor stretching from the Katahdin Iron Works north to **Baxter State Park** (baxterstateparkauthority.com). One of the largest and least known woodland preserves surrounds the chain of lakes in Washington County, extending into New Brunswick. The **Grand Lake Stream**–based **Downeast Lakes Land Trust** (downeastlakes.org) has worked with other conservation groups to protect some 445 miles of shore along 60 lakes on both sides of the border, more than a million contiguous acres in this region. The Bureau of Parks and Lands website (parksandlands.com) is helpful in locating public preserves scattered throughout the state, including the North Maine Woods.

OYSTERS Feasting on raw oysters is a 2,000-year-old tradition in Maine, as evidenced by heaps of empty oyster shells ("middens") still to be seen in Damariscotta. By the mid-1800s native oyster beds had all but disappeared, but thanks to seeding methods these sweet and salty oysters are back. Check out **Pemaquid Oyster Co.**, **Glidden Point Sea Farm**, **Mook Sea Farms**, **Muscongus Bay Aquaculture**, and **Norumbega Oyster Co.**

PARKS AND FORESTS, NATIONAL

Acadia National Park (207-288-3338; nps.gov/acad), which occupies roughly half of Mount Desert Island, plus scattered areas on Isle au Haut, Little Cranberry Island, Baker Island, Little Moose Island, and Schoodic Point, adds up to more than

CHRIS AND JOHN DAVIS SERVE UP PEMAQUID OYSTERS

Christina Tree

40,000 acres offering hiking, ski touring, swimming, horseback riding, canoeing, and a variety of guided nature tours and programs, as well as a scenic 27-mile driving tour. Note that an entry fee is charged to drive the Park Loop Road. Camping is by reservation only at Blackwoods, and first come, first served at Seawall. The **White Mountain National Forest** encompasses 41,943 acres in Maine, including five campgrounds under the jurisdiction of the Evans Notch Ranger District (207-824-2134).

PARKS, STATE The **Maine Bureau of Parks and Lands** (207-287-3821; parksandlands.com) can send you "Outdoors in Maine"—a map/guide to each of the 32 parks, 12 of which offer camping facilities. We have described parks as they appear geographically. In 2011 day-use fees are between $3 and $6.50 per adult for non-Maine-residents, $2–4.50 for residents; all children 2–12 are $1; all Maine seniors are free, and others pay $1–2. Seasonal park passes are $35 per individual, $70 per vehicle, $30 for seniors (maine stateparkpass.com). **Twelve state parks offer camping** (campwithme .com); the fee per site is $11–15 for residents, $19–25 for nonresidents.

BUREAU OF PARKS AND LANDS LOGO

Maine Office of Tourism

BAXTER STATE PARK

There is an additional fee for trailer hookups in the two parks that now offer them, Camden Hills and Sebago, also a $2-per-night reservation fee for camping. Call the reservations hotline (within Maine, 1-800-332-1501; from out of state, 207-624-9950) at least two days in advance to make a campground reservation, or use the real-time online registration system, which opens at the beginning of February (campground.reservations@maine.gov). There have been substantial improvements in many state park facilities—such as bathhouses and wheelchair accessibility—in recent years. Check the website for details, as well as for current programs and events.

PETS Throughout this book, lodgings and selected other places that accept pets are indicated with the dog-paw symbol 🐾. Most lodgings require a reservation and an additional fee. Always call ahead when traveling with your pet.

PLOYE This traditional Acadian pancake/flat bread, as delicate as a crêpe, is a specialty throughout the St. John Valley. The **Bouchard Family Farm** (1-800-239-3237) produces a line of French Canadian food products.

POPULATION 1,328,361, according to the 2010 census. It has grown 4.2 percent since 2000, enough to hold on to its two congresswomen.

PUFFIN-WATCHING Atlantic puffins are smaller than you might expect. They lay just one egg a year and were almost extinct at the turn of the 20th century, when the only surviving birds nested on either Matinicus Rock or Machias Seal Island. Since 1973 Audubon has helped reintroduce nesting on Eastern Egg Rock in Muscongus Bay, 6 miles off Pemaquid Point, and since 1984 there has been a similar puffin-restoration project on Seal Island in outer Penobscot Bay, 6 miles from Matinicus Rock. The best times for viewing puffins are June and July or the first few days of August. The only place you are allowed to view the birds on land is **Machias Seal Island**, where visitors are permitted in limited numbers. Contact Andrew Patterson (**boldcoast.com**) in Cutler. With the help of binoculars (a must), you can also view the birds from the water via tours with Cap'n Fish (**mainepuffin.com**) from Boothbay Harbor, Hardy Boat Cruises (**hardy**

Yogi Morgan

SEE PUFFINS UP CLOSE ON MACHIAS SEAL ISLAND

boat.com) from New Harbor, and the Monhegan Boat Line (**monhegan boat.com**) from Port Clyde. The **Hog Island Audubon Camp** (maine audubon.org) also offers guided boat cruises to Eastern Egg Rock. For those who can't make time to get out on the water, the **Project Puffin Visitor Center** (projectpuffin.org) in Rockland uses live-streaming mini cams and audio to provide a virtual visit with nesting puffins on Seal Island.

RAIL TRAVEL See *Amtrak* for passenger service on the Downeaster from Boston to Portland. The seasonal **Maine Eastern Railroad** runs between Brunswick and Rockland; see *Railroad Excursions.*

RAILROAD EXCURSIONS AND MUSEUMS Boothbay Railway Village (railwayvillage.org) delights small children and offers railroad exhibits in its depot. The **Maine Eastern Railroad** (maineeasternrailroad.com) offers 54-mile seasonal runs between Rockland and Brunswick, stopping in Bath and Wiscasset. It's a beautiful trip along the coast in plush 1940s and '50s coaches and a dining car, pulled by a 1950s diesel electric engine. Check the website for current information. In

Bill Davis

Portland the **Maine Narrow Gauge Railroad Company & Museum** (mngrr.org) combines displays and a 3-mile shoreside excursion. Inland, the **Sandy River & Rangeley Lakes Railroad** (srrl-rr.org) in Phillips operates short excursions several times a month, June through October. Near Wiscasset the **Waterville Farmington Railway Museum** (wwfry.org) at Sheepscot Station, Alna, preserves the history of another 2-foot narrow-gauge railroad with seasonal 37-minute roundtrip runs on 2.6 miles of track; it displays an 1891 2-footer locomotive billed as the oldest in the United States. Rail buffs also find their way to **Maine Central Model Railroad** (207-497-2255) in Jonesport.

RATES Please do not regard any prices listed in *Lodging* as set in stone. Call ahead to confirm them. Rates are those in effect as we go to press. *MAP* stands for "Modified American Plan": breakfast and dinner included in rate. *AP* stands for "American Plan": three meals included in rate. *EP* stands for "European Plan": no meals. *B&B* stands for "bed & breakfast": Breakfast is included.

MAINE EASTERN RR

Christina Tree

RENYS Billed as "A Maine Adventure," and as "a part of the state's culture since 1949," Renys (renys.com) is a family-owned chain of 14 discount stores that, like hermit crabs, occupy spaces vacated by previous owners. The **Farmington** Renys fills a former music hall, the **Madison** space was an opera house, and in **Damariscotta** Renys Underground was a bowling alley. Several Renys fill former supermarkets, and in Bath, Gardiner, Dexter, and Damariscotta the shops effectively fill the void left by small-town clothing and department stores. Listing what Renys stocks is harder than saying what it doesn't. There are linens and shoes, name-brand clothing and toys, electronics, clamming and camping gear, stationery, Maine-made products, and always surprises. Renys has recently become less about odd lots (that niche is now filled by **Marden's**, Maine's other discount chain), and more about quality, service, and good value. For big-time discounts hit any Renys on the first Saturday in November at 6 AM. The biggest discounts are during the first hour, with diminishing but still substantial savings every hour until 9 AM.

ROCKHOUNDING Maine is a famous source of pink and green **tourmaline**, especially plentiful in the Bethel area; see that chapter for a complete listing of mine tours and rockhounding activities. Thanks to the high price of gold, prospectors are back panning Maine streambeds. The **Maine Geological Survey** (207-287-2801) offers an online introduction to Maine minerals and their sources.

SAILING Windjammers and yacht charter brokers aside, there are a limited number of places that will rent small sailing craft, fewer that will offer lessons to adults and children alike.

Christina Tree

RENYS

Linekin Bay Resort (linekinbay resort.com) in Boothbay Harbor is billed as the only surviving full-service sailing resort on the East Coast. Qualified sailors can rent Rhodes 19 foot sailboats, and sailing lessons are offered for all abilities. The **Mansell Boat Rental Company** (mansellboat rentals.com), Southwest Harbor, rents sailboats by the day or longer. **Buck's Harbor Marine** (207-326-8839), South Brooksville, rents sail- and motorboats. Inquire about sailing lessons. Learn-to-sail programs are offered by **WoodenBoat School** (woodenboatschool.com) in Brooklin, the **Camden Yacht Club** (camden yachtclub.org), which offers a junior sailing program to nonmembers, and **Bay Island Sailing School** (sailme .com) based in Rockland. **Sawyer's Sailing School** (sawyerssailingschool .com), geared to adults, is based at the Dolphin Marina in Harpswell. **Old Quarry Ocean Adventures** (old quarry.com) in Deer Isle rents a variety of sailboats and offers lessons. Other rentals and daysails are listed throughout the book. (Also see *Windjammers*.)

SCENIC HIGHWAYS AND BYWAYS Books have been written

about Maine's most scenic roads. Those officially recognized as **National Scenic Byways** include **the Old Canada Road**, 78 miles of Rt. 201, from Solon north to the Canadian border; the 52 glorious miles of Rt. 17 from Byron on up through **Rangeley Lakes**; and the 29 miles of Rt. 1 from Sullivan to **Schoodic**. Check the excellent **exploremaine.org** website maintained by Maine DOT for details about nine more official "Maine Scenic Highways" and the Acadia Scenic Byway, an "All-American Road." Within each chapter we describe our own picks under *Scenic Drives*.

SHAKERS Sabbathday Lake Shaker Village and Museum (shaker .lib.me.us) in New Gloucester is the country's last functioning Shaker religious community. Visitors are welcome to walk the grounds, take seasonal tours of 6 of the 18 existing structures on 1,800 acres, visit the museum reception center and gift shop, and attend seasonal Sunday services in the meetinghouse. Frequent workshops and special events are scheduled March through December. *Note:* With the exception of service dogs, no pets are allowed in the village, not even in a car.

LINEKIN BAY RESORT SPECIALIZES IN SAILING LESSONS AND RENTALS

Bill Davis

SKIING, CROSS-COUNTRY Some 20 cross-country ski centers are listed at **skimaine.com**—and there are more. The **Sugarloaf Outdoor Center** is the state's largest commercial Nordic network. **Bethel**, with three trail networks (Sunday River Inn, Bethel Inn, and Carter's Farm X-C Ski Center), offers varied terrain. **Rangeley Lakes Trails Center** at Lower Saddleback Mountain offers 55 groomed kilometers, and the town of **Millinocket** maintains extensive trail networks that enjoy dependable snow cover. The **Birches Resort** (birches .com) in Rockwood is a major cross-country destination. The AMC-owned **Little Lyford**, **Medawisla**, and **Gorman Chairback Lodges and Cabins** near Greenville offer guided lodge-to-lodge tours (details at outdoors.org) in conjunction with **West Branch Pond Camps**. **Chesuncook Lake House** (chesuncooklakehuse.com), **Nahmakanta Lake Camps** (nahmakanta .com), and **Katahdin Lake Wilderness Camps** (katahdinlakewilderness camps.com) all cater to cross-country skiers. Also see *Maine Huts and Trails* in the Sugarloaf area for progress on an evolving system maintained year-round

SUGARLOAF

exclusively for nonmotorized traffic with full-service, winterized huts.

SKIING, DOWNHILL Ski Maine Association (207-773-SNOW; ski maine.com) provides information about 18 mountains in Maine. **Sugarloaf** in the Carrabassett Valley and **Sunday River** in the Bethel area vie for the title of Maine's number one ski resort. The two are very different and actually complement each other well. Sugarloaf is a high, relatively remote mountain with New England's only lift-serviced snowfields on its summit and a classy, self-contained condo village at its base. Sunday River, just an hour north of Portland, consists of eight adjoining (relatively low-altitude) mountains; snowmaking is a big point of pride, and facilities include a variety of slope-side condo lodgings. **Saddleback Mountain** in Rangeley has an enthusiastic following and is currently undergoing its first major development in decades. **Mount Abram** (in the Bethel area) is a true family area with a strong ski school and some fine runs. **Shawnee Peak** in Bridgton, in business since 1938, is a medium-sized, family-geared area that offers night as well as day skiing. The **Camden Snow Bowl** in Camden is small but satisfying.

SKIERS NEAR GORMAN CHAIRBACK AMC CAMP

Kevin Bruenig, courtesy AMC

SNOWMOBILING Maine has reciprocal agreements with nearly all states and provinces; for licensing and rules, contact the **Department of Inland Fisheries and Wildlife** (maine.gov /ifw). You can renew a registration online. The **Maine Snowmobile Association** (MSA; mesnow.com) represents more than 290 clubs and maintains some 14,000 miles of an ever-expanding cross-state trail network. **Aroostook County**, given its reliable snow conditions, is an increasingly popular destination. The **Upper Kennebec Valley** and **Jackman** as well as the entire **Moosehead, Katahdin**, and **Rangeley Lakes** areas are snowmobiling meccas.

Maine Office of Tourism

SNOWMOBILING

SPORTING CAMPS The Maine sporting camp—a gathering of log cabins around a log hunting lodge by a remote lake or stream—is a distinctly Maine phenomenon that began appearing in the 1860s. "Sports" (guests) were met by a guide at a train or steamer and paddled up lakes and rivers to a camp. With the advent of floatplanes, many of these camps became more accessible (see *Air Services*), and the proliferation of private logging roads has put most within reach of sturdy vehicles. True sporting camps still cater primarily to anglers in spring and hunters in fall, but since summer is neither a hunting season nor a prime fishing season, they all host families who just want to be in the woods. True sporting camps still include a central lodge in which guests are served all three meals; boats and guide service are available. The **Maine Sporting Camp Association** (maine sportingcamps.com) maintains lists and links with some 50 members.

THEATER, SUMMER The **Ogunquit Playhouse** (ogunquitplayhouse .org) is among the oldest and most

prestigious summer theaters in the country. Along the South Coast also check out the **Arundel Barn Playhouse** (arundelbarnplayhouse.com) in Kennebunk, the **Hackmatack Playhouse** in Berwick (hackmatack.org), and The **Legacy Theater Company** (legacytheatercompany.org) at Thornton Academy in Saco. In Portland note the **Portland Stage Company** (portlandstage.com); in Brunswick the **Maine State Music Theater at Bowdoin College** (msmt.org) is a big draw. Farther along the coast look for the **Camden Civic Theatre** (camden civictheater.com), based in the refurbished Opera House in Camden, the **Belfast Maskers** in Belfast (belfast maskerstheater.com), the **Acadia Repertory Theatre** in Somesville (acadiarep.com), and **Downriver Theater Productions** in Machias. Inland you'll find the **Theater at Monmouth** (theateratmonmouth.org), **Lakewood Theater** in Skowhegan (lakewoodtheater.org), **Deer-Trees Theatre** in Harrison (deertrees theatre.com), and **Celebration Barn Theater** in South Paris (celebration barn.com). All are detailed in their respective chapters.

THEATER, YEAR-ROUND Penobscot Theatre Company in Bangor offers a variety of winter productions (penobscottheatre.org), as do **The Portland Players** (portlandplayers .org) and the **Portland Stage Company** (portlandstage.com). Year-round venues include the **Camden Civic Theatre** in Camden (camdencivic theater.com), the **Waldo Theatre** in Waldoboro, the **Public Theatre** (thepublictheatre.org) in Auburn, and **City Theater** (citytheater.org) in Biddeford. Most universities and colleges also offer performances throughout the school year. Also see maineperforms.com.

TRAFFIC AND HIGHWAY TRAVEL TIPS Maine coastal travel has its sticky wickets. By far the worst is the backup at the tolls at the entrance to the Maine Turnpike as well as those not far south in New Hampshire. Get E-ZPass (ezpassmaineturn pike.com), or avoid passing through these tolls, if at all possible, at obvious peak travel times. Within their respective chapters we suggest ways around bottlenecks at Brunswick, Wiscasset, and Camden. Note that it takes no longer to reach a Down East than a Midcoast destination, thanks to the way the highways run. The quickest way to reach Rockland or Camden from points south is up I-295 to Brunswick and then coastal Rt. 1. Belfast and destinations east through the Blue Hill Peninsula, however, can be reached in roughly the same time by taking I-295 to Augusta and then Rt. 3 to coastal Rt. 1. You can reach Ellsworth (gateway to Mount Desert and points east) in equal time by traveling I-295 to I-95 to Bangor and then heading down Rt. 1A. For current information on road conditions and delays dial 511 in Maine, call 1-866-282-7578 from out of state,

or check 511maine.gov. Also see maineperforms.com.

TRAFFIC RULES Seat belts are the law in Maine, and turns on a red light are permitted—unless otherwise stated—after a stop to check for oncoming traffic. **Headlights** should be turned on with windshield wipers.

WABANAKI means "people of the dawn." Native Americans have lived in Maine and eastern Canada for many thousands of years, judging from shell heaps and artifacts found in areas ranging from the coastal Damariscotta/ Boothbay and Blue Hill areas to the Rangeley Lakes in western Maine. Ancient pictographs can be found on the Kennebec River and around Machias Bay. An excellent exhibit, *12,000 Years in Maine*, in the **Maine State Museum** (mainestatemuseum .org) in Augusta, depicts the distinct periods in this history and features the Red Paint People, named for the red pigments found sprinkled in their burial sites. They flourished between 5,000 and 3,800 years ago and are said to have fished from large, sturdy boats. The **Abbe Museum** (abbemuseum .org) in Bar Harbor is dedicated to showcasing the cultures of Maine's Wabanaki, the less than 7,000 members of the Penobscot, Passamaquoddy, Micmac, and Maliseet tribes who live in the state. The permanent collection of 50,000 objects ranges from 10,000-year-old artifacts to exquisite basketry and craftswork from several centuries. The time line begins with the present and draws visitors back through 10,000 years and to its core, "the Circle of Four Directions." Two North Maine Woods sites are said to have been sacred: the **Katahdin Iron Works**, in Brownville Junction, source of the pigments found in burial sites; and **Mount Kineo** on Moosehead Lake, source of the flintlike volcanic stone widely used for arrowheads. Early French missions at Mount Desert and Castine proved battlegrounds between the French and English, and by the end of the 17th century thousands of Wabanaki had retreated either to Canada or to the Penobscot community of Old Town and to Norridgewock, where Father Sebastian Rasle insisted that the Indian lands "were given them of God, to them and their children forever, according to the Christian oracles." The mission was obliterated (it's now a pleasant roadside rest area), and by the end of the French and Indian Wars only four tribes remained. Of these the **Micmacs** and **Maliseets** made the unlucky choice of siding with the Crown and were subsequently forced to flee (but communities remain near the Aroostook County–Canadian border in Presque Isle and Littleton, respectively). That left only the **Penobscots** and the **Passamaquoddys**.

In 1794 the Penobscots technically deeded most of Maine to Massachusetts in exchange for the 140 small islands in the Penobscot River, and in 1818 Massachusetts agreed to pay them an assortment of trinkets for the land. In 1820, when Maine became a

state, a trust fund was set aside but ended up in the general treasury. The state's three reservations (two belonging to the Passamaquoddys and one to the Penobscots) were termed "enclaves of disfranchised citizens bereft of any special status." Indians loomed large in Maine lore and greeted 19th-century tourists as fishing and hunting guides in the woods and as snowshoe and canoe makers and guides, while Native American women sold their distinctive sweetgrass and ash-splint baskets and beadwork at the many coastal and inland summer hotels and boardinghouses.

In 1972 the Penobscots and Passamaquoddys sued to reclaim 1.5 million acres of land allegedly illegally appropriated by the state, and in 1980 they received an $80.6 million settlement, which they have since invested in a variety of enterprises. The Indian Island Reservation in Old Town is presently home to 500 of the tribe's 2,000 members, and the **Penobscot Nation Museum** (penobscotnation .org/museum) there, while small, is open regularly and well worth checking. The Passamaquoddy tribe today numbers 3,369 members, roughly divided between the reservations at **Indian Township** on Schoodic Lake and at **Sipayik**, also known as **Pleasant Point** (wabanaki.com), near Eastport, site of the **Indian Ceremonial Days**, held annually in mid-August to celebrate Passamaquoddy culture and climaxing in dances in full regalia. Exhibits at the **Wabanaki Culture Center** (207-454-2126) in Calais currently focus on Passamaquoddy history and craftsmanship, including a 20-foot vintage-1872 birch-bark canoe, but plans call for the story of all four Wabanaki tribes to be told here. There is also a small **Passamaquoddy Cultural Heritage Center** in Indian Township, Princeton, north on Rt. 1.

DISPLAY OF PASSAMAQUODDY BASKETS AT THE WABANAKI CULTURE CENTER, CALAIS

Christina Tree

The 1,000-member Aroostook Band of Micmacs are headquartered in Presque Isle; tribal offices for the 800-member Houlton Band of Maliseet Indians are in Littleton. The **Hudson Museum** at the University of Maine–Orono has a small display on local tribes. Members of all four tribes form the **Maine Indian Basketmakers Alliance** (maineindianbaskets.org), which publishes *Wabanaki Cultural Resource Guide*, and makes and markets traditional ash-splint and sweet-grass baskets at special sales events, held in July in Bar Harbor and December at the University of Maine–Orono. The **L. C. Bates Museum** in Hinckley displays ancient artifacts and 19th- and early-20th-century craftsmanship, and **Nowetah's American Indian Museum** in New Portland (see "Sugarloaf and the Carrabassett Valley") displays a large collection of authentic basketry.

WATERFALLS The following are all easily accessible to families with small children: **Snow Falls Gorge** off Rt. 26 in West Paris offers a beautiful cascade (ask for directions at Perham's Gem Store); **Small's Falls** on the Sandy River, off Rt. 4 between Rangeley and Phillips, has a picnic spot with a trail beside the falls; **Jewell Falls** is located in the Fore River Sanctuary in the heart of Portland; **Step Falls** is on Wight Brook in Newry off Rt. 26; and just up the road in Grafton Notch State Park is **Screw Auger Falls**, with its natural gorge. Another Screw Auger Falls is in Gulf Hagas (see *Gorges*), off the Appalachian Trail near the Katahdin Iron Works Rd., north of Brownville Junction. **Kezar Falls**, on the Kezar River, is best reached via Lovell Rd. from Rt. 35 at North Waterford. An extensive list of "scenic waterfalls" is detailed in the *Maine Atlas and*

Gazetteer (DeLorme). Check out 90-foot **Moxie Falls** at The Forks.

WEDDINGS At this writing no one conduit exists for information about the ever-increasing number of services (photographers, musicians, carriage operators, caterers, and florists, as well as inns and venues) geared to helping couples wed near Maine water. Several chambers of commerce, notably York, Kennebunkport, Boothbay, and Camden, are particularly helpful. Within the book we note properties that specialize in weddings with our ring symbol ♂.

WHALE-WATCHING Each spring humpback, finback, and minke whales migrate to New England waters, where they remain until fall, cavorting, it sometimes seems, for the pleasure of excursion boats. One prime gathering spot is **Jefferies Ledge**, about 20 miles off Kennebunkport, and another is the **Bay of Fundy**. For listings of whale-watch cruises, see "The Kennebunks," "Portland Area," "Bar Harbor," and "Washington County." The East Quoddy (Campobello) and West Quoddy (Lubec) Lighthouses are also prime viewing spots. Whales are sighted more often than not on the ferry ride from Black Harbor, New Brunswick, to the island of Grand Manan, another hub for whale-watch cruises.

WHITEWATER RAFTING In Maine this phenomenon's beginnings coincided with the last log drive on the Kennebec River. Logs were still hurtling through Kennebec Gorge on that day in spring 1976 when fishing guide Wayne Hockmeyer (and eight bear hunters from New Jersey) plunged through it in a rubber raft. At the time Hockmeyer's rafting know-how stemmed solely from having seen *River of No Return*, in which Robert

WHITEWATER RAFTING

Northern Outdoors

Mitchum steered Marilyn Monroe down the Salmon River.

Hockmeyer went on to found **Northern Outdoors**, and there are now a dozen outfitters positioned around The Forks, near the confluence of the Kennebec and Dead Rivers, all skilled in negotiating the rapids through nearby 12 mile-long Kennebec Gorge. Numbers on the river are now strictly limited, and rafts line up to take their turns riding the releases—which gush up to 8,000 cubic feet of water per second—from the Harris Hydroelectric Station above the gorge. Several rafting companies—notably Northern Outdoors (northern outdoors.com), **Crab Apple** (crab appleinc.com), and **Magic Falls Rafting Company** (magicfalls.com)—have built fairly elaborate base facilities in and around The Forks. **New England Outdoor Center** (noec.com) and **Three Rivers White Water** (three-rivers.com) have established food and lodging facilities for patrons who want to raft the Penobscot near Baxter State Park. *Note:* Online promotions project images in which all outfitters seem to offer the same experience and to differ only in price. This isn't true. Read about the real differences among out-

fitters in the "Upper Kennebec" and "Katahdin" chapters.

WINDJAMMERS In 1936 artist Frank Swift outfitted a few former fishing and cargo schooners to carry passengers around the islands of Penobscot Bay. At the time these old vessels were moored in every harbor and cove, casualties of progress. Swift's fleet grew to include more than a dozen vessels. Competitors also prospered throughout the 1950s, but the entire windjammer fleet appeared doomed by rigorous Coast Guard licensing requirements in the 1960s. The 1970s and 1980s saw the rise of a new breed of windjammer captain. Almost every one of those now sailing has built or restored the vessel he or she commands or acquired it from the captain who did. Members of the current Maine windjammer fleet range from the *Stephen Taber* and the *Lewis R. French*, both originally launched in 1871, to the *Heritage*, launched in 1983.

Former *Taber* co-captain Ellen Barnes recalls her own discovery of windjammers: "No museums had gobbled up these vessels; no cities had purchased them to sit at piers as public relations gimmicks. These vessels were the real thing, plying their trade as

PARADING

Bob Angell and the Maine Windjammer Association

they had in the past with one exception: The present-day cargo was people instead of pulpwood, bricks, coal, limestone, and granite."

Choosing which vessel to sail on is the most difficult part of a windjammer cruise. All have ship-to-shore radios and sophisticated radar; some offer more in the way of creature comforts; some are known for their food. Windjammers accommodate between 6 and 40 passengers. Excessive drinking is discouraged on all the vessels, and guests are invited to bring musical instruments. Children under 14 are permitted only on some. In relevant chapters we have described each vessel in the kind of detail we devote to individual inns. Questions you might like to ask in making your reservation: (1) What's the bunk arrangement? Double bunks and cabins for a family or group do exist. (2) What's the cabin ventilation? Some vessels offer cabins with portholes or windows that open. (3) What's the rule about children? Several schooners schedule special family cruises with activities geared to kids. (4) What's the extent of weatherproof common space? It varies widely. (5) Is smoking allowed? (6) Is there evening entertainment of any kind? The Maine Windjammer Association (1-800-807-WIND; **sailmainecoast.com**) represents most windjammers.

WINE AND SPIRITS Prohibition began in Maine, and before Bob and Kathe Bartlett could open Maine's first winery, in 1982, they had to get the law changed. Just off Rt. 1 in Gouldsboro, **Bartlett Maine Estate Winery** (bartlettwinery.com) offers tastings of its prizewinning fruit wines utilizing Maine apples, blueberries, raspberries, and honey as well as regional pears and peaches, and has added **Spirits of Maine** to its name, pear eau de vie

Bill Davis

TASTING ROOM SIGN

and Calvados-style apple brandy to its labels. Currently the website **maine winetrail.com** lists upward of 20 visitor-friendly wineries, utilizing a variety of hardy grapes as well as fruit. **Cellardoor Vineyard** (mainewine .com) in Lincoln offers wine tastings in their 18th-century barn beside their vineyard in Lincoln and at "The Villa," Rt. 1 in Rockport. **Breakwater Vineyards** (breakwatervinerads.com) in Owls Head has planted some 3,000 vines; its tasting room commands a glorious view of Penobscot Bay. In this area also check out **Oyster River Winegrowers** (oysterriverwinegrowers .com) in Thomaston; in Union, **Sweetgrass Farm Winery and Distillery** (sweetgrasswinery.com) uses fruit to craft gins and rum as well as fruit brandies and wine; **Savage Oakes** (savageoakes.com) produces apple and grape wines. **Blacksmiths Winery** (blacksmithwinery.com) on Rt. 302 in South Casco produces both prizewinning grape and fruit wines. We also recommend **Cold River Vodka** (coldrivervodka.com), which has won national recognition in the few years since brothers from an Aroostook farm found a new use for their potatoes. The distillery/tasting room is on Rt. 1 in Freeport.

Southern Coast

Christina Tree

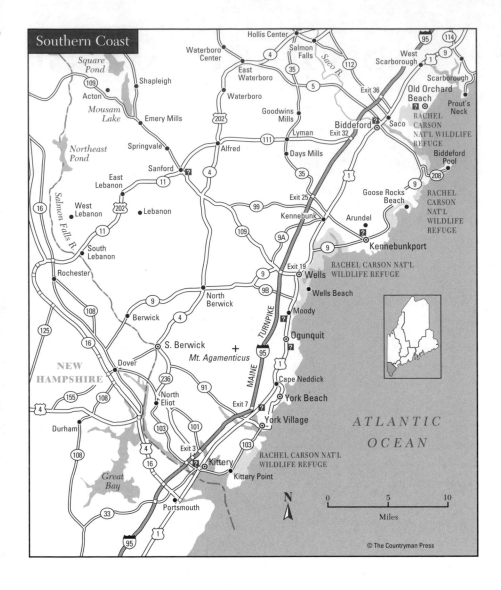

Southern Coast

Hollis Center

Waterboro
Center

Square
Pond

Shapleigh

East
Waterboro

Salmon
Falls

Saco R.

West
Scarborough

109

Acton

Mousam
Lake

Emery Mills

Waterboro

202

Goodwins
Mills

Lyman

Exit 36

Old Orchard
Beach

Scarborough

Prout's
Neck

Biddeford

Saco

RACHEL
CARSON
NAT'L WILDLIFE
REFUGE

Northeast
Pond

Springvale

Alfred

Days Mills

111

Exit 32

1

Biddeford
Pool

208

Sanford

East
Lebanon

11

4

35

Exit 25

Goose Rocks
Beach

9

RACHEL
CARSON
NAT'L
WILDLIFE
REFUGE

16

Salmon Falls R.

West
Lebanon

202

Lebanon

11

99

Kennebunk

Arundel

109

9A

9

Kennebunkport

South
Lebanon

Rochester

108

Berwick

4

North
Berwick

9

Exit 19

9

9B

Wells

Wells Beach

RACHEL CARSON NAT'L
WILDLIFE REFUGE

125

16

Moody

TURNPIKE

S. Berwick

Mt. Agamenticus

95

Ogunquit

MAINE

1

NEW
HAMPSHIRE

Dover

236

91

North
Eliot

Exit 7

Cape Neddick

York Beach

155

108

York Village

Durham

4

103

101

103

RACHEL CARSON NAT'L
WILDLIFE REFUGE

108

Exit 3

Kittery

ATLANTIC
OCEAN

4

16

Kittery Point

Great
Bay

33

Portsmouth

95

1

N

0   5   10
Miles

© The Countryman Press

95

114

9

1

© The Countryman Press

SOUTHERN COAST

The smell of pine needles and salt air, the taste of lobster and saltwater taffy, the shock of cold green waves, and, most of all, the promise of endless beach—this is the Maine that draws upward of half the state's visitors, those who never get beyond its Southern Coast. The southern Maine coast makes up just 35 of the state's 3,500 coastal miles but contains 90 percent of its sand.

The early histories of these towns differ sharply, but all have been shaped since the Civil War by the summer tide of tourists. York Village and Kittery are recognized as the oldest communities in Maine; Wells dates to the 1640s, and Kennebunkport was a shipbuilding center by the 1790s. All were transformed in the second half of the 19th century, an era when most Americans—not just the rich—began to take summer vacations, each in his or her own way.

Maine's Southern Coast was one of the country's first beach resort areas, and it catered then—as it does today—to the full spectrum of vacationers, from blue-collar workers to millionaires. Before the Civil War, Old Orchard Beach rivaled Newport, Rhode Island, as the place to be seen; when the Grand Trunk Railroad to Montreal opened in 1854, it became the first American resort to attract a sizable number of Canadians.

While ocean tides are most extreme way Down East, the ebb and flow of tourist tides wash most dramatically over this stretch of Maine. Nowhere are the 1930s-era motor courts thicker along Rt. 1, now sandwiched between elaborate condo-style complexes with indoor pools and elevators. Most of the big old summer hotels vanished by the 1950s, the era of the motor inns that now occupy their sites. But in the past few decades many former sea captains' homes and summer mansions have been transformed into small inns and bed & breakfasts, rounding out the lodging options. Luckily, the lay of the

YORK HARBOR

Christina Tree

land—salt marsh, estuarine reserves, and other wetlands—largely limits commercial clutter.

GUIDANCE The Maine Beaches Association (mainebeachesassociation.com) publishes a guide and maintains an umbrella website linking to all the Southern Coast chambers.

The Maine Tourism Association's Kittery Information Center (207-439-1319; mainetourism.com). Open daily (except Christmas, Easter, and Thanksgiving), 8–6 in summer months, otherwise 9–5:30 (bathrooms open 24 hours daily). Maine's gatehouse in a real sense is on I-95 northbound in Kittery, with exhibits and rack cards from all Maine regions. The staffed information desk is good for local as well as statewide advice on lodging, dining, and attractions. You can also check regional websites and lodging by computer. The rest area includes vending machines and picnic tables under the pines.

KITTERY, SOUTH BERWICK,
AND THE YORKS

The moment you cross the Piscataqua River you know you are in Maine.
Kittery and York both have their share of deep coves and rocky ocean paths and both towns claim to be Maine's oldest community. Technically Kittery wins, but York looks older . . . depending, of course, on which Kittery and which York you arew talking about.

Kittery Point, an 18th-century settlement overlooking Portsmouth Harbor, boasts Maine's oldest church and some of the state's finest mansions. The village of Kittery itself, however, has been shattered by so many bridges and rotaries that it initially seems to exist only as a gateway, on the one hand for workers at the Portsmouth Naval Shipyard and on the other for patrons of the outlet malls strung along Rt. 1. However, don't overlook the shops and restaurants around downtown Wallingford Square, or the strolling and swimming spots along coastal Rt. 103.

In the late 19th century artists and literati gathered at Kittery Point. Novelist and *Atlantic Monthly* editor William Dean Howells, who summered here, became keenly interested in preserving the area's colonial-era buildings. Novelist Sarah Orne Jewett, a contributor to the *Atlantic*, spearheaded restoration of the magnificent 18th-century Hamilton House in her hometown, nearby South Berwick. Her friend Sam Clemens (otherwise known as Mark Twain), who summered in York, was involved in the effort to buy up that town's splendid old school, church, burial ground, and abundance of 1740s homes, recognizing York as Maine's oldest surviving community.

In 1896 Howells suggested turning York Village's "old gaol" into a museum. At the time you could count the country's historic house museums on your fingers. The Old Gaol today is one of eight Museums of Old York. Stop by the visitors center at the Remick Barn to learn about the town's bizarre history, including its origins as a Native American settlement called Agamenticus, one of many wiped out by a plague in 1616. In 1631 it was settled by English colonists, and in 1642 it became Gorgeana, America's first chartered city. It was then demoted to the town of York, part of Massachusetts. Fierce Native American raids followed, but by the middle of the 18th century the present colonial village was established, a crucial way station between Portsmouth and points east.

York is divided into so many distinct villages that Clemens once observed, "It is difficult to throw a brick . . . in any one direction without danger of disabling a

Kittery & The Yorks

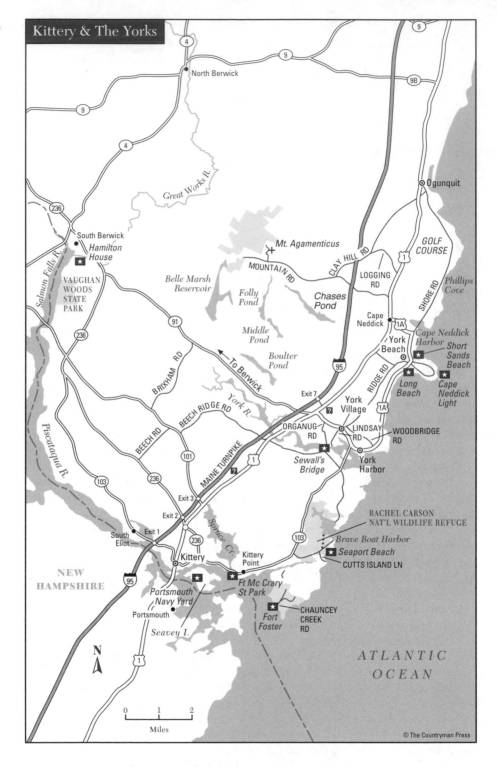

ATLANTIC OCEAN

© The Countryman Press

Miles

0   1   2

N

NEW HAMPSHIRE

Portsmouth

Portsmouth Navy Yard

Seavey I.

South Eliot

Kittery

Kittery Point

Ft Mc Crary St Park

Fort Foster

CHAUNCEY CREEK RD

Piscataqua R.

Spruce Cr.

Exit 1

Exit 2

Exit 3

103

236

236

95

1

103

CUTTS ISLAND LN

Seaport Beach

Brave Boat Harbor

RACHEL CARSON NAT'L WILDLIFE REFUGE

MAINE TURNPIKE

101

BEECH RD

BEECH RIDGE RD

BRIXHAM RD

91

236

BEECH RD

York R.

To Berwick

Exit 7

Sewall's Bridge

ORGANUG RD

York Village

York Harbor

LINDSAY RD

WOODBRIDGE RD

RIDGE RD

1A

95

Long Beach

Cape Neddick Light

Short Sands Beach

Cape Neddick Harbor

York Beach

Cape Neddick

1A

LOGGING RD

SHORE RD

Phillips Cove

GOLF COURSE

1

Ogunquit

9B

9

9

4

9

4

North Berwick

236

Salmon Falls R.

South Berwick

Hamilton House

VAUGHAN WOODS STATE PARK

Great Works R.

Belle Marsh Reservoir

Folly Pond

Middle Pond

Boulter Pond

Chases Pond

Mt. Agamenticus

MOUNTAIN RD

CLAY HILL RD

postmaster." Not counting Scotland and York Corners, York includes York Village, York Harbor, York Beach, and Cape Neddick—such varied communities that locals can't bring themselves to speak of them as one town; they refer instead to "the Yorks."

The rocky shore beyond York Village was Lower Town until the Marshall House was opened near the small gray-sand beach in 1871 and its address was changed to York Harbor. Soon the hotel had 300 rooms, and other mammoth frame hotels appeared at intervals along the shore. Now most of the old hotels are gone, with the exception of the relatively small Union Bluff and recently resurrected Atlantic House in York Beach. There is also Cliff House, a resort that, although physically in York, has long since changed its address to Ogunquit, better known these days as a resort town.

Still, York Harbor remains a delightful, low-key retreat. The Marshall House has been replaced by the contemporary Stage Neck Inn, and several dignified old summer "cottages" are now part of the York Harbor Inn; others are now inns and B&Bs. York Harbor's mile-or-so-long shore path was first traced by fishermen and later smoothed and embellished with small touches such as the Wiggly Bridge, a graceful little suspension bridge across the river and through Steedman Woods.

Landscaping and public spaces were among the consuming interests of the 19th-century summer residents, who around the turn of the century also became interested in zoning. In *Trending into Maine* (1935) Kenneth Roberts noted York Harbor's "determination to be free of billboards, tourist camps, dance halls and other cheapening manifestations of the herd instinct and Vacationland civilization."

A York Harbor corporation was formed to impose its own taxes and keep out unwanted development. The corporation's biggest fight, wrote Roberts, was against the Libby Camps, a tent-and-trailer campground on the eastern edge of York Harbor that "had spread with such fungus like rapidity that York Harbor was in danger of being almost completely swamped by young ladies in shorts, young men in soiled undershirts, and fat ladies in knickerbockers."

Libby's Oceanside Camp still sits on Roaring Rock Point, its trailers neatly angled along the shore. Across from it is matching Camp Eaton, established in 1923. No other village boundary within a New England town remains as clearly defined as this one between York Harbor and York Beach.

Beyond the campgrounds stretches 2-mile Long Sands Beach, lined with a simpler breed of summer cottage than those in York Village or York Harbor. There is a real charm to the strip and to the village of York Beach, with its Victorian-style shops, boardwalk amusements, and the Goldenrod— known for its taffy Goldenrod Kisses. This restaurant is still owned by the same family that opened it in 1896, about the time the electric streetcar put York Beach within reach of the "working class."

YORK HARBOR CLIFF PATH

Christina Tree

During this "trolley era" half a dozen big hotels accommodated 3,000 summer visitors, and 2,000 more guests patronized boardinghouses in York Beach. Today's lodgings are a mix of motels, cottages, and B&Bs. There are beaches (with metered parking), Fun-O-Rama games and bowling, and York's Wild Kingdom, with exotic animals and carnival rides. York Beach, too, has now gained "historic" status, and Museums of Old York sponsors York Beach walking tours.

GUIDANCE Greater York Region Chamber of Commerce (207-363-4422; via the Southern Maine link, 1-800-639-2442; gatewaytomaine.org), 1 Stonewall Lane, York 03909. On Rt. 1 just off I-95 exit 7 northbound (York), this handsome information center (with restrooms) modeled on a Victorian summer "cottage" is open daily, year-round, high season daily 9–5, shorter hours off-season.

The Maine Tourism Association Welcome Center (207-439-8281), I-95 northbound in Kittery, is well stocked with local as well as statewide information, with access to Rt. 1 from the rear of the parking lot. Open daily spring–fall, Sun.–Thu. 8–6, Fri.–Sat. 8–8; winter 9–5:30.

At **Sohier Park**, overlooking Nubble Light on York Beach, a seasonal information center with restrooms is open May–mid-Oct., 10 AM–sunset. A seasonal center is also operated by volunteers on Railroad St. in York Beach.

GETTING THERE York is off I-95 exit 7, the last exit before the Maine Turnpike tolls. The nearest bus service is to Portsmouth, NH, and the nearest train stop is Wells, Maine. The I-95 exits for Kittery are 1, 2, and 3. **Beach Taxi** (207-451-4031) services the York area with rides to the airport, train, and bus as well as beach.

GETTING AROUND York Trolley Company (207-363-9600; yorktrolley.com). Late June–Labor Day, trolleys circle all day along the beaches and around the Nubble. Inquire about special narrated tours and service to the Kittery Outlet Malls. $8 all-day pass, $4 for ages 10 and under; free under age 2.

WHEN TO COME With the exception of York Beach, which is highly seasonal, this area can be an appealing seaside getaway June through December. It's packed on July and August weekends. Thanks to the sizable year-round population, most restaurants remain open year-round. The Kittery outlets and Stonewall Kitchen draw holiday shoppers.

✳ To See

In Kittery
& **Kittery Historical and Naval Museum** (207-439-3080; kitterymuseum.com), Rt. 1, just north of the Rt. 236 rotary. Open June–Columbus Day, Tue.–Sat. 10–4, and by appointment. Admission charged. A fine little museum filled with ships' models and exhibits about the early history of this stretch of the Southern Coast. Displays include archaeological finds, early shipbuilding tools, navigational instruments, and mariner folk art, including samples of work by Kittery master ship's carver John Haley Bellamy (1836–1914). The lens from Boon Island Light is also displayed.

FORT MCCLARY

Christina Tree

Fort McClary, Rt. 103. A state park open seasonally (grounds accessible year-round). A hexagonal 1846 block-house on a granite base, it was the site of fortifications in 1715, 1776, and 1808. Its picnic area is across the road, but on a fine day the grounds of the fort itself, with a spectacular view of Portsmouth Harbor, are far more inviting. This site was first fortified to protect Massachusetts's vessels from being taxed by the New Hampshire colony. Contribution requested.

In York Harbor and York Beach

First Parish Church, York Village. An outstanding, mid-18th-century meeting-house with a fine cemetery full of old stones with death's heads and Old English spelling.

Civil War Monument, middle of York Village. Contrary to the local legend that this was a Civil War memorial meant for a town in the South (the uniform suggests a Confederate rather than a Union soldier), it's intended to honor all the town's "fallen heroes." Admittedly it's confusing: This particular soldier is wearing a Spanish-American War uniform, but the only years chiseled into its base are 1861–65.

Sayward-Wheeler House (207-384-2454; historicnewengland.org), 79 Barrell Lane, York Harbor. Open June–Oct. 15, second and fourth Sat. of the month, 11–4; tours on the hour, $5, $4 seniors, $2.50 students. This fine, circa-1718 house was built by a merchant, shipowner, judge, and representative to the Massachusetts General Court, who earned the respect of the community despite his Tory leanings. It remained in the same family for 200 years and retains its Queen Anne and Chippendale furnishings, family portraits, and china brought back as booty from the expedition against the French at Louisburg in 1745.

Note: Historic New England also maintains the **Hamilton House** and the **Sarah Orne Jewett House** in South Berwick, described in *Scenic Drives.*

Nubble Light, York Beach. From Rt. 1A (Long Beach Ave.), take Nubble Rd. out through the Nubble (a cottage-covered peninsula) to Sohier Park at the tip of the peninsula. The 1879 Cape Neddick Lighthouse Station

NUBBLE LIGHT

Christina Tree

MUST SEE
The Museums of Old York (207-363-1756; off-season 207-363-4974; oldyork
.org). This nonprofit group maintains nine historic buildings, open to the public early June–Columbus Day weekend, Mon.–Sat. 9:30–4. Admission is $6
adults for one building, $12 for all, $1 less for seniors; children and family
rates. It's best to pay the umbrella price and spend several hours wandering
through the 17th- and 18th-century buildings scattered through the village.
Begin with the orientation film screened in the **Virginia Weare Parsons Education Center's** 1830s **Remick Barn**, attached to the vintage-1754 **Jefferds
Tavern**, corner of Lindsay Rd. and York St. (parking is on Lindsay Rd.).
Exhibits change but are dependably outstanding; this is also a venue for
special programs, and by arrangement there's cooking on the hearth at the
tavern kitchen. If you have time to visit only one building, pick the **Old Gaol**
with its dank and dismal cells and stories of luckless patrons, many of them
women. Dating in part to 1719, this was the jail for the entire province of
Maine until 1760. In the vintage-1742 **Emerson-Wilcox House** on York St.
(tours by appointment) you'll find period rooms and changing exhibits. The
Elizabeth Perkins House, Southside Rd. (at Sewall Bridge), is our favorite
building, a 1730 house by the York River, and may be toured by appointment.
It is filled with Colonial Revival antiques, with decorative arts, and with the
spirit of Elizabeth Perkins, the real powerhouse behind the Colonial Revival
movement and the original Society for the Preservation of Historic Landmarks in York County. Nearby at 140 Lindsay Rd. are the 18th-century **John
Hancock Warehouse and Wharf** and **George Marshall Store**, which was

(better known as "Nubble Light") is perched on a small island of its own—but
that's all the better for taking pictures from the park, which offers parking and a
seasonal information center with restrooms and a small gift shop.

♂ ☁ **York's Wild Kingdom** (207-363-4911; yorkzoo.com), York Beach. In July and
Aug. the zoo is open daily 10–6 and the amusement area, noon–9:30; varying hours
in shoulder seasons, so call ahead to check. This is an old-fashioned amusement
area and zoo with goats, bears, ducks, swans, a white Bengal tiger, and a number of
unhappy-looking exotic animals. You'll also find mini golf, a butterfly kingdom, and
both pony and elephant rides. $21.25 adults, $16.25 ages 4–10, and $4.75 ages 3
and under for zoo/ride admission; less for zoo or rides only.

SCENIC DRIVES Kittery Point, Pepperrell Cove, and Gerrish Island.
From Rt. 1, find your way to Rt. 103 and follow its twists and turns along the harbor until you come to the white **First Congregational Church** and a small green
across from a striking, privately owned Georgian-style house. An old graveyard
overlooking the harbor completes the scene. Park at the church (built in 1730,
Maine's oldest), notice the parsonage (1729), and walk across the road to the old

built in 1869 as a chandlery for the large schooners that once docked here; it's now a contemporary art gallery. Also on Lindsay Rd., the **Ramsdell House**, a 1740s farm laborer's home, is presently a work in progress (tours by appointment), and the **Old School House** (1745) has exhibits on mid-18th-century education. The museums also sponsor walking tours and special events and offer a local historical research library (open year-round) and archives in the headquarters, a former bank building at 207 York St. in the middle of York Village.

THE MUSEUMS OF OLD YORK

graveyard. The magnificent neighboring house was built in 1760 for the widow of **Sir William Pepperrell**, the French and Indian Wars hero who captured the fortress at Louisburg from the French. Knighted for his feat, Pepperrell went on to become the richest man in New England. For a splendid view of the harbor, continue along Rt. 103 to **Fort McClary**. Four large hotels once clustered in this corner of Kittery, but today it's one of the quietest spots along the Southern Coast. At the back of the parking lot across from Enoteca (formerly Frisbee's), a seemingly forgotten tomb is inscribed with a plaque commemorating **Colonel William Pepperrell**, born in Devonshire in 1646, died in Kittery in 1734. Just beyond you can still see the foundations of one of the former summer hotels. Turn right beyond Pepperrell Cove and follow Gerrish Island Lane to a T; then take Pocahontas (the name of another vanished hotel) to World War I–era **Fort Foster**, now a park. Also check out Chauncey Creek Lobster Pound and **Seapoint Beach**. Rt. 103 winds on by the mouth of the York River and into York Harbor.

South Berwick. A short ride north of the Rt. 1 outlets brings you to a bend in the Salmon Falls River that is anchored by a splendid 1780s Georgian mansion, restored through the efforts of local author Sarah Orne Jewett; a formal garden

HAMILTON HOUSE

Christina Tree

and riverside trails through the woods add to the unusual appeal of this place. From Kittery, take either Rt. 236 north from the I-95 Eliot exit or more rural Rt. 101 north from Rt. 1 at exit 3 (turn right at its junction with Rt. 236). From York, take Rt. 91 north. Hamilton House and **Vaughan Woods State Park** are the first left after the junction of Rts. 236 and 91 (Brattle St.); follow signs. **Hamilton House** is open June–Oct. 15, Wed.–Sun. 11–4, with tours on the hour ($8 adults, $7 seniors, $4 children); grounds open every day dawn to dusk. The foursquare Georgian mansion built in 1785 on a promontory above the Salmon Falls River had fallen into disrepair by the time Jewett (1849–1909) was growing up in nearby South Berwick; she used it as the setting for her novel *The Tory Lover* and persuaded wealthy Boston friends to restore it in 1898 (during that same period William Dean Howells was involved in restoring nearby York Village). Historic New England (207-384-2454; historicnewengland.org) also maintains the **Sarah Orne Jewett House** farther up Rt. 236, at its junction with Rt. 4 (5 Portland St.), in the middle of the pleasant village of South Berwick (open Fri.–Sun. 11–4, with tours on the hour; $5, $4 seniors, $2.50 students). This is another fine 1774 Georgian house. Jewett, who is best known for her classic novel *The Country of the Pointed Firs*, grew up in the clapboard house next door, now the delightful town library. Here you learn that in the mid-19th century this picturesque village was home to extensive mills. The brick **Counting House Museum** (207-384-0000) by the Salmon Falls on Main St. (Rt. 4 at the bridge) is open July 1–Oct. 1, weekends. It houses the Old Berwick Historical Society collection with exhibits on 17th- through 19th-century rural life in southern Maine. Inquire about monthly lectures and events.

✳ To Do

BICYCLING Mount Agamenticus (see *Green Space*) is webbed with trails beloved by mountain bikers. **Berger's Bike Shop** (207-363-4070) in York Village and the **Daily Grind** (207-363-3040) in York Beach rent mountain and hybrid bikes.

BOAT EXCURSIONS Isles of Shoals Steamship Co. (603-431-5500 or 1-800-441-4620; islesofshoals.com), Portsmouth, New Hampshire. Daily cruises in-season stop at **Star Island**, site of a vast old white summer hotel that's now a Unitarian conference center. Visitors are welcome to this barren but fascinating place, webbed with walking trails. The ride on the 90-foot replica of an old steamboat takes one hour each way.

Captain & Patty's Piscataqua River Tours (207-439-8976), Town Dock, Pepperrell Rd., Kittery Point. June–Oct. 15, frequent daily departures for a tour aboard the launch *Sir William Pepperrell*.

BOAT RENTALS York Harbor Marine Service (207-363-3602; yorkharbormarine.com), 20 Harris Island Rd., York. Boston Whalers and other runabouts can be rented to explore the river and nearby coast.

FISHING Check with the Greater York Region Chamber of Commerce about the half a dozen deep-sea-fishing boats operating from York Harbor and Kittery. **Surf casting** is also popular along Long Sands and Short Sands Beaches and from Sohier Park in York. **Eldredge Bros. Fly Shop** (207-363-9269; eldredgeflyshop .com), 1480 Rt. 1, Cape Neddick, is a full-service outfitter offering guided freshwater and saltwater trips.

FRIGHTS Ghostly Tours (207-363-0000), 11 Railroad Ave., York Beach. Late June–Halloween. Check for days and times for guided strolls with tales of shipwrecks, mermaids, and more.

GOLF The Ledges Golf Club (207-351-3000; ledgesgolf.com), 1 Ledges Dr. (off Rt. 91), York. This is a destination course for much of southern Maine: 18 holes, carts, pro shop, favored by local residents.

Cape Neddick Country Club (207-361-2011; capeneddickgolf.com), Shore Rd., Cape Neddick. Designed in the early 1900s by Donald Ross, redesigned by Brian Silva in 1998, the 18 holes feature rolling fairways integrated with ledge outcroppings and wetlands. A pro shop and restaurant, **The Cape Neddick Grille** (207-361-2112).

The Links at Outlook (207-384-4653), Rt. 4, South Berwick. An 18-hole Scottish-style course and driving range.

SEA KAYAKING The tidal York River, stretches of the Piscataqua around and above Eliot, and the Salmon Falls River (accessible from Vaughan Woods State Park in South Berwick) are particularly appealing to kayakers. **Harbor Adventures** (207-363-8466; harboradventures.com), based in York Harbor, and **Excursions** (207-363-0181; excursionsinmaine.com), Rt. 1, Cape Neddick, offer guided tours and rentals; **Eldredge Bros. Fly Shop** (see *Fishing*) also offers rentals.

SPAS The Cliff House Resort & Spa (207-361-1000; cliffhousemaine.com), Shore Rd., on the York–Ogunquit line. A variety of massage, face care, and body care services are offered and include use of the fully equipped fitness area as well as large indoor and outdoor pools. Exercise classes are also offered.

Portsmouth Harbor Inn & Spa (207-439-7060; innatportsmouth.com), 6 Water St., Kittery. A full-service spa housed in the attractive carriage house of this waterside inn, offering facials, body treatments, massage, manicures, and pedicures. Inquire about both day and two-night packages.

The Spa at Stage Neck Inn (207-363-3850; stageneck.com) is geared to guests at this York Harbor resort but also a day spa, offering access to the hotel's indoor pool and Jacuzzi along with services.

✳ Green Space

BEACHES

In Kittery

Seapoint Beach is long with silky soft sand. Parking is residents-only.

❦ **Fort Foster**, Gerrish Island, is shallow a long way out and also has low-tide tidal pools with crabs and snails.

In York

Long Sands is a 2-mile expanse of coarse gray sand stretching from York Harbor to the Nubble, backed by Rt. 1A and summer cottages, great for walking. Metered parking the length of the beach and a bathhouse midway. Lifeguard in high season.

❦ **Short Sands** is a shorter stretch of coarse gray sand with a bathhouse, parking lot (meters), and playground, just in front of the village of York Beach.

York Harbor Beach is small and pebbly, but pleasant, with restrooms. Limited parking for nonresidents on Rt. 1A.

PARKS Fort Foster Park, Kittery. Beyond Pepperrell Cove, look for Gerrish Island Lane and turn right at the T onto Pocahontas Rd., which leads, eventually, to this 92-acre town park. The World War I fortifications are ugly, but there is a choice of small beaches with different exposures (one very popular with sailboarders), extensive walking trails, and picnic facilities. Fee.

Piscataqua River Boat Basin (207-439-1813), Main St., Eliot. Open May–Oct. Boat launch, picnic area, beach, restrooms.

Mount Agamenticus (207-361-1102; agamenticus.org), York. Just 691 feet high but billed as the highest hill on the Atlantic seaboard between York and Florida. On a clear day, it's said, you can see Mount Washington from this summit. We couldn't, but the view is definitely expansive: On one side lies a sweep of coastal communities and ocean; on the other, hills roll off to distant mountains. Once part

LONG SANDS BEACH, YORK BEACH

Nancy English

of a ski area, now part of a 10,000-acre wooded preserve maintained by the Mount Agamenticus Conservation Region, a nonprofit collaborative that includes surrounding towns and furnishes trail maps (check the website). Easiest access is from Mountain Rd. off Rt. 1 (turn at Flo's Hot Dogs). The summit is cluttered with satellite dishes and cell towers, but there are viewing platforms, especially popular for tracking hawks in spring and fall. Bring a picnic.

Vaughan Woods State Park (207-384-5160), South Berwick. Seasonal. $2 ages 12 and above. Take Old Fields Rd. off Brattle St. A 250-acre preserve on the banks of the Salmon Falls River; picnic facilities and 3 miles of nature trails. The first cows in Maine are said to have been landed here at Cow Cove in 1634. See directions under South Berwick in *Scenic Drives*.

Sohier Park, Rt. 1A, York. See Nubble Light under *To See*. A popular picnic spot.

Goodrich Park, York. A good picnic spot on the banks of the York River, accessible from Rt. 1 south; look for the entrance just before the bridge.

Hartley Mason Harbor Park, Rt. 1A, York Harbor, adjoining Harbor Beach. Created in 1998 when several classic York Harbor cottages were destroyed in accordance with the wills of their former owners, this is a great spot for a picnic and a favored venue for weddings.

WALKS Cliff Path and Fisherman's Walk, York Harbor. For more than a mile, you can pick your way along the town's most pleasant piece of shorefront. Begin at the George Marshall Store and walk east along the river and through the shady Steedman Woods. Go across the Wiggly Bridge (a mini suspension bridge), then continue across Rt. 103, past the Sayward House, along the harbor, down the beach, and along the top of the rocks. Continue east from the parking circle at York Harbor Beach until the path ends at a private property line. This portion is a bit rough, and walkers are advised to keep to the path. Returning the way you've come is no hardship.

✳ Lodging

Note: York Beach offers many summer cottage rentals, and rentals can also be found elsewhere in town. Check with the Greater York Region Chamber of Commerce for individual rentals as well as reliable Realtors. Also see seasiderentals.com.

INNS AND RESORTS *Note:* For details about the largest local resort, **The Cliff House** resort and spa, which sits on the Ogunquit–York line, see the "Ogunquit" chapter.

✪ ✑ ♿ **Dockside Guest Quarters** (207-363-2868 or 1-800-270-1977; docksidegq.com), 22 Harris Island Rd., York 03909. Open Apr.–mid-Nov. Sited on a peninsula in York Harbor, this family-run inn faces a harbor outlet. From the porch and front rooms of the gracious, 19th-century Maine House, the view usually includes fishing boats, sailing yachts, and kayakers; always gulls and the Boon Island Light. The inn forms the centerpiece of a 7-acre compound that includes four contemporary, multi-unit cottages. In all there are 25 guest rooms—including several with gas fireplace and six apartment/suites with kitchenette—all with private deck and water views. Breakfast is served buffet-style in the Maine House, a morning gathering place for guests who check the blackboard weather forecast and plan their day. Guests have access to fishing equipment, bicycles, and Boston whalers. River tours are also offered by innkeeper Eric Lusty. Two-night minimum stay during July and Aug. $232–278 in high season, $133–165 off-season; $248–325 for a suite with living room and kitchenette. Phil Lusty serves lunch and dinner in the neighboring Dockside Restaurant (see *Dining Out*).

Stage Neck Inn (207-363-3850 or 1-800-222-3238; stageneck.com), 8 Stage Neck Rd., York Harbor 03911. Open year-round. An attractive 1970s resort built on the site of the 19th-century Marshall House. The 58 rooms have either two double beds or one single, king-sized bed. Located on its own peninsula, the inn offers water views, a formal dining room (see Harbor Porches in *Dining Out*), the less formal **Sandpiper Grille**, tennis courts, an outdoor pool, a small indoor pool and Jacuzzi, and a full-service spa. Grounds adjoin Harbor Beach. $145–385 per room, no meals included. Geared to groups off-season. Inquire about packages.

VIEW FROM DOCKSIDE GUEST QUARTERS
Christina Tree

♂ ఉ **York Harbor Inn** (207-363-5119 or 1-800-343-3869; yorkharborinn.com), P.O. Box 573, York St., Rt. 1A, York Harbor 03911. Open year-round. A full-service inn with a beamed common area said to have been built in 1637 on the Isles of Shoals. An exclusive men's club in the 19th century, this is now a popular dining spot (see *Dining Out*). The 54 rooms are air-conditioned and furnished handsomely. Several have a working fireplace, some in the Harbor Hill Inn have a Jacuzzi, and most have water views. The neighboring Harbor Cliffs B&B, a former summer mansion, and 1730 Harbor Crest hold elegant common rooms, all the amenities, and several suites. Geared to groups and conferences in cooler months. High season $149–349, off-season $99–279 per couple, continental breakfast included.

Atlantic House (207-363-0051; atlantichouseyorkbeach.com), 2 Beach St., P.O. Box 1300, York Beach 03910. Open year-round. Built rather grandly in 1888, this rehabbed inn now offers 15 elevator-accessed units, 8 of them fully equipped one- and two-bedroom condos, available for nightly as well as weekly rental. The Blue Sky restaurant (see *Dining Out*) is on the second floor; the ground level is occupied by shops. Summer-season rates are $250–300 per night for rooms, $425–675 for condos; $1,500–4,100 per week. From $100 off-season.

♂ **The Union Bluff** (207-363-1333 or 1-800-833-0721; unionbluff.com), 8 Beach St., P.O. Box 1860, York Beach 03910. Open year-round. First opened in 1868, this landmark has been totally renovated. There's not much of a lobby, but the elevator accesses comfortable rooms with a view of the ocean and Short Sands Beach. All

Christina Tree

ATLANTIC HOUSE, YORK BEACH

three meals are served, and there's a choice between the **Union Grill** and an informal pub. The 70 units are divided among the original hotel, a three-story motel-like annex with balconies, and the more recently added Meeting House, which also houses a function hall. $199–309 for ocean-view rooms mid-June–Labor Day, from $89 for street side, Sun.–Thu. From $59 off-season.

BED & BREAKFASTS

In York Harbor 03911

Inn at Tanglewood Hall (207-351-1075; tanglewoodhall.com), 611 York St., P.O. Box 490. Open year-round. In this shingled 1880s summer mansion, onetime home of bandleader Tommy Dorsey, owners Su and Andy Wetzel offer six nicely decorated and air-conditioned guest rooms, all with queen beds and private bath, three with gas fireplace or porch. The York Harbor Suite holds hand-painted flowers on its floors and porch. Guests mingle on the wraparound veranda overlooking the wooded garden. A full breakfast is served between 8 and 10 on the veranda or in the dining room, or brought to your room. Although the house has no water views, the most

dramatic stretch of the Cliff Path is just down the road. $165–235 in high season, otherwise $95–155.

Edwards' Harborside Inn (207-363-3037; edwardsharborside.com), P.O. Box 866. Open year-round. Location! Location! Sited across from York Harbor Beach with a wharf of its own, this solidly built summer mansion is owned by Jay Edwards, a third-generation innkeeper. Breakfast is served in one of the sunporches with a view of the harbor. Many of the 10 guest rooms (all with private bath) also have water views; all are air-conditioned and have TV and phone. The York Suite is a lulu, with water views on three sides and a Jacuzzi overlooking the water, too. In July, Aug. $200 for rooms, $300 for suites; shoulder months $170–240; off-season $130–220 per couple.

Chapman Cottage (207-363-2059 or 1-877-363-2059; chapmancottage bandb.com), 370 York St. Open year-round. Neil Archibald welcomes guests to this three-story 1899 summer home with its four exceptional guest rooms and two suites. The suites each have two gas fireplaces, one to enjoy from your Jacuzzi, but our favorite is the third-floor Elizabeth's Room, bright and simple with a deck. All rooms have air-conditioning and a welcoming fruit basket, water, and sherry. The ground-floor parlors serve as dining room and lounge. Dinner is available to by reservation Fri. and Sat. There's a porch set high above the sloping lawn with distant water views. $175–225 per couple in high season, otherwise $160–225, includes breakfast.

Inn at Harmon Park (207-363-2031; sueantal@gmail.com), P.O. Box 495. Open for B&B Sept.–early June and by the week in summer. Sue Antal's hospitable 1899 Victorian is within walking distance of Harbor

Beach and the shore paths. She offers a comfortable living room with wood-burning fireplace and four guest rooms, from cozy Celia Thaxter with its water view (nice if you are alone) to the suite with fireplace (nice if you aren't). All have private bath and are furnished in wicker and antiques, with radio, small TV, and VCR. Sue is a justice of the peace and knows all the likely local wedding venues inside and out. $89–139 ($79–119 in winter) includes a great breakfast served in the dining room by the fire or on the delightful sunporch.

In York 03909
✪ **Morning Glory Inn** (207-363-2062; morninggloryinnmaine.com), 129 Seabury Rd. Veteran innkeepers Bonnie and Bill Alston have designed this unusually comfortable oasis to conform to their idea of what a B&B should be. What began more than 200 years ago as a post-and-beam cottage on the Isles of Shoals now has the feel of contemporary house, banked in flower gardens and squirreled away down a rural road half a mile from the ocean. There are three guest rooms, each with a patio or deck, new bath (one with jets), TV, DVD, and mini fridge. Our favorite is Sandpiper: The spacious living/dining area has plenty of space to relax plus a wood-burning fireplace. From $175–235 July–Oct., $155–215 early spring and late fall. Rates include a full breakfast.

🐾 **Bittersweet Bed & Breakfast** (207-3007; bittersweetbednbreakfast .com), 167 Cape Neddick Rd. Beyond York beach and handy to Cape Neddick Beach, a rambling, welcoming country house with seven guest rooms and pleasant common space, including a screened porch. Reasonable rates ($150 in July and August, otherwise $75), and no minimum-stay requirement, only add to the appeal.

In York Beach 03910
🐾 🖋 **The Katahdin Inn** (207-363-1824), 11 Ocean Ave. Extension, P.O. Box 93. Open year-round. "Bed and beach" is the way innkeepers Bob and Rae LeBlanc describe their golden-colored 1890s guest house overlooking Short Sands Beach and the ocean. Rae's parents ran the old York Beach casino, and she knows about as much about York Beach as there is to know. The couple now live here year-round, and there's an unusually hospitable and well-kept feel to the place. Eight of the nine guest rooms have water views. Number 9 on the third floor is small and white with a window and skylight that seem to suspend it above the water. All rooms have a small fridge. The porch is lined with rockers. From $95 (shared bath) to $145 for a large room (private bath). No breakfast, but morning tea and coffee are served.

🖋 **Candleshop Inn** (207-363-4087; candleshopinn.com), 44 Freeman St., P.O. Box 1216. Open May–Nov. 1. Barbara and Michael Sheff have turned an old summer home into a tasteful, restful B&B geared to group and do-your-own retreats. The 10 guest rooms offer a range of beds (from twin to king) and come with and without private bath; many have water views. $125–195 per couple includes a full vegetarian breakfast. Children under age 5 stay free, then it's $10 to age 12; otherwise $20 per extra person.

In Kittery and the Berwicks
✪ **The Portsmouth Harbor Inn and Spa** (207-439-4040; innatportsmouth .com), 6 Water St., Kittery 03904. Open year-round. Lynn Bowditch maintains this 1890s redbrick inn just off the Kittery green, across from the Piscataqua River and within walking distance (across the bridge) of the theaters, shops, and restaurants of downtown Portsmouth, NH. Common

PORTSMOUTH HARBOR INN

rooms are cheerful and spacious, and the six guest rooms are carefully, imaginatively furnished; all have private bath (some with claw-foot tub), air-conditioning, ceiling fan, phone, and cable TV/VCR (there's an extensive video library). Add to all this a full-service day spa in the carriage house. $165–195 in-season includes a full breakfast. From $125 off-season.

✪ **The Academy Street Inn** (207-384-5633), 15 Academy St., South Berwick 03908. Open year-round. We highly recommend this 1903 mansion, adjacent to the attractive village that's home to Maine's oldest private school and to the several historic houses associated with author Sarah Orne Jewett (1840–1909). Paul Fopeano displays his antique snowshoe collection, and restaurant manager Lee Fopeano knows how to organize excellent breakfasts. The twin parlors are richly paneled with carved mantels. Five spacious guest rooms have private bath and solid furnishings. A full breakfast is served at the dining room table under the crystal chandelier. Early coffee is set out upstairs, within steps of the guest rooms. $105–118. Inquire about the two-bedroon, two-bath carriage house, available for extended stays (pets okay).

Angel of the Berwicks Bed & Breakfast (207-676-2133; angelofthe berwicks.com), 2 Elm St., North Berwick 03906. Open year-round. Sited a ways off the tourist trail, this is an impressive, 27-room, 1880s Queen Anne Eastlake mansion painted several shades of lavender. Think 11-foot, hand-painted ceilings, stained-glass windows, original chandeliers, and richly paneled common rooms. This isn't the first Victorian mansion that Sally and Benn Gunn have restored as a B&B—they are obviously skilled and enjoy the work. The five guest rooms are spacious, two of them furnished with appropriate antiques and tasteful contemporary pieces. We especially like the second-floor former master bedroom and the third-floor, two-room Salmon Falls Suite. Common space includes a parlor, library, and upstairs TV room. Handy to summer theater and golf, this is at least a 15-minute drive inland from the shore, where its rates would unquestionably be higher. $119–159 in summer/fall includes breakfast; from $99 off-season.

OTHER LODGING View Point (207-363-2661; viewpointhotel.com), 229 Nubble Rd., York 03909. Office open

ACADEMY STREET INN

Nancy English

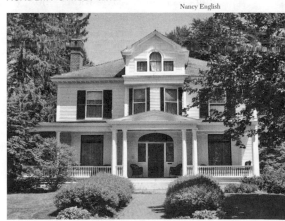

daily in summer, selected days off-season. A nicely designed oceanfront, condominium-style complex overlooking the Nubble Lighthouse. Units have a living room, kitchen, porch or patio, gas fireplace, phone, cable TV, CD stereo, VCR, and washer-dryer, and vary from one to three bedrooms. In summer from $275 (for a couple) with a two-night minimum; $1,795–3,495 per week. From $145 off-season. Specials.

♪ (ŵ) **Cutty Sark Motel** (207-363-5131 or 1-800-543-5131), 58 Long Beach Avenue, York Beach 03910. Location! This is the only lodging on the beach side of the road in York Beach. The 42 rooms are housed compactly in multistory clapboard buildings wedged into a corner of the beach, above a private lawn overlooking the ocean. All units have picture windows with this water view. We recommend an upper-level room for privacy. Lowest rates are for unrenovated rooms without AC or phones and either a king or two double beds; those in the newest wing each have two queen beds, and one has a Jacuzzi. $165–265 in-season, $99 off-season, includes a continental breakfast.

♪ & **The Anchorage Inn** (207-363-5112; anchorageinn.com), Rt. 1A, Long Beach Ave., York Beach 03910. A total of 179 motel-style rooms, most with water views across from Long Sands Beach, a good choice for families. Facilities include indoor and outdoor pools; some rooms sleep four, some have TV, small fridge. High season $187–435 (for a four-person spa suite), low season $68–226; inquire about packages.

♪ & **Sands by the Sea & Rose Suites** (207-363-2211), 15 Ocean Ave., York Beach. Open May–late Oct. This 60-unit 1950s motel is family-run and a find for families. Spanking clean,

recently renovated. Standard rooms have two double beds, AC, a microwave, coffeemaker, and fridge; some include pullout sofas. There's a new pool with waterfall. Short Sands Beach is across the road. $169–209 in high season, $99–139 in spring and fall. Inquire about Sea Rose Condo suites and cottages with one to three bedrooms, kitchen and living room.

🐾 **Country View Motel & Guesthouse** (207-363-7160 or 1-800-258-6598; countryviewmotel.com), 1521 Rt. 1, Cape Neddick 03902. Open mid-Apr.–Oct. Owner Scott MacNeil welcomes canines with home-baked dog biscuits and a fenced dog run. With or without pets, the standard and efficiency units, varying from studios to two-bedrooms, are up to snuff. The five guest rooms in the original 19th-century house are reserved for humans only. All have private bath and include the two spacious rooms that were once parlors. Reasonable rates.

✳ Where to Eat

DINING OUT ✪ **Anneke Jans** (207-439-0001; annekejans.net), 60 Wallingford Square, Kittery. Open nightly from 5. This dramatically dark dining room creates the illusion of sitting in a theater. The drama unfolds in the well-lit kitchen, visible beyond a stainless-steel framed counter. The chefs perform well. The signature Bangs Island mussels with Great Hill blue cheese, bacon, shallots, and pommes frites ($21) beg for an encore. Entrées $15–34. Fully licensed with a wide selection of wines by the glass.

♂ **Clay Hill Farm** (207-361-2272; clayhillfarm.com), 220 Clay Hill Rd., Cape Neddick. Open year-round for dinner but generally closed Mon. and Tue. in winter. Call for off-season hours and reservations. A gracious old farmhouse set in landscaped gardens halfway up Mount Agamenticus, with valet parking and an elegant decor, the farm is geared to functions. You might begin with escargots in puff pastry and dine on roasted half duckling or Maine-lobster-stuffed shrimp. Entrées $19–35.

The York Harbor Inn (207-363-5119; yorkharborinn), Rt. 1A, York Harbor. Open year-round for dinner and Sunday brunch. Dine either in the pleasant dining rooms with water views or downstairs in the less formal **Ship's Cellar Pub** (open 11:30 AM–11 PM), evoking the paneled saloon of a luxurious sailing yacht. The menu is large, but fresh seafood is the specialty. Dinner entrées might include Yorkshire lobster supreme (lobster stuffed with a scallop-and-shrimp filling) and seafood ravioli, but there are also salads, sandwiches, and flat breads. From $8.50 for a burger; entrées $18.95–28.95.

Harbor Porches (207-363-3850; stageneck.com), Stage Neck Rd., York Harbor. Open year-round for breakfast, lunch, dinner, and Sunday brunch. Glass-walled, with unbeatable ocean views, this attractive dining room has shed its white tablecloths and offers a menu with light as well as serious entrées. Patrons can opt for an open-faced grilled eggplant sandwich ($10) as well as a Maine seafood bouillabaisse ($28) or boneless roast crisp duck à l'orange ($26).

✐ **Robert's Maine Grill** (207-439-0300; robertsmainegrill.com), Rt. 1 north, Kittery. Open year-round, 11:30–8 or 9. Same ownership as Bob's Clam Hut but a newer, upscale version with an expanded menu, including a raw bar and ranging from lobster bruschetta to seafood paella. Family-geared, this has quickly become a local favorite. Chef Craig Spinney is a stickler for not just the freshest but also the best seafood (like scallops from Winter Harbor); ditto for produce. Try the mussels with sausage, fennel, and cream, or the baked haddock with sherry and lobster broth. Entrées $15.95–26.95.

Blue Sky on York Beach (207-363-0050; blueskyonyorkbeach.com), 2 Beach St., York Beach. Open year-round for dinner, Sun. brunch., but check. A spacious, glittery dining room with an open kitchen, housed in the second floor of the Atlantic House. Reviews are mixed. Wood-fired pizzas are $14–24, entrées $24–35. Live jazz brunch on weekends is popular.

✐ **Cape Neddick Inn Restaurant and Tavern** (207-351-1145; cape neddickinn.com), 1273 Rt. 1, Cape Neddick, York. Open for dinner from 4 PM, year-round. Originally opened in 1926, burned to the ground in 1984 and rebuilt, this establishment has had numerous owners and names. Both the dining room and tavern now have fieldstone fireplaces—it was the glowing hearth that drew us to the tavern on an unseasonably cool evening. The menu ranges from a $10 bruchetta bruge to a $28 filet mignon. Children's menu $10.

✪ *✐* **Dockside Restaurant** (207-363-2722; docksidegq.com), Harris Island Rd. off Rt. 103, York Harbor. Open for lunch and dinner late May–Columbus Day. Reservations suggested for dinner. Docking as well as parking. The view of yacht-filled York Harbor from Phil and Anne Lusty's glass-walled dining room and screened porch is hard to beat. At lunch try the seared tuna salad or garlic shrimp spaghettini; at dinner, the specialties are seafood, such as drunken lobster sauté with shrimp, and roast stuffed duckling. Dinner entrées $19–32. Children's menu.

✪ **Frankie & Johnny's Natural Foods** (207-363-1909), 1594 Rt. 1, Cape Neddick. Open for dinner

Wed.–Sun. in July and Aug., Thu.–Sun. off-season, closed Jan. No credit cards. BYOB. This colorful place offers vegan and vegetarian dishes but also plenty of seafood and meat. It can hit the spot if you're in the mood for a blackened salmon salad, toasted-peppercorn-seared sushi-grade tuna on gingered vegetables, or homemade "harvest" pasta. Daily specials. Entrées $16.75–27.75.

✍ **Sun 'n' Surf Restaurant** (207-363-2961), 165 Long Sands Beach Ave. (Rt. 1A), York Beach. Open for three meals. Location, location! Smack on the beach with a seasonal deck. Still owned by the Ramsey family who opened a snack bar on this prime spot on Long Sands Beach in 1963, this is now a popular full-service restaurant. Breakfast specials, lunch salads and sandwiches, seafood and steak for dinner. Dinner entrées $16.99–39.99 (steak & lobster).

Pepperland Café (207-384-5535; pepperlandcafe.com), 279 Main St., South Berwick. Open lunch–dinner Tue.–Sat.; Sun. brunch 9–3. A destination for brunch, known for corned beef hash, crabcake Benedict, and many other things you will never make at home; creative soups, sandwiches and salads at lunch, locally sourced sinner entrées include fish stew, pork schnitzel and house-made porcini pappardelle with portobello mushroom, swiss chard and garlic. Full bar. Dinner entrées: $17–22.

LOBSTER

✪ **Cape Neddick Lobster Pound and Harborside Restaurant** (207-363-5471; capeneddick.com), 60 Shore Rd. (Rt. 1A), Cape Neddick. Open Mar.–Nov. for lunch and dinner—but call for hours in shoulder seasons. In August come early or be prepared to wait. Sited by a tidal river, this attractive building with dining inside and on a deck is a local favorite. Besides lobster and clams, the menu offers a variety of choices, from vegetable stir-fry to soups and salads to filet mignon and bouillabaisse. Dinner entrées $16–market price, but you can always get a lobster roll or a fried haddock sandwich. Fully licensed.

✪ **Chauncey Creek Lobster Pier** (207-439-1030; chaunceycreek.com), 16 Chauncey Creek Rd., Kittery Point. Open Mother's Day–Labor Day daily, 11–8; post Labor Day–Columbus Day, daily 11–7, closed Mon. Owned by the Spinney family since the 1950s, specializing in reasonably priced lobster dinners with steamers, served at brightly painted picnic tables (also indoor eating) right on a pier on a tidal river walled by pine trees. Also available: lobster in rolls and in the rough, chowders, baked beans, a chicken dinner, and a raw bar. Coleslaw, corn, baked beans, and individual pizzas, pies, and cheesecake are served. On summer weekends expect a wait. BYOB.

✍ **The LobsterBarn** (207-363-4721; thelobsterbarn.com), 1000 Rt. 1, York. Open year-round for lunch and dinner. An informal dining room with wooden

Also see **Arrows** in "Ogunquit and Wells."

EATING OUT

Along Route 1 in Kittery and York (south to north)

✪ **Beach Pea Baking Co.** (207-439-555), 59 State Rd. (Rt. 1 south), Kittery, south of the exit 2 Kittery traffic circle. Open Tue.–Sat. 7:30–6. The aromas alone are worth a stop. Known for artisan breads—from roasted garlic boules through country French and baguettes to focaccia—and fabulous cakes, also a source of great sandwiches to go or eat on the deck.

Bob's Clam Hut (207-439-4233; bobsclamhut.com), Rt. 1 south, next to the Kittery Trading Post, Kittery. Open

Christina Tree

BOB'S CLAM HUT IN KITTERY

daily year-round, 11–9. Here since 1956 and definitely the best fried clams on the strip—some say the

booths and a full menu. Steak and lobster are what this is about. In summer lobster dinners (in the rough) are served under a tent out back. Salad bar and fresh-made bread. Early-bird and daily specials. Children's menu. Lobster bakes for groups.

⚓ **Warren's Lobster House** (207-439-1630; lobsterhouse.com), 1 Water St., Kittery. Open year-round for lunch, dinner, and Sun. brunch; docking facilities. Call for hours off-season. The rambling, knotty-pine dining room and canopied deck overlook the Piscataqua River and Portsmouth, NH, beyond; a dining landmark with 1940s decor. The salad bar, with more than 60 selections, provides a meal in itself. The specialty is "Lobster, Lobster, and More Lobster." The menu is large, however, and includes several beef dishes and plenty of seafood. Entrées $14–18, more for lobster.

Fox's Lobster House (207-363-2643; foxslobster.com), 8 Sohier Park Rd., Nubble Point, York Beach. Open daily in-season 11:45–9. A large, tourist-geared place near the Nubble, with a water view and a menu ranging from fried clam rolls to lobster.

Foster's Clambake (207-263-3255 or 1-800-552-0242), 5 Axholme Rd., Rt. 1A, York Harbor. Open in-season with a full menu, from hot dogs to lazy lobster—but this place is all about lobster bakes for groups, at their place or yours, anywhere in the world (including the White House).

entire coast. The menu includes all the usual fried (using "cholesterol-free oil") seafood plus burgers and sandwiches. Order at the takeout and look for seating either inside or at the picnic tables around back.

Bosn'n's Landing (207-363-4116), 150 Rt. 1, York. Open Mar.–Nov., Thu.–Sun. 8 AM–9 PM. With views of the York River 2 miles north of the Kittery outlets, this is a tried-and-true favorite with reasonably priced broiled as well as fried fish, sandwiches, and lobster, good breakfasts.

When Pigs Fly Wood-Fired Pizzeria (207-438-7036), 460 Rt. 1, Kittery. Open daily 11:30–9 Sun.–Thu.; until 10 Sat–Sun. Ron Siegel began baking this artisanal bread not far from here, and a bakery that now supplies retail outlets throughout the Northeast is just up the road. This latest venture of the Siegel brothers includes a company store and a restaurant featuring not only pizza but also other dishes that beg for bread, like steamed mussels and Portuguese-style red chowder; also sandwiches and salads.

Stonewall Kitchen Café (207-351-2713), 2 Stonewall Lane, just off Rt. 1, beside the chamber of commerce, York. Open Mon.–Sat. 8–6, Sun. 9–6. Shorter hours off-season. At the Stonewall Kitchen flagship store (see *Selective Shopping*) you order from the espresso bar or deli and a server will find you in the café or (weather permitting) at an outside table. Breakfast breads and house granola for breakfast, daily soups and deli sandwiches (like roasted apple chicken salad) and salads all afternoon.

✔ **Wild Willy's Burgers** (207-363-9924), 765 Rt. 1, York. Daily (except Sun.) 11–7:30. This wildly popular family eatery features 100 percent certified Angus ground chuck hand

shaped daily into burgers, topped with more combinations than you thought possible, and served with "country fair" fries.

Roost Café & Bistro (207-363-0266; roostcafeandbistro.com), 1300 Rt. 1, Cape Neddick, York. Open daily except Tue. for breakfast and lunch mid-June–mid-Sept., Fri.–Sun. the rest of the year; also for dinner Wed.–Sun. year-round. This is an attractive space with over-the-top breakfasts (three-egg omelets with crabmeat and Granny Smith apples, lemon ricotta pancakes) and a dinner menu that ranges from tempura-battered fish to lamb loin with herbed spaetzle ($23). Full bar. At lunch a "turkey and all the fixings sandwich" on from-scratch multigrain bread was amazing. We took it to the top of Mount Agamenticus, accessed just up the road.

✪ **Flo's Hot Dogs**, Rt. 1 north, Cape Neddick. Open only 11–3 and not a minute later. The steamers are bargain-priced, but that doesn't explain the long lines, and it's not Flo who draws the crowds because Flo has passed away. Her daughter-in-law Gail carries on. Request the special sauce and hold the mustard and ketchup.

In York Village

Fat Tomato Grill (207-36-5333), 241 York St. Mon.–Sat. 11–8. Basic sandwiches, multiple kinds of burgers and dogs, kids' menu, cheap, cheerful, and handy.

Rick's All Seasons Restaurant (207-363-5584), 240 R York St. Open daily from 5 AM for breakfast until 2 PM weekdays, closing earlier on weekends; for dinner only Wed. and Thu., until 8 PM. A reasonably priced local hangout; specialties include omelets, quiche, corned beef hash, and hot apple pie with cheese.

Christina Tree

THE GOLDENROD, YORK BEACH

In York Beach

✪ 🐾 ✎ **The Goldenrod** (207-363-2621; thegoldenrod.com), Rt. 1A. Open Memorial Day–Columbus Day for breakfast, lunch, and dinner. Still owned by the Talpey family, who first opened for business here in 1896—just in time to serve the first electric trolleys rolling into York Beach from Portsmouth and Kittery. One of the best family restaurants in New England; same menu all day 8 AM–10:30 PM, but lunch and dinner specials are served up at time-polished, wooden tables in the big dining room with a fieldstone fireplace as well as at the old-style soda fountain. Their famous Goldenrod Kisses are made from saltwater taffy cooked and pulled in the windows. A wide selection of homemade ice creams and yogurts, good sandwiches. (Where else can you still get a cream cheese and olives or nuts sandwich?) The dinner menu features basics like meat loaf, broiled haddock, and chicken teriyaki.

✎ **Lobster Cove** (207-351-1100), 756 York St. Open for breakfast through dinner. Just west of Long Sands Beach with an upstairs deck and water views. The Talpey family, owners of the Gold-enrod, have created this moderately priced eatery. No surprises, but a good dinner bet for broiled haddock or baked stuffed shrimp. Burgers all day plus a children's menu.

Shore Road Restaurant & Deli/ Market (207-363-6533; shoreroadrestaurant.net), junction of Rt. 1A and Shore Rd. Open seasonally 8–3; dinner Fri., Sat. A friendly market up front with plenty of seating in back, a deli and grill. The $8.99 lobster roll comes with homemade slaw, and it's fine if you aren't too hungry ($16.99 for double meat).

Elsewhere

✎ **Captain & Patty's** (207-439-3655; capandpatty.com), 80 Pepperrell Rd. (Rt. 103), Kittery Point. Open for lunch, dinner, and Sun. brunch; call for off-season hours. Formerly Cap'n Simeon's, still pretty similar. You enter through the original Frisbee's Store (the building is said to date back to 1680). The dining area's picture windows overlook the cove and beyond to Portsmouth Harbor; now there is also seasonal patio dining outside by the water. Seafood is the specialty but you can also just have a grilled cheese sandwich at lunch. The dinner menu features fried seafood, including fried oysters shrimp and scallops. Reviews are good. Inquire about traditional clambakes and Cap'n Neil's boat excursions.

Loco Cocos Tacos (207-438-9322; lococos.com), 36 Walker St. (Rt. 103), Kittery. Open Mon.–Sat. 11–9, Sun. 11–7. Cal-Mex fare, expanded from the original truck to a roomy restaurant with lounge, heated patio. Cheap and cheerful, tasty *enchiladas con mole*, chile, soups and salads, guacamole, cabbage slaw, four kinds of free salsa (try the green avocado sauce).

❧ **Fogarty's Restaurant and Bakery** (207-384-8361), South Berwick Village. Open daily 11–8, until 9 Sat. and Sun. Closed Mon. in Jan. Big, casual, and friendly, a local institution with sandwiches, salads, and burgers served for dinner along with Yankee pot roast, tenderloin tips, and ham steak, all at digestible prices. Indian pudding and Aunt Pat's pies for dessert. Children's menu.

✪ **Hebert Brothers Seafood** (207-703-0431), 2 Badgers Island, Kittery. Open daily 10–9. A local secret! A fabulous fish store with a few tables, picnic benches outside by the river, and a menu that includes steamers, a fisherman's platter, salmon sandwiches, and a great crab roll, also lobster rolls that are a find at $13.95 ($5.99 on Wed.!).

SNACKS, TREATS, AND TAKEHOME Brown's Ice Cream (207-363-4077), Nubble Rd., 0.25 mile beyond the lighthouse, York Beach. Seasonal. Family-owned, all extra-

creamy ice creams—55 flavors—are made on the premises. Try the "Maine Survivor." From $2.75 for a kiddy cone. "Small" is enormous. Picnic tables but no view.

Pie in the Sky Bakery (207-363-2656), Rt. 1, Cape Neddick. Open Thu.–Mon. except Jan.; hours vary off-season. The purple house at the corner of River Rd. is filled with delicious smells and irresistible muffins, pies, and scones baked here by John and Nancy Stern.

Terra Cotta Pasta Company (207-375-3025), Rt. 1 north, below the Kittery traffic circle. Open Mon.–Sat. 9–6. Freshly made parsley and garlic linguine and wild mushroom lasagna are a sampling of what's offered, along with dozens of full-bodied sauces. It's also a good spot to pick up a sandwich for a picnic at nearby Fort McClary.

Enoteca (207-703-0153), 88 Pepperrel Rd. (Rt. 103), Kittery Point. Open Mon.–Sat.7–7, Sun. 8–7. The former Frisbee's Store now houses this popular source of Italian wine, cheese, and specialty items, previously in downtown Kittery in 2010. Take-out sandwiches on fresh-baked bread include caprese (fresh mozzarella, roasted tomatoes, and red peppers with marinated onions and garlic spread).

PIE IN THE SKY BAKERY, CAPE NEDDICK
Nancy English

✳ Entertainment

Ogunquit Playhouse (see *Entertainment* in "Ogunquit and Wells") is the nearest and most famous summer theater. Special children's presentations.

Hackmatack Playhouse (207-698-1807; hackmatack.org), in Berwick, presents summer-stock performances most evenings; Thu. matinees.

Seacoast Repertory Theatre (603-433-3372; seacoastrep.org), 125 Bow St., Portsmouth, NH. Professional theater productions.

The **Kittery Art Association** (see *Art Galleries*) offers a summer series of Friday concerts and lectures.

✳ Selective Shopping

ANTIQUES Half a dozen antiques dealers can be found along Rt. 1 between **Bell Farm Antiques** in York and **Columbary Antiques** (a group shop) in Cape Neddick. Stop in one and pick up the leaflet guide to the couple dozen member shops between York and Arundel.

TJ's (207-363-5673), 1287 Rt. 1, Cape Neddick. In a class of its own. All reproduction antiques, including fine arts and fabrics. Operated by interior designers Jerry Rippletoe and Tony Sienicki.

ART GALLERIES York Art Association Gallery (207-363-4049 or 207-363-2918), Rt. 1A, York Harbor. Annual July art show, films, and workshops.

George Marshall Store Gallery, 140 Lindsay Rd., York. Open mid-June–mid-Oct., Thu. 11–4, Sun. 1–4. Housed in an 18th-century store maintained by the Museums of Old York. Exhibits feature regional contemporary art and fine crafts. Free.

Kittery Art Association (207-451-9384; kitteryart.org), 8 Coleman Ave., Kittery Point. Open seasonally Thu. 3–6, Sat. noon–6, Sun. noon–5. Housed in a former firehouse marked from (and just off) Rt. 103, changing shows by member artists. The website lists Friday-night music and other events.

FARMER'S MARKET Gateway Farmer's Market (207-363-4422; gatewayofmaine.org), behind the visitors center for the Greater York Region Chamber, 1 Stonewall Lane, Rt.1 at I-95 exit 7 northbound.

June–mid-Oct., Sat. 9–1; July–Sept. also Thu. 11–2. Many local products, crafts, produce, and food.

SPECIAL STORES Kittery Trading Post (207-439-2700; kitterytrading post.com), Rt. 1, Kittery. A local institution since 1926, this sprawling store completed a major expansion in 2004 and is always jammed with shoppers in search of quality sportswear, shoes, children's clothing, firearms, outdoor books, and fishing or camping gear. The summer-end sales are legendary, and many items are often discounted, but this is not an outlet store.

In York

Stonewall Kitchen (207-351-2712; stonewallkitchen.com), Stonewall Lane, Rt. 1, beside the chamber of commerce visitors center, York. Open 8–8 in high season, except 9–6 Sun.; check for off-season hours. What began as a display of offbeat vinegars at a local farmer's market in 1991 is now a mega specialty food business with a big wholesale and mail-order component. Owners Jonathan King and Jim Stott are quick to claim, however, that all their products—from roasted garlic and onion red pepper jelly to raspberry peach champagne jam, sun-dried tomato mustard, fresh lemon curd, and dozens of vinegars, chutneys, and barbecue sauces—still represent homemade care. Sample them in the open-kitchen-style shop, pick up free recipes, and find kitchen supplies and more. There's also a café (see *Eating Out*) and a cooking school with a calendar of varied classes, some taught by celebrity chefs; check the website.

Rocky Mountain Quilts (207-363-6800 or 1-800-762-5940), 130 York St., York Village. Open by appointment. Betsey Telford restores quilts and sells antique quilts (more than 450 in stock, "from doll to king"), blocks, and fabrics from the late 1700s to the 1940s.

Knight's (207-361-2500; mainequilt shop.com), 1901 Rt. 1, Cape Neddick. Bright fabrics, quilt supplies, and small quilted gifts (but no quilts) are sold here. Inquire about quilting classes.

When Pigs Fly (207-439-3114; send bread.com), 40 Brickyard Court in York and 460 Rt. 1, Kittery. The first is the headquarters (closed Tue.) and the second is a company store (daily) and restaurant (see *Eating Out*), both sources for these widely distributed, all-natural breads.

Woods to Goods (207-363-6001; woodstogoods.com), 891 Rt. 1, York. Open daily 10–6; 10–5 off-season. Not all but many of the lamps, ships' models, and other decorative items in this roadside shop are made by inmates of Maine prisons. The PRISON BLUES T-shirts and sweatshirts with the catchy line MADE ON THE INSIDE TO BE WORN ON THE OUTSIDE are produced by Oregon inmates.

In Kittery
OUTLET MALLS Kittery Outlets (1-888-548-8379; thekitteryoutlets .com). Open daily year-round, Mid-Mar.–Dec., Mon.–Sat. 9–9, Sun. 10–6; off-season Sun.–Thu. 10–6, Sat. 10–8. Take I-95 exit 3. At this writing more than 170 discount stores within a 1.3-mile strip of Rt. 1 in Kittery represent a mix of clothing, household furnishings, gifts, and basics. All purport to offer savings of at least 20 percent on retail prices.

✳ **Special Events**
Note: Be sure to pick up the area's unusually lively Calendar of Events at the Greater York Region Chamber of Commerce (gatewaytomaine.org).

June: **Strawberry Festival**, South Berwick.

July: **Ellis Park Concerts** almost nightly, and band concerts Wednesday evening at Short Sands Pavilion, York Beach. Sunday Concerts at Hamilton House, South Berwick (historicnew england.org).

Late July/early August: **York Days Celebration**—flower show, church supper, concerts, square dances, parade, and sand-castle contest. **Decorator's Show House** (oldyork.org).

August: **Mainely Grill'n & Chill'n BBQ Festival** (celebratemainefestival .com), Raitt Farm, Eliot.

Labor Day weekend: **Old York Antiques Show** (oldyork.org) fills Remick Barn, the Museums of Old York visitors center, York.

September–October: **Zach's Corn Maze** (zachscornmaze.com) in York.

October: **Artfest** (first two weekends)—studios and galleries from Kittery to Ogunquit host special events. **Harvestfest** (the weekend after Columbus Day weekend, usually coinciding with peak foliage here), York Village—an ox roast, oxcart races, hay- and horse rides, music, and live entertainment.

Saturday of Thanksgiving weekend: **Lighting of the Nubble, Sohier Park**, 5:45–7, with a shuttle bus from Ellis Park (207-363-1040). The famous lighthouse is illuminated in sparkling white lights for the Christmas season.

December: **Christmas Open House Tours**. **Kittery Christmas Parade and Tree Lighting** and **York Festival of Lights Parade** (first weekend).

OGUNQUIT AND WELLS

Ogunquit and Wells share many miles of uninterrupted sand, and the line between the two towns also blurs along Rt. 1, a stretch of restaurants, family attractions, and family-geared lodging places. The two beach resorts are less and less different as Wells becomes more sophisticated, though it was once the more down-market of the two communities.

Named for the English cathedral town, Wells was incorporated in 1653 and remains a year-round community of 10,000 with seasonal cottages, condo complexes, and campgrounds strung along the beach and Rt. 1—parallel strips separated by a mile-wide swatch of salt marsh.

Ogunquit was part of Wells until 1980 but seceded in spirit long before that, establishing itself as a summer resort in the 1880s and a magnet for artists in the 1890s through the 1940s. It remains a compact, walk-around resort village clustered between its magnificent beach and picturesque Perkins Cove; these two venues are connected by the mile-long Marginal Way, an exceptional shore path. The village offers a vintage movie house and the Ogunquit Playhouse, one of New England's most famous summer theaters.

With the 1980s came condos, B&Bs, more restaurants, and boutiques. Luckily, the decade also brought trolleys on wheels to ease traffic at Perkins Cove and the beach. With a year-round population of 1,100 and 3,000 rooms for rent, Ogunquit regularly draws 40,000 on a summer weekend, 80,000 on holiday weekends year-round. A reservation on summer weekends, or even on a weekday in August, is wise—but call the Ogunquit Chamber (listed below) if you are without one; they can usually help.

GUIDANCE Ogunquit Chamber of Commerce (207-646-2939; ogunquit.org), P.O. Box 2289, Rt. 1, Ogunquit 03907 (beside the Ogunquit Playhouse). Open year-round, Mon.–Fri. 9–5, Sat. 10–3; more hours on Fri., Sat., and Sun. in July and Aug. Staff are helpful, and this large visitors center (with restrooms) is well stocked with pamphlets, including *This Week in Ogunquit* with entertainment and more. The Ogunquit Chamber offers 90-minute walking tours in summer; call 207-967-2939 for schedule.

Wells Chamber of Commerce (207-646-2451; wellschamber.org), 136 Post Rd. (Rt. 1, northbound side) in Moody. Open year-round Mon.–Fri. 9–5; weekends in-season.

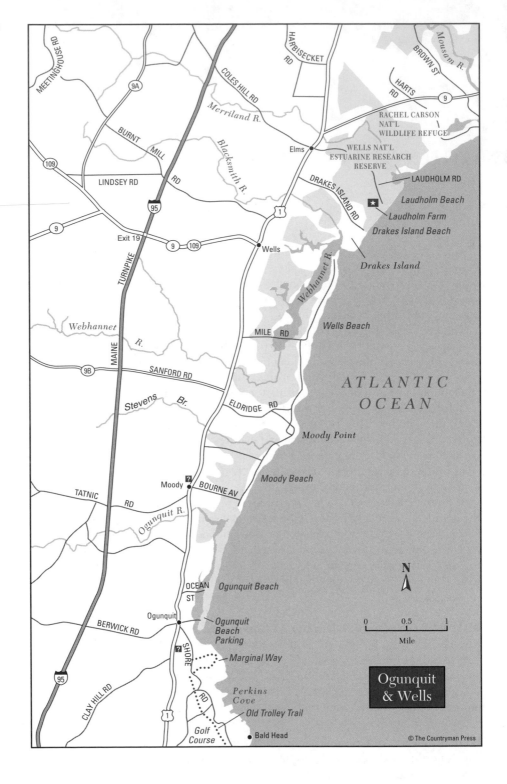

MEETINGHOUSE RD

9A

COLES HILL RD

HARBISECKET RD

BROWN ST

Mousam R.

HARTS RD

9

RACHEL CARSON
NAT'L
WILDLIFE REFUGE

Merriland R.

BURNT MILL RD

109

LINDSEY RD

95

9

Exit 19

Blacksmith R.

Elms

WELLS NAT'L
ESTUARINE RESEARCH
RESERVE

DRAKES ISLAND RD

LAUDHOLM RD

Laudholm Beach

★ Laudholm Farm

Drakes Island Beach

9

109

Wells

Webhannet R.

Drakes Island

Webhannet R.

MILE RD

Wells Beach

MAINE TURNPIKE

9B

SANFORD RD

Stevens Br.

ELDRIDGE RD

Moody Point

**ATLANTIC
OCEAN**

TATNIC RD

Moody ?

BOURNE AV

Moody Beach

Ogunquit R.

N

OCEAN ST

Ogunquit Beach

Ogunquit

BERWICK RD

Ogunquit
Beach
Parking

0   0.5   1
Mile

95

CLAY HILL RD

SHORE RD

? Marginal Way

*Perkins
Cove*

1

Old Trolley Trail

*Golf
Course*

● Bald Head

**Ogunquit
& Wells**

© The Countryman Press

By car: Coming north on I-95, take exit 7 (York) and drive up
Rt. 1 to the village of Ogunquit. Coming south on the Maine Turnpike/I-95, take
turnpike exit 19 (Wells).

By train: The **Downeaster** (amtrakdowneaster.com), Amtrak's popular Boston–
Portland service, makes five roundtrips daily, year-round. The Wells Transportation
Center stop is at 696 Sanford Rd. (Rt. 109) near the exit 19 tollbooth of the Maine
Turnpike (I-95).

Brewster's Taxi (207-646-2141), billed as serving Ogunquit since 1898, offers
local and long-distance service.

Coastal Taxi (207-229-0783; mainetaxicab.com). Friendly service available year-
round.

GETTING AROUND Mid-May–Columbus Day **open-sided trolleys** circle
through the village of Ogunquit, Perkins Cove, and out Rt. 1 in Wells, stopping at
the main entrance to Ogunquit Beach and at Footbridge Beach. Fare is nominal.
Trolley stops are mapped, and maps are available from the chambers of commerce.
They run weekends in June and daily from July 1 to Columbus Day.

PARKING Park and walk or take the trolley. In summer especially, the trolley is
the easiest way to get around. There are at least seven public lots; call the chamber
for rates. There is also free parking (one-hour limit) on Rt. 1 across from the Leavitt Theatre just north of Ogunquit Square or adjacent to Cumberland Farms. Parking at the main entrance to Ogunquit Beach is $4 per hour ($20 weekdays in good
weather, maybe less if it's raining, per day). In Wells parking at the five public lots
was $15 per day in 2011; 10-visit punch cards, $75, are available from the town
office. Perkins Cove parking has a minimum charge of $3 for an hour, with a three-
hour maximum.

PUBLIC RESTROOMS *In Ogunquit:* At Footbridge Beach, Main Beach, Perkins
Cove, Jacob's Lot, the Dunaway Center, and the Ogunquit Chamber Welcome
Center.
In Wells: At the jetty, Wells Harbor Pier, Wells Beach, and Drakes Island parking
areas.

WHEN TO COME Ogunquit and Wells slow down in winter, though more and
more restaurants are staying open through the year. But since the height of summer is so busy in both places, visiting in September and October or June makes for
a more leisurely experience with far less traffic.

✳ To See

Perkins Cove, Ogunquit. Maine's most painted fishing cove, with restaurants and
shops now housed in weathered fish shacks. It is the departure point for the area's
excursion and fishing boats, based beside the famous draw-footbridge. Parking is
nearly impossible in summer, but public lots are nearby, and the trolley stops here
regularly. The cove can also be reached on foot via the Marginal Way.

Ogunquit Museum of American Art (207-646-4909; ogunquitmuseum.org),
Shore Rd., Ogunquit (0.4 mile west of Perkins Cove). Open May–Oct., Mon.–Sat.

Nancy English

THE DRAW-FOOTBRIDGE SPANNING
PERKINS COVE

10–5, Sun. 1–5. Closed Labor Day. $7 adults, $5 seniors, $4 students, free under 12. Founded in 1952 and built superbly of local stone and wood, with enough glass to let in the beauty of the cove it faces, the museum displays selected paintings from its permanent collection, which includes the strong, bright oils of Henry Strater and other onetime locals such as Reginald Marsh; also Thomas Hart Benton, Marsden Hartley, Edward Hopper, Rockwell Kent, and William and Marguerite Zorach. Special exhibitions feature nationally recognized artists.

Ogunquit Heritage Museum (207-646-0296; ogunquitheritagemuseum .org), 86 Obeds Lane, Ogunquit. Open June–Sept., Tue.–Sat. 1–5. Set inside the Captain James Winn House, an 18th-century Cape with a unique Federal staircase and original paneling and flooring, this museum exhibits artifacts of Ogunquit's artistic and fishing history and houses the Littlefield Genealogical Library.

&. **Historical Society of Wells & Ogunquit** (207-646-4775; wells ogunquithistory.org), 936 Post Rd. (Rt. 1, opposite Wells Plaza). Open mid-May–mid-Oct., Tue.–Thu. 10–4; off-season, Wed.–Thu. 10–4. $2 donation per adult. Housed in a historic meetinghouse still used for weddings, concerts, and numerous special events; also a genealogy library, old photos, memorabilia, ships' models, and a gift shop.

✧ &. **Wells Auto Museum** (207-646-9064; wellsautomuseum.com), Wells. Open Memorial Day–Columbus Day, daily 10–5. Admission fee. More than 80 cars dating from 1900 to 1963, including a 1919 Stutz Bearcat and a 1941 Packard convertible, plus nickelodeons, toys, and bicycles.

✶ To Do

APPLE, BLUEBERRY, AND VEGGIE PICKING Spiller Farm U-Pick (207-985-2575; spillerfarm.com), 85 Spiller Farm Lane, Wells. Pick apples (including Northern Spy), blueberries, strawberries, and more—like your own buttercup squash, or other vegetables—and pay by the pound or piece. Hayride farm tours on fall weekends at this 130-acre farm that got its start in 1894. No credit cards. **Spillers' Farm Store** (207-985-3383), 1054 Branch Rd., Wells, does accept cards and is open year-round with farm products, Angus beef, pizza, and more.

BICYCLING Wheels and Waves (207-646-5774; wheelsnwaves.com), 365 Post Rd. (Rt. 1), Wells. Rentals include mountain bikes, hybrids, and kids' bikes.

BOAT EXCURSIONS Finestkind Cruises (207-646-5227; finestkind cruises.com) offers scenic cruises and "lobstering trips." The *Bunny Clark* (207-646-2214; bunnyclark.com) offers deep-sea-fishing trips from Perkins Cove.

Christina Tree

OGUNQUIT MUSEUM OF ART

FISHING FROM SHORE Tackle can be rented at Wells Harbor; bait is available as well. The obvious fishing spots are the municipal dock and harbor jetties. There is surf casting near the mouth of the Mousam River. Also see "Kittery" and "The Kennebunks."

GOLF The area's major 18-hole golf courses are described in "Kittery."
Merriland Farm (207-646-0508; merrilandfarm.com), 545 Coles Hill Rd. (off Rt. 1), Wells. Nine-hole, par-three course on a working farm. Also a café (207-646-5040; merrilandfarmcafe.com).

MINI GOLF ✇ ♿ **Wells Beach Mini-Golf** (1-800-640-2267; wellsbeach.com), 1000 Post Rd. (Rt. 1), Wells. Open daily mid-May–mid-Oct.
✇ **Wonder Mountain Fun Park** (207-646-9655), 270 Post Rd. (Rt. 1), Wells. Open Memorial Day–Labor Day. A human maze, two 18-hole courses—including Mountain Mania, complete with waterfalls—and an arcade with skee ball and video games.
✇ **Sea-Vu Mini Golf** (207-646-7732; sea-vucampground.com) is another Rt. 1 option in Wells. 18 holes.

SEA KAYAKING World Within Sea Kayaking (207-646-0455; worldwithin .com), Wells. Registered Maine Guide Andrew French offers guided estuary and ocean tours from the Ogunquit River Inn and Suites, on the Ogunquit–Wells line, in kayaks and also on stand-up paddleboards (lessons offered).

SURFING AND STAND-UP PADDLEBOARDS Wheels and Waves (207-646-5774; wheelsnwaves.com) 365 Post Rd. (Rt. 1), Wells. Rentals include surfboards and wet suits. Two-hour lesson with equipment is $60; offered year-round but in winter generally only those 13 and older can find equipment that fits. Summer surf camps. Anyone can get on the big paddleboards; speed paddleboards offer an incredible workout.

TENNIS Three public courts in Ogunquit. Inquire at **Dunaway Center** (207-361-9538). **Wells Recreation Area**, Rt. 9A, Wells, has four courts.

❋ Green Space

BEACHES Three-mile-long **Ogunquit Beach** offers surf, soft sand, and space for kite flying, as well as a sheltered strip along the mouth of the Ogunquit River for toddlers. It can be approached three ways: (1) The most popular way is from the foot of Beach St. There are boardwalk snacks, changing facilities, and toilets, and it is here that the beach forms a tongue between the ocean and the Ogunquit River (parking in the lot here is $4 per hour in-season). (2) The Footbridge Beach access (take Ocean St. off Rt. 1 north of the village) offers restrooms and is less crowded. $15 a day weekdays, $20 weekends for parking. (3) Moody Beach parking lot, Wells. Be sure to park in the lot provided; $20 a day. Walk west onto Ogunquit Beach, not to Moody Beach, now private above the high-water mark.

Wells Beach. Limited free parking right in the middle of the village of Wells Beach; also parking at the east end by the jetty. Wooden casino and boardwalk, clam shacks, clean public toilets, a cluster of motels, concrete benches—a gathering point for older people who sit while enjoying the view of the wide, smooth beach.

Drakes Island, Wells. Take Drakes Island Rd. off Rt. 1. There are three small parking areas on this spit of land lined with private cottages.

NATURE PRESERVES AND PARKS Wells Reserve at Laudholm (207-646-1555; wellsreserve.org), Laudholm Rd. (off Rt. 1, just south of its junction with Rt. 9; look for the blinking yellow light just south of the Maine Diner on Rt. 1), Wells. This 2,250-acre reserve on two estuaries, an area formed where ocean tides meet freshwater currents, is a National Estuarine Research Reserve with headquarters listed on the National Register of Historic Places. The reserve consists of two parts: the meadows, salt marshes, woodlands, and two barrier beaches at the mouth of the Little River; and Laudholm Farm, a former estate that began as a saltwater farm in the 1640s. Owned by the Lord family from 1881 until 1986 (George C. Lord was president of the Boston & Maine Railroad), it was farmed until the 1950s. Today it's a birder's mecca. A visitors center is open year-round (weekdays 10–4; also May–Oct., Sat. 10–4 and Sun. noon–4), with a exhibits, restrooms, and parking. Seven miles of trails meander through fields, woods, and wetlands (bring a bathing suit if you want to swim at the beach). The Wells Reserve is open daily year-round (gates open daily 7 AM–sunset); entrance fee Memorial Day–Columbus Day is $3 adults, $1 ages 6–16; no dogs allowed. Guided trail walks and programs for adults and kids ages 6–9. The Laudholm Nature Crafts Festival is held the weekend after Labor Day. Punkinfiddle (punkinfiddle.org) in early fall is a celebration of National Estuaries Day with fiddle bands, artisan demonstrations like butter churning, apple pressing, and pumpkin rolling, and more.

Rachel Carson National Wildlife Refuge, off Rt. 9 on the Wells–Kennebunk line. See the description in "The Kennebunks."

Dorothea Grant Common. Hidden away between Rt. 1 and the Dunaway Center, this quiet park surrounds the Ogunquit Heritage Museum at Winn House (see *To See*).

WALKS Marginal Way. In 1923 Josiah Chase gave Ogunquit this windy path along the ocean. A farmer from the town of York, just south of here, Chase had driven his cattle around rocky Israel's Head each summer to pasture on the marsh grass in Wells, just to the north. Over the years he bought land here and there until, eventually, he owned the whole promontory. He then sold off sea-view lots at a tidy profit and donated the actual ocean frontage to the town, thus preserving his own right-of-way. There is very limited parking at the mini lighthouse on Israel's Head.

✄ ♿ **Wells Harbor**. Here is a pleasant walk along a granite jetty and a good fishing spot. There is also a playground, and a gazebo where concerts are held.

Old Trolley Trail. An interesting nature walk and cross-country ski trail that begins on Pine Hill Rd. N., Ogunquit.

WHALE WATCH See First Chance under *Whale-Watching* in "The Kennebunks."

✳ Lodging

Note: Ogunquit's 2,500 "rooms" include many family-geared efficiencies, especially along Rt. 1. We do not attempt to critique them here, but all are listed on the Ogunquit Chamber of Commerce website (ogunquit.org) and in its Four Season Destination Resource Guide.

All listings are in Ogunquit 03907, or have an Ogunquit mailing address, and are most convenient to Ogunquit, unless otherwise noted

RESORT ✄ ♿ **The Cliff House** (207-361-1000; cliffhousemaine.com), Shore Rd., P.O. Box 2274. Open mid-April–Nov. Over the last few years the Cliff House, opened in 1872 with a single building on the top of its spectacular location, now features a monumental spa facility and 32 large rooms that feature gas fireplaces and of course ocean views. Guests ages 18 and older can use the "vanishing edge" pool (set out on the terrace, it gives swimmers the illusion of a sea dip without the low temperature of Maine ocean water). The spa, open to the public as well as to guests, gives guests access to luxurious massages and facials.

Innkeeper Kathryn Weare is the great-granddaughter of the woman who opened this 194-room hotel, and hospitality remains her focus. Although the decor in the main building rooms is undistinguished, furnishings are good quality. Every amenity you need is close at hand, from a dining room with that great view and good food (see *Dining Out*) to nearby golf courses, two indoor heated pools, and an exercise room.

This place rose from its own ashes after being run down during the temporary, exclusive use of the U.S. military, which used it as a lookout for Nazi submarines in World War II. Innkeeper Charles Weare tried to sell it for

THE CLIFF HOUSE

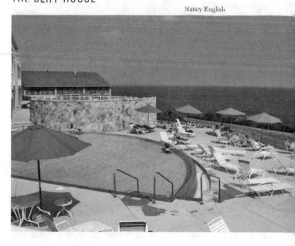

Nancy English

$50,000 in 1946 with an ad in *The Wall Street Journal*, but received no offers.

High-season summer rates range $265–360 with no meals; $175–250 off-season.

RESORT MOTOR INNS Our usual format places inns before motels, but in the 1960s some of Ogunquit's leading resorts replaced their old hotel buildings with luxury "motor inns."

🖉 **Sparhawk** (207-646-5562; the sparhawk.com), 85 Shore Rd., P.O. Box 936. Open mid-Apr.–late Oct. Fifty-two-unit Oceanfront overlooks the confluence of the Ogunquit River and the Atlantic Ocean, as well as Ogunquit Beach (waves lap below the balconies). Twenty units in neighboring Ireland House (with balconies canted toward the water) are combination living room/bedroom suites. The Barbara Dean and Jacobs Houses, formerly village homes, add another 11 suites and four apartments, some with gas fireplace and Jacuzzi. The two-bedroom Little White House overlooks the ocean. Guests register and gather in Sparhawk Hall. Amenities include outdoor pool (heated mid-June–mid-Sept.),

AERIAL VIEW OF BEACHMERE INN
Courtesy of Beachmere Inn

shuffleboard, croquet, tennis, and privileges at the local golf course and fitness center. One-week minimum stay July–mid-Aug.; $195–315 per night in high summer, $105–250 in spring and fall.

Parsons Post House Inn (207-646-7533; parsonsposthouse.com), 62 Shore Rd. Thirteen bright and comfortable rooms, all with private bath, TV, AC, and cushy beds, along with a suite and "The Penthouse" with an ocean-view living room. Rooms $125–229, depending on season.

INNS AND HOTELS 🖉 ♿ **The Beachmere Inn** (207-646-2021 or 1-800-336-3983; beachmereinn.com), 62 Beachmere Place. Open year-round. Beachmere Inn consists of a rambling, updated mansion and a streamlined building that border a huge lawn overlooking Ogunquit Beach. The inn, owned by female members of the same family since 1937, has 39 rooms and 33 suites; Number 35 is a blue aerie set over Marginal Way and ocean waves, with handmade furniture and gas fireplace. All rooms have kitchenette and cable TV, and most have a private balcony, deck, or terrace. Four handicapped-accessible rooms are available, as are a breakfast area, bar, and function space. A huge indoor hot tub, cedar sauna, massage rooms, exercise rooms, and children's play area are available to guests. Attention to detail and high-level hospitality make a stay here a pleasure. High-season rates, $160–395, drop in the off-season after the last weekend in October to $65–195.

The Grand Hotel (207-646-1231 or 1-800-806-1231; thegrandhotel.com), 276 Shore Dr. Open Mar.–Nov. Twenty-eight suites in this hotel, originally a condominium complex, each have two rooms, wet bar, fridge, cable

TV, a king-sized bed, and a private deck or balcony; fireplace in top-floor rooms. There's an elevator, an interior atrium, an indoor pool, and an outdoor hot tub. $180–240 in high season, $95–210 right after Labor Day, from $70 off-season.

BED & BREAKFASTS The Trellis House (207-646-7909 or 1-800-681-7909; trellishouse.com), 2 Beachmere Place, P.O. Box 2229. Open year-round. Pat and Jerry Houlihan's shingled, turn-of-the-20th-century summer cottage offers appealing common areas, including a wraparound screened porch and comfortable seating around the fireplace. Upstairs are three guest rooms, all with full private bath, one with a water view; the English Suite has an enclosed porch and is furnished with antiques. A romantic cottage in the garden is private. This is one of those places where guests feel at ease, because the Houlihans are genuine hosts. $155–225 in-season, from $95 off-season, includes a breakfast that might include sour cream waffles with whipped cream and blueberry sauce. The inn is handy both to the village and to Perkins Cove via Marginal Way.

Marginal Way House and Motel (207-646-8801; in winter, 207-361-4321; marginalwayhouse.com), Wharf Lane, P.O. Box 697. Open late Apr.–Oct. Just a short walk from the beach and really in the middle of the village, this delightful complex is hidden down a waterside lane; its landscaped lawn has a water view. Geoffrey Blake and his family have run this property since 1968. There are old-fashioned guest rooms—Number 8 has flowered wallpaper and a beach view—in the Main and Wharf Houses, each with private bath. Dockside houses six standard motel units, and there are seven (high-season weekly rental) apartments. High season $104–216, low $49–94.

Morning Dove (207-646-3891; the morningdove.com), 13 Bourne Lane, P.O. Box 1940. On a quiet side street off Shore Rd., within walking distance of everything, this is a handsome, spotless 1860s farmhouse. We like the living room with its white marble fireplace; there are two suites, one with gas fireplace, and four guest rooms. Innkeeper Rob Leary took over in 2007. $160–225 in-season, $75–135 off-season, full breakfast included.

Above Tide Inn (207-646-7454; abovetideinn.com), 66 Beach St. Open May 15–Oct. 15. Right at the start of the Marginal Way and steps from the bridge leading over to Ogunquit Beach, also steps from village shops and jutting right out into the water. Meghan and John Hubacz offer nine rooms, each with an outdoor sitting area, small fridge, TV, and shower or bath. All but one room have water views, and local artists painted the pictures hanging inside. Mid-July–Labor Day rates are $190–235; $100–140 off-season, continental breakfast included.

The Beauport Inn on Clay Hill (207-361-2400; beauportinn.com), 339 Clay Hill Rd. Open Apr.–mid-Dec. A two-minute drive from town and quiet, this stone manor set by a river has vintage-1835 English oak floor-to-ceiling paneling in its great room. Each room has a gas fireplace, cable TV, and DVD; there's also a two-room suite and a fully equipped apartment. A lap pool, steam room, and Jacuzzi are shared by guests. $95–240 (depending on the season) includes a full breakfast.

Beach Farm Inn (207-646-8493; beachfarminn.com), 97 Eldridge Rd., Wells 04090. Open Apr.–Nov. This handsome restored farmhouse has been taking in guests since the 19th century, when it was a working salt-marsh farm.

Today loyal repeat customers and many French Canadians appreciate the hospitality of Nancy Swenson and Craig White. Victorian upholstery by Nancy and furniture by Craig give the interior panache. A full breakfast featuring apple-baked French toast or homemade pierogi is served on the bright sunporch. The guest pantry stocks Carpe Diem coffee, and a swimming pool beckons from the lawn. Eight attractive bedrooms, three with private bath—others can be rented with an unattached bath for private use—and two efficiency cottages. $100–150 per couple June–Sept. and holiday weekends, including breakfast; $80–115 off-season.

COTTAGES *Note:* We have noted just a few of the dozens of the area's summer rentals, especially plentiful in Wells. Contact the Wells Chamber of Commerce, which keeps track of rental cottages and condos. **Garnsey Bros. Rentals** (207-646-8301; garnsey .com) offers cottage rentals throughout the area.

 ✍ **Dunes on the Waterfront** (207-646-2612; dunesonthewaterfront.com), 518 Main St., P.O. Box 917. Open May–Oct. Owned by the Perkins family for more than 70 years, this is really a historic property, the best of the coast's surviving "cottage colonies," as well as a great family find. The 36 units include 19 old-style white cottages with green trim, many with fireplace, scattered over well-kept grounds fronting on the Ogunquit River, with direct access to Ogunquit Beach by rowboat at high tide and on foot at low tide. All rooms have refrigerator and color TV. Minimum stay in July and Aug. in the larger cottages. $255–315 in-season, $170–195 off-season.

 ✍ **Cottage in the Lane Motor Lodge** (207-646-7903; cottageinthe lane.com), 84 Drakes Island Rd., Wells 04090. There are 10 housekeeping cottages, all facing landscaped grounds under the pines (an artistic play structure and a pool form the centerpiece); salt marsh beyond. It's a 0.75-mile walk or bike ride to the beach. The quiet setting borders the Rachel Carson Wildlife Refuge and Laudholm Farm (see *Green Space*). A two-bedroom cottage runs $990 per week in-season, $560–750 off-season.

 ✍ **The Seagull Inn and Condominiums** (207-646-5164; seagullvacations .com), 1413 Post Rd. (Rt. 1), Wells 04090. Open May.–Oct. Two three-story town houses (available year-round), 27 two-bedroom cottages, 1 one-bedroom cottage, all with a screened porch, fill what used to be an open field. Private driveway and gas grills; new cottages have ocean views. The seven remaining old cottages have been updated with bathrooms and kitchens. Two heated pools, one with hot tub, the other with a wading pool for children. Rentals by the week in summer (three-night minimum off-season), $800–1,500 for the housekeeping cottages; $2,800 a week for town houses.

MOTEL Riverside Motel (207-646-2741; riversidemotel.com), Shore Rd., P.O. Box 2244. Open mid-Apr.–Oct. Just across the draw-footbridge and overlooking Perkins Cove is this trim, friendly place with 42 units; also four rooms in the 1874 house. The property had been in the Staples family for more than 100 years before Geoff Scimone took over in 2009. All 4 acres are nonsmoking. All rooms have cable TV and full bath, most tiled, and all overlook the cove; fresh muffins, Congdon's Doughnuts, yogurt, and cereal served in the lobby 7:30–11 around the fireplace, with outdoor seating.

Nancy English

THE RIVERSIDE MOTEL OVERLOOKING PERKINS COVE

$79–199, depending on season and location of room.

✳ Where to Eat

DINING OUT Technically in Cape Neddick but just as handy to Ogunquit, **Clay Hill Farm** is described in "Kittery and the Yorks."

Arrows (207-361-1100; arrows restaurant.com), Berwick Rd., Ogunquit. Open Wed.–Sun. in July and Aug. at 6 PM, fewer days of the week off-season, and closed Jan.–Mar. Winners of the 2010 Best Chefs Northeast Award from the James Beard Foundation, Mark Gaier and Clark Frasier run Arrows with mastery; the food is sometimes extraordinary. Friday night is Bistro Night, served year-round ($39.95 for three courses). The big wine list is expensive, as are the wines by the glass. A strict dress code is enforced (no one in shorts or jeans will be seated), and 24-hour notice is required for cancellations; without that a $50-per-person fee is charged on the credit card required to make

the reservation. Immaculate gardens surround the old house, and guests often tour the garden before dinner, when some of the produce they have observed will be on their plates. Prix fixe $85 and up.

✪ **98 Provence** (207-646-9898; 98provence.com), 262 Shore Rd., Ogunquit. Open Apr.–Dec. 1, daily except Tue. for dinner (5:30–9:30) in summer, and now serving weekend breakfast. This classic French Provençal restaurant gets all the details right. Over the winter of 2011–12 a renovation created a new look. The wine list is dominated by France, and some lovelies are sold by the glass. Reservations advised. Entrées $22–32.

✪ & **Joshua's Restaurant** (207-646-3355; joshuas.biz), 1637 Post Rd. (Rt. 1), Wells. Open for dinner daily in summer, closed Sun. The buzz about Joshua's just keeps getting better. The Mather family farm grows its own vegetables, and chef Joshua Mather puts them to spectacular use as sides for grilled rack of lamb, pork tenderloin with plum chutney, and haddock with caramelized onion crust. An elegant, refurbished farmhouse dining room and bar. Entrées $21–35.

✪ **Angelina's Ristorante** (207-646-0445; angelinasogunquit.com), 655 Main St., Ogunquit. Open daily 4:30–10. Reservations recommended. Owner-chef David Giarusso Jr. might be tired, but he's scrupulously polite whenever you encounter him on a busy night at this deservedly popular Italian restaurant, and that's part of why people love it here. A garden terrace feels cool in the hot summer and the bustling rooms are always comfortable, but what's most important is on the plate, and it is wonderful. Good wine list. Entrées $16–29.

The Cliff House (207-361-1000; cliff housemaine.com), Shore Rd., Ogunquit. Open daily for dinner late Mar.–Dec. No jeans, shorts, sneakers, sweat suits, or T-shirts are allowed on diners in the restaurant; "gentlemen need a collared shirt." Diver scallops come with baked beans and mini corn cake. Swordfish, halibut with blueberry gastrique, and naturally raised sirloin with mushroom confit are from a summer menu. The view over the water from

the high cliff is mesmerizing. Entrées $22–36.

MC Perkins Cove (207-646-6263; mcperkinscove.com), Perkins Cove. Lunch and dinner daily in summer, closed some days of the week off-season. Wonderful water views and live Thu.-night entertainment. Owned by the inventive chefs of Arrows (see above), this is a casual place for fresh raw oysters, grilled steak and fish, fried trout, and other seafood with splendid touches. Choose your own "evil carbos" and sauces. The even more casual bar menu is a deal. Entrées $19–32.

Five'O Shore Road (207-646-5001; five-oshoreroad.com), 50 Shore Rd., Ogunquit Village. Open for dinner in-season nightly, light fare served until 11 PM; Thu.–Sun. in winter. The beef tenderloin brochette we tried remains a high point of dining out, and the skilled preparation of everything else was memorable, too. Lamb porterhouse with mint champagne chimichurri, as well as grilled veal chop, were on a summer menu, along with sides of grilled baby squash and pickled golden beets. Good wine and cocktails. Entrées $23–39.

Gypsy Sweethearts (207-646-7021; gypsysweethearts.com), 30 Shore Rd., Ogunquit. Open Apr.–Oct. for dinner Tue.–Sun. from 5:30; weekends off-season. Meals with a Caribbean twist are served in a charming old house that is the dependable neighborhood dinner spot for demanding locals. Chef-owner Judie Clayton's green secret pumpkinseed sauce is a tangy delight on the rack of lamb. Poblano rellenos, and shelled lobster with spinach tagliatelle. Many wines available by the glass. Entrées $18–29.

Prime (207-646-8600; primeogunquit .com), 331 Shore Rd., Ogunquit. Steaks, of course. Located near Perkins Cove with valet parking avail-

ANGELINA'S RISTORANTE

Nancy English

able, Prime offers the dedication to fine beef every area needs; the reasonable prices acknowledge the area's tastes as well. Two side dishes and a sauce, perhaps blue cheese and horseradish or the classic béarnaise, come with any steak ordered. Beef dry-aged in-house. Entrées $21–29.

The Front Porch Restaurant (207-646-4005; frontporchrestaurant.net), 9 Shore Rd., Ogunquit. A popular nightspot boasts a fine fish taco with cilantro slaw, good crabcakes, and burgers. Count on a crowd on summer weekends, with entertainment upstairs in the piano bar (see *Entertainment*). The menu is served in all three spaces except during shows. Steaks, pasta, and grilled fish, too. Entrées $17–27.

Jonathan's Restaurant (207-646-4777; jonathansrestaurant.com), 92 Bourne Lane, Ogunquit. Open year-round. There are two entirely distinct parts to this big place. The downstairs restaurant consists of a series of nicely decorated rooms (one with a 600-gallon tropical aquarium). The mainstream fare is well made, including grilled steak, scampi Provençal, and caramelized salmon fillet. Entrées $18–26. For more about what happens upstairs, see *Entertainment*.

Varano's Restaurant (207-641-8550; varanos.com), 60 Mile Rd., Wells. Open daily at 4. A family-owned Italian restaurant that combines a welcoming professional staff with good food. Fritto misto (fried seasonal vegetables) might be a summer appetizer, and whole wheat vegetarian pasta keeps up the good work. Grilled lamb, house pork sausage, and lobster with black fettuccine. Reservations not accepted.

Katie's Café on Shore Road (207-641-2780; katiescafeonshoreroad.com), 261 Shore Rd., Ogunquit. Pan-seared cod with salt cod potato cake, grilled

chorizo, and burnt lemon and baby spinach salad sounds like a good idea for dinner. Duck, New York strip, and shrimp scampi were also on a fall menu. $16–32.

LOBSTER *Note:* Maine's southernmost beach resorts are the first place many visitors sample real "Mane Lobstah" the way it should be eaten: messily, with bib, butter, and a water view.

✄ **Barnacle Billy's, Etc.** (207-646-5575 or 1-800-866-5575; barnbilly .com), Perkins Cove. Open May–Oct. for lunch and dinner. What began as a no-frills lobster place (the one that's still next door) has expanded over 50 years to fill a luxurious dining space created for a more upscale waterside restaurant. Lobster and seafood dishes remain the specialty, and it's difficult to beat the view combined with comfort, which frequently includes the glow from two great stone fireplaces. Full bar; dinner entrées from $16.75, higher for a big boiled lobster. You can also order lobster at the counter and wait for your number, dine on the outdoor deck, or order burgers.

✪ 🦞 ✄ ♿ **Lobster Shack** (207-646-2941), end of Perkins Cove. Open mid-Apr–mid-Oct., 11–9 in-season. A family-owned, old-style serious lobster-eating place since the 1940s (when it was known as Maxwell and Perkins). The tables are wide slabs of shellacked pine with plenty of room for lobster by the pound, steamer clams, good chowder, house coleslaw; also reasonably priced burgers, apple pie à la mode, wine, beer.

✄ **Ogunquit Lobster Pound** (207-646-2516), Rt. 1 (north of Ogunquit Village). Open April–Oct. Expanded gradually over the years, this log landmark retains its 1930s atmosphere and is still all about selecting your lobster and watching it (if you so choose) get steamed in the huge outdoor pots. "Steamers" (steamed clams) are the other specialty. The large menu, however, now includes angel-hair pasta, fried foods, and sirloin steaks. Beer and wine are available. Entrées $14–30 and up for lobster.

🦞 🐟 **Fisherman's Catch** (207-646-8780; fishermanscatchwells.com), 134 Harbor Rd., Wells Harbor. Open May–Columbus Day, daily 11:30–9 in summer, closing earlier off-season. Set in a salt marsh, with rustic tables; a traditional seafood place with unbeatable prices. Good chowder and really good lobster stew, homemade crabcakes, lobster dinners, children's menu, beer on tap, all provided by a family that takes good care of you. Try the bread pudding with whiskey sauce. Entrées $12–18 plus.

EATING OUT Féile Restaurant and Pub (207-251-4065; feilerestaurant andpub.com), 1619 Post Rd. (Rt. 1), Wells. Fish-and-chips is perfectly made with a battered crust and hand-cut potatoes. Sandwiches, burgers, and seafood are also served. The Smithwicks, an Irish red ale, is lively and thirst quenching, and the Guinness is almost as good. Live entertainment includes local musicians playing traditional Irish music with fiddle, accordion, or whatever instruments they bring along at this well-loved pub with a knack for hospitality.

Amore Breakfast and Café Amore (207-646-6661; amorebreakfast.com), 309 Shore Rd., Ogunquit. Open early spring–mid-Dec., in-season 7 AM–1 PM daily, closed Wed. and Thu., extended hours in the café and evening hours in summer. Relaxed and pleasant, this restaurant makes exuberant omelets and a lobster eggs Benedict as pretty as an ocean sunrise. Also panini and sandwiches including a lobster roll,

and a place to park. Breakfast $4–14; lunch $6–12.

Caffé Prego (207-646-7734; caffe pregoogt.com), 44 Shore Rd., Ogunquit. Pizza, well-made pasta and panini, Italian pastries and desserts, cappuccino and espresso all vie for your appreciation. In any case, you can finish with house gelato in compelling flavors like kiwi and chocolate. Entrées $9–19.

Oarweed Oceanside Restaurant (207-646-4022; oarweed.com), Perkins Cove. This seaside restaurant has outdoor seating in warm weather, but inside or out you can feast your eyes on the water—and on your plate, where you might choose good crab roll, lobster roll, crabcakes, steamed lobster, roast chicken, or the perfectly done steamers, an essential ingredient in the shore dinner.

Lord's Harborside Restaurant (207-646-2651; lordsharborside.com), Harbor Rd., Wells Harbor. Open end of Apr.–Oct. for lunch and dinner; closed Tue. A big, ungarnished dining room with a harbor view serving fried and broiled fish and seafood. Lobster boiled and baked. Entrées $15–26. A midafternoon (2–4 PM) 15 percent discount was offered in 2011.

The Steakhouse (207-646-4200; the-steakhouse.com), Rt. 1, Wells. Lobster and seafood, but the emphasis is on corn-fed prime and choice beef, and all steak dinners include a choice of two: baked beans, fries, baked potato, pasta with meat sauce, vegetable, salad, applesauce, or cottage cheese with pear. Entrées $14–26.

Jake's Seafood (207-646-6771), 127 Post Rd. (Rt. 1), Moody. Open for all three meals Apr.–Oct., breakfast and lunch Nov.–Mar. Specializes in good American cooking, fresh seafood, ice cream.

Congdon's Donuts Family Restaurant (207-646-4219; congdons.com), 1090 Post Rd. (Rt. 1), Wells. Open 6–3 daily in summer, fewer days in winter. Fresh muffins, breads, pastries, doughnuts, and a full menu for breakfast and lunch. The doughnuts are fried in lard; this place is one of the very few left that do so, and it makes a great doughnut.

Mike's Clam Shack (207-646-5999; mikesclamshack.com), 1150 Post Rd. (Rt. 1), Wells. Open daily in-season 11:30 to closing. An enormous place with enormous crowds, with a reputation for good fried clams. Sandwiches, burgers, pasta, and fried seafood, $10–22.

✿ **Billy's Chowder House** (207-646-7558; billyschowderhouse.com), Mile Rd., Wells. Open daily mid-Jan.–early Dec. Overlooking Wells Harbor and a salt marsh, a family favorite with famous chowder and a selection of fried seafood, steamed shellfish, broiled scallops, and, of course, boiled lobster. There's also plenty of meat on the menu, including a hot dog and fries. Entrées $13–21.

Maine Diner (207-656-4441; mainediner.com), 2265 Post Rd. (Rt. 1), Wells, near the junction of Rts. 1 and 9. Open year-round 7 AM–9 PM. This packed place can still boast about its seafood chowder, made with shrimp, scallops, lobster, and clams in a milky broth. Avoid the chicken potpie. Entrées $5–21.

✿ **Village Food Market and Cafe** (207-646-2122; villagefoodmarket .com), 230 Main St., Ogunquit. This landmark grocery store has changed with the times, adding daily baked goods, soups, salads, a deli—and a summer takeout called Fancy That, with an outdoor eating area. Call before 11 for a picnic order to avoid the line.

✿ **Sundaes at the Beach** (207-646-5424; sundaesatthebeach.com), 231 Post Rd. (Rt. 1), Wells. Make your own sundaes, enjoy a burger or a lobster roll, or do both at this casual spot on Rt. 1. The ice cream is made here.

SNACKS Bread & Roses Bakery (207-646-4227; breadandrosesbakery .com), 28 Main St., Ogunquit. Over the years Mary Breen's pleasant bakery has expanded into an attractive café serving muffins and coffee, irresistible cinnamon butter puffs, and other delectable pastries. Lunch on panini, big salads, and fresh thick-crust pizza.

Scoop Deck (207-646-5150; scoop deck.com), Eldridge Rd. (just off Rt. 1), Wells. Open Memorial Day–Columbus Day. Mocha chip and Dinosaur Crunch (blue vanilla) are among the more than 55 flavors; the ice cream is from Thibodeau Farms in Saco. Also yogurt, brownies, and hot dogs.

Borealis Breads (207-641-8800; borealisbreads.com), Rt. 1, Wells. Open daily. Great bread and sandwiches—don't overlook the fabulous bread sticks—and the brownies and other treats are excellent. More than 100,000 pounds of whole wheat flour for the breads is milled from wheat grown in Aroostook County.

✳ Entertainment

THEATERS Hackmatack Playhouse (207-698-1807; hackmatack.org), 538 School St. (Rt. 9), Berwick, stages live performances throughout the season.

Arundel Barn Playhouse (207-985-5552; arundelbarnplayhouse.com), 53 Old Post Rd., Arundel. Mid-June–Labor Day. Professional musical theater in a restored 1800s barn.

🎭 ✿ **Booth Theater** (207-646-8142; boothproductions.com), 13 Beach St.,

Ogunquit. A black-box theater with productions Tue.–Sat., June–Aug. The theater seats 60, and the productions vary from musicals to dramas.

Leavitt Fine Arts Theatre (207-646-3123; leavittheatre.com), 259 Main St., Ogunquit Village. An old-time theater with new screen and sound; showing first-run films since 1923.

Ogunquit Playhouse (207-646-5511; ogunquitplayhouse.org), Rt. 1 (just south of Ogunquit Village). Open June–Oct. Billing itself as "America's Foremost Summer Theater," this grand old summer-stock theater opened for its first season in 1933 and is now owned by the Ogunquit Playhouse Foundation. It continues to feature top stars in productions staged Tue.–Fri. at 8 PM, Sat. at 8:30 PM; matinees are offered several days of the week.

OTHERS Jonathan's Restaurant (207-646-4777; jonathansrestaurant .com), 92 Bourne Lane, Ogunquit. Year-round. You can check the current schedule on the website. Spiro Gyra, the Jon Pousette-Dart Band, Paula

OGUNQUIT PLAYHOUSE

Kim Grant

Poundstone, and Leon Redbone headlined in 2011.

Ogunquit Performing Arts (207-646-6170) sponsors the Chamber Music Festival in June and the Capriccio annual summer arts festival; also film, social dances, and theater year-round.

The Front Porch Restaurant (207-646-4005; frontporchrestaurant.net), 9 Shore Rd., Ogunquit. Performances and piano and the chance to join in the show tunes; special events with live entertainment.

Hope Hobbs Gazebo at Wells Harbor Park is the site of Sat.-night concerts in summer.

✳ Selective Shopping

ANTIQUARIAN BOOKS Boston book lovers drive to Wells to browse in the cluster of exceptional bookstores along Rt. 1. **Douglas N. Harding Rare Books** (207-646-8785; hardings books.com), 2152 Post Rd., open year-round, is huge and excellent with some 200,000 titles, including rare finds, maps, and prints. **The Arringtons** (207-646-4124), 1908 Post Rd. (Rt. 1), specializes in military subjects as well as vintage paperbacks and postcards.

ANTIQUES SHOPS Rt. 1 from York through Wells and the Kennebunks is studded with antiques shops, among them: **MacDougall-Gionet** (207-646-3531; macdougall-gionet.com), open Tue.–Sun. 10–5, a particularly rich trove of formal and country furniture in a barn; 60 dealers are represented. **R. Jorgensen Antiques** (207-646-9444; rjorgensen.com) has nine rooms filled with antique furniture, including fine formal pieces from a number of countries. Open Mon.–Sat. 10–5, Sun. noon–5.

BARN GALLERY

Nancy English

ART GALLERIES In addition to the
Ogunquit Museum of Art there is the
Barn Gallery, home of the **Ogunquit
Art Association** (207-646-8400; barn
gallery.org, ogunquitartassociation
.com), Shore Rd. and Bourne Lane,
Ogunquit. Open late May–early Oct.,
Mon.–Sat. 11–5 and Sun. 1–5. The
Barn Gallery showcases work by mem-
bers; also stages frequent workshops,
lectures, Wed.-night films about artists,
Tue.-night workshops working with a
model, and concerts. **Shore Road
Gallery** (207-646-5046), 294 Shore
Rd., open Memorial Day–Columbus
Day weekend, daily July–Aug, offers
fine arts, jewelry, and fine crafts by
nationally known artists. **Van Ward
Gallery** (207-646-0554; vanwardgallery
.com), 49 Shore Rd., Ogunquit.

SPECIAL SHOPS Perkins Cove,
the cluster of former fish shacks by
Ogunquit's famous draw-footbridge,
harbors more than a dozen shops and
galleries.

Ogunquit Camera (207-646-2261), at
the corner of Shore Rd. and Wharf
Lane in Ogunquit Village. Open year-
round and featuring digital photo
printing. A great little shop that's been
here since 1952, this spot is also a

trove of toys, towels, windsocks, beach
supplies, and sunglasses.

Harbor Candy Shop (207-646-8078;
harborcandy.com), 26 Main St., Ogunquit. Open since 1956, this family-
owned store makes turtles with
Belgian chocolate and handmade
caramel (made from cream and sugar
and no preservatives); they are their
most popular item. Also small-batch
fudge made with cream, brittles, and
coconut "snowflakes"—coconut shreds
in chocolate.

Lighthouse Depot (207-646-0608;
lighthousedepot.com), 2178 Post Rd.
(Rt. 1), Wells. Look for the lighthouses
outside (just before the turnoff for
Laudholm Farm). Open daily in summer, fewer days in winter. Billed as
"the largest selection of lighthouse gift
items in the world," this is two floors
filled with lawn lighthouses, lighthouse
books, ornaments, jewelry, paintings,
replicas, and much more.

Pine Tree Farm Market and Café
(207-646-7545; bloomsflowershoppe
.com), 411 Post Rd., Wells. A fine
place to find a good sandwich, fine
breakfast, or wine, cheese, pickles, and
more, like pumpkins in fall and flowers
year-round.

STATUE GARDEN AT BARN GALLERY

✳ Special Events

February: **Mardi Gras**, Ogunquit.

April: Big **Patriot's Day celebration** at Ogunquit Beach.

June: **Ogunquit Chamber Music Festival** (first week). **Laudholm Farm Day** (midmonth). **Wells Week** (end of the month)—a weeklong celebration centering on Harbor Park Day, with boat launchings, a chicken barbecue, a sand-sculpture contest, and a crafts fair.

July: **Fireworks** on July 4, sand-castle building, family fun day, and three-day **Harbor Fest** in Wells.

August: **Sidewalk art show** in Ogunquit.

September: **Open Homes Day**, sponsored by the Wells Historical Society. **Nature Crafts Festival** (second weekend) at Laudholm Farm. **Capriccio**, a celebration of the performing arts, and **Kite Day** in Ogunquit. **Punkinfiddle** (punkinfiddle.org), a celebration of National Estuaries Day.

Third week of October: **Ogunquit Fest**—ghost tours and costume parade.

November: **Celebrations by the Sea Wedding Expo**, Ogunquit.

December: **Christmas parade** in Wells. **Christmas by the Sea** in Ogunquit.

Nancy English

PINE TREE FARM MARKET AND CAFÉ

THE KENNEBUNKS

T he Kennebunks began as a fishing stage near Cape Porpoise as early as
1602, but the community was repeatedly destroyed by Native American raids. In
1719 the present "port" was incorporated as Arundel, a name that stuck through
its lucrative shipbuilding and seafaring years until 1821, when it became Kennebunkport. Later, when the novel *Arundel*, by Kenneth Roberts (born in Kennebunk), had run through 32 printings, residents gave the old name to North
Kennebunkport.

That the Kennebunks prospered as a shipbuilding center is obvious from the
quantity and quality of its sea captains' and shipbuilders' mansions, the presence of
its brick customhouse (now the library), and the beauty of its churches.

In his 1891 guidebook *The Pine-Tree Coast*, Samuel Adams Drake noted that
"since the beginning of the century more than eight hundred vessels have been
sent out from the shipyards of this river." He recalled: "When I first knew this
place, both banks of the river were lined with shipyards . . . all alive with the labor
of hundreds of workmen." But by the 1890s, Drake noted, shipbuilding was "mori-
bund" and Kennebunkport had become "a well-established watering-place."

In 1872 this entire spectacular 5-mile stretch of coast—from Lords Point at the
western end of Kennebunk Beach all the way to Cape Porpoise on the east—was
acquired by one developer, the Sea
Shore Company. Over the next couple
of decades no fewer than 30 grand
hotels and dozens of summer mansions
evolved to accommodate the summer
visitors that train service brought. The
Kennebunks then shared the 1940s-to-
1960s decline suffered by all Maine
coastal resorts, losing all but a scattering of old hotels.

According to the locals, the Kennebunks developed an almost countercul-
tural feel in the 1960s and '70s. Then
the tourist tide again turned, and over
the past few decades the area has
grown increasingly upscale: Surviving
hotels have been condoed, inns have

ON THE BRIDGE BETWEEN KENNEBUNK
AND KENNEBUNKPORT

Nancy English

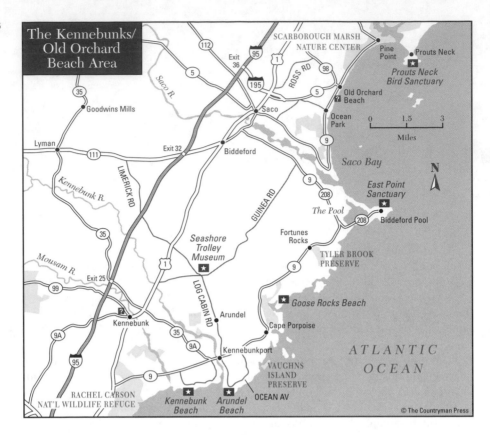

The Kennebunks/
Old Orchard
Beach Area

© The Countryman Press

been rehabbed, and dozens of B&Bs and inns have opened. Still, if you look beyond the clichés, you'll discover the real Maine here, too. Dock Square's world-class shopping district now rivals those in Palm Beach (where many retail stores have sister shops) and other swanky spots, but a walk through the historic streets of Kennebunkport is free and quite idyllic. And a meal at one of the lobster shacks is as rustic, delicious, and affordable as any on the Maine coast.

You can bed down a few steps from Dock Square's lively shops and restaurants, 2 miles away in the quiet village of Cape Porpoise, or out at Goose Rocks, where the only sound is the lapping of waves on endless sand. Most B&Bs are, however, the former sea captains' homes grouped within a few stately streets of each other, many within walking distance of both Dock Square and the open ocean.

GUIDANCE Kennebunk/Kennebunkport Chamber of Commerce (207-967-0857 or 1-800-982-4421; visitthekennebunks.com), P.O. Box 740, Kennebunk 04043. Open Mon.–Fri. year-round, plus Sat. and Sun. late May–late Oct. The information center, a yellow building on Rt. 9 just east of its junction with Rt. 35 (at the light in Lower Village), offers plenty of parking in the rear, but the turn is abrupt so go slow. Staff are unusually helpful, and the chamber publishes an excellent free guide.

DOCK SQUARE, KENNEBUNKPORT

Nancy English

GETTING THERE *By air:* You can fly your own plane into **Sanford Airport**; otherwise, **Portland International Jetport** (see "Portland Area") is served by various airlines and taxi services.

By car: Drive up I-95 to exit 25 and take Rt. 35 into Kennebunk, on to Kennebunkport and the Kennebunk Beaches. Coming up Rt. 1, take Rt. 9 east from Wells.

By train: See *Amtrak* in "What's Where." The **Downeaster** service from Boston's North Station takes about two hours and stops in Wells. Transportation is available from the station to the Kennebunks.

GETTING AROUND Kennebunk is a busy commercial center straddling the strip of Rt. 1 between the Mousam and Kennebunk Rivers. A 10-minute ride down Summer St. (Rt. 35) brings you to Kennebunkport. Then there are the Kennebunk Beaches, Cape Porpoise, Goose Rocks Beach, Cape Arundel, and Kennebunk Lower Village. Luckily, free detailed maps are readily available.

Intown Trolley (207-967-3686; intowntrolley.com), Kennebunkport, offers narrated sightseeing tours; $15 adults, $6 ages 3–17, free for those 2 and under. The tickets are good for the day, so you can also use them to shuttle between Dock Square and Kennebunk Beach.

Bicycles work well here and are a good way to handle the mile between Dock Square and the Kennebunk Beaches.

PARKING A municipal fee parking lot is hidden behind the commercial block in Dock Square. You can find free parking at 90 North St., a short walk to Dock Square, and another fee lot near the bridge in Lower Village. Good luck!

WHEN TO COME One nice side effect of the Kennebunk tourist trade: This is the least seasonal resort town on the Southern Coast. Most inns and shops stay open through Christmas Prelude in early December, and many never close. Visit in fall, when crowds thin out and the colorful foliage makes the old mansions and crashing waves even more picturesque.

✷ To See

MUSEUMS The Brick Store Museum and Archives (207-985-4802; brick storemuseum.org), 117 Main St., Kennebunk. Open year-round, Tue.–Fri. 10–4:30, Sat. 10–1. Admission is by donation. This block of early-19th-century commercial buildings, including William Lord's **Brick Store** (1825), hosts a permanent exhibit documenting the region from the days of Native Americans, the arduous settlement years, and the subsequent colonial era through the period of shipbuilding glory. Changing exhibits focus on a wide variety of subjects. Visitors can research local history in the archives by appointment. Walking tours of the historic district are offered by appointment May–Oct.

✎ **Seashore Trolley Museum** (207-967-2800; trolleymuseum.org), 195 Log Cabin Rd., located 3.2 miles up North St. from Kennebunkport or 2.8 miles north on Rt. 1 from Kennebunk, then right at the traffic light. Open daily, rain or shine, Memorial Day–Columbus Day, weekends in May and through Oct.; $10 adults, $7.50 ages 6–16, $8 seniors over 60, children under 6 free. This nonprofit museum

Nancy English

MANSION ON SUMMER STREET IN THE HISTORICAL DISTRICT

preserves the history of the trolley era, displaying more than 250 vehicles from all over the world. The impressive collection began in 1939, when the last open-sided Biddeford–Old Orchard Beach trolley was retired to an open field straddling the old Atlantic Shore Line from Kittery to Biddeford. Five million passengers traveled this line in 1907. A 3-mile trolley excursion takes visitors through woods and fields. An 8,000-hour effort restored an electric locomotive that sometimes operates and is always on display; the vehicle is on the National Historic Register and is the subject of an exhibit about public transportation in the first half of the 20th century. Ask what car is most recently restored.

Kennebunkport Historical Society (207-967-2751; kporthistory.org) has three facilities. **Pasco Exhibit Center**, 125 North St., free, is open year-round (the Benson Blacksmith Shop and Clark Shipwright Office hours vary); Tue.–Fri. 10–4; July–Aug., Sat. 10–1. The **Town House School**, at 135 North St., is used for research ($10 an hour) and open year-round, Wed. and Fri. 10–1. Free on-site parking at both. The society also maintains the **Nott House**, 8 Maine St. (no parking), a Greek Revival mansion with Doric columns, original wallpaper, carpets, and furnishings. Open mid-June to Labor Day, Tue.–Fri. 1–4, Sat. 10–1; Labor Day to Columbus Day, Thu.–Fri. 1–4, Sat. 10–1. Guided walking tours July and Aug., Thu. 2; Sat. 11; Sat. only till Columbus Day; $10 adults. Call ahead to confirm hours.

HISTORIC SITES Wedding Cake House, Summer St. (Rt. 35), Kennebunk. This privately owned 1826 house is laced up and down with ornate white gingerbread. Legend has it that a local sea captain had to rush off to sea before a proper wedding cake could be baked, but he more than made up for it later.

South Congregational Church, Temple St., Kennebunkport. Just off Dock Square, built in 1824 with a Christopher Wren–style cupola and belfry; Doric columns added in 1912.

Louis T. Graves Memorial Library (207-967-2778), 18 Maine St., Kennebunkport. Built in 1813 as a bank, which went bust, it later served as a customhouse. It was subsequently donated to the library association by artist Abbott Graves, whose pictures alone make it worth a visit. You can still see the bank vault and the sign from the custom collector's office. At the Perkins House next door, the book saleroom is full of bargains and open during the library's hours.

First Parish Unitarian Church, Main St., Kennebunk. Built between 1772 and 1773 with an Asher Benjamin–style steeple added between 1803 and 1804, along with a Paul Revere bell. In 1838 the interior was divided into two levels, with the church proper elevated to the second floor. Popular legend holds that the pulpit was carved from a single log found floating in the Caribbean Sea and towed back to Maine.

SCENIC DRIVE Ocean Avenue, starting in Kennebunkport, follows the **Kennebunk River** for a mile to Cape Arundel and the open ocean, then winds past many magnificent summer homes. Stop along **Parson's Way**, located off Ocean Ave. on the right just after the Colony Hotel, and enjoy the park benches that take advantage of the magnificent view of the mouth of the Kennebunk River and **Gooch's Beach**. Continue north and east to **Walker's Point**, former president George H. W. Bush's summer estate (it fills a private 11-acre peninsula). Built by his grandfather in 1903, its position is uncannily ideal for use as a president's summer home, moated by water on three sides yet clearly visible from pullouts along the avenue. Continue along the ocean (you don't have to worry about driving too slowly, because everyone else is, too). Follow the road to **Cape Porpoise**, site of the area's original 1600s settlement. The cove is still a base for lobster and commercial fishing boats, and the village is a good place to lunch or dine. Continue along Rt. 9 to **Clock Farm Corner** (you'll know it when you see it) and turn right onto Dyke Rd. to **Goose Rocks Beach**; park and walk. Return to Rt. 9 and cross it, continuing via Goose Rocks Rd. to the Seashore Trolley Museum and then Log Cabin Rd. to Kennebunkport.

✳ To Do

BICYCLING Aquaholics (207-967-8650; aquaholicsurf.com), 166 Port Rd., Kennebunk, and **Coastal Maine Kayak** (207-967-6065; coastalmainekayak.com) 8 Western Ave., Kennebunk, rent bikes. **Kennebunkport Bicycle Co.** (207-251-3135), 34 Arundel Rd. (off North St.), Kennebunkport, rents a variety of bikes. Open seasonally. The Kennebunks lend themselves well to exploration by bike, a far more satisfying way to go in summer than by car since you can stop and park wherever the view and urge hit you.

BOAT CRUISES The **Rugosa** (207-468-4005; rugosacharters.com), at The Nonantum Resort, Ocean Ave., Kennebunkport. Several daily trips to Goat Island Lighthouse, where you can visit the tower, at high tide only. Lobstering demonstrations with traps pulled, and a cocktail cruise in the evening.

BOATBUILDING SCHOOL The Landing School of Boat Building and Design (207-985-7976; landingschool.edu), 286 River Rd., Arundel, offers a Sept.–June program in building and designing sailing craft. Visitors welcome if you call ahead.

CARRIAGE RIDES Rockin' Horse Stables (207-967-4288; rockinhorsemaine .com), 245 Arundel Rd., Kennebunkport. Tour Kennebunkport's historic district (25 minutes) in a spiffy white vis-à-vis carriage with burgundy-colored velvet seats and antique lanterns. Sleigh rides all winter and wagon and carriage rides at Christmas Prelude (see *Special Events*).

FISHING Stone Coast Anglers, Inc. (207-985-6005; stonecoastanglers.com), Kennebunk. Captain Paul J. Rioux specializes in chartered boat trips along the coast for up to three guests as well as guided wading trips for saltwater and game fish.

GOLF Cape Arundel Golf Club (207-967-3494; capearundelgolfclub.com), 19 River Rd., Kennebunkport, 18 holes. The local links former president George H. W. Bush frequents are open to the public daily. Three-day advance tee time reservations accepted. **Webhannet Golf Club** (207-967-2061; webhannetgolfclub .com), 26 Golf Club Dr., off Sea Rd., Kennebunk Beach, 18 holes. Open to the public but semi-private, with limited tee times especially in July and Aug. **Dutch Elm Golf Course** (207-282-9850; dutchelmgolf.com), Arundel, 18 holes; cart and club rentals, lessons, pro shop, snack bar, putting greens. ✍ **Hillcrest Golf** (207-967-4661), Rt. 9, Kennebunk. Open daily 8 AM–dark; balls and clubs furnished.

KAYAKING Harbor Adventures (207-363-8466; harboradventures.com), Kennebunkport. Guided sea kayak tours for individuals and groups. **Coastal Maine Kayak** (207-967-6065; coastalmainekayak.com), 8 Western Ave., Kennebunk (next to Federal Jack's), offers kayak tours, rentals, a sea kayak guide course, a women's retreat, and kayak rolling sessions. The trip to Cape Porpoise Lighthouse is good for beginners and old hands.

SAILING Schooner *Eleanor* (207-967-8809; gwi.net/schoonersails). Two-hour sailing trips aboard a traditional, gaff-rigged, 55-foot schooner set sail from the docks at the Arundel Wharf Restaurant.

The Pineapple Ketch (207-468-7262; pineappleketch.com), 95 Ocean Ave., Kennebunkport. Daily 2-hour tours and private charters at 11, 2, and sunset, mid-May–Oct. on this 38-foot ketch with red sails and a black hull. $40 per person. Book tours in-season at 207-967-4050.

SURFING Aquaholics (207-967-8650; aquaholicsurf.com), 166 Port Rd., Kennebunk, is the place for a surf lesson, whether you are 3 or 73. Weeklong Surf Camps run right into winter, and with a wet suit on, the cold is nothing compared with the fun. Stand-up paddle clinics and tours, surf shop, and a full line of rentals.

WHALE-WATCHING AND OCEAN TOURS This is a popular departure point for whale-watching on Jefferies Ledge, about 20 miles offshore. If you have any tendency toward seasickness, be sure to choose a calm day or take anti-nausea medication. Chances are you'll see more than a dozen whales. Frequently sighted species include finbacks, minkes, rights, and humpbacks. **First Chance** (207-967-5507 or 1-800-767-2628; firstchancewhalewatch.com), 4 Western Ave. in the Lower Village (at the bridge), also offers a scenic lobster cruise.

☀ Winter Pastimes

CROSS-COUNTRY SKIING Harris Farm (207-499-2678; harrisfarm.com), 252 Buzzell Rd., Dayton. A 500-acre dairy farm with more than 20 miles of trails. Equipment rentals available, including snowshoes and ice skates. Located 1.5 miles from the Rt. 5 and Rt. 35 intersection.

SLEIGH RIDES Rockin' Horse Stables (207-967-4288), 245 Arundel Rd., Kennebunkport, offers 30- to 40-minute sleigh rides on a 100-acre farm.

☀ Green Space

BEACHES The Kennebunks discourage day-trippers by requiring a permit to park at major beaches. Day, week, and seasonal passes must be secured from the chamber of commerce, town hall, police department, or local lodging places. You can also park in one of the town lots and walk, bike, or take a trolley to the beach.

Goose Rocks Beach, a few miles north of Kennebunkport Village on Rt. 9, is the area's most beautiful beach: a magnificent wide, smooth stretch of silver-white sand backed by high dunes. Children here seem to mimic their less frenetic 19th-century counterparts, doing wonderfully old-fashioned things like flying kites, playing paddleball, and making sand castles.

Kennebunk and **Gooch's Beaches** in Kennebunk are both long, wide strips of firm sand backed by Beach Ave., divided by Oak's Neck. Beyond Gooch's Beach, take Great Hill Rd. along the water to **Strawberry Island**, a great place to walk and examine tidal pools. Please don't picnic. Keep going and you come to **Mother's Beach**, small and very sandy.

Arundel Beach, near the Colony Hotel at the mouth of the Kennebunk River, offers nice rocks for climbing and good beachcombing for shell and beach-glass enthusiasts.

NATURE PRESERVES ✿ ♿ **Rachel Carson National Wildlife Refuge** (207-646-9226; fws.gov/northeast/rachelcarson). Headquarters for this almost 50-mile, 5,000-acre preserve is just south of the Kennebunkport line at 321 Port Rd. (Rt. 9) in Wells. The refuge is divided among 10 sites along Maine's Southern Coast. Pick up a leaflet guide to the mile-long, wheelchair accessible nature trail here. Kayakers can enter the refuge traveling up the rivers, but no put-ins or takeouts allowed to avoid disturbing the wildlife. (Also see Laudholm Farm in "Ogunquit and Wells.")

Kennebunkport Conservation Trust (207-967-3465; kporttrust.org), P.O. Box 7004, Cape Porpoise 04014, maintains a number of properties. These include the **Tyler Brook**

CAPE ARUNDEL INN

Nancy English

Nancy English

CARSON INTERPRETIVE TRAIL

Preserve near Goose Rocks, the 148-acre **Emmons Preserve** along the Batson River (access from unpaved Gravelly Rd., off Beachwood Rd.), the nearly 1,000-acre **Kennebunkport Town Forest**, and the **Vaughns Island Preserve**, which offers nature trails on a wooded island separated from the mainland by two tidal creeks. Cellar holes of historic houses are accessible by foot from 1½ hours before to 1½ hours after low tide. The trust also maintains historic **Goat Island Lighthouse**.

The Nature Conservancy (207-729-5181) owns 135 acres of the **Kennebunk Plains Preserve** and assists in the management of 650 state-owned acres in West Kennebunk (take Rt. 99 toward Sanford) with nearly 4 miles of shoreline on the Mousam River in Kennebunk.

WALKS Henry Parsons Park, Ocean Ave., is a path along the rocks leading to Spouting Rock and Blowing Cave, both sights to see at midtide. A great way to view the beautiful homes along Ocean Ave.

St. Anthony Monastery and Shrine (207-967-2011), Kennebunk. Some 44 acres of peaceful riverside fields and forests on Beach Ave., now maintained by Lithuanian Franciscans as a shrine and retreat. Visitors are welcome; gift shop. (See the Franciscan Guesthouse in *Other Lodging*.)

✳ Lodging

The Kennebunks represent one of the Maine coast's largest concentrations of inns and B&Bs, with more than 80 lodging places, or 1,400 rooms. We list a number of options in different price ranges, but still just a fraction of what's available. These places tend to stay open at least through the first two weekends in December, when the town celebrates Christmas Prelude, and many are open year-round.

All listings are in Kennebunkport 04046 unless otherwise noted
TOP-DOLLAR INNS AND B&BS
Captain Lord Mansion (207-967-3141 or 1-800-522-3141; captainlord .com), P.O. Box 800, at the corner of Pleasant and Green Sts. Open year-round. This three-story Federal home, built in 1812, is topped with a widow's walk from which guests can contemplate the town and sea. All 16 rooms

have a gas fireplace and private bath; large high beds are equipped with steps to climb into them. The decor here is possibly the most elaborate in the state, and the Merchant Captain's Suite may have the most elaborate bathroom, including its gas fireplace. The Captain's Garden House holds four more ornate rooms. This is home when what you covet is perfection and every amenity. $289–499 per room in high season, $149–399 off-season, breakfast and tea included. Spa services include massage for couples and facials.

White Barn Inn (207-967-2321; whitebarninn.com), 37 Beach Ave., P.O. Box 560C, Kennebunk 04043. Open year-round. The "barn" is an elegant dining room (see *Dining Out*) where guests have breakfast and can dine. Built in the 1860s as a farmhouse, later enlarged as the Forest Hills House, this complex lies midway between Dock Square and Kennebunk Beach. Courteous staff wear black, a sleek hotel version of the brown-robed Franciscan friars nearby (see the Franciscan Guesthouse in *Other Lodging*). Choose an antiques-furnished room in the farmhouse; a suite in the carriage house with four-poster king bed, fireplace, and marble bath; a cottage suite with specially crafted furnishings, a double-sided fireplace, Jacuzzi, and steam shower. Room 8 in the main house—with a king bed, enormous bathroom, and steam shower—held a fruit bowl ready for guests checking in. Tea sandwiches and cookies are on a sideboard in the afternoon. $320–860 per couple for rooms includes breakfast, tea, and use of touring bikes. The yacht *True Blue* can be rented by the day, and meals arranged on board. Three waterfront cottages are also for rent. A 5.35 percent housekeeping fee is added.

MODERATELY EXPENSIVE INNS AND B&BS

On the water
Cape Arundel Inn (207-967-2125; capearundelinn.com), 208 Ocean Ave.,

---

RESORT HOTEL

🐾 ✆ **The Colony Hotel** (207-967-3331 or 1 800-552-2363; thecolonyhotel.com), 140 Ocean Ave. and King's Hwy. Open May–Oct. With 124 rooms (all with private bath) in three buildings, this is among the last of New England's coastal resorts maintained in the grand style. The Colony is also environmentally conscious, placing recycling bins in guest rooms, composting, and earning the accolade "Certified Wildlife Habitat" from the National Wildlife Federation. None of these practices, however, diminishes the luxuriousness of the hotel with historic Waverly wallpaper and handsome old furniture. Set on a rise overlooking the point at which the Kennebunk River meets the Atlantic, it's been owned by the Boughton family since 1948; many guests have been coming for generations. Amenities include a heated saltwater pool, a private beach, an 18-hole putting green, and a social and nature walk program. A three-night minimum is required for weekend reservations for July and Aug. $159–319 high season per day includes a full buffet breakfast. Pets are $30 per day.

P.O. Box 530A. Open mid-Feb.–New Year's Eve. The most dramatic location in town, facing the open ocean with just the estate of former president George H. W. Bush interrupting the view. Rich Malconian bought this inn in 2011. Seven rooms in the main house and six in an addition as well as a carriage house make up the accommodations; those in the addition all have picture windows and deck facing the water, parking in back, and TV. The carriage house water-view suite (up a flight of stairs) has a deck and sitting area. The living room is hung with interesting art, some of it by Jack Nahil, the inn's precious owner. The dining room, which is open for dinner to the public (see *Dining Out*), is deservedly well loved. $320–425 in-season, from $135 off-season, includes a continental breakfast.

🐾 🌿 **The Captain Jefferds Inn** (207-967-2311 or 1-800-839-6844; captain jefferdsinn.com), 5 Pearl St., Box 691. Erik and Sarah Lindblom are your hosts at this handsome Federal-era mansion with two suites and 13 rooms; 9 have wood or gas fireplace, and all have air-conditioning, feather beds, and down comforters. Baxter, in the carriage house, is decorated in a "Maine camp" style—except for the two-person whirlpool with a round-stone surround. A screened porch is one feature of the suites. First-floor Chatham has a four-poster and two wingback chairs by the fireplace. The spacious common rooms include a sunporch where tea and coffee are always available. $149–379, depending on season.

🌿 **Maine Stay Inn and Cottages** (207-967-2117 or 1-800-950-2117; mainestayinn.com), 34 Maine St., Box 500A. Open year-round. The inn offers six guest rooms in the main house and 11 suites in five cottages nestled in

Nancy English

THE CAPE ARUNDEL INN OVERLOOKS THE OCEAN

nicely landscaped grounds. The house was built in 1860 by Melville Walker and given to his wife as a Christmas present five years later. The cottages are simple on the outside but handsomely outfitted in with efficiency kitchens, deep whirlpool tubs, some with gas fireplaces. A full breakfast, perhaps baked eggs with cheddar and Parmesan, and afternoon tea are offered by friendly owners Judi and Walter Hauer, who bought the inn in 2008. Order breakfast delivered, if in a cottage, or join the other guests in the pretty dining room. $229–329 in-season, $129–259 off-season, when there might be a discount on offer midweek.

Tides Beach Club (207-967-3757; tidesbeachclubmaine.com), 252 Kings Hwy., Goose Rocks Beach. Open late

May–Oct. Twenty-one renovated rooms, some overlooking Goose Rocks Beach, are painted in pastels and outfitted with comfortable beds and high-tech amenities. Fans of the previous owners' Tides-Inn-By-the-Sea will be in for a shock because the Victoriana has vanished, traded in for cool colors and modern graphic prints. Fans of contemporary style will be thrilled. The beach across the narrow road remains its eternal self, a wide sweep of white sand banded by a ribbon of dunes. Rates $235–500 in-season.

Seaside Inn & Cottages (207-967-4461; kennebunkbeach.com), 80 Beach Ave., Kennebunk 04043. Open year-round. A modern 22-room inn set on a quiet stretch of one of Maine's best public beaches is the only one in the area directly on the ocean. This property has been in the Gooch-Severance family for nine generations, beginning in the 1640s when King Charles II conveyed the land to John Gooch, who ferried folks across the river. All of that seems to makes this the oldest inn in the country—and the history is detailed on the website. The cheery breakfast room is an 1850 former boathouse for the 19th-century inn that stood here until the 1950s. Inn rooms feature two queen beds, air-conditioning, cable TV, phone, mini fridge, and balcony or patio. Three-day minimum in oceanfront rooms in high season. $105–259 per night, including extended continental breakfast with stuffed French toast on Thu. and access to a local fitness center. Great off-season packages.

Bufflehead Cove Inn (207-967-3879; buffleheadcove.com), Box 499, off Rt. 35. Open May–Nov. This hidden gem, sequestered on 6 acres at the end of a dirt road and overlooking an 8-foot-deep tidal cove, sits a mile from the village of Kennebunkport. Harriet Gott, a native of nearby Cape Porpoise, her husband, Jim, and their son Erin offer four good-looking guest rooms, a suite, and a separate deluxe cottage. River View cottage lies off by itself with a deck, kitchen, wood-burning fireplace, and whirlpool tub. The inn's living room has a hearth and deep window seats. $155–395 includes a full breakfast on the white porch if the weather is fine, and afternoon wine and cheese.

Kennebunkport Inn (207-967-2621 or 1-800-248-2621; kennebunk portinn.com), 1 Dock Square, P.O. Box 111. Open year-round. Owners Debbie Lennon and Tom Nill have redecorated the 50 rooms; Number 303 is a "mansion room" with canopy four-poster, gas fireplace, and bathtub. The inn has four sections—the main house (originally an 1890s mansion), a 1980s Federal-style addition, a 1930s river house with smaller rooms, and the Wharfside, with 14 rooms including 3 family suites. In summer a small, enticing pool on the terrace offers respite from the Dock Square hubbub, and guests can dine in **One Dock** year-round. The cocktail lounge with a huge old bar offers evening piano music. High-season rates $205–349 per room, less off-season.

The Captain Fairfield Inn (207-967-4454 or 1-800-322-1928; captainfair field.com), P.O. Box 3089, corner of Pleasant and Green Sts. Open year-round. Owners Rob and Leigh Blood bought the inn in 2004, adding a wine list and small plates to serve guests afternoon or evening. Homemade cookies, included, are served in the afternoon, and the three-course breakfast features local ingredients. The lawn with two "fire tables" stretches back across the width of the block, where guests make themselves comfortable. Notable among the nine handsome rooms, the Library features a private porch and garden and double whirlpool; Sweet Liberty has a tiled rainfall shower; and the Breakwater Room is contemporary. $256–409 in high season, $156–300 in low.

& **The Breakwater Inn, Hotel and Spa** (207-967-5333; thebreakwater inn.com), 127 Ocean Ave., P.O. Box 560C, across from Mabel's Lobster Claw. A 19th-century riverside complex, open year-round. The 37 rooms are split among three buildings, each equipped with CD player, TV, phone, air-conditioning, and a granite-and-tile bath; rooms vary in view and size. The inn, made up of two buildings, has rooms on four floors and no elevator; only the hotel has an elevator. Guests can dine at Stripers Waterside Restaurant (see *Eating Out*). In-season rates, as high as $449 at the inn and $609 for a suite in the hotel, include continental breakfast and afternoon tea; $189–319 off-season. Waterside Cottage is $750 a night in summer. Some handicapped units.

✪ **Old Fort Inn** (207-967-5353 or 1-800-828-FORT; oldfortinn.com), 8 Old Fort Ave., P.O. Box M. Open mid-Apr.–mid-Dec. Stepping into David and Sheila Aldrich's quiet respite is like falling into a plush wing chair—or a magnificent, carved antique bed. The inn, set on 15 acres, feels miles away from humming Dock Square, but it's little more than a mile's walk. The 16 guest rooms in the stone-and-brick carriage house are filled with elegant furnishings, and all include TV, DVD, phone, wet bar with microwave and refrigerator, dishes and flatware for meals, and air-conditioning—and the tiled bathroom floors are heated. The property includes a heated pool, tennis court, horseshoes, and shuffleboard. Spa services by reservation. Two-night minimum in-season. $190–390; less

off-season. Rates include buffet breakfast on a heated porch. An antiques and gift shop in the entrance is filled with charming old china and stylish modern tchotchkes.

& **The 1802 House** (207-967-5632 or 1-800-932-5632; 1802inn.com), 15 Locke St., P.O. Box 646-A. Open year-round. Linda Van Goor and Jay Durepo offer six guest rooms, all with queen four-poster bed, five with fireplace, and four with whirlpool tub. A three-room suite with a fireplace, fridge, double shower, Roman garden room, and double whirlpool tub overlooks a private deck. The house, shaded by large pines and on the 15th fairway of the Cape Arundel Golf Course, has an out-in-the-country feel; golf packages available. $167–219 in high season, $146–189 in low, includes full breakfast.

MODERATELY PRICED INNS AND B&BS 🏵 🐾 ✎ & **The Green Heron** (207-967-3315; greenheron inn.com), 126 Ocean Ave., P.O. Box 2578. Open Apr.–Dec. A friendly little hotel with a casual atmosphere, owned and run by Tony Kusuma and Dan Oswald, The Green Heron has 10 small but pleasant rooms and a cove-side cottage with private bath, air-conditioning, and TV; some also have a refrigerator and a fireplace. Portland Head, with oak furniture, shares a deck on the inlet on the inn's west side, where herons and other water-birds find their own breakfast. In-season $190–225 for a double, off-season $145–175, cottage higher, includes a fantastic full breakfast and afternoon refreshments.

Chetwynd House Inn (207-967-2235; chetwyndhouse.com), 4 Chestnut St., P.O. Box 130. Open year-round. In 1972 Susan Chetwynd opened Chetwynd, Kennebunkport's first B&B. Now owned by Robert Knowles, her son, it remains a gracious 1840s home near Dock Square. The four antiques-furnished guest rooms have private bath, TV, refrigerator, and air-conditioning; a top-floor junior suite has skylights and a river view. Generous breakfasts—with eggs cooked to order and a quarter melon with peaches, blueberries, and bananas or other fruit—are served family-style at the dining room table. $210–240 in-season; off-season specials.

Harbor Inn (207-967-2074; harborinn kennebunkport.com), 90 Ocean Ave., P.O. Box 538A. Open year-round. Kathy and Barry Jones, longtime Port residents, fill this fine old house with flowers and their warm friendliness. The five rooms and two-room suite (all with private bath) feature a mix of family antiques, paintings, and prints, and the long front porch is lined with wicker. It's a short walk to the ocean, a longer but pleasant walk to Dock Square. $155–225 for rooms in-season, $125 off-season. Woodbine Cottage in-season is $225 a night or $1,500 weekly.

The Waldo Emerson Inn (207-985-4250 or 1 877-521-8776; waldo emersoninn.com), 108 Summer St (Rt. 35), Kennebunk 04043. This special house was built in 1784 by a ship-builder who inherited the land and original 1753 cottage (the present kitchen) from Waldo Emerson, the great-uncle of the famous poet and essayist. The building was later a stop on the Underground Railroad. John and Kathy Daamen offer four cozy guest rooms with private bath and air-conditioning, each with a wood-burning fireplace. Each is handsomely decorated with antique wallpaper and period details. A quilt store is on the property, and the Wedding Cake House is next door and now available

for weddings. $165–175 high season per couple includes a full gourmet breakfast and afternoon tea in one of the two handsome 18th-century parlors (one with a large-screen TV).

OTHER LODGING The Franciscan Guest House (207-967-4865; franciscanguesthouse.com), 26 Beach Ave., Kennebunk 04043. Open mid-March to mid-Dec. With private bath, air-conditioning, and television, the 65 rooms here have the feeling of Maine the way it used to be. This 1908 estate on the Kennebunk River was converted to a guesthouse in the 1960s; the friars live in the Tudor great house. The 44-acre garden is open to the public year-round during daylight hours (no pets), and walking the riverside trails might take half an hour, past formal gardens and the Stations of the Cross, Our Lady of Lourdes, and other shrines and fountains. A modern abstract statue, with colored glass from the Vatican Pavilion at the 1964 World's Fair, stands beside the monastery. Maps of the trees and shrubs planted under Frederick Law Olmsted's design, and of the shrines, are available. $80–165 in-season, $60–90 off-season, with breakfast often made by the Lithuanian cook, a cross between a European and an American breakfast that might include home-made farmer's cheese, raisin bread, carrot bread, and potato bread. A moderately priced buffet dinner is served most nights in the height of summer.

🐾 🦀 ✒ ♿ **Yachtsman Lodge and Marina** (207-967-2511; yachtsman lodge.com), Ocean Ave., P.O. Box 560C. Open May–early Dec. This 30-room inn is great for the cruising crowd, who can sail right up the Kennebunk River to the lodge and take advantage of its 59-slip marina. The Yachtsman features rooms decorated to resemble the inside of a yacht, with private riverside patios. $179–399 includes continental breakfast in the marble-tiled breakfast room or under the pergola. Children and pets are okay, and wheelchair access is easy. Bicycles and canoes are available for guests.

✷ Where to Eat

DINING OUT ✪ **Cape Arundel Inn** (207-967-2125; capearundelinn.com), Ocean Ave., Kennebunkport. Open daily mid-Feb.–Dec. for dinner, closed Mon. off-season. This dining room, matching its great location facing the ocean, presents skilled cooking and fine service. Chef Rich Lemoine extols his "fabulous staff," many of whom have worked here for decades. Certainly a dinner feels seamless, and the care is both genuine and unaffected. Lobster stew is equally perfect, as are grilled Australian lamb chops and poached halibut, perhaps with coconut curry broth and scallion couscous. A pianist plays every night in summer. $28–43.

✪ ♿ **Pier 77** (207-967-8500; pier77restaurant.com), Pier Rd., Cape Porpoise. Open daily for lunch and dinner June–Sept.; Wed.–Mon., St. Patrick's Day–May and Columbus Day–Dec.; the Ramp is open noon–8 Wed.–Sun., Jan.–mid-March. Well-made dinners upstairs and lunches downstairs in the **Ramp**, a bar filled with sports memorabilia, deserve the big following they've earned. Duck cassoulet, chicken and dumplings, and seafood stew were on a fall menu, and pulled pork sandwiches or fried clams—perhaps dug by the man you spotted on the flats as you came inside—might be for lunch. Entrées $17–30.

THE RAMP AT PIER 77

Nancy English

White Barn Inn (207-967-2321; whitebarninn.com), 37 Beach Ave., Kennebunkport. Open for dinner year-round Mon.–Sat. (except Jan.), daily in summer. Reservations required with credit card; $25 per-person fee charged if canceled less than 24 hours in advance. This award-winning restaurant is set in two restored 19th-century barns with a three-story glassed rear wall, exposed beams, and extravagant seasonal floral displays. Original art, hotel silver, and fine linens are accessories to extraordinary meals. The four-course prix fixe menu, under chef Jonathan Cartwright, changes frequently. In 2011 menu items started with the phenomenal lobster bisque; went on to seafood minestrone; and culminated in local venison with wild mushroom tapioca. One dessert was pear soufflé with dark chocolate sauce. Jackets required. $98 prix fixe plus tax, beverage, and gratuity.

On the Marsh Bistro (207-967-2299; onthemarsh.com), Rt. 9, Kennebunk Lower Village. Open daily for dinner May–Oct.; closed Mon. and Tue. offseason. Continental dining with style overlooking a lovely salt marsh. Executive chef Jeff Savage takes pride in his high-quality ingredients. Grilled bison New York strip sirloin with chive popovers and seared scallops with lobster risotto were on a fall menu, when the bar menu listed house creton (a French Canadian pork spread) and a meatball sub. The wines are wonderful, with hundreds to choose from. Entrées $21–37.

Tides Beach Club (207-967-3757), Goose Rocks Beach, 6 miles northeast of Dock Square. Open late May–Oct. 1 for dinner. Under new ownership and with a completely new decor, Tides Beach Club serves signature cocktails alongside its raw oysters; steamed mussels with tomato, citrus, and saffron; and fried chicken with cheesy grits. Of course you can also get a lobster, or a steak, or a steak with lobster. Entrées $19–42.

&. **Bandaloop** (207-967-4994; bandaloop.biz), 2 Dock Square. Open daily for dinner in summer, less often in winter. Entrées and sauces can be paired as you like; but the menu always offers several entrées and specials. Seared scallops with pistachio-cilantro pesto might appeal more than the fantastic mac-and-cheese (half portion is still large); a rack of lamb with buttermilk sweet potato mash hit the spot one fall. Desserts like dark chocolate torte or fruit crisp deserve to be enjoyed. Entrées $17–31.

Grissini Italian Bistro (207-967-2211; restaurantgrissini.com), 27 Western Ave., Kennebunk. Open year-round, except Jan., for dinner. A 120-seat northern Italian trattoria with seasonal outdoor terrace dining and an à la carte menu. You might dine on cannelloni or gnocchi con verdure with roasted eggplant, or try the woodfire-grilled chicken with cipollini onions. Large portions. Entrées $13–30. A fall special offered three courses for $35. The drinks and wine lists are excellent.

50 Local (207-985-0850; localkennebunk.com), 50 Main St., Kennebunk. For anyone hungry for something

grown nearby, this is the place; anyone else who simple likes to dine well will be equally satisfied. Try mussels, Taunton Bay oysters, and lobster spring rolls to start; steak frites, fish stew, and vegan noodle bowl are some entrée possibilities. Entrées $14–29.

Lucas on 9 (207-967-0039; lucason9.com), 62 Mills Rd. (Rt. 9), Cape Porpoise. Open May–mid-Dec. This cheerful, family-owned place cooks up 10 to 12 specials at both lunch and dinner. Baked stuffed haddock, lobster ravioli, and Mediterranean haddock with kalamata olives, tomatoes, and feta, or salmon with Cajun seasoning, are prepared by Jonathan Lane, who makes his own Cajun rub. Locally picked lobster stuffs the fine lobster rolls; bread pudding with warm whiskey sauce is the signature dessert. Deborah Lane, the chef's mother, and Corey Lane, his sister, run the dining room. Entrées $7–29.

&. **Academe at the Kennebunk Inn** (207-985-3351; thekennebunkinn.com), 45 Main St., Kennebunk. Open Wed.–Sat. for dinner; daily for the more informal tavern menu, lunch on weekdays. Chef-owners Brian O'Hea and Shanna Horner O'Hea make high-quality meals at a moderate price. Braised beef short rib with garlic and Parmesan Tater Tots, or famous lobster potpie, were on a fall menu. Entrées $11–35.

&. **Stripers Waterside Restaurant** (207-967-3625), 131–133 Ocean Ave., Kennebunkport. Open in-season daily for lunch and dinner. This upscale seafood place has a long, thin aquarium harboring little blue fish that match pale blue slipcovered chairs. But the real view is out the window where the river flows by. Pork porterhouse with onion jam and yellowfin tuna with grilled squash and poached lobster were on one menu. Entrées $20–34.

The Landing Restaurant (207-967-4221; landingintheport.com), 21 Ocean Ave., Kennebunkport. A completely new building houses a steak house scheduled to open in 2012. Innkeepers say guests often want a good steak, and this is their destination.

LOBSTER AND CLAMS

✪ ✐ ♿ **Nunan's Lobster Hut** (207-967-4362), Rt. 9, Cape Porpoise. Open for dinner weekends in May and then daily June–mid-Oct. A long telescope of a building full of old benches, with buoys hanging from the rafters, Nunan's has been feeding lobster lovers since 1953 when Bertha Nunan started working here. Her two sons and their wives are in charge, with decades of experience to guide them. The place can fill up by 5:15; people outside get a number and wait for a table. A 1½-pound lobster comes with melted butter, potato chips, a roll, and pickles. Grilled cheese and a hamburger supply other tastes, and pie, brownies, and cheesecake are on the dessert list. Beer and wine. No credit cards.

✐ **Mabel's Lobster Claw** (207-967-2562), Ocean Ave., Kennebunkport. Open Apr.–early Nov. daily for lunch

THE CLAM SHACK

Nancy English

and dinner. An informal favorite with locals, including former president Bush. Reservations recommended for dinner. Specialties include stuffed lobster Savannah, lobster stew, and shore dinner (clam chowder, lobster, and steamed clams). The lunch special is a lobster roll in a buttery, grilled hot-dog roll, and the mussels marinara is great anytime. Dinner entrées $13–30.

✐ ♿ **The Clam Shack** (207-967-3321 or 207-967-2560), Kennebunkport (at the bridge). Clams, lobsters, and fresh fish. A year-round seafood market and Mother's Day–Columbus Day take-out stand that's worth the wait. Other seafood markets include **Cape Porpoise Lobster Co.** (207-967-4268) in Cape Porpoise, where the locals get their fish and steamed lobster to go, and **Port Lobster** (207-967-2081), 122 Ocean Ave., Kennebunkport, which offers live or cooked lobsters packed to travel or ship, and lobster, shrimp, and crab rolls to go (several obvious waterside picnic spots are within walking distance). Other local businesses get their picked lobster here; it won't be fresher anywhere else.

EATING OUT Old Vines (207-207-967-2310; oldvineswinebar.com), 173 Port Rd., Kennebunk. Open Wed.–Mon. from 5. A popular wine bar that opened in 2009, Old Vines serves snacks and small plates with its glasses of wine from featured vineyards. More than 20 are sold by the glass; try the Noemus Rioja from Spain or Château Bousquette, a sparkling rosé from France. Small plates of spiced almonds, cheeses, and cured meats might be the start of a delicious meal centered on a soppressata panini or quiche of the day, $6–21.

♨ ✐ **The Wayfarer** (207-967-8961), 1 Pier Rd., Cape Porpoise. Open

Tue.–Sat. for breakfast, lunch till 2; Sun. breakfast–noon. Closed Mon. The chowder comes with high praise, and the lobster roll we enjoyed was the best of its kind, on a toasted hot-dog bun with lots of sweet fresh lobster meat and not too much mayonnaise. Pies are homemade.

🦞 ✒ **Alisson's** (207-967-4841; alissons .com), 5 Dock Square, Kennebunkport. Open at 11 for lunch and 5 for dinner. Casual dining in this busy, family-run spot features standards with occasional outstanding twists, like the Dee Dee Burger with blue cheese. Count on reliably good casual food. **The Market Pub** is Dock Square's meeting place. Entrées $8–22.

♿ **Seafood Center** (207-985-7391; seafoodcenterofmaine.com), 1181 Portland Rd. (Rt. 1), Arundel. Open Wed.–Sun. 11–8 in summer, but call to confirm hours off-season. The locals say this is the best place for fried seafood, with a high degree of cleanliness and frequently changed oil. You will taste the delicate fish, clams, or shrimp, and the onions in the onion rings, and not the oil.

🦞 ✒ ♿ **Federal Jack's Restaurant & Brewpub** (207-967-4322; federaljacks .com), 8 Western Ave., Kennebunk Lower Village. Open from 11:30 for lunch and dinner, offering a variety of handcrafted ales. This is the original Shipyard Ale brewery with parking right in the thick of things. The spacious and sunny restaurant is upstairs, with a seasonal terrace dining on the river. There are lobster rolls, burgers, seafood and pasta dishes, and the Blue Fin stout might go with the Captain Jack's Feast—chowder, lobster, and mussels. Live acoustic music on weekends. The pub fare is the best way to go.

✒ **Bartley's Dockside** (207-967-5050; bartleysdining.com), by the bridge, Kennebunkport. Lunch and dinner daily. Since 1977 this friendly, family-owned place has been a reliable bet for meals that range from lunchtime chowders and stews to a dinner bouillabaisse. The juicy blueberry pie comes in a bowl. Items tend to be on the expensive side.

Cape Porpoise Kitchen (207-967-1150; kitchenchicks.com), 1 Mills Rd., Cape Porpoise. Open year-round. Takeout and catering are the focus, but this is the right place to go for a fabulous BLT or many other delicious sandwiches, salads, and baked goods for a picnic on the beach. Wine, beer, cheese, and gifts, with a small seating area if the weather is bad. No restroom.

✳ Entertainment

✒ **Arundel Barn Playhouse** (207-985-5552; arundelbarnplayhouse.com), 53 Old Post Rd. (just off Rt. 1), Arundel. Opened in 1998 in an 1800s revamped barn, this is a thoroughly professional, classic summer theater with performances June–Labor Day: Tue.–Sat., some Sundays, , matinees Wednesdays and some Fridays. Tickets $28–39.

✒ **Hackmatack Playhouse** (207-698-1807; hackmatack.org), 538 Rt. 9, Beaver Dam, Berwick. Local actors, rave reviews.

✒ **River Tree Center for the Arts** (207-967-9120; rivertreearts.org), 35 Western Ave., Kennebunk. Encompassing the Chappell School of Music and the Irvine Gallery and School of Art, this multifaceted organization stages local concerts, productions, and happenings, as well as workshops in the visual and performing arts for all ages.

Also see **Federal Jack's** under *Eating Out*, and *Entertainment* in "Ogunquit and Wells."

✳ Selective Shopping

ANTIQUES SHOPS The Kennebunks are known as an antiques center, with half a dozen shops, most on Rt. 1, representing a number of dealers. One on Rt. 9 that's sure to offer endless interest is **Antiques on Nine** (207-967-0626), 81 Western Ave. (Rt. 9), Kennebunk, overflowing with things strange and wonderful.

ART GALLERIES You'll find some 50 galleries, many seasonal; **Mast Cove Galleries** (207-967-3453) on Maine St., Kennebunkport, is touted as the largest gallery in Maine, with more than 100 artists represented. Pick up a free copy of the annual *Guide to Fine Art, Studios, and Galleries*, published by the **Art Guild of the Kennebunks** (207-324-4912) and available at the chamber of commerce and most galleries.

ANTIQUES ON NINE, KENNEBUNK

Nancy English

FARMS 🐄 **Harris Farm** (207-499-2678; harrisfarm.com), Buzzell Rd., Dayton. July–Oct. Visitors are welcome to tour the dairy barn; fresh milk, eggs, produce, and maple syrup are sold. Pick-your-own pumpkins on the last Sunday in Sept. and the first two Sundays in Oct., with hayrides offered to the pumpkin patch. A half-hour ride through beautiful, wooded forest and farms, this farm is 1 mile down Buzzell Rd. from Rt. 35.

Blackrock Farm (207-967-5783; blackrockfarm.net), 293 Goose Rocks Rd., Kennebunkport. A beautifully planted perennial garden and nursery with unusual plants and trees, and a pick-your-own raspberry patch. Bring a picnic and feast your eyes on the stone walls, grape arbor, and sculpture.

SPAS The Breakwater Inn, Hotel and Spa (207-967-5333; thebreakwaterinn.com), 127 Ocean Ave., P.O. Box 560C, Kennebunkport. Full-service spa, with massage, facials, and body wraps, along with steam room and fitness center. All facilities are open to the public. **Cottage Breeze Day Spa** (207-967-2259; cottagebreeze.com), 31 Western Ave., Kennebunk. Full-service spa. With any luck Judy will be your massage therapist, and what fine therapy it will be. Utterly comfortable treatment rooms and an array of body products.

SPECIAL SHOPS Kennebooks (207-967-6136; kennebooks.com), 149 Port Rd., Lower Village Kennebunk. Open daily in summer, closed Mon. off-season. A big, full-service book store with events, more than 11,000 books, comfortable seating, and a woodstove. Trish and Gary Koch renovated a farmhouse and hired a crack crew of local literati to assist customers with finding the perfect book.

KBC Coffee & Drygoods (207-967-1261; federaljacks.com), 8 Western Ave., Kennebunkport. Hidden beneath Federal Jack's, this is a source of Kennebunk Brewing Company ales (bottled or in a returnable "Growler") and brew gear as well as souvenir clothing and gifts; also good for cappuccino and homemade fudge.

Hearth and Soul (207-985-7466; hearthandsoulme.com), 35 Main St., Kennebunk. Open Tue.–Sat. "Primarily Primitives" is the motto at this quirky, charming place. Braided rugs, furniture, a folk art wall mural, and bricks of milk paint.

Daytrip Society (207-967-4440; daytripsociety.com), 4 Dock Square, Kennebunkport. Essentials and fripperies in good taste, from Pendleton blankets and good thermoses to old books and new cards. Around the corner, ✄ **Daytrip Jr.** (207-967-8345; daytripjr.com), 9 Ocean Ave., sells fine toys and games, some perfect for a long drive.

✳ Special Events

Many of the events below are listed with the Kennebunk/Kennebunkport Chamber of Commerce (207-967-0857 or 1-800-982-4421; visitthekennebunks .com), P.O. Box 740, Kennebunkport 04043.

February: **Winter Carnival Weekend** with hay- and sleigh rides in Kennebunk. Weekend **"February Is for Lovers"** events (207-967-0857).

May: **May Day Festival** on Main Street, Kennebunk.

Summer: **Farmer's Market** (kennebunk farmersmarket.org) during the growing season.

June: **Métis of Maine Annual Pow-wow**—dance, rituals and crafts made by people of Native American ancestry. **The Kennebunkport Festival**, with food, wine, and works of art.

July: **Bed & Breakfast Inn and Garden Tour**. Old-fashioned **July 4** picnic, fireworks, and band concert.

First Saturday in August: **Riverfest**.

September: **Harvest Fest**—parades, music, and good food.

October: **Presidential Road Race** (presidentialroadrace.com).

November: **Holiday Auction**. **Holiday Presents Weekend**.

December: **Christmas Prelude** (first full and second weekends)—Dock Square is decked out for Yuletide, and there are champagne receptions, church suppers, concerts, carols, holiday fairs, and house tours.

OLD ORCHARD BEACH, SACO, AND BIDDEFORD

Old Orchard's name stems from an apple orchard, one of the first in Maine, planted in 1657 by pioneer settler Thomas Rogers. It was also one the first Maine towns to prosper by catering to tourists.

In 1837 a canny local farmer, Ebenezer C. Staples, recognized the region's summer playground potential. Initially taking in boarders on his farm for $1.50 a week, he later opened the first hotel, the still-operating Old Orchard Beach Inn. Staples's instincts proved right: The new railroads soon brought a wave of tourists from both the United States and Canada to frolic on Old Orchard's superb 7-mile-long white-sand beach.

Thanks to the Grand Trunk Railroad, Old Orchard became the closest ocean beach resort to Montreal. The area, which has a large Franco-American population, is still a popular destination for French Canadian visitors, and in summer you are likely to hear Quebec-accented French spoken almost anywhere you go.

When the first pier at Old Orchard Beach was built in 1898, it stood 20 feet above and 1,800 feet out over the water and was constructed entirely of steel. The pavilions housed animals, a casino, and a restaurant. In the decades that followed, the original pier was rebuilt many times after being damaged by fire and storms, until a wider and shorter wooden pier was built in 1980.

An amusement area appeared in 1902 and grew after World War I. The 1920s brought big-name bands such as those led by Guy Lombardo and Duke Ellington to the Pier Casino, and thousands danced under a revolving crystal ball.

Fire, hard economic times, and the decline of the railroad and steamboat industries all took their toll on Old Orchard Beach over the years, but then a major revitalization plan widened sidewalks, added benches and streetlights, and passed and enforced ordinances that prevent "cruising" (repeatedly driving the same stretch of road). The result is a cleaner, more appealing, yet still lively and fun vacation spot. For families, it can't be beat, with the beach, amusement park rides, mini golf just down the road, and reasonable lodging rates.

The area is also well known for the camp meetings that began in the mid-1800s, first by Methodists, then by Baptists and the Salvation Army. These meetings continue throughout the summer in the Ocean Park community today.

Biddeford and Saco, separated by the Saco River, are often called "the twin cities." Saco is a classic Yankee town with white-clapboard mansions, a prestigious museum, and a long, dignified main street. However, it also has a rather garish strip of amusement and water parks along Rt. 1 that is a big draw in summer for families with young children.

Although it also includes the stately old seaside resort village of Biddeford Pool, the city of Biddeford is essentially a classic mill town with a strong French Canadian heritage and mammoth 19th-century brick textile mills that have largely stood idle since the 1950s.

Pine Point in Scarborough and its surrounding area is the easternmost tip of Old Orchard Beach and is often a less crowded, quieter spot to visit. A large saltwater marsh in Scarborough is also good for quiet relaxation and exploring by foot, bike, and canoe.

GUIDANCE Old Orchard Beach Chamber of Commerce (207-934-2500; to get a free vacation planner by mail, 1-800-365-9386; oldorchardbeachmaine.com), P.O. Box 600 (1st St.), Old Orchard Beach 04064, maintains a year-round walk-in information center (open 8:30–4:30 weekdays, also Sat. and Sun., June–Aug.) and offers help with reservations.

Biddeford-Saco Chamber of Commerce & Industry (207-282-1567; biddeford sacochamber.org), 110 Main St., Saco Island, Suite 1202, Saco 04072. Stocks many local brochures; helpful, friendly staff.

GETTING THERE *By air:* **Portland International Jetport** is 13 miles north, and rental cars are available at the airport. You can also fly your own plane into **Sanford Airport**.

By hired car: **Maine Limousine Service** (207-883-0222 or 1-800-646-0068; mainelimo.com), P.O. Box 1478, Scarborough 04070, can also pick you up and bring you to the region.

THE PIER AT OLD ORCHARD BEACH

Nancy English

By car: Exits 36 and 42 off the Maine Turnpike (I-95) take you easily to Rt. 9 and the center of Old Orchard Beach. You can also find the town from Rt. 1.

By train: The **Downeaster** (1-800-USA-RAIL; thedowneaster.com), Amtrak's train service between Boston and Portland, makes five stops a day year-round at Saco and seasonally, May–Oct., at Old Orchard Beach.

GETTING AROUND From many accommodations in Old Orchard Beach, you are close enough to walk to the pier, the town's center of activity. **Shuttle Bus**, the local transportation service, connects the downtowns of Biddeford, Saco, Portland, and Old Orchard Beach. Call 207-282-5408 or go to shuttlebus-zoom.com for schedules.

PARKING There are a number of privately owned lots in the center of Old Orchard Beach and one municipal lot. Most charge $5–15 for any length of time— 10 minutes or all day. There are meters on the street if you don't mind circling a few times to catch an available one, but at 15 minutes for a quarter, you're better off in lots if you plan to stay long.

WHEN TO COME Biddeford is especially worth visiting during La Kermesse, the colorful four-day Franco-American festival in late June. This festival—which features a colorful parade (some marching bands wear snowshoes), concerts, dances, fireworks, and public suppers with traditional stick-to-the-ribs French Canadian food—is one of the largest ethnic events in New England. Old Orchard Beach quiets way down after Columbus Day, but there are still many places to stay and four year-round restaurants for off-season visitors. The pier closes after Columbus Day weekend.

✳ Villages

Ocean Park is a historic community founded in 1881 by Free Will Baptists and well known for its outstanding religious, educational, and cultural programs. The Ocean Park Association (207-934-9068; oceanpark.org) sponsors lectures, concerts, movies, and other events throughout the summer in the cluster of old buildings known as Temple Square. Within the community you'll also find a recreation hall, shuffleboard and tennis courts, an old-fashioned ice cream parlor, and a smattering of gift shops. The entire community is a state game preserve, and you can find great walking trails through cathedral pines. A comprehensive guide to programs and recreation is put out by the association.

Pine Point. This quiet and less crowded end of the beach offers a selection of gift shops, restaurants, lobster pounds, and places to stay.

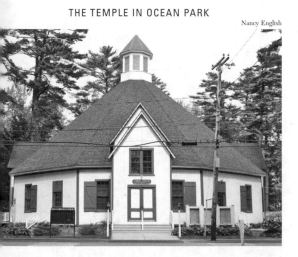

THE TEMPLE IN OCEAN PARK

Nancy English

Nancy English

THE BREAKWATER AT CAMP ELLIS, SACO

Camp Ellis. At the end of a peninsula where the Saco River blends with the ocean. Residents fight a constant battle with beach erosion, and some of the homes are frighteningly close to the shore. Fishing trips, whale-watching, a long breakwater great for walking, interesting shops, and a couple of restaurants.

Biddeford Pool. A small yachting port with lots of low-key charm where well-to-do families have been summering in the same big old shingled houses for generations. You'll find a few shops, a lobster pound, and a small restaurant, but not much else. Although politically part of blue-collar Biddeford, "the pool" is socially closer to fashionable nearby Kennebunkport.

✳ To See and Do

APPLE PICKING ✐ **Snell Farm** (207-929-6166; snellfamilyfarm.com), 1000 River Rd. (Rt. 112), Buxton. Pick-your-own-apples in Sept. and Oct., when the farm stand here moves from its summer spot across the street over toward the farmhouse, and the greenhouse is jammed with pumpkins ready for carving. In summer and fall the farm stand is stuffed with the best produce imaginable.

FOR FAMILIES The Rt. 1 strip in Saco and nearby Old Orchard Beach makes up Maine's biggest concentration of "family attractions." Kids go wild. Parents fear they may go broke.

✐ **Funtown/Splashtown USA** (207-284-5139; funtownsplashtownusa.com), Rt. 1, Saco. Open daily (depending on the weather) mid-June–Labor Day, weekends in spring and fall. Water activities and a large amusement park. In addition to the 100-foot wooden roller coaster Excalibur, the park has bumper cars, New England's largest log flume, plenty of carnival rides, a hydrofighter, kiddie rides, antique cars.

✐ **Aquaboggan Water Park** (207-282-3112; aquaboggan.com), Rt. 1, Saco. Open mid-June–Labor Day. Several waterslides, including a high-thrills slide with mats or tubes, Aquasaucer, swimming pool, bumper boats, mini golf, arcade, shuffleboard, toddler area, wave pool.

✐ **Monkey Trunks** (603-452-8812; monkeytrunks.com), 1 Cascade Rd., Saco. A high ropes and ziplines park that opened in the summer of 2011, Monkey Trunks was an immediate hit. A giant swing, a 50-foot leap, and more for $39 to $49, depending on height.

✐ **Pirate's Cove Adventure Golf** (207-934-5086; piratescove.net), 70 1st St., Old Orchard Beach. Two 18-hole up-and-down mini golf courses, waterfalls, ponds.

🖌 **Palace Playland** (207-934-2001; palaceplayland.com), 1 Old Orchard St., Old Orchard Beach. Open daily June–Labor Day; arcade open through Columbus Day on weekends. For more than 60 years fun seekers have been wheeled, lifted, shaken, spun, and bumped in Palace Playland rides. There's a carousel (though it no longer contains the original 1906 horses), a Ferris wheel, a 60-foot-high (Maine's largest) waterslide, and a roller coaster. You can pay by the ride or buy an all-day pass.

Courtesy of the Saco Museum

A LANDSCAPE BY GOOKIN AT THE SACO MUSEUM

GOLF Dunegrass (207-934-4513; dunegrass.com), 200 Wild Dunes Way, Old Orchard Beach, 18 holes. **Biddeford-Saco Country Club** (207-282-5883), 101 Old Orchard Rd., Saco, 18 holes. **Deep Brook Golf Course** (207-282-3500; deepbrookgolfcourse.com), 36 New County Rd. (Rt. 5), Saco, nine holes. **Cascade Golf Center** (207-282-3524), 955 Portland Rd., Saco, driving range.

MUSEUMS Saco Museum (207-283-3861; sacomuseum.org), 371 Main St., Saco. Open year-round Tue., Wed., Thu. noon–4; Fri. noon–8; Sat. 10–4; Sun. noon–4 June–Dec. 15. $5 adults, $3 seniors, $2 students, under 6 free (free to all 4–8 Fri.). Larger than it looks from the outside, and very well maintained and organized. An exhibit about art and industry fills the first floor, and one room presenting a Factory Girl Bedchamber is furnished with the artifacts of a millworker—including a racy novel. A dress-up trunk allows visitors to try on mid-1800s fashion. Original paintings include 13 portraits by deaf painter John Brewster Jr.—whose subjects seem tenacious and inured to suffering—furniture, tools, and natural history specimens. Lectures and special exhibits. The institute's **Dyer Library** next door has an outstanding Maine history collection.

Harmon Historical Museum, (207-934-9319; harmonmuseum.org), 4 Portland Ave., Old Orchard Beach, is open June–Sept., Tue.–Fri. 11–4, Sat. 9–noon; winter hours by appointment. Home of the Old Orchard Beach Historical Society, the building is full of exhibits from the town's past. Each year, in addition to the regular school, fire, and aviation exhibits, there is a special exhibit. Pick up the time line of the area's history and the walking map of historic sites.

SCENIC DRIVE From Saco there's a loop that heads up Rt. 112, past the Way-Way General Store. On the left a few miles out is the Saco Heath Preserve, worth a stop to explore. From there, continue on Rt. 112 until it intersects with Rt. 202. Turn left and stay on 202 until you see the intersection with Rt. 5. Turn left again and follow Rt. 5 along the river, back to the center of Saco.

TENNIS The **Ocean Park Association** (207-934-9068; oceanpark.org) maintains public tennis courts, open to the public for a fee in summer.

Nancy English

PINE POINT

✳ Green Space

BEACHES Obviously, **Old Orchard Beach** is the big draw in this area, with 7 miles of sand and plenty of space for sunbathing, swimming, volleyball, and other recreation.

Ferry Beach State Park is marked from Rt. 9 between Old Orchard Beach and Camp Ellis, in Saco. The 100-plus-acre preserve includes 70 yards of sand, a boardwalk through the dunes, bike paths, nature trails, a picnic area with grills, lifeguards, changing rooms, and pit toilets. Even in the middle of summer it isn't terribly crowded here. $6 per nonresident, $1 ages 5–11, free under 5 or over 65 with identification. Off-season the Iron Ranger (a green pole with a green can beside the booth) collects reduced fees on the honor system.

Bay View Beach, at the end of Bay View Rd. near Ferry Beach, is 200 yards of mostly sandy beach; lifeguards, free parking.

Camp Ellis Beach, Rt. 9, Saco. Some 2,000 feet of beach backed by cottages; also a long fishing pier. The commercial parking lots fill quickly on sunny days.

Pine Point, off Rt. 9, Scarborough, has a small and uncrowded beach near the fisherman's co-op. The larger beach area, closer to Old Orchard, with snack bar, changing room, and bathrooms, charges fees in summer for parking in the adjacent lot.

HIKING Saco Bay Trails (sacobaytrails.com), P.O. Box 720, Saco 04072, publishes a trail guide for Saco, Biddeford, and Old Orchard Beach. Copies are sold for $10 in local shops and at the Biddeford-Saco Chamber of Commerce.

Saco Heath Preserve (nature.org), Rt. 112 (2 miles from I-95 exit 36), Saco. This small Nature Conservancy preserve shouldn't be overlooked. The sign is hard to spot; look for it on the right a few miles out of Saco. A quiet, peaceful stroll through a peat bog on a 1-mile wooden boardwalk and woodland trail through the 1,223-acre preserve brings visitors close to heathland plants like Labrador tea and sheep laurel. Atlantic white cedar nurtures rare-in-Maine Hessel's hairstreak butterflies.

East Point Sanctuary, off Rt. 9 (east of Goose Rocks Beach) in Biddeford Pool. A 30-acre Maine Audubon wildlife sanctuary well known to birders, who flock here during migrating seasons. Beautiful any time of year. From Rt. 9 turn right just beyond Goose Rocks Beach onto Fortune Rocks Beach Rd. to Lester B. Orcutt Blvd.; turn right, drive almost to the end, and look for a chain-link fence and AUDUBON sign. The trail continues along the golf course and sea.

LIGHTHOUSE TOUR Wood Island Lighthouse (207-286-3229; woodisland lighthouse.org), Biddeford Pool. Tours are offered by the Friends of Wood Island Lighthouse departing from Vines Landing in Biddeford Pool, by phone reservation only. The tours last 1½ hours and are offered July and Aug.; donations of $10 encouraged. The 42-foot stone tower, attached keeper's house, and stone oil house can be entered on this 35-acre island where seabirds nest and others rest on their migrations. A half-mile boardwalk takes visitors from the boat landing to the lighthouse.

✴ Winter Sports

CROSS COUNTRY SKIING ✐ **Harris Farm Cross Country Ski Center** (207-499-2678; harrisfarm.com), 280 Buzzell Rd., Dayton. Open daily 9 AM–dusk when there's snow. This 500-acre dairy and tree farm offers 40 kilometers of groomed trails, from easy to difficult, over hills, by ponds and streams, and through the woods. Rentals available, and they include snowshoes.

✴ Lodging

INNS AND BED & BREAKFASTS

The Atlantic Birches Inn (207-934-5295 or 1-888-934-5295; atlanticbirches .com), 20 Portland Ave., Old Orchard Beach 04064. A Victorian, shingle-style home, built in the area's heyday. Five guest rooms in the main house are named for former grand hotels; they're cheerful, with a mix of old and new furnishings. The "cottage" offers three rooms and two kitchenette suites with separate entrances. The in-ground pool is perfect on a hot day. $131–192 in high season includes continental breakfast with fresh muffins, fruit salad, and whole-grain bread.

Hobson House Celtic Inn (207-284-4113; hobsonhouse.com), 398 Main St., Saco 04072. A big yellow mansion in the heart of Saco's historic district, Hobson House was built in the 1820s by Joseph Hobson, Saco's first mayor. Owner Frank Zayac rents four pleasant and comfortably furnished bedrooms, two with a private bath (the Alice May Hobson Suite also has a canopy bed, fireplace, and sitting area) and two sharing a bath, by reservation only. Common space includes a back garden with a large, free-form swimming pool. $115–180 with full breakfast.

✐ **Old Orchard Beach Inn** (207-934-5834 or 1-877-700-6624; oldorchard beachinn.com), 6 Portland Ave., Old Orchard Beach 04064. Ebenezer Staples's original hostelry, part of this inn dates from the 1730s, and the building is on the National Register of Historic Places as Maine's oldest continually operated inn. Now updated, it retains traditional wide-pine floorboards, antique furnishings, and a lot of period touches; some rooms have ventless fireplace. All 18 rooms, one a two-bedroom suite, have air-conditioning, cable TV, and private bath. $125–450 high season, $89–225 off-season, with a continental breakfast that includes homemade muffins and breads.

OTHER LODGING Old Orchard Beach offers an overwhelming number of motel, cottage, and condominium complexes both along the beach and on main roads. The chamber of commerce publishes a helpful *Old Orchard Beach Vacation Planner*.

Aquarius Motel (207-934-2626; aquariusmotel.com), 1 Brown St., Old Orchard Beach 04064. A small, family-owned and -operated 14-unit motel that's exceptionally clean, and right on the beach. The patio is a great place to relax after a day of sightseeing. $159 for a double with kitchenette in-season. Family-sized units also available. Many special rates in early spring and late fall.

Ocean Walk Hotel (207-934-1716 or 1-800-992-3779; oceanwalkhotel.com), 197 E. Grand Ave., Old Orchard Beach 04064. Forty-four well-kept rooms, from studios to oceanfront suites. The top-floor rooms in one building have very high ceilings, giving them a light, airy, spacious feel. Barbecue grills are available for guests to use, and there's an indoor pool. $175–300 in-season, $75–200 off-season.

&. **Sea View Motel** (207-934-4180 or 1-800-541-8439; seaviewgetaway.com), 65 W. Grand Ave., Old Orchard Beach 04064. Forty-nine rooms, some with ocean views. Pretty landscaping, with an outdoor pool and a beautiful fountain in front. The simple rooms, some with kitchenette, are modern, bright, and well maintained. Two-bedroom suites with kitchenette are also available. $98–290 in-season, $57–125 off-season.

⌀ **The Gull Motel, Inn & Cottages** (207-934-4321; gullmotel.com), 89 W.

Grand Ave., Old Orchard Beach 04064. An attractive motel with an outdoor pool, immaculate and family-oriented. The inn is right on the beach, with a great porch. Cottages also available by the week. Inn rates $80–150 per night; motel rates $75–160; cottages $1,250 per week.

⌀ &. **Billowhouse** (207-934-2333 or 1-888-767-7776; billowhouse.com), 2 Temple Ave., Ocean Park 04063. This 1881 Victorian seaside guesthouse is Mary Kerrigan's retirement project, completely renovated yet with old-fashioned charm. There are three ground-level efficiency apartments and six kitchenette units in the adjoining motel. The four B&B units include a large three-room suite with private deck, in-room Jacuzzi, and full kitchen; a two-room suite with private deck and outside hot tub; two oceanfront rooms with private bath share a deck

SEA VIEW MOTEL

Nancy English

overlooking the ocean. The beach is just steps away. $135–250 in-season, less for extended stays, breakfast included for B&B guests only; $95–155 off-season.

The Nautilus by the Sea (207-934-2021 or 1-800-981-7018; nautilusbythe sea.com), 2 Colby Ave., Ocean Park 04063. This 12-room B&B, built in 1890 as a private home, is smack up against the beach. A couple of rooms share baths, but all have beach or ocean views, with the most dramatic vista from the fourth-floor "penthouse suite," where you can lie in bed at night and watch the beam of Wood Island Light play across the water. Owners Dick and Patte Kessler have kept the decor simple and traditional, much as it would have been when the house was built. $85–175 in-season, $65–125 off-season, with continental breakfast including fresh muffins.

CAMPGROUNDS Camping is a budget-minded family's best bet in this area. There are at least a dozen camp-grounds here (more than 4,000 sites in the area), many geared to families and offering games, recreational activities, and trolley service to the beach in-season. Following are a few recommendations; check with the chamber for a full listing.

Silver Springs Campground and Cottages (207-283-3880; silversprings campgroundandcottages.com), 705 Portland Rd. (Rt. 1), Saco. May–mid-Oct. Thirteen cottages and 130 sites (with full RV hookups) keep Mary Ann and Bryce Ingraham busy. "Most people who come, come back," Mary Ann said. The framework for the cottages is still from the 1930s, but inside and out they are new, with interiors finished with V-match pine boards and all new appliances. Two swimming pools and a rec hall. The Ingrahams

host family reunions. Camping sites $42–48, cottages $80–175 in-season. Discounts off-season.

✑ & **Bayley's Camping Resort** (207-883-6043; bayleys-camping.com), 52 Ross Rd., Scarborough 04074. Just down the road from Pine Point are paddleboats, swimming pool, Jacuzzi, fishing, game room, special programs for children and adults—and a shuttle to take you to Pine Point Beach and Old Orchard's downtown. More than 400 sites and 50 rental trailers. $47–86 depending on hookups.

✪ ✑ & **Powder Horn** (207-934-4733; mainecampgrounds.com), P.O. Box 366, Old Orchard Beach 04064. A 450-site campground with plenty of recreation options—playgrounds, shuffleboard, horseshoes, volleyball, rec hall and game room, activities pro-gram, mini golf, trolley service to the beach in-season. $50–65 per night in-season, $40–50 off-season. **Hidden Pines** is a sister campground next door for basic to premium sites.

✱ Where to Eat

DINING OUT Mia's at Pepperell Square (207-284-6427; miasatpepperell square.com), 17 Pepperell Square, Saco. Open for dinner Mon.–Sat. Excellent cooking is the lure for visi-tors, starting with buttercup bisque or crabcakes made with lots of crab, then butter-poached lobster, grilled pork chops with mustard fruit compote, or seared scallops with potato pierogi, all from a fall menu. Roast chicken with risotto is so reasonable at $15. Good wine and cocktails. Entrées $15–24.

& **Joseph's by the Sea** (207-934-5044; josephsbythesea.com), 55 W. Grand Ave., Old Orchard Beach. Open Apr.–Dec. Serving breakfast and din-ner daily in-season; hours vary the rest of the year, so call ahead. The dining

Nancy English

JOSEPH'S BY THE SEA

rooms overlook the water, or you can dine on the garden patio. This family-run restaurant is one of the few to keep high standards over years of operation. While not as formal as in years past, the dinners are still as polished and well made. Wonderful grilled steaks, seared scallops, and the popular Pasta Maison—Maine shrimp, scallops, salmon, and mussels on angel-hair pasta with real cream—for once the cream is light, enhancing and not overwhelming the seafood. Entrées $18–29

Run of the Mill (207-571-9648; therunofthemill.net), 100 Main St., Saco. This microbrewery set on Saco Island in the Saco River has a fabulous outdoor deck in good weather and finely crafted ales and good food year-round. The hand-cut fries are memorable, and of course what could be better with "Basement Bitter"? Fourteen barrels ferment what's on tap, while shepherd's pie and bangers and smash keep the UK close at hand. Entrées $9–20.

❦ **The Landmark** (207-934-0156; landmarkfinedining.com), 28 E. Grand Ave., Old Orchard Beach. Open at 5 for dinner Apr.–Dec.; daily June–

Columbus Day; call for hours off-season. Fine dining in a 1910 Victorian house, and on an outdoor terrace in fine weather. Menu specialties include a creamy lobster stew, garlicky pasta with mussels, lacquered duck, and barbecued ribs, all quite good. Entrées $18–27. Early-bird specials.

Bufflehead's (207-284-6000; buffle headsrestaurant.com), 122 Hills Beach Rd., Biddeford. Open year-round, daily for lunch and dinner in summer; call for hours off-season. Offering indoor and outdoor seating with a terrific ocean view, this great family place makes quality food. Try the fried sole with Creole meunière sauce, or baked scallops. Baked manicotti with a side of Italian sausage or hazelnut-crusted rack of lamb could do for someone ready to switch from seafood. Entrées $11–28.

RUN OF THE MILL, SACO

Nancy English

EATING OUT Bebe's Burritos (207-283-4222), 140 Main St., Biddeford. Open Tue.–Sun. for lunch and dinner. Great burritos with all the fixings, including homemade beans and slow-cooked beef and chicken. Live entertainment Thu.–Sat. nights.

Huot's Restaurant (207-282-1642; huotsseafoodrestaurant.com), Camp Ellis Beach, Saco. Open mid-Apr.–mid-Sept. Tue.–Sun. 11–9. The third generation of the Huot family is carrying on the tradition of good fresh seafood at this clean, simple spot in Camp Ellis, begun in 1935. Entrées $7–25.

Traditions (207-282-6661), 162 Main St., Saco. A cozy little restaurant specializing in pasta and traditional Italian meat and seafood dishes. Open for lunch and dinner. Entrées $8–16.

Wormwoods (207-282-9679), 16 Bay Ave., Camp Ellis Beach, Saco. Open daily year-round for lunch and dinner. An old-fashioned place, with dark green booths, by the breakwater. They go all-out decorating for the seasons—watch out for the screeching skull in October—and can be counted on for fried seafood.

OLD CAR WEEKEND AT WORMWOOD'S
Nancy English

BREAKFAST AND LUNCH Cole Road Café (207-283-4103; coleroadcafe.com), 1 Cole Rd., Biddeford. Open for breakfast and lunch Wed.–Sat. 7 AM–1:45 PM; breakfast only on Sun., same hours. Deservedly popular, this colorful, friendly place makes all the breakfast standards; specials might include blueberry-stuffed French toast with cream cheese or Granny Smith apple pancakes topped with granola; for lunch, perhaps a butternut squash goat cheese tart. Six specials daily for each meal. Joyce Rose has run Cole Road Café for 20 years. Breakfast $3–10.

The Blue Elephant (207-281-3070; blueelephantcatering.com), 12 Pepperell Square, Saco. Open Mon.–Fri. 8–3 for breakfast and lunch, but call first because hours vary. A former Philadelphia caterer and restaurant manager serve fine breakfast sandwiches; house-made croissants, scones, and cinnamon rolls; and Carpe Diem coffee. Lunch features chowder, panini, Cubans, and mac-and-cheese. Lunch $4–7.

LOBSTER POUND Lobster Claw (207-282-0040), 4 Ocean Park Rd. (Rt. 5), Saco. Lobsters cooked outside in giant kettles, stews and chowders, cozy dining room, and takeout available. Twin lobster specials, also steamers, fried seafood. Lobster packed to travel.

BAKERY Coastal Cakes (207-282-7516; coastalcakes.com), 8 Pepperell Square, Saco. Coffee and tea are served, but the main attractions are the specialty cakes, cupcakes, and muffins.

TAKEOUT Near Old Orchard Beach's pier and on the main drag are an abundance of take-out stands and informal restaurants serving pizza, burgers, hot dogs, fried seafood, fried dough, pier fries, ice cream, and more. Our

Nancy English

COASTAL CAKES IN SACO

favorites are **Bill's** for pizza, **Lisa's** for pier fries.

Goldthwaite's (207-284 5000; pool lobster.com), 3 Lester B. Orcutt Blvd., Biddeford Pool, is good for a lobster roll or something else at the counter; enjoy your food at a picnic table in back near the water.

Rapid Ray's (207-282-1847), 179 Main St., Saco. Open daily until around midnight. A local icon since 1953. Quick and friendly service from people who seem to know everyone who walks through the door. Burgers, hot dogs, lobster rolls, fries, onion rings, and the like at great prices.

✳ Entertainment

City Theater (207-282-0849; city theater.org), Main St., Biddeford. This 500-seat, 1890s theater offers a series of live performances.

Saco Drive-In (207-284-1016), Rt. 1, Saco. Double features in spring and summer.

✳ Selective Shopping

Cascade Flea Market, 885 Portland Rd. (Rt. 1), Saco. One of Maine's largest outdoor flea markets, open daily in summer.

Stone Soup Artisans (207-283-4715; stonesoupartisans.com), 228 Main St., Saco. Quality crafts from more than 50 Maine artisans. Pottery and jewelry all made in Maine.

✳ Special Events

January: **Annual Lobster Dip**— hundreds of participants dip into the chilly Atlantic to benefit Special Olympics of Maine, in Old Orchard Beach.

Late June: **La Kermesse**, Biddeford— parade, public suppers, dancing, and entertainment highlighting Franco-American culture and traditions. **Saco Sidewalk Arts Festival**, Saco.

GOLDTHWAITE'S AT BIDDEFORD POOL

Nancy English

Early July: **Greek Heritage Festival**, St. Demetrius on Bradley St. in Saco.

Late July: **The Lobster Bowl Shriners Football Game** in Biddeford.

June–Labor Day: **Fireworks** at the Old Orchard Beach square Thursday at 9:45 PM.

August: **Ocean Park Festival of Lights** and **Salvation Army camp meetings** under the pavilion in Ocean Park. **Beach Olympics**—three days of competitions, music, displays, and presentations to benefit the Special Olympics of Maine. Annual **5K Race and Kids' Fun Run**, scholarship fund-raiser.

September: **Annual Car Show**—with a car lineup and parade, Old Orchard Beach.

October: **Saco Pumpkin Fest**.

December: **Celebrate the Season by the Sea**—a tree-lighting ceremony with horse-drawn hay-wagon rides, refreshments, a holiday bazaar, caroling, and a bonfire on the beach, in Old Orchard.

Casco Bay 2

PORTLAND AREA

FREEPORT

PORTLAND AREA

Lively, walkable, sophisticated, Maine's largest city is also a working port. Greater Portland accounts for one-quarter of Maine's total population, but Portland's most populated area is a 3.5-mile-long peninsula facing Casco Bay. Visitors head down Congress Street to the Old Port, more than five square brick and stone blocks built exuberantly during the city's peak shipping era and now laced with restaurants, cafés, shops, and galleries.

Portland's motto, "Resurgam" (I shall rise again), could not be more appropriate. The 17th-century settlement was expunged twice by Native Americans, then torched by the British. Finally it prospered as a lumbering port in the 1820s—as still evidenced by its many Federal-era mansions and commercial buildings, like the granite-and-glass Mariner's Church in the Old Port, built in 1820 to be the largest building in the capital of a brand-new state. Then on Independence Day in 1866 a firecracker flamed up in a Commercial Street boatyard and quickly destroyed most of the downtown. Again the city rose like the legendary phoenix, rebuilding quickly and beautifully, this time in sturdy brick, to create the core of northern New England's shipping, rail, and manufacturing businesses.

PORTLAND'S OLD PORT

Kim Grant

These very buildings, a century later, were "going for peanuts," in the words of a real estate agent who began buying them up in the late 1960s, when its handsome Grand Trunk Station was demolished. Down by the harbor artists and craftspeople were renting shopfronts for $50 per month. They formed the Old Port Association, hoping to entice people to stroll through the no-man's-land. That first winter they strung lights through upper floors to convey a sense of security, and they shoveled their own streets, a service the city had ceased to provide to that area. At the end of the winter they celebrated their survival by holding the first Old Port Festival, a street fair that is still held each June.

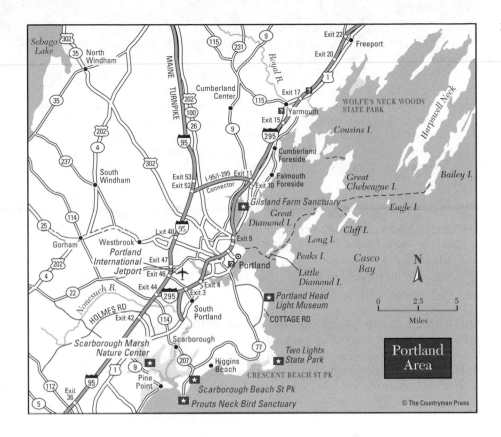

Lining a ridge above the Old Port, Congress Street was the city's fashionable shopping and financial strip in the first half of the 20th century. The present Maine Bank & Trust Building was the tallest in all New England when it was built in 1909. By the mid-1990s, however, the three department stores here had closed and foot traffic had shifted to the Maine Mall. Now some of it is back.

The Maine College of Art (MECA) has replaced Porteus Department Store in a five-story Beaux Arts building and maintains the street-level Institute of Contemporary Art. With a student body of more than 400 and a far larger continuing-education program, MECA has had a visual impact up and down Congress Street, which is now called the Arts District. Contemporary art galleries proliferate around the Portland Museum of Art.

Scattered throughout the city are members of Portland's growing immigrant community, with families from Bosnia, Russia, Somalia, Sudan, Congo, Vietnam, Puerto Rico, and Mexico, making this Maine's most diverse city.

Longfellow Square abuts the gracious residential blocks of the West End. Spared by the fire that destroyed the Old Port, its leafy streets are lined with town houses and mansions in a range of graceful architectural styles (several are B&Bs).

The Western Promenade was laid out as an overlook for the West End way back in 1836; the Eastern Promenade was at the opposite end of the peninsula, along the verge of Munjoy Hill, overlooking Casco Bay. In 1879 the city gained Deering Oaks Park and was blessed by the design of city civil engineer William Goodwin.

In 1917, with turn-of-the-century plans by Frederick Law Olmsted, a dream of James Phinney Baxter, a mayor of Portland, came true when the Baxter Boulevard along Back Cove was opened to pedestrians.

Commercial Street, with condominiums and fish-processing plants, is a departure point for the fleet of Casco Bay Lines ferries that regularly transport people, mail, and supplies to nearby Peaks Island—offering rental bikes, guided sea kayaking, lodging, and dining—and to the Diamond Islands, Chebeague, and Cliff Island, more than an hour's ride. A boat trip also visits Eagle Island, preserved as a memorial to Arctic explorer Admiral Peary. The waterfront is, moreover, the departure point for deep-sea fishing, harbor cruises, whale-watching, and daysailing.

South Portland's waterfront has become far more visitor-friendly in recent years, with the Spring Point Lighthouse and recently restored Bug Light as focal points, along with a burgeoning Greenbelt Trail system.

Beyond South Portland lies Cape Elizabeth, home of the vintage-1791 Portland Head Light and its museum. Nearby Scarborough to the south and both Falmouth and Yarmouth, just north of the city, also offer secluded seaside reserves for walking, boating, and birding.

GUIDANCE Greater Portland Convention and Visitors Bureau (207-772-5800; visitportland.com) publishes *Visit Portland Maine*, listing restaurants, sights, museums, and accommodations, including cottages. **Visitors information centers** are at 14 Ocean Gateway Pier (east of the end of Commercial St.), Portland 04101, open March–Oct. July–Columbus Day the schedule is Mon.–Fri. 9–5, Sat.–Sun. 9–4. Another center is at the **Portland International Jetport** (207-775-5809), open daily 10–10:30 through the summer, opening 10:30 AM the rest of the year. **Deering Oaks Visitor Center** (207-828-0149) is located in Deering Oaks Park just off the State St. extension and Forest Ave., and is open daily in summer and winter. The website has updated schedules.

Portland's Downtown District (207-772-6828; portlandmaine.com), 549 Congress St., Portland 04101, offers information about performances, festivals, and special events. They publish a guide to services, attractions, dining, and lodging.

For current entertainment, weather, and dining ratings, click onto one of several local newspaper websites: **pressherald.com**, the *Portland Press Herald* site, or the *Portland Phoenix's* page, **portlandphoenix.com**. The

MONUMENT SQUARE

Nancy English

Nancy English

OCEAN GATEWAY

Portland Forecaster, **theforecaster .net**—a free weekly available in street vending boxes and at coffeehouses and shops—carries listings for galleries, music, and events. A website, **port landfoodmap.com**, holds the most complete listing of Portland restaurants, and is the best source for food-related events in the city.

The Maine Tourism Association (207-846-0833) staffs a major state information center on Rt. 1 in Yarmouth, just off I-295 exit 17.

Also see **Greater Portland Landmarks** under *To See*.

GETTING THERE *By air:* **Portland International Jetport** (207-774-7301; portlandjetport.org) is served by AirTran (1-800-247-8726; airtran.com), Air Canada (1-888-247-2262; aircanada.com), Continental Airlines (1-800-523-3273; continental.com), Delta Air Lines (1-800-221-1212; delta.com), JetBlue (1-800-538-2583; jetblue.com), United (1-800-864-8331; ual.com), and U.S. Airways (1-800-428-4322; usair.com). Car rentals at the airport include National, Avis, Hertz, Budget, Enterprise, and Alamo.

By bus: **Concord Coach Lines** (207-828-1151 or 1-800-639-3317; concordcoach lines.com) stops en route from Boston to Bangor and coastal points at a modern station just off I-295 exit 5A (it's also the new train station—see *By train*); the buses offer movies, music, and a nonstop express to Boston and its Logan Airport. It's a $10 taxi ride or $1.50 by METRO Bus 5 from the bus station to downtown. **Vermont Transit** (207-772-6587 or 1-800-552-8737; vermonttransit.com) and Greyhound (1-800-231-2222; greyhound.com) offer frequent service among Portland, Boston, and Maine's coastal and inland points, using the Greyhound terminal, which unfortunately is dingy and offers little parking.

By car: From I-95, take I-295 to exit 44 (Portland Waterfront) and follow signs for the ferry.

By train: Amtrak service (1-800-USA-RAIL; thedowneaster.com or amtrak.com). The **Downeaster** is so successful, it now runs five times daily between Boston's renovated North Station and Portland's clean new rail–bus station on outer Congress St.; the trip takes about 2½ hours. Paid parking is available, and even when cars overflow the big lots, helpful attendants seem to find a space for you. The trip is tranquil and the view of Scarborough Marsh beautiful. Stops in Old Orchard Beach (seasonal), Saco/Biddeford, and Wells give another option to Portland visitors who would like to skip driving. The trip to Old Orchard Beach, for instance, takes just 15 minutes, and drops you off next to the amusement park and beach.

GETTING AROUND Portland, like many interesting small cities, holds beautiful 18th- and 19th-century facades, engaging street musicians, and creative window displays. It's a great place for walking.

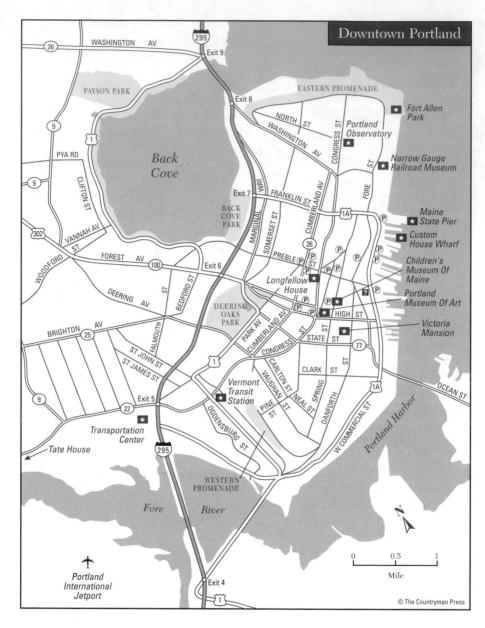

Downtown Portland

The Metro (207-774-0351; gpmetrobus.com) bus transfer system serves Greater Portland. Metro city buses connect airport and city, and offer convenient routes around the city. $1.50 one-way, or $5 for a day pass; 75¢ for seniors over 65 and those with disabilities; $1 high school students.

PARKING Portland meters are 50¢ per half hour, but, as we have discovered the hard way, you get a $15 ticket after two hours, which climbs higher if you are caught feeding the meter. The city urges visitors to use its many parking garages.

The **Fore Street Garage** (439 Fore St.) puts you at one end of the Old Port, and the **Custom House Square Garage** (25 Pearl St.) at the other. The **Casco Bay Garage** (Maine State Pier) and **Free Street Parking** (130 Free St., just up from the art museum) are also handy. Fisherman's Wharf, one block from Long Wharf, the site of many boat tour companies, offers all-day parking for $8.

WHEN TO COME Portland, with its thriving restaurant and museum scene, makes a great destination any time of year. The Victoria Mansion, Longfellow House, and the Tate House dress up in Christmas finery and offer holiday tours, though a whale-watching trip would have to be scheduled in the months of better weather. And the winter wind can blow bitterly cold on Portland streets—even when some of us are still out skating on Deering Oaks pond.

✳ To See

MUSEUMS

All listings are in Portland unless otherwise noted

✔ **Museum of African Culture** (207-871-7188; museumafricanculture.org), 13 Brown St. Open Tue.–Fri. 10:30–4, Sat. noon–4. With more than 1,500 pieces representing more than 1,000 years of African history and art, including masks, bronzes, batiks, and wooden sculptures, this museum is devoted to sub-Saharan arts and culture. Founder Oscar Mokeme conducts workshops on the healing practices of Nigerian Igbo people; he is a descendant of Igbo royal family healers.

Maine Historical Society (207-774-1822; mainehistory.org), 485 Congress St. Maine Historical Society's offices are here, as are **Wadsworth-Longfellow House**, **MHS Museum**, and **MHS Research Library**, as well as the **Maine memory network** (maine memory.net). The Wadsworth-Longfellow House is open May–Oct., Mon.–Sat. 10:30–4, Sun. noon 4 (closed July 4 and Labor Day), when the museum is open Mon.–Sat. 10–5, Sun. noon–5; the library is open year-round, Tue.–Sat. 10–4. $12 adults for the house and museum, $10 seniors and students, $3 children. Call for hours for a 45-minute guided tour of the house. Built in 1785 by the grandfather of Henry Wadsworth Longfellow, this was the first brick dwelling in town. Peleg Wadsworth was a Revolutionary War hero, and the entire clan of Wadsworths and Longfellows was prominent in the city for nearly two centuries. A small garden is hidden behind the house; another is a couple of blocks down Congress beside the

WADSWORTH-LONGFELLOW HOUSE

Nancy English

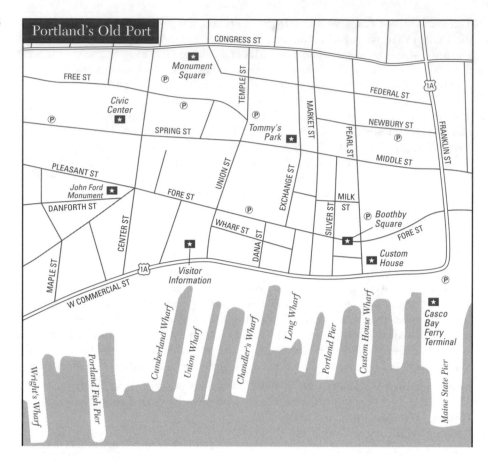

Portland's Old Port

granite First Parish Church (No. 425), marking the site on which Maine's constitution was drafted in 1819.

🖊 ♿ **The Museum at Portland Head Light** (207-799-2661; portlandheadlight .com), 1000 Shore Rd. in Fort Williams Park, Cape Elizabeth. Open daily Memorial Day–Oct., 10–4; Columbus Day–mid-Dec. and mid-Apr.–Memorial Day weekends, 10–4. $2 adults, $1 ages 6–18. This is the oldest lighthouse in Maine, first illuminated in 1791 per order of George Washington. It is now automated, and the former keeper's house has been transformed into an exceptional lighthouse museum.

Institute of Contemporary Art/MECA (207-879-5742; meca.edu/ica), 522 Congress St. Changing exhibits frequently worth checking; free. The ICA is a street-level gallery at the Maine College of Art (MECA), with more than 350 full-time students and many more in continuing-studies programs.

🖊 **The International Cryptozoology Museum** (207-518-9496; cryptozoology museum.com), 11 Avon St., Portland. $7 admission ages 13 or older, $5 ages 12 and under, "infants-in-arms" free. Meet the "Feejee Mermaid," a haunting movie prop, and the 8-foot-tall Crookston Bigfoot. This collection of mysterious creatures is the lifework of Loren Coleman and includes a life-sized colossus squid; 14 feet

✏ & PORTLAND MUSEUM OF ART

(207-775-6148; for a weekly schedule of events and information, 207-773-ARTS; portlandmuseum.org), 7 Congress Square. Open Tue., Wed., Thu., Sat., and Sun. 10–5, Fri. 10–9; Memorial Day–Columbus Day open Mon. 10–5; closed New Year's Day, Thanksgiving, and Christmas. $10 adults, $8 students and seniors (with ID), and $4 ages 6–17; under 6 free. Free admission Fri. 5–9 PM. Tours daily—inquire about times. Maine's largest art museum is a striking building designed by I. M. Pei's firm. Featured American artists include Winslow Homer, Edward Hopper, Rockwell Kent, Louise Nevelson, Andrew and N. C. Wyeth, John Singer Sargent, and Marguerite Zorach; the museum also has interesting European works by Renoir, Degas, Prendergast, Matisse, and Picasso. Neighboring McLellan House, the lovely Federal-period home of the museum's original collection, along with the Sweat Memorial Galleries, showcases an impressive collection of 19th-century American paintings and decorative arts. The museum owns the Winslow Homer Studio on Prouts Neck in Scarborough. This studio is undergoing a major restoration and is closed to the public, but it is scheduled to open in 2012. Check the website for updated information.

PORTLAND MUSEUM OF ART

Nancy English

long, was made by a local artist. A fecal sample from a Yeti in 1959 and a preserved foot from the Terror of Turner are more of the major attractions.

✏ **Maine Narrow Gauge Railroad Co. & Museum** (207-828-0814; mainenarrowgauge.org), 58 Fore St. Open May–Oct., daily 10–4, trains on the hour, and seasonally for special events. A 1.5-mile roundtrip excursion along Casco Bay is offered regularly May–Oct. Leading up to Christmas, you can take the Polar Express, a train trip to the North Pole. Entrance to the museum and gift shop is free if you buy a train ticket; excursion fares are $10 roundtrip adults, $9 seniors, $6 ages 3–12. Drive through the complex of brick buildings and park on the waterside. The museum sells the tickets. From the 1870s to the 1940s, five narrow-gauge lines carrying visitors linked rural Maine communities.

✎ ♿ **Children's Museum and Theatre of Maine** (207-828-1234; kitetails.com), 142 Free St. Open Memorial Day–Labor Day, Mon.–Sat. 10–5, Sun. noon–5; otherwise, closed Mon. but open 9–11 for members; $9 per person (under 18 months free). Next door to the Portland Museum of Art, this fun museum features three levels of interactive, hands-on exhibits designed to help the young and old learn together. Permanent exhibits include *Have a Ball*, in which kids make ramps and set balls in motion, a car repair shop and lobster boat, an ATM, a climbing wall, and a shipyard outside good for a picnic lunch in nice weather. There's also a science center, a toddler area, and a black-box room that's a walk-in camera obscura.

✎ ♿ **Portland Fire Museum** (207-772-2040; portlandfiremuseum.com), 157 Spring St. (near the corner of State). Open through the year during First Friday Art Walk, the first Friday of each month, at 6; call for more hours. The only remaining firehouse in Portland with horse stalls, this wonderful old brick structure was built in 1837 and originally housed a girls' grammar school. The artifacts, photos, paintings, and fire equipment (including a 1938 pumper truck) chronicle the city's contentious relationship with fire, from the fire department's humble beginnings in 1768 and the city's destruction by fire at the hands of the British in 1775, to the Great Fire of 1866.

HISTORIC SITES

All listings are in Portland unless otherwise noted

✎ **Victoria Mansion**, the Morse-Libby House (207-772-4841; victoriamansion .org), 109 Danforth St. (at the corner of Park St.). Open for tours May–Oct., daily 10–4 (closed major holidays); $15 adults, $13.50 seniors, $5 students 6–17, under 6 free. Christmas hours and rates: day after Thanksgiving–first week of Jan., open daily; $15 adults (no senior discount), $5 students. Ruggles Sylvester Morse, a Maine native who made his fortune as a New Orleans hotelier, built this elaborately gilded, frescoed, carved, and many-mirrored mansion in 1858 as a summer home after relocating south just before the Civil War. The Italianate brownstone palazzo features a three-story grand hall with stained-glass windows, a stunning skylight, and a flying staircase with 377 balusters hand carved in black walnut. It was rescued from destruction and opened to the public in 1941. The gift shop sells well-chosen Victoriana. In December the house is dressed to the hilt.

Tate House Museum (207-774-6177; tatehouse.org), 1267 Westbrook St. Follow Congress St. (Rt. 22) west

PORTLAND SQUARE

Nancy English

✒ PORTLAND OBSERVATORY

(207-774-5561, ext. 104; portlandlandmarks.org), 138 Congress St. Open Memorial Day–Columbus Day, daily 10–5. $8 adults, $7 students and seniors, $5 ages 6–16. Built in 1807, this imposing, octagonal, 86-foot-high shingled landmark atop Munjoy Hill is the last surviving 19th-century maritime signal station in the country. Interpretive displays. Climb the 103 steps to the top of Captain Lemuel Moody's masterpiece, and watch the ships entering Casco Bay.

across the Fore River and turn left on Westbrook St. Open mid-June–mid-Oct., Wed.–Sat. 10–4, Sun. 1–4. $8 adults, $6 seniors, $3 ages 6–12, under 6 free. George Tate, mast agent for the Royal Navy, built this Georgian house in 1755 to reflect his important position. Both the interior and exterior are unusual, distinguished by clerestory windows, a gambrel roof, wood paneling, and elegant furniture. An 18th-century herb garden is part of the historic landscape. Gift shop.

Neal Dow Memorial (207-773-7773; mewctu.org), 714 Congress St. Open year-round, Mon.–Fri. 11–4. Donation requested. Currently the headquarters of the Maine Women's Christian Temperance Union, this handsome Greek Revival mansion was built in 1829 by Neal Dow, the man responsible for an 1851 law that made Maine the first state to prohibit alcohol. He also championed women's rights and abolition.

GUIDED TOURS ✪ **Greater Portland Landmarks Center for Architecture and Preservation**, Safford House (207-774-5561; portlandlandmarks.org), 93 High St., Portland 04101. Greater Portland Landmarks fills a 1858 bow-fronted Italianate building, designed by architect Charles Alexander, which was saved from destruction by this nonprofit organization in the 1970s after a block of historic homes was demolished to widen Spring Street. The Frances W. Peabody Library is inside, along with exhibit space. Landmarks has lead downtown walking tours of Portland's historic neighborhoods in the past; check the website for updated offerings. Also note the organization's excellent books and its series of walking guides available at the observatory, the center, or online. Landmarks runs the Portland Observatory (see the sidebar).

✒ **Portland Discovery Land and Sea Tours** (207-774-0808; portland discovery.com), 170 Commercial St., Portland. Mid-May–Oct. One trip is a narrated, 90-minute trolley tour that begins on Commercial St. in the Old Port and includes Portland Head Light. $19 adults, $13 children. Boat tours take in lighthouses, or Eagle Island, the former estate of Arctic explorer Admiral Robert E. Peary (see *Boating*).

CONGRESS STREET

Nancy English

Downeast Duck Tours (207-774-3825; downeastducktours.com), departing from Commercial St., by Casco Variety. The Duck Tour, about an hour long, takes you around Portland and into Casco Bay after the amphibious vehicle rolls into the harbor. Narrated tours run from mid-May to mid-Oct., daily, with five a day before Labor Day and fewer in fall. $24 adults, $20 seniors, $17 ages 6–12, $5 under 5.

SCENIC DRIVES Cape Elizabeth and Prouts Neck. From State St. in downtown Portland, head south on Rt. 77 across the Casco Bay Bridge to South Portland, turn right at the fourth light onto Cottage St., which turns into Shore Rd. Enter 94-acre **Fort Williams Park** (4 miles from downtown) to see the **Museum at Portland Head Light**. There are also picnic tables with water views and a beach, as well as the ruins of the old fort. Many people like to come here early in the morning. (Stop at **Terra Cotta Pasta Co.**, 501 Cottage Rd., for gelato and

ISLAND EXCURSIONS

No one seems quite sure how many islands there are in Casco Bay. Printed descriptions range from 136 to 222. Seventeenth-century explorer John Smith dubbed them the Calendar Islands, saying there was one for every day of the year. Regardless of the actual number, there are plenty of offshore places for poking around. Regular year-round ferry service runs to six of the islands, five of which invite exploration.

CHEBEAGUE ISLAND is the largest in Casco Bay: 4.5 miles long and 2 miles wide. Its population of 350 swells to eight times that in summer. A bike is the best way to explore. Mack Passano (207-846-7829), 168 South Rd., is known as the Bike Man of Chebeague and was written up in *Down East* magazine. He offers more than 100 secondhand bikes for free. **The Sunset House** (207-846-6568), 74 South Rd., is no longer a B&B but is offered for rent by the week or month. **The Chebeague Island Inn** (207-846-5155; chebeagueislandinn.com), the island's dowager lodging and an elegant place for a summer meal, is likely to be open from late May to mid-Oct. with 21 rooms available at $188–390. Call first to confirm. **The Niblic** (207-846-1015) is a little store next to the boatyard where visitors can buy local crafts and snacks and drinks, as well as a good lunch. You can pick up takeout at **Doughty's Island Market** (207-846-9997). To relax and enjoy the scenery, head to **Chandler's Cove**, a white-sand beach, or the beach near **Coleman's Cove**. Golfers will want to try the **Chebeague Island Golf Club** (207-846-9478; chebeague.org), a beautiful nine-hole course founded in 1920, where non-members can play anytime except Mon. or Thu. morning. Facilities on the island include a recreation center with an Olympic-sized outdoor heated swimming pool, indoor gym, weight room, and outdoor tennis/basketball courts. The **Chebeague Island Historical Society** has restored the old Dis-

cannoli and terrific take-out Italian meals and salads.) Follow Shore Rd. south to
Rt. 77 and turn left to continue through Pond Cove, the main village in residential
Cape Elizabeth, and on to **Two Lights State Park**, with its views of Casco Bay
and the open Atlantic, good for fishing and picnicking. **Crescent Beach State
Park**, just beyond, is a mile of inviting sand, the area's premier beach.

Rt. 77 continues through **Higgins Beach**, a Victorian-era summer community of
reasonable rentals and lodging with plenty of beach but limited parking. At the
junction of Rts. 207 and 77 continue on Black Point Rd., past **Scarborough
Beach State Park**, and on to exclusive **Prouts Neck**. Unless you are staying or
eating at the **Black Point Inn**, parking in-season is all but impossible here. Park
back at Scarborough Beach and walk or bike to the **Cliff Walk**, site of the
Winslow Homer Studio. Return by the same route (you are just 15 miles from
downtown). A short and rewarding detour: At the junction of Cottage Rd. and

trict No. 9 Schoolhouse, open all day in summer with a visitors center and
museum. Call 207-846-5237 for more details. **Casco Bay Lines** ferries dock at the
southern end of the island, and **Chebeague Transportation Company** (207-846-
3700; chebeaguetrans.com) runs the ferry that travels between Cousins Island
and Chebeague. Call for directions and parking details.

LONG ISLAND Three miles long and approximately a mile wide, Long Island,
like the others, has a thriving summer population. **Cushing Homestead Bed &
Breakfast** (207-766-2846), 21 Homestead Lane, sits in the village, offering comfortable rooms and casual hospitality. **Chestnut Hill Cottage Rentals** (email
chestnuthillrentals@yahoo.com) rents two houses, one a seven-room (four bedrooms with private bath) house, in season.

GREAT DIAMOND ISLAND A pleasant half-hour ferry ride from downtown,
this 2-mile-long island is the site of Fort McKinley, built sturdily of brick in the
1890s, now restored as **Diamond Cove** (diamondcove.com), a resort-style development featuring 121 town houses. A rental agency, Great Diamond Rentals
(207-766-3005; greatdiamondrentals.com), can be contacted for summer
rentals—but unless you are staying there, or take a guided tour (given by Diamond Cove management company), the resort grounds are not open to the public. **Diamond's Edge** (207-766-5850; diamondsedge.com) is the big attraction here,
a casually elegant restaurant open late May–Sept., dinner only except mid-
June–Labor Day, when lunch is also served. A popular place for weddings.

CLIFF ISLAND Cliff Island is a full 1½-hour ride down the bay. It is the most
rustic of the islands, with 8 miles of dirt roads, no overnight accommodations, a
peaceful feel, and sandy beaches. There's a seasonal sandwich shop on the
wharf, and the general store sells sandwiches year-round. For **cottage rentals**
check with the Greater Portland CVB.

Broadway, turn right onto Broadway to Southern Maine Community College. A granite breakwater leads to the **Spring Point Light**, overlooking Casco Bay. Look for signs for the **Spring Point Shoreway Path**, which follows the bay 3 miles to **Willard Beach**.

❀ **Falmouth Foreside**. From downtown Portland, take Rt. 1 north across the mouth of the Presumpscot River. Signs for the Governor Baxter School for the Deaf direct you down Andrews Ave. and across a causeway to 100-acre **Mackworth Island**. Park and walk (dogs permitted) the 1.5-mile path that circles the island. Views are off across the bay, and a small beach invites strolling. Return to Rt. 1 and continue north, looking for signs for **Gilsland Farm Audubon Center**, headquarters for Maine Audubon. The sky-blue sign comes up in less than 0.5 mile; follow the dirt road to the visitors center.

Yarmouth. From downtown Portland, take I-295 to exit 17. Commercial and tourist-geared businesses are relegated to Rt. 1, leaving the inner village lined with 18th- and 19th-century homes. The village green retains its round railroad station, and **Royal River Park** offers recreation (the Royal River is popular with sea kayakers) in all seasons. Also check out **Lower Falls Landing**, a former sardine cannery that now houses interesting shops. Don't miss the DeLorme Map Store on Rt. 1 with "Eartha," the world's largest rotating and revolving globe.

✴ To Do

BALLOONING Hot Fun (207-799-0193; hotfunballoons.com), P.O. Box 2825, South Portland. Hot-air balloon rides for up to six passengers.

BICYCLING Map Adventures (1-800-891-1534; mapadventures.com) makes very readable small maps of bike routes. **Portland Trails** (207-775-2411; trails .org) prints a *Map and Trail Guide*. The Maine Department of Transportation publishes a spiral-bound book with bike routes in Maine; separate tours are published in smaller books. These maps are stocked at **Back Bay Bicycle** (207-773-6906; backbaybicycle.com; 333 Forest Ave., Portland) and **Cycle Mania** (207-774-2933; cyclemania1.com; 59 Federal St., Portland), which sponsor weekly group rides. Cycle Mania and **Gorham Bike and Ski** (207-773-1700; gorhambike.com; 693 Congress St., Portland) are the city bike shops that rent bicycles. They recommend you make a reservation, and also stock DOT bike trail booklets and Portland Trails maps. **Wheelie Good Bike Rentals** (207-318-4660; wheeliegoodbikerental.com). Sean Hegarty delivers his rental bicycles within an hour's drive of Portland, seven days a week. $15 for half day, $25 for full day, includes delivery, fee charged when more than 20 miles from Portland.

Eastern Trail (207-284-9260; easterntrail.org) is an ambitious trail system that will someday connect Casco Bay to Kittery (and Maine to Florida) with a 68.8-mile off-road greenway. Parts of the route now stretch through Scarborough Marsh, with its flocks of birds and summer scenery, up through South Portland where it is also called the **Greenbelt Trail**. That section, while interrupted by intersections, features a quiet and safe ride from Big Light Park, Madison St., off Broadway, through Mill Creek and its duck pond, along Fore River. One section follows Chestnut St. before resuming its off-road paved quiet along a total of 5.7 miles.

Mountain Division Trail (mountaindivisiontrail.org), Standish. Running from Standish through Gorham to Windham, the Mountain Division Trail is packed gravel with some paved sections. Four intersections take you across roads, but the 5-mile-plus trail is off-road. Horses travel on it, too. The trail starts at Johnson Field, Rt. 35, Standish, and runs to Gambo Recreational Center, Gambo Rd., Windham.

BOATING Chebeague Transportation Company (207-846-3700; chebeague trans.com) runs the ferry that travels between Cousins Island and Chebeague. Call for directions and parking details.

Casco Bay Lines (207-774-7871; cascobaylines.com), Casco Bay Ferry Terminal, 56 Commercial St. at the foot of Franklin Arterial, Portland. Founded in 1845, this business was said to be the oldest continuously operating ferry company in the country when it went bankrupt in 1980. The present, quasi-municipal Casco Bay Island Transit District now carries 870,000 passengers and 26,000 vehicles out to the bay's beautiful islands every year. The brightly painted ferries are still lifelines to six islands, carrying groceries and lumber as well as mail. The year-round, daily mail-boat run (three hours) puts in to all the islands in the morning and again in the afternoon. A variety of seasonal, special excursions includes a 5½-hour Bailey Island Cruise and a Moonlight Run at 9:15 PM. Also year-round, daily car ferry service to Peaks Island. Bring your own picnic lunch and beverages.

Portland Discovery Land and Sea Tours (207-774-0808; portlanddiscovery .com), Long Wharf, Portland. Runs mid-May–Oct. Visit the former home of Admiral Peary, now maintained by the state as a historic site and nature preserve; the company also offers Lighthouse Lovers and sunset cruises. Group charters available. Land and Sea Tour includes tickets for the Portland Discovery trolley (see *Guided Tours*) run by the same family.

🖋 *Lucky Catch* **Lobstering** (207-761-0941; luckycatch.com), 170 Commercial St., Portland. Instead of just eating them, why not land one of those tasty crustaceans yourself? Memorial Day–Columbus Day, Captain Tom takes tourists and locals out to haul traps on the *Lucky Catch* five times daily Mon.–Sat., with side trips to Portland Head Light and White Head Passage. Each 80- to 90-minute cruise costs $25 per adult, $20 ages 13–18, and $22 seniors; $15 ages 12 and under.

✪ *Odyssey* **Whale Watch** (207-775-0727; odysseywhalewatch.com), Long Wharf, Portland. Whale-watches daily at 10 AM June–Oct. in the *Odyssey*, a 93-passenger boat. $48 adults, $38 children 12 and under, $9 infants 2 and under. Harbor cruises and deep-sea fishing are also offered.

BOAT CRUISES American Cruise Lines (1-800-814-6880; americancruise lines.com), 741 Boston Post Rd., Ste. 200, Guilford, Connecticut. This cruise company offers an eight-day cruise called Maine Coast and Harbors, with stops in Belfast, Camden, Castine, Rockland, Bar Harbor, Boothbay Harbor, and Portland. The 104-passenger ship *Independence* is scheduled to make 17 trips in the summer of 2012.

BREWERY TOURS Like its namesake city in Oregon, Portland is famous for its microbreweries, and many feature restaurants alongside them. Most give tours, either on a regular basis or by appointment. For information, contact individual breweries: **Allagash Brewing** (207-878-5385 or 1-800-330-5385; allagash.com), 100 Industrial Way, Portland; **Casco Bay Brewing** (207-797-2020; cascobay brewing.com), 57 Industrial Way, Portland; **D. L. Geary Brewing** (207-878-BEER; gearybrewing.com), 38 Evergreen Dr., Portland; **Gritty McDuff's Brew Pub** (207-772-2739; grittys.com), 396 Fore St., Portland; and the largest of all, **Shipyard Brewing** (207-761-0807; shipyard.com), 86 Newbury St., Portland.

FOR FAMILIES ✏ **Southworth Planetarium** (207-780-4249; usm.maine.edu /~planet), University of Southern Maine, 96 Falmouth St., Portland. Astronomy shows throughout the year. Special shows for young children in summer and on holidays, including an astronomical exploration of the biblical Star of Bethlehem, Friday-evening shows, and children's matinees on Saturday.

GOLF There are several popular 9- and 18-hole courses in the area, notably **Sable Oaks Golf Club** (207-775-6257), South Portland, considered among the most challenging and best courses in Maine (18 holes); **Riverside North** (18 holes, 207-797-3524) and **Riverside South** (9 holes, 207-797-5588), in Portland; **Val Halla** (18 holes, 207-829-2225), in Cumberland; and **Twin Falls** (9 holes, 207-854-5397), in Westbrook.

Willowdale Golf Club (207-883-9351; willowdalegolf.com), off Rt. 1, Scarborough, has 18 holes. **Nonesuch River Golf Club** (207-883-0007; nonesuchgolf .com), off Rt. 114, Scarborough, also has 18 holes.

RACING Scarborough Downs (207-883-4331; scarboroughdowns.com), off I-95 exit 6 in Scarborough. From Apr. to Dec. Scarborough Downs, the largest facility of its kind in New England, has live harness racing with betting windows; year-round thoroughbred and harness racing is available via simulcast with Off-Track Betting. **Downs Club Restaurant** (207-883-3022) is open for dinner Mon., Tue., Sat., and Sun. in-season, and you can place your bets from the top of the multilevel dining room with great views of the track.

Beech Ridge Motor Speedway (207-883-5227; beechridge.com), Holmes Rd., Scarborough. Summer stock-car racing Thu.–Sat., May–Oct.

SAILING *Bagheera* (207-766-2500 or 1-87-SCHOONER; portlandschooner .com), Maine State Pier, Portland. Built in 1924 of long-leaf yellow pine, oak, and mahogany, this vintage Alden sailed all over the world before making Casco Bay her home port in 2002. She can carry as many as 48 passengers. Four cruises daily, Memorial Day–Labor Day, three daily till Columbus Day. $35; $10 ages 3–12. *Wendameen*, a schooner built in 1912, is available for private charters and overnight cruises.

Portland Schooner (207-766-2500; portlandschooner.com), Maine State Pier, offers sails on a historic John Alden schooner.

The *Frances* (207-749-9169; mainesailingadventures.net) offers three cruises daily Memorial Day to Columbus Day.

SEA KAYAKING ✏ **Maine Island Kayak Co.** (207-766-2373 or 1-800-796-2373; maineislandkayak.com), 70 Luther St., Peaks Island. Late May–Oct. We love this company for many reasons, including its exceptional guides, its state-of-the-art equipment, and its commitment to the leave-no-trace philosophy, crucial in heavily

SAILING CLASS IN CASCO BAY

trafficked Casco Bay. MIKCO offers a limited schedule of trips; call for information and instruction in kayaking throughout the summer.

✳ Green Space

BEACHES ✍ ♿ **Crescent Beach State Park** (207-799-5871), 66 Two Lights Rd., Cape Elizabeth; 8 miles from Portland on Rt. 77. A mile of sand complete with changing facilities, a playground, picnic tables, and a snack bar. Fee charged for adults and ages 5–11. Good for young children because it's protected from heavy surf.

✍ ♿ **Wolfe's Neck Woods State Park** (207-865-4465; off-season, 207-865-6080), 426 Wolfe's Neck Rd. (take Bow St., across from L.L. Bean), Freeport. Open Apr.–Oct. Day-use fee. A 233-acre park with shoreline hiking along Casco Bay, the Harraseeket River, and salt marshes, as well as excellent birding with ospreys the local stars. Guided nature walks, and scattered picnic tables and grills.

Kettle Cove is just down the road from Crescent Beach—follow the road behind the (excellent) ice cream shop on Rt. 77. There is no admission fee to this rocky end of Crescent Beach, but parking is limited. This spot is good for bird-watching during migration seasons.

Higgins Beach, farther down Rt. 77 in Scarborough, is an extensive strand within walking distance of lodging—but there is no parking on the street. Private lots charge a fee. The swell can kick up quite a bit here, so beware the undertow. Surfers are always here when the waves are high.

Scarborough Beach State Park, 414 Black Point Rd. (Rt. 207), 3 miles south of Rt. 1 on Prouts Neck. Open Memorial Day–Sept. ($5 admission), also for walking year-round. A 243-acre park with a superb beach, but only a 65-foot stretch is technically public. Get there early because parking is minimal and open-ocean lovers like this one best. See *Scenic Drives* for the best route from Portland.

PARKS ✍ **Deering Oaks**, Portland's 51-acre city park, designed by city civil engineer William Goodwin, has a pond, ducks and, rarely, a beaver and a moose, a fountain, a playground completely rebuilt in 2009, a fine grove of oak trees, a beautifully cared-for rose garden, and a refurbished urban "ravine" complete with a wading pool and spray jets for summertime frolicking. A farmer's market is held here Sat. morning May–Nov. Ice skating on the pond in winter. No admission fee. The winter lights hung by Pandora LaCasse are fabulous. The Greater Portland Convention & Visitors Bureau staff a year-round Visitor Information Center in the renovated "Castle" (along with restrooms).

Two Lights State Park, 66 Two Lights Rd., Cape Elizabeth, is open year-round. No swimming, but 40 acres of shore with stunning water views for picnicking and fishing.

Also see **Fort Williams Park** in *Scenic Drives* and **Fort Allen Park** under Eastern Promenade in *Walks*.

NATURE PRESERVES ✍ **Gilsland Farm Audubon Center** (207-781-2330; maineaudubon.org), 20 Gilsland Farm Rd., Falmouth (3 miles east of Portland). Open Mon.–Sat. 9–5, Sun. noon–5 in warm weather, 2–5 in cold weather. Maine Audubon's headquarters are located at this 65-acre wildlife sanctuary, along with trails, rolling fields, river frontage, and salt marsh. The education center features exhibits throughout the year, a wildlife discovery room for children, and a Maine Audubon Nature Store selling binoculars and great books. The education center hosts day and evening wildlife-related programs year-round, including preschool year-round and children's day camps during summer and school breaks. The sanctuary is also open year-round for walking, sunrise to sunset.

Scarborough Marsh Audubon Center (207-883-5100), Pine Point Rd. (Rt. 9), Scarborough. Open daily mid-June–Labor Day, 9:30–5:30. The largest salt marsh (3,000 acres) in Maine, this is a great place for quiet canoe and kayak exploration. This Maine Audubon center offers canoe and kayak rentals, exhibits, a Maine Audubon Nature Store, and guided walking and canoe and kayak tours throughout the summer.

VIEW OF THE PRESUMPSCOT RIVER
ESTUARY FROM GILSLAND FARM
Courtesy of Maine Audubon

Fore River Sanctuary, (207-775-2411; trails.org). Located near Maine Turnpike exit 8, off Brighton Ave., Portland, and managed by Portland Trails. This 85-acre preserve is hidden behind a suburban neighborhood where explorers may not think to look. The 2.5 miles of hiking trails offer access to Portland's only waterfall,

THE SCARBOROUGH MARSH AUDUBON CENTER

Nancy English

Jewell Falls. A set of railroad tracks (be careful—they are active) marks the beginning of a trail that leads you through woods and marshland.

Prouts Neck Cliff Walk and Wildlife Sanctuary. Winslow Homer painted many of his seascapes in a small studio here (now owned by Portland Museum of Art and scheduled to open to the public sometime in 2012). This exclusive community on Prouts Neck is not far from the Black Point Inn. Winslow Homer Road marks the start of the Cliff Path (unmarked), a beautiful stroll along the rocks, around Eastern Point, and back almost to the inn. You can also walk through the sanctuary between Winslow Homer Road (just east of St. James Episcopal Church) and Library Lane, donated by Winslow's brother Charles.

WALKS Portland Trails (207-775-2411; trails.org), 305 Commercial St., Portland, an organization committed to developing hiking and walking trails in the city, sells a map describing several city parks and more than 50 miles of trails as well as bus routes to take you there. The *Portland Trails Map* costs $4.95 and can be bought from the website. A favorite walk is the Presumpscot River trail, full of wildflowers and wildlife.

✔ **The Eastern Promenade**. Follow Congress St. east to the Portland Observatory atop Munjoy Hill and then continue the extra block to the Eastern Promenade, a park-lined street high on this same bluff with sweeping views of Casco Bay. Follow it around, back toward the harbor, to 68-acre **Fort Allen Park**, which dates to 1814, set on a blustery point above the bay. Down along the bay itself the paved **Eastern Promenade Trail** runs along the base of Munjoy Hill, good for biking and walking. (The railroad museum's excursion train runs alongside it.)

🐾 ♿ **The Western Promenade**. It's ironic that Munjoy Hill (see above), the poorer (but vibrant) section of town, has the million-dollar view while the Western Promenade overlooks the airport and gas holding tanks. Still, this is Portland's most architecturally interesting residential neighborhood. Pick up a copy of the Portland Landmarks leaflet *Guide to the Western Promenade* from the seasonal visitors bureau at Ocean Gateway.

EAST END TRAIL BY PORTLAND TRAILS

Nancy English

☕ ✒ ♿ **Baxter Boulevard**. A 3.5-mile path around the tidal flats of Back Cove connects with the Eastern Promenade Trail. It's a popular spot for dog walking, jogging, and biking. Adjacent fields provide good kite-flying and soccer venues. Park across from the Hannaford Bros. store.

Eastern Cemetery, Congress St. and Washington Ave. (near the Portland Observatory on Munjoy Hill). The oldest cemetery in Portland, it is listed by the National Trust for Historic Preservation. Its 6 acres hold more than 4,000 headstones dating from the mid-17th century to the early 19th; some are embellished with angels and death's heads. **Spirits Alive** (spiritsalive.org) runs guided tours here ($10 adults, $5 children under 12) usually on weekends in summer, a Halloween Walk Among the Shadows tour, and others. The group restores gravestones, and is installing botanical markers. They also choose a subterranean celebrity of the month. Over 100 trees have been planted with the assistance of the City of Portland, and granite benches placed for meditation.

Portland Freedom Trail (207-591-9980; portlandfreedomtrail.org). A granite-and-bronze marker at the Eastern Cemetery on Congress St. was the first of a series of 13 markers at places in the city where abolitionists lived, preached, and harbored escaping slaves on the Underground Railroad. The website offers a Freedom Trail Map for a self-guided walking tour, which starts at Franklin Street Wharf, where slaves who had stowed away were known to have arrived in the North. The Abyssinian Church on Newbury St. was Maine's first black church when it was built in 1829, and is undergoing restoration. A pro-slavery riot erupted after a sermon criticizing slavery in 1842, at First Parish Church at the head of Temple St.

FREEDOM TRAIL MARKER

Nancy English

Clark's Pond Trail, maintained by the South Portland Land Trust (splandtrust .com). Home Depot in South Portland is located at the trailhead of this plunge into the woods, a 1.1-mile trail located near the Maine Mall with a secret waterfall and turkeys and deer. South Portland's master plan will someday connect many neighborhoods with walkways and bike trails.

Cape Elizabeth Land Trust (207-767-6054; capelandtrust.org), 330 Ocean House Rd., Cape Elizabeth. The Cape Elizabeth Land Trust has preserved 566 acres of the town's land, and developed many miles of trails on those acres and via rights-of-way that connect the scattered parcels. The Cape Elizabeth Town and Trail Map is sold at the office and the IGA and can be downloaded from the website. The trails provide a fine way to explore and to cross-country ski in this pretty town.

✳ Lodging

HOTELS There are more than 2,000 hotel and motel rooms in and around Portland.

In the Old Port 04101

🐾 ♿ **Portland Regency** (207-774-4200 or 1-800-727-3436; theregency .com), 20 Milk St. We like the Regency for its quiet stateliness in the midst of the Old Port, even though some of the rooms don't have much in the way of windows. Stay in one of 95 rooms (including suites) housed in a century-old armory. Rooms come with reproduction beds (a king or two doubles) white down comforters, cable TV, and air-conditioning; some suites feature a whirlpool tub. **Twenty Milk Street** is a good steak house with a formal dining room, the **Armory Lounge** offers cocktails and lighter fare in an upscale bar (martinis are a deal on Monday), and the outside **Garden Café** serves summer lunch, brunch, and dinner. There's a downstairs gym and day spa with luxurious locker rooms, each with private sauna; also coed sauna and steam room, and 10-person, tiled whirlpool with a waterfall. Complimentary van service and $12 valet parking $139–189 Nov.–Apr.; in-season (Memorial Day weekend–Oct.), $249–329.

🐾 🐕 ♿ **Portland Harbor Hotel** (207-775-9090 or 1-888-798-9090; the portlandharborhotel.com), 468 Fore St. The choice of granite-look-alike rigid foam garnered some controversy when this hotel was being built, but the exterior is holding up well. An enviable location in the heart of the Old Port and an in-hotel restaurant and elevators make it a good bet. Amenities include cable TV and radio, marble bath, European-style glass shower, granite counters, and free pickup service from the Jetport or train station based on availability.

Jacuzzi suites feature an oval spa tub and separate sitting area with sofa bed. Fitness center. **Eve's at the Garden** serves fine dinners. $129–399, depending on view and season. Pets are allowed with a $25 fee per day, on the first and second floors.

🐾 🐕 ♿ **Hilton Garden Inn Portland Downtown Waterfront** (207-780-0780; hiltongardeninnportland.com), 65 Commercial St. Portland's corporate and leisure hotel rents 120 rooms, all with a bath, refrigerator, and microwave. Two corner suites with views and a sitting area are also available. A small indoor pool and fitness center, and impressive views of the harbor from half of the rooms—the inn is located across from Casco Bay Lines in the Old Port—make this a fun place to stay. Rates $259–359 in summer, as low as $149 in winter.

🐾 ♿ **Residence Inn Portland Downtown/Waterfront** (207-761-1660; marriott.com), 145 Fore St., Portland. This hotel opened in July 2009 as part of a revamping of the city's northern waterfront area, allowing visitors to enjoy its service and comfortable rooms, many overlooking

GARDEN CAFE AT THE PORTLAND REGENCY
Nancy English

the harbor. One hundred thirty-seven studios, 34 one-bedroom suites, and 8 two-bedroom suites all have full kitchen and sleeping area with king bed; a hot breakfast buffet is included. Mon.–Wed. barbecue in good weather, plus a bar. Indoor pool and fitness center. Guest laundry room. On-site parking $12 daily. Onetime $100 fee for pets. Rates $169–349.

Hampton Inn Downtown Portland (207-775-1454; hamptoninn.com), 209 Fore St., Portland. New in 2011, this hotel was built on the site of the old Jordan's Meats factory, famous for its red hot dogs. Now the good-sized rooms, some with harbor views, are proving restful. Other perks include the free breakfast and Sebago Brewing Company on the first floor.

In midtown Portland

♂ & **Holiday Inn by the Bay** (207-775-2311 or 1-800-HOLIDAY; innbythebay.com), 88 Spring St. 04101. Portlanders love to hate this ugly, 11-story, downtown high-rise, especially since it took over a beautiful neighborhood. But perhaps someday we'll regard its utilitarian architecture fondly, and the harbor and skyline views are great from the inside. Amenities include an indoor pool, small fitness center, cable TV with in-room movies, free parking, laundry facility, and a restaurant and lounge. Two suites and 239 rooms range from $180 in high season to $240.

Note: Portland does host the major chains, many located by I-95 at exit 8 in Westbrook or in South Portland.

Beyond Portland

✪ ♂ & **Black Point Inn** (207-883-2500 or 1-800-258-0003; blackpointinn.com), 510 Black Point Rd., Prouts Neck 04074. Open May–Nov. 1. This vintage-1878 summer hotel underwent a renovation that tore down newer additions; it's now quite small with just

25 rooms. The oldest elevator in the state of Maine is still hand operated by a polite staff member, and there is a wonderful widow's walk with 360-degree views of Scarborough, Old Orchard Beach, and the blustery Atlantic Ocean. Guests use the Prouts Neck Country Club's 18-hole golf course and 14 tennis courts, and use kayaks, moorings, or rental boats at the local yacht club; bikes are available at the inn. Two sandy beaches, an outdoor heated pool, a room with exercise equipment, and in-room massages by appointment. Afternoon tea, evening cocktails, and both casual and formal dining rooms (see *Dining Out*). In high season $500–620 for double MAP per night plus 18 percent guest service charge (covers all gratuities); from $400–500 MAP and $250–350 bed & breakfast off-season. Live jazz on the porch at brunch.

🐾 ♂ & **Inn by the Sea** (207-799-3134; innbythesea.com), 40 Bowery Beach Rd., Cape Elizabeth 04107. Open year-round. A 15-minute drive from downtown Portland, this shingled complex maintains a high reputation for great hospitality and beautiful rooms. Fifty-seven accommodations include 14 traditional guest rooms with gas-burning fireplace and mini fridge, 18 two-bedroom cottages with kitchens, and 25 suites with a bedroom and living area, mini fridge, and microwave. All of the suites have large bathroom and large tub. The suites and cottages have a porch or balcony and water views. Many amenities are lined up for guests, including a pool, a bocce court, a fitness center, and walking and jogging trails. A spa with six treatment rooms and golf privileges at nearby Purpoodock Club are also available. A boardwalk leads to the tip of Crescent Beach State Park to start or end the day, perhaps after dinner in the inn's **Sea Glass Restaurant** or before an aperitif in the lobby bar. $189–709 depending on season and accommodation, plus 5 percent hotel fee.

✒ **Higgins Beach Inn** (207-883-6684; higginsbeachinn.com), 34 Ocean Ave., Scarborough 04074 (7 miles south of Portland). Open mid-May–mid-Oct. A well-cared-for 1890s three-story wooden summer hotel near sandy, gorgeous Higgins Beach. The dining room, **Garofalo's**, features seafood and pasta dishes from owner Diane's Sicilian family recipes (entrées $16–27). There is also a cocktail lounge and a sunporch. Upstairs the 22 guest rooms are archetypal summer hotel rooms—simple, clean, and airy—13 with private bath. Full breakfast available but not included in the room rates: $85–150 double with private bath, $50–125 with shared bath, with a minimum two-night stay likely most weekends.

INNS AND BED & BREAKFASTS

Pomegranate Inn (207-772-1006 or 1-800-356-0408; pomegranateinn .com), 49 Neal St., Portland 04102. In eight amazing rooms, bold, hand-painted walls by Heidi Gerquest, a Portland artist, create an energetic atmosphere; all rooms have discreet TV and private bath, and five have a gas fireplace. Big, bold flowers fly across bright-colored walls, and the fireplace surround and columns in the dining room are painted a faux stone that mimics green onyx. Consider yourself assured of a fantastic breakfast from innkeeper Dana Moos, author of *The Art of Breakfast*. Breakfast might be an egg roulade with leeks, Parmesan, and lobster. $185–295 per room in-season, $120–190 off-season, of course including breakfast.

Morrill Mansion Bed & Breakfast (207-774-6900; morrillmansion.com),

249 Vaughan St., Portland 04102. Seven bedrooms are named for local neighborhoods and old families in this elegant, even luxurious B&B, next to Maine Medical Center and on the edge of the West End, an easy walk to midtown. The building was completely done over by owner David Parker, and all rooms have queen beds, private bath, and cable TV/DVD. The dark blue Burnham Room has a whirlpool bath in a room with an original tin ceiling painted gold. $89–239 includes a breakfast buffet with an egg custard, French toast, warm fruit crisp and yogurt, fresh fruit, cereals, and more. Afternoon treats, perhaps whoopie pies, are served in the second-floor guest living room.

🐾 ✒ ((ᵖ)) **Wild Iris Inn** (207-775-0224 or 1-800-600-1557; wildirisinn.com), 273 State St., Portland 04101. This small Victorian on the hill below Portland's main street, Congress, is the favorite stop for visitors who like a quiet place with all the basic comforts. Six rooms, all with private bath, have been furnished by owner Diane Edwards with attractive quilts and furniture; all are air-conditioned. A Shaker-inspired dining room holds biscotti and tea at all hours, as well as a breakfast of granola, yogurt, fruit, and muffins in the morning. The inn is certified green. Downtown is a short walk, and a computer and printer are available for visitors. $89–175.

Inn on Carleton Bed & Breakfast (207-775-1910; innoncarleton.com), 46 Carleton St., Portland 04102. A beautiful building in the hands of a hospitality professional. Buddy Marcum has revitalized this town house in Portland's West End, updating the beds and the rooms with modern furniture and embellishing the classic structure to make it a fine addition to Portland's small inns. Marcum is a flight attendant; when he's working part-time, his well-trained staff cater to his guests. $99–195.

West End Inn (207-772-1377 or 1-800-338-1377; westendbb.com), 146 Pine St., Portland 04102. This 1871 brick town house combines natural elegance with colorful decor. The most popular of the six rooms is Cliff Island, with 12-foot ceilings, private deck, and white and blue accents, but this inn's three traditional and three contemporary rooms give visitors a comprehensive choice of styles. All have private bath, cable TV, ceiling fan, and air-conditioning. $100–225 includes full breakfast—perhaps butter-poached eggs with pesto or coconut, or ricotta silver dollars with ginger syrup—and afternoon tea in the handsome parlor.

Inn at Park Spring (207-774-1059 or 1-800-437-8511; innatparkspring.com), 135 Spring St., Portland 04101. At one of the most convenient locations in town, Nancy and John Gonsalves offer six well-appointed guest rooms with private bath and sitting area. The handsome Museum Room is painted yellow and furnished with two wing chairs and a four-poster queen bed. A breakfast is served in the formal dining

INN AT PARK SPRING

Nancy English

room with floor-to-ceiling windows, when a French toast croissant stuffed with marmalade and cream cheese could be on the menu. June–Oct. $149–180, otherwise $99–149.

The Chadwick Bed & Breakfast (207-774-5141 or 1-800-774-2137; thechadwick.com), 140 Chadwick St., Portland. Under the management of innkeeper E. Scot Fuller. Four rooms on the second floor have cushy beds, flat-screen TV and DVD, and private bath (but two are across the hall). A full breakfast completes the experience; oatmeal chocolate chip cookies or another baked good are set out for afternoon tea. The back garden and a big sitting room with capacious chairs and couches are ideal for relaxation. Rates $99–200.

♂ **The Danforth** (207-879-8755 or 1-800-991-6557; danforthmaine.com), 163 Danforth St., Portland. Fitted out with new wall-to-wall carpets and repainted walls, The Danforth, a historic mansion and an inn since 1993, reopened in 2009 after a brief hiatus. The nine rooms, seven with fireplace and all with private bath, are indeed attractive. Although every room is comfortable, many are large, and the decor is handsome. $195–295 in-season, $145–255 off.

🕯 🐾 ✿ ♿ **Inn at St. John** (207-773-6481 or 1-800-636-9127; innatstjohn .com), 939 Congress St., Portland 04102. A 39-room hotel built in 1897 to accommodate railroad passengers arriving at Union Station (unfortunately long gone), this place has undergone a renovation that brings many of its rooms into the modern age. Convenient for guests arriving by Greyhound and Vermont Transit, it's a hike to downtown, but the moderate rates and quality make up for the distance. Attractive rooms are well managed by innkeeper Paul Hood. $60–250

Nancy English

THE DANFORTH SITTING ROOM

(depending on season) includes continental breakfast, air-conditioning, and cable TV; $10 fee per pet, but not to exceed a maximum of $20.

✳ Where to Eat

The quality of the dining is exceptional in Portland. Some of the chefs have national reputations, with an award from *Food and Wine* magazine to Steve Corry of five fifty-five, and from the James Beard Foundation to Sam Hayward of Fore Street; one local star has won awards from both—Rob Evans of Hugo's.

But many more chefs are distinguished by incredibly consistent, reliably wonderful dinners. Several women have made their marks with their new restaurants, including Abby Harmon of Caiola's, a great neighborhood spot in the West End, and Krista Kern, whose petite Bresca is the scene of simple brilliance.

DINING OUT

In Portland
✪ **Back Bay Grill** (207-772-8833; backbaygrill.com), 65 Portland St. It's always a good night for dinner at Back Bay Grill, a comfortable, elegant restaurant with a lively menu. A lot of history hasn't made this dining room stiff, perhaps because the mural on the wall always provides such a good example of bon temps—but you can be assured of fine service and excellent wine. The Maine crabcake is excellent, seared foie gras with pickled cherries divine. Scottish salmon with chanterelles in-season, braised pork chops with fava beans, and organic Maine chicken might be on the always appealing menu. Entrées $24–36.

✪ **Bresca** (207-772-1004; restaurant bresca.com), 111 Middle St. A 20-seat mocha dining room is usually stuffed with Krista Kern's happy customers, who might have a fetish for the wilted greens, pancetta, and a six-minute egg. Raves in the national press crowded the little room in 2009. Steak and fish are made with precision and flair; the homemade pasta is tender and

BRESCA

Nancy English

seasoned with invention. Desserts by the chef-owner, a former pastry chef, pull out all the stops. Entrées $20–26.

Fore Street (207-775-2717; fore street.biz), 288 Fore St. Open for dinner nightly. Reservations a must in summer, but there are open tables at 5:30 when the dining room opens. Sam Hayward oversees meals full of his signature integrity. Great roast pork, turned on a spit in the open kitchen, or wood-fired oven-roasted fish, or roast quail, or just a few chicken livers quickly sautéed, and the best steamed mussels with garlic almond butter. The local vegetable side dishes are not to be missed. Desserts like chocolate soufflé cake and peach tarte tatin are favorites on the menu. Entrées $18–35.

Hugo's (207-774-8538; hugos.net), 88 Middle St. Rob Evans came to Portland in 2000. An original, adventurous menu of small plates creates an evening packed with revelations. Combinations of flavors and quirky juxtapositions, perhaps watermelon rind and BBQ skate or Cortland apple agnolotti, absorb thought and leave diners in a reverie. Other combinations showcase Evans, winner of the James Beard Foundation's Best Chef: Northeast Award in 2009. Evans's casual Duckfat is farther down on Middle St. (see *Eating Out*). Plates $13–22 with the recommendation that you order several.

✪ **Miyake** (207-871-9170; miyake restaurants.com), 468 Fore St. Open for lunch and dinner Mon.–Sat., Sun. 1–9. In-season a variety of wild salmon allows a taste of the Pacific's best; all the sushi is fresh and perfectly cut. Uni, cracked fresh from the urchin shell, and ankimo are exceptional, and even the miso soup is of the highest quality. Omakase nigiri, $36, presents 10 pieces of the freshest fish possible. You will be thoroughly amazed.

& **five fifty-five** (207-761-0555; five fifty-five.com), 555 Congress St. Chef-owner Steve Corry smiled from the July 2007 cover of *Food and Wine* magazine, named one of 10 best new chefs. His skills make even hamburgers an unusual pleasure. But try black pepper ice cream, or other flavors the evening menu offers, for real adventure. A fall menu offered paper-wrapped flounder, served with couscous and black olive tangerine butter; a steak might come with crispy potatoes. Entrées $13 (from the bar menu)–32. Reservations advised.

✪ **Caiola's** (207-772-1110; caiolas .com), 58 Pine St. A short walk into the West End, this professional kitchen is run by Abby Harmon, head of the kitchen at Street and Co. for 16 years. Her sure touch makes scallops perfect and grilled swordfish even better. The burger is a moist marvel, and the steak, pork chop, house cannelloni, and more are, too. The fine wine list and well-run dining room, managed by Lisa Vaccaro, makes the atmosphere welcoming. Entrées $15–25.

Paciarino (207-774-3500; paciarino .com), 470 Fore St. Fabiana de Savino and Enrico Barbiero make fresh pasta daily, to be enjoyed at lunch with fresh tomato sauce or with pesto, or enjoyed at dinner in somewhat larger portions. The light, deft touch with fine olive oil (the gold-foil-wrapped bottle is an elixir, friends assert) and other fine imported products also for sale make a meal here utterly refreshing and *saporito*—which is "tasty" in Italian. Entrées $16–18.

Cinque Terre (207-347-6154; cinque terremaine.com), 36 Wharf St. Northern Italian food is served in an open-plan dining room with tile floors and a second-floor gallery. Lee Skawinski runs the kitchen, turning out homemade gnocchi, each like a cheesy, buttery little soufflé. Any of the home-made stuffed pasta dishes will be wonderful, and mussels, baby octopus, and monkfish work wonders in a spicy tomato broth with crostini. Great, if expensive, Italian wine. Entrées $18–24, vegetable sides ordered separately.

&. **Local 188** (207-761-7909; local 188.com), 685 Congress St. Open Tue.–Sat. for dinner, and Sunday brunch. A tapas bar and dinner restaurant with a great lounge and bar. The Spanish bias is evident, as is local produce and a stray influence from Turkey or elsewhere. Spanish wines are a specialty. Try the gazpacho, and the garlic shrimp, grilled chorizo, and paella. Entrées $18 and up; tapas $4–14.

Ribollita (207-774-2972; ribollita maine.com), 41 Middle St. Open for dinner Mon.–Sat. The classics are the draw at this welcoming place, with pansanella, crispy calamari, handmade pasta in butternut squash ravioli, good wine, and main dishes of osso buco or seared rib eye. Bean and bread soup, the ribollita of its name, is always available. Desserts include the creamiest flan in town. Entrées $12.50–20.

The East Ender (207-879-7669; east enderportland.com), 47 Middle St. A cider-brined local pork chop and a plate of baby back ribs argued for a return visit to this friendly, comfortable place with an affection for good meat and Wed.-night half-off wine by the bottle. Entrées $16–22.

&. **Street & Company** (207-775-0887; streetandcompany.net), 33 Wharf St. Open for dinner daily at 5:30. Reservations recommended. The noisy, packed dining rooms here, and a comfortable bar with upholstered seats, are filled with lovers of the wonderful fish, inventive specials, and comfortable standards like lobster diavolo for two, mussels Provençal, and scallops in Per-

nod and cream. The raw bar serves up the best oysters in town. Bourbon pecan pie and peach crisp might be on the dessert menu. Entrées $18–32.

The Corner Room (207-879-4747; thefrontroomrestaurant.com), 110 Exchange St. Harding Lee Smith has always made sure the menu items at his three "Rooms" (see the two others below) are affordable, but at The Corner Room, with half portions of pasta, they will also exactly fit your appetite. Fresh pasta in all shapes and sizes with lamb ragu, mushrooms and cream, or all'Amatriciana can be counted on for lunch or dinner. Pizza, dinner specials, terrific cocktails, and a long antipasto list of cheeses and cured meats. $15 and up.

The Grill Room (207-774-2333; thefrontroomrestaurant.com), 84 Exchange St. Harding Lee Smith takes care of grilled steaks with The Grill Room, where you can also order wood-oven pizza and, depending on the season, grilled swordfish, skewered scallops with rosemary and mushroom risotto, and a grilled rib eye with béarnaise and frites. The bar is a good place to meet a friend. Entrées $12–37.

On Munjoy Hill

&. **The Front Room** (207-773-3366; thefrontroomrestaurant.com), 73 Congress St. Open daily for all three meals. Bustling and hectic on weekends, this neighborhood mainstay serves a wide range of fine dinners, from meat loaf to roast pork chops, grilled flatiron steak to mushroom ragu with polenta. Easy to understand why it's full, but the noise can overwhelm some. Entrées $15–21.

✪ &. **Bar Lola** (207-775-5652; barlola .net), 100 Congress St. Open Wed.–Sat. for dinner. Little dishes offer customers a chance to tailor dinner to their appetite, with the smallest being really just a taste, and even the largest courses modestly sized. Owners Guy and Stella Hernandez take pride in the changing menu, and its respect for seasonal meat and fish, but each season will be sure to be an inspiration, perhaps seared strip steak with creamed corn or oven-roasted tomato stuffed with cheese and herbs. Entrées $18, with a prix fixe five-course dinner sometimes offered for $39. Try the elegant Manhattan with brandied cherries.

& **Blue Spoon** (207-773-1116), 89 Congress St. Open for lunch and dinner Tue.–Sat., brunch on Sat. This small restaurant at the top of Munjoy Hill cooks up straightforward dishes with skill and keeps them reasonably priced. Local stuff in-season, and seasonal dishes. The juicy burger and large bowls of mussels with lemon and garlic are popular mainstays on an otherwise changing menu. Entrées $15–20.

Sonny's (207-772-7774; sonnysportland .com), 83 Exchange St. Open daily. A magnificent renovation in a great Portland space, Sonny's bar area is perfect for an inventive cocktail, and its tables and booths are a fine place to enjoy South and Central American and southwestern flavors. Dishes might include beef brisket enchiladas or a roasted poblano cheeseburger. Entrées $14–24.

Boda (207-347-7557; bodamaine.com), 671 Congress St. Closed Mon. "Very Thai" means fragrance and flavors turned up a notch from the typical Thai restaurant; it also means exceptional dishes anyone can love. Romelo salad with betel leaves, a range of skewered meats and vegetables, and entrées like pork hock with star anise. Dine for less after 9:30 PM on Sun. Entrées $12–14.

Zapoteca (207-772-8242; zapoteca restaurant.com), 505 Fore St. Eat at

the lively bar or in the dining room and enjoy seviche with crab and Maine shrimp; enchiladas stuffed with the same under green chili sauce; or a local rib eye with lime, oregano, and cilantro salsa.

Figa (207-518-9400; figarestaurant .com), 249 Congress St. Lee Farrington presides over this rustic and elegant restaurant, mixing Asian and South American elements to create spicy, complex entrées and appetizers well worth sampling. Entrées $18–26, with half portions available.

Outside Portland

& **The Point Restaurant at The Black Point Inn** (207-883-2500 or 1-800-258-0003; blackpointinn.com), 510 Black Point Rd., Prouts Neck. Open May–Jan. 1, reservation required in the formal restaurant. This inn has revived its reputation for great dinners. (Fine casual entrées in the **Chart Room**, no reservations accepted, range $12–30; Sun. brunch.) The cocktails on the porch, overlooking the coastline stretching south, were always fine, but with new management the dinners are delightful, too. Entrées $17–34.

& **SeaGrass Bistro** (207-846-3885; seagrassbistro.com), 305 Rt. 1, Yarmouth. Stephanie Brown takes her obsession with fresh and local straight from spring and summer into fall and winter, with roasted rack of lamb or seafood minestrone with lobster. Entrées $23–26.

✍ & **Saltwater Grille** (207-799-5400; saltwatergrille.com), 231 Front St., South Portland. Open daily for lunch and dinner, with fabulous views across the bay to Portland. The food has steadied and improved here. Entrées include marinated hanger steak with mashed potatoes, smoked tamarind baby back ribs, and roast salmon— all in enormous portions. Entrées $19–30.

restaurants described under *Dining Out* also serve a reasonably priced lunch.

In and around the Old Port

El Rayo (207—780-8226; elrayo taqueria.com), 101 York St. Tacos, of course, like *al pastor*, filled with braised pork with grilled pineapple salsa and great side and beginners like seviche, fried plantains, and fundido, baked cheese with chorizo. Big burritos, daily specials; and finish with *dulces suenos*, mocha milk with tequila and Kahlúa. Excellent margaritas and a fine selection of tequila, too.

Vignola (207-772-1330; vignolamaine .com), 10 Dana St. Open Thu.–Sat. for lunch, daily for dinner, and on Sun. for brunch. The casual sister restaurant of Cinque Terre (see *Dining Out*), Vignola focuses on pizza, cured meats, and straightforward entrées like grilled skirt steak, pork loin, and a cassoulet with cotechino. Entrées $10–20.

Petite Jacqueline (207-553-7044; bistropj.com), 190 State St. French bistro fare priced right. Quiche, roast chicken, perhaps choucroute garnie on Friday for the plat du jour, and always tarte tatin. Entrées $13–26.

Duckfat (207-774-8080; duckfat.com), 43 Middle St. Open daily at 11 AM through dinner. Sister restaurant to Hugo's (see *Dining Out*), with the soul of a gourmand on a budget. Incredible fries rise from a mix of duckfat and vegetable oil. Panini are crisp cases of vegetable ratatouille or bacon, goat cheese, and tomatoes. Rich milk shakes, tender beignets, sweet dessert sandwiches of brioche and jam. Salads and iced coffee for a light lunch. Panini $6–13.50.

Pai men Miyake (207-541-9204; miyakerestaurants.com), 188 State St. Deep bowls of miso broth with pork belly and noodles might be the main attraction, but the pork buns and crab and scallop hamayaki with eel sauce will have you licking your chops. The sake list is elaborate and worth your while. $9–14.

PepperClub (207-772-0531; pepperclubrestaurant.com), 78 Middle St. Open for dinner Sun.–Thu. 5–9, Fri. and Sat. 5–10. A creative menu is written on two large blackboards and smaller table versions. Choose from six vegetarian, three fish, and three meat entrées every night, perhaps the wonderful meat loaf, organic salmon, Indian curry with dal and chutney, or roasted vegetables with orzo. Entrées $13.50–17.50. Free parking across the street.

Flatbread Pizza (207-772-8777; flatbreadcompany.com), 72 Commercial St. Open daily at 11:30 AM through dinner. One of a small chain of pizza joints (nine others include one in Paia Maui, Hawaii). Flatbread bakes its pies in a clay, wood-fired oven shaped like a low igloo—right in the middle of the restaurant. Kids are always sitting on a stone, mesmerized by the fire. Our favorite pizza features house maple-fennel sausage, sun-dried tomatoes, onions, mushrooms, mozzarella, and Parmesan, but everything here is good, including the salads and desserts. Outside deck overlooks the ferry terminal.

Shulte & Herr (207-773-1997), 349 Cumberland Ave. Open Tue.–Sun. 8–3. Fresh German food, from crisp potato pancakes with house lox, to tangy cucumber salad and spaetzle with Emmentaler, to a poppy-seed cake with vanilla sauce that was authenticated by our critical German companion.

Taco Escobarr (207-541-9097), 548 Congress St. Closed Sun. A quick, cheap meal of three crisp, puffy, or soft tacos wrapped around braised chicken or carne asada is a welcome thing. The hot salsa is guaranteed to raise your temperature.

🍴 **Gilbert's Chowder House** (207-871-5636; gilbertschowderhouse.com), 92 Commercial St. Open for lunch and dinner. As the name implies, Gilbert's serves filling chowders, but they also have a nice range of seafood appetizers and entrées, like lovely steamed mussels with garlic butter. The decor is Early Dive, but you can sit outside on the wharf in-season.

🍽 **Federal Spice** (207-774-6404), 225 Federal St. (across from the downtown post office). Open Mon.–Sat. from 11 AM. The soups du jour zing with flavor, as does the chili. Homemade falafel, yam fries, and sweet potato jalapeño corn bread round out the creative menu of hot and cold wraps and soft tacos.

Japanese, Korean, and Indian

Little Seoul (207-699-4326), 90 Exchange St. How can you beat the consoling, invigorating heat of the pork bulgogi, sizzling on its plate, teamed up with a bowl of nutty rice and beans, Korean-style? The kimchee tastes of its long marination.

Korea House (207-771-2000), 630 Congress St. The spicy tofu stew with an egg cooking in its bubbling stock is an antidote to cold Maine weather. The beef bipimbop feeds the soul. Inexpensive.

Benkay (207-773-5555; sushiman .com), 2 India St. A happening sushi bar with Western- and Japanese-style tables (one in the shape of a dory).

Restaurant Sapporo (207-772-1233; sappororestaurant.com), 230 Commercial St. Open for lunch and dinner daily. Portland's oldest sushi place has kept its high standards. You can count on Sapporo for a great dinner.

Yosaku (207-780-0880), 1 Danforth St. Open daily for lunch and dinner. High-

quality sushi and other good Japanese meals.

Fuji (207-773-2900; fujimaine.com), 29 Exchange St. Open daily for lunch and dinner, with fine sushi and Japanese dishes. Japanese steak-house-style meals are served on hibachis in the lower dining room; a reservation is a good idea for three or more.

🍽 **Tandoor** (207-775-4259), 88 Exchange St. Open daily for lunch and dinner. Choose from classics like chicken and lamb cooked in the tandoor oven, or vegetarian favorites like dal (yellow lentils sautéed with cream and spices) and sag paneer (spinach with homemade cheese).

Around Portland

🍽 🍴 ♿ **Becky's Diner** (207-773-7070; beckys.com), 390 Commercial St. Open daily 4 AM–9 PM, this is a genuine local favorite, known for soups and pies. Breakfast on fruit salad, a granola-and-yogurt bowl, and delicious grilled, homemade corn and blueberry muffins. Also reasonably priced lunch and dinner specials, and good chowder.

🍽 🍴 **Artemisia Café** (207-761-0135), 61 Pleasant St. (just behind and to the east of Holiday Inn by the Bay). Lunch Mon.–Fri., brunch Sat. and Sun., dinner Thu.–Sat. Salads, wraps, and sandwiches, from salade Niçoise to the Tuscan grill with portobello mushrooms, pesto, and goat cheese. A friendly spot for a quiet and good brunch or dinner.

Bonobo (207-347-8267; bonobo pizza.com), 46 Pine St. Open for lunch Wed.–Fri. 11:30–2:30, Sat. noon–4; dinner Sun.–Thu. 4–10, Fri.–Sat. 4–11. A wood-fired oven bakes pizza with a thin crust made with wet dough; many organic ingredients are used. Sausage and onion is one popular pie. The house pizza, Bonobo, holds mushrooms, prosciutto, spinach, cream,

Fontina, and thyme. Pizza $12.50–16.50.

✪ **Otto and Enzo** (207-773-7099; ottoportland.com), 576 Congress St. Exceptional pizza by the slice ($3.50) or pie. This is the spot to satisfy an appetite for thin-crust, remarkable pizza, perhaps with mashed potato and bacon, or grilled eggplant and tomato, or just wonderful pepperoni. Takeout on the left, eat-in on the right. Sister restaurant **Otto** (207-358-7870), 225 Congress St., is bigger and even more convivial; same terrific pizza.

The Bayou Kitchen (207-774-4935; bayoukitchen.com), 543 Deering Ave. (across the street from Big Sky Bakery and an excellent art supply store). Serving breakfast and lunch daily; call for dinner hours. This hole-in-the-wall off Forest Ave. offers the best grits and eggs in town, plus decent jambalaya, crawfish po'boys, and Cajun burgers.

Beyond Portland

✪ **158 Pickett Street Café** (207-799-8998), 158 Benjamin Pickett St., South Portland. Breakfast and lunch Tue.–Sun. They make the bagels so exactly right: chewy, slightly sour, utterly delicious, and golden brown. A variety of original soups in winter, local salads in summer, and sandwiches like ham and Brie with roasted grapes on baguette, Anestes Fotiades's favorite (and see portlandfoodmap.com, his work of art).

✆ **The Lobster Shack at Two Lights** (207-799-1677; lobstershacktwolights.com), 225 Two Lights Rd., Cape Elizabeth (off Rt. 77 at the tip of the cape, near Two Lights State Park). Open Apr.–late Oct., 11–8. Dine inside or out at this local landmark built in the 1920s, set below the lighthouse and next to the foghorn. Herb and Martha Porch have gotten their line management down to a science. Lobsters, chowders and lobster stew, fried

Maine shrimp, scallops, clams, and the lobster and crabmeat rolls.

🦞 ✆ **The Good Table** (207-799-4663; thegoodtable.net), 526 Ocean House Rd. (Rt. 77), Cape Elizabeth. Open Tue.–Sun. for breakfast, lunch, and dinner 8 AM–9 PM in summer, from 11 AM in winter, with 3 PM Sun. closing year-round. Beloved by its loyal regulars, the restaurant serves home-style entrées for lunch and dinner, but the specials board is where some of the best meals can be found. Weekend brunch menu might include eggs Benedict and interesting quiches.

Ken's Place (207-883-6611), 207 Pine Point Rd., Scarborough. Open daily for lunch and dinner Apr.–Oct. You can depend on David Wilcox to make sure things are running smoothly here, and that the kitchen is scrupulous about changing the oil and serving the freshest seafood. Great fried clams, and wonderful seafood.

First and Last Tavern (207-883-8383), 240 Pine Point Rd. (Rt. 9), Scarborough. Open Tue.–Sun. in summer, fewer days off-season, closed Jan.–Apr. A family branch of the well-known First and Last Tavern in

THE LOBSTER SHACK AT TWO LIGHTS

Nancy English

Nancy English

KEN'S PLACE

Hartford, Connecticut. The Italian dishes here deliver flavor; pizza is crisp and wonderful. Homemade gelato. Entrées $10–17.

Jewel of India (207-828-2001; the jewelofindia.com), 45 Western Ave., South Portland. Owned by the same family that made its reputation in Biddeford, this branch serves the same aromatic dishes and adds a big-screen

ARABICA

Nancy English

TV with Bollywood movies running nonstop.

COFFEE BARS Coffee by Design (207-772-5533; coffeedydesign.com), 620 Congress St., is the first in this friendly local chain (now also at 67 India St.), a cheerful spot with plenty of tables (sidewalk tables in summer), local art on display (and for sale), and all the usual coffee and espresso choices. **Arabica** (207-879-0792; arabicacoffee.com), 2 Free St. We like this place's baked goods, high ceilings, and cinnamon toast. The coffee is the best in town. Of course, people who flock to **Bard Coffee** (207-899-4788; bardcoffee.com), 185 Middle St., would say the same for their favorite spot with its expert espresso.

ICE CREAM AND GELATO Beal's Ice Cream (207-828-1335; bealsice cream.com), 12 Moulton St., is in the middle of the Old Port (and has four other locations), making 17 percent butterfat premium ice cream. **Mount Desert Island Ice Cream** (207-210-3432; mdiic.com), 51 Exchange St., just up the street, makes its own terrific ice creams, some spiked with hot chili—but who can resist the salted caramel? **Gorgeous Gelato** (207-699-4309; gorgeousgelato.com), 434 Fore

St., calls itself the only authentic gelato in Portland and uses cream and whole milk in its brilliantly flavored confections. Mariagrazia Zanardi and her husband Donato Giovine, from Milan, make gelato with "70 percent less fat" than premium ice cream. **Gelato Fiasco** (gelatofiasco.com), 425 Fore St., moved in across the street in late 2011. Time to take a stroll and compare them all.

✳ Entertainment

All listings are in Portland unless otherwise noted
Cumberland County Civic Center (207-775-3458; theciviccenter.com), 1 Civic Center Square. An arena with close to 8,000 seats, the center hosts year-round concerts, ice-skating spec-

BEAL'S ICE CREAM

Nancy English

taculars, Portland Pirates hockey games, and more.

Top of the East (207-775-5411; eastlandparkhotel.com), Eastland Park Hotel, 157 High St. Open for dinner daily 5–10, drinks till late. Portland's only rooftop lounge, with a marble bar, leather banquettes, and floor-to-ceiling windows taking in views of the city and Casco Bay.

MUSIC Portland Symphony Orchestra (207-773-6128; portlandsymphony.com), Merrill Auditorium, 20 Myrtle St. (just off Congress St. behind city hall). The winter series runs Sept.–May; in summertime, outdoor pops concerts at different locations along the shores of Casco Bay.

PORT Opera Repertory Theatre (207-879-7678; portopera.org), Merrill Auditorium. This critically acclaimed company enters its 18th season in 2012. Past productions include The Barber of Seville and Faust.

Portland Ovations (207-773-3150; portlandovations.org). A series of orchestra, jazz, and musical theater performances staged in fall and winter at Merrill Auditorium. Everything from *Mamma Mia!* to Indian Jazz Suites.

Port City Music Hall (207-899-4990; portcitymusichall.com), 504 Congress St. Jane's Addiction, the Clash, and Paranoid Social Club were on the schedule in late 2011.

PROFESSIONAL SPORTS The **Portland Pirates** (207-828-4665; portlandpirates.com), a professional minor-league hockey team, play their home games at the Cumberland County Civic Center. The **Portland Sea Dogs** (1-800-936-3647; portlandseadogs.com), a double-A baseball team and Boston Red Sox affiliate, play in Hadlock Stadium on Park Ave. (next to the Expo). The **Maine Red Claws** (207-210-6655; nba.com/dleague /maine), a National Basketball Association Development League affiliated with the Boston Celtics, had their first season in 2009–10, playing in the Portland Expo Building on Park Ave.

THEATER Portland Stage (207-774-0465; portlandstage.com) is based in the city's old Odd Fellows Hall (25A Forest Ave.), now an elegant, intimate, 290-seat theater. This Equity group stages a variety of shows Oct.–Apr.

Portland Players (207-799-7338), Thaxter Theater, 420 Cottage Rd., South Portland. An excellent community theater, the Players put on productions Sept.–June.

Lyric Music Theater (207-799-6509), Cedric Thomas Playhouse, 176 Sawyer St., South Portland. Four musicals each winter.

St. Lawrence Arts & Community Center (207-775-5568; stlawrencearts .org), 76 Congress St. An umbrella performance space for musicians, filmmakers, dance companies, and other artists. **The Good Theater** (207-885-5883), a resident theater company, performs four stage productions and one musical each season. The schedule changes constantly, so call to see what's doing.

✳ Selective Shopping

All listings are in Portland unless otherwise noted

Angela Adams (207-774-3523; angela adams.com), 273 Congress St. This store sells the swirling, colorful carpets and handbags designed by Angela Adams. Her work has won praise from all kinds of designers, and her pricey rugs are now coveted items. Sales held at the end of the retail seasons.

Ferdinand (207-761-2151; ferdinand homestore.com), 243 Congress St. Just

steps from Angela Adams, Ferdinand is stuffed with low chic—T-shirts with charming animals, and cheap pins, earrings, and jewelry, all infused with owner Diane Toepfer's eccentric aesthetic.

Rogues Gallery (207-553-1999; roguesgallery.com), 41 Wharf St. A line of T-shirts, jackets, and outerwear from a company created by designer Alex Carleton, whose work, also part of L.L. Bean's spring 2010 "Signature" line (fitted hunting jackets?), tends to be bohemian and very attractive.

ANTIQUES Allen and Walker (207-772-8787), 600 Congress St. A mix of 1960s modern and older antiques, with some Japanese pottery.

ART GALLERIES Art Walks are held the first Friday of every month, when galleries citywide hold open house.

Greenhut Galleries (207-772-2693 or 1-888-772-2693; greenhutgalleries .com), 146 Middle St. Peggy Golden Greenhut represents many of Maine's top artists and sculptors.

June Fitzpatrick Gallery (207-772-1961; fitzpatrickgallery.com), 112 High St. Well established and showcasing contemporary and fine art.

Susan Maasch Fine Art (207-478-4087; susanmaaschfineart.com), 1 Forest Ave. Established and new artists.

Aucocisco Galleries (207-775-2222; aucocisco.com), 89 Exchange St. Andres Verzosa's gallery showcases Maine artists like well-known Dozier Bell and Bernard Langlais, the fantastical work of Portland's Michael Waterman, and the extraordinary miniatures of Mary Hart.

Salt Gallery (207-761-0660; salt.edu), 561 Congress St. The Salt Institute for Documentary Studies brings students from all over the United States and abroad to study photography, nonfiction writing, and documentary radio. The gallery exhibits their photographic work, mostly about Maine.

CRAFTS GALLERIES 9 Hands Gallery (ninehandsgallery.com), 615A Congress St. Featuring the jewelry by Elizabeth Prior, fish and other creature sculptures by T. J. McDermott, and lyrical tapestries by Carolyn Spies.

Edgecomb Potters Gallery (207-780-6727; edgecombpotters.com), 49 Exchange St. One of three in the state; a fine collection of reasonably priced, interesting pottery.

Abacus (207-772-4880; abacusgallery .com), 44 Exchange St. A fascinating array of fine glass, ceramics, jewelry, textiles, and home furnishings.

Maine Potters Market (207-774-1633; mainepottersmarket.com), 376 Fore St. Work by 15 Maine potters.

BOOKSTORES Longfellow Books (207-772-4045; longfellowbooks.com), 1 Monument Way, is Portland's literary hot spot, stocking a full range of titles and hosting frequent readings by local and national authors. The website lists the busy schedule of readings; Maine authors in particular are worth checking out. **BAM** (207-253-5587; books amillion.com), 430 Gorham Rd., sells books, toys, games, and electronics and is Books-A-Million store No. 851.

Antiquarian-book lovers should check out **Carlson-Turner Books** (207-773-4200; carlsonturnerbooks.com), 241 Congress St. **Yes Books** (207-775-3233), 589 Congress St., founded by Pat Murphy, is considered by some to be the best used-book store in Maine.

FOOD Public Market House (207-228-2056; publicmarkethouse.com), 28 Monument Square. Open Mon.–Sat. 8–7, Sun. 10–5. **K. Horton Specialty Foods** with fine cheeses, many from Maine, **Maine Beer and Beverage Company** with beers, many from Maine's great breweries, and **Big Sky Bread** with its good bread and terrific granola. Coffee shop upstairs and

LONGFELLOW BOOKS

Nancy English

Kamasouptra, a fabulous, inexpensive food stand that serves terrific soup.

❂ **The Rosemont Markets** (rosemont market.com) are each a treasure cave stuffed with local produce, fresh meat, the best cheeses, wines from all over the world, and fresh-baked excellent bread, including chewy bagels, and pies, cakes, and cookies. The first **Rosemont Market and Bakery** (207-774-8129) is located at 559 Brighton Ave., Portland. The **Munjoy Hill Rosemont Market** (207-773-7888) is at 88 Congress St., Portland. The **Yarmouth Rosemont Market** (207-846-1234) at 96 Main St. in Yarmouth also sells fresh fish.

Two Fat Cats (207-347-5144; twofat catsbakery.com), 47 India St., Portland. Cupcakes, terrific blueberry pie, red velvet cake, and many other delectables.

Maine's Pantry (207-228-2028; mainespantry.com), 111 Commercial St. Many of the best food products made in Maine can be found here—like Stanchfield Farms high-quality jams and jellies, and Captain Mowett Blue Flame hot sauce, made with blueberries—and they are all perfect souvenirs.

Len Libby's Candies (207-883-4897; lenlibby.com), 419 Rt. 1, Scarborough. The candies made here are good, but the real draw is the enormous moose named Lenny—made with 1,700 pounds of milk chocolate, the only life-sized chocolate moose in the world. You can watch a video about how he was put together in 1997.

Standard Baking Co. (207-773-2112), 75 Commercial St. (below Fore Street restaurant). Open Mon.–Fri. 7–6, weekends 7–5. Artisanal French and Italian breads are exceptional, and so are the rolls, baguettes, brioches, and pastries. Small ginger-bread cakes, brownies, morning buns

with or without nuts, croissants, and pain au chocolat.

Scratch Baking Company (207-799-0668; scratchbakingco.com), 416 Preble St., South Portland. Opens on the weekend at 7 AM, when people begin to line up for the fresh, crusty, and phenomenal bagels. If you arrive when they are gone, any of the other fine breads will feed you well; also cakes, pastries, granola, wine, cheese, and milk.

Browne Trading Market (207-775-7560; brownetrading.com), 260 Commercial St. Open Mon.–Sat. 10–6. Formerly a fish wholesaler serving upscale restaurants throughout the United States, now selling their own smoked salmon, trout, shrimp, scallops, mussels, fresh seafood, and caviar, along with a wide assortment of cheeses and wine.

Portland Farmer's Market (portland mainefarmersmarket.org), May–Nov., Wed. 7–2 at Monument Square, and Sat. 7–noon in Deering Oaks Park. Produce, flowers, seeds, baked goods, and more, some organic and all grown and made in Maine. Visit the wading pool nearby in the park.

Harbor Fish Market (207-775-0251 or 1-800-370-1790; harborfish.com), 9 Custom House Wharf. Open Mon.–Sat. 8:30–5:30. The epicenter of fish, lobster, crabs, oysters, clams, eels, and squid, to name a few, which you can ship anywhere you like.

MORE SPECIAL SHOPS Portmanteau (207-774-7276; portmanteauon line.com), 11 Free St. Nancy Lawrence began by stitching canvas bags but has long since established a reputation for the distinctive tapestry hand-bags, totes, backpacks, luggage, and cloaks fabricated in her store.

Leroux Kitchen (207-553-7665; lerouxkitchen.com), 161 Commercial

St. Everything you could possibly need to make a gourmet meal, from marble mortars and pestles and Henckels knives to Viking cookware and wines and prepared foods.

☙ **Fetch** (207-773-5450; fetchportland .wordpress.com), 195 Commercial St. Fetch sells all-natural pet foods, supplements, and litter, as well as a smattering of chew toys and shampoos. Pets welcome.

Beyond Portland proper is the **Maine Mall** (exit 45 off I-95), whose immediate complex of more than 100 stores is supplemented by large shopping centers and chain stores.

Cabela's (cabelas.com), Haigis Pkwy., Scarborough 04070. Located at I-95 exit 42. Cabela's, a nationwide chain, opened this new 130,000-square-foot showroom in spring 2008. A competitor of Freeport's L.L. Bean, Cabela's offers a huge array of sporting equipment and clothing, along with wild game displays, an indoor archery range, an aquarium of native fish, and re-creations of habitats with trophy animals.

✳ Special Events

Mid-March: **Maine Jewish Film Festival** (mjff.org).

Second Sunday in June: **Old Port Festival**—a celebration that began in the 1970s with the revival of the Old Port; includes a parade, various performances, street vendors, and special sales.

Mid-July: **Yarmouth Clam Festival**—arts and crafts, plenty of clams, performances, more.

August: **Cumberland Crafts Fair**, Cumberland Fairgrounds. **Sidewalk Art Festival**, Congress St.

September: **Cumberland County Fair**, Cumberland.

October: **Harvest on the Harbor**.

First weekend in November: **Maine Brewer's Festival**. Each year this event grows in size, due to the increasing number of Maine microbreweries.

Post-Thanksgiving–Christmas: **Victorian Holiday Portland**—with tree lighting, the arrival of Father Christmas, costumed carolers, special events through Christmas.

FREEPORT

T hink of Freeport, and you'll likely think of shopping. This is one coastal town that welcomes visitors every day of the year, even on Christmas morning, when the famous L.L. Bean store is open for business. A 24-hour, 365-day-a-year superstore, L.L. Bean has been a landmark since the famous boot was developed back in 1912. The store grew in popularity in 1951 when it opened around the clock, and is now re-creating itself as an activity center, offering activities and tours with its Outdoor Discovery Schools. But it was with the influx of seconds and factory stores in the early 1980s that the reputation of Freeport as a shopping mecca took hold.

Freeport is definitely a bargain shopper's dream, but it has always featured upscale retailers as well, such as Cole-Haan and Coach and famous furniture makers like Thomas Moser.

The retail facades, however, belie a rich and varied history dating back more than 200 years. The first known residents of the area were several tribes of the Wabanaki. Attempts by colonists to settle in the area resulted in a series of wars throughout the 1600s and early 1700s. By 1715 epidemics of European diseases and the settlers' persistence ended the Native American hold on the area, and a peace treaty with the Penobscots was signed in 1725.

Originally a part of North Yarmouth, Freeport was granted a charter, separating it from the town in 1789. A longtime legend (somewhat controversial, because there is no documented evidence of the occurrence) holds that in 1820 the papers separating Maine from Massachusetts were signed in the historical Jameson Tavern.

Early citizens made a living through agriculture and timber. During the War of 1812, shipbuilding became an important industry, with one famous boat inspiring Whittier's poem "The Dead Ship of Harpswell." In the 1880s shoe factories sprouted up in Freeport, adding another industry to its economy.

Transportation advances also had their effect on Freeport's history. When an electric trolley was built to connect Portland and Yarmouth with Brunswick and Lewiston, it passed through Freeport. Many trolley companies built parks to encourage ridership; likewise a developer built the Casco Castle Hotel to draw tourists to South Freeport. The hotel burned down, but a stone tower remains (on private property) and can be best viewed from Winslow Memorial Park or from the harbor.

Despite the proliferation of shops, the village has retained the appearance of older days—even McDonald's has been confined to a gracious old house, with no golden arches in sight. The Freeport Historical Society operates a research library and museum in a historic house, in the midst of the retail sector. You can take a self-directed walking tour of Freeport historic sites.

Some come to the area simply to stroll wooded paths in Wolfe's Neck Woods State Park and the Mast Landing Audubon Sanctuary. Bradbury Mountain is just a short drive, and Pettengill Farm offers a look at 19th-century coastal life. The Desert of Maine is a quirky attraction as well.

GUIDANCE FreeportUSA (207-865-1212 or 1-800-865-1994; freeportusa.com), P.O. Box 452, Freeport 04032, operates a visitors center in a relocated historic hose tower on Depot St. Brochures, information, and restrooms can be found here. Among their materials is an excellent, free visitors walking map with a list of stores, restaurants, accommodations, attractions, and other services.

The Maine Tourism Association's welcome center in Kittery stocks some Freeport brochures, and there is another state information center on Rt. 1 just south of Freeport, in Yarmouth, at exit 17 off I-95.

GETTING THERE A number of **bus tour companies** also offer shopping trips to Freeport from Boston and beyond. Most people drive, which means there can be a shortage of parking spaces in peak season. One solution to this problem is to stay at one of the dozen or so inns or B&Bs within half a mile of L.L. Bean and leave your car there. The Amtrak **Downeaster** brings you from Boston to Portland, where you can get a bus, or just take one from Boston until the line is extended. Excellent bus service on **Concord Coach Lines** (see *Getting There* in "Portland Area") runs from Boston to Brunswick. If all goes according to schedule, the Amtrak **Downeaster** will offer service through to Brunswick with stops in Freeport starting in late 2012.

DOWNTOWN FREEPORT

Nancy English

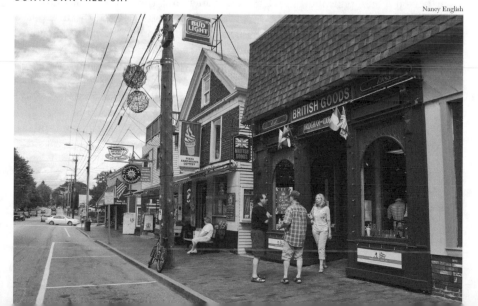

WHEN TO COME The holiday shopping season is one of Freeport's busiest times, and a special "Sparkle Weekend" celebrates it in December. For hiking and swimming, summer months are best.

✳ Villages

South Freeport has been a fishing center from its beginning, when it was known as Strout's Port. Between 1825 and 1830 up to 12,000 barrels of mackerel were packed and shipped from here each year. Later the area specialty became lobster packing. Offering a very different feel from the chaotic shopping frenzy of downtown Freeport, the harbor features great seafood. From here you can take a cruise to explore Eagle and Seguin Islands in summer.

Porter's Landing. Once the center of commercial activity, this now quiet residential neighborhood nestles amid rolling hills, woods, and streams. The village is part of the Harraseeket Historic District on the National Register of Historic Places.

✳ To See and Do

🦐 🐾 ✎ ♿ **Desert of Maine** (207-865-6962; desertofmaine.com), 95 Desert Rd., Freeport. Open daily, early May–mid-Oct., 9–5. Admission runs $10.50 adults, $7.75 ages 13–16, $6.75 ages 4–12. Visit the new butterfly room. Narrated tram tours and self-guided walks through 40 acres of sand that was once the Tuttle Farm. Heavily farmed, then extensively logged to feed the railroad, the topsoil eventually gave way to the glacial sand deposit beneath it, which spread . . . and spread until entire trees sank below the surface. It is an unusual sand, rich in mineral deposits that make it unsuitable for commercial use but interesting to rockhounds. Children love it, especially the gem hunt, when you sluice for gems from a bag of "tailings" guaranteed to contain small or large gemstones or fossils ($6, $8.50, and $8.50 respectively). Camping available (see *Lodging*).

BOAT EXCURSIONS *Atlantic Seal* (207-865-6112; atlanticsealcruises.com), Town Wharf, South Freeport. Memorial Day–mid-Oct. Captain Thomas Ring (former owner of the charming Atlantic Seal B&B) runs daily narrated trips (if the eight-person minimum is met) into Casco Bay, including three-hour cruises to Eagle Island, the former summer home of Admiral Robert E. Peary, the first person to reach the North Pole; Thu. six-hour cruises from South Freeport to Seguin Island Lighthouse to see—and climb inside—the fascinating first-order Fresnel lens, and a visit to the museum run by the Friends of the Seguin Lighthouse Caretakers (with 50-foot humpback whale and porpoise sightings on the trip to the island); this is one of the few Maine lighthouses open to the public. Seal- and osprey-sighting group tours of 10 or more; and fall foliage cruises mid-Sept. and Oct. Lobstering demonstrations usually included, except on Sunday in June, July, and Aug., when lobstering is prohibited by Maine law. Fee for state historical site is included. Trips leave Tue. and Fri. from Cook's Lobster House on Bailey Island, and Mon., Wed., Sat., and Sun. from South Freeport.

CANOEING The **Harraseeket River** in Freeport is particularly nice for canoeing. Start at Mast Landing, the northeastern end of the waterway; there are also launching sites at Winslow Memorial Park on Staples Point Rd. and at South

Freeport Harbor. Nearby lake canoeing can be found at **Run Around Pond** in North Pownal (the parking lot is off Lawrence Rd., 1 mile north of the intersection with Fickett Rd.).

CROSS-COUNTRY SKIING The areas listed under *Green Space* are good cross-country skiing spots; rent or purchase equipment from L.L. Bean, which also offers classes (see *Special Learning Programs*).

GOLF Freeport Country Club (207-865-0711; harrisgolfonline.com), 2 Old County Rd., Freeport. With nine holes, golf clinics, driving range, pro shop, and snack bar.

JEWELRY MAKING ✍ **The Beadin' Path** (207-865-4785; beadinpath.com), 15 Main St., Freeport. Choose beads and findings from a wide variety (including vintage and contemporary Swarovski crystals), then sit at the table and create your own jewelry pieces. Prices are based on the beads you choose, so this can be a good, inexpensive rainy-day activity for kids (and adults).

MUSEUM ✍ **Harrington House** (207-865-3170; freeporthistoricalsociety.org), 45 Main St., Freeport. Hours vary depending on season; check the website under VISIT US. Donations appreciated. Built of local brick and granite, this 1830 house with its garden is maintained by the Freeport Historical Society as a museum, research library, and archive.

SPECIAL LEARNING PROGRAMS L.L. Bean Outdoor Discovery Schools (1-888-552-3261; llbean.com/walkon), Rt. 1, Freeport. You can get your toes wet— literally, if you're kayaking—with L.L. Bean's Walk-On Adventures program. For a fee starting at $10, participants can take a shuttle bus from the downtown store to enjoy 1½ to 2½ hours of (Memorial Day–Columbus Day) fly casting, kayaking, archery, and clay shooting—and, when the snow permits, till March, cross-country skiing and snowshoeing. All you need to do is sign up at the store on the day of the program; all equipment is provided. Schedules at the Freeport store are listed online.

The Outdoor Discovery School offers half-day or longer tours and classes that cover the basics—the Women's Kayak Touring Essentials II, for instance, covers advanced strokes and boat handling. A Maine bike tour involves a two-day trip on coastal roads with camping at the private L.L. Bean Freeport waterfront campground ($299 in 2011, minimum age 10, all equipment provided). A family camping trip with kayaks to Maine islands is another possibility.

✳ Green Space

✍ **Winslow Memorial Park** (207-865-4198; freeportmaine.com), Staples Point Rd., South Freeport. Open Memorial Day–Sept. A 90-acre municipal park with a sandy beach and large grassy picnicking area; also boating and 100-site oceanside campground ($20–27 per night for nonresidents). Facilities include restrooms with showers. $2 nonresident admission fee.

✍ **Mast Landing Audubon Sanctuary** (207-781-2330; maineaudubon.org), Upper Mast Landing Rd. (take Bow St. south), Freeport. Maintained by Maine

Audubon, this 140-acre sanctuary offers trails through apple orchards, woods, meadows, and along a millstream. Several paths radiate from a 1-mile loop trail. You might even get lucky and see mink, deer, or porcupines.

♥ ♂ Bradbury Mountain State Park (207-688-4712; bradburymountain .com), Rt. 9, 528 Hallowell Rd., Pownal (6 miles from Freeport: from I-95, take exit 20 and follow signs). Open year-round. $4.50 nonresidents ages 12 and older, $1 ages 5–11, under 5 free. The summit, accessible by an easy (even for young children) 0.5-mile hike, yields a splendid view of Casco Bay and New Hampshire's White

> **♂ ♿ WOLFE'S NECK WOODS STATE PARK**
> (207-865-4465), 425 Wolfe's Neck Rd. (take Bow St., across from L.L. Bean), Freeport. Open Apr.–Nov. A 233-acre park with shoreline hiking along Casco Bay, the Harraseeket River, and salt marshes, with excellent birding. Ospreys nest here, and an eagle is nearby. Guided nature walks and scattered picnic tables and grills. $4.50 dayuse fee for nonresident adults.

Mountains. Facilities in the 800-acre park include a small playground, a softball field, hiking trails, toilets, and a 35-site overnight camping area.

♂ Pettengill Farm (207-865-3170; freeporthistoricalsociety.org), Pettengill Rd., Freeport. Managed by the Freeport Historical Society (which conducts periodic guided tours), the grounds are open anytime. A saltwater farm with 140 acres of open fields and woodland that overlooks the Harraseeket Estuary, with a totally unmodernized vintage-1810 saltbox house. Come the weekend after Labor Day for the annual Pettengill Farm Days celebration.

✳ Lodging

All listings are in Freeport 04032 unless otherwise noted
INN ♥ ♂ ♿ Harraseeket Inn (207-865-9377 or 1-800-342-6423; harraseeketinn.com), 162 Main St. The Gray family—Nancy, her son Chip, and daughter Penelope (all former Maine Guides)—have a passion for Maine expressed through meticulous and warm innkeeping. Two blocks north of L.L. Bean, their luxury hotel is the largest in the area, with 84 rooms (including 5 suites) plus nine town houses. The inn began as a fiveroom B&B in the 1800 Federal house next door. Many of the rooms feature antiques and reproductions, canopy bed, and Jacuzzi; 20 have a fireplace. The inn has formal dining rooms (see *Dining Out*), conference spaces (one

with outdoor terrace), and the casual and popular Broad Arrow Tavern (see *Eating Out*). Other public spaces include a drawing room, library, gym, ballroom, and a pretty, glassed-in pool overlooking the gardens. Rates inseason are $185–315, full buffet breakfast and afternoon tea included.

Hilton Garden Inn Freeport (207-865-1433; hiltongardeninn.com), 5 Park St. Reliable and with all the best amenities, this Hilton Garden Inn has 99 rooms, indoor pool, hot tub, exercise room, restaurant, and bar. A gas fireplace burns in the lounge, where you can enjoy a drink. The inn is a fiveminute walk to the shops.

BED & BREAKFASTS ♥ ♂ White Cedar Inn (207-865-9099 or 1-800-

853-1269; whitecedarinn.com), 178 Main St. Open year-round. This restored Victorian is the former home of Arctic explorer Donald B. MacMillan, who traveled nearly to the North Pole with Admiral Peary—till frostbite set in. Seven bedrooms come with private bath, down comforters, and airconditioning; some have a fireplace. A spiral staircase leads down to the Bowdoin Room, with a private entrance, sitting area, and TV (pets are welcome here). Owners Rock Nadeau and Monica Kissane, who are constantly updating the inn's rooms and common spaces, serve a full breakfast at small tables in the sunroom. Doubles $130–200 in-season, $105–175 off-season.

Brewster House (207-865-4121; brewsterhouse.com), 180 Main St., Freeport. The bright, warm colors of the tasteful and well-appointed rooms and immaculate bathrooms at Brewster House will put any traveler at ease. Scott and Ruth Thomas have practiced professional hospitality here since 2006. Room 3 with its coffee-and-cream walls has a four-poster queen bed, handsome dark wood upholstered chairs, and a tub in its tile-floored bathroom—but all the rooms look inviting. $179–199 for the rooms, depending on season, and a two-bedroom suite is $209–269, including breakfast that might be blueberry-stuffed French toast.

The James Place Inn (207-865-4486 or 1-800-964-9086; jamesplaceinn .com), 11 Holbrook St. Victoria and Robin Baron have furnished their pretty B&B with charm, luxury, beautiful furnishings, and a relaxed atmosphere. Single women enjoy a stay in the Rose Room, with a stunning spool bed and a single whirlpool bath. All seven rooms have air-conditioning and cable TV; one features a kitchenette,

four have a whirlpool bath, and the Pine Room has a wood-burning fireplace and deck. Enjoy the full breakfast at the café tables on the deck or in the pretty glassed-in breakfast room. $135–195 double depending on season.

☕ **Applewood Inn** (207-865-9705; applewoodusa.com), 8 Holbrook St. Jay and Jennifer Yilmaz have 11 rooms in well-kept, modern buildings for nightly rentals, one with kitchenette, another with a full kitchen. Local artists are the creators of much of the engaging decor, all available for purchase. Two blocks south of L.L. Bean, the inn sits far enough off Rt. 1 to be quiet. Private bath in each room; some have a fireplace, skylights, Jacuzzi, and TV/DVD. Full breakfast included in the $165–300 in-season rates; longer-term rentals available. The family also operates several AJ Dogs food stands and an ice cream stand on Freeport's busy Main Street.

Kendall Tavern (207-865-1338; kendalltavern.com), 213 Main St. This 200-year-old farmhouse, owned by Loree and Tim Rudolph, features seven rooms, all with private bath and air-conditioning. Pastel walls, quilts, and antiques, like hand-painted armoires and four-poster beds, make the rooms attractive; two are under the eaves on the top floor. Sit in one of two parlors with fireplaces, or hang out on the lovely front porch in summer; the shops are a 10-minute walk away. Rates range up to $175 in-season, and include a full breakfast. Children over 8 welcome.

✪ ☕ ✿ ♿ **Royalsborough Inn at the Bagley House** (207-353-6372 or 1-800-765-1772; royalsboroughinn.com), 1290 Royalsborough Rd., Durham 04222. A 10-minute drive from downtown Freeport in a serene country setting, this is the oldest house in town, built as a public house in 1772. The town's first worship services were held here, and this was the site of the first schoolhouse. Marianne and Jim Roberts have furnished eight rooms with antiques and down and alpaca comforters. Emma's Room, brilliant with red and white bedding, is enchanting, but all the rooms show off classic style. $139–179 double in-season includes full breakfast and afternoon refreshments. Alpacas graze behind the house; alpaca fiber goods and cashmere yarns from the farm's cashmere goats are for sale in the store. You can also pet the angora rabbits. Massage therapy available and programs for women.

🐾 **Captain Briggs House** (207-865-1868 or 1-888-217-2477; captainbriggs .com), 8 Maple Ave. Simple, pleasant rooms with private bath, all botanically named. Evergreen has a large full bath with beadboard wainscoting. This place is quieter than some because it's set well off Rt. 1. $120–230 in-season includes full breakfast made with local eggs.

MOTELS The Village Inn (207-865-3236; reservations only, 1-800-998-3649; freeportvillageinn.com), 186 Main St., has rates starting at $75 and is within easy walking distance of all the shops. The very basic decor is perfectly clean, and the owners since 1986, Lewis and Jackie Corliss, are down-home Mainers who can tell you the history of their transformed town or help you get your disabled car fixed, as they did for us.

On Rt. 1 south of Freeport near the Yarmouth town line are a number of modern motels. Among these is the 🐾 **Best Western Freeport Inn** (207-865-3106 or 1-800-99-VALUE; freeportinn.com), 31 Rt. 1. Set on 25 acres of lawns and nature trails, this place offers an upscale motel ambience at reasonable prices. All rooms have sheet-covered comforters on the Serta beds, carpeting, cable TV, air-conditioning, and phone. Outdoor swimming pool and playground. Pets are allowed in 32 of the 80 rooms. Doubles are $130–199 in-season. The Freeport Café (see *Eating Out*) serves breakfast all day (seasonal hours).

CAMPGROUNDS 🐾 ✎ ♿ **Cedar Haven Campground** (207-865-6254; reservations only, 1-800-454-3403; cedarhavenfamilycampground.com), 39 Baker Rd. Open May–Oct. Fifty-eight mostly wooded sites, each with fireplace and picnic table. Water and electricity hookups, five with sewer and cable TV as well. Ten tent sites. Store with wood, ice, and groceries; mini golf, playground, and pond for swimming. Two miles from Rt. 1 and downtown Freeport. $22–50 per night.

🐾 ✎ ♿ **Desert Dunes of Maine Campground** (207-865-6962; desert ofmaine.com), 95 Desert Rd. Located next to a kitschy attraction with a natural glacial sand deposit (see *To See and Do*), this campground offers 50 wooded and open sites with hookups, hot showers, laundry, convenience store, propane, fire rings, picnic tables, horseshoe pits, nature trails, and swimming pool. Campsites are $25–39 per night.

✳ Where to Eat

All listings are in Freeport unless otherwise noted

DINING OUT ♿ **Harraseeket Inn Maine Dining Room** (207-865-9377 or 1-800-342-6423), 162 Main St. Open year-round for dinner and Sun. brunch 11:30–2. Continental cuisine and elegant service in three formal dining rooms. The chefs use fresh, in-season, and often organic ingredients

Nancy English

HARRASEEKET LUNCH & LOBSTER CO.

from local gardeners and farmers to create mouthwatering entrées like five-spice scallops with leek cream, and châteaubriand for two carved at the table. Entrées $24–38. The Harraseeket is also known for its Sunday brunch, which can feature such delicacies as caviar, oysters on the half shell, lobster, and a crêpe station.

✪ **Azure Café** (207-865-1237; azurecafe.com), 123 Main St. Alfresco dining in good weather allows careful surveillance of the shoppers, but warm, handsome rooms and a bar inside make sure you can enjoy the good food year-round. The focus is on Italy with ravioli stuffed with butternut squash and ricotta, or grilled filet mignon skewers glazed with roasted garlic balsamic. Maine seafood risotto marries the best of both coastlines. Steamed lobster is sold for the best price in town, guaranteed. The classic pasta dishes are worth exploring. Entrées $13–32.

Mediterranean Grill (207-865-1688; mediterraneangrill.biz), 10 School St. Open daily in summer for lunch and dinner, closing earlier off-season. A Turkish dinner awaits you here: everything from falafel and stuffed eggplant to kebabs, moussaka, and lamb shanks.

Choose from Turkish wines as well as the usual from California, and baklava or rice pudding to end. Entrées $16–23.

✂ & **Jameson Tavern** (207-865-4196; jamesontavern.com), 115 Main St. Open daily 11:30–9, till 10 on Fri.–Sat. The 1779 building has an interesting

AZURE CAFÉ

Nancy English

history: Locals claim that the papers separating Maine from Massachusetts were signed here in 1820. Dine on the outside patio in summer, or by one of several indoor fireplaces during cold months, on salmon Oscar, steak, or a lazy man lobster. If there's a wait, order from the same menu in the neighboring Tap Room (see *Eating Out*). $10–27.

EATING OUT ✎ ♿ **The Broad Arrow Tavern** (207-865-9377), Harraseeket Inn, 162 Main St. Open 11:30–10:30, with drinks till midnight. A ground-floor dining room overlooking the terrace, this place is packed with locals, tourists, and guests, who come for the delicious food, unstuffy pub atmosphere, and collection of stuffed animals on the wall (moose, fisher, deer). The open kitchen has a wood-fired oven and grill, and serves up everything from pizzas, sandwiches, and grilled steak to a Caesar salad that can be ordered with anchovies. A dessert might be a double chocolate chip cookie, hot out of the oven, with double vanilla ice cream and chocolate sauce. Lunch entrées $10–30.

Freeport Chowder House (207-865-3403), 4 Mechanic St. Fried clams, hand-cut french fries, and excellent lobster and crabmeat rolls.

❖ **Jacqueline's Tea Room** (207-865-2123; jacquelinestearoom.com), 201 Main St. Open 10:30–3 Tue.–Fri. and every other weekend. Try the "Cream Tea" ($12) without a reservation, or make a reservation for tea with all the trimmings ($29.50) with seatings between 11 and 1; four courses and unlimited tea, with tea sandwiches of smoked salmon or cucumber, delicate, crumbling scones with clotted cream and lemon curd, and cakes, tarts, and English toffee. Tea is chosen from a list of 88 teas (also available to pur-

chase) and served in 2-cup teapots during a leisurely two hours.

Conundrum (207-865-0303), 117 Rt. 1, South Freeport. This bistro, set right under the Big Indian, serves good burgers and other casual meals in an intimate, dark blue room decorated with local artists' work. We like the varieties of pâté and cheese (also sold in the neighboring shop, Old World Gourmet; see *Snacks*), which you can order as entrées, and the wine selection is amazing. More than 500 bottles are available here; 60 wines are offered by the glass. You can get a taste before deciding on a glass, or half glass, to drink. The best place in Maine to taste wine. Entrées $10–27.

Tap Room (207-865-4196; jameson tavern.com), Jameson Tavern, 115 Main St. This informal tavern to the rear of the building serves the full Jameson Tavern menu plus pub fare from 11:30 AM until late in the evening.

✎ ♿ **Gritty McDuff's** (207-865-4321), 187 Lower Main St. The only brewpub in Freeport, this branch of the popular Portland pub offers outdoor dining, lobster, seafood, pizza, and pub food. Great ales brewed right here, and a tasty lamb burger with feta, too.

✎ ♿ **Muddy Rudder** (207-846-3082; muddyrudder.com), Rt. 1, Yarmouth. Operated by the nearby Freeport Inn, this popular restaurant overlooks Cousins River and visiting deer, heron, and seagulls. It serves a wide selection of seafood dishes plus steaks, sandwiches, and salads. You can have a full clambake on the deck. Completely renovated in 2007, the Rudder holds the piano played in 1976, when the business opened, and still played nightly, making for a romantic atmosphere.

❖ ✎ **Harraseeket Lunch & Lobster Co.** (207-865-4888), foot of Main St.,

South Freeport (turn off Rt. 1 at the giant wooden Indian, then turn right at a stop sign a few miles down). Open May–Columbus Day. At this traditional lobster shack in the middle of the Harraseeket boatyard, order lobsters and clams on one side, fried food on the other, and eat at picnic tables (of which there are never enough at peak hours) overlooking a boat-filled harbor. Lobsters are fresh from the pound's boats; homemade desserts. There is also a small inside dining room. Be aware that it is a busy place; you may have to wait to eat.

✐ **The Lobster Cooker** (207-865-4349; lobstercooker.net), 39 Main St. Steamed lobster, excellent fresh-picked lobster and crabmeat rolls, sandwiches, and chowders; cafeteria-style dining on the outdoor patio; beer and wine. Chefs earn their stripes at this busy spot, learning speed and skill.

✿ ✐ & **The Freeport Café** (207-865-3106), Rt. 1 (next to the Freeport Inn). Open daily 6 AM–9 PM. A bona fide local hangout, this small café makes up for its unappealing location right on Rt. 1 with good food at great prices. Extremely friendly service, great dinner specials, and a children's menu.

SNACKS AND TAKEOUT Old World Gourmet (207-865-4477), Rt. 1 (next to the Big Indian). Foreign cheese, pâté, prepared food, and wine are ready to fill picnic baskets or take over dinner duty. Eat lunch here at one of the tables nestled next to the shop's shelves. Try one of their grilled panini, vegetarian sandwiches, composed salads, baked goods, Italian sodas, or lattes with Torani syrup.

Royal River Natural Foods (207-865-0046; rrnf.com), 443 Rt. 1. A great place to buy vegetarian snacks for the road, such as organic fruits and local vegetables, freshly made soups, pasta

and green salads, sandwiches, and muffins, which you can eat in the café, too. Full line of natural grocery items.

✳ Selective Shopping

FREEPORT FACTORY OUTLETS

✿ As noted in the chapter's introduction, Freeport's 74-plus downtown factory outlets, with more on the edges of town, constitute what may have become Maine's mightiest tourist magnet. *Boston Globe* writer Nathan Cobb called it "A shoppers' theme park spread out at the foot of L.L. Bean, the high church of country chic."

A $45 million open-air commercial center, Freeport Village Station, opened in 2009 on more than 3 acres of L.L. Bean–owned land in the middle of town with a plaza surrounded by three large and several smaller buildings, each sized for a boutique. It's open Mon.–Sat. 9–9, Sun. 10–6, and holds factory outlets for Calvin Klein, Talbot's, Nike, Coach, Izod, Pacsun, VanHeusen, Brooks Brothers, and the L.L. Bean Outlet itself.

L.L. Bean contends that it attracts at least three million visitors annually— almost three times the population of Maine. In the early 1980s neighboring property owners began to claim a portion of this traffic. Instead of relegating the outlets to malls, they have deftly draped them in brick and clapboard, actually improving on the town's old looks (although longtime shopkeepers who were forced to move because of skyrocketing real estate prices might well disagree). Ample parking lots are sequestered behind the Main Street facade, and the new construction has added a parking garage for 550 cars.

In summer a festive atmosphere reigns, with hot-dog and ice cream vendors on key corners. But it's the

L.L. BEAN

(1-877-755-2326, press 7; llbean.com), 95 Main St. Open 24 hours a day, 365 days a year, as are the three other stores listed below (but not the outlet). With a kids' department, a camping department, a pond stocked with brown or brook trout, and a trail "rock" to test new hiking boots, the building resembles a fancy shopping mall more than it does a single store. Back in 1912 Leon Leonwood Bean developed his boot, or Maine Hunting Shoe, a unique combination of rubber bottom and leather top. "You cannot expect success hunting deer or moose if your feet are not properly dressed," Bean wrote in his very first catalog. Ninety out of the first 100 boots he built literally fell apart at the seams, so Bean refunded the purchasers' money and began a company tradition of guaranteed customer satisfaction, including all-night hours for the outdoorsmen who passed through in the wee hours. Bean himself died in 1967, but his grandson Leon Gorman, chairman of the board, and company president Christopher McCormick now oversee an empire of outdoor equipment.

L.L. Bean Hunting and Fishing Store (1-877-755-2326, press 4; llbean.com), 95 Main St. All the fishing equipment is here, along with archery gear and hunt-

L.L. BEAN BIKE, BOAT & SKI

Nancy English

quality of the shops that ensures a year-round crowd, with well-known clothing, accessories, or home furnishing line factory stores. The following is a selected list of the more interesting outlets. Many stores claim 20 to 70 percent off suggested retail prices, and even L.L. Bean has a separate outlet,

L.L. BEAN

ing rifles. Bean also sells used guns, and will buy guns in good condition. Fish and game mounts are hung around the store, giving the place a hunting lodge atmosphere. With 33,000 square feet, L.L. Bean is showing off more of its equipment in one space than it ever has. Hunting clothing and boots to outfit anyone.

L.L. Bean Bike, Boat & Ski Store (1-877-755-2326, press 5; llbean.com), 95 Main St. When the weather warms up, the bike and boat displays bloom; when it's getting colder it's time for all the ski equipment, snowshoes, toboggans, and sleds to take a bigger share of the space. You can bring a bike in for repair, or get bindings mounted to skis. A wide selection of kayaks, paddles, and accessories.

L.L. Bean Home Store (1-877-755-2326, press 6; llbean.com), 12 Nathan Nye St., Freeport. Opened in the summer of 2009, the Home Store stocks attractive, inexpensive quilts based on vintage designs, good-quality flannel and cotton sheets, towels, hooked-wool pillows, and furniture like a wicker side table. Vintage items and antiques are interspersed among the new merchandise, ready to furnish your dream of a mountain lodge, or just your comfortable house.

which you should check for bargains before heading to the main store.

L.L. Bean Outlet Store, 1 Freeport Village Station. Seconds, samples, and irregular merchandise of all kinds. You never know what you'll find, but it's always worth a look. Unlike the main store, the outlet is open only during the hours for Freeport Village Station: Mon.–Sat. 9–9, Sun. 10–6.

Thomas Moser Cabinetmakers (207-865-4519 or 1-800-708-9041; thosmoser.com), 149 Main St. Open Mon.–Sat. 10–6, Sun. 11–5. Fine furniture inspired by Shaker, Arts and Crafts, Japanese, Danish, and art deco designs. This family business has been a Freeport institution for more than 35 years.

Dooney & Bourke (207-865-1366; dooney.com), 56 Main St. (in back). Stylish pocketbooks, shoulder bags, belts, wallets, and portfolios.

& **Cuddledown of Maine Factory Store** (207-865-1713; cuddledown .com), 554 Rt. 1. Comforters, pillows, gift items, all filled with goose down. The annual sale in mid-July is worth the trip.

& **Maine Wreath & Flower Factory Outlet** (207-865-3019 or 1-800-973-4987; mainewreath.com), 13 Bow St. Quality Maine-dried flowers and wreaths at discount prices.

Cole-Haan Footwear and Accessories (207-865-6321; colehaan.com), 66 Main St. Beautiful shoes, handbags, and socks. Pricey, but their quality is famous.

SPECIAL SHOPS

All listings are in Freeport unless otherwise noted

Brown Goldsmiths (207-865-4126; browngoldsmiths.com), 11 Mechanic St. Open Mon.–Sat. Original designs in rings, earrings, and bracelets.

Bridgham & Cook, Ltd. (207-865-1040 or 1-800-UK-BUYER; british goods.com), 116 Main St. Packaged British and Irish foods, toiletries, teas, gifts—a must for the Anglophile, who might also like Jacqueline's Tearoom and the Harraseeket Inn (see *Where to Eat*) for a proper cup of tea.

Cold River Vodka (207-865-4828; coldrivervodka.com), 437 Rt. 1, south of Rt. 295 exit 20. Open daily in-season, closed Sun. and Mon. off-season. Using Maine potatoes grown on his

COLD RIVER VODKA

Nancy English

farm in Fryeburg, Donnie Thibodeau and his brother, neurosurgeon Lee Thibodeau, teamed up with a professional brewer and former Olympic ski coach Bob Harkins to open Maine's first vodka distillery in 2005. A gallery dramatizes the history of Maine potato farming. Tours are offered noon–5 in-season, with free tastings.

✍ **DeLorme's Map Store** (207-865-4171), Rt. 1 (south of downtown Freeport). A good place to spend a couple of rainy hours watching the world turn—literally—and sifting through DeLorme's impressive offerings. Check out the publishing company's maps, atlases, pamphlets, and guidebooks of the United States and the world, as well as some interesting educational toys. A large bank of computers invites visitors to try mapping software. Many people come just to see Eartha, the world's largest rotating and revolving globe, which spins quietly in a glassed-in lobby.

Edgecomb Potters/Hand in Hand Gallery (207-865-1705 or 1-800-343-5529; edgecombpotters.com), 8 School St. Fine contemporary American crafts, including colorful porcelain made in Maine, jewelry, blown glass, and iron.

✪ ✍ ⅋ **Mangy Moose** (207-865-6414 or 1-800-606-6517; themangymoose.com), 112 Main St. Moose, moose, and more moose. Susan Culkins has put together a fun store filled with clothing, books, art, and mounts—meaning stuffed moose, mountain lion, bobcat, caribou, and bear heads. A beautiful rustic quilt with machine-embroidered pinecones was reasonably priced, but the moose antler chandelier rings up at $6,000.

✍ **Island Treasure Toys** (207-865-7007; islandtreasuretoys.com), 20 Bow St. Locally owned, Island Treasure Toys is located on the second floor and holds baby gifts, and finely made dolls, trucks, puzzles, and more. It's the kind of toy shop that makes you want to be a kid.

Sherman's Book & Stationery Store (207-869-9000; shermans.com), 128 Main St. A branch of the Maine bookseller (also in Bar Harbor, Camden, and Boothbay Harbor), featuring Maine books and gifts, cards, and toys.

Simply Divine Brownies (207-865-3961; simplydivinebrownies.com), 7 Mill Street, Floor 2. Hand-cut and decorated brownies made from scratch. From gluten-free to cappuccino to chocolate pecan, these are the perfect hostess gift.

✳ Special Events

Mid-February: **L.L. Bean Kids Winter Fun Week**; **Winter Festivities and Flavors of Freeport** (freeportusa.com).

Early June: **L.L. Bean Paddlesport Weekend**.

Summer: Frequent musical and comedy performances in the **L.L. Bean Discovery Park**.

Labor Day weekend: **Sidewalk Sale**, with sales galore.

Fall: **Pettengill Farm Days**—living history demonstrations, horse-drawn wagon rides, inside/outside house tours, children's days, fresh-pressed cider. **Fall in the Village Art and Music Festival**.

November: **Girlfriends Getaway**. **Moonlight Madness—Black Friday**, with overnight shopping and activities.

December: **Sparkle Weekend** (*first full weekend*)—caroling, horse-drawn wagons, Santa arriving in a Maine yacht, musical entertainment, holiday readings, storytelling, complimentary refreshment and hot-cocoa stops, and **Tuba Concert**.

Midcoast and the Islands

3

BRUNSWICK AND THE HARPSWELLS

BATH AREA

WISCASSET AREA

BOOTHBAY HARBOR REGION

DAMARISCOTTA/NEWCASTLE/
WALDOBORO AND PEMAQUID AREA

ROCKLAND/THOMASTON AREA

MIDCOAST ISLANDS
Monhegan; The Fox Islands: Vinalhaven and North Haven; Matinicus

CAMDEN/ROCKPORT AREA
Isleboro

BELFAST, SEARSPORT,
AND STOCKTON SPRINGS

Christina Tree

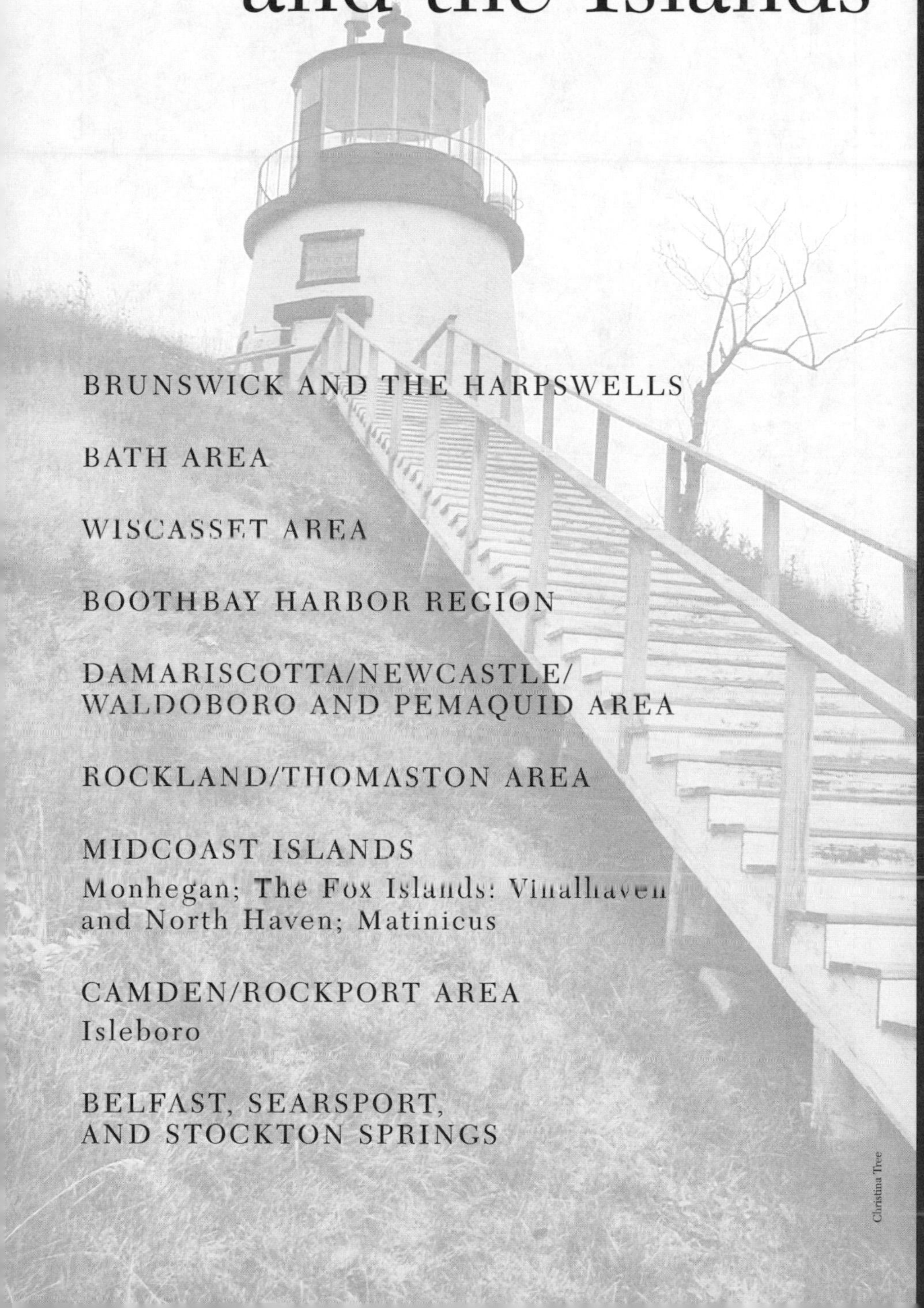

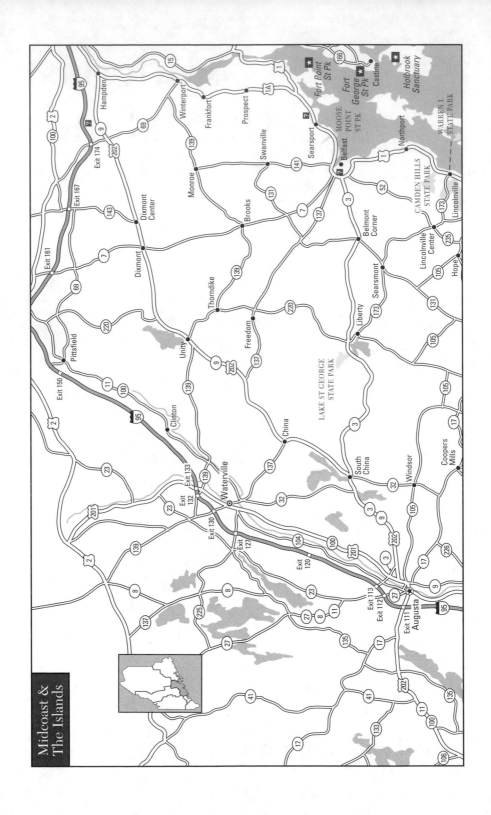

Midcoast &
The Islands

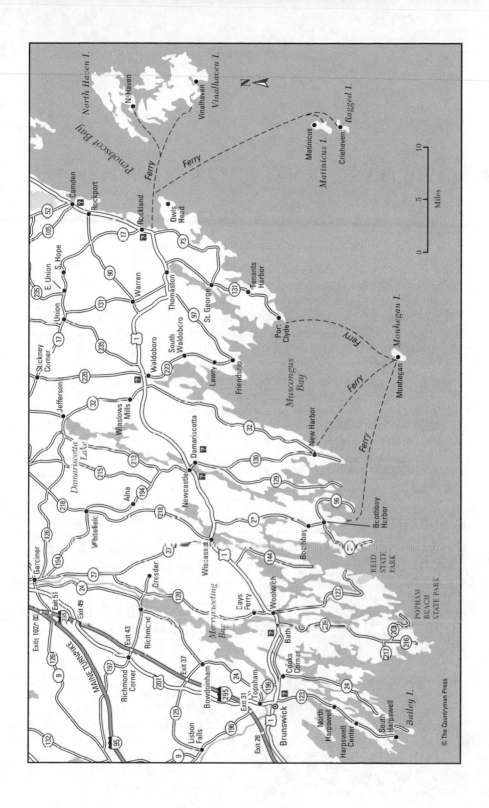

© The Countryman Press

MIDCOAST AND THE ISLANDS

Beyond Casco Bay the shape of Maine's coast changes—it shreds. In contrast with the sandy arc of shoreline stretching from Kittery to Cape Elizabeth, the coast between Brunswick and Rockland comprises a series of more than a dozen ragged peninsulas extending like so many fingers south from Rt. 1, creating countless big and small harbors, coves, and bays. Scientists tell us that these peninsulas and the offshore islands are mountains drowned by the melting of the same glaciers that sculpted the many shallow lakes and tidal rivers in this area.

The 100 miles of Rt. 1 between Brunswick and Bucksport are generally equated with Maine's Midcoast, and its depth is greater than the name suggests. It extends south of Rt. 1 to the tips of every peninsula, from Potts Point in South Harpswell and Land's End on Bailey Island; to Popham Beach on the Phippsburg Peninsula and Reid State Park in Georgetown; and on through the Boothbays to Pemaquid Point, Friendship, Port Clyde, and Spruce Head. Along with Rockland, Camden, Belfast, Searsport, and the islands of Monhegan, Vinalhaven, North Haven, and Islesboro, these communities have all catered to summer visitors since steamboats began off-loading them in the mid-19th century. Each peninsula differs in character from the next, but all offer their share of places to stay and eat in settings you rarely find along Rt. 1.

BELFAST WATERFRONT

Nancy English

North of Rt. 1, this Midcoast region also extends inland. Above Bath, for instance, five rivers meld to form Merrymeeting Bay, and north of Newcastle the tidal Damariscotta River widens into 13-mile-long Damariscotta Lake. This gently rolling, river- and lake-laced backcountry harbors a number of picturesque villages and reasonably priced lodging places.

We hope that no one who reads this book simply sticks to Rt. 1.

BRUNSWICK AND THE HARPSWELLS

What you see of Brunswick from Rt. 1 is an uninspired commercial strip, then a particularly annoying light at which the highway angles off to the left. Continue straight instead, up Pleasant St., and you are in for a pleasant surprise. Brunswick is Maine's premier college town, home to Bowdoin College with its venerable campus and museums, and to more than the usual quantity and quality of restaurants.

The Civil War began and ended in Brunswick, or so say local historians. A case can be made. Harriet Beecher Stowe was attending a service in Brunswick's First Parish Church when she is said to have had a vision of the death of Uncle Tom and hurried home to begin penning the book that has been credited with starting the war. Joshua Chamberlain, a longtime parishioner in this same church, was the Union general chosen for the honor of receiving the surrender of General John Gordon, commander of the Confederate infantry, at Appomattox.

Thanks largely to the Ken Burns PBS series *The Civil War*, and to the film *Gettysburg*, Joshua Chamberlain has been rediscovered. Annual admissions to his house have soared, fueling its restoration. This scholar-soldier-governor also presided as president of Bowdoin College, after serving four terms as governor of Maine.

Brunswick began as an Indian village named Pejepscot, at the base of the Androscoggin River's Great Falls. In 1688 this site became a Massachusetts outpost named Fort Andross, and subsequently it has been occupied by a series of mills. Its current population of 20,000 is a mix of Franco-Americans whose great-grandparents were recruited to work in mills, of Bowdoin-related families and retirees and professionals who commute to work in Portland or Augusta (Brunswick is halfway between).

Brunswick's Maine Street is the state's widest, laid out in 1717 with a grassy "mall"—a long strip of greenery that's the scene of concerts and of farmer's markets—at the upper end, near the neo-Gothic First Parish Church and the Bowdoin College campus.

A prestigious college, chartered in 1794, Bowdoin is the July and August venue for the Bowdoin International Music Festival, and for the Maine State Music Theatre. The recently expanded Bowdoin College Museum of Art and the Peary-

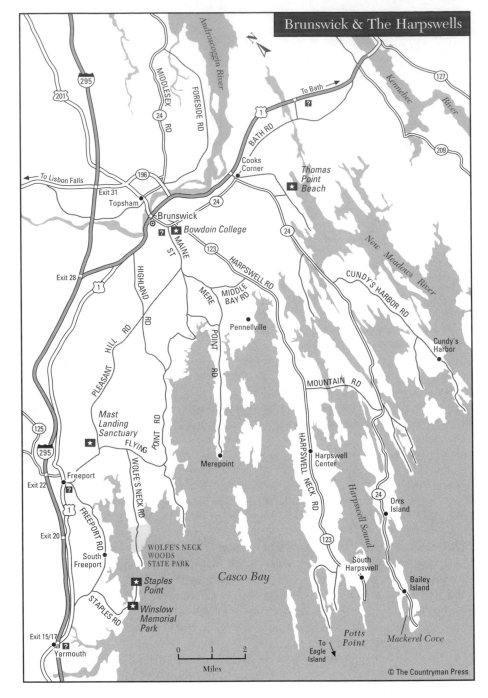

Brunswick & The Harpswells

© The Countryman Press

are also well worth a stop.

Brunswick isn't a tourist town. No kiosk proclaims the schedule of plays and concerts, because patrons know enough to read about them in the Thursday edition of the *Times Record*. Maine Street's shops, galleries, and restaurants cater to residents, and the Eveningstar Cinema and Frontier Café and Cinema screen art films for local consumption. Freeport's nearby outlet stores seem light-years away.

South of Brunswick one peninsula and several bridge-linked islands stretch seaward, defining the eastern rim of Casco Bay. Collectively they form the town of Harpswell—better known as "the Harpswells" because it includes so many coves, points, and islands (notably Orrs and Bailey)—which claims more shoreline than any other town in Maine. Widely known for their seafood restaurants, these peninsulas are surprisingly sleepy, salted with crafts, galleries, and some great places to stay. These are Maine's most convenient peninsulas, yet seem much farther Down East.

GUIDANCE Brunswick Downtown Association Visitor Center (207-721-0999; brunswickdownton.org), 16 Station Ave, just off upper Maine St. (look for the railroad tracks). Open daily year-round, 9:30–5 in summer, until 3 off-season. From Rt. 1 north turn right onto Maine St. and follow the "?" to the visitors center parking and restrooms.

Southern Midcoast Maine Chamber (1-877-715-8797; midcoastmaine.com) maintains an excellent website and publishes a free visitors guide.

Harpswell Business Association (harpswellmaine.org), P.O. Box 125, Harpswell 04079, publishes a useful map/guide pinpointing lodging and the many restaurants and galleries on the peninsulas south of Brunswick. Map/guides are available at the Black Sheep Wine Shop (see *Selective Shopping*).

GETTING THERE *By bus:* **Concord Coach** (concordcoachlines.com) offers 2½-hour service from Boston's Logan International Airport and South Station to the Brunswick Visitors Center.

By car: The I-295 (formerly I-95) exit for Brunswick and coastal points north is exit 28 to Rt. 1. Continue straight ahead up Pleasant St., which forms a T with Maine St. Turn right for the Bowdoin College campus and the Harpswells. For Topsham, the new exits are 31 northbound and 31A southbound.

By train: Plans call for Amtrak's *Downeaster* to extend service from Boston by fall 2012. In summer months you can currently come by rail from Rockland and points between. See the **Maine Eastern Railroad** under *To Do*.

By air and limo: **Mid-Coast Limo** (1-800-937-2424; midcoastlimo.com) makes runs by reservation from Portland International Jetport. **Mermaid Transportation** (1-800-696-2463; gomermaid.com) picks up at Boston's South Station and from Logan, Manchester, and Portland airports.

GETTING AROUND *Brunswick Explorer* (207-721-9600; brunswickexplorer.org) makes hourly stops throughout the area ($1 per trip/$2 per day). With the ease of public transport from Boston and Portland and choice of downtown lodging, dining, shopping, and attractions, this service further enhances Brunswick as a car-free destination.

WHEN TO COME Brunswick is a lively year-round community. If you want to visit all its museums and take advantage of summer music and theater, come in July or August—but never on Monday.

✳ To See

Bowdoin College (207-725-3100; bowdoin.edu), Brunswick. Tours begin at the admissions office. Visitors may park in lots off Bath Rd., College St., and Sills Dr. Maine was part of Massachusetts when the college was founded in 1794, and the school is named for a Massachusetts governor. Nathaniel Hawthorne and Henry Wadsworth Longfellow were classmates here in 1825; other notable graduates include U.S. president Franklin Pierce and North Pole explorer Robert Edwin Peary. Founded as a men's college, the school has been coed since 1971, and the current student body of 1,723 is 51 percent female. Bowdoin ranks among the nation's top both in status and in cost (the college provides substantial financial aid). It isn't necessary to take a tour to see its two outstanding museums.

& **Bowdoin College Museum of Art** (207-725-3275; bowdoin.edu/artmuseum), Park Row. Open year-round, Tue.–Sat. 10–5, Thu. till 8:30, Sun. 2–5. Closed Mon. and holidays. Free. A recent $20.8 million renovation has significantly increased gallery space. The entrance to this 1894 copper-domed building designed by McKim, Mead & White is now through a discrete glass pavilion facing the street. There are seven galleries and a rotunda with murals by Abbott Thayer, Kenyon Cox, and John LaFarge. Current collections include more than 14,000 objects ranging from Assyrian bas-reliefs and Far Eastern works, to American portraits by Gilbert Charles Stuart and Thomas Eakins, to Maine-based works by Winslow Homer, Rockwell Kent, John Sloan, and Andrew Wyeth. Check the website for current exhibits, which include contemporary artists.

For the college's **Peary-MacMillan Arctic Museum**, see the Peary sidebar.

Pejepscot Historical Society Museums (207-729-6606). Founded in 1888 and named for an ancient Indian settlement, this is one of Maine's oldest historical societies. It maintains three downtown Brunswick museums. For the first—the Joshua L. Chamberlain Museum—see the sidebar. The **Pejepscot Historical Society Museum**, 159 Park Row (Tue.–Fri. 10–5; free), is a massive, cupola'd mansion that displays changing exhibits on the history of Brunswick, Topsham, and Harpswell. The adjoining **Skolfield-Whittier House** is open seasonally for tours Thu.–Sat. 11 and 2. Its high-Victorian drawing room is hung with crystal chandeliers and heavy velvet drapes, furnished in wicker and brocade, and filled with the photos, books, and paintings of three generations. A combination ticket for all three museums is available. Inquire about walking tours.

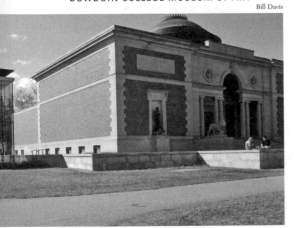

BOWDOIN COLLEGE MUSEUM OF ART

Bill Davis

CRIBSTONE BRIDGE

The First Parish Church (UCC) (207-729-7331), Maine St. at Bath Rd., Brunswick. Open for noon-time summer organ concerts and tours July–mid-Aug., Tue. 12:10–12:50; for Sunday services; and by chance. This graceful neo-Gothic building was designed in the 1840s by Richard Upjohn, architect of New York City's Trinity Church. A dramatic departure from its Puritan predecessors, it's open-beamed, is mildly cruciform in shape, and has deeply colored stained-glass windows. The large sanctuary window was donated by Joshua Chamberlain, one of the first people to be married here. The Hutchings-Plastid tracker organ was installed in 1883.

SCENIC DRIVE A tour of the Harpswells, including Orrs and Bailey Islands. Allow a day for this rewarding peninsula prowl. From Brunswick, follow Rt. 123 south past Bowdoin College 9 miles to the picturesque village of Harpswell Center. The white-clapboard Elijah Kellogg Church faces the matching Harpswell Town Meeting House, built in 1757. The church is named for a former minister who was a prominent 19th-century children's book author. Continue south through West Harpswell to Potts Point, where multicolored 19th-century summer cottages cluster on the rocks like a flock of exotic birds that have wandered in among the gulls.

Retrace your way up Rt. 123, and 2 miles north of the church turn right onto Mountain Rd., leading to busier Rt. 24 on Great (also known as Sebascodegan) Island. Drive south along **Orrs Island** across the only remaining cribstone bridge in the world, a National Historic Civil Engineering Landmark. (Its granite blocks are laid in honeycomb fashion—without cement—to allow tidal flows.) This bridge

JOSHUA LAWRENCE CHAMBERLAIN

Joshua Lawrence Chamberlain (1828–1914) was Maine's greatest Civil War hero, a college professor who became one of the most remarkable soldiers in American history.

Pejepscot Historical Society

JOSHUA LAWRENCE CHAMBERLAIN

An outstanding scholar—he had a graduate degree in theology and was teaching rhetoric and languages (he spoke or could read eight) at his alma mater, Bowdoin College, when the war began— Chamberlain proved to be an even better soldier. He fought in some of the bloodiest battles of the war, had horses shot out from under him five times, and was wounded six times, once so severely that he was given up for dead and his obituary appeared in Maine newspapers.

Of all his military achievements Chamberlain is best remembered for his valor and leadership on the second day of the Battle of Gettysburg, July 2, 1863. A lieutenant colonel commanding an inexperienced and understrength regiment, the 20th Maine Volunteer Infantry, he defended Little Round Top, a key position on the extreme left of the Union line. Repeatedly attacked by a much larger Confederate force, he refused to retreat; when defeat seemed imminent—there was no more ammunition and most of his men were dead or wounded—he ordered an unorthodox bayonet charge that routed the Confederates.

Had the southerners taken Little Round Top they could have outflanked the Union army and won the battle—and with it, possibly, the war. Eventually, more than 30 years later, Chamberlain received the nation's highest military award, the Medal of Honor, for his "daring heroism and great tenacity" at Gettysburg.

He ended the war a major general and was chosen by General Ulysses S. Grant to accept the surrender of the Confederate Army of Northern Virginia following General Robert E. Lee's capitulation at Appomattox. As the Confederate regiments marched into the Union camp to lay down their arms, Chamberlain had his troops salute them, a gesture of respect that infuriated some northerners but helped reconcile many southerners to their defeat.

After the war Chamberlain served four one-year terms as governor of Maine. From 1871 to 1883 he was president of Bowdoin College, where he introduced science courses to modernize the curriculum and tried unsuccessfully to make military training compulsory. (Students rioted in protest.) He died in 1914, "of his wounds," it was said. Late in life he wrote *The Passing of the Armies*, an account of the final campaign of the Union's Army of the Potomac from the point of view of its Fifth Corps, which he commanded. Filled with vivid descriptive passages, the book is still in print.

A household name in his day, Chamberlain's memory eventually faded. That began changing in 1975 with the publication of Michael Shaara's best-selling and Pulitzer Prize–winning novel about the Battle of Gettysburg, *Killer Angels*, in which Chamberlain was a major protagonist. In 1990 the story of his desperate defense of Little Round Top was a highlight of the acclaimed PBS television series *The Civil War*. A few years later actor Jeff Daniels convincingly portrayed Chamberlain, drooping handlebar mustache and all, in *Gettysburg*, the epic film based on Shaara's novel. Daniels played Chamberlain again in a 2003 Civil War movie, *Gods and Generals*.

The Pejepscot Historical Society maintains Chamberlain's old home at 226 Main St., across from the Bowdoin campus. On display are Chamberlain's uniforms, medals, sword, bullet-dented boots, and the ornate chair he used as governor and college president. Note the statue depicting him as a major general, set in the small park beside the house. Seemingly as tenacious and enduring after death as he was in battle, Chamberlain appears to have now finally won from posterity the full recognition he deserves. The Chamberlain House is open late May–Columbus Day, Tue.–Sat. 10–4. Guided tours are on the hour; the last begins at 3. $5 adults, $2.50 children.

JOSHUA LAWRENCE CHAMBERLAIN HOUSE AND MUSEUM

Pejepscot Historical Society

⚓ ADMIRAL ROBERT EDWIN PEARY JR.

In the 1890s the North Pole was the equivalent of the moon in the 1960s. The race was on among nations to be the first to reach it. On April 6, 1909, Robert E. Peary (1856–1920) was that man. Peary was a naval engineer who sailed south to help survey a possible Nicaraguan canal route in 1880s but became obsessed with the Far North. On his own time and financing, he began leading Greenland-based expeditions in 1886. His wife, Josephine, came along twice, and their daughter Marie Ahnighto, widely celebrated as "Snow Baby," was born on the second trip. Working with native Inuit and their dog teams, Peary pushed steadily north in subsequent expeditions. He designed the *Roosevelt*, a steam and sail vessel with a shallow draft, to navigate among icebergs, and on its second voyage it is said to have sailed to within 150 miles of the North Pole. The remaining distance was cov-

photograph by Sears/The Arctic Museum, Bowdoin College

ADMIRAL ROBERT E. PEARY GREETS THE CROWDS IN NOVA SCOTIA ON HIS RETURN FROM THE NORTH POLE

ered on sled and foot during the following spring, when light was sufficient but snowfields still solid enough to travel. Dismissing their support team, Peary with his African American assistant Matthew Henson and four Inuit finally reached the geographic pole, taking measurements and photographs to document the feat. Controversy continues to dog the accuracy of their final position, but this was unquestionably a saga that entranced the world.

That September it was on Eagle Island that Josephine Peary finally received the news of her husband's triumph. Peary had bought the 17-acre Casco Bay island soon after graduating from Bowdoin because its rocky headland resembles the prow of a ship. The shingled summer home he built here is positioned atop this bluff, facing northeast. Peary designed the three-sided living room hearth, made from island stones and Arctic quartz crystals, and stuffed many of the birds on the mantel. The player piano is one octave short because it had to fit aboard the *Roosevelt*.

The **Eagle Island State Historic Site** (207-624-6080; pearyeagleisland.org) is open mid-June–Labor Day, 10–sunset. The house offers a rare glimpse into era as well as the life of an unusual man and his family. Bedrooms appear as though someone has just stepped out for a walk, and the dining room is strewn with photos of men and dogs battling ice and snow. A nature path circles the island, passing pine trees filled with seagulls (trails open July 15, after bird nesting season). There are also picnic sites and a small beach. The island is accessible from South Freeport with Captain Thomas Ring via **Atlantic Seal Cruises** (207-865-6112), from Portland's Long Wharf via **Eagle Island Tours** (207-774-6498; eagleislandtours), from Card Cove in Harpswell via **Captain's Watch Sail Charters** (207-725-0969), and from Bailey Island with **Sea Escape Charters** (207-833-5531). There are guest buoys and a dock; this is a popular destination for rental and private boats. There is a nominal landing and admission charge.

In Brunswick on the Bowdoin College campus look for Hubbard Hall, home to the **Peary-MacMillan Arctic Museum** (207-725-3416), open year-round, Tue.–Sat. 10–5, Sun. 2–5; closed Mon. and holidays. Free. A colorful, well-displayed collection of clothing, trophy walruses and seals, polar bears and caribou, and other mementos showcases expeditions to the North Pole by both Robert Peary and Donald Baxter MacMillan (class of 1898), who assisted Peary on his 1909 expedition and went on to dedicate his life to exploring Arctic waters and terrain. Displays include an interactive touch screen, photo blowups, and artifacts to tell the story.

EAGLE ISLAND STATE HISTORICAL SITE

Christina Tree

brings you to **Bailey Island**, with its restaurants, lodging places, picturesque **Mackerel Cove**, and rocky **Land's End**, with a statue honoring all Maine fishermen. To find the **Giant's Staircase** (see *Walks*), turn off Rt. 24 at Washington Ave. and park at the Episcopal chapel Otherwise continue on Rt. 24 and take Cundy's Harbor Rd. 4.3 miles to another picturesque fishing harbor with a couple of good little restaurants.

✳ To Do

BICYCLING The **Androscoggin River Bicycle Path**, a 2.6-mile, 14-foot-wide paved bicycle/pedestrian trail, begins at Lower Water St. in Brunswick and runs along the river to Grover Lane in Cooks Corner. It connects with Topsham along the way via a bicycle lane on the new Merrymeeting Bridge.

BOAT EXCURSIONS Casco Bay Lines (207-774-7871) offers a daily seasonal excursion from Cook's Lobster House on Bailey Island. It takes an hour and 45 minutes to circle around Eagle Island and through this northern end of Casco Bay.

Captain's Watch Sail Charters (207-725-0969). From Card Cove (off Rt. 24) in Harpswell, Captain Ken Brigham offers morning and full-day sails as well as overnight charters on his *Symbion II*, a 38-foot Hunter sailboat. This is a great way to visit Eagle, sailing down along Orrs and Bailey Islands and out into Casco Bay.

Sea Escape Charters (207-833-5531; seaescapecottages.com) offers Bailey Island–based fishing charters for mackerel & stripers in Casco Bay, also scenic cruises aboard the 35-foot ketch *Tevake*.

GOLF Brunswick Golf Club (207-725-8224), River Rd., Brunswick. Incorporated in 1888, an 18-hole course known for its beauty and challenging nature. Snack bar, lounge, and cart rentals.

Mere Creek Golf Club (207-721-9995) is a nine-hole course at the Brunswick Naval Station open to the public.

SEA KAYAKING H₂Outfitters (207-833-5257; h2outfitters.com). Based just north of the cribstone bridge on Orrs Island, this is one of Maine's oldest kayaking outfitters. No rentals. Lessons for all abilities, from beginners to instructor certification; guided day trips and overnight excursions are also offered.

Seaspray Kayaking (207-443-3646; seaspraykayaking.com), with a base on the New Meadows River in Brunswick, offers rentals and a variety of guided trips and rentals.

✳ Green Space

BEACHES AND SWIMMING HOLES ✍ **White's Beach** (207-729-0415), Durham Rd., Brunswick. Open mid-May–mid-Oct. A pond in a former gravel pit (water no deeper than 9 feet). Facilities include a small slide for children. Sandy beach, lifeguards, picnic tables, grills, and a snack bar. Inquire about campsites.

✍ **Thomas Point Beach** (207-725-6009), off Thomas Point Rd., marked from Rt. 24, Cooks Corner. Open Memorial Day–Labor Day, 9 AM–sunset. Admission fee. The beach is part of an 85-acre private preserve on tidal water overlooking the New Meadows River and Thomas Bay. It includes groves for picnicking (more

RAILROAD EXCURSION

✄ **The Maine Eastern Railroad** (1-866-637-2457; maineeasternrailroad.com) runs Fri. and Sat. Memorial Day weekend through late June, then Wed.–Sun. through mid-Oct., plus special off-season runs. The best excursion train in New England! The 54-mile run from Brunswick to Rockland—with stops in Bath and Wiscasset—takes just over two hours, traveling along the coast in plush, streamlined 1940s and '50s coaches and dining car, pulled by a 1950s diesel electric engine. Check the website for current schedule and fares. At this writing you can depart Brunswick at 10:20 AM and arrive in Rockland at 12:25 PM. That gives you plenty of time of see that community's museums before returning at 6:30. Alternatively, one family member can drive and meet the train at any of its stops. Note that it's now once more almost possible to travel by train from Washington, DC, to Brunswick. Amtrak's Downeaster now comes as far as Portland, 30 miles south of Brunswick. Plans call for that gap to be closed by late 2012.

MAINE EASTERN RAILROAD

than 500 picnic tables plus a main lodge snack bar, playground, and arcade) and 75 tent and RV sites. It's the scene of a series of August events, including the Maine Highland Games and Bluegrass Festival.

✄ **Coffin Pond** (207-725-6656), River Rd., Brunswick. Open mid-June–Labor Day 10–7. Admission fee. A strip of sandy beach surrounding a circular, spring-fed pond. Facilities include a 55-foot-long waterslide, a playground, and changing rooms maintained by the town.

WALKS Giant's Staircase, Bailey Island. Turn off Rt. 24 at Washington Ave., park at the Episcopal church, and walk down to Ocean St.; follow the path along the water and follow the small sign to the well-named "stairs."

Brunswick Topsham Swinging Bridge. This restored footbridge spans the Androscoggin River, and was originally built in 1892 by John A. Roebling Sons Co., the firm that built the Brooklyn Bridge, for workers walking to the Cabot Mill.

Brunswick-Topsham Land Trust (207-729-7694; btlt.org), 108 Maine St., Brunswick. The land trust has preserved more than 700 acres in the area. Pick up a map and guides to the nature loops at Skolfield Nature Preserve, Rt. 123, Brunswick (4 miles or so south of town), adjoining an ancient Indian portage between Middle Bay and Harpswell Cove; to the Bradley Pond Farm Preserve in Topsham, a 2.5-mile trail system in a 162-acre preserve; and to Crystal Spring Farm Trail, a 2.5-mile trail on the 160-acre farm on Pleasant Hill Rd. in Brunswick.

Town of Harpswell Walking Trails. By far the most famous of these leads to the **Giant Stairs** (see above), but there are half a dozen more options. Stop by the town offices on Mountain Rd. (between Rts. 24 and 123) and pick up a trail map to seven local properties with walking trails. Check out the **Cliff Trail**, which begins around back. This 2.3-mile loop features a shore walk along tidal Strawberry Creek, two "fairy house" zones, and a view from 150-foot cliffs over Long Reach.

Swan Island (207-547-5322; mefishwildlife.com). At the head of Merrymeeting Bay, the island is 4 miles long and less than a mile wide, a haven for wood ducks, mergansers, bald eagles, wild turkeys, and more. It was the site of an Indian village, and in 1614 Captain John Smith visited here. It's open by self-access year-round; limited transport and tours are offered seasonally by reservation. No pets allowed. Managed by the Maine Department of Inland Fisheries and Wildlife, which requires reservations for overnight camping. The landing is in Richmond Village.

✴ Lodging

In and around Brunswick

✪ 🐾 (📶) **Middle Bay Farm Bed & Breakfast** (207-373-1375 or 1-800-299-4914; middlebayfarm.com), 287 Pennellville Rd., Brunswick 04011. Open year-round, this handsome clapboard farmhouse dates to the 1830s and overlooks a tidal cove. Sited at the end of a country road, it's minutes from downtown Brunswick and also from seafood restaurants in the Harpswells. In the early 1900s it was a summer boardinghouse (Helen Keller is said to have stayed here), but it had stood empty for 10 years when the Truesdells bought and then devoted two years to renovating it. Phyllis Truesdell is a warm and skilled hostess who makes guests feel invited. There's a living room with a baby grand, a gracious dining room, and a big country kitchen. The four spacious guest rooms are decorated with many bright and tasteful touches; our current favorite is the Star Room with its stenciled floor and writing desk. All have private full

Christina Tree

MIDDLE BAY FARM BED & BREAKFAST

bath, water view, sitting area, and cable TV/VCR hidden in an armoire. There's also a porch from which to survey lawn, sky, and water. The neighboring Sail Loft Cottage houses two rustic suites, each with a living area, cooking facility, and two small bedrooms. The 5 landscaped acres are on a rise above Middle Bay tidal cove; kayaks and canoes are available. $170–190 in-season, $160–175 off-season, includes a full breakfast.

✪ ✐ ♿ (ᵛᵖ) **Brunswick Inn** (207-729-4914 or 1-800-299-4914; thebrunswick inn.com), 165 Park Row, Brunswick 04011. This 1840s Greek Revival home with long windows and a pillared porch offers the charm of a gracious country inn but within easy walking distance of both the Bowdoin campus and downtown restaurants. It's buffered from traffic by the town's wide green mall. Innkeeper Eileen Horner has hung common spaces and guest rooms with well-chosen art by local artists (most of it for sale), added a flowery patio, and decorated the double parlors invitingly. On cool days wood fires glow in the parlors, the breakfast room, and the Great Room

at the rear of the house, a space with comfortable seating and a full-service bar (open to the public Tue.–Sat. evenings). The 15 guest rooms are divided among the original house, a contemporary Carriage House with its own common space, and a self-contained "Garden Cottage." Each room is equipped with phone, desk, and clock-radio; TV on request. $145–260 includes a full breakfast.

BRUNSWICK INN

Gary Pennington

♂ & (ɣ) **The Inn at Brunswick Station** (207-837-6565; theinnatbrunswick station.com), 4 Noble St., Brunswick 04011. Opened in 2011, steps from the Bowdoin campus and the new station complex, this is a three-floor, 48-room, four-suite facility obviously geared to Bowdoin parents, alums, and hopefuls. Rooms are comfortably, sleekly furnished, most with two queens. Decor is notably masculine, featuring earth colors and pictures of polar bears (the college mascot). The Tavern serves all meals. Rooms run $159–300; breakfast is $15.

♂ & (ɣ) **Captain Daniel Stone Inn** (207-373-1824 or 1-877-373-2374; captaindanielstoneinn.com), 10 Water St., Brunswick 04011. Totally renovated in 2009, the inn is linked to a Federal-era mansion (as yet unrestored) and has a matching facade. There are 24 elevator-accessed guest rooms and suites—some with two double beds, others with queens or kings, several with whirlpool baths, all furnished in reproduction antiques. Amenities include cable TV, phone, and mini fridges. A fitness center and a hot tub room with an adjoining sauna are also available to guests, and a full-service spa is planned. The inn's restaurant, **No. 10 Water**, is open to the public for dinner. It's an ambitiously large space with a varied menu—from tapas and tavern fare to entrées such as apple and cranberry-stuffed game hen ($23–28). Room rates run $169–209 per couple, continental breakfast included. Handy to the Androscoggin River Recreation Path (a great place to walk and jog), it's minutes by car from downtown but not an easy walk.

(ɣ) **The Black Lantern** (207-725-4165 or 1-888-306-4165; blacklanternbandb .com), 57 Elm St., Topsham 04086. Open year-round. Longtime local B&B owners Tom and Judy Connelie offer comfortable rooms, a view of the Androscoggin River and direct access to the bike path (also good for jogging) along its banks, as well as a dock with good access for kayakers. Just across the river from downtown Brunswick, this hospitable old house has three cheerful guest rooms, all with private bath, two with river views, and the third with a gas fireplace. $110–125, $95–100 off-season, includes a full breakfast. Quilters are particularly welcome.

In Harpswell

❂ ☀ (ɣ) **Harpswell Inn** (207-833-5509 or 1-800-843-5509; harpswellinn .com), 108 Lookout Point Rd., Harpswell 04079. Open year-round. Innkeepers Richard and Anne Mosley have deep ties to Harpswell and a keen interest in its history, in which their gracious three-story white-clapboard B&B has played a significant part. It was built as the cookhouse for an adjacent boatyard (there's still a bell you can ring from the stairwell), and subsequently became the Lookout Point House, one of no less than 52 summer hotels and boardinghouses to be found in Harpswell during the steamboating era. The nine guest rooms vary widely and come with and without hearth, deck, and water views; there are also three suites with kitchens. The large living room has a massive stone fireplace, ample seating, and plenty to read. Lawns slope to the shore with plenty of comfortable spots from which to view Middle Bay. Allen's, one of the area's best sources for lobster and clams (see *Where to Eat*), is just down at the end of the road. In high season $120–170 for rooms, $235–259 for suites, with a very full breakfast, including Anne's blueberry cake if you're lucky. Richard, a professional chef, caters for groups of 50 inside and

150 with an outdoor tent. Pets are accepted in four cottages, available for weekly rental. Many off-season packages.

✪ ☼ The Captain's Watch B&B (207-725-0979), 926 Cundy's Harbor Rd. and Pinkham Point Rd., Harpswell 04079. Open most of the year. Donna Dillman and Ken Brigham offer four spacious guest rooms with water views in a former Civil War–era inn with an octagonal cupola, set on a 250-foot-high bluff. Upstairs rooms are handsome, furnished with antiques (two share access to the cupola); a first-floor barnboard-sided room with a king bed and picture window is equally attractive. Full breakfasts are served in the paneled dining room or, weather permitting, on the deck. Walk down to the picturesque, working harbor. There is also easy access to Captain Ken's splendid daysails aboard the 38-foot *Symbion II* (see *Boat Excursions*), moored by a contemporary house that the couple also rent on a weekly basis on nearby Card Cove.

The Log Cabin, An Island Inn (207-833-5546; logcabin-maine.com), Rt. 24, Bailey Island 04003. Open Apr.–Oct. Built decades ago as a lavish

DRIFTWOOD INN

Christina Tree

log summer home with a huge hearth (a moose head, of course, hangs above), this was for many years a popular restaurant, but the owners refitted it to offer nine rooms—four with kitchen, two with hot tub, all with private bath, fridge, coffee machine, and waterside deck—and access to the heated swimming pool. Breakfast is included for high-season rates of $179–299; $329 for the Harpswell Room, really a fully equipped cottage. Dinner is still served, but the restaurant's no longer open to the public (entrées $17.95–32.95).

☼ ☼ ☼ ((•)) Driftwood Inn and Cottages (207-833-5461; thedriftwoodinnmaine.com), 81 Washington Ave., Bailey Island 04003. Open late May to mid-Oct.; the dining room (which is open to the public) is open June–Labor Day. Location, location! Sited on a rocky point within earshot of a foghorn and walking distance of the Giant's Staircase, Driftwood is classically "Maine rustic." This term was once generally understood to mean naturally air-conditioned, heated by fireplaces (there are also gas stoves in the common rooms), with shared baths (some guest rooms now feature private), and this 1905 complex is one of the last of its breed along Maine's coast. Breakfast and a full-course dinner (BYOB) are served in a classic, pine-walled dining room; dinner is $16–30 depending on the entrée, and choices vary with the night (Sunday is always turkey). The child's menu is $8. The cottages contain a total of 16 doubles (some now have queen beds) and eight singles (nine with half-bath); there are also six housekeeping cottages. We recommend Rooms 6 and 7 in Driftwood, pine-walled with a firm queen bed, a half-bath, and windows on the water. There is a small saltwater swimming pool set in the rocks. Innkeeper David Conrad's family has owned Driftwood for more than 60 years. $80–145 per couple (no minimum stay). Housekeeping cottages, available by the week, are $675–720. On a per-diem basis, breakfast is $7.25. Inquire about weekly rates. No credit cards. Pets are accepted in the cottages ($25 fee).

♂ ✦ **Bailey Island Motel** (207-833-2886; baileyislandmotel.com), Rt. 24, Bailey Island 04003. Open mid-May–mid-Oct. Located just over the cribstone bridge. A real find, an attractive two-story gray-shingled building on the water's edge, offering water views and landscaped lawns with rocks and a dock to walk out on. Kudos to owner Chip Black. The 11 rooms are fresh, clean, and comfortable, with cross-ventilation from windows front and back, also cable TV. No smoking. Morning coffee and muffins are included in $100–145. Guests are welcome to tie their boat up to the dock or a mooring or push off in their kayaks. Walk next door to lunch or dinner at Morse's Cribstone Grill or across the way to Cook's Lobster House.

COTTAGES The Southern Midcoast Maine Chamber (see *Guidance*) lists cottage rentals on Orrs and Bailey Islands.

✴ Where to Eat

DINING OUT

In Brunswick
Note: This is a college town, and the quality of the food is higher than prices imply.

✪ **Clementine Restaurant** (207-721-9800; clementinemaine.com), 44 Maine St. Reserve. Experienced chefs Dana and Nancy Robicheaw offer a sophisticated menu, white-tablecloth ambience, and well-selected wine list. The walls are hung with local art, and the small bar at the back of the room invites you to sample a glass of wine and the house-made country pâté. Entrées might include Provençal seafood stew or salmon in bric pastry; desserts, a delicately balanced lavender flan with orange syrup and almond praline. Food is beautifully plated. Entrées $19–26; a three-course tasting menu is $27.

✪ **Henry & Marty** (207-721-9141; henryandmarty.com), 61 Maine St. Open for dinner Tue.–Sun. Reservations recommended. Filling two warmly colored and decorated storefronts, chef Aaron Park offers a welcoming ambience, whether you come for a glass of wine and thin-crust pizza or paella Valencia ($14–26). This is a long-established favorite with a full bar that's an oasis for single diners.

✪ **Trattoria Athena** (207-721-0700), 25 Mill St. Open for dinner Tue.–Sat. 5–9, Sun. 3–7, family-style. Lunch Tue.–Sat. in summer. Seating just 30 (reservations are a must), this is as genuine as a trattoria can be in Maine, locally sourced as much as possible with from-scratch pastas. The Italian and Greek menu includes stuffed grape leave and carpaccio as well as mussels of the day. Entrées range from moussaka to a grilled whole stuffed Mediterranean sea bass served with herbed couscous, saltimbocca alla Romana, and braised lamb ($18–24). Mill St. parallels and is accessible from Rt. 1 north.

Bacari Bistro (207-725-2600; bacaribistro.com), 212 Maine St. Open for dinner Tue.–Sat. A casual, frequently packed bistro at the upper end of Maine St. The menu includes a choice of "small plates" like lobster risotto with asparagus ($10), and "featured tastings" such as scallops pan-seared with an apple brandy cream sauce ($17) or panko-encrusted eggplant blended with assorted cheeses ($14). Full bar.

❂ 🖤 The Great Impasta (207-729-5858), 42 Maine St. Open daily (except Sun.) for lunch and dinner. A great stop even if you're simply traveling up or down Rt. 1, but arrive early to get a booth (plaques honor booth regulars). Specialties include pasta dishes like seafood lasagna; try the butternut-squash-stuffed ravioli in a pine nut, raisin, and pesto sauce. Wine and beer served. Dinner entrées $13.50–18.50.

❂ El Camino (207-725-8228), 15 Cushing St. Open for dinner Tue.–Sat. An unpromising exterior disguises a hip, funky interior, the setting for highly inventive Mexican food, with a dedication to using chemical-free seafood and meats as well as organic—local wherever possible—produce. Vegans as well as vegetarians have options, and everything is spicy and good. The chips are warm, the selection of beers large, and the margaritas famous. Entrées $12.50–19.

Back Street Bistro (207-725-4060; backstreetbistro.net), 11 Town Place. Open nightly. Just off Maine St. by the fire station. A dependable local favorite with a menu that changes weekly. The fish and shellfish gumbo varies nightly, but always comes with a deeply flavored broth. Entrées $16–29. Full bar.

EATING OUT

In and near Brunswick
❂ 🖤 ♪ Frontier Café & Cinema Gallery (207-725-5222; explore frontier.com), 14 Maine St. (Fort Andross). Open Mon.–Thu. 9–9, Fri. 9–10, Sat. 11–10. A theater, gallery, and café is a winning combination that's difficult to pigeonhole. In the café huge windows along two walls overlook the Androscoggin River, its dam, and the picturesque Bowdoin Mill in Topsham. Tables by these windows maximize light and views, which frequently include ospreys, sometimes eagles and peregrine falcons. There are coffees and teas, wine, and beer; a menu of soups and salads, sandwiches and panini, changes weekly. There are reasonably priced cheeses and "marketplates" representing different parts of the world. Check the website for wine tastings and other special events. Owner Michael "Gil" Gilroy, who traveled the world for his previous work, has used largely salvaged and recycled materials to turn this raw factory space into his vision of a cultural crossroads. Also see *Entertainment*. Parking is less complicated than it looks. Evenings are okay in the big lot up front; also look for the rear entrance lot just before the bridge.

❂ Scarlet Begonias (207-721-0403), 16 Station Ave. Open Mon.–Sat. For lunch- dinner. . The first and still one of the most popular Brunswick bistros, now in Brunswick Station. Doug and Colleen Lavallee serve up some great sandwiches (we recommend the turkey spinach with mozzarella and basil mayo, grilled on sourdough bread) and chunky, fresh-herbed pastas like rose

FRONTIER CAFÉ

Christina Tree

LOBSTER

Note: The peninsulas stretching south from Brunswick into Casco Bay have been a destination for lobster lovers since steamboatin' days. All are accessible by boat. Cook's Lobster House is a seasonal noon stop for Casco Bay Liners out of Portland.

✍ **Dolphin Marina & Restaurant** (207-833-6000; dolphinchowderhouse.com), 515 Basin Point Rd., South Harpswell (marked from Rt. 123, it's 2.5 miles; also accessible by water). Open daily May 1–Nov. 1 for lunch and dinner. In 2011 Chris Saxton, grandson of the couple who opened a coffee shop/chowder house in this boatyard in 1966, opened an entirely new restaurant up the road at the very tip of Basin Point. Twice as large as the old facility, this nicely designed building maximizes sweeping views of Casco Bay. The draw remains the same lobster stew, fish chowder, lobster and crab rolls, and broiled seafood that have been luring patrons nightly from Brunswick (15 miles) and beyond. All dinners continue to include a blueberry muffin. Nightly specials. Fully licensed. Dinner entrées $9.95–$24.95.

Morse's Cribstone Grill (207833-7775), Rt. 24 at the Cribstone Bridge, Bailey Island. Cathy and Sheldon Morse are local lobster dealers and lobster pound managers who have moved like horseshoe crabs from seasonal site to site in recent years, ever since the popular lobster shack at their own lobster pier was closed due to zoning. Their current home in another former restaurant by the Cribstone Bridge is a winner—a glass-walled tavern right on the water. How can you beat fresh lobster meat cooked and picked in-house, mixed with just the right amount of mayonnaise and served in a buttered and grilled roll (from $9.99)—while watching cormorants and gulls on an island just offshore? Nothing fancy here, just steamers, lobster, broiled and fried scallops, haddock, chowders, and stews.

✍ **Cook's Lobster House** (207-833-2818), Bailey Island. Open year-round, 11:30–10. The area's most famous and heavily touristed landmark lobster barn of a place right on the water (beyond the parking lots) with knotty-pine walls, booths, and a classic Maine seafood menu and seasonal outdoor dining. Founded in 1955 and little changed since, it overlooks the Cribstone Bridge. If there's a line and you don't mind settling for light fare, head for the deck where there's open seating. In July and August try to get here before noon, when the Casco Bay liner arrives with its load of day-trippers. Chowders and fried seafood are reasonably priced but we find their lobster prices high: $34.95 for a 1-pound lobster dinner, $42.95 for a shore dinner.

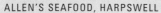 **Allen's Seafood & Takeout** (207-833-2828), 119 Lookout Point Rd., Harpswell. Open Apr.–Oct, Tue.–Sun. 11–7. This longtime seafood wholesaler has added a trailer kitchen with a take-out menu and picnic benches to take advantage of the glorious view. The steamed clams are locally picked and processed on the spot, served with broth and butter. The lobster couldn't be fresher. There are plenty of fried seafood options, but this is the place for lobster. Order from the stand and eat at picnic tables, some with umbrellas. BYOB.

 Holbrooks (207-729-9050), Cundy's Harbor. Open Memorial Day–mid June on weekends, then daily until Labor Day, 11–8. A nicely sited lobster landmark with its harbor view, currently operated by the Morse family. Tables are topped with umbrellas and banked in flowers, and lobster is available right off the boat in all the usual ways. BYOB.

Note: Inquire about **Estes Lobster House** near Potts Point, Harpswell. This venerable landmark closed early in the 2011 season and its future seemed uncertain, but it's a great spot and hopefully will survive.

ALLEN'S SEAFOOD, HARPSWELL   Christina Tree

begonia, also fabulous pizzas and pasta. Wine and beer served.

⌐ **Sea Dog Brewing** (207-725-0162; seadogbrewing.com), Great Mill Island, 1 Main St., Topsham. Open daily 11:30–1 AM. Music Thu.–Sat. Housed in a picturesque (former) paper mill, vintage 1868. A big, friendly brewpub with seasonal outdoor dining overlooking the churning Androscoggin. This is a good bet for families. Specialties include fried scallops, grilled or teriyaki sirloin, potato-crusted haddock, and cioppino (seafood stew). The wide choice of beers includes house ales.

⌐ **Joshua's Restaurant & Tavern** (207-725-7981), 121 Maine St. Open 11:30 AM–11 PM. Named for General Joshua Chamberlain, reliably good for burgers and basics, including a first-rate crab salad. Don't be put off by the downstairs pub; head upstairs for the deck or dining room. It's a big menu—plenty of fried and broiled fish, soups, stews, and a wide choice of beers.

Bangkok Garden Restaurant (207-725-9708), 14 Maine St. (Fort Andross). Open daily for lunch and dinner, Sun. 4–9. This attractive restaurant gets good reviews for classic dishes like green curry and pad Thai.

✪ ⌐ **Wild Oats Bakery and Café** (207-725-6287), Tontine Mall, 149 Maine St. Open Mon.–Sat. 7:30–5, Sun. 8–3. Set back from Maine St. with tables on the terrace and inside. A town meeting place serving coffees and teas, from-scratch pastries and breads, healthy build-your-own sandwiches and salads. For those too impatient to stand in line, there are freshly made salads in the cooler. Yum! Outside seating, too, weather permitting.

Fat Boy Drive-In (207-729-9431), Old Rt. 1. Open for lunch and dinner, late Mar.–mid-Oct. This is no 1950s reconstruct, just a real drive-in with carhops that's survived because it's so good and incredibly reasonably priced. If you own a pre-1970 car, you can come to the annual "sock hop."

Little Dog Coffee Shop (207-721-9500), 87 Maine St. Open 6 AM–8 PM. An inviting way stop with soothing eggplant-colored walls, widely spaced tables, a couch or two. The daily changing menu includes soup and grilled panini. We recommend the mushroom, avocado, and tomato combo. Also coffees, teas, smoothies, pastries, and newspapers.

The Barn Door Café (207-721-3229), 4 Bowdoin Mill Island. Open Mon.–Fri. 7–6, Sat. 9–2. A small café, just off Rt. 1 and well known to locals for soups and sandwiches, like "crunchy tuna" (with slivered Granny Smith apples) and crunchy Thai chicken (marinated chicken with veggies and peanut sauce).

Miss Brunswick Diner (207-729-5948), 101 Pleasant St. (Rt. 1 northbound). Open daily 5 AM–9 PM. A convenient road-food stop, a remake of a diner that originally stood in Norway (Maine) but has now been here several decades; the neon lights, booths, and jukebox are all new, but the food is what it claims to be: "home cooking at a down-home good price."

Gelato Fiasco (207-607-4002), 74 Maine St. Open daily 11–11. Owners Josh and Bruno make a couple dozen flavors of their irresistible ice cream from scratch, daily.

Block & Tackle (207-725-5690), 842 Cundy's Harbor Rd, (off rt. 24), harpswell. Open seasonally, 11–8, breakfast from 7 AM on weekends. A family-run and -geared restaurant. Try shrimpster stew or real homemade clam cakes. The Friday special is corned hake.

⌐ **Railway Café** (207-737-2277), 64 Main St. Open Mon.–Thu. 6:30 AM–8 PM, Fri. and Sat 6:30 AM–9 PM; Sun.

7–4. Minutes off I-295 exit 43, Richmond. This pleasant restaurant makes a good road-food stop: a wide choice of morning omelets and lunchtime sandwiches, burgers, salads, and pizzas, and a huge, reasonably priced dinner menu includes "Just for Kids." (Warning: Skip the onion rings.) Allow a few minutes to walk around this historic Kennebec River town.

✳ Entertainment

MUSIC Bowdoin International Music Festival (207-373-1400; bowdoinfestival.org), Brunswick. Famed in classical music circles since 1964, this late-June through early-August festival brings together talented young performers and internationally acclaimed musicians for six concert series of both classical and contemporary works. Wednesday- and Friday-evening concerts, featuring festival faculty and guest artists, are staged in Crooker Theater at Brunswick High School. Daily student concerts and the Gamper Festival of Contemporary Music are held in the new, state-of-the-art Studzinski Recital Hall on the Bowdoin College campus. Additional concerts, staged throughout the local community, are free, as are all student and Gamper Festival concerts.

Music on the Mall (207-729-4439). July–Aug., concerts at 7 PM Wed. on Brunswick's grassy downtown mall. Free.

Also see First Parish Church under *To See*.

THEATER 🎷 **Maine State Music Theatre** (207-725-8769; msmt.org), Bowdoin College, Brunswick. Summer performances at 8 PM, Tue.–Sat.; matinees Tue., Thu., and Fri. Special children's shows. Air-conditioned Pickard Theater is housed in Memorial Hall, an 1873 memorial to the Bowdoin students who fought and died in the Civil War—ordered built, of course, by Joshua Chamberlain. It's a fit stage for Maine's premier performing-arts group. This highly professional Equity company strives for a mix of classics and new scripts and frequently gets rave reviews.

FILM Eveningstar Cinema (207-729-6796 or 1-888-304-5486), Tontine Mall, 149 Maine St., Brunswick. The specialty is alternative film: foreign, art, biography, documentary, and educational. Also a monthly venue for folk, jazz, and other music performances.

Frontier Café & Cinema Gallery (207-725-5222; explorefrontier.com), 14 Main St. (Fort Andross). Check the website for frequent films and lectures in the 75-seat cinema (seats are recycled from the Biddeford Theater, converted into swivel/rocking chairs and coffee tables). Visual storytelling, workshops, and special events, too (also see *Eating Out*).

✳ Selective Shopping

ART AND CRAFTS GALLERIES

In Brunswick and Topsham **Second Friday Art Walks** (207-798-6985; fiveriverartsalliance.org),

THE PICKARD THEATER AT BOWDOIN COLLEGE

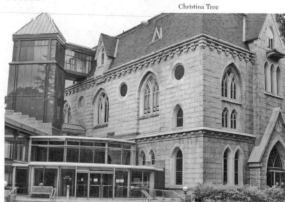

Christina Tree

May–Dec., are major events, with open houses at many studios as well as galleries and a total of 20 art venues.

Bayview Gallery (207-729-5500), 58 Maine St., features traditional Maine landscapes. **Icon Contemporary Art** (207-725-8157), 19 Mason St., just off the Rt. 1 end of Main St., is open year-round, Wed. 1–5, Sat. 1–4. A serious contemporary gallery with changing exhibits of sculpture, original drawings and paintings.

Spindleworks (207-725-8820; spindle works.com), 7 Lincoln St., an artists' cooperative for people with disabilities that produces some striking handwoven fiber clothing and hangings, quilts, accessories, paintings, prints, T-shirts, rag rugs, and more.

Maine Fiberarts (207-721-0678; fiberarts.org), 13 Main St., Topsham, open weekdays and for special events, exhibits work and serves as a resource center for this active statewide association of farmers, artists, and craftsmen.

In the Harpswells

The Gallery at Widgeon Cove (207-833-6081; widgeoncove.com). Open most of the year, but call before coming. This waterside gallery features Georgann Kuhl's watercolors and monotypes, mostly landscapes, on her handmade papers, and the gold and silver jewelry and sculptures of Condon Kuhl; it's worth a detour. **Ash Cove Pottery** (207-833-6004), farther down the road, displays a variety of hand-thrown and -glazed functional stoneware by Susan Horowitz and Gail Kass. On Rt. 24 (north of Mountain Rd.) the former Gunpoint Church now serves as a gallery for **Sebascodegan Artists** (named for the island on which it stands), a cooperative with 20 members. It's open July 4–Labor Day, Mon.–Sat. 10–5.

FARMER'S MARKET **Brunswick Farmer's Market** (brunswickfarmers market.com), May–Nov., Tue. and Fri. 8–2 on "the Mall"—the park-like green strip on upper Maine St. Local produce and products.

SPECIAL STORES

In Brunswick

Gulf of Maine Books (207-729-5083), 134 Maine St., Brunswick. A laid-back, full-service bookstore with a wide inventory, particularly rich in Maine titles, poetry. The owners (they

BRUNSWICK FARMER'S MARKET ON THE MALL

Christina Tree

have been called "curators") are photographer Beth Leonard and Gary Lawless, founder of Blackberry Press (note the full line here), which has reissued many out-of-print Maine classics. A true Renaissance man, Lawless is a well-known poet with an international following. Also great cards.

Cabot Mill Antiques (207-725-2855; cabotiques.com), 14 Maine St. (at Rt. 1; Fort Andross), Brunswick. Open daily 10–5. A vast, 140-dealer space with quality antiques; flea markets on summer weekends.

Wyler Gallery (207-729-1321), 150 Maine St., Brunswick, is a great mix of quality pottery, glassware, jewelry, and clothing.

Vinylhaven (207-729-65139, 141A Maine St., Brunswick. Open weekdays. Vinyl rules. LPs are bought and sold, and turntables repaired.

Wilbur's of Maine Confections (207-729-4462; wilburs.com), 143 Main St., Brunswick. Open daily. We dare you to pass up "double decadence" (a dark chocolate truffle with hazelnuts). The chocolate is handmade in Freeport, and there's a large inventory of other candies.

In Harpswell
Black Sheep Wine Shop (207-725-9284; blacksheepwine.com), 105 Mountain Rd., Harpswell. With more than 600 different labels, a range of prices (at least 90 under $12), friendly service, and frequent tastings, dinners, and classes, this has become a destination for wine lovers. Easy to find, it's on the road connecting Harpswell's two major routes (24 and 123) and also serves as the Harpswell Visitor Information Center.

Hawke's Lobster (207-721-0472) in Cundy's Harbor is a seasonal source of not only live lobster but also the work of local craftspeople. It may be the world's only gift shop with a tank full of freshly caught lobsters as its centerpiece.

Island Candy Company (207-833-6639), Rt. 24, Orrs Island. Open 11–8 in summer, fewer hours, fewer days off-season. Closed in snow season. Melinda Harris Richter makes everything from lollipops to truffles. Try the almond cups.

✳ Special Events
Check the Thursday edition of Brunswick's *Times Record* for current happenings.

Mid-May–June: **Fishway Viewing Room** (207-795-4290), Brunswick–Topsham Hydro Station, next to Fort Andross. Open during the spawning season, Wed.–Sun. 1–5. Watch salmon, smallmouth bass, and alewives climb the 40-foot-high fish ladder that leads to a holding tank beside the viewing room.

June: **Taste of Brunswick** (brunswick downtown.org).

July: **Bailey Island Fishing Tournament** (to register, phone Cook's Lobster House at 207-833-2818). **Harpswell lobster-boat races**.

August: **Topsham Fair** (first week)—a traditional agricultural fair complete with ox pulls, crafts and food competitions, a carnival, and livestock; held at Topsham Fairgrounds, Rt. 24, Topsham. **Maine Highland Games**, Thomas Point Beach (third Saturday), a daylong celebration of Scottish heritage, with piping, country dancing, sheepdog demonstrations, and Highland fling competitions.

September: **Annual Thomas Point Bluegrass Festival,** Labor Day weekend (thomaspointbeach.com).

October: **Downtown Brunswick Fall Festival**. (brunswickdowntown.org).

Late November: **Annual Tree Lighting** (brunswickdowntown.org)

BATH AREA

Over the years some 5,000 vessels have been built in Bath. Think about it: In contrast with most communities—which retain what they build—here an entire city's worth of imposing structures have sailed away. Perhaps that's why, with a population of fewer than 9,000, Bath is a city rather than a town, and why the granite city hall, with its rounded, pillared facade and cupola (with a Paul Revere bell and a three-masted schooner for a weather vane), seems meant for a far larger city.

American shipbuilding began downriver from Bath in 1607 when the 30-ton pinnace *Virginia* was launched by Popham Colony settlers. The tradition continues with naval vessels regularly constructed at the Bath Iron Works (BIW).

BATH CITY HALL

Christina Tree

With around 5,700 workers, BIW employs fewer people than worked in Bath's shipyards in the 1850s. At its entrance a sign proclaims: THROUGH THESE GATES PASS THE WORLD'S BEST SHIPBUILDERS. This is no idle boast, and many current employees have inherited their skills from a long line of forebears.

Obviously, this is the place for a museum about ships and shipbuilding, and the Maine Maritime Museum has one of the country's foremost collections of ships' models, journals, logs, photographs, and other seafaring memorabilia. It includes a 19th-century working shipyard and offers tours of BIW as well as river and coastal cruises.

Both BIW and the Maine Maritime Museum are sited on a 4-mile-long reach of the Kennebec River where the banks slope at precisely the right

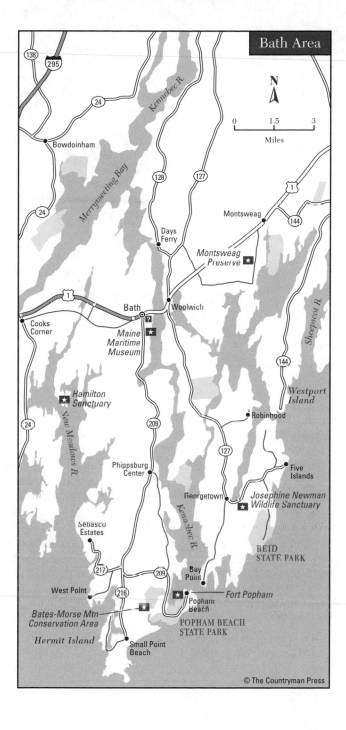

Bath Area

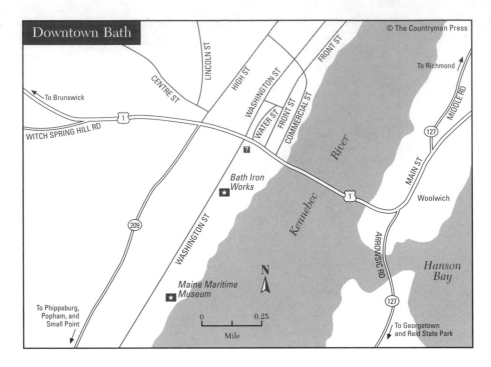

Downtown Bath

© The Countryman Press

To Richmond

To Brunswick

LINCOLN ST

CENTRE ST

HIGH ST

WASHINGTON ST

WATER ST

FRONT ST

FRONT ST

COMMERCIAL ST

FRONT ST

MIDDLE RD

To Richmond

127

MAIN ST

WITCH SPRING HILL RD

Bath Iron
★ Works

Kennebec River

1

Woolwich

209

WASHINGTON ST

ARROWSIC RD

Hanson
Bay

Maine Maritime
★ Museum

N

To Phippsburg,
Popham, and
Small Point

0   0.25

Mile

127

To Georgetown
and Reid State Park

gradient for laying keels. Offshore, the channel is 35 to 150 feet deep; the open Atlantic is 18 miles downriver.

Bath's 19th-century prominence as "City of Ships" is reflected in the blend of Greek Revival, Italianate, and Georgian Revival styles in the brick storefronts along Front Street and in the imposing wooden churches and mansions in similar styles along Washington, High, and Middle Streets. Front Street offers a healthy mix of shops and restaurants.

Today BIW with its 400-foot-high towers at the end of Bath's Front Street still dominates the city's economy, but Bath now styles itself "Maine's Cool Little City." Its downtown hums with newfound energy, a visitor-friendly mix of culture and commerce. Take the plunge from Rt. 1, down the steep northbound exit ramp just before the soaring Sagadahoc Bridge. Pick up walking and parking maps at the visitors center in the former rail station and explore shops and restaurants along Front Street.

Save a day to explore the Phippsburg Peninsula south of Bath. Phippsburg's perimeter is notched with coves filled with fishing boats, and Popham Beach near its southern tip is a grand expanse of sand. Reid State Park on Georgetown Island, just across the Kennebec River, is the Midcoast's other major sandy strand. North of Bath, Merrymeeting Bay is a major flyway well known to birders.

GUIDANCE Maine Street Bath (207-442-7291; visitbath.com) operates a visitors center (207-443-1513) in the rehabbed Bath Railroad Station, 15 Commerical St. Open May–Oct., daily in high season, Thu.–Sun. in shoulder seasons. Restrooms and a manned info desk. From Rt. 1 take Historic Downtown Bath exits.

GETTING THERE *By car:* Rt. 1 barrels through the city, with views only from high on the Sagadahoc Bridge, too late if you're heading north. Take the downtown exits just south of the bridge. From points south take I-95 to I-295 (formerly I-95) to either exit 28 (Brunswick) or exit 31 (Topsham) and the connector (Rt. 196) to Rt. 1. We prefer exit 28 (it's less confusing), but if it's a peak traffic time try your luck with 31.

By bus: **Concord Coach** (1-800-639-3317; concordcoachlines.com), en route to and from Boston, stops in Bath at Coastal Plaza off Rt. 1.

By air and limo: **Mid-Coast Limo** (1-800-937-2424; midcoastlimo.com) makes runs by reservation from Portland International Jetport.

By train: **The Maine Eastern Railroad** (1-866-636-2457; maineeasternrailroad .com) offers 54-mile seasonal runs between Brunswick and Rockland, stopping in Bath and Wiscasset. See *To Do.*

GETTING AROUND Bath Trolley operates a loop throughout the city, daily July–Labor Day, weekends in the shoulder seasons. $1 per ride.

WHEN TO COME Bath itself remains lively year-round, but the Popham and Georgetown areas are June–Columbus Day destinations.

✳ To See

Bath Historic District. In the 18th and 19th centuries Bath's successful families built impressive mansions. **Sagadahoc Preservation, Inc.** (207-443-2174; sagadahocpreservation.org), publishes an excellent brochure: *Architectural Tours—Self-Guided Walking and Driving Tours of the City of Bath.*

✐ **Woolwich Historical Society Museum** (207-443-4833; woolwichhistory.org), Rt. 1 and Nequasset Rd., Woolwich. Open during summer months, several days

POPHAM BEACH VILLAGE

Christina Tree

⚓ MAINE MARITIME MUSEUM

(207-443-1316; www.maine maritimemuseum.org), 243 Washington St., Bath (watch for the turnoff from Rt. 1). Open daily year-round 9:30–5 except Thanksgiving, Christmas, and New Year's Day. $12 adults, $11 seniors, and $9 ages 4–16. Docking and mooring available. Sited just south of Bath Iron Works on the banks of the Kennebec River, this extensive complex—10 riverside acres—includes the brick-and-glass Maritime History Building and the Percy & Small Shipyard, the country's only surviving wooden shipbuilding yard (its turn-of-the-20th-century belts for driving machinery have been

MAINE MARITIME MUSEUM EXTERIOR   Christina Tree

restored). Museum exhibits focus on the era beginning after the Civil War when 80 percent of this country's full-rigged ships were built in Maine, almost half of these in Bath.

The pride of Bath, you learn, were the Down Easters, a compromise between the clipper ship and the old-style freighter that plied the globe from the 1870s through the 1890s, and the big multimasted schooners designed to ferry coal and local exports like ice, granite, and lime. A fine example, the six-masted *Wyoming* was the largest wooden sailing vessel ever built. A full-scale steel sculpture suggests its mammoth size and height.

The museum's permanent collection of artwork, artifacts, and documents totals more than 20,000 pieces, and there is an extensive research library. Permanent exhibits include *Distant Lands of Palm and Spice*, a fascinating, occasionally horrifying glimpse of where and why Maine ships sailed beginning in the 18th century with the West Indies sugar and slave trade, on around Cape Horn to the Pacific and Asia as well as Europe in 19th centuries. You hear the wind whistling in the rigging and follow the individual stories of multiple captains.

Beyond the Maritime History Building exhibits are housed in half a dozen buildings, widely scattered on the museum grounds. One of our favorites chronicles the history of Maine's lobstering business, including displays on the 19th-century canning boom and a vintage 1954 film, *The Maine Lobsterman*,

Christina Tree

THE MAINE MARITIME
MUSEUM'S EXHIBITS
INCLUDE A KID-
FRIENDLY PILOTHOUSE,
MARINE PAINTINGS,
AND FIGUREHEADS

Christina Tree

written and narrated by E. B. White. The Donnell House, the late-Victorian home of a prominent Bath family, is open seasonally.

Exhibits aside, this museum involves visitors in the significance of the surroundings. A one-hour trolley tour of the neighboring General Dynamics' Bath Iron Works is not to be missed. You can also choose from half a dozen regularly offered cruises (see *To Do*) with historic narrations down the Kennebec and around into Sheepscot Bay. There's plenty for children, too, from a hands-on pilothouse and elaborate pirate-boat climbing structure to summer mariners' and boatbuilders' camps. Check the website for frequent lectures, workshops, concerts, and special events.

TROLLEY TOUR OF BATH IRON WORKS

Bath Iron Works

per week. Volunteer-run, this 19th-century rural life museum displays antique clothing, quilts, and seafaring memorabilia from local attics. Special events.

SCENIC DRIVES The **Phippsburg Peninsula**. From the Maine Maritime Museum drive south on Rt. 209, down the narrow peninsula that's the town of Phippsburg. Pause at the first causeway you cross. This is Winnegance Creek, an ancient shortcut between Casco Bay and the Kennebec River; look closely to your left and you'll see traces of the 10 tide mills that once operated here.

Continue south on Rt. 209 until you come to the **Bisson's Center Store** on your right. Turn left on Parker Head Rd. into the tiny hamlet of Phippsburg Center. This is one of those magical places, far larger in memory than in fact—perhaps because it was once larger in fact, too, as you can see in the **Phippsburg Historical Society** (open July–Sept., Mon.–Sat. 2–4). Notice the giant linden tree planted in 1774 between the white-clapboard Congregational church (1802) and its small cemetery. Another surviving linden was also planted in 1774, the year the striking Georgian mansion next door (now **The 1774 Inn**) was built. Also look for the stumps of piers on the river shore beyond, remnants of a major shipyard. Continue along the peninsula's east shore on the Parker Head Rd., past a former millpond where ice was once harvested. At the junction with Rt. 209, turn left and note the entrance to **Popham Beach State Park** with its 3 miles of sand. Rt. 209 ends shortly beyond at **Fort Popham**, a granite Civil War–era fort (with picnic benches) at the mouth of the Kennebec River, 15 miles below Bath. It's a favorite spot for fishermen and a destination for eating seafood by the water at **Spinney's Restaurant** and **Percy's General Store** (see *Eating Out*). This is also a departure point for excursions to **Sequin Island Light**. A pedestrian wooded road leads to World War I and II fortifications that constitute **Fort Baldwin Memorial Park**; a six-story tower yields views up the Kennebec and out to sea.

Along the shore at Popham Beach, note the pilings, in this case from vanished steamboat wharves. Around the turn of the 20th century, two big hotels served the passengers who transferred here from Boston to Kennebec River steamers, or who simply stayed a spell to enjoy the town's spectacular beach.

Returning back up Rt. 209, you have two detours to consider. The first is a left on Rt. 216, which runs south to Small Point with limited beach access and camping on **Hermit Island** at its end. Note access to the **Morse Mountain** preserve (great walk, great beach) almost at the beginning.

A few curves north on Rt. 209, turn left on Sebasco Rd. (Rt. 217) to find Sebasco Estates and Anna's Water Edge, the reason many drive out this way from Bath.

Arrowsic and Georgetown Islands. Just east of the Sagadahoc Bridge (at the Dairy Queen that's been there forever), turn south on Rt. 127. Cross a shorter bridge and you are on Arrowsic Island. Note Robinhood Rd., which leads to two of the area's top restaurants (see *Dining Out*). Farther down Rt. 127 in Georgetown Center look for **Georgetown Pottery**; the general store has a snack bar and is good for sandwiches. The **Georgetown Historical Society and Cultural Center** (207-371-9200; georgetownhistoricalsociety.org), open weekends, is just south at 20 Bay Point Rd.; check the website for a schedule of lectures and events. Continue on Rt. 127 to **Reid State Park**, the big draw (see *Swimming*). The road ends at the **Five Islands Lobster and Grill** (see *Eating Out*).

BIRDING Hamilton Sanctuary, West Bath. A Maine Audubon Sanctuary (maine audubon.org) situated on a peninsula in the New Meadows River, offering a 1.5-mile trail system and great bird-watching. Look for common eiders and snowy egrets in the cove and shorebirds in the mudflats at low tide. In spring there are bobolinks, red-winged blackbirds, meadowlarks, and several species of warblers. Take the New Meadows exit off Rt. 1 in West Bath; turn left on New Meadows Rd., which turns into Foster Point Rd.; follow it 4 miles to the sanctuary sign.

Thorne Head Preserve, Bath. Follow High St. 2 miles north to the end and you will find easy, wooded paths in this 96-acre Kennebec Estuary Land Trust's preserve with views of the Kennebec River, rich in common warblers and vireos. The trust publishes a widely available guide to all nine of its preserves; contact them at 207-442-8400; lkrlt.org.

Also see *Green Space*.

BOAT EXCURSIONS Maine Maritime Museum (mainemaritimemuseum.org; see *To See*) offers an extensive choice of regularly scheduled one- to three-hour narrated tours down the Kennebec River and Merrymeeting Bay, heading along the coast to Boothbay Harbor to view lighthouses (as many as 10 of them) and several more destinations.

The **M/V Ruth**, based at Sebasco Estates (207-389-1161); the **M/V Yankee** (207-389-1788), based at Hermit Island Campground at Small Point; and **Kennebec Charters** (207-389-1883) at Popham Beach all offer coastal excursions.

Maine Island Touring Company (207-371-9930) offers tours to see birds and seals. **Gillies & Fallon Guide Service** (207-389-2300) also offers scenic cruises, lobster hauling, and sportfishing.

River Run Tours (207-442-7028; riverruntours.com), based in Woolwich. Captain Ed Rice offers charter tours for up to 15 people throughout this area.

Seguin Island Light Station (seguinisland.org). Guarding the mouth of the Kennebec River, this 186-foot granite lighthouse stands on a bluff on a 64-acre island. Commissioned by George Washington in 1795, it's one of the oldest lighthouses in the country. It's accessed regularly by **Mid-Maine Water Taxi** (207-371-2288), **Atlantic Seal** (877-285-7325), and local charter boats.

CANOE AND KAYAK RENTALS This area's many coves and quiet stretches of smaller tidal rivers lend themselves to kayaking, and outfitters have multiplied in recent years. **Seaspray Kayaking** (207-443-3646; seaspraykayaking.com), with bases at Sebasco Harbor, Georgetown Center, and on the New Meadows River between Bath and Brunswick, offers rentals and daily tours, also inn-to-inn trips and multilevel instruction. **Up the Creek** (207-442-4845), 39 Main Rd. (Rt. 209), is sited beside a put-in not far south of Bath, renting Old Town canoes and kayaks. **Sea Taylor Rentals** (207-725-7400), 271 Bath Rd., Brunswick, rents canoes to explore Merrymeeting Bay.

FISHING Kennebec Angler (207-442-8239), 97 Commercial St., Bath, is fishing central for the area, a referral service for guides and charter boats. The shop is filled with tackle and gear and offers demo rods for full-day trials before purchasing.

Surf fishing is popular at Popham Beach. Nearly 20 boats offer fishing on the river, while **Obsession Sportfishing Charters** (207-442-8581) offers deep-sea-fishing charters. Also see *Boat Excursions*.

GOLF Bath Country Club (207-442-8411), Whiskeag Rd., Bath, has 18 holes and a pro shop; lessons available. **Sebasco Harbor Resort Golf Club** (207-389-9060) is a recently renovated, waterside nine-hole course open to the public. Reservations advised. Also see the Brunswick chapter.

⊘ **RAILROAD EXCURSION** The **Maine Eastern Railroad** (1-866-636-2457; maineeasternrailroad.com) offers 54-mile seasonal runs between Brunswick and Rockland, stopping in Bath and Wiscasset. Travel along the coast in plush 1940s and '50s coaches and a dining car, pulled by a 1950s diesel electric engine. Check the website for current information. The Bath stop is in the renovated RR station at the foot of Main St.

SWIMMING 🐾 If you're traveling with a dog, it's important to know that they're allowed only in picnic areas, not on the beaches.

⊘ **Popham Beach State Park** (207-389-1335; for current parking and tide updates, 207-389-9125), Rt. 209, Phippsburg; 14 miles south of Bath. One of the best state park swimming and walking beaches in Maine: 3 miles of sand at the mouth of the Kennebec River, a small part of the park's 519 acres. Facilities include bathhouses, showers, and picnic areas with grills. Also a sandbar, tidal pools, and smooth rocks. It can be windy; extra layers are recommended. Day-use fees ($4 adults, $1 ages 5–11, under 5 free) are charged mid-Apr.–Oct.

⊘ **Reid State Park** (207-371-2303), Rt. 127, Georgetown (14 miles south of Bath and Rt. 1). Open daily year-round. A 766-acre preserve with rock ledges, woodlands, and salt marshes as well as sand beaches. Good for year-round walking and birding. The bathhouse and snack bar overlook 2 miles of sand in three distinct beaches that seldom become overcrowded, although the limited parking area does fill by noon on summer weekends. You can choose surf or slightly warmer sheltered backwater. Little River, around the corner from Half-Mile Beach, is a tidal estuary that warms on sunny days, especially good for children. Entrance fee ($4.50 under age 65) charged mid-Apr.–mid-Oct.

⊘ **Charles Pond**, Rt. 127, Georgetown (about 0.5 mile past the turnoff for Reid State Park; 15 miles down the peninsula from Rt. 1). Often considered the best all-around swimming hole in the area, this long and narrow pond has clear water and is surrounded by tall pines.

⊘ **Sewall Pond**, Arrowsic. This large pond is visible from Rt. 127, but the beach is on the far side. Heading south, turn left on Old Post Rd.; the parking area is a mile or so on your left. It's another 0.25 mile to the pond.

⊘ **Pleasant Pond** (207-582-2813), **Peacock Beach State Park**, off Rt. 201, north of Richmond. Open Memorial Day–Labor Day. A sand-and-gravel beach with lifeguards on duty. Water depth drops off gradually to about 10 feet in a 30-by-50-foot swimming area removed from boating and enclosed by colored buoys. Picnic tables and barbecue grills.

Also see *Birding*.

A year-round resource center for people who want to build or retrofit their own energy-efficient home, offering a wide variety of classes.

Halcyon Yarn (see *Special Shops*) offers classes in fiber arts, including weaving, knitting, felting, spinning, crocheting, and rug hooking.

Art classes and workshops are offered by more than a dozen local artists. The oldest and most prominent of these are based at Rock Gardens Inn (see *Resorts*).

✳ Green Space

✐ **Fort Baldwin Memorial Park**, Phippsburg. Follow the short, narrow road around a one-lane corner to Point Sebago, the site of the Popham Colony. An interpretive panel in the parking lot details the remarkable extent of the 1607–08 settlement here. An undeveloped area with a six-story tower to climb (steep stairs, but the railing is sturdy) for a beautiful view up the Kennebec and, downriver, out to sea. There are also remnants of fortifications from World Wars I and II.

✐ **Fort Popham Historic Site** (207-389-1335), Hunniwell's Point at Popham Beach. Open Memorial Day–Sept. Picnic sites are scattered around the ruins of this 1861 granite fort, built to guard the Kennebec during the Civil War. Beach and ocean fishing access.

Josephine Newman Wildlife Sanctuary, Georgetown. Bounded on two sides by salt marsh, the 119 acres maintained by Maine Audubon provide good birding along 2.5 miles of walking trails. Look for the sign on Rt. 127, 9.1 miles south of Rt. 1.

Morse Mountain Preserve consists of some 600 acres extending from the Sprague to the Morse River and out to Seawall Beach. Allow two hours for the 2-mile hike over a hill and from this unspoiled private beach. Pack a picnic, a towel, and some water (or pick it up at North Creek Farm)—but please, no radios or beach paraphernalia: Seawall Beach is an important nesting area for piping plovers and least terns. There's a great view from the top of Morse Mountain, which is reached by an easy hike, just over a mile along a partially paved road. Look for the small sign on the left to Morse Mountain Rd. soon after the Small Point Road veers off from Rt. 209. Parking is very limited so come early, especially on busy weekends; don't park on the road or you will get a ticket.

Montsweag Preserve, Montsweag Rd., Woolwich. A 1.5-mile trail takes visitors through woods, fields, and a salt marsh, and along the water. This 45-acre preserve is owned by The Nature Conservancy (207-729-5181). You will have to watch carefully for the turns (right onto Montsweag Rd. about 6.5 miles from Bath on Rt. 1, then 1.3 miles and a left into the preserve).

Note: The **Phippsburg Land Trust** protects a constantly evolving number of preserves and offers guided walks throughout summer and fall. See phippsburg landtrust.org.

Also see **Reid State Park** under *Swimming* and Hamilton Sanctuary under *Birding*.

✳ Lodging

RESORTS ♂ 🐾 ✐ ♿ ((ᵞ)) **Sebasco Harbor Resort** (207-389-1161 or 1-800-225-3819; sebasco.com), P.O. Box 75, 29 Kenyon Rd., Sebasco Estates 04565. Open May–Oct. This 550-acre, 133-room, family-geared waterside resort dates back to 1930, featuring a nine-hole golf course, tennis courts, a large swimming pool, kayaking, and full children's and adult activities programs. Sailing lessons and excursions, lobster cookouts, and live entertainment are also offered. The newest additions are luxury Harbor Village Suites ($319–459) and the Fairwinds Spa Suites ($319–399), handy to the full-service **Fairwinds Spa**. Lodging is otherwise divided among the main lodge ($189–319), a lighthouse-shaped annex ($259–359), and 22 widely scattered and differing cottages, some with fireplace and kitchenette ($375–1,890). Rates drop in shoulder seasons. All rates are based on two people, $15 per extra person. Add $48 per person MAP

(breakfast and dinner), another $20 for golf. Weddings and family reunions are specialties. Informal dining is at **The Ledges**, more formal at **The Pilot House** (entrées $14–23). A spa menu is also available. Children under 10 dine at no charge when accompanied by an adult and ordering from the children's menu. Inquire about golf, spa, and other special packages. Pets are accepted in some cottages ($25 per night).

✪ ✐ **Rock Gardens Inn** (207-389-1339; rockgardensinn.com), Sebasco Estates 04565. Open mid-June–late Sept. A hidden gem, sited on its own narrow peninsula between a cove and bay, within but beyond the Sebasco Harbor Resort grounds. Accommodating just 60 guests, it offers a more intimate atmosphere but access to all of Sebasco Harbor Resort's facilities as well as to its own pool and dock with kayaks. Rock Gardens dates back to 1911, and Ona Barnet has preserved the old-style atmosphere of the dining

THE DOCK AT ROCK GARDENS INN

Christina Tree

room with its painted tables and library with its well-thumbed books. Traditions include a weekly lobster bake and cocktail party. The 10 cottages (accommodating three to eight) and three inn rooms are tastefully furnished and constantly updated. Request one with a water view. August is family-geared. In June, July, and September a series of Sebasco Art Workshops feature some surprisingly well-known teachers (Ona's father, Will Barnet, is a prominent artist). In high season $115–200 per person MAP, $15 less in June and September in low (ask about children's rates), includes a four-course dinner (BYOB) as well as breakfast; five-night minimum in July and Aug., but check for cancellations; add 15 percent for service.

BED & BREAKFASTS

In Bath 04530

✪ ⍟ 🐾 ♂ ♿ (ᵂ) **The Inn at Bath** (207-443-4294 or 1-800-423-0964; innatbath.com), 969 Washington St. Open year-round. Elizabeth Knowlton is the hospitable keeper of Bath's leading inn. A restored 1840s Greek Revival home in the city's historic district, the inn features elegantly comfortable twin living rooms with marble fireplaces, eight luxurious guest rooms with private bath, including a two-bedroom suite. Four rooms have a wood-burning fireplace; two of these also feature a Jacuzzi. Most rooms have a writing desk and small niceties that add up to comfort but differ a lot in decor. Our favorites are the Lavender Room with its Hitchcock dressing table, a rocker, and a king bed with a spool headboard; and the Sail Loft with buttery yellow walls, a high four-poster, and a comfy armchair beside a well-stocked bookcase. All guest rooms have air-conditioning, phone, cable TV, DVD, and clock-radio. There's also a guest computer. $170–200, from $150 off-season, with a breakfast that includes homemade granola and fresh fruit and always a hot entrée, perhaps quiche. $25 per additional guest. Children (over 5) and dogs are welcome, $15 fee.

(ᵂ) **Pryor House** (207-443-1146 or 1-866-977-7969; pryorhouse.com), 360 Front St. Don and Gwenda Pryor offer two crisp, attractive guest rooms with air-conditioning and private bath in this late-Federal-style home. The Tall Chimney Room features a small deck and big Jacuzzi. Common space is inviting. Breakfast, which may feature tomato basil quiche, banana crêpes, or blueberry French toast, is included ($125–160, from $110 off-season). Forest, the brown greyhound, will undoubtedly greet you. Guest pets are possible but carefully screened.

(ᵂ) **Benjamin F. Packard House** (201-443-6004 or 1-888-361-6004; benjaminpackard.com), 45 Pearl St.

BREAKFAST AT THE INN AT BATH

Christina Tree

This striking, Italianate house was built solidy to house a local shipbuilder in 1790 and remained in the same family until 1985. Amy and Mark Hranicky are enthusiastic hosts, assisted by Lupi, their sheepdog. They have created an extensive, brick-floored garden as an option to the more formal gathering room with its working hearth. The four guest rooms include two that work well as a family suite. $140–180 in-season, from $90 off-season, includes a choice of a full breakfast.

Kismet Inn (207-443-3399; kismet innmaine.com), 44 Summer St. Open year-round. You know the world is shrinking when a former lumber baron's mansion is the setting for organic Middle Eastern food and Japanese-style baths. "I like color," is the way innkeeper Shadi Towfighi explains the deep reds, lavenders, and yellows on the walls and the brightly patterned fabrics. Born in Iran, Towfighi has decorated with handwoven Iranian fabrics and hangings but also commissioned local craftspeople to reupholster locally found antiques and to create beds of her own design. Guests are welcome to just come for the night and enjoy an organic breakfast, but this is far from your average B&B. Shadi offers a very personal hospitality and the option of a deep exfoliation treatment in your own 3-foot-deep tub, or of a very special tea or dinner. Couples or small groups are also welcome simply for tea or dinner, both combining locally sourced organic ingredients with traditional Iranian recipes. $200–255 for B&B. Inquire about tea and dinner, exfoliation treatments, and yoga. No credit cards.

Hampton Inn (207-386-1310; bathbrunswickarea.hamptoninn.com), 140 Commercial St. This four-story, 94-room inn fills a long-vacant spot right downtown, a welcome addition to Bath's lodging options. Elevator-accessed rooms come with a king or two queens; facilities include a lap pool and Jacuzzi as well as a fitness center and laundry room. $99–209 depending on the season. On the June day we stopped by a standard room was $169. Rates includes a full breakfast.

On the Phippsburg Peninsula south of Bath

The 1774 Inn at Phippsburg (207-389-1774; 1774inn.com), 44 Parker Head Rd., Phippsburg 04562. Open year-round. Ranked among the most beautiful houses in Maine, this is an imposing cupola-topped, foursquare mansion, built in 1774 at the heart of picturesque Phippsburg Center by the Kennebec River. The home of Maine's first U.S. congressman, this landmark was thoroughly restored in 2009 by Brits Jacqueline Hogg and John Atkinson. Guests can choose from four splendid Federal-style guest rooms furnished with antiques, three smaller but thoughtfully decorated rooms in an el, and the open-timbered but luxurious "Woodshed" with its own porch and steps out into the garden. The

1774 INN AT PHIPPSBURG

Christina Tree

Christina Tree

COVESIDE BED & BREAKFAST

paneling is original throughout, and rooms are furnished with an eye to elegance and comfort. A full breakfast is served at a common table by the hearth in the original kitchen. Grounds slope to the river. $150–214. No credit cards at this writing.

On the Georgetown Peninsula
✪ ❀ **Coveside Bed and Breakfast** (207-371-2807 or 1-800-232-5490; covesidebandb.com), Georgetown (Five Islands) 04548. Open Memorial Day–mid-Oct. Twelve miles down Rt. 127 from Rt. 1, beyond the turnoff for Reid State Park. Tucked into a corner of a quiet, lobster-filled cove, Carolyn and Tom Church have created a rare retreat. The seven guest rooms are divided between a century-old farmhouse and a matching, shingled (built from scratch) cottage with its own common space and screened porch. All of the many-windowed rooms face the

water; those in the cottage have French doors opening onto decks. Some have a gas fireplace and/or a Jacuzzi, but really any room here is special. All have high, angled, or cathedral ceilings with fans, and there's a sense of uncluttered spaciousness, real comfort. Weather permitting, the multicourse breakfast is served on the brick terrace from which the lawn slopes away down beneath high trees to the shorefront. Carolyn and Tom are consummate hosts who go way beyond the norm in helping guests with local dining and sightseeing. Beach passes, a canoe, and bikes are free to guests, and there's exercise equipment in a rec room with TV. $140–205.

♂ **The Mooring** (207-371-2790; the mooringb-b.com), 132 Seguinland Rd., Georgetown 04548. Open May–Oct. Paul and Penny Barabe, the great-granddaughter of Walter Reid—donor of the land for his namesake state park—share their home as a B&B. The five guest rooms all have private bath; there are gracious common spaces and a great wicker-furnished porch overlooking the lawns and water. Weddings are a specialty. $150–200 in high season, from $100 off-season, includes a full breakfast.

♂ **Grey Havens** (207-371-2616 or 1-855-473-9428; greyhavens.com), 96 Seguinland Rd., P.O. Box 308, Georgetown 04548. Open early May–Oct. The donor of the land for neighboring Reid State Park also built this turreted, gray-shingled summer hotel, opened in 1904 as the Seguinland. A huge parlor window—said to be the first picture window in Maine—as well as most of the 13 guest rooms and the long veranda command views of Sheepscot Bay. In 2011 this old landmark received a much-needed overhaul from new owners. Rooms and baths were renovated, the spacious old parlor with its dark tongue-and-groove paneling has been lightened with bright, contemporary furnishings, and the restaurant has taken on new status. Now "Blue," it's open to the public for breakfast and dinner (see *Dining Out*). Rooms are $195–350 (the turret rooms are $295) mid-June–mid-Oct, $160–295 in shoulder weeks. Weddings are a specialty.

OTHER LODGING 🐾 🎣 **Hermit Island Campground** (207-443-2101; hermitisland.com), 6 Hermit Island Rd., Phippsburg 04562; winter mailing address: 42 Front St., Bath 04530. This 255-acre almost-island at Small Point offers 275 nicely scattered campsites, 51 on the water. Only tents, small to medium pop-ups, and small pickup campers are permitted. Owned since 1953 by the Sewall family, Hermit Island also has a central lodge with a recreation room and snack bar where kids can meet. Beyond the camping area are acres of private beach and hiking trails through unspoiled woods and meadows. $35–57 per night; less off-season. Repeat customers tend to mail in their reservations Jan. 2, but it's always worth a try. No pets.

🐾 **EdgeWater Farm** (207-389-1322 or 1-877-389-1322; ewfbb.com), 71 Small Point Rd., Phippsburg 04562. Year-round. A former B&B, this circa-1800 farmhouse, set in 4 acres of gardens and fruit trees, offers six individual guest rooms with private bath, kitchen privileges, and access to a large dining/living room. It's well suited to small-group gatherings. There's also an apartment sleeping 7 to 13, and an indoor pool. Call for rates.

Cottage rentals are listed with the Southern Midcoast Maine Chamber at midcoastmaine.com.

✳ Where to Eat

DINING OUT Also see "Brunswick and the Harpswells."

The Robinhood Free Meetinghouse (207-371-2188; robinhood meetinghouse.com), 210 Robinhood Rd. (off Rt. 127), Robinhood. Open nightly mid-May–Oct., Thu.–Sat. off-season. Reservations advised. Michael Gagné, known regionally for his fresh, innovative dishes, has turned the vintage-1855 Robinhood Free Meetinghouse into an attractive dining space. The second-floor chapel, with a 16-foot ceiling and 10-foot windows, seems designed for wedding parties. There's also an intimate ground-floor dining room, a totally different feel with contemporary art. The soup of the day might be cream of mushroom hazelnut; as an entrée, you might select seared duck breast with potato pancake and strawberry rhubarb peach compote, or lobster Newburg with cream and sherry in a puff pastry shell. Entrées $24–28. The irresistible dessert menu runs from homemade ice creams to raspberry vanilla soufflé. Inquire about lower-priced "Pub Nights."

✪ **Solo Bistro** (207-443-3373; solo bistro.com), 128 Front St., Bath. Open at 5 nightly in summer, closed Sun. in shoulder seasons; Mon., too, in winter and spring. Reserve. The Scandinavian decor is contemporary, and so is the chef's way with locally sourced ingredients. The menu changes monthly, but there's always a wide choice, from a bistro burger to oven-roasted sea scallops ($25). Entrées from $16, and the three-course prix-fixe special is $22.99. Live jazz Friday.

The Osprey (207-371-2530; robinhood marinecenter.com), 340 Robinhood Rd. (just off Rt. 127, near Reid State Park). Open May–Oct., 11–11, but

THE OSPREY RESTAURANT AT ROBINHOOD MARINE CENTER

check in shoulder seasons. Named for an osprey nest offshore, this attractive restaurant with water views is squirreled away in the Robinhood Marine Center, a full-service yacht yard. The varied dinner menu ranges from steak tips to seafood fettuccine with lobster, smoked mussels, scallops, and Maine shrimp. Entrées $15–26; pizza and light fare also available.

"Blue" at Grey Havens Inn (207-371-2616), Seguinland Rd. (marked from Reid State Park). Open seasonally Wed.–Sat. 5–9, nightly in high season. White-clothed tables are well spaced in this large, classic old summer hotel tongue-and-groove-paneled dining room with views out across Sheepscot Bay. New in 2011, the restaurant offers traditional fine dining, from baked haddock and stuffed chicken breast to rack of lamb and lazy man's lobsters. Entrées $21–32, but there's also a tavern fare menu. We dined happily on a loaded seafood chowder and fried calamari. Breakast is also open to the public.

✪ **Kennebec Tavern and Marina** (207-442-9636), 119 Commercial St., Bath. Open for lunch through dinner

until 10 weekdays, 11 Fri. and Sat.; Sun. brunch 11–2. A spacious, casual oasis with booths and tables overlooking the Kennebec River, and a seasonal waterside deck. The choice of seafood, chicken, steak, and combos is wide. It can hit the spot either after or during a long day of driving—anytime you want to sit down to a meal by the water. Easy access from Rt. 1. Dinner entrées $12–36. It fits under both *Dining* and *Eating Out*.

EATING OUT

In Bath

♪ **Beale Street Barbeque and Grill** (207-442-9514; mainebbq.com), 215 Water St. Open for lunch and dinner. No reservations. Mark, Mike, Rebecca, and John Quigg have built their slow-cooking pits and are delivering the real Tennessee (where Mark lived for six years) goods: pulled pork, ribs, sausage, a big Reuben; also nightly specials (frequently fish) to round out the menu.

♪ & **Mae's Cafe** (207-442-8577; maescafeandbakery.com), 160 Center St. (corner of High), Bath. Open 8–3, until 2 Sun. Breakfast omelets and specials like lobster Benedict are available all day, and the lunch menu has a loyal following. Try a crab melt or a flatbread pizza with sautéed lobster, onion, spinach, and mozzarella. Andy and Kate Winglass have created an unusually attractive café. The upstairs dining room at this writing is open primarily for functions. The downstairs bakery case is filled with delectable cakes—most patrons walk away with at least a cookie. Fully licensed.

Byrnes Irish Pub (207-443 6776; byrnesirishpub.com), 38 Centre St. Touting the area's best single-malt whiskeys and selection of Maine and imported beers, this is also a surprisingly great place to eat. The soup of the day might be black bean, and the daily printed menu may feature a smoked salmon BLT; there are also blackboard specials like the best dinner salad of our summer. Live music Thu. and Fri. evenings.

✪ **Starlight Café** (207-443-3005; starlightcafe.me), 15 Lambard St. Open weekdays 7–2; also Sat. June–Christmas. This bright, funky eatery and bakery is a real find. Large, luscious sandwiches. Create your own by picking bread, meat, cheese, veggies, and daily specials. Come early at lunchtime or be prepared to wait. Limited indoor seating, but it's a short walk to a bench by the Kennebec River.

✎ **J. R. Maxwell &Co.** (207-443-2014), 122 Front St., Bath. Open year-round for lunch and dinner daily. In the middle of Bath's shopping street, in a renovated 1840s building, originally a hotel. Try the popcorn shrimp and blueberry pie; dependably good burgers, sandwiches, and prime rib. Children's menu. Dinner entrées $14–23.

Admiral Steakhouse (207-443-2555; admiralsteak.com), 798 Washington St. Open from 4:30 daily. Under the same ownership as Byrnes Irish Pub (see

SPINNEY'S RESTAURANT, POPHAM BEACH

Christina Tree

Eating Out), this upscale restaurant beside the Chocolate Church is getting raves. You might begin with an oyster shooter and dine on your choice of cut of Black Angus or seafood, vegetarian dishes or an Angus burger.

✪ **The Cabin** (443-6224), 552 Wastington St., across from the Bath Iron Works. The extrerior is a bit shabby but inside it's a great local spot boasting "the only real pizza in Maine." Booths, patio seating in warm weather, pitchers of beer plus terrific good pizza. A good road-food stop, just off Rte. 1. Best in evening, after BIW workers have gone home.

On the Phippsburg Peninsula

✪ ✿ ✎ **Anna's Water's Edge** (207-389-1803), Black's Landing Rd., Sebasco Estates. Open daily May–Sept., 11–9. Reservations accepted but last orders taken at 8:45 PM. Well marked from Rt. 209. Sited on a commercial fishing wharf 13 miles south of Bath—but worth the drive on a summer evening—this is a great place to eat steamed lobster or clams, with a full menu ranging from sandwiches to surf and turf. A shore dinner with chowder, steamed clams, and a lobster is $31.95. Less well known and crowded than Spinney's but with a great view from the attractive dining room as well as from outdoor seating. Standout chowder and crabcakes. Nightly specials. Beer and wine served.

✎ **Spinney's Restaurant** (207-389-1122), at the end of Rt. 209, 987 Popham Rd. Open weekends Apr.–Nov.; call to check before July, then it's daily until Labor Day for lunch and dinner. Our kind of beach restaurant: a pleasant atmosphere, a basic chowder-and-a-sandwich menu, and (if you're lucky) a table on the glassed-in porch with water views. Glen and Diane Theal specialize in fresh fish and seafood, fried, steamed,

Christina Tree

VIEW FROM FIVE ISLANDS LOBSTER

and broiled; good lobster and crabmeat rolls. Fully licensed.

Percy's General Store (207-389-2010), Popham Beach. Locals head for the back room with its water-view booths, good for breakfast on through lobster rolls, fried clams, and lobster dinner specials.

North Creek Farm (207-389-1341; northcreekfarm.org), 24 Sebasco Rd., Phippsburg. Open year-round 9–6:30. Suzy Verrier's nursery and extensive perennial gardens (see *Selective Shopping*) are also the setting for a great little eatery with limited inside seating and picnic benches. The tables by the woodstove are especially inviting off-season, as are the freshly made soups. Homemade pies are another draw.

On the Georgetown Peninsula
✪ ✿ **Five Islands Lobster and Grill** (207-371-2990; fiveislandslobster.com), Georgetown. Fourteen miles south of Rt. 1 at the end of Rt. 127 on Five Islands wharf. Open Mother's Day–Columbus Day 11:30–8. It's hard to beat the view from this end-of-the-road commercial lobster wharf. A genuine, old-style lobster pound, it's all outdoors and all about steamed lob-

sters and clams with corn and potatoes, lobster rolls, fried clams, and fried seafood. Blackboard specials in the "Lovenest Grill" here usually include Jenny's special crabcake sandwich (two crabackes, mostly crab) and a grilled haddock sandwich. Onion rings are also a specialty.

Georgetown Country Store (207-371-2106), Rt. 127 just before Bay Point Rd. Open 7 AM–8 PM in July–Aug. A friendly general store but with a counter and picnic tables out back, also good for takeout to bring to to town-owned Five Islands Wharf down the road. A great lobster roll for $10.99 and good onion rings.

✷ Entertainment

✿ **Chocolate Church Arts Center** (207-442-8455; chocolatechurcharts .org), 804 Washington St., Bath. Year-round presentations include plays, concerts, and a wide variety of guest artists. Special children's plays and other entertainment are included on the schedule. Bowdoin International Music Festival concerts take place Sundays at 2 PM in July (bowdoin festival.org).

Gazebo Series band concerts. July and Aug., Tue. and Fri., 7 PM, Library Park, Bath.

Live music can be found at **Solo Bistro** (Fri.-night jazz), at **Byrnes Irish Pub** (Thu.–Sun. evenings), and at the **Kennebec Tavern** Sun. afternoons.

✳ Selective Shopping

ANTIQUES Look for antique stores at the upper end of Front Street. Of special note: **Brick Store Antiques** (207-443-2790), 143 Front St.

ART AND ARTISANS Five River **Arts Alliance** (207-798-6964; fiveriver artsalliance.org) is a source of information about **Third Friday Art Walks**, involving some 20 local galleries and studios.

Georgetown Pottery (207-371-2801; georgetownpottery.com), Rt. 127, Georgetown (some 9 miles south of Rt. 1). Open daily 8:30–5, later in summer. Jeff Peters has been handcrafting his distinctive style of pottery here since 1972. There are branches in Brunswick and Freeport, but this is a showroom worth a drive. An extensive selection of dishes, mugs, and other practical

MARKINGS GALLERY, BATH

Christina Tree

pieces in a variety of hand-painted and deeply colored designs, from casseroles to ikebana "Zen pots."

Saltbox Pottery (207-443-5586; salt boxpottery.com), 4 Shaw Rd., Woolwich. Open daily year-round, 10–5:30. Traditional-style stoneware.

Markings Gallery (207-443-1499; markingsgallery.com), 50 Front St., Bath. Open 10–5, closed Sun., Mon. off-season. This gallery, owned by five local artists/craftspeople and showing three times that number, is exceptional not only for the quality of what it shows but also for the careful blend of clay, glass, jewelry, woodworking, mixed media, and more. There's plenty here but the shop isn't cluttered. It's a delight and a significant addition to Front St.

Old Post Office Gallery (207-371-2015; leapetersonart.net), 833 Five Islands Rd. (Rt.127), Georgetown. Open late May–mid-Sept., Wed.–Sun. Owned by several local artists and displaying work by a select number, this is well worth a stop, if just to pick up locally inspired cards by Lea Peterson.

Sarah Greenier Studio & Gallery (207-443-3936; sarahgreenier.com), 428 Middle St., Bath. Open Memorial Day–Labor Day, Wed.–Sun. 11–5. Greenier paints Maine coastal landscapes, available in prints as well as originals.

BOOKSTORES Bath Book Shop (207-443-9338), 96 Front St., Bath. Connie Butson's well-stocked independent bookstore offers personalized service. Plenty of Maine children's and summer reading titles, Maine authors, and locally made cards.

Open Door Books (207-443-8689; opendoorbooks.us), 178 Front St., Bath. John Ring has a great selection of used, rare, and out-of-print books.

FARMER'S MARKET Bath Farmer's Market (bathfarmersmarket.com) is held Sat. mornings; check the website for precise times and venue.

FLEA MARKET Montsweag Flea Market (207-443-2809), Rt. 1, Woolwich. Open Wed. and Fri.–Sun., 6:30–3. A field filled with tables weighted down by every imaginable collectible and curiosity. Wednesday is Antique Day; on weekends look for collectibles, crafts, and good junk. Come early.

SPECIAL SHOPS Halcyon Yarn (207-442-7909 or 1-800-341-0282; halcyonyarn.com), 12 School St., Bath. Warehouse open Mon.–Sat. 10–4, Wed. until 8. A destination and mecca for knitters, spinners, and rug hookers with yarns distributed worldwide. Inquire about workshops.

Bath's Front Street is lined with mid-19th-century redbrick buildings. Among the clothing and specialty shops, don't overlook **Renys** (46 Front St.), one in a chain of Maine department stores good for genuine bargains and good value in an amazing range of things. **Springer's Jewelers** (76 Front St.) is a vintage emporium with mosaic floors, chandeliers, and ornate glass sales cases. **Now You're Cooking** (207-443-1402; acooksemporium.com) is a major kitchen supply store with a wide following and cooking classes. **Lisa-Marie's Made in Maine** (207-443-2225) fills three storefronts with work by more than 100 Maine artisans. Also see **Markings Gallery** above.

North Creek Farm (207-389-1341; northcreekfarm.org), 24 Sebasco Rd. (junction of Rts. 217 and 209). Open year-round 9–6:30. Suzy Verrier, an authority on *Rosa rugosa* and the author of two books on roses, maintains an extensive nursery and perennial gardens through which visitors are invited to wander. The store sells her organically grown produce, eggs, cut flowers, wine and beers, cheese, gardening implements, and gifts (also see *Eating Out*).

Five Islands Farm (207-371-9383; fiveislandsfarm.com), Rt. 127, Five Islands. Open mid-May–Dec., Wed.–Mon. 10:30–6. Heidi Klingelhofer's small, shingled emporium overflows with flowers and is a seasonal trove of Maine cheeses, wines, local produce, and specialty foods. Cheese is Heidi's passion, and she carries one of the largest selections of Maine artisan cheeses available anywhere.

Native Arts (207-442-8399), Rt. 1, Woolwich. Open 10–6 daily, year-round. Native American art and craftwork from throughout the country.

BATH'S FRONT STREET

Christina Tree

✳ Special Events

Details for most events are at visitbath.com.

June: **Bath House and Garden Tour**, sponsored by Sagadahoc Preservation, Inc. (207-443-2174; sagadahoc preservation.org).

Three days surrounding the Fourth of July: **Bath Heritage Days**—a grand celebration with an old-time parade of antique cars, marching bands, clowns, guided tours of the historic district, crafts sales, art shows, musical entertainment in two parks, a triathlon, a strawberry shortcake festival, a carnival, a train, and Fireman's Follies featuring bed races, bucket relays, and demonstrations of equipment and firefighting techniques. Fireworks over the Kennebec.

August: 🐾 **Dog Days**. Special events for dogs and their owners.

Saturday of Columbus Day weekend: **Autumn Fest**.

December: **Old-Fashioned Christmas** (all month), with competitions and special events.

WISCASSET AREA

Sea captains' mansions and mid-19th-century commercial buildings line Rt. 1 in this historic village—and on July and August weekends motorists have plenty of time to study them as they inch along. The wide bridge across the Sheepscot River here was to have eased the traffic snarl, but Wiscasset is the only village through which cars heading up and down the Midcoast on Rt. 1 must all file, stopping at pedestrian crossings.

It's an obvious stop. The places to eat are varied and good, antiques stores abound, and the historic buildings are worth visiting.

Still the shire town of Lincoln County, Wiscasset is only half as populous as it was in its shipping heyday—which, judging from the town's clapboard mansions, began after the Revolution and ended around the time of the Civil War. Lincoln County Courthouse, built in 1824 on the town common, is the oldest functioning courthouse in New England.

From Wiscasset, Rt. 27 runs northwest to Dresden Mills. From there it's just a few miles to the haunting Pownalborough Court House and on to Dresden, the Kennebec River, and Swan Island at Richmond. Rt. 218 veers northeast, paralleling the Sheepscot River through backcountry to Alna, home of the Wiscasset, Waterville & Farmington Railway and Head Tide Village. Rt. 144 heads south down the spine of the quiet Westport Island to the Squire Tarbox Inn.

GUIDANCE Southern Midcoast Maine Chamber (207-725-8797; midcoast maine.com). **Wiscasset Area Chamber of Commerce** (wiscassetchamber.com) publishes a walking guide and maintains a useful website.

GETTING THERE *By bus:* **Concord Coach** (1-800-639-3317; concordcoachlines .com) stops twice daily.

By car: Note the shortcut around traffic northbound: Turn right on Lee St., continue to Fore St. and Water St., and either park or continue north (right) on Rt. 1.

By air and limo: **Mid-Coast Limo** (1-800-937-2424; midcoastlimo.com) makes runs by reservation from Portland International Jetport.

PARKING is surprisingly easy. You can usually find a slot in the parking lot or along Water St.

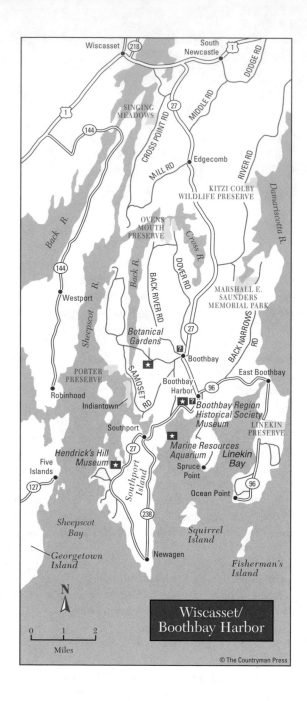

Wiscasset/
Boothbay Harbor

© The Countryman Press

PUBLIC RESTROOMS are in the Waterfront Park, corner of Water and Fore Sts. *Note:* This is also a great spot for a picnic.

✳ To See

In Wiscasset Village

Nickels-Sortwell House (historicnewengland.org), 121 Main St. (Rt. 1). Open June 1–Oct. 15, Fri.–Sun. Tours every half hour, 11–4. Admission $5, $4 seniors, $2.50 students. This classic Federal-era mansion in the middle of town was built by a shipowner and trader. After he lost his fortune, the house became a hotel for many years. In 1895 a Cambridge, Massachusetts, mayor purchased the property; some of the furnishings date to that time. It's now maintained by Historic New England.

Castle Tucker (603-436-3205, historicnewengland.org), Lee and High Sts. Same nonprofit owner as the Nickels-Sortwell House, same season, tour hours, and admission price but open Wed.–Sun. Castle Tucker was built in 1807 by Judge Silas Lee, who overextended his resources to present his wife with this romantic house. After his death it fell into the hands of his neighbors, to whom it had been heavily mortgaged, and passed through several owners until it was acquired in 1858 by Captain Richard Holbrook Tucker, whose descendants owned the house until 1997. Highlights include a freestanding elliptical staircase, Victorian furnishings, and original wallpapers.

Old Lincoln County Jail and Museum (207-882-6817; lincolncountyhistory.org), 133 Federal St. (Rt. 218). Open July and Aug., Tue.–Sat. 10–4, Sun. noon–4. Weekends only in June and Sept. $3 adults, $2.50 seniors and students. The museum consists of a chilling 1811 jail (in use until 1930) with damp, thick granite walls (some bearing interesting 19th-century graffiti), window bars, and heavy metal doors. The jailer's house (in use until 1953) displays tools and changing exhibits.

Musical Wonder House (207-882-7163 or 1-800-336-3725; musicalwonderhouse.com), 18 High St. Open Memorial Day–Halloween, Mon.–Sat. 10–5, Sun. noon–5. No admission charge for the gift shop or for the Entrance Hall, with its 23 antique coin-operated music boxes; guided tours are $20 for the ground floor, $40 for a tour of the entire 32-room mansion. A truly magnificent collection covering two centuries of musical his-

NICKELS-SORTWELL HOUSE

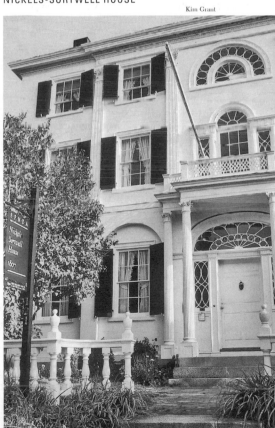

Kim Grant

Christina Tree

POWNALBOROUGH COURT HOUSE

tory. There are some 5,000 music boxes, player grand pianos and organs, spring-wound phonographs, musical birds, porcelains, furniture, clocks, steins, whistlers, and a musical painting—all displayed with period furniture in a fine 1852 sea captain's mansion. Inquire about concerts and special events. Music box repairs, restoration, and appraisals are offered year-round.

In Dresden

⚓ **Pownalborough Court House** (207-882-6817; lincolncountryhistory.org), Rt. 128. Same hours and admission as the county jail, and worth the drive. Maine's only surviving pre–Revolutionary War courthouse, this striking three-story building, which includes living quarters upstairs for the judge, gives a sense of this countryside along the Kennebec in 1761, when it was built to serve as an outpost tavern as well as a courtroom. The courthouse is on the second floor, and the third floor is a museum of rural life. Bring a picnic (there are tables). Special events include a mustering of the militia and wreath-laying ceremonies on Memorial Day, and a cider pressing in October. From Wiscasset take Rt. 27 north for 8 miles to Dresden Mills, then Rt. 127 south for 3.7 miles to Rt. 197 and on to Rt. 128, where you head north for 1.3 miles.

In Edgecomb

⚓ **Fort Edgecomb State Memorial** (207-882-7777), 66 Fort. Rd.; the turnoff from Rt. 1 is just across the Sheepscot River. The fort is open Memorial Day–Labor Day, daily 9–6. Nominal donation. This 27-foot, two-story octagonal blockhouse (built in 1808) overlooks a narrow passage of the Sheepscot River. For the same reasons that it was an ideal site for a fort, it is today an ideal picnic site, and tables are provided.

FOR FAMILIES ⚓ **Wiscasset, Waterville, and Farmington Railway Museum** (207-882-4193; wwfry.org), 97 Cross Rd., Sheepscot Station, Alna (just off Rt. 218, 4.5 miles north of Wiscasset). The museum is open 9–5 on Sat. year-round, also Sun. Memorial Day–Columbus Day. Trains run most weekends, departing on the hour, Apr.–Dec., but check the website; inquire about Halloween and Victorian Christmas runs. Volunteers preserve the history of this 2-foot narrow-gauge railroad. The museum's pride is Engine No. 9, an 1891 2-footer locomotive, billed as the oldest in the United States. Volunteers have built replicas of the engine house and shop, original station, and freight shed, which now houses the gift shop and museum. It's a 37-minute roundtrip run on 2.6 miles of track. Trains are usually pulled by a diesel locomotive, but on special occasions a vintage-1904 steam engine is used. Rides are $6 per adult, $5 seniors, $4 ages 12 and under.

Monkey C Monkey Do (207-882-6861; monkeycmonkeydo.com), 698 Bath Rd. (corner of Rt. 1 and Rt. 144), Wiscasset. Open daily mid-June–Labor Day, weekends from Memorial Day Weekend–Columbus Day. Full course: $25 ages 4–13, $35 older students, $40 adults. Three zip lines and a great swing with 30 obstacles to navigate at heights of 12–40 feet. This is Maine's first zip line and it got rave reviews in its initial season.

SCENIC DRIVE From the WW&FR (see above) cross Rt. 218 to Sheepscot Village, a picturesque gathering of early-19th-century buildings. The 32-acre Bass Falls Preserve, maintained by the Sheepscot Valley Conservation Association (207-586-5616), is 1.2 miles east of Rt. 218; from the parking lot a mile-long trail leads down to the river. Back on Rt. 218 continue north past the Alna Meeting House to Head Tide Village, another quiet cluster of old homes around the Old Head Tide Church (1858). Note the swimming hole beneath the milldam. The Alna Store (open until 7 PM except Sun.) on Rt. 218 just south of Head Tide is a great source of sandwiches and hot specials.

✳ Green Space

The **Back River Trail at Eaton Farm** (chewonki.org/about/nature trails.asp). This is a 4.5-mile coastal trail. From Route 1 turn right onto Old Ferry Road in Wiscasset (at Norm's Used Cars). Take the 3rd right onto Ready Point Rd. (Ready Point Rd. is 0.5 mile past Chewonki Neck Rd.) Follow Ready Point Rd. until you see a well-marked sign on the right for Eaton Farm Trail. There is ample parking there and a kiosk for hikers.

Sunken Garden, Main St., Wiscasset. Down a few steps, easy to miss, but a wonderful little garden surrounded by a stone wall. Planted by the Sortwell family in the foundation of an old inn, the property was donated to the town in 1959.

Sherman Lake Rest Area, Rt. 1 between Edgecomb and Newcastle. Pick up the fixings in Wiscasset and picnic at this scenic rest area. Since the dam broke, this "lake" is now a tidal river. It's still a lovely spot, though, complete with rest rooms.

✐ **Morris Farm** (207-882-4080; morrisfarm.org) 156 Gardiner Rd. (Rt. 27), Wiscasset. A 60-acre organic working farm, with trails open to the public during daylight hours; phone to check on current programming, which includes day camps and farm tours.

✳ Lodging

INN Squire Tarbox Inn (207-882-7693 or 1-800-818-0626;), 1181 Main Rd. (Rt. 144; turn off Rt. 1 south of Wiscasset), Westport 04578. Open mid-Apr.–Dec. "A good country inn must be tasted" maintains Swiss chef Mario De Pietro, and food is indeed what draws most patrons to his handsome Federal-style farmhouse, a full 8 miles down a winding country road from Rt. 1. Those who come as guests also savor one of the quietest country

SQUIRE TARBOX INN

Christina Tree

locations to be found on the coast.
Boards and timbers in the low-
ceilinged dining room date to 1763,
while the parlor and four largest guest
rooms, all with working fireplace, are
in the "new" (1825) section of house.
The remaining seven, more rustic
guest rooms are in the converted
1820s Carriage Barn, off an inviting
sitting room with a gas fireplace,
books, and games. De Pietro and his
wife, Roni, perpetuate the inn's reputation for hospitality as well as food,
encouraging guests to follow walking
paths on their 13 acres, row on the
saltwater pond, or explore Westport
Island on a mountain bike. $139–199
per couple; off-season $115–179 per
couple. Breakfast is included, and features freshly baked croissants, homemade muesli, and a hot dish prepared
by the chef, with fresh-laid eggs from
his hens. In a previous life De Pietro
was corporate chef of NYC-based
Restaurant Associates, overseeing 50
restaurants. Inquire about cooking
classes. Also see *Dining Out*.

BED & BREAKFASTS

✪ ✿ ✐ (ᵒᵖ) **Snow Squall Inn** (207-882-
6892 or 1-800-775-7245; snowsquall
inn.com), 5 Bradford Rd., Wiscasset
04578. Open more or less year-round.
Melanie, a trained yoga instructor and

massage therapist, and Paul Harris, a
professional chef, met in Bermuda,
where Paul owned a popular restaurant. They offer comfortably elegant
accommodations in this 1850s house
(named for a clipper ship) with ample
common space, gardens, and lounges
with hearths and TV. The four guest
rooms in the main house, each named
for a clipper ship, have a private bath,
king or queen bed, phone, and air-
conditioning. White Falcon is particularly spacious, with a king-sized pencil-
post bed and working fireplace. Each
of the three suites in the Carriage
House has two bedrooms (one and a
half baths) and a private entrance, good
for families. $107–160.50 for rooms,
from $160 for suites, less off-season. A
fabulous full breakfast is included.
Inquire about massage and yoga.

♨ (ᵒᵖ) **Marston House** (207-882-6010
or 1-800-852-4137; marstonhouse
.com), Main St., P.O. Box 517, Wiscasset 04578. Open May–Oct. The front
of the house is Paul and Sharon
Mrozinski's antiques shop, specializing
in 18th- and early-19th-century textiles
and painted furnishings. In the carriage house behind—well away from
the Rt. 1 traffic noise—are two exceptional guest rooms, each with private
entrance, each with working fireplace
and private bath. Breakfast is served in
the flowery gardens or in your room
and features fresh fruit, yogurt, home-
baked muffins, and fresh orange juice.
$110, $125 if just for one night.

Highnote (207-882-9628; wiscasset
.net/highnote), 26 Lee St., Wiscasset
04578. "You have to love high Victorian," John Reinhardt tells anyone who
inquires about this hospitable B&B.
The name is appropriate, he explains,
because he also manages the Pocket
Opera Players. John and Marie offer
three comfortable guest rooms furnished with authentic Victorian
antiques; shared bath. $85 per room

includes a European-style breakfast with cheese, meat, fruit, and homemade scones.

OTHER ❧ **Wiscasset Motor Lodge** (207-882-7137; wiscassetmotorlodge .com), 596 Bath Rd. (Rt. 1), Wiscasset 04578. Open Apr.–Nov. An unusually attractive, clean, comfortable motel with either a queen or two queen beds and air-conditioning. $79–108 in high season, from $65 in shoulder seasons.

✳ Where to Eat

DINING OUT Squire Tarbox Inn (207-882-7693; squiretarboxinn.com), 1181 Main Rd. (Rt. 144; turn off Rt. 1 south of Wiscasset), Westport (see *Lodging*). Open daily (except Mon.) Memorial Day–Oct.; Thu.–Sat. in Apr., May, Nov., and Dec., when Thu. is Swiss night. Reserve. Dinner is served 6–8:30 PM in an 18th-century former summer kitchen with a large colonial fireplace and ceiling timbers that were once part of a ship. In warm-weather months there's an attractive screened and canopied deck. Swiss chef-owner Mario De Pietro could start you off with Scandinavian dill-cured salmon, then serve entrées like rosemary roasted rack of lamb or sautéed sliced veal with Swiss-style roesti potatoes. Several nightly specials feature the freshest available produce. Strawberries (served with double cream) along with salad greens and many vegetables come from the inn's extensive organic farm. Entrées $23.50–30. A 15 percent gratuity is added.

✪ ♿ **Le Garage** (207-882-5409; legaragerestaurant.com), 15 Water St., Wiscasset. Open from 11 am–dinner (closed Mon.); Sunday brunch 9:30–3. A 1920s-era garage, now an outstanding restaurant with a glassed-in porch overlooking the Sheepscot River (when you make reservations, request a table

on the porch). Frequently less crowded for lunch than restaurants on the main drag. Owner Cherl Lee Rust's family transformed the place into a restaurant in 1974 and has been known for its seafood chowders, stews, Newburgs, crêpes, and creamed finnan haddie. More recently Swedish executive chef Mikael Andersson has expanded the locally sourced menu with more steak dishes and vegetarian options like French-style ratatouille and eggplant napoleon. Dinner entrées $16–24.

EATING OUT ✪ ♪ **Sarah's** (207-882-7504; sarahscafe.com), Main and Water Sts., Wiscasset. Open daily year-round, 11–8, with an outdoor deck for summer dining. Everything in this popular way stop is prepared from scratch, and the extensive menu includes good pizza (try the Greek pizza with extra garlic), salads, sandwiches in pita pockets or baked in dough, vegetarian dishes, Mexican fare, and lobster more than 15 different ways. Well known for their soup and bread bar, a godsend if you are trying to get a quick but tasty bite on your way up or down the coast. We can never pass up the Cobb crab salad.

♪ **Red's Eats** (207-882-6128), Rt. 1 and Water St., just before the bridge, Wiscasset. Open Apr.–Sept. until 2 AM on Fri. and Sat., until 11 weeknights, and noon–6 on Sun. The lines can be an hour long and the seating is at picnic benches, but the lobster rolls—packing an entire lobster into one small hot-dog roll—continue to get rave reviews. Whether or not this is "Maine's #1 Lobster Roll" is a matter of taste. The lobster is cold, fresh from the fridge, served with a choice of hot butter or mayo. With hot butter it's good, but we prefer warm lobster freshly picked from the shell, available at a number of traditional lobster pounds. There are also fried clams, crabcakes, hot dogs, fried zucchini, and more. Al Gagnon, who opened this classic hot-dog stand in 1977, passed away in 2008, but his daughters Debbie and Cindy ably carry on.

Sprague's Lobster (207-882-7814), Water St. just before the bridge, Wiscasset. Open seasonally. Picnic tables on a pier beside the river are the other great place to sample fresh, bargain lobsters with all the fixings, or crab rolls and road-food staples. No legend, no lines, a great view, and really good clam fritters.

❦ **The Sea Basket** (207-882-6581), 303 Bath Rd. (Rt. 1), Wiscasset. Open Wed.–Sun. 11–8. A long-established, attractive road stop, known for fresh seafood; a lot of it is fried, but with an eye to keeping it hearth-healthy. Known for lobster stew; other seafood choices include lobster rolls and sea scallops. The kids menu includes a PB&J sandwich for $1.50.

Montsweag Roadhouse (207-443-6563; montsweagroadhouse.com), 942 Rt. 1, Woolwich, nearer to Wiscasset than Bath. Open 11–1 AM. Serving food until 9, until 10 Fri. and Sat. This

distinctive red building is an old apple storage barn, part of a large farm and orchard owned for many years by Bath's Sewall family, who turned the barn into a restaurant in the 1930s, eventually closing it down. Reopened several years ago, it presently has a pleasantly split personality. Come on a weeknight and it's a quiet, spacious family-geared place with booths and a large, reasonably priced menu and full bar. We can speak for the haddock taco. On Fri. and Sat. this place hops with live bands upstairs.

Treats (207-882- 6192), 80 Main St. Open Mon.–Sat. 8–6, Sun. 10–4. A gourmet food store also known for baked goods plus terrific soups and sandwiches, with an eat-in table. The town's picnic source.

✳ Selective Shopping

ANTIQUES SHOPS Antiques are everywhere in Wiscasset. On and just off Water Street, in or attached to attractive old homes, more than 20 shops by our last count. Pick up a map (available in most shops) and browse the day away; many specialize in nautical pieces and country primitives. **Avalon Antiques Market** (207-882-4029; avalonantiquemarket.com), Rt. 1, 2 miles south of Wiscasset Village, open daily 9–7, represents more than 100 dealers. See the Bath chapter for details about the Montsweag Flea Market, south of Wiscasset on Rt. 1, open seasonally on Wed. and weekends.

ART GALLERIES Wiscasset Bay Gallery (207-882-7682; wiscassetbaygallery.com), 67 Main St., Wiscasset. Changing exhibits in attractive, spacious exhibit rooms. Specializes in 19th- and 20th-century Maine and New England marine and landscape paintings.

RED'S EATS

Christina Tree

Maine Art Gallery (207-882-7511; maineartgallery.org), 15 Warren S. Open June–Nov., Tue.–Sat. 10–4, Sun. 11–4. Housed in a vintage-1807 brick schoolhouse, a nonprofit gallery since 1954. Frequently changing exhibits. Worth finding.

OTHER Sheepscot River Pottery (pastel, floral designs), Rt. 1 just north of Wiscasset in Edgecomb, home base for one of Maine's major potteries.

Wiscasset Old General Store (207-882-6622), 49 Water St., Wiscasset Maine souvenirs, and products, gifts, cards, book, garden accessories and more.

Big Al's Supervalues (201-882-6423; bigalssupervalues.com), south of Wiscasset Village on Rt. 1. An odd-lots trove of everything you don't need and a few things you might. Toys, gadgets, Maine souvenirs, party supplies etc. Free coffee.

Winters Gone Farm (207-882-9191), 145 Alna Rd. (Rt. 218), Wiscasset. Open daily 10–6. An alpaca farm with nature trails and picnic areas, a store selling sweaters, scarves, jackets, teddy bears, toys, and more.

BOOTHBAY HARBOR REGION

The water surrounding the village of Boothbay Harbor is more than just a view. You must cross it—via a footbridge—to get from one side of town to the other, and you can explore it on a wide choice of excursion and charter boats and in sea kayaks. It is obvious from the very lay of this old fishing village that its people have always gotten around on foot or in boats. Though parking has increased in recent years, cars don't have room to pass each other, and still feel like an intrusion. In the peninsula's other coastal villages, Southport and East Boothbay, roads are walled by pines, permitting only occasional glimpses of water, and offer little or no shoulder for pedestrians or cyclists.

Boats are what all three of the Boothbays have traditionally been about. Boats are built, repaired, and sold here, and sailing and fishing vessels fill the harbors. Excursions range from an hour-long sail around the outer harbor to a 90-minute crossing (each way) to Monhegan Island. Fishermen can pursue giant tuna, stripers, and blues, and nature lovers can cruise out to see seals, whales, and puffins.

In the middle of summer Boothbay Harbor itself is chockablock full of tourists licking ice cream cones, chewing freshly made taffy and fudge, browsing in shops, looking into art galleries, listening to band concerts on the library lawn, and, of course, eating lobster. You get the feeling it's been like this every summer since the 1870s.

Boothbay Harbor is just a dozen miles south of Rt. 1 as the road (Rt. 27) runs, down the middle of the peninsula. The coastline is, however, a different story, measuring 100 miles as it wanders down the Sheepscot, around Southport Island and up into Boothbay Harbor, out around Spruce Head, around Linekin Bay, out Ocean Point, and back up along the Damariscotta River.

Thanks to the fervor of developers from the 1870s on, this entire coastline is distinguished by the quantity of its summer cottages, many of which can be rented by the week for much less than you might think. Still, thanks to the Boothbay Region Land Trust, there are now over 30 miles of accessible waterside preserves, with trails meandering through hundreds of acres of spruce and pine, down to smooth rocks and tidal pools. It was precisely this landscape that inspired Rachel Carson, who first summered on the peninsula in 1946 and built a cottage on the Sheepscot River in 1953, to write much of *The Edge of the Sea* (1955) and then *Silent Spring* (1962), the book that changed global thinking about human beings' relation to basic laws of nature.

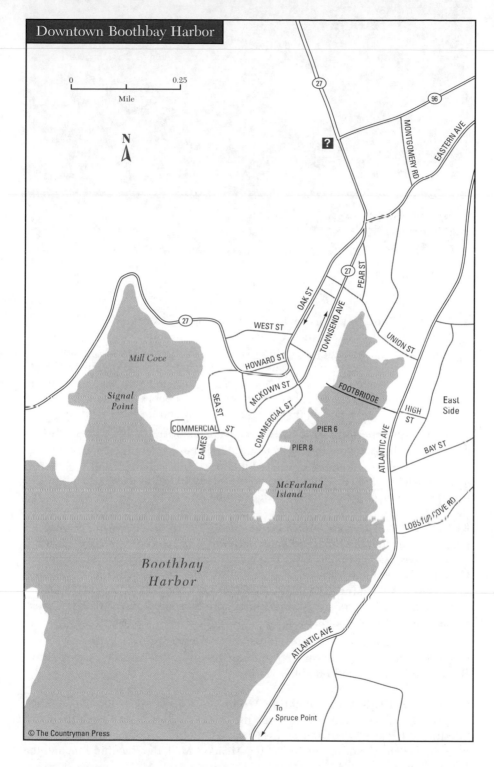

Downtown Boothbay Harbor

0   0.25
        Mile

N

27

96

MONTGOMERY RD

EASTERN AVE

?

27

PEAR ST

OAK ST

TOWNSEND AVE

WEST ST

UNION ST

HOWARD ST

Mill Cove

Signal
Point

MCKOWN ST

SEA ST

FOOTBRIDGE

HIGH ST

East
Side

COMMERCIAL ST

COMMERCIAL ST

EAMES ST

PIER 6

PIER 8

ATLANTIC AVE

BAY ST

McFarland
Island

LOBSTER COVE RD

Boothbay
Harbor

ATLANTIC AVE

To
Spruce Point

© The Countryman Press

Christina Tree

BOOTHBAY HARBOR

GUIDANCE Boothbay Harbor Region Chamber of Commerce (207-633-2353 or 1-800-266-8422; boothbayharbor.com), 192 Townsend Ave. (Rt. 27), southbound, just before the light but north of Hannaford Supermarket at the junction with Rt. 96. Open weekdays year-round, also weekends June–Columbus Day. Pick up the chamber's annual *Visitor & Resource Guide* and (indispensable) map detailing local parking lots. The chamber also keeps detailed books of cottage listings and photos, and tracks availability for cottages weekly and for lodgings daily.

Boothbay Information Center (207-633-4743; boothbay.org/bcc), Rt. 27, Boothbay, after the fire station. Open daily 9–9 (until 6 on Sun.) late June–Columbus Day, also Fri.–Sun. Memorial Day–late June. A friendly walk-in center that does its best to help people without reservations find places to stay. It keeps an illustrated scrapbook of options, also a cottage rental list.

GETTING THERE *By air or bus:* Private planes can fly into the Wiscasset Airport. If you fly into the **Portland International Jetport**, take **Concord Coach Lines** to Wiscasset, 14 miles away. **Harbor Tour and Shuttle** (207-443-9166), **Country Coach Charters** (207-380-7201), **Bo-Mar Transportation** (207-725-7189), **D&P Associated Limousine Services** (207-865-0203), **Executive Car Service** (207-228-3715), and **Maine Limousine Service** (207-883-0222) all pick up and deliver to the Boothbays.

By car: Take I-295 from Portland, getting off at exit 28 (Brunswick) or exit 31 (Topsham). Follow signs to Rt. 1 north through Bath and Wiscasset, turning onto Rt. 27 into Boothbay and Boothbay Harbor.

GETTING AROUND The Rocktide Trolley (on wheels) runs every 30 minutes daily, 10–5, mid-June–Labor Day. From the east side of town, starting at the Rocktide Inn, to Brown's Wharf Inn, across to the heart of the Boothbay Harbor Region, up onto 27 north, stopping at the Meadow Mall, the Flagship Inn, and the Boothbay Region YMCA.

PARKING Finding a spot in the center of Boothbay Harbor can mean circling the block a couple of times. Still, we had little trouble on an August weekend, armed with a local map showing parking lots (see *Guidance*). Boothbay offers free street parking for two- or four-hour increments and has eight parking lots in the downtown area.

WHEN TO COME Many Some B&Bs and restaurants stay open year-round, even in midwinter when the gas fireplaces are on high. But if it's bright warm days on the water you're looking for, summer can't be beat.

✳ Must See

FOR FAMILIES ✿ **Maine State Aquarium** (207-633-9559), McKown Point Rd., West Boothbay Harbor. Open Memorial Day weekend–Sept. daily 10–5; in Sept., Wed.–Sun. $5 adults, $3 ages 5–18 and over 60; 4 and under free. At this octagonal waterside aquarium, kids and adults alike can view tanks filled with sea creatures found in Maine waters such as striped bass, cod, alewives, and a 14-pound lobster. Dip your hands into the touch tank and view "chained sharks," skates, and alewives (larger than we'd thought). Presentations several times a day in summer, but get there early (except Sept.) to ensure a good view.

✿ ♿ **Boothbay Railway Village** (207-633-4727; railwayvillage.org), Rt. 27 (about 3 miles north of Boothbay Harbor). Open daily 9:30–5, June–Columbus Day; special rides for Halloween and Thanksgiving, plus a Polar Express in early Dec. Regular admission $9 adults, $5 ages 3–16. A 2-foot narrow-gauge railway wends its way through a miniature village made up of several restored buildings, including vintage railroad stations, the Boothbay Town Hall (1847), and the Spruce Point chapel (1923). Displays include a general store, a doll museum, and a 1920s-era home with an authentic 1929 GE refrigerator and period furniture. More than 55 antique autos (1907–49) are also on display. Many special events, including a weekend antique auto meet (more than 150 cars) in late July.

🐚 ✿ **Kenneth Stoddard Shell Museum** and **Dolphin Mini-Golf** (207-633-4828), Hardwick Rd. off Rt. 27 (turn at the lighthouse), Boothbay Harbor. Open daily May–mid-Sept .The museum boasts one of the world's largest private collections of seashells, including lobster claws and sand dollars (free). The 18 holes of mini golf include lakes stocked with fish and a covered bridge.

✿ **The By-Way**. Don't miss Boothbay Harbor's old-fashioned harborside boardwalk area. Walk from the By-Way down to the footbridge across the harbor.

Romar Bowling Lanes (207-633-5721), at the By-Way, Boothbay Harbor. Open summer months only. In business since 1929, under the same ownership since 1946, this log-sided pleasure hall with its sandwich bar, pool tables, and video games is a genuine throwback. A great rainy-day haven.

✳ Also See

✿ **Boothbay Region Historical Society Museum** (207-633-0820; boothbay historical.org), 72 Oak St., Boothbay Harbor. Open year-round Wed.–Sat. 10–2. Free. Seven rooms are filled with vintage lobster traps, Native American artifacts, ships' bells, a Fresnel lens from Ram Island, and genealogical resources. The gift shop stocks books, maps, coins, photos, and more.

✔ ♿ **Coastal Maine Botanical Gardens** (207-633-4333; mainegardens.org), 132 Botanical Garden Dr., off Barter's Island Road, Boothbay. Grounds open daily 9–5 year-round; buildings closed on weekends Jan.–Mar. $12 adults, $10 seniors 65 and over, $6 ages 7–17, under 3 free. This gorgeous public garden on 120 shorefront acres contains more than 80,000 plants from more than 1,300 species, 350 of them native. The visitors center, with a gift shop and café, sits near the Kitchen Garden, Garden of the Five Senses, Children's Garden, and Rose Garden. Count on the café for meals made with produce picked just outside the door in summer. The Garden of the Five Senses adds the scent of grosso lavender and other aromatic plants, the texture of lamb's ears and creeping thyme, the noise of flowing water and frogs and wooden boards underfoot, and the tastes of herbs like Russian tarragon to the beauty you can drink in with your eyes. Geology lessons, like one about layered schist, are presented in signage along the winding paths. A downward-sloping path brings you to the Meditation Garden, centered on a magnificent stone basin. From here the path can connect with the Shoreland Trail, along which you can find the Fern Garden and a Fairy House Village. The tranquil Huckleberry Trail loops back up to the Woodland Garden Area. Outdoor sculpture of wildlife by Wendy Klemperer conveys the spirit of those longtime inhabitants, wolves and deer. At the other end of the property a growing rhododendron collection is set off by waterfalls and terraced paths above ponds. The Maine Woods Trail highlights mosses, lichens, heaths, and ferns. The Children's Garden is themed from children's books and includes a lupine meadow, story barn, maze, tree house, and shallow

✔ **Burnt Island Lighthouse Program** (for Maine gov., 207-633-9559; maine.gov /dmr/education; for reservations, 207-633-2284; balmydayscruises.com). Please call to confirm. Once a day Monday and Thursday July–Aug. $22 adults, $12 under 12. This three-hour living history tour of Burnt Island Light Station is a must-do on a visit to the Boothbay region. Guides in 1950 wardrobes portray the family that once maintained the light in the lantern room; the family children give tours of the island's 5 acres and surrounding water. Volunteers from many organizations have turned this formerly abandoned site into a well-maintained destination good for walks on trails as well as learning about the past and the hazards of navigation on the coast of Maine.

✔ **Hendricks Hill Museum** (207-633-1102; hendrickshill.org), 419 Hendricks Hill Rd., Rt. 27, Southport Island. Open July 1–Labor Day, Tue., Thu., and Sat. 11–3. The house looks much as it did in 1810, with a period kitchen including a beehive oven, pictures of Southport's grand hotels as well as other village memorabilia, wooden boats, and farm implements. While in Southport, visit the Southport Memorial Library, which has an impressive butterfly collection. Southport lies in the narrow heart of the migratory route of the monarch butterfly.

pond as well as a place for children to learn about gardening. The Bosarge Family Education Center is the venue for a wide variety of programs (check the website). Free, seasonal shuttles ease the way from multiple parking lots, and guided Cart Tours are available by reservation. Pets are allowed only in the parking area; there is a dog walk and water spigot. Plan to arrive early in summer as the many lots can fill by midday.

COASTAL MAINE BOTANICAL GARDENS

Christina Tree

✴ To Do

BICYCLING Tidal Transit Co. (207-633-7140; kayakboothbay.com), by the foot bridge, Boothbay Harbor, rents bikes in-season. Our favorite bike route begins at Boothbay Village and follows lightly trafficked Barter's Island Rd. past Knickerbocker Lake and Knickerkane Island Park to Hodgdon Island, and then on to Barter's Island and the Porter Preserve. **Oak Street Provisions** (207-633-1290), 43 Oak St., Boothbay Harbor, also rents bikes.

BOAT EXCURSIONS ❧ **Balmy Days Cruises** (207-633-2284 or 1-800-298-2284; balmydayscruises.com), Pier 8, Boothbay Harbor. *Balmy Days II* offers sails to Monhegan every morning early June–early Oct. and weekends in shoulder seasons (see "Monhegan" in "Midcoast Islands"). The crossing takes 90 minutes each way, and you have close to four hours on the island (a 30-minute boat ride around the island is also possible on the way back). Bring a picnic and hit the trail. *Novelty* makes one-hour Boothbay Harbor tours all day. Party fishing boat *Miss Boothbay* is another great family option. Also see **Burnt Island Lighthouse** under *To See*.

✒ **Boothbay Whale Watch** (207-633-3500 or 1-888-942-5363; whaleme.com), Fisherman's Wharf, Pier 6, Boothbay Harbor. This company offers guaranteed whale-watches: If you don't see a whale, your next trip is free. They also run Sunday reggae and Thursday classic oldies evening cruises with full bar and galley.

🐾 ✒ **Cap'n Fish Boat Cruises** (207-633-3244 or 1-800-636-3244; mainewhales .com), Pier 1 (red ticket booth), Boothbay Harbor. Operates mid-May–mid-Oct. daily. A variety of cruises: whale-watch, puffin, Pemaquid Point Lighthouse, seal-watch, Kennebec River–Bath, and a sunset sail. Coffee, snacks, soft drinks, and a full bar are available on board (don't bring your own). Dogs allowed on board.

Schooner Lazy Jack (207-633-3444; sailschoonerlazyjack.com), Pier 1, Boothbay Harbor. Captain Joe Tassi operates May–mid-Oct., offering two-hour trips, and can accommodate 13 passengers.

Bay Lady (207-633-2284; balmydayscruises.com), Pier 8, Boothbay Harbor. This 31-foot Friendship sloop can take as many as 13 passengers on 30- and 60-minute excursions past lighthouses and island in the harbor.

BOAT RENTALS Charger Charters (207-380-4556), 80 Commercial St., Boothbay Harbor, and **Finest Kind Wooden Boats** (207-633-5082), West Boothbay, offer both power- and sailboat rentals.

FISHING The Tackle Shop at the White Anchor (207-633-3788; whiteanchor innboothbay.com), Rt. 27, Boothbay, is one of the largest tackle shops on the Maine coast. Open daily 9–7; call for hours in winter. Rod and reel rentals, bait, plus a full line of fishing gear.

All the following can be accessed from Boothbay Harbor: **Charger Charters** (207-380-4556; chargersportfishing.com), 80 Commercial St. The *Charger* runs four fishing trips daily for mackerel, stripers, and bluefish. Also half- and full-day private charter options for cod, cusk, pollack, and shark. **Blackjack Sportfishing & Charters** (207-633-6445), Pier 7, next to Whale Park. Captain Dan Stevens offers charters on his six-passenger, 28-foot bass boat for sportfishing, sightseeing, and transportation. **Redhook Charters** (207-633-3807) leaves from Tugboat Inn Marina. Captain Mark Stover provides tackle for charters, sightseeing, and transportation. **Shark Six Charters** (207-633-5929; salt watermaine.com), Brown's Wharf Inn & Marina, 121 Atlantic Ave. Captain Barry Gibson has spent more than 40 years fishing striped bass; tackle provided when on his 28-foot center-console boat. **Sweet Action Charters** (207-633-4741; sweetactioncharters .com), Kaler's Crab and Lobster House, 48 Commercial St.. Inshore fishing for mackerel, stripers, and bluefish on a 19-foot Seaway T-top, gear

BOOTHBAY OFFERS PLENTY OF WAYS TO GET OUT ON THE WATER

Christina Tree

included. **Hay Val Charters** (207-319-8123; hayvalcharters.com), 92 Cape Newagen Rd., Southport. A day, an afternoon, or an hour for up to six. Captain Bruce White offers custom tours aboard his 37-foot boat. He picks you up. **Go Lobstering F/V Sea Swallow** (207-380-7677), Boothbay Harbor. Captain Clive Farrin offers one-hour trips aboard his working lobster boat. **The Lobstah' Haul** (207-563-2709, lobstahhaul.com) offers a chance to haul traps plus a good old-fashioned lobster bake. Cash only.

GOLF AND MINI GOLF Boothbay Region Country Club (207-633-6085; boothbaycountryclub.com), Country Club Dr. (off Rt. 27), Boothbay. Open April–Nov. Eighteen holes, restaurant and lounge, and carts and clubs for rent. Open to the public.

RECREATIONAL FACILITY ✔ **Boothbay Region YMCA** (207-633-2855; brymca.com), Townsend Ave., Rt. 27 (on your left as you come down the stretch that leads to town). An exceptional facility open to nonmembers (user fee charged) with two new swimming pools and other programs for children. Tennis, racquetball, gymnastics, aerobics, soccer, swimming in a heated six-lane indoor pool, saunas, exercise and weight-lifting rooms, and a fieldhouse with a three-lane track.

SEA KAYAKING ✔ **Tidal Transit Company** (207-633-7140; kayakboothbay .com), 18 Granary Way, Boothbay Harbor, in the "Chowder House" building by the footbridge, offers guided tours as well as hourly, half-day, and full-day rentals (basic instruction included). Offerings include a lighthouse tour, wildlife tours, and sunset tours. They also rent bikes. **Gray Homestead Camping** (207-633-4612; graysoceancamping.com) on Southport Island (rentals only) and **East Boothbay Kayak Company** (207-633-7411; eastboothbaykayaks.com) can deliver kayaks and arrange kayak tours anywhere in the Boothbay region.

TENNIS Public tennis courts are located across Rt. 27 from the YMCA, which also has indoor courts.

SAILING Linekin Bay Resort (207-633-2494 or 1-866-847-2103; linekinbay resort.com), 92 Wall Point Rd., Boothbay Harbor 04538. Overnight moorings (all chain), onshore facilities. Qualified sailors can rent 19-foot Rhodes sailboats, and sailing lessons are offered for all abilities. We hadn't sailed in decades and couldn't say more for our hour spent fitting and hoisting the sail, then taking the tiller and tacking back and forth in this sheltered bay.

(((ɥ))) **Boothbay Harbor Yacht Club** (207-633-5750), 156 Western Ave., West Boothbay Harbor 04575. Moorings available for sailing/cruising to visitors. Launch service 8–2, heads, showers, laundry, dining room/lounge access. Closed Mon. Free WiFi wireless Internet access at mooring, ice available, plus other amenities.

WALKING Ocean Point, at the tip of the East Boothbay peninsula, offers beautiful views of the ocean and several windswept islands, but parking can be tricky. Leave your car in the lot operated by the Linekin Preserve (part of Boothbay Region Land Trust, see *Green Space*) or in designated parking areas and walk the point by foot, being mindful of NO TRESPASSING signs. Explore the rocky beach and its tidal pools. On a clear day you can see both Ram Island and the Cuckolds lighthouses.

Red Cloak Haunted History Tours (207-380-3806) offers lantern-lit walking tours of Boothbay Harbor and other nearby commuities.

Also see *Green Space*.

✴ Green Space

BEACHES 🐾 Beaches are all private, but visitors are permitted in a number of spots:

Hendricks Head Beach. Follow Rt. 27 toward Southport, across the Townsend Gut Bridge to a circle (white church on your left, monument in the center, general store on your right); turn right and follow Beach Rd. to the beach, which offers roadside parking and calm, shallow water. Limited parallel parking.

🐾 **Grimes Cove** has a little pebble beach with rocks to climb at the very tip of Ocean Point, East Boothbay. Follow Rt. 96 to the end.

🐾 **Barrett Park**, Lobster Cove (turn at the Catholic church, east side of Boothbay Harbor), is a place to picnic and get wet.

🐾 **Knickerkane Island Park**, Barter's Island Rd., Boothbay. Paths lead from the parking lot onto a small island with picnic tables and swimming. You can also turn in at the sign for **Knickerbocker Lake**, near the park. The road in is a bit rough, but that seems to keep crowds away from this small beach with a dock.

NATURE PRESERVES **Boothbay Region Land Trust** (207-633-4818; bbrlt.org), 137 Townsend Ave., Boothbay Harbor. Open Mon.–Fri. 9:30– 4:30. The trails are open year-round and free of charge although donations are appreciated.

Pick up a copy of the handy, spiral-bound, illustrated *Take a Hike* ($15) published by the land trust—a guide to 18 major preserves with a total of 30 miles of trails. The 1,700 acres of land under the trust's protection include several islands. Free map/guides are also available at trailheads. In the **Porter Preserve** (23 wooded acres, including a beach) on Barters Island, an osprey peered at us from its nest atop a marker along a ledge just off-shore, and another ledge was so thick with seals that they seemed like some kind of brown growth—until a dog barked and the entire ledge seemed to heave and rise, then flop and splash off in different directions. The **Ovens Mouth Preserve** is a narrow passage between the Sheepscot and Back Rivers and a tidal basin. Separated by the two peninsulas that constitute this preserve is **Ice House Cove**, and across it are the remnants of the 1880s dam that once turned it into a freshwa-ter pond. Schooners once moored out-side the dam, loaded their hulls with ice, and sailed for the Caribbean. The pond has reverted to salt marsh and

HENDRICKS HEAD BEACH

Christina Tree

teems with wildlife. Our Wiscasset/Boothbay area map shows the location of major trust preserves; for a full listing, go to their website.

✳ Lodging

The chamber of commerce lists more than 100 lodging places in its regional guide, from resorts to B&Bs to campgrounds and cottages, and keeps a list of vacation rentals. Because the chamber is open year-round, it's possible to contact the people there in time to reserve well in advance. See *Guidance*.

RESORTS ♂ ♪ ⅃ **Newagen Seaside Inn** (207-633-5242 or 1-800-654-5242; newagenseasideinn.com), Rt. 27, Southport Island, Cape Newagen 04576. Open mid-May–mid-Oct. When the original resort opened in the 1920s, owner Joshua Brooks,—founder of the Eastern States Exposition—had both electricity and Rt. 27 extended to this southern tip of Southport Island to serve it. In 1943 the original inn burned in a fire said to be set as a sig-

IN BOOTHBAY HARBOR

Bill Davis

nal to German U-boats. Brooks then had the present large, admittedly plain-faced facility built, painted, and open within three months. Rachel Carson frequented the inn and its splendid grounds; her ashes were scattered here. Even if you don't stay here, be sure to find your way to the property's pine-shaded shore. The 25 rooms and three suites in the main inn all have private bath; first-floor rooms have private deck. The Little Inn building houses three more junior suites. Take a chilly plunge in the bay off the dock, then hightail it to the heated freshwater pool and finish in the hot tub overlooking the little harbor. Amenities include tennis courts, bicycles, lawn games, rowboats, and the Pine Room, which houses two funky 1940s-era candlepin bowling lanes, pool table, and Ping-Pong. Weddings tend to fill the place on weekends. Rooms $150–295 and suites $189–305, depending on room and season. Inquire about condos and three cottages.

♂ 🐾 ♪ **Spruce Point Inn Resort & Spa** (207-633-4152 or 1-800-553-0289; sprucepointinn.com), 88 Grandview Ave., Boothbay Harbor 04538. Open mid-May–mid-Oct. A full-service resort at the end of a 57-acre landscaped peninsula jutting into Boothbay Harbor, the inn offers 9 guest rooms in the main building; 12 rooms with Maine traditional decor, some with cathedral ceilings and hardwood floors; 56 deluxe rooms featuring unusually large bedroom and marble bath, TV, gas fireplace, and balcony with water views; and five cottages, two oceanfront, perfect for families. We loved swimming in the cold saltwater pool and warming back up again in the hot tub, both on the edge of the sea. Large living room, TV room and study, recreation room (geared to kids), heated freshwater pool, clay tennis courts, lawn games, fitness center, full-service spa, and private pier. Organized children's programs in July and Aug. High season $169–560 for guest rooms, cottages, and condos. A service charge, 10 percent on rooms and 15 percent on cottages, is added for use of amenities, including kayaks, 42 acres for hiking, and bicycles.

Sprucewold Lodge (207-633-3600 or 1-800-732-9778; sprucewoldlodge.com), 4 Nahanada Rd., Boothbay Harbor 04538. Open late May–mid-Oct. Richard Paiser runs this vintage 1920s, 30-room log lodge, with three stone fireplaces for chilly weather. No water views but surrounded by spruce, pine, oak, and birch in a rare wooded part of Boothbay Harbor, it's tucked away but just a 20-minute walk to the village. A buffet breakfast is served in the cathedral-ceilinged dining hall, with eggs, peach French toast, bacon, breads, and pastries. $85–160, depending on room and season.

✔ ♿ **Ocean Point Inn** (207-633-4200 or 1-800-552-5554; oceanpointinn .com), 191 Shore Rd., P.O. Box 409, East Boothbay 04544. Open Memorial Day–Columbus Day. Owner David Dudley has worked at Ocean Point since 1969, and he bought the inn in 1985—he even met his wife here! He has outfitted many of the 61 rooms, suites, cottages, and apartments with pretty wallpaper borders, king and queen four-posters, and botanical prints. All rooms and cottages have private bath, air-conditioning, cable TV, mini refrigerator, and phone; some have a fireplace, ocean view, and porch. Guests relax in the heated pool with a hot tub or the Adirondack chairs overlooking the ocean. The inn has an oceanfront dining room (see *Dining*

Out). $99–219 in-season. Breakfast is extra.

☀ (⸘) **Ocean Gate Resort** (800-221-5924 or 207-633-3321; oceangateinn .com), P.O. Box 673, Boothbay Harbor 04538. Several multistory buildings with water views are ranged along the shore, and attractive cottages come with and without views on this 45-acre wooded property. A breakfast buffet and use of canoes and kayaks is included in the rates: $134–310 in summer, less in shoulder months. Facilities include a heated pool, miniature golf, fishing pond, tennis, and more. Maine lobster bake every Wed. in July and Aug.

INNS AND BED & BREAKFASTS

✪ (⸘) **Five Gables Inn** (207-633-4551 or 1-800-451-5048; fivegablesinn.com), 107 Murray Hill Rd. (off Rt. 96), P.O. Box 335, East Boothbay 04544. Open Memorial Day weekend–mid-Oct. Hosts De and Mike Kennedy have created a very special oasis combining luxury with unstuffy relaxation. Fifteen of the 16 rooms offer views of Linekin Bay; most have queen-sized beds (many with handmade quilts), and 5 have a working fireplace. Try one of the smaller third-floor gable rooms, which offer some of the best views of the water. What we love best about this place is the expansive living room/dining area with a wraparound porch that extends the common area. It's spacious enough for guests to find their own corner, but the books, hearth, and conversation (frequently sparked by Mike draw in anyone who wants in. An extensive buffet breakfast, prepared by Mike, a Culinary Institute of America graduate, is included in $165–240 double. Afternoon tea comes with home-baked goodies.

✪ ✔ ♿ **Topside Inn** (207-633-5404 or 1-888-633-5404; topsideinn.com), 60 McKown St., Boothbay Harbor 04538.

🪢 ✪ 🐾 ✎ ((ᵗ)) **Linekin Bay Resort** (207-633-2494 or 1-866-847-2103; linekin bayresort.com), 92 Wall Point Rd., Boothbay Harbor 04538. Open Memorial Day–Columbus Day weekends. Styled as the last all-inclusive sailing resort on the East Coast, Linekin Bay has been owned by the same family since 1909. It's been evolving ever since, which explains its range of lodging—35 rooms in five different lodges (a family or group of friends numbering up to 12 can rent a lodge, each with a sitting room and kitchen), along with 30 cottages (one or two rooms), 8 with water views and the rest scattered through the woods. High-season rates—$120–170 per adult, less for children (free under 3) or more than three adults traveling together—include the use of a fleet of Rhodes 19s or a 30-foot sailboat (also used for cruises). Lessons are offered by more than a dozen instructors. Three really good meals (manager Mark Osburn has run popular restaurants), served family-style in the open-timbered central lodge, are included. Also included: weekday Kids Camp and the use of canoes, kayaks, rowboats, and tennis and fishing gear. During our stay guided morning walks into downtown Boothbay Harbor were offered by a resident naturalist/historian. Spring and fall B&B rates are $129 per couple; group rates also available. Facilities include a heated bay-side saltwater pool and tennis court, a TV room (nightly movies), an old-fashioned game/library area, and a bar and deck in West Lodge as well as kids' rec room and play areas. Weddings for up to 150 in shoulder months.

PORCH AT LINEKIN BAY RESORT

Christina Tree

Open May 1–mid-Oct. Brian Lamb and Ed McDermott host water excursions, hiking trails, and visits to art galleries. With a great location at the top of McKown Hill, more than half of the 21 rooms in the 1864 house and a pair of two-story motel-style annexes have water views of the lighthouses and islands; all have private bath and cable TV. Room 4 sits at the top of the stairs, with views of the water, a large bathroom, and a king bed. Reasonable rates: $155–225, including a breakfast with great house granola, yogurt, a bowl packed with all kinds of fruit, and a hot entrée as well as fresh muffins.

✪ (((•))) **Hodgdon Island Inn** (207-633-7474 or 1-800-314-5160; boothbaybb.com), 374 Barter's Island Rd., Boothbay 04537. Open year-round. Pamela and Richard Riley came from Kentucky to Boothbay on their honeymoon and kept returning. Finally they made the leap and have created a colorful, comfortable, and warmly welcoming bed & breakfast a mile from the Coastal Maine Botanical Gardens (see *Must See*) and handy to the Porter Preserve (see *Green Space*) on Barter's Island. The handsome 19th-century home

VERANDA AT FIVE GABLES

Christina Tree

overlooks a cove and one of Maine's few hand-cranked drawbridges. Each of the nine air-conditioned rooms has a water view, private bath, refrigerator, and ceiling fan, and each is individually decorated with a sure eye to color and fabrics; two of the rooms share a balcony. Richard's paintings are hung throughout. Inquire about the huge model of a sailboat in the parlor's bay window. The heated swimming pool is set in a landscaped garden. Guests enjoy a four-course breakfast, served in the sunny breakfast room or on the front porch overlooking the cove, included in $139–215, along with afternoon treats. Guests also gather for dessert in the evening.

The Inns at Greenleaf Lane (207-633-3100 or 1-888-950-7724; innsatgreenleaflane.com), 65 and 71 Commercial St., Boothbay Harbor 04538. Open year-round. These two neighboring sea captains' houses are both steps from the harbor. In No. 65 a library full of games and books centers on a stone wood-burning fireplace. The seven rooms at No. 71 all have private bath, cable TV, air-conditioning, fireplace, and deck with a view of the harbor, and some overlook little McFarland Island. The sitting room is a solarium with a gas fireplace. Room 1 features a charming murals of a garden. Room details show the painstaking innkeeper at work, from glass-doored showers to pretty glasses by the sink. Room 8 is a suite good for long stays. A fitness room has free weights, treadmill, and stationary bicycle, and there are yoga mats for use on the deck. $155–265 includes full breakfast.

Blue Heron Seaside Inn (207-633-7020 or 1-866-216-2300; blueheronseasideinn.com), 65 Townsend Ave., Boothbay Harbor. Laura and Phil Chapman returned from overseas with a container of fine furniture, ready to furnish this inn. Their six rooms are outfitted with refrigerator/freezer, private bath, air-conditioning, and cable TV; all share a deck set above the harbor. Admiral's Rest, with a king bed, is spacious—but so are all the rest. Kayaks sit at the inn's little dock ready to explore the harbor. $165–265 in-season includes a full breakfast, perhaps Vickery French toast with baked apples. Then walk out the door for a stroll through the village.

((ᵩ)) **Linekin Bay Bed & Breakfast** (207-633-9900 or 1-800-596-7420; linekinbaybb.com), 531 Ocean Point Rd., East Boothbay 04544. Open April–Oct. A haven overlooking Linekin Bay, with four charming rooms, all with water views, fireplace, and private bath. Owners Larry Brown and Marti Booth take pride in helping guests take advantage of what the area offers. All rooms have views of Linekin Bay beyond perennial gardens. In the Holbrook Suite you can take in this view from a king four-poster; in the Linkein Loft suite, a staircase above the bedroom leads to an airy loft sitting room with the best water views. $145–190 in-season, $125–140 off, includes a full breakfast, perhaps blueberry cinnamon French toast stuffed with blueberry jam. Brown also makes a great brownie and sweets in the afternoon.

MOTELS Boothbay Harbor has number of inviting motels, many on the water, but we defer to the Mobil and AAA guides.

♿ **Flagship Inn** (207-633-5094 or 1-800-660-5094; boothbaylodging.com), 200 Townsend Ave. (Rt. 27), Boothbay Harbor 04538. Open year-round. This completely renovated, affordable motel offers 82 rooms and family suites. Amenities include a swimming pool,

hot tub, and cable TV. $74–149, depending on the season. On-site restaurant.

✪ 🐾 ⊘ ♿ **Ship Ahoy Motel** (207-633-5222; shipahoymotel.com), Rt. 238, Southport Island (mailing address: P.O. Box 235, Boothbay Harbor 04538). Open Memorial Day weekend–Columbus Day. Great views at a sensational price. A family-owned motel with 54 units, all with TV and air-conditioning, 30 with a private balcony right on the water, others tucked into the granite ledges and pines of the island. Guests who hanker for 1960s decor are in for a real treat; others might find it all a little bare. Amenities include an unheated freshwater pool, coffee shop, and dock on 0.75 mile of waterfront. $49–89 in high season; $39–59 off-season; breakfast extra.

COTTAGES The following are variations on old-style cottage colonies, still a good option, especially with children and/or pets.

🐾 **Harborfields on the Shore** (207-633-5082; harborfields.com), 24 McKown Point Rd., West Boothbay Harbor 04575. A friendly, quiet family resort on a 10-acre harborfront property. Cozy cottages feature woodstoves, full kitchens, and great views of harbor. Floats for boating, swimming, and fishing are available, as are moorings and a small tidal beach. Pets welcome. From $808 per week.

🐾 ♿ ((ᵩ)) **The Boothbay Resort** (207-633-3411; boothbayresort.com), 301 Adams Pond Rd., Boothbay 04537. Open May–Oct. Lori and Win Mitchell have completely updated 5 one-bedroom kitchenette cottages, 6 two-bedroom full-kitchen cottages, and, in The Evergreen, 2 three-bedroom, two-bath, full-kitchen family suites. The swimming pool in front of the smaller, sweet cottages on the front lawn is a draw, and guests can golf at nearby private Boothbay Country Club or stay close to their accommodations on the putting greens, bocce court, or horseshoe pit. $99–239. Wine, beer, and cheese shop on site.

Note: Contact the chambers of commerce for lists of rental cottages. In addition, the locally based Cottage Connection of Maine (1-800-823-9501; cottageconnection.com) represents dozens of properties.

Thompson Cottages (207-633-5304; thompsoncottages.com), 7 Thompson's Hill Rd., Southport 04576. Three 1-bedroom cottages and one 3-bedroom cottage come fully equipped, located on Townsend Gut. Alice and Dick Thompson have been hosting guests here since 1968. From $700 per week.

VACATION RENTALS Boothbay Region for Rent by Owner (207-633-5026 summer or 508-358-3439; www .brfrbo.com; brfrbo@brfrbo.com). Cottages, condos, homes, and apartments in the Boothbay region for rent. Deal directly with the owner and save. P.O. Box 140, East Boothbay 04544 in winter.

Cottage Connection of Maine, Inc. (207-633-6545 or 1-800-823-9501; cottageconnection.com), Boothbay 04537. From small two-person cottages to full homes.

CAMPING ✿ ✍ ໒ Gray Homestead Campground (207-633-4612; grays oceancamping.com), 21 Homestead Rd., Southport Island 04576. Open mid-May–Columbus Day. You can't beat the location—301 acres on the east coast of Southport Island. Forty sites for tents and RVs. Stephen Gray's family has been here since 1800. $37–52 per night for RVs, tent sites starting at $38 for a family of four.

✿ ✍ **Shore Hills Campground** (207-633-4782; shorehills.com), 553 Wiscas-

set Rd., Boothbay. Open May 1–Columbus Day, with 150 sites, some on the waterfront. Amenities and recreation opportunities, and the motto "No Rig Too Big." Tent sites $27, full-service RV sites $45 in summer.

✳ Where to Eat

DINING OUT ✪ ✍ Ports of Italy (207-633-1011; portsofitaly.com), 47 Commercial St., Boothbay Harbor. Open for dinner daily from 4:30, Apr.–mid-Oct. Sante Calandri carries on the tradition of real Italian meals with homemade pasta in this bright upstairs dining room. An outdoor dining area is lovely in summer. *Tagierini alle vongole* tosses angel hair with clams, white wine, and olive oil. Grilled fish and meat, too. Entrées $9–29.

✪ **The Boathouse Bistro & Tapas Bar** (207-633-4074; theboathouse bistro.com), 12 By-Way, Boothbay Harbor. Open mid-March–Christmas for lunch and dinner. We love this place! Three different atmospheres— all casual—on each of the three floors, and the view improves as you climb (the top deck is open). Lunch on hot tapas like lobster and corn brûlée or duck confit crêpes; Maine mussels in a buttery wine broth or on a warm ratatouille tartlet, each about the price of a sandwich most places in town. Austrian chef Karin Guerin offers a vast menu, and this is one of those places where everyone orders a different dish and shares. The menu ranges from dinner salads, to a wide choice of vegetarian dishes, to seafood paella. $6–29.

The Thistle Inn (207-633-3541; thistleinn.com), 55 Oak St., Boothbay Harbor. Open year-round for dinner. Reservations recommended. No water views, but attractive dining rooms and seasonal deck. The focus is on local seafood and produce, a place to feast on Glidden Point oysters, pan-seared scallops, or lobster paella. Entrées $18–29. Pub menu also available.

*⚹ ♿ **Newagen Seaside Inn** (207-633-5242 or 1-800-654-5242), Rt. 27, Southport Island, Cape Newagen. Open for breakfast and dinner seasonally; usually closed Sat. night. A pleasant, old-fashioned dining room with ocean and sunset views, and splendid grounds to walk off the meal. The Cape Harbor Grill, the inn's dining room, might serve veal Oscar with crabmeat and béarnaise sauce, or salmon with chervil spaetzle and lime, cucumber, and raspberry coulis. A pub menu offers casual meals. Entrées $18–28.

The Rocktide Inn (207-633-4455 or 1-800-762-8433; rocktideinn.com), 35 Atlantic Ave., Boothbay Harbor. Open daily for breakfast 7:30–9:30 AM, dinner 5:30–9 PM, or drinks 4–11 PM; until 8:30 after Labor Day. Closed Columbus Day–mid-June. Come by boat or car for dinner (jackets required in the formal dining room, not in the casual dining room) or a Rocktide martini in the **On the Rocks Bar**. The view of the sunset is magnificent, and locals rate the dinners highly.

*⚹ **Andrews' Harborside Restaurant** (207-633-4074; andrewsharborside.com), 12 Bridge St., Boothbay Harbor (downtown, next to the municipal parking lot and footbridge). Open for breakfast, lunch, and dinner, daily May–Oct.; off-season closed Sun. afternoon. The chef-owner specializes in creative seafood and traditional New England dishes. Wonderful cinnamon rolls at breakfast, crab rolls and burgers at lunch, Round Top ice cream and seafood entrées at dinner. Entrées $14–29.

*⚹ ♿ **Ocean Point Inn Restaurant** (207-633-4200 or 1-800-552-5554),

East Boothbay. Open mid-June–Columbus Day weekend. Full breakfast buffet, and dinner. Reservations suggested. More than 110 years of tradition in these three informal dining rooms with ocean views. Choices usually include duckling, rib eye, and Delmonico steak. Entrées $18–29. Children's and tavern menus also available.

*⚹ **Lobsterman's Wharf** (207-633-3443), Rt. 96, East Boothbay (adjacent to a boatyard). Open mid-May–Columbus Day, serving 11:30–9, until 10 on weekends. The large menu includes all the usual seafood, lobster stew, and crabcakes, as well as spinach salad and pastas. Entrées $7–30.

EATING OUT ✪ *⚹ Ebb Tide (207-633-5692), Commercial St., Boothbay Harbor. Open year-round, 7 AM–7:30 PM; until 9:30 PM Fri. and Sat., closing 7:30 off-season. Nothing fancy about this place, but they offer breakfast all day, plus lobster rolls, milk clam chowder, fisherman's platters, and more. The raspberry pie is excellent. Old-fashioned, but with air-conditioning and knotty-pine booths.

McSeagull's (207-633-5900; McSeagullsOnline.com), 14 Wharf St., Boothbay Harbor. Open daily 11:30–closing. Wharfside dining and so popular it can get packed in high season. It's a local gathering place off-season because it's good. The book-sized menu ranges from pizzas to grilled as well as fried seafood platters. Try the northern white beans stewed in lobster stock, served with poached lobster. $6–36.

✪ **Baker's Way** (207-633-1119), 89 Townsend Ave., Boothbay Harbor. Open 6 AM–9 PM daily. Just the place for fried apple dumpling, you think, and then you smell lemongrass cooking and wonder where you are. There are two worlds here: a full bakery, very

LOBSTER

🦞 🍴 ♿ **The Lobster Dock** (207-633-7120; thelobsterdock.com), 49 Atlantic Ave., Boothbay Harbor, at the east end of the footbridge. Open 11:29–8:31 Memorial Day weekend–early Oct. This is our in-town place for a lobster roll, either hot with drawn butter or cold with a dab of mayo. Also lobster and shore dinners, steamed clams, mussels, steaks, and prime rib. Lobster spring rolls, and seared, exceptional tuna might be specials. Some people love the seafood fra diavolo: shrimp, scallops, mussels, and an entire lobster, simmered in a zesty broth with herbs, garlic, bay leaf, tomato, red pepper flakes, and wine ($25).

🍴 ♿ **Robinson's Wharf** (207-633-3830; robinsonswharf.net), Rt. 27, Southport Island (just across Townsend Gut from West Boothbay Harbor). Open mid-June–Columbus Day for lunch and dinner daily; children's menu. On a sunny day sit on the dock at one of the picnic tables and watch the boats unload their catch. Lobsters and lobster rolls, fried shrimp, clams, scallops, fish chowder, lobster stew, sandwiches, and homemade desserts.

🍴 **Clambake at Cabbage Island** (207-633-7200; cabbageislandclambakes .com). Late June–early Sept., the boat departs Pier 6 at Fisherman's Wharf daily, twice on Sat. and Sun., carrying passengers to 6-acre Cabbage Island in Liniken Bay. This is a traditional clambake with lobsters, clams, corn, and potatoes steamed in seaweed then served on picnic tables. In bad weather a circa-1900 lodge seats up to 100 people by a huge fireplace. About $60 per person including boat ride and tax.

Trevett Country Store (633-1140), 381 Barters Island Rd., Boothbay. Open daily 7 AM–8 PM, a mile up the road beyond the botanical gardens. Several knowledgeable friends had recommended this as the area's best lobster roll, but we were disappointed. The setting is great: Tables on the deck overlook the Barter's Island bridge. And there's a generous serving of lobster on a toasted hot-dog bun ($13.99). But the lobster meat was very cold and tasteless, lying heavily in our stomachs all day. Still, give it a try. Let us know what you think.

popular with locals, and a restaurant that serves traditional Vietnamese foods. Available 11 AM–closing, the Vietnamese menu includes appetizers like steamed buns with ground pork, onion, garlic, peas, eggs, and scallions, and fresh spring rolls. Try the fabulous stir-fried squid—or chicken or shrimp—and dine in the back garden by the magnolia.

Blue Moon Café (207-633-2220), 54 Commercial St., Boothbay Harbor. Open seasonally, Mon.–Sat. 7:30 AM–2:30 PM, Sun. 8–1, Apr.–Oct. This little café with a seaside deck makes perfect crabcakes, and the side salad is filled with fresh greens. The Thai crunchy veggie wrap comes with a great dipping sauce. Order at the counter.

Kaler's Restaurant Crab & Lobster House (207-633-5839; fax 207-633-4923; www.kalers.com), 48 Commercial St., Boothbay Harbor. Casual, reliable.

Dunton's Doghouse, Sea St., Boothbay Harbor. Open May–Sept., 11–8. Good, reasonably priced take-out food, including a tasty crabmeat roll.

SNACKS ✍ **Down East Ice Cream Factory** (207-633-3016), the By-Way, Boothbay Harbor. Homemade hard ice cream and frozen yogurt, and a make-your-own sundae bar; all sorts of toppings, including real hot fudge. Open 10:30–10:30 in the height of summer; hours vary off-season.

✍ **Daffy Taffy and Fudge Factory** (207-633-5178), the By-Way, Boothbay Harbor. No credit cards. Watch taffy being pulled, designed, and wrapped—then chew! The fudge is made with fresh cream and butter. Open 10–10 in the height of the season, fewer hours off-season.

WINE & BEER 1828 Vintage House Beer, Wine and Cheese Shop (207-633-3411), 301 Adams Pond Rd., Boothbay 04537, open May–Oct., has more than 100 brands of beers and hosts beer and wine tastings. Boothbay Craft Brewery opens here in 2012.

Oak Street Provisions (207-633-1290; oakstreetprovisions.com), 43 Oak St., Boothbay Harbor, offers fresh seafood, meats, beer, wine, and specialty foods.

The East Boothbay General Store (207-633-7800), 255 Ocean Point Rd.,

East Boothbay. Open mid-May to mid-Oct. Tucked into the big bend of Rt. 96, this is a popular stop to grab an apple Brie bacon wrap for breakfast, or a sandwich from the deli to bring down to Ocean Point. Wine, beer, a variety of cheeses, and soft serve are also draws.

✷ Entertainment

The Boothbay Playhouse (207-633-3379; boothbayplayhouse.com), Rt. 27, Boothbay. Late June–late Sept., popular musicals are the rule in this air-conditioned theater.

The Opera House at Boothbay Harbor (207-633-5159; boothbay operahouse.com), 86 Townsend Ave., Boothbay Harbor. This vintage-1894 theater is a nonprofit performance center, staging roughly 100 events annually. Check the website for current concerts, lectures, community events, and more.

Carousel Music Theater (207-633-5297; carouselmusictheater.org), 196 Townsend Ave. (Rt. 27), Boothbay. July 4–Labor Day, 7:30 PM. Patrons are asked to come at 6:30 and have a drink, order supper, and then sit back with dessert and coffee to watch a musical revue ($36 for the show, a sandwich, dessert, and coffee).

Lincoln Arts Festival (207-633-3913; lincolnartsfestival.org). Concerts throughout the summer in varied locations.

Thursday-evening concerts by the Hallowell Band on the library lawn, Boothbay Harbor.

✷ Selective Shopping

ART GALLERIES First Friday Art Tours (artwalkmaine.org/boothbay). June–Oct. the first Fri. of each month a dozen local studios hold open house.

Gleason Fine Art (207-633-6849; gleasonfineart.com), 31 Townsend Ave., Boothbay Harbor. Tue.–Sat. 10–5. Museum-quality paintings by Fairfield Porter and James Fitzgerald, paintings of birds by Scott Kelley, and more of the best contemporary artists in Maine.

Gold/Smith Gallery (207-633-6252), 41 Commercial St., Boothbay Harbor. Contemporary art and jewelry.

Boothbay Region Art Foundation (207-633-2703; boothbayartists.org), 1 Townsend Ave., Boothbay Harbor. Open May–late Oct., Mon.–Sat. 10–5, Sun. noon–5. Six juried shows are held each season.

The Art District by Allen David (207-633-0003; allendavidgallery.com), 15 Townsend Ave. Featuring work by Allen Bunker and 15 other artists.

ARTISANS Abacus Gallery (207-633-2166; abacusgallery.com), 12 McKown St., Boothbay Harbor. We love this shop, which since its 1971 opening has spawned sister stores in four Maine towns. Check out the jewelry, whimsical wooden sculptures, hand-painted furniture, and unusual gifts.

Boothbay Harbor Artisans (207-633-1152; mainecraftcoop.org/boothbay), 4 Boothbay House Hill Rd., Boothbay Harbor. A cooperative crafts market featuring quilts, soap, stained glass, pottery, maple syrup, jewelry, and more.

The Silver Lining (207-633-4103; asilverlining.com), 17 Townsend Ave., Boothbay Harbor. Working metalsmiths. Original, exceptional sculpture and jewelry in brass, sterling, and gold.

Edgecomb Potters (207-882-9493 or 1-800-343-5529; edgecombpotters .com), Rt. 27, Edgecomb. Open year-round. One of Maine's largest, most famous pottery stores (with branches in Portland and Freeport). A two-tiered gallery filled with deeply colored pots, vases, and table settings, lamps, bowls, cookware, and jewelry. There's also a sculpture garden and a small seconds corner.

Macdonald Stained Glass, Ltd. (207-633-4815; macdonaldglass.com), 7 Wall Point Road, Boothbay Harbor. Housed in a converted vintage garage (call for directions), this studio-gallery is a source of stained glass in many shapes. Visitors welcome.

SPECIAL SHOPS Sherman's Book & Stationery Store (1-800-371-8128; shermans.com), 5 Commercial St., Boothbay Harbor. A two-story emporium filled with souvenirs, kitchenware, and games, as well as a full stock of books; specializing in nautical titles. Art and school supplies.

The Palabra Shop (207-633-4225; palabrashop.com), 53 Commercial St., Boothbay Harbor. Open in summer, Sun.–Thu. 9–6, opening later on weekends. A warren of 10 rooms offering everything from kitschy souvenirs to handcrafts and jewelry to a few antiques.

Rare Books at Vagabond's House (207-633-7518), 5 Lincoln St., East Boothbay. Pam and Ron Riml stock rare and used books, and specialize in travel, nautical, and maritime books.

MacNab's Premium Teas (207-633-7222 or 1-800-884-7222; macnabstea .com), Back River Rd. (first driveway on your left), Boothbay. Open Tue.–Sat. 10–4. More than 100 varieties of teas and tisanes sold. Rowan yarns, multicolored sock yarn, local alpaca yarn, and hand-dyed yarns.

✳ Special Events

January: **The Penguin Plunge**, East Boothbay.

April: **Fishermen's Festival**—contests for fishermen and lobstermen, cabaret ball, crowning of the Shrimp Princess, tall-tale contest, boat parade, and blessing of the fleet.

May: **Rocky Coast 10-K Road Race and Bunny Run**.

June: **Windjammer Days**—parade of windjammers into the harbor, fireworks, band concert, parade of floats and bands up Main St., visiting U.S. Navy and Coast Guard vessels, live music on the waterfront, food, children's activities, and two crafts shows. Celebrating 50 years in 2012, this is the big event of summer.

July: **Antique Auto Days**, Boothbay Railway Village, Rt. 27. Also **Antique Tractor Show and Engine Meet**. **Boothbay in Bloom** celebrates the season with summer merchandise, a fashion show, flower box competitions, special nature tours, pink lady's slipper count, pooches on parade, and more. Maine Brewer's Guild "**Craft Beer Comes to Boothbay**" at the Boothbay

Resort & Craft Brewery is held in mid-July with over 20 of Maine's top breweries represented.

Boothbay Region Fish and Game Saltwater Fishing Tournament, Boothbay Harbor (207-633-3788). **YMCA Southport Regatta** entails a variety of ways of circling Southport Island.

September: **Restaurant Week** (207-633-2353), third week in September, participating restaurants offering a three-course meal for a great price.

October: **Fall Foliage Festival**—foliage cruises, crafts sales, live entertainment, steam train rides.

November: **Early-bird sale**. Stores open early to tempt shoppers. Stroll the streets in your pajamas as part of the pajama parade and then watch the fast-paced fun of the bed races.

Early December: **Harbor Lights Festival**. Mr. and Mrs. Claus arrive by boat; parade, crafts, holiday shopping.

SHERMAN'S BOOK & STATIONERY STORE

Christina Tree

DAMARISCOTTA/NEWCASTLE/
WALDOBORO AND PEMAQUID AREA

Damariscotta is a small region of large, quiet lakes, long tidal rivers, and almost 100 miles of meandering coastline, all within easy striking distance of Rt. 1. It encompasses the Pemaquid Peninsula communities of Bristol, Pemaquid, New Harbor, and Round Pond, as well as communities around Lake Damariscotta, the exceptional twin villages of Damariscotta and Newcastle, and neighboring Waldoboro.

Damariscotta's musical name is an Algonquian word meaning "meeting place of the alewives," and in spring spawning alewives can indeed be seen climbing more than 40 feet up a fish ladder from Great Salt Bay to the fresh water in Damariscotta Lake.

The area's first residents also found an abundance of oysters here, judging from the shells they heaped over the course of 2,400 years, on opposite banks of the river just below Salt Bay. Recently, the local oyster industry has been revived.

Native Americans also had a name for the peninsula jutting 10 miles seaward from this spot: Pemaquid, meaning "long finger." Its protected harbors loomed large on 16th- and 17th-century maps, the the nearest mainland havens for Monhegan, a busy fishing center for European fishermen. It was from these fishermen that the Pemaquid Native American Samoset learned the English with which he welcomed the Pilgrims at Plymouth in 1621. It was also from these fishermen that Plimoth Plantation, the following winter, secured supplies enough to see it through to spring. Pemaquid, however, lacked a Governor William Bradford. Although it is occasionally referred to as this country's first permanent settlement; its history remains murky.

The site of Maine's "Lost City" is a mini peninsula bordered by the Pemaquid River and Johns Bay (named for Captain John Smith, who explored here in 1614). At one entrance stands a round stone tower, a re-creation of part of a fort built here in 1692. In recent years more than 100,000 artifacts have been unearthed in the adjacent meadow, many of them now on display in a small state-run museum. An old cemetery full of crooked slate headstones completes the scene.

Since 19th-century steamboats began bringing guests, this region has supported summer inns and cottages. It is especially appealing to families with young children since it offers warm-water lakes, including 15-mile-long Damariscotta, which

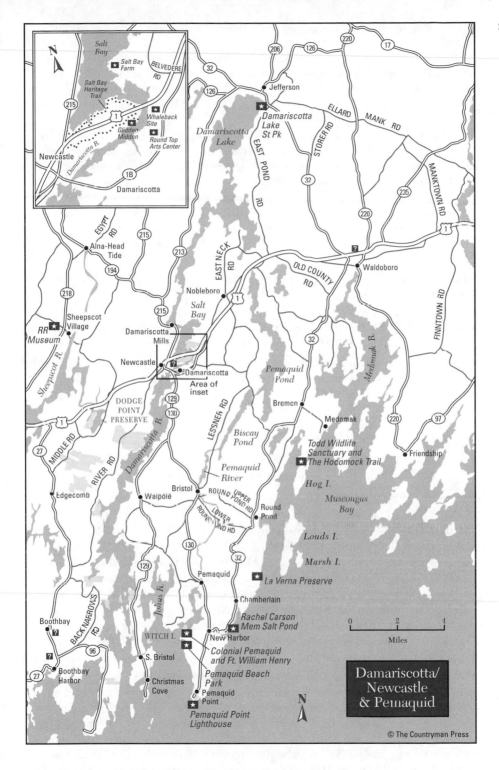

Damariscotta/
Newcastle
& Pemaquid

© The Countryman Press

has the kind of clarity and largely wooded shore you'd expect to find much farther inland.

Pemaquid Light is pictured on Maine's quarter as well as on countless calendars and books because it looks just like a lighthouse should and stands atop dramatic but clamber-friendly rocks. These are composed of varied seams of granite schist and softer volcanic rock, ridged in ways that invite climbing, and pocked with tidal pools that demand stopping.

While there is plenty to see and to do (and to eat), it's all scattered just widely enough to disperse tourist traffic. The villages are small. Damariscotta, with easy off/on access to Rt. 1, is just a few waterside streets built of mellow old local brick; it's the region's compact shopping, dining, and entertainment hub.

GUIDANCE Damariscotta Region Chamber of Commerce (207-563-8340; damariscottaregion.com). The chamber office is open year-round weekdays 9–5 at 15 Courtyard St., just off Main St. beside the Salt Bay Café. Inquire about cottage rentals.

The Damariscotta Region Information Bureau at the eastern end of Main St., junction of Rt. 1B and Vine St., is a walk-in center. Open seasonally.

GETTING THERE *By bus:* **Concord Coach** (concordcoachlines.com) stops in Damariscotta and Waldoboro en route from Portland to Bangor.

By air: **Mid-Coast Limo** (within Maine, 1-800-834-5500; outside the state, 1-800-937-2424) runs to and from the Portland International Jetport. Most inns on the peninsula will pick up guests in Damariscotta, but you do need a car—or a boat—to get around.

By car: The obvious way is up Rt. 1.

PARKING in Damariscotta is much better than it first looks. Large lots are sequestered behind buildings on both sides of Main Street.

✳ Villages

Damariscotta/Newcastle. The twin villages of Newcastle (pop. 1,950) and Damariscotta (1,910 residents) are connected by a bridge and form the commercial center of the region. Damariscotta's Main Street is the commercial hub here, flanked by fine brick buildings built after the fire of 1845. It's studded with shops and restaurants, and more of the same are tucked down alleyways and around parking lots. Note the towns' two exceptional churches, and check the program of downtown concerts and art openings listed in the *Lincoln County News*. Damariscotta Mills, a short drive up Rt. 215 from Newcastle, on Lake Damariscotta, is worth a visit.

Waldoboro (pop. 1,337). An inscription in the cemetery of the Old German Church (see *Historic Churches*) relates the deceptive way in which landholder General Samuel Waldo lured the town's first German settlers here. The church and much of the town overlook the tidal Medomak (pronounced with the emphasis on *med*) River. Bypassed by Rt. 1, this village includes some architecturally interesting buildings, and the **Waldo Theatre** (see *Entertainment*). The **Waldoborough Historical Society Museum** (waldoborohistory.us), 1664 Main St. (Rt. 220,

NEW HARBOR

just south of Rt. 1), is open regularly in summer months. It includes a vintage school, a barn, and a hall housing plenty of colorful local memorabilia.

Round Pond, Bristol. The name was obviously inspired by the village's almost circular harbor, said to have been a pirate base. This was once a major shipbuilding spot and then a quarrying center. It remains a working fishing harbor with competing lobster pounds, a good restaurant, several interesting shops, and a famous Independence Day parade.

New Harbor, Bristol. As picturesque a working harbor as any in Maine. Take South Side Rd. to Back Cove and walk out on the wooden pedestrian bridge for a great harbor view. Note the Samoset Memorial, honoring the Native American who greeted the Pilgrims at Plymouth and also sold land here, creating the first deed executed in New England. The village itself is far bigger than it looks at first. Hanna's Garage looks like a gas station but inside is a serious hardware and marine supply store with an upstairs (past the huge moose head) stocked with clothing and hunting and clamming gear. C. E. Reilly & Son (established 1828) offers far more than most supermarkets.

South Bristol. Chances are you will be stopped at "The Gut," the narrow channel spanned by the busiest swing bridge in Maine. This is the place to photograph lobster and fishing boats, always in view. Rt. 129 continues south to Christmas Cove, a long-established summer colony.

Jefferson, the village at the head of Damariscotta Lake, also at the junction of Rts. 126, 32, and 206. Old farmhouses, a general store, and summer homes along the river now form the core of the village, and Damariscotta Lake State Park, with its sandy beach, is on the fringe. Be sure to drive west a couple of miles on Rt. 213 to Bunker Hill, with its old church commanding a superb panorama down the lake.

✳ Must See

✪ ✿ **Colonial Pemaquid State Historic Site** (207-677-2423; friendsofcolonial pemaquid.org). Marked from Rt. 130, this 8-acre complex includes a state-maintained visitors center and museum, **Fort William Henry**, and the **Old Fort**

✪ ✎ PEMAQUID POINT LIGHTHOUSE

(lighthousefoundation.org), Rt. 130 (at the end), Pemaquid Point. The tower is open Memorial Day–Columbus Day 10:30–5, but closed on rainy days. Pemaquid Point is owned by the town, which charges a per-person entry fee during summer. The lighthouse, built in 1824 and automated in 1934, is a beauty. It's just a 39-step climb to the top of the tower, but the light looms high above the rocks below and the real place to appreciate it is gained by climbing down, not up. The rocks offer a wonderfully varied example of geologic upheaval, with tilted strata and igneous intrusions. The tidal pools are exceptional, but take care not to get too close to the dangerous waves. The rocks stretch for half a mile to Kresge Point. **The Fishermen's Museum** (207-677-2494) in the former lighthouse keeper's home (open Memorial Day–Columbus Day, daily 9–5:30) contains photographs, ships' models, and other artifacts related to the Maine fishing industry and lighthouses. Donations are requested. The complex also includes the **Pemaquid Art Gallery**, picnic tables, and public toilets. Another fabulous site, even when the museum is closed.

PEMAQUID LIGHT

Christina Tree

House. Open Memorial Day–Labor Day, 9–6; nominal fee. This small peninsula at the mouth of the Pemaquid River offers a glimpse into many layerings of history, beginning with a circa-1610 seasonal English fishing station that evolved into a year-round fur-trading outpost circa 1630–50. In recent decades archaeologists have uncovered the foundations of homes, a customhouse, and a tavern, all of which are now on view. The 17th-century tools and pottery, Spanish oil jars, and wampum found in these cellar holes are displayed in the museum.

Local farmers had filled in the foundations, but in the late 19th century, when this area became a popular steamship stop and summer colony, the series of forts at the very mouth of the river were excavated. In 1908 the state re-created a portion of 1692 Fort William Henry, the second and most substantial of these, intended to be "the most expensive and strongest fortification that has ever been built on American soil" and destroyed by the French a year later. The crenellated stone tower contains exhibits on the early explorations of Maine and on the French and Indian Wars, and enshrines the "Rock of Pemaquid," obviously meant as a rival to Plymouth Rock, suggesting that settlers alighted on it long before the Pilgrims ever got to Plymouth. Both the proven and possible history of this place are fascinating. The distinctive square clapboard Fort House, beside the tower, contains a library, restored parlor, changing exhibits, and a gift store that sells, among other things, a DVD about the settlement's long history. Picnic tables on the grounds command water views. For a schedule of frequent summer lectures, tours, and reenactments check the website. Even if the museum and fort are closed, this is a beautiful, haunting site. A burial ground, dating to the early 1700s, overlooks the quiet inner harbor.

✳ Also See

Shell middens. The upper Damariscotta River is known for its enormous heaps ("middens") of oyster shells, amassed over 1,000 years by Native Americans who camped on the sites now occupied by the villages of Newcastle and Damariscotta. A trail to the Glidden Midden, now on the National Register of Historic Places, 30 feet deep and said to date back 2,400 years, begins beside the Newcastle Post Office on Rt. 215. This is the **Glidden Point Trail**, maintained by the Damariscotta River Association (207-563-1393). Visit its nearby headquarters (see *Green Space*) for more about this and the **Whaleback Shell Midden State Historic Site**, with access well marked on Business Rt. 1, just north of Round Top Ice Cream. A path leads to the riverbank; the surviving midden, mostly covered with vegetation, is directly across the river. This bank was once the site of an even larger shell heap that was substantially removed in the 1880s to supply a factory, built on the spot, to process oyster shells into chicken feed. The factory is gone and, once more, this is a great picnic spot.

Damariscotta Mills Fish Ladder, maintained by the Damariscotta River Association (see above), Rt. 215 near the intersection of Austin Rd. and behind the old fish plant, parking available. Originally built in 1807 and recently rebuilt, a stone-lined series of stepped pools and raceways. For roughly a month beginning in early May, alewives—also known as river herring—climb the 50-foot from Salt Bay up to Damariscotta Bay while gulls, cormorants, ospreys, and eagles circle.

FORT WILLIAM HENRY

Christina Tree

Thompson Ice House, Rt. 129 in South Bristol. Open July and Aug., Wed., Fri., Sat. 1–4. A 150-year-old commercial icehouse is preserved, displaying traditional tools for cutting ice from an adjacent pond, and a video presentation on how ice continues to be harvested here by volunteers on Presidents' weekend. Small blocks of this ice can be found all summer in the outside cooler, $1 on the honor system. On the Sunday closest to July 4 this is scene of a ice cream social, with hand-churned ice cream made with the ice.

✍ **Old Rock Schoolhouse**, Bristol (halfway between Bristol Mills and Round Pond; follow signs from Rt. 130 to Rt. 132). Dank and haunting, this 1835–99 rural stone schoolhouse once was one of 20 one-room schoolhouses scattered through town. On summer Wednesdays and Sunday afternoons costumed volunteers offer to teach all comers.

Chapman-Hall House, 270 Main St., Damariscotta. Open July–Labor Day, weekends noon–4, volunteer-dependent. Built in 1754, this is the oldest home-stead in the region. The house has been restored with its original kitchen, and an herb garden.

HISTORIC CHURCHES This particular part of the Maine coast possesses an unusual number of fine old meetinghouses and churches, all of which are open to the public.

Old German Church (207-832-5100), Rt. 32, Waldoboro. Open daily during July and Aug., 1–4. Built in 1772 with square-benched pews and a wineglass pulpit; note the inscription in the cemetery: "This town was settled in 1748 by Germans who immigrated to this place with the promise and expectation of finding a pros-perous city, instead of which they found nothing but wilderness." Bostonian Samuel Waldo—owner of a large tract of land in this area—had not been straight with the 40 German families he brought to settle it. This was the first Lutheran church in Maine and is the setting of one of Andrew Wyeth's most famous Helga paintings.

St. Patrick's Catholic Church (207-563-6038), Academy Rd., Newcastle (Rt. 215 north of Damariscotta Mills). Open year-round daily, to sunset. This is the oldest surviving Catholic church (1808) in New England. It's an unusual building: brick construction, very narrow, and graced with a Paul Revere bell. The pews and stained glass date to 1896, and there's an old graveyard out back. It's used for daily Mass, but a spacious, unusually tasteful new addition with a clerestory roof and glass-walled sanctuary is now used on Sunday.

St. Andrew's Episcopal Church (207-563-3533), Glidden St., Newcastle. A charming half-timbered building on the bank of the Damariscotta River. Set among gardens and trees, it was the first commission in this country for Henry Vaughan, the English architect who went on to design the National Cathedral in Washington, DC.

Old Walpole Meeting House, Meeting House Rd., off Rt. 129, South Bristol. Open Sun. during July and Aug. for 3 PM services. A 1772 shingled meetinghouse with box pews and a pulpit with a sounding board.

Harrington Meeting House, 278 Harrington Rd., Pemaquid. Open during July and Aug., Mon., Wed., Fri., and Sat. 2–4:30. Donations accepted. The 1775 build-ing with its original box pews has been restored and serves as a museum of Old

INSIDE HARRINGTON MEETING HOUSE

Christina Tree

Bristol. A nondenominational service is held here once a year, usually on the third Sunday in August.

OTHER ((·)) **Skidompha Library** (207-563-5513; skidompha.org), 184 Main St., Damariscotta. Open Tue.–Sat. from 9 AM; until 7 PM Thu. and 1 PM on Sat., otherwise until 5 PM. This stunning library forms the heart of town, the scene of many programs geared to visitors as well as regulars. There are also frequent authors' nights and classic films.

Fawcett's Antique Toy & Art Museum (207-832-7398), 3506 Rt. 1., Waldoboro. Memorial Day–Columbus Day, open Thu.–Mon. 10–4, then weekends noon–4 until weekend before Christmas. $5 admission. Comic-book and antique-toy lovers alert: This is a major collection of original cartoon art, billed as the finest Lone Ranger collection in the world, also antique Disneyana, space toys, and the like. Antique toys bought and sold.

SCENIC DRIVES Damariscotta Lake. From Newcastle, Rt. 215 winds along past the newly rebuilt and landscaped Alewife Fishladder in Damariscotta Mills. Continue by St. Patrick's Church through farm country on Rt. 213 when 215 jogs west (note the scenic pullout across from the Bunker Hill Church, with a view down the lake) to Jefferson for a swim at Damariscotta Lake State Park.

Sheepscot Village and Alna Head Tide. From Rt. 215 beyond St. Patrick's Church (see above) turn left at "Cowshit Corner" (there's a sign) onto W. Hamlet Rd and then right on Old Country Rd. through rolling, open country to the picturesque village of Head Tide. (You can also reach this point directly from Rt. 1 on Sheepscot Rd. in Newcastle.) This is a cluster of old buildings around the river and its reversing falls. Cross the river and turn north on Rt. 218 to the **Alna Store** (207-586-5515), open except Sun. until 7 PM, good for hot specials as well as sandwiches, local meat and eggs. Continue on to Head Tide, another scenic village with a beautiful church and

HARRINGTON MEETING HOUSE

Christina Tree

overlook at a small dam. Cut back to the store and turn down Dock Rd. (it's on the corner) and then right (south) on Rt. 194, which becomes Rt. 215. This is a lovely loop, one of the best in the area for bicycling.

Pemaquid Peninsula. Follow Rt. 129 south from Damariscotta, across the South Bristol Bridge to Christmas Cove. Backtrack and cross the peninsula via Harrington Meeting House Rd. to Colonial Pemaquid and Pemaquid Beach (glorious at sunset). Turn south on Rt. 130 to Pemaquid Point and return via Rt. 32 and Round Pond; take Biscay Rd. back to Damariscotta or continue on Rt. 32 into Waldoboro.

Christina Tree

COWSHIT CORNER

✳ To Do

BIRDING ✍ **Audubon Camp**, Hog Island (hogisland.audubon.org). The center, 0.25 mile offshore at the head of Muscongus Bay, is a venue for nature and ornithology programs, including seasonal sessions sponsored by Audubon's Project Puffin, which reintroduced Atlantic puffins to nearby islands. Five miles of spruce trails, wildflower and herb gardens, and mudflats surround rustic bungalows. The dining room is in a restored 19th-century farmhouse. For puffin-watching and birding cruises, see Hardy Boat Cruises (below). Also see *Green Space*.

BOAT EXCURSIONS ✍ **Hardy Boat Cruises** (Stacie and Captain Al Crocetti: 207-677-2026 or 1-800-278-3346; hardyboat.com), Shaw's Wharf, New Harbor, May–Oct. The 60-foot Maine-built *Hardy III* offers daily (twice daily in high season) 50-minute-long runs to **Monhegan Island** (for a detailed description, see "Midcoast Islands"). Pick a calm day. It doesn't matter if it's foggy, but the passage is no fun if it's rough. Another cruise circles **Eastern Egg Rock**, one of only five Maine islands on which puffins breed, with narration by an Audubon naturalist. There are also seal-watching, lighthouse (Pemaquid Light), and harbor cruises. Parking is $3 per day and roughly 0.25 mile back up the road (Gosnold Arms guests park for free, steps from Shaw's Wharf).

Midcoast Kayak (207-563-5732; midcoastkayak.com), 47 Main St., Damariscotta, offers a variety of guided paddles in and around Muscongus Bay, also rentals. **Maine Kayak** (1-866-624-6352; mainekayak.com) offers guided trips, rentals, and packages from a variety of bases, including New Harbor.

BOAT RENTALS Lake Pemaquid Camping (207-563-5202; lakepemaquid .com), Egypt Rd., Damariscotta, rents canoes, kayaks, and paddle- and motorboats. **Bay Sail** (207-242-6292; baysaillc.com), based in Round Pond, rents 22-foot sailboats by the hour, day, or week.

FISHING Damariscotta Lake is a source of bass, landlocked salmon, and trout. See Mill Pond Inn under *Bed & Breakfasts*.

GOLF Wawenock Country Club (207-563-3938), Rt. 129 (7 miles south of Damariscotta), Walpole. Open May–Nov. A nine-hole course with 18 tee boxes and a full-service clubhouse.

Sheepscot Links (207-549-7060), 822 Townhouse Rd., Whitefield. A rural, nine-hole golf course set on a former dairy farm. Clubhouse, pull carts.

HIKING Monhegan Island, easily accessible from New Harbor (see *Boat Excursions*), is webbed with coastal shore and cliff trails beloved by hikers and birders. A day trip gives you a sampling, but it's best to spend the night for a full exploration.

SWIMMING Pemaquid Beach Park (207-677-2754), Rt. 130, Pemaquid. A town-owned area open Memorial Day–Labor Day, 9–5. Nominal admission. Bathhouse, restrooms, refreshment stand, and picnic tables. This is also a great place to walk and watch the sunset in the evening.

Damariscotta Lake State Park (207-549-7600), Rt. 32, Jefferson. A fine sandy beach with changing facilities, picnic tables, and grills at the northern end of the lake. No pets allowed. $4 per Maine car, $6 per out-of-state car, $2 out-of-state seniors.

On Pemaquid Peninsula the big freshwater swimming holes are at **Biscay Pond** (from Rt. 1 take Biscay Rd. 3 miles) and **Bristol Dam** on Rt. 130, 5 miles south of Damariscotta.

✳ Green Space

NATURE PRESERVES Damariscotta River Association (207-563-1393; draclt.org), based at 115-acre Heritage Center Farm, 110 Belvedere Rd., 0.25 north of Rt. 1 in Damariscotta. Open year-round. Sited on 100-acre Salt Pond Farm with hay fields, salt- and freshwater marshes, and woods, laced with walking/skiing paths, this is also the site of seasonal Friday farmer's markets, a summer concert series, special programs, and tours. DRA properties total more than 1,200 acres in over a dozen easily accessible places, including Great Salt Bay Preserve Heritage Trail, which loops around Glidden Point and leads to the Glidden Midden (see *To See*). Dodge Point Preserve is a 506-acre property on Newcastle's River Rd. (2.6 miles south of Rt. 1), which includes a sand beach as well as a freshwater pond, a beaver bog, and trails.

✄ **Rachel Carson Memorial Salt Pond**, Rt. 32, north of New Harbor. The pond is on the opposite side of the road from the parking lot. There's a beautiful view of the open ocean from here, and at low tide the tidal pools are filled with tiny sea creatures. Look for blue mussels, hermit crabs, starfish, and green sea urchins. Here Rachel Carson researched part of her book *The Edge of the Sea*. Inland from the pond, the preserve includes fields and forest.

Griggs Preserve, Newcastle, is maintained by the Sheepscot Valley Conservation Association (207-586-5616). A loop trail through 56 acres brings you to a view of the reversing falls at Sheepscot Village. Take Rt. 1 south to Cochran Rd. (turn

Christina Tree

DAMARISCOTTA LAKE

right at Skip Cahill's Tires). After a mile turn left onto Trails End Rd. to the trail-head (on the left, before the bridge).

Todd Wildlife Sanctuary and the Hocomock Trail, Bremen (take Keene Neck Rd. off Rt. 32). A visitors center (207-529-5148) is open June–Aug., daily 1–4. The nature trail leads down to the beach. This is a great family picnic spot, accessible with short legs.

Witch Island, South Bristol. An 18-acre wooded island lies 0.25 mile offshore at the east end of "the Gut," the narrow channel that serves as South Bristol's harbor. A trail around the island threads through oaks and pines, and there are two sheltered beaches.

Hidden Valley Nature Center (hvnc.org), 131 Egypt Rd., Jefferson (0.5 mile south from Rt. 215). Nearly 1,000 acres of diverse land, 25 miles of trails to Little Dyer Pond, good for cross-country skiing and snowshoeing. Three cabins and several campsites, ongoing programs.

✳ Lodging

INNS 🐾 ♿ **Bradley Inn** (207-677-2105 or 1-800-942-5560; bradleyinn .com), 3063 Pemaquid Point, New Harbor 04554. Open Apr.–Dec. Warren and Beth Busteed are energetic innkeepers who have established a culinary reputation for this turn-of-the-20th-century inn (see *Dining Out*), now the area's only inn serving dinner. The 14 guest rooms and two suites are divided among the main house, the carriage house, and a cottage, all nicely furnished (each with private bath). Clunker bicycles are free, and the inn is less than a mile from Pemaquid

Lighthouse and Kresge Point. Amenities include a spa with sauna and treatment rooms. High-season rooms are $175–375 (for a carriage house suite); off-season $135–375; $50 pet fee; special birding and spa weekends.

✪ 🍴 ✎ ♿ (((•))) **Gosnold Arms** (207-677-3727; winter, 561-575-9549; gosnold .com), 146 Rt. 32, New Harbor 04554. Open mid-May–mid-Oct. Sited at the entrance to a picturesque working harbor, steps from Shaw's Wharf, a traditional lobster pound and a departure point for the Hardy Boat cruises to Monhegan Island and around Egg

Rock. Originally a saltwater farm, this friendly inn has been owned by the Phinney family for more than three decades. It rambles on along the water with rockers on the porch and ample rainy-day space. There are 10 simple but comfortable guest rooms upstairs (all private bath, 8 with water views) and 20 cottage units, 6 with deck or sunporch, smack-dab on this working harbor. The Hillside units, squirreled away at the top of the property, are good for families. Breakfast on the enclosed porch is served buffet-style, the better to catch the boat. Guests who overnight on Monhegan are permitted to keep their car in an upper lot. Inn rooms $118–152, cottages $138–216 B&B; $330 for a two-bedroom and -bath waterside cottage with a living room, fireplace, and kitchen; 15 percent less before July and after Labor Day.

& **The Hotel Pemaquid** (207-677-2312; hotelpemaquid.com), 3098 Bristol Rd., New Harbor 04554. Open mid-May–mid-Oct. A vintage-1888 summer hotel a short walk from Pemaquid Point but without water views. The 30 rooms are divided among the main house and new annexes. Most rooms have private bath (four rooms in the inn itself share two baths). Coffee is set out at 7, and the nearby Sea Gull Shop (see *Eating Out*) serves three meals. From $85 off-season to $250 for a suite in Aug.; a four-bedroom housekeeping cottage is $825–875 per week. No credit cards.

BED & BREAKFASTS

In Newcastle/Damariscotta
✪ ✿ ✑ **Mill Pond Inn** (207-563-8014; millpondinn.com), Rt. 215, Damariscotta Mills (mailing address: 50 Main St., Nobleboro 04555). Open year-round. Two-person hammocks swing under the willow trees beside a pond.

Enter the red door of this much-expanded 1780 gray-clapboard house and you immediately feel at home. Sherry and Bobby Whear have been welcoming guests since 1986, and many have returned many times. The six rooms—including three 2-bedroom suites, one with its own entrance—all have private bath and are so different from one another that you might want to ask for descriptions, but all cost $140 per couple (from $110 off-season). Breakfast might be a crabmeat omelet with veggies from the garden. In winter pack a picnic lunch and skate across the lake to an island, accessible in summer with the inn's canoe. The lake warms up by July, and you can take a dip off the dock or ask for a ride in the 16-foot restored antique motorboat. Bobby, a Registered Maine Guide and co-host of *Wuzzup?*—a weekly series on Lincoln County TV (lctv.org)—enjoys tuning guests into local secrets as well as dining and all the more obvious things to do and see in this amazingly varied area. No credit cards please.

☀ (ᵩ) **Newcastle Inn** (207-563-5685 or 1-877-376-6111; newcastleinn.com), 60 River Rd., Newcastle 04553. Open

GOSNOLD ARMS, NEW HARBOR

Christina Tree

MILL POND INN

year-round. Julie Bolthuis offers 14
tasteful and comfortable rooms, all
with private bath, some with water
views, several with four-poster beds, 8
with gas fireplace, and 2 with Jacuzzi.
An inviting little bar with French doors
opens onto a wide deck with water
views—the breakfast venue weather
permitting. The grounds overlook the
Damariscotta River. $180–255 in high
season, $135–195 in low, includes a
three-course breakfast. $30-per-day
charge for dogs. Inquire about special
getaway weekends.

Alewives & Ales (207-563-1561;
alewivesandales.com), P.O. Box 809, 22
High St., Damariscotta 04543 This is a
Federal-style mid-19th-century house
on a quiet street south of town, a B&B
with three guest rooms. Host Mimi
McConnell tells us that the name honors Damariscotta's spring alewife
migration, and brewing "Ale" is her
husband's Ray's hobby. A very full
breakfast, served at the dining room
table, is included in $150, $250 for a
two-room suite.

(ʔ) **Oak Gables** (207-563-1476 or 1-
800-335-7748; oakgablesbb.com), 36
Pleasant St., Damariscotta 04543.
Open year-round. Set on 9 acres on
the Damariscotta River, with a heated

swimming pool and boathouse (with a
tournament-quality Ping-Pong table),
Martha Scudder's gracious house has
four second-floor rooms, shared bath
($95–120 with breakfast). Inquire
about weekly rentals for the riverside
three-bedroom cottage, a two-person
studio, an apartment in the guest wing,
and a river-view apartment in the
main house. Well-behaved children
welcome.

On the Pemaquid Peninsula south of Damariscotta

🐾 🐾 🐾 (ʔ) **Brannon-Bunker Inn**
(207-563-5941 or 1-800-563-9225;
brannonbunkerinn.com), 349 Rt. 129,
Walpole 04573. Open April–Dec. We
like the feel of this 1820s inn, which at
one point became a Prohibition-era
dance hall. Your hosts are the Hovance
family, and children are welcome. In
the main house there are five guest
rooms, one on the first floor with private bath, four upstairs (two with
shared bath). The neighboring Carriage House includes a suite with two
bedrooms and a kitchen/living room,
also two more rooms with private bath.
There's ample common space, with a
big fieldstone fireplace for foggy mornings and a screened porch for sunny
afternoons. The upstairs sitting area
walls are hung with memorabilia from
World War I, and all rooms are tastefully furnished in country antiques.
$90–100 for rooms; $110–180 for the
Carriage House suite. Pets are $10.
Breakfast features freshly baked
muffins and fresh fruit.

✪ (ʔ) **The Inn at Round Pond** (207-
809-7386; theinnatroundpond.com),
1442 Rt. 32, Round Pond 04564. Sue
and Bill Morton have brought new life
to this 1830s Colonial with its
mansard-roofed third floor, added
around the turn of the last century,
when it became the Harbor View
Hotel. This remains the only place to

stay in this picturesque waterside village. There's a gas stove in the parlor; rooms are furnished in great colors and comfortable antiques, hung with original art. Guest rooms have been reduced to three delightful suites. Our favorite is the third-floor Monhegan Suite with a king-sized iron bed and a sitting area. An adjoining room with twins is available for an additional charge. Check out the Garden Cottage, a hideaway for all guests to share, fitted with books, puzzles, wicker, and a daybed. A full breakfast is included in $165–185 mid-June–mid-Sept.; $145 in spring and fall, $120 in winter.

In Waldoboro 04572

✪ ☙ **Blue Skye Farm** (207-832-0300; blueskyefarm.com), 1708 Friendship Rd. (Rt. 220). Open year-round. What a treasure! This is an exquisite house, dating back to 1775 but with an elegant Federal facade. It retains all its original woodwork and working fireplaces (in two of the five guest rooms as well as in common rooms); the stenciling in the front hall is thought to be by Moses Eaton. Stenciling aside, walls are all painted white because, as innkeeper Jan Davidson, explains, "We had the luxury of living in empty rooms for four months, waiting for our furniture to come from England. I loved the glow of the light on walls and realized that I didn't want these rooms to be busy. I wanted to create a restful, peaceful place in which people would look out the window and see the marsh." Small-paned windows are thinly veiled in European-style lace café curtains.

Peter and Jan Davidson spent a year restoring the house, which dates from 1775 and is set in 100 acres of marsh, meadows, and woods. Original detailing includes Indian shutters and a scalloped cupboard as well as paneling and mantels. Rooms are tastefully, comfortably furnished in antiques, and tempting, well-thumbed books line walls between the five guest rooms.

The two upstairs front rooms and one downstairs (the former North Parlor) are classically proportioned; a smaller downstairs guest room (the Library) overlooks the marshes. A room tucked under the eaves has a loft bed as well a two doubles. A full breakfast is served, but because their hosts live in an adjoining cottage, guests have access to the kitchen as well as outdoor grills for other meals. The property includes gardens, hiking trails, and a skating pond. This is a great house to rent in its entirety. Candlelit lobster dinners can be arranged when booking This happens frequently in winter when guests tend to come from nearby Portland or Boston for a weekend of hiking or cross-country skiing "This house hums in winter when all the fireplaces are lit," Jan observes. $125–145 in-season, less off-season.

Le Vatout Bed and Breakfast (207-832-5150; levatout.com), 218 Kaler's Corner. *La va tout* is French for "everything," Dominika Spetsmann will tell you, suggesting the total experience—good food, conversation, garden, art, books, Yodi the small cat, and Chimbo the large dog—that

BLUE SKYE FARM IN WALDOBORO

Christina Tree

Dominika (a novelist) and partner Linda Mahoney (an artist and fine photographer) share with guests. The rambling house also includes four guest rooms, two with private bath. $130 with private bath, from $95 with shared. Dominika prides herself on flavorful breakfasts.

North of Damariscotta Lake in Jefferson 04348

🐾 (𝚙) **Blueberry Hill Farm** (207-549-7448), 101 Old Madden Rd. Another find: a secluded 125-acre organic farm with a 1774 farmhouse, tastefully restored and furnished with antiques and original art. JoAnn Tribby and Ellis Percy offer three guest rooms in their house, one with a fireplace and one a small single (all shared bath). This is an organic farm raising registered Jersey heifers, Shetland ponies, and chickens, along with a kitchen garden. Clary Lake, within walking distance, is good for swimming, canoeing, and fishing. Damariscotta Lake State Park is also near. This is an ideal place for people interested in organic gardening and/or looking for complete quiet. The downside is the distance from restaurants. $65 for the single room, $80 per couple for the doubles, $15 for extra children, full breakfast included.

COTTAGES 🐾 🖊 Many rental properties are listed with the Damariscotta area chamber. **Newcastle Square Vacation Rentals** (207-563-6500; mainecoastcottages.com), 87 Main St., Damariscotta, handles some 150 area cottages and houses.

🐾 🖊 **The Thompson House and Cottages** (207-677-2317; thompson cottages.net), New Harbor 04554. Open May–Nov. Merle and Karen Thompson are the third generation of a family that's been offering hospitality since they began taking guests in an

1874 house in 1920. There are still two sparkling-clean rooms in the house, but the big attractions are the 21 equally tidy housekeeping cottages (maximum of five people), many with ocean views and facing New Harbor or Back Cove, all with fireplace (wood supplied). $400–1,700 per week in-season.

Ye Olde Forte Cabins (207-677-2261; yeoldefortecabins.com), 18 Old Fort Rd., Pemaquid Beach 04554. Nostalgia buffs take note: Eight classic 1922 cabins (sleeping one to four) stepped roof-to-roof along a wide central lawn sloping to a private beach on John's Bay. There's a cookhouse equipped with everything you need to make meals, along with immaculate men's and women's shower houses. $108–210 per day, $550–675 per week; less if you bring your own linen. A neighboring cottage with bath, kitchen, living room, fireplace, and deck is $1,225 per week. Many families have been coming for 50 years. Guests bring kayaks, canoes, and fishing rods. Moorings, $18 per day, $95 per week.

🐾 🐾 🖊 **Moody's Motel** (207-832-5362; moodysdiner.com), P.O. Box 864, Rt. 1, Waldoboro 04572. Open May–Dec. Moody's Diner is a Rt. 1 icon; less well known is the vintage

YE OLDE FORTE CABINS

Christina Tree

CABINS AT MOODY'S MOTEL

Christina Tree

motor court squirreled away behind the eatery, up a wooded drive in a quiet hilltop meadow. P. B. and Bertha Moody built the first cabins in 1927 when this was Rt. 1. Still in the family with Debbie Bellows as manager, there are 18 spanking-clean units. Each of the cottages has a screened porch, bath with shower, cable TV, and heat; five have kitchens. The grounds include lawn games and swings. Best of all is the handy access to the diner and then an uphill walk that's just enough to settle your pie. $54 for a one-bedroom unit with twins, $64 for a two-bedroom, sleeping four, $59–74 for kitchenette units, $700 a week for "Letta's House" with three bedrooms and two baths, sleeping six to nine. Pet charge.

CAMPING 🛶 ㅤ **Lake Pemaquid Camping** (207-563-5202; lake pemaquid.com), Box 967, Damariscotta 04543. Off Biscay Rd. More than 200 tent and RV sites, also cabin and cottage rentals on 7-mile Lake Pemaquid. Facilities include tennis, a pool, 18-hole mini golf, a game room, laundry facilities, a sauna, Jacuzzi, a snack bar, and store, along with a marina with boat rentals.

Note: Wherever you eat in this area, sampling **Damariscotta oysters** is a must. It's a 2,000-year-old tradition here, as evidenced by the famous shell middens (see *To See*), and the area once more offers some of the world's best oysters. By the mid-1800s native oyster beds had about disappeared due to overharvesting, but thanks to the University of Maine's Darling Marine Center on the Damariscotta River in Walpole, seeding began. The resulting firm, distinctively sweet and salty oysters are served in the world's best restaurants. They have been popularized by **Pemaquid Oyster Co**. (207-446-8923; pemaquidoysters.com), founded in 1986, spawned in late winter in a nearby hatchery, then planted as "seeds" in the Damariscotta River. This company stages the September **Pemaquid Oyster Festival** at Schooner Landing, featuring oyster shucking. At **Glidden Point Sea Farm** (207-633-3599; oysterfarm .com), 707 River Rd., Edgecomb, the roadside retail stand is usually open daily 8–8; shucking knives, gloves, and condiments are supplied. Other local oyster companies include Mook Sea Farms, Muscongus Bay Aquaculture, and Norumbega Oyster Co.

DINING OUT

In Damariscotta/Newcastle
🍴 🍴 **Damariscotta River Grill** (207-563-2992), 155 Main St. Open for lunch and dinner. A brick-walled, two-floor, middle-of-Main-Street gem under the same ownership as the long and justly popular Anchor Inn in Round Pond. Head upstairs to a seat by the window or at the copper bar. Begin either meal with an order of oysters on the half shell, served with the house horseradish. At dinner feast on lobster cakes on sweet corn sauce;

seared yellowfin tuna and tempura shrimp with orange miso chili sauce; or wakame salad with eggplant. Children's menu. Dinner entrées $16.97–21.68. Add $7.97 for a three-course prix fixe. All entrées are available as small plates.

Schooner Landing (207-563-7447), Schooner Wharf, Main St. Open May–Sept. daily for lunch and dinner, just weekends in Apr. and Oct.; the pub remains open for live music on weekends through winter. A harborside restaurant on the Damariscotta River; the view is the big draw here, along with the informal feel and draft brews. Pemaquid oysters are the feature, fresh on the half shell, baked, stewed, or fried. Plenty of other seafood, sandwiches, burgers, and beers. The best location in town, but service can be slow. Inquire about Free Oyster Fridays and Sunday music.

✐ **Salt Bay Café** (207-563-3302; salt baycafe.com), 88 Main St. Open Mon.– Thu. 7:30 AM–8 PM, Fri. and Sat. until 9, Sun. 8–8. What this chef-owned restaurant lacks in a view, it makes up for in comfort, reliably good food, and service. Lunch features soups, salads, and sandwich combos. The large dinner menu ranges from pasta dishes to fresh-cut steaks and includes the widest variety of vegetarian dishes around. Children's menu. Entrées $14–25, and you can always have a sandwich.

✐ **King Eider's Pub** (207-563-6008; kingeiderspub.com), 2 Elm St. Open year-round 10:30 AM–11 PM. The downstairs pub is a good foggy-evening spot for light grub and a boutique brew. Crabcakes are also the specialty in the pleasant upstairs restaurant, and they're bigger than the norm: The two offered as an appetizer can work as dinner for most appetites, especially if you begin with Damariscotta River

oysters and add the house salad. The dinner menu is large, ranging from burgers to char-grilled steaks. Entrées $6–20.

✐ **Newcastle Publick House** (207-563-3434; newcastlepublickhouse .com), 52 Main St., Newcastle. Housed in a landmark brick building at the junction of Rts. 1 and 125 and just across the bridge from Damariscotta, this is an invitingly informal family-friendly pub. Here you can feast on the town's famed oysters, then dine on shepherd's pie or wild mushroom fettuccine or a veggie burger. A dozen draft beer selections. Dinner entrées $6–26.

On the Pemaquid Peninsula

🦞 ✐ **Anchor Inn** (207-529-5584), Round Pond. Open daily for lunch (11–2), dinner (from 5), and Sunday brunch (noon–3), mid-May–Labor Day, then Wed.–Sun. until Columbus Day. Jean and Rick Hirch's tiered dining room overlooking the harbor is a real standout. Reservations are necessary for dinner; ask for a table on the porch, hanging over the harbor. At either meal try the Italian seafood stew, loaded with fish, scallops, and mussels, served with garlic bread ($18.64). Dinner options include shrimp and scallops baked with crabmeat, and chicken sautéed with dried tomatoes and baby spinach, finished with melted Gruyère and fresh basil cream. Children's menu. Dinner entrées $8–20. Shore dinners and lobster priced to market.

Bradley Inn (207-677-2105; bradley inn.com), Pemaquid Point Rd., New Harbor. Open by reservation for dinner year-round: Call to check but generally open Thu.–Tue. in-season; Thu.–Sun. Nov.–Mar. Fine dining is what these two attractive dining rooms are about. The rooms are decorated in nautical antiques and soothing colors;

tables are well spaced and candlelit. The à la carte menu changes nightly but might include lavender risotto with black mission figs and roasted corn, or Maine crabcakes with a lobster corn compote, peas, and fava beans. Entrées $34–38. The inviting bar features house cocktails and grilled flat breads.

Coveside Restaurant & Marina (207-644-8282; covesiderestaurant .com), Christmas Cove, South Bristol. Open seasonally, 11–9. Geared to customers arriving by yacht (call for moorings) and to the neighboring old summer colony, this is a good excuse to drive all the way down to Christmas Cove—but check to make sure they are open. The big, open-timbered, pine-paneled dining room has picture windows and a deck on the water. Even the lunch menu is sophisticated, with such offerings as bouillabaisse and calamari salad in addition to burgers and baskets. Dinner choices include orange horseradish-crusted grouper, and scallop and shrimp linguine with spicy ham and mushrooms. Entrées $19–34.

EATING OUT

In Damariscotta
Mediterranean Kitchen (207-563-2882), 189 Main St. Open for lunch and dinner except Sun. year-round. Greek-style pizzas are the house specialty, but the lamb and beef gyros with the house sauce get rave reviews. Dinner options include moussaka and all the classic Greek salads and side dishes.

Weatherbird Café (207-563-8993), 72 Courtyard St. If you are browsing the shops and want a quick but delicious lunch, this bakery and market serves up deli sandwiches on fresh-baked breads and panini.

✪ ❦ **Larson's Lunch Box** (207-563-57550), 430 Upper Main St. (Business

Rt. 1). May–late Oct., daily except Wed. 11–4; until 7 in July and August. Beloved by locals, this roadside stand is known for its fresh and generous crab and lobster rolls. Billy and Barbara Ganem have installed a serious restaurant kitchen and also pride themselves on from-scratch clam chowder, sweet potato fries, and cookies. Burgers, too. Picnic tables. Inquire about and "picnic baskets."

Paco's Tacos (207-563-5355), off Main St. in the alley beside Sheepscot River Pottery. Open weekdays 11–4. Better than average and handy to the public landing (parking and a picnic spot).

S. Fernald's Country Store (207-563-8484), 50 Main St. Owner Sumner Richards opened his store in Damariscotta 20 years ago, moved to Waldoboro for 10, and now is back in suitably weathered digs near the landing. There's a soda fountain and limited seating, a full breakfast menu, and a large choice of hot and cold sandwiches (whole and half), soups, and salads. Decor includes one of Maine's largest collection of Moxie memorabilia.

On or just off Route 1
✪ ❦ ✿ ♿ **Moody's Diner** (207-832-7785), Rt. 1, Waldoboro. Open Mon.–Sat. 5 AM–10 PM, Sun. 6 AM–10 PM. A clean and warm, classic 1930s diner run by several generations of the Moody family along with other employees who have been here so long they've become part of the family. Renovated and expanded, it retains all the old atmosphere and specialties, including killer pies and family-style food—corned beef hash, meat loaf, and stews—at digestible prices. You can buy T-shirts and other Moody's paraphernalia, but you can also still get chicken or turkey potpie and a great crabmeat roll. Prices haven't soared with fame.

LOBSTER POUNDS

Muscongus Bay is a particularly prime lobster source, and genuine lobster pounds are plentiful around the harbors of the Pemaquid Peninsula.

✔ **Harbor View Restaurant at the Pemaquid Fisherman's Co-op** (207-677-2801; pemaquidlobsterco-op.com), off Pemaquid Harbor Rd., Pemaquid Harbor. Open Memorial Day–Columbus Day, 11–8. Operated by Maine's oldest continuously run fishermen's cooperative. Lobster, steamed clams and mussels, shrimp, shore dinners, and baskets, enjoyed at indoor and outdoor tables with a great view across John's Bay to Colonial Pemaquid. There's a play area for kids while you wait for your lobster.

Broad Cove Marine (207-529-5186; broadcovemarine.com), 371 Momak Rd. (look for the BCMS sign on Rt. 32), Bremen. Open daily in-season 10–6. You can't get closer to a working harbor. Lobster and clams, live and cooked, oysters on the half shel, and lobster and clam rolls, as fresh as they come. Dockside deck on the Medomak River.

✔ **Shaw's Wharf** (207-677-2200), Rt. 32, New Harbor. Open early May–mid-Oct., daily for lunch and supper. This is a popular, long-established lobster pound on one of Maine's most picturesque harbors. It's also departure point for the Hardy Boat Cruises and can get busy. Pick your lobster out of the pool below and feed on it upstairs at picnic tables, either inside or out. Chowders and stews, a wide choice of sandwiches, dinner salads, sides, and fried and seafood dinners are also on the menu—but there's no corn. Fully licensed.

✔ **Bullwinkle's Family Steakhouse** (207-832-6272), Rt. 1, Waldoboro. Locally loved and a good bet for road food. Steaks are the specialty, along with baby back ribs, seafood baskets, and subs.

✪ ✔ **Narrows Tavern** (207-832-2210), 15 Friendship St., Waldoboro. Open 11:30 AM–1 AM, dinner until 9. A welcoming village pub with picnic-style tables and an unobtrusive TV screen in back, also local art on old brick walls. Good chowder, salads, and pastas with fresh veggies and fish, also burgers and sweet potato fries. Great pies. Good

MOODY'S DINER

Nancy English

On the dock at Round Pond two competing lobster shacks are both open daily for lunch through dinner in-season:

Muscongus Bay Lobster Company (207-529-5528). Still pretty basic but expanded in recent years with plenty of picnic tables on the deck. Sample the area's oysters on the half shell, as well as the freshest of crabmeat, lobsters, corn, and fixings.

Round Pond Lobster (207-529-5725). Really no-frills but locals swear by it. Check out the nightly special and BYOB and salad.

BROAD COVE MARINE, BREMEN Christina Tree

selection of wine by the glass as well as brews.

Rising Tide Co-op (207-563-5556), 323 Main St., Damariscotta. This long-established local food co-op has moved across the road into palatial new quarters with an expanded deli and café. For health-conscious visitors it's a source of good things to fill a cooler.

On the Pemaquid Peninsula: Route 130

⚓ **Country Cupboard** (207-677-3911), 137 Huddle Rd., New Harbor. Open Tue.–Sat. 8–3, Sun. 8–noon; until 7 Tue.–Sat in summer. A family-run log eatery specializing in from-scratch baking (try the cinnamon buns). Given its local fame, we were disappointed in the chowder but agree this is a great food option within striking distance of Pemaquid Light and the beach. Luncheon options include blackboard specials as well as salads, burgers, and sandwiches. Sunday is breakfast only, with table service.

Sea Gull Shop (207-677-2374), next to the Pemaquid Lighthouse at Pemaquid Point. Open daily in-season, 7:30 AM–8 PM, serving all three meals. The Monhegan Room, hidden behind the shop but overlooking the water, is delightfully old-fashioned. Standard menu. Entrées $5–20. BYOB.

The Contented Sole (207-677-3000) at Colonial Pemaquid. Open seasonally for lunch and dinner, this large wharfside restaurant is dependably less crowded than anywhere else in the area. Managed by the Bradley Inn, food and service are good. Full license.

On the Pemaquid Peninsula: Along Route 129 to Christmas Cove

Harborside Café (207-644-8751), South Bristol. Open year-round for breakfast, lunch, supper. Just north of the drawbridge at "the Gut," this is a general store that we passed many times before noticing all the pickups gathered at noon. Inside we found a six-stool counter and several booths, a standard road-food menu—fresh-dough pizza, omelets all day, sandwiches, fried seafood, daily specials—plus standout chowder and fresh fruit pies.

Miss Ashley's On the Wharf (207-644-8101), Rt. 129 at the South Bristol drawbridge. Open daily, year-round, 7 AM–10 PM, until 8 on Sun. We wish Miss Ashley luck! The old restaurant-store here at "the Gut" seems to change ownership frequently but remains a great spot for a sandwich, pizza, or sub. An excuse to stop and watch boat traffic.

Island Grocery (207-644-8552; islandgrocery.net), 12 West Side Rd., South Bristol. Open May–Labor Day. Just off Rt. 129, serving the Christmas Cove summer community. Beth Fisher has totally rehabbed an old building to create this bright combination store-café with fresh-baked muffins, scones, a deli menu with sandwiches (the turkey is house-baked), wine, gourmet items, organic produce, and yummy frozen custard.

Elsewhere

⚓ **Morse's Kraut House** (207-832-5569; morsessauerkraut.com), 3856 Washington Rd. (8 miles north of Rt. 1, on Rt. 220), Waldoboro. Open year-round, daily except Wed., 9–4. Lunch served 10:30–4. Breakfast Thu.–Sun. 8–10:30. Since 1918 sauerkraut has been made from fresh cabbage and sold on the premises, which now include a store and a restaurant. Lunch entrées include choucroute garni, pork schnitzel, and house-made pierogi filled with minced sausage or cheese plus potato, sauerkraut, porcini mushrooms, and onions. Desserts include Black Forest liqueur cakes and apple strudel. The store sells many of the house specialties and more. See *Special Stores*.

ICE CREAM ⚓ **Round Top Ice Cream** (207-563-5307), Business Rt. 1, Damariscotta. Open early Apr.–Columbus Day, 11:30–10, until 8 off-season. You'll find delicious Round Top Ice Cream, made with 15 percent butterfat, offered at restaurants throughout the region, but this is the original shop just up the road from the farm where it all began in 1924. The ice

MORSE'S IS DESTINATION DINING AND SHOPPING

Bill Davis

cream comes in 60 flavors, including fresh blueberry.

✳ Entertainment

Lincoln Theater (207-563-3424; lcct.org), entrance off Main St., Damariscotta. The biggest hall east of Boston in 1875, later boasting the largest motion-picture screen in the state. A second-floor theater has been restored (with elevator access) by the Lincoln County Community Theater, which stages its own productions here. Also first-run films and special programs.

Waldo Theatre (207-832-6060; waldotheatre.org), Main St., Waldoboro. Mar.–Dec., a schedule of films, concerts, and live performances.

Also check the film and lecture schedule at Damariscotta's Skidompha Library (see *To See*).

⌘ **Colonial Pemaquid State Historic Site** (207-677-2423; friendsof colonialpemaquid.org) is a venue for frequent reenactments, lectures, and other special events (see *Historic Sites*).

✳ Selective Shopping

ANTIQUES *Antiquing in the Mid coast Pemaquid Region*, an annually produced, widely available free pamphlet guide, lists more than two dozen dealers in this small area. Check local papers for auctions or call **Robert Foster** (207-563-8110), based at his auction gallery on Rt. 1, Newcastle.

ART, CRAFTS, AND MORE

In Damariscotta unless otherwise noted

River Arts (207-563-1507; riverarts .org), 170 Main St. The library's former clapboard home is now is now home to a 300-member arts cooperative gallery

with changing exhibits; also an arts center with lectures and classes.

River Gallery (207-563-6330), Main St. Open in-season Mon.–Sat. 10–3; features 19th- and early-20th-century landscapes.

Tin Fish Etc. (207-563-8204), above the Weatherbird Store, Northey Square. Dana Moses fashions remarkable art pieces in all sizes from recycled metal, mostly corrugated iron.

Damariscotta Pottery (207-563-8843), around back of the Weatherbird. Open year-round except Sun. Majolica ware, decorated in floral designs. You won't see this advertised. It doesn't have to be. Watch it being shaped and painted.

The Stable Gallery (207-563-1991; stablegallerymaine.com), 26 Water St. Open daily mid-May–mid-Oct. A cooperative showing works of member artists and a variety of craftspeople.

Watershed Center for Ceramic Arts (207-882-6705; watershed ceramics.org), 19 Rick Hill Rd., Newcastle. An old brickworks serves as a seasonal studio in which artists use the local clay to create work. Inquire about studio tours and Salad Days.

Sheepscot River Pottery (207-882-9410 or 1-800-659-4794), Main St. The big shop is on Rt. 1 in Edgecomb, but this gift shop features the distinctive hand-painted dinnerware, plates, lamps, and more.

In New Harbor and Pemaquid Point

Pemaquid Craft Co-Op (207-677-2077), Rt. 130, New Harbor. Open May–Oct., daily 10–6, then Fri.–Sun. until Dec. 24. Fifteen rooms filled with varied work by 50 Maine crafters.

Saltwater Artists Gallery (207-677-2490; saltwaterartists.com), corner of Rt. 30 and Lighthouse Rd. Open Memorial Day–Columbus Day, 10–5.

A nonprofit cooperative featuring 30 local artists in a wide variety of media.

Pemaquid Art Gallery (207-677-2753), Pemaquid Lighthouse Park, displays the work of local artists.

North Country Wind Bells (207-677-2224; mainebuoybells.com), 544 Rt. 32, Chamberlain. Open daily June–Labor Day, weekdays off-season. North of New Harbor on the pretty coastal road to Round Pond. Buoy wind bells, wilderness bells, and lighthouse bells are made and sold, along with garden and home accessories.

SPECIAL SHOPS

In Damariscotta

✪ 🐾 ✎ **Renys** (207-563-3177; renys .com), Main St. First opened in Damariscotta in 1949, family-owned Renys has since become a small-town Maine institution with 14 stores from Wells to Ellsworth as well as many inland. Corporate headquarters are

DOWNTOWN DAMARISCOTTA

Christina Tree

south of town. Main Street hosts two stores: The original sells quality clothing, while Renys Underground offers everything from tea to TVs, bedding, china, toys; a wide assortment of canned and boxed foodstuffs at amazing savings; also a wide assortment of shoes, sandals, and boots; beach equipment and all manner of staples and things you didn't realize you needed. The antithesis of Walmart, Renys has been the subject of two Maine musicals. The biggest sales of the year here begin at 6 AM on the first Saturday of November.

✎ **Maine Coast Book Shop** (207-563-3207), 158 Main St. One of Maine's best bookstores, with a large children's section and knowledgeable staff members who delight in making suggestions and helping customers shop. It now fills the entire first floor of the Lincoln Theater building and includes an inviting cyber café with a blackboard menu and freshly made soups as well as espressos and teas.

Intarwut (207-563-8899; intarawut .com), 136 Main St. Open daily year-round. This gorgeous store features ethnic silver jewelry and deeply colored textiles, clothing, and accessories from northern Thailand. For more than a decade Hathaihip Intarwut has been designing handbags, jackets, and other clothing stitched in her native Chiang Mai; this store expands on her former shop in Cambridge, Massachusetts.

Weatherbird on Main (207-563-1177), 132 Main St. An exceptional women's clothing store, expanded from the corner it previously occupied at Weatherbird's Courtyard Street store (see *Eating Out*).

Damariscotta Fresh Fish (207-563-5888), 49 Main St., Damariscotta. Daily 8:30–6. Best source of of fresh fish and seafood. Inquire about oysters on the half shell.

GRANITE HALL STORE

Christina Tree

Elsewhere

✦ **Granite Hall Store** (207-529-5864), Rt. 32, Round Pond. Open daily in-season 10–8:30. This distinctive, mansard-roofed building was constructed as a dance hall in the 1880s at the center of a busy little coastal port. Check out the movie screen and piano upstairs, relics of its silent-movie days. Sarah and Eric Herndon have preserved this sense of the past but filled it with reasons to explore, from the penny candy up front to Scottish scarves, Irish hats, and Maine-made woolens, books, and cards, plus an ice cream take-out window.

✦ **Morse's Kraut House** (207-832-5569; morsessauerkraut.com), 3856 Washington Rd. (8 miles north of Rt. 1, on Rt. 220), Waldoboro. Open year-round, daily except Wed., 9–6. A dozen years ago Morse's was sold to an enterprising couple, David Swetnam and Jacqueline Sawyer, who assumed that the secret sauerkraut made here since 1918 would be part of the deal. Not so. Several 50-pound batches of kraut later, they figured it out. The restaurant here remains small (see *Eating*

Out) but the store has morphed into a major source of European deli meats, cheeses, and delicacies, especially in the pre-Christmas season. Judging from an almond-stuffed croissant, the traditional European and especially German-style pastries, baked here daily, are well worth the drive.

Borealis Breads Store (207-832-0655; borealisbreads.com), 1860 Rt. 1 (across from Moody's Diner), Waldoboro. Open Mon.–Fri. 8:30–5:30, Sat. and Sun. 9–4. Maine's most popular bread, made from all-natural ingredients, including local grains, and baked here on a stone hearth; more than a dozen kinds are widely distributed.

Alewives (207-563-5002), Rt. 215, Damariscotta Mills. Open daily, year-round. Two miles north of Rt. 1, a red barn houses one of the state's outstanding fabric stores. The selection is outstanding, including Marimekko, batik, and Asian. Also quilting supplies. We stopped because we were looking for and found pillow forms.

I'm Puzzled (207-563-5719), Nobleboro, marked from Rt. 1. Jigsaw puzzle buffs should follow the signs to Robert Havenstein's two-car garage, filled to overflowing with jigsaw puzzles, more than 850 different offerings ranging from $2 yard-sale rejects to antique wooden puzzles prized by collectors.

Jean Gillespie Books (207-529-5555), Rt. 32 south of Round Pond. Open seasonally 1–5, or by appointment. An exceptional antiquarian bookstore since 1961. Some 20,000 titles line shelves in a barnlike annex to the house. Specialties include the Civil War, cookbooks, and Maine.

FARMER'S MARKET The Damariscotta Farmers' Market (damariscottafarmersmarket.org) is held mid-May–Oct., Fri. 9–noon at the

Damariscotta River Association, Belvedere Rd. (see *Green Space*); also Mon. late June–Oct. at **Rising Tide Market** (see *Eating Out*).

✳ Special Events

Note: See damariscotta.com for details.

February: Annual ice harvest at the Thompson Ice House, South Bristol.

May–early June: Alewives climb the fish ladder in Damariscotta Mills to spawn in Damariscotta Lake.

Memorial Day weekend: **Alewives Festival**.

July: Annual July 4 fireworks in Damariscotta and Wiscasset and a famously unorthodox parade in Round Pond. **Great Salt Bay Music Festival** at Damariscotta River Association.

Early August: **Olde Bristol Days**, Old Fort Grounds, Pemaquid Beach—

parade, fish fry, chicken barbecue, bands, bagpipers, concerts, pancake breakfast, road race, boat race, firemen's muster, crafts, and the annual Bristol Footlighters Show.

September: **Pemaquid Oyster Festival** at Schooner Landing, Damariscotta.

First weekend of October: **Annual Pumpkinfest & Regatta** has become the most one of the biggest events of the year; it includes a parade of river-worthy pumpkins.

First Saturday in November: **Early Bird Sale at Renys** and at stores throughout town. Free coffee, doughnuts, and bargains. From 6 AM.

December: **Coastal Christmas Fest**.

ROCKLAND/THOMASTON AREA

Long billed as the "Lobster Capital of the World," Rockland is now better known as home of the Farnsworth Museum, with its exceptional collection of Maine-based paintings, and for the galleries, shops, attractions, and restaurants lining its mile-long, floridly brick Main Street. Departure point for ferries to the islands of Vinalhaven, North Haven, and Matinicus, it is also home port for the majority of Maine's windjammers, as well as for several daysailers and excursion boats.

In the past couple of decades this city of nearly 7,300 has been transformed almost completely. Never a "tourist town" like Camden or Boothbay, Rockland is fiercely proud of its working waterfront. Its sardine-packing and fish-processing plants are, however, gone, and the huge harbor, protected by a nearly mile-long granite—and walkable—breakwater, is now sparkling clean and equipped to accommodate pleasure boats. Old waterside industrial sheds have disappeared, replaced by offices and restaurants. The harborside walking trail lengthens with every edition of this book. A former newspaper plant is now the chamber of commerce visitors center and the Maine Lighthouse Museum.

Still, Rockland prides itself on its grit. The city's industrial base still includes FMC Bio-Polymer (processing carrageenan from seaweed) and home-grown Fisher Snowplow. The harbor, Maine's second largest after Portland, remains home to a sizable fishing and lobstering fleet along with tugs and U.S. Coast Guard and commercial vessels.

Rockland has remade itself several times over the centuries. Initially known for its shipbuilding, the city became synonymous in the late 19th century with the limestone it quarried, burned, and shipped off to be made into plaster. When wallboard replaced plaster, Rockland quickly switched to catching and processing fish. In the 1990s, with fishing on the decline, city

DOWNTOWN ROCKLAND

Christina Tree

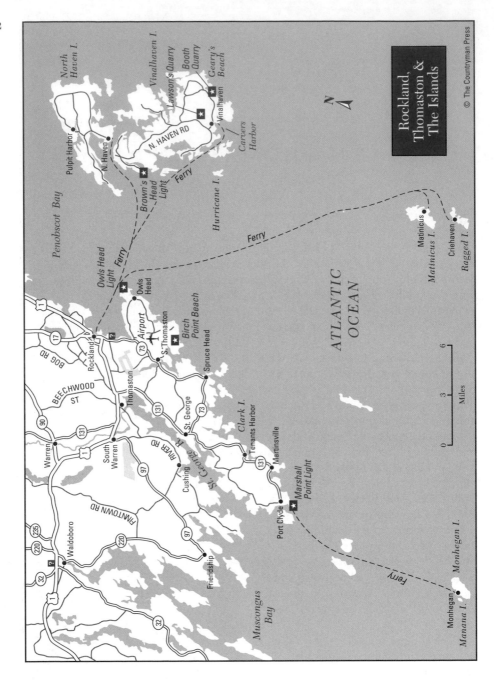

entrepreneurs once more looked to widening their base. Initially MBNA, the national credit card company, seemed a gift from the gods, tidying the southern rim of the harbor into an office "campus" and building a public boardwalk along its rim. In 2005, however, MBNA sold out and disappeared.

Truly amazing is the way Rockland's resurgence has continued to be powered by the economic engines of fine art, food, and cultural attractions, barely losing momentum despite the departure of MBNA. The vacated office space was filled, and restaurants moved in to take advantage of waterfront views.

A century ago summer people heading for Bar Harbor, as well as the islands, took the train as far as Rockland, switching here to steamboats. Today a similar summer crowd rides the bus to the ferry terminal or flies into Knox County Regional Airport on Owls Head, just south of town, transferring to rental cars, air taxis, or windjammers, to charter boats as well as ferries. The old train terminal on Union Street is now a restaurant and terminus of the popular Maine Eastern Railroad excursion train from Brunswick.

Southwest of Rockland, two peninsulas separate Muscongus Bay from Penobscot Bay. One is the fat arm of land on which the villages of Friendship and Cushing doze. Nearer is the skinnier St. George Peninsula with Port Clyde at its tip, departure point for the year-round passenger ferry service to Monhegan Island. The peninsulas are divided by the 10-mile-long St. George River, on which past residents of Thomaston launched their share of wooden ships.

GUIDANCE Penobscot Bay Regional Chamber of Commerce (207-596-0376 or 1-800-562-2529; therealmaine.com), 1 Park Dr., Rockland. Open daily Memorial Day–Labor Day, Mon.–Fri. 9–5 and Sat. 10–4; then weekdays and 10–2 Sat. through the Columbus Day weekend. The chamber's Maine Discovery Visitor Center serves the Rockland area, which includes Owls Head, Thomaston, the peninsula villages, and the islands. It also lists cottage and vacation rentals.

GETTING THERE *By air:* **Knox County Regional Airport** (207-594-4131), at Owls Head, just south of Rockland. Frequent daily service is via **Cape Air** (1-866-227-3247; capeair.com) to Boston's Logan Airport, with baggage connections to major carriers. **Penobscot Island Air** (penobscotislandair.net) offers both scheduled and charter service to Vinalhaven, North Haven, and Matinicus. Rental cars are available at the airport. Also see *By taxi* under *Getting Around*; all offer service to Portland International Jetport (see "Portland Area"). **Mid-Coast Limo** (1-800-937-2424; midcoastlimo.com) also serves Boston's Logan Airport.

By bus: **Concord Coach** (1-800-639-3317; concordcoachlines.com) stops in Rockland at the Maine State Ferry Terminal.

By boat: For moorings contact the harbormaster (office, 207-594-0312; dock, 207-594-0314).

By train: **The Maine Eastern Railroad** (1-866-637-2457; maineeasternrailroad .com) offers seasonal Wed.–Sun. service from Brunswick (ample parking).

GETTING AROUND *By taxi:* **Schooner Bay Limo & Taxi** (207-594-5000), **Hit the Road Driver Service** (207-230-0095; cell, 207-691-0295), and **Joe's Taxi** (207-975-3560) will get you there. **All Aboard Trolley** (207-594-9300; aatrolley .com) offers seasonal, narrated service on a loop around Rockland. Call to check times.

By ferry: Frequent service from the **Maine State Ferry Service Terminal** (207-596-2022 or 1-800-491-4883) to Vinalhaven, North Haven, and, less frequently, to

Matinicus (see "Midcoast Islands").
Monhegan Boat Line (207-372-8848) serves Monhegan from Port Clyde.

Note: Rockland can be accessed and thoroughly enjoyed without a car.

PARKING Try to park in a free, all-day municipal lot off Tillson Ave. Note that street parking is limited to two hours and strictly enforced.

WHEN TO COME Rockland stages a series of festivals that draw weekend

Christina Tree

A MAINE STATE FERRY HEADS OUT FROM ROCKLAND

crowds from mid-July through September. The biggest is the Maine Lobster Festival, first weekend in August. The Farnsworth Museum, major galleries, restaurants, and lodging all remain open year-round.

✳ Villages and Islands

Friendship (pop. 1,200). Best known as the birthplace of the classic Friendship sloop, first built by local lobstermen to haul their traps (originals and reproductions of this sturdy vessel hold races here every summer), Friendship remains a quiet fishing village. The **Friendship Museum** (207-832-4852), housed in a former brick schoolhouse at the junction of Rt. 220 and Martin Point Rd., is open late June–Labor Day, Mon.–Sat. 1–4 and Sun. 2–4, also weekends March–Columbus Day. Displays feature Friendship sloops.

St. George is a town composed of several distinct villages along Rt. 131 on the St. George Peninsula, a 15-mile-long land finger between the tidal St. George River and the Atlantic. The most visible of these is **Tenants Harbor**, a fishing village with a terrific sculpture of St. George and the Dragon in front of the town office. There's a good little library and, beyond, rock cliffs, tidal pools, old cemeteries, and the kind of countryside described by Sarah Orne Jewett in *The Country of the Pointed Firs*. Jewett lived just a few bends down Rt. 131 in Martinville while she wrote the book.

Port Clyde marks the end of Rt. 131 and the tip of the peninsula. The departure point for the year-round ferries to Monhegan, it's tranquil and picturesque—with the exception of ferry departures and arrivals, when it's chaotic. The Ocean House is a great place to spend the night before boarding the ferry. Linda Bean (as in L.L. Bean) owns the working wharf, offers guest buoys and a launch service for yachtsmen (207-372-6543). She also owns the Dip Net restaurant, the Port Cylde General Store, and the neighboring Seaside Inn and gallery. This is a great spot for kayaking (see *To Do*), and **Marshall Point Light** (see *To See*) is around the bend.

Thomaston (pop. 2,800). Passing through Thomaston on Rt. 1 you notice the handsome brick downtown and line of handsome captains' homes, evidence of early-19th-century wealth from shipbuilding. In the 1840 census, three of the nation's seven millionaires lived in town. To dramatize its history Thomaston has installed 25 plaques along Main, Knox, and Water Sts., each with a photo taken at

Christina Tree

PORT CLYDE

that spot a century ago with text in both English and French. Leaflet guides to this **Museum in the Streets** are available at the library and most businesses. The **Thomaston Historical Society** (207-354-2314; thomastonhistoricalsociety.com) at the foot of Knox St. is open June–Aug., Tue.–Thu. 2–4. For many years Thomaston was known as the home of the state prison, which has since moved but left behind its popular **Maine State Prison Showroom** (see *Selective Shopping*). Montpelier, ttThe **General Knox Museum** (see *To See*), is just north of town at the junctions of Rts. 1 and 131.

Union (pop. 2,350) is 15 miles west of Rockland via Rt. 17, a little less if you follow Rt. 131 north along the St. George River. It's sited between Round Pond and Seven Tree Pond and surrounded by gentle hills and farm country. Union Common with its bandstand and Civil War monument is the oldest public common in the state. The **Union Fair** in August has been held since 1892. This place is also a good spot to swim, eat, and explore the **Matthews Museum of Maine Heritage** (matthewsmuseum.org) at the fairgrounds, open Wed.–Sat. in July and Aug., noon–4. Two vineyards (see *Selective Shopping*) welcome visitors for tastings.

Islands. An overnight or longer stay on an island is far preferable to a day trip. From Rockland you can take a Maine State (car) Ferry to **Vinalhaven** and **North Haven**. Together these form the Fox Islands, divided by a narrow passage. Vinalhaven is Maine's largest offshore island, with its largest year-round population and lobstering fleet. A number of shopping, eating, and lodging options cluster around Carver's Harbor, a 10-minute walk from the ferry. North Haven offers fewer and more seasonal places to eat, shop, and stay, but a more open landscape. **Matinicus**, also accessible from Rockland, is the most remote of Maine's island communities, and quietly beautiful. Tiny **Monhegan**, accessible from Port Clyde, offers the most dramatic cliff scenery and the most hospitable welcome to visitors. For details, see the descriptions of each island in the next chapter.

✳ To See

✪ ⅄ **Farnsworth Art Museum and Wyeth Center** (207-596-6457; farnsworth museum.org), 16 Museum St., Rockland. Open year-round. Memorial Day weekend–Oct. 31, daily 10–5, also Wed. and First Fridays 5–8 (free); Nov.–Dec. 31,

WHARF SCENE BY GEORGE BELLOWS

closed Mon.; Jan–Memorial Day weekend, Wed.–Sun. 10–5. Admission to the museum and Farnsworth Homestead (see below) is $12 adults, $10 senior citizens, $10 students over 17; no charge under 17; free for all Wed. 5–8. This exceptional art museum was established by Lucy Farnsworth, who amazed everyone when, on her death at age 97 in 1935, she left $1.3 million to preserve her house and build a library and art gallery to honor the memory of her father. From the beginning the collection included paintings of Maine by Winslow Homer, George Bellows, and a (then) little-known local summer resident, Andrew Wyeth.

Since the early 1990s the Farnsworth has more than doubled its space and now occupies 3 acres in the middle of downtown Rockland. The collection numbers over 14,000 objects housed in five buildings with 28 galleries. The museum remains Maine-focused. A permanent exhibit traces the evolution of Maine landscape paintings with Hudson River School artists like Thomas Cole and 19th-century marine artist Fitz Henry Lane; American impressionists Frank Benson, Willard Metcalf, Childe Hassam, and Maurice Prendergast; early-20th-century greats like Rockwell Kent and Charles Woodbury; and such "modernists" as John Marin and Marsden Hartley. Rockland-raised painter and sculptor Louise Nevelson is also well represented. In recent years contemporary art holdings have been significantly expanded to include works by Alex Katz, Neil Welliver, Janet Fish, Bernard Langlais, and Robert Indiana, along with such photographers as Elliot Porter and Rockland native Kosti Ruchomaa.

The Farnsworth's original Georgian Revival library and the Jamien Morehouse Wing house changing exhibits of reference materials and regularly scheduled lectures and concerts. Gardens connect the main museum with the Wyeth Center, a two-story exhibit space in a former church, displaying works by N. C. Wyeth (1882–1945) and Jamie Wyeth (born 1946). Exhibits vary. Andrew Wyeth's paintings are shown in the main museum.

Farnsworth Homestead (207-596-6457), 21 Elm St., Rockland. Open late May–mid-Oct., Tue.–Sun. 11–5. Tours on the hour. Free with museum admission. Built in 1850 for successful

TURKEY POND BY ANDREW WYETH, 1944

Farnsworth Art Museum

CHILDREN WITH A DOCENT

businessman William A. Farnsworth and his growing family, this was the nearly lifelong home of his daughter and museum founder Lucy Copeland Farnsworth. The Greek Revival–style Farnsworth Homestead has a richly decorated Victorian interior, with original furniture, carpets, wallpaper, paintings and prints, gas lighting fixtures, and many of the family's original belongings.

The Olson House (207-596-6457), Hawthorn Point Rd., Cushing. Open Memorial Day–Columbus Day, daily 11–4. $10 adults, $8 seniors and students over 17. Administered by the Farnsworth Art Museum, this house served as a backdrop for many works by Andrew Wyeth, including *Christina's World*. It's been intentionally left unrestored except for interpretive materials. On Pleasant Point, accessed by quiet back roads, this saltwater farm makes a good bicycle destination. Built in the late 1700s, it was remodeled in 1872 but remained in the same family, ultimately passing to Alvara and Christina (1892–1968) Olson. It has been owned by the Farnsworth since 1991. The house, both inside and out, evokes the familiar painting.

MUSEUMS AND HISTORIC HOMES *⚓* **General Henry Knox Museum** (Montpelier) (207-354-8062; knoxmuseum.org), 30 High St., Thomaston. Guided tours Memorial Day–Columbus Day, Tue.–Sat. 10–3:30. Admission $7 adults, $6 seniors, $4 ages 5–14 (family: $18). A 1926 re-creation of the grand mansion built (on another spot) in 1794 by General Henry Knox (1750–1806), the portly 5-foot-6-inch, 300-pound Boston bookseller who became a Revolutionary War hero, then our first secretary of war. He married a granddaughter of Samuel Waldo, the Boston developer who owned all of this area and for whom the county is named. The re-creation was financed by *Saturday Evening Post* publisher and Camden summer resident Cyrus Curtis.

THE OLSON HOUSE

Farnsworth Art Museum

Owls Head Transportation Museum (207-594-4418; owls head.org), 117 Museum St., Owls Head. Off Rt. 73, 2 miles south of Rockland, adjacent to the Knox County Regional Airport. Open daily year-round (except Christmas, Thanksgiving, and New Year's Day) 10–5. Check the website for frequent special-event days. On non-event days admission is $10 adults, $8 seniors, free under 18 (a couple dollars more on special-event days such as antique air shows, or antique car and motorcycle auctions). One of the country's outstanding collections of antique planes and automobiles, and everything works. In the

Owls Head Transportation Museum

EVERYTHING AT THE OWLS HEAD TRANSPORTATION MUSEUM WORKS

exhibition hall you can take a 100-year journey through the evolution of transportation, from horse-drawn carriages to World War I fighter planes; from a 16-cylinder Cadillac to a Rolls-Royce; from the Red Baron's Fokker triplane to a vintage 1923 popcorn wagon from Old Orchard Beach. Exhibits are constantly changing and evolving. If you haven't been here in a few years, you are in for a pleasant surprise. On weekends there are special demonstrations of such magnificent machines as a 1901 Oldsmobile, and visitors can take a ride in Model T Fords.

Project Puffin Visitor Center (207-596-5566; projectpuffin.org), 311 Main St., Rockland. Open daily June–Oct. 10–5 (until 7 Wed in July and Aug.), then weekends until Dec; call for off-season hours. Free. Live-streaming mini cams and audio provide a virtual visit with nesting puffins. A joint project of National Audubon and Maine Audubon, this is a must-stop, with exhibits cleverly designed for children, like the "burrow" into which they can crawl and observe puffins feeding their chicks in a similar burrow. Exhibits include a video chronicling the decades-long effort to restore these seabirds to the Maine coast.

CAPTAIN JIM SHARPE AT HIS SAIL, POWER & STEAM MUSEUM

Bill Davis

Sail, Power & Steam Museum (207-701-7627; sailpowerandsteam.org), 75 Mechanic St., Sharps Point South. Open May–Nov.; check the web or call for hours. $5 adult, $3 ages 7–16. Free over 65. Nineteenth-century sail and steam vessels are the focus of this evolving museum, sited in the historic, still-working Snow Family Shipyard. It's the brainchild of Captain Jim Sharp, who helped restore Maine windjammer *Stephen Taber* and Arctic explorer Donald MacMillan's schooner *Bowdoin* (now owned by the Maine Maritime Academy). The growing collection includes half models, marine paintings and prints, a vintage-1674 brass navigational instrument owned by Nathaniel Bowditch, a room full of tools, another dedicated to Rockland's lime rock history, and much more. Inquire about requent concerts and lectures, also harbor cruises.

✄ **The Coastal Children's Museum** (207-975-2530; coastalchildrensmuseum .org), 75 Mechanic St. at Sharps Point South. $5 adults, $3 ages 3–9. Wed.–Sat. 10–4, Sun. 1–4. More than 16 hands-on, interactive displays include a touch tank, a full-sized sailboat, and a lobster trap you can crawl through.

✳ To Do

BICYCLING Bikesenjava (207-596-1004; haybikesenjava.com), 481 Main St., Rockland, now sited conveniently near the ferry terminal, is a source of rental hybrid and mountain bikes, as well as tag-a-longs, 21-speed kids' mountain bikes, car racks, coffees, and chai.

Georges River Bikeways is the name of a free map/guide that traces routes along the river and in its watershed area from Thomaston north into Liberty. Check with the Georges River Land Trust (207-594-5166), 328 Main St., Rockland.

Note: Both Vinalhaven and North Haven are popular biking destinations. Please ride single-file. Roads are narrow.

BOAT EXCURSIONS Check with the chamber of commerce for a complete list of current excursions. Also see the Maine State Ferry Service under *Getting Around.* The ferry rides to both North Haven and Vinalhaven are reasonably priced and a good way to get out on the water. Both islands make good day trips, but Monhegan is far more walkable. See the Midcoast Islands chapter for details about all three islands.

Monhegan Boat Line (207-372-8848; monheganboat.com) in Port Clyde offers frequent 50-minute service to the island using its two boats, the *Elizabeth Ann* (built in 1995 for this run, with both open top and lower enclosed decks) and the smaller *Laura B* (built in 1943 for World War II duty). The same boats are also used for seasonal "Puffin/Nature" cruises to Eastern Egg Rock and to view the area's lighthouses.

Captain Jack Lobster Boat Adventure (207-542-6852; captainjacklobstertours .com), 130 Thomaston St., Rockland. Memorial Day–Columbus Day. Lobster-boat tours that may include a onboard lobster dinner.

Daysails and longer

Summertime Cruises (1-800-562-8290; schoonersummertime.com), 115 South St., Rockland. Captain Bill Brown offers three- and six-day cruises on a 53-foot pinky schooner for up to six passengers throughout the summer, plus day sails in spring and autumn.

A Morning in Maine (207-691-7245; amorninginmaine.com), Rockland Middle Pier. A classic coastal ketch with an overall length of 55 feet, captained by marine biologist Bob Pratt, offers sails ranging from a few hours to overnights for up to 21 people.

LIGHTHOUSES

Penobscot Bay boasts the largest concentration of Maine's 68 lighthouses. Three in the Rockland area are accessible by land.

Rockland Breakwater Light (207-542-7574; rocklandlighthouse.com). Wear sensible shoes for the glorious but uneven almost-mile-long granite breakwater (turn off Rt. 1 onto Waldo Ave. just north of Rockland, then right onto Samoset Rd.; follow this to the end). The squat brick light- and foghouse attached to a gabled keeper's house is presently under renovation as a museum. It's open Memorial–Columbus Day weekends, Sat. and Sun. 10–5, weather and volunteers permitting.

Owls Head Light State Park, a classic, white conical tower 20 feet high, built in 1825 atop sheer cliffs, nonetheless has safe trails down one side to the rocks below—good for scrambling and picnicking. Open Memorial–Columbus Day weekends, Sat.–Sun. 10–4, weather and volunteers permitting. From Rockland or the Owls Head Transportation Museum, take Rt. 73 to North Shore Dr. After about 2 miles you come to a small post office at an intersection. Turn left onto Main St., and after 0.25 mile make a left onto Lighthouse Dr. Follow signs to Owls Head Light State Park.

Just north of the village of Port Clyde (turn off Rt. 131 onto Marshall Point Rd.) is the **Marshall Point Lighthouse Museum** (207-372-6450; marshall point.org), open Memorial Day–Columbus Day, Sun.–Fri. 1–5 and Sat. 10–5; during May, weekends 1–5. Built in 1885, deactivated in 1971, this is a small light on a scenic point; part of the former lighthouse keeper's home is now a lively museum dedicated to the history of the town of St. George in general and the light station (established in 1832) in particular. Even if the lighthouse isn't open, this is a great spot to sit, walk, and picnic.

Goose Rocks Lighthouse (207-867-4747; beaconpreservation.org) is a freestanding "spark-plug-style" light 10 miles off Rockland in the Fox Islands Thorofare between Vinalhaven and North Haven, built in 1890. It offers two bedrooms and a bunkroom, bath, kitchen with an Aga stove, and dining "snug," as well as balconies. "Keeper stays" are available with a donation.

⚓ **Maine Lighthouse Museum** (207-594-3301; mainelighthousemuseum .com), Maine Discovery Center, 1 Park Dr., Rockland. Open daily Memorial Day–Oct., Mon.–Fri. 9–5, Sat. and Sun. 10–4. Check the website for winter hours. $5 adults, $4 seniors. Billed as the country's largest exhibit of lighthouse lenses and lifesaving artifacts, the display showcases more than a dozen Fresnel lenses. Most of these were amassed by Kenneth Black, former commander of the Rockland Coast Guard Station. Black realized that with the automation of lighthouses, historic lenses and other mechanical gear would largely be scrapped. He created the Shore Village Museum—known as "Mt. Lighthouse"—in a former Civil War veterans' hall, where he delighted in demonstrating the working foghorns. He lived to see the collection installed in this spacious hall, named in his memory. Note the LEDs locating Maine's working lighthouses. Exhibits include flashing lights, search-and-rescue gear, buoys, bells, rescue boats, and half models.

American Lighthouse Foundation (207-594-4174; lighthousefoundation.org), 464 Main St., Rockland. This is a nonprofit umbrella for the organizations supporting many lighthouses in need of preservation and/or renovation since automation. Thanks to these "Friends" groups, a number of lights have also become visitor-friendly. The foundation maintains a helpful information center picturing ad mapping lights; gift items benefit restoration efforts. Check the ALF website for the latest about individual lighthouses.

MARSHALL POINT LIGHT, PORT CLYDE Nancy English

✪ 🐾 WINDJAMMERS

In three days aboard a windjammer you can explore islands and remote mainland harbors that would take hundreds of miles of driving and several ferries to reach. Two-, three-, four-, five-, and six-day cruises are offered late May–mid-Oct. and run from $365 for two-day to $1,995 for nine-day trips. This includes all meals and—for our money—the most relaxing way to experience Penobscot Bay. All these vessels are inspected and certified each year by the Coast Guard. Most are members of the **Maine Windjammer Association** (1-800-807-WIND; sailmainecoast.com). Also see *Windjammers* in "What's Where" and "Camden/Rockport Area."

Schooner *American Eagle* (207-594-8007 or 1-800-648-4544; schooneramerican eagle.com), North End Shipyard, Rockland. One of the last classic Gloucester fishing schooners to be launched (in 1930), this 92-foot vessel continued to fish (minus her original stern and masts, plus a pilothouse) off Gloucester until 1983, when Captain John Foss brought her to Rockland's North End Shipyard and spent the next two years restoring and refitting her. The *Eagle* was built with an engine (so she still has one) as well as sails, and she offers some comfortable belowdecks spaces. The *Eagle* sails farther out to sea (to see whales and seabirds) than other windjammers and also offers a July cruise to Canada and a Labor Day sail to Gloucester (Massachusetts) to participate in a race. Most cruises are four to six days, accommodating 26 guests in 14 double cabins.

Schooner *Heritage* (207-594-8007 or 1-800-648-4544; schoonerheritage.com), North End Shipyard, Rockland. Captain Doug Lee likes to describe the graceful, 95-foot, 30-passenger vessel he designed and built as "the next generation of coasting schooner rather than a replica." He notes that schooners were modified over the years to suit whatever cargo they carried. Here headroom in the cabins and the top of the companionways was raised to accommodate upright cargo, and the main cabin is an unusually airy, bright space in which to gather. Lee is a marine historian who, with his wife and co-captain, Linda, designed and built the *Heritage* in Rockland's North End Shipyard. Their two daughters, Clara and Rachel, sometimes sail as crew. Both captains are unusually warm hosts.

Schooner *Stephen Taber* (207-594-0035 or 1-800-999-7352; stephentaber.com) was launched in 1871 and is the oldest documented U.S. sailing vessel in continuous use. She is 68 feet long and accommodates 22 passengers. Cabins have windows; two are singles, four have full-sized double beds, and six have twins; all have sink with running water. Heads and showers are on deck. Captain Noah Barnes is the first second-generation windjammer captain, taking over the helm from his parents (both licensed captains), who restored the vessel and sailed her for 25 years. The *Taber* continues to have an enthusiastic following, known for her exceptional food, also for wine-tasting and other special-interest cruises.

Schooner *Victory Chimes* (207-594-0755 or 1-800-745-5651; victorychimes.com). "There was nothing special about this boat in 1900 when she was built," Captain Kip Files is fond of telling his passengers at their first breakfast aboard. "But now she's the only three-masted American-built schooner left. And she's the largest commercial sailing vessel in the United States." The *Chimes* is 132 feet long, accommodating 40 passengers in a variety of cabins (four singles, two quads, one triple, 12 doubles).

Schooner *Nathaniel Bowditch* (207-596-0401 or 1-800-288-4098; windjammer vacation.com) was built in East Boothbay as a racing yacht in 1922. Eighty-two feet long, she took special honors in the 1923 Bermuda Race and served in the Coast Guard during World War II. She has since been rebuilt. Captain Owen Dorr's great-grandfather was mate aboard one of the last five-masted schooners to sail the East Coast; in the 1940s Owen's parents worked for Captain Frank Swift, creator of the Maine windjammer tradition. Captain Owen and Cathie Dorr met aboard a Maine schooner (she was a passenger, he, a crew member). The *Bowditch* accommodates 24 passengers in 11 double-bunked cabins and two single "Pullmans"; in-cabin sinks.

Schooner *Isaac H. Evans* (207-594-7956 or 1-877-238-1325; isaacevans.com). A trim 22-passenger schooner dating (in part) to 1886, built for oystering in Delaware Bay, now back in service with owner-captain Brenda Thomas. There are 11 double berths, some side-by-side, some upper–lower bunks. Three- and four-day and weeklong cruises are offered. Specializes in family trips; children 6 and over welcome on all cruises.

SCHOONER *AMERICAN EAGLE*
Greg Cramma, courtesy of Maine Windjammer Association

Schooner *J&E Riggin* (207-594-1875 or 1-800-869-0604; mainewindjammer .com) was built in 1927 for the oyster-dredging trade. A speedy 90-footer, she was extensively rebuilt in the 1970s before joining the windjammer trade. Captains Jon Finger and Anne Mahle take 24 passengers in nine double and two triple cabins. Mahle is an outstanding chef, author of the cookbook *At Home, At Sea*. The *J&E Riggin* welcomes families with children ages 6 and up on special family cruises.

BOAT RENTALS Johanson Boatworks (207-596-7060 or 1-877-456-4267), 11 Farwell Dr., Rockland, offers sailboat charters. **Bay Sailing** (207-831-8425; bay-sailing.com), the Pier at the Pearl, Rockland, offers yacht charters, boat rentals, and an ASA sailing school.

SEA KAYAKING Breakwater Kayak (207-596-6895; breakwaterkayak.com), behind Landings Restaurant (see *Eating Out*) on Commercial St., Rockland. Two-hour to multiday guided kayaking tours.

Port Clyde Kayaks (207-372-8100; portclydekayaks.com), Port Clyde. Based at an outfitting shop near the Port Clyde wharf. Guided tours take you across Port Clyde Harbor to Marshall Point Light and among the nearby Georges Islands.

FISHING, HUNTING, AND CANOEING The **Penobscot Bay Regional Chamber of Commerce** (see *Guidance*) offers information on fishing (both salt- and freshwater) and registered duck-hunting guides, among them **Saltwater Fishing & Guide Service** (207-542-8915), **Cramer Guide Services** (207-233-3979), and **Ten Mile Guide Service** (207-542-8777).

Maine Outdoors (207-785-4496; maineoutdoors.biz), 69 Beote Rd., Union, offers fishing and other paddling adventures.

GOLF Rockland Golf Club (207-594-9322; rocklandgolf.com), 606 Old County Rd., Rockland. Open Apr.–Oct. This 18-hole public course gets high marks from pros; complete with a modern clubhouse serving meals from 7 AM.

For the local resort that specializes in golf, see **Samoset Golf Course** in "Camden/Rockport Area."

RAILROAD EXCURSION ☙ **The Maine Eastern Railroad** (1-866-636-2457; maineeasternrailroad.com) offers 54-mile seasonal runs between Rockland and Brunswick, stopping in Bath and Wiscasset. It's a beautiful trip along the coast in plush 1940s and '50s coaches and a dining car pulled by a 1950s diesel electric engine.

✳ Green Space

BEACHES ☙ **Johnson Memorial Park**, Chickawaukee Lake, Rt. 17, 2 miles north of downtown Rockland. Restrooms, picnic area, a sand beach, and warm water add up to the area's best swimming, good for small children.

☙ **Birch Point Beach State Park**, also known as Lucia Beach, off Ash Point Rd. in Owls Head. Sandy, with smooth boulders for sunning, wooded walking trails, and picnic benches. Marked from Rt. 73 (Dublin Rd. to Ballyhac Rd.).

Drift Inn Beach in Port Clyde, down Drift Inn Rd. by the Harpoon Restaurant, just off Rt. 131; a small beach in a great spot.

WALKING/PICNICKING Rockland waterfront. The area's most spectacular stretch of the **Rockland Harbor Trail** begins on the Samoset Hotel property just over the Rockport line and runs 1.7 miles out along the Rockland Breakwater to the lighthouse. There's always plenty of boat traffic.

ROCKLAND HARBOR TRAIL

Christina Tree

Harbor Park at the public landing marks the beginning of the trail south along the water past Sandy Beach Park (picnic benches) to Mechanic St. and on to Snow Marine Park. Along the way you'll find benches, flowers, a gazebo, and harbor views.

Owls Head Light State Park. This classic lighthouse is set into a beautiful point with walks and views on both the bay and harbor sides, picnic tables. See *Lighthouses* for directions.

Waldo Tyler Wildlife Sanctuary, Buttermilk Lane (off Rt. 73), South Thomaston, is a birding spot on the Weskeag River.

The Georges River Land Trust (207-594-5166), 8 N. Main St., Rockland, publishes a map/guide to the Georges Highland Path, a foot trail through the hills of the Georges River watershed. Maps are available at the chamber of commerce.

✴ Lodging

INNS AND BED & BREAKFASTS

In Rockland 04841

((ᵠ)) **Berry Manor Inn** (207-596-7696 or 1-800-774-5692; berrymanorinn .com), 81 Talbot Ave., P.O. Box 1117. This expansive 19th-century shingle-style mansion is a sumptuous retreat. The 12 guest rooms, divided among the second and third floors of the mansion and the second floor of the Carriage House, all have queen- or king-sized bed, flat-screen TV, phone, air conditioning, and luxurious bath with soaking or whirlpool tub; almost all have a gas fireplace. A two-room, two-bath suite in the Carriage House has a separate living room. Morning coffee and juice available at 7 AM. $115–275 for rooms, $400 for the suite mid-June–mid-Oct., less off-season, including a five-course breakfast and a guest pantry stocked with goodies that include homemade pies.

((ᵠ)) **LimeRock Inn** (207-594-2257 or 1-800-546-3762; limerockinn.com), 96 Limerock St. P. J. Walter and Frank Isganitis are the innkeepers of this 1890s Queen Anne–style mansion on a quiet residential street with a wraparound front porch and two living rooms to relax in. The eight guest rooms, all with private bath, are opulently furnished with antiques. The turret room is over the top, but our favorite is the airy Island Cottage room at the back of the house, opening on the garden. Amenities include a 24-hour guest pantry and computer. $159–239 ($119–165 off-season) includes a full breakfast.

✿ 🐾 & ((ᵠ)) **Granite Inn** (207-594-9036 or 1-800-386-9036; oldgraniteinn.com), 546 Main St. An 1840s mansion built of local granite, set in a flower garden, across from the Maine State Ferry Terminal (also the Concord Coach stop). Ideal if you come without a car and are bound for an island, but innkeepers Edwin and Joan Hantz have added plenty of other reasons to stay here. Joan is a graphic artist with an eye for blending contemporary furnishings and antiques, creating uncluttered, comfortable spaces. Both the living room and dining room are unusually inviting. There are eight guest rooms, including two suites. Two front second-floor bedrooms—the largest—overlook the water and ferry terminal. We also like the simply but elegantly decorated rooms (with spiffy new baths) in the quieter back of the house; the two-room suites (the second bedrooms have twin beds) represent good value for families or couples who don't mind sharing a bath. $100–200 per night includes a breakfast featuring fresh fruit, from-scratch baked goods, bacon or sausage, and a hot entrée, maybe crab fritters, traditional Maine strata, or lemon crêpes with wild blueberry compote.

○ ♿ (((•))) **The Captain Lindsey House** (207-596-7950 or 1-800-523-2145; lindseyhouse.com), 5 Lindsey St. This was built in 1837 as one of Rockland's first inns, and the feel is that of a small, boutique hotel. With richly paneled public rooms and nine spacious guest rooms (one handicapped accessible), it's a gem, and the most convenient lodging to the Farnsworth

THE GRANITE INN, ROCKLAND

Christina Tree

Museum and Main Street shops. It's the creation of schooner captains Ken and Ellen Barnes, who also restred and operated the windjammer *Stephen Taber* for more than 25 years. Each guest room is different, but all have air-conditioning, phone, TV, and private bath. $159–239 includes a full buffet breakfast, served in the garden, weather permitting. Captain Ken Barnes is a justice of the peace familiar with local wedding venues.

❦ ✿ **Ripples** (207-594-2771 or 1-800-375-5771; ripplesinnattheharbor.com), 16 Pleasant St. Open year-round. Sandi Dillon has restored this pleasant house with imagination and skill. Rooms are not overly fussy but nicely decorated with an eye to comfort. There are four rooms and a family suite (accommodating four) with a whirlpool tub and private entrance. In addition to the usual common spaces, an "UN-common room" has a microwave, fridge, and TV. $100–240 (for a two-bedroom suite) with full breakfast.

On Spruce Head and on the St. George Peninsula

❦ (((•))) **Craignair Inn** (207-594-7644 or 1-800-320-9997; craignair.com), Clark Island Rd., Spruce Head 04859. Main building, open year-round. Michael and Joann O'Shea are breathing new life into this pleasant three-story inn, sited on 4 shorefront acres. Built in the 1920s as a boardinghouse for quarry workers, it has a comfortably old-fashioned feel. The 20 guest rooms are divided between the main house (Room 12 is a corner room with a queen and three windows with water views) and the Vestry, a former chapel set in gardens in the rear with water views from the second floor. The dining room overlooks the water and is open to the public for dinner (see *Dining Out*). Walk across the causeway to the Clark Island shoreline and a granite quarry that's good swimming. In high season from $105 for a room with shared bath to $175 for a private room with water view, $90–140 off-season, including a full breakfast. $10 extra for a pet.

🐾 (ᵗᵖ) **East Wind Inn** (207-372-6366 or 1-800-241-8439; eastwindinn.com), Mechanic St., P.O. Box 149, Tenants Harbor 04860. Open May–Oct. This tall, distinctive, 19th-century building has been an inn since the 1920s, when patrons arrived at the landing by steamboat. For more than 35 years it's been owned by Tim Watts, who is retiring, but we trust that this beloved landmark will continue to offer its expansive waterside grounds and its superlative views from the veranda and sunny dining room, as well as from comfortable rooms. From $118 in high season with shared bath; otherwise $176–206, from $99 before June 18 and after Labor Day. All rates include a full breakfast. Some guests still sail in.

✐ (ᵗᵖ) **Weskeag Inn** (207-596-6676 or 1-800-596-5576), Rt. 73, P.O. Box 213, South Thomaston 04858. Open year-round. Handy to the Owls Head Transportation Museum and to Knox County Regional Airport (pickups provided, perhaps in one of Gray Smith's antique cars). A handsome and hospitable 1830s home overlooking the Weskeag estuary in the tiny village of South Thomaston. There's inviting space to relax throughout the ground floor, out on the deck, and on the lawn (available for weddings) that sweeps to the river's edge. Six attractive guest rooms have private bath; two share or are rented as a suite. Our pick would be the third floor with recently enlarged dormers and water views. $135–150 in-season, $100–112 off-season, with full breakfast, frequently crab quiche.

🦞 ✐ (ᵗᵖ) **Ocean House** (207-372-6691 or 1-800-269-6691; oceanhousehotel .com), P.O. Box 66, Port Clyde 04855. Open May–Oct. This friendly old village inn is the logical place to spend the night before or after taking the neighboring ferry to Monhegan. Built to board local mariners in the 1820s, it's earned a loyal following under long-time ownership by the Murdock family. Second- and third-floor rooms include one apartment. This is a good place for a single traveler, thanks to the single rates and the ease of meeting fellow guests, but families are welcome. Rooms from $110, $125–145 with private bath, less solo, full breakfast included. The adjacent cottage is available weekly. No credit cards.

(ᵗᵖ) **Seaside Inn & Barn Café** (207-372-0700; seasideportclyde.com), 5 Cold Storage Rd., Port Clyde 04855. Open May–Oct. This 1850s captain's house offers nine clean, attractive guest rooms, and living and breakfast rooms with picture windows overlooking the garden and Monhegan Store. Under the same ownership as the neighboring general store, restaurant, and gallery, managed by resident

EAST WIND INN, TENANTS HARBOR

Christina Tree

innkeepers. $139–179 with breakfast, from $89 off-season.

Mill Pond House Bed & Breakfast (207-372-6209; millpondhouse.com), 453 Port Clyde Rd., Tenants Harbor 04860. Leslie Korpinen's rambling 1860s farmhouse is a homey, attractive B&B with three second-floor guest rooms, from $70 single (shared bath) to $105 double (private bath), morning muffins and fruit included.

MOTELS ㅎ ((ꞯ)) **Trade Winds Motor Inn** (207-596-6661 or 1-800-834-3139; tradewindsmaine.com), 2 Park Dr., Rockland 04841. Open year-round. This locally owned 120-unit motel is composed of several wings, obviously added over the decades. Units vary from "non-view" basics (from $64 off-season) to balcony rooms ($134–154) and "deluxe suites" ($214–234 in high season). Amenities include a health club, pool, and restaurant.

ㅎ ((ꞯ)) **Navigator Motor Inn** (207-594-2131 or 1-800-545-8025; navigatorinn .com), 520 Main St., Rockland 04841. Open June–Oct., this is a five-story motor inn with 80 rooms and suites (cable TV, AC, phones), same ownership as Trade Winds. Geared to families bound for the islands, it's across the street from the Maine State Ferry Terminal. You can park your car in line for the early-morning ferry and walk back to your room. There is a restaurant/lounge on the premises. $79–169 with continental breakfast.

COTTAGES AND EFFICIENCIES Rental listings are available from the **Penobscot Bay Regional Chamber of Commerce** (see *Guidance*).

✱ Where to Eat

DINING OUT ✪ **Primo** (207-596-0770; primorestaurant.com), 2 S. Main St. (Rt. 73), Rockland. Open May–Jan.,

daily in summer, otherwise Wed.–Mon. 5:30–9:30 or less; call first. Reservations are a must. This very special restaurant, rated among the best in Maine, grows much of what it serves. "Primo" was chef and co-owner Melissa Kelly's grandfather, a butcher. Kelly raises her own pork and makes several kinds of sausages as well as preparing cuts of meats and overseeing the gardens, greenhouses, and beehives on the 4-acre, intensely cultivated property. Some water-view tables, but most patrons have their eyes on their plates. The menu changes nightly depending on what's available locally. You can dine on wild mushroom pizza—but it's difficult to resist entrées like sautéed pork scaloppine with prosciutto in sage-mushroom Madeira. The house cannoli are crisp, rich, and excellent. Delectable pastas are $26–36, entrées $27–40. The menu, along with a pizza and small plates, is also available upstairs, a lively space with a long copper bar. Inquire about $1-per-oyster nights.

✪ ✿ **Café Miranda** (207-594-2034; cafemiranda.com), 15 Oak St., Rockland. Open year-round 5–9:30. Reserve for dinner. In 1993 Kerry Altiero was the first chef in Rockland to offer the

MELISSA KELLY GROWS HER OWN GREENS AT PRIMO, ROCKLAND'S LEADING RESTAURANT

Christina Tree

Christina Tree

KERRY ALTIERO USES HIS WOOD-FIRED
OVEN IN CREATIVE WAYS AT CAFÉ
MIRANDA

hip kind of dining for which the city
has since become known. His small
restaurant has, however, neither
expanded (unless you count seasonal
café tables) nor moved from its side
street. Single diners sit up at the
counter watching an amazing variety of
food emerge from the brick oven
(fueled by logs from Altiero's farm).
One side of the menu lists more than
40 entrées while the other offers about
the same number of appetizers and
lighter, eclectic fare to mix and match.
On our last visit we began with a
delectable kale dish roasted with
mushrooms, garlic, and feta, followed
by mussels roasted with curry. Full bar
and beer on tap. Entrées
$19.50–28.50.

✪ **Rustica** (207-594-0015), 315 Main
St. Open Mon.–Sat. 11–3 and 5–10,
Sun. 11–8; Tue.–Sat. off-season. No
reservations. High quality at reasonable prices, a pleasant atmosphere, and
decent wine are a winning combination for this "cucina Italiana." Chef-
owner John Stowe serves up a hearty
soups and a wide choice of mouthwatering pastas, like wild mushroom and
three-cheese lasagna (house-made
pasta layered with portobello, crimini,
and shiitake mushrooms, Swiss chard,

and three cheeses, served on a bed of
marinara). Pizza, too. Entrées from
$12 for pizzas; $17–21 for pasta and
entrées such as veal Marsala and pan-
roasted cod.

Lily Bistro (207-594-4141; lilybistro
maine.com), 421 Main St., Rockland.
Reserve. Open daily in-season, 5–9.
Chef-owners Robert Krajewski and
Lynette Mosher are well-known Midcoast chefs whose newest venture was
an instant success. We prefer the
street-level space. The limited, locally
sourced menu might include fennel-
crusted duck with tabouli, sheep's-milk
yogurt, and cucumber salad, or halibut
with lobster potato salad. Entrées
$24–27.

Amalfi on the Water (207-596-0012;
amalfionthewater.com), 12 Water St.,
Rockland. Open daily year-round
(except Mon.) for lunch and dinner. In
2009 chef David Cooke moved from
his longtime downtown site to the harbor's edge, expanding from 34 to 134
seats. It's spacious and sleek with a seasonal deck. The menu is drawn from
all sides of the Mediterranean. Paella
is the specialty, in the traditional mix of
seafood, chorizo, and chicken, but
there are also all-seafood and vegetarian versions. Dinner entrées $16–36.

Suzuki's Sushi Bar (207-596-7447;
suzukisushi.com), 419 Main St. Open
Tue.–Sat. for dinner. Where better to
sample the full variety of the ocean's
yield than a sophisticated Japanese
restaurant? Keiki Suzuki's extensive
menu includes raw nigiri dishes and
spicy sushi rolls, entrées such as
shrimp with shiitake, and many delectable salads and vegetarian dishes.
Entrées $10–30.

In Good Company (207-593-9110;
ingoodcompany.com), 415 Main St.,
Rockland. Open from 4:30 except
Mon. No reservations. A wine bar in a
living-room-like setting, serving salads,

cheeses, nibbles, and light meals such as cedar-planked salmon and cold sliced beef tenderloin. $5–20.

Archer's on the Pier (207-594-2435), 58 Owen St., Rockland. Open Mon.–Sat. 11–10, and for jazz brunch on Sun. Chef-owner Lynn Archer, the dynamo powering the Brass Compass Café, has opened this new restaurant on a prime site overlooking both the harbor and bay (formerly the Boathouse). Plenty of seafood choices. $25 for lazy lobster, $21 for seafood pie, $10 for a creamy crab quesadilla.

Elsewhere

✪ **The Slipway** (207-542-1829; maine -slipway.com), 24 Public Landing, Thomaston. Open May–Oct., lunch and dinner except Tue. Scott Yakovenko enjoyed an enthusiastic following during the years that he owned the Dip Net in Port Clyde before acquiring this larger, waterside venue (formerly the Harborside). We recommend the fried oysters, crisp and still juicy, then sautéed scallops and cod with red pepper sauce, fresh vegetables, and grilled swordfish with pesto, topped off with perfect blueberry pie, made by Scott's mother, a dessert staple. The chef's specialty remains a seafood-studded bouillabaisse. The dining room is good looking but best views are from the porch and seasonal deck. Lunch on a blackened haddock sandwich or lobster BLT. Dinner entrées $18.50–24.

Thomaston Café and Bakery (207-354-8589; thomastoncafe.com), 154 Main St., Thomaston. Open year-round Mon.–Sat. 7:30–2, Sun. brunch 8:30–2. Dinner Fri. and Sat. 5:30–8. Chef-owners Herbert and Eleanor Peters have won many awards and acquired a strong following. Lunch on fresh-made soups, great sandwiches, specials like fish cakes with home fries, salads. The dinner menu might include lobster ravioli with brandied lobster cream sauce. Wine and beer are served. Dinner entrées $17–25.

Craignair Inn & Restaurant (207-594-7644), Clark Island Rd., off Rt. 73, Spruce Head. Open May–Oct. for dinner; Fri., Sat. in spring and fall. Walk the shore before dining by a water-view window. Since 2010, when ownership changed, we're hearing raves about the food. Signature dishes include Craignair crabcakes served with risotto with Dijon rémoulade and fresh vegetables ($18); seared scallops and black Japonica rice ($23); and crispy pan-seared duck breast with cranberry orange reduction. Wines are limited but reasonably priced.

EATING OUT

In Rockland

Atlantic Baking Co. (207-596-0505), 351 Main St. Open Mon.–Sat. 1–6, Sun. 8–4; Tue.–Sat. in winter. Sited across from the Farnsworth Museum, this busy place seduces passersby with the aroma of fresh-baked bread. There's a blackboard sandwich menu and plenty of help-yourself salads and such in deli cases. Yummy soups and breads. The plastic and Styrofoam do seem at odds with the from-scratch, PC ethos of the place.

✪ **The Brass Compass Café** (207-596-5960), 305 Main St. Open Mon.–Sat. 5–3, Sun. 6–3. Lynn Archer's friendly eatery is a find. Seafood stews, sandwiches, and salads, generous portions, good value. Yummy onion rings and fries. The house special is a lobster club, with 1¼ lobsters, bacon, lettuce, and tomato on Lynn's toasted, fresh-made white bread. Beer and wine.

✪ ((ฅ)) **Rock City Café** (207-594-4123), 316 Main St., open 7–7, until 9 Thu.–Sat. Rock City Coffee—chai and teas, too—along with bagels, scones, and pastries baked on premises. The

LOBSTER

Miller's Lobster Company (207-594-7406; millerslobster.com), Wheeler's Bay, off Rt. 73, Spruce Head. Open 11–7, late June–Labor Day. This is our hands-down favorite: on Wheeler's Bay, family-owned and -operated, with a loyal following. Tables are on the wharf; lobsters and clams are cooked in seawater, served with fixings, topped off with fresh-made pies. BYOB.

✎ **Cod End** (207-372-6782) on the wharf, Tenants Harbor. Open July, Aug. daily. Hidden down a lane, a combination fish shop and informal wharfside eatery (tables inside and out) right on Tenants Harbor with a separate cookhouse: chowders and lobster rolls, lobster dinners, steamed clams and mussels. Also burgers and sandwiches. Children's menu. Beer and wine served.

Waterman's Beach Lobsters (207-594-7819; watermansbeachlobster.com), off Rt. 73, South Thomaston. Open mid-June to Sept., Wed.–Sun. 11–7. Oceanfront feasting on the deck: lobster and clam dinners, seafood rolls, homemade ice cream and pies. BYOB.

Ship to Shore Lobster Co. (207-594-4604), 7 Wharf St., Owls Head. Open June–Sept., 10–6. Live or cooked, this place is all about lobster. Picnic tables on the wharf.

Linda Bean's Perfect Maine Lobster Roll (207-563-9388), corner of Park and Main Sts. Open May–Oct. The concept is a standardized "quarter pounder" of lobster on a toasted bun, seasoned with an herbed mixture. It's available in Rockland from a takeout (outdoor seating) at the corner of Park and Main. We sampled it at Bean's **Dip Net Restaurant** in Port Clyde (see *Eating Out*). The lobster was cold and tasteless, served with a paper cup of coleslaw so tiny that we paid $2 for an extra side. It came with a bag of strongly flavored chips, and three thin slices of sweet pickle. The combo was far from perfect.

WATERMAN'S BEACH LOBSTERS, SOUTH THOMASTON

Jim Dugan, courtesy of Maine Windjammer Association

Christina Tree

ATLANTIC BAKING CO. IS A POPULAR CAFÉ

soups and wraps are exceptional, and sandwiches come on Borealis sourdough. We feasted on a summer-veggie grilled panini loaded with roasted eggplant, squash, red onion, and tomatoes. Local beer and wine. In sleek new quarters, still the town meeting/gathering place. Live music, weekends.

Sunfire Mexican Grill (207-594-6196), 488 Main St. Open for lunch Tue.–Sat. 11–3, for dinner Wed. and Sat. 5–8. This is exceptional Mexican fare, all the basics but with very fresh veggies (try the mango avocado salad) and just the right taste. Beer, wine.

𝒮 **Rockland Café** (207-596-7556; rocklandcafe.com), 441 Main St. Open daily 5:30 AM–9 PM. This is a reliable family eatery, good for fish-and-chips, soups, salad, clam rolls, and daily specials. Warning: The crabcakes are more like crab pancakes. Look for the green-and-white-striped awning.

The Brown Bag (207-596-6372), 606 Main St. (north of downtown). Open Mon.–Sat. 6:30 AM–4 PM. This expanded storefront restaurant is a local favorite, with an extensive breakfast and sandwich menu, soups, chowders, and daily specials. Make your selection at the counter and carry it to your table when it's ready.

𝒮 **The Landings Restaurant & Marina** (207-596-6563), 1 Commercial St. Open year-round. On the harbor with outside as well as inside seating; serves 11:30–9 from a menu that ranges from a hot dog to steak, lobster, and a full-scale clambake. Fried clams, fish-and-chips, and a good selection of sandwiches.

𝒮 **Trackside Station** (207-594-7500), 4 Union St. Open daily for lunch and dinner. Ironically this is just off the beaten track unless you are coming on the Maine Eastern, the excursion train from Brunswick. As a result it's either briefly mobbed or relatively empty. The vintage railroad station makes an attractive dining space. It's decorated with blowup photos from Rockland's past. We lunched happily on a fresh crabmeat cheese melt.

𝒮 **Wasses Wagon**, 2 N. Main St. A local institution for hot dogs.

✱ Entertainment

The Strand Theatre (207-594-0070; rocklandstrand.com), 345 Main St., Rockland. Vintage 1923, a beautifully restored classic downtown 350-seat theater offering films, concerts, and live performances including a summer Wednesday-evening series of Bay

ROCK CITY CAFÉ IS ROCKLAND'S GATHERING SPOT

Christina Tree

ELSEWHERE

Port Clyde General Store (207-372-6543), end of Rt. 131. A full-service deli with limited seating and picnic tables on the dock. Hot specials available. Guest moorings and shuttle service, delivery to boats, showers, all part of Linda Bean's Port Clyde Wharf. Next door the **Dip Net Restaurant** (207-372-112), open seasonally noon–9, offers limited indoor seating, more on the wharf (the only area in which wine and beer are served). The menu features locally sourced seafood. The **Barn Café** across the way (open seasonally from 4:30) offers a full bar and some delectable light fare such as crabcakes and "lobster traps" (lobster-stuffed pasta). It's part of the neighboring Seaside Inn, also owned by Linda Bean.

The Harpoon (207-372-6304), corner of Drift Inn and Marshall Point Rds. (just off Rt. 131, around the corner from the harbor), Port Clyde. Open May–mid-Oct. for dinner, Wed.–Sat. in shoulder months. This is the local hangout.

Keag General Store (207-596-6810), Rt. 73, South Thomaston. Open Mon.–Sat. 5 AM–9 PM, Sun. 6–8. A general store with a counter in back, good for breakfast, pizza and sandwiches, shepherd's pie, lobster stew, and one of the best lobster rolls around.

Owls Head General Store
(207-596-6038), 2 South Shore Dr., Owls Head. Open except Feb., 6 AM–7 PM, from 7 on Sun. Handy to transportation and the lighthouse, this great little store prides itself on everything that comes out of its open kitchen. Still, what you have to try are the beef burgers, widely acclaimed as Maine's best.

OWLS HEAD GENERAL STORE BOASTS MAINE'S BEST BURGER

Christina Tree

Chamber Concerts, also streamed performances ranging from the Metropolitan Opera to the Super Bowl.

The Farnsworth Art Museum (207-596-6457; farnsworthmuseum.org) in Rockland stages a year-round series of Sunday films and other weekly cultural events.

✳ Selective Shopping
ART AND CRAFTS GALLERIES

In Rockland
Arts in Rockland (AIR; artsinrockland.com) publishes a widely available downtown map of the two dozen galleries hosting **First Friday** Receptions (5–8) during the seasonal **Art Walks**. Galleries include the oldest (since

1982) and prestigious **Caldbeck Gallery** (caldbeck.com), at 12 Elm St.; goldsmith Thomas O'Donovan's **Harbor Square Gallery** (harborsquare gallery.com), filling three floors of a former bank building (374 Main St.) with art but also featuring fine jewelry. The **Dowling Walsh Gallery** (dowling walsh.com) is another highlight. Others to check: **Art Space Gallery** (207-594-8784; artspacemaine.com), 342 Main St. Also check out **Playing with Fire! Glassworks and Gallery** (playing withfireglassworks.com), 497 Main St.; **Lucky Dog Gallery** (luckydoggallery .com), 373 Main St.

✪ **Eric Hopkins Gallery** (erichopkins .com), 21 Winter St. This spacious but low-key gallery just off Main St. is in a class by itself. It showcases work by one of Maine's most prominent contemporary artists. The son of North Haven fishermen, Eric Hopkins conveys a sense of land, sea, and air around his island home. He is known for bold, distinctive paintings of clouds, deep blue water, spiky green islands, and fish. His work in blown glass is also stunning.

ERIC HOPKINS GALLERY

Eric Hopkins Gallery

ALSO DON'T MISS

In Rockland

Archipelago Fine Arts (thearchipelago .net) at the Island Institute (386 Main St.) represents roughly 300 artists and craftspeople on "hinged" as well as real islands. Changing exhibits. The **Island Institute** (207-594-9209; islandinstitute.org) is a nonprofit organization focusing on the human dimension of Maine's 15 surviving year-round island communities (a century ago there were 300). The idea initially was to get residents of different islands talking to one another. The monthly *Working Waterfront* newspaper, as well as the glossy *Island Journal*, focus on shared concerns ranging from fisheries to schools to mapping.

The Museum Store at the Farnsworth Art Museum (207-596-5789; shop.farnsworthmuseum.org) is itself a standout trove of quality gifts including jewelry, books, and toys as well as art books, cards, and prints.

MORE SELECTIVE SHOPPING

Along Main Street in Rockland
Hello Hello Books (207-593-7780; hellohellobooks.com), No. 316. In the rear of the Rock City Café but with its own side-street entrance. Open daily except Tue. Lacy Simons offers a wide but obviously selective stock of used and new books. The **Black Parrot** (No. 328) specializes in its colorful fleece-lined reversible garments but carries a mix of clothing, toys, cards, and more. **The Grasshopper Shop** (No. 400) is a major link in a small Maine chain featuring clothing but a widely eclectic and colorful inventory. **The Reading Corner** (207-596-6651; No. 408), is a full-service bookstore with an unusual interior. **The Store** (No. 435) features a wide selection of cooking supplies and stocks a wide assortment of other things; **Sea Street**

Graphics (No. 475) specializes in silk-screened designs on T-shirts and clothing (made here, widely distributed) **Fiore Artisan Olive Oils and Vinegars** (207-596-0276; No. 503), is all about extra-virgin unfiltered olive oils and aged balsamic vinegars from the world over; sample them in the tasting room.

South from the junction of Routes 1 and 73, which begins as the southern end of Main Street, Rockland

Rock City Coffee Roasters (207-594-5688; rockcitycoffee.com), 252 Main St. Roasted on the spot, the source of this widely distributed brew.

((ŋ)) **Sweets & Meats Market** (207-594-2070), 218 Main St. Coffee, fresh baked goods, and terrific sandwiches. Daily specials.

✪ **Trillium Soaps** (207-593-9019; trilliumsoaps.com), 216 S. Main St. A find for all of us with dry skin. Using organic olive oil, Peter and Nancy Digirolamo make small batches on the spot in some two dozen varieties, like rosemary-lime, clove, and bay rum. Also moisturizing bath soap including palm and coconut. Reasonably priced.

✪ **Jess's Market** (207-593-5068; jessmarket.com), 118 S. Main St. This is definitely the place in Rockland to buy lobster and a wide variety of very fresh fish, clams, mussels, oysters, and crab. Also the best take-out crab rolls.

Breakwater Vineyards (207-594-1721; breakwatervineyards.com), 35 Ash Point Dr., Owls Head (turn off Rt. 73 onto North Shore Dr.). Open Memorial Day–Columbus Day weekends, Wed.–Sun. noon–5. This 32-acre estate, with expansive views of across the harbor and bay to the Camden Hills, has been planted in some 3,000 vines of hardy vinifera grapes. Bill and Jean Johnson presently offer oaked and unoaked Chardonnays, a dry Riesling,

a Pinot Noir, and a blueberry wine. We can attest to the Pinot. Tastings are offered in the retail shop.

Also see **Owls Head General Store** and **Keag General Store** under *Eating Out*.

Art of the Sea Galleries (207-594-9396; artofthesea.com), 5 Spruce Head Rd. (Rt. 73), displays nearly 100 museum-quality, full-rigged ships' models; also half models and hundreds of nautical paintings and prints.

Along Route 131 to Port Clyde

Check out **St. George Pottery** (4.5 miles south of Rt. 1), George Pearlman's combination studio and contemporary ceramics gallery. **Noble Clay** (529 Port Clyde Rd.) in Tenants Harbor, open year-round, displays Trish and Steve Barnes's white-and-blue-glazed porcelain pottery with whimsical and botanical designs. **Mars Hall Gallery** (marshallgallery.net), 621 Port Clyde Rd., Tenants Harbor, is well worth a stop. **Ocean House Gallery** (207-372-6930; oceanhousegallery.com), end of Port Clyde Rd., is a seasonal gallery in the inn. **The Store Upstairs** over the Port Clyde General Store is worth a look: kitchenware and gadgets, oilcloth, children's books and toys, gifts. **The Sea Star Shop** in the Monhegan Boat Line ticket office next door is also worth checking for its selection of gifts and books.

In Thomaston

Maine State Prison Showroom (207-354-9237), Main St. (Rt. 1), Thomaston, at the south end of town. Open daily 9–5. A variety of wooden furniture—coffee tables, stools, lamps, and trays—and small souvenirs, all carved by inmates. The prison has moved to Warren but, happily, the shop is still here. Prices are reasonable, and profits go to the craftsmen.

✐ **The Personal Book Shop** (207-354-8058), 144 Main St., Thomaston.

Open year-round 10–5. Marti Reed's shop is more like a book-lined living room than your ordinary bookstore: plenty of places to sit and read but also a large selection of titles; many Maine authors, and a well-stocked children's room. Also check out the adjoining Frost-Gully Gallery, featuring Maine artists.

Oyster River Winegrowers (207-354-7177; oysterriverwinegrowers.com). The Tasting Room, 12 Oyster River Rd. (Rt. 131 north), Thomaston, is open May–Halloween, usually noon–6. Brian Smith is an experienced vintner who is just beginning to harvest his own vines. In the meantime he's souring Merlot grapes from the Finger Lakes and Petite Syrah from California.

In Union

Savage Oaks Vineyard & Winery (207-785-2828; savageoaks.com), 174 Barett Hill Rd. (north of the junction of Rts. 17 and 131). Tasting room open Mother's Day–Oct., then weekends until Christmas, 11–5. Elmer (Buddy) and Holly Savage have been growing grapes on their 95-acre farm for a decade. A variety of red and white wines are available for sampling, along with three blueberry wines made from their 15 acres of wild blueberries.

Sweetgrass Farm Winery & Distillery (207-785-3024; sweetgrasswinery .com), 347 Carroll Rd., marked from Rt. 17 west of Union village. Tasting room open daily 11–5. Keith and Constance Bodine produce fruit wines and spirits using Maine-grown apples, cranberries, blueberries, and peaches. Best sellers: Back River gin, Cranberry Smash, and apple wine. The property also includes the **Carroll Farm Trail**, part of the Medomak Valley Land Trust; visitors are welcome to hike, snowhoe, and ski.

✳ Special Events

June: **Summer Solstice Night**, a Main Street Rockland street fair.

July: **Thomaston Fourth of July** festivities include a big parade, footraces, live entertainment, a crafts fair, barbecue, and fireworks. The **North Atlantic Blues Festival** (mid-July), Harbor Park, Rockland (northatlantic bluesfestival.com) is huge. **Maine Windjammer Parade of Sail** (mid-month), Rockland Harbor. **Friendship Sloop Days** (last weekend) includes a regatta and festivities in Rockland and a parade, BBQ, and children's activities in Friendship.

August: **Maine Lobster Festival** (first weekend, plus the preceding Wed. and Thu.), Harbor Park, Rockland (maine lobsterfestival.com). This is probably the world's biggest lobster feed, prepared in the world's largest lobster boiler. Patrons queue up on the public landing to heap their plates with lobsters, clams, corn, and all the fixings. King Neptune and the Maine Sea Goddess reign over the event, which includes a parade down Main Street, concerts, an art exhibit, contests such as clam shucking and sardine packing, and a race across a string of lobster crates floating in the harbor. **Maine Boats, Homes & Harbor Show** (midmonth), Harbor Park, Rockland. **Union Fair and State of Maine Wild Blueberry Festival** (third week) (unionfair.org)—a real agricultural fair with tractor- and ox-pulling contests, livestock and food shows, a midway, the crowning of the Blueberry Queen, and, on one day during the week, free mini blueberry pies for all comers.

November–December: **Rockland Festival of Lights** begins on Thanksgiving—parade, Santa's Village, sleigh rides.

MIDCOAST ISLANDS

MONHEGAN; THE FOX ISLANDS: VINALHAVEN AND NORTH HAVEN; MATINICUS

MONHEGAN

This island is endless and wonderful in its variety. It's possessed of enough beauty to supply a continent.

—Artist George Bellows, on first seeing Monhegan

Eleven miles at sea and barely a mile square, Monhegan is a microcosm of Maine landscapes, from 160-foot sheer headlands to pine woods, from wildflower-filled inland meadows to the smooth, low rocks along Lobster Cove. "Beached like a whale" is the way one mariner in 1590 described the island's shape: headlands sloping down to the small off-island of Manana, a blip on Monhegan's silhouette.

Monhegan is known for the quality and quantity of its artists and the grit of its lobstermen, who fish October through June. The island's first recorded artist arrived in 1858, and by the 1870s a hotel and several boardinghouses were filled with summer guests, many of them artists. In 1903 Robert Henri, a founder of New York's Ashcan School and a well-known art teacher, discovered Monhegan and soon introduced it to his students, among them George Bellows and Rockwell Kent. The island remains a genuine art colony. Jamie Wyeth owns a house built by Rockwell Kent, and Rockwell Kent has passed his studio on to James Fitzgerald. More than 20 artists regularly open their studios to visitors.

The island continues to draw artists in good part because its beauty not only survives but also remains accessible. Prospect Hill, the only attempted development, foundered around 1900. It was Theodore Edison, son of the inventor, who amassed property

THE ROPE SHED, MONHEGAN ISLAND'S BULLETIN BOARD

Christina Tree

317

Christina Tree

COMING ASHORE ON MONHEGAN ISLAND

enough to erase its traces and keep the island's cottages (which still number just 130 or so) bunched along the sheltered harbor, the rest preserved as common space and laced with 17 miles of footpaths.

In 1954 Edison helped organize Monhegan Associates, a nonprofit corporation dedicated to preserving the "natural, wild beauty" of the island. Ironically, this was one of the country's few communities to shun electricity until relatively recently. A number of homes and one inn still use kerosene lamps. Vehicles are limited to a few trucks for those with businesses and golf carts for those with medical needs.

Petroglyphs on Manana Island (just offshore) are said to have been carved by Norsemen, but a plaque beside the schoolhouse states that the island was discovered by Captain John Smith in 1614. Native American artifacts on display in the Monhegan Museum may date back 8,000 years. The island's present settlement has been continuous since 1790; it's been a "plantation" since 1839. The year-round population of less than 50 swells in summer to a little more than 600, not counting roughly 100 seasonal employees, 300 overnight guests, and up to 300 day-trippers. Visitors come to walk, to paint, to bird, and to reflect. A number of them come alone.

PLEIN-AIR PAINTING

Christina Tree

Monhegan has three inns, a B&B, several nightly rentals, and a limited number of weekly rental cottages. Fog and a frequently rough passage insulate it to some degree, but on summer days a high tide of day-trippers from Boothbay Harbor and New Harbor, as well as Port Clyde, washes over this small, fragile island. More worrisome still are skyrocketing real estate prices. Monhegan Island Sustainable Community

SWIMMERS IN GULL COVE

Christina Tree

Association (MISCA) is now dedicated to ensuring affordable housing for year-round residents.

GUIDANCE *A Visitor's Guide to Monhegan Island, Maine*, a free 10-page leaflet, comes with every boat ticket to the island in the hope that visitors will read about the dangers and rules as well as the obvious beauty of the cliff-side trails on the island's backside. The Monhegan Associates Trail Map, also available on the boats, is well worth a $1 (see *Hiking*), and the free Studio Locations sheet (see the chapter intro) is also handy if you want to meet resident artists. Also check out monhegan.com, the site for Monhegan Commons, not your usual chamber of commerce (there isn't one).

GETTING THERE Monhegan Boat Line (207-372-8848; monheganboat.com) operates both the sleek *Elizabeth Ann* and the beloved old *Laura B* from Port Clyde; reservations a must. Service is three times daily in-season, less frequent in spring and fall, and only Mon., Wed., and Fri. in winter. It's a 50- or 70-minute trip, depending on which boat you catch. Mid-May–Columbus Day weekend **Hardy Boat Cruises** (1-800-278-3346; hardyboat.com) offers a 50-minute run from New Harbor with two daily roundtrips early June–September. **The Ocean House** in Port Clyde and the **Gosnold Arms** in New Harbor are within walking distance of these two services, taking the sting out of making morning boats. The *Balmy Days II* (1-800-298-2284; balmydaycruises.com) also offers seasonal roundtrips from Boothbay.

EQUIPMENT AND RULES Come properly shod for the precipitous paths. Hikers should wear long pants and socks against poison ivy; bring sweaters and windbreakers. Wading or swimming anywhere but Swim Beach (on the harbor) can be lethal. During our last visit in 2011 a young man was washed away by a rogue wave. Kayaking is also dangerous. Flashlights, hiking boots, and rain gear are also good ideas. Public phones are few; cell phone reception has improved, thanks to an intrusive tower that now dwarfs the lighthouse, but is still undependable. Smoking is prohibited beyond

CLIFF COMBER

Christina Tree

Christina Tree

THE VIEW FROM THE LIGHTHOUSE

the village. So is camping. Do not bring bicycles. Dogs must be leashed at all times. And *please* don't pick the flowers.

PUBLIC RESTROOMS The two public pay toilets are on a lane behind the Monhegan House.

GETTING AROUND Several trucks meet each boat as it arrives and provide baggage service. Otherwise visitors have no access to motorized transport.

WHEN TO COME The spring migration season brings birds and birders. June can be rainy and foggy—but also glorious and always flowery, with wild strawberries to be found along hiking paths. July and August are prime time, but September is best for hiking; birds and birders return.

✳ To See

Monhegan Island Light, built of granite in 1850 and automated in 1959, caps a hill that's well worth climbing for the view alone. The **Monhegan Historical & Cultural Museum** (207-596-7003; monheganmuseum.org) is a real gem. In July and Aug. it's open daily 11:30–3:30; in late June and all Sept. it's 1:30–3:30. $4 suggested donation. A spellbinding display of island art, including prints by George Bellows and Rockwell Kent, and annual special exhibits in the neighboring gallery.Flora, fauna, some geology, lobstering, and island history are interpreted through artifacts, including documents dating back to the 16th century. The neighboring **Art Gallery** houses annually changing exhibits.

THE FITZGERALD STUDIO IS OPEN TO VISITORS

Christina Tree

The **Kent-Fitzgerald-Hubert House**. Horn Hill. Open seasonally, Tue. and Sat. 1–3. Built by Rockwell Kent, it later served as a home and studio for James Fitzgerald (1899–1971), one of the most distinctive and prominent artists for whom Monhegan has been a home and inspiration.

✴ To Do

BIRDING Positioned in the middle of the Atlantic flyway, Monhegan is one of the best birding places on the East Coast. Your local Audubon Society may have a trip going in May or mid- through late September.

HIKING Pick up a current Monhegan Associates Trail Map before setting out on the island's 17-mile network. Day-trippers are advised to take the **Burnt Head Trail** (No. 4) and loop back to the village via the **Whitehead Trail** (No. 7), descending by the lighthouse, or vice versa. This way you get a sense of the high bluffs and the unusual rocks in Gull Cove. Beyond this well-trod loop, trails are marked with few guideposts. It's easy to get turned around in **Cathedral Woods** (justly famed and known for its "fairy houses"), which, along with **Pulpit Rock**, should be reserved for an unhurried day. The path along the southern outer tip of the island, from Burnt Head to Christmas Cove, is ledgy and unsuitable for children and shaky hikers. The relatively flat trail from the village to **Lobster Cove** at the southern tip of the island is a favorite and has recently been improved. It can, however, be the muddiest and slipperiest of all after rains. Be sure to bring a flashlight if you are setting out toward evening, just in case you get lost—the fate of our brother-in-law, who wandered around all through the night.

HIKING THE BACK SIDE OF MONHEGAN

Christina Tree

✴ Lodging

All listings are on Monhegan Island 04852

Note: Lodging is limited but remarkably varied.

INNS Island Inn (207-596-0371; islandinnmonhegan.com). Open Memorial Day–Columbus Day weekend. This shingled, cupola-topped, gabled, classic 1907 summer hotel with a long, rocker-lined veranda is steps from the ferry dock and overlooks the boat-filled harbor and Manana Island. In recent years it has been steadily renovated, and public rooms are a winning mix of old-fashioned and chic, with a comfortable living room and book-stocked side porches. The nicely decorated dining room has the harbor view (see *Dining Out*). The 28 rooms and four suites are divided between the main inn and Pierce Cottage behind it. Opt for a room with a view in the inn itself. Eight rooms still share baths. In high season (late July–Labor Day), from $165 per couple (shared bath, meadow view) to $350–395 for suites. Otherwise $130–285, depending on room and week. $5 gratuity added per day and $10 charge for one-night stays. Children under 5 are free if no extra bedding is required. All rates include a full breakfast, served buffet-style, usually featuring lobster casserole.

✐ **Monhegan House** (207-594-7983; monheganhouse.com), P.O. Box 345. Open Memorial Day–early Oct. Holden and Susan Nelson have revived Monhegan's oldest continuously operating summer hotel, upgrading both infrastructure and decor. Two suites with bath and a deck have been added, and more are planned. Built in 1870s in the middle of the village, it offers 28 rooms on four floors. No closets, and most baths and showers (plentiful and immaculate) are in a wing off the middle of the second floor. For couples and families we recommend the third floor; for singles the bargain-priced fourth-floor rooms have the best views (coveted by artists). The downstairs lobby is tastefully decorated, hung with art, warmed by a gas fireplace, and equipped with books and games. On sunny days guests opt for the porch, watching the comings and goings of everyone on the island. Children are welcome and free under age 3. A full breakfast is included in the rates ($87–171 in high season, $190–221 for suites; $77–171 in low). Head in for breakfast before 8 AM, because it's open to the public and very popular. Dinner is also excellent (see *Dining Out*).

🐾 ☀ ✐ **The Trailing Yew** (207-596-6194; trailingyew.com). Open mid-May–mid-Oct. This quirky institution has a loyal following among artists and writers. New England's last genuine 19th-century-style "summer boardinghouse," it's the place for the many solo travelers drawn to Monhegan. The 33 rooms are divided among the main house and adjacent annexes and cottages on the grounds and The Mooring Chain (good only for groups) up the road. Each building has its own sitting room. Guest rooms are comfortable, lit with kerosene lamps. With the exception of The Cabin, baths are shared but clean, numerous enough to go around, and they have electricity—which, with the advent of cell phones and laptops, does mean competition for the outlets. In shoulder seasons it's advisable to bring a sleeping bag. Dining is at 5:45 at shared tables, and the conversation is usually lively (BYOB). Dinner is open to the public: $32 for four courses, tax and gratuity included. Two rooms in Lower Seagull are geared to families. $120 per person solo, $210 double includes breakfast and dinner; sliding scale ages 2–12. $10 pet fee. No credit cards.

BED & BREAKFAST ✪ ✔ Shining Sails (207-596-0041; shiningsails.com), P.O. Box 346. Open year-round. Lobsterman John Murdock and his wife, Winnie, offer two rooms and five exceptional apartments in their welcoming village home overlooking the water. All five water-view units have a deck, the better to savor the sunset and stars. All rooms are tastefully decorated, featuring original island art. On foggy days a woodstove warms the living room, where an ample continental breakfast is served daily, May–Columbus Day. The Murdocks are helpful hosts and this place is so justly popular, it's advisable to book far in advance for July and August, but there are always some openings. $145–220 per night, $110–165 off-season. Also see *Rentals*.

GUESTHOUSES AND DAILY RENTALS

Hitchcock House (207-594-8137; hitchcockhouse.com), Horn's Hill. Open year-round. Hidden away on Horn's Hill with a delightful garden and a large, sheltered deck, which serves as common space for guests. In the house itself Barbara Hitchcock offers two appealing housekeeping units, both with decks with views down across the meadow to the village and water. There are also two upstairs guest rooms, each with a small fridge and a hot pot, sharing one bath; a "cabin" in the garden has a full kitchen, living room, and bath. July–Labor Day weekend efficiencies are $120–130 per night, $760–840 per week; rooms are $85 per night, $520 per week, less off-season.

Tribler Cottage (207-594-2445; triblercottage.com). Open mid-May–mid-Oct. On the edge of the Meadow, at the base of Lighthouse Hill, this remains in the same family that has been welcoming visitors since the 1920s. Richard Farrell offers four housekeeping apartments and one housekeeping room. All have private bath; one apartment (Hillside) has a sundeck and living room with fireplace, while another (accommodating three) has a gas heater and is available off-season. $85–140 per couple per night based on two-night stay; $560–945 weekly, less off-season.

Fish & Maine (207-596-0041; shiningsails.com). Four attractive apartments in the middle of the village, just off Fish Beach, two with harbor views and decks. From $165 per night ($1,055 per week) for a one-bedroom with a full kitchen and gas fireplace to $235 ($1,510 per week) for a two-bedroom with deck and harbor view. Less off-season.

WEEKLY RENTALS

Cooking facilities come in handy here: You can buy lobster, good fresh and smoked fish, and a limited line of vegetables (bring meat and staples). **Shining Sails Cottage Rental** (207-596-0041; shiningsails.com) manages more than 30 rental cottages, available by the week. Demand is high, and it's wise to get in your bid in early January for the summer. $840–2,900 per week, less off-season.

FISH BEACH

Nancy English

✳ Where to Eat

Note: Restaurants are BYOB, but wine is readily available in island stores.

DINING OUT The Island Inn (207-596-0371). Open to the public Memorial Day–Columbus Day for breakfast and dinner, also for lunch July 4–Labor Day. This classic, turn-of-the-20th-century dining room has contemporary decor and water views. The breakfast frequently features lobster casserole. Reserve for dinner and request a table overlooking the water. Appetizers usually include lobster stew. We can vouch for pan-seared scallops on a bed of mixed greens and tangy Maine crab-cakes with the house herb and chive aioli. Both came with Israeli couscous and crisp green beans. Entrées $19–36.

Monhegan House Open nightly late June–Labor Day, then weekends. The attractive, many-windowed dining room at the back of the inn overlooks the village and meadow. Breakfasts feature house-made breads and

omelets. The dinner menu changes nightly and always includes a vegetarian option. You might dine on a house-made onion and lavender sausage, haddock en papillote, honey brined chicken, or cumin-scented scallops. Dessert might be lemon mousse with blueberry sauce and Chantilly cream. Entrées $22–27.

EATING OUT ✪ The **Fish House Market**, Fish Beach. Open daily. The seasonal source of the freshest of seafood for anyone with cooking facilities. Better yet, anyone can enjoy Damariscotta oysters, steamed clams, the island's best crab and lobster rolls, and daily specials to eat at picnic tables on Fish Beach with the island's best view of the sun setting behind Manana Island (BYOB).

The Barnacle. Sited beside the ferry wharf and owned by the Island Inn, the Barnacle offers limited seating on the deck and inside. Sandwiches, soups, and pastries; also espresso and prepared sandwiches. Wine and beer sold.

The Novelty, behind Monhegan House. Pizza, soups and sandwiches, quiche, salads and hot wraps. Freshly made cookies are great hiking fuel as you set off up Horn's Hill. Hand-dipped ice cream and frozen yogurt hit the spot on the way down. Wine, beer, splits of champagne. Outside seating.

Black Duck Emporium. Open Memorial Day–Columbus Day in the former general store. Sited at the center of the village, next to the post office, this is the current island gathering place, good for snacks and pastry as well as coffee, tea, etc.

✳ Selective Shopping

ART GALLERIES The Lupine Gallery (207-594-8131; lupinegallery.com), 48 Main St. Open early May–

THE VILLAGE

Liam Davis

Columbus Day, 11–4:30. Bill Boynton and Jackie Bogel offer original works by 100 artists who paint regularly on the island. This is a very special gallery, showcasing the work of many professional artists within walking distance. Sited just uphill from the ferry dock, it's a good place to judge which studios you want to visit. Great cards, prints, and art books, also artists' supplies and framing.

Open studios. More than 20 resident artists welcome visitors to their studios; pick up a map/guide and schedule, check "The Rope Shed," or look for shingles hung outside listing the hours they're open. Don Stone is the current dean of Monhegan painters, and his studio on the way to Burnt Head is open by chance or appointment.

SPECIAL SHOPS Black Duck Emporium. Open Memorial Day–Columbus Day. This longtime island gift store has expanded to fill the former general store, offering cappuccino and pastries as well as a selection of imaginative T-shirts, books, kitchenware, pottery, jewelry, and more.

Carina. Groceries, a few booths over coffee, tea, and fresh-baked goods. It's also a prime source of wines, produce, and daily newspapers.

Winterworks. Open more or less daily Memorial Day–Labor Day, by the ferry dock. A former fish house is now the island co-op, filled with work produced by the island's craftspeople: a surprising variety and quality of knitted goods, jewelry, cards, Christmas decorations, and more.

THE FOX ISLANDS: VINALHAVEN AND NORTH HAVEN

The Fox Islands Thorofare is a rowable stretch of yacht-filled water that separates Vinalhaven and North Haven, two islands roughly a dozen miles off Rockland that differ deeply, even geologically. It's said that they were once oceans apart. While you can get from one island to the other, no ferry stops at both.

Vinalhaven is heavily wooded and marked by granite quarries that include two public swimming holes. Life eddies around the village of Carver's Harbor, home to Maine's largest lobster fleet. In 1880, when granite was being cut on Vinalhaven to build New York's Customs House, 2,855 people were living here on the island, a number now reduced to less than 1,300—a mix of descendants of 18th-century settlers and the stonecutters who came here from Sweden, Norway, Finland, and Scotland. In recent years the island has also attracted a number of artists, including Robert Indiana. Summer visitors now equal year-round residents, but there is no yacht club or golf course. This is Maine's largest offshore island and its largest year round island community. It's not a resort island, and yachtsmen will be hard-put to find a guest mooring among the lobster boats in Carver's Harbor.

North Haven is half as big, with just 350 year-round residents, some 1,500 in summer. Founded well over a century ago by Boston yachtsmen, its summer colony now includes some of the country's wealthiest and most influential families. Over the years some members of these families have married islanders, while others have settled or retired here. The result is a creative mix. Its K–12 school, the smallest in New England, has produced a play (*Islands*) that has been performed on Broadway. The former general store by the ferry dock is now Waterman's Community Center, with a 140-seat state-of-the-art theater, the venue for summer lectures, concerts, and plays.

Christina Tree

NORTH HAVEN VILLAGE

The village of North Haven offers several gift shops and galleries, two seasonal restaurants, and recently restored Nebo Lodge, with gracious year-round lodging and dining (see *Lodging* and *Dining Out*). Beyond the village a 10-mile loop beckons bicyclists through rolling, open fields, spotted with buttercups and idyllic farmhouses, most of them summer homes. Unusually sheltered Pulpit Harbor is a favorite mooring for windjammers and yachtsmen. There's also a public golf club and a private yacht club, the North Haven Casino, home to the island's distinctive dinghies.

It was British explorer Martin Pring who named the Fox Islands in 1603, ostensibly for the silver foxes he saw there. A dozen miles out in Penobscot Bay, these islands are understandably protective of their considerable beauty, especially in view of their unusual—by Maine island standards—accessibility by Maine State Ferry. Be it said that there is a terrific, seasonal inn on North Haven, and a limited but real choice of lodging on Vinalhaven. The current news here is the installation of three 1.5-megawatt wind turbines on the north side of Vinalhaven, capable of generating all the electricity needed for both islands. Reviews are mixed. Islanders who live within earshot are understandably upset and some have sued, reducing the promised savings from wind power.

For anyone who loves islands, especially less crowded islands with ample places to walk, Vinalhaven is a find. And contrary to rumor, it's possible to cross the Thorofare (see *Getting Around*) to spend the day on North Haven, though you may have to wait a little while for transport. Islands dictate their own terms.

Vinalhaven makes sense as a day-trip destination only if it's a nice day and if you take the early boat. Pick up a map and don't be discouraged by the walk into Carver's Harbor, along the island's least attractive half mile. Don't miss the Historical Society Museum, and walk or bike out to Lane's Island. It's better as a destination for a couple of days or more, and it's a great place to be on the Fourth of July.

GUIDANCE Town offices on North Haven (207-867-4433) and Vinalhaven (207-863-4471) field most questions. The Vinalhaven Chamber site is vinalhaven.org. On-island, pick up a free copy of *The Wind*, the island's newsletter.

GETTING THERE The **Maine State Ferry Service** (in Rockland: 207-596-2202). The islands are serviced by different ferries, and neither ferry stops at both.

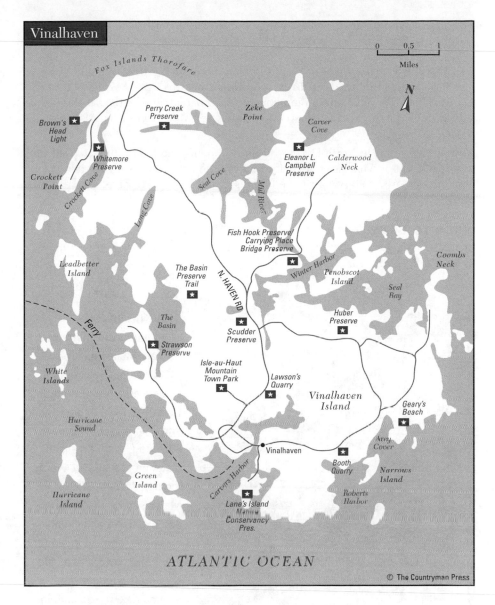

Vinalhaven

From Rockland it's a 75-minute ride, and service is frequent. Day-trippers never have a problem walking on; the bike fee is nominal. Each ferry takes a set number of cars, and only a handful of these spaces can be reserved; otherwise, cars are taken in order of their position in line. For the morning boats, it's wise to be in line the night before. During the summer season, getting off the island can be nerve racking. It doesn't make sense to bring a car unless you plan to stay awhile.

Note: **Concord Coach Lines** (concordcoachlines.com) stops daily at the Rockland Ferry Terminal.

Penobscot Island Air (207-596-7500; penobscotislandair.net) will fly you in from Portland or Boston as well as Rockland to either Vinalhaven or North Haven.

GETTING AROUND *By boat:* Shuttle service between North Haven and Vinal-haven is possible through **J. O. Brown & Sons Boatyard** (207-867-4621) in North Haven. Try calling from the phone on the boat landing on the Vinalhaven side of the Thorofare. On Vinalhaven the Tidewater Motel rents cars. Also see *Bicycling*.

Note: Day-trippers to North Haven will find shopping and food within steps of the ferry dock, but on Vinalhaven it's 0.4 mile from the ferry to Carver's Harbor. It's another mile or so to the quarries and Lanes Island Nature Preserve. A bike comes in handy.

WHEN TO COME Only in July and August can you count on all visitor-geared facilities being open on both these islands. June and September, however, can be as beautiful.

Christina Tree

THE FORMER STAR OF HOPE LODGE IN CARVER'S HARBOR, VINALHAVEN, IS HOME AND STUDIO FOR ARTIST ROBERT INDIANA

ON VINALHAVEN
The Vinalhaven Historical Society Museum (207-863-4410; vinalhavenhistorical society.org), top of High St. Open Tue.–Sat. noon–5, mid-June–mid-Sept.; daily in July, Aug. Within walking distance of the ferry, worth the uphill climb. One of Maine's most welcoming and extensive community museums, housed in the former church, which has also served as a theater and skating rink. It was built in 1838 in Rockland as a Universalist church, and floated over on a barge in 1878. Displays feature the island's granite industry, with photos of St. John the Divine's massive columns, for instance, quarried here.

The first order for Vinalhaven granite, you learn, was shipped to Boston in 1826 to build a jail, but production really skyrocketed after the Civil War, when

✳ To See

On North Haven

North Haven Village. The village itself is charming, with several shops, galleries, and a choice of places to eat. **Pulpit Harbor**, the island's second, much smaller community, several miles away, is the site of the general store and the **North Haven Historical Society's North Island Museum** (open Sun. in July and Aug., 2–4:30). A general store, period kitchen and living room, special exhibits.

✳ To Do

BICYCLING If you take care to keep to the roadside, both North Haven and Vinalhaven are suited to bicycling. Bike rentals are available at **Bikesenjava** (see *Bicycling* in "Rockland") near the ferry terminal. A more limited selection is available at **Tidewater Motel** on Vinalhaven and **Nebo Lodge** on North Haven.

On North Haven we recommend the North Shore Rd. On Vinalhaven we recommend the Granite Island Rd. out along the Basin or following Main St. the other

granite was the preferred building material for the country's building boom. On an island map, 40 red pins mark the sites of major quarries, but there are also countless "motions," or backyard pits.

Museum displays also depict island life and other industries, like fishing (the Lane-Libby Fisheries Co. was once one of Maine's largest fish-processing companies) and lobstering (in the 1880s the Basin, a large salt-water inlet, was used as a giant holding tank, penning as many as 150,000 lobsters until prices peaked). Knitting horse nets (to keep off flies) in intricate designs was yet another island industry.

Check out the nearby Carver Cemetery. A Galamander, a huge wagon such as those used to carry stone from island quarries to schooners, stands in the small park at the top of the hill on the other side of town (junction of Main, Chestnut, Carver, and School Sts. and Atlantic Ave.).

The Victorian-style town of Carver's Harbor is picturesque and interesting, its downtown a single street straddling a causeway and narrow land strip between the harbor and Carver's Pond, its estuary. A boomtown dating from the 1880s when Vinalhaven was synonymous with granite, the village is built almost entirely of wood, the reason why many of the best of its golden-era buildings are missing. The strikingly Victorian Star of Hope Lodge, owned by artist Robert Indiana, is one of two surviving Second Empire mansard buildings (there were once four) marking the center of town.

Brown's Head Lighthouse, now automated, commands the entrance to the Thorofare from the northern end of Vinalhaven, more than 8 miles from Carver's Harbor.

direction out to Geary's Beach (see *Green Space*). The North Haven Rd. is an 8-mile slog up the middle of Vinalhaven, but the rewards are great: Browns Head Light, the Perry Creek Preserve, and views of North Haven.

GOLF **North Haven Golf Club** (207-867-2054), open June–Sept. A waterside course, nine holes.

SEA KAYAKING **Tidewater Motel** in Carver's Harbor, Vinalhaven, rents kayaks.

Christina Tree

BOOTH QUARRY, VINALHAVEN

SWIMMING On Vinalhaven, **Lawson's Quarry**. From the middle of Carver's Harbor, turn (uphill) at the Bank Building and continue up and up High St., past the historical society, and then turn right on the North Haven Rd. for 0.5 mile. For **Booth Quarry** continue east (uphill) on Main St. 1.5 miles past the Union Church. This is a town park and swimming hole.

✱ Green Space

On Vinalhaven

Lane's Island Preserve, on the southern side of Carver's Harbor (cross the Indian Creek Bridge and look for the sign on your left). Little more than a 15-minute walk from town, this is 40 acres of fields, marsh, moor, and beach. It's a great spot to picnic or to come in the evening. Stroll out along the beach and up into the meadows facing open ocean and filled with wild roses and beach peas.

Armbrust Hill is on the way to Lane's Island, hidden behind the medical center. The first place from which the island's granite was commercially quarried, it remained one of the most active sites on the island for many decades. Notice the many small pits ("motions") as well as four major quarries. The main path winds up the hill for a splendid view.

Grimes Park, just west of the ferry terminal, is a 2-acre point of rocky land with two small beaches. Note the rough granite watering trough once used by horses and oxen.

VIEW FROM TIDEWATER MOTEL, CARVER'S HARBOR

Christina Tree

Geary's Beach. Turn right off Main St. a bit farther than the Booth Quarry, just after the Coke Statue of Liberty (you'll see), and bear left for this stony town-owned beach, its trails, and picnic table. The view is off to Isle au Haut, Brimstone, and Matinicus.

The Vinalhaven Land Trust (207-863-2543; vinalislandtrust.org) maintains several of the preserves mapped on island handouts. This list is just a sampling.

✳ Lodging

On Vinalhaven 04863

✪ 🐾 🐕 ⟨⟨ᵞ⟩⟩ **Tidewater Motel and Gathering Place** (207-863-4618; tidewatermotel.com), P.O. Box 546, 15 Main St., Carver's Harbor. Open except Jan.–Feb. "I don't want to leave this room," we wrote about Room 16, an aerie with a skylight (with shade) above the bed, a window above the raceway, and a deck overlooking a harbor full of lobster boats, all turned into the wind like gulls. Creature comforts include a microwave, coffeemaker, small fridge, full bath, and small TV. Phil and Elaine Crossman's waterside motel (inherited from Phil's parents) has evolved into a remarkable place to stay in the heart of both the harbor and the village. It spans a tidal stream connecting the harbor with Carver's Pond. The water swooshing under your room once powered a blacksmith shop. The 19 units are divided between the original motel rooms (many with decks on the water) and adjacent buildings—also over the water—with varied suites and efficiencies. One has a full kitchen and living/dining room, "the Gathering Place," fit for reunions or a small conference. The Crossmans also loan guests bikes and kayaks, meet the ferry, and help them around the island. All the town's eating options are within steps. Elaine Crossman is a noted artist, and Phil is the island chronicler. His genuinely funny book of essays, *Away Happens*, captures island life. $165–195 for rooms, $295 for the Harbormaster's Berth, from $100 off-season. $8 for each additional person over two—but kids 10 and under are free, and families with more than one older kid are only charged for one. Rates include morning coffee, juice, and muffins. Inquire about Millstream Cottage.

Libby House (207-863-4696; libby house1869.com), Water St. Open April–Nov. This proud home was built in 1869 by T. E. Libby, namesake of an island ferry (he was responsible for brining the Maine State Ferry service to Vinalhaven). It's on the edge of the village, on the way to Lane's Island Preserve. Guests share the long sunporch with its rocking chairs and upright piano, as well as an old-fashioned living room with a fireplace and access to the dining room and kitchen fridge (no meals are served). There are four guest rooms, one downstairs and three on the second floor, all furnished in genuinely interesting but comfortable antiques, all with private bath. There's also a downstairs two-bedroom apartment with a full kitchen and deck. Longtime host Philip Roberts asks guests to remove their shoes on entering. $100–120 for rooms, $150 for the apartment. Pets accepted Sept.–June.

On North Haven 04853

✪ 🐾 🐕 **Nebo Lodge** (207-867-2007; nebolodge.com), 11 Mullins Lane, P.O.

NEBO LODGE, NORTH HAVEN

AmazingMaine.com

Box 358. Open May–Dec.; winter rooms by chance (no breakfast). Built handsomely in 1912 as an inn but privatized in 1956, reopened in 2006 by a dedicated local group of women to serve both as a place for residents to dine together and as an island entrée for visitors. There are eight crisp guest rooms, four with shared bath, many with tufted wool rugs, throw pillows, and linens by nationally known designer and island native Angela Adams. Two third-floor rooms are the brightest and most attractive, both with private bath. The sitting room is delightful, with a rosy Angela Adams rug. There's a strong commitment here to all things green and local. The dining room with its working fireplace is justly busy (see *Dining Out*). Your cell phone may not work, but there is wireless Internet. Bikes are available, and the innkeeper can arrange a boat trip. $125–250 includes a delicious breakfast, as organic as possible. Pets are accepted on a case-by-case basis; $25 cleaning fee.

COTTAGE RENTALS Davidson Realty (207-863-2200; maineisland living.com) specialize in summer rentals. The **Island Group** (207-863-2554) offers both sales and rentals for both islands.

✳ Where to Eat

On Vinalhaven

The Haven Restaurant (207-863-4969), 49 Main St. Open Tue.–Sat. June–Dec. unless Tory Pratt is catering, with a 6 and 8:15 seating harborside; reservations required. On the street side (Wed.–Sat.––9) you can eat from a lighter menu, pub-style, and do not need a reservation. This island mainstay serves a variety of entrées that change almost nightly. You might begin with crabcakes with a sherry cayenne mayonnaise, then dine on baked fresh scallops with crème fraîche, Gruyère, Parmesan, and bread crumbs, or roast pork tenderloin. There's always at least one steak and a pasta dish. Entrées $15.75–22.50.

✐ **The Harbor Gawker** (207-863-9365), Main St., middle of the village. Open mid-Apr.–mid-Nov., Mon.–Sat. 11–8. Lobster rolls, crabmeat rolls, and baskets of just about anything. Owned by the Morton family since 1975, this is a great, casual spot with views of the millrace and Carver's Pond. Order at the counter: from-scratch soups and chowders, seafood baskets, and blueberry pies, along with ice cream and a dairy bar for dessert. It's a big menu with everything from hot dogs through salads and wraps to quesadillas, flat bread, and lobster dinners.

Surfside (207-863-2767), Harbor Wharf, W. Main St. Donna Webster opens at 4 AM for the lobstermen and technically closes at 11 AM on weekends; lunch until 1:30 weekdays. A great harborside breakfast spot with tables on the deck, and specials like a crabmeat or lobster omelet, or a tomato herb cheese omelet with fish cakes.

(ᵗᵖ) **ARCafe** (207-863-4191; vharc.org), 50B Main St. Open 7–11 for breakfast, 11–5 for soups and sandwiches. Sunday brunch in summer. Check the website for off-season hours. Coffees, smooothies, teas, and island produce all day. This student-run "Community Learning Center & Local Foods Market" is an attractive, welcoming space with free WiFi and good food.

Trickerville Sandwich Shop (207-863-9344), Water St., Mon.–Sat. 5 AM–4 PM, Sun. 11–4. Closed Sun. off-season. Off Main St. on the way to Armbrust Hill, this eatery is tucked down by the harbor, the place lobster-

men stop for breakfast, good sandwiches, lobster and crab rolls.

🍴 **The Pizza Pit** (207-863-4311), 36
West Main St., is open daily 4–9 PM,
serving more than pizza. Kids love it.

On North Haven
Coal Wharf Restaurant (207-867-
4739), hidden away in the J. O. Brown
& Sons Boatyard, overlooking the Fox
Islands Thorofare. Open for dinner
(except Mon.) in July and Aug.; check
in June. Specializing in local seafood
and on-island organic produce. Dinner
entrées $15–25. Reservations advised.

Nebo Lodge (207-867-2007; nebo
lodge.com), 11 Mullins Lane, North
Haven Village. Open July and Aug.,
Tue.–Sat.; also Fri. and Sat. in May,
June, and Sept.–Dec. Reserve. This is
a very special inn (see *Lodging*) right
in the village with a menu that changes
nightly. Chef Amanda Hallowell is
committed to using as much locally
grown produce as possible. A "first
taste" might be butter-poached lobster
with baby lettuce, fried lemon, and
fresh tarragon, or fried green tomatoes
with slab bacon and homemade aioli.
On a June evening we dined on homemade "torn" pasta, fresh crabmeat,
local pea shoots, and lemon crème
fraîche, topped off with rhubarb pie
and cardamom-ginger ice cream. It's
an à la carte menu with most entrées
under $30 and a full bar. Free trans-
port across the Thorofare is offered to
patrons coming from Vinalhaven.

Cooper's Landing (207-867-2060)
Open July–Aug. for lunch and dinner,
check in June and Sept. Mickey
Campbell now runs this handy little
restaurant, which offers offers seating
inside and out at the summer heart of
the village. Burgers, fried foods, lobster and crab rolls, fish cakes, chowder
and salads, full bar.

Waterman's Community Center
(watermans.org), North Haven Village.
Open daily year-round 7–4 for coffee,
tea, muffins, sodas, and bagels in an
airy, nonprofit community center with
couches, tables, board games, and
newspapers.

✳ Entertainment
Waterman's Community Center
(207-867-2100; watermans.org), North
Haven Village. This exceptional center
right at the ferry dock includes a theater, the venue for frequent productions, concerts, and presentations.
Check the calendar for contra dance,
workshops, and children's activities.

Smith Hokanson Memorial Hall at
Vinalhaven High School is the stage for
lectures, theater, and a variety of community activities.

✳ Selective Shopping
In Carver's Harbor on Vinalhaven
🍴 **The Paper Store** (207-863-4826) is
the nerve center of the island, the
place everyone drops by at least once a
day. Carlene Michael is as generous
about dispensing directions to visitors
as she is news to residents. This is also

NEW ERA GALLERY, CARVER'S HARBOR

Christina Tree

the place to check for current happenings like plays and concerts, and to get a chart of the island.

New Era Gallery (207-863-9351; neweragallery.com), Main St. Open Memorial Day–Dec. Painter and printmaker Elaine Austin Crossman's gallery shows work by some of Maine's most prominent painters, sculptors, photographers, and fiber artists. Check out the sculpture garden and special exhibits in the barn.

✎ **Go Fish** (207-863-4193), Main St. Open year-round, Tue.–Sat. 10–4:30. A cheerful kids-geared shop with books, games, and candy.

Second Hand Prose, Main St. Open Mon.–Sat. 9–4:30. Run by Friends of the Library and featuring secondhand books. Good selection of Maine and maritime titles.

Island Spirits (207-863-2192), 32 Main St. Open Mon.–Sat. 11–6:30. Some of the "best cheeses you can ever hope for," great wines, beer, olives, freshly ground coffee, and breads; first Friday wine tastings.

In North Haven Village
North Haven Gift Shop and Gallery (207-867-4444). Open Memo-

COSTUMED EAGLE ATOP GRANITE EAGLE DURING ARTS CELEBRATION, CARVER'S HARBOR

AmazingMaine.com

rial Day–mid-Sept. (but closed Sun.), 9:30–5. Since 1954 June Hopkins (mother of Eric) has run this shop with rooms that meander on and on, filled with pottery, books, accessories, jewelry, and much more, including bags by the island's famous young designer, Angela Adams. Gallery exhibits change frequently. Hopkins keeps running accounts for summer families and knows the names of members of as many as six generations of a family when they walk in.

Calderwood Hall and North Island Fiber Shoppe (207-867-2265). Open seasonally. Housed in a weathered building that has served as movie theater and dance hall, featuring paintings by owner Herbert Parsons; also offering an interesting mix of clothing and gifts, many island-made, and Mickey Bullock's lustrous yarns, hand spun from her sheep. Wine, beer, and water are also sold.

Hopkins Wharf Gallery (207-867-2229). Open seasonally. This is a contemporary gallery operated by David Hopkins, brother of the artist Eric.

✳ **Special Events**

Year-round: **North Haven Arts Enrichment Presentations** include exceptional plays, concerts, and lectures performed in Waterman's Community Center in North Haven Village at the ferry landing. For details, phone 207-867-2100; watermans.org.

Summer season: Concerts, primarily classical, chamber, and jazz, are staged on both islands, sponsored by Fox Islands Concerts.

July 4: **Parade** in Vinalhaven.

July–August: **Saturday Farmer's Market** at the ball field, North Haven Village, features crafts as well as produce. **Saturday Flea Market**, 10 AM in the field next to the Galamander,

Carver's Harbor, Vinalhaven. **Union Church Baked Bean Supper** (every other Thursday), Vinalhaven. Check **vinalhavenlandtrust.org** for the schedule of frequent morning walks and evening talks.

For details about other regular occurrences on both islands, consult *The Wind*, a weekly newsletter published on Vinalhaven.

MATINICUS

Home to fewer than 40 hardy souls in winter, most of whom make their living lobstering, Matinicus's population grows to about 200 in summer. Maine's outermost island, it lies 22 miles at sea beyond the outer edge of Penobscot Bay. Quiet and unspoiled, it's a haven for birds and birders with some 650 species identified. Walking trails thread the meadows and shore, and there are two sand beaches—one at each end of the 750-acre island. Matinicus Rock is offshore, a protected nesting site for puffins, a lure for birders in June and July. Matinicus and neighboring Ragged Island (better known as Criehaven, the name of its seasonal village) are the setting for Elizabeth Ogilvie's trilogy, *High Tide at Noon*, *Storm Tide*, and *Ebb Tide*.

GUIDANCE For an informative mailing or answers to general questions contact Harriet Williams (207-354-8354), 45 Thatcher St., Thomaston 04861. Williams is a former islander who is helpful with cottage rental options.

GETTING THERE The flying time via **Penobscot Island Air** (207-596-7500) from Owls Head is 15 minutes, but flights may be canceled because of weather—and the fog can hang in there for days. That's when you contact **George Tarkleson** (207-691-9030; matinicusexcursions.com), June 22–Oct. 20; it's a 70-minute ride. Inquire about puffin-, whale-, and seal-watching trips. **The Maine State Ferry** (207-596-2022) takes 2¼ hours to ply between Matinicus and Rockland, four times a month May–Oct., and once a month the rest of the year. Other water taxis include **Equinox Island Transit** (207-236-6890; cell, 691-6891) and **Penobscot Ferry Transport** (207-691-6030; cell, 594-5163). For a longer list of water of water taxis, see *Guidance*.

✳ Lodging

☗ ✍ **Tuckanuck Lodge** (207-366-3830; tuckanuck.com), Shag Hollow Rd., P.O. Box 217, Matinicus 04851. Open year-round. Well-behaved children and pets welcome. Nantucket native Bill Hoadley offers five rooms (two shared baths), some with a view of Old Cove and the ocean; $100 double, $70 off-season including breakfast and tax; half rate for children 12 and under; weekly rates available. Guests have kitchen privileges for lunch (bring your own fixings); the lodge offers supper ($18–21 including salad and dessert; BYOB). Baked goods are available on-island.

The Fisherman's Wife, operated by Donna Rogers (207-366-3011), sells books, paintings, crafts, and handmade items.

CAMDEN/ROCKPORT AREA
ISLESBORO

Smack on Rt. 1, Camden is the most popular way station between Kennebunkport or Boothbay Harbor and Bar Harbor. Seemingly half its 19th-century captains' homes are now B&Bs. Shops and restaurants line a photogenic harbor filled with private sailing and motor yachts. It's also a poor man's yacht haven—open year-round—with a thriving fishing industry. The ski area would make a good winter vacation destination as well as a summer tour.

Here, in 1936, artist Frank Swift refitted a few former fishing and cargo schooners to carry passengers around the islands in Penobscot Bay. He called the boats windjammers. Half a dozen members of Maine's current windjammer fleet are still based here (the rest are in neighboring ports), and several schooners offer daysails. You can also get out on the water in an excursion boat or a sea kayak.

From the water you can see two aspects of Camden not apparent from land. The first is the size and extent of the Camden Hills. The second is the size and number of the palatial old waterside "cottages" along Beauchamp Point, the rocky promontory separating Camden from Rockport. Here, as in Bar Harbor, summer residents were wise and powerful enough to preserve the local mountains, seeding the creation of the present 6,500-acre Camden Hills State Park, one of Maine's more spectacular places to hike.

Camden's first resort era coincided with those colorful decades during which steam and sail overlapped. As a stop on the Boston–Bangor steamboat line, Camden acquired a couple of big (now vanished) hotels. In 1900, when Bean's boatyard launched the world's first six-masted schooner, onlookers crowded the ornate neighboring steamboat wharf to watch.

In contrast with Boothbay and Bar Harbor, Camden has always been a year-round town and never overdependent on tourism. Camden's early business was, of course, building and sailing ships. By the mid-1800s half a dozen mills lined the series of falls on the Megunticook River, just a block or two from the waterfront. The vast wooden Knox Woolen Company—the "Harrington Mill" portrayed in the movie *Peyton Place*—made the felts used by Maine's paper mills to absorb water from paper stock. It operated until 1988, and now holds a hodgepodge of restaurants, businesses and homes.

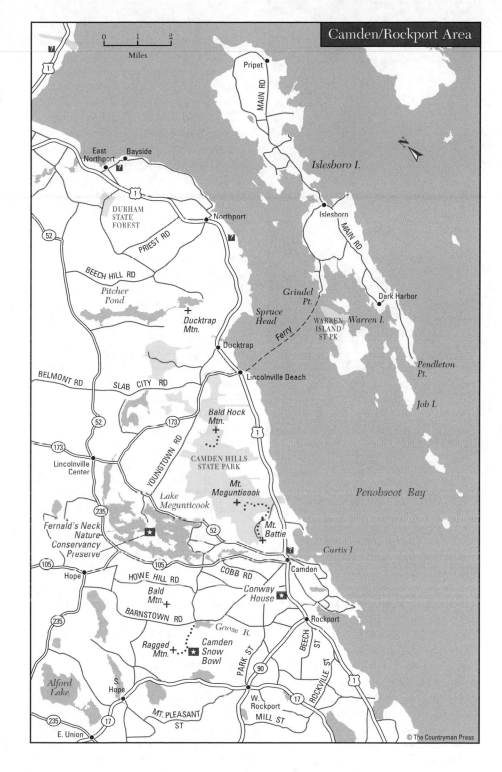

Camden/Rockport Area

© The Countryman Press

Kim Grant

WINDJAMMERS IN CAMDEN HARBOR

Culturally enriched by its sophisticated populace—workaday residents, retired diplomats, military and intelligence officers, and summer people alike—Camden (along with Rockport) offers a bonanza of music, art, and theatrical productions, all of surprising quality. There are also world-renowned programs in filmmaking, computer science, woodworking, and photography.

Ironically, only a small fraction of the thousands of tourists who stream through Camden every summer take the time to discover the extent of its beauty. The tourist tide eddies around the harborside restaurants, shops, and galleries and continues to flow on up Rt. 1 toward Bar Harbor. Even in August you are likely to find yourself alone atop Mount Battie (accessible by car as well as on foot) or Mount Megunticook (highest point in the Camden Hills), or in the open-sided Vesper Hill Children's Chapel, with its flowers and sea view. Few visitors see, let alone swim in, Megunticook Lake or set foot on the nearby island of Islesboro.

A decade or two ago you could count on your fingers the number of places to stay here, but Camden has since become synonymous with B&Bs. A total of some 1,000 rooms can now be found in hotels, motels, inns, and cottages as well as the B&Bs between Camden and neighboring Lincolnville and Rockport.

GUIDANCE Penobscot Regional Chamber of Commerce, Camden Office (207-236-4404 or 1-800-223-5459; visitcamden.com), 2 Public Landing (behind Cappy's), P.O. Box 919, Camden 04843. Open year-round, Mon.–Fri. 9–5 and Memorial Day–mid-Dec. Sat. 10–4; also open Sun. 10–4, Memorial Day–Columbus Day. You'll find all sorts of helpful brochures here, plus maps of Camden, Rockport, and Lincolnville, along with knowledgeable people to send you in the right direction. The chamber keeps tabs on vacancies during the high season, as well as on what's open off-season and cottages available to rent (a list is ready for requests each year by Jan.). Be sure to secure the 184-page *Discover the Jewel of the Maine Coast*. Events are listed on the website. The Camden-Rockport Historical Society's *A Walking Tour*, which outlines tours of historic districts in Camden and Rockport, is an essential publication that includes a bike and car route.

GETTING THERE *By air:* **Knox County Regional Airport**, at Owls Head, about 10 miles from Camden, offers daily flights to and from Boston. **Bangor International Airport** and **Portland International Jetport** offer connections to all parts of the country.

By bus: **Concord Coach Lines** (1-800-639-3317; concordcoachlines.com) stops on Rt. 1 at the Maritimes Farm, just south of Camden en route from Bangor to Portland and Boston and vice versa.

By limo: **MidCoast Limo** (207-236-2424 or 1-800-937-2424; midcoastlimo.com) makes runs from Portland International Jetport by reservation. **Schooner Bay Limo** (207-594-5000; schoonerbaytaxi.com) goes to Portland and elsewhere.

By car: Our preferred route, to bypass Rt. 1 traffic, is to take I-295 to Gardiner, then follow signs to Rt. 226. When this road ends, take a right onto Rt. 17, which winds through pretty countryside to Rt. 90, and then intersects with Rt. 1 leading into Camden.

PARKING is a problem in July and August. In-town parking has a stringently enforced two-hour limit (just 15 minutes in a few spots, so be sure to read the signs). There is parking just a two- to five-minute walk away; the chamber recommends parking on Chestnut St., Union St., Mechanic St., and Washington St. The chamber has a map that highlights all-day parking areas.

WHEN TO COME Camden and Rockport are open year-round with a thriving fishing industry; the ski area makes this area a good winter destination as well as a summer tour. But for sailing and swimming, summer is the time to come, and fall foliage contrasts beautifully with the blue water.

✳ Villages

Rockport's harbor is as picturesque as Camden's, and the small village is set high above it. Its quiet, subdued charm provides a nice respite from the hustle of Rt. 1. Steps (you have to look closely for them) lead down to Marine Park, a departure point in 1816 for 300 casks of lime shipped to Washington, DC, to help construct the Capitol. In the small park you'll see the restored remains of a triple kiln, a saddleback steam locomotive, and a granite sculpture of André the Seal, the legendary performer who drew crowds every summer in the early and mid-1980s. The village (part of Camden until 1891) includes the restored Rockport Opera House, site of Bay Chamber Concerts, the Center for Maine Contemporary Art, the Maine Media Workshops program, and restaurants and shops.

Lincolnville's landmarks—the Lobster Pound Restaurant, Maine State Ferry to Islesboro, and the Whale's Tooth Pub, formerly a customhouse, with a big fireplace—serve as centerpieces for proliferating shops, restaurants, and B&Bs. The beach offers a nice swimming spot on hot days.

✳ To See

LIGHTHOUSE Curtis Island Light. A public park, the island is nevertheless accessible only by boat, and the lighthouse is not open to the public. The best views are from sightseeing cruises out of Camden Harbor, but if you walk down to where Bayview St. connects with Beacon, there's a good lookout.

MUSEUMS ✍ ♿ **Old Conway Homestead and Cramer Museum** (207-236-2257; crmuseum.org), Conway Rd. (off Rt. 1 at the Camden–Rockport town line). Open July and Aug., Mon.–Fri. 11–3; admission $5 adults, $4 seniors 60-plus, $2 students 6–18, children 5 and under free; 10 percent AAA discount. Open June and Sept. by appointment. Administered by the Camden-Rockport Historical Society, this restored early-18th-century farmhouse features antiques from several periods. The barn holds collections of carriages, sleighs, and early farm tools; don't miss the Victorian privy, blacksmith shop, and 1820 maple sugar house, where sugaring demonstrations are held each spring. **The Cramer Museum** displays local memorabilia and changing exhibits.

Schoolhouse Museum (207-789-5445), Rt. 173, Lincolnville Beach. Open Mon., Wed., and Fri. 1–4 June–Oct., other times by appointment. Admission is free. A small museum detailing the history of Lincolnville, with exhibits that change often and include stereoptics and tintypes, early settlers' tools, and Native American artifacts. The museum also publishes *Ducktrap: Chronicles of a Maine Village*, an excellent book on local history, and *Staying Put in Lincolnville, Maine*, both by local author Diane O'Brien.

SCENIC DRIVE Drive or, better yet, bicycle around **Beauchamp Point**. Begin on Chestnut St. in Camden and follow this peaceful road by the lily pond and on by the herd of **belted Galloway cows** (black on both ends and white in the middle). Take Calderwood Lane through the woods and by the **Vesper Hill Children's Chapel**, built on the site of a former hotel and banked with flowers, a great spot to get married or simply to sit. Continue along Beauchamp Ave. to Rockport Village to lunch or picnic by the harbor, and return via Union St. to Camden.

OTHER SITES Cellardoor Vineyard (207-763-4478; mainewine.com), 367 Youngtown Rd., Lincolnville, 11–6 daily, May–Oct, and **Cellardoor Winery at the Villa** (207-236-2654), aka The Yellow House, Rt. 1 (at Rt. 90), Rockport; 11–6 daily, April–Oct. Call for off-season hours. Vines in this 7-acre Lincolnville vineyard were completely removed in 2008 and 2009. Some were dead and others didn't produce the best wines, according to Bettina Doulton, who purchased the business in 2007. New grape varietals planted, better suited to the climate, include Seyval Blanc, Frontenac Gris, and Marquette, and are now being harvested. To supplement the crop, the business buys grapes from the West Coast, to make, for instance, its excellent Viognier, which can be tasted along with more than a dozen others at both sites listed, and in the 18th-century barn in Lincolnville.

CELLARDOOR WINERY AT THE VILLA

Nancy English

BICYCLING ⌀ **Camden Hills State Park**, Rt. 1, Camden, has a 10-mile (round-trip) ride through the woods on a snowmobile trail. Bikes are not allowed on hiking trails. The **Camden Snow Bowl** also offers a number of rides through woods and swamps, as well as riding on ski trails. It's a hearty ride, but the views from the top are terrific.

⌀ **Georges River Bikeways**. The Georges River Land Trust (207-594-5166) puts out a pamphlet highlighting several good biking routes, with many scenic spots within the Georges River watershed.

Maine Sport Outfitters (207-236-7120 or 1-800-722-0826; mainesport.com), Rt. 1, Rockport, rents Raleigh hybrids, as well as bike trailers and car racks for a day or extended periods. Rentals include helmet, lock, water bottles, and cable. **Map Adventures** (1-800-891-1534; mapadventures.com) makes a very readable small map of bike routes and trails in the Camden Hills, stocked here.

BOAT EXCURSIONS See also *Windjammers*.

Yacht charters are offered spring to autumn along the Maine coast. Most charters run for a week, although sometimes it's possible to charter a boat just for a long weekend, with or without crew. For more information, contact **Johanson Boat-works** (207-596-7060 or 1-877-4-JOHANS), which rents everything from J-40 sloops to Ericson 38s. **Rockport Charters** (207-691-1066; rockportcharters.com) offers, with advance notice, 20-passenger, three-hour wildlife charters to see puffins, eagles, ospreys, and more. Leaving from both Camden and Rockland, as well as Rockport, Captain Robert Iserbyt also provides transportation for workers out to North Haven.

It would be a shame to be in Camden and not spend some time on the water. The two-hour sailing excursions are a wonderful way to get a taste of what the harbor has to offer if your time is limited. Remember to bring a jacket, because the air can get chilly once you're offshore, even on a sunny day. Wander down the wooden boardwalk and check the offerings, which include:

⌀ **Schooner** *Appledore II* (207-236-8353 or 1-800-233-PIER, appledore2.com), an 86-foot schooner (the largest of the daysailing fleet), has sailed around the world and now offers several trips daily, including sunset cruises.

Schooner *Surprise* (207-236-4687; camdenmainesailing.com), a traditional, historic, 57-foot schooner, offers entertaining, informative two-hour sails. Captain Jack and wife Barbara Moore spent seven years cruising between Maine and the Caribbean, educating their four children on board in the process.

Schooner *Olad* (207-236-2323; maineschooners.com), a 57-foot schooner, offers two-hour sails and charters.

Schooner *Heron* (207-236-8605 or 1-800-599-8605; woodenboatco.com), runs lobster lunch, midafternoon, and evening sails (BYOB, with hors d'oeuvre served) out of Rockport for a maximum of 36 passengers. With typically 8 to 20 passengers on the regular sails, this 65-foot schooner, built in 2003 in Camden by its owners, is available for private trips.

⌀ *Betselma* (207-236-4446), a motor launch, provides one-hour coastal and two-hour island trips (owner Les Bex was a longtime windjammer captain) out of the harbor and down the coast.

⚓ *Lively Lady Too* (207-236-6672 or 418-839-7933; livelyladytoo.com), a traditional lobster boat, takes passengers on two-hour ecotours that can include watching lobster traps being hauled and swinging in close to an island for bird-watching. A monitor shows video of the ocean floor.

Schooner *Lazy Jack II* (207-230-0602). Two-hour sails and private charters from Camden Harbor, with Captain Sean O'Connor.

⚓ **Maine State Ferry** from Lincolnville Beach to Islesboro (207-734-6935). At $10 roundtrip per passenger, $27.50 per vehicle, and $8.50 per bicycle, this is the bargain of the local boating scene. An extra $12 each way secures your reservation. (See *Getting There* under "Islesboro.")

BOWLING Oakland Park Bowling Lanes (207-594-7525), 714 Commercial St., Rockport. Susan and Joe Plaskas have updated this old-fashioned bowling alley with refinished lanes, air-conditioning, and tile flooring, retaining the 1950s decor. Video games, air hockey, and VDR, too.

GOLF Goose River Golf Club (207-236-8488; gooseriver.com), Simonton Rd., Rockport. Nine holes, but you can play through twice using different starting tees. Cart rentals; clubhouse. Tee times recommended any time of the week; you can request up to a week in advance.

⚓ **Golfers Crossing Miniature Golf** (207-230-0090); water hazards and obstacles complete this mini golf experience on Rt. 1 in Rockport.

Samoset Resort Golf Course (clubhouse, 207-594-1431), Rockport, has an 18-hole, par-70 course with seven oceanside holes and ocean views from 14 holes. A renovation includes a redesigned 18th hole featuring a stone seawall, a remodeled 185-yard, par-three 5th hole, and renovations to hole 4. The clubhouse has a pro shop, locker rooms, and the **Clubhouse Grille**. Carts are available.

HIKING Bald Rock Mountain. This 1,100-foot mountain in Lincolnville once had a ski area at the top. Great views of Penobscot Bay and the Camden Hills. You'll find the trailhead 1.25 miles down a dirt road from the gate on Ski Lodge Rd. (off Youngtown Rd.). The climb is about 0.5 mile long and moderate. Ask about overnight camping at the Camden Hills State Park headquarters on Rt. 1 in Camden.

Georges Highland Path is a 40-mile trail network created and maintained by the Georges River Land Trust (207-594-5166; grlt.org). Trails wind through the Oyster River Bog, a magnificent semi-wilderness area with a 7.2-mile trail that links the Thomaston Town Forest with the Ragged Mountain section. A map put out by the trust details distances and hiking times and shows where the trailheads are.

Coastal Mountain Hiking (207-236-7731), Camden, offers guided hikes and packed lunches.

See also **Beech Hill** and **Camden Hills State Park** in *Green Space*.

SEA KAYAKING Ducktrap Sea Kayak Tours (207-236-8608; ducktrapkayak .com), Lincolnville Beach, offers two-hour and half-day guided tours in Penobscot Bay. No experience is necessary; in fact, most patrons are first-time kayakers. Group and family tours, rentals, and lessons.

Maine Sport Outfitters (207-236-8797 or 1-800-722-0826; mainesport.com), on Rt. 1 just south of Rockport, is no mere outfitter—it's a phenomenon. They offer courses in kayaking, guided excursions around Camden Harbor and out into Penobscot Bay, and island-based workshops. They also rent kayaks and canoes (also see *Special Learning Programs*).

SPECIAL LEARNING PROGRAMS ✍ **Camden Yacht Club Sailing Program** (207-236-4575; off-season, 207-236-7033), Bayview St., Camden, provides sailing classes for children and adults, boat owners and non-boat-owners, during late June, July, and Aug.

Maine Media Workshops (207-236-8581; theworkshops.com), Rockport. This nationally respected year-round school for photography, cinematography, television production, and related fields offers a choice of 200 programs that vary in length from one week to three months for every skill level. The faculty includes established, recognized professionals from across the country; the students come from around the world. Housing is provided for most of the students, and the school helps arrange accommodations for others. Also a gallery with changing exhibitions, open to the public.

The Center for Maine Contemporary Art (207-236-2875; artsmaine.org; see *Entertainment* and *Selective Shopping*), 162 Russell Ave., Rockport (formerly Maine Coast Artists). Exhibits and professional development for artists, including workshops and lectures for visual artists. The winter of 2009–10 proved to be a financial challenge for this organization, so call first to confirm programming.

Maine Sport Outfitters (207-236-8797; mainesport.com), Rockport. This Rt. 1 complex is worth a stop whether you're up for adventure sports or not. The place has evolved from a fly fishing and canvas shop into a multi-tiered store that's a home base for a wide variety of local kayaking tours and multiday kayaking workshops geared to all levels of ability, based at facilities on Gay Island.

Center for Furniture Craftsmanship (207-594-5611; woodschool.com), 25 Mill St., Rockport. June–Oct. Hands-on one- and two-week workshops for novice, intermediate, and advanced woodworkers and cabinetmakers. Twelve-week intensive courses are also offered three times a year. A nine-month comprehensive course runs from Sept. to June.

SWIMMING ✍ Saltwater swimming from Camden's **Laite Memorial Park and Beach**, Upper Bayview St.; at **Lincolnville Beach**, Rt. 1 north of Camden; and in Rockport at **Walker Park**, across the road from Marine Park. Freshwater swimming at **Megunticook Lake**, Lincolnville (**Barret Cove Memorial Park and Beach**; turn left off Rt. 52 northwest of Camden), where you'll also find picnic grounds and a parking area; **Shirttail Beach**, Camden (Rt. 105); and at the **Willis Hodson Park** on the Megunticook River, Camden (Molyneaux Rd.). At the **Penobscot Bay YMCA** (207-236-3375), Union St., visitors can pay a day-use fee that entitles them to swim in the Olympic-sized pool (check hours for family swimming, lap swimming, and other programs), use the weight rooms, use the rock-climbing gym, use the sauna, and play basketball in the gym.

TENNIS There are two public tennis courts at the **Camden Snow Bowl** on Hosmer Pond Rd. (first come, first served). In addition, **Samoset Resort** (207-593-

1545), Rockport, has outdoor courts, as does the **Rockport Recreation Park** (207-236-9648).

WALKING TOUR **The Camden-Rockport Historical Society** (207-236-2257) has prepared a brochure (available at the chamber of commerce and the Cramer Museum) with a 2.5-mile walk past historic buildings. The brochure includes historical details and a sketch map. An expanded bicycle or car tour encompassing two towns is also included.

WINDJAMMERS ✐ Windjammer cruises are offered late May–mid-Oct. Twelve traditional tall ships sail from Camden, Rockport, and Rockland on three- to six-day cruises throughout Penobscot Bay. For brochures and sailing schedules, contact the **Maine Windjammer Association** (1-800-807-WIND; sailmainecoast.com).

Angelique (207-785-3020 or 1-800-282-9989; sailangelique.com), Camden, is a 95-foot ketch that was built expressly for the windjammer trade in 1980. Patterned after 19th-century English fishing vessels, she offers 15 passenger cabins, a pleasant deck-level salon with piano, belowdecks showers, and rowboats for exploring the coast.

Lewis R. French (207-594-2241 or 1-800-469-4635; schoonerfrench.com), Camden, was launched on the Damariscotta River in 1871 and is the oldest documented vessel in America's windjammer fleet. Before becoming a passenger vessel, the French carried cargo such as lumber, firewood, bricks, granite, lime—even Christmas trees—along the coast. She had three major rebuilds, the most recent in 1976 when she was brought into passenger service. Sixty-five feet long, the *French* accommodates 21 passengers in 13 private cabins with freshwater sinks and portholes that open. Hot, freshwater shower on board. Captain Garth Wells enjoys getting his guests actively involved in the experience of sailing an authentic 19th-century schooner.

Mary Day (1-800-992-2218; schoonermaryday.com), Camden, was the first schooner built specifically for carrying passengers. At 90 feet, she's among the swiftest; Captains Barry King and Jen Martin have extensive sailing experience. Features include a fireplace and parlor organ and hot, freshwater showers on the deck. The *Mary Day* accommodates up to 28 passengers, and meals include a New England boiled dinner, baked goods made in the galley's woodstove, and a lobster bake on every cruise.

WINDJAMMER *GRACE BAILEY*

Barbara Hatch

Grace Bailey*, Mercantile, and *Mistress (207-236-2938 or 1-800-736-7981; mainewindjammercruises.com), Maine Windjammer Cruises, Camden. For years known as the *Mattie*, *Grace Bailey* took back her original name following a thorough restoration in 1990. Built in 1882 in New York, the 81-foot

Grace Bailey once carried cargo along the Atlantic coast and to the West Indies. She has belowdecks showers. *Mercantile* was built in Maine in 1916 as a shallow-draft coasting schooner; 78 feet long, she has been in the windjammer trade since its beginning in 1942. There are belowdecks showers. *Mistress*, the smallest of the fleet at 46 feet, carries just six passengers. A topsail schooner built in 1960 along the lines of the old coasting schooners, she is also available for private charter. All three cabins have private heads, but there is no shower on board.

Timberwind (207-236-0801 or 1-800-759-9250; schoonertimberwind.com), Rockport. Built in Portland in 1931 as a pilot schooner, this pretty 96-foot vessel was converted to passenger use in 1969. She has an enclosed handheld shower on deck and room for 20 passengers. The only windjammer sailing out of Rockport Harbor, the *Timberwind* welcomes families with children ages 5 and up on most cruises.

❋ Winter Sports

CROSS-COUNTRY SKIING Camden Hills State Park (207-236-3109) marks and maintains some trails for cross-country skiing, and there's a ski hut on Mount Battie (see *Green Space*).

Tanglewood 4-H Camp (207-789-5868 or 1-877-944-2267), 1 Tanglewood Rd., off Rt. 1 near Lincolnville Beach. Ungroomed, scenic cross-country trails that wend through woodlands and along streams. Maps with a description of trails are at the kiosk at the trailhead on the loop of the road.

DOWNHILL SKIING ✍ **Camden Snow Bowl** (207-236-3438; camdensnow bowl.com), Hosmer Pond Rd., Camden. The only place you can ski overlooking views of the Atlantic Ocean! With an 850-foot vertical drop, 10 trails for beginners through experts, and night skiing, this is a comfortably sized area where everyone seems to know everyone else. Facilities include a base lodge, rental and repair shop, ski school, and cafeteria, plus the Jack Williams Toboggan Chute ($5 per person/per hour) and tube sliding ($5 per person/per hour). In early February the Snow Bowl hosts the hilarious annual U.S. National Toboggan Championship Races at the toboggan chute (right next to the ski area). Outlandishly costumed teams make mad runs down the chute at 40-plus miles an hour, bottoming out on the ice-covered Hosmer Pond. $35 full-day adult weekend pass, $26 students.

❋ Green Space

✍ ♿ **Camden Hills State Park** (207-236-3109; off-season, 207-236-0849), 280 Belfast Rd., Rt. 1, Camden. $4.50 nonresident adults, $3 Mainers, $1 ages 5–11; free under 5 and 65 and older for residents, $1.50 nonresidents 65 and older. In addition to Mount Battie, this 6,500-acre park includes Mount Megunticook, one of the highest points on the Atlantic seaboard, and a shoreside picnic site. You can drive to the top of Mount Battie on the road that starts at the park entrance, just north of town. At the entrance pick up a Camden Hills State Park brochure, which outlines 19 trails with distance and difficulty level. In winter many of the trails convert to cross-country ski runs, given snow. There are 106 campsites available May 15–Oct. 14.

Warren Island State Park, also administered by Camden Hills State Park, is just a stone's throw off the island of Islesboro. The park features picnic tables, trails, and tent sites. Accessibility is the problem: You can arrange to have a private boat carry you over from the mainland, rent your own boat in Camden, or paddle out in a sea kayak. Because of this, the island boasts a peace and quiet often hard to find on the mainland in high season.

Marine Park, off Russell Ave. (just after you cross the bridge), Rockport. A nicely landscaped waterside area with sheltered picnic tables. Restored lime kilns and a locomotive remind visitors of the era when the town's chief industry was processing and exporting lime. During a stroll you're likely to see several painters capturing the picturesque harbor on canvas.

Merryspring Nature Center (207-236-2239; merryspring.org), Camden. Open to the public year-round during daylight hours. A 66-acre private preserve with walking trails; herb, daylily, demonstration, and rose gardens; raised beds; and an arboretum. The Goose River borders the preserve, accessible via Conway Rd. from Rt. 1 in Camden. Birders frequent the gardens on the lookout for barred owls and warblers. If you're lucky you'll see white-tailed deer, ermine, porcupine, raccoon, rabbit, and even moose. Weekly talks in summer. Free to members, $5 for nonmembers.

Fernald's Neck Preserve (207-236-7091; coastalmountains.org). Owned by the Coastal Mountains Land Trust, located at the end of Fernald Neck Rd. off Rt. 52, past Youngtown Rd., Lincolnville and Camden. Open dawn till 7:30 PM, no pets allowed. The preserve's 326 acres cover most of a wooded peninsula that juts into Lake Megunticook. Signs showing walking trails are at the trailhead kiosk and trail intersections. Trails lead to stunning water views. Trails can be boggy: Wear boots or old shoes.

Amphitheatre and Camden Harbor Park (207-236-3440), Atlantic Ave., Camden. The amphitheater, designed by Fletcher Steele in 1929, has been nominated as a National Historic Landmark; it's a magical setting for summertime concerts or weddings, and a good place to sit, think, or read anytime. Across the street Harbor Park covers a manicured slope down to the water, with the Megunticook River waterfall in its midst. Picnic on one of the benches overlooking Camden Harbor.

MERRYSPRING NATURE CENTER

Nancy English

CAMDEN AMPHITHEATER

Nancy English

The Beech Hill Preserve (207-236-7091; coastalmountains.org), Beech Hill Rd., Rockport. Coastal Mountains Land Trust cares for 295 acres on this hilltop preserve, bare of trees and the perfect place to drink in the intricate coastline of Midcoast Maine. More than 100 species of birds stop here at some point in the year, feasting on the organic blueberries that attract people, too—although access is limited to the annual free picking days. The berries are harvested and sold to support the preserve. A sod-roofed stone house at the top of the hill called Beech Nut is on the National Register of Historic Places. A trail map is available by download, or with a call to the land trust.

Curtis Island, in the outer harbor. A small island with a lighthouse that marks the entrance to Camden, this is a public picnic spot and a popular sea kayaking destination.

✴ Lodging

All listings are in Camden 04843 unless otherwise noted
Note: If you choose one of the many B&Bs in historic houses on Elm, Main, or High Sts. (all are Rt. 1), you might want to ask what has been done to muffle the sound of passing traffic.

Camden Accommodations (207-236-6090 or 1-800-344-4830; camdenac.com), 43 Elm St., is a vacation rental agency with more than 85 private properties in the Camden area.

Camden Bed & Breakfast Association (camdeninn.com), Camden. The brochure lists 13 members with descriptions of each and contact information.

RESORT ✔ ♿ **Samoset Resort** (207-594-2511 or 1-800-341-1650; samoset.com), 220 Warrenton St., Rockport 04856. Open year-round. The original Samoset lodge burned down in 1972; a renovation in 2011 brought this resort closest yet to its luxurious beginnings. Set on 230 oceanfront acres, the Samoset holds 178 rooms and suites, many with ocean views, balcony, or patio; all have private bath, TV, and air-conditioning. Four cottages, including the two-bedroom Flume Cottage perched on a rocky outcropping above the water, are also available. The Samoset has a world-class 18-hole golf course and golf pro shop, outdoor tennis courts, fitness center, spa, sauna, and indoor and heated, handicapped-accessible outdoor pools. Samoset takes wonderful care of families with young children with a children's program during July and August and other school holidays. The dining room, La Bella Vita (see *Dining Out*), and the adjacent Enoteca (see *Eating Out*) have a large fireplace and floor-to-ceiling windows overlooking the water. Rooms $249–479, off-season $129–329.

INNS ♿ **Inn at Ocean's Edge** (207-236-0945; innatoceansedge.com), P.O. Box 258, Lincolnville 04849. Look for the entrance off Rt. 1 a couple of miles north of the Camden line. Open May–Oct. This modern hotel features a main inn with three common areas and 18 guest rooms; the Hilltop building with 12 rooms, each with a balcony, sits up the hill; also a restaurant and a spa. Almost every single room features a water view, and all have a Jacuzzi, gas fireplace, TV, VCR, stereo, and more. The Spa building holds two luxury suites. Steps lead down to a private shingle beach. Breakfast, served in the restaurant, might include Grand Marnier French toast. An elegant heated pool, spa with treatment rooms, sauna, and whirlpool are available to guests, and a casual and fine-dining restaurant stands next door (see The Edge in *Dining Out*). $195–425 includes breakfast. Children 14 and up welcome.

Camden Harbour Inn (207-236-4200 or 1-800-236-4266; camden harbourinn.com), 83 Bayview St., Camden. This luxury inn names its rooms for former Dutch ports and colonies, and each room's decor takes flight from the places evoked—like Java, with an orange-red headboard and green-gold pillows. Views of the harbor, some fireplaces, thick feather beds, TV/DVD, CD player, and much more, like a vintage 1962 Bentley and a private chauffeur that could take you to Acadia National Park for a day tour, and arrange a lobster picnic on the beach, too. Natalie's is the site of breakfast, included in the rates, $175–375, and fine dining (see *Dining Out*).

♂ ঘ **Whitehall Inn** (207-236-3391 or 1-800-789-6565; whitehall-inn.com), 52 High St. (Rt. 1). Open mid-May–Oct. Owners Russ and Rebecca Miller run this old inn with comfortable parlors are fitted with sofas, games, and three guest computers.

The Millay Room, with its vintage-1904 Steinway, looks much the way it did on the summer evening in 1912 when a local girl, Edna St. Vincent Millay, read her poem "Renascence" to assembled guests; you can learn about the evening in the words hung on the walls. One of the guests, swept away by Millay's verse, paid for her Vassar education. Forty guest rooms in the main inn and several two-bedroom suite hold old-fashioned furnishings, but the Italian sheets and duvet covers are ironed daily. Most rooms have private bath and nonworking old hotel phone; all have AC and flat-screen TV. The bar called Gossip is decorated with *Peyton Place* memorabilia; some of the movie was filmed here. Outsiders can enjoy the good breakfast, included in the rates for guests, for $15. A "sneaker" beach (wear shoes because of the rocks) is nearby. Rooms $139–219; $99–159 off-season.

Hartstone Inn (207-236-4259 or 1-800-788-4823; hartstoneinn.com), 41 Elm St. Open year-round. Mary Jo and Michael Salmon and their innkeepers are in charge of three properties: the first building on Rt. 1, the Hideaway House, and the Manor House. Some of the 11 guest rooms and 12 suites (all with private bath) offer a fireplace and canopy bed. Dinner is served by in the main inn (see *Dining Out*). In high season $125–285 double with full breakfast and afternoon tea and cookies; low season $105–185. Spa services offered. Guests can sign up for the inn's "Chef for a Day" package and prepare the multicourse dinner, or take a group cooking class between Nov. and May.

Cedarholm Garden Bay Inn (207-236-3886; cedarholm.com), Rt. 1, Lincolnville Beach 04849. The pleasures of privacy and setting make a stay extraordinary. Down a road set in the

Courtesy of Cedarholm Garden Bay Inn

FROM THE DECK OF TERN AT CEDARHOLM
GARDEN BAY INN

midst of the landscaped grounds are
the four cottages, Osprey, Puffin, Tern,
and Loon, with fireplace, Jacuzzi,
queen (or king) bed, wet bar with
microwave oven, small fridge, and a
fabulous view of the ocean from a private deck. Two upper cottages, closer
to Rt. 1, have a private bath, wet bar,
and mini fridge. Continental breakfast
includes muffins baked with berries
grown here, in-season. All guests have
access to a shared deck right on the
beach. Upper units begin at $175 per
night; luxury cottages, $300–495 per
night.

**BED & BREAKFASTS The Cam-
den Maine Stay** (207-236-9636;
camdenmainestay.com), 22 High St.
(Rt. 1). Open year-round. Innkeepers
Claudio and Roberta Latanza welcome
guests to this 1802 Greek Revival
house, one of the best known in Camden's High Street Historic District.
Stay in one of four standard rooms and
four suites with names like the Common Ground Room, which has a
cathedral ceiling and private deck over
the garden. The lower-level Carriage
House Room, with well-stocked, built-
in bookshelves, a woodstove, and

French doors opening onto a private
patio with lawn and woods beyond, is
painted in lovely colors. The 2-acre
property is embellished with impecca-
ble gardens. Breakfast in the formal
dining room or on the sunporch overlooking the gardens. Afternoon tea
included. $155–270 double room rate,
in-season; $110–170 off.

✪ ✍ **The Hawthorn** (207-236-8842;
camdenhawthorn.com), 9 High St. (Rt.
1). Open year-round. Owner Maryanne
Shanahan has renovated each of the 10
guest rooms at this Victorian mansion,
a short walk from Camden village and
its harbor. The spacious carriage house
rooms each have a double Jacuzzi,
TV/VCR or DVD, fireplace, and private deck or patio. The Queen Anne
Tower holds two bedrooms, a Victorian
slipper tub, and four shades of violet
that make the walls luminous. Breakfast made with local and organic ingredients may include house hazelnut
granola. A landscaped garden spreads
out beyond the two-tiered deck and
terrace, where breakfast is served in
fine weather. Children are welcome in
rooms that accommodate more than
two people. $140–290 in high season.

TEATIME, THE HAWTHORN

Nancy English

The Blue Harbor House (207-236-3196 or 1-800-248-3196; blueharbor house.com), 67 Elm St. Open year-round. This friendly 11-room inn serves cocktails and hors d'oeuvres to guests (by reservation, starting at $10 per person); breakfast, included in the rates, is served on the spacious sun-porch and might include poached pears and raspberry to start and quiche Florentine for a main course. Fresh Scottish shortbread was baking for the afternoon snack on our visit. Rooms are pleasantly decorated with country antiques and handmade quilts; all have private bath, telephone, air-conditioning, and TV/VCR. The Captain's Quarters has a kitchenette. Doubles $95–205.

Norumbega (207-236-4646 or 1-877-363-4646; norumbegainn.com), 63 High St. (Rt. 1). Open year-round. With one of the most imposing facades of any B&B anywhere, this turreted stone "castle" has long been a landmark just north of Camden. Inside you'll find an ornate staircase with fireplace and love seat on the landing, formal parlor, and dining room with blue-tiled fireplace. Ten guest rooms and two suites named for European castles come with king or queen bed, private bath, antiques, phone, and TV. Doubles $105–575, including full breakfast and evening hors d'oeuvres. The inn welcomes children 7 and up, and offers murder mystery weekends.

The Camden Windward House (207-236-9656 or 1-877-492-9656; windwardhouse.com), 6 High St. (Rt. 1). Open year-round. Kristen and Jesse Bifulco have added a cozy wine bar upstairs with a second-floor deck overlooking Mount Battie; they have been entertaining guests since 2005. The five guest rooms and three suites all have private bath, air-conditioning, cable TV, and clock-radio with CD player. The Quarterdeck Room with skylights has its own entrance, fireplace, TV/DVD, library, sofa, Jacuzzi whirlpool tub, and separate shower. Ironed linens and feather beds make for blissful sleep. Breakfast, perhaps orange yogurt pancakes and sausage, is a choice of several dishes from a menu. $125–280 high season, $99–199 low.

A Little Dream (207-236-8742; little dream.com), 60 High St. (Rt. 1). Open year-round except March. Raised up on a hill over busy Rt. 1, this place feels wonderfully secluded and intimate. Seven guest rooms include a carriage house suite called the Isle Watch. Overlooking the harbor and Curtis Island, it has a gas fireplace, king canopy bed, soaking tub, and covered porch complete with porch swing. If you stay here or in Treetops July 4, you can view three separate fireworks displays from your rooms; in 2009 tree clearing opened up the view, and the Parade of Sails on Windjammer Days is spectacular. $159–295 double includes breakfast, perhaps an apple cheddar omelet or lemon ricotta pancakes. Two-night minimum on holiday weekends. Foreign guests are always welcome: Innkeeper JoAnna Ball speaks Italian, German, and French. Her husband, Bill Fontana, is a sculptor.

🐾 ✍ **Inns at Blackberry Common** (207-236-6060 or 1-800-388-6000; blackberryinn.com), 82 Elm St. Open year-round. Cyndi and Jim Ostrowski's two buildings hold some of the prettiest interiors in town. Settees covered in silk damask, ornate Oriental rugs, and decorative swords set the style. Stay in the Bette Davis, where the movie star slept after the cast party for *Peyton Place*, with a queen brass bed and antique lighting fixture. In-house dinners offered Nov.–June on Sat.

nights, and cooking classes are a monthly feature. Children are welcome in rooms that can accommodate them. $129–249 in-season, $149–189 off, including a full breakfast served in the dining room or in the courtyard.

The Inn at Sunrise Point (207-236-7716 or 1-800-435-6278; sunrisepoint .com), Sunrise Point Rd., P.O. Box 1344, Camden, 04843. Open May–Oct. Set on a 4-acre waterfront estate just over the town line in Lincolnville, this small, luxurious B&B is now run by Daina Hill. Five cottages named for Maine painters and writers—among them Winslow Homer and Richard Russo—have an incredible view, fireplace, private deck, and Jacuzzi. The three rooms in the main house each hold a fireplace. The Wyeth Loft Suite offers king bed, gas fireplace, small deck, and TV/DVD; an attached bedroom can be rented. Count on fine linens on all the sumptuous beds. Common rooms include a snug, wood-paneled library with fireplace perfect for cooler days. Three rooms and the loft are $300–445, cottages $330–595, full breakfast, perhaps poached eggs with asparagus and chive oil, included.

The Belmont (207-236-8053 or 1-800-238-8053; thebelmontinn.com), 6 Belmont St. Open mid-May–Oct. This inn, with a peaceful location a few blocks off Rt. 1, has been undergoing a renewal under the ownership of Anita Zeno. An 1890s Edwardian house with a wraparound veranda with a blue ceiling, the Belmont has six guest rooms with private bath and several with a gas fireplace. Full breakfast, afternoon tea always available. $129–259 per night in-season. Diglet is the resident cat.

✿ **The Victorian by the Sea** (207-236-3785 or 1-800-382-9817; victorian bythesea.com), Lincolnville Beach 04849. Open year-round. Jeanne and Rob Short own this 1889 shingle-style Victorian "cottage" overlooking the water, away from Rt. 1. Seven guest rooms each have a queen bed, private bath, and fireplace. The Victorian Suite, with a turret room, chaise longue, and fireplace, overlooks Penobscot Bay. The $165–250 in-season rate includes full breakfast with, perhaps, blueberry buttermilk scones. Walk down the private path to a viewpoint 30 feet above the sea.

OTHER LODGING 🔍 🐾 ✿ **High Tide Inn** (207-236-3724 or 1-800-778-7068; hightideinn.com), Rt. 1. Open May–late Oct. Set far enough back from Rt. 1 to preclude traffic noise, this no-frills, easygoing complex appeals to singles and couples (who tend to choose one of the five rooms in the inn) and families (who opt for a cottage, two-bedroom deck house, or motel unit, five with connecting sleeping rooms). Most of the very clean 31 rooms have breathtaking views—especially for the price. The complex fills 7 quiet acres of landscaped grounds that slope to the water and more than 250 feet of private ocean beach. A generous continental breakfast includes just-baked popovers and muffins. Pets allowed in only four of the cottages. The living room and bar have working fireplaces. $65–195.

🐾 ✿ ♿ **Lord Camden Inn** (207-236-4325 or 1-800-336-4325; lordcamden inn.com), 24 Main St. Open year-round. This inn is named for the British nobleman who championed the American cause in the House of Lords during the Revolutionary War. Occupying a restored 1893 brick Masonic hall, the Lord Camden sits smack dab in the center of town and takes up several floors above a row of Main St. shops. Six luxury rooms with balconies line the top floor. The 36 rooms offer cable TV, private bath, telephone, air-conditioning, and elevator. Most rooms have two double beds and private balcony overlooking the town and harbor or the hills beyond. June–Nov., rates include a full breakfast with a make-your-own waffle stand; continental breakfast off-season. Owner Marianne Smith's painted still lifes hang on many walls in the inn. $99–289, depending on season.

CAMPING ✓ 🐾 ♿ **Megunticook Campground by the Sea** (207-594-2428; campgroundbythesea.com), P.O. Box 375, Rockport 04856. Open May 15–early or mid-Oct. Wooded, ocean-front campground with 100 sites and 10 rustic camping cabins. Facilities include a store, recreation hall, fishing, heated pool, and oceanfront picnic area and gardens for Saturday-night lobster bakes. $35–45 in-season. **Camden Hills RV Resort** (207-236-2498), 30 Applewood Rd. in Rockport, is a sister park.

✳ **Where to Eat**

DINING OUT ❂ **Francine Bistro** (207-230-0083; francinebistro.com), 55 Chestnut St., Camden. Open Tue.–Sat. 5:30–10; reservations recommended. Small, intimate, and a little noisy. Chef-owner Brian Hill has been earning high praise since 2003. Chewy, moist bread with a marvelous crust is one mark of excellence. The dry-aged steak has an astonishingly good flavor, as does the venison, and the seared line-caught Chatham cod is both moist and crisp. Count on Hill to seek out the best ingredients in Maine. Excellent wine list. Entrées $24–29.

The Edge (207-236-4430), P.O. Box Stone Coast Rd., Rt. 1, Lincolnville. Open daily May–Oct. You can sit on the oceanside outdoor patio for a casual menu, or inside by the wood fire in one of the 66 seats at this elegant, high-design restaurant next to a luxurious inn (see *Inns*). The inn promised another season in 2010 of $1 oysters during happy hour. Sunday night is pizza night, a great time to savor the chef's inventions. On other nights finely made entrées fill the menu, like rib eye with truffle and leek gratin, or seared cod with potato gnocchi. Dessert might be sticky toffee pudding. Entrées $18–30.

Natalie's (207-236-7008; camden harbourinn.com), at the Camden Harbour Inn, 82 Bayview St., Camden. Open daily for dinner 5:30–9. Executive chef Geoffroy Deconinck employs the coast's best seafood and farm products to make his inventive, French-inspired meals, perhaps seared duck breast with turnip puree and black mission figs or halibut with crushed cauliflower and royal trumpet mushrooms. Fine wine list. Entrées $34–49.

Paolina's Way (207-230-0555; paolinas way.com), 10 Bayview Landing, Camden. Open for lunch Fri.–Sun., dinner Thu.–Tue. Recycled pizza boxes and homemade napkins display certain important virtues, but the excellent pizza inside is what really counts. You will want to try another pizza after the first—perhaps the funghi or the shrimp and zucchini with pesto. House pasta makes lasagna and ravioli tender and resilient; dinner specials, too. Gelato is made with local milk. $14–26.

Atlantica (207-236-6011; atlantica restaurant.com), 1 Bay View Landing, Camden. Open for dinner year-round, closed Tue. and Wed.; reservations suggested. Ken and Del Paquin serve creative dishes, like butter-poached lobster or grilled filet mignon with potato strudel. A wonderful deck on the harbor makes summer evenings here charming. Good cocktails, wine, and beer. Dinner $25–30.

The Gallery Café (207-230-0061; prismglassgallery-cafe.com), 297 Commercial St., Rockport. Open Wed.–Sat. 11–3 for lunch and 5–9 for dinner; Sunday brunch 10–3, dinner 4–8. This glassblowing gallery and studio can show off its craft, but even if the artist is absent, the food is so good you might not mind—especially since her work is always on display. A meal of pork chops with Vidalia onion jam or haddock stuffed with crab might end with blueberry fritters. Entrées $14–21.

✪ ✦ ♿ **Chez Michel** (207-789-5600), Lincolnville Beach (across from the beach). Open Apr.–mid-Nov., dinner Tue.–Sun., lunch and dinner on Sun. This restaurant serves French food, and has been winning repeat loyal customers since 1989. The mussels marinière with garlic, onion, and white wine are a great appetizer, and even better for dinner (with salad, potato, and French bread). New England–style fisherman's chowder, with haddock, Maine shrimp, clams, and scallops, and steak au poivre are always good. Raspberry pie in-season inspires requests with reservations. Dinner entrées run $17–24.

Hartstone Inn (207-236-4259 or 1 800-788-4823; hartstoneinn.com), 41 Elm St., Camden. Open year-round. The menu for the five-course, prix fixe dinner ($45) changes nightly—with only one available each night. Menus are on the website, so you can choose what you prefer, perhaps finding seared duck breast with sweet potatoes or grilled swordfish with pesto. Chocolate almond soufflé with crème Anglaise might be dessert. In the off-season, Mon. and Tue. are $24.50 bistro nights.

La Bella Vita Ristorante (207-593-1529; labellavitaristorante.com), Rockport (at Samoset Resort). Open daily for breakfast, dinner, and Sunday brunch, year-round. Veal or chicken Parmigiana is the most popular, but tuna puttanesca, steak, and East Coast halibut with artichokes, capers, and cherry tomatoes on taglialini are also on the menu. Count on a wonderful view. $20–38. Reservations suggested.

EATING OUT

In Camden

✦ ♿ **Peter Ott's** (207-236-4032), 16 Bayview St. Open year-round for casual dinner, with a large menu that features grilled sirloin steak and salmon with maple chipotle glaze. Entrées are served with the salad bar, unless you choose a lighter entrée. $17–31.

✦ ♿ **Camden Deli** (207-236-8343; camdendeli.com), 37 Main St. Open

VIEW FROM THE BACK DECK OF CAMDEN DELI

Nancy English

7 AM–10 PM daily. Breakfast, and more than 40 sandwich choices, combining all the regular deli meats and cheeses as well as some less expected choices, like a pressed Cubano or a Monte Cristo, for lunch. The back dining room overlooks the waterfall in downtown Camden, and another dining room upstairs, with a deck open in summer, does too.

🍴 ♿ **Camden Bagel Café** (207-236-2661), 25 Mechanic St. Open Mon.–Sat. 6:30 AM–2 PM, Sun. 7:30–2. Bagels with substance are baked here, some in whole wheat. The plain interior makes a good refuge as you enjoy a bagel with cream cheese or with an egg and bacon for breakfast. Soups and chili when things cool down.

🍴 ♿ **Cappy's Chowder House** (207-236-2254; cappyschowder.com), 1 Main St. Open year-round—for more than 30 years. Lunch and dinner daily in summer; closing some days in winter. Croissant sandwiches, burgers, and full meals for lunch; seafood entrées, pasta, and meat dishes for dinner.

🍴 ♿ **Elm Street Grill** (207-236-7722), Cedar Crest Motel, 115 Elm St. Open Tue.–Sun. 7 AM–9 PM, fewer days off-season. A great breakfast spot, with a black coffee carafe that stays at your table, house bread with real flavor, and responsive servers quick to help you. For dinner and lunch you can find highly praised pizza and seafood. Entrées $12–16.

🍴 ♿ **The Waterfront Restaurant** (207-236-3747; waterfrontcamden .com), Bayview St. Open for lunch and dinner; you can watch the activity in the harbor. Popular and with a well-trained staff, this place fills up fast and doesn't take reservations, so be prepared to wait. Dinners include a shore dinner (clam chowder, corn on the cob, steamers, mussels, and a lobster) and steaks. $18–24.

🍴 **Boynton-McKay Food Co.** (207-236-2465; boynton-mckay.com), 30 Main St. (in the heart of downtown). Open daily year-round for breakfast, lunch, and takeout, closed Mon. Labor Day–late June. A fun place to have a skillet breakfast, roast turkey wrap, and sometimes fresh croissants. Sit in one of the tall booths in this 1890s-era former apothecary designed by the owner, and relax.

In Rockport

Shepherd's Pie (207-236-8500; shepherdspierockport.com), 18 Central St. A gastropub devised by Francine Bistro chef-owner Brian Hill that serves excellent food. Chefs Mark Senders and Patrick Duffy are in charge of the shepherd's pie made with lamb shanks braised with Madeira, served with buttermilk potato puree; a duck, smoked peanut butter, and hot pepper jelly sandwich was driving people wild in the fall of 2011. Skillet-roasted mussels on fresh cedar fronds gives a new twist to this mainstay. Seasonal tartd tatin. Entrées $13–22.

Sweet Sensations and 3 Dogs Café (207-230-0955; mainesweets.com; 3dogscafe.com), 309 Commercial St. (Rt. 1). Open daily and early in summer; shorter hours in winter. A big, modern building with outdoor seating makes this a great stop. The café and bakery offer dinosaur cookies, meringues, and much, much more. Lunch is soup, salad, and sandwiches— perhaps the Vinalhaven, a BLT with applewood-smoked bacon on organic whole wheat bread. Lunch $7–14.

Enoteca (207-593-1529), at Samoset Resort. Open daily for breakfast, dinner, and Sunday brunch, year-round. Brick-oven fired pizza and Italian-American menu, with a large fireplace indoors and an outdoor firepit on the terrace (open till mid-Sept.) and floor-to-ceiling windows overlooking the water.

LOBSTER ♂ ♿ **Lobster Pound Restaurant** (207-789-5550), Rt. 1, Lincolnville Beach. Open every day for lunch and dinner from the first Sun. in May to mid-Oct. This is a mecca for lobster lovers—some people plan their trips around a meal here. Features lobster, boiled or baked, also clams, other fresh seafood, roast turkey, ham, steaks, and chicken. A family-style restaurant that seats 246 inside and has an outside patio near a sandy beach. Takeout and picnic tables offered across the beach.

Graffam Brothers Seafood (207-236-8391), 211 Union St., Rockport. Open late spring to sometime in Oct. Across the street from the fish store are picnic tables where you can enjoy lobsters, clams, and more. This takeout-only spot serves hand-cut french fries, lobster rolls made with freshly picked lobster, and lobster dinners, with hot dogs, chicken fingers, and salads for alternatives.

TAKEOUT **The Market Basket** (207-236-4371), Rts. 1 and 90, Rockport.

SCOTT'S PLACE, A SOURCE OF FIRST-RATE LOBSTER ROLLS

Nancy English

Open Mon.–Fri. 7–6:30, Sat. 8–6:30, Sun. 9–4. This specialty food store offers a wide variety of creative salads, French bread, soups, entrées, sandwich specials for takeout, more than 500 wines from around the world, and more than 75 varieties of cheese. Baked goods like double chocolate mini cakes are another reason to visit.

🦞 **Scott's Place** (207-236-8751), Elm St. (Renys parking lot), Camden. Open 10:30–4, Mon.–Sat. Since 1974 this tiny building in the parking lot of a small shopping center has served thousands of toasted crabmeat and lobster rolls, chicken sandwiches, burgers, veggie burgers, hot dogs, and chips. Prices are among the best around, and it's open year-round.

✳ Entertainment

Bay Chamber Concerts (207-236-2823; baychamberconcerts.org), 58 Bay View St., Suite 1, Camden 04843. This renowned organization has presented outstanding concerts since 1961. In July and August they sponsor Thursday-evening chamber music concerts in the Rockport Opera House with its gilded interior, and Wednesday-evening concerts at the beautifully restored Strand in Rockland. The series celebrated its 50th year in 2010. Winter-season selections include classical and jazz music concerts and dance performances.

Camden Civic Theatre (207-236-2281; camdencivictheatre.com), Main St., Camden. A variety of theatrical performances are presented in the restored Camden Opera House, a second-floor theater with plum seats and cream-and-gold walls. Tickets are reasonably priced.

♂ ♿ **The Center for Maine Contemporary Art** (207-236-2875; cmcanow.org), 162 Russell Ave., Rockport. Open year-round, Tue.–Sat. 10–5;

also open Sun. 1–5. Call for details about special exhibits. $5 admission for nonmembers; members, children under 18, and Rockport residents free. Promoting contemporary Maine art and artists since 1952 through exhibitions and education. The building, which started out as a late-19th-century livery stable, then became a firehouse, then the town hall, now showcases contemporary Maine art. The gallery sponsors more than 20 shows each season, an art auction, a crafts show, gallery talks, a shop, and an evening lecture series. The shop features a mix of objects for gifts and home use. T-shirts that read FEAR NO ART go for $22.

Everyman Repertory Theatre (207-236-0173; everymanrep.org), Rockport. Noel Coward's *Blythe Spirit* was performed in June 2012 at this nonprofit, professional theater dedicated to fine acting, inspired playwrights, and reasonable ticket prices.

✳ Selective Shopping

Avena Botanicals (207-594-0694; avenabotanicals.com), 219 Mill St., Rockport. Open in summer Mon.–Fri. 9–5, off-season Mon.–Thu. 9–5, Fri. 9–1. Walk in the botanical garden in growing season, when you can drink in the scents serenaded by the chorus of crickets and honeybees. At the apothecary you can purchase creams, salves, teas, and tinctures, during the same hours, year-round. You can also purchase items online. Check the website for the summer schedule of free herb walks with Deb Soule, the herbalist founder of this company, and workshops about herbs.

ANTIQUES At the chamber of commerce, pick up the leaflet guide to antiques shops scattered among Camden, Rockport, and Lincolnville.

ART GALLERIES Bay View Gallery (207-236-4534; bayviewgallery.com), 33 Bayview St., Camden. One of the largest galleries in the Midcoast area. Original paintings and sculptures by contemporary artists working in Maine. Custom framing.

A Small Wonder Gallery (207-236-6005; smallwondergallery.com), 1 Public Landing (across from the chamber of commerce), Camden. A small gallery with well-chosen, limited-edition graphics, watercolors, hand-painted tiles, porcelain, and original sculpture. Custom framing.

Prism Glass Gallery (207-230-0061; prismglassgallery-cafe.com), 297 Commercial St., Rockport. Open Wed.–Sat. 10 AM–9 PM, Sun. 10–8 with exhibits of hand-blown glass.

ARTISANS Windsor Chairmakers (207-789-5188; windsorchair.com), Rt. 1, Lincolnville Beach. Filling two floors of an old farmhouse are Windsor chairs and tables, highboys, and four-poster beds, all offered in a selection of finishes. A gallery in a wing of the connected farmhouse shows a line of Shaker-style furniture. Visitors can tour the workshop to see furniture being made.

Maine Artisans (207-789-5376), Rt. 1, Lincolnville Beach. Open daily May–Oct., this charming store sells work by weavers, potters, and sock makers, among others.

The Foundry (207-236-3200; remsen .com), 531 Park St., West Rockport (next to the Baptist church). Richard Remsen makes 20-inch-long fishing lures out of handblown glass that are outfitted with metal hardware, some shaped like Hawaiian tube fish.

Michael Good Gallery (1-800-422-9623; michaelgood.com), 325 Commercial St. (Rt. 1), Rockport. Original and extraordinary pottery, jewelry, sculpture, and accessories.

BOOKSTORES ㅎ **Down East** (207-594-9544), Rt. 1, Rockport. The headquarters for Down East Enterprises (publishers of *Down East*, *Fly Rod & Reel*, and *Shooting Sportsman* magazines, as well as a line of New England books) is located in a handsome old mansion that includes a bookshop, open 8–5 Mon.–Fri. year-round.

♪ **The Owl and Turtle Bookshop** (207-236-4769 or 1-800-876-4769), 32 Washington St. (one block north of Rt. 1 on Rt. 105), Camden. One of Maine's best bookstores, located in an old mill with old maple floors and dark wood bookcases, and a reading corner by a fireplace. The children's room has a little wishing well with a Plexiglas window children can peer through to the Megunticook River. One room holds one of the best selections of marine books on the East Coast, along with nautical charts for sailors. Maine history, travel, and art. Frequent author book signings.

Sherman's Books (207-236-2223 or 1-800-803-5049; shermans.com), 14 Main St., Camden. Another in the fine chain of Sherman's bookstores on the Maine coast, Camden's branch has expanded in its new, sun-filled location and is packed with books, toys, puzzles, cards, and gifts.

Book Case Mystery Book Shop (207-236-4457), 28 Bay View St., Camden. Selling mostly new mysteries, this shop specializes in complete series—the books by Daniel Silva, whose Israeli spy operates undercover as an art restorer, are an especially popular purchase.

SPA The Spa at Samoset (207-593-1575; samosetresort.com), Rockport. Four treatment rooms for services that

include couple's massage, an outdoor retreat for after-treatment relaxation, and an indoor room that allows meditation and tea sipping, overlooking Penobscot Bay.

SPECIAL SHOPS

All shops are in Camden and open year-round unless otherwise noted

♪ **Once a Tree** (207-236-3995; once atree.net), now on 31 Main St. Fine woodworking, with Maine-made wooden bowls, cutting boards, American-made products from the functional to the unusual.

Chocolatier Blue (207- 619-3932; chocolatierblue.com/location.aspx), 12 Bayview St. Berkeley, Nebraska, and now Maine enjoy this fine chocolate maker's products, made with raw organic butter and Italian Domori chocolate and featuring maple syrup, apple cider, and cardamom in some of the assortments.

♪ **The Smiling Cow** (207-236-3351; smilingcow.com), 41 Main St. Seasonal. Three generations ago a mother and five children converted this stable into a classic gift shop, one with unusual warmth; members of the fifth generation are now employed inside. We like the Maine-themed items like fragrant, locally made soaps.

The Cashmere Goat (207-236-7236; thecashmeregoatknit.com), 20 Bayview St. Drop-in classes will get you started on the project the soft irresistible cashmere will inspire you to undertake. Alpaca fiber, wool, cotton, too.

♨ **Heavenly Threads** (207-236-3203), 57 Elm St. (Rt. 1). Open Mon.–Fri. 10–4, Sat. 10–1, closed Mon. off-season. Wealthy summer folks and locals both donate to this extremely clean shop full of surprising finds. We found clothes by Ann Taylor, Calvin Klein, and others for under $5 per garment, as well as books and housewares in excellent shape. Also men's and children's clothing, jewelry, gift items, and coffee-table books. Proceeds benefit Habitat for Humanity, Coastal Hospice, Rockland Soup Kitchen, and others. Call with an email address to receive notices of sales.

Ducktrap Bay Trading Company (1-800-560-9568; ducktrapbay.com), 37 Bayview St. Many of these pieces—decoys, wildlife and marine art, scrimshaw, and paintings—have earned awards for their creators.

Danica Candleworks (207-236-3060), 569 West St. (Rt. 90), West Rockport. In a building with a Scandinavian-inspired exterior especially pretty when it snows, you'll find a candle factory and a shop that sells high-quality hand-dipped and scented candles and accessories.

✳ Special Events

February: **US National Toboggan Championships**—teams from all over the country compete in two-, three-, and four-person races, often in costume (Camden Snow Bowl); **Winterfest**; and **Camden Conference**.

March: **Maine Maple Sugar Sunday**.

Mid- to late July: **Annual Open House and Garden Day**, sponsored by the Camden Garden Club. Very popular tour of homes and gardens in Camden and Rockport held every year for five decades. **Summer Harbor-**

Arts, a juried arts and crafts show (third Saturday and Sunday), Camden Harbor Park. **The Annual Hope Jazz Festival**, Hope.

August: **The Center for Maine Contemporary Art's Annual Art Auction**—Maine's largest exhibit and auction of quality contemporary Maine art. **Merryspring's Annual Kitchen Tour**—see uniquely designed kitchens in Camden, Rockport, and Lincolnville, plus demonstrations and tastings.

Late August: **Union Fair** and **Blueberry Festival**, Union Fairgrounds (see "Rockland/Thomaston Area").

Labor Day weekend: **Camden Windjammer Festival**, Camden Harbor. A celebration of the windjammer industry, featuring a parade of boats, music, nautical history, fireworks, and the Schooner Bum Talent Contest.

October: **Fall HarborArts**, a juried arts and crafts show, Camden Harbor Park—75 artisans displaying work for sale. **Work of the Hand**, juried crafts show and sale at Center for Maine Contemporary Art (207-236-2875; cmcanow.org), Rockport. **VinFest**, Cellardoor Winery, Lincolnville. **Lincolnville Fall Festival**, Lincolnville. **POP!Tech!**, Camden.

First weekend in December: **Christmas by the Sea**—tree lighting, Santa's arrival, caroling, holiday house tour, refreshments in shops.

December: Rockport Garden Club **Holly Berry Fair**.

A 14-mile-long, string-bean-shaped island just 3 miles off Lincolnville Beach (a 20-minute ferry ride), Islesboro is a private kind of place, best visited with a car or a bicycle.

There are three distinct communities on the island. The town of Islesboro with the necessary services (town office, post office, health center, and fire department) sits in the center between Dark Harbor and Pripet. Dark Harbor (described by Sidney Sheldon in his best seller *Master of the Game* as the "jealously guarded colony of the super-rich") has long been a summer resort village, where huge "cottages" peek from behind the trees along the road to Pendleton Point. Pripet is a thriving year-round neighborhood of boatbuilders and fishermen.

GETTING THERE Take the car-carrying **Maine State Ferry** (207-789-5611 or 207-734-6935); $10 roundtrip per passenger, $27.50 per vehicle, and $8.50 for a bicycle, with reservations from the mainland or island available for a fee. The ferry lands mid-island at Grindle Point. The crossing is a 3-mile, 20-minute ride, the schedule depending on the season. If you go for a day trip only, pay close attention to when the last ferry leaves the island to avoid being stranded. At the landing you'll find a clean ferry terminal with public restrooms. When you board the Maine State Ferry, ask for a map and schedule. The detailed and informative island map shows a full view of the island as well as business locations, a ferry schedule, a brief description of the island, and a historical society events calendar.

GUIDANCE The **Islesboro town office** (207-734-2253), 150 Main Rd., is a great source of information, with friendly service both on the phone and in person.

WHEN TO COME Only in summer will visitors be able to visit a bookstore, one café, and a historical society museum with a gallery.

✳ To See and Do

The old lighthouse on **Grindle Point** (built in 1850, now automated) and keeper's cottage now house the seasonal **Sailors' Memorial Museum** (207-734-2253), open July–Labor Day, 9:30–4:30, closed Wed. and Sun. Look for summer musical and theatrical performances at the **Free Will Baptist Church**. Check out the **Up Island Church**, a fine old structure with beautiful wall stencils and fascinating old headstones in the adjacent graveyard.

The layout of the island makes at least a bicycle necessary to get a real feel for the place. The roads are narrow, winding, and have no shoulder. Bicyclists should use great caution. Even so, after both driving and biking the island, we prefer biking. A drive from one end of the island to the other is a nice way to spend a couple of hours, but on bicycles, it'll take you most of a day. In Dark Harbor you'll see huge "cottages" and impressive architecture. In summer you'll also find a very few shops for browsing, including the **Dark Harbor Shop** (207-734-8878), with souvenirs, gifts, ice cream, and a deli. "We haven't changed in 35 years—it's disgusting," said owner Bill Warren, laughing. Open daily the Friday of Memorial Day weekend to Labor Day. A picnic area and town beach at Pendleton Point have spectacular views. The trip down the other side of the island will take you past the **Islesboro**

Historical Society (207-734-6733) in the former high school, a beautiful stone building, which houses an annual arts and crafts show and weekly exhibits on the first floor and a permanent collection upstairs.

✳ Lodging

The Islesboro town office (207-734-2253) can refer you to local real estate agents who handle cottage rentals. As of late 2011, there were no inns or B&Bs open on the island.

✳ Where to Eat

You can often pick up a snack (breakfast specials, burgers, lobster rolls, and such for lunch and dinner) at a take-out stand at the far end of the ferry terminal parking lot. The luncheonette in the **Dark Harbor Shop** (207-734-8878), open daily from the Friday of Memorial Day weekend to the Sunday before Labor Day, serves ice cream, deli sandwiches, and breakfast items, with gifts and souvenirs for sale. It's a local gathering place for breakfast, lunch, and ice cream sundaes all summer long. **Durkee's General Store** (207-734-2201) and **The Island Market** (207-734-6672) both sell sandwiches and pizza. The Island Market also has a big wine selection.

✳ Selected Shopping

Artisan Books and Bindery (207-734-6852; artisanbooksandbindery .com), 111 Derby Rd., Dark Harbor Village on Islesboro. Open year-round. A nice little bookstore with new books and some used books, with coffee and muffins served, cigars for sale, and custom binding done at the small bindery. Used and rare books. Open summer afternoons and differing hours off-season. Call ahead.

BELFAST, SEARSPORT, AND STOCKTON SPRINGS

B elfast's long, Victorian brick Main Street slopes steadily downward, away from Rt. 1, toward the confluence of the tidal Passagassawakeag River and Belfast Bay.

With just 7,100 residents and a small-town feel, Belfast is a city and the seat of Waldo County. Magnificent Greek Revival and Federal homes, proof of early prominence, line High and Church Streets. Lower blocks suggest a checkered commercial history that included a sarsaparilla company, a rum distillery, a city-owned railroad, and, most recently and memorably, poultry slaughtering and shipping.

An artist in one of Belfast's burgeoning galleries observes: "You have to want to come here. People who turn off Rt. 1 and take the downhill plunge are looking for something." What they find is a mix of boutiques and basic shops, cafés, restaurants, and hometown eateries, a supermarket-sized health food store, a funky old movie house, and live theater, as well as B&Bs that could charge twice as much down the road in Camden.

High above downtown Belfast, Rt. 1 crosses the Passagassawakeag River into East Belfast, threading a string of shops, restaurants, and a mix of 1940s motor courts and motor inns with water views.

In Searsport Rt. 1 becomes, suddenly and briefly, a mid-19th-century brick-and-granite downtown. Stop at Mosman Park, with its picnic tables and playground right on Penobscot Bay (just down Water Street), for a sense of place. Then visit the Penobscot Marine Museum to learn that more than 3,000 different vessels have been built in and around Penobscot Bay since 1770. Searsport alone launched eight brigs and six schooners

DOWNTOWN BELFAST

Kim Grant

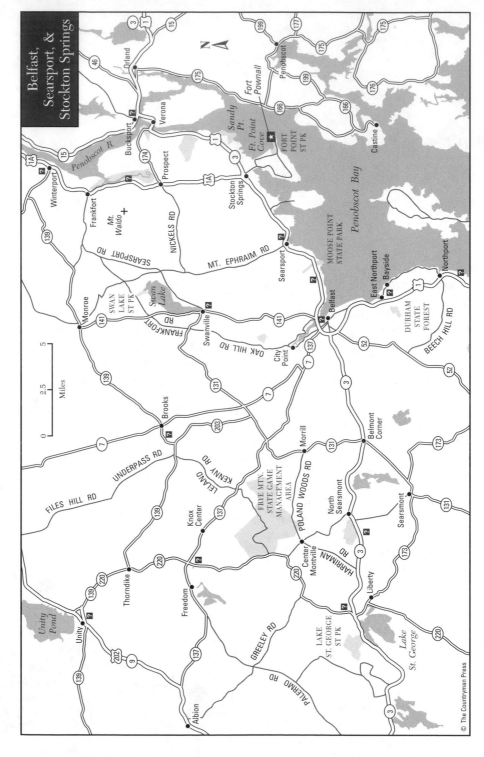

Belfast, Searsport, & Stockton Springs

© The Countryman Press

BELFAST WATERFRONT

Nancy English

in one year (1845), and for many years boasted more sea captains than any other town its size, explaining the dozens of 19th-century mansions lining Rt. 1. What you don't see from the highway is Sears Island and its deepwater harbor, for which a series of projects has been planned in recent decades.

If you have the time, take the scenic route to this region from Augusta, poking through the communities of Unity, Thorndike, and Brooks, detouring to Liberty then down to Belfast. Rt. 1 continues to shadow the shore as it narrows into what seems more like a broad river.

GUIDANCE **The Belfast Area Chamber of Commerce** (207-338-5900; belfast maine.org), P.O. Box 58, Belfast 04915, maintains an information center at 14 Main St. near the waterfront; open daily June–mid-Oct., 10–6; mid-Oct.–May, Mon.–Fri. 9–2.

GETTING THERE *By air:* For commercial service, see "Rockland/Thomaston," "Bangor," and "Portland."

By car: The most direct route to this region from points south and west is via I-95, exiting in Augusta and taking Rt. 3 to Belfast. Exit 113 on I-95 accesses a connector to Rt. 3, offering motorists bound for the Midcoast a way around Augusta. If you're coming up Rt. 1, take the first turnoff for downtown Belfast. The approach is down Northport Ave. and Belfast City Park, then down High St.

By bus: **Concord Coach Lines** (1-800-639-3317; concordcoachlines.com) stops in both Searsport and Belfast.

PUBLIC RESTROOMS At the public landing at the bottom of Main Street, open May to mid-Oct.

WHEN TO COME The town chugs along through winter, with most inns and restaurants open throughout the year; still, the summer season gives the ocean a friendlier look and fills the farm stands. Come to Belfast anytime to enjoy the downtown, but wait for warm weather to sail, visit the wonderful museum, and eat seafood along the shore.

✳ Villages

Brooks. In the center of this quiet county, surrounded by hills, this town has the most scenic golf course around.

Liberty, straddling Rt. 3, is home to Lake St. George State Park and to the extraordinary **Liberty Tool Company** (207-589-4771; jonesport-wood.com), Main St. Open June–mid-Oct., daily, fewer days off-season, closed Jan. and Feb. and reopening in Mar. with a big sale on the first Saturday. Antique and used tools, and every other thing that you can imagine—clocks, lanterns, books, postcards. Tools for sale can be looked at Sat. morning or call 888-405-2007. The octagonal Liberty post office, located across the street from Liberty Graphics, dates to 1867 and houses the Liberty Historical Society (207-589-4393), open weekend afternoons in July and Aug. **Liberty Graphics** (207-589-4035; libertygraphicstshirts.com), Main St., open daily in summer, fewer days off-season, sells T-shirts, including organic cotton versions, printed with water-based designs from nature and designs by Frank Lloyd Wright.

Northport. A low-key community with pleasure boats in the harbor and golf clubs, as well as a mid-19th-century former Methodist campground with hundreds of gingerbread cottages on the bay.

Unity. Home to a rural college, a raceway, and the fairgrounds for the popular late-September Common Ground Fair.

Stockton Springs. Rt. 1 now bypasses this former shipbuilding town. Follow East St. down to Fort Point.

✴ To See

MUSEUMS ✐ **Penobscot Marine Museum** (207-548-2529; penobscotmarine museum.org), Rt. 1, Searsport. Open May–mid-Oct., Mon.–Sat. 10–5 and Sun. noon–5. $8 adults; children 7–15 are $3. Family rate $18. (The library is open Mon.–Fri. 9–1.) The 13 buildings include 8 on the National Register of Historic Places. The museum shop is at the entrance to the complex on Rt. 1. More than 50 small craft, one of the largest collections in New England, are on display, including peapods, dories, canoes, and lobster boats. A meticulously restored ship captain's home re-creates prosperous Maine coast life in the 19th century, while a commercial fishing exhibit in Searsport's original town hall shows the working side of the maritime community. Other artifacts show the changing faces of Maine, from the Wabanaki natives to the shipbuilders of the 1800s. Gorgeous nautical paintings convey the ship-worship of a time when fortunes were made when the ships came in. The galleries in the **Captain Jeremiah Merithew House** hold a world-class collection of paintings by father, son, and grandson marine artists Thomas Buttersworth (Sr. and Jr.) and James Buttersworth, whose depictions of ships in storm and calm are luminous and exciting. The museum displays scrimshaw-carved whales' teeth, ships' models, and artifacts of the China trade. Tours include scheduled visits to the adjacent First Congregational Church to view glorious stained-glass windows and a 100-year-old organ with over 1,000 pipes. Three children's activity areas include a "marine science lab," a ship's capstan, and a large-scale model of a square-rigger's mast and sails that kids can manipulate. Other exhibits focus on the working-class people who made their living in the granite, lime, ice, lumber, and tourism industries; a "visible storage" area gives visitors a look at a rotating display of items.

Davistown Museum (207-589-4900; davistownmuseum.org), 58 Main St., Liberty. Skip Brack, meticulous owner of Liberty Tool Company, has sorted out the finest antique tools of his collection to create this museum above Liberty Graphics. Its specialty is a collection of signed shipbuilders' edge tools. The marriage of tools, art, and history is the theme of this unique collection. Contemporary Maine artists, 108 artists in total, exhibit their work in this space, and a permanent collection is also on display, most in the top floors. As the website states, the art and artifact combination at Davistown Museum "is unique among Maine's museums and galleries." Native American artifacts. Children can make a sculpture out of odds and ends gathered from the tool store. Suggested donation $3.

Belfast Historical Society and Museum (207-338-9229; belfastmuseum.org), 10 Market St., Belfast. Open mid-June–mid-Oct.; in summer Tue.–Sat. 11–4, from Labor Day Fri.–Sat. 11–4; by appointment year-round. Local artifacts, paintings, and changing exhibits. A ship's model of the *Charlotte W. White* has been restored for display. A self-guided "Museum-in-the-Streets" walking tour is installed downtown.

Safe Harbor Church, Rt. 1, Searsport. Phone 207-548-6663 or pick up the key across the street and check out the fabulous stained-glass windows in this church, built in 1815. It's now maintained as a meditation space, and holds regular services.

Bryant Wood Stove Museum (207-568-3665; bryantstove.com), 27 Stovepipe Alley (junction of Rts. 220 and 139), Thorndike. Open year-round, Mon.–Sat. 8–4:30. What began as a stove shop has evolved into a fascinating museum. The front room is crammed with restored woodstoves (for sale). Walk through these to the doll circus, with its array of mechanical, musical dolls from Barbie to Disney characters and everything in between. The back room houses a collection of player pianos, nickelodeons, and vintage automobiles. Worth the drive.

SCENIC DRIVE Rt. 3, past Lake St. George and Sheepscot Pond, through the China Lakes region, is the most direct path between Belfast and Augusta, but take time to detour down Rt. 173 to **Liberty** to see the octagonal post office and the **Liberty Tool Company** and **Davistown Museum** (see *Museums*). For a leisurely tour of the villages between Belfast and Augusta, head north from East Belfast on Rt. 141 to Monroe. Ask for directions to **Stone Soup Farm** to see their gardens, then check out **Monroe Falls**, just off Rt. 139, and maybe have a picnic. Head out on Rt. 139, through Brooks, and then on toward Thorndike, where you'll want to stop at the **Bryant Museum**. Continue on Rt. 139 to Unity, where you'll pass the new home of the Common Ground Fair. Follow Rt. 139 into Kennebec County to Fairfield to meet up with I-95, or detour yet again onto Rt. 202, which will bring you through the China Lakes region to Augusta.

✳ To Do

BERRY PICKING Staples Homestead Blueberries (207-567-3393 or 207-567-3703), 302 Old County Rd., Stockton Springs. Turn at the ball field on Rts. 1/3, then drive 3 miles to the T at County Rd.; turn right. Open 8–5 daily while its certified organic berries are in-season (Aug.). Friendly owners Basil and Mary Staples will instruct you in the mysteries of blueberry raking, then let you go to it, or you can pick by hand.

BOAT EXCURSIONS Downeast Windjammer Cruises (207-546-2927; downeastwindjammer.com), Thompson Wharf, Belfast. The *Patience* cruises Penobscot Bay daily June–Sept., offering a choice of itineraries.

Miss Nina (207-505-1618; sailingmissnina.com), Belfast Harbor. June–Oct. 1, sail this 61-foot wooden ketch with Captain Dan and Amy Miller for half- and full-day charters; six-passenger maximum.

GOLF Country View Golf Club (207-722-3161) in Brooks is the most scenic in the area: nine holes, par 36, cart and club rentals, lessons, clubhouse. **Northport**

Golf Club (207-338-2270), Northport. A fully irrigated nine-hole course, pro shop, snack bar, driving range, and rentals.

KAYAKING Water Walker Sea Kayaks (207-338-6424; touringkayaks.com), Belfast. Ray Wirth, a Registered Maine Guide and ACA-certified open-water instructor, offers tours ranging from several hours in Belfast Harbor or around Sears Island to full-day trips to other islands to overnight trips.

SWIMMING Lake St. George State Park (207-589-4255), Rt. 3, Liberty. Open May 15–Oct. 15. A great way station for travelers going to or from Down East. A deep, clear lake with a small beach, lifeguard, bathhouse, parking facilities, 38 campsites with a new shower facility, and a boat launch. **Swan Lake State Park**, Rt. 141, Swanville (north of town; follow signs), has a beach with picnicking facilities. **Belfast City Park**, Rt. 1, Belfast (south of town), holds a swimming pool, tennis courts, picnicking facilities, and a gravel beach. **Sandy Point Beach**, off Rt. 1 north of Stockton Springs (it's posted HERSEY RETREAT; turn toward the water directly across from the Rocky Ridge Motel).

TRAINS Belfast and Moosehead Lake Railway (brookspreservation.org), Upper Bridge Station, High St., Belfast. Train rides leave the station twice a day on weekends in summer, taking passengers over 7 miles of track and bridges along the harbor and river.

WINERY Winterport Winery (207-223-4500; winterportwinery.com), 279 S. Main St., Winterport. Open May–Dec., Tue.–Sat. 11–5; Mar.–Apr., Fri.–Sat. 11–5; closed Jan.–Feb. Taste the wine and ales from Penobscot Bay Brewery. A line of ice cream made with Half Moon Stout is worth sampling, too.

✳ Green Space

Also see Lake St. George State Park and Belfast City Park under *Swimming*.

Moose Point State Park, Rt. 1, south of Searsport. Open May 30–Oct. 15. A good spot for picnicking; cookout facilities are in an evergreen grove and an open field overlooking Penobscot Bay. Also check out **Mosman Park** in downtown Searsport with its playground and picnic benches by tidal pools and the public landing.

Fort Pownall and Fort Point State Park, Stockton Springs (marked from Rt. 1; follow the 3.5-mile access road). The 1759 fort built to defend the British claim to Maine (the Penobscot River was the actual boundary between the English and French territories) was burned twice to prevent its being taken; only earthworks remain. The adjacent park, on the tip of a peninsula jutting into Penobscot Bay, is a fine fishing and picnic spot.

CANOEING BY BELFAST HARBOR

Nancy English

Sears Island. After decades of debate about the future of this island (it was slated to be a container port, nuclear power plant site, LNG port, and more), it's open to the public. There are 940 acres and around 5 miles of shorefront to explore, just as migratory birds do. Good for walking, biking, kayaking, and fishing; visit the sand beaches to view the Camden Hills. It's connected to the mainland by a causeway. Off Rt. 1, take Sears Island Rd.

Carleton Pond Waterfowl Production Area, Troy. Part of the Maine Wildlife Refuge System. One thousand acres are accessible by canoe or kayak. Unstaffed. Contact the Maine Coastal Islands Wildlife Refuge Rockport office (207-236-6970), P.O. Box 495, Rockport 04856, for information and for regulations on duck and geese hunting.

✻ Lodging

RESORTS ☙ Point Lookout (207-789-2000 or 1-800-515-3611; visitpoint lookout.com), 67 Atlantic Hwy., Northport (on the Lincolnville line). Open year-round. The 106 luxurious one-, two-, and three-bedroom cabins at Point Lookout, a gorgeous setting, started their existence as a corporate retreat, built by MBNA in the mid-1990s. In 2008 these pine-paneled cabins were transformed into a resort. Each one holds a cable TV/DVD, a propane fireplace, and a screened porch, and more than half have cooking facilities; a small number have ocean views. **Copper Pine Café** takes care of breakfast and lunch, perhaps a panini with fresh mozzarella and tomatoes. Catered meals can be arranged for 5 to 300. Fitness center with massage and Zumba and yoga classes offered, plus bowling, racquetball, virtual golf, an artificial turf soccer field, a baseball field, and hiking trails. Bone-density tests and more, part of the Erickson Institute of Vital Aging Assessment Program, are a specialty. $129–189 off-season, $189–299 in high season.

INNS AND BED & BREAKFASTS

In Belfast 04915
The Belfast Bay Inn (207-338-5600; belfastbayinn.com), 72 Main St. Ed and Judy Hemmingsen, former owners of the Bluenose Inn in Bar Harbor, have transformed a brick building on Main Street into a boutique hotel that pulls out all the stops. The eight luxury rooms are filled with gorgeous upholstered furniture and plush beds, art, refrigerators, cable TV/DVD; some have views of the harbor, fireplace, dining area, and/or a balcony. Suite 301 has a two-sink granite bathroom, and 303 includes a deck overlooking rooftops. Breakfast in a garden courtyard. Spa services. $198–378.

The Alden House (207-338-2151 or 1-877-337-8151; thealdenhouse.com), 63 Church St. This gracious 1840 Greek Revival mansion holds Italian marble mantels and sinks and a circular staircase inside its substantial walls. Larry Marshal and Rosemarie Cyr are the innkeepers overseeing the six guest rooms—five with private bath—a charming open porch, and comfortable furnishings. A working fireplace is the Hiram Alden Room. $129–179 includes a full breakfast, served at separate tables.

The Jeweled Turret Inn (207-338-2304 or 1-800-696-2304; jeweledturret .com), 40 Pearl St. Open year-round. A handsome 1890s gabled and turreted house that's ornate inside and out, with a fireplace in the den said to be made of stones from every state in the Union at that time. This now lovely house suffered neglect before Carl and Cathy Heffentrager began transforming it in 1986, reviving its first glory and restoring the wood stairs and decking of the stone-edged verandas, where guests love to lounge in rockers and a swing. The Topaz Turret Room lies inside the octagonal turret with a window seat, and the Amethyst Turret Room has a cannonball four-poster bed. Full breakfast and afternoon sherry with cheese and crackers. $130–169.

The White House (207-338-1901 or 1-888-290-1901; mainebb.com), 1 Church St. The pillared facade of this 1840 Greek Revival mansion with its octagonal cupola is strikingly handsome, set off by a triangular front lawn in the V between Church and High Sts. Diana and Santiago Rich are proud hosts of the six, elaborate guest rooms, all with phone, private bath, Frette linens, and a cable TV/DVD. The Coastal Escape Room is the most modern; Belfast Bay has an enormous bathroom and crystal chandeliers. (The Bates bedspread comes from Bates Mill in Lewiston, another great Maine

THE WHITE HOUSE

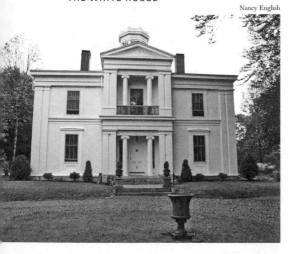

Nancy English

spot.) Rates are $175–250 per couple, including a full breakfast.

In Searsport 04974

○ **Carriage House Inn** (207-548-2167; carriagehouseinmaine.com), 120 E. Main St. (Rt. 1). Three rooms with private bath are available in this 1874 Victorian home built by sea captain John McGilvery. It was later owned by impressionist Waldo Peirce, whose friend Ernest Hemingway visited often. Peirce painted Hemingway's portrait many times during their 40-year friendship. Two of the painter's works hang in the room named for him, which also has a view of the sea. A loft space, Peirce's studio—paneled with oak and pine, with full kitchen and bath and room for six—rents for $750 a week. Gardens and 200 books on tape. Rates $115–140, less Nov.–mid-May, with full breakfast.

1794 Watchtide By the Sea (207-548-6575 or 1-800-698-6575; watchtide.com), Rt. 1. This bright house faces the sea with a 19-windowed sunporch. The five guest rooms each have a private bath, TV, AC, and small fridge. Eleanor Roosevelt slept here several times when this was the College Club Inn (opened in 1917), and her namesake ocean-view room has a two-person Jacuzzi and skylight. $140–190 in high season, $125–175 off-season, includes breakfast. Owners Frank and Patricia Kulla, chefs in former lives, might serve sweet potato pancakes with nectarine butter and spiced pecans.

Captain A. V. Nickels Inn (207-548-1104; captain-a-v-nickels-inn.com), 127 E. Main St. (Rte. 1), Searsport. Open Mar.–Dec. Brenda and Michael Liston bought this inn in 2011 and gave it a complete renovation, upgrading the seven bedrooms and suites (all with private bath) with European antiques, flat-screen TV, and more. Each room is named for a city: Paris, with a four-posterbed, wine-red walls, and white moldings, is our top choice. Twin parlors, a library, and a porch are fine places for relaxation. Overnight guests receive three-course breakfast and wine and cheese in the afternoon. $135–195. Two resident terriers.

COTTAGES ✦ **Bayside Village**, built in the 1800s, has about 50 cottages on Penobscot Bay in Northport rented by the week by Bayside Cottage Rentals (207-338-5355; baysidecottagerentals .com). Margaret Lacoste's agency is open spring, summer, and fall, renting the cottages out for between $550 and $1,595 a week May–mid-Oct. Originally a Methodist campground, the cottages are ornately trimmed with Victorian gingerbread, some with stone fireplace. The village offers a main common, a swim float and dock on the pebble beach, sailing lessons, and a little yacht club with children's activities in summer.

MOTELS 🐾 ✦ **Ocean's Edge Comfort Inn** (207-338-2090 or 1-800-303-5098), 159 Searsport Ave. (Rt. 1), Belfast 04915. Usually we wouldn't include a Comfort Inn in our listings, but the location of this three-story facility is terrific. All 83 units (with two queen beds, king beds, or suites) have a balcony overlooking the bay; amenities include a full-service restaurant, guest laundry, indoor "mineral" pool (no chlorine) with sauna and hot tub, and lobby computer. $89–329 in summer includes continental breakfast; less off-season. Try the two-night specials in winter midweek—the pool is heated to 86 degrees.

🐾 ✦ **Belfast Harbor Inn** (207-338-2740 or 1-800-545-8576; belfastharbor inn.com), 91 Searsport Ave. (Rt. 1), Belfast 04915. Set back from Rt. 1 on 6 acres of lawn that stretch to the rim

of the bay, this is an inviting, independently owned two-story motel with 61 units. Price depends on location—from (heated) poolside to ocean view. A generous continental breakfast is included for all rooms. Top rate of $159 in high season, less late Sept.–late June.

✳ Where to Eat

DINING OUT Delvino's Grill & Pasta House (207-338-4565; delvinos .com), 52 Main St., Belfast. Open daily. The Italian classics are made well at Delvino's, where you can also dine on a blue cheese burger, fresh fish, or rib eye. Local buffalo and Maine beef are usually offered. Or try the mushroom sacchetti—pasta stuffed with portobello and porcini mushrooms and cheeses, topped with peppered cream sauce. House desserts change daily. Entrées $8–22.

The Captain's Table and **The Captain's Wine Lounge at Captain A. V. Nickels Inn** (207-548-1104; captain-a -v-nickels-inn.com), 127 E. Main St. (Rt. 1), Searsport. Open Mar.–Dec. Reservations recommended; no table is turned over at this restaurant dedicated to relaxed, fine dining. Three- and four-course meals from a changing menu might include Captain's Pepper Steak with cognac cream sauce, or champagne chicken. $30–40 depending on the number of courses. Entrées from The Captain's Table or a cheese plate or sandwiches ($5–20) can be enjoyed in the lounge, with has a fabulous view of the ocean. The business is building a fine wine list.

EATING OUT Chase's Daily (207-338-0555), 96 Main St., Belfast. Breakfast and lunch Tue.–Sat., dinner Fri. from 5:30, Sun. brunch 8–1. This high-ceilinged restaurant features enticing produce from the owners' Chase Farm in Freedom, sold in the back. The freshness of the ingredients and the great cooking combine to make the vegetarian fare wonderful. Thin-crusted Marguerite pizza with fresh tomatoes and pools of melted mozzarella is great in late summer, as are soft corn tacos stuffed with black beans, spicy pepitas, feta, crema, shredded cabbage, and lime. Freshly baked bread and treats like sunken chocolate cake for dessert. Meals $7–19.

✪ **Three Tides** (207-338-1707; 3tides .com), 2 Pinchy Lane, Belfast. Open Tue.–Sat. from 3 PM, Sun. 1–8, later opening in winter. A fun spot with a serpentine concrete bar and an outdoor deck over the river, where you can drink special cocktails and eat pizzettes ($8.50), salads, and quesadillas. The oysters, mussels, steamers, and lobsters are very fresh; the lobsters are from their own lobster pound. The **Marshall Wharf Brewing Company**, on the premises, offers exceptional micro-brews; Cant Dog Imperial IPA is a "hops monster," exhilarating and bitter.

✐ ♿ **The Ocean's Edge Restaurant** (207-338-2090), 159 Searsport Ave., Belfast. Open daily 4–9, closed Sun. off-season. Not just an amenity for the Comfort Inn to which it's attached, this spot is a local favorite given the view, the service, and the menu, which ranges from chicken and broccoli Alfredo with fettuccine to surf and turf. Entrées $10–28. Children's menu.

Darby's Restaurant and Pub (207-338-2339), 155 High St., Belfast. Open daily for lunch and dinner. A storefront café with tin ceilings and local artwork. A reasonably priced dinner might include pecan haddock with mojito sauce, or a black bean enchilada "smothered in cheddar and Ranchero sauce." Soups, salads, and sandwiches are served all day. Entrées $8–22.

Nancy English

CHOCOLATE PEAR TARTS AT CHASE'S DAILY

Papa J's & The Lobster Bar (207-338-6464), 191 Searsport Ave., Belfast. Open Tues.–Sat. 4–9 in-season only. The Pemaquid mussels grow on a platform visible from the dining room, and are served steamed with garlic. Lobster pizza is "serious comfort food," says Kelley Marston, manager. Feta lobster is in the same category, mixed with penne pasta. Over 100 wines are on the list, priced from low to high.

✐ **Anglers** (207-548-2405), Rt. 1, Searsport. Open daily 11–8. Buddy Hall's Maine-style diner serves seafood that ranges from chowder to fried and broiled fish dinners to lobster every which way. "Land Lovers" get chicken Parmesan, barbecued ribs, and prime rib, and the Minnow Menu is for "the smaller appetite" (you don't have to be small). Entrées $7–30.

Bay Wrap (207-338-9757; baywrap .com), 20 Beaver St. (off Main), Belfast. Open daily for lunch and dinner, except Sun., closing earlier in winter. An eatery with a next-door coffee shop called the Hub, where you can eat the wraps. On a foggy day we feasted on warm grilled eggplant with roasted red peppers, ricotta and feta cheeses, mint, field greens, and salsa verde ($7.95 for large).

Bell the Cat (207-338-2084), Renys Plaza, Rt. 3, Belfast. Open 7:30–7:30, Sun. 9–5. Set inside a spacious upfront corner of Mr. Paperback, this is the local, very casual favorite for designer sandwiches; from breakfast sandwiches to a fat Reuben. Also good for salads, soups, and ice cream. Coffees and teas. This little café has a cultlike following—among adults.

Seng Thai (207-338-0010), 139 Searsport Ave. (Rt. 1), Belfast. Open daily (except Mon.) from 11:30. Not your ordinary Thai. Residents warn you not to try level-five spiciness. Newly established in a larger building with a great view of the bay, Seng Thai is as creative and brilliant in the kitchen as ever. Dinner entrées $9–14.

Also see **Belfast Co-op** under *Selective Shopping*.

ICE CREAM Scoops (207-338-3350), 35 Lower Main St., Belfast. A comfortable place to rest and recoup with ice cream. The (homemade) chocolate chip cookie sundae with Round Top Dairy ice cream and hot fudge is $5.50, and a fruit-filled crêpe topped with honey ice cream is $5.75. In Liberty, Maine, on Rt. 3, you will find possibly the best ice cream in the state of Maine at **John's Ice Cream** (207-589-3700), 510 Belfast Augusta Rd. (Rt. 3) This is why you may very well choose to drive to this area via I-95 to Augusta and Rt. 3. Lemon custard; mandarin orange chocolate; strawberry rhubarb; espresso anise swirl.

BEER AND SUPPLIES Marshall Wharf Brewing Store (207-338-1707; marshallwharf.com), 2 Pinchy Lane, Belfast. Call for hours. This is the brewery store for Marshall Wharf Brewery, selling growlers or half gallons of whatever is on tap, as well as kegs by special order.

Nancy English

JOHN'S ICE CREAM, LIBERTY

LOBSTER POUND ❂ **Young's Lobster Pound** (207-338-1160), Mitchell Ave. (posted from Rt. 1 just across the bridge from downtown Belfast), East Belfast. Open in-season 7–9, and year-round (winter closing at 5:30) for live and cooked lobsters, crabs, clams, and mussels, or takeout. A pound with as many as 30,000 lobsters, and seating (indoor and outdoor) to accommodate 500. The view of Belfast across the Passagassawakeag River is beautiful. They pick the lobster meat here fresh every day for the lobster rolls

DANNY MCGOVERN, BREWER AT MARSHALL WHARF

Nancy English

✳ Entertainment

Marsh River Theater (207-722-4110; marshrivertheater.com), Rt. 139, Brooks. Community theater performed in historic Union Hall. This group formed in the mid-1990s and has been offering performances ever since.

🎭 **The Playhouse** (207-338-5777), 107 Church St., Belfast. A cozy 36-seat theater offering plays for adults as well as children. Founder Mary Weaver teaches acting, directs, and performs.

The Colonial Theater (207-338-1930; colonialtheater.com). The new home of the outsized carved elephants from a local landmark, Perry's Nut House; three screens with nightly showings in a restored theater in downtown Belfast.

✳ Selective Shopping

ANTIQUES SHOPS Searsport claims to be the Antiques Capital of Maine. **The Searsport Antique Mall**, 149 E. Main St., open more or less daily year-round, is a cooperative of more than 70 dealers, spread over two floors. **The Pumpkin Patch Antiques Center** (207-548-6047), 15 W. Main St., a 12-dealer shop, has been in business since 1975, run by Phyllis Sommer, and is widely respected. Cindy Gallant runs the **Hobby Horse Flea Market** (207-548-2981, 379 E. Main St.), which fills a 3-acre complex with five retail stores. A flea market surrounds it every day but Tue., and it's open May–Columbus Day. Two other Searsport flea markets are held weekends in-season. **Captain Tinkham's Emporium** (207-548-6465; jonesport-wood.com), 34 Main St., next to the Penobscot Marine Museum store, is where you can find antique and functional tools, as well as books, records, sheet music, and other finds from the cellars, attics, and workshops of New England. Open daily in summer, Sat. year-round.

BlueJacket Ship Crafters (207-548-9974 or 1-800-448-5567; bluejacketinc .com), 160 E. Main St., (Rt. 1), Searsport. The to-scale ship models, from starting kits to custom commissions, are made in Maine. Beginners undertaking the *Red Baron*, a Holland 32 lobster boat built in Belfast, for instance, will be able to call Charlie Cook if they need advice assembling the kits. The company began in 1904 under the name of the founder, H. E. Boucher. The radio-controlled pond yacht *Osprey* can go for a spin, a voyage that will be guided by Michael de Lesseps's expert, engaging instruction.

BOOKSTORES 🐾 **Left Bank Books** (207-548-6400; leftbankbookshop .com), 21 E. Main St. (Rt. 1), Searsport. A cup of tea or coffee is waiting for you here, along with 5,000 select titles, from great mysteries to Arctic explorations. This handsome and welcoming bookstore also sells reproduction maps and vintage cards. Well-mannered dogs always welcome.

Penobscot Books (207-548-6490; penobscotbooks.com), 164 W. Main St., Searsport. Open May–Oct., and Christmas. With art, architecture, and photography books, more than 50,000 titles, this store sells to universities and libraries all over the world.

Victorian House/Book Barn (207-567-3351), 290 Main St., Stockton Springs. Open every day of the year. A landmark collection of 20,000 antiquarian books, and a special find for mystery-book buffs.

GALLERIES, ETC. A leaflet guide to all current Belfast galleries is available at any one of them. Don't miss **The Art Alliance Gallery** (207-338-9994), 39 Main St., a cooperative gallery for 7 to 10 very different and interesting artists; the **Parent Gallery** (207-338-1553; nealparent.com), 92 Main St., displaying fine black-and-white photographs by Neal Parent, and pastels and oils by daughter Joanne; **High Street Studio and Gallery** (207-338-8990; highstreetgallery.com), 149 High St., featuring Susan Tobey White's many-peopled landscapes and amazing doll sculptures. **Waterfall Arts** (207-338-2222; waterfallarts.org), 256 High St., is an arts organization offering classes, residencies, and exhibits in Belfast at Clifford Gallery and Fallout Shelter Gallery. **Aarhus Gallery** (207-338-0001; aarhusgallery.com), 50 Main St., contemporary and unique art.

SPECIAL SHOPS

In Northport
Swan's Island Blankets (207-338-9691; swansislandblankets.com), 231 Atlantic Hwy. (Rt. 1), Northport. The old looms are in use in the back room, visible through a window from the elegant showroom, near which a few of the natural sources of dye stand in jars. But the real draw is the soft, beautiful, expensive blankets. Sheep may be grazing in the field near the store, but their wool isn't used in the blankets. Organic, naturally dyed, imported merino yarn is for sale.

In Belfast
Belfast Co-op Store (207-338-2532; belfast.coop), 123 High St. Open daily 7:30 AM–8 PM. Everyone needs something in this store and café with its standout deli and lunches. **Coyote Moon** (207-338-5659), 54 Main St., is a nifty, reasonably priced women's clothing and gift store. **All About Games** (207-338-9984), 78 Main St., is a great place to buy traditional board games; **The Game Loft**, 78A Main, over the store, is a youth center where kids can play non-electronic games for free. **Colburn Shoe Store** (207-338-1934), 79 Main St., bills itself as the oldest shoe store in America, open

Nancy English

SWAN'S ISLAND BLANKETS DYED WOOL

since 1832. **Renys** (207-338-4588), Renys Plaza, Rt. 3 just north of the junction with Rt. 1, is one in Maine's chain of distinctive outlet stores. Always worth a stop (good for everything from TVs to socks).

North along Route 1
Perry's Nut House (207-338-1630), Rt. 1 just north of the Belfast Bridge. Reopened and working on being what it used to be. The nut collection is in the Smithsonian. The man-eating clam cannot be located. **Mainely Pottery** (207-338-1108; mainelypottery.com), 181 Searsport Ave. (Rt. 1), features the

SWAN'S ISLAND BLANKET SHOWROOM

Nancy English

work of owner Jamie Oates and carries varied work by 30 other Maine potters.

In Searsport

Silkweeds (207-548-6501), Rt. 1, Searsport. Specializes in "country gifts": tinware, cotton afghans, wreaths. **Waldo County Craft Co-op** (207-548-6686), 307 E. Main St. (Rt. 1), Searsport Harbor. Open mid-May–mid-Oct. daily 9–5, weekends till Christmas. A showcase for the local extension service. Eclectic birdhouses, baskets, wooden crafts, quilts, pillows, jams, ceramics, and more.

✳ Special Events

May–October: **Belfast Farmer's Market** 9–1 on Friday on Front Street by the waterfront.

June–October: **Friday Night Art Walk**.

July: On the 4th, parade, fairs, and fireworks in Searsport; **Arts in the Park**; and the **Celtic Festival**.

July–August: Free Thursday-night **street concerts** in downtown Belfast.

August: **Searsport Lobster Boat Races** and related events; **Marine Heritage Festival & Boatbuilding Challenge**.

September: ✪ **Common Ground Fair** in Unity—organic farm products, children's activities, sheepdog roundup, crafts, entertainment.

ORGANIC PRODUCE AT BELFAST FARMER'S MARKET

October: First Sat., **Church Street Festival** and parade; **Fright at the Fort**, when Fort Knox is haunted.

Columbus Day weekend: **Fling into Fall celebration**—parade, bonfire, church suppers.

December: **Searsport Victorian Christmas**—open houses at museums, homes, and B&Bs; **New Year's by the Bay**.

Down East 4

EAST PENOBSCOT BAY REGION
Bucksport/Orland Area; Castine;
Blue Hill Area; Deer Isle, Stonington,
and Isle au Haut

ACADIA AREA
Mount Desert Island; Acadia National
Park; Bar Harbor and Ellsworth;
The Quiet Side of Mount Dessert

EAST HANCOCK COUNTY

WASHINGTON COUNTY
AND THE QUODDY LOOP
The Bold Coast: Steuben to Campobello
Island (New Brunswick); Eastport,
Cobscook Bay, and Passamaquoddy Bay;
Calais and the Downeast Lakes Region;
St. Andrews and Grand Manan
(New Brunswick)

Nancy English

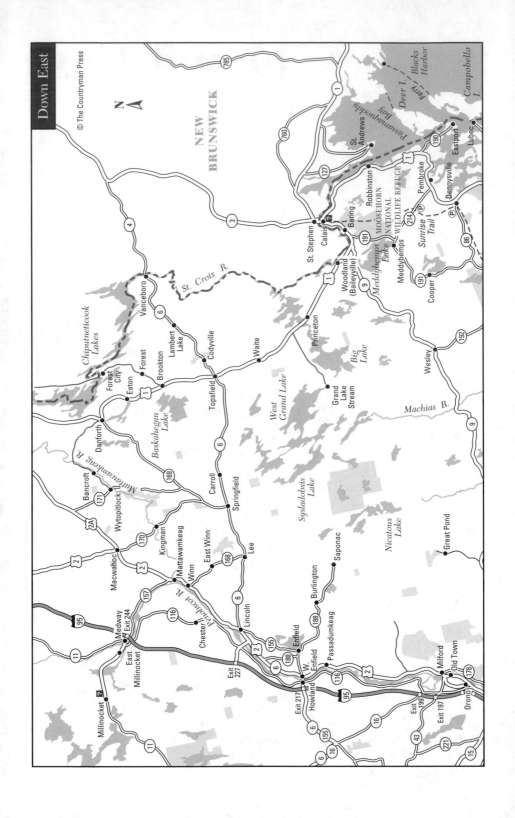

© The Countryman Press

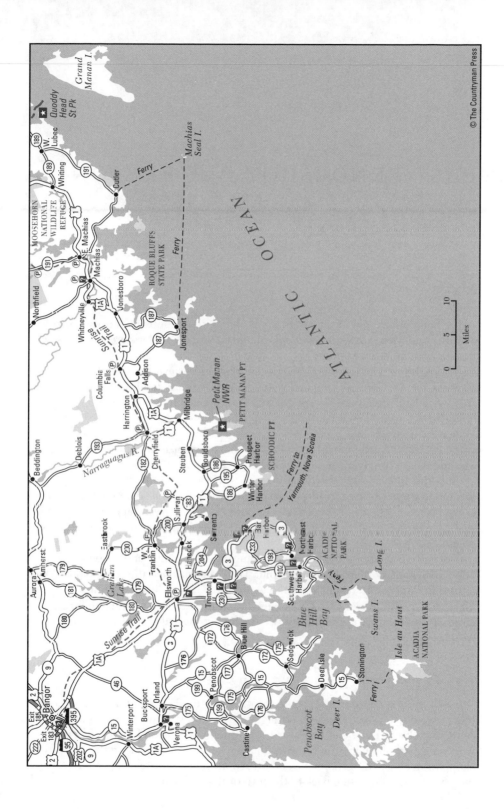

© The Countryman Press

Grand Manan I.

Quoddy Head St Pk

W. Lubec

Whiting

Ferry

Machias Seal I.

Cutler

MOOSEHORN NATIONAL WILDLIFE REFUGE

Northfield

E. Machias

Machias

Jonesboro

ROQUE BLUFFS STATE PARK

Whitneyville

Sunrise Trail

Ferry

ATLANTIC OCEAN

Jonesport

Beddington

Columbia Falls

Addison

Harrington

Milbridge

Petit Manan NWR

PETIT MANAN PT

Deblois

Narraguagus R.

Cherryfield

Steuben

Gouldsboro

Prospect Harbor

SCHOODIC PT

Eastbrook

Sullivan

Sorrento

Winter Harbor

Ferry to Yarmouth, Nova Scotia

Aurora

Amherst

W. Franklin

Hancock

Bar Harbor

Northeast Harbor

ACADIA NATIONAL PARK

Graham Lake

Ellsworth

Trenton

Southwest Harbor

Long I.

Sunrise Trail

Blue Hill Bay

Swans I.

Isle au Haut

Bangor

Exit 185

Exit 183

Winterport

Bucksport

Orland

Penobscot

Blue Hill

Sedgwick

Deer Isle

Stonington

ACADIA NATIONAL PARK

Verona

Castine

Penobscot Bay

Deer I.

Ferry

0   5   10
Miles

EAST PENOBSCOT BAY REGION

BUCKSPORT/ORLAND AREA; CASTINE; BLUE HILL AREA; DEER ISLE, STONINGTON, AND ISLE AU HAUT

The dramatic new Waldo-Hancock bridge at the Penobscot Narrows links two counties and Midcoast with Downeast Maine. It visually underscores the sense of turning a major coastal corner.

The series of peninsulas and islands defining the eastern rim of Penobscot Bay—an intermingling of land and water along ponds and tidal rivers, as well as bays—is a landscape that's exceptional, even in Maine. Seasonal home to the state's largest concentration of artists and craftspeople, writers and musicians, it's no longer the undiscovered backwater described in earlier editions of this book. On summer days the gallery- and shop-lined main streets of Blue Hill, Castine, and Stonington are thronged, and reservations are essential at the best restaurants.

Still, the area is webbed with narrow roads threading numerous land fingers, leading to studios of local craftspeople and artists. What you remember afterward is the beauty of clouds over fields of wildflowers, quiet coves, some amazing things that have been woven, painted, or blown, and conversations with the people who created them.

Getting anywhere here takes longer than you'll anticipate, and it's best to allow a few days here, perhaps one on the Blue Hill Peninsula, another on Deer Isle and a third in Castine . In recent years the wealth of places to hike has greatly increased, and it's easier than ever to get out on the water, via excursion boat or kayak. Do try to get to Isle au Haut with its hiking trails at Dark Harbor, part of Acadia National Park.

BUCKSPORT/ORLAND AREA

Whoosh and the elevator sets you 45 stories above the Penobscot River, atop one of the two obelisk-like pylons anchoring Maine's newest bridge at the confluence of the Penobscot River and Penobscot Bay. Bucksport, beyond the bridge, is a workaday river and paper mill town with a mile-long walkway along the waterfront, shopping, a choice of restaurants, and a 1916 movie theater/museum showcasing New England films dating back to the turn of the 20th century.

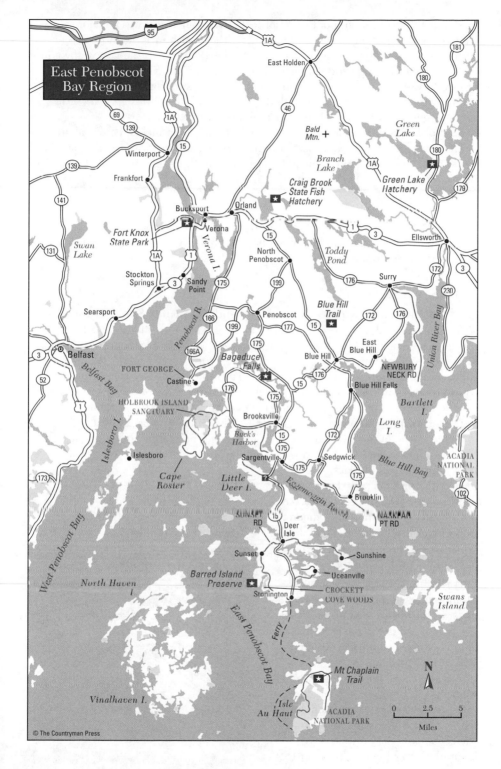

East Penobscot Bay Region

95

1A

1A

181

East Holden

180

69

139

180

Green Lake
Lake

139

15

Winterport

180

Bald
Mtn. +

Branch
Lake

1A

Green Lake
Hatchery

179

141

Frankfort

Craig Brook
State Fish
Hatchery

1A

Bucksport

Orland

1

3

Ellsworth

Verona I.

Fort Knox
State Park

Verona

North
Penobscot

Toddy
Pond

172

3

131

Swan
Lake

1A

1

15

15

199

176

Surry

230

Stockton
Springs

3

Sandy
Point

175

Blue Hill
Trail

172

176

Searsport

Penobscot R.

166

199

Penobscot

177

15

East
Blue Hill

Union River Bay

3

Belfast

166A

Bagaduce
Falls

175

Blue Hill

NEWBURY
NECK RD

52

FORT GEORGE

Castine

176

176

15

Blue Hill Falls

Bartlett
I.

Belfast Bay

HOLBROOK ISLAND
SANCTUARY

Brooksville

172

Long
I.

Isleboro I.

Buck's
Harbor

15

175

Blue Hill Bay

ACADIA
NATIONAL
PARK

Islesboro

Sargentville

175

Sedgwick

175

173

Cape
Rosier

Little
Deer I.

?

Eggemoggin Reach

NASKEAG
PT RD

102

Brooklin

SUNSET
RD

15

West Penobscot Bay

North Haven
I.

Deer
Isle

Sunshine

Sunset

Barred Island
Preserve

Oceanville

Swans
Island

CROCKETT
COVE WOODS

Stonington

East Penobscot Bay

Ferry

Mt Chaplain
Trail

N

Vinalhaven I.

Isle
Au Haut

ACADIA
NATIONAL PARK

0   2.5   5

Miles

© The Countryman Press

Positioned at the mouth of the Penobscot River, Bucksport was a major ship-ping port in 1764, the reason it was burned by the British in 1799 and was then occupied by them during the War of 1812. In the 1820s it was the largest town in eastern Maine (its population is currently just over 3,800). Note the former Jed Prouty Tavern in the middle of Main Street, a dining stop for Daniel Webster and half a dozen presidents down through the years. Bucksport overlooks New Eng-land's biggest fort, dwarfed by its most dramatic bridge.

East of Bucksport the town of Orland offers more than meets the eye along Rt. 1. The village itself overlooks the Narramissic River, and in East Orland, Alamoo-sook Lake is just north of the highway, accessible to the public from the Craig Brook National Fish Hatchery with its innumerable salmon, visitors center, swim-ming, and hiking trails.

GUIDANCE Bucksport Bay Area Chamber of Commerce (207-469-6818; bucksportchamber.org), 52 Main St. Open May–Sept. Mon.–Fri. 10–5; Mon., Wed., Fri. off-season. Brochures available 24 hours.

✳ To See and Do

𝄂 ✎ ♿ **Penobscot Narrows Observatory and Fort Knox State Historic Site** (207-469-6553 or 207-469-7719; fortknox.maineguide.com), Rt. 174 (off Rt. 1), Prospect. The observatory is open daily May–Oct. 31, 9–5, until 6 in July and Aug. $7 adults ($5 for Maine residents), $3 ages 5–11; fort only: $5 adults, $2 seniors, $3 children. West of the Waldo-Hancock bridge a traffic light eases access to the Fort Knox grounds, site of the elevator up to the observatory. Access is limited to 49 vis-itors at any one time, so at the parking-lot gate you receive a ticket stamped with a "go time." In July and August expect a wait. On a sunny Sunday we just had time to picnic at one of the tables overlooking the river, but a larger group might well have had time to explore the fort first. The elevator whisks you to the top in a minute (it's had its off days). Far below, Bucksport is a toy town, and from another window Penobscot Bay sweeps away to the horizon. Theoreti-cally you can see 40 miles in all direc-tions. This is the only bridge with an observatory in the country.

Fort Knox guided tours are available Memorial Day–Labor Day, then week-ends. In the visitors center interpreta-tive panels tell the story: Built in 1844 of granite cut from nearby Mount Waldo, the fort includes barracks, storehouses, a labyrinth of passage-ways, and picnic facilities. The fort was to be a defense against Canada during the Aroostook War with New Bruns-wick. The boundary dispute was ignored in Washington, and so in 1839 the new, lumber-rich state took matters

PENOBSCOT NARROWS BRIDGE

Christina Tree

Bill Davis

VIEW OF FORT KNOX FROM BUCKSPORT WATERFRONT

into its own hands by arming its northern forts. Daniel Webster represented Maine in the 1842 treaty that formally ended the war, but Maine built this fort two years later, just in case. It was never entirely completed and never saw battle. Troops were, however, stationed here during the Civil War and again during the Spanish-American War. This is a great fort with plenty of tunnels and turrets to explore. It's a venue for reenactments and a wide variety of events, sponsored by Friends of Fort Knox, every weekend, beginning with a Civil War cannon firing in June, ranging from Shakespeare performances to a pirate invasion, ending with "Fright of the Fort" nights on the two weekends before Halloween. Check the website. This is also a weddings venue.

Northeast Historic Film/The Alamo Theatre (207-460-0924; oldfilm.org), 85 Main St., Bucksport (entrance on Elm). This 125-seat, vintage-1916 restored theater is open year-round, featuring first-run movies, Dolby digital sound, low prices, and real buttered popcorn. It is also a venue for concerts and live performances. Call for showtimes. The theater was restored by nonprofit Northeast Historic Film, New England's only "moving-image" archive. Stock footage, technical services, and sales of videos of life in New England are all available. The theater store is open during business hours (weekdays 9–4) as well as weekends in July and Aug. during films and

ALAMO THEATRE, BUCKSPORT

Christina Tree

performances. The office is at 279 Main St. (207-469-0914); check the website for available films.

Bucksport Historical Society Museum, Main St., Bucksport. Open July–Aug., Wed.–Fri. 1–4, and by appointment: 207-469-3284. Housed in the former Maine Central Railroad Station by the water with some genuinely interesting displays, including one about town founder Colonel Jonathan Buck, whose grave (Rt. 1, north of downtown, across from Hannaford's Supermarket), a granite obelisk, is a longtime tourist attraction. The outline of a leg on the stone has spurred many legends, the most popular being that a woman whom Judge Buck sentenced to death for witchcraft is carrying through on a promise to dance on his grave.

Craig Brook National Fish Hatchery, (207-469-2803), 306 Hatchery Rd., East Orland (marked from Rt. 1). First opened in 1871, this is the country's oldest salmon hatchery. A visitors center (open daily 8–3) offers videos and interactive displays on Maine rivers, watersheds, and salmon. A small Atlantic Salmon Museum (open daily noon–3 in summer) exhibits salmon industry memorabilia. The facility also includes a boat launch on Alamoosook Lake, a picnic area and swim beach on Craig Pond, and hiking/skiing trails.

✳ Lodging

🐾 ✪ 🖊 ((ᵧ)) **Alamoosook Lakeside Inn** (207-469-6393 or 1-866-459-6393; alamoosooklakesideinn.com), 229 Soper Rd., Orland 04472. Open year-round. A few miles north of Rt. 1, this log lodge—built as a corporate retreat by the local paper company—feels much farther away. Grounds stretch for a quarter mile along the lake and you can swim off the beach or push out, as we did before breakfast, and

VIEW OF BUCKSPORT FROM FORT KNOX
Bill Davis

paddle out among the islands offshore. Innkeeper Gina Bushong, a former environmental scientist with the EPA, likes to help guests explore off the beaten path. There are six attractive guest rooms, all in a row, with easy access to the outdoors. The lake is good for fishing; in winter it's cleared for ice fishing and cross-country skiing. $95–139 per couple with full breakfast. The dining room, jutting out into Alamoosook Lake, is a popular spot for weddings.

Fort Knox Park Inn (207-469-3113; fortknoxparkinn.com), 64 Main St., Bucksport 04416. Open year-round. Built as a modern annex to the old Jed Prouty Inn, offering motel-style rooms with two double beds and several queen suites. Request a water view. It includes Fort Knox across the mouth of the Penobscot River. $79–149 per couple, depending on the season, includes continental breakfast.

✳ Where to Eat

🖊 ((ᵧ)) **MacLeods** (207-469-3963), 63 Main St., Bucksport. Open Tue.–Sun.

4–close, also lunch from 11:30 Tue.–Fri. Dependable dining in a pubby atmosphere with booths. Dinner entrées ($11–22) range from comfort food like baked meat loaf and barbecued ribs to specials like a baked scallop strudel.

⌗ Harbor View Grille (207-469-3396), 96 Main St., Bucksport. Open daily 6 AM–8 PM. Sited on the town dock, it overlooks water, Fort Knox, and the bridge. Reasonably priced seafood baskets and specials and a full road-food menu. Kids' menu, too.

Wahl's Dairy Port (207-469-3697), 79 Main St., Bucksport. Open Apr.–late Sept., 11–8. For more than 50 years this old-fashioned ice cream stand has been dishing it up: many flavors of ice cream (Giffords), also soft serve, frozen yogurt, sherbet, shakes, more.

✳ Selective Shopping

h.o.m.e. co-op (207-469-7961; home coop.net), Rt. 1, Orland. Open daily 9–5. A remarkable complex that includes a crafts village (visitors can watch pottery making, weaving, leather work, woodworking); a museum of old handicrafts and farm implements; a large crafts shop featuring handmade coverlets, toys, and clothing; and a market stand with fresh vegetables, herbs, and other garden produce.

Book Stacks (207-469-8992 or 1-888-295-0123; bookstacksmaine.com), 71 Main St., Bucksport. Open Mon.–Sat. 9–6 (later in summer), Sun. 9–4. Not what you would expect to find on this brief Main Street: an inviting full-service bookstore with a cyber café.

Rosen's (207-374-2227), 3 Main St., Bucksport. In business since 1910, an old-fashioned family clothing stores. We finally found the socks we were looking for.

✳ Special Events

Note: Check with **Friends of Fort Knox** (fortknox.maineguide.com) for colorful events at the fort, staged most weekends Apr.–Oct. Halloween is huge here.

Late July: **Bay Festival**—parade, plus a variety of events on the river; at the fort and along the Bucksport waterfront.

July–August: **Bucksport Riverfront Market** every Sat. 9–3. Art, crafts, baked goods, and produce.

August: h.o.m.e.'s **Annual Craft & Farm Fair and Benefit Auction** (207-469-7961; homecoop.net) A Saturday blueberry pancake breakfast, poetry readings, music, fish-fry supper, street dance, BBQ, children's games, crafts, and more.

CASTINE

In Maine, *Blue Hill* refers to a specific hill, a village, a town, and a peninsula—also to an unusual gathering of artists, musicians, and craftspeople. A shade off the beaten path, one peninsula west of Mount Desert, Blue Hill has its own following—especially among creative people.

While the bulk of the Blue Hill Peninsula wanders away to the southeast, one finger of land points down along the Penobscot River toward the bay. Rt. 175, the first turnoff from Rt. 1 for the Blue Hill Peninsula, shadows the river, leading to a mini peninsula with Castine at its tip. Sited at the confluence of the Penobscot and Bagaduce Rivers, the town still looms larger on nautical charts than on road maps. Yacht clubs from Portland to New York visit annually.

Christina Tree

CASTINE

Castine has always had a sense of its own importance. According to the historical markers that pepper its tranquil streets, it has been claimed by four different countries since its early-17th-century founding as Fort Pentagoet. It was an early trading post for the Pilgrims but fell into the hands of Baron de Saint Castine, a young French nobleman who married a Penobscot Indian princess and reigned as a combination feudal lord and Indian chief over Maine's eastern coast for many decades.

Since no two accounts agree, we won't attempt to describe the outpost's constantly shifting fortunes—even the Dutch owned it briefly. Nobody denies that in 1779 residents (mostly Tories who fled here from Boston and Portland) welcomed the invading British. The Commonwealth of Massachusetts retaliated by mounting a fleet of 18 armed vessels and 24 transports with 1,000 troops and 400 marines aboard. This small navy disgraced itself absurdly when it sailed into town in 1779. The British Fort George was barely in the making, fortified by 750 soldiers with two sloops as backup, but the American privateers refused to attack and hung around in the bay long enough for several British men-of-war to come along and destroy them. The surviving patriots had to walk back to Boston, and many of their officers, Paul Revere included, were court-martialed for their part in the disgrace. The town was occupied by the British again in 1814.

Perhaps it was to spur young men on to avenge this affair that Castine was picked (150 years later) as the home of the Maine Maritime Academy, which occupies the actual site of the British barracks and keeps a training ship anchored at the town dock, incongruously huge beside the graceful, white-clapboard buildings of a very different maritime era.

In the mid-19th century, thanks to shipbuilding, Castine claimed to be the second wealthiest town per capita in the United States. Its genteel qualities were recognized by summer visitors, who later came by steamboat to stay in the eight hotels. Many built their own seasonal mansions. Castine remains one of Maine's most photogenic coastal villages, the kind writers describe as "perfectly preserved." Even the trees that arch high above Main Street's clapboard homes and shops have managed to escape the blight that felled elms elsewhere, and Castine's post office is the oldest continuous operating post office in the country (since 1833). Current population hovers around 1,300, including the 700 Maine Maritime Academy students, but it roughly doubles in summer. Two of the hotels survive, and one baronial mansions is now an inn. The town dock is unusually welcoming, complete with picnic tables, parking, and restrooms. It remains the heart of this walking town, where you can amble uphill past shops or down along Perkins Street to the Wilson

Museum. While the remainder of the Blue Hill Peninsula has become notably more touristed in recent years, Castine seems to have become less so.

GUIDANCE Castine Merchants Association produces a helpful map/guide, available on request from the town office (207-326-4502) or around town. Also check the town's website, **castine.me.us**, as well as penobscotbay.com. A good place to begin exploring is the **Castine Historical Society** on the common.

GETTING THERE See "Blue Hill Area," but turn off Rt. 1 onto Rt. 175 in Orland and follow signs for Castine.

WHEN TO COME Museums are highly seasonal, but the Maritime Academy contributes to the sense of a college town, a pleasant place to stay through October.

✴ To See

Historic District. All of downtown Castine is on the National Register of Historic Places. Pick up the pamphlet *A Walking Tour of Castine*—it's free, available at shops—and walk out along Perkins Street and up along Maine to Battle Avenue. Don't miss:

Castine Historical Society (207-326-4118; castinehistoricalsociety.org), Abbott School Building, Castine town common. July–Labor Day, Tue.–Sat. 10–4; from 1 on Sun. The permanent exhibit here is a multimedia presentation about the 1779 Penobscot Expedition (see chapter introduction). Special exhibits and events throughout the summer.

The Wilson Museum (207-326-8545; wilsonmuseum.org), 120 Perkins St. Open daily May 27–Sept. 30, 10–5 weekdays, 2–5 weekends; free. This handsome waterside building houses the amazing collections amassed by geologist J. Howard Wilson, a summer resident. These include prehistoric artifacts from North and South America, also ancient artifacts from Africa and Oceana, vintage-1926 dioramas depicting life in prehistoric and Native American cultures, collections of minerals, stones, and shells, early firearms, tools, and farm equipment, an 1805 kitchen, and a Victorian parlor. The complex also includes a 19th-century **Blacksmith Shop** and the **John Perkins House**, open July and Aug., Wed. and Sun. 2–5 (admission for Perkins House): a pre–Revolutionary War home, restored and furnished in period style. Check the website for changing exhibits, wood-turning and blacksmithing demonstrations, frequent special events.

Fort George, Battle Ave. Open May 30–Labor Day, daylight hours. The sorry tale of its capture by the British during the American Revolution (see the chapter introduction) and again during the War of 1812, when redcoats occupied the town for eight months, is told on panels at the fort—an earthworks complex of grassy walls (great to roll down) and a flat interior where you may find Maine Maritime Academy cadets being put through their paces.

State of Maine (207-326-4311), town dock. When in port, the training vessel for Maine Maritime Academy is usually open to visitors daily from the second week in July until mid-Aug.; 30-minute tours on the hour 10–6 are conducted by midshipmen (allow an hour), subject to security checks and alerts. Tours on weekends during the academic year. If this is your prime reason for coming to Castine, call to check if tours are being offered.

✳ To Do

GOLF AND TENNIS Castine Golf Club (207-326-8844), Battle Ave. Offers nine holes and four clay courts.

SEA KAYAKING Castine Kayak Adventures (207-866-3506; castinekayak .com), Sea St., beyond Dennett's Wharf. Karen Francoeur offers half- and full-day trips plus a number of "unique adventures" such as sunrise and phosphorescent paddles, and "intermediate adventures" to the Bagaduce reversing falls and around Cape Rosier. Also overnight camping and B&B tours and workshops ranging from beginning skills to advanced coastal navigation. This is also the area's only source of **bike rentals**.

SAILING EXCURSIONS Vintage Yacht *Guildive* (207-701-1421; guildive cruises.com), Dennett's Wharf. Launched in 1934, this 56-foot vessel has sailed far and wide, mostly as a private yacht. She's now based at Dennett's Wharf restaurant, offering two and three-hour sails and full-day excursions to the Penobscot Marine Museum in Searsport.Seating in both the pilothouse and on deck.

✳ Green Space

Witherle Woods is an extensive wooded area webbed with paths at the western end of town. The ledges below Dyce's Head Light, also at the western end of town, are great for clambering. The Castine Conservation Commission sponsors nature walks occasionally in July and Aug.; check local bulletin boards.

✳ Lodging

In Castine 04421

Three inns, each different enough from the others to offer very real choices.

🐾 (ᵀ) **Pentagoet Inn** (207-326-8616 or 1-800-845-1701; pentagoet.com), 26 Main St., P.O. Box 4. Open May–Oct. A very Victorian summer hotel with a three-story turret, gables, wraparound porch, and striped awnings. Over the past dozen years Jack Burke and Julie VandeGraaf have restored this vintage-1894 Queen Anne–style building room by room. They've added exceptional food, and created inn with rare warmth and personality. Jack presides behind an oak counter in the **Passports Pub**, one of Maine's more unusual rooms. It's papered floor-to-ceiling in photos, paintings, and memorabilia depicting the likes of Lenin, Gandhi, and Queen Elizabeth, collected during this innkeeper's previous life in the foreign service. Guest rooms are unusually shaped and furnished in comfortable, period antiques—ornately carved headboards and marble-topped dressers— but there's nothing creaky here: good mattresses, serious showers. In all there are 16 guest rooms, most on the second and third floors of the inn, several in the neighboring 18th-century "cottage." There's a cheerful sitting room, a flowery veranda, and a garden. $125–285 during high season with full buffet breakfast. $25 for pets. Amenities include bicycles and a guest computer. (Also see *Dining Out*.)

Castine Inn (207-326-4365; castine inn.com), P.O. Box 41, 33 Main St. Open May–Oct. Also dating from the 1890s, but with an entirely different look and feel than the Pentagoet. Guests enter a wide, welcoming hallway

Christina Tree

PENTAGOET INN, CASTINE

spacious Pine Tree with its king canopy bed, fireplace, and sitting porch. Both are hands-on hosts with Tom at the front desk (or behind the bar) and Nancy presiding over the kitchen. She is also respected Iyengar yoga teacher, and guests are permitted to participate in scheduled classes (we slid into the back row and heartily recommend doing likewise). Rates include a full breakfast and drop to $95–165 in spring and fall, less in winter. Pets are $25 per stay. See *Dining Out* for the restaurant and pub.

Rental cottages are available through Jean de Raat Realty (207-326-8448; deraatrealty.com) and Castine Realty (207-326-9392).

✳ Where to Eat

All listings are in Castine
DINING OUT Pentagoet Inn (207-326-8616), 26 Main St. Open for dinner in-season. Reservations advised. The rose-colored dining room glows with candlelight in the evening. There are white tablecloths and garden flowers on the well-spaced tables, with more seating, weather permitting, on the veranda. Tables are also set for dinner in **Passports Pub** (see *Lodging*). Chef Gina Melita is well known for preparing locally sourced seafood and produce in unpretentiously delicious ways. We split a big bowl of rope-cultured mussels, steamed in white wine with garlic, shallots, fresh herbs, and chili flakes, followed by seared scallops served on potato puree with curry butter, green apple relish, and braised vegetables. House specialties include lobster linguine and lobster bouillabaise. Entrées $24–28; "Bistro plates" ($12–16) are also available. Don't pass up dessert.

The Manor Inn (207-326-4861), Battle Ave. Open for dinner Valentine's Day–New Year's, Thu.–Sat. off-season. A former enclosed porch has been

with an old-style check-in desk. There's a pleasant sitting room and a pub, both with frequently lit fireplaces. A mural of Castine by a previous innkeeper covers all four walls of the dining room, and French doors open onto a broad veranda overlooking the extensive garden. The village slopes away below and the 10 rooms on this side of the building all enjoy harbor views. All 19 second- and third-floor rooms have private bath; renovation is planned over the winter of 2011–12 for all. $110–195 for rooms, $175–195 for two-room suites (with a sleep sofa in the second room), including a full breakfast.

☃ (ᵂⁱ) **The Manor Inn** (207-326-4861; manor-inn.com), 76 Battle Ave. Open year-round except Christmas–Valentine's Day. This expansive 1890s stone-and-shingle mansion sits off above the village on its own lawns, which border conservation land. Tom Ehrman and Nancy Watson have restored and maintain this Gilded Era "cottage" with 14 guest rooms. These range widely in size and price, from $110 for twin-bedded Dices Head to $295 for expanded into an appealing dining room overlooking the sweeping front lawn and gardens. Co-owner Nancy Watson is the chef. The crabcakes are a family recipe, served as an entrée with mustard and aioli sauces. Other choices on the daily-changing menu might include seared sesame-wasabi-crusted tuna and aged beef from the local butcher. Entrées $15–33. Full liquor license, and pub food in the appealing **Pine Cone Pub**.

Stella's Restaurant (207-326-9710), 26 Water St. Open for dinner daily in July and Aug.; Tue.–Sat. in shoulder months. Reservations advised. There's seating for 40 in this attractive new dining and music space above Bah's Bake House (see *Eating Out*). The menu ranges from light to elaborate fare, and the specialty of the house is frequent live jazz. Entrées $20–30.

EATING OUT Dennett's Wharf (207-326-9045), Sea St. (off the town dock). Open daily May–Columbus Day, 11–11. An open-framed, harbor-side structure said to have been built as a bowling alley after the Civil War, this is the town's informal gathering place. There's a big all-day menu with plenty of salads as well as seafood and BBQ back ribs. The home brew is Wharf Rat Ale. Entrées $16–25.

Bah's Bake House (207-326-?), Water St. Open 7 AM–3 PM daily in-season. A few tables and a great deli counter featuring sandwiches on baguette bread, daily-made soups, salads, and baked goods.

✪ **The Breeze** (207-326-9200), Town Dock. May–Sept. 6 AM–8 PM. When the summer sun shines, this tiny takeout is the best place in town to eat—and not just lobster rolls, fried clams, hot dogs, and soft serve. Native Hawaiian owner Snow Logan offers unexpected delicacies: Hawaiian "Lokomoko," Japanee

chicken salad, miso soup, and combinations like fresh crabmeat and avocado. The public facilities are next door and, with luck, you can dine at the picnic tables on the dock.

T&C Grocery (207-326-4818), 12 Water St. Open 7–9, until 8 Sun. This well-stocked market has a first-rate deli, source of great picnic fixings.

✳ Selective Shopping

In Castine
Leila Day Antiques (207-326-8786), 53 Main St. An outstanding selection of early American furniture; also paintings, quilts, and Maine-made Shard Pottery. The shop is in the historic Parson Mason House, and the approach is through a formal garden.

✎ **Compass Rose Bookstore & Café** (207-326-9366 or 1-800-698-9366), 3 Main St. Open Mon.–Sat. 10–6. Sharon Biggie is the owner of this local institution, featuring children's titles, summer reading, nautical and regional books. The café serves drinks, snacks, and soups.

Four Flags (207-312-8526), 19 Water St. A long-established gift shop with an eclectic mix of Maine-made and exotic gifts.

Adam Gallery (207-326-8272), 140 Battle Ave. Open weekends in July and Aug., also most days by appointment. Susan Paris Adams's oils are worth a stop.

Tarratine Gallery (207-326-8444), 5 Main St. Maine landscapes are the specialty.

Farmer's market June–Oct., Thu. 7–noon on Castine Common.

✳ Special Events
May: Memorial Day Parade.

July: Independence Day parade and fireworks.

Over the entrance of the Bagaduce (sheet music) Lending Library, a mural depicts the area as the center of concentric creative circles. Helen and Scott Nearing, searching for a new place to live "the Good Life" in the 1950s (when a ski area encroached on their seclusion in southern Vermont), swung a dowsing pendulum over a map of coastal Maine. It came to rest on Cape Rosier. For many decades the small town of Brooklin was a familiar byline in *The New Yorker* thanks to E. B. White, who also wrote *Charlotte's Web* and *Stuart Little* here at about the same time millions of children began to read about Blueberry Hill in Robert McCloskey's *Blueberries for Sal* and about Condon's Garage (still a South Brooksville family-owned landmark) in the 1940s classic *One Morning in Maine*.

Energy lines or not, this peninsula is exceptionally beautiful, with views to the east toward Mount Desert as well as back across Penobscot Bay. Pause at the turnout on Caterpillar Hill, the height-of-land on Rt. 15/175 (just north of the Deer Isle Bridge), to appreciate the panorama. Then plunge down the hill to an improbably narrow, soaring suspension bridge.

The 1939 bridge spans Eggemoggin Reach, a 10-mile-long passage dividing the Blue Hill Peninsula from Deer Isle but linking Penobscot and Jericho Bays. A century ago this was a busy thoroughfare, a shortcut from Rockland to points Down East for freight-carrying schooners and passenger steamboats. It remains a popular route for windjammers, yachts, and, increasingly, sea kayakers. Rt. 175 winds along "the Reach" on its way through Sedgwick to Brooklin.

GUIDANCE The **Blue Hill Peninsula Chamber of Commerce** (207-374-3242; bluehillpeninsula.org), 107 Main St., Blue Hill, covers the six peninsula towns, publishing a booklet guide. It maintains a year-round information center open Mon., Tue., Thu., and Fri. 9–3, with additional summer hours that vary with volunteers. Pick up a copy of the **East Penobscot Bay Region map** (also at penobscot bay.com). This can come in handy, as roads here can be seriously confusing. Also pick up the current free copies of the ***Browser's Trail***, the ***Arts Guide***, and the ***Bay Community Register***.

GETTING THERE *By car:* From points south take I-95 to Rt. 295 to I-95 (briefly again) to exit 213: Rt. 3 to Belfast and Rt. 1 to Rt. 15 to Blue Hill. There are many shortcuts through the confusing web of roads on this peninsula; ask directions to your lodging.

By air: The nearest commercial airports are **Bangor International** (fly bangor.com) and **Hancock County & Bar Harbor Airport** (between Ellsworth and Bar Harbor).

WHEN TO COME Blue Hill is very seasonal, but several inns and restaurants remain open year-round.

VIEW OF PENOBSCOT BAY FROM CATERPILLAR HILL, SEDGWICK, BY JILL HOY

✳ To See

MUST SEE A dozen miles south of Rt. 1 via Rt. 15, the town of Blue Hill (blue hill.gov) is cradled between its namesake hill and bay. In the walkable center of town you'll find a pillared town hall, a handsome WPA library, two Federal-era historic houses (see *Also See*), and several outstanding shops and galleries. While this is the hub of the peninsula, to come as far as Blue Hill Village and go no farther would be like walking up to a door and not opening it. The beauty of the peninsula lies beyond—via roads that wander southwest to **Brooksville** (Rt. 15 south to Rt. 176 north to Rt. 176/175) and across the **Bagaduce River** at the **Reversing Falls** (see Bagaduce Lunch under *Eating Out*); head south on Rt. 176 (never mind) and, if time permits, turn off at the sign for Cape Rosier to see **Holbrook Island Sanctuary** (see *Birding*) and **Forest Farm** (see *Also See*). Return to Rt. 176 and continue into the village of South Brooksville (don't miss **Buck's Harbor**). Rt. 176 rejoins Rt. 175 and then Rt. 15; turn south and follow Rt. 15 south over **Caterpillar Hill**, where a pullout permits space to enjoy one of the most spectacular panoramas available from any coastal road, south across Penobscot Bay to the Camden Hills. From this height Rt. 15 plunges downhill. Turn left at the bottom, following Rt. 175 as it shadows **Eggemoggin Reach**, through Sargentville, winds up around the Benjamin River in Sedgwick, and down along the Reach again, into Brooklin, home to **WoodenBoat School** (see *Special Programs*). Check *Selective Shopping* for tempting stops along the way.

ALSO SEE Johnathan Fisher Memorial (207-374-2459; jonathanfisherhouse .org), 0.5 mile south of Blue Hill Village on Rt. 15/176. Open July–mid-Oct., Thu.– Sat. 1–4. A house built in 1814 by Blue Hill's first pastor, a Harvard graduate who augmented his meager salary with a varied line of crafts and by teaching (he founded Blue Hill Academy), farming, and writing. His furniture, paintings, books, journals, and woodcuts are exhibited. Antiques show, mid-Aug. Admission.

Holt House, 3 Water St., Blue Hill. Open July–mid-Sept., Tue. and Fri. 1–4, Sat. 11–2. Open year-round on Thu. for research. Donation. The Blue Hill Historical Society collection is housed in this restored 1815 Federal mansion near the harbor and noted for its stenciled walls. Don't pass this by if it's open: a lovely old house filled with images and tokens evoking Blue Hill's past.

Blue Hill Library (207-374-5515; bhpl.net), 5 Parker Point Rd., Blue Hill. Open daily except Sun. A handsome WPA building with periodicals and ample reading space; changing art shows in summer.

Bagaduce Music Lending Library (207-374-5454; bagaducemusic.org), 5 Music Library Lane, Rt. 172, Blue Hill. Open Mon.–Fri. 10–3. This Blue Hill phenomenon features roughly 250,000 sheet music titles (instrumental, keyboard, and vocal), some more than a century old and most special for one reason or another— all available for borrowing. The collection includes more than 1,400 pieces about Maine, by Maine composers, or published in Maine. Stop by just to see the mural over the entrance.

The Good Life Center (207-326-8211; goodlife.org), 372 Harborside Rd., Harborside, on Cape Rosier. Open mid-June–Aug., Thu.–Mon 1–4; weekends only in Sept.; and by appointment. Forest Farm, with its stone home built in 1953 by Helen (d. 1995) and Scott Nearing (d. 1983), coauthors of *Living the Good Life*

Christina Tree

THE GOOD LIFE CENTER

and seven other books based on their simple, purposeful lifestyle, is now maintained by a nonprofit trust. Through a stewardship program a couple maintains the property year-round. The grounds include an intensively cultivated organic garden, a greenhouse, and a yurt. Check the website for workshops.

Sedgwick-Brooklin Historical Society & Museum (207-359-8958), Rt. 172, Sedgwick. Open July–Aug., Sun. 2–4. This complex includes the town's original parsonage, a restored schoolhouse, and an 1820s cattle pound. It is part of the Sedgwick Historic District. Note the old cemetery.

✳ To Do

BIRDING Holbrook Island Sanctuary State Park (207-326-4012), 172 Indian Bar Rd. (off Rt. 176 in West Brooksville on Cape Rosier), is a state wildlife sanctuary of 1,350 acres, including 2.3 miles of shore and 115-acre Holbrook Island. No camping is permitted, but a lovely picnic area adjoins a pebble beach. A network of old roads, paths, and animal trails leads along the shore and through marshes and forest. It's the creation as well as the gift of Anita Harris, who died in 1985 at age 92, the sole resident of Holbrook Island. Her will stipulated that her mansion and all the other buildings on the island be demolished. She was also responsible for destroying all homes within the sanctuary. Wildlife is plentiful and birding is exceptional, especially during spring and fall migrations. Great blue herons nest around the pond and the estuary. Bald eagles and peregrine falcons and an eagle's nest may also be seen. Inquire about guided nature walks in July and Aug.

BOATING Buck's Harbor Marine (207-326-8839), South Brooksville, rents sail- and motorboats. Inquire about sailing lessons.

Summertime (1-800-562-8290; schoonersummertime.com). Captain Bill Brown offers daysails in early summer and fall; three- and six-day midsummer cruises on his 30-foot pinky schooner depart from Rockland.

Sand Dollar Sailing (207-266-1686; sanddollarsailing.com) out of Brooklin. Captain Peter Niehoff offers charters aboard the 52-foot *Adelaide*; instruction and consultation offered.

BUCKS HARBOR IS A SAILING CENTER
Christina Tree

✍ **MERI Summer Eco-Cruises** (207-374-2135; meriresearch.org). During summer months regularly scheduled eco-cruises and Island Explorer programs are held aboard a 12-passenger, lobster-boat-style excursion boat, also Island Explorer programs for children (see *Special Learning Programs*).

Also see *Sea Kayaking, Canoeing*.

FISHING Eggemoggin Guide Service (207-359-2746; eggemogginguideservice .net), Sedgwick. Captain Pete Douvarjo offers half-day trips for striped bass and full-day float trips on the Penobscot River. Fly-fishing and handcrafted fishing rods are specialties.

SEA KAYAKING, CANOEING The Activity Shop (207-374-3600; activityshop .com), 61 Ellsworth Rd. (Rt. 172), north of Blue Hill Village. Old Town canoes, kayak and bicycle rentals. **Rocky Coast Outfitters** (207-374-8866), on Grindleville Rd. off Rt. 15 in Blue Hill, rents and offers free delivery of kayaks, canoes, and bicycles. The Bagaduce River north from Walker Pond is a favorite flatwater run for novices, with some popular whitewater at Blue Hill Falls, a reversing falls accessible off Rt. 175. Also see *To Do* in "Deer Isle, Stonington" and "Castine."

SPECIAL LEARNING PROGRAMS WoodenBoat School (207-359-4651 or 1-800-273-7447; woodenboat.com), off Naskeag Point Rd., south of the village of Brooklin. A spinoff from *WoodenBoat* magazine, this seafaring institute of national fame offers summer courses that range from building your own sailboat, canoe, or kayak to navigation and drawing and painting. Accommodations available. The store is a shopping destination in its own right; open weekdays 7:30–6, Sat. 9–5.

✍ **Marine Environmental Research Institute** (MERI) (207-374-2135; meri research.org), 55 Main St., Blue Hill. Visitors center is open year-round except Sun.; weekdays only in the off-season. This nonprofit research organization focuses on marine mammals, especially harbor seals. MERI offers a summer schedule of educational, guided cruises plus hands-on ocean science programs, some specially geared to youngsters ages 6–12 and others to older kids. The center is also the scene of lectures, videos, and children's story hours.

Also see **Haystack Mountain School of Crafts** in "Deer Isle, Stonington."

✳ Green Space

Blue Hill. Our friends at the Blue Hill Bookstore tell us that this was not the setting for the children's classic *Blueberries for Sal*, by Robert McCloskey—a long-time summer resident of the area. But we choose to disbelieve them. It looks just like the hill in the book and has its share of in-season blueberries. The big attraction, however, is the view of the Mount Desert mountains from the 934-foot summit. From Rt. 172 take Mountain Rd. to the parking area (on your right). It's a mile to the top via the Hayes Trail through town conservation land, and a little longer if you loop back down to the road via the Osgood Trail through Blue Hill Heritage Trust land. A trail right from town begins behind the post office.

Blue Hill Heritage Trust (207-374-5118; bluehillheritagetrust.org) is steadily increasing the amount of preserved open space throughout the peninsula.

✐ **Blue Hill Town Park**. Follow Water St. past the hospital to this pleasant water-side park with picnic tables and great rocks for kids.

393

EAST PENOBSCOT BAY REGION

✲ Lodging

INNS AND BED & BREAKFASTS

In Blue Hill 04614

✪ 🐾 ♿ **Blue Hill Inn** (207-374-2844 or 1-800-826-7415; bluehillinn.com), 40 Union St. The inn open mid-May–Oct.; the Cape House is open year-round. A classic 1830s New England inn on a quiet, elm-lined street in the village. Wisconsin-bred innkeeper Sarah Pebworth preserves a sense of comfortable elegance in the gracious sitting room and library and the 11 guest rooms, some with sitting room and/or working fireplace. The handicapped-accessible Cape House, a neighboring cottage, is divided into two units, each with kitchen facilities, one with a fireplace; it accommodates families and pets. In warm weather guests may gather for cocktails in the garden, but more often it's in the living room. Hors d'oeuvres are served, and guests can order drinks and exchange their day's adventures. A full breakfast with a choice of entrées is served at individual tables in the large, sunny dining room. It's included along with afternoon tea and evening nibbles in rates of $195–225 double in high season, from $145 before July. Cape House suites are $280–305 in-season; from $170 in winter. Also see *Dining Out*.

((ᵠ)) **Barncastle Hotel + Restaurant** (207-374-2300; barncastlehotel.com), 125 South St. A fanciful shingle-style summer mansion, for many years an inn called Arcady Downeast, has been totally renovated by Lori and Isaac Robbins. The guest area is nicely removed from the busy restaurant, but this is on a main drag. The feel is of a boutique hotel rather than an inn. The four rooms vary in size; all have a king bed, flat-screen TV, coffeemaker, and private bath. $100–160 includes breakfast. (Also see *Dining Out*.)

Elsewhere on the Blue Hill Peninsula

The Brooklin Inn (207-359-2777; brooklininn.com), 22 Reach Rd., P.O. Box 25, Brooklin 04616. A casual, friendly, year-round inn in the middle of a coastal village. Chip (a former tugboat captain) and Gail Angell are clearly the right innkeepers for this landmark that's well known for its restaurant (see *Dining Out*) with a separate, inviting pub. There are five pleasant upstairs bedrooms, four with private bath. $95–125 includes full breakfast; a $145 winter special adds all you can eat for two. *Note:* Brooklin offers sheltered moorings to yachters, and the inn picks up guests.

🐾 **Brass Fox Bed and Breakfast** (207-326-0575; brassfox.com), 907 Southern Bay Rd. (Rt. 175), Penobscot 04476. Open year-round. This 19th-century farmhouse is filled with antiques. Common space includes two dining rooms (with original tin ceilings), a small library with TV, and a parlor. All the second-floor guest rooms (each with bath and one with a sleep sofa) share balconies with views off across fields and woods. Breakfast includes a fruit course, an entrée, and homemade bread and pastries; the Bagaduce Lunch (see *Eating Out*) is nearby. Gerry and Dawn Freeman are helpful hosts. $110–130, from $85 off-season. Pets $40 per day (donated to Greyhound Rescue).

Surry Inn (207-667-5092; surryinn .com). Box 25, Surry 04684. Open Memorial–Columbus Day weekends. Longtime innkeepers Peter and Anne-lise Krinsky offer eight moderately priced, old-fashioned, spanking-clean rooms, six with private bath, many with water views. Lawns sloping to Contention Cove are ideal for launching and paddling a kayak. Sited on Rt. 172 between Blue Hill and Ellsworth, this is a good location from which to explore both Mount Desert and the Blue Hill Peninsula. $88–102 before June 20, then $88–112. Also see *Dining Out*.

COTTAGES AND MORE

🐟 🏕 🐾 ⚓ (((ŋ))) **Hiram Blake Camp** (207-326-4951; hiramblake.com), Cape Rosier, Harborside 04642. Open May–Columbus Day weekend. Well off the beaten track, operated by the same family since 1916, this is the kind of place where you come to stay put. All cottages are within 200 feet of the shore, with views of Penobscot Bay. Under the able management of Deborah Venno Ludlow and her husband, David, all have been recently renovated. There are five one-bedroom cottages, six cottages with two bedrooms, and three with three bedrooms; each has a living room with a wood-burning stove, a kitchen, a shower, and a porch. Guests with housekeeping cottages cook for themselves in the shoulder months, but in July and August everyone eats in the dining room, which doubles as a library because thousands of books are ingeniously filed away by category in the ceiling. There are rowboats at the dock and kayaks for rent, a playground, and a recreation room with table tennis and board games; also trails. In high season, from $600 per week with breakfast and dinner for the one-room Acorn Cottage to $3,000 for a three-bedroom cottage (up to five guests); linens are $20 per person. Rates drop during "housekeeping months" to $660–940 per week.

♂ **Oakland House Cottages** (207-359-8521; oaklandhouse.com), 435 Herrick Rd., Brooksville 04617. Sadly this venerable resort has closed, but a dozen cottages, each different, with cooking facilities, living room, and fireplace, accommodating up to nine, are still available as rentals, scattered through the woods and shorefront with a beach near the entrance to Eggemoggin Reach, handy to both the Blue Hill Peninsula and Deer Isle. This grounds remain a wedding site.

♂ **The Lookout** (207-359-2188; thelookoutinn.biz), 455 Flye Point Rd., Brooklin 04616. Seven cottages are scattered over this spectacular property that's been in the same family since 1891. This is also a great venue for a wedding (see *Dining Out*) with seriously old-fashioned but clean rooms upstairs in the inn.

Peninsula Property Rentals (207-374-2428; peninsulapropertyrentals .com), Main St., Blue Hill 04614. A range of area rentals. Also see **Maine Vacation Rentals** (207-374-2444; mainevacationrentalsonline.com), 105 Main St., Blue Hill.

✳ Where to Eat

DINING OUT Arborvine (207-374-2119; arborvine.com), Main St. (Rt. 172), south Blue Hill Village. Open for dinner Tue.–Sun. in-season, Fri.–Sun. off-season. Few Maine restaurants are as widely acclaimed, and reservations may be necessary a couple of days in advance. Chef-owner John Hikade was already the area's most respected chef when he and his wife, Beth, restored the handsome 1820s Hinckley homestead, retaining its original Dutchman's pipe vine above the door. The several open-beamed dining rooms with fireplaces, once the parlors, are simple and elegant. The menu presents local produce in memorable ways. For starters try Bagaduce River oysters on the half shell with a frozen sake mignotte ($12), then dine on roast native halibut with grilled polenta, lemon butter crumb crust, baby bok choy, and garlic beurre blanc ($28), or grilled native lamb chops with creamy risotto, mushrooms, herb gremolata, and apple ginger chutney. Entrées $27–30. The wine list is extensive and reasonably priced. Also see **The Vinery** under *Eating Out.*

✪ **Buck's Restaurant** (207-326-8688), Buck's Harbor Market, center of South Brooksville, Rt. 176. Open seasonally except Sun. 5:30–8; check nights off-season. Reserve. Chef Johnathan Chase has a wide following and gets great reviews. The informal dining room behind the village market is decorated with local sculpture and art and is all about turning local ingredients into tasty dishes. On a September night the limited menu included a Greek lemon soup for starters; seared duck breast with red wine, orange, and cranberry reduction sauce; and—the payoff—Johnathan's Kettle of Fish, a seafood jumbo stew with shrimp, lobster, scallops, littlenecks, and haddock in fennel-and-saffron-infused broth. Entrées $19–24.

The Blue Hill Inn (207-374-2844; bluehillinn.com), 40 Union St., Blue Hill. Dinner served seasonally, Mon.–Fri. After a few years' hiatus dinner is served again in this classic inn dining room, and the reviews are all raves. Chef Devin Finigan is passionate about using local produce; the lobster comes straight from her husband's traps. Begin with Bagaduce River oysters and/or mussels, then feast on butter-poached lobster ravioli, veal osso buco with squash risotto and crispy kale, or delicata squash stuffed with wild rice, dried cranberries,

greens, and apple cider reduction. Entrées $19–30. Breakfast is also open to the public.

⌁ **66 Steak & Seafood** (207-374-1055), 66 Main St. Each year there seems to be a new restaurant on this prime site in the middle of Blue Hill. We hope this one sticks. We sampled it for lunch, served out front on a beautiful day. The Cobb salad was huge and delicious ($11.66), and service was fast and friendly. Light fare (there's a children's menu) keeps the street-level pub and café area busy all day; more formal dining is downstairs at tables along the pleasant enclosed porch above a stream. Dinner entrées $15.66–36.66 (for a 32-ounce rib-eye steak).

The Brooklin Inn (207-359-2777; brooklininn.com), 22 Reach Rd. (Rt. 175), Brooklin Village. Reservations advised. Open nightly in summer, closed Mon. and Tue. in winter. This restaurant religiously serves only wild fish and produce that's organic and local, or organic if it isn't local. This is a justly popular and hospitable small village inn with a menu that changes nightly. Chefs do tend to change, but quality has been consistent. In 2011 entrées ranged from $18 for chicken Marsala to $28 for scallops with herb risotto, Swiss chard, and fruit salsa. With a menu featuring Guinness beef stew and chicken potpie, burgers, and pizza, the downstairs pub is a favorite local gathering spot.

The Lookout Inn & Restaurant (207-359-2188; thelookoutinn.biz), 455 Flye Point Rd., Brooklin. Open for dinner Tue.–Sat. mid-June–mid-Oct.; call off-season. Butch Smith has a talent for finding superb chefs, year after year. The setting is one of Maine's oldest family-owned summer hotels, set above gardens and a meadow that slope to the water, a stunning wedding venue. The à la carte menu might include salmon grilled with crab, asparagus, and hollandaise, or seared venison with boysenberry port sauce. Entrées $21–26.

Surry Inn (207-667-5091; surryinn .com), Rt. 172, Contention Cove, Surry. Open nightly for dinner except Tue.; just Fri.–Sat. in winter. This pleasant dining room overlooking a cove is well known locally for reasonably priced fine dining, under the same ownership and management for many years. The menu changes often but always includes interesting soups— maybe Hungarian mushroom or lentil vegetable—and a wide entrée selection that might include veal sautéed with sun-dried tomatoes, blueberry duckling, spicy garlic frogs' legs, and lobster with corn cakes and a scallop mousseline. Entrées $13.50–23.

Also see *Dining Out* in "Deer Isle, Stonington," and in "Castine."

EATING OUT

In Blue Hill

The Vinery & Deep Water Brewing Co. (207-374-2441; arborvine.com), behind the Arborvine (see *Dining Out*), Blue Hill Village. Open seasonally, Wed.–Sun. for supper; bar open until 10. No reservations. With partner Chrissy Allen, Tim Hikade, son of the Arborvine owners, has transformed this piano bar into a more casual brewpub (the beer is crafted in Brooklin) with a one-page, reasonably priced menu featuring burgers, ribs, calamari, salads, and the like.

⌀ **Boatyard Grill** (207-374-3533; the boatyardgrill.com), 13 E. Blue Hill Rd. Open June–mid Sept., Tue.–Sat. for lunch and dinner. Eat inside or out, in a pavilion sited in a working boatyard. This welcome new restaurant offers water views. Chef-owner Annelise Riggal serves up the basics, including local

Bill Davis

THE BOATYARD GRILL IS REALLY IN A BLUE HILL BOATYARD

mussels and lobster in forms that range from pizza and mac-and-cheese to a shore dinner.

⌀ **Marlintini's Grill** (207-374-2500), 89 Mines Rd. (Rt. 15/176) south of Blue Hill Village. Local favorite, open for all three meals. There's a sports bar but plenty of space to get away from it. Grilled and fried meat and seafood, salads, hot sandwiches, and nightly specials.

Barncastle (207-374-2300), 125 South St., Blue Hill. Open daily 11–9. This former mansion is an unlikely but delightful venue for the area's best pizza. What you need to know is that most of the staff here come from Pie in the Sky, the area's previously best but now defunct pizza source. The centerpiece of this sleek restaurant is its wood-fired oven, producing pizza with a choice of more than 30 toppings. The menu also includes sandwiches, subs, and salads featuring local farm ingredients. Wine and beer served.

Blue Hill Food Co-op Café (207-374-2165), Rt. 172 in Green's Hill Place, a small shopping center just north of the village. Open weekdays

8–7, Sat. 8–6, Sun. 10–5. This attractive café is part of a well-stocked market specializing in organic and local produce as well as wines, general health foods, and vitamins. Good organic coffees and teas and a selection of baked goods, soups, sandwiches, and specials. Also a source of premade sandwiches and quiche. *Note:* This is the obvious place to eat and sip while washing clothes at the Laundromat across the street.

The Fish Net (207-374-5240), Blue Hill Village, Rt. 15, across from the turnoff (Rt. 176) to East Blue Hill. Open seasonally 11–8, until 9 on Fri.–Sat. Known for lobster rolls; also a convenient place to feast on lobster and steamers or to buy a cooked lobster to take home, plus the usual fried seafood, burgers, and sandwiches. Seating inside and out with a playground for kids.

✪ **Blue Hill Hearth** (207-610-9090), 58 Main St., Blue Hill Village. Open 8–8 in July and Aug., otherwise 8–6; 9–3 Sat.–Sun. Kathleen McCloskey, locally beloved for her former bakery, Pain de Famille, is producing her artisan breads (focaccia is a specialty), pizzas, terrific sandwiches (including vegetarian delights such as walnut-cheddar loaf), and great desserts. Limited indoor seating, also outdoor in summer with surprisingly good views of the water.

Elsewhere on the Blue Hill Peninsula

✪ 🍴 **Bagaduce Lunch**, Rt. 176, South Penobscot at the reversing falls and the bridge to North Brooksville. This seasonal, hugely popular lunch stand, recently rebuilt, is a must. Fried seafood baskets are the big draw, and they will spoil you for seafood baskets anywhere else forever. Picnic tables are scattered over a lawn that slopes to the Bagaduce River.

Buck's Harbor Market (207-326-8683), Cornfield Hill Rd. (Rt. 176), Brooksville Village. Open weekdays 7–7, weekends 8–7. Soups and sandwiches. The market has a lunch counter, open year-round for breakfast and lunch. Baking is done here, and the stuffed pockets and breads make great picnic fare.

✎ **El El Frijoles** (207-359-2486; elelfrijoles.com), 41 Caterpillar Hill Rd. (Rt. 15), Sargentville. Open Memorial Day–Sept., Wed.–Sun. 11–8. We love the takeoff on L.L. Bean. Takeout and three inside tables, plenty more seating outside at a mix of covered and open picnic tables, a great space for kids with a play structure, sandbox, and and badminton court. This is California/Mex food with local ingredients, right down to the black beans. Fillings for tacos and burritos include grilled veggies and carnitas (slow-braised, shredded pork with chilies, onions, and spices). The house special is spicy lobster. Mini burritos and a PB&J quesadilla for kids. Owners Michael Rossney and Michele La Vesque also

BAGADUCE LUNCH HAS BEEN NAMED "AN AMERICAN CLASSSIC" BY THE JAMES BEARD FOUNDATION

Christina Tree

welcome patrons to the **Coast to Coast Fine Arts**, the art gallery in their home, and in winter there's a twice-monthly supper club.

✪ **Perry's Lobster Shack** (207-667-1955) 1076 Newbury Neck Rd, Surry. Open May to mid-Oct. but call to check in shoulder months. The only lobster shack on the entire Blue Hill Peninsula is near the tip of a long skinny sliver of land dangling off the peninsula proper in Surry. It was almost dark by the time we found it and there wasn't much to see, just a gray-shingled shack—with steam billowing from it, Caribbean music blaring, and picnic tables on the dock below. Then we saw the view, with the sun setting over Acadia. Great lobster and crab rolls, plus local sweet corn-on-the-cob—and homemade ice cream sandwiches. BYOB.

🍴 **Morning Moon Café** (207-359-2373), Rt. 175, Brooklin. This beloved little eatery in the middle of Brooklin is closed at this writing but the promise is that it will reopen by the time you may need it.

Also see *Eating Out* in "Deer Isle, Stonington."

PICNIC FIXINGS Don't waste a nice day by eating inside! For picnic sites, see *Green Space*. **Merrill & Hinckley** on Union St., middle of Blue Hill, is an old-fashioned general store, making good sandwiches fresh each morning and keeping them in a cooler way in back. Also see **Buck's Harbor Market** in Brooksville and the **Blue Hill Food Co-op**, above, as well as **The Cave** in Brooklin (*Special Shops*) and the **Brooklin General Store**.

✳ Entertainment

MUSIC 🎶 **Kneisel Hall Chamber Music School and Festival** (207-374-2811; kneisel.org), Pleasant St. (Rt.

15), Blue Hill. One of the oldest chamber music festivals in the country (dating back to 1924). Faculty present string and ensemble music in a series of Sunday-afternoon and Friday-evening concerts, June–Aug.; inquire about Young Artist Concerts.

WERU (207-469-6600; weru.org) is a major nonprofit community radio station based in East Orland (89.9 FM) known for folk and Celtic music, jazz, and reggae.

Bagaduce Chorale (207-667-6084; bagaducechorale.org), Blue Hill. A community chorus staging several concerts yearly, ranging from Bach to show tunes.

Flash in the Pans Community Steel Band (peninsulapan.org) performs throughout the Blue Hill Peninsula with special performances elsewhere. Check their schedule on the website.

✳ Selective Shopping

In Blue Hill

ART GALLERIES Leighton Gallery (207-374-5001; leightongallery.com), Parker Point Rd. Open June–Columbus Day. One of Maine's oldest and most

LEIGHTON GALLERY

prominent contemporary art galleries, with exhibits in the three-floor space changing every few weeks. Judith Leighton passed on in 2011 but this remains a must-stop for art lovers. Don't miss the expansive sculpture garden.

Jud Hartman Gallery and Sculpture Studio (207-374-917; judhartman gallery.com), 79 Main St. Open mid-June–mid-Sept. daily. Hartman exhibits his nationally known realistic bronze sculptures of northeastern Native Americans as well as the work of other well-known local artists.

Randy Eckard (207-374-2510; randy eckardpaintings.com), 29 Pleasant St. Open July–Sept., Tue.–Sat. 11–4. Limited-edition prints of the artist's precise, luminous landscapes.

Liros Gallery (207-374-5370; liros gallery.com), Parker Point Rd., specializes in fine paintings, old prints, and Russian icons; appraisals.

Blue Hill Bay Gallery (207-274-5773; bluehillbaygallery.com), 11 Tenney Hill. Open 10–5 Memorial Day–Labor Day; weekends thereafter. Changing exhibits of 19th-century and contemporary art, featuring northern landscapes and the sea.

ARTISANS Rackliffe Pottery (207-374-2297; rackliffepottery.com), Rt. 172, Blue Hill Village. Open Mon.–Sat. 8–4; also Sun. in July and Aug., noon–4. Since 1968 Phyllis and Phil Rackliffe have produced their distinctive pottery, featuring local clay and their own glazes. Their emphasis is on individual small pieces rather than on sets. Visitors are welcome to watch.

✪ **Handworks Gallery** (207-374-5613; handworksgallery.org), 48 Main St., Blue Hill. Open Memorial Day–late Dec., Mon.–Sat. 10–5. A middle-of-town space filled with stunning work by Maine artists and arti-

Christina Tree

LEIGHTON GALLERY, BLUE HILL

sans: handwoven clothing, jewelry, furniture, rugs, and blown glass and art.

North Country Textiles (207-374-2715; northcountrytextiles.com), corner of Main and Union Sts., Blue Hill. Woven clothing, custom rag rugs, pottery, handcrafted woodwork, and much more.

HANDWORKS GALLERY, BLUE HILL

Christina Tree

SPECIAL SHOPS ⊙ **Blue Hill Books** (207-374-5632; bluehillbooks.com), 26 Pleasant St (Rt. 15). Open Mon.–Sat. 10–5:30, also Sun. June–Aug., Blue Hill. A long-established, independent, full-service, two-floor, family-run bookstore with a separate room for children's titles. One of the best bookstores in Maine, with frequent readings by the many local authors.

Blue Hill Wine Shop (207-374-2161), Main St., Blue Hill. Open Mon.–Sat. 10–5:30. A long-established shop dedicated to the perfect cup of tea or coffee, a well-chosen wine, and the right blend of tobacco. Great finds for wine lovers at reasonable prices, also morning coffee and muffins.

Blue Hill Antiques (207-374-8825; bluehillantiques.com), 8 Water St., Blue Hill. Open May–Oct. and by appointment. This is a large shop, featuring French and American antiques 1750–1950.

Blue Hill Yarn Shop (207-374-5631), Rt. 172 north of Blue Hill Village. Open Mon.–Sat. 10–4. A mecca for knitters in search of a variety of wools and needles. Lessons and original hand knits.

New Cargoes (newcargoes.com), 49 Main St., Blue Hill. Lots of everything, from clothing to housewares to gifts.

On and off Route 175 along Eggemoggin Reach

Eggemoggin Textile Studio (207-359-5083; chrisleithstudio.com), 497 Reach Rd. (Rt. 175), Sargentville. Open seasonally Tue.–Sat. Exceptional woven scarves, wraps, hangings, and pillows from hand-dyed silks and wool.

Reach Road Gallery (207-359-8803; reachroadgallery.com), 62 Reach Rd., Sedgwick. Open June–mid-Sept., Wed.–Sat. 10–5. Holly Meade makes striking wood block prints, also prints

of her illustrations from children's books.

Sedgwick Antiques (207-359-8834), 775 N. Sedgwick Rd. (Rt. 172), Sedgwick. May–Sept., Wed.–Sat. 10–5, and by appointment. Jill Knowles and Bill Perry run an old-fashioned shop with a wide range of furniture, rugs, ceramics, and lighting, emphasis on formal styles.

Pushcart Press & Bookstore (207-669-5335), Rt. 172 behind Sedgwick Antiques. Claiming to be the "world's smallest bookstore," this self-serve cottage is crammed with books, and there's space to read on the porch overlooking a meadow. Annually since 1976 Pushcart Press has published *The Pushcart Prize*, a collection of short stories, poetry, and essays selected from hundreds of small presses. Current and past editions of the anthology are sold, along with other small-press titles and thousands of books from publisher Bill Henderson's personal library.

The Cave (207-359-8008; thecavebrooklin.com), 123 Reach Rd., Brooklin. Open year-round. Closed Sun.–Mon. off-season. Laura Cramer's shop is a find for wine, cheese (150 vari-

PUSHCART PRESS

Christina Tree

eties, 25 from Maine), and chocolate lovers. Fresh breads and house-roasted coffees, too. Not a place to pass up.

Handmade Papers (207-359-8345), 113 Reach Rd., Brooklin. Open summer, Wed.–Sun. noon–5. Virginia Sarsfield fashions exquisite lamp shades and other creations from a variety of fibers, including tufts of cattail and bits of lichen.

Betsy's Sunflower (207-359-5030), 12 Reach Rd., Brooklin. Unusual but handy kitchen and garden gadgets and other nifty things for cottages and boats; also home furnishings, toys, gifts, books, sailcloth totes, local music, more.

Maine Hooked Rugs, (207-359-2812), 6 Naskeag Rd., Brooklin. Open in summer Tue.–Sat. 10–5. A selection of colorful hooked rugs, plus hooking supplies and classes.

Cape Rosier

Four Season Farm (fourseasonfarm .com), 609 Weir Cove Rd., Harborside. Open June–Sept. Mon.–Sat. 1–5. Barbara Hamrosch and Eliot Coleman have both authored popular gardening books, and Barbara writes a weekly "Cook's Garden" column for *The Washington Post*. Their greenhouse produce vegetables year-round, and their farmstand carries a wide variety of seasonal produce. Also check out their Cape Rosier Artists Collective here and their vege-mobile, which travels to the Blue Hill, Brooksville, and Deer Isle Farmer's Markets.

Architectural Antiquities (207-326-4942; archantiquities.com), 52 Indian Pt. Lane, Harborside. Call for directions and to let them know what you're looking for. Specialties include brass lighting, hardware and fireplace items, Victorian plumbing fixtures, windows, doors, weather vanes, hand-hewn beams, and more.

Tinder Hearth Wood-Fired Bread (207-326-8381 or 326-9266),1452 Coastal Rd. (Rt. 176), West Brooksville. Look for the sign. This is a source of terrific, wood-fired breads. Inquire about open-mike nights in summer.

The Sow's Ear Winery (207-326-4649), junction of Rt. 176 and Herrick Rd. The winery tasting room is theoretically open Tue.–Sat. 10–5. For many years Tom Hoey has produced dry, organic blueberry, chokeberry, and rhubarb wines, but on our last visit no one was around and the place was pretty dusty.

Thomas Hinchcliffe Antiques (207-326-9411), Graytown Rd. (Rt. 176), West Sedgwick. Open 10–5 most days in-season. Call ahead. Early furniture, decoys. Quilts, nautical and country accessories.

FOUR SEASON FARM

Christina Tree

✳ Special Events

Memorial Day–mid-October: **Blue Hill Farmer's Market**, Sat. 9–11:30 AM, Blue Hill Fairgrounds, Rt. 15 until mid-Aug., then in the Congregational church parking lot. Crafts, food, and baked goods as well as seasonal produce and flowers. Guest artists in July and Aug. In **Brooklin**, Thu. 3–5 beside Friend Memorial Library. **Brooksville**: Tue. 9–11, Commuity Center, Cornfield Rd. **Surry**: Sweet Pea Gardens (center of town), Thu., 3–6.

July: **Blue Hill Pops** (July 4 weekend) at the Bagaduce Lending Library. **Touring Through Time** (fourth weekend)—All the local historical sites hold open house. The **Blue Hill Crafts Show** at the Blue Hill Consolidated School is held the same weekend.

August: **Mountain Day** (first Saturday) begins with yoga on the summit of Blue Hill; children's activities, music, food day take place in the field at the base. **Academy Antiques Fair** (first weekend), George Stevens Academy, Blue Hill, is big. **Downeast Antiques Fairs** (midmonth). The **Annual St. Francis Fair**, midmonth at the Blue Hill Fairgrounds, is bigger, also about antiques.

Labor Day weekend: **Blue Hill Fair** (207-374-3701; bluehillfair.com) at the fairgrounds—harness racing, a midway, livestock competitions; one of the most colorful old-style fairs in New England. Best view of the fireworks is from the top of Blue Hill.

Early October: Foliage **Food & Wine Festival**. Wine dinners, special tastings, area chefs as well as crafters, writers, and musicians (bluehillpeninsula.org).

DEER ISLE, STONINGTON, AND ISLE AU HAUT

The narrow, half-mile-long suspension bridge across Eggemoggin Reach connects the Blue Hill Peninsula with Little Deer Isle, linked in turn by causeways and bridges to Deer Isle and its wandering land fingers. This intermingling of land and water is characterized by the kind of coves, spruce, and lupine-fringed inlets usually equated with "the real Maine." It's divided between the towns of Deer Isle and Stonington, and there are the villages of Sunset and Oceanville and of Sunshine, home of the nationally respected Haystack Mountain School of Crafts. Galleries display outstanding work by dozens of artists and craftspeople who live, or at least summer, in town.

Stonington, almost 40 miles south of Rt. 1, remains a working fishing harbor, but with more than its share of galleries. Most buildings, scattered on smooth rocks around the harbor, date from the 1880s to the World War I boom years, during which Deer Isle's pink granite was shipped off to face buildings from Rockefeller Center to Boston's Museum of Fine Arts. The Deer Isle Granite Museum depicts Stonington at the height of the granite boom when its population was 5,000, compared with 1,143 in 2010.

In Stonington life still eddies around Billings Diesel and Marine, and the Commercial Pier, home base for one of Maine's largest fishing/lobstering fleets. The town is also home to a pioneering lobster hatchery. The tourist season is short but busy enough to support a string of seasonal galleries and visitor-geared shops along waterside Main Street. The restored Opera House stages frequent films, live performances, and readings, and the Reach Performing Arts Center is also active year-

Christina Tree

STONINGTON HARBOR

round. Hundreds of new houses have been built in recent decades, and property values have soared. Happily, the number of nature preserves has also multiplied.

Stonington is departure point for the mail boat to Isle au Haut, a wooded, mountainous island with more than half its acreage preserved as a part of Acadia National Park. The boat makes seasonal stops at Duck Harbor, near the island's southern tip, accessing rugged, coastal hiking trails. The remaining half of the island, which supports fewer than 80 year-round residents and an old summer colony, is vividly depicted in *The Lobster Chronicles* by Linda Greenlaw.

GUIDANCE Deer Isle–Stonington Chamber of Commerce (207-348-6124; deerisle.com) maintains an "Information Building" (with facilities) on Rt. 15 at Little Deer Isle, south of the bridge. Open 10–4 mid-June–Labor Day, sporadically after that for a few weeks. Be sure to pick up the chamber's current map/guide (an outside box is kept stocked), an invaluable tool.

Note: Pick up a copy of *Island Advantages*, Stonington's weekly paper, since 1882.

GETTING THERE Follow directions under *Getting There* in "Blue Hill Area"; continue down Rt. 15 to Deer Isle.

RESTROOMS are on the public landing in Stonington.

EGGEMOGGIN REACH BRIDGE

Christina Tree

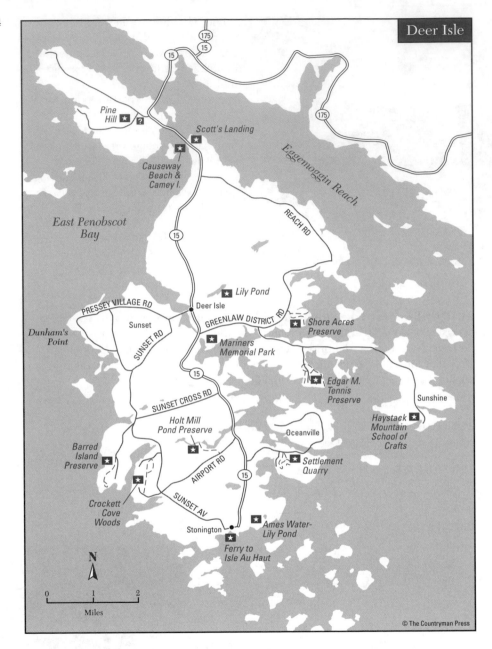

Deer Isle

© The Countryman Press

✽ To See

✐ ♿ **Deer Isle Granite Museum** (207-367-6331), Main St., Stonington. Open theoretically Memorial Day–Labor Day, Mon.–Sat. 9–5, Sun. 10–4, but call to check. Housed in the former pharmacy, this small museum features an 8-by-15-foot working model of quarrying operations on Crotch Island and the town of Stonington in 1900. Derricks move, and trains carry granite to waiting ships. Photo blowups and a video also dramatize the story of the quarryman's life during the height of the boom (see the chapter introduction).

Isle au Haut (pronounced *eye-la-HO*) is 6 miles long and 3 miles wide. More than half the island is part of **Acadia National Park** (see *Green Space*), but this is a quiet, working island with limited facilities for visitors. Samuel de Champlain named it "High Island" in 1605, and the highest hill (543 feet) is named for him. Most visitors come to hike the 20-mile network of trails around Dark Harbor and along the cliffy southern tip. To really enjoy the island, to swim in Long Pond and explore without the pressure of needing to catch a boat, you need to spend a couple of days. On the other hand, given a beautiful day the 45-minute boat ride is its own reward and a 15-minute walk from the town dock can be a pleasure (see *Lodging* and *Selective Shopping*).

Haystack Mountain School of Crafts (207-348-2306; haystack-mtn.org), Deer Isle (south of Deer Isle Village; turn left off Rt. 15 at the gas station and follow signs 7 miles). This is one of the country's outstanding crafts schools, and the campus itself is a work of art: a series of spare, shingled buildings, studios with a central dining hall and sleeping quarters, all weathered the color of surrounding rocks and fitted between trees, connected by steps and terraced decks, floated above the fragile lichens and wildflowers on land sloping steeply toward Jericho Bay. Given the brevity and intensity of each session (see *Special Learning Programs*), visitors are permitted in the studios only on weekly tours (Wed. at 1 PM) and during the "walk-throughs," in which student and faculty work is displayed (4–6 on the second Thu. of each session, followed by a 7:30 PM auction). The public is also welcome in the Gateway Building auditorium for frequent 8 PM slide lectures, visiting artists' presentations, and occasional concerts. There are also biweekly auctions.

The Penobscot East Resource Center (207-367-2708; penobscoteast.org), 13 Atlantic Ave., operates this pioneering **Zone C Lobster Hatchery** hatchery for the waters from Penobscot Bay to Jonesport. Visitors welcome.

The Salome Sellers House (207-348-2897), 416 Sunset Rd. (Rt. 15A), Sunset. Open late mid-June–mid-Sept., Wed. and Fri. 1–4. Salome Sellers herself lived to be 108 years old in this snug 1803 red Cape, now the home of the Deer Isle–Stonington Historical Society, displaying ships' models, Native American artifacts, and old photos; interesting and friendly.

LIGHTHOUSES Pumpkin Island Light, at the entrance to Eggemoggin Reach, visible from the end of Eggemoggin Rd. on Little Deer Isle, now a private home. **Eagle Island Light** can be viewed from Sylvester Cove in Sunset or, better yet, from the Eagle Island mail boat, from which you can also see the **Heron Neck**, **Brown's Head**, and **Goose Rocks Lights**. From Goose Cove Lodge in Sunset you can see and hear the now automated **Mark Island Light** (its old bronze bell sits on the resort's lawn);

ISLE AU HAUT

Christina Tree

the **Saddleback Ledge Light** is also visible on the horizon. (For details about reaching the **Isle au Haut Light**, or about Old Quarry Ocean Adventures, which offers a lighthouse cruise, see *Boat Excursions*.)

✴ To Do

BICYCLE RENTALS Old Quarry Ocean Adventures rents mountain bikes (see *Boat Excursions*), but we advise using two wheels only on quieter side roads, please, not Rt. 15. **Isle au Haut Ferry Service** rents bikes at the island's town dock.

BOAT EXCURSIONS 🐾 ⌀ **Isle au Haut Ferry Service** (207-367-5193; isleau haut.com) links Stonington with Acadia/Duck Harbor twice daily early June–Labor Day. This is the only regularly scheduled direct service to this dramatic, trail-webbed part of the island, and it's limited to 50 daily passengers. See *Green Space* for more about logistics. $37 (roundtrip) adults, $19 children, $4 pets (must be leashed). This mail boat also stops at the island's town dock on these runs and several more during summer, daily (except Sun.) but less frequently off-season. It takes kayaks and canoes ($22 one-way) and bicycles ($10 one-way), but not to Duck Harbor. The ferry service also offers seasonal scenic cruises aboard the *Miss Lizzie* (2 PM), with lobster hauling. The Isle au Haut Dock is at the end of Seabreeze Ave. at the eastern end of the village ($20 adult,$8 per child).

Old Quarry Ocean Adventures (207-367-8977; oldquarry.com), 130 Settlement Rd. off the Oceanville Rd., Stonington. Captain Bill Baker offers seasonal 9 AM runs aboard his 38-foot lobster-boat-style *Nigh Duck* to the Isle au Haut town dock (returning 5 PM), carrying bikes and kayaks gratis ($35 roundtrip adult, $18 per child); guided kayaking around the island is also available. Stay aboard until noon for an ecotour. A variety of other cruises are offered throughout the day, as are sailboat rentals and lessons. Old Quarry has also become the area's prime source of kayak rentals, lessons, and both half- and full-day guided trips, also multiday island camping. The **Old Quarry Campground**, with its platform tent sites and camp store, caters to kayakers. The waters off Stonington and Merchant's Row—the many islands just offshore—are among the most popular along the coast, but it's imperative for novice kayakers to explore these waters with a guide. Rental row-boats, canoes, and a bunkhouse are also available. Inquire about lobster bakes and weddings.

Eagle Island mail boat. Operated by the **Sunset Bay Company** (207-348-9316), the *Katherine* leaves Sylvester's Cove in Sunset mid-June–mid-Sept., Mon.–Sat. at 9:30 AM. Three miles off Sunset, Eagle Island is private, roughly a mile long with rocky ledges, a sandy beach, and a working lighthouse. Inquire about island rentals. Kayaks are carried. Passengers are welcome aboard just for the ride. The passage each way is only 20 minutes, but frequently there's a stop at Spruce Head and the captain takes time to point out local sights and seals, $20 adults roundtrip, $10 children under 12.

GOLF AND TENNIS Island Country Club (207-348-2379), 442 Sunset Rd. (Rt. 15A), Deer Isle, welcomes guests mid-May–mid-Oct. Nine holes; Fairway Café opens Memorial Day for lunch except Mon. Lessons, carts, also **tennis courts** and lessons.

(207-348-2306; haystack-mtn.org), Deer Isle. One- and two-week sessions, June–Labor Day, attract some of the country's top artisans in clay, metals, wood, fibers, graphics, and glass. From its beginnings in 1950, Haystack has been equated with cutting-edge design rather than traditional craft, and the architecture underscores the school's philosophy. It's intimate and self-contained, like the summer sessions themselves, each limited to no more than 90 students. Workshop topics are determined by faculty members, and these, like the students, change every two weeks. Each group is carefully balanced to include young (minimum age 18) and old, neophytes as well as master craftsmen; repeaters are kept to a third. Visitors are welcome to tour the campus, but not classes; tours are offered Wed. at 1 PM.

The Stonington Painter's Workshop (207-367-2368; off-season, 617-776-3102). Nationally prominent artist and art teacher Jon Imber coordinates and teaches this July series of weeklong landscape workshops.

🍃 **Seamark Community Arts** (207-348-5308; seamarkcommunityarts.com), 11 Church St., Deer Isle. Year-round classes and workshops for residents and visitors of all ages.

SWIMMING ✪ 🍃 Lily Pond, off Rt. 15 north of Deer Isle Village. The island's freshwater swimming hole offers a shaded, grassy beach that's a great spot for small children, also for long swims. With relief we can report that the beach and access have been preserved forever by the Island Heritage Trust. Turn in at Deer Run Apartments; it's a 5- to 10-minute walk to the pond.

Sand Beach in Burnt Cove, Stonington. Turn off Rt. 15A on the fire road across from Bunt Cove Market (the sign says NO ENTRANCE AFTER DARK).

Reach Beach off Reach Rd. in Deer Isle is accessible via Sunshine Rd. to Greenlaw District Rd.

Causeway Beach, Rt. 15. South of the information booth (see *Guidance*), this roadside strand can fill the bill at low tide on a hot day, especially if there are children in the car. Also see **Scott's Landing** in *Green Space*.

✱ Green Space

Island Heritage Trust (207-348-2455; islandheritagetrust.org), which maintains an office at 420 Sunset Rd., publishes detailed maps of the following walking trails, also sponsors walks and talks.

Settlement Quarry, Stonington. A 0.25-mile walk from the parking area follows an old road to the top of this former working quarry for a view off across Webb Cove and west to the Camden Hills. Side trails loop back through woods. It's on Oceanville Rd., 0.9 mile from Rt. 15 (just beyond the turn marked for Settlement Quarry Ocean Adventures); turn at Ron's Mobil.

Scott's Landing. A small sign along the causeway points the way to the parking area. Trails web this historic 24-acre point on Eggemoggin Reach, leading to a vintage 1807 dock and a sandy beach. Great views of the bridge and the Reach.

Pine Hill Preserve, Little Deer Isle. The trail from this easy-to-find parking area (0.2 mile down Blastow Cove Rd.) is a short, rugged climb to a bald summit with a sweeping view. It's also of particular interest to geologists, and its vegetation is remarkably varied, some of it rare. Please keep to the path.

Edgar M. Tennis Preserve. Three miles of wooded and shore trails with shore views. Access is off Sunshine Rd., Fire Rd. 523.

Crockett Cove Woods Preserve (a Maine Nature Conservancy property) consists of 100 acres along the water, with a nature trail. Take Rt. 15 to Deer Isle, then Sunset Rd.; 2.5 miles beyond the post office, bear right onto Whitman Rd.; a right turn at the end of the road brings you to the entrance, marked by a small sign and registration box. From Stonington, take Sunset Rd. through the village of Burnt Cove and turn left onto Whitman Rd.

Barred Island Preserve is a 2-acre island owned by The Nature Conservancy, just off Stinson Point, accessible at low tide (only) by a wide sandbar; parking is on the road to Goose Cove Lodge. Owned by landscape architect Frederick Law Olmsted around the turn of the 20th century and bequeathed to The Nature Conservancy by his grandniece, this is a very special place, a good walk with small children.

Shore Acre Preserve. A 38-acre preserve with a loop trail to and along the shore with views of Oak Point and Goose Island. Take Sunshine Rd. 1.2 miles, bear left at the fork onto Greenlaw District Rd., and continue 0.9 mile to the parking area.

More public spaces

Ames Pond, east of Stonington village on Indian Point Rd., is full of pink-and-white water lilies in bloom June–early Sept.

Holt Mill Pond Preserve. A walk through unspoiled woodland and marsh. The entrance is on Stonington Cross Rd. (Airport Rd.)—look for a sign several hundred feet beyond the medical center. Park on the shoulder and walk the dirt road to the beginning of the trail, then follow the yellow signs.

Mariner's Memorial Park, Deer Isle. This is a delightful picnic and bird-watching spot with views of Long Cove. Take Fire Rd. 501 off Sunshine Rd., just east of Rt. 15.

Acadia National Park/Isle au Haut (see *To See* and *Boat Excursions*). In summer months the mail boat arrives at Duck Harbor at 11 AM, allowing time to hike the island's dramatic Western Head and Cliff Trails before returning on the 4 PM boat. The logistics are more difficult if you are coming from the town dock. Plan to catch the earliest boat and return on the latest. It's a short walk to the park ranger station (207-335-5551), where you can use the facilities (&) and pick up a map, but 4 miles to Duck Harbor. You should allow four hours to enjoy the dramatic cliff trails at Duck Harbor and around Western Head, Deep Cove, and Barred Harbor. The Duck Harbor trail from the ranger station is through the woods. With a bike you can get there faster on the unpaved road. Bikes are not permitted on the trails, which are largely pine-needle-carpeted and shaded but demanding with cliffy outcroppings. Camping is permitted at Duck Harbor mid-May–mid-Oct. in the five Adirondack-style shelters (each accommodating six people). Reserve on or as soon after April 1 as possible (207-288-8791, or download a form at nps.gov/acad).

❋ Lodging

INNS AND BED & BREAKFASTS

In Deer Isle 04627

✪ ☀ (ᵒ) **Pilgrim's Inn** (207-348-6615
or 1-888-778-7505; pilgrimsinn.com),
20 Main St. Open mid-May–mid-Oct.
Built as a private home in 1793, this
gracious, four-story, hip-roofed inn
stands in the middle of Deer Isle Village yet both fronts and backs on
water. It was built in 1793 by Ignatius
Haskel, who sailed to Deer Isle from
Newburyport to take advantage of
the island's ready supply of lumber.
According to innkeeper Tina Oddleif-
son, he built this expansive home to
house his wife and nine children, and
in 1889 another Haskell (Lizzie)
turned the house into an inn named
The Ark. It accommodated summer
guests who had begun arriving by
steamer from Boston, Portland, and
Rockland.

Pilgrim's Inn has been lucky in its subsequent owners. The wide pumpkin
pine floors and the 8-foot-wide original
fireplaces in the common and tap
rooms survive, along with working
hearths and paneling in the Game
Room and library, and the original
hardware in most of the dozen guest
rooms. In our room (No. 4) the wide
floorboards sloped away from the
hearth. Tasteful but unfussy furnishings underscored rather than upstaging
the 18th-century feel of the space, and
the view of the millpond. On the other
hand, the jetted tub and bracing
shower were welcome additions.
Rooms vary in size but all have water
views and private bath, and are furnished in antiques. There are also
three nicely decorated, two-bedroom
cottages with kitchens and living
rooms. The Whale's Rib (see *Dining
Out*) is open to the public. Inn rooms
$129–249 in-season, $119–189 in

shoulder months, including breakfast.
$50 charge for pets allowed in cottages.

Goose Cove Resort (207-348-2600 or
348-2300; goosecoveresortmaine.com),
300 Goose Cove Rd., Sunset. Open
late May–Columbus Day. This 21-acre
beachside property adjoins a Nature
Conservancy preserve and is well
known to birders and hikers. It is
presently owned by summer resident
Donald Sussman and managed by
locally known Azorean-born chef
Suzen Carter (see *Dining Out*). The
lodge is now primarily a restaurant.
The five rooms in the main lodge and
16 cabins have all been redecorated.
The cabins vary widely; some have
kitchenette, and several are waterfront
or have ocean views. $100–125 for
rooms in the lodge, $125–200 for
cabins.

✪ ∅ **The Inn at Ferry Landing**
(207-348-7760; ferrylanding.com), 77
Old Ferry Rd., RR 1, Box 163. Open
year-round. Overlooking Eggemoggin
Reach, Jean and Gerald Wheeler's
1840s seaside farmhouse offers magnificent water views, spacious rooms,
patchwork quilts, and a great common
room with huge windows and two
grand pianos that Gerald plays and

PILGRIM'S INN, DEER ISLE VILLAGE

Christina Tree

uses for summer recitals and spontaneous music sessions. The six guest rooms include a huge master suite with a woodstove and skylights. $130–140 for double rooms, $185 for the suite; less off-season. The Mooring, a two-story, two-bedroom, fully equipped housekeeping cottage, perfect for families, is $1,700 per week. Room rates include a full breakfast; minimum of two nights in high season.

In Stonington 04681

✪ **Pres du Port** (207-367-5007; pres duport.com), 91 W. Main and Highland Ave., P.O. Box 319. Open June–Oct. A find. We relax the moment we walk into this cheery, comfortable B&B in an 1849 home built on a rise above Greenhead Cove. The light- and flower-filled sunporch with a big picture window overlooks the harbor, filled with as many as many as 400 lobster boats, and the library/sitting room has a wood-burning hearth. There are three imaginatively furnished guest rooms, one with a cathedral ceiling and loft, kitchenette, deck access, and private bath. The other two share two baths (each room also has its own sink) and have harbor views, plus there's an outdoor hot tub overlooking the water and a crow's nest—"Charlotte's Folly"—for the best view of all. Charlotte Casgrain is a warm, knowledgeable hostess who enjoys speaking French and helping guests to fully explore the island. The generous buffet breakfast—perhaps crustless crabmeat and Parmesan quiche—is served on the sunporch. $125–150 per couple, less per single, tax included.

✪ **The Inn on the Harbor** (207-367-2420 or 1-800-942-2420; innonthe harbor.com), 45 Main St., P.O. Box 69. Open year-round. Guest rooms come with binoculars, the better to focus on lobster boats and regularly on the schooners in the Maine windjammer

fleet, for which each of the 14 comfortable rooms (private bath, phone, cable TV) is named. The inn backs on Stonington's bustling Main Street, but most rooms, some with balcony, face the working harbor, one of Maine's most photographed views. Our favorite rooms: the Heritage, with working hearth; the Stephen Taber, a freestanding room retaining its tin ceiling (it used to be a barbershop); and the American Eagle suite with two bedrooms, an open kitchen, dining area, and living room. A flowery ground-floor deck is shared by all. $145–230 summer, $65–135 off-season, includes continental breakfast. In-room spa services are available.

On Isle au Haut 04645

((ᵧ)) **The Inn at Isle au Haut** (207-335-5141; innatisleauhaut.com), P.O. Box 78. Open June–late Sept. This mansard-roofed Victorian-era cottage has four guest rooms, one downstairs with private bath and three upstairs that share. The house faces east, with views of the Mount Desert hills. Diana Santospago greets guests at the 4:30 mail boat and serves them a five-course dinner. A full breakfast, a packed lunch, and use of bicycles is also included in $300–375, less for single visitors. The inn is nicely situated for biking to town, to Long Pond, and to the hiking trails in the Acadia National Park section of the island, but Diana cautions that her bikes are fat-tired and single-speed. You need to be in good shape to enjoy this island, and you need to spend a couple of days. No need, however, to travel farther than the front porch. No children under age 16.

MOTEL 🐾 ✈ **Boyce's Motel** (207-367-2421 or 1-800-224-2421; boyces motel.com), P.O. Box 94, Stonington 04681. In the heart of Stonington Village, Barrett Gray has expanded on this appealing motel, run by his family run for four decades. This is a bit of a local secret, far bigger than it looks from the street. Most of the 11 units line a quiet lane that angles off from Main Street. They have queen or twin beds, and there are several efficiency units—one with two bedrooms, a living room, and kitchen. All are clean, and comfortable, with in-room coffee, water views from some decks, free long-distance, popular with families and kayakers. $69–135 per in high season, $49–90 off-season; $10 per pet per stay.

COTTAGES Check listings at the chamber website: deerisle.come.

✳ Where to Eat

DINING OUT Whale's Rib Tavern in Pilgrim's Inn (207-348-5222; pilgrimsinn.com), 20 Main St., Deer Isle Village. Open mid-May–Oct., daily 5–9 for dinner; closed Tue. in shoulder seasons. Reservations advised. Co-

innkeeper Tony Lawless, a graduate of the Culinary Institute of America, maintains the reliable quality of dining in this many-windowed old barn on the garden level of the Pilgrim's Inn, overlooking a millpond. We feasted with friends on Deer Isle clams steamed in beer and on locally raised mussels in a butter and cream sauce with roasted garlic and fried leeks, mopped up with freshly baked breads and followed by a seafood stew that included mahogany clams and calamari as well as a half lobster. Daily specials. Dinner entrées $13 (for a burger) $30 (boiled 1½-pound lobster). The wine list is respectable, and there's a choice of Maine microbrews.

Seasons of Stonington (207-367-2600; seasonsofstonington.com), 27 Main St., Stonington. Open daily June–Sept. for lunch, Wed.–Sun. for dinner. Check off-season. Reservations advised. Local residents Graham and Sue Bolton now own this prime harborside dining spot with its unbeatable view and tables, weather permitting, on a lower deck. We had heard rave reviews but our dinner was a letdown, from the tepid tap water and cold, hard rolls, through the gooey tasteless wild mushroom risotto ($19.95) and baked haddock (a small portion of fish on a few beans and dollop of mashed potato, $23.95). Admittedly this was a rainy September weeknight and the star chef was off. We'll give it a try at lunch this summer. Beer and wine.

Cockatoo Portuguese Restaurant at Goose Cove (207-348-2300 or 207-367-0900), marked from Rt. 15 west of Stonington in Sunset, Deer Isle. Open daily in-season, noon–9. Sunday buffet on the deck, 11–3 ($15). The woods road ends in an open green expanse overlooking a beach and the ocean—but that's not the call of seagulls you hear. It's the throaty screech and

BOYCE'S MOTEL, STONINGTON

Bill Davis

chatter of Peaches and Mango, Suzen Carter's pet cockatoos, whom many patrons know from Suzen's previous restaurant, Carter's Seafood, across the island in Sunrise. The dining room in this classic old lodge is spacious, with a many-windowed view of the water, and there's dining on the deck. It features the freshest of fish but also meat prepared in interesting ways by Azorean chefs. At lunch try a cup or bowl of Portuguese kale soup; chowder with a scallop roll; or a chouriço and pepper sandwich. The house specialty is Portuguese paella ($45 for two), but this is also the place to try an authentic bacalhau (shredded codfish with onions, crispy potatoes, and peppers). Dinner entrées $17–35.

EATING OUT ✪ ✐ Harbor Café, Stonington. Open year-round, Mon.–Sat. 6 AM–8 PM; in summer, open later on Fri. and Sat., plus Sun. 6–2. Spanking clean and friendly; booths and dependable food. Soups and salads. Seafood rolls, sandwiches and subs, fried and broiled seafood. Friday night it's a good idea to reserve for the all-you-can-eat seafood fries.Checkout the two-for-one lobster specials. Spirits available.

✦ ✐ The Fisherman's Friend Restaurant (207-367-2442), 5 Atlantic Ave., Stonington. Open year-round, 11–9 in summer months, until 10 Sat., check off-season. This vast waterfront restaurant (next to the quarryman statue) can seat more than 200 with a second-floor deck. A wide choice of fried and broiled fish, chowders and stews, burgers, and all the usual sandwiches. Lobster many ways. Children's menu.

(ᵧ) **Suzy Q's** (207-367-2415), 40 School St., Stonington. Open June–Oct., 8–3. The former Fisherman's Friend remains in the family, now a home

bake shop with plenty of space to sample the blackboard menu of soups and sandwiches.

(ᵧ) **Madelyn's Drive-in** (207-348-9444), 495 N. Deer Isle Rd. (Rt. 15), Deer Isle. Roadside takeout with burgers, fried seafood, hard and soft ice cream.

Stonington Ice Cream Co. next to G. Watson Gallery (68 Main St., Stonington). A seasonal takeout known for its lobster rolls, Gifford's ice cream, daily specials.

✐ Harbor Ice Cream (348-9949), 11 Main St., Deer Isle Village. A casual oasis good for sandwiches, wraps, Gifford's ice cream, and lobster rolls.

✐ Nervous Nellie's Jams and Jellies and Mountainville Café (207-348-6182; nervousnellies.com), 598 Sunshine Rd., Deer Isle. Open May–Oct. 10–5. Sculptor Peter Beerits displays his whimsical life-sized sculptures, sells his jams and jellies (wild blueberry preserves, blackberry-peach conserve, hot tomato chutney), and serves tea, coffee, and scones. Children of all ages love the sculptures, including a big red lobster playing checkers as a 7-foot alligator looks on. From Rt. 15, follow directions for Haystack (see *To See*).

Sophie's Cup (207-348-5667), 7 Main St., Deer Isle Village. Daily 7:30–4. For those who need their morning cappuccino, this is an unexpected find, especially in a shop that also sells handcrafted jewelry (fibulajewelry.com).

Espresso Bay at the Inn on the Harbor (207-367-2420), 45 Main St., Stonington. Open daily in-season. Espresso, iced drinks, homemade ice cream, and desserts. In good weather this is a must, an excuse to sit a spell on the inn's flower-filled harborside deck.

Note: ✪ **Lily's Café** (207-397-5936), Rt. 15 at Airport Rd. This beloved island restaurant is closing for the 2012 season. Check it out in 2013.

✷ Entertainment

Stonington Opera House (207-367-2788; operahousearts.org), School St., Stonington. Open year-round. This shingled building with its skinny, four-story "fly tower" dates to 1912. It stages a full calendar of reasonably priced concerts and original theatrical productions. Movies Fri.–Sun. at 7 PM. Call for schedules of movies and live performances.

Reach Performing Art Center (207-348-6301; atthereach.com), 249 N. Deer Isle Rd. at the elementary school, a venue for theater, dance, and musical performances.

✷ Selective Shopping

ART GALLERIES AND ARTISANS

Note: Studio crawling is a popular local pastime. Because local galleries feature work by local artists, it's frequently possible to trace a piece to its creator. Handout studio maps and postcards that picture individual artists' works are also readily available. The following is a partial listing.

In Deer Isle Village
Deer Isle Artists Association (207-348-2330; deerislertists.com), 15 Main St. Open Memorial Day weekend–Columbus Day daily 10–6; until mid-Dec. noon–5. A stunning, middle-of-village cooperative gallery with exhibits changing every two weeks.

Turtle Gallery (207-348-9977; turtlegallery.com), Rt. 15, north of Deer Isle Village. Open daily in summer, year-round by appointment. Artist Elena Kubler's gallery showcases exceptional jewelry as well as biweekly changing shows featuring fine art and contemporary crafts. It's housed in the barn in which Haystack faculty work was first

displayed, back when adjoining Centennial House was home to Francis ("Fran") Sumner Merritt, the school's founding director, and his wife, Priscilla, a noted weaver.

Red Dot Gallery (207-348-2733; reddotgallery.net), 3 Main St. Open June–Columbus Day, daily, then less often until Christmas. A cooperative showcase for the work of 10 established local artists in mixed media, painting, fibers, jewelry, and clay.

The Blue Heron (207-348-2267; blueherondeerisle.com), 22 More Farm Dr. off the Sunshine Rd. (just east of Rt. 15). Open June 15–Columbus Day weekend. Call for hours. Sue Wilmot's long-established gallery now fills a wing of her own home. Works by faculty and students of Haystack Mountain School in many media are featured.

The Lester Gallery (207-348-2676; tlesterphotography.com), 4 Main St. Open in-season Mon.–Sat. 10–5; off-season by chance or appointment. Ginger Lester features Terrell Lester's striking local "lightscapes," also photography by other locally based photographers.

Greene-Ziner Gallery (207-348-2601), 73 Reach Rd. (off Rt. 15 north of the village). Open July–Sept. In a barn surrounded by meadows, iron sculptor Eric Ziner displays his ornate and whimsical creations and potter Melissa Greene, her thrown earthenware pots suggesting Greek amphorae in shape but decorated with designs evoking tribal themes. Their **Yellow Birch Farm Stand** (Tue.–Sat. 10–5) sells fruit, veggies, herbs, eggs and dairy products.

In Stonington
Note: A dozen galleries now fill many of Stonington's old shopfronts. Check stoningtongalleries.com for receptions and special events.

✪ ♿ **Hoy Gallery** (207-367-2368; jill hoy.com), 80 Thurlow Hill. Open daily July–Columbus Day. Don't miss this big white barn set back up from the street, filled with Jill Hoy's bold, bright Maine landscapes.

G. Watson Gallery (207-367-2900; gwatsongallery.com), 68 Main St. Open May–Oct., Mon.–Sat. 10–5, Sun. 1–5. This is a serious gallery, showing contemporary painting and sculpture, featuring prominent East Coast artists.

Isalos Fine Art (207-367-2700; isalos fineart.com), 26 Main St. Open May–Oct., Mon.–Sat. 10–5, Sun. noon–5. Contemporary painting, sculpture, photography, and mixed media art by more than a dozen local artists.

SEAFOOD Stonington Lobster Co-op (207-367-2286 or 1-800-315-6625), 51 Indian Point Rd. Since 1948, the largest co-op in Maine of its type, wholesale and retail.

Carter's Seafood (207-367-0900), 24 Carter Lane, off Oceanville Rd. at Webb Cove. Open Mon.–Sat. 10–5. Very fresh fish, clams, lobsters, mussels, and shrimp.

Stonington Sea Products (207-367-200), 100 N. Main St. (Rt. 15). New ownership, specializing in clams and shrimp, whole and shelled.

Christina Tree

AT THE G. WATSON GALLERY

SPECIAL SHOPS

In Deer Isle
The Periwinkle, Deer Isle Village. Open June–Sept., a tiny shop with a vintage-1910 cash register, crammed with books and carefully selected gifts, great cards.

In Stonington
Dockside Books and Gifts (207-367-2652), 62 W. Main St. Seasonal. Al Webber's waterside bookstore has an exceptional selection of Maine and marine books, also gifts, sweaters by local knitters, and a great harbor view from the deck.

The Dry Dock (207-367-5528), Main St. Open daily mid-May–Oct., 9–5. Tempting clothing and craftwork; an outlet for Deer Isle granite products.

Prints & Reprints (207-367-5821), 31 Main St. Virginia Burnett's landmark shop featuring framed art, antiquarian books, and unexpected treasures.

Seasons (207-367-6348; seasonsof stonington.com), 6 Thurlow's Hill Rd. Graham and Sue Bolton have created an interesting mix of art, wine, and gifts.

V&S Variety Stores (207-367-5570), Rt. 15A, Burnt Cove. The many bou-

STONINGTON, BY JILL HOY

tiques and galleries have displaced the basic stuff of life—like groceries and everything a five-and-dime once carried. It's all moved out to Burnt Cove, where you'll also find the recycle shop, gas, and plenty of parking. Beside Burnt Cove Market (the supermarket, open daily until 9 PM) stands this huge but homespun "variety store," which stocks everything you forgot to bring.

Harbor Farm (207-348-7713 or 1-800-342-8003; harborfarm.com), the causeway on Little Deer Island. An eclectic emporium featuring local pottery, hand-rubbed wooden bowls, jewelry, plumbing and lighting fixtures, and a wide variety of gadgets and gifts.

Also see Nervous Nellie's Jams and Jellies under *Eating Out*. The shop is open year-round, producing 15 flavors of jam, chutney, marmalade, and much more.

On Isle au Haut

(ꄼ) **Black Dinah Chocolatiers** (207-335-5010; blackdinahchocolatiers.com), 1 Moor's Harbor Rd. Open daily in July and Aug., fewer days in Sept. A café with wireless Internet, serving drinks and pastries as well as delectable chocolates, isn't what you expect to find on a hike. In 2007 Kate and Steve Shaffer began making amazing fresh cream truffles and other chocolates, featuring ingredients from Maine farms, marketing them through mail order. The venture is named for the

rock face above their house. The chocolates are also available in Stonington at The Seasons and at The Cave in Brooklin.

✳ Special Events

Note: The weekly *Island Advantages* (islandadvantages.com) lists and details many more current happenings. Unless otherwise noted the contact is the chamber of commerce: 207-348-6124; deerislemaine.com.

Late January: **Winterfest**—three days include fireworks and bonfire.

May–October: Fri.-morning (10–noon) **farmer's market** at the Island Community Center (the former elementary school) in Stonington. This is huge.

May: **Wings, Waves & Woods**, "birding by land, by sea and by art"—puffin and pelagic trips, walks, lectures, food. **Memorial Day Parade**.

June: **Lupine Festival**—garden tours, open studios, boat, plane, and schooner trips.

July: **Independence Day** features island-wide festivities—a parade in Deer Isle Village, fireworks at Stonington Fish Pier. **Lobster-boat races** are usually the next Saturday, and **Fisherman's Day** (slippery cod contest, wacky boat races, and family fun) is the following week, sponsored by the Island Fishermen's Wives Association.

ACADIA AREA

MOUNT DESERT ISLAND; ACADIA NATIONAL PARK; BAR HARBOR AND ELLSWORTH; THE QUIET SIDE OF MOUNT DESERT

MOUNT DESERT ISLAND

Mount Desert (pronounced *dessert*) is New England's second largest island, one conveniently linked to the mainland. Two-fifths of its 108 square miles are maintained as Acadia National Park, laced with roads ideally suited for touring by car, more than 50 miles of "carriage roads" specifically for biking and skiing, and 120 miles of hiking trails.

The beauty of "MDI" (as it is locally known) cannot be overstated. Twenty-six mountains rise abruptly from the sea and from the shores of four large lakes. Mount Cadillac, at 1,532 feet, is the highest point on the U.S. Atlantic seaboard; a road winds to its smooth, broad summit for a 360-degree view that's said to yield the first view of dawn (which usually attracts a crowd) in the United States. Sunset, however, attracts a far larger crowd. There are also countless ponds and streams, an unusual variety of flora, and more than 300 species of birds.

Native Americans populated the island for at least 6,000 years before 1604, when Samuel de Champlain sailed by and named it L'Isle de Monts Deserts. In 1613 two French Jesuits attempted to establish a mission on Fernald Point near present Southwest Harbor. They were welcomed by the local Wabanaki chief Asticou but massacred by sailors from an English ship, and for 150 years this part of Maine remained a war zone between French and English. Finally settled in the second half of the 18th century, this remained a peaceful, out-of-the-way island even after a bridge was built in 1836, connecting it to the mainland.

In the 1840s landscape painters Thomas Cole and Frederic Church began summering here, and their images of the rugged shore were widely circulated. Summer visitors began arriving by steamboat, and they were soon joined by travelers taking express trains from Philadelphia and New York to Hancock Point, bringing guests enough to fill more than a dozen huge hotels that mushroomed in Bar Harbor. By the 1880s many of these hotel patrons had already built their own mansion-sized "cottages." These grandiose summer mansions numbered more than 200 by the time the stock market crashed. Many are now inns.

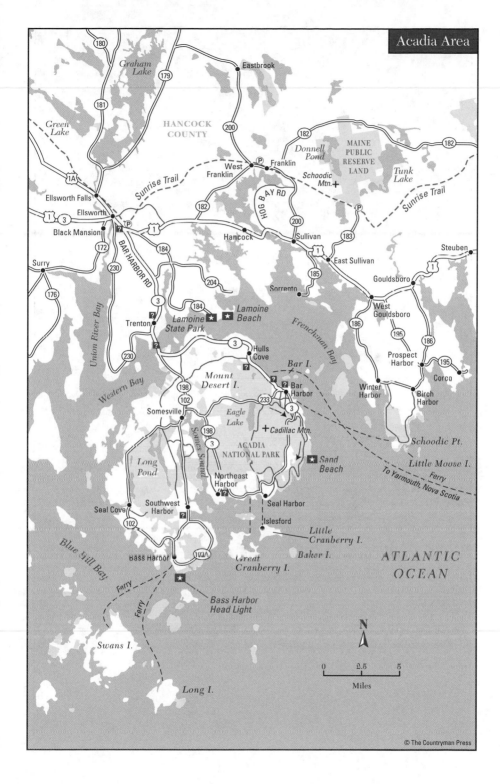

Acadia Area

180
Graham Lake
179
Eastbrook
181
Green Lake
HANCOCK COUNTY
200
182
Donnell Pond
MAINE PUBLIC RESERVE LAND
Tunk Lake
182
Sunrise Trail
West Franklin
Franklin
Schoodic Mtn.
Sunrise Trail
1A
Ellsworth Falls
1
3
Ellsworth
Black Mansion
182
HOG BAY RD
200
Sullivan
183
Steuben
1
172
204
Hancock
East Sullivan
1
Surry
230
BAR HARBOR RD
185
Gouldsboro
176
Sorrento
West Gouldsboro
195
3
184
Lamoine Beach
Frenchman Bay
186
Prospect Harbor
195
Trenton
Lamoine State Park
Corea
230
3
Hulls Cove
Winter Harbor
Birch Harbor
Western Bay
198
Mount Desert I.
Bar I.
102
233
Bar Harbor
Somesville
Eagle Lake
3
Schoodic Pt.
198
Cadillac Mtn.
Little Moose I.
Long Pond
Somes Sound
ACADIA NATIONAL PARK
Sand Beach
Ferry
To Yarmouth, Nova Scotia
Northeast Harbor
Seal Cove
102
Southwest Harbor
Seal Harbor
Islesford
Blue Hill Bay
Little Cranberry I.
Bass Harbor
102A
Great Cranberry I.
Baker I.
ATLANTIC OCEAN
Ferry
Bass Harbor Head Light
Ferry
Swans I.
N

0   2.5   5
Miles

Long I.

© The Countryman Press

Union River Bay

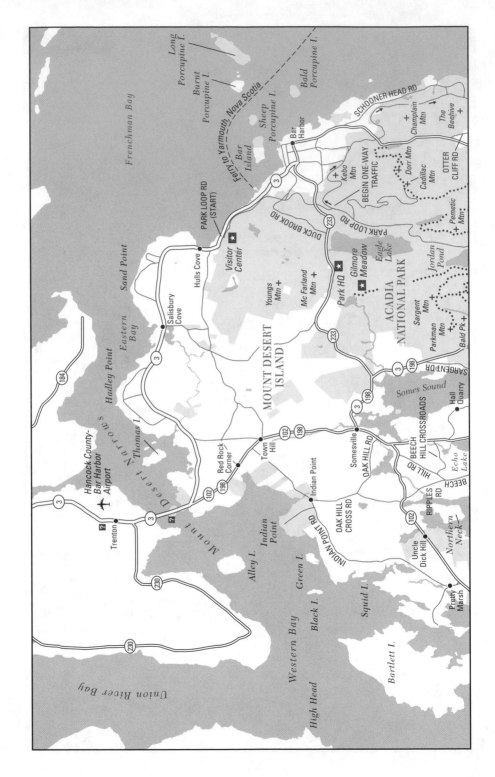

Long Porcupine I.

Burnt Porcupine I.

Bald Porcupine I.

Sheep Porcupine I.

Ferry to Yarmouth, Nova Scotia

SCHOONER HEAD RD

Champlain Mtn

The Beehive

Bar Harbor

Frenchman Bay

Bar Island

Kebo Mtn

Dorr Mtn

Cadillac Mtn

BEGIN ONE-WAY TRAFFIC

OTTER CLIFF RD

PARK LOOP RD (START)

DUCK BROOK RD

233

PARK LOOP RD

Pemetic Mtn

Sand Point

Hulls Cove

Visitor Center

Youngs Mtn +

Mc Farland Mtn +

Park HQ

Gilmore Meadow

Eagle Lake

ACADIA NATIONAL PARK

Jordan Pond

Salisbury Cove

Eastern Bay

Hadley Point

233

Sargent Mtn

Parkman Mtn +

Bald Pk +

184

MOUNT DESERT ISLAND

233

198

SARGENT DR

Somes Sound

Hall Quarry

Desert Narrows

Thomas I.

3

102

198

Red Rock Corner

Town Hill

Somesville

BEECH HILL CROSSROADS

OAK HILL RD

Echo Lake

Hancock County-Bar Harbor Airport

198

102

Indian Point

OAK HILL CROSS RD

BEECH HILL RD

RIPPLES RD

3

Trenton

3

Mount

Alley I.

Indian Point

INDIAN POINT RD

Uncle Dick Hill

Northern Neck

230

Green I.

Black I.

Squid I.

Pretty Marsh

Western Bay

Bartlett I.

230

High Head

Union River Bay

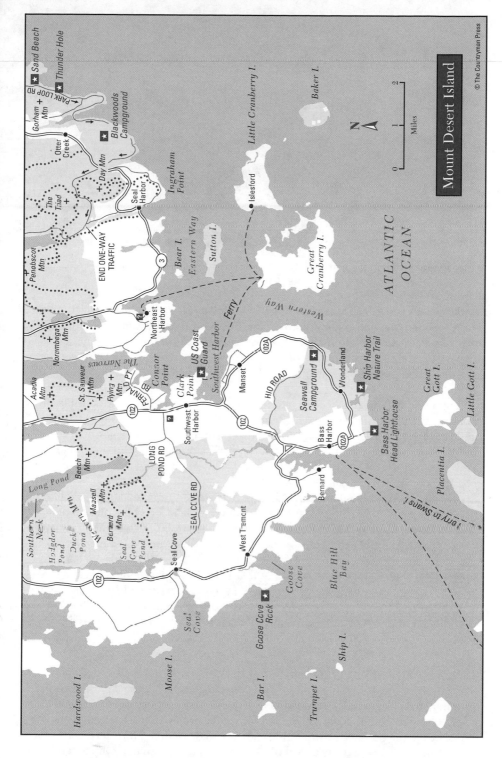

Mount Desert Island

© The Countryman Press

Nancy English

"THE BUBBLES" AT JORDAN POND

Mount Desert Island seems far larger than it is because it's almost bisected by Somes Sound, the only natural fjord on the East Coast, and because its communities vary so in atmosphere. Bar Harbor lost 67 of its 220 summer mansions and five hotels in the devastating fire of 1947, which also destroyed 17,000 acres of woodland, but both the forest and Bar Harbor have recovered, and then some, in recent decades.

Politically the island is divided into four townships: Bar Harbor, Mount Desert, Southwest Harbor, and Tremont. Northeast Harbor (a village in Mount Desert) and Southwest Harbor, the island's other two resort centers, also enjoy easy access to hiking, swimming, and boating within the park. Compared with Bar Harbor, however, they are relatively quiet, even in July and August, and the several accessible offshore islands are quieter still.

Mount Desert's mountains with "their gray coats and rounded backs look like a herd of elephants, marching majestically across the island," travel writer Samuel Adams Drake wrote in 1891, describing the first impression visitors then received of the island. They were, of course, arriving by steamboat instead of traveling down the unimpressive commercial strip that's Rt. 3. Today it's harder to get beyond the clutter and crowds—but not that hard. The memorable march of rounded mountains is still what you see from excursion boats and from Little Cranberry Island, as well as from the eastern shore of Frenchman Bay, the area described in this section as "East Hancock County."

ACADIA NATIONAL PARK

The legacy of Bar Harbor's wealthy "rusticators" is Acadia National Park. A cadre of influential citizens, who included Harvard University's President Charles W. Eliot, began to assemble parcels of land for public use in 1901, thus protecting the forests from the portable sawmill. Boston textile heir George Dorr devoted his fortune and energy to amassing a total of 11,000 acres and persuading the federal government to accept it. In 1919 Acadia became the first national park east of the

Mississippi. It is now a more-than-47,000-acre preserve, with 30,300 acres and more than another 10,000 in easements encompassing almost half of Mount Desert Island.

Almost two-thirds of the park's more than two million annual visitors get out of their cars and hike the park's trails. Many take the free, white-and-blue Island Explorer buses. They usually begin by viewing the introductory film in the Hulls Cove Visitor Center and then drive the 27-mile Park Loop Rd., stopping to see the obvious sites and noting what they want to explore more fully (see below). The park has much more to offer, from simple hikes to rock climbing, horse-drawn carriage rides to swimming, bicycling, canoeing, and kayaking.

Within the park are more than 45 miles of carriage roads donated by John D. Rockefeller Jr. These incredible broken-stone roads take bikers, hikers, joggers, and cross-country skiers through woods, up mountains, past lakes and streams. The paths also lead over and under 17 spectacular stone bridges. In recent years volunteers have rallied to refurbish and improve this truly spectacular network. Isle au Haut (see "East Penobscot Bay Region") and the Schoodic Peninsula (see "East Hancock County") are also part of Acadia National Park, but they are not located on Mount Desert Island and are much quieter, less traveled areas.

FEES The entrance fee for vehicles is $20 for a weekly pass. The fee is $10 from May 1 to June 22, and the day after Columbus Day to the end of October, when the Island Explorer is not running. Free Nov.–Apr. For individuals on foot, on the Island Explorer, or on a bicycle, the fee is $5 for a weekly pass.

GUIDANCE The park maintains **Hulls Cove Visitor Center** (207-288-3338; nps.gov/acad), just north of Bar Harbor. It's open mid-Apr.–Oct. In July–Aug., hours are 8–6 daily; Sept. 8–5; during shoulder seasons, 8–4:30. The glass-and-stone building, set atop 50 steps, shows a 15-minute introductory film and sells books, guides, and postcards. Pick up a free map and a listing of all naturalist activities, and sign up for the various programs scheduled June–Sept. at the amphitheaters in Blackwoods and Seawall Campgrounds. Children of all ages are eligible to join the park's Junior Ranger Program; inquire at the Hulls Cove Visitor Center. The park headquarters at Eagle Lake on Rt. 233 (207-288-3338) is open throughout winter, daily 8–4:30. **Map Adventures** (1-800-891-1534; mapadventures.com) makes very readable small maps of bike routes.

EAGLE LAKE

Nancy English

✷ To See

MUSEUM AND GARDENS Robert Abbe Museum at Sieur de Monts Spring (207-288-3519), 2 miles south of Bar Harbor, posted from Rt. 3 (south of Jackson Laboratory). The spring itself is encased in a Florentine-style canopy placed there by park founder George B. Dorr, who purchased the property to prevent enterprising islanders from opening a springwater business here. It stands in a garden, and beyond is the original **Abbe Museum**, open mid-May–mid-Oct., daily 10–5. On exhibit at Sieur de Monts are Dr. Robert Abbe's original collections of stone and bone tools, representing the Native American people in Maine, from the archaic periods. Admission to this octagonal, Mediterranean-style building, built by Abbe in 1928, is $3 adults, $1 ages 6–15. The rest of Abbe's collection is exhibited in the downtown Bar Harbor Abbe Museum (see "Bar Harbor"). The park museum is accessible through the **Wild Gardens of Acadia**, a pleasant walk where more than 300 species of native plants are on display with labels. The **Park Nature Center** here (open mid-May–Sept., daily 9–5) has displays on park wildlife; children can record the animals they have seen in the center's logbook.

✷ To Do

BICYCLING The more than 45 miles of broken-stone carriage roads make for good mountain biking. Several outfitters in Bar Harbor (see "Bar Harbor") rent equipment and can help you find good trails.

CAMPING The two campgrounds within the park are Blackwoods, 5 miles south of Bar Harbor, and Seawall, on the quiet side of the island, 4 miles south of Southwest Harbor. Both are in woods and close to the ocean. One vehicle, up to six people, is allowed on each site. Neither campground has utility hookups. Facilities include comfort stations, cold running water, a dump station, picnic tables, and fire rings. Showers and a camping store are within 0.5 mile of each. There are also four group campsites at Blackwoods and five at Seawall, for up to 15 people, which must be reserved through the park. Call 207-288-3338 for details.

Blackwoods (207-288-3274 answered May–Oct. only), open all year. Reservations required May–Oct. through the National Recreation Reservation Service (1-877-444-6777; recreation.gov). Cost of sites is $20 per night during the reservation period; fees vary during the off-season, when you need a special use permit and must walk 0.75 mile to the campsite. The road is not plowed.

MDI CARRIAGE ROAD, EAGLE LAKE
Nancy English

Seawall (207-244-3600), near Southwest Harbor, open late May–late Sept. Sites at Seawall are meted out on a first-come, first-served basis; but call to see if some sites are reservable, as this may change. Cost is $20 with a vehicle, $14 if you walk in.

HIKING The park is a mecca for hikers. Several detailed maps are sold at the Hulls Cove Visitor Center, which is also the source of an information sheet that profiles two dozen trails within the park. These range in difficulty from the **Jordan Pond Loop Trail** (a 3.3-mile path around the pond) to the rugged **Precipice Trail** (1.5 miles, very steep, with iron rungs as ladders). There are 17 trails to mountain summits on Mount Desert. **Acadia Mountain** on the island's west side (2 miles roundtrip) commands the best view of Somes Sound and the islands. The **Ship Harbor** on Rt. 102A (near Bass Harbor) offers a nature trail that winds along the shore and into the woods; it's also a great birding spot.

HORSE-DRAWN CARRIAGE TOURS ✍ **Wildwood Stables** (1-877-276-3622; carriagesofacadia.com), 0.5 mile south of the Jordan Pond House. One- and two-hour horse-drawn tours in multiple-seat carriages are offered six times a day.

RANGER PROGRAMS A wide variety of programs—from guided nature walks and hikes to birding talks, sea cruises, and evening lectures—are offered throughout the season. Ask at the Hulls Cove Visitor Center for a current schedule.

ROCK CLIMBING Acadia National Park is the most popular place to climb in Maine; famous climbs include the **Precipice**, **Great Head**, and **Otter Cliffs**. See "Bar Harbor" for guide services.

PARK LOOP ROAD

The 27-mile Loop Road is the prime tourist route within the park. There is a weekly fee of $20 per car on the road in summer ($10 off-season May–June 22, and Tue. after Columbus Day–Oct. 31; no fee Nov. and Apr.). The road always closes on Dec. 1, reopening mid-Apr., weather permitting.

The Loop Road officially begins at the Hulls Cove Visitor Center but may be entered at many points along the way. Most of the road is one-way, so be alert to how traffic is flowing. Places of interest along the Loop Road include Sieur de Monts Spring, a stop that could include the Wild Gardens of Acadia, the Abbe Museum, and Park Nature Center as well as the covered spring itself; Sand Beach, which is actually made up of ground shells and sand and is a great beach to walk down and from which to take a dip, if you don't mind 50- to 60-degree water (there are changing rooms and lifeguards); Thunder Hole, where the water rushes in and out of a small cave, which you can view from behind a railing; Jordan Pond House, popular for afternoon tea and popovers; and Cadillac Mountain. From Cadillac's smooth summit (accessible by car), you look north across Frenchman's Bay, dotted with the Porcupine Islands, which look like giant stepping-stones, and way beyond Down East. To the west, Jericho and Blue Hill Bays are directly below, and beyond the Blue Hill Peninsula you see Penobscot Bay and the Camden Hills. Many visitors come at sunrise, but sunset can be far more spectacular, a sight not to be missed.

SWIMMING Within Acadia there is supervised swimming at **Sand Beach**, 4 miles south of Bar Harbor, and at **Echo Lake**, a warmer, quieter option, 14 miles west of Bar Harbor (see "The Quiet Side").

WINTER SPORTS More than 45 miles of carriage roads at Acadia National Park are maintained as cross-country skiing and snowshoeing trails. Request the Winter Activities leaflet from the park headquarters (write to Information, Acadia National Park, P.O. Box 177, Bar Harbor 04609).

BAR HARBOR AND ELLSWORTH

Bar Harbor is the island's resort town, one of New England's largest clusters of hotels, motels, inns, B&Bs, restaurants, and shops—all within easy reach of the park's Hulls Cove Visitor Center and main entrance on the one hand, and an array of water excursions and the ferries to Nova Scotia on the other.

Ellsworth is the shire town and shopping hub of Hancock County, a place with a split personality: the old brick downtown blocks along and around the Union River and its falls, and the strip of malls and outlets along the mile between the junctions of Rts. 1A and 1 and of Rts. 1 and 3. If you're coming down Rt. 1A from Bangor, you miss the old part of town entirely, and it's well worth backtracking. Downtown Ellsworth offers the restored art deco Grand Auditorium, several good restaurants and one standout called Cleonice, as well a sense of the lumbering-boom era in which the Colonel Black Mansion, arguably the most elegant in Maine, was built.

The 6 miles of Rt. 3 between Ellsworth and Bar Harbor are lined with a mix of commercial attractions (some of which are vacation savers if you are here with children in fog or rain), 1920s motor courts and 1960s motels, newer motor inns and hotels.

In Bar Harbor itself shops and restaurants line Cottage, Mount Desert, West, and Main Streets, which slope to the Town Pier and to the Shore Path, a mile walk between mansions and the bay. On sunny days most visitors tend to be out in the park or on the water; half an hour before sunset (the time is announced each day in local publications), folks gather on and near the top of Cadillac Mountain for a show that can be truly spectacular. Dinner reservations are advisable because everyone then converges on restaurants at the same time, then walks around; most shops stay open until 9 PM.

BAR HARBOR VILLAGE GREEN

Nancy English

GUIDANCE Bar Harbor Chamber of Commerce (year-round 207-288-5103 or 1-888-540-9990; barharbor maine.com), 1201 Bar Harbor Rd.,

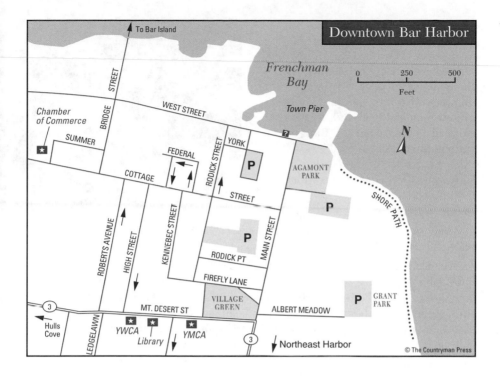

Downtown Bar Harbor

To Bar Island

Frenchman Bay

Town Pier

Chamber of Commerce

WEST STREET

BRIDGE STREET

SUMMER

COTTAGE

FEDERAL

RODICK STREET

YORK

STREET

AGAMONT PARK

SHORE PATH

ROBERTS AVENUE

HIGH STREET

KENNEBEC STREET

RODICK PT

MAIN STREET

FIREFLY LANE

MT. DESERT ST

VILLAGE GREEN

ALBERT MEADOW

GRANT PARK

Hulls Cove

LEDGELAWN

YWCA

Library

YMCA

3

Northeast Harbor

0   250   500

Feet

N

© The Countryman Press

Trenton 04605, maintains year-round and a seasonal information booth on Cottage Street in Bar Harbor.

Mount Desert Island Information Center (207-288-3411) is open daily mid-May–mid-Oct. (8:30–6 during high season) on Thompson Island, just after Rt. 3 crosses the bridge. This is the island's most helpful walk-in center, with restrooms and help with lodging reservations on all parts of the Island. It keeps track of vacancies at Seawall Campground; park rangers are usually there to sell passes to the park. The in-town **Bar Harbor Information Center** is at the corner of Main and Cottage Sts., open May till the last cruise ship in October.

Ellsworth Chamber of Commerce (207-667-5584 or 207-667-2617; ellsworthchamber.org), 163 High St., Ellsworth 04605, is an information center in the Ellsworth Shopping Center on the Rt. 1/3 strip; look for Wendy's.

Also see "Acadia National Park."

COLONEL BLACK MANSION

Nancy English

GETTING THERE *By air:* **Colgan Air** (1-800-428-4322; colganair.com) has been absorbed by U.S. Airways but still serves the **Hancock County & Bar Harbor Airport** in Trenton (between Ellsworth and Bar Harbor) from Boston and Rockland. Rental cars are available at the airport. **Bangor International Airport** (207-947-0384; flybangor.com), 26 miles north of Ellsworth, offers connections with most American cities.

Nancy English

ELLSWORTH FARMER'S MARKET

By private boat: For details about moorings, contact the Bar Harbor harbormaster at 207-288-5571.

By bus: **Concord Coach Lines** (1-800-639-3317; concordcoachlines.com) offers unbeatable year-round service from Boston's Logan Airport and South Station (five hours) to Bangor. The **Bar Harbor Shuttle** (207-479-5911; barharborshuttle.com) stops at the Bar Harbor Villager Motel and can pick up passengers by reservation elsewhere. The 10-passenger van provides transportation to and from the airports and the bus depots in Bangor, with other stops in Ellsworth and Somesville.

By car: From Brunswick and points south (including Boston and New York), the shortest route is I-295 to I-95 in Augusta, to Bangor to I-395 to Rt. 1A south to Ellsworth. A slightly slower route that includes some coastal views is I-95 to Augusta, then Rt. 3 east to Belfast (stop for a swim at Lake St. George State Park), and north on Rt. 1 to Ellsworth.

GETTING AROUND Jump on the **Island Explorer** buses operated by Downeast Transportation (207-288-4573; exploreacadia.com). The free, propane-powered buses travel eight routes around the island and carry bikes front and back. They will stop on request wherever it's safe. Readers have informed us that you can park at the Hulls Cove parking lot as long as you put the receipt on view in your car after buying the pass. Hikers take note: You can get off at one trailhead and be picked up at another. Bus schedules are timed to coincide with ferry departures to Nova Scotia, Swans Island, and the Cranberry Isles. The bus service starts June 23 every year and ends Columbus Day.

ISLAND EXPLORER

Nancy English

PARKING In high season, parking here is a pain. Note the lots on our Downtown Bar Harbor map. Much of the lodging is downtown (with parking), and the village is compact. Park and walk.

WHEN TO COME Since this is the most crowded summer place on the coast, everyone who lives nearby, from Portland north, prefers a visit in the off-season, preferably early fall. Although the Island Explorer bus schedule is reduced and the nights are chilly, the scenery is spectacular and the museums are still open. Winter is quiet indeed.

✳ To See

In Bar Harbor

✪ ✎ ♿ **Abbe Museum** (207-288-3519; abbemuseum.org), 26 Mount Desert St. Open May–Oct. daily 10–5, off-season Thu.–Sat. 10–4. $6 per adult, $2 ages 6–15, under 6 free. Museum members and Native Americans are free, too. The downtown Abbe in the heart of Bar Harbor, facing the village green, is more than eight times the size of its original, seasonal facility. The museum is dedicated to showcasing the cultures of Maine's Wabanaki, the 7,000 members of the Penobscot, Passamaquoddy, Micmac, and Maliseet tribes who live in Maine and the Maritimes. The permanent collection of 50,000 objects ranges from 10,000-year-old artifacts to exquisite basketry and crafts from several centuries. The orientation gallery and time line begin with the present and draw visitors back slowly and skillfully through 10,000 years to the core, a circular three-story tower, the "Circle of Four Directions." Exhibits include a fabricated copy of the 1794 treaty between Massachusetts and the Wabanaki that deeded much of Maine to its Native people. Much of the museum space is devoted to changing exhibits.

✎ **College of the Atlantic** (207-288-5395; coa.edu), Rt. 3. Housed in the original Acadia National Park headquarters, the **George B. Dorr Museum of Natural History** is a good stop (open 10–5 Tue.–Sat., closed Sun.–Mon.). Admission by donation, suggested $3 adults, $1.50 children. Exhibits include a tidal pool tank with marine animals visitors can touch and student-created dioramas of plants and animals of coastal Maine. "Study skins" from animals and birds can be touched as well. The **Ethel H. Blum Gallery** (open Tue.–Sat. 11–4) holds changing exhibits. Founded in 1969, COA is a liberal-arts college specializing in ecological studies. Its waterside acreage, an amalgam of four large summer estates, is now a handsome campus for 350 students.

Bar Harbor Historical Society (207-288-0000; barharborhistorical.org), 33 Ledgelawn Ave. Open June–Oct., Mon.–Sat. 1–4. In winter, open by appointment. Free. Well worth finding. A fascinating collection of early photographs of local hotels, Gilded Era clothing, books by local authors and about Bar Harbor, and the story of the big fire of 1947.

In Hulls Cove

✎ **Hulls Cove Sculpture Garden** (207-288-5126; jonesport-wood.com), 17 Breakneck Rd., Hulls Cove. This is the Bar Harbor branch of the

THE GEORGE B. DORR MUSEUM

Nancy English

Davistown Museum in Liberty. Two acres with a path and signage thread through grounds full of work by contemporary Maine artists like Melita Westerlund, who works with polychrome steel, David McLaughlin, who does assemblage art, painter Phil Barter, sculptor Obadiah Buell, and other artists. A picnic area, tree house, and playhouse for children are all open sunrise to sunset (Rocky Mann's studio is next door). You can also park here to walk into the Breakneck Hollow entrance to Acadia National Park and find a beaver pond.

In Ellsworth

Woodlawn: Museum, Garden & Park (207-667-8671; woodlawnmuseum.org), Surry Rd. (Rt. 172). Open June–Sept., daily 10–5; May and Oct., Tue.–Sun. 1–4. Audio tours $10 adults, $5 ages 12 and older, children under 12 free. The stone walls are shipshape around this outstanding 1824 Federal mansion based on a design by Asher Benjamin and built by John Black, who moved in with his wife and his three youngest children (five older children had already left home). The rooms are furnished as they were when the last Mr. Black and his family lived here. Stroll the formal gardens, walk the 2 miles of walking trails open dawn to dusk year-round, or reserve the croquet court for a match. The Ellsworth Antiques Show is held each August.

Birdsacre/Stanwood Wildlife Sanctuary (207-667-8460; birdsacre.com), Rt. 3. Old homestead and gift shop open May–Oct., daily 10–4; sanctuary open year-round with outdoor shelters that house non-releasable (injured) hawks and owls. This 200-acre nature preserve is a memorial to Cordelia Stanwood (1865–1958), a pioneer ornithologist, nature photographer, and writer. The 1850 homestead contains a collection of Stanwood's photos.

The Telephone Museum (207-667-9491; thetelephonemuseum.org), 166 Winkumpaugh Rd., marked from Rt. 1A north of Ellsworth. Open July–Sept., Thu.–Sun. 1–4. $5 adults, $2.50 children. The evolution of telephone service, from 1876 to 1983 (when the museum was founded), is the subject of this quirky museum. Switchboards and phones are hooked up ready for people to place calls—within the museum.

FOR FAMILIES ✕ **Acadia National Park Junior Ranger Programs** (207-288-3338) are the best thing going here for youngsters: First complete the activities in the Junior Ranger booklet, then join a ranger-led program or walk to receive a Junior Ranger patch. Books are for 7 and younger, and 8 and older; the senior ranger book for 18 and older contains much harder activities.

✕ **Family Nature Camp at College of the Atlantic** (see above) offers one- and two-week programs, Summer Field Studies, for children, and a one-week session for families who live in dorms and spend days on field trips, led by naturalists in Acadia National Park.

Route 3 attractions

You'll find waterslides, mini golf, and go-carts, as well as:

✕ **Mount Desert Oceanarium** (207-288-5005; theoceanarium.com), 1351 Rt. 3, Bar Harbor 04609. Open 9–5 daily, except Sun., mid-May–mid-Oct. $10–12 adults, $6–7 ages 4–12, depending on what you want to see and do. Tour the lobster hatchery and the Thomas Bay Marsh Walk.

Kisma Preserve (207-667-3244; kismapreserve.org), Rt. 3, Trenton. Open mid-May to late fall. $25 adults, under 3 free, but check if allowed. Tours are geared toward adults and more mature children. Make your reservation in advance and consider choosing an animal encounter with a wolf, moose, or primate. Thirty-five-acre nonprofit animal preserve with native and non-native animal species. The moose is a draw for tourists who want to see one, but animals from 60 other species are also living here, many retired, injured, or abused.

𝒮 **The Great Maine Lumberjack Show** (207-667-0067; mainelumberjack.com), Rt. 3, Trenton. Mid-June–Labor Day, nightly at 7 rain or shine, in fall on Sat. and Sun. The 1¼-hour show includes ax throwing, log rolling, speed climbing, and more.

✱ To Do

AIRPLANE RIDES Scenic Flights of Acadia (207-667-6527; mainecoastalflight .com), Rt. 3, Hancock County Airport, Trenton. Sightseeing flights in a Cessna 172 take four different routes over MDI.

Acadia Air Tours (207-667-7627; acadiaairtours.com), located at both the Hancock County–Bar Harbor Airport and on the pier in downtown Bar Harbor, offers scenic airplane, biplane, and glider flights sunrise to sunset, by appointment, weather permitting. The biplane and the glider flights are extremely popular. "No one's done this up here before," says owner Steve Collins. "It's simply the best way to experience the beauty of Acadia National Park."

AMUSEMENT PARK 𝒮 **Wild Acadia Fun Park** (207-667-3573; wildacadia .com), 233 Bar Harbor Rd., Trenton. Open end of May to Labor Day. Waterslides and splash pool, 18-hole mini golf, Indy-style go-carts, 32-foot rock climbing wall, slingshot trampoline, and water wars with water balloons and catapults.

BICYCLING The network of gravel carriage roads constructed by John D. Rockefeller Jr. in 1915 lends itself particularly well to mountain biking. In Bar Harbor, **Bar Harbor Bicycle Shop** (207-288-3886, barharborbike.com), 141 Cottage St., is the oldest bike outfitter in town and still rents only bikes: mountain, tandem, and everything that goes with them. **Acadia Bike** (207-288-9605 or 1-800-526-8615; acadiabike.com), 48 Cottage St., rents mountain and hybrid bikes and offers a full bike shop for sales and service. **Acadia Outfitters** (207-288-8118), 106 Cottage St., offers rentals of mountain and hybrid bikes, sea kayaks, and scooters. **Map Adventures** (1-800-891-1534; map adventures.com) makes very readable small maps of bike routes, stocked at these shops.

ACADIA BIKE

Nancy English

Nancy English

BICYCLING NEAR EAGLE LAKE, ACADIA NATIONAL PARK

BIRDING ✔ **Downeast Nature Tours** (207-288-8128; downeastnaturetours
.com), 150 Knox Rd., Bar Harbor. Michael J. Good offers guided bird-watching
and nature tours daily, and is a leader in ecotourism. Birders can strengthen field
identification skills and encounter neotropical migrants in-season along with birds
of the Gulf of Maine. Three Pines Bird Sanctuary includes wetland habitat for
Canada warblers and wood thrushes, and can be part of the tour.

For special programs led by park naturalists, visit the Hulls Cove Visitor Center.

BOAT CRUISES American Cruise Lines (800-814-6880; americancruiselines
.com), 741 Boston Post Rd., Ste. 200, Guilford, Connecticut. This cruise company
offers an eight-day cruise called the Maine Coast and Harbors, with stops in
Belfast, Camden, Castine, Rockland, Bar Harbor, Boothbay Harbor, and Portland.
The 104-passenger ship *Independence* is scheduled to make 17 trips in the summer of 2012.

BOAT EXCURSIONS Bar Harbor Ferry Co. (207-288-2984; barharborferry
.com) sails from the Bar Harbor Inn Pier, crossing Frenchman Bay to Winter Harbor several times a day; bring a bicycle and bike around Schoodic. **Lulu Lobster
Boat Ride** (207-963-2341; lululobsterboat.com), Harborside Hotel and Marina,
offers sightseeing (*le capitaine parle français*) on Frenchman Bay, with lobstering
demonstrations and seal-watching. **Dive-in-Theater** (207-288-3483; divered.com)
operates the *Seal*, an excursion boat from which passengers can watch Diver Ed
(through an underwater camera) probe the depths of Frenchman Bay, and then
get to touch what he fetches.

BREWERY TOURS Atlantic Brewing Company (207-288-BEER; atlantic
brewing.com), 15 Knox Rd., in Town Hill (across from the Town Hill Market), has
re-created an indoor–outdoor European brewery-pub. Daily tours and tastings at
2, 3, and 4, Memorial Day–Columbus Day; the barley wine is a wonderful thing to
try, and so are the rest of the brews. Try **The Knox Road Grille** for its great barbecue next door; all-you-can-eat Saturdays.

Bar Harbor Brewing Co. and Sodaworks (207-288-4592; barharborbrewing .com), 8 Mount Desert St., also offers tours Memorial Day–Columbus Day at 10, with changing seasonal hours.

CANOEING AND SEA KAYAKING Most ponds on Mount Desert offer easy access. **Long Pond**, the largest lake on the island, has three access points. Boats can be launched at **Echo Lake** from **Ike's Point**, just off Rt. 102. **Seal Cove Pond** is less used and accessible from fire roads north of Seal Cove. **Bass Harbor Marsh** is another possibility at high tide. Canoe rental sources offer suggestions and directions. **National Park Canoe Rentals** (207-244-5854) on Long Pond near Somesville offers tours as well as rentals, including kayaks. In Bar Harbor, **Aquaterra Adventures** (207-288-0007; aquaterra-adventures.com), 1 West St., does guided sea kayak tours and sells gear. **National Park Sea Kayak Tours** (207-288-0342 or 1-800-347-0940; acadiakayak.com), 39 Cottage St., gives guided kayak trips on the remote, west side of MDI. **Coastal Kayaking Tours** (207-288-9605 or 1-800-526-8615; acadiafun.com), 48 Cottage St., operates guided sea kayaking tours 2½–7 hours long, and multiday camping excursions. It also rents touring sea kayaks.

GOLF Kebo Valley Club (207-288-3000; kebovalleyclub.com), Rt. 233, Bar Harbor. Open daily May–Oct. Eighteen holes. "Eighth oldest golf grounds in America," since 1888. **Bar Harbor Golf Course** (207-667-7505; barharborgolfcourse .com), Rts. 3 and 204, Trenton. Eighteen holes.

FISHING Several charter boats offer deep-sea fishing. **Downeast Windjammer Cruises** (207-288-4585; downeastwindjammer.com) offers a four-hour fishing trip once or twice a day, with bait and tackle provided, leaving from the Bar Harbor Inn pier.

HIKING See "Acadia National Park."

HORSE-DRAWN CARRIAGE TOURS See "Acadia National Park."

ROCK CLIMBING Acadia Mountain Guides (207-288-8186; acadia mountainguides.com), 198 Main St., and **Atlantic Climbing School** (207-288-2521), 67 Main St., offer instruction and guiding for beginner through advanced climbers. (Also see "Acadia National Park.")

SAILING The *Margaret Todd* (207-288-4585) sails from the Bar Harbor pier from late May to mid- to late Oct. This 151-foot four-masted schooner, designed and built in 1998 by Captain

VIEW ACROSS BAR HARBOR GREEN AND THE *MARGARET TODD*

Nancy English

Steve Pagels, cruises through Frenchman Bay three times a day in high season, less frequently in late October.

SWIMMING 🐚 **Lake Wood** near Hulls Cove is a pleasant freshwater beach, ideal for children. Also see "Acadia National Park."

WHALE-WATCHING The big operator is **Bar Harbor Whale Watch Co.** (207-288-2386; barharborwhales.com), 1 West St., Bar Harbor, which also offers seal-watching and lobstering tours. Bring a jacket, sunblock, binoculars, and a camera. Ask how long it takes to get out to the whales and about weather—and sea—conditions on the day you book.

✳ Lodging

Many of Bar Harbor's nearly 2,400 beds, ranging from 1920s motor courts to large chain hotels and motels, are strung along Rt. 3, north of the walk-around town—where a few surviving summer mansions are now B&Bs commanding top dollar. Reservations are not as crucial as they used to be, with a surge in the number of rooms here, but still a good idea. We cannot claim to have inspected every room in town, but we have checked out the most appealing options.

WATER-VIEW BED & BREAKFASTS

In Bar Harbor 04609
Ullikana Bed & Breakfast (207-288-9552; ullikana.com), 16 The Field. Open May–Oct. This is our top pick in downtown Bar Harbor, steps from both Main Street and the Shore Path, yet with an away-from-it-all feel. Innkeepers Helene Harton and her husband, Roy Kasindorf, combine a rare flair for decorating with a genuine warmth that sets guests at ease. They bought Ullikana, a vintage-1885 Tudor-style summer mansion, in 1990 and transformed it with vivid colors and stylish, artful decor. The neighboring Yellow House, another classic Bar Harbor "cottage," flaunts their touch with tiled baths and pretty colors. Breakfast, perhaps a light berry-stuffed soufflé

pancake, is served on the terrace overlooking the water or in Ullikana's attractive dining room, where you will feel as if you've returned to the home you always wished for. The 10 guest rooms all have private bath; 3 have a fireplace. $165–295, varying with room size and view.

🐚 **The Shore Path Cottage** (207-288-0643; shorepathcottage.com), 24 Atlantic Ave. Open May–Oct. Lisabeth Chester Oxman has taken over management of this delightful Bar Harbor "cottage" and comfortable B&B previously run by her mother, Roberta Chester, since 1973. The dining room has a kind of authentic elegance that can't be imitated, with lovely china and

THE FOUNTAIN AT ULLIKANA BED & BREAKFAST

Nancy English

decor. Seven guest rooms (just one without with private bath, a few with claw-foot tub) are named for the youngsters who grew up in them. The house is filled with books, art, and classic videos. Both kosher and vegetarian breakfasts are served, and solo travelers and children are particularly welcome. $140–280 in-season, $110–200 low-season.

&. **The Bass Cottage Inn** (207-288-1234 or 1-866-782-9224; basscottage .com), 14 The Field, P.O. Box 242. Open mid-May to the end of Oct., this 10-room inn was completely redone before reopening in 2004, adding whirlpool tubs, gas fireplaces, and TVs with DVD players (which will be removed if you ask). Teri Anderholm oversees the cuisine featuring lobster quiche or crème brûlée French toast for breakfast served in a bright, elegant sunporch, and wine with fine hors d'oeuvres in the early evening. She and her husband, Jeff Anderholm, run things smoothly in the handsome and comfortable inn, where rates range $225–365 in season, less before and after.

❖ **Balance Rock Inn** (207-288-2610 or 1-800-753-0494; balancerockinn .com), 21 Albert Meadow. The original mansion, built in 1903 for a Scottish railroad tycoon, is augmented by a heated pool. Fourteen rooms, most with ocean view, private balcony, whirlpool bath; some with fireplace. The three suites have a kitchen, living room, and sauna. Rooms and suites, all with breakfast, range $125–525 depending on season. $40 fee for pets.

Saltair Inn (207-288-2882; saltairinn .com), 121 West St. Set on the street that overlooks Frenchman Bay and close to the center of things, Saltair Inn provides traditional accommodations with excellent extras, like the heated Travertine tile floor in

Sedgewick Room. Stroll down the sweep of green lawn to the seats overlooking the sea and back to enjoy breakfast on a deck close to the inn in fine weather. $95–355 depending on season.

OTHER DOWNTOWN B&BS

In Bar Harbor 04609

Manor House Inn (207-288-3759 or 1-800-437-0088; barharbormanor house.com), 106 West St. Open mid-Apr.–Oct. No real water views, but a short walk from Bar Island. Nine comfortable rooms with private bath are in the vintage-1887 "Manor" with its rich woodwork. The full acre of landscaped grounds also includes Acadia Cottage with whirlpool, the Chauffeur's Cottage with three guest rooms and two suites, and two garden cottages with gas fireplace. $83–250 includes full breakfast and afternoon tea.

Seacroft Inn (207-288-4669 or 1-800-824-9694; seacroftinn.com), 18 Albert Meadow. Open mid-May–Oct. Bunny Brown's gracious, many-gabled old "cottage" is sequestered on a quiet street, steps from the Shore Path. Extended stays are the norm; all seven rooms have a fridge and a microwave, or a kitchen. $89–129 in season, substantially less off season, with housekeeping $10 extra and a complimentary coffee bar and towel exchange. A "Breakfast Basket" with fruit, muffin, juice, and yogurt is $5.

Primrose Inn (207-288-4031 or 1-877-TIME-4-BH; primroseinn.com), 73 Mount Desert St. Open mid-May–Oct. This is a spiffy 1878 stick-style "painted lady" Victorian summer cottage owned by Catherine and Jeff Shaw. The 15 guest rooms are bright with floral wallpaper and Victorian decor; several have a gas fireplace and private balcony. The nicest rooms in the house have a "bubble massage"

Kohler bathtub. Every room has a flat-panel TV with DVD player. Rooms are $159–249, less off-season, including a great breakfast and afternoon tea, perhaps with apple pie. Free soda and water in the guest refrigerator, and the loan of a GPS to find Thurston's Lobster Pound.

The Maples Inn (207-288-3443; maplesinn.com), 16 Roberts Ave. Open May–Oct. Mark Dresser bought this inn in 2005 and has been decorating with his and his family's antiques; his architectural books are a resource at this pleasant 1903 house on a quiet side street within walking distance of shops and restaurants. The six rooms (all with private bath) are crisply decorated, furnished with a high, antique bed and down comforter. Red Oak, under the eaves, has its own tranquil deck. $160–215 per couple; $115–150 off-season, with a fine breakfast.

🐾 **Canterbury Cottage** (207-288-2112; canterburycottage.com), 12 Roberts Ave. Open year-round. This architecturally interesting Victorian house (its original owner was the B&M stationmaster, and its architect specialized in railroad stations) has a canine welcome committee. Rooms each hold a private bath and cable TV. One has a small balcony. $145–155 double in-season, $89–99 off-season, includes full breakfast served in the pretty dining room.

Cleftstone Manor (207-288-4951; cleftstone.com), 92 Eden St. Open May–Oct. Located a short drive from downtown, this 1880 mansion once owned by wealthy summer visitors has been an inn for 50 years. One smallish room called Benjamin Stanwood has a huge bathroom; four have a sofa bed. Joseph Pulitzer summered here, and a few of the original antiques are still in place, like two crystal chandeliers in the dining room. Seventeen rooms

with private bath, two with whirlpools, five with fireplace. Pool and spa services are shared with neighbor **Bluenose Inn**. In-season rates $130–195, less off-season.

Anne's White Columns Inn (207-288-5357 or 1-800-321-6379; annes whitecolumns.com), 57 Mount Desert St. Open May–Oct. Built in the 1930s as a Christian Science church, hence the columns. The 10 rooms have private bath, air-conditioning, and cable TV. $110–165 July–mid-Oct. (less off-season), including full breakfast and afternoon wine and cheese.

♿ **Mira Monte Inn and Suites** (207-288-4263 or 1-800-553-5109; mira monte.com), 69 Mount Desert St. Open May–mid-Oct. Bar Harbor native Marian Burns offers 13 comfortable guest rooms and four suites in her gracious 1864 mansion. Many, like Malvern, have a private balcony overlooking the deep, peaceful lawn in back or the gardens on the side. All rooms have private bath, phone, clock-radio, voice mail, and flat-screen cable TV; some have a gas fireplace. Rates include a full breakfast buffet and afternoon refreshments. $188–256 for rooms and suites; $95–165 off-season.

HOTELS AND MOTELS

In Bar Harbor 04609

♿ **Bar Harbor Inn** (207-288-3351 or 1-800-248-3351; barharborinn.com), Newport Dr. Open Mar.–Nov. With 153 units, this landmark hotel gets its share of groups, but its downtown waterside location is unbeatable. It's a genuinely gracious hotel, with a 24-hour front desk, bellhops, a restaurant, and room service. The hotel-sized lobby with seating near the fire is quite grand. Reading Room Restaurant (see *Dining Out*), begun as an elite men's social club in 1887, offers fine dining with water views. The 51 guest rooms

Nancy English

BAR HARBOR INN

rant, lies off the main lobby (and has the same branding as The Samoset's 2011 version in Rockport). The spa is located in the neighboring Bar Harbor Club with its own restaurant. Tennis courts and a saltwater pool. Standard rooms $275–425, suites $399–1,700 in-season; off-season $99–199, $299–800.

✍ **Wonder View Inn** (207-288-3358 or 1-888-439-8439; wonderviewinn .com), 50 Eden St., P.O. Box 25. Open May–Oct. Children are welcome in the 75-unit motel built on 14 acres, the site of an estate once owned by Mary Roberts Rinehart, author of popular mystery stories. Near downtown Bar Harbor, the motel overlooks French-man Bay and includes a swimming pool. $109–249 in summer, less off-season. Most rooms have a balcony with an ocean view.

🐾 ✍ **Bar Harbor Villager Motel** (207-288-3211 or 1-888-383-3211; barharborvillager.com), 207 Main St. This reasonably priced motel provides immaculately clean and comfortable rooms within an easy walk of every-thing Bar Harbor offers, along with a turquoise, heated pool tucked into a back corner of the parking lot. The **Bar Harbor Shuttle** (207-479-5911; barharborshuttle.com) stops here, going to the airports and the bus depot in Bangor. Summer rates $99–138, $79–108 off-season, children under 10 free.

✍ **Sea Breeze Motel** (207-288-3565 or 1-800-441-3123; seabreeze.us), 323 Rt. 3. Open mid-May–mid-Oct. Watch the sun rise over Frenchman Bay all summer long from the motel's 7-acre hillside location, 4 miles from town. Thirty-six clean, comfortable rooms, most with ocean view, have private bath, mini fridge, cable TV, air-conditioning, and in-room coffee. Heated swimming pool and hot tub. $64–254, depending on season.

in the Main Inn were the first new hotel rooms available in town after the 1947 fire. Of these, 43 were com-pletely rebuilt in 1998; balconies, jet-ted tubs, and fireplaces were added. The grounds also include a 64-unit Oceanfront Lodge with private bal-conies on the bay, and the Newport Building—38 equally comfortable rooms without views. All rooms have phone, cable TV, and access to the pool, Jacuzzi, fitness room, and 7 acres of manicured lawns on the water. $199–379 in-season, continental break-fast included.

Harborside Hotel & Marina (207-288-5033 or 1-800-328-5033; the harborsidehotel.com), 55 West St. Open May–Oct. Views of the harbor and Porcupine Islands in some rooms. Luxuriously furnished and accented with marble baths and marble-tiled floors, many rooms and suites are equipped with full kitchens; some have a fireplace in the master bedroom and Jacuzzi on the porch. One deluxe oceanfront room has upscale hotel fur-niture and a balcony. The on-site marina can dock a 175-foot yacht. **La Bella Vita**, a high-end Italian restau-

In Ellsworth 04605

🐾 ✿ **Twilite Motel** (207-667-8165 or 1-800-395-5097; twilitemotel.com), Rts. 1 and 3. In 2007 Chuck and Ariela Zucker took over this charming motel with flowers spilling out in between the 1950s-style, updated rooms, all with private bath and a little outdoor seating area. Children's play area, continental breakfast served in the breakfast room, and coin-operated laundry with games and books for guests to enjoy. Rates $82–119, less off-season.

COTTAGES ✿ **Acadia Cottage Rentals** (207-288-3636; acadiarental.com) offers camps, cottages, private homes, and estates for a minimum of one week (Sat.–Sat.).

✿ **Emery's Cottages on the Shore** (207-288-3432 or 1-888-240-3432; emeryscottages.com), Sand Point Rd., Bar Harbor 04609. Open May–late Oct. In the family since 1969, these 22 cottages and an apartment on Frenchman Bay offer electric heat, shower, and cable TV; 14 have a kitchen. Linens, dishes, and cooking utensils provided. Serene, private pebble beach. Telephone available for local calls. No pets. Hikers like to use these cabins as a launching place from which to set out on day trips in Acadia National Park. $560–1,075 per week late June–late Aug.; $470–820 late Aug.–Oct.; less in May and June.

PUBLIC CAMPGROUNDS
Lamoine State Park (207-667-4778; campwithme.com), Rt. 184, Lamoine. Open mid-May–mid-Oct. Minutes from busy Rt. 3 (between Ellsworth and Bar Harbor), this 55-acre waterside park offers a boat launch and 62 campsites (no hookups, but hot showers in a bathhouse), two-night reservation minimum, $25 per night for nonresidents in-season, $15 for residents. Neighboring Lamoine Beach is great for skipping stones. *Note:* There are occasionally vacancies here in July and Aug. when Acadia National Park campsites are full, and about 20 sites are on a first-come, first-served basis. (For reservations, out-of-state call 207-624-9950; in-state call 1-800-332-1501; or visit maine.gov/doc/parks/reservations.)

Also see *To Do* in "Acadia National Park." There are more than a dozen commercial campgrounds in this area; check local listings.

✳ Where to Eat

DINING OUT

All listings are in Bar Harbor unless otherwise noted
The Burning Tree (207-288-9331), Rt. 3, Otter Creek. Open June–Columbus Day 5–10; closed Tue., also Mon. after Labor Day. Reservations recommended. Admired for its fresh fish and its own organically grown produce from five gardens. Dine inside or on a lattice-enclosed porch on a wide choice of seafood, chicken, and vegetable entrées, but no red meat. You might begin with crispy kale and oven-roasted littleneck clams with garlic, pine nuts, and chèvre ($12.50), then dine on a cashew, brown rice, and Gruyère cheese terrine ($23.50) or basil and chèvre stuffed organic chicken breast with homemade tomato jam ($24). Entrées $20–29.

Cleonice (207-664-7554; cleonice.com), 112 Main St., Ellsworth. Open year-round for dinner, lunch, daily in summer. Chef Rich Hansen is a master of Mediterranean seafood and meat dishes. Perfect fish cakes, steak frites with grass-fed beef from nearby, paella, and poached halibut with Pernod velouté were one fall day's specials, but don't skip the tapas, like grilled baby octopus with piri piri sauce and Sicilian-style meatballs. The dark wood bar adds to the illusion of being farther south and east, but the food makes you feel like this is the center of the universe. Entrées $21.50–29.50.

Mache Bistro (207-288-0447; mache bistro.com), 135 Cottage St. Kyle Yarborough has made Mache Bistro a place to count on for vibrant flavors and great cooking. His excellent lobster cakes, a special, with cracked green olive relish, and mussels with chorizo get dinner started perfectly, and the bistro hanger steak with Gorgonzola butter is just as good. Entrées $16–27.

&. **Café This Way** (207-288-4483; cafethisway.com), 14½ Mount Desert St. Open seasonally for breakfast and dinner. Tucked just off the village green, this is a winner. Start dinner with a smoked salmon "parcel" that wraps up goat cheese and pickled jalapeños, then try fish-and-chips made with tempura ahi tuna. Entrées $15–26. Reservations a good idea. Breakfast is just as good (see *Eating Out*).

✐ **Jordan Pond House** (207-276-3316, jordanpond.com), Park Loop Rd., Seal Harbor. Open mid-May–late Oct. for lunch and tea 11:30–6 in summer, 5:30 early and late in the season, and for dinner 6–9. Reservations advised. First opened in the 1870s, this landmark was beautifully rebuilt after a 1979 fire, with dining rooms overlooking the pond and mountains. It's best known for popovers and outdoor tea (see *Afternoon Tea*) but is least crowded at dinner. Prime rib, fresh fish, and baked scallops. Dinner entrées $15–24.

&. **Havana** (207-288-CUBA; havana maine.com), 318 Main St. Open from 5 nightly; reservations suggested. The menu changes weekly, and the accent ranges from the Caribbean to Africa and farther east. Dinners have

included braised beef short ribs in soy sauce, apple cider, and brown sugar with avocado guasaca, a spicy Venezuelan spread, and local squash curry. Entrées $19–34.

Galyn's (207-288-9706; galynsbar harbor.com), 17 Main St. Lunch and dinner. Easy to miss among the shops near the bottom of Main St., this is bigger than it looks, with dining rooms upstairs and down. Try the crabcakes or lobster enchilada. Entrées from $16.

Café Bluefish (207-288-3696; cafebluefishbarharbor.com), 122 Cottage St. Dark wood, books, cloth napkins with varying designs, and mismatched china create a pleasant atmosphere. Chef-owner Bobbie Lynn Hutchins, a fourth-generation Bar Harbor native, prepares meat, vegetarian, vegan, and seafood entrées, plus (Food Network famous) lobster strudel. $16–32.

McKay's Public House (207-288-2002; mckayspublichouse.com), 231 Main St. Two floors (with live music upstairs) fill up with dedicated local customers at this year-round place. Farm stand salad, Maine étouffée, roasted organic chicken, and brandy-braised pork are possibilities. Entrées $16–21.

JORDAN POND HOUSE

Nancy English

The Reading Room (207-288-3351; barharborinn.com), Bar Harbor Inn, Newport Dr. Opened in 1887 as an elite men's club, the horseshoe-shaped formal dining room commands a splendid harbor view; frequent piano music at dinner. Open for breakfast and dinner (lunch at The Terrace Grill). Dinner entrées range from a Dijon-roasted rack of lamb to lobster pie ($24–37).

✔ **Testa's** (207-288-3327; testas restaurants.com), 53 Main St. Open 8 AM–10 PM, June–Aug., closing earlier off-season (the family moves to its Palm Beach restaurant in Nov.). In Bar Harbor since 1934. Extensive menu, including Italian and seafood specialties. Dinner entrées $17–30.

LOBSTER POUNDS Lobster pounds are the best places to eat lobster. The easiest to find are the clutch around the Trenton Bridge on Rt. 3. The **Trenton Bridge Lobster Pound** (207-667-2977; trentonbridgelobster .com), open Memorial Day–Columbus Day 8–8, or for live lobsters year-round, has been in George Gascon's family a long time. The view and the aromas are unparalleled.

& **Bar Harbor Lobster Bakes** (207-288-4055; barharborlobsterbakes.com), Rt. 3, Hulls Cove, is a twist on the traditional lobster pound. Reservations are a must. Choices are lobster or steak. Watch the lobsters being steamed with your potatoes and corn in the large steel cookers.

Also see **Union River Lobster Pot** under *Eating Out*, as well as *Lobster Pounds* in "The Quiet Side."

EATING OUT

In Bar Harbor
The Black Friar Pub (207-288-5091; blackfriarinn.com), across from the Shop and Save. The Black Friar Pub serves pub fare that was winning loyalty in 2009, like sweet potato fries, crab fritters, and fish-and-chips. Of course the big beer selection, with many Maine brews on tap, is another draw, with Black Fly Stout from Gritty's at the top of the list of stouts. Meals $10–17.50.

Café This Way (207-288-4483), 14½ Mount Desert St. Open for breakfast 7–11 Mon.–Sat., 8–1 Sun. The menu ranges from scrambled tofu to steak and includes omelets, eggs Benedict with smoked salmon, and many other appetizing dishes.

Lompoc Café (207-288-9392; lompoc cafe.com), 36 Rodick St. Open daily with lunch 11:30–3 in the summer and 5–9:30 for dinner, till 1 for drinks. Billed as the original home of Bar Harbor Real Ale (the Atlantic Brewing Company itself has outgrown its birthplace), this is a congenial oasis with an open knotty-pine dining room, plus porch and terrace tables by a bocce court. Entrée choices include pizzas and salads; live music on weekends.

🍴 ✔ **Rosalie's Pizza** (207-288-5666), 46 Cottage St. Locals head for a booth at Rosalie's when they want excellent pizza. Calzones, salads, and baked subs are also served.

Morning Glory Bakery (207-288-3041; morningglorybakery.com), 39 Rodick St. Open weekdays 7–7, Sat.–Sun. 8–7. Smoothies, espresso, savory and sweet baked goods, soup, sandwiches. Local meats, produce, and dairy products on the menu; the bacon and fresh eggs are local, Smith Family Farm yogurt, and Sunset Acres Farm goat cheese.

🍴 & **Poor Boy's Gourmet** (207-288-4148), 300 Main St. Open for dinner from 4:30 nightly. Count on a decent dining experience at reasonable prices. Choices range from vegetarian entrées to a full lobster dinner—including brownie à la mode. Wine and beer.

UNION RIVER LOBSTER POT

Epi Sub & Pizza (207-288-5853), 8 Cottage St. Open 11–9 June–early Nov., fewer hours off-season, may be closed in winter. Tops for food and value but zero atmosphere. Cafeteria-style salads, freshly baked calzones, pizza, quiche, pasta, and crabmeat rolls.

Jordan's Restaurant (207-288-3586), 80 Cottage St. Open 4:30 AM–2 PM. Under David Paine's ownership (since 1976), this remains an old-style diner: breakfast all day, specializing in blueberry pancakes and muffins and a wide variety of three-egg omelets. The place to fuel up for a hike.

In Hulls Cove
Chart Room (207-288-9740), Rt. 3. Open for lunch and dinner. A dependable, family-geared waterside restaurant with seafood specialties; good quiche and Caesar salads.

In Ellsworth
Union River Lobster Pot (207-667-5077; lobsterpot.com), behind Rooster Brothers at the western edge of Ellsworth. Open daily June–Aug., 11:30–8:30, dinner only through Oct. Brian and Jane Langley own this pleasant riverside restaurant and serve a full menu, including ribs, but the specialty is lobster and seafood cooked four

ways. Leave room for pie. Beer and wine, and an eagle overhead at a beautiful setting.

Riverside Café (207-667-7220), 151 Main St. Open 6 AM–3 PM weekdays, 7–3 Sat., 7–2 Sun. for breakfast and lunch in expanded, bright, spacious quarters. Good food and coffees.

AFTERNOON TEA Jordan Pond House (207-276-3316; jordanpond .com), Park Loop Rd., Seal Harbor. Tea on the lawn at the Jordan Pond House (served 11:30–6 mid-July–Aug., till 5:30 early and late mid-May to mid-Oct.) has been de rigueur for island visitors since 1895. The tea comes with freshly baked popovers and homemade ice cream. Reservations suggested.

SNACKS AND ICE CREAM Mount Desert Island Ice Cream (for information call 207-460-5515; mdiic.com). Stores are at (207-801-4007) 7 Firefly Lane and (207-801-4006) 325 Main St., both in Bar Harbor. Ice cream, chocolate made with Callebaut

MOUNT DESERT ISLAND ICE CREAM

chocolate, vanilla with vanilla beans, and sorbet, like lemon made with hand-squeezed lemons. Blueberry basil sorbet and salted caramel ice cream were both hits. Linda Parker started this business in 2005.

J. H. Butterfield Co. (207-288-3386), 152 Main St., Bar Harbor. FANCY FOODS SINCE 1887, the sign says, and John Butterfield preserves the atmosphere of the grocery that once delivered to Bar Harbor's summer mansions. Now featuring Maine specialty foods. Carry sandwiches to a bench on the village green, or to Grant Park overlooking the water. Try the chocolate and lemon cake.

Rooster Brother (207-667-8675; roosterbrother.com), Rt. 1, Ellsworth. Just south of the bridge. Gourmet groceries, cheese, fresh-roasted coffee blends, take-out sandwiches.

✳ Entertainment

MUSIC Bar Harbor Music Festival (207-288-5744, off-season 212-222-1026; barharbormusicfestival.org), the Rodick Building, 59 Cottage St., Bar Harbor. Late June–late July. For more than 40 years this annual series has brought up-and-coming young artists to the island, with opera, jazz, new composers, the Bar Harbor Festival String Orchestra, and more. The evening concerts are staged at a variety of sites around town.

Also see *Entertainment* in "The Quiet Side."

FILM Criterion Movie Theater (207-288-3441), Cottage St., Bar Harbor. This vintage-1932, art deco, 891-seat nonprofit performing-arts theater was in financial limbo at press time in 2011; call for an updated status.

Reel Pizza Cinema (207-288-3811), 22 Kennebec Place, Bar Harbor. Pizza

and art, foreign, and independent films in a funky setting (beanbag chairs and big sofas). Films at 6 and 8:30 nightly, year-round.

The Grand Auditorium (207-667-9500; grandonline.org), Main St., Ellsworth. A classic theater, recently restored, offers live performances, musical theater; live opera from the Met; art and independent films.

THEATER See **Acadia Repertory Theatre** in "The Quiet Side" and **Grand Auditorium**, above.

✳ Selective Shopping

ART AND FINE-CRAFTS GALLERIES Eclipse Gallery (207-288-9048; eclipsegallery.us), 12 Mount Desert St., Bar Harbor. Seasonal. A quality gallery specializing in contemporary handblown American glass, ceramics, and fine furniture; also showing metal sculpture.

Island Artisans (207-288-4214; islandartisans.com), 99 Main St., Bar Harbor. Open May–Dec. Featuring Maine artists and craftspeople: textiles, pottery, Native American baskets. Glass, silver, and more.

Alone Moose Fine Crafts (207-288-4229), 78 West St., Bar Harbor. A long-established collection of "made in Maine" crafts, specializing in wildlife sculpture in bronze and wood.

The Hulls Cove Tool Barn (207-288-5126; jonesport-wood.com), Hulls Cove. Open Wed.–Sun. year-round, closed in Jan. Owned by Jonesport Wood Company, this store holds a huge selection of hand planes and other old woodworking tools. Books, old postcards, and more are also stocked. The store is next to the Sculpture Garden of the Davistown Museum. (See Liberty Tool Company in the Searsport chapter.)

Rocky Mann Studio Potter and Gallery (207-288-5478; rockymann .com), Breakneck Rd., Hulls Cove. Turn off Rt. 3 at the Hulls Cove General Store. In summer open daily 10–5; off-season 11–4, closed Mon. After Christmas by appointment. Rocky Mann's ever-evolving work is worth a trip, with his raku and charming frogs and turtles, and Acadia starry night series. Paintings and cards by Carol Shutt.

In Ellsworth
The Sand Castle/Hands Gallery (207-667-9399), 163 Main St. Open daily year-round. Hand-blown glass, jewelry and artwork from and about the ocean and nature by more than 120 Maine artists and craftspeople, 100 more from around the country. Also books, DVDs, music, and chimes.

BOOKSTORES Sherman's Bookstore and Stationery (207-288-3161; sherman.com), 56 Main St., Bar Harbor. Open 9 AM–10:30 PM in summer, 9–6 daily in winter. A great browsing emporium; really a combination five-and-dime, stationery store, gift shop, and well-stocked bookshop.

Big Chicken Barn Books and Antiques (207-667-7308; bigchicken barn.com), Rt. 1/3 south of Ellsworth. Open daily year-round; call for hours. Maine's largest used-book store fills the vast innards of a former chicken house. Annegret Cukierski has 150,000 books in stock: hardbacks, paperbacks, magazines, and comics; also used furniture and collectibles.

✳ Special Events

Throughout the summer: **Band concerts**, Bar Harbor village green (check current listings).

June: **Acadia Birding Festival**—lectures, walks and boat tours. **Working Waterfront Celebration** (second Sunday) includes the Blessing of the Fleet. **Legacy of the Arts** (mid-month), a week of art and culture with concerts, artists' events, and, at the week's end, **Bar Harbor Chamber of Commerce Art Show**, displaying original work on the Bar Harbor village green (207-288-5103).

July: **Bar Harbor Music Festival** (see *Entertainment*).

July 4 weekend: **Independence Day**—blueberry pancake breakfast, town parade, seafood festival focused on lobster and mussels, and strawberry shortcake. Live music, kids' games, and fireworks from the pier at night. **Native American Festival**—dances and a big sale by the Maine Indian Basketmakers at the College of the Atlantic (207-288-5744).

August: **Ellsworth Antiques show at Woodlawn**, Ellsworth.

Late September: **Acadia Night Sky Festival** (acadianightskyfestival.com) will celebrate its fourth year in 2012. **Art in the Park** on the Bar Harbor village green throughout a weekend.

October: **Woodlawn Golf Croquet Tournament**, Colonel Black Mansion, Ellsworth.

CROQUET AT COLONEL BLACK MANSION
Nancy English

November: **Shopping in your PJs** downtown for extra discounts, with a parade and fashion show at 9 PM, prize for craziest sleepwear.

First Friday in December: **Midnight Madness Sale and Village Holidays**, Santa arrives, lights the tree. Discounts from 8 PM to midnight.

First weekend of December: **Island Arts Association Holiday Fair** sponsored by YWCA (207-288-5008).

THE QUIET SIDE OF MOUNT DESERT

The Quiet Side has come to refer to the longer, thinner arm of land that's divided by Somes Sound from the part of Mount Desert that's home to Bar Harbor, the Acadia National Park visitors center, and Park Loop Road. The name generally also applies to Northeast Harbor.

"Northeast" is a yachting village, with a large marina geared to visiting yacht owners, summer residents, and ferries to the Cranberry Islands. A 2008 fire destroyed several Main Street buildings and some priceless art in one of Maine's oldest, most established galleries. Soon, however, the village was bright and humming again. It's flanked by a mile of mansions hidden along Somes Sound. The splendid, public Thuya Gardens are just east of town. Try to get to Islesford (Little Cranberry Island), and be sure to follow Sargent Drive (rather than Rt. 3/198) along the sound. The Mount Desert Historical Society in Somesville is well worth a stop. Some of Acadia's best hiking, as well as its best public swimming beach (at Echo Lake) and canoeing (on Long Pond), are found west of Somes Sound.

Southwest Harbor is a boatbuilding center, home of the Hinckley Company—the Rolls-Royce of yacht builders—and to a substantial commercial fishing fleet. In the neighboring town of Tremont, Bass Harbor is a classic fishing village. It's also the departure point for Swans, a destination in its own right, and several other islands that were once far busier.

Ironically, back in the 1840s Mount Desert's first summer visitors—artists in search of solitude—headed for the Bar Harbor area precisely because it was then far less peopled than the villages on this western side of the island. Much as the

SEAWALL, MDI

Nancy English

Rt. 1 town of Ellsworth is today, Southwest Harbor back then marked the crossroads of Down East Maine, and several island harbors were as busy as any on the mainland today.

Nancy English

SW HARBOR FISH TRUCK

GUIDANCE ⅁ (ᵖ) **Mount Desert Chamber of Commerce** (207-276-5040; mountdesertchamber.org), Sea St., Northeast Harbor. A walk-in cottage (with wireless Internet, accessible restrooms, and showers), geared to visitors arriving by water, is open daily Memorial Day–Sept., 9–4, at the town dock. Pick up a copy of the current *Northeast Harbor Port Directory*.

Southwest Harbor/Tremont Chamber of Commerce (207-244-9264 or 1-800-423-9264; acadiachamber.com), 20 Village Green Way, behind the library in the middle of the village. The walk-in info center is open June–Labor Day, weekdays 9–noon and 1–5; Sat. 9–3, Sun. 10–2.

GETTING THERE *By air and bus:* See *Getting There* in "Bar Harbor."

Note: **Airport & Harbor Car Service** (207-667-5995) meets planes, buses, and boats; serves the entire area.

By boat: Contact the harbormasters in Northeast Harbor (207-276-5737) and Southwest Harbor (207-244-7913) about guest moorings.

By car: From Ellsworth: Fork right off Rt. 3 as soon as it crosses the Mount Desert narrows; follow Rt. 102/198 to Somesville and Rt. 198 to Northeast Harbor, or Rt. 102 to Southwest Harbor.

GETTING AROUND This is one place in Maine where water transport is still as important as land. **Beal & Bunker** (207-244-3573) offers year-round mail and ferry service from Northeast Harbor to the Cranberry Islands, and the **Maine State Ferry Service** (207-244-4353 or 1-800-491-4883) services Swans Island and Frenchboro.

Island Explorer Bus Service (207-288-4573 or 1-866-282-7558), late June–Columbus Day. Free. This bus stops frequently along the routes from Southwest Harbor to Bernard, up and down both sides of Somes Sound, and into the park and Bar Harbor, connecting with service from Northeast Harbor. Donations welcome.

✳ To See

In Northeast Harbor
Thuya Garden and Lodge (207-276-5130). This is a very special place. Parking is marked on Rt. 3, just east of the junction with Rt. 198. Cross the road and climb the steps with Asticou Terraces, carved in granite beside them. These wind up

THUYA GARDEN

Christina Tree

Asticou Hill, offering a splendid view of Northeast Harbor. Thuya Lodge (open late June into Sept., 10–4:30), a botanic library and a lovely spot to read, is the former home of Joseph Henry Curtis, a landscape architect who began this exquisite system of paths and shelters around 1900 and donated the 140-acre property to the public. It's now maintained by the Mount Desert Land and Garden Preserve, to which visitors are asked to donate $3. The 2-acre Thuya Garden, behind the lodge, was designed by the Asticou Inn's longtime former innkeeper, Charles Savage, who also designed the 2.3-acre **Asticou Azalea Garden** (junction of Rt. 3 and Rt. 198), a spectacular show of azaleas and laurels mid-May–mid-June. Stroll down winding paths and over ornamental bridges. Those not wishing to climb the Asticou Terrace steps can take Thuya Drive (just past the parking lot) up to the garden and lodge. Also note the 1.4-mile **Eliot Mountain Trail** behind Thuya Garden, leading up through blueberry bushes to a sweeping view.

Great Harbor Maritime Museum (207-276-5262; greatharbormaritimemuseum .org), 125 Main St. in the Old Firehouse. Open seasonally, Tue.–Sat. 10–5. $3. The permanent collection is of model ships, small boats, and historical maritime artifacts from Mount Desert Island; there are also notable changing exhibits on a variety of subjects.

Petite Plaisance (207-276-3940; petiteplaisance@acadia.net), South Shore Rd. Open mid-June–Aug., 9–4 by appointment. The former home of French author Marguerite Yourcenar has long been a destination for her fans.

In Mount Desert

The tiny white wooden village of **Somesville** at the head of Somes Sound is a National Historic District; be sure to check out **Brookside Cemetery** and the **Somesville Museum** (207-244-5043; mdihistory .org), Rt. 102. Open mid-June to mid-Oct., Tue.–Sat. 1–4 (donation), this lively museum is maintained by the **Mount Desert Historical Society**. Two tidy buildings, one dating back to

GREAT HARBOR MARITIME MUSEUM

Christina Tree

1780, connected by a moon bridge, house many artifacts and photographs of the island's vanished hotels and the shipyards for which this village was once widely known. An heirloom garden shows off MDI plants and herbs. The MDI Historical Society's headquarters is on the other side of Somes Sound in the vintage 1892 **School House and Museum**, Rt. 3/198 between Somesville and Northeast Harbor, open June–Sept., Tue.–Sat. 10–4; Sept.–May, weekdays 10–4. It houses changing exhibits, a children's program, library, and year-round activities relating to MDI history.

In Southwest Harbor

Wendell Gilley Museum (207-244-7555; wendellgilleymuseum.org), Rt. 102. Open June–Dec., 10–4 (10–5 in July and Aug.), daily except Mon.; Fri.–Sun. only in May, Nov., and Dec. $5 adults, $2 ages 5–12. Wendell Gilley was a local plumber who began hand carving birds as a hobby in the 1930s, over more than 50 years carving some 10,000 birds and acquiring a reputation as a master. Friend and patron Steven Rockefeller helped develop this first-rate, handsome museum, housing more than 200 of Gilley's works and changing art exhibits.

GREAT HARBOR MARITIME MUSEUM

Nancy English

In Bass Harbor

Tremont Historical Society (207-244-9753), Shore Rd. near the Swans Island Ferry. Open July–Columbus Day, Mon. and Wed. 1–4. If you are lucky enough to find this restored country store open, don't pass it by. It's now filled with historic artifacts and photos and sells bargain-priced copies of the novels like *The Weir*, *Spoonhandle*, and *Speak to the Winds*, written in the 1940s by longtime local resident Ruth Moore, vividly capturing life on the offshore islands here. Archival records, available by appointment.

In Seal Cove

⌀ **Seal Cove Auto Museum** (207-244-9242; sealcoveautomuseum.org), Pretty Marsh Rd. (Rt. 102), between Bass Harbor and Somesville. Open May–Oct., daily 10–5. $5 adults, $2 children 12 and under. Squirreled away in a little-trafficked corner of the

BASS HARBOR LIGHT

island across from Cove Pond and Western Mountain, this collection is a real find: more than 100 gleaming antique cars and 30 motorcycles, including the country's largest assemblage of pre-1915 cars—the lifework of a private collector.

SCENIC DRIVES **Sargent Drive**, obviously built for carriages, runs from Northeast Harbor north half a dozen miles right along Somes Sound.

Route 102A loop. This isn't the quickest way between Southwest and Bass Harbors, but it's beautiful, following the shore through a section of Acadia National Park that includes the Seawall Campground (note the oceanside picnic tables) and the Ship Harbor Nature Trail down to gorgeous, flat pink rocks. A short way beyond, be sure to turn onto Lighthouse Rd. to see Bass Harbor Light, a photographer's delight. Continue on into Bass Harbor and Bernard.

✴ To Do

✍ **Acadia Ranger Programs**. Pick up a copy of *Acadia's Beaver Log* at Seawall Campground (Rt. 102A) if you can't find it in local chambers or shops. The free handout *Acadia Weekly* also lists programs ranging from guided walks and cruises to evening programs. Definitely worth doing.

BICYCLING The network of gravel carriage roads constructed by John D. Rockefeller Jr. in 1915 lends itself particularly well to mountain biking. The fire roads are also good for mountain biking, as is Swans Island. **Southwest Cycle** (207-244-5856; southwestcycle.com), 370 Main St., Southwest Harbor, rents mountain and touring bicycles, children's bikes, baby seats, car racks, and jog strollers.

BIRDING For special programs led by park naturalists, consult Acadia's Beaver Log; also see the **Wendell Gilley Museum** under *To See*, and **Island Cruises**, below.

BOAT EXCURSIONS

From Bass Harbor
Island Cruises (207-244-5785; bassharborcruises.com), Little Island Marine, Bass Harbor. Mid-June–mid-Sept. Kim Strauss offers daily (weather-dependent) lunch cruises aboard 40-foot *R. L. Gott* to Frenchboro, also afternoon and cruises to see wildlife—a wide variety of birds, including several bald eagles, porpoises and many harbor and gray seals on and around Placentia and Black Islands as well as Great and Little Gott Islands, all depicted in novels by Great Gott native Ruth Moore (1903–89). In *The Weir*, *Speak to the Winds*, and *Spoonhandle*, Moore describes the poignant ebb of life from these islands in the 1930s and 1940s. These are exceptional cruises, given the quality of the historical narration and scenery.

Maine State Ferry (207-244-3254) makes the 40-minute run to Swans Island several times a day, twice weekly to Frenchboro, carrying cars.

From Northeast Harbor
Beal & Bunker (207-244-3575) offers year-round mail-boat and ferry service to the Cranberries and Sutton Island. **Sea Princess Cruises** (207-276-5352; bar harborcruises.com) offers seasonal regular cruises with naturalists, including Somes Sound, sunset, and Islesford historical cruises.

Cranberry Cove Boating (207-244-5882) offers frequent service to the Cranberries from both Lower Town Dock in Manset and Upper Town Dock on Clark Point Rd., both in Southwest Harbor. **Downeast Friendship Sloop Charters** (207-266-5210; sailacadia.com) offers daysails and private charters. **Schooner *Rachel B. Jackson*** (207-288-2216; downeastsail.com) and **Friendship sloop *Surprise*** both offer daysails from Southwest Harbor.

BOAT RENTALS In Southwest Harbor both **Manset Yacht Service** (207-244-4040) and **Mansell Boat Rental Company** (207-244-5625) rent power- and sailboats and offer sail lesson cruises.

CANOEING AND KAYAKING Long Pond, the largest lake on any Maine island, has three access points. Boats can be launched at Echo Lake on Ike's Point, just off Rt. 102. Seal Cove Pond is less used and accessible from fire roads north of Seal Cove. Bass Harbor Marsh is another possibility at high tide. Canoe rental sources offer suggestions and directions. **National Park Canoe/Kayak Rentals** (207-244-5854; nationalparkcanoerental.com), on Long Pond near Somesville, offers guided paddles and instruction. Guided half- and full-day paddles are offered by **Maine State Sea Kayak** (207-244-9500; mainestatekayak.com), 254 Main St., Southwest Harbor.

GOLF Causeway Golf Club (207-244-3780), Fernald Point Rd., Southwest Harbor. Nine-hole waterside course, clubhouse and pull carts, pro shop.

HIKING The highest mountains on the western side of Somes Sound are Bernard and Mansell, but both summits are wooded. The more popular hikes are up Acadia Mountain (3.5 miles roundtrip, off Rt. 102) with an east–west summit trail commanding a spectacular view of the sound and islands. Admittedly we have only climbed **Flying Mountain**, a quick hit with a great view, too. The trail begins at the Fernald Cove parking area. Don't miss **Asticou Terraces** (see *Thuya Garden* under *To See*) and the **Indian Point Blagden Preserve** (see *Green Space*). **Ship Harbor Nature Trail** (off Rt. 102A) winds along the shore and into the woods, with good birding. If a sunny Friday is promised, take advantage of the once-weekly service to **Frenchboro** (207-244-5785; see *Boat Excursions*) and spend the day hiking in the Frenchboro Preserve. There are some 110 miles of maintained, marked trails on MDI. *A Walk in the Park* (10th edition) by Tom St. Germain is a useful companion.

SAILING Mansell Boat Rentals (207-244-5625), Rt. 102A, Manset (near Southwest Harbor), offers sailing lessons; also rents small sailboats. All-day sailing trips offered with Captain Robert Wellborn; bring some wine and cheese and spend the day on the water. Also check **Hinckley Yacht Charters** (207-244-5008), Southwest Harbor, and **Manset Yacht Service** (207-244-4040) in Manset.

SWIMMING Echo Lake offers a beach with a lifeguard, restrooms, and parking (Rt. 102 between Somesville and Southwest Harbor). Another favorite spot is known as "the bluffs" or "the ledges." Park in the Acadia Mountain parking area

ISLANDS

The Cranberry Isles (cranberryisles.com). There are five Cranberry isles just southeast of Mount Desert.

LITTLE CRANBERRY The most visitor-friendly of the islands is 400-acre Little Cranberry (islesford.com), located 20 minutes offshore. The official "sight-to-see" is the incongruously brick and formal **Islesford Historical Museum** (207-244-9224; open daily mid-June–Sept., 9–noon and 12:30–3:30), built in 1928 with funds raised by Bangor-born, MIT-educated summer resident William Otis Sawtelle to house his fascinating collection of local, historical objects. Acadia National Park maintains the museum (and restrooms), featuring it as part of a ranger-narrated **Islesford Historical Cruise**. We prefer to come by mail boat, taking our time to exploring the island and beating the crowd to **Islesford Dock Restaurant** (see *Dining Out*), the island's gathering spot and a great place to eat. Stop in at the **Islesford Dock Galley** and walk on up the road to Danny and Kate Fernald's **Islesford Artists Gallery** (207-244-3145; islesfordartists.com), specializing in Maine's many excellent island artists. At the dock look for the **Alleyway**, Cari Alley's white truck selling reasonably priced fresh lobster and shrimp rolls (her husband is a lobsterman/shrimper), hot dogs, island desserts, and more. **Winter's Work** showcases island-made crafts, and Marian Baker's **Islesford Pottery** (207-244-5686) is worth a stop. The **Islesford Market** (207-244-7667) has been open sporadically in recent years. Stop by at least to meet island-bred postmistress Joy Sprague, who sells more stamps per year from her window here than any other post office in Maine, despite the fact that Islesford has less than 80 year-round and some 400 summer residents. Requests for Sprague's "Stamps by Mail" come from as far as Fiji, Iceland, and Istanbul—perhaps because with each order she encloses one of her island photos and a monthly newsletter (her address is USPO, Islesford 04646). Sprague also operates **Joy of Kayaking** (207-244-4309), renting one- and two-person kayaks. For a wide choice of summer rentals see islesford.com. To get there see *Boat Excursions*.

GREAT CRANBERRY—the largest of the islands—is a lobstering and boatbuilding island with a year-round population of around 40 that swells to 300 in summer. The **Seawich Café & Cranberry General Store** (207-244-0622) at the ferry landing offers salads, sandwiches, and daily specials. About 0.3 mile down the road is **Cranberry House**, start of the trail to Whistler Cove, and home to the **Historical Society Museum** (207-244-7800) and **Hitty's Café** (207-244-7845), serving meals and ice cream on a cheerful deck ((☈)). Another 0.25 mile farther on is the library ((☈)) in the currently inactive

AmazingMaine.com

THE VIEW FROM LITTLE CRANBERRY ISLAND

school. Just beyond that look for **The Whale's Rib** (207-244-5153), offering a selection of crafts and art.

SWANS ISLAND (04685; swansisland.org). At the mouth of Blue Hill Bay, 6 miles out of Bass Harbor, with frequent car ferry service (see *Getting Around*), this is a large lobstering and fishing island with a year-round population of 300, a library, a general store (no alcohol), seasonal restaurants, Quarry Pond to swim in, and Fine Sand Beach to walk. With a bike it's a possible day trip, but be forewarned: The ferry dock is 4 hilly miles from **Burnt Coat Harbor**, the picturesque island center with **Hockamock Light** (built in 1872) at its entrance. Swans works better as an overnight, given its choice of places to stay and the beauty of local hiking trails (check out the shore path at the light).

Swans Island is divided into three areas: **Atlantic**, where the ferry docks; **Minturn**, by the quarry pond and grocery store; and **Swans Island Village**, with the beach and lighthouse. The island was named for James Swan, the original owner. Maili Bailey arranges seasonal rentals of cottages, houses and apartments at **Swans Island Vacation** (swansislandvacation.com). **Harbor Watch Motel** (207-526-4563; swansisland.com) is open year-round on Burnt Coat Harbor. The **Island Bake Shop** (207-526-4578) serves breakfast and lunch and is known for its pastries. **Carrying Place Market and Take-out** (207-526-4043) is another welcome place for prepared food; you can buy lobsters and clams from **Traftons** (207-526-4427). It's wonderful to arrive in your own boat; Kevin Staples (207-526-4323) rents moorings.

The Sweet Chariot Festival (sweetchariotmusicfestival.com) gathers folksingers from across the country and starts with a serenade of the boats in the harbor, many of them Maine windjammers, usually in the first week of August.

The **Swans Island Library** (207-526-4330) has historic displays and summer speakers; **Swans Island Lobster & Marine Museum** (207-526-4423), open mid-June to mid-Sept., displays ships' models, fishing equipment, and photos. **Iverstudio** (207-526-4350) offers weeklong workshops in woodblock printing.

FRENCHBORO The town of Frenchboro (frenchboroonline.com) is composed of 12 islands, but the name is usually applied to Long Island, 8 miles out of Bass Harbor, home to 70 year-round residents (up from 38 in 2000), most in Lunts Harbor. Two-thirds of the island (nearly 1,000 acres) is preserved by the Maine Coast Heritage Trust as the Frenchboro Preserve. A network of hiking trails runs along the shoreline, and the birding is terrific. See *Boat Excursions* for access via the **Maine State Ferry** and **Island Cruises**. The seasonal **Lunt's Dockside Deli** (207-334-2902) serves the basics, from veggie wraps to a lobster dinner; the fish chowder is good. The **Frenchboro Historical Society** (207-334-2932), open daily in-season 12:30–5, displays old tools, furniture, and local memorabilia, also sells crafted items. *Note:* One day a year (early in August) the island welcomes visitors for the **Annual Lobster Festival**, a lobster feed with plenty of chicken salad and pies. The Lunt & Lunt Lobster Co. sells fuel, water, and live lobsters, also rents moorings.

FRENCHBORO

(about 3 miles south of Somesville on Rt. 102). A short path leads down to the lake.

TENNIS The courts at the **Northeast Harbor Marina** are open to the public, and the Mount Desert Chamber of Commerce (see *Guidance*) offers racquets and balls.

✳ Green Space

Indian Point Blagden Preserve, a 110-acre Nature Conservancy preserve in the northwestern corner of the island, includes 1,000 feet of shorefront and paths that wander through the woods. It offers a view of Blue Hill Bay and is a tried-and-true seal-watching spot. From Rt. 198 north of Somesville, turn right on Indian Point Rd., bear right at the fork, and look for the entrance; sign in and pick up a map at the caretaker's house.

Seal Cove. An unpublicized waterside park with picnic tables, a beach at low tide, a kayaking put-in. From Rt. 102 turn at the red buoy onto the waterside extension of Seal Cove Rd.

See also Thuya Garden and Islands under *To See*; *Hiking*; and the "Acadia National Park" section of this chapter.

✳ Lodging

INNS AND BED & BREAKFASTS

In Southwest Harbor 04679
✿ **Cranberry Hill Inn** (207-244-5007; cranberryhillinn.com), 60 Clark Point Rd. Open mid-May–mid-Oct. We like the feel of this B&B with its lovely long, bright living room and the easy hospitality of hosts Patti and Jerry Selig. The five rooms each has a private entrance and bath (two with Jacuzzi), and all are tastefully, cheerfully furnished. Request a harbor view. $95–155 includes a three-course breakfast.

The Inn at Southwest (207-244-3835; innatsouthwest.com), Main St., P.O. Box 593. Open May–Oct. Built in 1884 as a Victorian-style annex to a now vanished hotel, this delightful B&B is furnished with comfortable Arts and Crafts antiques. Of the seven guest rooms, all with private bath and named for lighthouses, Cape Elizabeth, a huge room with four-poster, and the third-floor Pemaquid Point suite with its chapel-style window and window seat stand out. In the fall, Sandy Johnson's breakfast might be pumpkin pecan pancakes with ginger butter. $135–200 per couple in high season; from $120 up in shoulder seasons.

Lindenwood Inn (207-244-5335 or 1-800-307-5335; lindenwoodinn.com), 118 Clark Point Rd., P.O. Box 1328. This turn-of-the-20th-century sea captain's home set by the harbor among stately linden trees is open Apr.–Nov. 1. Australian-born owner Jim King has a sure decorating touch in the 15 rooms (all with private bath), in the main inn and the Rosebrook House, many with water views, balcony, and fireplace. The pool and hot tub are appreciated after hiking or biking. A full breakfast is served in the paneled dining room, where the fire is lit in cool weather. A full bar is also available. $175–295 double in-season, $125–225 in low. The high end rents the penthouse suite, with its own hot tub and a great view.

Harbour Cottage Inn and Pier One (207-244-5738 or 1-888-843-3022; harbourcottageinn.com), 9 Dirigo Rd., P.O. Box 258. Don Jalbert and Javier Montesinos have revamped this old landmark to feature creature comforts and romance. The eight standard rooms are equipped with phone and cable TV; some have whirlpool bath or steam-sauna shower. The Southwester (sleeping six) and Carriage House (sleeping four), both neighboring cottages, have full kitchen. Five skillfully furnished weekly rental units ($1,155–1,715) with kitchens are clustered by the water, collectively known as Pier One. $165–245 for standard rooms, $205–269 for suites, $225–279 for cottages. Rates include breakfast at separate tables in a sunny dining room.

The Kingsleigh Inn (207-244-5302; kingsleighinn.com), 373 Main St. Open seasonally. The check-in desk is the counter of a large, open kitchen, and the living room has a wood-burning fireplace; wicker chairs fill the wraparound porch and several rooms have decks to maximize harbor views. We like the Chelsea, Abbott, and Hawthorne Rooms more than the three-room third-floor suite. Innkeepers Pamela Parker and Bryan Stevens offer a multicourse breakfast that's a true event; afternoon tea is another. $150–305 mid-June–mid-Oct., $305 for the three-room, third-floor suite; from $130 off-season.

✔ **Penury Hall** (207-244-7102; penuryhall.com), Main St., P.O. Box 68. Open year-round. An attractive village house with three guest rooms (private bath). With the first B&B on the island. Gretchen Strong takes her job seriously and delights in helping guests figure out what's happening on the island. Breakfast may be blueberry pancakes or a "penurious omelet" (eggs, cheese, and salsa with no meat) served with

popovers. $145 May–Oct., otherwise from $100 includes modest use of the fridge, laundry facilities, library, music, games, and sauna. There are also two frisky, friendly black cats.

✔ ♂ **The Birches** (207-244-5182; thebirchesbnb.com), Fernald Point Rd., P.O. Box 178. Open year-round. A very special place. Dick and Susi Homer's home, built in 1916, commands a waterfront view from its spacious living room with formal gardens, which include a croquet court. The three guest rooms (private bath) are furnished in family antiques. $149–189 includes a full breakfast. Inquire about moorings and ski specials.

Moorings Inn (207-244-5523 or 1-800-596-5523; mooringsinn.com), 133 Shore Rd., Rt. 102A, Manset. Overlooking the entrance to Somes Sound, this rambling old inn stands beside the fabled Hinkley boat (as in yacht) yard. Leslie Watson, the fourth generation of her family to run the inn, has made major and tasteful renovations in the Main House, which dates in part to 1784. The inviting living room features a telescope aimed at the spread of mountains and water beyond the picture window. There are 13 rooms in the house itself, ranging from a couple of small "lawn view" rooms to suites with spectacular views. Three rooms in the Lighthouse Wing have a deck, microwave, and fridge. The complex also includes six cottages, most with a living room, fireplace, and kitchenette. Bikes, canoes, and kayaks are available, and sailing lessons are offered through Mansell Boat Rentals, also on the property. $95–195 for the rooms.

In Northeast Harbor 04662
❧ **Harbourside Inn** (207-276-3272; harboursideinn.com), P.O. Box 178. Open June–Sept. A gracious 1880s shingle-style inn set on 4 wooded acres, with 11 guest rooms and three

suites (two with kitchenette) on three floors, all with phone and private bath, some with kitchen. There are also nine working fireplaces in first- and second-floor guest rooms. This very special place has four generations of Sweet family living on the premises. Flowers from the garden brighten every guest room. Guests mingle at breakfast over fresh-baked blueberry muffins, served on the sunporch. The Asticou Azalea Gardens, extensive woodland walks, shops, and the town landing with its water excursions are all within walking distance. $150–180 for a room; $250–295 for a suite with kitchen.

🐾 **Asticou Inn** (207-276-3344 or 1-800-258-3373; asticou.com), Rt. 3, Northeast Harbor 04662. Mid-May–mid-Oct. The inn offers rooms with and without water views, public rooms with Oriental rugs, and a porch overlooking formal gardens and the harbor. The 48 rooms and suites, all with private bath, are divided among the main house and annexes, which include Cranberry Lodge across the road and the Topsider suites in modern water-view cottages. Facilities include a cocktail lounge, tennis courts, bike rentals and a heated swimming pool. Since the 1960s the inn has been owned by a consortium of summer residents and business people. The current feel is impersonal and a bit tired. Groups and weddings are specialties. Along with many of the area's shingle-style "cottages," the inn was designed by Fred Savage, son of A. C. Savage, the original innkeeper. It was another Savage (Charles) who developed the neighboring Asticou Azalea Garden (see *To See*). $225–375 per couple in high season, from $155 in shoulder months, plus 10 percent gratuity, including a continental breakfast buffet. Inquire about family rates. Also see *Dining Out*.

🐾 **Bass Harbor Inn** (207-244-5157), P.O. Box 326. Open May–Oct. In an 1870 house with harbor views, within walking distance of village restaurants and the ferry to Swans Island, Barbara and Alan Graff offer six rooms ranging from doubles with shared baths to a fabulous top-floor studio with kitchenette. One room with half-bath has a fireplace; two open onto the side deck. $90–135 in-season, $70–115 off-season, including continental breakfast.

Ann's Point Inn (207-244-9595, annspointinn.com), P.O. Box 398. This secluded, contemporary waterfront home packs some unusual luxuries, like a hot tub, sauna and 32-by-12-foot indoor pool. The four large rooms have water views and extras like gas fireplace and king bed; three have private terrace. Jeannette and Alan Feuer are hospitable hosts. $250–350 includes a full breakfast with the inn's own vegetables and afternoon nibbles and evening cookies.

MOTELS 🐾 ♿ **Kimball Terrace Inn** (207-276-3383 or 1-800-454-6225; kimballterraceinn.com), 10 Huntington Rd., P.O. Box 1030, Northeast Harbor 04662. Open May–late Oct. Replacing its predecessor hotel of the same name, this pleasant motor inn occupies a prime site on the harbor by the Northeast Harbor Yacht Marina. It offers 70 large rooms, 52 with sliding doors opening onto private patio or balcony. Amenities include a full-service restaurant, outdoor pool, and tennis courts. $155–205 in high season, from $70 single off-season.

🐾 🐈 🐾 **Harbor View Motel & Cottages** (207-244-5031 or 1-800-538-6463; harborviewmotelandcottages.com), P.O. Box 701, Southwest Harbor 04679. Open mid-May–mid-Oct. Lorraine and Joe Saunders have

✪ ❦ ✐ ♿ **CLAREMONT HOTEL** (207-244-5036 or 1-800-244-5036; theclaremonthotel.com), 22 Claremont Rd., Southwest Harbor 04679. Open May–mid-Oct. Gracious but not stuffy, Mount Desert's oldest hotel has the grace and dignity but not the size of a grand hotel. It also has the best views on the island and has benefited from the fact that, since its 1884 opening, there have been just three owners. Walking into the comfortably sized lobby, you pour yourself a glass of ice water, ease into a wing chair by the wood fire or a rocker on the porch, and feel at home. Upstairs the original 35 second-and third-floor rooms

Christina Tree

GUESTS ON THE FRONT LAWN OF THE CLAREMONT

have been reduced to 24, all with closets and baths, furnished with refinished original pieces and graceful reproductions, all with phones and fresh flowers. Wood floors gleam around thick carpets in sitting rooms, the wraparound porch is lined with rockers, and every table in the dining room has a view. Visitors are welcome to lunch at The Boathouse (see *Eating Out*), to dine at Xanthus (see *Dining Out*), and to attend Thursday-evening lectures (see *Entertainment*). There are large suites in Phillips, Clark, and Cole Cottages, as well as individual cottages, each with living room and fireplace, all

owned this 20-unit harborside motel for more than 42 years. In July and Aug. rooms with decks right on the water are $116–128, while others are $84–97 including continental breakfast, less in Sept., for solo travelers, and by the week. A third-floor apartment and seven cottages are available in high season by the week.

Seawall Motel (207-244-3020 or 1-800-248-9250; seawallmotel.com), 566 Seawall Rd., Southwest Harbor 04679. Open year-round. Twenty clean, quiet rooms with two queen beds and cable TV, right across the road from the

ocean. The free, seasonal Island Express shuttle bus stops outside. From $65 in winter to $115 in high season, when rates include a generous continental breakfast.

OTHER LODGING ✐ **Appalachian Mountain Club's Echo Lake Camp** (207-244-3747; amcecholakecamp.org), AMC/Echo Lake Camp, Mount Desert 04660. Open late June–Labor Day weekend. Accommodations are platform tents; family-style meals are served in a central hall. There is a rustic library and reading room, and an with kitchenette. Facilities include tennis on clay courts, two croquet courts, badminton, and water sports; bicycles and rowboats are available. The Croquet Classic in August is the social high point of the season. The McCue family, current owners, have been summering on Mount Desert since 1871. "We didn't expect to make money, just to keep it going and to improve it" is how the late Gertrude McCue explained what she and her late husband, Allen, were thinking when they bought the hotel in 1968. $125–300 B&B in the hotel; the 12 rooms on the water side are priced slightly higher than those overlooking the tennis courts. Cottages are $155–335 with a three-day minimum. Before July 15 and after Labor Day rates drop, and there are children's and weekly rates. A 15 percent gratuity is added.

CROQUET AT THE CLAREMONT

Christina Tree

indoor game room, but more to the point are boats for use on the lake, daily hikes, and evening activities. Reservations should be made on April 1. Rates for the minimum one-week stay (Sat.–Sat.) are inexpensive per person but add up for a family. All meals included.

☙ **Bass Harbor Cottages** (207-244-3460; bassharborcottages.com), 95 Harbor Dr. (Rt. 102A), Bass Harbor. Open year-round. This is a classic old farmhouse with three guest rooms and three more assorted cottages scattered in the meadow below, above the water.

It's a great spot for families and kayakers. All accommodations offer housekeeping. $80–175 per couple in the inn, $100–400 daily and $800–3,000 weekly in the cottages. Sorry, no pets.

VACATION RENTALS Both chambers of commerce listed under Guidance keep and publish lists.

✴ Where to Eat
DINING OUT

In the Southwest Harbor area
Red Sky Restaurant (207-244-0476; redskyrestaurant.com), 14 Clark Point

Rd., Southwest Harbor. Open nightly June–Columbus Day, and year-round, when hours vary; closed Jan. The toast of this restaurant town, a comfortably low-key bistro with locally sourced food to come back and back for: appetizers like mussels with white wine and Dijon, and crispy polenta with mushrooms and beet greens; entrées like braised baby back ribs and lobster with risotto. Ingredients are all as fresh and local as possible. Owners Elizabeth and James Lindquist are both owners and chefs. Entrées $19–30.

& **Xanthus at the Claremont** (207-244-5036; theclaremonthotel.com), Clark Point Rd., Southwest Harbor. Open for dinner June–Oct. Here most tables have some water view. Both decor and service are traditional, with white tablecloths and wall sconces spilling fresh flowers, the kind of place where it's appropriate (but not required) to dress up. The restaurant is named for Xanthus Smith, who painted the 1885 portrait of the inn hung here. In 2011 the chef was Daniel Sweimler, and the food was excellent. Grilled tiger shrimp with lobster mushroom risotto and golden tomatillo salsa or grilled sirloin with horseradish mashed potatoes and roasted root vegetables are from a fall menu; as always there is an emphasis on seasonal vegetables, natural meats, and earthy, deep rich flavor. Dessert maintains the standard. Plan to come on Thursday and stay for a lecture (see *Entertainment*). Entrées $24–27.

XYZ Restaurant & Gallery (207-244-5221; xyzmaine.com), end of Bennett Lane off Seawall Rd. (Rt. 102A), Manset. Open high season nightly for dinner, varying hours shoulder seasons. Ask directions when you call to reserve. Janet Strong and Robert Hoyt have made XYZ well-loved for its "classical food from the Mexican interior" (*X* is for "Xalapa," *Y* for "Yucatán," and

Z for "Zacatecas"). Robert is the chef, Janet the hostess, and they live in Mexico in winter. The atmosphere is intimate (just 30 seats) and colorful with Mexican folk art. Entrées change constantly but always include pork and chicken dishes, all $24 in 2011, including salad. The fresh lime margaritas are legendary. The chiles rellenos con queso remain indelibly delicious in recollection.

Café 2 (207-244-4344), 326 Main St., Southwest Harbor. Dinner served Tue.–Sun. 5–9, May–mid-Oct. Reserve a booth. A vintage car dealership transformed into an informal, colorful café with a patio bar offers a wide-ranging menu, from pasta to sesame-crusted tuna or rack of lamb. The dinner salads are generous; signature dishes include a seafood pot au feu and sage-rubbed tenderloin of pork. You can also get a burger or lobster roll. Full-service bar with specialty drinks. Entrées $17–26.

Fiddler's Green (207-244-9416; fiddlersgreenrestaurant.com), 411 Main St. Open seasonally for dinner except Mon., 5:30–9. Chef-owned with harbor views and a casual decor. Dine on a mix of "small plates" such as salt cod fritters and broiled oysters or on entrées ranging from an Asian vegetable hot pot to a choice of steaks ($16–32). Full bar.

In Northeast Harbor
Redbird Provisions Restaurant (207-276-3006), 11 Sea St. Open for lunch and dinner June–mid-Oct., Tue.–Sat. in July and Aug., fewer days in shoulders. Terrace and inside dining overlooking the marina and harbor. Lunch on a lobster BLT or warm prosciutto sandwich with fresh mozzarella. Chef Jesse Perrin's dinner menu changes often, but you might dine on chicken scaloppine or veal chop with morels and bone marrow vinaigrette. Entrées $22–30.

Asticou Inn (207-276-3344), Rt. 3. Open for dinner May–mid-Oct., also for lunch and brunch in July and Aug. Grand old hotel atmosphere with water views. Dinner entrées might include baked stuffed lobster and beef tenderloin with parsnip and potato puree ($24–37). Reservations required.

Islesford Dock (207-244-7494; islesforddock.com), Islesford. Open mid-June–Labor Day except Mon. for lunch (11–3), Sunday brunch (10–2), and dinner (5–9). Another great reason to come to the Cranberry Islands (see the *Islands* sidebar), this is also a spectacular place to watch the sun set behind the entire line of Mount Desert's mountains. Check the website before making the trip for any dates "closed for a private event." Owners Cynthia and Dan Lief grow herbs and vegetables behind the restaurant and secure most of their seafood and produce from close by or from Maine wonders like Tide Mill Farm far downeast, an eighth-generation farm. The dinner menu includes the Dock burger (served with fresh-cut fries or a salad) and a crabcake sandwich, "small plates" of Maine mussels or salt cod sliders, as well as entrées like Gulf of Maine halibut with white beans and fennel, or pork ragu pacchari (large tube-shaped pasta) with broccoli rabe. Save room for blueberry crisp. Buy a bottle of South African wine and $2 benefits Ubuntu, the educational and health center in Cape Elizabeth, South Africa, founded by Cynthia and Dan's son Jacob Lief, currently serving over 40,000 children. We can vouch for this venue as magical for a wedding reception. Entrées $9–38. An attached gallery showcases artists and craftsmen, some from the Cranberry Isles and some from away but all with an aesthetic connection to the islands of Maine.

EATING OUT

In Southwest Harbor

❧ **Café Drydock** (244-5842), 357 Main St. Open daily 11–9:30, Sun. brunch 10–2. Convenient, pleasant, predictable, and dependable. The lounge offers many hospitable corners, and the same menu is served in the quieter dining room. If it's on the menu at dinner try the mussels with lime, cilantro, carrots, and chive cream sauce served over linguine, or the Portuguese poached haddock. Fully licensed. Dinner entrées $19–22, and you can always get a burger.

❧ **Gilley's Head of the Harbor** (207-244-5222), 433 Main St. This long, diner-shaped place overlooks the harbor. Sharon and Michael Gilley, owners of Thurston's in Bass Harbor, serve thick, creamy seafood chowder studded with scallops, clams, shrimp, and lobster. As at Thurston's, lobster is the big draw; also fried seafood and steaks. Children's menu.

❧ **Sips** (207-244-4550), 4 Clark Point Rd. Open 7 AM–9 PM in summer, shorter hours off-season. Sips opens early for fresh-brewed coffee, espresso, and full breakfasts, from bagels with homemade spreads to crêpes and all-natural egg

ISLESFORD DOCK RESTAURANT

AmazingMaine.com

omelets. Lunch options include unusual sandwiches and salads. The dinner menu includes crêpes, risotto, vegetarian pastas, and polentas as well classic meat loaf and baked haddock stuffed with crabmeat. Wine and beer. Kids' menu. Dinner entrées $10–24.

Chow Maine (207-669-4142; chowmaine.com), Post Office Building, Clark Rd. in Southwest Harbor village. Open year-round except Sun., 10:30–9. Taiwan native Ciaolin is well known on MDI, with her Chow Maine Asian Specialties available in many markets. Opened in 2009, this is great lunch and dinner option, a pleasant space to lunch on drunken noodles or shrimp spring rolls at lunch, or to dine on Thai curry mussels over buckwheat noodles or sweet ginger shrimp over rice with fresh greens. The sushi menu is available all day. BYOB.

Little Notch Café (207-244-3357), 340 Main St. Open late May–Columbus Day 8–8 for coffees, breads, and light meals. The aroma of freshly baked bread is almost impossible to resist. Arthur and Katherine Jacobs specialize in soups and sandwiches like grilled tuna salad with cheddar on wheat; also great pizza. Seating inside and out, takeout.

EAT-A-PITA CAFÉ, SOUTHWEST HARBOR

Christina Tree

The Captain's Galley at Beal's Lobster Pier (207-244-3202; bealslobster pier.net), Clark Point Rd. Open daily Memorial Day–Columbus Day, 11–8. The dining room on this working pier is all about lobster, crabmeat rolls, chowder, fresh fish specialties, and lobster. This is also a place to buy lobster to ship.

The Boathouse at the Claremont Hotel (207-244-3512), Clark Point Rd. Open July–Aug., serving lunch until 2 PM. This informal dockside facility on the grounds of the island's oldest hotel arguably offers the island's best view, east across the mouth of Somes Sound, with Acadia's mountains rising beyond. Sandwiches, salads, and burgers; also good for drinks at sunset.

Eat-a-Pita (207-244-4344), 326 Main St. Open daily May–mid-Oct. from 8 AM; at dinner this spot turns into Café 2 (see *Dining Out*). A lively, bright café with a patio, soups, salads, and pastas, specialty coffees, and pastries, fully licensed.

✍ **DuMuro's Top of the Hill Restaurant** (207-244-0033), 1 Main St., Rt. 102 north of town. Open seasonally. We have had only good reports about this family-run and -geared place with a very reasonably priced menu ranging from fried chicken and salad plates to mussels marinara.

In Northeast Harbor

🏵 ✍ **Docksider** (207-276-3965), Sea St. Open Memorial Day–Columbus Day, 11–9. Bigger than it looks, with a no-frills, knotty-pine interior, amazingly efficient, friendly waitresses. The light and crispy onion rings are simply the best anywhere, one serving enough for two. Good chowder and Maine crabcakes; also salads, burgers, clam rolls, and a shore dinner. Wine and beer; lunch all day; early-bird specials.

THURSTON'S LOBSTER POUND, BERNARD

🐚 **The Colonel's Restaurant** (207-276-5147), Main St. Open early Apr.–late Oct. Serving breakfast 6:30–11:30, lunch and dinner 11:30–9. A big, informal eatery, rebuilt after the 2008 fire. There's a deli-style storefront section as well as the more formal dining area. Still good for fresh-dough pizzas, burgers, also reasonably priced seafood dinners.

Pine Tree Market (207-276-3335), 121 Main St. Open daily 1–1, Sunday 8–6. Geared to boaters and summer residents, this classic old market prides itself on its meats, wines, and baked goods. Good picnic makings. There's a coin-operated laundry in the cellar.

The Full Belly Deli (207-276-4299), 5 Sea St. A handy source of picnic fixings as you head down to the harbor. Imaginative sandwiches as well as the basics plus baked goods. A few tables.

In Bass Harbor
🐚 🐚 **Thurston's Lobster Pound** (207-244-7600; thurstonslobster.com), Steamboat Wharf Rd., Bernard. Open Memorial Day–Columbus Day, daily 11–8:30. Weatherproofed, on a working wharf overlooking Bass Harbor and just far enough off the beaten path not to be mobbed. Fresh and tender as lobster can be, plus corn and pie, also seafood stew, sandwiches, and blueberry cheesecake. Wine and beer.

🐚 **Seafood Ketch** (207-244-7463; seafoodketch.com), on Bass Harbor. Open mid-May–mid-Oct., daily 11–9. Longtime ownership by Stuart and Lisa Branch has given this place a solid reputation for homemade breads and desserts, and fried seafood. Eat inside or out on the new deck. Dinner entrées $19–30.

✳ Entertainment

MUSIC Mount Desert Festival of Chamber Music (207-276-3988; mtdesertfestival.org), Neighborhood House, Main St., Northeast Harbor. A series of six concerts presented for more than 48 seasons mid-July–mid-Aug.

See "Bar Harbor" for the Bar Harbor Music Festival.

Saturday Evening Concerts at the Claremont Hotel (207-244-5036), Claremont Rd., Southwest Harbor. Summer concerts have included the Jerks of Grass and the Gilbert and Sullivan Society of Hancock County.

THEATER Acadia Repertory Theatre (207-244-7260; acadiarep.com), Rt. 102, Somesville. Performances during July and Aug., Tue.–Sun. at 8:15 PM; matinees at 2 on the last Sun. of each run. A regional repertory theater group performs in the Somesville Masonic Hall, presenting several popular plays in the course of the season. Tickets are reasonably priced.

The Claremont Hotel Thursday Evening Lecture Series (207-244-5036), Claremont Rd., Southwest Harbor. July and Aug. An impressive array of authorities speak on a variety of topics (like "Writing for a Living and Other Mistakes I Have Made" by Alex Beam), as well as talks on jazz, mountain climbing, and Mount Desert history. All lectures are at 8:15.

✴ Selective Shopping

Along Main Street in Northeast Harbor

Island Artisans (207-276-4045; islandartisans.com), 119 Main St. Open mid-June–mid Oct., an offshoot of the Bar Harbor shop, showcasing exceptional work by more than 100 area craftspeople working with textiles, pottery, baskets, paper, wood, glass, silver, metal, and stone. **Shaw Contemporary Jewelry** (207-276-5000; shawjewelry.com), 126 Main St., open year-round, is an outstanding gallery featuring Sam Shaw's own work but also displaying work by artists from throughout the United States and Europe, genuine eye candy, priced $20–2,000. A village anchor is the **Kimball Shop & Boutique** (207-276-3300; kimballshop.com), an upscale mini department store geared to summer residents' needs since 1935 and an amazing trove of home furnishings, gadgets, clothing, children's items, and gifts. The other anchor is the **Pine Tree Market** (see *Eating Out*). **McGrath's Store** (207-276-5548), Main St., is an old-fashioned newspaper/stationery store with some surprises, while long-established **Wikhegan Books** (208-276-5079), 117 Main St., is a trove of early history and guidebooks as well as fiction relating to the MDI region, including the legendary Red Book directory of Northeast Harbor summer residents; also nautical titles, Eastern Woodland Indians, poetry, antiques, and much more.

In Southwest Harbor

Aylen & Son Fine Jewelry (207-244-7369; peteraylen.com), 320 Main St. Open mid-April–Christmas Eve. Peter Aylen fashions gold, silver, pearl, and Maine gemstone jewelry with botanical themes; Judy Aylen creates bead necklaces and works with a variety of stones.

Under the Dogwood Tree (207-244-3089), 326 Main St. Women's clothing, fabric, accessories, and pretty rugs.

Carroll Drug Store (207-244-5588), just off Main St. at the north end of the village. A supermarket-sized store with a genuine general-store/five-and-dime feel.

Sawyer's Market (207-244-3315), 344 Main St. This is a great old grocery store with a good deli counter and good soups on tap.

In Bernard and Seal Cove

Seal Cove Pottery and Gallery (207-244-3602; sealcovepottery.com), Kelly Town Rd., Seal Cove. Marked from Rt. 102. Open Apr.–mid-Nov., 10–5. Lisbeth Faulkner and Ed Davis create handsome, functional pottery (glazes are made from scratch), worth a special trip. Davis is a fifth-generation (both sides) MDI native.

Also see the **Cranberry Isles** sidebar under *To See* for more galleries and studios.

✴ Special Events

July: **Independence Day fireworks** on Somes Sound. **Quietside Festival** and **Annual Pink Flamingo Canoe Race** at Seal Cove in Tremont (207-244-3713).

Early August: **Sweet Chariot Festival** on Swans Island. **Frenchboro Days** in Frenchboro. **Annual Art Show on the Green**, Southwest Harbor (1-800-423-9264).

September: **Mount Desert Island Garlic Festival** (207-288-0269), 20 Main St., Southwest Harbor, at Smugglers Den Campground, with local restaurants, brewers, musicians and garlic growers.

EAST HANCOCK COUNTY

At the junction of Rts. 3 and 1 in Ellsworth, it's Rt. 3 that continues straight ahead and Rt. 1 that angles off, the road less taken. Within a few miles you notice the absence of commercial clutter. Nowhere in Maine does the coast change as abruptly as along this rim of Frenchman Bay.

On the western side of the bay is Mount Desert Island with busy Bar Harbor, magnet for everyone from everywhere. The northern and eastern shores are, however, a quiet, curving stretch of coves, tidal bays, and peninsulas, all with views of Acadia's high, rounded mountains. This is an old but quiet resort area with high mountains, hidden lakes, fishing villages, fine inns, and a rich cultural life.

In 1889 the Maine Central's Boston & Mount Desert Limited carried passengers in less than eight hours from Boston's North Station to Mount Desert Ferry, the name of the terminal in Hancock. Briefly billed as the fastest train in New England, it connected with ferries to several points on this far side of Frenchman

THE VIEW FROM COREA

Christina Tree

Bay, as well as Bar Harbor. That era's huge old summer hotels are long gone, and only the surviving summer colonies in Sorrento, Grindstone Neck, and Hancock Point evoke the era of steamboats and railroads.

The 27 miles along Frenchman Bay that begin on Rt. 1 at the Hancock/Sullivan bridge and loop around the Schoodic Peninsula to Prospect Harbor are now a National Scenic Byway. Beyond the bridge across the tidal Taunton River, Rt. 1 shadows the bay, offering spectacular views. Be sure to stop at the scenic turnout (the site of a former inn) just before Dunbar's Store.

It's said that on a clear day you can see Katahdin as well as the Acadia peaks from the top of Schoodic Mountain, some 20 miles inland, back up between Sullivan and Franklin and handy to swimming at Donnell Pond. Most travelers who come this far are, however, bound for the Schoodic Point loop around a 2,100-acre headland that's part of Acadia National Park.

Schoodic is the name that has come to apply to the entire coastal area along the eastern side of Frenchman Bay. *Schoodic Peninsula*, however, applies only to the fat finger of land pointing seaward that's now part of the national park—which is just the tip of what's commonly referred to as the Gouldsboro Peninsula. This larger peninsula is divided between the towns of Winter Harbor and the several villages, including Prospect Harbor and Corea, that together make up the town of Gouldsboro. Sensibly, Louise Dickinson Rich titled her 1958 classic about this area *The Peninsula*.

At the entrance to the park, Winter Harbor serves the old summer colony on adjacent Grindstone Neck. Formerly it was home to a U.S. naval base that sent and intercepted coded messages from ships and submarines; the 100-acre campus within the park is now the Schoodic Education and Research Center (SERC), a venue for public programs and an information center for the park. Prospect Harbor, at the eastern end of the park, is a fishing village known for red-flashing Prospect Harbor Light. Corea, beyond on Sand Cove, is a photogenic fishing village set on pink granite rocks.

Possibilities for hiking and paddling in the hilly, lake-specked woodland north of Rt. 1 have been greatly increased in recent years, thanks to thousands of acres acquired by the Maine Bureau of Parks and Lands. Signage for trailheads and lake access has also improved now that a stretch of Rt. 182 has become the Blackwoods Scenic Byway.

Many visitors day-trip to Winter Harbor and Schoodic Point, especially since access has been eased by the seasonal ferry from Bar Harbor. Given the choice of attractive places to stay and to eat, the widely scattered but outstanding art and crafts galleries, the arts festivals, and all the hiking, biking, and kayaking possibilities, this should be a busier area than it is. Those who discover it are grateful that it isn't.

GUIDANCE Schoodic Peninsula Chamber of Commerce (207-963-7658; acadia-schoodic.org).

GETTING THERE *By car:* For a shortcut to Hancock from Bar Harbor, take Rt. 3 north to Rt. 204, posted for Lamoine State Park. Turn left onto Rt. 184, immediately right at the town hall onto Pinkham Rd., left after a mile or so at the sign for Rt. 1 (Mud Creek Rd.). From points south, see *Getting There* in "Bar Harbor."

By boat: The **Bar Harbor Ferry** (207-288-2984; barharborferry.com) offers five-times-a-day service late June–Aug. across Frenchman Bay between Bar Harbor and Winter Harbor; $29.50 roundtrip per adult, $19.50 per child. Bring a bike ($6).

GETTING AROUND Island Explorer (exploreacadia.com). Late June–Aug. this fabulous, free bus meets the Bar Harbor Ferry and makes an hourly circuit from Winter Harbor around Schoodic Point and back through Birch and Winter Harbors. Bicycles are a great way to explore the park itself.

✳ To See

Acadia National Park, **Schoodic Peninsula** (nps.gov/acad) Accessed from Rt. 186 just east of Winter Harbor, this is a one-way shore road, 6 miles of it within the park. **Frazer Point Picnic Area** (with comfort station) is a good first stop, a place to unload bikes if you want to tour on two wheels. It's said to have been an Indian campsite for thousands of years.

Farther along this stretch note the turnouts with views of the **Winter Harbor Light** (1856) and across French Bay to Cadillac Mountain.

A little more than 2.5 miles farther along, the unmarked, unpaved road up to **Schoodic Head** may or may not be open. Visitors are clearly encouraged to access the long views from this rocky 400-foot summit via hiking trails (see *Hiking*).

Bear right at the intersection for Schoodic Point (this portion of the road is two-way). You can pick up a map and hiking advice at the **Schoodic Gatehouse** (open daily in seasonally, weekends in winter) at the entrance to the **Schoodic Education and Research Center** (207-288-1310; sercinstitute.org). Plans call for a visitors center with displays about the park to open here in Rockefeller Hall by late summer 2013. Check the SERC website for year-round lectures, discussions, and ranger-led programs. The former 100-acre former U.S. Navy campus (established in 1935 and operating until 2002) is now managed jointly by Acadia National Park and SERC, a private nonprofit organization

Schoodic Point (plenty of parking) thrusts into the Atlantic, and on sunny days tidal pools invite clambering. On stormy days surf and spray can shoot as high as 40 feet, a popular spectacle. That surf can be deadly, so be careful. Bear right along the drive to the **Blueberry Hill Parking Area** (about a mile beyond Schoodic Point) with its views of Moose and Schoodic Islands and access to most of the area's hiking trails. Continue along the drive 2 more miles to Rt. 186 in the village of Birch Harbor.

SCENIC DRIVES Schoodic Scenic Byway (see the description in this chapter's introduction and at byways.org). Federal funding has improved signage and turnouts along this breathtakingly beautiful 29-mile stretch of coast with views back across the bay to Acadia's mountains.

Blackwoods Scenic Byway (Rt. 182; blackwoodsbyway.org). Newly resurfaced, Rt. 182 is the mostly wooded, inland shortcut from Hancock to Washington County (you save 9 miles vs. Rt. 1). Recently the 12.5 easternmost miles—between **Franklin** and **Cherryfield** (see the Washington County chapter)—has been declared a scenic byway, meaning better signage and turnout areas, and boat launches to access to the 14,000 acres of woods and water now maintained by the Maine Bureau of Parks and Lands as the Donnell Pond Unit. It includes **Tunk Lake**, **Donnell Pond**, and **Spring River Lake** as well as other backwaters. From Rt. 1 it's 6 miles to Rt. 182 via Rt. 200 from Hancock, past outstanding crafts galleries (see *Selective Shopping*).

✳ To Do

BIKING The 12-mile loop from Winter Harbor around Schoodic Point is a popular bike route. Rentals available from **SeaScape Kayaking** (below). Also check out the **Down East Sunrise Trail** (sunrisetrail.org), a converted railbed that begins in Hancock and runs east across this area.

BOATING Bar Harbor Ferry (see *Getting There*).

Robertson Sea Tours (robertsonseatours.com), departing from Milbridge Marina (see *To Do* in "Washington County"), cruises the 50 miles east of Schoodic.

Shaw Marine Brokerage & Water Taxi (207-963-7007), 22 Harbor Rd., offers winter water taxi service to Bar Harbor, also rents sail- and motorboats.

FISHING Donnell Pond is known for salmon; Tunk Lake and Spring River Lake are good for trout (togue). Look for launch sites along Rt. 182.

KAYAKING Hancock Point Kayak Tours (207-422-6854; hancockpointkayak .com), 58 Point Rd., Hancock. Antonio Blasi offers guided paddling in Frenchman and Taunton Bays, also overnight camping and guided snowshoeing.

SeaScape Kayaking (207-963-5806 or 207-963-5806), 18 E. Schoodic Dr., Birch Harbor. Kayak and canoe rentals, good for quiet coves and lakes only, along with guided tours of Flanders Bay and the Corea area, more.

GOLF Grindstone Neck Golf Course (207-963-7760), Gerrishville. A nine-hole course dating to 1895 as part of this summer colony; open to the public June–Sept.

Blink Bonnie Golf Course (207-422-3930), Rt. 185, Sorrento. A nine-hole walking course with an open layout and views of Flanders Bay. Golf-cart rentals.

HIKING Acadia National Park, Schoodic Peninsula (see *To See*), offers several short hikes, all best accessed from the Blueberry Hill Parking Area. The gentle 0.6-mile Alder Trail leads to the steeper 0.6-mile **Schoodic Head Trail** to the summit of Schoodic Head (440 feet), a vantage point also accessed by the relatively demanding 1.1-mile Anvil Trail. While it's not marked, another popular hike at low tide is out on Little Moose Island. Check the tide and pick up a map at the Schoodic Gatehouse.

Schoodic Mountain, off Rt. 183 north of Sullivan, provides one of eastern Maine's most spectacular hikes, with 360-degree views. Maine's Bureau of Parks and Lands (207-287-5936) has improved the parking area and trail system here. Take the first left (it's unpaved) after crossing the **Sunrise Trail** (sunrisetrail.org) on Rt. 183; bear left at the Y and in 2 miles reach the parking lot (outhouse facility). The hike to the top of Schoodic Mountain (1,069 feet) should take around 45 minutes; a marked trail from the summit leads down to sandy **Schoodic Beach** at the southern end of **Donnell Pond** (good swimming and half a dozen primitive campsites). Return to the parking lot on the old road that's now a footpath (0.5 mile). From the same parking lot, you can also follow a dirt path down to Donnell Pond or hike to the bluffs on Black Mountain, a mesmerizingly beautiful hike with summit views north to Tunk Lake and east across Washington County. Another trail descends to **Schoodic Beach**. This is now part of 14,000 acres known as **Donnell Pond Public Preserved Land**, which also includes Tunk and Spring River Lakes and primitive campsites. **Tucker Mountain** rewards a mile's hike with panoramic views. The trail begins on old Rt. 1, across from the Long Cove scenic turnout on Rt. 1 in Sullivan.

SWIMMING Jones Beach on Jones Pond in West Gouldsboro offers a family playground, swimming and picnic areas, changing rooms, and a boat launch. Take Recreation Rd. off Rt. 195 just south of Rt. 1. Along Rt. 183 there's Flanders Pond (turn left 2.9 miles north of Rt. 1); **Little Tunk Lake** offers a sandy beach. Look for blue FBC sign on your left at 4.7 miles (it's 0.4 mile to the beach). Ask locally about **Molasses Pond** in Eastbrook. Also see **Donnell Pond** under *Hiking*.

✳ Green Space

The **Schoodic** section of **Acadia National Park** is detailed under *To See*. In addition, the **Frenchman Bay Conservancy** (frenchmanbay.org) maintains a dozen outstanding preserves; check out SHORT HIKES on their website and look for their blue diamond-shaped trail sign. Outstanding: **Tidal Falls**, formerly a popular lobster pound, is now a great picnicking site from which to watch eagles, herons, seals, and kayakers playing in the whitewater of the reversing falls in the Taunton River. From Rt. 1 turn right just before the Hancock/Sullivan bridge on Eastside Rd., then left on Tidal Falls Rd. (0.7 mile down).

Corea Heath is an excuse to drive, as everyone should, out scenic Corea Rd. (Rt. 195); look for the FBC sign beyond the junction with Rt. 186 and park in the National Wildlife Refuge lot a short ways beyond on the right. The path loops around a peat bog and beaver flowage. Great for bird-watching, as is the adjoining 600-acre wildlife refuge, formerly owned by the navy, which includes Grand Marsh and Grand Marsh Bay.

Also see *Hiking* and *Swimming* for more about the 14,000-acre mountain and lake-spotted **Donnell Pond Public Preserved Land**, maintained by the **Maine Bureau of Parks and Lands**.

✳ Lodging

✪ ☻ ✍ ♿ **Crocker House Country Inn** (207-422-6806 or 1-877-715-6017; crockerhouse.com), Hancock Point 04640. Open daily May–Oct., weekends Nov.–New Year's Eve. Billed as "a little out of the way and out of the ordinary," this handsome, shingled inn is midway between the sections of Aca-dia National Park on Mount Desert and Schoodic Point. Sited at the center of a charming 1880s summer colony, complete with a chapel, tiny post office, octagonal library, and tennis courts, it's the lone survivor among several once-larger hotels. Since 1980 it's been owned by Richard and Elizabeth

Malaby, and the welcome is genuine. There are nine antiques-furnished rooms in the inn itself, two in the carriage house, all with private bath and phone, and in addition to the inn's parlor, there's a den with TV (adjoining a room with a hot tub) in the carriage house. The inn is set among flowers and trees, but water is a short walk in most directions. $110–165 mid-June–mid-Oct., $85–100 off-season includes a full breakfast. Moorings are available, and a few touring bikes are kept for guests. The restaurant is a major draw (see *Dining Out*).

🐾 **Le Domaine** (207-422-3395 or 1-800-554-8498; ledomaine.com), 1513 Rt. 1, Hancock 04640. Open mid-June–mid-Oct. Best known for its dining room (see *Dining Out*), this elegant little inn offers three rooms and two suites. Provençal antiques, fabrics, original paintings, and small niceties create real charm and a high comfort level. Bathrooms have a porcelain soaking tub and separate shower as well as a heated towel rack, lighted vanity mirror, and fluffy towels; the suites have a gas fireplace and cathedral ceilings, and all rooms have phone, bed light, and access to the balconies on which you can enjoy the flakiest of croissants with homemade honey and jam and French-roast coffee. Pets are accepted for an additional $30. $150 per room, $225 per suite B&B. Guests receive 10 percent off on dinner.

✪ 🐾 (📶) **The Black Duck** (207-963-2689; blackduck.com), P.O. Box 39, Corea 04624. Barry Canner and Robert Travers offer their fine old house overlooking one of Maine's most picturesque working harbors. Their four guest rooms and ample common areas are all comfortably, imaginatively furnished with antiques and contemporary art. The sunny dining room is a

Christina Tree

THREE PINES B&B, HANCOCK

venue for morning feasts and good conversation. The working harbor is just across the road—unless you happen to be renting one of two housekeeping cottages that sit right on it. You can walk to sand beaches, but the nearby pond is more inviting for swimming. One host can perform weddings. There's a pleasant upstairs room with a harbor view, a first-floor room with deck plus queen and twin beds, a two-bedroom suite, and Harbor Studio (one bed and a kitchenette). $140–200 includes a full breakfast. Inquire about Harbor Cottage, a weekly rental.

🐾 ✎ **Three Pines B&B** (207-460-7595; threepinesbandb.com), 274 Eastside Rd., Hancock 04640. Open year-round. Turn in at this organic farm and follow a private road down through 40 acres of woods and meadow to the shore. Here Ed and Karen Curtis have built a shingled, timber-frame, passive solar dream house with a separate wing housing two delightful B&B guest rooms, each with a sitting room and water view. Breakfast includes eggs from the farm's chickens, and frequently home-grown vegetables and fruit, too. Farm animals also include sheep, ducks, and roosters. $85–125 per couple, $15 per extra person.

Acadia View Bed & Breakfast (1-866-963-7457; acadiaview.com), 175 Rt. 1, P.O. Box 247, Gouldsboro 04607. Aerospace engineers in a previous life that took them many places, Pat and Jim Close have designed and built this mansion specifically as a B&B. The Great Room, with its wood-burning fireplace, and two of the four guest rooms (private bath) all share splendid views across Frenchman Bay to Acadia. All rooms have private deck with water views. $139–169 in high season, otherwise from $119, includes a full breakfast.

🐾 **Island View Inn** (207-422-3031; maineus.com/islandview), 12 Miramar Ave., Sullivan Harbor 04664. Open June–mid-Oct. This is a spacious, gracious 1880s summer "cottage" with a massive central hearth and airy sitting room set well back from Rt. 1 with splendid views of Frenchman Bay and the mountains on Mount Desert. Evelyn Joost offers seven nicely decorated

guest rooms, all with private bath and water views. There is a well-equipped guest pantry; a very full breakfast in the dining area overlooking the water is included. $155–175.

🎨 ♿ **Oceanside Meadows Inn** (207-963-5557; oceaninn.com), P.O. Box 90, Prospect Harbor 04669. Open May–Oct., off-season by special arrangement. This 200-acre property (a nature preserve) includes an 1860s sea captain's home and neighboring 1820s farmhouse overlooking well-named Sand Cove. Sonja Sundaram and Ben Walter, passionate conservationists who met at an environmental research center in Bermuda, have renovated both houses, with a total of 15 guest rooms, including several suites good for small families. All are within earshot of waves. The farmhouse in particular lends itself to rental as a whole, ideal for family reunions. The meadows and woods are webbed with trails leading to a salt marsh, good for spotting wildlife ranging from moose to eagles. A rehabbed open-timbered barn is the venue for a full schedule of concerts, lectures, and live performances and

VIEW OF ACADIA FROM ISLAND VIEW INN

Bill Davis

Christina Tree

ELSA'S INN ON THE HARBOR

also works as a conference or wedding reception center. $149–189 for rooms, $189–209 for suites July–Labor Day weekend, including Sonja's three- to four-course breakfasts. Less in May, June, Sept., Oct. See *Entertainment* for details about the Oceanside Meadows Institute for the Arts and Sciences.

✪ ☀ ✐ ♿ **Elsa's Inn on the Harbor** (207-963-7571; elsasinn.com), 179 Main St., Prospect Harbor 04669. This gabled, mid-1800s house overlooks a working harbor, the last in Maine to retain its sardine cannery. Jeff Alley, a sixth-generation lobsterman, was raised in this house, which is named for his mother. Jeff, his wife Cynthia, daughter Megan Alley Moshier (a veteran of management jobs at hotels from Hawaii to DC), and her husband Glenn have together totally renovated the old homestead, creating six bright, spiffy guest rooms with handmade quilts, private bath, and water views, as well as a comfortable living room, veranda, and patio. In all 16 guests can bed down. $130–165 June 25–Oct.15, from $115 off-season, including a full breakfast that might feature crabmeat strata. Lobster bakes ending with blueberry cobbler can be arranged for in-house guests. Space to relax includes a back patio as well as the bright, comfy living room and long veranda with rockers.

♂ ☀ ✐ ((ᵖ)) **Bluff House Inn** (207-963-7805; bluffinn.com), 57 Bluff House Rd., South Gouldsboro 04607. Open year-round. Mary Moshier is the friendly innkeeper at this modern lodge with a dining room featuring floor-to-ceiling windows, a screened porch overlooking the water, and a comfortable sitting area by a stone hearth. The eight guest rooms line the upstairs hall; three have water views. It's set off by itself above the pink granite shore; there's a road down to a beach from which you can launch a kayak onto Frenchman Bay. Inquire about Saturday-night lobster dinner and other evening meals. $85–140 varying by the season includes a continental breakfast. A two-bedroom efficiency apartment is $150 per couple with a three-night minimum.

Taunton River Bed & Breakfast (207-422-2070; tauntonriverbandb .com), 19 Taunton Dr., Sullivan 04664. Open Apr.–Oct. Just east of the Hancock Sullivan bridge, set back from Rt. 1 behind the common, Dottie Mace's comfortable house offers three guest rooms, a good way stop. $140–150 per couple in-season includes a full breakfast; from $115 off-season.

COTTAGES ☀ **Sullivan Harbor Farm** (207-422-3735 or 1-800-422-4014; sullivanharborfarm.com), Rt. 1, P.O. Box 96, Sullivan 04664. Three particularly attractive cottages cluster on a nicely sited property with a landscaped pool and a resident host who delights in turning guests on to local hiking, biking, and paddling possibilities. **Cupcake**, a bright year-round cottage with two working fireplaces, has water views and can sleep six ($1,600 per week; less off-season).

Another cottage, **Milo**, sleeps four adults ($1,075 per week); **Guzzle Cottage** ($1,800) is a newly renovated three-bedroom, two-bath 1810 Cape with all conveniences and views across Frenchman Bay. A kayak is available.

✦ **Albee's Shoreline Cottages** (207-963-2336), Rt. 186, P.O. Box 70, Prospect Harbor 04669. Open Memorial Day–mid-Oct. The 10 rustic cottages, 5 directly on the shore, are classic old Maine motor court vintage, but each has been painstakingly rehabbed; all have gas heater, woodstove, or fireplace. Richard Rieth enjoys orienting guests to the best of what's around. $79–132 per night.

✳ Where to Eat

DINING OUT **Le Domaine** (207-422-3395; ledomaine.com), Rt. 1, Hancock (9 miles east of Ellsworth). Open for dinner early June–Oct., Tue.–Sun. 6–9, and for Sunday brunch. Reservations recommended. Many summer residents on MDI know the shortcut to Le Domaine (see *Getting There*). Tables are nicely spaced in the softly lit dining rooms, decorated in Provençal prints with fresh flowers from the cutting garden; there's frequently a glowing fire reflected in gleaming wood and copper. The meal might begin with the lightly sautéed sweetbreads ($14) and feature crispy-skinned duck with fresh berry gastrique ($29), ending with a frozen hazelnut soufflé ($9.50). A tempting five-course prix fixe menu is $45.

Crocker House Country Inn (207-422-6806; crockerhouse.com), Hancock Point. Open nightly Apr.–Jan., weekends off-season, for dinner 5:30–9. The main dining room, with its 19th-century leaded-glass windows, is a pleasant setting for reliably fine dining, popular among a wide circle of summer residents. The menu daily to take full advantage of local produce and fish. Staples include Crocker House scallops, sautéed with mushrooms, scallions, garlic, and tomatoes with lemon and wine sauce, and farm-raised semi-boneless roast duckling with Grand Marnier ginger sauce. Entrées $26–34, including fresh bread, salad, starch, and a fresh vegetable. Desserts include homemade ice creams and gelato as well as a sinful Crocker House mousse (layered white and dark chocolate, laced with Myers's rum).

Chippers Restaurant (207-422-8238), 1239 Rt. 1, Hancock. Open year-round for dinner Tue.–Sun. 5–10 in summer months, otherwise Fri.–Sat. 4–8. It's a good idea to reserve. Chef-owner Chip Butterwick's place isn't much from the road, but inside there's a serious dining atmosphere and menu, also a new lounge with a pub menu. For the fewer than 40 patrons in the dining room, all meals begin with a very small bowl of rich haddock chowder. Entrée choices might include rack of lamb and Cajun seafood Alfredo. Entrées $18–31. Pub menu, too.

Fisherman's Inn Restaurant (207-963-5585), 7 Newman St., Winter Harbor. Open Apr.–Oct. for lunch 11:30–2; dinner is 4:30–8:30. Chef owner Carl Johnson's booth filled restaurant is pleasant and dependable, with a full menu ranging from pasta to char-grilled filet mignon. Seafood is the specialty. Signature dishes: lobster several different ways, a Winter Harbor seafood casserole, and haddock in a creamy lobster sauce. Dinner entrées $17–28; early-bird specials 4:30–5:30.

Bunker's Wharf (207-963-7488), 206 E. Schoodic Dr., Birch Harbor. Open Mother's Day–Oct. from 4, also lunch July 4–Labor Day. Nathan Hall's attractive waterside restaurant is back after a year's hiatus. Dine on chicken and sausage farfalle or caramelized

scallops, linguine and veggies with walnut basil pesto. Entrées $18–32.

EATING OUT

Along Route 1

☞ **Ruth & Wimpy's Kitchen** (207-
422-3723), Rt. 1, Hancock. Open year-
round. Look for "Wilbur the Lobster."
Wimpy Wilbur is a former long-haul
truck driver, and this family-run mainstay is decorated with his collection of
miniature trucks, license plates, beer
bottles, and more. The menu includes
burgers and steaks, overstuffed sandwiches, and seafood, including lobster
with all the fixings.

The Mexican Restaurant (207-422-
3723), 1166 Rt. 1, Hancock. Open
seasonally, 11-8 daily. This authentic
Mexican cantina has migrated down
Rt. 1 from Harrington where it served
the area's seasonal blueberry harvesters.

The Galley (207-422-2059), Rt. 1 on
the Sullivan end of the bridge. Open
year-round for lunch and dinner, daily
in summer, Thu.–Sun. off-season. This
handy way stop offers a dining room
with views of the Taunton River south
to Tidal Falls. Standout crab rolls and

cakes, house-made slaw, rolls, and
fries. Seafood chowder is thick with
shrimp, scallops, and haddock. Reasonably priced specials frequently include
lobster. Beer and wine.

Chester Pike's Galley (207-422-
8200). 2336 Rt. 1, Sullivan. Open 6–2
Tue.–Sat.; also 4:30–8:30 Fri., 7–2 Sun.
Generous road food, good pies.

On the Schoodic Peninsula

((ᵧ)) **Gerrish For Schoodic** (207-963-
7320; gerrishforschoodic.org), 352
Main St., Winter Harbor. This middle-
of-the-village gathering spot is now
community-owned, better than ever,
and open year-round., Thu.–Mon. 8–4;
daily 7–5 in summer. From-scratch
soups and sandwiches (with yummy
homemade chips), salads and panini,
ice cream. Beer and wine. Dinner Fri.
and Sat. by reservation.

((ᵧ)) **The HarborGirl Emporium &
Café** (207-963-5900), 4 Duck Pond
Rd., Birch Harbor. Open (except
Feb.–Mar.) Tue.–Sun. 11–8. Audrey
Keller and Alexis Souders are known
for the best pizza and macaroons in
town. This is a homey combo diner/gift
shop, a source of picnics, also lobsters
boiled while you wait.

☀ ☞ **Chase's Restaurant** (207-963-
7171), 193 Main St., Winter Harbor.
Open all year for all three meals. A
convenient local hangout on Rt. 186
near the entrance to the park. Booths,
fried lobsters and clams, good chowder; will pack a picnic.

**SMOKED SALMON Sullivan Har-
bor Salmon** (1-800-422-4014; sullivan
harborfarm.com), Rt. 1, Hancock Village. Open 9–5 Mon.–Sat.; weekdays
only off-season. The salmon is carefully
chosen, top of the line, and visitors can
view the smokehouse through windows
in the retail area. Fish are cured in
small batches, hand rubbed with a

RUTH & WIMPY'S

Nancy English

blend of salt and brown sugar, then rinsed in springwater and slowly smoked over a smudge fire of hickory shavings in the traditional Scottish way. No preservatives or additives. Mustards, crackers, breads, and Maine-made items also sold. Tasty samples.

Grindstone Neck of Maine (207-963-7347 or 1-800-831-8734; grindstone neck.com), 311 Newman St. (Rt. 186), Winter Harbor. A source of smoked mussels, oysters, scallops, and seafood spreads as well as salmon.

✳ Entertainment

&. **Schoodic Arts for All** (207-963-2569; schoodicarts.org), Hammond Hall, 427 Main St., Winter Harbor. This grassroots nonprofit sponsors music, art, crafts, dance, theater, and film through most of the year. Check the website for ongoing events, such as Friday concerts, coffeehouses, community theater, and a summer chorus. See *Special Events* for more about the **Schoodic Arts Festival**, two weeks in early August crammed with cultural events.

Also see *Special Events*.

Christina Tree

BARTER FAMILY GALLERY AND SHOP, SULLIVAN

✳ Selective Shopping

ART AND FINE-CRAFTS GALLERIES

Listed geographically, more or less, heading east along Route 1
Gull Rock Pottery (207-422-3990), Eastside Rd. (1.5 miles off Rt. 1), Hancock. Open year-round, Mon.–Sat. 9–5. Akemi Wray maintains this fabulously sited gallery known for wheel-thrown stoneware and now, too, for Japanese glazes. The sculpture garden offers a spectacular view of Frenchman Bay, and seats to enjoy it from. Akemi's husband, Russell, showcases his figurative wood carvings and bronzes at **Raven Tree Art Gallery** (207-422-8273; raventreegallery.com) nearby at 536 Point Rd., Hancock (open Mon.–Sat. 9–5:30), with etchings and sterling silver as well as sculpture; pottery by Akemi Wray can be found both places.

✪ **Barter Family Gallery and Shop** (207-422-3190), 318 Taunton Bay Rd., Sullivan. Open July into Sept.,

SCULPTURE AND VIEW AT GULL ROCK POTTERY, HANCOCK

Christina Tree

Tue.–Sat. 10–5, or by appointment. Posted from Rt. 1 at Sullivan's common (it's 2.5 miles). "We never get busy here," Priscilla Barter will tell you. Never mind that her husband's paintings hang in museums and fetch big money in the best galleries. Attached to the small house that Philip Barter built and in which the couple raised seven children, this is easily the most colorful gallery in Maine, but remote enough to keep browsers and buyers to a trickle. Here, added to dozens of distinctive Barter mountains, houses, and harbors, are off-the-wall pieces, wood sculptures, and Barter-made furniture. The gallery also features Matthew Barter's paintings, Priscilla's braided rugs, family-made jewelry, cards, and other reasonably priced gifts.

Lunaform (207-422-0923; lunaform .com), 66 Cedar Lane, marked from Rt. 1 at the Sullivan common. Open year-round, Mon.–Fri. 9–5. Striking handmade, steel-reinforced concrete garden urns (some are huge) as well as pots and planters are made in this former granite quarry.

Bill Davis

DON'T MISS WORKS OF HAND & WINTER HARBOR ANTIQUES, WINTER HARBOR

Also worth a detour

✪ **Hog Bay Pottery** (207-565-2282; hogbay.com), 245 Hog Bay Rd. (Rt. 200, 4 miles north of Rt. 1), Franklin. Open Apr.–Nov.; call off-season. This shop/studio is a find, the kind of place patrons return to again and again. Susanne Grosjean's bright, multicolored, hand-dyed and -woven, award-winning rugs complement distinctive table- and ovenware by Charles Grosjean (great seconds).

Moosetrack Studio (207-422-9017), 388 Bert Gray Rd. (Rt. 200, 1.8 miles north of Rt. 1), Sullivan. Open May–Oct., Fri.–Mon. 10–6 or by appointment. Camilla Stege's work is exquisite, ranging from handbags to shawls and rugs.

Spring Woods Gallery (207-442-3007; springwoodsgallery.com), Rt. 200, 0.25 mile off Rt. 1, Sullivan. Open May–Oct. Mon.–Sat. 10–6. This gallery features work by *National Geographic* cartographer and illustrator Paul Breeden and paintings by Ann Breeden as well as work by other members of the Breeden family. The adjoining garden alone is worth a stop.

SUSANNE GROSJEAN, AN AWARD-WINNING WEAVER, IS ANOTHER REASON TO VISIT HOG BAY POTTERY

Bill Davis

Christina Tree

LITTLEFIELD GALLERY

On the peninsula

Maine Kiln Works (207-963-5819), Rt. 186, West Gouldsboro (0.5 mile off Rt. 1). Over the years Dan and Elizabeth Weaver have come to specialize in distinctive stoneware sinks and towel bars, flameware platters and plates, as well as tableware.

Lee Art Glass Studio (207-963-7280), Rt. 186, 3 miles south of Rt. 1. Open June–Oct., 10–4. It's difficult to describe this fused-glass tableware, which incorporates ground enamels and crocheted doilies or stencils. Wayne Taylor has acquired the secret of creating these distinctive pieces, which he makes and sells in a former post office in South Gouldsboro.

✪ **Works of Hand & Winter Harbor Antiques** (207-963-7900;), 424–426 Main St., Winter Harbor. Open June–Oct., daily 10–5. This antiques shop and neighboring gallery are set back from the street across from Hammond Hall, and visitors are invited to sit a spell in the flowery garden. The two-floor gallery is well

worth a look, presenting the work of more than 50 local area artists, craftsmen in a wide range of media, and a selection of author-signed books.

Littlefield Gallery (207-838-2156; littlefieldgallery.com), 145 Main St., Winter Harbor. Sited just before the turnoff for the park, this is an exceptional contemporary gallery, a mix of paintings and pieces by prominent sculptors.

U.S. Bells and Watering Cove Pottery (207-963-7184; usbells.com), Rt. 186, Prospect Harbor. Open weekdays 9–5, Sat. 9–2, and by appointment. Richard Fisher creates (designs and casts) bells that form musical sculptures, and Liza Fisher creates wood-fired stoneware and porcelain.

SPECIAL SHOPS ✍ **Darthia Farm** (207-963-2770; darthiafarm.com), 51 Darthia Farm Rd. off Rt. 186 (east), Gouldsboro. Open June–late Sept. Mon.–Fri. 8–5, Sat. 8–noon. A 150-acre organic farm on West Bay with resident sheep, pigs, and turkeys, where much of the farmwork is powered by drafthorses. Cynthia and Bill Thayer's farm stand is justly famed for

HATTIE'S SHED AT DARTHIA FARM

Christina Tree

its vinegars, jams, salsas, and cheeses; Hattie's Shed, a weaving shop also at the farm, features coats, jackets, scarves, shawls, and Cynthia Thayer's well-respected, locally set novels.

✪ **Winter Harbor 5&10** (207-963-7927; winterharbor5and10.com), 349 Main St., Winter Harbor. Open daily, year-round. Peter Drinkwater will tell you it isn't easy operating a genuine, old-style five-and-dime these days. While it sells some souvenirs, this is the genuine article with just about everything you come looking for; also the local stop for keys, photo developing, digital printing, UPS, a copier, fax, and newspapers.

Chapter Two: Corea Rug Hooking Company & Accumulated Books Gallery (207-963-7269), 611 Corea Rd., Prospect Harbor. Open year-round, Thu.–Mon. 11–4.; daily July, Aug. Rosemary's hand-hooked designs and Gary's extraordinary accumulation of books are a winning combination. Many local products, like Prospect Harbor Soap, are featured.

WINTER HARBOR 5&10

Christina Tree

WINE AND SPIRITS ✪ **Bartlett Winery and Spirits of Maine** (207-546-2408; bartlettwinery.com), just off Rt. 1, Gouldsboro. Open for tastings June into Oct., Tue.–Sat. 11–5 and by appointment. Before Bob and Kathe Bartlett could open Maine's first winery back in 1982, they had to get the law changed. "Prohibition began in Maine," Bob Bartlett will remind you. An architect by training, he designed this low-slung winery sequestered in firs. The wines, which utilize Maine apples, blueberries, raspberries, and honey as well as regional pears and peaches, continue to win top honors in national and international competitions. They also offer pear eau de vie and Calvados-style apple brandy, both of which have fetched top international competition honors.

Shalom Orchard Organic Farm and Winery (207-565-2312; shalom orchard.com), 158 Eastgroon Rd. (Rt. 200 north of Rt. 182). The peaceful old hilltop farm includes a 1,000-plus apple orchard, also blueberries, cherries, and raspberries that are all made into organic wines. The farm store sells eggs, meat, and homespun yarns as well as tanned pelts and fleece from Rambouillet sheep. A reasonably priced apartment in the farmhouse (sleeping six) is also available by the night or week (🐾 ✑ (ⁱ)).

✶ Special Events

Also see *Entertainment*.

June–July: **Pierre Monteux Memorial Concert Hall** (207-422-3931; monteuxschool.org), off Rt. 1, Hancock. In June and July the internationally respected Pierre Monteux School for Conductors, founded in 1943, hosts a series of symphony concerts (Sun. at 5) and chamber music concerts (Wed. at 7:30) presented by faculty and students in the school's Forest Studio.

Late June–Labor Day: **Winter Harbor Farmers Market**, Tue. 9–noon, corner of Rt. 186 and Main St.

Late June–early September: **Schoodic International Sculpture Symposium** (schoodicsculpture.org), based at the Schoodic Education and Research Center (SERC), next held in 2013, involves prominent sculptors from throughout the world producing works in granite to be placed throughout eastern Maine. Note the striking *Cleat* by Don Justin Meserve, in the water off the town landing (Rt. 186) in Winter Harbor. Visitors are welcome to watch artists at work at SERC.

July–August: **Frenchman Bay Conservancy Monday-night concerts** at Tidal Falls Preserve, Hancock (207-422-2328; frenchmanbay.org; also see *Green Space*). **Ocean Meadows Innstitute for the Arts and**

Sciences (oceaninn.com) stages lectures and concerts throughout the summer; check their website for a complete list of cultural events in the area.

August: ♿ The **Schoodic Arts Festival** (schoodicarts.org) held annually the first two weeks in August, is a destination extravaganza with dance, theater, visual arts, writing and crafts workshops, and evening performances staged throughout the area, but otherwise the venue is Hammond Hall—renovated, heated, and handicapped-accessible. **Sullivan Daze** (first Saturday) is a daylong celebration in Sullivan. The **Winter Harbor Lobster Festival** (acadia.schoodic.org) (second Saturday), is the biggest day of the summer here: crafts fair, lobster-boat races, a parade, live music, and a huge lobster feed.

WASHINGTON COUNTY
AND THE QUODDY LOOP
THE BOLD COAST: STEUBEN TO CAMPOBELLO ISLAND (NEW BRUNSWICK); EASTPORT, COBSCOOK BAY, AND PASSAMAQUODDY BAY; CALAIS AND THE DOWNEAST LAKES REGION; ST. ANDREWS AND GRAND MANAN (NEW BRUNSWICK)

As Down East as you can get in this country, Washington County is a ruggedly beautiful and lonely land unto itself. Its coastline harbors some of the most dramatic cliffs and deepest coves—certainly the highest tides—on the eastern U.S. seaboard, but relatively few tourists. Lobster boats and trawlers far outnumber the few pleasure craft to be seen.

Created in 1789 by order of the General Court of Massachusetts, Washington County is as large as the states of Delaware and Rhode Island combined. Yet it's home to less than 34,000 people, widely scattered among fishing villages, logging outposts, Native American reservations, and saltwater farms. Many people (not just some) survive here by raking blueberries in August, making balsam wreaths in winter, and lobstering, clamming, digging sea worms, harvesting sea cucumbers, diving for sea urchins, and "winkling" the remainder of the year. Washington County is the world's largest source of wild blueberries.

A fraction of Maine's visitors get this far. The only groups you see are scouting for American bald eagles or ospreys in the Moosehorn National Wildlife Refuge; for puffins, auks, and arctic terns on Machias Seal Island; or for whales in the Bay of Fundy. You may also see fishermen angling for landlocked salmon and smallmouth bass in the Downeast Lakes, and perhaps meet a few people looking to buy some of the most reasonably priced coastal property in Maine. Ecotourism—hiking and birding, especially puffin-watching and kayaking—is increasingly important.

This is former lumbering country. Maine writer Wayne Curtis has noted that it's here that the North Woods meets the shore, and "you can set off in search of moose and whales on the same hike." Curtis has also written in *Down East* magazine about the little-noted preservation of more than a million acres of former commercial woodland in this area: "The defining characteristic of inland Washington County

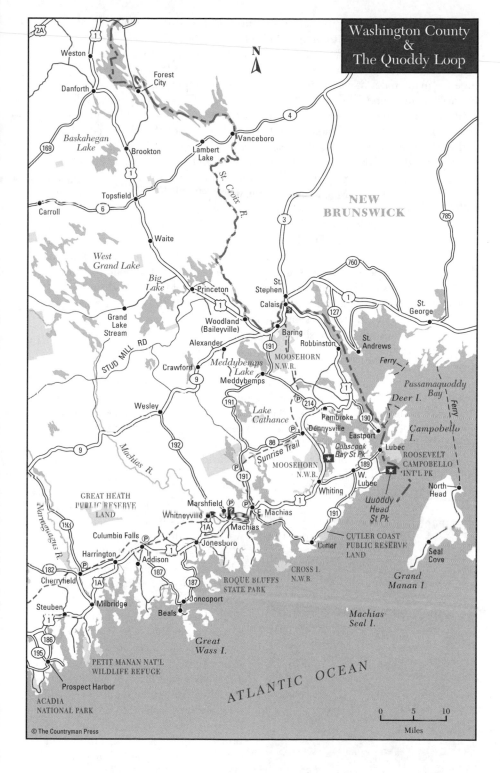

Washington County
&
The Quoddy Loop

© The Countryman Press

isn't mountains or rushing rivers or even endless forests. It's wetlands—vast primeval places fringed with pine and hemlock and birch."

For exploring purposes, we divide Washington County into three distinct regions: (1) the 60-mile stretch of Rt. 1 from Steuben to Lubec (with roughly 10 times as many miles of wandering coastline) and Campobello Island, New Brunswick, just across the bridge from Lubec, site of Roosevelt Camopobllo International Park, the only major attraction, per se, in this region. (2) Eastport and Cobscook Bay, the area of the highest tides and an end-of-the-world feel. (Lubec and Eastport are less than 3 miles apart by water, connected by a seasonal ferry, but separated by 43 land miles.) (3) Calais and the Downeast Lakes, the lake-splotched backwoods largely accessible from Grand Lake Stream. (4) We include St. Andrews and Grand Manan, New Brunswick, part of the Quoddy Loop and well worth exploring for anyone who has come this far.

Wherever you explore in Washington County—from the old sardine-canning towns of Eastport and Lubec to the coastal fishing villages of Jonesport and Cutler, and the even smaller villages on the immense inland lakes—you find a Maine you thought had disappeared decades ago. You are surprised by the beauty of old buildings, such as the 18th-century Burnham Tavern in Machias and Ruggles House in Columbia Falls. You learn that the first naval battle of the Revolution was won by Machias men; that some local 18th-century women were buried in rum casks (because they were shipped home that way from the Caribbean); and that pirate Captain Richard Bellamy's loot is believed to be buried somewhere near Machias.

What happened along this particular coastline in prehistoric times has also taken on new interest to scientists studying global warming. Apparently the ice sheet stalled here some 15,300 years ago, evidenced by the region's extensive barrens and number of bogs, eskers, and moraines. A free map/guide to 46 stops on *Maine's Ice Age Trail Down East* (iceagetrail.umaine.edu) is widely available.

Happily, you don't drop off the end of the world beyond Eastport or Campobello Island, even though—since the boundary was drawn across the face of Passamaquoddy Bay—New England maps have included only the Maine shore and Campobello Island and Canadian maps have detailed only the New Brunswick side of the bay. In summer when the ferries are running, the crossing from either Eastport or Campobello to L'Etete, near the resort town of St. Andrews, NB, is among the most scenic in the East. This circuit, the Quoddy Loop, includes a drive up along the St. Croix River to Calais, and a ferry trip that involves transferring from a small to a larger (free) Canadian ferry on Deer Island in the middle of Passamaquoddy Bay. St. Andrews itself probably offers a greater number and variety of "rooms" and dining than all Washington County combined. We also

JONESPORT

Bill Davis

include the magnificent island of Grand Manan, which lies off Maine's Bold Coast but is part of New Brunswick, accessible from Blacks Harbour not far from St. Andrews.

With the border tightening after 9/11 the international flow of tourists ebbed for several years, but we are happy to report that it's on the rise again, with an ever-increasing number of events, excursions, websites, and print handouts encompassing both sides of Passamaquoddy Bay.

GUIDANCE DownEast & Acadia Regional Tourism (1-888-665-DART; downeastacadia.com) is the umbrella tourism organization for Hancock and Washington Counties. Also see chambers of commerce for specific regions.

The **Maine Tourism Association** maintains a full-service visitors center (207-454-2211) at 39 Union St. (the Wabanaki Cultural Center), Calais. Open July–Oct., daily 8–6, otherwise 9–5:30.

A Quoddy Loop Tour Guide (quoddyloop.com) has information and a map of the area from Machias to Calais as well as Campobello Island, Grand Manan, and other communities around Passamaquoddy Bay in Maine and New Brunswick.

GETTING THERE *By air:* See "Bar Harbor" and "Bangor Area" for scheduled airline service.

By bus: **Concord Coach** (1-800-639-331; concordcoachlines.com) offers the quickest service to Bangor from Augusta, Portland, and Boston. **West's Coastal Connection** (1-800-596-2823; westbusservice.com) offers daily, regularly scheduled service year-round between Bangor Airport (stopping at both bus terminals) and Calais, with stops in Machias and Perry, and flag-down stops (call ahead) in between.

By car: From points south take I-95 to Rt. 295 to I-95 to Bangor. For the westernmost towns take Rt. 1A to Ellsworth, then Rt. 1. For coastal points east of Harrington, you save 9 miles by cutting inland on Rt. 182 from Hancock to Cherryfield, but for most easterly points from Bangor, take the **Airline Highway** (Rt. 9) from which many roads connect to coastal communities. Rt. 9 runs for 100 miles, straight through the blueberry barrens and woods, to Calais.

GETTING AROUND East Coast Ferries Ltd. (506-747-2159 or 1-877-747-2159; eastcoastferries.nb.ca), based on Deer Island, serves both Campobello Island (30 minutes) and Eastport (20 minutes). Generally these run every hour from around 9 AM (Atlantic Time, or AT) to around 7 PM

EAST COAST FERRY

Christina Tree

(AT), late June–early Sept., but call to check. $16 per car and driver, $3 per passenger (free ages 12 and under). The Campobello ferry takes 15 cars, and the Eastport ferry takes 8 but gets fewer passengers. "It's not what you usually think of as a ferry," says Velma Lord, about the shape of the two vessels her family operates. *Bay of Fundy* and *Island Hopper* are both tugs with long, hydraulically operated arms linked to barges. Passengers and bikes, cars, and even buses board on ramps lowered to the beach. Once back in deep water the steel arm turns the barge, reversing direction. The Lords go back at least four generations on **Deer Island** (pop. 900), the largest island in Passamaquoddy Bay. It offers lodging and dining, but most ferry passengers use it as a stepping-stone to the Canadian mainland, accessed from Butler's Point at the opposite end of the island via the free, larger **New Brunswick Department of Transportation** ferries (506-453-3939). These make the 20-minute run, usually every half hour, 6 AM–10 PM, to L'Etete, New Brunswick, handy both to St. Andrews and to Blacks Harbour (departure point for ferries to Grand Manan). Theoretically the ferry from Campobello to St. Andrews is 100 miles shorter than the drive around the bay, but the two trips may well take the same amount of time. On a beautiful day, however, there's no comparison.

The Eastport Ferry (207-853-2635 or 546-2927; eastportferry.com) connects Lubec and Eastport seasonally.

CROSSING THE BORDER Passports or NEXUS cards are required for reentry to the United States from Canada by land. For details see getyouhome.gov. Children 15 and under need a birth certificate. For questions about pets and what you can bring back and forth see cbp.gov. U.S. Immigration in Lubec (207-733-4331) can also answer questions about the crossing there and in Calais. Canadian citizens are required to present a passport or a NEXUS card.

Note: Do not bring a radar detector into Canada; they are illegal in the Maritime Provinces. Also, if you're driving a vehicle other than your own, you must have the owner's written permission. An Immigration official greets arriving ferries in Eastport, but there is virtually no line because this is not a commercial crossing. The Calais crossing has been eased since the opening of the International Avenue crossing—on Rt. 1 north of town—and of there is also a Milltown crossing.

THE BOLD COAST: STEUBEN TO CAMPOBELLO ISLAND (NEW BRUNSWICK)

GUIDANCE The Machias Bay Area Chamber of Commerce (207-255-4402; machiaschamber.org). A walk-in information center on Rt. 1 is sequestered between Helen's Restaurant and the Irving station, in the back of the Wall's Appliance building. Open weekdays 10–3, it's well stocked with brochures and serves the coastal and lake area extending from Milbridge to Whiting.

West Quoddy Head Visitors Center (207-733-2180; westquoddy.com). Open daily Memorial Day weekend to mid-Oct., 10–4.

Cobscook Bay Area Chamber of Commerce (207-733-2201; cobscookbay.com) overlaps in area with the Machias chamber and extends through towns north along the bay to Eastport. Also look for the volunteer-run seasonal information center in the **Lubec Historical Society**, 135 Main St., a former general store, as you enter town on Rt. 189.

Christina Tree

THE FISH IS IN LUBEC, THE LIGHTHOUSE
ON CAMPOBELLO

The Campobello Welcome Center (506-752-7043) at the entrance to the island is open daily May–Columbus Day. New Brunswick tourist information is available from 1-800-561-0123; tourismnbcanada.com.

WHEN TO GO Memorial Day weekend kicks off the season with the **Down East Birding Festival** (downeastbirdfest.org). The best months to view **puffins on Machias Seal Island** are May–early July (boldcoast.com). **Milbridge Days**, last weekend in July, and the **Wild Blueberry Festival** in Machias, third weekend in August, are the big summer events. September usually brings the clearest weather—but the ferries from Eastport and Campobello to Deer Island (esatcoastferries.nb.ca) usually stop running soon after Labor Day. By mid-September and into early October the blueberry barrens turn red, adding their brilliance to foliage.

✸ To See

Entries are listed geographically, heading east
Steuben, the first town in Washington County, is known as the site of the **Maine Coastal Islands Refuge**. See *Green Space.*

Milbridge (visitmilbridge.com). A Rt. 1 town of less than 1,300 residents, with a wandering coastline, is the administrative home of Jasper Wyman and Sons, one of the oldest wild blueberry processors. The town also supports a Christmas wreath factory and a good little movie theater.
McClellan Park (207-546-2422), overlooking Narraguagus (pronounced *nair-a-GWAY-gus*) Bay, offers picnic tables, fireplaces, campsites, restrooms, and drinking water. The **Milbridge Historical Museum** (207-546-4471; milbridgehistorical society.org) is open June–Aug., Sat.–Sun. 1–4, also Tue. 1–4 in July and Aug. It's a delightful window into this spirited community, with ambitious changing exhibits and displays on past shipyards, canneries, and 19th-century life. **Milbridge Days** in late July has attracted national coverage in recent years; the highlight is a codfish relay.

Cherryfield (pop. 1,080). A few miles up the Narraguagus River, Cherryfield

CHERRYFIELD GENERAL STORE

Bill Davis

boasts very early and stately houses (see *Lodging*), built on the proceeds of early lumbering. The **Cherryfield-Narraguagus Historical Society**, 88 River Rd., is generally open July and Aug., Fri. 1–4. Cherryfield (why isn't it called Berryfield?) bills itself Blueberry Capital of Maine; there are two major processing plants in town. It's presently enjoying a renaissance as a shopping center.

Columbia Falls (pop. 560) is an unusually picturesque village with one of Maine's most notable houses at its center: **Ruggles House** (207-483-4637; ruggleshouse .org; 0.25 mile off Rt. 1; open June–mid-Oct., Mon.–Sat. for guided tours, 9:30–4, Sun. noon–4; $5 adults, $2 children 6–12) is a Federal-style mansion built by wealthy lumber dealer Thomas Ruggles in 1818. It is a beauty, with a graceful flying staircase, a fine Palladian window, and superb woodwork. Legend has it that a woodcarver was imprisoned in the house for three years with a penknife, and there is an unmistakably tragic feel to the place. Mr. Ruggles died soon after its completion. The house had fallen into disrepair by the 1920s, and major museums were eyeing its exquisite flying staircase when local pharmacist Mary Chandler, a Ruggles descendant, galvanized local and summer people to save and restore the old place. Neighboring **Columbia Falls Pottery** is also worth the 0.5-mile detour from Rt. 1. This is also the site of a Wild Salmon Research Center (207-483-4336; mainesalmonrivers.org), which welcomes visitors weekdays 8–4.

Jonesport (pop. roughly 1,400) sits at the tip of a 12-mile-long peninsula facing Moosabec Reach, which is, in turn, spanned by a bridge leading to Beals Island (pop. 600). Both communities are all about fishing. Together Jonesport and Beals are home to eastern Maine's largest lobstering fleet, and the bridge is a popular viewing stand for the July 4 lobster-boat races. **Beals Island**, populated largely by Alleys and Beals, is known for the distinctive design of its lobster boats, and it's not hard to find one under construction. Beals is connected, in turn, to **Great Wass Island**, a hiking destination with trails through a 1,579-acre tract maintained by The Nature Conservancy (there's good picnicking on the rocky shore, when you finally reach it). Turn right just before the Conservancy parking to visit the **Downeast Institute for Applied Marine Research and Education** (207-497-5769; open to the public year-round, daily 9–4). This facility at Black Duck Cove produces millions of seed clams annually for distribution to local clam flats, also thousands of lobsters; old photos depict the history of local clamming and (May–Sept.) there are aquarium tanks to check out in the Education Center.

North of the village of Jonesport, be sure to stop by the **Maine Coast Sardine History Museum** (207-497-2961), 34 Mason Bay Rd. (Rt. 187). Open Memorial Day weekend, then the third Sunday in June through Sept., Tue.– Sat. noon–4. $4 adults, $2 students, school-aged children and under free. Ronnie Peabody blows a sardine cannery whistle when he opens up at 10 AM, and visitors must punch in. Exhibits includes hundreds of original cans, labels, crates, as well as canning equipment. Ronnie himself worked for Ray Packing Co. in Milbridge and will tell you that every Downeast town had one or two sardine canneries right up until the 1970s, when a New Brunswick firm began buying them out "one by one," and then, just as systematically, shutting them down. Farther up Rt. 187 look for Buz and Helen Beal's **Maine Central Model Railroad** (call ahead: 207-497-2255), where 380 cars traverse 3,000 feet of tracks that wind through hand-built miniature replicas of local towns and scenery. Also in Jonesport: ((ᵩ)) The **Peabody Memorial Library** offers WiFi, restrooms, and art exhibits. It's home to the

Jonesport Historical Society (207-497-2395; jonesporthistoricalsociety.org) with exhibits, lectures, and computer access to visual and oral histories of over 65,000 residents (present, past, and related). It's also the venue for concerts.

Jonesboro (pop. roughly 600) is represented on Rt. 1 by blueberry barrens, a church, and a post office. The beauty of this town, however, is its shoreline, which wanders in and out of points and coves along the tidal Chandler River and Chandler Bay on the way to **Roque Bluffs State Park**, 6 miles south of Rt. 1. A **public boat launch with picnic tables** is 5 minutes south of Rt. 1; take the Roque Bluffs Rd. but turn right onto Evergreen Point Rd.

Machias (pop. 1,331) is the county seat, an interesting old commercial center with the Machias River running through town and over the Bad Little Falls. The **Burnham Tavern** (207-255-6930; burnhamtavern.com), just off Rt. 1 on Rt. 192, is open mid-June–Sept., Mon.–Sat. 9:30–3:30 and by appointment. $5-per-adult donation requested. A 1770s gambrel-roofed tavern, it's filled with period furnishings and tells the story of British man-of-war *Margaretta*, captured on June 12, 1775, by townspeople sailing the small sloop *Unity*. This was the first naval battle of the American Revolution. Unfortunately, the British retaliated by burning Portland. The **University of Maine at Machias** enrolls roughly 1,000 students, and its 43-acre campus is just south of downtown. Its **Art Gallery** is usually open weekday afternoons for special events check umm.maine.edu. Inquire about use of the fitness center and pool. There is summer theater and music in Machias, including concerts in the graceful 1836 Congregational church (centerpiece of the annual **Wild Blueberry Festival**, the third weekend in August). Also note the picnic tables and suspension bridge at the falls and the many headstones worth pondering in the neighboring cemetery. Early in the 19th century Machias was second only to Bangor among Maine lumber ports. In 1912 the town boasted an opera house, two newspapers, three hotels, and a trotting park. Today Main St. (Rt. 1) is pocked with empty storefronts but still offers good places to shop and to eat.

Machiasport (pop. 1,071). Turn down Rt. 92 at Bad Little Falls Park in Machias. This picturesque village includes the **Gates and Cooper Houses** (open July and Aug., Tue. Fri. 12:30–4:30, free), Federal-style homes with maritime exhibits and period rooms. Neighboring **Fort O'Brien** consists of earthen breastworks with cannons and includes the grass-covered remains of the ammunition powder magazine used during the American Revolution and the War of 1812. We recommend that you continue on down this road to the fishing village of Bucks Harbor and on to **Jasper Beach**, so named for the wave-tumbled and polished pebbles of jasper and rhyolite that give it its distinctive color. The road ends with great views and a beach to walk in part of town known as Starboard.

Cutler (pop. less than 600). From East Machias, follow Rt. 191 south to this small, photogenic fishing village that's happily shielded from a view of the U.S. Navy communications station's 26 antenna towers (800 to 980 feet tall), which light up red at night and can be seen from much of the county's coast. A portion of this former base is now Beachwood Bay Estates, a housing development with an enterprising general store (see *Selective Shopping*). The **Little River Lighthouse** (see *Other Lodging*) at the mouth of its harbor has been restored. This area was initially about lumbering, not fishing. In 1835 Massachusetts investors built a dam across the upper part of the harbor and a tidal mill to turn spruce into laths and shingles. In the 1850s fires destroyed what was left of the original forest. In 1883 a steamboat wharf and hotel were built for the Boston–St. John ferry. This remains the departure point for **Bold Coast puffin cruises** to Machias Seal Island, 9.7 miles offshore (see *Birding*). Beyond Cutler, Rt. 191 follows the shoreline through moorlike blueberry and cranberry country, with disappointingly few views from the road but splendid panoramas from the **Bold Coast Trails** (see *Hiking*).

In South Trescott bear right onto Boot Cove Rd. instead of continuing north on Rt. 191 and follow the coast, keeping an eye out for the **Hamilton Cove Preserve**, with a walk to a cobble beach. Continue on to **West Quoddy Light** (below), one of the jewels of the entire Maine coast. Take time to hike and/or get out on the water.

CUTLER WATERFRONT

Christina Tree

Lubec (pop. 1,508). The direct route from Machias to **Quoddy Head State Park** (207-733-0911) in South Lubec is via Rt. 1 to the marked Rt. 189 turnoff. The 532-acre park is open mid-May–mid-Oct., sunrise to sunset, with a staffed **visitors center** (&) in the **Keepers House** (207-733-2180; westquoddy.com), open Memorial Day–mid-Oct., 10–4. Displays tell the story of the lighthouse, which dates back to 1858, and of local industries; there's also a gift shop and a gallery with changing art exhibits. Despite its name, the red candy-striped **West Quoddy Head Lighthouse** marks the easternmost tip of the United States (see the *Campobello Island* sidebar for the East Quoddy Head Lighthouse). There are benches for those who come to be among the first in the United States to see (fog permitting) the sunrise, a fine view of Grand Manan Island, and a pleasant picnic area.

WEST QUODDY LIGHT

Christina Tree

Best of all is the spectacular 2-mile **Coastal Trail** along the cliffs to Carrying Place Cove. Between the cove and the bay, roughly a mile back down the road from the light, is an unusual coastal, raised-plateau bog with dense sphagnum moss and heath.

Water Street is presently transitioning from sardine cannery row to an interesting lineup of shops, restaurants, and galleries, and many trails (see *Hiking*) access some of the most scenic stretches of the town's widely wandering shoreline. The **Lubec Historical Society Museum** (207-733-2274), 135 Main St. (Rt. 189), open seasonally, selected weekdays 9–3, fills the old

Columbian Store and doubles as an information center. It's also base for nonprofit **Tours of Lubec and Cobscook** (1-888-347-9302; toursof lubecandcobscook.com), offering local eco- and historic tours, including one of **McCurdy's Smokehouse** (open June–late Sept., Thu.–Tue.) on Water St., restored by Lubec Landmarks (207-733-4959) to evoke the era in which Lubec was home to 20 canneries. Stop by the old town landing with its public boat launch, breakwater, and a view of **Mulholland Point Light** on Campobello Island. The tide rushes in and out through the narrows, and frequently you can see seals playing and

Christina Tree

WATER STREET, LUBEC

fishing in the water. Another light, Lubec Channel Light, better known as the **Sparkplug**, can be viewed from **Stockford Park**, along the water south of the bridge. **SummerKeys** (see *To Do*) offers musical, writing, art, and photogrpahy workshops and a series of free Wednesday-evening concerts all summer long.

✳ To Do

BICYCLING Down East Sunrise Trail. An 85-mile railbed, paralleling Rt. 1 as far as East Machias then turning inland, has been surfaced to serve bicyclists, ATVs, and pedestrians. Best access: from Cherryfield, off Rt. 193 at Matthews Grocery; in Columbia Falls: off Rt. 1 on Tibbettstown Rd. north; in Machias: at the boxcar just south of the Dike (causeway); in East Machias: off Rt.1 on Willow St. next to the gas station, and on Rt. 191, 7 miles north of Rt. 1. Ideal for mountain bikes. **Bicycle rentals** are avable from **The Wharf** (207-733-4400, theinnon thewharf.com), Lubec.

MCCURDY'S SMOKEHOUSE, LUBEC

Christina Tree

BOATING AND PADDLING
Robertson Sea Tours Adventures (207-483-6110; cell phone, 207-461-7439; robertsonseatours.com). Captain Robertson offers a variety of cruises, including whale-watching and island lobster bakes, from Milbridge Marina on the 30-foot lobster boat *Mairi Leigh*. The focus is on the 50 miles of coast west to Schoodic.

Downeast Coastal Cruises (207-546-7720; downeastcoastalcruises.com), Milbridge Town Landing. Mid-May–

MUST-SEE: CAMPOBELLO ISLAND

Campobello Island, New Brunswick, is easily accessible from Lubec via the FDR Memorial Bridge. You have to pass through Canadian and U.S. Customs, but there's rarely a wait. Franklin D. Roosevelt's "Beloved Island" (the family sum-mered here for six

CAMPOBELLO ISLAND   Joyce Morell

decades) is 9 miles long with some 1,200 year-round residents living primarily in the fishing villages of **Wilson's Beach**, **Welshpool**, and **North Road**. Granted to Captain William Owen in the 1760s, much of the island remained in the family until 1881, when a large part was sold to Boston developers who built three large (long-gone) hotels. Another major real estate development in the 1980s and '90s by the same Arkansas-based company that developed Whitewater (the Clintons were not involved in this one) failed.

     ✐ **Roosevelt Campobello International Park** (506-752-2922; fdr.net), Welsh-pool, Campobello Island, New Brunswick. Open Memorial Day weekend–mid-Oct., daily 9–5 EDT (10–6 Canadian Atlantic daylight time). This manicured 2,800-acre park with a visitors center and shingled "cottages" is the number one sight to see east of Bar Harbor. The house in which Franklin Delano Roo-sevelt summered as a boy has disappeared, but the airy 34-room **Roosevelt Cot-tage**, a wedding gift to Franklin and Eleanor, is sensitively maintained just as the family left it, charged with the spirit of the dynamic man who was felled by polio here on August 25, 1921. (They are quick to tell you that he had contracted it several weeks before at a Boy Scout jamboree in New York.) The house is filled with many poignant objects, such as the toy boat FDR carved for his children. During his subsequent stints as governor of New York and then as president of the United States, FDR returned only three times. Neighboring **Hubbard Cottage**, with its oval picture window, gives another slant on this turn-of-the-20th-century resort. Afternoon tea is offered here to the 20 visitors a day (free). The **visitors center** offers excellent historical exhibits and a 15-minute introductory film. Beyond stretch more than **8 miles of trails** to the shore and then inland through woods to lakes and ponds. There are also 15.4 miles of **Carriage Road Drives** modified from the network that the wealthy "cottagers" maintained on the island. Detailed trail maps and advice is available at the visitors center. We rec-ommend the trail from **Southern Head to the Duck Ponds**. Seals frequently sun

ROOSEVELT COTTAGE

Christina Tree

on the ledges off Lower Duck Pond, and loons are often seen off Liberty Point. Along this dramatic shoreline at the southern end of the island, also look for whales July–Sept. Neighboring 1,049-acre **Herring Cove Provincial Park** (506-561-7010), open mid-May to mid-Nov., also offers trails, a beach, **restaurant** (open 8 AM–11 PM) and **golf course** with nine holes, a clubhouse, and rentals, also a **campground** with 76 campsites, 40 hookups.

Head Harbour Light, as it's known in Canada (in the U.S. it's **East Quoddy Head Lighthouse**) is a 51-foot-high tower built in 1829, at the northern tip of the island. Its wooden, shingled exterior, painted white with a distinctive red cross, has recently been restored, thanks to its "Friends." The cast-iron lantern is vintage 1887. This is a popular whale-watching station but demanding to reach and accessible only at low tide, then only if you are physically fit. Visitors have died when caught by the incoming tide. There's a great viewing spot from just across the narrow channel. From the international park follow Rt. 774 to the end.

WHALE-WATCH CRUISES Campobello is a prime departure point for seasonal whale-watching. **Capt. Riddle's Whale Watch Cruises** (1-877-finback; finback.com), tickets: 727 Friar's Bay Rd., and **Island Cruises** (1-888-249-4400; bayoffundy whales.com), from **Head of Harbour Wharf**, both offer several cruises a day.

((ᵧ)) **Campobello Public Library & Museum** (506-752-7082), 3 Welshpool St., Welshpool (Tue.–Fri.), is a waterside gem with free WiFi and Internet access. *Note* that June–early Sept., **East Coast Ferries** (*Getting Around*) run from Campobello to Deer Isle with a free connection to mainland New Brunswick. Also check **Owen House** under *Lodging*; it's outstanding.

HEAD OF HARBOR LIGHT, CAMPOBELLO

Christina Tree

mid-Oct., Capt. Buzzy Shinn offers 1½-to 3-hour cruises, which can include an island lobster feast.

Coastal Cruises and Dive Downeast Maine (207-598-7473; cruisedowneast .com), 117 Kelley Point Rd., Jonesport. Captain Laura Fish and her brother Harry,

PUFFIN-WATCHING AND OTHER BIRDING

This region is said to have every northern forest habitat, from thick stands of boreal softwood to marsh and bog wetlands, clam flats, rocky cliffs, meadows, and blueberry barrens. Thinly populated, it also has two national wildlife refuges and is home or a migratory stop for hundreds of species, many now rare (see mainebirdingtrail.com /Downeast). The **Annual Down East Spring Birding Festival**, Memorial Day weekend (downeastbirdfest.org), with an associated **Road Scholar** (formerly Elderhostel) program, is growing year by year; more than 171 species of birds are usually spotted. By far the area's most famous bird is the puffin, and the place to see it is Machias Seal Island, 9.7 miles off Cutler.

Puffins are alcids, seabirds that come to land only to breed. Just about 12 inches tall, these colorful "sea parrots" converge in spring on 15-acre **Machias Seal Island**, a rodent-free outcropping of rocks with crevices seemingly designed for birds to lay and nurture eggs. On the June day we visited, Captain Andy Patterson

Christina Tree

PUFFINS

MACHIAS SEAL ISLAND

Christina Tree

whose family have been in this area since 1773, are themselves seasoned guides to Moosabec Reach and its islands. Their cabin cruiser *Aaron Thomas* accommodates up to six passengers on three- and five-hour cruises. Special charters and dive trips are also offered.

CAPTAIN ANDY ABOARD THE *BARBARA FROST*

Bold Coast Charters

estimated it was home to 3,000 pairs of nesting puffins, 2,000 pairs of razorbills, 300 arctic terns, and 800 common murres. Visitors are strictly limited to formal groups and herded into blinds, which tend to be surrounded by birds. It's an unforgettable sight—and sound (a chorus of puffins sounds just like a chain saw). The birds are pretty much gone by late August. Although it's just 9 miles off Cutler, Canada maintains and staffs a lighthouse station as well as the wildlife refuge. Reservations are usually required well ahead of time with any of the three outfits that have landing permits for the island.

Bold Coast Charter Company (207-259-4484; boldcoast.com) is based in Cutler. Captain Andrew Patterson offers daily five-hour puffin-watching trips (weather permitting) May–Aug. Captain Andy also uses his partially enclosed 40-foot passenger vessel *Barbara Frost* to cruise the Bold Coast, the stretch of high, rocky bluffs east of Cutler.

Sea Watch Tours offers similar tours from Grand Manan (see *To Do* in that chapter). Also see Pleasant River Boat Tours (in *Boating and Paddling*), with puffin tours to the island of Petit Manan.

For any of these trips come prepared with windbreakers, hats, and mittens for the early-morning ride out, usually in fog. Also see *Green Space*.

Pleasant River Boat Tours (207-483-6567; pleasantriverboattours.com), South Addison Town Landing. Captain Paul Ferriero offers coastal tours on his 34-foot lobster boat, the *Honey B*. Six people max.

✪ **Bold Coast Charter Co.** (see *Birding*) also offers coast sightseeing cruises and nature/hiking tours to Cross Island Wildlife Refuge.

✪ **Sunrise Canoe & Kayak Tours** (207-255-3375; sunrisecanoeandkayak.com), based just off Rt.1 in Machias. Rob and Jen Scribner offer kayak rentals and guided tours out in Machias Bay to see the Indian petroglyphs on several private islands. Conditions permitting, tours are also offered of the Bold Coast, Wass Island Archipelago, and Roque Bluffs. Shuttles and logistical support for private parties also offered.

Multiday canoe expeditions are on the Machias and St. Croix Rivers. For rigorous spring Whitewater Weekends or weeks with wilderness camping, contact Bangor-based Martin Brown at **Sunrise Expeditions International** (sunrise-exp.com).

Wharf Rentals (207-773-4400), 69 Johnson St., Lubec, offers full- and half-day kayak and bike rentals.

Eastport Ferry (207-853-2635 or 546-2917; eastportferry.com) offers four roundtrips daily between Lubec and Eastport late June–Labor Day. $19.50 roundtrip adult, $10 children under 12, $6 bikes.

The Wharf (207-733-4400; theinnatthewharf.com), 69 Johnson St., Lubec, rents kayaks and is the departure point for whale-watching aboard the *Tarquin*.

Downeast Charter Boat Tours (207-733-2009; downeastharterboattour.com), 31 Johnson St., Lubec. The 25-foot lobster "yacht" *Lorna Doone* offers tours of Passamaquoddy, Cobscook, and Fundy Bays.

Also see **East Coast Ferries** departing Campobello under *Getting Around*.

FISHING Sea-run Atlantic salmon, long the draw for fishermen to the **Narraguagus** and **Machias Rivers**, are currently illegal to catch and will be until stocks have been replenished. Landlocked salmon are, however, still fair game and can be found in **Schoodic Lake** (8 miles north of Cherryfield), **Bog Lake** in Northfield on Rt. 192 (10 miles north of Machias), **Gardner Lake** in East Machias (look for the new boat ramp and parking area), and **Cathance Lake** on Rt. 191 (some 18 miles north of East Machias with a nice boat landing). Trolling lures, streamer flies, or bait from a boat is the most popular way to catch landlocked salmon.

Brook trout can be caught in May and June in local rivers and streams, but in warm weather they move to deeper water like **Six Mile Lake** in Marshfield (6 miles north of Machias on Rt. 192), Indian Lake along Rt. 1 in Whiting, and **Lily Lake** in Trescott. Brown trout are found in **Simpson Pond** in Roque Bluffs (park in Roque Bluffs State Park), as well as in the lakes listed above.

Saltwater and tidewater fishing is usually for striped bass or mackerel. For information about licenses, guides, and fish, check with the regional headquarters of the **Inland Fisheries and Wildlife Department** in Jonesboro.

GOLF Great Cove Golf Course (207-434-7200), 387 Great Cove Rd., Roque Bluffs, offers nine holes, water views, a clubhouse, rental clubs, and carts.

Barren View Golf Course (207-434-7651), Rt. 1, Jonesboro. This new course offers nine holes with views of the blueberry barrens and boasts Maine's largest sand trap. Facilities include a clubhouse plus rental carts and clubs.

Also see the *Campobello Island* sidebar.

HIKING Within the past 15 years the number of coastal hiking options has increased dramatically. See *Green Space*.

PICNICKING McClellan Park, in Milbridge, 5 miles south of town at Baldwin's Head, overlooks the Atlantic and Narraguagus Bay (from Rt. 1, follow Wyman Rd. to the park gates). It's a town park on 10.5 acres donated in 1926 by George McClellan, a onetime mayor of New York City. There's no charge for walking or picnicking.

Roosevelt Campobello International Park's large natural area on Campobello Island, **Quoddy Head State Park** in Lubec, and **Roque Bluffs State Park** also all have picnic areas.

SPECIAL PROGRAMS (ADULT) ☻ SummerKeys (207-733-2316; in winter, 973-316-6220; summerkeys.com), 6 Bayview St., Lubec. Mid-June–Labor Day. In 1992 New York piano teacher Bruce Potterton began offering weeklong programs in Lubec. The program has ballooned to cover a wide variety of instruments, but especially piano for beginners to advanced students. Plein-air summer art workshops are now also offered, along with writing and photography. Lodging is at local B&Bs.

Road Scholar (formerly Elderhostel) programs on varied subjects are held on Campobello Island (roadscholar.org).

Sunrise Senior College (207-255-1384ssc.umm.maine.edu), an all-volunteer program with widely varied courses and workshops, is based at the University of Maine at Machias, geared to people 50-plus. "Summer Shorts," two- to three-day workshops, include guided hikes along the shore, in the woods, history walks, astronomy, much more. A onetime $25 membership covers it.

Tours of Lubec and Cobscook (207-733-2997 or 1-888-347-9302; toursofcobscook .com), 135 Main St. (Lubec Historical Society). Guided history and nature tours by foot and van, from intertidal zone and bogs to Tide Mill Farm (see *Selective Shopping*).

SWIMMING ⚓ Roque Bluffs State Park, Roque Bluffs (6 miles off Rt. 1). The pebble beach on the ocean is frequently windy, but a sheltered sand beach on a freshwater pond is good for children—though the water is cold. Tables, grills, changing areas with vault toilets, and a playground.

Sandy River Beach in Jonesport (off Rt. 187) is a rare white-sand beach marked by a small sign, but the water is frigid. On Beals Island the Backfield Area, **Alley's Bay**, offers equally bracing saltwater swimming.

Gardner Lake, Chases Mills Rd., East Machias, offers freshwater swimming, a picnic area, and a boat launch. **Six Mile Lake**, Rt. 192 in Marshfield (north of Machias), is good for a dip.

Campobello Memorial Aquatic Park, Welshpool, Campobello Island. Changing rooms, toilets; this is landlocked saltwater swimming, so it's relatively warm.

✳ Green Space

Entries are listed geographically, heading east, and are continued under Green Space in the next two subchapters

Pigeon Hill and Petit Manan. From Rt. 1 in Steuben turn onto Pigeon Hill Rd.; after some 5 miles, look for a small graveyard on your left. Stop. The well-trod path up Pigeon Hill begins across the road. The climb is fairly steep in places, but it's nonetheless a pleasant 20-minute hike, and the view from the summit reveals the series of island-filled bays that stretch away to the east, as well as mountains inland. Drive another mile down Pigeon Hill Rd. and past the sign announcing that you have entered a 2,166-acre preserve, part of **Maine Coastal Islands Refuge** (fws.gov/northeast/mainecoastal), which includes two other parcels and 47 offshore islands. There are two **loop trails**, and you can drive to the parking lot for the second. This is a varied area with pine stands, cedar swamps, blueberry barrens, marshes, and great birding (more than 250 species have been identified here). Maps are posted at the parking lots. A 0.5-mile shore path hugs the woods and coastline.

Great Wass Island. The Maine chapter of The Nature Conservancy owns this 1,579-acre tract at the southern tip of the Jonesport-Addison peninsula. Trail maps are posted at the parking lot (simply follow the island's main road to its logical end). The interior of the island supports one of Maine's largest stands of jack pine and is a quite beautiful mix of lichen-covered open ledge, wooded path, and coastal peatland. Roughly a third of the 5-mile loop is along the shore. Little Cape Point is a great picnic spot. Wear rubber-soled shoes.

Western Head, off Rt. 191, 11 miles south of East Machias, is maintained by the Maine Coast Heritage Trust, Brunswick (207-276-5156). Take the first right after the Baptist church onto Destiny Bay Rd. and follow it to the sign. The 3- to 4-mile loop trail is through mixed-growth woods and spruce to the shore, with views of the entrance to Cutler Harbor and high ledges with crashing surf, large expanses of open ocean, as well as the high, sheer ledges of Grand Manan to the northeast and Machias Seal Island to the southeast.

HIKING THE BOLD COAST

Christina Tree

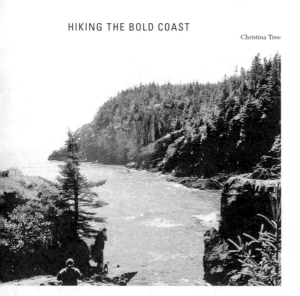

Bold Coast Trails. Look for the trailhead marked CUTLER COAST UNIT TRAILS some 4 miles east of Cutler Harbor on Rt. 191. Maine's Bureau of Parks and Lands (207-287-4920) has constructed inner and outer loop trails (one 5 miles, one 10 miles) from the road to the rugged cliffs and along the shore overlooking Grand Manan Channel. The **Coastal Trail** begins in deep spruce-fir forest, bridges a cedar swamp, and 1.5 miles from the parking lot climbs out of the woods and onto a promontory, continuing to rise and dip along the cliffs to Black Point Cove, a cobble beach. (*Note:* The cliffs are high and sheer, not good for children or shaky adults.) Bring a picnic and allow at least five hours. The trail continues from Black Point Cove to Fairy Head, site of three primitive campsites.

The Quoddy Regional Land Trust (207-733-5509; qrlt.org), with the help of the Maine Coast Heritage Trust, publishes a thick, ever-expanding booklet titled *Cobscook Trails: A Guide to Walking Opportunities Around Cobscook Bay and the Bold Coast.* It's available locally and from the trust. Descriptions include trails in Lubec to **Morong Cove**, **Mowry Beach** to **Horan Head**, and trails in the **Pike Lands**, in the **Hamilton Cove Preserve** and the **Boot Head Preserve**, and to **Comissary Point** in Trescott.

Quoddy Head State Park, Lubec (follow signs from Rt. 189). The candy-striped lighthouse and visitors center (see *To See*) are as far as most people come, but the **Coastal Trail**, along the cliffs, is one of the most dramatic in Maine. The views from the trail and from well-placed benches are back to the lighthouse, down the coast, and across to the sheer cliffs of Grand Manan 7 miles offshore. Bring a picnic.

✴ Lodging

INNS AND BED & BREAKFASTS

Entries are listed geographically, heading east

🐾 **The Englishman's Bed and Breakfast** (207-546-2337; englishmans bandb.com), 122 Main St., Cherryfield 04622. This is a beautifully restored four-square 1793 Federal-style mansion (on the National Register) set above the Narraguagus River, with a wide back deck and screened gazebo. Kathy and Peter Winham offer two guest rooms (1½ baths) in the house itself and a delightful "guesthouse" unit with a fridge, microwave, toaster, and hot plate. A full breakfast is served by the 18th-century hearth in the dining room. Teas and cream teas are also available on request. Per-couple rates: $95 for either room, $155 for both; $120 for the guesthouse, less before July 1 and after mid-Oct.; less for singles and longer stays.

⌀ **The Guagus River Inn** (207-546-9737; guagusriverinn.com), 376 Kansas Rd., Milbridge 04658. Currently up for sale but still welcoming visitors at this

writing. Billy and Jackie Majors's contemporary house has a hot tub and overlooks a meadow with paths down to the Narraguagus River. The five rooms (three private baths) are each themed: Deer, Fish, Bear, et cetera. The Moose suite features a log bed and stained glass above the Jacuzzi. In-season: $75–85; the Moose $150, with a two-night minimum. A one-bedroom apartment is $450 per week. Set in

ENGLISHMAN'S BED AND BREAKFAST, CHERRYFIELD

Bill Davis

meadows, the B&B is 1.8 miles up a quiet road from Rt. 1A and the shore. Rates include a full breakfast.

✪ ❀ ✿ **Pleasant Bay Bed & Breakfast** (207-483-4490; pleasantbay.com), 386 West Side Rd., P.O. Box 222, Addison 04606. Open year-round. After raising six children and a number of llamas in New Hampshire, Leon and Joan Yeaton returned to Joan's girlhood turf, cleared this land, and built this gracious house with many windows and a deck and porch overlooking the tidal Pleasant River. A living room is well stocked with puzzles and books for foggy days; there's a hammock down by the river for pleasant weather. This is a working llama farm, and guests can meander the wooded trails down to the bay with or without their companionship. The four upstairs guest rooms with views include one family-sized room with private bath and a lovely two-room suite with a living room, kitchenette, and deck overlooking the water. There are moorings for guests arriving by water. $55–95 per couple ($10 per child) and $150 for the suite includes, if you're lucky, Joan's popover/pancake. $15 charge for llama walks.

✿ **Moose-A-Bec Manor** (207-497-2121), 40 Old House Point, P.O. Box 557, Jonesport 04659. Open year-round for weekly rentals. Charlie and Abby Alley have renovated an 1875 waterside house that's been in Abby's family for generations, turning it into two large waterside apartments, each with two bedrooms plus a sleeper-sofa and full kitchen, including dishwasher, washer-dryer, and cable TV. Views are of Moosabec Reach. $100–125 per night includes linens.

Chandler River Lodge (207-434-2540; chandlerriverlodge.com), 654 Rt. 1, Jonesboro 04648. Open year-round, this comfortable old house welcomed

guests in decades past, and it's nice to see it restored. Set back in its grounds from Rt. 1, it offers four rooms, one with a king-sized bed and spa bath, the others with queens and private bath, although one is down the hall. $100–150 in-season includes a continental breakfast. There's no common space, as the first floor is a restaurant (see *Dining Out*).

The Inn at Schoppee Farm (207-255-4648; schoppeefarm.com), RR 1, Box 314, Machias 04654. David and Julie Barker are Machias natives and have spent many years away but returned to buy this landmark farm, set on a 40-acre meadow rise above the Machias River. There are two antiques-furnished rooms, both with whirlpool bath, satellite TV, air-conditioning, a fridge, sitting area, and river view. $85–110, depending on season. David and Julie also operate Helen's, the town's most famous restaurant (see *Eating Out/Dining Out*), and guests receive a 10 percent discount there.

✪ ❀ ✿ **Micmac Farm Guesthouses and Gardner House** (207-255-3008; micmacfarm.com), 47 Micmac Lane, Machiasport 04655. Open Memorial

MICMAC FARM IN MACHIASPORT DATES TO 1776

Christina Tree

Day weekend–Oct. This classic Cape, built by Ebenezer Gardner above the Machias River in 1776, is the oldest house in Machias and a real treasure. It's home to Anthony Dunn, Bonnie, his wife, and their small daughter; in summer they occupy a separate wing and offer guests the large downstairs bedroom off the living room. Very private—with a deck overlooking the river and a bath with whirlpool tub—it's furnished in family antiques, a desk, and a life's collection of books. Three comfortable, well-designed housekeeping cabins (we had boiled lobsters for five, and feasted on them, in one) each has two double beds and overlooks the river. $80–95 daily for either the guest room or cabin; $495–595 per week. Children and pets are welcome in the cabins. Ebenezer Gardner was born in Roxbury, Massachusetts, and moved to Nova Scotia in 1763, but because he sided with the Americans in the Revolution he moved back down the coast. He is buried in the family cemetery on the property.

Captain Cates (207-255-8812; captain cates.com), 309 Port Rd. (Rt. 92), Machiasport 04655. Open year-round. This 1820s sea captain's house overlooks the tidal river and offers guests six cheerful, antiques-furnished rooms on the second and third floors, sharing three baths. Downstairs there's a lilac-colored front parlor, a library, and a dining room. From $65 for a small single to $85 for rooms with queens, with full breakfast that may well include grits. Rick and Mary Bury offer hospitality with a southern accent: The library now features portraits of Confederate generals and battlefield prints as well as cable TV, books, and games. Discounts for extended stays and for groups.

🦆 **Riverside Inn** (1-888-255-4344; riversideinn-maine.com), Rt. 1, P.O. Box 373, East Machias 04630. Open year-round. The heart of this vintage-1805 house—actually the first thing guests see—is the kitchen. Innkeepers Ellen McLaughlin and Rocky Rakoczy will probably be there preparing for the evening meal (see *Dining Out*). We recommend one of the two suites (one with a living room, bedroom, and kitchen facilities; the other with two bedrooms) in the Coach House, nearer the river and with decks. There are also two nicely decorated upstairs guest rooms with private bath in the house, which was Victorianized in the 1890s; the clear glass in its fan lights was replaced with red and tin ceilings were added. $99–135 includes a full breakfast.

West Quoddy Station (1-877-535-7414; quoddyvacation.com). The former U.S. Coast Guard station within walking distance of Quoddy Head State Park has been transformed into six attractive units, nicely furnished with antiques, fitted with phones and TV; upstairs units have a sea view. From $95–130 per day and $700 per week for a one-bedroom to $1,500 per week for the five-bedroom Station House.

🦆 ♿ **Peacock House** (207-733-2403; peacockhouse.com), 27 Summer St., Lubec 04652. Open May–Oct. A gracious 1860s house on a quiet side street, home to four generations of the Peacock family, owners of the major local cannery. There are three carefully, comfortably furnished guest rooms and four suites, one handicapped-accessible. The most luxurious suite, the Peacock, is especially spacious and has a gas fireplace. Innkeepers Dennis and Sue Baker have the right touch. Children ages 7 and up. Rates, which include a full breakfast served at the dining room table (two sittings, 8 and 9), run $95–135.

Home Port Inn Bed and Breakfast
(207-733-2077 or 1-800-457-2077;
homeportinn.com), 45 Main St., P.O.
Box 50, Lubec 04652. Open May–
mid-Oct. Happily, this long-established
inn is flourishing under owners
Dave and Suzannah Gale. The large,
raspberry-colored living room is a great
space to read or watch TV, and each of
the seven guest rooms (private bath)
has been tastefully decorated. We like
Room 5, melon-colored with a canopy
bed. $95–115 per couple; $20 per extra
person.

Inn on the Wharf (207-733-4400;
theinnonthewharf.com), 69 Johnson
St., Lubec 04652. Open May–Oct. 20.
Victor and Judy Trafford have transformed the town's last surviving sar-
dine-processing plant into a waterside
inn with 12 spacious suites and 3 two-
bedroom, two-bath apartments (suitable for four). There's a common
gathering space with a kitchen, dining
areas, and two-level deck. Suites $100,
apartments $150 daily; inquire about
weekly rates.

❀ **BayViews** (207-733-2181; off-season, 718-788-2196), 6 Monument St.,
Lubec 04652. Open mid-May–Labor
Day. An 1894 Victorian with not just
bay views but also a porch, hammock,
and lawn sloping to Johnson Bay. The
house has been lovingly restored by
Kathryn Rubeor, filled with period furniture, prints, books, and collectibles,
and fitted with two pianos, the better
to serve participants in SummerKeys.
There are five guest rooms (shared
baths): a family suite with a double
bed, twins, a child's bed, and private
bath; a room with its own piano and
bath (twin beds); and three more
rooms with double beds, sharing one
bath. $60–100 includes a full breakfast.

& **Betsy Ross Lodging** (207-733-
8942; atlantichouse.net), 61 Water St.,
Lubec 04652. Open most of the year.
This shingled building, replicating the
Betsy Ross House in Philadelphia, fits
into the eclectic lineup on this funky
old street. Bill and Dianna Meehan
offer four pleasant rooms with private
bath. $95–115 in-season includes a
credit for breakfast at the Atlantic
House Coffee House and Deli across
the street (see *Eating Out*).

✪ ✿ **The Owen House** (506-752-
2977; owenhouse.ca), 11 Welshpool
St., Welshpool, Campobello, New
Brunswick, Canada E5E 1G3. Open
late May–mid-Oct. This delightful inn
is reason enough to come to Campobello. Built in 1835 by Admiral William
Fitzwilliam Owen, son of the British
captain to whom the island was
granted in 1769, this is probably the
most historic house on the island, and
it's a beauty, set on a headland overlooking Passamaquoddy Bay. Joyce
Morrell, a watercolor artist who maintains a gallery here, inherited the
house from her parents and with an
able assist from Jan Meiners maintains
the B&B beautifully. The nine guest
rooms (seven with private bath) are
furnished with friendly antiques, handmade quilts, and good art. Room 1 is

BAYVIEWS B&B, LUBEC

Christina Tree

OWEN HOUSE, CAMPOBELLO ISLAND

really a suite with a single bed in the adjoining room; Room 2, the other front room, is a favorite. Guests gather around the formal dining room table for a full breakfast and around one of several fireplaces in the evening. Paths lead through the 10-acre property to the water, and the Deer Island ferry leaves from the neighboring beach. From $110 (Canadian) for the shared-bath third-floor rooms to $210 for the water-view suite; $115–178 for a private room with bath, plus the 13 percent tax.

COTTAGES Check with the **Machias Bay Area** and **Cobscook Bay Chambers of Commerce** (see *Guidance*). Summer rentals in this area still begin at around $600 per week.

MOTELS AND COTTAGES
🐾 🐕 **Machias Motor Inn** (207-255-4861; machiasmotorinn.com), Rt. 1 next to Helen's Restaurant, Machias 04654. Larry Barret maintain a two-story, 35-unit motel; most rooms are standard units, each with two double, extra-long beds, cable TV, coffee, fridge, microwave, and phone. Rooms feature decks overlooking the Machias River. $89 double, more for the seven

efficiencies, less off-season. Dogs (no cats) are $10 per night each.

Robinson's Log Cottages (207-726-9546; robinsonscottages.com), 231 King St., off Rt. 86, Edmunds Twp. 04628. Open spring–Thanksgiving. These are third-generation sporting-camp-style cottages on the Dennys River, fully equipped, heated, most with stone fireplace, direct access to the multiuse Sunrise Trail, good for mountain biking. Amenities include canoes. $65–75 per night, from $500 per week. Inquire about a cottage on Cathance Lake, also Denny's River Guide Service.

CAMPGROUNDS McClellan Park, marked from Rt. 1, Milbridge. Open Memorial Day–Columbus Day. This waterside town park is free for day use; a nominal fee is charged to stay at one of the 14 campsites (showers available). For details, call the town hall at 207-546-2422.

Henry Point Campground (207-497-9633), Kelley Point Rd., Jonesport 04649. Open May–Nov. Surrounded on three sides by water. No showers. This is a put-in place for sea kayaks.

Also see **Cobscook Bay State Park** under *Lodging* in "Eastport."

OTHER LODGING Little River Lighthouse (207-259-3833; littleriverlight.org). For reservations in July and Aug. contact Friends of Little River Light, P.O. Box 671, East Machias 04630. This 1847 lighthouse is set on a 15-acre trail-webbed island at the mouth of Cutler Harbor (see Cutler under *To See*). Three guest rooms in the keeper's house are $125–150 per night (two guests maximum per room). The Friends offer transport but it's BYO linens, towels, sleeping bag, food, beverages, and bottled water. There are cooking facilities, cooking utensils, and blankets. The grounds are also available for day use for weddings and gatherings.

✳ Where to Eat

DINING OUT

Entries are listed geographically, heading east

Kitchen Garden Restaurant (207-546-4269; thekitchengardenrestaurant.com), 335 Village Rd., Steuben. Open Sat.–Sun. at 6 PM; also Fri. in winter. This is a long-established dining option, but a bit of a local secret. Jessie King and Alva Lowe welcome guests to their house to savor authentic Jamaican dishes like curried goat, jerk chicken, and rabbit in a wine sauce laced with prunes and shallots. Entrées $23–25. BYOB.

Chandler River Lodge (207-434-2540; chandlerriverlodge.com), Rt. 1, Jonesboro. Open by reservation for dinner July–Sept., Wed.–Sat. 5–8; off-season, Thu.–Sat.; closed Mar.–Apr. Chef-owner Beth Foss is well known locally as a good cook, having honed her skills at her family-owned Bluebird Ranch Restaurant in Machias. Two candlelit dining rooms with white-clothed tables are the setting for a dinner menu that changes every few weeks. You might begin with white wine and garlic steamed mussels ($8), then dine on veal saltimbocca or sea scallops sautéed in vermouth with mushrooms and garlic, topped with sharp cheddar cheese cream sauce (both $30).

Riverside Inn (207-255-4134; riversideinn-maine.com), 622 Main St. (Rt. 1), East Machias. Open for dinner except Jan. Innkeepers Ellen McLaughlin and Rocky Rakoczy have expanded the dining area in their winterized wrap-around porch. Still, space is limited, demand is large, and reservations are a must. Rocky is the chef and offers a choice of 30 entrées, ranging from a salmon with crab and shrimp stuffing through dinner salads to steak and halibut. House specialties include lobster and scallops in champagne sauce. Entrées $23–30, including a salad and herbed bread. Full liquor license.

EATING OUT/DINING OUT ✪ ✎

44 Degrees North (207-546-4440; 44-deegrees-north.com), 17 Main St., Milbridge. Open daily 11–9 and Fri.–Sat. year-round, otherwise until 8 in winter. Bright, attractive, affordable, this is a great road-food stop. Soups and salads, burgers and slow-roasted prime rib, Bourbon Street chicken, grilled swordfish, beer-batter-fried shrimp, pasta, daily specials, homemade pies, and a full bar (blueberry martinis). However, if you order grilled or baked fish and don't like it dry, say so. Chldren's menu.

✪ ✎ **Helen's Restaurant** (207-255-8423), 111 E. Main St., Machias (just before the Dike, on the water). Open 6

HELEN'S RESTAURANT, MACHIAS

Bill Davis

AM–8 PM, Fri. and Sat until 8:30. The town's landmark restaurant since 1950 has a new lease on life thanks to David and Julie Barker, who literally grew up in the family business, eventually purchasing the Schoppe Dairy (visible from the restaurant) and turning it into an inn (see *Lodging*) At this writing they are focusing their considerable skill and energy on Helen's. Head for the far dining room with the hearth and grab a booth by the water. The fish chowder is made daily with haddock, onions, Maine potatoes, butter, and cream. Options range from a (local) goat cheese or crab salad to a hot roast beef sandwich on homemade bread, from hot dogs, burgers, and pot roast to rib-eye steak and lobster dinners. Whatever you do, don't pass up a piece of pie. Fully licensed. Children's plates.

Frank's Dockside (207-733-4484), 20 Water St., Lubec. Open year-round for lunch and dinner, daily except Wed. in summer, check days off-season. Seafood chowders, soups, and baskets at lunch, Italian menu at dinner, plenty of pasta and veal dishes plus chicken Leanna, baked with seasoned crabmeat. There's a welcoming feel and reliably good taste to this place, a cheery dining room and a back deck overlooking the water. Dinner entrées $11.99–17.99.

Water Street Tavern & Inn (207-733-2477; watersttavernandinn), 12 Water St., Lubec. Open 11–8. A prime spot with a great water view, but two of us had lousy lunches here. It's a frequently changing and varied menu: southwest chicken eggrolls to scallop po'boys and turkey with cranberries at lunch; tavern pie, lobster mac-and-cheese, and Brazilian seafood stew with coconut lime broth at dinner, when entrées are $12–19. We'll give it another try.

Fisherman's Wharf Seafood & Restaurant (207-733-4400; innonthewharf), 68 Johnson St., Lubec. Open May–Oct., 11:30–8. Reservations suggested for dinner in high season because this—the newest dining room in town—is relatively small, walled in windows overlooking the water. Lobster, steamers, and local seafood are the specialties, also available for takeout.

EATING OUT

Listed geographically, heading east

❀ **Joshy's Place**, Rt. 1, Milbridge. Good seasonal takeout. Having researched crab rolls up and down the coast, we think Joshy's rates an 8 on a scale of 1–10. Gifford's ice cream.

Milbridge House (207-246-5504), 20 Main St., Milbridge. Open Tue.–Sun. 6–2. Village breakfast and lunch place.

✪ **Fisherman's Wife Café** (207-546-7004) School St. (hidden by the water at the junction of Rts.1 and 1A). Open year-round, Mon.–Sat. 6–6, 2–7 weekdays in summer, Sat. 5 AM–8 PM. A welcome new addition to local options. Great breakfasts, seafood rolls, baskets,

FISHERMAN'S WIFE RESTAURANT, MILBRIDGE

Bill Davis

wraps, sandwiches, subs, and burgers, all from scratch; daily specials.

Hungry Bear Lunch Counter at Downeast Convenience (207-951-9537), 3 Campbell Hill Rd. (junction of Rts. 1 and 193). Daily except Sun. The only place to eat in Cherryfield and a good one. Heidi whips up from-scratch daily specials such as meat loaf and shepherd's pie. Counter inside, picnic tables out by the Narraguagus River.

The Seafood Shack, Rt. 1, Columbia. Open daily except Mon. 11–8. Formerly Perry's Seafood, a spanking-clean diner on a rise with a view of the barrens. Good seafood and road food. We hit this one every time.

Jonesport Pizza (207-497-2187), 187 Main St., Jonesport. Open early for breakfast–dinner. The only place to eat in town and it's good. Pizza, great shakes, other options, too.

Bayview Takeout (207-596-5471), just over the bridge on Beal's Island (by the co-op). In 2011 this was the best bet around for a lobster or crab roll.

Whole Life Natural Market & Café (207-255-8855), 4 Colonial Way, Machias. Open year-round; summer hours Mon.–Sat. 9–6, Sun. 10–2; closed Sun. off-season. A comfortable, window-side corner of the market is furnished with tables. Pick a sandwich or salad from the deli or have one made. Daily soups, too. Our spanako-pita, warm and flaky, came on a real (not plastic) plate.

Fat Cat Deli & Pizzeria (207-255-6777), 291 Main St., Machias. Open daily 11–8. The decor is all about the blues, and the sandwiches, pizza, and salads are above average. Try the Broken Record Cheesecake, frozen on a stick and hand-dipped in milk chocolate.

🦞 🍴 **Blue Bird Ranch** (207-255-3351), Lower Main St. (Rt. 1), Machias. Open year-round for all three meals. Family-owned with a diner atmosphere and good food. Plenty of fried fish and steak choices, fresh-made chowders and seafood stews, burgers and sandwiches, pies and puddings. Fully licensed.

Village Restautant (207-733-4440), 122 Main St. (Rt. 189), Lubec. Open daily year-round, 7 AM–2:30 PM. Mary Sue Thompson own this local gathering place serving "traditional Downeast home-style cooking." It's breakfast all day long, fresh seafood, and home-made pies. Fully licensed.

Uncle Kippy's Seafood Restaurant (207-733-2400), Rt. 189, Lubec. Open daily 11–8. Closed Mon.; also Tue. off-season, when hours are 11–7. A local dining landmark known for steak, seafood, and the area's best pizza.

Cohill's Inn (207-733-4300), 7 Water St., Lubec. Open year-round from 11. Blackboard menu and microbrews. We had a lousy lunch experience here but can see that this would be a great place for a brew and burger on a foggy evening.

Atlantic House Coffee Shop (207-733-0906), 52 Water St., Lubec. Open seasonally, daily 7–7. Check out the back deck on the water: pastries, pizza, lobster rolls, stromboli, calzones, sandwiches, 30 flavors of ice cream.

Family Fisheries (506-752-2470), Rt. 774, Wilson's Beach, Campobello Island, New Brunswick. Open from 11:30 through at least 8:30; June–Oct., until 10 CDN (an hour later than Lubec). This is a combination fish market, takeout, and sit-down dining room, a good bet for fish-and-chips, fried clams, chowder, and lobster boiled outside over a wood fire. The dining room is small, and there can be a wait—avoid it by ordering takeout and eating in the pleasant screened porch area on the other side of the building, which most tourists don't seem to find. BYOB.

Barrell Well Restaurant and Bakery (506-753-2220), 1001 Rt. 774, Campobello Island. Open for breakfast and lunch. From-scratch baking, great cinnamon buns, chili and soups, pleasant atmosphere.

✳ Entertainment

🦞 ♪ **Milbridge Theater** (207-546-2038), Main St., Milbridge. Open nightly May–Nov., 7:30 showtime. A refurbished movie house featuring first-runs at affordable prices. Fresh popcorn.

Down River Theatre Co. (207-255-8862) stages plays June–Aug. at the University of Maine–Machias. Community theater productions—a mix of safe musicals and original plays. Tickets are very affordable.

Machias Bay Chamber Concerts (207-255-3889), Center Street Congregational Church, Machias. A series of six chamber music concerts, July–early Aug., Tue. at 7:30 PM. Top groups such as the Kneisel Hall Chamber Players and the Vermeer Quartet are featured.

Mary Potterton Memorial Piano Concerts, Sacred Heart Church Parish Hall, Lubec. Wed. evenings (7:30) all summer. Free. Featuring SummerKeys faculty and guest artists (summerkeys.com).

✳ Selective Shopping

Entries are listed geographically, heading east

A&M Chain Saw Sculptures (207-546-3462), Rogers Point Rd., Steuben. Arthur Smith's wooden animals are truly amazing and exhibited in widely

respected galleries for many times the price that he will sell them to you for from his roadside house-gallery. Marie Smith is responsible for painting the sculptures.

Milbridge Farmers Market (207-546-2395), center of town across from Kelco Industries. June–Oct., Sat. 9–noon.

In Cherryfield

River Bank Gallery and Antiques (207-546-3718), 8 Main St. Open May, Sept., and Oct., Thu.–Sat. 10–4, also Tue. and Wed. in July and Aug. A colorful vintage 1894 Queen Ann little "painted lady" filled with an eclectic mix of art, antiques and more.

4 Main Street Antiques (207-546-2664), 4 Main St. Two floors, an eclectic mix including furniture, large decorative items.

Cherryfield Maine General Store (no phone), 7 Main St. Open year-round, daily 10–5. This vintage-1865 store has once more become the heart of the village, thanks to Royal Montana who returned to his mother's birthplace after 20 years teaching poor children in India. Stock includes local art (representing some 40 artists), eggs,

CHERRYFIELD HAS BECOME AN ANTIQUES CENTER

Christina Tree

Bill Davis

RIVERLILY, A BOUTIQUE IN CHERRYFIELD

blueberry pies, crafted items, some antiques, teas, jewelry, Cherryfield-made dark chocolate with blueberries . . . and then there's the second floor.

Riverlily (207-546-7666), 2 Wilson Hill Rd. (at the Rt. 1 bridge). Open summer–Christmas, Tue.–Sat. 10–5. Billed as "A shop for your senses," with

APRIL ADAMS AT COLUMBIA FALLS POTTERY

Christina Tree

a wide selection of cards, scarves, Christmas ornaments, gifts.

Tunk Mountain Arts & Crafts (207-546-8948; tunkmountainartsandcrafts .com), 639 Blackwoods Rd. (Rt. 182). Open June–Nov., Wed.–Sat. 10–5, Sun. 10–4. A ways out on Rt. 182, handy to hiking trails and swimming (see the East Hancock chapter). This home/gallery displays art and decorative crafts.

Intervale Farm (207-546-2589; intervalebluebewrryfarm.com). In Cherryfield head north on Rt. 193 for 2.2 miles; it's No. 199. A family farm growing and packing certified organic wild blueberries, also making juice, jam, and chutney.

On and off Route 1

✪ **Columbia Falls Pottery** (207-483-4075 or 1-800-235-2512; columbiafalls pottery.com), 150 Main St., Columbia Falls (0.5 mile off Rt. 1). Open June–Oct., daily 10–5, otherwise call ahead. Striking bright, sophisticated pottery featuring lupines and other wildflowers; custom Delft-style bird- and sea-themed tiles, lamps and tide clocks by April Adams; sculpture by Dana McEacharn.

Wild Blueberry Land (207-483-3583), Rt. 1, Columbia Falls. The blue geodesic dome suggests a squashed blueberry and houses an assortment of berries—fried, in freshly made pies, jam, syrup, juice, frozen (will ship), and actual blueberries beyond the usual season.

In Jonesport

Nelson Decoys Gallery and Gifts (207-497-3488), Cranberry Lane, open May–Dec., sells prizewinning decoys, local art, and Maine-made gifts. At **Downeast Quilting & Interiors** (207-497-2251; downeastquilting.com), 178 Main St., Sarah Davis sells quilts, also makes draperies and much more.

MAINE BLACKFLY BREEDER'S ASSOCIATION (WWW.MAINEBLACKFLY.ORG)

You may have seen bumper stickers proclaiming SAVE THE BLACKFLY and T-shirts boasting WE BREED 'EM, YOU FEED 'EM. The puzzling message can be traced to Machias's Woodwind Gallery, where owner Holly Garner-Jackson's standard greeting is "May the swarm be with you." She explains that the nonprofit association traces its conception to the length and boredom level of Washington County winters. Proceeds from the sale of all products benefit Washington County charities. For $1 the association will send you a "certificate of membership" designed by artist Marilyn Dowling, featuring a blackfly striking an eagle-like pose. Dowling personally renders your name in flowing calligraphy. The source: **Woodwind Gallery** (207-255-3727), 104 Dublin St. (Rt. 1 south of the bridge), Machias. Open year-round, Tue.–Sun. in July and Aug.; closed Sun. off-season The combination framery and gallery shows some 40 local artists and sculptors. Work includes glass, pottery, photography, paintings, and metal; art supplies, too.

MAINE BLACKFLY BREEDER'S ASSOCIATION CERTIFICATE

Christina Tree

Machias Laundromat (207-255-6639). Open in summer daily 8–8, closing in winter at 6. Spanking clean and sited next to the river (just across the bridge as you come into town) so that you can dump your stuff, poke around, lunch, and come back. For a nominal fee they will also wash, dry, and fold for you.

Machias Hardware Co. (207-255-6581), 25 Main St., Machias. An old-fashioned hardware store that's also an

Christina Tree

WILD BLUEBERRY LAND, RT. 1, COLUMBIA FALLS

unexpected source of reasonably priced herbs and spices in 2-ounce and 1-pound packages. Also local products like those by A. M. Look's Canning (see below).

((◦)) **Whole Life Natural Market** (207-255-8855), 80 Main St., Machias. Open year-round; summer hours Mon.–Sat. 9–6, Sun. 10–2. Finally, a first-class market featuring organic and local produce and environmentally safe products, beauty aids, and supplements. There's also a resource/lending library and café with wireless Internet (see *Eating Out*).

Machias Valley Farmer's Market (machiasvalleyfarmersmarket.com), Rt. 1 across from Helen's Restaurant, May–Oct., Fri. 10–4, Sat. 9–1.

Unique Possibilities of Maine (207-255-3337), Causeway Commons, Rt. 1, Machias. Open Tue.–Sun. 10–5. Crafted items from Maine, books, more.

Connie's Clay of Fundy (207-255-4574), Rt. 1, East Machias. Open year-round. Connie Harter-Bagley's combination studio-shop is filled with her distinctive glazed earthenware in deep colors. Bowls, pie plates, platters, lamps, and small essentials like garlic jars and ring boxes, also "healing spiritual jewelry."

Maine Sea Salt Company (207-255-3310; maineseasalt.com), 11 Church Lane, Marshfield, 2 miles up Rt. 192 from downtown Machias. Salt is produced in shallow pools of seawater inside greenhouses. Tours are offered daily. Open 8–6 most days, salt tastings.

Look's Gourmet Food Co. (207-259-3341 or 1-800-962-6258), Rt. 191 south of East Machias. Retail shop open year-round weekdays 8–4. Said to be the first company to successfully can crabmeat and the first to bottle clam juice (the product for which it's most famous) under the Atlantic label, Look's now produces a whole line of specialty products, from lobster spread to Indian pudding, under both the Atlantic and Bar Harbor labels.

A2Z General Store (207-259-3800), Beachwood Bay Estates, Rt. 191, Cutler. Open except Sun. (10–2). This much-needed general store has opened in the former Cutler Naval Base. In addition to groceries, pizza, sandwiches, and gas, it carries local products.

In Lubec

✪ **Bold Coast Smokehouse** (1-888-733-0807; boldhousesmokehouse.com), 224 County Rd. (Rt. 189), Lubec. Open year-round, Mon.–Sat. 8:30–5. Be sure to stop at Vinny Gartmayer's fine smokehouse to pick up some delectable smoked salmon kebabs, finnan haddie, smoked mussels, or smoked lobster pâté.

✪ **Monica's Chocolates** (207-733-4500 or 1-866-952-4500; monicas chocolates.com), 100 County Rd. (Rt. 189), Lubec. Open daily. Monica Elliott, a native of Peru, pioneered (so to speak) chocolate making in Lubec, where she now creates truffles, crèmes, and bonbons with her father's special recipe.

Bayside Chocolates (207-733-8880), 37 Water St., Lubec. Super-dark chocolate, handmade truffles, chocolate-covered blueberries.

Laughing Raven Gallery (207-773-4776), 41 Water St. Open Memorial Day weekend–Oct., 10–5, less frequently until Christmas. Gretchen Mead's stunning new in-town shop features Maine and fair-trade crafts, also landscapes by Michael Chesley Johnson. Check out the Asian costume exhibit in the rear room.

✪ **Northern Tides Art and Gift Gallery** (207-733-2500), 24 Water St., Lubec. Debra and Jerry Kasunic's attractive shop featuring original prints, weaving, wood and stone carving, jewelry, cards, pottery, and more.

Quoddy Mist Sea Salt (207-733-4847; quoddymist.com), 72 Water St., Lubec. Occupying the former R. J. Peacock Canning Building, Quoddy Mist revives a tradition of harvesting salt from the Bay of Fundy. Its plant is strategically sited along the Lubec Narrows, fed twice daily by extreme tides. It's possible to arrange a tour and see how the brine from the boiled-down seawater crystallizes on tables, with high trace minerals, low sodium chloride levels, and a fine flavor.

Dianne's Glass Gallery (207-733-2458; diannesglass.com), 72 Water St. (Peacock Canning Building), open daily June–Sept. Truly exceptional glass jewelry and fused accent plates using recycled glass.

Campobello Island Gift Shop (506-752-2233), Rt. 774, Welshpool, Campobello Island, NB. The specialty of the house is New Brunswick and Celtic folk music CDs but there's plenty of everything else, from souvenirs (especially lighthouse stuff) to books and local crafts, especially jewelry.

Friar's Bay Studio Gallery (575-267-2450; friarsbaygallery.com), 822 Rt. 774, Welshpool, Campobello. Open July–Labor Day. The gallery features works by Michael Chesley Johnson, who also offers plein-air outdoor painting workshops.

CHRISTMAS WREATHS More than half of Maine's Christmas wreaths are made in Washington County. You can order in fall and take delivery of a freshly made wreath right before Christmas. Prices quoted include delivery. The **Wreath Shoppe** (207-483-4598), Harrington (wreaths decorated with cones, berries, and reindeer moss), and **Flo's Wreaths** (1-800-321-7136; floswreaths.net), Marshfield, are a couple among dozens of purveyors.

✳ Special Events

Memorial Day weekend: **Down East Birding Festival**—guided hikes, cruises, lectures (downeastbirdfest.org).

July: **Independence Day** celebrations in Jonesport/Beals Island (lobster-boat races, easily viewed from the bridge); **Cherryfield** (parade and fireworks); and **Steuben** (firemen's lobster picnic and parade); **Lubec** goes all-out with a grand parade, contests, and fireworks; **Cutler** and **Machias** also celebrate. Campobello celebrates **Canada Day** (July 1) in a big way. Also see the Eastport section for the state's biggest celebration. **Milbridge Days** (last weekend) (visitmilbridge.com) includes a parade, a dance, a lobster dinner, and the famous codfish relay race.

August: **Wild Blueberry Festival** and Machias Craft Festival (third weekend) in downtown Machias—concerts, food, a major crafts fair, and live entertainment.

September: **Lights Across the Border** is a day of coordinated activities at all the area's lighthouses.

October: **Hot Air Balloon Festival** (machiaschamber.org), Machias Airport.

EASTPORT, COBSCOOK BAY, AND PASSAMAQUODDY BAY

Eastport is just 3 miles north of Lubec by boat but 43 miles by land around Cobscook Bay. Cobscook is said to mean "boiling water" in the Passamaquoddy tongue, and tremendous tides—a tidal range of more than 25 feet—seemingly boil in through this passage and slosh up deep inlets divided by ragged land fingers along the north and south shores. One gap between the opposite shores is just 300 yards wide, and the tides funnel through it at 6 to 8 knots, alternately filling and draining the smaller bays beyond. For several hours the incoming tide actually roars through these "Cobscook Reversing Falls."

The force of the tides in Passamaquoddy Bay on Eastport's eastern and northern shores is so powerful that in the 1930s President Roosevelt backed a proposal by hydroelectric engineer Dexter Cooper to harness this power to electrify much of the northeast coast, including Boston. The sardine-canning process in Maine began in Eastport in 1875 and a boom era quickly followed, but today the population of this island "city" has dropped to below 2,000 (from more than 5,000 in 1900). Still, Eastport—which once rivaled New York in shipping—remains a "city" and a working deepwater port, the deepest on the U.S. East Coast. Large freighters regularly dock at the new shipping pier near Estes Head to take on woodland products, a reminder (as is the surviving Federal and Greek Revival architecture) that by the War of 1812 this was already an important enough port for the British to capture and occupy it.

Today there are many gaps in the old waterfront, now riprapped in pink granite to form a seawall. With its flat, haunting light, Eastport has an end-of-the-world feel and suggests an Edward Hopper painting. It's a landscape that draws many artists, and there are growing number of galleries along Water Street as well as art workshops and open studios. It's also the venue for a series of home repair homicide mysteries by resident Sarah Graves.

Eastport consists entirely of islands, principally Moose Island, which is connected to Rt. 1 by Rt. 190 via a series of causeways (actually, tidal dams built in the 1930s for the failed tidal power project), linking other islands. In warm-weather

EASTPORT WATERFRONT

Christina Tree

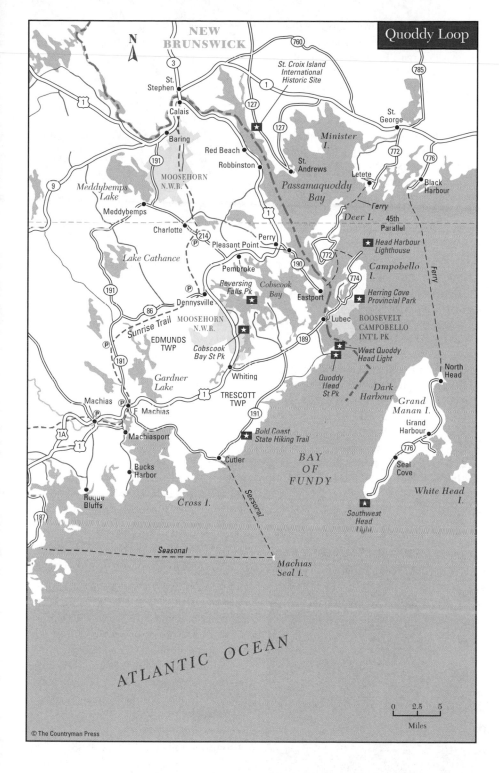

Quoddy Loop

NEW BRUNSWICK

760
785
3
St. Stephen
St. Croix Island International Historic Site
1
Calais
127
Baring
Red Beach
127
St. George
191
Robbinston
Minister I.
772
776
MOOSEHORN N.W.R.
St. Andrews
Letete
Black Harbour
9
Meddybemps Lake
Passamaquoddy Bay
Meddybemps
Ferry
Charlotte
214
Pleasant Point
Perry
Deer I.
45th Parallel
Lake Cathance
Head Harbour Lighthouse
Pembroke
190
772
Campobello I.
191
Reversing Falls Pk
Cobscook Bay
Eastport
774
86
Dennysville
Herring Cove Provincial Park
Ferry
Sunrise Trail
MOOSEHORN N.W.R.
Lubec
ROOSEVELT CAMPOBELLO INT'L PK
EDMUNDS TWP
Cobscook Bay St Pk
189
West Quoddy Head Light
North Head
191
Gardner Lake
Whiting
Quoddy Head St Pk
Dark Harbour
Grand Manan I.
Machias
TRESCOTT TWP
1
Grand Harbour
1A
E Machias
191
1
Machiasport
Bold Coast State Hiking Trail
776
Seal Cove
Bucks Harbor
Cutler
BAY OF FUNDY
White Head I.
Roque Bluffs
Cross I.
187
Seasonal
Southwest Head Light
Seasonal
Machias Seal I.

ATLANTIC OCEAN

0   2.5   5
Miles

© The Countryman Press

months it's a departure point for the small car ferry to Deer Island, New Brunswick, with links onward to St. Andrews or to Campobello Island. Frequently there are whales to be seen, and always there's Old Sow, a whirlpool between Eastport and Deer Island said to be 230 feet in diameter and the largest in the Western Hemisphere. Thanks to the extreme tides and currents, marine life is more varied than in other places. Nutrients that elsewhere settle to the bottom shoot here to the surface and nourish some forms of life that exist nowhere else. The fact that you can see only a short distance down into the water around Eastport is due not to pollution but to this rich nutrient life.

Christina Tree

FISHERMAN STATUE, EASTPORT

Rt. 190 runs through the center of Sipayik (pronounced *zeh-BAY-igh*), the Pleasant Point Indian Reservation, home to some 700 members of the Passamaquoddy Indian tribe. The three-day Indian Ceremonial Days in early August fully celebrate Passamaquoddy culture.

Unfortunately, the 20 miles of Rt. 1 between Whiting (turnoff for Lubec) and Perry (turnoff for Eastport) offer few glimpses of Cobscook Bay. Be sure to take the short detour into Cobscook Bay State Park and into the village of Pembroke to find your way to the Reversing Falls Park.

GUIDANCE Eastport Chamber of Commerce (207-853-4644; eastport.net). **Cobscook Bay Area Chamber of Commerce** (207-733-2201; cobscookbay .com). Also check the website eastportme.info. For more about the Quoddy Loop, circling both sides of Passamaquoddy Bay see quoddyloop.com.

MUSIC AT THE PEAVEY LIBRARY, EASTPORT

Christina Tree

GETTING AROUND East Coast Ferries Ltd. (506-747-2159; eastcoast ferries.nb.ca.), departs late June–early Sept. every hour from the beach beside Eastport Chowder House. Be sure to take it at least to Deer Island, NB. We strongly suggest you go the whole way to L'Etete near St. Andrews, NB. (see *Getting Around* in the "Washington County" introduction).

Eastport Ferry (207-853-2635; eastportferry.com) offers seasonal service, Tue.–Sun., between Eastport and

Lubec. The 35-passenger *Quoddy Dam* departs Lubec four times between 11 and 5 with special 6:30 PM runs on Wednesday for the SummerKeys Concerts in Lubec. $19.50 roundtrip adult, $10 children under 12. Inquire about shuttle van from Lubec to Roosevelt International Park.

✳ To See

✪ **The Tides Institute and Museum of Art** (207-853-4047; tides.institute .org), 43 Water St., Eastport. Open seasonally Tue.–Sun. 10–4. In 2002 the city's ornate, vintage-1887 bank building came up for sale and seemed in danger of demolition. Still evolving, it's now an impressive cultural center committed to collecting and exhibiting art, photography, and archival pictures of local architecture and landscape, focusing particularly on the region surrounding Passamaquoddy Bay on both sides of the border. The institute is also committed to creating new work and has installed letterpress and printmaking facilities, offering a series of workshops. Check the website for lectures, workshops, and changing exhibits, also culturepass.net for arts events aound the bay. The permanent collection is on the second floor.

✪ **Raye's Mustard Mill and Pantry** (207-853-4451 or 1-800-853-1903; rayes mustard.com), Rt. 190 (Washington St.). Open daily 9–5 in summer, 10–4 off-season. Closed Sun. off-season. In business since 1900, this company is the country's last remaining stone-ground-mustard mill. It's the mustard in which Washington County's sardines were once packed, and it's sensational. Sample the many varieties in The Pantry, where soup, salads, and sandwiches are also served; limited seating. Tours of the mustard mill are offered year-round, daily on the hour (except the lunch hour).

Quoddy Dam Museum, 72 Water St., Eastport, open Memorial Day–Sept., usually open daily 10–4. A 14-by-16-foot concrete model of the Passamaquoddy Tidal Power Project (see the introduction). The storefront also houses a crafts cooperative and information center.

Barracks Museum (207-853-6630), 74 Washington St., Eastport. Open June–Aug., Wed.–Sat. 1–4. Originally part of Fort Sullivan and occupied by the British during the War of 1812, this house has been restored to its 1820s appearance as an officers' quarters and displays old photos and memorabilia about Eastport. Free.

Waponahki Museum and Resource Center (tribal office 207-853-2600; wabanaki.com), 59 Passamaquoddy Rd. off Rt. 190, Pleasant Point, upstairs in the Sipayik Youth Center.

HUGH FRENCH AT THE TIDES INSTITUTE AND MUSEUM OF ART, EASTPORT

Christina Tree

Baskets, beaded artifacts, historical photos, and crafts.

Reversing Falls Park. Turn off Rt. 1 at Rt. 214 into the village of Pembroke; follow the slight jog in the road then Leighton Point for 3.3 miles, and turn right onto Clarkside Cemetery Rd. (the sign may or may not be there), then left at the T. This last road turns to dirt before it ends at a parking area for a town park with two short trails to the water. Try to time your visit to coincide with the couple of hours before the height of the incoming tide, which funnels furiously through the gap between Mahar's Point and Falls Island. As the salt water flows along at 6 to 8 or more knots, it strikes a series of rocks, resulting in rapids. At low water this is a great place to hunt for fossils, and it's well worth finding anytime.

Christina Tree

RAYES IS MAINE'S DESTINATION MUSTARD MILL

Old Sow. What's billed as the largest whirlpool in the Western Hemisphere, and one of five significant whirlpools in the world, is sited between the tips of Moose and Deer Islands. It's said to be produced by 70 billion cubic feet of water rushing into Passamaquoddy Bay, much of which finds its way around the tip of Deer Island and an underwater mountain at this narrow point. The area's smaller whirlpools are called Piglets. See *Boat Excursions* for viewing. The Old Sow is visible from the ferry crossing. We once saw a small cruise ship heel over dramatically when it came too close to the vortex; small craft beware.

✳ To Do

BIRDING Moosehorn National Wildlife Refuge (see *Green Space*) is a prime spot for spotting bald eagles. Vast tidal flats in Eastport are good places to watch migrating plovers, sandpipers, and other shorebirds. For details about the late-May **Down East Spring Birding Festival**, see downeastbirdfest.org, and for puffin-watching on Machias Seal Island see boldcoast.com.

DOWNTOWN EASTPORT

Christina Tree

BOAT EXCURSIONS Schooner *Ada C. Lore* (207-853-2500; eastportwindjammers.com), 104 Water St. Mid-June–October. This vintage-1923, 118-foot schooner offers whale-watching, afternoon, and sunset cruises. Lobster cruises are also offered aboard the 37-foot *Lady H*.

Fundy Breeze Charters (207-853-4660), 109 Water St. Captain Skip

Harris offers deep-sea fishing as well as lighthouse-, puffin-, and whale-watching tours abourd his six-passenger, 33-foot sportfishing boat *Vonnie and Val.*

Cobscook Hikes & Paddles (207-726-4776; cobscookhikesandpaddles .com). Registered Maine Guides Stephen and Tess Forek, based in Robbinston, offer guided two- and three-hour kayaking paddles from Whiting to Calais.

Also see **East Coast Ferries** (car) to Deer Isle and the New Brunswick mainland and the **Eastport Ferry** (passengers only) to Lubec under *Getting Around.*

MINI GOLF 🐾 **Downeast Adventure Golf** (207-853-9595), Rt. 1, Perry. An oversized putting course with 2 acres of terrain including a pond, splash fountains, arched bridges, and a batting cage.

WALKS Shackford Head State Park (posted from Rt. 190 near downtown Eastport) is a 90-acre peninsula with several trails including a roughly 0.7-mile path from the parking lot to a 173-foot-high headland overlooking Campobello Island and Lubec in one direction and Cobscook Bay in the other. Another 0.25-mile-long trail leads down the headland and permits access to the shore. Views are of the bay with its floating salmon pens. Look for fossils at low water.

Eastport Walk-About. Pick up a copy of the leaflet walking guide at the Quoddy Dam Museum (see *To See*) and follow it at east along Water St. for a sense of the city's fascinating history.

SPECIAL LEARNING PROGRAMS Eastport Arts Center (see *Entertainment*) offers a variety of arts workshops ranging from outdoor painting to storytelling and soap making. **The Tides Institute** (see *To See*) offer workshops in printmaking, letterpress, and photography.

✳ Green Space

The Quoddy Regional Land Trust (207-733-5509) publishes *Cobscook Trails* (see *Green Space* in the Bold Coast subchapter)

Moosehorn National Wildlife Refuge (fws.gov/northeast/moosehorn) consists of two divisions. Trails in the first—the Baring section (Unit 1)—are maintained; see "Calais." The second division, the Edmunds, is threaded by Rt. 1 between Dennysville and Whiting. Some 7,200 acres are bounded by Whiting and Dennys Bays and the mouth of the Dennys River. North Trail Rd. is 2.5 miles long and leads to a parking area from which canoes can be launched into Hobart Stream. South Trail Rd. covers 0.9 mile and leads to a parking area for a 10-mile unmaintained trail network.

⊙ **Cobscook Bay State Park** (207-726-4412), S. Edmunds Rd., just off Rt. 1 between Dennysville and Whiting. The 880-acre park includes a 2-mile nature trail with water views, and a 0.5-mile Shore Trail. Wildlife and birds are plentiful. The campground is open mid-May–mid-Oct.; there are 150 campsites, most of them for tents and many with water views. It also offers a boat-launch area, picnic benches, and a hiking and cross-country ski trail. Birding is superb.

Gleason's Point State Park, Perry. On Rt. 1 look for Shore Rd., across from the New Friendly Restaurant. After a short way turn right on Gleason Cove Rd. This is a great place for walking, sunbathing, and picnics (tables provided).

✳ Lodging

INNS AND BED & BREAKFASTS

In Eastport 04631

🍴 **Kilby House Inn** (207-853-0989 or 1-800-853-4557; kilbyhouseinn.com), 122 Water St. Open year-round. This Queen Anne–style house is on the quiet end of the waterfront, an easy walk from shops and rstaurants, also from the Deer Island ferry. The attractive double parlor with a fireplace and grand piano invites you to sit down and read. Innkeeper Gregg Noyes's passions include playing the Estes reed organ and refinishing antiques. He clearly relishes his role as full-time innkeeper after many years of also teaching down in Steuben. There are five pleasant antiques-furnished upstairs guest rooms, three with private bath. Our favorite is the sunny master with its four-poster canopy bed and water view. $75–95 includes a very full breakfast.

🍴 **Weston House** (207-853-2907; westonhouse-maine.com), 26 Boynton St. Open year-round. Jett and John Peterson's elegant Federal-style house was built in 1810. Two large front guest rooms share a full bath. One of these has a working fireplace and a tall four-poster, views of the bay and gardens, and antiques, but it was in the other—equally spacious and gracious—room that John James Audubon slept on his way to Labrador in 1833. A small room, tucked into the back of the ell, is perfect for solo travelers. There's also a a bricked terrace and a rose garden with gazebo. $85–95 double includes breakfast in the formal dining room.

Chadbourne House (1-888-853-2728; chadbournehouse.com), 19 Shackford St., P.O. Box 191. Open May–Oct. Jill and David Westphal ask guests to shed their shoes on entering their 1821 Federal-style mansion, furnished with antiques. Three of the four guest rooms

are suites, one occupying the entire third floor, with skylights, a king bed, and a sitting area. The remaining suites have fireplace. Breakfast is served in a formal dining room. $130–175 per night, $25 per extra person.

🍴 🐾 ✂ ♿ **Todd House** (207-853-2328), 1 Capen Ave. Open year-round. A restored 1775 Cape, the oldest house in Eastport, with water views. In 1801 men met here to charter a Masonic order, and in 1861 the house became a temporary barracks. Three large double rooms with kitchenettes are tucked away in various corners, along with one double room with twin beds. Our favorites are the ground-floor Cornerstone Room and the Masonic Room, with a working fireplace. Grandmotherly innkeeper Ruth McInnis presides in the living room, welcoming well-behaved children and pets; her own pets include four cockatiels. $75–100 in-season, otherwise from $50. $10 per stay for pets.

🐾 ✂ **The Milliken House** (207-853-2955 or 1-888-507-9370; eastport-inn.com), 29 Washington St. Mary Williams is the owner of this 1840s house, which retains Victorian charm with a large double parlor, ornate detailing, and some original furniture. There are six guest rooms, all with private bath. $80–90 year-round includes a full breakfast.

MOTEL ✂ ♿ **The Motel East** (207-853-4747), 23A Water St., Eastport 04631. Owen Lawler's two-story motel has 16 units, some handicapped accessible, all with water views, some with balcony. Amenities include direct-dial phones, cable TV, eight kitchenettes. We recommend Friar Roads, the adjoining, freestanding efficiency, and the upper-floor units with shared balconies. No charge under 18 years. $105–120 per night, less off-season. Guest cottage next door.

The Commons (207-853-4123; thecommonseastport.com), 51 Water St., P.O. Box 255, Eastport 04631. Two second-floor units in an 1880s brick commercial building. Each offers two bedrooms, bath, kitchen, sitting area, balcony overlooking the harbor, and laundry facilities. $770–1,150 per week.

Cobscook Property Management (207-853-6179; cobscookpm.com), based in Eastport, offers a wide selection of weekly and monthly rentals.

✳ Where to Eat

In Eastport unless otherwise noted

The Pickled Herring (207-853-2323; thepickledherring.com), 32 Water St. Open Wed.–Sun. 5–closing. Closed Jan.–March. Eastport native Gary Craig has renovated this prime downtown dining spot. It's an attractive space with an open kitchen and wood-fired grill, from which comes a wide choice of pizzas as well as Black Angus sirloin strip, ahi tuna, sweet and spicy haddock, chicken or duck breast. Mixed reviews lately. Entrées run $17–26. Local beers and produce are featured.

❧ **Eastport Chowder House** (207-853-4700), 167 Water St. Open seasonally, daily 11–9. A good location, on what's said to be the site of the country's first fish and sardine cannery. The downstairs pub on Cannery Wharf is informal, and it's possible to get take-out (and thus park in line) for the ferry that departs from the adjacent beach. The restaurant is barnlike and can be noisy; the outside deck is a blessing. The reasonably priced menu runs from fried haddock and eggplant Parmesan to lobster.

✪ **Quoddy Bay Lobster Co.** (207-853-6640), 7 Sea St. Open seasonally Tue.–Sat. 10–6, Sun. 11–4. It's well worth finding your way down to this fish store/eatery. The rewards are fresh fish and fabulous lobster rolls drizzled with butter, great homemade chowder and coleslaw, fried clam rolls so thick you have to eat them with a fork. This is also the place to try a grilled seared scallop roll with garlic pepper seasoning. Scallops are the local specialty. Then there is the smoked lobster wrap: lobster and smoked lobster pâté, cream cheese, lettuce, tomato, and onion. Owner Sarah Griffin's family operates four fishing boats, and both the quality and prices reflect a lack of middlemen. Picnic tables, sheltered pavilion.

Rose Garden Café (207-853-9598), 9 Dana St. Open year-round from 3 PM with live music most weekends. A funky eclectic restaurant and antiques shop. Linda Salleroli is a locally respected cook, known for her stir-fries, chili, and root beer floats, also steaks and low, slow barbecue. Meals come with baked beans, roasted potato wedges, and from-scratch corn bread.

Liberty Cafe (207-853-2080), 64 Water St. Open Mon.–Sat. 11–7. A welcome edition to local food options. Genuine Greek gyros with seasoned lamb and beef, shish kebab, moussaka, spanakopita, and souvlaki salad. Also homemade macaroni-and-cheese and galaktabouriko, an irresistible dessert: layers of phyllo filled with custard, topped with honey/sugar syrup.

❧ **The Happy Crab Downeast Grill and Sports Bar** (207-853-9400), 35 Water St. Open daily 11:30–8:30. There are two sides to this place, one a cheerful family-geared restaurant with a selection of burgers, pizza, seafood baskets, wraps, and sandwiches all made with the specially flavored house mayo. The other is a sports bar with a pool table, also popular dining with a deck.

The Blue Iris Restaurant (207-853-2440), 31 Water St. Open year-round 8–2. In early morning a group of men assemble here so regularly that they're known as the "Knights of the Round Table." We can see why: good omelets, friendly service, and a water view.

(ⵘ) **Moose Island Bakery** (207-853-3111; mooseislandbakery.com), 75 Water St. Open year-round, 7–5. Cream puffs, carrot cakes, coffees, drinks, a great deck with water views. Hope it lasts.

(ⵘ) **Dastardly Dicks** (207-853-2090), 62 Water St. Open 7–3 (or later); Sun. 9–1. Espressos, teas, frappes, smoothies, snacks, and sweets, a welcome gathering spot in the middle of town.

WaCo Diner (207-853-4046; wacodiner.com), Water St. Open year-round; in summer 6 AM–11 PM, bar until 1 AM. This local landmark has a great view from its Schooner Room and a deck, but it has been getting poor reviews.

Bank Square Pizza & Deli (207-853-2709), 24 Water St. Open 11–closing. The Mexican fare we sampled here was terrible and the owner, rude. We have, however, heard raves.

Rosie's Hot Dog Stand at the breakwater. Open seasonally for decades.

Also note: **Raye's Mustard** (see *Selective Shopping*) offers salads and sandwiches.

✪ ♪ **The New Friendly Restaurant** (207-853-6610), Rt. 1, Perry. Open daily 11–8. Great road food. A homey restaurant with booths and food that's known as the best around: fish stews and chowders, basics like liver and onions, not-so-basics like an elegant crab salad and the most lobster in a lobster sandwich. Desserts include Grape-Nut pudding as well as pies. Beer and wine served.

The Hansom House (726-4466), 45 Main St., Dennysville (the former Lincoln House), just off Rt. 1. Open Fri. and Sat. year-round from 5 PM. John Jacques is a sculptor who operated larger nightclubs elsewhere and here has created "the world's most absurd bar" with a living room ambience in an expanded version of the former inn's Woodshed Pub. Locally sourced pub and finger foods are served, and silent films are shown at one end of the bar while musicians perform at the other. Wine and beer.

✸ Entertainment

Eastport Arts Center (207-853-5803; eastportartscenter.com), 36 Washington St., Eastport. The vintage-1837 Washington Street Baptist Church has been restored and fitted with a new heating system as home to six arts organizations, including the **Northern Lights Film Society** (Thu.-evening films at 7 on a large screen, great sound) as well as frequent performances by the **Passamaquoddy Bay Symphony Orchestra** and other concerts, performances by **Stage East** (stageeast.org), a terrific community theater, plus puppetry, more. Check the website for the current schedule.

Also see Lubec for Wed.-evening **Mary Potterton Memorial Piano Concerts** (summerkeys.com). The **Eastport Ferry** (see *Getting Around*) offers service over and back for the concerts.

For live music also see **Hansom House** and **Rose Garden Café** in *Eating Out*.

✸ Selective Shopping

In downtown Eastport
ART AND CRAFT GALLERIES
✪ **The Commons** (207-853-4123; thecommonseastport.com), 51 Water St. Open year-round; in summer, Mon.–Sat. 9–6, Sun. 1–5, otherwise Mon.–Sat. 10–6. An outstanding

Bill Davis

THE EASTPORT GALLERY

gallery displaying the work of more than 90 Passamaquoddy Bay area artists and artisans: botanical and wildlife paintings, fabric art, carved burl bowls, jewelry, hand-knit sweaters, wooden ware, pottery, and Passamaquoddy sweetgrass baskets.

The Eastport Gallery (207-853-4166; eastportgallery.com), 74 Water St. Open early June–Oct. 1 daily, 10–5, Sun. noon–5. Eastport's oldest and most established art gallery, a cooperative representing local artists

Crow Tracks (207-853-2336; crowtracks.com), 11 Water St. Open year-round. R. J. LaVallee carves a variety of birds, whales, and fantasy figures, from decoys to Christmas ornaments.

Eastport School of Arts & Gallery (207-853-4777), 3 Dana St. Heidi Reidell offers classes, also shows work by local artists.

Dancing Dogs Pottery & Art (207-853-6229), 107 Water St. An impressive array of wheel-thrown porcelain and stoneware pottery, also oils, acrylics, and watercolors.

Note: Galleries and antiques stores multiply each summer; this is only a sampling. Check out the **Arts and**

SPECIAL SHOPS Port O'Call (207-853-0800; portofcalleastport.com), 38 Water St. Cards, alpaca gifts, PJs, jewelry and bags, books and toys.

Quoddy Crafts. Sharing space the Quoddy Dam Museum (see *To See*), a local crafts outlet worth checking out.

S. L. Wadsworth & Sons (207-853-4343; slwadsworth.com), 42/44 Water St. Billed as the country's oldest ship chandlery and Maine's oldest merchandiser (no one really noticed until the present generation took over), this marine-geared store has recently added "nautical gifts" to hardware. There's no question that it was founded in 1818 by Samuel Wadsworth, son of General Peleg Wadsworth and uncle of poet Henry Wadsworth Longfellow. Buy a rod and fish from

THE SHOP AT THE COMMONS, EASTPORT

Christina Tree

the breakwater (you don't need a license).

Along Route 1, heading north from Whiting

○ **Tide Mill Farm** (207-733-2551; tidemillfarmorganic.com), 91 Tide Mill Rd., Edmunds. This 200-year-old working farm on Whiting Bay and Crane Mill Stream has been in the Bell family since 1765. It is set on 1,600 acres with 6 miles of shorefront. Terry and Cathy Bell are maintaining the property as a working organic farm with Hereford cattle, chickens, pigs, and an organic dairy herd. The seventh through ninth generations raise organic produce and animals, with milk, vegetables, and eggs available in summer season. Check the website to order winter wreaths and for current open farm says and farmstand hours.

Mainely Smoked Salmon Company (207-853-4794; mainelysmokedsalmon .com), 555 South Meadow Rd., Perry. Hot and cold smoked salmon.

○ **The Red Sleigh** (207-853-6688; kendallfarmcottages.com), Rt. 1, North Perry. Open Tue.–Sun. 10–6. Georgiana Kendall has created a very special outlet for local arts and edibles. There's meat and organic produce from Tide Mill Farm (see above),

RED SLEIGH IS A MUST-STOP BETWEEN EASTPORT AND CALAIS

Bill Davis

locally produced milk, yogurt, and cheese, fair-trade coffee, knit goods, veggies from the garden out front, and work by local artists including Earth Forms Pottery by Donald Sutherland, a widely respected Eastport sculptor who died in 2011.

✳ Special Events

February: **Valentine's Day Speedo Run** down Water Street raises funds for heating oil.

Memorial Day weekend: **Down East Birding Festival**—guided hikes, boat tours, presentations (downeast birdfest.org).

July: **Independence Day** is celebrated for an entire week in Eastport, with parades, a military flyover, and fireworks. Eastport's is the first flag in the United States to be raised on July 4 at dawn (eastport4th.com).

Mid-August: **Annual Indian Ceremonial Days**, Pleasant Point Reservation—a celebration of Passamaquoddy culture climaxing with dances in full regalia (wabanaki.com).

September: **Eastport Salmon Festival** (eastportsalmonfestival.com) (first weekend) celebrates Eastport's salmon industry with great food, boat tours of area fish farms, walking tours, live entertainment, games, concerts. **Eastport Pirate Festival** (eastportpirate festival.com) is now a weeklong celebration beginning Labor Day with an invasion of Lubec; there's plenty of music, a parade, a bed race, cruises and more. **Two Countries, One Bay Art Studio Tour** (twocountriesart .com) (midmonth)—self-guided tour of 40 studios on both sides of the border around Passamaquoddy Bay.

December: **Festival of Lights**, Eastport. **New Year's Eve** is also big in Eastport, the first American city to welcome in the new year.

Calais (pronounced *CAL-us*), the largest city in Washington County, is the sixth busiest point of entry into the United States from Canada, just across the St. Croix River from St. Stephen, New Brunswick. The two communities are inextricably linked, celebrating a nine-day International Festival together in August.

The city's present population is less than 3,160, far fewer than in the 1870s, the decade in which its fleet of sailing vessels numbered 176. The brick downtown was built soon after an 1870 fire had wiped out the previous city center. Happily, the city's wooden residential district seems largely to have escaped the fire and remains the best testament to the city's most prosperous era.

The Wabanaki Cultural Center, showcasing the history and culture of the Passamaquoddy Nation, has reopened and is not to be missed. The museum was created in 2004 to celebrate the 400th anniversary of the settling of nearby St. Croix Island, 8 miles downstream in the middle of the river. Rarely mentioned in American schoolbooks, St. Croix looms large in Canadian and French history. It was the first European settlement north of Florida and the beginning of the French presence in North America.

This area was first settled by Passamaquoddy Indians, who migrated up from the Bay of Fundy along the inland waterways. North on Rt. 1 from Calais, the small town of Princeton, flanked by Big Lake and Grand Falls Lake, is home to a number of fishing camps and to the Passamaquoddy community of Odeneg. The center of this Indian township reservation is, however, in Motahkomiqkuk at Peter Dana Point on Big Lake, a village with an Indian cemetery beside the Catholic mission church of St. Anne's. To visit Dana Point you have already turned off Rt. 1 on the road to Grand Lake Stream, a plantation that's a famous fishing outpost, with access to a vast chain of lakes.

Grand Lake Stream is a community of some 100 residents scattered along neighboring lakes, who tend to meet up in the Pine Tree Store, the hub of their barely visible village. The town's namesake stream links Big Lake with West Grand Lake, which flows into Pocumcus Lake and on into Sysladobsis, with water links to Junior and Scraggly Lakes on the north and to Wabassus and Third Machias Lakes on the south. Big Lake links to Long Lake, which links to Lewy Lake, which links to Grand Falls, and so on. For more than a century the area has been a sportsman's paradise, especially for fishermen lured by landlocked salmon, lake trout, smallmouth bass, pickerel, and white perch. The lakes are ringed by wooded shorefront that were owned for more than a century by timber companies with no interest in developing them. In the 1990s, however, these companies began selling off woodland. Georgia-Pacific sold almost half a million acres surrounding the village to a holding company.

Writer and summer resident Wayne Curtis has chronicled the David-versus-Goliath tale that ensued.

DOWNTOWN CALAIS

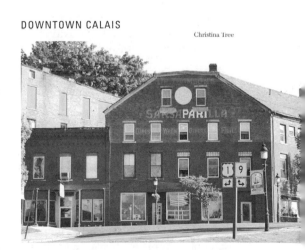

Christina Tree

Residents rallied to raise funds to buy the land along the river and subsequently formed the Downeast Lakes Land Trust (downeastlakes.org), which has worked with other conservation groups to protect some 445 miles of shorefront along 60 Maine lakes and a total of more than a million contiguous acres on both sides of the border.

The symbol of Grand Lake Stream remains the Grand Laker, an unusually long canoe with a distinctive square stern, designed to hold a small outboard motor that can be easily flipped up when the paddling gets rough or shallow. The community continues to boast the state's largest concentration of fishing guides. Its fishing lodges and camps are typically open from ice-out through hunting season. In July and August they cater to families. Inquire about hiking and guided kayaking. The Grand Lake Stream Folk Festival in late July draws visitors from far and wide.

The St. Croix River actually rises in another chain of lakes to the north and forms the boundary with Canada as it flows south 110 miles. It's one of the East's great paddling rivers.

GUIDANCE Maine Tourist Information Center in the Wabanaki Culture Center (207-454-2211), 39 Union St., Calais. Open year-round; July–Oct. 15, daily 8–6, otherwise 9–5:30. This center, operated by the Maine Tourism Association, is a source of brochures for all of Maine as well as the local area. The staff are friendly and eager to help, and there are public restrooms.

St. Croix Valley Chamber of Commerce (1-888-422-3112; visitstcroixvalley.com) is helpful.

Note the new visitors center at the **St. Croix International Historic Site Overlook** (see *To See*).

For the **Grand Lake Stream area** check grandlakestream.org.

GETTING THERE *By car:* The direct route to Calais from Bangor and points west of Washington County is Rt. 9, the Airline Highway. From the Machias area, take Rt. 191. The slower but more scenic drive is along coastal Rt. 1.

WHEN TO COME Fly-fishers converge on Grand Lake Stream and the many lakes and ponds of the St. Croix Valley in May and June. The tourist season begins in July, and winter comes early, as Samuel de Champlain discovered. The area's two big events—the **Grand Lake Stream Festival** in late July and the **Calais/St. Stephen International Festival** in August—are as colorful as only big celebrations in small places can be.

BORDER CROSSING See the "Washington County" introduction.

✳ To See

✪ St. Croix International Historic Site Overlook, Rt. 1, 8 miles south of Calais in Red Beach. A **visitors center**, with restrooms, is open May–Columbus Day weekend, 9–5; 8:40–6 in July, Aug. It's staffed by rangers, with changing exhibits. A path leads to a bronze replica of the settlement. Along the way you encounter half a dozen haunting, life-sized bronze statues, here an elaborately dressed Frenchman, there a young Passamaquoddy girl. The French expedition was drawn here by the fur trade, and its leader, Pierre Dugua, Sieur de Monts, retained Samuel de Champlain as his mapmaker and chronicler. Probably the first European expedi-

Christina Tree

ST. CROIX INTERNATIONAL HISTORIC SITE
OVERLOOK, RT. 1, RED BEACH

tion to push up into Passamaquoddy Bay, they chose this 6½-acre island for their settlement in June 1604 and set about building a storehouse and dwellings, despite the blackflies. The waters teemed with fish, and the native inhabitants were friendly—but the first snow came in early October, the river froze, and 35 of the 79 settlers died. Finally, on June 15, supply vessels arrived, and Dugua sailed south in search of a better settlement site. He instead returned to Port Royal, Nova Scotia, seeding French culture in Canada.

Wabanaki Cultural Center (207-454-2126), 39 Union St. Calais. Open daily, hours of the Maine Tourist Information Center. Built in 2004 by the National Park Service to commemorate the 1604 settlement on St. Croix Island, then closed for several years, recently reopened with a focus on telling the story of the of all four Wabanaki tribes. Walk in through the info center and down the stairs to the museum area. At present most of the numerous exhibits are about the local Passamaquoddy tribe. They include an original vintage-1872 ,20-foot birch-bark canoe. A replica, crafted here by tribal members using traditional techniques, is presently on display in the **Passamaquoddy Cultural Heritage Center** in Indian Township, Princeton north on Rt. 1.

The Chocolate Museum (506-466-7847; chocolatemuseum.ca), 73 Milltown Blvd. (Rt. 1), downtown St. Stephen, New Brunswick. Open June–early Sept., Mon.–Sat. 1 4. Admission. This interesting museum tells the story of the Ganong Bros. Ltd. Company. Displays of old candy boxes, hand-dipping demonstrations, videos, a game to test your packing speed, and free samples. The Ganong Chocolatier sells the tempting goodies.

Dr. Holmes Cottage/Museum (207-454-2604), 245 Main St., Calais. Open July and Aug., Mon.–Sat. 1–4. The oldest existing house in Calais, built in 1805 by Artemus Ward. Restored to its 1850 look and maintained by the St. Croix Historical Society. Pick up a

WABANAKI CULTURE CENTER, CALAIS

Bill Davis

Walking Tour Guide to the Calais Residential Historic District, which includes several Gothic Revival gingerbread houses on S. Main St.

Whitlock Mills Lighthouse. The northeasternmost lighthouse in the country is best viewed from the Pike Woods Rest Area on Rt. 1, 3 miles south of Calais.

✳ To Do

BIRDING **Moosehorn National Wildlife Refuge** is a prime birding center with some 190 species recorded, as well as resident bald eagles (see *Green Space*).

FISHING The Downeast Lakes are famed for their abundance of landlocked salmon, square-tailed trout, and some of the finest smallmouth bass fishing in Maine. Best May–mid-June. When ice is out in spring, trolling starts on **West Grand Lake, Big Lake**, and **Pocumcus Lake**. **Grand Lake Stream** itself, fast-flowing water linking West Grand and Big Lakes, is one of the country's premier fly-fishing spots for landlocked salmon. Fishing licenses, covering three days to a full season (also necessary for ice fishing), are available, along with lodging and supplies, in the woodland village of Grand Lake Stream (**grandlakestream.org**), the focal point of the region and base for the state's largest concentration of fishing guides (**grandlakestreamguides.com**). Princeton, on the way to Grand Lake Stream, is also worth noting for its waters: Big Lake and Grand Falls Lake. Both once ran freely into the St. Croix River, but thanks to a series of 19th-century industrial dams they're now known for their shallows and flowage, great for trout as well as moose-watching and canoeing. Within **Moosehorn National Wildlife Refuge** (see *Green Space*). Several lakes and streams within the refuge are open for fishing.

GOLF St. Croix Country Club (207-454-8875), River Rd., Calais. A tricky nine-hole course on the banks of the St. Croix River.

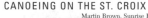

PADDLING Sunrise Expeditions International (sunrise-exp.com). Since 1973 Martin Brown has been offering multiday camping and canoeing trips down the St. Croix River. These may begin by exploring the quiet bays in Lake Spednik before heading down the St. Croix with its many Class I and II (one Class III) rapids. We can vouch for the skill of the guides, and their good cooking. It's a glorious trip.

Grand Lake Stream Outdoor Adventures (207-796-5557; glsoutdoor adventures.com). Al and Sue Le Plante offer guided paddling on the St. Croix and Little Rivers, also tours in their Grand Laker on Big Lake.

Cobscook Hikes & Paddles (207-726-4776; off-season, 207-454-2130). Registered Maine Guides Stephen and Tess Forek, based in Robbinston, offer guided two- and three-hour kayaking paddles from Whiting to Calais. Also see *Lodging* entries for Princeton and Grand Lake Stream; all fishing camps offer boat rentals.

SWIMMING Red Beach on the St. Croix River is named for the sand on these strands: pulverized deep red granite. There is also swimming in dozens of crystal-clear lakes. Round Pond in Charlotte has a free beach and boat launch. North of Calais, follow the Charlotte Rd. 8 miles to the pond.

✳ Green Space

Moosehorn National Wildlife Refuge (207-454-7161; moosehorn.fws.gov). This area is the northeast end of a chain of wildlife and migratory bird refuges extending from Florida to Maine and managed by the U.S. Fish and Wildlife Service. The 23,000-acre refuge is divided into two sections some 20 miles apart. The larger, 17,200-acre area is in Baring, 5 miles north of Calais on Rt. 1. Look for eagles, which nest each spring at the intersection of Charlotte Rd. and Rt. 1. The Edmunds Division is found by heading south on Rt. 1 from Calais, between Dennysville and Whiting (see "Eastport"). This 7,200-acre area lies on the border of the tidal waters of Cobscook Bay. Volunteer-dependent programs—guided hikes, bike tours, and van tours, which sometimes take you down roads you wouldn't be able to explore on your own—are offered late June–Aug.

Downeast Lakes (downeastlakes.org). Evolving preservation efforts safeguard some 340,00 forested acres one of the largest wilderness areas in the East (see this section introduction). It's with best explored by canoe or kayak with a guide (readily available at local lodging places) but there are also trails (see *Walks* below). Look for loons, bald eagles, herons, ruffed grouse, and many kinds of warblers as well as fish.

WALKS

In the Calais area
Calais Waterfront Walkway. A 1.5-mile path follows a former railbed along the river, beginning at city landing parking lot. Formally a part of the East Coast Greenway, it's a good venue from which to appreciate the daily 25-foot tidal changes.

Devil's Head. A trail leads to a promontory, said to be the highest point west of Cadillac Mountain; great views. Look for the sign on Rt. 1 south of Heslin's Motel.

Downeast Lakes (downesastlakes.org)
Little Mayberry Trail begins in the village of Grand Lake Stream and runs some 2.5 miles along the western shore of West Grand Lake.

Pocumcus Lake Trail offers a choice of 1.3- or 3.6-mile loops to the shoreline. Look for the trailhead 7.5 miles west of Grand Lake Stream. This is a rough footpath. Hikers can expect to hear vireos, thrushes, and warblers as well as loons. Watch for bear and moose.

Wabassus Mountain Trail. A 1-mile, moderately steep path climbs to the summit following a small brook, with views of surrounding lakes. The trailhead (yellow blazes) is on Wabassus Mountain Rd.

Redclyffe Shore Motor Inn (207-454-3270; redclyffeshoremotorinn
.com), Rt. 1., Robbinston 04671. Open mid-May–mid-Oct. Twelve miles south of Calais on Rt. 1, this one-story motel with 16 units is set high above the wide mouth of the St. Croix, many rooms (request one) with river views. It's attached to an 1860s Carpenter's Gothic house with a restaurant open only for dinner (see *Eating Out*). $85–95 per couple.

In Calais 04619
✪ Greystone Bed & Breakfast (207-454-2848; greystonecalaisme.com), 13 Calais Ave. This 1840s Greek Revival mansion is set back on a quiet street, within walking distance of downtown shops. Alan and Candace Dwelley offer two attractive upstairs guest rooms with private bath and TV; common space includes a double parlor with black marble fireplace mantels and Corinthian columns separating the two rooms. Breakfast is served at 8 at the dining room table. $95 ($130 for a two-room family suite with shared bath) includes breakfast; $89 off-season.

THE BEACH AT LEEN'S LODGE

Christina Tree

🐾 ✎ The International Motel (207-454-7515 or 1-800-336-7515; the internationalmotel.com), 626 Main St. The best lodging views in town are from the 19 Riverview units in this 61-unit motel owned and operated by three generations of the Thomas family. From $65, $85 per couple for water views, more for efficiency units with whirlpool tubs. Dogs accepted but not in Riverview. Meals are next door at the Wickachee (see *Eating Out*).

🐾 ✎ Calais Motor Inn (1-800-439-5531; calaismotorinn.com), 663 Main St. A friendly, locally owned 70-unit motel with a licensed restaurant (see *Dining Out*). $79 per couple in-season, $59 off-season.

In Grand Lake Stream 04637
Leen's Lodge (207-796-2929 or 1-800-995-3367; leenslodge.com), P.O. Box 40. Open May–Oct. This traditional sporting camp faces West Grand Lake. According to guide and owner Charles Driza, this area represents the best woodcock hunting in the United States. July and August are family season, a good time just to fish, kick back, and relax by the lake. Lights are doused by 9 PM, the better to see the amazing sky. The nine cabins (50 beds) are scattered along the wooded shore, ranging in size from one to eight bedrooms, each with a full bath, fireplace or Franklin stove (with gas heat as a backup), and fridge. The dining room overlooks the water. The Tannery, a pine-paneled gathering space with a picture window, is equipped with games, books, and a TV. BYOB. $145 per person per day double occupancy AP, $165 per person single occupancy, $175 for a single-night stay, includes all meals. Less in spring and fall. A 15 percent gratuity is added; lunch, boat rentals, and guide service are extra.

✪ ✎ Grand Lake Lodge (207-796-5584; grandlakelodgemaine.com), P.O.

GRAND LAKE LODGE

Christina Tree

Box 8. Open from ice-out to Oct. 20. Six classic Maine camp-style, well-equipped housekeeping cottages are nestled under the pines on the shore of West Grand Lake, just above the headwaters of Grand Lake Stream. Each is different (some with lofts), but all have electric heat, good showers, and screened porches from which to take in the expanse of lake and listen to the loons. Chris and Lindsay Wheaton have added many small touches to each. Guests are also welcome on the big sunporch of their neighboring house, with its rockers and computer. Fishing/hunting licenses and guides, boats and bikes are available. We weathered a hurricane comfortably in Cabin 1 (it sleeps seven). $50 for the first person, $45 per person for two or more, half price under 12 years. $450–675 per week in July and Aug.

☀ ✐ **Chet's Camps** (207-796-5557; chetscamps.com). Open late Apr.–Nov. deer season. Al and Sue Le Plante's five lakeside cabins and a central lodge overlook Big Lake, with its 52 island and 105 miles of shoreline. They serve as a base for fly-fishing workshops and canoe expeditions as well as laid-back family vacations. Cabins can accommodate 4 to 10 people, each with a screened porch and dock. They can be booked on a housekeeping basis ($50–55 per person, minimum $100–165) with meals available. Inquire about guided ATV treks, backcountry canoe trips, flat- and whitewater canoeing and kayaking workshops, boats, licenses, and guides.

☀ ✐ **The Pines** (207-557-7463; off-season, 207-825-4431; thepineslodge .com), P.O. Box 158. Open May 15–Oct. 1. Twelve miles and a century in atmosphere away from Grand Lake Stream on Lake Sysladobsis, part of the Grand Lake Stream chain. It's the oldest sporting camp in the area; past guests include Andrew Carnegie and Calvin Coolidge. There are five cabins, also two housekeeping cottages on small islands. The oldest cabin dates to 1883 and the large, double-porched white-clapboard house, to 1884. The upright piano in the living room was ferried over on the *Manhattan*, the launch that served the camp until the 1950s, when the 12 miles of logging roads were built (the last mile or so is a narrow dirt track that peters out into a trail along the edge of the lake). The cabins are heated by woodstoves and have gas lights and a chemical toilet. The main house (which offers flush toilets) and bathhouse are electrified. Cabins are $85 per person per night with three meals, including a packed lunch, $65 for children 3–10. Housekeeping cottages are $600 per week for four or less, $140 per day ($150 for more than four people). Steve and Nancy Norris have managed The Pines for the past 19 years.

☀ ✐ ♿ **Weatherby's** (207-796-5558; in winter 207-926-5598; weatherbys .com), P.O. Box 69. Open early

May–Oct. Fishing is what this place is about (fly-fishing only—Weatherby's is now Orvis-sponsored). Jeff McEvoy and Elizabeth Rankin are the owners of this rambling white 1870s lodge. Each of the 15 cottages is different, but most are log-style with screened porches, a bath, and a Franklin stove or fireplace. $145–165 per person double occupancy (family rates available) plus 15 percent gratuity. Rates include three meals; motorboats are $50 per day; a guide, $250 for two people for Orvis-endorsed fly-fishing on the stream or smallmouth fishing on the lakes. Inquire about scheduled fly-fishing schools for novices and women as well as pros. Pets are $10 per day. Kayaks and canoes available. The big, old-fashioned **dining room** is open to the public for dinner by reservation—and in 2011 it was the best dining to be had for hundreds of miles around.

Elsewhere

🐾 🏕 ⚲ **Lakeside Country Inn and Cabins** (207-796-2324 or 1-888-677-2874; thelakeside.org), P.O. Box 36, 14 Rolfe St., Princeton 04668-0036. Open year-round; cabins May–Nov. Built in 1854, the inn offers eight guest rooms. There are also five housekeeping cabins on Lewy Lake (the outlet to Big Lake). Rooms in the inn are simple, nicely furnished; each has a sink, TV, fridge, toaster oven, and microwave; some share a bath. Hosts Gary and Jennifer Dubovick seem right for this place, hospitable outdoorspeople who are gardeners and good cooks. Inn rooms are $35 single, $50 double, $65 per person with three meals (box lunch); camps are $65–85 per couple. $80 for a two-bedroom cabin. $20 per extra person, $10 under age 10; pets $15 per stay. Facilities include spa and game rooms. Guide service, boat rentals, and hunting/fishing licenses are available.

Bellmard Inn (207-796-2261), 86 Main St. (Rt. 1), Princeton 04668. This big, rambling 19th-century house, a tourist home since 1951, is now a bed & breakfast run by Andrea Smith and Doug Clements. Guests share the dining room and sitting room; there's one guest room on the ground floor, four on the second, both shared and private baths. From $35 for one person, $50 double with private bath. Meals available.

✳ Where to Eat

EATING OUT Redclyffe Shore Dining Room (207-454-3270), Rt. 1, Robbinston. Open May–Oct., 5–9 for dinner. The dining room overlooks the St. Croix River. The menu offers pasta, steaks, chicken, and seafood; specialties include baked haddock with lobster sauce.

Heslin's (207-454-3762), Rt. 1, Calais (south of the village). Open May into Oct., 5–9. A popular local dining room high above the river, specializing in steak ("the thickest cuts in town!") and seafood entrées; homemade desserts, fully licensed. Most entrées under $20.

❂ ⚲ 🖧 **Border Town Subz** (207-454-8562), 313 Main St., Calais. Open weekdays 10–6, Sat. from 11. Dynamic mother–daughter team Gail Cottrell and Glorian Phillips operate this homey restaurant, serving from-scratch soups, breads, rolls, and cookies, and Grandpa's homemade chili; also sandwiches, subs and wraps, PB&J for kids, and a seasonal adult-sized lobster sub with mayo and lettuce.

Wickachee (207-454-3400), 282 Main St. (Rt. 1), Calais. Open year-round 6 AM–10 PM. Steak and seafood (with a big salad bar) are the dinner specialties. Spacious, clean, and friendly; tiny restrooms.

Calais Motor Inn Restaurant (207-454-7111), 293 Main St. (Rt. 1), Calais.

Open for lunch and dinner. A large, comfortable dining room specializing in steak and seafood at dinner.

Bistro on the Boulevard (506-466-2322), 73 Milltown Boulevard, St. Stephen, NB. Open for lunch and dinner. Hours vary with season. This the best dining bet in the area, an attractive restaurant opened by Diane Gagnon of family-owned Gagnon Bros. Ltd. and their Chocolate Museum across the way. Soups, sandwiches, and specialty coffees, the best dinner option on either side of the border (it's just on the other side from Calais). Daily specials.

✳ Selective Shopping

✪ 45th Parallel (207-853-9500), "halfway between the Equator and the North Pole," Rt. 1, Perry. Open seasonally. Chicago designers Britani and Philip Pascarekka have filled this space—from floor to 12-foot-high ceilings—with an eclectic mix of gifts and home decor accents and furnishings: stained glass and antique beds, drawer pulls and lamps, jewelry, bird feeders, and much more, gathered from around the world.

Katie's on the Cove (207-454-8446; katiesonthecove.com), Rt. 1, Mill Cove, Robbinston. All handmade and hand-dipped chocolates. Favorites, the luscious truffles aside, include Passamaquoddy Crunch, Maine Potato Candy, and Maine Black Bear Paws, even mustard chocolates using Raye's.

✪ Calais Bookshop (207-454-1110), 405 Main St., Calais. This is Washington County's only genuine bookstore and it's a treasure. Carol Heinlein stocks new, used, and rare titles and serves a wide circle of loyal patrons.

Marden's (207-454-1421), 189 Main St. and Rt. 1, Calais. Two representatives of the chain of Maine discount centers, which has been doing business in the state since 1964. Big-time bargains can be found here, from furniture to fabrics, housewares to clothing.

Pine Tree Store (207-796-5027), Water St., Grand Lake Stream. Open daily ice-out through Jan. 1, when it closes to make maple bark baskets, sold through L.L. Bean. Kurt and Kathy Cressey's outpost oasis offers one of the largest selections of fishing flies in Maine; also tackle, clothing, hunting and fishing licenses, groceries, a selection of wines, plus pizza and great sandwiches to go. It's up for sale . . .

✳ Special Events

Last weekend of July: **Grand Lake Stream Folk Art Festival**—bluegrass and folk music, woodsmen's skills demonstrations featuring canoe building, crafts, dinner cooked by Maine Guides. See downeastlakes.org for lectures and other events in Grand Lake Stream throughout the summer.

August: **International Festival**, Calais and St. Stephen, New Brunswick—a week of events on both sides of the border, including pageants, a parade, entertainment, and more.

THE PINE TREE STORE, GRAND LAKE STREAM

Christina Tree

ST. ANDREWS AND GRAND MANAN (NEW BRUNSWICK)

Beyond Eastport and Calais, you don't drop off the end of the world. Instead you cross the Canadian border—either via Rt. 1 at Calais or via ferry across Passamaquoddy Bay—into coastal New Brunswick. Suddenly it's an hour later, distance is measured in kilometers, signs are in French as well as English, gas is priced by the liter. Most tourists here are, of course, Canadian.

Historically and geographically, in this area Maine and Canada are intrinsically linked. Both St. Andrews (New Brunswick's liveliest resort town) and the island of Grand Manan (a haven for whale-watchers, birders, and hikers) were settled by loyalists during the Revolution, and Grand Manan, which lies just 9 miles off West Quoddy Light, is geographically closer to Maine than to Canada.

GUIDANCE Complete lodging listings for both St. Andrews and Grand Manan are detailed in the *New Brunswick Touring Guide*, available by calling 1-800-561-0123 (toll-free in Canada and the United States) or by visiting tourismnbcanada.com. A large Provincial Tourist Information Centre (506-466-7390), 5 King St., St. Stephen, is housed in a grand old railroad station a few blocks beyond the border crossing, surrounded by banks at which you can exchange American for Canadian dollars.

GETTING THERE In good weather the car ferry ride across Passamaquoddy Bay from Eastport or Campobello via Deer Island is a delight, certainly the way to go at least one way to St. Andrews (see "Washington County"). If you're heading directly to Grand Manan, however, it makes more sense to drive to Blacks Harbour and board that island's ferry. From the Calais–St. Stephens border, it's 19 miles to St. Andrews and 35 miles to Blacks Harbour. See "Grand Manan" for details about the ferry.

TIME Note that New Brunswick's Atlantic time is one hour ahead of Maine's eastern time (1 PM ET is thus 2 PM AT). Both Maine and New Brunswick observe Daylight Saving Time.

CROSSING THE BORDER See the "Washington Country" introduction.

ST. ANDREWS

St. Andrews retains a genteel 19th-century charm. It's a pleasant resort town with shops lining well-named Water Street, plenty of choices for lodging, several restaurants, and a range of activities from historical tours to day adventures.

The big hotel is the Fairmont Algonquin, a 240-room, many-gabled, neo-Tudor resort dating to 1915. It sits enthroned like a queen mother above this tidy town with loyalist street names like Queen, King, and Princess Royal. St. Andrews was founded in 1783 by British Empire loyalists, American colonists who so strongly opposed breaking away from the mother country that they left the new United States after independence was won. Most came from what is now Castine, many of them unpegging their houses and bringing them along. Impressed by this display of loyalty, the British government made the founding of St. Andrews as painless as possible, granting the settlers a superb site. British army engineers dug wells, built a dock, constructed a fort, and laid out the town on its present grid. Each loyalist family was also given a house lot twice the usual size. The result is an unusually gracious, largely 19th-century town, hauntingly reminiscent of Castine. The focal point remains Market Wharf, where the first settlers stepped ashore—now the cluster point for outfitters offering whale-watching, sailing, and kayaking tours—and Water Street, lined with shops.

GUIDANCE Visitor Information Center (townofstandrews.ca), corner of Reed and Harriet Sts. in the Arena Building, is open June–Oct. 9–5, until 9 in July and Aug.

GETTING THERE *By car:* Rt. 1 via Calais. From the border crossing at Calais, it's just 19 miles (25k) to St. Andrews.

By car ferry: Late June–mid-Sept. only. See the "Washington County" introduction. The ferry docks in L'Etete, and the road curves up the peninsula through the town of St. George, where you pick up Canadian Rt. 1, following it 13 unremarkable miles to the turnoff (Rt. 127) for St. Andrews.

WHEN TO COME The summer season is late June–September, but December is also big in St. Andrews, with many special events.

✳ To See

Note: Prices are in Canadian dollars.

✪ ♿ **Kingsbrae Horticultural Garden** (506-529-3335; kingsbraegarden.com), 220 King St., St. Andrews. Open mid-May–mid Oct., daily 9–6. Also open Nov.–Jan. with trees decorated for Christmas. $14 adults, $10 seniors and students, free ages 6 and under; $32 per family. Even if you aren't a garden buff, this glorious, elaborate 27-acre site is a must-see. Walking paths, a delightful café, an art gallery, and a gift shop Built on the grounds of several long-gone estates, the garden uses mature cedar hedges, flower beds, and old-growth forest in the new design. Specialized areas include display gardens with rare and native plants, a fantasy garden with animals made from moss, demonstration gardens, a woodland trail through the old-growth forest, a therapy garden, bird and butterfly gardens, and much more. For more about the café, see *Eating Out*.

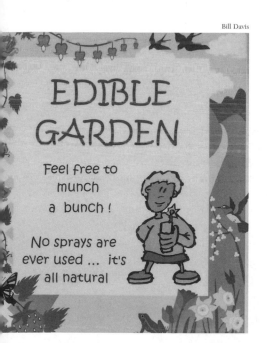

Bill Davis

Ministers Island Historic Site (506-529-5081; ministersisland.net), Bar Rd., St. Andrews. Open June–mid-Oct. $15 adult ($25 per couple), $10 seniors

Christina Tree

KINSBRAE GARDEN

and students, free ages 6 and under; $45 per family. One of the grandest estates around, built around 1890 on an island connected by a "tidal road" to St. Andrews, Covenhoven is a 50-room mansion with 17 bedrooms, a vast drawing room, a bathhouse, and a gigantic and ornate livestock barn. The builder was Sir William Van Horne, the driving force in construction of the Canadian Pacific Railway. This is a real island, accessible at low tide; otherwise wait for the shuttle boat or kayak across.

Ross Memorial Museum (506-520-5124; rossmemorialmuseum.ca), corner of King and Montague Sts., St. Andrews. Open mid-June–mid-Oct., Mon.–Sat. 10–4:30. Donations welcomed. An 1824 mansion displaying the fine decorative art collection of the Reverend and Mrs. Henry Phipps Ross of Ohio, world travelers and collectors who fell in love with the area while on a picnic on Chamcook Mountain. They purchased the 1824 house and donated it, along with their collections, to the town.

Sheriff Andrews House Historic Site (506-529-5080), King St., St. Andrews. Open late May–mid-June, Mon.–Fri. 9:30–4:30, also Sat. mid-June–late Sept. An 1820 house that belonged to Elisha Andrews, high sheriff of Charlotte County; fine detailing. Costumed guides offer tours and demonstrate open-hearth cooking techniques and traditional domestic handiwork, such as quilting.

Fundy Discovery Aquarium at the Huntsman Marine Science Centre (506-529-1200; huntsmanmarine.ca), Brandy Cove Rd. (off Rt. 127), St. Andrews. Open year-round, hours varying with the season. A brand-new 20,000-square-foot aquarium opened in Sept. 2011, replacing the former facility and offering four viewing galleries with more than 80 Bay of Fundy marine species to be seen. This is a nonprofit aquaculture research center sponsoring educational programs and cruises.

♦ **Atlantic Salmon Interpretive Centre** (506-529-1384; asf.ca), Chamcook, 5 miles east of St. Andrews on Rt. 127. Open mid-May–mid-Oct., daily 9–5. Admission. These undervisited post-and-beam buildings include the Atlantic Salmon International Hall of Fame—which resembles an old river lodge complete with great room. Exhibits examine the history, geography, and distressingly dwindling numbers of wild salmon. Chamcook Stream flows through the room, and salmon of all sizes can be seen in an aquarium.

St. Andrews Blockhouse (506-529-4270), Centennial Park, St. Joe's Point Rd., St. Andrews. Open June–Aug., 9–8; until mid-Sept., 9–5. Erected during the War of 1812, partially restored but also partially original, this is one of the few such blockhouses that's survived in North America. Interpretive panels tell the story.

Green's Point Lighthouse Museum, L'Etete. After leaving the ferry landing, turn right and drive to the parking area near the keeper's garage. The official name of the light station is L'Etete Passage Light.

✴ To Do

GOLF ○ Algonquin Signature Golf Course (see *Lodging*). Open May–Oct. The resort's golf course, recently completely redesigned. Thomas McBroom, an award-winning architect, laid out the 18 holes. From oceanfront to forest holes, the natural flow of the course and the scenic views make this an unforgettable golfing experience. Clubhouse, pro shop.

SAILING Tall Ship Whale Adventures (506-529-8116; jollybreeze.com), St. Andrews Wharf. June–Oct. Three-hour sails travel Passamaquoddy Bay and up the St. Croix River of the Bay of Fundy, where you can see whales, dolphins, and other wildlife. Passengers are welcome to take the helm or help hoist sails.

SEA KAYAKING AND CANOEING In St. Andrews, **Seascape** (506-529-4866; seascapekayatours.com) offers half- and full-day guided tours as well as longer expeditions and lessons. **Eastern Outdoors** (1-800-56-KAYAK; easternoutdoors .com), 165 Water St., also offers guided half- and full-day tours; beginners welcome.

SWIMMING Katy's Cove (506-529-3433), Acadia Rd., St. Andrews, has (relatively) warm water, a sandy white beach, and a newly renovated clubhouse; nominal fee.

WHALE-WATCHING Fundy Tide Runners (506-529-4481; fundytiderunners .com). Hurricane boats, and clients wear flashy orange, full-length flotation suits; **Quoddy Link Marine** (506-529-2600; quoddylinkmarine.com) offers Whale Search and Island Cruises aboard two larger, slower vessels with enclosed, heated viewing areas as well as outdoor decks; **Jolly Breeze Tall Ship Whale Adventures** (506-529-8116; jollybreeze.com) offers whale-watching on a pirate-themed tall ship.

✴ Lodging

All listings are in St. Andrews, New Brunswick, Canada
Note: Rates are in Canadian dollars (CAD). Add 13 percent tax.

RESORT ♂ & **The Algonquin Hotel** (506-529-8823; in the U.S., 1-800-441-1414; fairmont.com), 184 Adolphus St.,

E5B 1T7. Fully open mid-Apr.–mid-Nov., but some 50 rooms in the new wing remain open year-round. The last of the truly grand coastal resorts in northeastern America. A 240-room (including 13 suites), Tudor-style hotel with formal common and dining rooms, this hotel was built in 1889 with

Christina Tree

THE ALGONQUIN HOTEL

its castle facade, but only 80 rooms. Ownership began with the St. Andrews Land Company and passed to the Canadian Pacific Railway Company, then to the province of New Brunswick; this is now a Fairmont-managed property. The golf course has undergone extensive renovations in recent years, and there are five dining options, a spa and fitness center, fitness classes year-round, a heated outdoor pool, tennis courts, shuffleboard, and a daily activity program for children in July and August. Bellhops wear kilts. The rack rates are $99–459, $299–1,100 for suites (Canadian) per couple, but there are many special packages. *Note:* Management changes in 2012.

INNS 🐾 ♪ **Kingsbrae Arms Relais & Chateaux** (506-529-1897; kingsbrae .com), 219 King St., E5B 1Y1. Canada's first five-star inn (as decreed by Canada Select) is this 1897 shingled mansion adjoining Kingsbrae Gardens. The innkeeper is Harry Chancey Jr. The softly colored drawing room is elegant with its grand piano and a pool in gardens beyond. A five-course meal is served (see *Dining Out*). Two rooms and eight suites are divided between the mansion and newer "wings." Those in the mansion are elegantly formal,

while newer units are more spacious and informal, some tailored for families. All have phone and air-conditioning; some have airpool bathtub, steam shower, and fireplace. The inn's landscaped grounds include a solar-heated pool. $595–995 (CAD), including a full breakfast and dinner. Minimum two-night stay. Check the website for special packages.

🍴 **Rossmount Inn** (506-529-3351; rossmountinn.com), 4599 Rt. 127, E5B 2Z3. East of town, this boxy three-story hilltop mansion is a period piece—high Victorian with ornate chandeliers, woodwork, and appropriate furnishings. Built at the turn of the

KINGSBRAE ARMS IS A MEMBER OF RELIAS & CHÂTEAUX

Christina Tree

20th century by the same Reverend and Mrs. Ross who endowed the Ross Museum in town, it has been revitalized by Chris and Graziella Aerni. A Swiss-born and -trained chef, Chris has established the inn as a prime dining destination (see *Dining Out*). The 18 rooms are now charmingly furnished with antiques and a choice of double, twin, queen-, and king-sized beds (private bath, flat-screen TV). The extensive property includes a swimming pool and walking trails up Chamcook Mountain, the highest point on this side of Passamaquoddy Bay. $139–239 (CAD) in high season, off-season from $119.

BED & BREAKFASTS Check with the chamber of commerce for other reasonably priced B&Bs, many of which seem to change each season.

✪ ❧ **Treadwell Inn** (1-888-529-1011; treadwellinn.com), 129 Water St., E5B 1A7. Open year-round. A real find. Annette and Jerry Mercer offer seven spacious rooms, imaginatively furnished in antiques, each with private bath. Four rooms have a balcony overlooking the water (35 feet away). Two third-floor efficiency suites have a sitting area and whirlpool bath with private waterside balcony. Originally built in 1820 by a ship's chandler, eventually the building served as the town's customhouse. $149–250 (CAD), $99–180 off-season, with breakfast available. Two-night minimum stay in waterfront rooms. Unfortunately Annette and Jerry have firm retirement plans, so come quickly.

Harris Hatch Inn Bed & Breakfast (506-529-4995; harrishatchinn.ca), 142 Queen St., E5B 1E2. Open year-round, this stately 1840 brick mansion is the longtime home of Jura and Bob Estes. They offer three suites with full bath, two with a fireplace; also a garden apartment. Full breakfast.

$100–135 CAD per couple in-season, from $75 in winter.

OTHER 🐾 ✿ **St. Andrews Motor Inn** (506-529-4571; standrewsmotorinn.com), 111 Water St., E5B 1A3. A three-story motel with 37 units and a heated indoor swimming pool. All rooms have two queen-sized beds and color TV, some have kitchenette, and all have private balcony overlooking Passamaquoddy Bay. $160–230 (Canadian) plus tax in high season includes coffee. From $80 off-season.

🐾 ✿ **Seaside Beach Resort** (506-529-3846 or 1-800-506-8677; seaside.nb.ca), 339 Water St., E5B 2R2. Open early spring through autumn. We like the feel and location of this complex: 24 one- and two-bedroom housekeeping units (towels changed daily) in a mix of old houses and cabins that's been evolving since the 1940s, fronting—with a big shared deck—on Passamaquoddy Bay. Either Beth Campbell or David Sullivan is in the office to meet, greet, and help. High season $130–220, off-season $90–150; $10 per extra person, $5 per child.

CAMPING Ocean Front Camping (506-529-3439), Indian Point Rd. Maintained by the Kiwanis Club of St. Andrews, this is a beautifully sited campground with full hookups as well as tent sites.

Island View Campground (506-529-3787), Rt. 127, with sites featuring full hookups and tent sites, pool, and beach access overlooking historic St. Croix Island.

✳ Where to Eat

All listings are in St. Andrews unless otherwise noted
DINING OUT Rossmount Inn (506-529-3351; rossmountinn.com), 4599

Rt. 127. East of town, this landmark inn (see *Lodging*) is a fabulous place to eat, thanks to Swiss-born and -trained chef-owner Chris Aerni. Reservations a must. The emphasis is on local ingredients—organic when possible—and all pastries are made here. The many-windowed yellow dining room is large and gracious, with crystal chandeliers, stained glass, and contemporary art. There's also a small, ornately comfortable bar. On our most recent visit we began with an heirloom tomato salad with chèvre and black olive tapenade and dined on prosciutto-wrapped pork tenderloin with shiitake truffle risotto. Somehow we also managed a lavender-lemon crème brûlée with berry sorbet and citrus gingersnap. Entrées $17–30. Fully licensed.

Kingsbrae Arms (506-529-1897; kingsbrae.com), 219 King St. Open for dinner by reservation May–Oct. and during the Christmas season. We celebrated our 35th wedding anniversary here. It's that kind of place. The current chef is from Provence and the menu is locally sourced, some ingredients from the inn's garden. Dinner is served in one of the inn's two elegant dining rooms, and it's a set menu: the "amuse," locally smoked sturgeon; the "debut," crabcakes from locally caught shellfish; "la suite," roasted leg of caribou with shallot popover; and a choice of "finale," a vanilla maple crème brûlée. $90 per person plus wine. Also see *Lodging*.

Europa Inn (506-529-3818; europa inn.com), 48 King St. Open in-season for dinner daily except Mon. Established as a fine restaurant with a German accent in 1983, it continues on both counts under owners master chef Markus Ritter and his wife, Simone, who moved to St. Andrews from Bavaria. Dine on duck à l'orange, or on Jägerschnitzel—milk-fed veal scallop-

pine in a creamy mushroom sauce with vegetables and homemade spaetzle. Entrées $21–27. Fully licensed.

The Algonquin Hotel (506-529-8823), 184 Adolphus St., offers two dining venues. In the **Veranda**, the long many-windowed sunroom overlooking the formal gardens, the menu features locally sourced ingredients in dishes ranging from goat cheese pizza to grilled lamb chops with roasted eggplant, or crispy chile- and panko-crusted scallops ($15–26). In the smaller, more formal **Library Lounge & Bistro** choices might range from roast cod with tomato and chorizo scalloped potatoes to tenderloin short ribs ($29–40).

Savour (506-529-1055; chefalexhaun .com), 4442 Rt. 127, Chamcook. New in 2009 and open limited days (check), this is a small restaurant—just 26 seats—in an attractive paneled room with an electric hearth or in a private dining room. It's chef Alex Haun's house, and his wife, Jennie, is the hostess. Guests are invited to savor a

LUNCH AT THE ALGONQUIN

Bill Davis

THE GABLES, ST. ANDREWS

Christina Tree

leisurely meal, as we did with old friends. We began with "salmon 3 ways," then feasted on seared sturgeon with beet-infused orzo and citrus cream, and Westphalian-wrapped scallops with an onion spaetzle cake; we finished by splitting a luscious orange tart. There were several small surprises between courses. The tab: $97.18 for two, including tax and a bottle of Pinot Grigio. A set menu is $60.

EATING OUT ✪ **The Gables** (506-529-3440), 143 Water St. Open 11–10. Reasonably priced good food, and a tiered, shaded deck with a water view make this a perennial favorite. Specialties include fresh fish ranging from fried haddock-and-chips to a seafood platter. The seafood chowder is full of shrimp and lobster, and we recommend the mussels. Fully licensed; wine by the glass and a wide selection of beers.

✪ ❧ **Kingsbrae Garden Café** (506-529-3335; kingsbraegarden.com), 220 King St. Open May–Oct, 10–6 in July, Aug., otherwise until 5. Housed in the original manor home on the grounds of a 27-acre formal garden, this delightful café is well worth knowing about before you get there, good for

ample but ladylike luncheon salads and sandwiches served on a choice of freshly baked croissant, seven-grain roll, or wrap. Wine and beer. Afternoon tea with scones, finger sandwiches, and a deluxe chocolate brownie is served from 2:30.

Niger Reef Tea House (506-529-8005), 1 Joe's Point Rd. Open May–Oct., 11–8. Reservations advised for dinner. The setting is delightful. Built in 1926 as a summer cottage but serving for many years as a meeting-house for the Daughters of the Empire, with murals picturing Shanghai, pleasant seating on the deck. Chef David Peterson's lunch menu includes fish cakes with lemon dill aioli and a potato tart with bacon, cheddar, and sour cream. The dinner menu varies nightly. We dined on planked salmon, served with greens and watermelon ($19.50). Beer and wine served.

✻ Selective Shopping

All listings are in St. Andrews
Cottage Craft Ltd. (1-800-355-9655; cottagecraftwoolens.com), 209 Water St. in Town Square. Open year-round, Mon.–Sat. Dating to 1915, Cottage

COTTAGE CRAFT, A ST. ANDREWS INSTITUTION

Christina Tree

Craft showcases yarns, tweeds, finished jackets, sweaters, and skirts; also distinctive throws handwoven in homes throughout Charlotte County. Upward of 150 knitters produce the sweaters, hats, scarves, and mittens, some wonderfully priced. The **Lobster Market** and **Rising Tides Wine Bar & Gallery** are recent additions to this landmark building store.

Serendipin' Art (506-529-3327; serendipinart.ca), 168 Water St. A large selection of handmade New Brunswick crafts, including jewelry, pottery, hand-painted silks, and more.

Christina Tree

LOCAL KNITTERS PRODUCE WOOLENS FOR COTTAGE CRAFT

GRAND MANAN

Little more than 15 miles long and less than 7 miles wide, Grand Manan is Canada's southernmost island, far enough at sea to be very much its own place, a rugged outpost at the mouth of the Bay of Fundy.

Right whales are what draw many visitors. These are the rarest of whales. Just 320 are known to exist worldwide, but many seem to be here in summer months, feeding on krill and other nutrients in the tide-churned waters. Birds are another draw: 240 species frequent the island. Machias Seal Island, the prime viewing place for puffins, is as easily accessible from Grand Manan as from Maine. A 40-mile network of hiking trails is another plus, many miles hugging cliffs that vary from 100 to almost 400 feet.

Fishing boats line the wharves the way they used to in New England. While fish are fewer than they once were here, too, fishing is more profitable than ever. Connors Brothers sardine factory at Seal Cove was the island's largest employer until it closed in the spring of 2005, but salmon farming remains big, along with lobster and clams, periwinkles, and that Grand Manan delicacy: dulse. The hundreds of herring smokehouses for which the island was once known are, however, either gone or standing unused, with one preserved as a sporadically open museum. A number of weirs, are, however, still in use to catch herring.

Grand Manan's population has hovered around 2,700 since the late 19th century, clustered in the sheltered harbors and coves along its gentle Bay of Fundy shore, which is protected by many small islands. In contrast, the northern and southern "heads" of the island are soaring cliffs, as is almost the entire western shore. It's a mirror image of Maine's Bold Coast, with only well-named Dark Harbour accessible by car. Trails and boats can make their way to Indian Beach, Money Cove, Bradfords Cove, and Little Dark Harbour.

In many ways Grand Manan remains as out-of-the-way and unspoiled as it was during the 20 summers (1922–42) that Willa Cather spent here, working on some of her most famous novels, including *Death Comes for the Archbishop*. Her cottage on Whale Cove is one among the island's many summer rentals.

GUIDANCE Grand Manan Tourism Association, 1141 Rt. 776. The seasonal Visitor Information Center (506-662-3442 or 1-888-525-1655; grandmanannb.com) is housed at the rear of the museum. Open July–mid-Sept., daily 9–5. The association publishes the inexpensive booklets *Grand Manan Trails* and *Grand Manan Guide*. The website is by far the island's best source of information.

GETTING THERE Coastal Transport (506-662-3724; coastaltransport.ca) operates ferries on the 20-mile, 90-minute sail between Blacks Harbour on the mainland and North Head on the island. During high season (late June–Labor Day), ferries run seven times a day, every two hours during summer months beginning at 7:30 AM. Service from the mainland is first come, first served, so allow an extra hour for the lineup. (Check; this policy may change.) Things we wish we'd known: (1) The ferry terminal is a couple of miles beyond the village of Blacks Harbour, so you may want to stock up on food and drink before you get in line. The new 380-passenger, 80-vehicle *Grand Manan Adventure* and the M/S *Grand Manan V* (carrying up to 64 vehicles) alternate runs, and most cars in line now get aboard. (2) If you are returning the following day, use the special wall phone in the terminal to reserve your space. Reservations are a must and available only a day in advance on trips back from the island (that's when you pay for the roundtrip). Food is available on both ferries. Pedestrians and bicyclists have no problem getting on. Parking is ample and free in Blacks Harbour, and whale-watching, sea kayaking tours, and rental bikes are also within walking distance of the ferry terminal on Grand Manan. From Calais, Maine, it's 35 miles to Blacks Harbour.

✳ To See

Swallowtail Light, North Head. One of the few surviving wooden lighthouses in Canada, dramatically sited on a point of land almost separated from the island by the "Sawpit," accessed by a footbridge. Notice the two herring weirs visible from this spot. Also look for seals and whales.

🐟 🕭 **The Grand Manan Museum** (506-662-3524; grandmananmuseum.ca), 1141 Rt. 776, Grand Harbor, across from the school. Open May–Sept., Mon.–Sat. 9–5. $5 adults, $3 seniors and students, free ages 12 and under. The Allan Moses Bird Collection, an exhibit of more than 300 mounted birds, documents the island's bird life, and the history of the island's smoked herring industry is dramatized in paintings, photographs, and memorabilia. Novelist Willa Cather's typewriter and manuscript table are also here. Inquire about evening slide shows and rainy-day programs.

Grand Manan Whale and Seabird Research Station (506-662-3804), 24 Rt. 776, North Head. Open June–Oct., 10–5. This marine natural history museum focuses on endangered right whales and the harbor porpoise.

Dark Harbour. The only road across the width of the island ends abruptly at the harbor (it's a tight turnaround at high tide), the one nick in what is otherwise a wall of cliffs that run the length of the western shore. This is a prime dulse-harvesting spot, but there are no commercial enterprises, just seasonal cottages that are inaccessible except by boat.

Southwest Head. Your first instinct is to drive the length of the island on the one north–south road, grandiosely numbered 776. It ends at Southwest Head Lighthouse, and a path leads along spectacular cliffs.

Hole in the Wall. The view of this much-photographed natural arch near the northern end of the island is most easily accessed via a fairly steep path, from a parking area that lies within Hole-in-the-Wall Park, a former airport that's now a commercial campground. Great viewing spots for whale-watching.

✳ To Do

BIRDING AND NATURE The island is visited annually by 240 species of birds and many, many more individual bird-watchers. Bird species are listed on the island website (grandmanannb.com). Castalia Marsh, accessible via a nature trail in Castalia Provincial Park, is a favorite spot at dawn and dusk. One of the first visitors was John James Audubon, who came in 1831 to check out the unlikely-but-true story that island seagulls nest in trees.

Sea Watch Tours (506-662-8332; seawatchtours.com) offers mid-June–early Aug. trips from Seal Cove Grand Manan to Machias Seal Island to see puffins, arctic terns, and razor-billed auks. Captain Peter Wilcox is a native of Grand Manan whose ancestors came here from New England during the Revolution. In 1969 his father began offering trips to Machias Seal, which is 10 miles south of the southern tip of in Grand Manan. Be sure to come prepared with windbreaker, wind pants, hat, and mittens for the early-morning ride out. For details about **Machias Seal Island** see *To Do* in the Bold Coast chapter. Also see *Whale-Watching*.

GOLF Brookside Golf Course (506-662-3253), Seal Cove. A 9-hole course beside an 18-hole mini golf.

HIKING Some 45 miles of marked hiking trails cover a variety of terrain along the shore. Pick up a copy of *Heritage Trails and Footpaths* (available in most island stores) and a picnic and you're set.

KAYAKING AND BIKE RENTALS Adventure High (506-662-3563 or 1-800-732-5492; adventurehigh.com), 83 Rt. 776. Guided tours range from a two-hour moonlight trip to six-hour explorations and include Seal Watch Tours and a Kayak Tour & Dinner on the beach. Mountain and hybrid bikes are also rented. Inquire about the solar-heated rental cottage on a remote cove.

WHALE-WATCHING Whales-n-Sails Adventures (506-662-1999 or 1-888-994-4044; whales-n-sails.com), North Head, Fisherman's Wharf, offers two daily trips, weather permitting, June–mid-Sept. Sailing and whale-watching are a great combination. The 56-foot, 47-passenger ketch *Elsie Menota* supplements sail with power to reach the deeps in the Bay of Fundy (12 miles northeast of Grand Manan), where Atlantic right whales feed and play, but then it's quiet and pleasant to tack and jibe among these huge creatures. Owner Allan McDonald points out bird and sea life en route.

Sea Watch Tours (see *Birding*) also offers whale-watch cruises, no whales, no charge. Also see *Birding* for tours to Machias Seal Island, the home of the puffins.

✳ Lodging

Note: The choice of lodgings and cottages is large, and most are listed on grandmanannb.com. The following represent the best of the Grand Manan inns and B&Bs we checked. Rates are in Canadian dollars.

⊙ 🐾 ∅ **The Inn at Whale Cove Cottages** (506-662-3181), 26 Whale Cove Cottage Rd., 35G 2B5. The gray-shingled Main House dates from 1816, overlooking a quiet cove with a large fish weir, backed by rugged Fish Head. It was here in picturesque Orchardside cottage ($1,000 per week) that Willa Cather first came to write in 1922, eventually building a replica of it a ways down the shore (also available for $950, a gem in which we celebrated a birthday). The inn and cottages are owned and operated by Laura Buckley. The Main House parlor has changed little since it began welcoming "rusticators" in 1910. The fireplace is large and usually glowing, and the walls are lined with books. Two-bedroom Cove View, with two decks and a full living room and library, is $900 per week; Coopershop features a huge fireplace and two upstairs bedrooms as well as a living room and kitchen/dining area ($850 per week). There are three delightful rooms in the Main House ($125 single, $135 double per night). Rates include a very full breakfast Dinner is also served (see *Dining Out*). Pets are also accepted, $10 per dog.

Compass Rose (506-662-8570; off-season, 613-471-1772; compassroseinn .com), 65 Rt. 776, North Head, E5G 1A2. Open June–Oct. Within walking distance of the ferry terminal, water excursions, and bike rentals, this is a gem of an inn, overlooking the busy harbor of North Head. Owner Nora Parker has renovated the entire inn. Each of the six guest rooms is furnished in antiques and has a private bathroom and harbor view, but they're also right on the road. The dining room, which is open to the public, is a must-stop for every visitor (see *Dining Out*). $99–139 per couple includes a full breakfast. Dinner is also served.

McLaughlin's Wharf Inn (506-662-8760), 1863 Rt. 776, E5G 3H1. Open July–Aug. A waterside former store in Seal Cove is now a reasonably priced B&B with six upstairs rooms, two shared baths, and a TV lounge. A full breakfast and dinner are served in the restaurant downstairs.

Marathon Inn (506-662-8488; marathoninn.com), North Head, E0G 2M0. Open year-round. This is a big white ark of a place on a hill overlooking the water in North Head. The rooms we saw (there are 24) were clean and cheerful, with tasteful prints and colorful quilts, and there's a pool. We've been warned to avoid the annex. The large, sunny dining room, serving

VIEW FROM THE WINDOW OF WILLA CATHER'S COTTAGE AT THE INN AT WHALE COVE

Christina Tree

all three meals, is popular with birding groups and Road Scholar (formerly Elderhostel). $65–120.

CAMPGROUNDS The Anchorage Provincial Park (506-662-7035 or 1-800-561-0123), 136 Anchorage Rd., E5G 2H4. The 100 sites vary from wooded to waterside; 24 accommodate trailers.

Hole-in-the-Wall (506-662-3152 or 1-866-662-4489; grandmanancamping .com), 42 Old Airport Rd., E5G 1A9. With 48 sites, there is a wide range in this sprawling property, from RV to wooded—some fairly spectacular.

✳ Where to Eat

DINING OUT The Inn at Whale Cove (506-662-3181), 25 Whale Cove Cottage Rd., near North Head. Open nightly in-season, 6–8:30. Reservations required. The dining room in the early-19th-century cottage seats just 30 people. It's candlelit and decorated with vintage willowware. Chef-owner Laura Buckley uses local ingredients imaginatively. The set menu changes nightly but always includes three to five courses. Fully licensed. Entrées $20–30.

Compass Rose (506-662-8570), 65 Rt. 776, North Head. Open June–Oct. for dinner (except Mon.). The harbor view is unbeatable, and even without it the dining room would strike you as unusually pleasant. Dinner might be seafood lasagna or pan-fried haddock; leave room for double chocolate cheesecake. Entrées $16–25.

Sailor's Landing (506-662-9620), 1 Ferry Wharf Rd., North Head. Open June–Oct. for breakfast (all day), lunch, and dinner, daily 6:30 AM–9 PM. Right there as you get off the ferry, an attractive place with local nautical decor. Full menu, featuring local seafood and homemade deserts.

McLaughlin's Wharf Inn (506-662-8760), 1863 Rt. 773, Seal Cove. Open July–Aug. A great waterside spot with a menu featuring fresh mussels steamed in garlic and butter and local fare like smoked salmon, scallops, and lobster.

EATING OUT ✍ Galloways Restaurant (506-662-8871), Rt. 776, North Head. A sports bar with plenty of room to get away from the bar, the obvious place for a burger and beer, also salads, fried seafood, a kids' menu.

North Head Bakery (506-662-8862), Rt. 776 south of the village. Open 6–6. Seasonal. Using organic flours, no bleach, this is a both a first and last stop for patrons: first stop in the morning for croissants and doughnuts (coffee is served); last stop when leaving the island, taking baguettes and breads home with them.

✳ Selective Shopping

Roland's Sea Vegetables (506-662-3866), 174 Hill Rd. (marked from the Dark Harbour Rd.), is a must-stop. Dulse and other seaweeds are hand harvested at Dark Harbour, then dried and packaged. We wish we had bought more bottles of dulse flakes.

Grand Manan Farmer's Market, 128 Rt. 776. Late June–mid-Sept., Sat. 10–noon. Showcasing local crafts and preserves as well as produce.

Western Mountains and Lakes Region

5

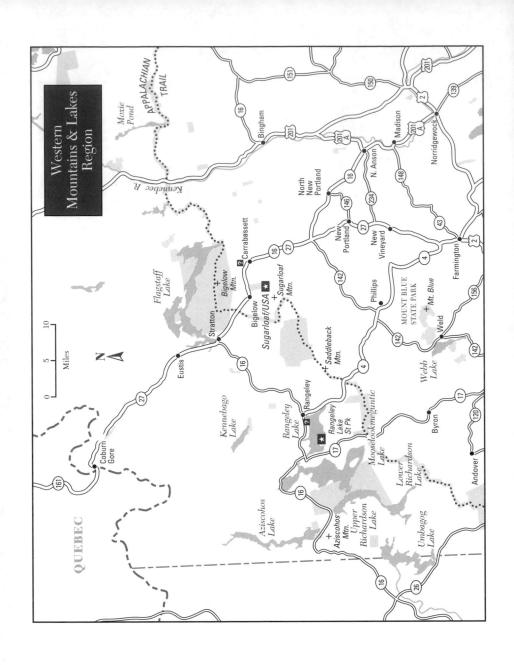

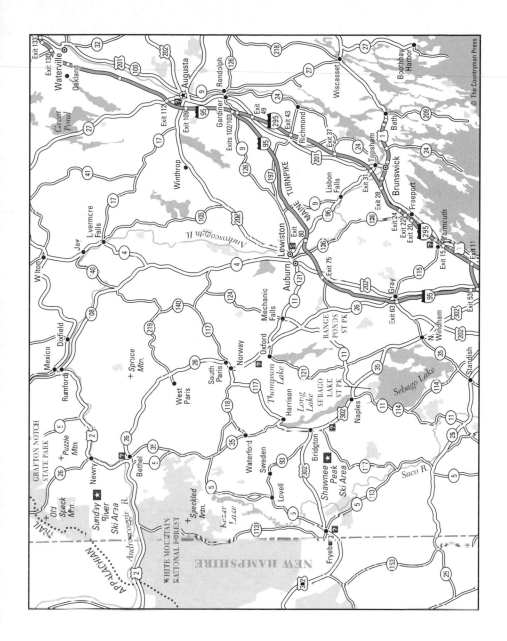

WESTERN MOUNTAINS
AND LAKES REGION

Inland Maine is the most underrated, least explored piece of New England, frequently perceived as an uninterrupted flat carpet of firs.

Larger than Vermont and New Hampshire combined, it is actually composed of several distinct and unique regions and distinguished by a series of almost continuous mountain ranges, more extensive than New Hampshire's White Mountains and higher than Vermont's Green Mountains, but lacking a name (why aren't they the Blue Mountains?).

In contrast with the coast, inland Maine was actually more of a resort area a century ago than it is today. By the 1880s trains connected Philadelphia, New York, and Boston with large resort hotels in Rangeley and Greenville, and steamboats ferried "sports" to "sporting camps" in the far corners of lakes. Many of these historic resorts survive but today require far more time to reach, unless you fly in.

Today inland Maine seems even larger than it is because almost a third of it lies beyond the public highway system, a phenomenon for which we can blame Massachusetts and its insistence that Maine sell off the "unorganized townships" (and divide the profits) before it would be permitted to secede in 1820. In the interim most of this land has been owned and managed by lumber and paper companies. Debate currently rages about the future of these woodlands (somewhere between a third and almost half of inland Maine); many environmental organizations would like to see a Maine North Woods National Park, but locals remain adamantly against such an initiative. The reality of the way public roads run—and don't run—continues to physically divide Maine's mountainous interior into several distinct pieces.

One of these pieces is the Western Mountains and Lakes Region, extending from the rural farmland surrounding the lakes of southwestern Maine, up through the Oxford Hills and into the foothills of the White Mountains and the Mahoosuc Range around Bethel, then on into the wilderness (as high and remote as any to be found in the North Woods) around the Rangeley Lakes and the Sugarloaf area—east of which public roads cease, forcing traffic bound for the Moosehead Lake region to detour south into the farmland of the Lower Kennebec Valley.

The five distinct areas within the Western Mountains and Lakes Region are connected by some of Maine's most scenic roads, with farmhouses, lakes, mountains, and unexpected villages around each bend. Many of these views are not generally appreciated because the area is best known to skiers, accustomed to racing up to Sunday River and Sugarloaf (Maine's most popular ski resorts) by the shortest routes from the interstate. They don't know what they're missing. The roads around Rangeley offer views so spectacular, stretches of two of them (Rts. 4 and 17) are a National Scenic Byway.

In summer and fall we suggest following Rt. 113 through Evans Notch or heading north from Bridgton to Bethel by the series of roads that threads woods and skirts lakes, heading east along Rt. 2, continuing north to Rangeley via Rt. 17 through Coos Canyon and over the spectacular Height o' Land from which you can see all five Rangeley Lakes and the surrounding mountains. From Rangeley it's just another 19 scenic miles on Rt. 16 (better known as Moose Alley) to the Sugarloaf area. You can return to Rt. 2 by continuing along Rt. 16 to Kingfield, then taking Rt. 142 through Phillips and Weld.

SEBAGO AND
LONG LAKES REGION

Fifty lakes can be seen from the summit of Pleasant Mountain, 10 within the town of Bridgton itself. These lakes are what draw summer visitors. They swim and fish, fish and swim. They cruise out in powerboats or paddle canoes and kayaks. On rainy days they browse through the area's abundant antiques and crafts stores. In winter visitors ski, downhill at Shawnee Peak (alias Pleasant Mountain) or cross-country almost anywhere.

Before the Civil War visitors could actually come by boat all the way to Bridgton from Boston. From Portland, they would ride 20 miles through 28 locks on the Cumberland & Oxford Canal, then across Sebago Lake, up the Songo River, Brandy Pond, and Long Lake to Bridgton. The first hotel atop Pleasant Mountain opened in 1850, and in 1882 the "2-footer" narrow gauge opened between Hiram and Bridgton, enabling summer visitors to come by train as well.

Today, as in the 1880s, most visitors waste little time getting onto or into water. The Naples Causeway is the base for water sports, and the departure point for cruises on Long Lake and through the only surviving canal lock. Sebago, Maine's second largest lake, is its most popular waterskiing area.

This southwestern corner of the state offers plenty on land, too: hiking, golf, tennis, mineral collecting, and such fascinating historic sights as Willowbrook in Newfield.

Fryeburg, just west of the lakes in the Saco River Valley, is the region's oldest community and the site of the state's largest agricultural fair. It is also headquarters for canoeing the Saco River. Sandy bottomed and clear, the Saco meanders for more than 40 miles through woods and fields, rarely passing a house. Too shallow for powerboats, it is perfect for canoes and

THE LIMINGTON RAPIDS

Nancy English

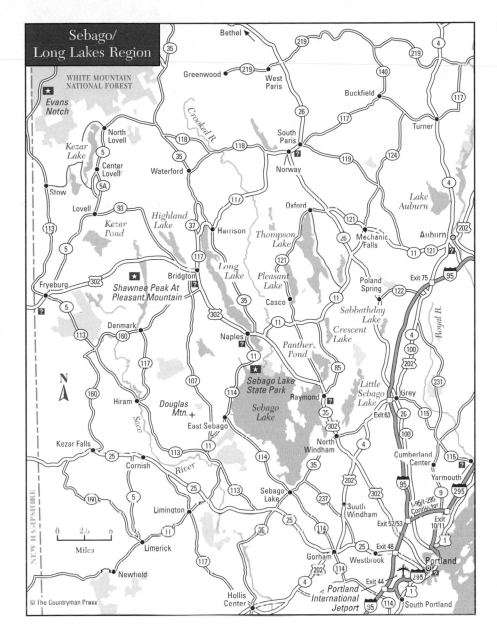

Sebago/Long Lakes Region

Bethel
219
4
219
140
Greenwood
219
West Paris
Buckfield
117
WHITE MOUNTAIN
NATIONAL FOREST
26
117
Turner
★ Evans Notch
South Paris
124
118
118
119
Crooked R.
North Lovell
Kezar Lake
5
Center Lovell
Waterford
Norway
Lake Auburn
5A
Stow
Oxford
4
Lovell
93
Highland Lake
Thompson Lake
121
Auburn
202
113
Kezar Pond
37
Harrison
121
26
Mechanic Falls
5
117
Long Lake
Pleasant Lake
Poland Spring
Exit 75
95
Fryeburg
302
Bridgton
Casco
122
Royal R.
★ Shawnee Peak At Pleasant Mountain
35
11
Sabbathday Lake
4
5
302
Crescent Lake
100
Denmark
160
Naples
11
Panther Pond
202
N
117
107
Sebago Lake State Park
85
231
Hiram
114
Raymond
Little Sebago Lake
Grey
Douglas Mtn.
Sebago Lake
35
Exit 63
26
115
East Sebago
302
100
Kezar Falls
113
11
North Windham
4
Cumberland Center
115
25
114
Yarmouth
Cornish
River
113
35
9
295
5
Sebago Lake
202
95
Limington
237
South Windham
Exit 52/53
Exit 10/11
11
25
114
Exit 48
1
Limerick
25
Gorham
Westbrook
Portland
117
202
114
Newfield
4
Portland International Jetport
295
1
Hollis Center
95
114
South Portland

Miles
© The Countryman Press

kayaks. There is usually just enough current to nudge along the limpest paddler, and the ubiquitous sandbars serve as gentle bumpers. Tenting is permitted most places along the river, and there are public campgrounds. Outfitters rent canoes and provide shuttle service.

In summer most families come for a week to stay in lakeside cottages—of which there seem to be thousands. Motels, inns, and B&Bs still fill on weekends with parents visiting their children at camps—of which there seem to be hundreds. As more travelers discover the beauty and tranquility of the region, the number of these types of lodgings, while nowhere near the glut of such establishments along the coast, is expanding every year.

GUIDANCE Greater Bridgton Lakes Region Chamber of Commerce (207-647-3472; mainelakeschamber.com), 101 Portland Rd. (Rt. 302), Box 236, Bridgton 04009. The chamber maintains a walk-in information center. Request a copy of the *Greater Bridgton–Lakes Region Area Guide*.

Sebago Lakes Region Chamber of Commerce (207-892-8265; sebagolakes chamber.com), 747 Roosevelt Trail (Rt. 302), Windham 04062, is open year-round (call for hours) and a seasonal information bureau next to the Naples Village Green on Rt. 302. It also publishes a information guide that covers the towns of Casco, Gray, Naples, Raymond, Sebago, Standish, Limerick, Limington, New Gloucester, and Windham.

Cornish Association of Businesses (207-625-8083; cornish-maine.org), P.O. Box 573, Cornish 04020. The website lists lodging, dining, shopping, and events, and relates the history of the town.

Fryeburg Information Center (207-935-3639; mainetourism.com), Rt. 302, Fryeburg 04037. The Maine Tourism Association staffs this spacious facility with AC and restrooms 500 feet from the New Hampshire line. Information on the entire state, with directions to every destination.

GETTING THERE *By air:* The **Portland International Jetport** is a 30- to 60-minute drive from most points in this area. Rental cars are available at the airport. (See "Portland.")

By bus and train: **Concord Coach Lines** (207-828-1151 or 1-800-639-3317) bus lines and **Amtrak's Downeaster** (1-800-USA-RAIL) serve the Portland area at its rail–bus station on Congress St. in Portland.

By car: From New York and Boston, take I-95 to the Westbrook exit (exit 48), then Rt. 302 to the lakes region. For Newfield and south of Sebago area, take Rt. 25 from I-95 at Westbrook (exit 48).

WHEN TO COME With some inns and B&Bs open year-round and good cross-country skiing available, this can be a place for a winter retreat. Ice fishing is another winter pastime some people love. Still, the big time here is summer.

✳ Villages

Bridgton has a plethora of antiques shops, including two country auction houses, making it a good way stop for browsers. Take time for a lovely hike on the trails newly developed inside Pondicherry Park (described under *Green Space*).

Cornish. The colonial and Victorian homes lining Main and Maple Sts. were moved here by teams of about 80 oxen in the 1850s after the arrival of a new stagecoach route. It's halfway between Portland and the Mount Washington Valley in New Hampshire.

Fryeburg is an interesting town that sees its share of traffic as travelers pass through en route to North Conway, New Hampshire, and the White Mountains. The traffic clog during the Fryeburg Fair (Maine's largest, most popular agricultural fair) can back up for more than an hour. The village is small and unassuming, with a smattering of historic homes (some now inns). Canoe trips down the Saco originate here.

✳ To See

MUSEUMS 19th Century Willowbrook Village (207-793-2784; willowbrook museum.org), off Rt. 11, Newfield. Open Memorial Day–Columbus Day, Thu.–Mon. 10–5. Admission $9 adults, $7.50 seniors, $4 students 6–18. Devastated by fire in 1947, the village was almost a ghost town when Donald King began buying buildings in the 1960s. The complex now includes 20 buildings displaying more than 10,000 items: horse-drawn vehicles, tools, toys, a vintage-1894 carousel, and many other artifacts of late-19th-century life. Linger in the ballroom, ring the schoolhouse bell, or picnic in the area provided. One Saturday each month ride the antique carousel.

Rufus Porter Museum (207-647-2828; rufusportermuseum.org), 67 N. High St. (Rt. 302), Bridgton. Open mid-June–mid-Oct.; call for hours. $5 adults, $4 seniors, 15 and under free. Dedicated to Rufus Porter, a multi-talented man, this house contains his 1828 original murals, an icon of folk art. Porter founded the *Scientific American* magazine and invented the Colt revolver; he patented a churn, corn sheller, fire alarm, and cheese press, among many other inventions; and in his spare time he painted murals in homes all over New England. A signed set of murals from Westwood, Massachusetts, is on display at the historic Wales and Hamblen building, renovated in 2007, 260 Main St., Bridgton. The museum will move to a new downtown location once a fund-raising campaign is successful; call or visit the website to for up-to-date information.

HISTORIC BUILDINGS AND MUSEUMS Daniel Marrett House (207-882-7169; historicnewengland.org), Rt. 25, Standish. Tours on the first and third Sat. of the month beginning at 11, June–mid-Oct. Admission $5. Money from Portland banks was stored in this Georgian mansion for safekeeping during the War of 1812. Built in 1789, it remained in the Marrett family until 1944; architecture and furnishings reflect the changing styles over 150 years. The formal perennial garden blooms throughout the growing season and is always open for a visit.

Narramissic (207-647-9954, summer only), Ingalls Rd. (2 miles south of the junction of Rts. 107 and 117), Bridgton. Open late June–Labor Day. Donation suggested. A Federal-period home and a Temperance Barn in a rural setting, this interesting site includes a working blacksmith shop and is the scene of frequent special events; check with the **Bridgton Historical Society Museum** (207-647-3699; bridgton history.org), Gibbs Ave., which also maintains a former fire station built in

DANIEL MARRETT HOUSE AND GARDEN, STANDISH

Nancy English

1902. The collection (open July and Aug., call for hours) includes slide images of the old narrow-gauge railroad.

Naples Historical Society Museum (207-693-4297), village green, Rt. 302, Naples. Open summer weekends and by chance. The brick complex includes a rooftop brake coach and great memorabilia on the Cumberland & Oxford Canal, photos of and information on the Sebago and Long Lake steamboats and the Songo Locks, and artifacts from vanished hotels, like the Bay of Naples Hotel.

Hopalong Cassidy in the Fryeburg Public Library (207-935-2731), 98 Main St., Fryeburg. Open Mon. Thu. 8–5, Sat. 9–noon. The library is housed in an 1832 stone schoolhouse and is decorated with many paintings by local artists. It also contains a collection of books, guns, and other memorabilia belonging to Clarence Mulford, creator of Hopalong Cassidy. The **Fryeburg Historical Society** (207-697-2044), 511 Main St., has a museum in the village and a research library in North Fryeburg on Rt. 113, open Wed. and Fri. 9–noon, Thu. 1–4.

Harrison Historical Society and Museum (207-583-2213), 121 Haskell Hill Rd., Harrison. Open July and Aug., Wed. 1–4 and by appointment; May–Dec., open the first Wed. of the month at 7 PM. The public is welcome at this small museum full of artifacts, cemetery records, town histories, and news clipping scrapbooks.

Raymond-Casco Historical Museum (207-655-8668; raymondcascohistory.org), Rt. 302, Casco. Open Memorial Day–Columbus Day, free. Exhibits of Victoriana, carriages, and old photographs are a few of the sights in the simple red building with a 60-foot mural on its side depicting 1800s summer visitors arriving on the Sebago Lake steamer and the Concord Coach—which was a horse-drawn covered carriage long before it was a bus.

OTHER HISTORIC SITES Songo Locks, Naples (2.5 miles off Rt. 302). Open May–Oct. Dating to 1830, the last of the 27 hand-operated locks that once allowed people to come by boat from Portland to Harrison still enable you to travel some 40 watery miles. Boat traffic is constant in summer.

✳ To Do

AIRPLANE TOURS North Country Scenic Rides (207-356-9924; north countryscenicrides.com), Naples Causeway. Floatplane rides for 15- or 30-minute tours of the area.

APPLE PICKING Five Fields Farm (fivefieldsski.com), 720 S. Bridgton Rd. (Rt. 107), South Bridgton. Fresh cider and seven varieties of apples for picking, with pumpkins for sale. In winter, cross-country ski trails lace through the 450 acres.

Apple Acres Farm (207-625-4777; appleacresfarm.com), 363 Durgintown Rd., South Hiram. Pick your own and check out the farm store at this pretty orchard near Cornish Village. Pumpkins, fresh cider, fudge, and more—like their own invention, Apple Crackle, fruit brittle that is simply delicious.

Douglas Mountain Orchard (207-787-2745), 42 Orchard Rd., Sebago. Apples, pears, and pumpkins.

And see Dole's Orchard and Libby U-Pick, below.

Nancy English

HARVEST AT APPLE ACRES FARM, CORNISH

BLUEBERRY (AND MORE) PICKING Crabtree's Pick-Your-Own Highbush Blueberries (207-787-2730; crabcoll.com), 703 Bridgton Rd., Rt. 107, Sebago. The multiple varieties of blueberries here make the picking season long—mid-July to the first frost, which can be as late as Oct. 15.

Dole's Orchard (207-793-4409; doles orchard.com), 187 Doles Ridge Rd., Limington. Blueberries, strawberries, raspberries, tart cherries, apples, plums, and peaches are pick-your-own. Call first to learn what's ripe and available. Fall hayrides and live music.

Libby & Son U-Picks (207-793-4749; libbysonupicks.com), Limerick. This popular inland spot for highbush blueberry picking grows more than 7,500 bushes. Even so, call in advance to make sure it's not closed for a day to let more berries ripen. In fall the apple orchard opens for picking, and there's berry picking into Oct. Freshly pressed cider and pumpkins, too.

BIKE RENTALS Wheelie Good Bike Rentals (207-318-4660; wheeliegoodbike rental.com). Sean Hegarty delivers rental bicycles within an hour's drive of Portland, seven days a week.

BOAT EXCURSIONS ✎ ♿ *Songo River Queen II* (207-693-6861), Naples Causeway. Operates daily July–Labor Day; reduced schedule in spring and fall. The *Queen* is a replica of a Mississippi River stern paddle wheeler, with accommodations for 300 passengers, a snack and cocktail bar, and restrooms. As of in 2012 she no longer travels through the last lock from the 1830 canal. Still, one-hour Long Lake cruises and moonlight charters remain popular during good weather.

BOAT RENTALS Available regionwide. Inquire at local chambers. (Also see *Canoeing and Kayaking*.)

THE *SONGO RIVER QUEEN II*

CANOEING AND KAYAKING **Saco River Canoe and Kayak** (207-935-2369; sacorivercanoe.com), 1009 Main St. (Rt. 5), Fryeburg (across from the access at Swan's Falls). Fred Westerberg, a Registered Maine Guide, runs Saco River Canoe and Kayak with the help of his wife, Prudy, and daughters, Beth and Chris. They offer shuttle service and canoe and kayak rentals, which come with a map and careful instructions geared to the day's river conditions.

Saco Bound (603-447-2177; sacobound.com), Rt. 302, Center Conway, New Hampshire (just over the state line, west of Fryeburg). The largest canoe outfitter around. With its sister company Northern Waters, Saco Bound offers rentals, guided day trips and whitewater canoeing on the Androscoggin River in summer, a campground at Canal Bridge in Fryeburg, and a shuttle service. Its base is a big glass-faced store stocked with kayaks and canoes, trail food and lip balm.

Sebago Kayak Company (207-935-4763; sebagokayakcompany.com), Naples Causeway. Canoes and kayaks rented by the day or week, with free delivery for multiday rentals.

Sportshaus (207-647-3000), 103 Main St., Bridgton, rents canoes and kayaks by the day or week.

Woodland Acres (207-935-2529; woodlandacres.com), Rt. 160, Brownfield. Full-facility camping, canoe rentals, and a shuttle service.

River Run (207-452-2500; riverruncanoe.com), P.O. Box 190, Brownfield. Canoe rentals, a shuttle, and parking Memorial Day–Labor Day weekends. They also have camping—see *Lodging*.

FISHING Licenses are available at town offices and online at mefishwildlife.com; check marinas for information. Salmon, lake trout, pickerel, and bass abound.

GOLF AND TENNIS **Bridgton Highlands Country Club** (207-647-3491; bridgtonhighlands.com), Highland Rd., Bridgton, has an 18-hole course, snack bar, carts, a resident golf pro, and tennis courts. Also 18-hole **Lake Kezar Country Club** (207-925-2462; lakekezargolf.com), Rt. 5, Lovell; and 18-hole **Naples Golf and Country Club** (207-693-6424; naplesgolfcourse.com), Rt. 114, Naples.

Point Sebago Golf Resort (1-800-530-1555; pointsebago.com), 261 Point Sebago Rd., Casco. This 18-hole, par-72 course on 500 acres of white birch forest was judged southern Maine's top course in *Golf Digest*, May 2003.

HIKING **Douglas Mountain**, Sebago. A Nature Conservancy preserve with great views of Sebago and the White Mountains. The trail to the top is a 20-minute walk, and there's a 0.75-mile nature trail at the summit; also a stone tower with an observation platform. Take Rt. 107 south from the town of Sebago and turn right on Douglas Mountain Rd.; go to the end of the road to find limited parking.

Pleasant Mountain, Bridgton. Several summits and interconnecting trails, the most popular of which is the Firewarden's Trail to the main summit: a relatively easy 2.5-mile climb from base to peak through rocky woods.

✒ **Jockey Cap**, Rt. 302, Fryeburg. Starts near the Jockey Cap Country Store and Motel under a small arch. A 15-minute climb up the path (steep near the top) accesses a bald, garnet-studded summit with a sweeping view of the White Mountains to the west, lesser peaks and lakes to the east and south, all ingeniously iden-

Nancy English

SEBAGO LAKE STATE PARK

tified on a circular bronze monument designed by Arctic explorer Admiral Peary.

HORSEBACK RIDING Secret Acres Stables (207-693-3441; secret acresstables.com), 185 Lambs Mill Rd. (1 mile off Rt. 302), Naples, offers trail rides and lessons.

☙ **Carousel Horse Farm** (207-627-4471; maine-horse-vacation.com), 69 Leach Hill Rd., Casco. Takes beginning through advanced riders on trail rides with views of lakes and the White Mountains.

MINI GOLF ☙ **Steamboat Landing** (207-693-6782; steamboatlanding minigolf.com), Rt. 114, Naples (0.25 mile off the causeway). Open daily Memorial Day weekend–Labor Day, 10–10. A lovely 18-hole course with a Maine theme in a wooded setting. Ice cream parlor with Gifford's ice cream, and game room for pinball and family-oriented video games.

☙ **Seacoast Fun Park** (207-892-5952; seacoastfunparks.com), Rt. 302, Windham. Open May–Oct. Elaborate mini golf, go-carts, bumper boats, arcade, hillside tubing, Ferris wheel, disk golf, trampoline, 32-foot rock climbing wall, and a 100-foot-plunge sky swing.

SAILING Sportshaus (in winter, 207-647-3000; in summer, 207-647-9528), 103 Main St., Bridgton, rents Sunfish and Rhumbas by the week.

SWIMMING ☙ **Sebago Lake State Park** (Memorial Day–Labor Day, 207-693-6613; otherwise, 207-693-6231; maine.gov), off Rt. 302 (between Naples and South Casco). A great family beach with picnic tables, grills, boat ramp, lifeguards, and bathhouses. Day use only; there is a separate camping area (see *Lodging*). No pets. **Tassel Top Beach**, just off Rt. 302 on Sebago Lake, is run by the town of Raymond. Picnic tables, 900 feet of sandy beach, nature trail, and roped-off swim area. Changing rooms but no lifeguards. The town of Bridgton maintains a tidy little beach on **Long Lake** just off Main St., another on **Woods Pond** (Rt. 117), and another on **Highland Lake**. The town of Fryeburg maintains a beach, with float, on the **Saco River**, and **Casco** maintains a small, inviting beach in its picturesque village.

✷ Winter Sports

CROSS-COUNTRY SKIING ☙ **Five Fields Farm X-C Ski Center** (207-647-2425; fivefieldsski.com), Rt. 107, 6 miles south of Bridgton. Open daily 9 AM–dusk. Trails loop around the 70-acre working apple orchard and connect to logging roads. You can snowshoe to the top of Bald Pate Mountain for spectacular views. Full- and half-day rates, rentals, warming hut. Mushers' Bowl, a dogsled race with 70 teams, is held here every year.

Sebago Lake State Park (207-693-6231), off Rt. 302 (between Naples and South Casco). Six miles of groomed trails open to the public, $1.50 per person, pay on the honor system at a trail "iron ranger."

DOWNHILL SKIING *⚡* **Shawnee Peak** (207-647-8444; shawneepeak.com), Rt. 302, Bridgton. An isolated 1,900-foot hump, 6 miles west of the center of town. Maine's oldest ski area has a vertical drop of 1,300 feet and offers 40 trails with 98 percent snowmaking capacity, a double, two triples, and a quad lift, plus a surface lift. Open until 9 PM (until 10 Fri. and Sat.), and night skiing is big here. Glades and freestyle terrain park. Ski and snowboard instruction, rentals, child care, and base lodge with pub. Rooms in a variety of lodging options include 10 with private bath in a comfortable self-service guesthouse that start at $79 per room weekdays.

Sportshaus (207-647-5100; sportshausski.com), rental facility on Rt. 302, also at 103 Main St., Bridgton, rents skis, snowshoes, and snowboards by the day or week.

✳ Green Space

Pondicherry Park (207-647-4352; lelt.org) is a 66-acre park that surrounds Bridgton, with 5 miles of trails that loop through the woods. Loon Echo Land Trust is in charge, with plans for a covered pedestrian bridge to access the parkland from downtown Bridgton. No pets, no bikes.

The **Lakes Environmental Association** (LEA; 207-647-8580; mainelakes.org), 102 Main St., Bridgton, has been working since 1970 to preserve the clear, unsullied lakes in western Maine from development, invasive species such as milfoil, and overuse. Trails and a boardwalk lead through the *⚡* **Holt Pond Preserve**, a watershed with a bog, a river, and other wetlands, and a boardwalk over a quaking bog full of sphagnum moss and orchids. The **Stevens Brook Trail** follows the water body from Highland Lake to Long Lake. Tour the LEA's **Harry & Eunice Bradley Lake Center**, 230 Main St., Bridgton, to see the water-testing lab, buffer gardens, and educational displays.

Sebago Lake Land Reserve (207-523-5421; pwd.org), Sebago Lake Ecology Center at Rts. 237 and 35, Standish. Wetlands, lakeside trails, and forests account for 1,700 acres under protection in this reserve. Sign in at any of 11 visitors permit kiosks at trailheads. The Ecology Center offers free lake maps that explain permitted uses; swimming is not allowed anywhere in the 2-mile shorefront of this reserve except one spot—where there is no fence. Camping, campfires, ATVs, and motorcycles are not allowed on the land of this watershed, which supplies Greater Portland with clean water.

Mountain Division Trail (mountaindivisiontrail.org) is a rail-trail under development. The Windham–Gorham–Standish section is completed from Rt. 202 in South Windham to Otter Ponds in Standish, with a 1-mile, unpaved section from Otter Ponds to Johnson Field on Rt. 35 in Standish, where you can park. On the other end, 1.5 miles of trail starts at the Fryeburg Visitors Center on Rt. 302 by the state line and heads to Portler Rd., south of town on Rt. 113, with parking at both ends and views of Burnt Meadow Mountains and the White Mountains.

In late 2012 another 2.5 miles will open between Porter Rd. and the access road to the Eastern Slope airport. Eventually the trail will connect Fryeburg with Portland.

Kezar Falls, reached from Lovell Rd. off Rt. 35, is a small, pretty waterfall on the Kezar River.

The Wilson Wing Moose Pond Frog Preserve, formerly Sucker Brook Preserve, has 0.5-mile signed, interpretive trails, one for both adults and children, and is part of the **Greater Lovell Land Trust** (207-925-1056; gllt.org), 208 Main St., Center Lovell. A view platform looks over the bog; and an evening program in March uses the platform to call owls—which usually respond. **The Heald Pond Preserve** and **Bradley Pond Reserve** total 801 acres in Lovell, with 7 miles of trails. The **Kezar Outlet Fen** in Lovell, a 250-acre wetland perfect for eagle-watching, has no vehicle access. Access by canoeing or kayaking. Trail maps are easy to download from the website.

✳ Lodging

RUSTIC RESORTS The Western Lakes area offers unusual old resort complexes, each with cabin accommodations, dining, and relaxing space in a central, distinctively Maine lodge. In contrast with similar complexes found farther north, these are all geared to families or to those who vacation here for reasons other than hunting and fishing.

✐ ♿ **Migis Lodge** (207-655-4524; migis.com), off Rt. 302, P.O. Box 40, South Casco 04077. Open early June–Columbus Day weekend. This classic Maine lakeside resort takes excellent care of its guests, tucking them under hand-sewn quilts at night, next to fully tiled baths, with arrival-day fresh flowers. A comforting fire burns constantly in the Main Lodge, fed from fences of stacked firewood that frame the pathways. Deluxe accommodations include six rooms in the two-story Main Lodge and 35 cottages with names like Skylark and Tamarack scattered throughout the pines on 125 acres. All cottages have a fireplace, with daily wood deliveries (and ice for the ice bucket). A private beach, tennis, lawn games, waterskiing, sailboats, canoes, and boat excursions while away the days. Because children

5 and under aren't allowed in the dining room during high season, they eat in a family dining room, and are offered supervised dining and playtime 5:55–8:30 PM; older children are welcome to join in. $215–385 per adult per night (cottages) includes three meals. $425 per adult in the lodge rooms. Children's rates available; 15 percent service charge. In-room massage and yoga, too.

✐ **Quisisana** (207-925-3500; off-season 914-833-0293; quisisanaresort.com), Lake Kezar, Center Lovell 04016. Mid-June–Aug. One-week minimum stay in high season. Guests and staff alike are passionate about this unique lodging, founded in 1917 as a place for music lovers to relax in the pines by one of Maine's clearest lakes. Each evening staff, many from music conservatories, perform in the lakeside hall, including perhaps the tenor who is the longtime business manager. But this lakeside refuge is a destination for everyone who loves to relax. The 75 guest quarters in one- to three-room pine-paneled cottages (some with fireplace) are scattered through the woods or near the soft beach. The lack of phone or TV in the cabins means more time for water-skiing, boating, fishing, croquet, tennis, and swimming. The white-frame central lodge includes a homey sitting room, a bar with tables on a deck, and the dining room, where lobster night and side dishes of local produce create alluring meals. $170–235 per person double occupancy includes all meals.

BED & BREAKFASTS

✪ ♂ ✎ **Noble House Inn** (207-647-3733 or 1-888-237-4880; noblehouse inn.com), 81 Highland Rd., Bridgton 04009. Open year-round. Rick and Julie Whelchel are innkeepers worth seeking out at this former senator's manor. Nine guest rooms (all with private bath) are divided between the original house and the former ell, with luxurious linens and beds in each one. The Highland Suite holds a sitting room and bed with matching painted headboard and dresser, perfect for a long stay. Most rooms in the ell open on a tranquil, private deck overlooking the flowers and lawn. The inn is across the street from a beach. Shawnee Peak stay-and-ski packages take care of winter. $135–265 double includes breakfast and use of the canoe or snowshoes, along with access to the bottomless cookie jar. Organic bread is baked

NOBLE HOUSE INN

Nancy English

fresh every morning, as is anything else served from this kitchen.

✪ ✎ **Center Lovell Inn** (207-925-1575 or 1-800-777-2698; centerlovell inn.com), Rt. 5, Center Lovell 04016. Open year-round. Innkeeper Janice Sage runs this striking old inn with a cupola and busy restaurant in-season (see *Dining Out*). The inn features four guest rooms on the second floor (the two with shared bath can be a suite), nicely furnished with antiques and art. In the 1835 Harmon House there are five cozy rooms, three with private bath. $95–245 with no meals; breakfast and dinner additional.

✎ **Oxford House Inn** (207-935-3442 or 1-800-261-7206; oxfordhouseinn .com), 548 Main St., Fryeburg 04037. Open year-round, but call first. Jonathan Spak and Natalie Knickerbocker Spak are in charge of this gracious 1913 house in the middle of Fryeburg, with its idyllic view across corn and potato fields and the placid Saco River to the White Mountains in New Hampshire. Four rooms are large, three with in-room sinks. The Porch Room, with a glassed-in porch, has a two-person air tub. Tile-floored baths, DVDs. $109–179 includes breakfast, perhaps butternut squash bread French toast, or crêpes, with a choice of six or seven entrée items, and coffee from friends who know South America.

✎ **Main Street Bed & Breakfast** (207-935-7171; mainstbandb.com), Fryeburg 04037. Margaret Cugini has transformed this 1820 farmhouse in the heart of Fryeburg into a stunning and luxurious B&B, with the original woodwork, pumpkin pine floors in the hallway, and oak balustrade. The inn's five guest rooms, three with immaculately tiled private bath, one with a 6-foot Jacuzzi, are furnished with antiques, updated beds, and lovely linens. Guests have use of a sitting room with a TV/DVD and shelves with books to choose from. Full breakfast and afternoon tea included. $109–219.

Admiral Peary House (207-935-3365 or 1-877-423-6779; admiralpearyhouse .com), 27 Elm St., Fryeburg 04037. Named for Robert E. Peary, Maine's famed Arctic explorer, this house holds seven well-appointed rooms named for Peary's partners, family, and others; each has a private bath and air-conditioning, three have a gas fire-place, and one has a whirlpool. Innkeepers Hilary Jones and Derrek Schlottmann, who brews his own bit-ter, can offer copious details about the area. Common space includes two spa-cious living rooms and an enclosed porch overlooking 2 acres of lawn and woods. $129–199 in-season includes a full breakfast, perhaps with oat scones; $119–159 off-season.

🐾 ♂ ✆ ♿ **Sebago Lake Lodge** (207-892-2698; sebagolakelodge.com), White's Bridge Rd., P.O. Box 110, North Windham 04062. A homey white inn opened in the mid-1980s, set on a narrows between Jordan Bay and the Basin, seemingly surrounded by water. Eight units have kitchenettes, and four standard rooms have kitchen privileges. There are also 12 cottages. An inviting beach, picnic tables, and grills; fishing boats, kayaks, canoes, and motorboat rentals. Pets are allowed in cottages rented by the week. $68 for a room in high season, $160–185 in the main lodge, continental breakfast.

✆ **The Inn at Long Lake** (207-693-6226 or 1-800-437-0328; innatlonglake .com), Lake House Rd., P.O. Box 806, Naples 04055. Innkeeper Keith Neu-bert offers 16 rooms, all named for stars and great musicians of the 1900s, and his skills as a chef at breakfast, which might be cinnamon bread French toast. The tall clapboard build-ing is just a block from the lake. Rooms include two suites, most with queen beds, all with private bath and AC, and a few with lake views. $110–200 with breakfast. Wine, beer, and cocktails are offered, to guests only.

Greenwood Manor Inn (207-583-4445; greenwoodmanorinn.com), 52 Tolman Rd., Harrison 04040. Open year-round. A former carriage house on 108 hillside acres sloping down to Long Lake, the inn features seven guest rooms and two suites, some with a gas log fireplace, some with whirlpool tub, and all with private bath. The dining and living areas over-look a landscaped garden. $140–245 in-season includes a full breakfast. *Note:* Although this B&B is technically in Harrison, much of its property lies in the town of Bridgton, and it is thus much closer to the Sebago/Long Lakes area than to the Oxford Hills; as a result, we're listing it in both chapters.

✆ **The Olde Saco Inn** (207-925-3737; theoldesacoinn.com), Fryeburg. Set in a grove of tall pines, along the quiet meandering Old Saco River, this secluded inn holds seven rooms and one suite, including two rooms that can link to a bunk room for children. A billiard table and trails for snowshoeing and cross-country skiing along with hiking trails on the 65-acre property could fill your days. Kayaks and canoes available for guests. Rates $85–169, include a full breakfast.

MOTELS ♣ **The Midway Country Lodging** (207-625-8835; maine midwaylodging.com), Rt. 25, Cornish. Clean rooms, views of the mountain, a TV, mini fridge and microwave, out-door pool, gardens, and deluxe room with (heart-shaped) whirlpool all at reasonable and low rates, add up to a find off the beaten track in western Maine. Rates $64–99.

🐾 ✂ ♿ **Jockey Cap Motel and Country Store** (207-935-2306), 116 Bridgton Rd., Fryeburg 04037. Open year-round. Located at the trailhead for Jockey Cap Mountain, this simple place is run by Allyson and Robert Quinn. Four rooms hold two doubles, and three have queens; all have private bath with tub and shower, air-conditioning, cable TV. $69–79.

COTTAGES The **Greater Bridgton Lakes Region Chamber of Commerce** (see *Guidance*) publishes a list of rental cottages, and many in this area are listed in the *Maine Guide to Inns and Bed & Breakfasts and Camps & Cottages*, free from the Maine Tourism Association (207-623-0363; mainetourism.com) and also easily browsed online.

OTHER LODGING 🐾 ✂ ♿ **Point Sebago Resort** (207-655-3821 or 1-800-655-1232; pointsebago.com), 261 Point Sebago Rd., Casco 04015. Open May–Oct. One hundred sites for RV hookups on a 775-acre lakeside site, plus hundreds of small, manufactured "park homes" for rent, some with linens and others empty, requiring you to stock the basics. Everyone has access to the beach, marina, pavilion, children's activities, excursion boats, soccer and softball fields, horseshoe pitches, 18-hole championship golf course, 10 tennis courts, video-game arcade, general store, and combination restaurant/nightclub, with DJs and teen dances. $200–250 for a park house per night.

CAMPGROUNDS See *Canoeing and Kayaking* for information about camping along the Saco River. In addition, the Appalachian Mountain Club maintains a campground at Swan's Falls. The Maine Camping Guide, available from the **Maine Campground Own-**

ers Association (207-782-5874; camp maine.com), 655 Main St., Lewiston 04240, lists private campgrounds in the area.

🦌 ✂ **Sebago Lake State Park** (Memorial Day–Labor Day, 207-693-6613; otherwise, 207-693-6231), off Rt. 302 (between Naples and South Casco). Open through Oct. 15. Visitors return year after year to these 1,300 thickly wooded acres on the northern shore of the lake, so make your reservations early if you want a good site. The camping area (with 250 campsites, many on the water) comes with its own beach, hot showers, a program of evening presentations such as outdoor movies, and nature hikes. For reservations, call 1-800-332-1501, or 207-624-9950 from outside the state. Go to campwithme.com to make reservations online. Ninety-five sites have water and electricity.

River Run (207-452-2500; riverrun canoe.com), Denmark Rd., P.O. Box 190, Brownfield 04010. Memorial Day–Labor Day, camp on more than 100 acres, with sites in the woods and along the Saco River. Amenities include public phone, group tenting area, swimming beaches, fire rings, picnic tables, and firewood and ice for purchase. $10 per person per night.

THE JOCKEY CAP, A CLEAN, SPRUCED-UP MOTEL

Nancy English

✳ Where to Eat

DINING OUT Oxford House Inn
(207-935-3442; oxfordhouseinn.com),
105 Main St., Fryeburg. Open for dinner Wed.–Mon. summer and fall; end
of Oct.–May, open Thu.–Sun. Reservations suggested. The most romantic
spot in western Maine when you sit in
the dining room's back porch, with
sunsets and wildlife sightings of an
albino woodchuck and passing deer.
The CIA-graduate chef Jonathan Spak
worked at The Water Club in New
York City and elsewhere in the United
States, and according to his wife and
business partner really loves what he
does. Sherman's Farm Stand is responsible for a lot of the sides in season;
seared Pekin Duck, a Long Island variety, seared scallops served with squash,
sage, and bacon risotto, and pumpkin
ravioli were on a fall menu. Entrées
$22–31.

Center Lovell Inn (207-925-1575),
Rt. 5, Center Lovell. Open for dinner
daily in summer; on weekends in winter, but daily again during holiday
weeks. Closed Nov.–mid-Dec. and
Apr.–mid-May. Call for reservations.
Specialties include a wild mushroom
crostini appetizer, and entrées like
seafood Norfolk—shrimp, scallops,
crabmeat, and lobster sautéed with
garlic and brandy. Bison from Beech
Hill Bison Farm in Waterford is served
occasionally, and there is always a fish
special. The rack of lamb with port
reduction was perfect. Entrées $23–32.

❂ Krista's (207-625-3600; kristas
restaurant.com), 2 Main St., Cornish.
Open Thu. 11:30–8, Fri. 11:30–9, Sat.
7 AM–9 PM, Sun. 7–8, different off-
season. The portions at dinner are
simply incredible—unless you are conducting a survey, one entrée will do
the trick. Prime rib, pork chops, seared
shrimp, and scallops all come with a
small salad, great mashed or other

potatoes, and generous amounts of
vegetables. Breakfast is all homemade,
with muffins and scones, and perhaps
Nutella-stuffed French toast, plus
elaborate fruit plates in-season.
Entrées $6–24.

❂ Ebenezer's Restaurant & Pub
(207-925-3200; ebenezerspub.net), 44
Allen Rd. Lovell. Thirty-five beers on
tap and more than 1,000 bottled beers
from an incredible cellar make this a
destination pub for the beer afi-
cionado—according to *Beer Advocate
Magazine*, it the best beer bar in
America. Burgers, one with Stilton garlic cream cheese, cheese steak, battered and fried cod in a sandwich, or
fish-and-chips—the frites are made
here—make it a destination for hungry
folks anywhere. The "sausage fest"
comes with house IPA mustard.

Venezia Ristorante (207-647-5333),
Bridgton Corners, Rts. 302 and 93,
Bridgton. Open for dinner Tue.–Sun.
5–9 in summer, Wed.–Sun. in winter.
Dependable, moderately priced Italian
dishes.

Olde Mill Tavern (207-583-9077;
oldemilltavern.com), 56 Main St., Harrison. Open daily at 4 for dinner year-
round. From prime rib to steak tips,
the meat eater will be well served.
Baked fish and seafood casserole, Mexican dishes, and grilled Thai beef salad,
too. Entrées $16–24.

Black Bear Café (207-693-4770; the
blackbearcafe.com), 215 Roosevelt
Trail (Rt. 302), Naples. Open daily in
summer, closed Tue. and Wed. off-
season. Susan Bohill has expanded
from her popular breakfasts and
lunches, with lobster Benedict and
burgers, to dinners of pizza and
lasagna and dinner specials that take
flight, like lobster risotto croquettes
with lemon caper aioli, or pork tenderloin with blueberry chutney. Entrées
$8–19.

Black Horse Tavern (207-647-5300; sunnysidevillagemaine.com/blackhorse tavern), Rt. 302, Bridgton. Open daily for lunch and dinner, Sunday brunch from 10 AM. A large filet mignon and honey-glazed ginger salmon are regulars on the changing menu. $11–19.

🐾 **Tom's Homestead** (207-647-5726), Rt. 302, Bridgton. Lunch and dinner are served (closed Mon.) in this 1821 historic home. The dining room may be a little tired, but the chef in the kitchen is making everything from scratch and diners consistently praise the food. House sausages makes the lunch a great deal, or you might find fried squash blossoms in summer.

EATING OUT Bray's Brew Pub (207-693-6806; braysbrewpub.com), 678 Roosevelt Trail, Rts. 302 and 35, Naples. Open year-round for lunch and dinner daily. Dinnertime in summer is busy, and there can be a wait. Mike Bray and brewer Rob Prindall brew excellent American ales using grains and malted barley, Oregon yeast, and Washington hops; a beer garden with horseshoe pits and a luxuriant hops vine is a pleasant place on warm nights. The dinner menu runs from grilled salmon to BBQ baby back ribs and smoked beef brisket; pub menu served till 9:30 PM.

Jonathan's (207-935-3442 or 1-800-261-7206; oxfordhouseinn.com), Oxford House Inn, 105 Main St., Fryeburg. Open for dinner Wed.–Mon. summer and fall; end of Oct.–May, open Thu.–Sun. Duck braised with an Asian sauce with hoisin is served in crispy scallion pancakes, or try house-smoked brisket and hand-cut fries served with garlic aioli. Cocktails feature Maine-made Cold River Vodka.

Beth's Kitchen Café (207-647-5211; bethskitchencafe.com), 82 Main St.,

Bridgton. Open daily 7–3. Salads and sandwiches can be relished at tables near Steven's Brook. Breakfast includes Belgian waffles, quiche, fruit, and more, and entrées like meat loaf and eggplant Parmesan arrive for lunch.

Chao Thai (207-647-4355), 112 Main St., Bridgton. This is the best Thai food that some customers have ever tasted—and they have been trying it all over. High praise indeed.

Center Lovell Market (207-925-1051), Rt. 5, Center Lovell. This place combines the best of an old-fashioned general store (clothing, groceries, Maine-made items) with a deli and café. Pizza, salads, and more served to go or to eat in the pleasant dining area.

Route 160 Ice Cream and Hot Dog Stand, north of Kezar Falls on Rt. 160. Locals swear by the dogs here, as well as the hamburgers and ice cream. A good place to stop for lunch when traveling between Cornish and Fryeburg.

Beef and Ski (207-647-9555), 243 Portland Rd. (Rt. 302), Bridgton. This North Conway take-out franchise serves everything from hot sandwiches to seafood dinners. Onion rings are hand cut, fish is fresh, turkey and beef are roasted here for sandwiches and dinners. Seating available. Entrées $6–16.

The Good Life Market (207-655-1196; thegoodlifemarket.com), 1297 Roosevelt Trail (Rt. 302), Raymond. Sandwiches like a classic Reuben or a steak-house wrap, salads, great coffee, and fine fresh-baked goods, with tables outside. Also wine, some local produce, and gourmet foods in the market.

SPECIALTY FOODS Weston's Farm & Sugar House (207-935-2567; westonsfarm.com), 48 River St.,

Fryeburg. Open mid-May–Dec. 24, daily 9–6. Fresh fruit and vegetables grown here, jams made from the farm's fruit, cider, and syrup made with the sap of the trees all around you. "Sustainable Agriculture Since 1799" is the motto at this seventh-generation farm. Cut your own bouquet outside.

✳ Entertainment

FILM The Magic Lantern (2207-647-5065; magiclanternmovies.com), 9 Depot St., Bridgton. Originally built in the 1920s, this old theater had to be torn down, but it was rebuilt and reopened in 2009, to the delight of the town. Three theaters show first-run and independent films, and **The Tannery** serves pub food. **Bridgton Drive-In** (207-647-8666), Rt. 302, shows movies in summer.

MUSIC Sebago–Long Lake Region Chamber Music Festival (207-583-6747), Deertrees Rd., Deertrees Theatre and Cultural Center, Harrison. A series of five world-class concerts held mid-July–mid-Aug.

The Saco River Festival Association (207-625-7116; sacoriverfestival .org) holds a chamber music festival in Cornish in July and Aug., and sponsors bandstand concerts in Parsonsfield in July.

Leura Hill Eastman Performing Arts Center at Fryeburg Academy (207-935-9232; fryeburgacademy.org), 745 Main St., Fryeburg. Opened in 2009, this new arts center with 400 seats hosts live broadcasts of Metropolitan Opera performances and concerts along with musicals performed by Fryeburg Academy students.

THEATER See **Deertrees Theatre and Cultural Center** in "Oxford Hills."

ANTIQUES SHOPS Rt. 302 is chockablock full of antiques shops, so stop anyplace that looks interesting. Cornish has also grown into an antiques haven, and we relish the lack of crowds.

The Smith Co. (207-625-6030), 24 Main St., Cornish. Specializes in country-store fixtures and memorabilia—including old Coca-Cola collectibles and advertising signs.

Cornish Trading Company (207-625-8387; cornishtrading.com), 19 Main St., Cornish. Open April–Oct., Wed.–Mon. 10–5; in Nov., Fri.–Sun. 10–5. A multidealer antiques shop with Americana, Persian carpets, garden sculpture, and more.

BOOKSTORES Bridgton Books (207-647-2122), 140 Main St., Bridgton. More than 20,000 titles, new and used books, books on tape, cards and stationery, as well as music.

SPECIAL SHOPS Harvest Gold Gallery (207-925-6502; harvestgold gallery.com), Rt. 5, Center Lovell. Crafts and original art, garden sculpture like a flock of pale fish, and lovely jewelry made by the owners.

Cornish Vintage Faire (207-625-7700), 51 Main St., Cornish. Three floors of vintage clothes and a few house goods, with fantastic examples of '50s and '60s styles, much of it very reasonably priced.

Kedar Quilt Gallery (207-693-5058; kedarquilts.com), 966 Roosevelt Trail (Rt. 302), Naples. This gallery sells quilts of all sizes made by Maine quilters in all sizes. Orders taken for custom quilts, too.

The Cool Moose (207-647-3957), 108 Main St., Bridgton. Handmade belts and leather goods, and other well-made and quirky inventory.

Craftworks (207-647-5436), 67 Main St., Upper Village, Bridgton. Open daily. Fills a former church. Selective women's clothing, shoes, pottery, books, linens, handmade pillows, crafted jewelry, Stonewall Kitchen–prepared foods, and wines from all over the world.

Cry of the Loon (207-655-5060; cry oftheloon.com), 90 Roosevelt Trail (Rt. 302), South Casco, is one of three businesses set together, with unique pottery, glassware, and handmade crafts. **The Nest** (207-655-5034) has country furniture and rugs, and **The**

Barn (207-655-5066) holds rustic furniture.

Blacksmiths Winery (207-655-3292; blacksmithswinery.com), 967 Quaker Ridge Rd., South Casco. May–Dec. 31, daily 11–6, tastings end at 5:30; Jan.–April, Fri.–Mon. 11–5, tastings end at 4:30. Visitors sample the surprisingly good Cabernet Sauvignon, Chardonnay, and blueberry wines, and an ice wine made with Ontario grapes. (Other grape juice is from New York and Washington State.)

✳ Special Events

January: **Mushers' Bowl**, a dogsled race at the Fryeburg Fairgrounds with

---

♿ STONE MOUNTAIN ARTS CENTER

(1-866-227-6523; stonemountainartscenter.com), 695 Dugway Rd., Brownfield. Musician Carol Noonan's 200-seat hall in Brownfield "literally picked up, moved and plopped onto a new foundation," as she describes it online. It's a phenomenon she wonders about sometimes. Though grateful to be able to stay home after growing weary of the road, she looks this gift horse in the mouth. "People are driving three hours to see a show," Noonan writes. "Why? There is something here bigger than me that drives this train."

Sold-out shows are held year-round in the open-raftered building, and dinner is served first if you can snag a dinner ticket, too. The meals are served quickly, with choices from a small menu like gourmet pizzas, salads with shrimp, salmon, or chicken, and chowder or chili. Beer and wine are served, but all service stops at 8 when the music starts. "It's a listening room first and foremost," says Katy Noonan, Carol's sister.

The business is booking a lot of shows, and some performers include the Neville Brothers, Robert Cray, Suzanne Vega, and Capitol Steps, national acts that found the way up the hilly road. At Stone Mountains Live Concerts Carol Noonan and the Stone Mountain Band host performers like Scottish master fiddler Alasdair Fraser.

The hall is in Brownfield, 20 miles east of Conway, New Hampshire. Whatever you do, do not use GPS to find it. Follow the precise directions available on the website. GPS and Google Maps will put you on rough roads.

participants from all over the United States. Includes sleigh rides, crafts, dancing, stargazing, ice skating, snow-shoeing, ice fishing, and more.

March: **March Maple Syrup Sunday**, with tapping and sugaring-off demonstrations around the area, including Pingree Maple Syrup and Highland Farms Sugar Works, both in Cornish, and Grampa Joe's Sugar House, Rt. 107, Sebago, among many.

April: **Sheepfest**, Denmark—demonstrations of spinning, carding, combing, knitting, dyeing, sheep shearing, hoof trimming, and more.

June: **Windham Summer Fest** (third weekend)—parade, contests, and food vendors. **Naples Blues Fest**, growing every year. **Wheels and Water Antique Transportation**, with chicken barbecue.

July: Independence Day is big in Bridgton and Naples, with fireworks, a parade, and the **4 on the Fourth Road Race**—a 5K walk/run/wheelchair race around Bridgton. In **Naples** the fireworks over the lake are spectacular. Harrison and Casco also hold their **Old Home Days** this month, and check out the **Waterford World's Fair**. **Strawberry Festival**, Thompson Park, Cornish.

August: In Lovell the **Annual Arts and Artisans Fair** (midmonth) is held at the New Suncook School—a juried crafts fair. The **Spinners and Weavers Show** at Narramissic has

grown in popularity in recent years (see *To See*).

September: **Chili Cook-Off and Road Race**, Waterford. **Cornish Apple Festival**, including crafts booths, food vendors, quilt show, antique auto parade, apple pie contest, and the **Apple Acres Bluegrass Festival**. **Brew Fest** at Point Sebago Resort, Casco, offers tastes from microbreweries; look at lakesbrewfest.com for details.

October: **Fryeburg Fair**, Maine's largest agricultural fair, is held for a week in early October, climaxing with the Columbus Day weekend.

November: **Early-Bird Shopping**, discounts at local retail shops, and **Snowflake Trail**, local crafts and open houses in Newfield, Limerick, and Limington.

Late November–early December: **Christmas in Cornish**—open houses, concerts, Cornish Historical Society Walking Tour, horse-drawn carriage rides, children's story time, poinsettia display, and caroling. **Bridgton's Festival of Lights**—a candlelight parade culminates with Santa Claus and tree lighting.

December: **Christmas Open House** and festivals in Harrison.

OXFORD HILLS AND
LEWISTON/AUBURN

Over the years many of Maine's small towns have banded together to form distinctive regional identities. One such area, a rolling gem- and lake-studded swatch of Oxford County, is known as the Oxford Hills. Technically made up of eight towns, the region seems to stretch to include many of the stops along Rt. 26, the region's traffic spine, as visitors pass through from Gray (an exit on the Maine Turnpike) to Bethel, an area with both summer attractions and winter ski resorts.

Its commercial center is the community composed of both Norway and South Paris, towns divided by the Little Androscoggin River but joined by Rt. 26. Off Rt. 26 is a quiet part of the Western Lakes and Mountains Region, with startlingly beautiful villages like Waterford and Paris Hill, and genuinely interesting places to see, such as the country's last living Shaker community at Sabbathday Lake.

The Oxford Hills are best known for their mineral diversity. The area's bedrock is a granite composed of pegmatite studded with semiprecious gemstones, including tourmaline and rose quartz. Several local businesses invite visitors to explore their "tailings," or rubble, and take what they find.

Otisfield is renowned for a unique summer camp devoted to healing the wounds of war, called Seeds of Peace Camp. It began with Palestinian and Israeli children, and now includes campers from Afghanistan, India, Pakistan, Iraq, and Iran, who spend the summer getting to know children they might have encountered otherwise only as enemies.

Lewiston and Auburn (Maine's "L/A"), just east of the Oxford Hills, are the "cities of the Androscoggin" but for most visitors are seen as "the cities on the turnpike," the exits accessing routes to the Rangeley and Sugarloaf areas. Both are worth a stop. By the 1850s mills on both sides of the river had harnessed the power of the Androscoggin's Great Falls, and the Bates Mill boomed with the Civil War, supplying fabric for most of the Union army's tents.

Today Lewiston is best known as the home of prestigious Bates College (founded in 1855), an attractive campus that's the summer site of the nationally recognized Bates Dance Festival. It's also the home of a growing number of Somali immigrants, who are bringing their own cultural flair to the region. The Bates Mill is now a visitor-friendly complex housing a museum and restaurants, and both Lewiston and Auburn offer a number of colorful festivals—some, like Festival de Joie, reflecting the rich diversity of the residents.

GUIDANCE Oxford Hills Chamber of Commerce (207-743-2281; oxfordhills maine.com), 4 Western Ave., South Paris 04281, publishes a comprehensive directory to the area.

Androscoggin County Chamber of Commerce (207-783-2249; androscoggin county.com), 415 Lisbon St., P.O. Box 59, Lewiston 04243.

GETTING THERE For the Sabbathday Lake–Poland Spring–Oxford area, take I-95 to Gray (exit 63) and Rt. 26 north. Auburn is exit 75 and Lewiston is exit 80 off the Maine Turnpike.

WHEN TO COME This is lovely country in winter, but dinner choices can be limited to weekends in the countryside. We love the Lilac Festival at the McLaughlin Garden on Memorial Day weekend.

✳ Villages

Harrison. Once a booming lakeside resort town, Harrison is now a quiet village resting between two lakes. Main Street has a popular restaurant and restored clock tower. In the 1930s many of the country's most popular actors came to perform at the Deertrees Theatre, which is again offering theater, dance, music, and children's shows to the area.

Norway. Making up part of the commercial center of the region, the downtown is quiet and quaint. L. M. Longley's hardware store has items from days gone by, the town is home to Maine's oldest newspaper, and there are interesting art exhibits held by the Western Maine Art Group in the Matolcsy Art Center. The Norway Sidewalk Arts Festival in July features close to 100 artists exhibiting along Main Street.

Paris is a town divided into sections so different, they don't feel like the same town at all. Paris Hill has views of the White Mountains and a number of historic houses and buildings, including the Hamlin Memorial Library.

Oxford, Home of the Oxford Plains Speedway, which attracts stock-car-racing fans throughout the season, and the Oxford County Fairgrounds (host to several annual events), Oxford is also the largest manufacturing base in the area, including manufactured homes, information processing, textiles, and wood products.

✳ To See

The International Sign. At the junction of Rts. 5 and 35 in the village of Lynchville, some 14 miles west of Norway, stands Maine's most photographed roadside marker, pointing variously to Norway, Paris, Denmark, Naples, Sweden, Poland, Mexico, and Peru—all towns within 94 miles of the sign.

FOR FAMILIES ✎ ♿ **Maine Wildlife Park** (207-657-4977), Rt. 26, Gray. Open Apr. 15–Nov. 11, daily 9:30–4:30 (no one admitted after 4 PM). $7 adults, $5 ages 61-plus, $5 ages 4–12, and free for those 3 and under. What started as a pheasant farm in 1931 has evolved into a wonderful haven for injured animals and other creatures that cannot live in the wild. It's a great opportunity to see more than 30 species of native Maine wildlife you might otherwise never glimpse. The park allows visitors to observe animals as they live in the wild. Nature trails and picnic facilities round out the experience. Animals include moose, lynx, deer, black bears, red foxes, mountain lions, and eagles. Also visit the nature store, snack shack, and a fish hatchery, which raises brook trout, where you can feed the fish.

𝒮 **Beech Hill Farm & Bison Ranch** (207-583-2515; beechhillbison.com), 630 Valley Rd. (Rt. 35), Waterford. Call for hours. Doretta and Ted Colburn are raising a breeding herd of North American bison here, and operate a shop with bison meat, buffalo hides, and a variety of gifts. For the most part the herd is visible, and you might see Chief Chadwick, who has produced champions.

Nancy English

THE INTERNATIONAL SIGN

HISTORIC BUILDINGS Poland Spring Museum (207-998-7143; polandspring.com), 115 Preservation Way, Poland Spring. Open Memorial Day–Columbus Day. Free admission. The original bottling plant from the early 1900s and springhouse for the well-known bottled water, Poland Spring, is its own branch in Preservation Park, with 4 miles of trails. The old spa had a renowned visitor list, and photos of some are displayed in the gallery here, like Mae West and Babe Ruth.

Maine State Building (207-998-4142; polandspringps.org), Rt. 26, Poland Spring. Open July and Aug., Tue.–Sat. 9–4, fewer hours off-season. Admission. A very Victorian building that was brought back from the 1893 World's Columbian Exposition in Chicago to serve as a library and art gallery for the now vanished Poland Spring Resort (today the water is commercially bottled in an efficient, unromantic plant down the road). Peek into the **All Souls Chapel** next door for a look at its nine stained-glass windows and the 1921 Skinner pipe organ.

Hamlin Memorial Library and Museum (207-743-2980), Hannibal Hamlin Dr. off Rt. 26, Paris Hill, Paris. Open seasonally, call for hours. The old stone Oxford County Jail now houses the public library and museum. Stop to see the American primitive art; also local minerals and displays about Hannibal Hamlin (who lived next door), vice president during Abraham Lincoln's first term; and the setting, a ridgetop of spectacular early-19th-century houses with views of the White Mountains.

MUSEUMS Sabbathday Lake Shaker Community and Museum (207-926-4597; shaker.lib.me.us), 707 Shaker Rd. (just off Rt. 26), New Gloucester (8 miles north of Gray). Open Memorial Day–Columbus Day for six 75-minute tours daily (except Sun.), 10–4:30; $6.50 adults, $2 ages 6–12. Self-guided tours of Spin House exhibits. The Sabbathday Lake Shaker Community was formally organized in 1794. Founded by Englishwoman Ann Lee in 1775, Shakers numbered 6,000 Americans in 18 communities by the Civil War. Today, with only two Shaker Sisters

Nancy English

SHAKER VILLAGE

and one Brother, this village is the only one in the world that still functions as a religious community. The Shakers here continue to follow the injunction of Mother Ann Lee to "put your hands to work and your heart to God." Guided tours are offered of some of the white-clapboard buildings; rooms are either furnished or filled with exhibits to illustrate periods or products of Shaker life. The **Shaker Store** and **Shaker Museum Reception Center**, a bookshop and exhibit area, sells Shaker-made goods, including oval boxes, knitted and sewn goods, homemade fudge, yarns, souvenirs, antiques, Shaker-style antique furniture, and Shaker herbs. During warm-weather months services are held at 10 AM on Sunday in the 18th-century meetinghouse just off Rt. 26, when Shakers speak in response to the psalms and gospel readings. Each observation is affirmed with a Shaker song—of which there are said to be 10,000. This complex includes an extensive research library housing Shaker books, writings, and records. Crafts workshops, demonstrations, and special events almost every weekend.

Museum L-A, Museum of Labor and Industry (207-333-3881; museumla.org), 35 Canal St., Box A7, Lewiston. Open Mon.–Sat. 10–4. $3 adults, $2 seniors and students. A 50-foot drop in the Androscoggin River powered the mills built alongside; in its heyday Lewiston had seven mills turning out elegant bedspreads for Bates Mills. George Washington spreads, matelasse spreads that sandwich fibers inside the weave, were one of their best products. Shoes and bricks were also made, and the mills prospered until cheaper electricity and labor moved the textile industry to the South in the mid-20th century. One last company still operates in

SHAKER VILLAGE STORE

Nancy English

the mills, and tours can be arranged with the museum; the Maine Heritage Weavers throws are also for sale in the gift store. Don't miss the jacquard loom, a model for early computers studied by IBM employees for functionality. Gallery space hosts changing exhibits, like a shoe industry exhibit on display in the summer of 2010.

Franco-American Collection, The University of Southern Maine Lewiston-Auburn College (207-753-6545; usm.maine.edu/lac/franco), 51 Westminster St., Lewiston. Hours vary; call for appointment. The curators of this collection research and promote interest in the French roots of many of the region's inhabitants. Changing exhibits have included one about textiles and embroidery.

Bates College Museum of Art, Olin Arts Center (207-786-6158; batescollege .edu), 75 Russell St., Lewiston. Open Tue.–Sat. 10–5. Hosts a variety of performances, exhibitions, and special programs. The museum also houses fine artworks on paper, including the Marsden Hartley Memorial Collection. Lovers of the artist won't want to miss this small but excellent collection of bold, bright canvases by Hartley, a Lewiston native (call ahead to find out what's on display).

Finnish-American Heritage Society of Maine (207-743-5677), 8 Maple St., West Paris. Open in July and Aug., Sun. 2–4, or by appointment; closed Jan.– March. A museum, library, and gift shop focused on the Finnish settlers in this area. The monthly meeting every third Sun., Sept.–June, includes a cultural program.

SCENIC DRIVES

Along Route 26

Patched with ugly as well as beautiful stretches, the 46 miles between Gray (Maine Turnpike exit 11) and West Paris don't constitute your ordinary "scenic drive," but this is the way most people head for Bethel and the White Mountains. The following sights are described in order of appearance, heading north:

Sabbathday Lake Shaker Community and Museum, New Gloucester (8 miles north of Gray), just off Rt. 26, is a must-stop (see *Museums*).

State of Maine Building from the 1893 World's Columbian Exposition in Chicago (see *Historic Buildings*). An abrupt right, up through the pillars of the old Poland Spring Resort.

✿ In Oxford two exceptional **farm stands** make ice cream from their own cows' milk. Northbound, don't miss hilltop **Crestholm Farm Stand and Ice Cream** (on your right; 207-539-8832), which has a petting zoo (sheep, goats, pigs, ducks, and more) as well as cheeses, honey, and great ice cream; also a nice view. Southbound, it's **Smedberg's Crystal Spring Farm** (see *Where to Eat—Snacks*).

✿ In South Paris highway hypnosis sets in big time after the light; it's easy to miss **Shaner's Family Dining** (see *Eating Out*).

Across from Ripley Ford, look for the **McLaughlin Garden** (see *Green Space*).

The **Oxford Hills Chamber of Commerce** (207-743-2281), 4 Western Ave., South Paris, is open year-round, and you can pick up the magazine guide to the area here.

Paris Hill is posted just beyond the second light in South Paris. The road climbs steadily up to Paris Hill common, a spacious green surrounded on three sides by early-19th-century mansions, with the fourth commanding a panoramic view of hills and valley and the White Mountains in the distance. Look for **Hamlin Memorial Library and Museum** (see *Historic Buildings*).

Christian Ridge Pottery (see *Special Shops*) is marked from Christian Ridge Rd., a way back to Rt. 26.

✐ **Snow Falls Gorge**, 6 miles south of the center of West Paris on Rt. 26, left as you're heading north. A great picnic and walk-around spot, a rest area with tables and a trail by a waterfall that cascades into a 300-foot gorge carved by the Little Androscoggin.

✐ **Trap Corner**, an area in West Paris (at the junction Rts. 219 and 26) is rock-hounding central.

Greenwood Shore Rest Area, Rt. 26 just north of Bryant Pond. A good water-side spot for a picnic.

STOCK-CAR RACING **Oxford Plains Speedway** (207-539-8865; oxfordplains .com), Rt. 26, Oxford. Weekend stock-car racing, late Apr.–Oct.

✳ To Do

APPLE PICKING ✐ **Ricker Hill Orchards** (207-225-5552; rickerhill.com), Turner. Maps show you where your favorite varieties can be picked in the big orchard here. Cranberries for sale at the farm stand, along with apple butter, fresh doughnuts, and, in-season, the best corn of the summer. Watch apple cider making and apple packing in process. In fall a corn maze can be explored. A petting "ranch" brings you close to goats, pigs, cows, donkeys, and horses.

BALLOONING **Rainbow's End** (207-782-1622), 69 Loring Ave., Auburn. Walter Crites, who has been involved in the Great Falls Balloon Festival since it started in 1993 and is a licensed commercial pilot, offers weekend trips by reservation and in good weather only.

Dream Song Ballooning (207-713-6578; dreamsongballooning.org), Reservoir Ave., Lewiston. Dave Gugnon, a licensed commercial pilot, offers a print-out of the ground track of your flight path; weekend trips by reservation.

Androscoggin Balloon Adventures (207-783-4574), 169 Ferry Rd., Lewiston. Jim Rodrigue, a licensed commercial pilot, offers weekend balloon rides by reservation.

BIRDING **Sabattus Pond**, Sabattus. The mudflats of autumn bring migrating ducks, sandpipers, and waterfowl, including American golden plovers. The boat access and beach at Martin's Point on the pond is the access point. See also Thorn-crag Nature Preserve in *Green Space*. Birding hot spots are listed at its sponsor's website, stantonbirdclub.org.

GOLF **Paris Hill Country Club** (207-743-2371), Paris Hill Rd., Paris, nine holes, founded in 1899, is the epitome of old-shoe; rental carts, snack bar. **Norway Country Club** (207-743-9840; norwaycountryclub.com), off Rt. 118 on Norway Lake Rd., nine holes, long views. Fourteen holes as well at **Summit Springs Golf Course** (207-998-4515), 292 Summit Spring Rd., Poland. **Spring Meadows Golf**

Club (207-657-2586; springmeadowsgolf.com), 59 Lewiston Rd., Gray. An 18-hole golf course with rentals and clubhouse.

HIKING ✂ **Streaked Mountain**. This is a short, occasionally steep hike with a panoramic view, good for kids. From Rt. 26, take Rt. 117 to the right-hand turnoff for Streaked Mountain Rd. and look for the trailhead on your left. The trail follows a power line up to an old fire tower at just 800 feet. A roundtrip, 1-mile hike takes about 1½ hours, longer to eat the blueberries in-season.

Singepole Mountain. Also off Rt. 117, nearer South Paris (see the *Maine Atlas and Gazetteer*, published by DeLorme), is a 1.5-mile walk up a dirt road (bear left) through the woods to a summit with a view of Mount Washington and the Mahoosuc Mountains.

MOUNTAIN BIKING Paris Hill Area Park, near the common. You can bike the ridge roads radiating from here; inquire about routes in Hamlin Memorial Library and Museum.

ROCKHOUNDING Rochester's Eclectic Emporium (207-539-4631), 403 Main St. (Rt. 26), Oxford. Nicholas Rochester has some of the finest mineral and crystal specimens you can see; he can steer you to local mines. Jewelry, beads, loose gems, and a large selection of tourmaline.

SWIMMING ✂ ⅙ **Range Pond State Park** (207-998-4104), Empire Rd., features a beach perfect for spreading out a picnic blanket. Lifeguards, playground, ball field, changing rooms, bathrooms, boat launch, swimming, and fishing, plus 2 miles of easy walking trails. The pond has a 10-horsepower limit—kayakers love it here. **Pennesseewassee Lake** in Norway is well off the road, but public and equipped with lifeguards.

✳ Winter Sports

CROSS-COUNTRY SKIING Carter's Cross Country Ski Center (207-539-4848; cartersxcski.com), 420 Main St. (Rt. 26), Oxford. Extensive acreage used to grow summer vegetables is transformed into a ski center in winter. Equipment rentals, lessons, 30 kilometers of groomed trails, and food.

Lost Valley Ski Area (207-784-1561; lostvalleyski.com), Lost Valley Rd., Auburn. One continuous trail is more than 5 miles long. Rentals. Tickets in 2009–10 cost $10.

DOWNHILL SKIING Lost Valley Ski Area (207-784-1561; lostvalleyski.com), Lost Valley Rd., Auburn. With 21 trails and two chairlifts, this small mountain is a favorite for schools and families. Night skiing every night till 9 except Sun. at 5.Weekend adult lift tickets are $45, junior $33, less for fewer hours on the slopes.

SNOW TUBING ⛄ ✂ **Oxford Plains Snow Tubing** (207-539-2454; oxford plains.com), Rt. 26, Oxford. A lighted 1,000-foot slope open Sat.–Sun., plus school vacation days. Tubes, helmets, and a T-bar are the ingredients of this low-tech, low-cost sport. Snowmaking keeps it open.

Nancy English

MCLAUGHLIN GARDEN IN SOUTH PARIS HOLDS A HUGE VARIETY OF LILACS

❋ Green Space

The McLaughlin Garden (207-743-8820; mclaughlingarden.org), 97 Main St., South Paris. Garden open daily May–Oct., 8–7. Free admission. Historic house and gift shop open, and educational programs offered, year-round, Mon–Sat. 10–5. In 1936 Bernard McLaughlin, who had no formal horticultural training, began planting his farmstead; now lilacs and established garden beds flourish next to stone walls and a massive barn. After his death in 1995, a nonprofit organization formed to preserve the home, barn, and 5-acre floral oasis. In lilac season, with more than 100 varieties, the annual Lilac Festival is a sensual delight, with tours and lilac workshops and sales. The gift shop is open year-round, and the café serving light lunches—including Provençal panini with prosciutto, artichoke hearts, and pesto—is open Memorial Day weekend–Labor Day, Wed.–Sun. 11–3.

Thorncrag Nature Sanctuary in Lewiston is 372-acre wildlife sanctuary, owned and managed by Stanton Bird Club (207-782-5238; stantonbirdclub.org). Six nature trails cross through meadows, forest, wetlands, and vernal pools, all good for bird watching or walking and jogging. This preserve is accessible through two gates, one at the end of East Ave., the other on Montello St. Open dawn to dusk, and free.

ORDWAY GROVE, NORWAY

Nancy English

The Ordway Grove, Pleasant St., Norway. These old-growth white pines, some 12 feet around and 140 feet or more tall, have been protected since 1789. The grove is a left turn heading north on Rt. 118, as you pass Lake Pennesseewassee. The grove of 250-year-old trees became a preserve in 1931.

✳ Lodging

INNS ✿ ♫ The Waterford Inne
(207-583-4037; waterfordinne.com),
turn off Rt. 37 at Springer's General
Store, Box 149, Waterford 04088. This
striking 1825 farmhouse with its double porch is sequestered up a back
road, set on 25 quiet acres of fields and
woods. Barbara Vanderzanden opened
her inn in July 1978; her unobtrusive
style will appeal to those who prefer
privacy. Four spacious rooms in an
addition and four upstairs, six with private bath, include the Chesapeake
Room, with a second-story porch. A
full breakfast is included. $120–200
per room; dinner is available by reservation (see *Dining Out*) at an additional cost. Pets are accepted; $15 fee.

Kedarburn Inn (207-583-6182 or 1-
866-583-6182; kedarburn.com), Valley
Rd. (Rt. 35), Waterford 04088. Open
June–Oct. London natives Margaret
and Derek Gibson offer English hospitality in their seven guest rooms, five
with private bath. Margaret's quilts
cover beds and the walls. The handsome Balcony Room has a queen bed
and loft with two twin beds. The quilt
shop on the ground floor is filled with
a rainbow of fabric. Quilting weekends
and retreats Sept.–June. $90–135 dou-
ble including breakfast.

♿ **King's Hill Inn** (207-744-0204 or 1-
877-391-5464; kingshillinn.com), 56
King Hill Rd., South Paris. Three
suites and three rooms, all with private
bath. Rooms 4 and 5 offer both a great
view of the White Mountains and a gas
log fire. Enjoy blueberry pancakes in
the morning before a tour of the
perennial gardens spreading out on the
lawn. Janice and Glenn Davis keeps
everything from the grass to the beds
in tiptop condition, including an
adorable wedding chapel. $95–150
per night for a double, depending on
season.

**BED & BREAKFASTS ♫ Bear
Mountain Inn** (207-583-4404; bear
mtninn.com), Rts. 35 and 37, South
Waterford 04081. Open year-round.
This 150-year-old farmhouse is set on
52 gorgeous acres next to Bear Pond.
Jim and Christie Kerrigan are the
innkeepers who can show you to the
beach, the trailhead, the hammocks,
canoes, kayaks, and more, all at your
disposal. Eleven rooms and suites,
most with private bath, each has its
own bear—Minnesota, Polar, and Polo
are three. The Great Grizzly Suite
offers a fireplace, two-person Jacuzzi,
views, and leather sofa along with TV,
DVD, and bath. The Sugar Bear Cottage has a fireplace, kitchenette, claw-
foot tub, and terrific views. $120–325
per room includes a full breakfast.

Greenwood Manor Inn (207-583-
4445; greenwoodmanorinn.com), 52
Tolman Rd., Harrison 04040. Open
year-round. A former carriage house
on 108 hillside acres sloping down to
Long Lake, the inn features seven
guest rooms and two suites, some with
a gas log fireplace, some with
whirlpool tub, and all with private
bath. The dining and living areas overlook a landscaped garden. $140–245
in-season includes a full breakfast.
Note: Although this B&B is technically
in Harrison, much of its property lies
in the town of Bridgton, and it is thus
much closer to the Sebago/Long Lakes
area than to the Oxford Hills; as a
result, we're listing it in both chapters.

Wolf Cove Inn (207-998-4976; wolf
coveinn.com), 5 Jordan Shore Dr.,
Poland 04274. Open year-round. A
romantic, quiet lakeside hideaway
holds 10 accommodations, each named
for a flower or herb, and nicely decorated. Eight rooms have private bath;
three have whirlpool tub and gas fireplace. Kayaks and canoes are available.
$100–250 in-season includes a full

breakfast. Light-filled sunporch or the grand room are the site of blueberry pancakes and pecan waffles for breakfast.

OTHER LODGING ✤ ♿ **Papoose Pond Resort and Campground** (207-583-4470; papoosepondresort.com), 700 Norway Rd. (Rt. 118), Waterford 04088 (10 miles west of Norway). Family-geared for 40 years, this facility is on 1,000 wooded acres with 0.5 mile of sandy beach on mile-long Papoose Pond. Cabins with or without bath, housekeeping cottages, bunkhouse trailers, tent and RV sites (some with electricity, water, and sewer); rates in high season range from $36 per night for a tent site and from $252 for a cottage. Amenities include a recreation hall, store, café, movie tent, canoes, rowboats, paddleboats, kayaks, fishing equipment, and a 1916 merry-go-round.

✷ Where to Eat

DINING OUT Fuel (207-333-3835; fuelmaine.com), 49 Lisbon St., Lewiston. Open for dinner Tue.–Sat. from 4:30. Fuel and an art gallery are now inside the renovated Lyceum Hall. The restaurant feeds appreciative locals bistro-style steak frites and braised short ribs, buttermilk-brined Cornish game hen and roasted scallops. Great wine list and elegant bar area, with bar menu. Entrées $18–26.

DiSanto's Italian Restaurant (207-428-4300; disantosrestaurant.com), 322 West Gray Rd, Gray. A vibrant marinara makes the Italian classics served here wonderful, and count on good veal and steaks, too. The house sausage is perfectly seasoned and can be enjoyed in an appetizer, but save room for the excellent cannoli and spumoni for dessert. Entrées $17–29.

Fishbones (207-333-3663; fishbonesag.com), 70 Lincoln St., Lewiston.

Grilled fish in a spacious room, with exposed brick and lively people. Seafood fra diavolo and linguine with clams, or blueberry-glazed roast pork tenderloin. Entrées $17–26.

The Waterford Inne (207-583-4037; waterfordinne.com), Waterford (turn off Rt. 37 at Springer's General Store). Open by reservation only. Come and enjoy a surprisingly sophisticated meal in this classic country inn. A four-course prix fixe dinner ($40) might include salmon with walnut crust, carrot Vichy, or pork à la Normande with apples and Calvados. BYOB.

Maurice Restaurant (207-743-2532; mauricerestaurant.com), 109 Main St., South Paris. Dinner Tue.–Sun. 4–8:30 PM, lunch Tue.–Fri. 11:30–1:30, Sunday brunch 11–2, closed Mon. Entrées include coquilles Saint-Jacques, sirloin Diane, and chicken roulade. Extensive wine list, $16 and up. Reservations recommended. $14–24.

✤ ♿ **The River Restaurant** (207-674-3800; riverrestaurant.com), nestled beside Snow Falls, Rt. 26 at West Paris. Open for lunch and dinner daily except Mon. Known for its creative fine dining at a reasonable price. All soups, dressings, and sauces are made

NEZINSCOT FARM STORE

Nancy English

in-house, and specialties include fettuccine Alfredo, beef Stroganoff, crabcakes, and prime rib au jus Fri. and Sat. Entrées $12–20, including soup or salad, and vegetable side dishes.

Sedgley Place (207-946-5990; sedgley place.com), off Rt. 202, Greene. Reservations required. A Federal-style house with a well-known dining room. Five-course dinners with entrées that change weekly but always include prime rib, fish, poultry, and a fourth selection. Prix fixe $19–29 includes salad and dessert, with greens, vegetables, meat, and berries from local farms.

Mother India (207-333-6777; mother indiamaine.com), 114 Lisbon St., Lewiston. Open in April 2009, Mother India is a draw for Indian-food lovers from all over the state.

EATING OUT ✪ Nezinscot Farm Store and Cafe (207-225-3231; nezinscotfarm.com), 284 Turner Center Rd., Turner. Food served Mon.–Fri. 7–4, Sat. 7–4, closed Sun., and also on Mon. Oct.–June. Exceptional

MELBY'S MARKET

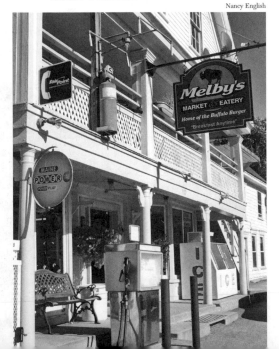

Nancy English

cheeses, jams, pickles, organic meats, eggs, and vegetables sold, and a café with a perfect organic hamburger on toasted, homemade bread. Gloria Varney, her husband, and her large family run this farm, providing eggs for omelets, organic cheese for lunch. The Tea House in the garden, with tea with clotted cream and scones, is open mid-May–Oct. amid the strolling chickens.

The Café Nomad (207-739-2249; cafenomad.com), 450 Main St., Norway. Open early AM though lunch. Scott Berk serves invigorating coffee drinks. Local produce and meat are on the menu, with breakfast burritos, omelets, weekend pancakes, along with a great caprese sandwich and soups. Chicken salad is a multiday process starting with marinade. Bottled wine, chocolate, and local jams and farm products for sale.

The Bread Shack (207-376-3090; thebreadshack.com), 1056 Center St., Auburn. Open Tue.–Fri. 7–6, Sat. 8–2. Carrot ginger and tomato basil soups were specials in fall, and oatmeal bread with a touch of molasses and pumpkin bread were coming out of the oven. Count on The Bread Shack for a hot Reuben sandwich or Brie and apple on a baguette with chutney.

Chick-A-Dee (207-225-3523; chickadeeresaurant.com), Rt. 4, Turner. Closed Tue. A longtime local favorite for lunch and dinner. Specialties include seafood like fried clams and beef. Entrées $6–20.

✐ Olde Mill Tavern (207-583-9077; oldemilltavern.com), Main St., Harrison. Open daily for dinner at 4. Popular with local residents and families. Chorizo burritos, chicken Parmesan, shrimp stir-fry with soba noodles, pasta, and burgers, among many other things on the varied menu. Entrées $9–24.

Cyndi's Dockside Restaurant (207-998-5008; polandspringinns.com

/Dockside.htm), 723 Maine St., Poland. Boat rentals in-season, open year-round. Enjoy an outside deck and outdoor pavilion on Middle Range Pond in good weather. Local beef burgers, fried clams, pulled pork sandwiches. Entrées $6–19.

☞ **Cole Farms** (207-657-4714; cole farms.com), 64 Lewiston Rd. (Rt. 100/202), Gray. Open Sun.–Thu. 6 AM–9 PM, Fri. and Sat. until 9:30. No credit cards; checks accepted with ID. Maine family recipes, including fried seafood, hot chicken sandwiches, Indian pudding, and daily specials like New England boiled dinner. No liquor. Playground with swings, and gift shop.

☞ **Melby's Market** (207-583-4447), 927 Valley Rd. (Rt. 26), North Waterford. Open 6 AM–9 PM except the last week of March. Paul and Kay Legare have run Melby's (formerly Tut's) for more than 20 years, making fresh bread and pastries, selling local honey and preserves, and cooking a fine buffalo burger. Breakfast served all day.

☞ ♿ **Val's Root Beer** (207-784-5592), 925 Sabattus St., Lewiston. Open daily mid-Apr.–mid-Sept., 11–8 except Sun., when they open at noon. A 1950s-style drive-in with carhops and a *Happy Days* theme. Greasy burgers, great onion rings, hot dogs, and the like, and their specialty, homemade root beer. Popular summer hangout among locals.

Shaner's Family Dining (207-743-6367), 193 Main St., South Paris. Open for breakfast, lunch, and dinner. A cheerful family restaurant with booths; specials like fried chicken, liver and onions, and chicken pie; creamy homemade ice cream in flavors like Grape-Nut, and ginger. Entrées $5–11.

SNACKS ☞ **Crestholm Farm Stand and Ice Cream** (207-539-2616), Rt. 26, Oxford. Open in season. Farm stand, cheeses, honey, ice cream, and a petting zoo: sheep, goats, pigs, ducks, and more.

Greenwood Orchards (207-225-3764; greenwoodorchards.com), 174 Auburn Rd., Turner. Open July–Dec. Fresh cider in fall, apples, house jams and jellies, and a bakery making pies and bread—100 percent whole wheat is one. Local produce fills this shop through the growing season.

Smedberg's Crystal Spring Farm (207-743-6723; smedburgfarm.com), Rt. 26, Oxford, sells its One Cow Ice Cream (there is actually a herd of beef cattle here); also jams, honey, maple syrup, fruits and vegetables, cheese, berries, home-baked pies, and home-grown grass-fed beef, pork, and lamb. Open-house country festival with a pig roast, free roast pork and samples, first Sun. of Nov.

Springer's General Store (207-583-2051), 1218 Waterford Rd., Waterford. This little country store makes pizza, chili, and soup to eat at one of the picnic tables, breakfast, lunch, and dinner, prime rib for dinner in fall, and 4-ounce lobster rolls. The gas pump is the only one in the area.

✹ Entertainment

☞ **Celebration Barn Theater** (207-743-8452; celebrationbarn.com), 190

SMEDBERG'S IN OXFORD

Nancy English

Stock Farm Rd. (off Rt. 117 north of South Paris). In 1972 theater and mime master Tony Montanaro founded a performance-arts school in this red racing-horse barn on Christian Ridge. Summer workshops in acrobatics, mime, voice, clowning, and juggling by resident New Vaudeville artists from around the world in summer.

& **Deertrees Theatre and Cultural Center** (207-583-6747; deertrees theatre.org), Deertrees Rd., Harrison. A 300-seat historic theater, built as an opera house in 1936, saved from being used as an exercise for the local fire department in the 1980s, and restored to its original grandeur complete with perfect acoustics. The nonprofit performing arts center, run by the Deertrees Foundation, is host to the Sebago–Long Lake Music Festival concert series (see below), and the venue for dance, music, and theatrical productions through the summer, as well as children's shows. Assisted audio for the hard of hearing. Fine arts and sculpture in the **Backstage Gallery**, open an hour before showtime.

Sebago–Long Lake Region Chamber Music Festival (207-583-6747), Deertrees Rd., Deertrees Theatre and Cultural Center, Harrison. Five world-class concerts held Tue., mid-July–mid-Aug.

The Public Theatre (207-782-3200; thepublictheatre.org), 2 Great Falls Plaza, Auburn. Professional Equity theater featuring high-quality productions of Broadway and off-Broadway shows.

L/A Arts (207-782-7228; laarts.org), 221 Lisbon St., Lewiston. A local arts agency bringing exhibitions, community arts outreach, dance and musical performances, and award-winning educational programs to the area. The new **Gallery 5**, 49 Lisbon St., has themed, group exhibits that change every six weeks.

The Maine Music Society (207-782-1403), 215 Lisbon St., Lewiston, is home to both the Maine Chamber Ensemble and the Androscoggin Chorale. A variety of performances throughout the year.

Bates Dance Festival (207-786-6381), Schaeffer Theater, Bates College, Lewiston. Mid-July–mid-Aug. Student, faculty, and professional performances at one of the best dance festivals in the country.

✳ Selective Shopping

ANTIQUES Orphan Annie's Antiques (207-782-0638; metiques .com/catalog/orphan.html), 96 Court St., Auburn. Open Mon.–Sat. 10–5, Sun. noon–5. If you're looking for art deco and art nouveau objects, this is the place. Tiffany, Steuben, Fiestaware, Depression glass, and much more. The vintage fashions are worth a long journey. Three-floor warehouse sale every Mon. 10–1.

BOOKSTORES ✐ **Books N Things** (207-739-6200; bntnorway.com), 430 Main St., Norway. Billing itself as "Western Maine's Complete Bookstore," this is a fully stocked shop with

MATOLCSY ARTS CENTER

Nancy English

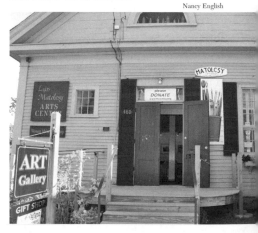

a good children's section. Coffee, muffins, and author events.

The Maine Bookhouse (207-743-9300; themainebookhouse.com), 1545 Main St. (Rt. 26), Oxford. A new- and used-book store in a charming, mustard-yellow building, with more than 13,000 well-organized titles. Specializing in Maine books, first editions, rare and out-of-print books, and children's classics. Coffee and tea are available. Check out the small art gallery, too.

GALLERIES **The Lajos Matolcsy Arts Center** (207-739-6161; thewmag .org), 480 Main St., Norway. From May to December, the Western Maine Art Group presents visual arts exhibits, with fine arts, artisan crafts, and sculpture; classes are offered throughout the year. Executive director Aranka Matolcsy is a resource for information about arts activity in the whole region.

The Frost Farm Gallery (207-743-8041; frostfarmgallery.com), 272 Pike's Hill Rd., Norway. Exhibits of area artists and special events.

The Commons Art Collective (207-743-9579; faresharecoop.org), 445 Main St., Norway. Exhibits of member artists; open during Fare Share Market hours and some weekends.

The Painted Mermaid (207-743-7744; paintedmermaid.com), 6 Briggs Ave., South Paris. Brenda Ellis Sauro's paintings and Michael Sauro's sculpture are on display.

GEM SHOPS See *To Do— Rockhounding.*

SPECIAL SHOPS **United Society of Shakers Store or Museum Reception Center** (207-926-4597), Rt. 26, New Gloucester. Open Mon.–Sat. 10–4:30, Memorial Day–Columbus Day. Sells Shaker herbs, teas, poultry seasoning, mulled cider mix, pumpkin pie spices, and handcrafted items.

The Barn on 26 (207-657-3470; barnon26.com), 361 Shaker Rd, Gray. Set inside a restored, 1870 Shaker-built barn, this business owned by Alice E. Welch features furniture, quilts, hoosiers, and more.

Artful Hands Fiber Studio (207-393-7664; artfulhands.net), 316 Main St., Norway. Wool yarns and hand-dyed wools for rug hooking and roving, wool for spinning. Classes in rug hooking, knitting, and spinning.

Christian Ridge Pottery (207-743-8419; applebaker.com), 210 Stock Farm Rd., South Paris (marked from Rt. 26 and from Christian Ridge Rd.). Open Memorial Day weekend–Dec., daily 10–5, except Sun. noon–5. Known for its functional, distinctive stippleware in ovenproof, microwave-safe designs, Christian Ridge Pottery makes coffee- and teapots, apple-baking dishes, and more.

Creaser Jewelers (207-744-0290 or 1-800-686-7633; creaserjewelers.com), 138 Main St., South Paris. Open daily 9–5; Jan.–June 1, Mon.–Sat. Original designs using Maine tourmaline and amethyst. A small room holds specimens of different gems and crystals. You can buy unset stones.

Kedar Quilts (207-583-6182; kedar quilts.com), 18 Valley Rd., Waterford 04088. Margaret Gibson began making quilts as a child in England. Now she makes them for her Kedarburn Inn and for this quaint shop. The inn hosts quilting retreats Sept.–June (see *Lodging*).

OUTLETS **Bates Mill Store** (207-784-7626 or 1-800-552-2837; batesmill store.com), 41B Chestnut St., Lewiston. Bedspreads, towels, and sheets, as well as blankets made by Maine Heritage Weavers are sold only over the phone and Internet. But go to the Museum of Labor and Industry (see Museum L-A in *To See*) to buy them in person.

Marden's Discount (207-786-0313; mardens.com), Northwood Park Shopping Center, Rt. 202, Lewiston. Like Renys (see "Damariscotta/Newcastle") this is a Maine original, the first store in a Maine chain. The founder died in 2002, but the legend lives on. A mix of clothing, staples, furnishings—whatever happens to have been purchased cheaply, after a hurricane like Katrina, or, memorably, after 9/11, when designer clothes here were going at 90 percent off.

Oxford Mill-End Store (207-539-4451), 971 Main St. (Rt. 26), Oxford. Open Mon.–Fri. 9–4, Sat. 9–1. First-quality woolen and quilting fabric store, flannel and fleece, too.

New Balance Factory Store (207-539-9022), Rt. 26, Oxford. Mon.–Sat. 9–7 Sun. 9–5. The running shoes you love at major discounts.

For more shops in this region, also see "Bethel."

✳ Special Events

February: **Norway-Paris Fish and Game Ice Fishing Derby**, on Norway Lake. **City of Auburn and Lost Valley Winter Festival**, Auburn.

May: **Maine State Parade**, Lewiston (first Saturday)—the state's biggest parade; theme varies annually. **Lilac Festival** at McLaughlin Garden.

Summer: **First Friday Gallery Hop** includes **The Lajos Matolcsy Arts Center** (207-739-6161; thewmag.org), 480 Main St., Norway, **The Frost Farm Gallery** (207-743-8041; frost farmgallery.com), 272 Pike's Hill Rd., Norway, **The Commons Art Collective** (207-743-9579; faresharecoop

.org), 445 Main St., Norway, **The Painted Mermaid** (207-743-7744; painted mermaid.com), 6 Briggs Ave., South Paris, **The Café Nomad** 739-2249; cafenomad.com), 450 Main St., Norway, **McLaughlin Garden** (see *Green Space*), and **Norway Library** (207-743-5309; norway.lib.me.us), 258 Main St., Norway.

July: **The Oxford 250 NASCAR Race** draws entrants from throughout the world to the Oxford Plains Speedway; Harrison celebrates **Old Home Days**. **Founders Day** (midmonth) on Paris Hill. **The Moxie Festival** (second weekend), downtown Lisbon, features live entertainment, plenty of food, and Moxie (Maine's own soft drink). The **Norway Sidewalk Art Show** has more than 100 exhibitors.

July–August: **Sebago–Long Lake Music Festival** at Deertrees Theatre, Harrison.

August: **Deertrees Theatre Festival**, award-winning plays with Equity casts and student acting workshops for all four weeks of the month (207-583-6747; deertreestheatre.org). **Gray Old Home Days** (beginning of the month)—parade, contests, and public feeds. **Festival de Joie** (first weekend), Lewiston—music, dancing, and cultural and crafts displays. **Great Falls Balloon Festival** (fourth weekend), Lewiston—music, games, hot-air launches.

September: **Oxford County Agricultural Fair** (usually second week), West Paris—all the usual attractions: horse pulls, 4-H shows, fiddling contests, apple pie judging, and a midway.

November: **The Biggest Christmas Parade in Maine**, Thanksgiving Saturday in South Paris and Norway.

December: Christmas Open House and Festivals in Paris Hill.

BETHEL AREA

Bethel is a natural farming and trading site on the Androscoggin River. Its town common is the junction of four routes—west to the White Mountains, north to the Mahoosuc Mountains, east to the Oxford Hills, and south to the lakes.

When the trains from Portland to Montreal began stopping here in 1851, Bethel also became an obvious summer retreat for city people. But unlike many summer resorts of that era, it was nothing fancy. Families stayed the season in the big white farmhouses, of which there are still plenty. They feasted on homegrown and home-cooked food, then walked it off on nearby mountain trails.

Hiking remains a big lure for summer and fall visitors. The White Mountain National Forest comes within a few miles of town, and trails radiate from nearby Evans Notch. Just 12 miles northwest of Bethel, Grafton Notch State Park also offers short hikes to spectacles such as Screw Auger Falls and to a wealth of well-equipped picnic sites. Blueberrying and rockhounding are local pastimes, and the hills are also good pickings for history buffs.

The hills were once far more peopled than they are today—entire villages have vanished. Hastings, for example, now just the name of a national forest campground, was once a thriving community complete with post office, stores, and a wood alcohol mill that shipped its product by rail to Portland, thence to England.

The Bethel Inn Resort, born of the railroad era, is still going strong. Opened in 1913 by millionaire William Bingham II and dedicated to a prominent neurologist (who came to Bethel to recuperate from a breakdown), it originally featured a program of strenuous exercise—one admired by the locals (wealthy clients actually paid the doctor to chop down his trees) as well as by the medical profession. The inn is still known for at least two forms of exercise—golf and cross-country skiing.

Bethel is best known these days as a ski town. Sunday River Resort, 6 miles to the north, claims to offer "the most dependable snow in New England."

WOODEN BRIDGE NEAR SUNDAY RIVER
Nancy English

577

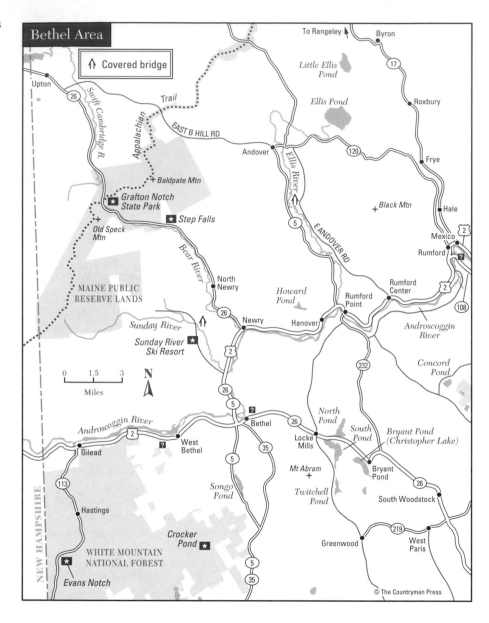

Bethel Area

↑ Covered bridge

Powered by its snow guns (powered in turn by snowmaking ponds fed continuously by the Sunday River), the family-geared resort doubled and redoubled its trails, lifts, and lodging regularly since 1980. Recent additions include winter and summer zipline tours, Chondola rides, and mountain biking. Snowmaking capacity continues to expand. Mount Abram Ski Resort, a few miles south of the village, remains an old-fashioned family ski area.

Bethel is also home to Gould Academy, a coed prep school with a handsome campus.

For Bethel, tourism has remained the icing rather than the cake. Its two mills and various wood product businesses manufacture pine boards, furniture, and more. Three dairy farms, including the six-generation Carter Farm, ship 7,000 gallons of milk per week. Brooks Bros. is still the name of the hardware store, not a men's clothier.

GUIDANCE Bethel Area Chamber of Commerce (207-824-2282 or 1-800-442-5826; bethelmaine.com), 8 Station Place, P.O. Box 1247, Bethel 04217, publishes an excellent area guide and maintains a large walk-in information center with restrooms in the depot-style Bethel Station, off Lower Main St. (Rt. 26). Open year-round, weekdays 9–5, varying hours on weekends. See *Lodging* for reservation services.

White Mountain National Forest Service (603-466-2713, dial 0 for help; fs.fed .us/r9/forests/white_mountain). The staff offers detailed information about camping, hiking, and other outdoor activities in the national forest and other nearby natural areas. You can pick up a pass for trailhead parking within the White Mountain National Forest at **Pleasant River Campground** (207-836-2000; pleasantriver campground.com), Rt. 2, West Bethel (see *Camping*).

GETTING THERE *By air:* The **Portland International Jetport**, served by several carriers, is 75 miles from Bethel. All major car rentals are available at the airport (see "Portland"). The **Bethel Airport** (207-824-2669) has a paved 3,818-foot runway, open year-round.

Northeast Charter & Tour (1-888-593-6328; northeastchartertour.com) is a charter and tour bus operator that runs a door-to-door bus service to and from the Portland International Jetport; Boston's Logan Airport; Manchester, New Hampshire; and all of New England.

By car: Bethel is a convenient way stop between New Hampshire's White Mountains and the Maine coast (via Rt. 2). From Boston, take the Maine Turnpike to Gray, exit 63; Bethel is 52 miles north on Rt. 26.

GETTING AROUND Mountain Explorer. Thanksgiving to Christmas weekends and then daily through the first weekend in April, this free 28-passenger van connects Sunday River with Bethel shops and inns.

WHEN TO COME The ski season, especially Christmas and February vacations, is high season here; given Sunday River's famous snowmaking, snow is fairly dependable through March. Except for whitewater rafting, April into June is very low season, and so is late fall. Summer is beautiful, with golf, hiking, swimming, llama trekking, horseback riding, mountain and road biking, canoeing, and kayaking all readily available. Fall is even more beautiful, the best season for hiking.

✳ To See

HISTORIC HOMES AND MUSEUMS ✪ Bethel Historical Society's Regional History Center's O'Neil Robinson House (207-824-2908; bethel historical.org), 10 Broad St., Bethel. Open year-round, hours seasonal and posted on the website. No charge for the changing (extensive) exhibits. Built in 1821, the O'Neil Robinson House was remodeled in the Italianate style in 1881 and also houses the museum shop. Next door is the **Dr. Moses Mason House** (open July and Aug., Tue.–Sat. 1–4). Ambitious, fascinating exhibits are on display in this exquisite Federal-style mansion built in 1813, proof of the town's early prosperity. Restored to its original grandeur, it has magnificent Rufus Porter–style murals in the front hall, fine furnishings in nine period rooms, and well-informed guides to tell you about the items you see throughout the house. Guided tours are $3 adults, $1.50 children. This complex has become a historical exhibit and research center for much of western Maine. Pick up a copy of the historical society's self-guided walking tour of town. Barn tours are usually offered every other year in Sept.

Maine Mineral and Gem Museum (mainemineralgemmuseum.org), 103 Main St., Bethel. First open July 1, 2012, this seven-years-in-the-making project has collected some of the best mineral discoveries in Maine at one building in Bethel. Mary McFadden and Larry Stifler are the founders and donors who make the collection possible, first buying Bumpus Mine in Albany and opening it for walking tours. A Hall of Gems, with more than 200 gemstones, holds the finest Maine gemstone collection ever put together, according to Jim Mann, owner of Mt. Mann Jewelers and curator of the museum.

One of the stars of the museum is the largest flawless 154-carat Morganite gemstone cut from the 50-pound "Rose of Maine." "From 50 feet away you can see its brilliance," Mann said. This fine mineral collection includes specimens from the Smithsonian National Museum of Natural History and the Harvard Museum of Natural History. Geological history displays will tell the story of the creation of the luminous stones, which lie buried underground and in the mountains around Bethel and are an ever more popular reason for visitors to make the trip.

COVERED BRIDGES Artists' Covered Bridge, Newry (across the Sunday River, 5 miles northwest of Bethel). A weathered town bridge built in 1872 and painted by numerous 19th-century landscape artists, notably John Enneking. A great spot to sun and swim. Other swimming holes can be found at intervals along the road upstream of the bridge.

Lovejoy Covered Bridge, South Andover, roughly 0.25 mile east of Rt. 5. Built across the Ellis River in 1867, another local swimming hole (it's more than 7 miles north of Rt. 2).

SCENIC DRIVES Evans Notch. Follow Rt. 2 west to Gilead and turn south on Rt. 113, following the Wild and then the Cold River south through one of the most spectacular mountain passes in northern New England.

Grafton Notch State Park. A beautiful drive even if you don't hike. Continue on beyond Upton for views of Lake Umbagog; note the loop you can make back from Upton along the old road (East B Hill Rd.) to Andover (look for the vintage-1867 Lovejoy Covered Bridge across the Ellis River), then south on Rt. 5 to Rt. 2.

Patte Brook Auto Tour, a 4-mile, self-guided tour with stops at 11 areas along Patte Brook near the national forest's Crocker Pond campground in West Bethel. The tour begins on Forest Rd. No. 7 (Patte Brook Rd.), 5 miles south of Bethel on Rt. 5. A glacial bog, former orchards and homesites, and an old dam and pond are among the clearly marked sites.

Rangeley and Weld loops. See the introduction to "Western Mountains and Lakes Region" for a description of these rewarding drives. You can access both by following Rt. 2 north from Bethel along the Androscoggin River, but back-road buffs may prefer cutting up the narrow rural valleys threaded by Rumford Rd. or Rt. 232 from Locke Mills (Greenwood); both join Rt. 2 at Rumford Point.

OTHER SITES Mount Zircon Bottle. Between Nos. 20 and 22 on Bethel's Broad St., you'll see this historic bottle-shaped lunch stand, built after the company's second bottling plant opened in 1922.

✳ To Do

BIRDING Birders will encounter waterfowl in Patte Marsh area of the **White Mountain National Forest**, and in **Grafton Notch State Park** (see *Hiking* for both areas) look for Philadelphia vireos near the Appalachian Trail parking lot, along with many more species.

BICYCLING/WALKING The **Bethel Pathway** offers a nearly 3.5-mile roundtrip along the Androscoggin River beginning in the Davis Park picnic area and playground on the eastern edge of town off Rt. 26., where you walk through a replica of the Artists' Covered Bridge (maps available at the Bethel chamber). ✎ **Bethel Bicycle** (207-824-2010; bethelbicycle.com), 53 Mayville Rd. (Rt. 2), Bethel. Bicycles sold, rented, and repaired. Group rides sponsored on Tuesday at 5:30 PM through summer and fall.

CAMPING In the **Evans Notch area** of the White Mountain National Forest there are five campgrounds: **Basin** (21 sites), **Cold River** (14 sites), **Crocker Pond** (7 sites), **Hastings** (24 sites), and **Wild River** (12 sites). All except Crocker Pond and Wild River, which take campers first come, first served, accept reservations mid-May–mid-Oct. through the National Recreation Reservation Service (1-877-444-6777; recreation.gov), but sites are often available without reservations. In addition, five private camping areas are within 8 miles of Bethel

CANOEING AND KAYAKING Popular local routes include the **Androscoggin River**, which has become far more accessible in recent years with 10 put-in points mapped and shuttle service offered between Shelburne on the New Hampshire line and the Rumford boat landing; the **Sunday River** (beginning at the covered bridge) also offers great whitewater trips in spring. A chain of water connects **North**, **South**, and **Round Ponds** and offers a day of rewarding paddling, with swimming holes and picnic stops en route.

Bethel Outdoor Adventure and Campground (207-824-4224 or 1-800-533-3607; betheloutdooradventure.com), Rt. 2, Bethel, offers shuttle service, canoe and kayak rentals, guided trips, and kayak clinics. An inn-to-inn weekend is one possibility; they will make all arrangements.

Sun Valley Sports (207-824-7533 or 1-877-851-7533; sunvalleysports.com), 129 Sunday River Rd., Bethel, offers guided (and nonguided) kayak and canoe tours and rentals on the Androscoggin River and on local lakes and ponds. They also offer ATV tours and weekly cabin rentals. This is a full-service authorized Orvis dealer, with Orvis-endorsed guides. Wading and driftboat fly-fishing trips.

Mahoosuc Guide Service (207-824-2073; mahoosuc.com), 1513 Bear River Rd., Newry 04261. One- to 10-day canoe trips, including a trip down the Allagash River in fall and spring, a trip with Cree Indians in Quebec, and western U.S. trips, too.

Pleasant River Campground (207-836-2000; pleasantrivercampground.com), Rt. 2, West Bethel, rents canoes and kayaks and offers shuttles.

CHAIRLIFT RIDE Sunday River Resort (207-824-3500; sundayriver.com), Newry 04261. The Chondola operates in summer and fall for rides to the North Peak, offering spectacular views of the Mahoosuc Mountains; Old Speck Mountain, the third highest peak in Maine, is visible from the summit. You can choose to ride up in an enclosed cabin or an open chair, and hike down on a trail.

FISHING Temporary nonresident licenses are available at the Bethel, Newry, and Woodstock town offices; also at **Bethel Outdoor Adventure** (207-824-4224 or 1-800-533-3607; betheloutdooradventure.com), Rt. 2, Bethel, and **Sun Valley Sports** (207-824-7533 or 1-877-851-7533; sunvalleysports.com), 129 Sunday River Rd., Bethel. Fly-fishing is a growing sport here, especially along the Androscoggin, which is increasingly known for the size of its trout. For guiding and fly-fishing instruction also check with **Aldro French**, based at Middle Dam in Andover (rapidriverflyfishing.com).

FOR FAMILIES ✍ **The BIG Adventure Center** (207-824-0929), Rt. 2 and North Rd. (adjacent to the Norseman), Bethel. A collection of arcade games, waterslide, miniature golf, and indoor rock climbing includes the largest laser tag arena in Maine. Call for information.

GOLF Bethel Inn Resort (207-824-2175; bethelinn.com), Broad St., Bethel. An 18-hole, 6,700-yard course and driving range. Mid-May–Oct. the Guaranteed Performance School of Golf (PGA) offers three- and five-day sessions (classes limited to three students per PGA instructor); golf-cart rentals are available.

Sunday River Golf Club (207-824-4653; sundayrivergolfclub.com). Top-rated by *Golf Week* and *Golf Digest*, Sunday River Golf Club has gracefully situated, wide fairways; each hole offers its own unique views of the surrounding five mountain ranges.

HIKING White Mountain National Forest, although primarily in New Hampshire, includes 41,943 acres in Maine. A number of the trails in the Evans Notch area are spectacular. Trail maps for the Baldface Circle Trail, Basin Trail, Bickford Brook Trail, and Caribou Trail are available from the **Bethel Chamber of Commerce** (207824-2282 or 1-800-442-5826; bethelmaine.com).

Grafton Notch State Park, Rt. 26, between Newry and Upton. From Bethel, take Rt. 2 east to Rt. 26 north for 7.8 miles. Turn left at the Bear River Trading Post (Newry Corner) and drive toward New Hampshire for 8.7 miles. **Screw Auger Falls** is 1 mile farther—a spectacular area at the end of the Mahoosuc Range. Other sights include **Mother Walker Falls** and **Moose Cave**, a 0.5-mile nature walk. The big hike is up **Old Speck**, the third highest mountain in the state; roundtrip is 7.8 miles. Also see *Green Space* for the new 35-mile Grafton Loop Trail.

Wight Brook Nature Preserve/Step Falls can be found just before the entrance to Grafton Notch State Park. From Newry Corner, drive 7.9 miles. On your right will be a white farmhouse, followed by a field just before a bridge. There is a road leading to the rear left of the field, where you may park. The well-marked trail is just behind the trees at the back.

In Shelburne there are hiking trails on **Mount Crag**, **Mount Cabot**, and **Ingalls Mountain**, and there are more trails in **Evans Notch**. For details, check the Appalachian Mountain Club's *White Mountain Guide* (subscribe online for $15 at outdoors.org) and John Gibson's *50 Hikes in Coastal and Inland Maine: From Burnt Meadow Mountains to Maine's Bold Coast* (Countryman Press).

Mount Will Hiking Trail. Developed by the Bethel Conservation Commission, this 3.25-mile loop is a good family trip; many people choose to climb only to the North Ledges (640 vertical feet in 0.75 mile), yielding a view of the Androscoggin Valley, which only gets better over the next 1.5 miles—climbing over ledges 1,450 feet and then descending the South Cliffs. The trailhead parking lot is opposite the recycling center on Rt. 2, just 1.9 miles east of the Riverside Rest Area (which is just beyond the turnoff for Sunday River).

HORSEBACK RIDING Deepwood Farm (207-824-2595; deepwoodfarm.com), Albany, offers trail rides and summer camps. **New England Riding and Carriage Driving** (207-731-6888; newenglandridinganddriving.com), Telemark Inn Wilderness Lodge, Mason. Leonarda Joost and Steve Crone offer "Learn to Carriage Drive" packages and riding instruction, as well as therapeutic riding and carriage for special-needs children.

LLAMA TREKKING ⚘ **Telemark Inn** (207-836-2703; newenglanddogsledding .com), 591 Kings Hwy., Mason Township, 10 miles west of Bethel. Treks offered Apr.–Oct. Primarily for guests of the Telemark Inn, but trips ranging from half a day ($50 for three hours, plus taxes and 10 percent gratuity) to three days ($750) into the surrounding wilderness are available to non-guests as well. Steve Crone offered the first llama treks in New England, and we took one of the first that he offered. The llamas carry your gear, but you walk beside them.

MOUNTAIN BIKING Sunday River Resort (207-824-3500; sundayriver.com), Newry 04261. Thirty trails with 20 miles of beginner, intermediate, and advanced terrain offer open dirt roads and singletrack trails with jumps, bridges, and berms. The bike park is reached by the Chondola lift; the trails cover the North Peak and South Ridge areas of the ski resort.

ROCKHOUNDING ⚘ This corner of Oxford County is recognized as one of the world's richest sources of some minerals and semiprecious gems. More than a third of the world's mineral varieties can be found here. Gems include amethyst, aquamarine, tourmaline, and topaz. Mining has gone on around here since tourmaline was discovered at Mount Mica in 1821. ⚘ Jim Mann's **Mt. Mann Jewelers** (207-824-3030; mtmann.com), 57 Main St., Bethel, includes a mineral museum. In the cellar kids (of all ages) can explore "Crystal Cave": a dimly lit "mine" in which rockhounds can fill their cardboard buckets (for a nominal fee) and then identify the stones back in the museum. **Songo Pond Mine** (207-824-3898), 433 Baker

Rd., Albany Township, is both a real mine open to the public with reservations and a rock shop, both open May–Nov. Reservations recommended.

Sunday River Gems (207-824-3414), Sunday River Rd., Bethel, is open daily 10–6, and sells local jewelers' one-of-a-kind pieces set with Maine gems, along with other gold and silver jewelry. **Mt. Mica Rarities** (207-875-3060; maine tourmalineonline.com), 162 Main St., Philbrook Place, Bethel, has a stockpile of tourmaline, amethyst, aquamarine, and smoky quartz, and a collection is on display. Phil McCrillis is the fourth generation of his family to mine Mt. Mica, which was owned by his family until 2003. **Maine Minerology Expeditions at Bethel Outdoor Adventure and Campground** (207-824-4224 or 1-800-533-3607;

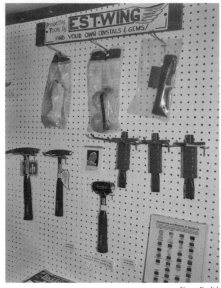

Nancy English

PROSPECTING TOOLS AT SUNDAY RIVER GEMS

rocksme.biz), Rt. 2, Bethel. May–Sept., dig from mine tailings, fill a bucket, and sluice it clean in search of gems. Tourmaline is the most exciting discovery, along with mica, rose and smoky quartz, and pretty lepidolite, according to Jeff Parsons, an owner. Every week several tours of the Bumpus Mine, famous for huge beryl crystals, are offered; closed-toe shoes required.

✍ **Western Maine Mineral Adventures** (207-674-3440; digmainegems.com), 1148 S. Main St. (Rt. 26), Woodstock. Zoltan and Jody Matolcsy offer mine tailings, purchased by the bucket, and a facility to screen the tailings and identify minerals. Field trips to area mines, mostly closed locations, are insured, and visitors can dig for up to 74 minerals. Call ahead to avoid the school field trips. Watermelon tourmaline and far more are at a new store in South Paris, scheduled to open in 2010.

The **Annual Gem, Mineral, and Jewelry Show** (second weekend in July) is a mega mineral event with guided field trips to local quarries. (For information contact the Bethel Area Chamber of Commerce, 207-824-2282.)

SWIMMING There are numerous lakes and river swimming holes in the area. It's best to ask the chamber of commerce about where access is currently possible. Reliable spots include:

Angevine Park and Swim Pond (207-824-2669). The town of Bethel has a swimming pond open to all free of charge. It is located on North Rd., 2.2 miles from Rt. 2 (turn in at Big Adventure Center and the Norseman Inn & Motel). Open daily 10–7, summer only.

Artists' Covered Bridge. Follow SUNDAY RIVER SKI RESORT signs north from Bethel, but bear right at two Y-intersections instead of turning onto either of the ski-area access roads. Look for the covered bridge on your left. Space for parking, bushes for changing.

Wild River in Evans Notch, Gilead, offers some obvious access spots off Rt. 113, as does the **Bear River**, which follows Rt. 26 through Grafton Notch.

✳ Winter Activities

CROSS-COUNTRY SKIING ✍ **Sunday River Outdoor Center** (207-824-5700; sundayriver.com), Newry 04261. Cross-country and snowshoeing trails with picnic areas, with equipment rentals available.

Bethel Nordic Ski Center (207-824-2175; caribourecreation.com), Bethel Inn, Bethel. More than 30 kilometers of groomed trails, wide enough for ski-skating and perfect for classic Nordic cross-country skiing. The trails offer beautiful mountain views, solitude, and challenges for all levels. Skating and classic trails, rental equipment, and lessons available.

Carter's Cross Country Ski Center (207-539-4848; cartersxcski.com), Intervale Rd. (off Rt. 26 south of the village), Bethel. Open daily during winter. Dave Carter, a member of one of Bethel's oldest families and a longtime cross-country pro, maintains 55 kilometers of wooded trails on 1,000 acres, meandering from 600 up to 1,800 feet in elevation; an easy loop connects two lodges and runs along the Androscoggin River. Reasonably priced equipment rentals and lessons; additional center on Rt. 26 in Oxford with 40 kilometers of trails.

DOGSLEDDING Mahoosuc Guide Service (207-824-2073; mahoosuc.com), 1513 Bear River Rd., Newry 04261. Polly Mahoney and Kevin Slater offer combination skiing and mushing trips along with lodgings at Mahoosuc Mountain Lodge. You can work with the dogs as much you want, for two- to three-day or longer trips.

Winter Journeys (207-928-2026), based in Lovell. Day, multiday, and custom programs.

New England Dogsledding (207-731-6888; newenglanddogsledding.com), 591 Kings Hwy., Mason, offers everything from one- to three-hour trips to multiple day "Learn to Dogsled" packages on trails in the Umbagog National Wildlife Refuge. Friday dogsledding is offered at the Bethel Inn Resort 5–7:30 PM.

✍ **Sunday River Outdoor Center** (207-824-5700; sundayriver.com), Newry 04261. A dogsledding and Iditarod team based in Michigan, Nature's Kennel Sled Dog Adventures, offer 30-minute dogsled rides on most weekends and holidays.

DOWNHILL SKIING ✍ ♿ **Sunday River Resort** (207-824-3500; resort reservations, 1-800-543-2754; sundayriver.com), Newry 04261. Sunday River has become synonymous with snow. A total of 132 trails now lace eight interconnected mountain peaks, including the Jordan Bowl. Challenges include a 3-mile easy run from a summit and White Heat, considered one of the premier bump runs in the East. The trails are served by 16 lifts including the only Chondola lift in New England: nine quad chairlifts (four high-speed detachable), three triple chairlifts, one double, and two surface lifts. The vertical descent is 2,340 feet, and the top elevation is 3,140 feet. Snowmaking covers more than 90 percent of the skiing and riding terrain. You'll also find one mini pipe, one super pipe, and five terrain parks, including the resort's signature Rocking Chair. Facilities include three base lodges and a Peak Lodge, ski shops, several restaurants, and a total of 6,000 slope-side

SUNDAY RIVER

beds (see *Lodging*). The Perfect Turn & Snowboard School offers Guaranteed Learn-to-Ski in One Day and specialty clinics, Mogul Munchkins for ages 4–6, Mogul Meisters for ages 7–14, and the Gould Academy Competition Programs. Sunday River is also home to the Maine Handicapped Skiing Program. Two lighted tubing runs are found at the White Cap Base Lodge along with a lighted skating rink, and the best spot for viewing fireworks on Saturday nights in-season is from South Ridge Base Lodge. Night skiing and riding Fri., Sat., and select holiday evenings 4–8. Two-day lift tickets are $146 adults, $122 young adults (13–18), and $100 for juniors and seniors.

✐ **Mount Abram Family Resort** (207-875-5000; mtabram.com), Locke Mills (Greenwood). Open 9–4 Thu.–Sun., Maine school vacation weeks, and holidays. With 44 trails and slopes, well-known learn-to-ski trails, many black-diamond trails, and a "cruiser" trail, most with snowmaking, Mount Abram offers all levels of skiers a great challenge on 650 acres of terrain and the charm of small crowds and local traditions. The vertical drop is 1,150 feet but well-designed trails create the sense of a big mountain. Facilities include two double chairlifts and two T-bars. A lightning strike and fire destroyed the base lodge in 2011; new facilities were constructed in 2012. A PSIA ski school with snowboard and telemark instruction. $49 adults, $37 seniors and juniors on weekends and holidays, $25 military; 80-plus and 5 and under free. Weekday specials include two lift tickets for the price of one Thu. and $75 "a carload" (everyone must be buckled into a seat belt) on Fri.

ICE SKATING Sunday River Resort (207-824-3500; resort reservations, 1-800-543-2754; sundayriver.com), Newry 04261. The lighted rink is free and open every day and evening that weather permits. Rentals are available in the White Cap Lodge during business hours. Call for rink conditions.

SLEIGH RIDES Bethel Inn Resort (see *Lodging*), Bethel, hosts sleigh rides with **Deepwood Farm** (207-824-2595; deepwoodfarm.com), Albany, 5–7:30 PM on Sat. and holiday periods. The farm also offers sleigh rides winter days and evenings. At the farm, the old-fashioned sleigh holds four to five people. The big sleigh, which operates at the Bethel Inn on Saturday night 5–7, holds eight.

SNOWMOBILING Contact the Bethel Area Chamber of Commerce for information on where to get maps of the trail system. Maine and New Hampshire also maintain 60 miles of trails in the Evans Notch District. **Sun Valley Sports & Guide Services** (207-824-7533 or 1-877-851-7533), 129 Sunday River Rd., Bethel, rents snowmobiles, offers guided snowmobile trips, and rents snowshoes.

ZIPLINE TOURS Sunday River Resort (207-824-3500; sundayriver.com), Newry 04261. Cross back and forth high above a deep ravine and streambed near the ski trails of Sunday River from a series of six lines from 100 to 300 feet long. Speeds of up to 25 miles per hour are achieved on the strong ziplines; your harness will keep you secure. Reservations are recommended for the tours, offered in summer, fall, and winter. The six-zipline tour was $49 for all ages in 2011 and takes about 2½ hours. There's also a twin zipline for paired travel.

✳ Green Space

The Mahoosuc Land Trust (207-824-3806; mahoosuc.org), P.O. Box 981, Bethel 04217. Formed in 1988 to preserve land in the Mahoosuc Range and the Androscoggin Valley, the trust owns islands, shoreland, and floodplain land, along with easements on land in the eastern foothills and on the banks of a large pond. Grafton Loop Trail, a trail about 35 miles long, is a collaborative partnership on land trust land with Maine Appalachian Trail Club (matc.org). It can be accessed at the Grafton Loop Trailhead on Rt. 26, or at the Appalachian Trail parking lot in Grafton Notch State Park. The Rumford Whitecap Mountain Preserve was purchased in 2007; the 2.5-mile trail is a popular day trip, and is accessed off the East Andover Rd. in Rumford. A map of the 42-mile Androscoggin Canoe Trail is available.

✳ Lodging

All listings are in Bethel 04217 unless otherwise noted
The **Bethel Area Chamber of Commerce** maintains a lodging reservations service for rooms on and off the mountain, year round· 1-800-442-5826; bethelmaine.com.

Sunday River Ski Resort maintains its own toll-free reservation number, 1-800-543-2SKI, good nationwide and in Canada; the service is geared toward winter and condo information. Many other condos and rental homes are available in the Bethel area through **Maine Street Realty & Rentals** (207-824-2114 or 1-800-824-6024), **Connecting Rentals** (207-824-4829), **Mahoosuc Realty & Rentals** (1-888-310-2771) and **Four Seasons Realty**

& Rentals (207-875-2414). Also the **Kedarburn Inn** in "Oxford Hills."

INNS 🐾 ♪ ᕘ **The Bethel Inn Resort** (207-824-2175 or 1-800-654-0125; bethelinn.com). This rambling, yellow wooden inn and its annexes frame a corner of the town common (for the history of this special resort, see the chapter introduction). Most Main Inn rooms have a gas fireplace. The formal dining room is truly elegant (see *Dining Out*), and Millbrook Tavern is more casual. The 49 rooms in the inn and guesthouses vary widely in size and view (request a larger room in back, overlooking the mountains), but all have air-conditioning, phone, cable TV, and private bath; some have a fireplace.

Families should opt for one of the 60 one-, two-, and three-bedroom town houses on the golf course and on Mill Hill Rd. There's an indoor–outdoor pool (heated to 92 degrees in winter) that's great year-round; also two saunas, an exercise room, a game room, and a lounge. The 18-hole golf course, with 7 holes dating to 1915 and 11 more added by Geoffrey Cornish, is a big draw, with golf-school sessions offered throughout the season. Other facilities also include a Har-Tru tennis court, a boathouse with canoes, and a sandy beach on Songo Pond, as well as an extensive cross-country ski and snowshoe network. From $50 per person in the inn including g breakfast; town houses, $110. Many packages are available, like Golf and Dine for an extra $40 per person. Children age 11 and under stay free in room with parent (plus $20 for the meal plan). Spa services. A concierge center offering Orvis fly-fishing, dogsledding, and canoe and kayak trips allows you to "choose your own adventure."

🐾 **Sudbury Inn** (207-824-2174 or 1-800-395-7837; sudburyinn.com), 151 Main St., P.O. Box 369. A nicely restored village inn built in 1873 to serve train travelers (the depot was just down the street). Innkeeper Scott Davis offers 11 guest rooms and six

Nancy English

WEDDING AT BETHEL INN RESORT

suites, all different shapes and decors. All have a private bath, TV, and air-conditioning, and two suites have whirlpool. The dining room is popular (see *Dining Out*). Suds Pub (see *Eating Out*) is a year-round evening gathering spot. Pets are accepted only in the Carriage House for $15 a night. The town house is available for rent year-round, $99–375; ski season, $109–475 double; includes breakfast.

The Briar Lea Inn at the Jolly Drayman English Pub (207-824-4717 or 1-877-311-1299; briarleainn.com), Rt. 2/26. Open year-round. One mile west of town, 5 miles east of Sunday River. Cindy Coughenour and Fred Seibert are innkeepers at this 1850s farmhouse, an attractive inn whose six rooms feature private bath, flat-screen TV, phone, and eclectic antique decor, all updated in 2011. The English pub is open to the public (see *Dining Out*). The sitting area with a fireplace is particularly attractive, a great place to enjoy a drink. $85–140.

♿ **The Victoria Inn** (207-824-8060 or 1-888-774-1235; thevictoria-inn.com), 32 Main St. Open year-round. High-Victorian details like silk-screened wallpaper make the high-ceilinged rooms at this inn posh. The inn has 14

SUDBURY INN, BETHEL

Nancy English

quiet and peaceful rooms, each with private bath, phone, TV, plush beds, and some with rocking chairs or sofas. A full breakfast is included. $109–279 depending on season.

✔ **Telemark Inn** (207-836-2703; telemarkinn.com), RFD 2, Box 800. It is a challenge to describe this unusual retreat, set among birch trees 10 miles from Bethel Village, 2.5 miles off the nearest back road and surrounded by national forest, with llamas, 60 huskies, and good riding and carriage horses. Steve Crone and staff offers horseback riding and carriage driving; winter brings the opportunity to try dog-sledding. Meals are served family-style. Six rooms share two baths and accommodate 10 to 17 guests. Two-day packages include room, breakfast, lunch, and guided day activities and start at $150 per person; three-day packages start at $475 adult, $375 child. Inn rates $125 per room include breakfast.

🐾 ✔ **Philbrook Farm Inn** (603-466-3831; philbrookfarminn.com), 881 North Rd., Shelburne, NH 03581. Open year-round, except Nov.–day after Christmas, and Apr. Twenty miles west of Bethel, just over the New Hampshire line. The long, meandering farmhouse, owned by the same family since 1861, sits above a floodplain of the

Androscoggin River with the Mahoosuc Range at its back, with 19 guest rooms furnished with the kind of hand-me-downs that most innkeepers scour the hills for. Second-floor rooms have a private bath; third-floor rooms share. The family-style meals are as old-fashioned as the rest of the place (fish on Friday, ham and beans on Saturday night; BYOB). There are also four housekeeping cottages and two seasonal cabins. $130–150 per couple MAP, plus a 15 percent service charge. B&B rates from $105–130. Higher for the cottages.

BED & BREAKFASTS Austin's Holidae House Bed and Breakfast
(207-824-3400 or 1-877-224-3400; holidaehouse.com), P.O. Box 1248, 85 Main St. A gracious turn-of-the-century Victorian built by a local lumber baron. Laurence Austin and Marcia Foster-Austin offer seven rooms furnished in comfortable antiques, with cable TV, private bath, and air-conditioning. $110–125 double, or $85 for guests who say "carpe diem" on the phone or in person on a day when there is an available room, includes a full breakfast made to order.

♿ **Bethel Hill Bed & Breakfast** (207-824-2461; bethelhill.com), 66 Broad St. Renovated with the needs of a B&B in mind, Scott and Carol Gould host three suites with whirlpool bath and cable TV, ceiling fans and air-conditioning, and soundproofing in the walls. $129–179 depending on season, includes complimentary pair of bikes; Scott Gould, a certified staff trainer and level 3 ski pro at Sunday River, can provide ski-tuning lessons.

✔ **Chapman Inn** (207-824-2657 or 1-877-359-1498; chapmaninn.com), 1 Mill Hill Rd. Fred Nolte and Sandra Frye bring years in the hospitality business to this rambling white wooden inn on the common. Eight comfortable

THE VICTORIA INN

Nancy English

units have private bath and two share; there's cable TV and air-conditioning in all rooms, and a phone in all, too. Common space in the barn includes a game room with a pool table and two saunas. $79–119 in summer, $89–139 in winter; $35 per person for the dorm, breakfast included, with fresh fruit, muffins, and omelet of the day.

✍ ♿ **Crocker Pond House** (207-836-2027; crockerpond.com), 917 North Rd. Off by itself on the Shelburne–Bethel Rd. (5 miles from downtown Bethel), facing south toward Evans Notch, this is a long, shingled, one-room-deep house designed and built by the architect-innkeeper Stuart Crocker. It's a beauty, filled with light and grace, and very quiet. Hiking and snowshoeing or just peace are what it offers, but no TVs. The five guest rooms, two with a loft for children, all have private bath. $150 per couple for one night, less for longer stays, includes a full breakfast, afternoon tea and cookies.

✍ ♿ **The Norseman Inn and Motel** (207-824-2002 or 1-800-824-0722; norsemaninn.com), Rt. 2, P.O. Box 934. An old farmstead with eight light, pleasant guest rooms, and 22 motel units in the renovated barn. Guests can sit by the common room's fireplace made from local stones. The motel units are spacious; amenities include a laundry room and game room, a deck, and walking trails. $58–158 depending on season.

🐾 ✍ ♿ **The Inn at the Rostay** (207-824-3111 or 1-888-754-0072; rostay .com), 186 Mayville Rd., Bethel. Kathy and Al Thrall's motel consists of units ranged behind a 19th-century house, with 19 rooms accommodating one to four people, including one two-room suite. Number 26 is a surprisingly cozy room in the older but nicely renovated 1950s section, with a queen bed and a

sofa. All rooms have phone, heat, TV and VCR, refrigerator, and microwave. Heated pool in summer, and outdoor hot tub year-round. Hot chocolate and cookies après ski. A full breakfast with a menu is served ($9 extra). The house has a guest parlor that doubles as a showcase for locally made quilts, sold in a quilt store in back. Dan Thrall, the owners' son, offers his expertise as a fly-fishing/hunting guide, and guided snowmobile tours with rentals are also available. $69–120 for rooms, $150–230 for two-bedroom suites.

SKI LODGES AND CONDOMINIUMS
✍ **Sunday River Ski Resort** (207-824-3500; resort reservations, 1-800-543-2SKI), P.O. Box 4500, now offers more than 6,000 "slope-side beds." There are condominium complexes ranging from studios to three-bedroom units. Each complex has access to an indoor pool, Jacuzzi, sauna, laundry, recreation room, and game room; **Cascades** and **Sunrise** offer large common rooms with fireplaces. **Merrill Brook Village Condominiums** have fireplaces, and many have a whirlpool tub. **South Ridge** also offers a fireplace in each unit, which range from studios to three bedrooms. The 68-room **Snow Cap Inn** has an atrium with fieldstone fireplaces, an exercise room, and an outdoor Jacuzzi; it also offers reasonably priced bunks. The 230-room **Grand Summit Hotel** has both standard and kitchen-equipped units, a health club with a pool, and conference facilities; it offers rooms and studios as well as one- and two-bedroom efficiency units. The 195-room **Jordan Grand Hotel** is off by itself but linked by ski trails as well as road, circled by the mountains of the Jordan Bowl; facilities include a health club, a swimming pool, and restaurants. Hotel prices start at $79. In winter, condo units are based on ski

packages, from $60 per night or $349 per person for five days. All winter lodging rates include a lift ticket and a ski school lesson.

CAMPGROUNDS 🐾 ⚓ **Littlefield Beaches** (207-875-3290; littlefield beaches.com), 13 Littlefield Lane, Greenwood 04255. Open mid-May–Sept. Arthur and Lisa Park run a clean, quiet family campground surrounded by three connecting lakes. Full hookups, a laundry room, miniature golf, a game room, swimming, kayak rentals. $32–40 daily, seasonal rates available.

🐾 ⚓ Ꮛ **Bethel Outdoor Adventure and Campground** (207-824-4224 or 1-800-533-3607; betheloutdoor adventure.com), Rt. 2. Jeff and Pattie Parsons offer RV and tent sites with a camp store on the Androscoggin River (where you can swim), within walking distance of downtown shops and restaurants. $20–32 daily.

⚓ **Pleasant River Campground** (207-836-2000; pleasantrivercamp ground.com), 800 West Bethel Rd. (Rt. 2). Wooded sites, restrooms, pool, playground, and many recreational possibilities. In addition to camping, Mike and Michelle Madoi offer canoe and kayak rentals, Androscoggin River access, shuttle service, and lobster boils, pig roasts, and barbecues. $22–30 daily.

🐾 Ꮛ **Stony Brook Recreation** (207-824-2846; stonybrookrec.com), 42 Powell Place, Hanover. Open year-round with open and wooded sites. $22–30 daily.

🐾 **Grafton Notch Campground** (207-824-2292; campgrafton.com), near the Bear River in Newry. Open May–Oct. The closest campground to Grafton Notch State Park. $25 a day.

Also see **Papoose Pond Resort and Campground** in "Oxford Hills." For

campgrounds in the White Mountain National Forest, see *To Do—Camping*.

SPECIAL LODGING ⚓ Ꮛ **The Maine Houses** (1-800-646-8737; themaine houses.com), Bryant Pond (reservations: P.O. Box 1138, Yarmouth 04096). Two of the four houses are located on or near Lake Christopher, with another just a short walk away; all four are near Sunday River Ski Area. These unique, self-service guesthouses are perfect for small groups or large reunions. The Maine House has nine bedrooms, six and a half baths, a steam room, and a wraparound porch. In the Maine Farmhouse there are seven bedrooms, each with a private bath. The Maine Country House has three bedrooms, two full baths, and a hot tub on its deck. The Maine Mountainview House features seven bedrooms, seven full baths, an indoor spa, and a fireplace. All four have fully equipped kitchen, access to the lake, canoes, and outdoor sports equipment, cable TV, DVD/VCR, and all bedding and towels. $20–50 per person per night, but groups of 20 to 94 are the main customers.

Androscoggin Home Rentals (207-824-2461; ahr-online.com), 66 Broad St. Scott and Carol Gould rent three cabins and vacation homes: fully outfitted, five-bedroom Village House; secluded River House; and Lake Cottage on remote Concord Pond, without electricity and only cold running water—it's the real thing. $150 and up per night, with weekly and multiday rates.

✴ Where to Eat

All restaurants are in Bethel unless otherwise noted
DINING OUT Sudbury Inn (207-824-2174 or 1-800-359-7837; sudbury inn.com), Main St. Open for dinner 5:30–9 Tue.–Sun. year-round except

Nov.–early Dec. and Apr.–early June. Attractive, traditional dining rooms and a sunporch in a 19th-century village inn. Widely respected chef Peter Bodwell has a fine reputation with a menu that changes seasonally with local ingredients. The chowder is the 2011 winner of both the judges' and the people's favorites awards from the annual Bethel Harvest Fest. Entrées $18–31.

❧ **The Jolly Drayman at the Briar Lea Inn** (207-824-4717), Rt. 2/26. The inn's welcoming dining room serves dinner daily. This English pub serves classics like fish-and-chips and bangers and mash along with Indian specialties like kormas, tikka masala, and vindaloos. Fine selection of draft and bottled beers. A reliably good and reasonably priced place for dinner. Entrées $10–20.

22 Broad Street (207-824-3496), 22 Broad St. This handsome inn holds an elegant dining room with an Italian-inspired menu that starts with carpaccio, escarole and bean soup, and more. A lovely primi, first course, might be the ravioli amatriciana, with pancetta, onions, and herbs. Among secondi there is osso buco, braised veal shank, and braciole alla Siciliana—beef rolls simmered in tomato sauce. Screened porch for summer dining, with 20-plus tables, plus a martini bar. Entrées $12.50–24.

♿ **The Bethel Inn Resort** (207-824-2175 or 1-800-654-0125), Bethel Common. Serves breakfast and dinner. An elegant formal dining room with a Steinway, hearth, and large windows overlooking the golf course and hills, plus a year-round veranda. The menu offers a choice of a dozen entrées that might include Maine lobster, Tuscan veal chop, and prime rib. Entrées $17–32.

S. S. Milton (207-824-2589), 43 Main St. Open for dinner 5–9, lunch in sum-

mer. Entrées ($16–23) might include scallops Nantucket with white wine, lemon, and cheddar cheese, topped with Ritz crackers, and Boothbay fettuccine with Maine lobster, scallops, and shrimp in a white cream wine sauce.

Sunday River Resort operates several "fine-dining" restaurants: **Legends** (207-824-5858; sundayriver.com) at the Grand Summit Resort Hotel, and **Sliders** (207-824-5000) at the Jordan Grand.

Phoenix House & Well (207-824-2222; phoenixhouseandwell.com), Skiway Rd., just before South Ridge Base Lodge at Sunday River. With windows on a great view, pick from a list of pasta and sauces, or go for a steak, beef, or tuna. Live music in the Well in winter. Entrées $16–22.

EATING OUT ✪ ✒ Café di Cocoa (207-824-6386; cafedicocoa.com), 125 Main St. A market and café with breakfast and lunch items; in winter an ethnic dinner is served by reservation only (call 207-824-5282) on Sat. night, BYOB. Cathy DiCocco's cheerful eatery specializes in vegan and vegetarian dishes. Full bakery, juice and espresso bars, and wonderful pain au chocolate. WE ARE A BAKERIE, NOT A FAKERIE, a sign proclaims, ONLY PURE, NATURAL INGREDIENTS. A calzone with cheese was crisp and savory, and stir-fry with tofu and bell peppers delicious.

Rooster's Roadhouse (207-824-0309; roostersroadhouse.com), 159 Mayville Rd., Rt. 2. Popular with locals and visitors alike, this roadhouse serves lunch and dinner all year round. Owners Steve Etheridge and Gary Szpara preside at this pub and family-style eatery. Entrées up to $28.

✒ **Suds Pub** (207-824-6558 or 1-800-395-7837), downstairs at the Sudbury Inn, 151 Main St. Open year-round, from 4:30 PM daily; lunch served in summer and between Thanksgiving and mid-Apr. A friendly pub with the largest number of beers on tap west of Portland, and a reasonably priced pub menu with a wide choice of pizzas. Burgers, soups and salads, ribs, lobster rolls, and pasta. Kids' menu.

Two Brothers Steakhouse (207- 824-4445), Sunday River Rd. Owners Rick and Ron Savage opened this family steakhouse in 2011, offering breakfast, lunch, and dinner year-round. Entrées $15–20.

The Funky Red Barn (207-824-3003; funkyredbarn.com), 19 Summer St. The Funky Burger is served on a huge Thomas's English muffin. Nasty Nachos include black olives and jalapeños to get the digestive turmoil up to speed. This newly reborn popular place used to be the Backstage Lounge, and sometimes features a DJ. Try the last-Thursday-of-the-month $8.50 roast beef dinner.

Crossroads Diner & Deli (207-824-3673), 24 Mayville Rd. (Rt. 2). Breakfast, lunch, and dinner. This is the hangout for the loyal locals.

The Sunday River Brewing Co. (207-824-4ALE; sundayriverbrewpub .com), junction of Sunday River Rd. and Rt. 2, North Bethel. Open from 11:30 daily for lunch and dinner. Live entertainment.

Bethel's Best Pizza Grille and Dairy Bar (207-824-3192; bethelsbest .com), just west of Bethel on Rt. 2. Open from 7 AM for a full breakfast. Will deliver, and the pizza is good. Homemade clam "chowdah," an excellent runner-up at the 2009 Harvest Fest chowder contest, chili, burgers, subs, salads, and "lobstah" rolls are also on the extensive menu. Entrées $7–14.

Matterhorn Ski Bar Wood-Fired Pizza and Fresh Pasta (207-824-6271; matterhornskibar.com), Sunday River Rd., ski season only, offers entertainment and steak, seafood, and brick-oven pizza.

Cho Sun (207-824- 7370; chosun restaurant.com), 141 Main St., Bethel. Open Wed.–Sun., 5:30–9. Authentic Japanese and Korean cuisine from owner Pok Sun Lane, who is Korean, including the Korean classics like savory and spicy beef bulgoki and kimchee stew, sushi and teriyaki steak.

Kowloon Village Chinese Restaurant (207-824-3707), Lower Main St. Simon and his wife are from Kowloon, and their Chinese food is good. Eat in or take out.

Smokin' Good BBQ (207-824-4744), in the parking lot of the Good Food Store, Rt. 2. Cooked "low and slow for up to 16 hours," according to Dave Nivus, the owner, these ribs taste tender and smoky. "You Don't Need Teeth to Eat Our Beef," says the motto. The T-shirt is a classic, too.

Milbrook Tavern and Terrace (207-824-2175; bethelinn.com), Bethel Common. The big inn has a comfortable barroom and outside terrace, serving pub food and basic dinners.

FARM STAND Middle Intervale Farm (824-2230), 758 Intervale Rd., Bethel. Open May–Dec. 1. Apples, salads greens, hot peppers, many varieties of garlic, and much more, in-season.

✳ Entertainment

Casablanca Cinema (207-824-8248; casablancatheater.com), a four-screen cinema in the new Bethel Station development (Cross St.), shows first-run films.

The Mahoosuc Arts Council (207-824-3575; mahoosucarts.org) presents the Mahoosuc Arts Council Summer Bandstand Series, Sun.-afternoon Aug. concerts on the Bethel common. Music begins at 4 PM.

Celebration Barn (207-743-8452; celebrationbarn.com), 190 Stock Farm Rd., off Rt. 117 north in South Paris. Programs year-round. In summer this restored barn, set on 10 acres, draws students from around the world for workshops in mime, voice, and clowning, with public performances by students and faculty.

Skye Theatre Performing Arts Center (207-562-4445; necelticarts .com), 2 Highland Dr., South Carthage. New England Celtic Arts sponsors year-round performances of renowned Celtic musicians, blues players, and country musicians.

✳ Selective Shopping

ANTIQUES Steam Mill Antiques (207-824-0844; steammillantiques .com), 155 West Bethel Rd. (Rt. 2), Bethel. Owner Jay Boschetti sells a huge range of antiques, with china, glass, art, furniture, and antique signs just a few categories of items for sale.

Peabody Tavern Antiques and Collectibles (207-836-2422), 695 Gilead Rd. (Rt. 2), Gilead, is set across from Bog Trail in a red house.

ARTISANS Bonnema Potters (207-824-2821; bonnemapotters.com), Lower Main St., Bethel. Usually open daily in summer, closed Wed. in winter, but call for hours. Distinctive stoneware and porcelain: lamps, garden furniture, dinnerware, produced and sold in Bonnema's big barn. Seconds are available.

Element's Gallery (207-357-0189; elementsartgallerymaine.com), 162 Main St., Bethel. Open Wed.–Sun., 10–5. Paintings, jewelry, pottery, photographs, and more, all handmade locally.

Artistic Endeavors (207-824-3273; artisticendeavors-llc.com), 312 Mayville Rd. (Rt. 2.), Bethel. Open Wed–

Sat. 10–4:30 or by appointment. Original art including watercolors, oils, gouache, fiber art, gourd art, and pottery.

GEM SHOPS This area is rich in semiprecious gems and minerals. Jim Mann at **Mt. Mann** (207-824-3030; mtmann.com), 57 Main St., Bethel, mines, cuts, and sets his own minerals and gems. **Sunday River Gems** (207-824-3414), Sunday River Rd., Newry, offers handcrafted pieces with Maine gems, gemstone carvings, and more. Also see *Rockhounding* in "Oxford Hills."

SPECIAL SHOPS Books-N-Things (207-824-0275 or 1-800-851-3219; books-n-things.com), 130 Main St., Bethel. A full-service bookstore in the Pok Sun Emporium.

Linda Clifford Scottish & Irish Merchants (207-824-6560 or 1-877-607-7787; lindaclifford.com), 91 Main St., Bethel. The Barbour line of elegant outerwear and fine handbags is sold here, along with tartans from both Scotland and Ireland. Kilts, crystal, and Celtic jewelry all offer something for the high percentage of us who have a Celtic ancestor or two; dozens of tartans are available online.

Brooks Bros. Inc. Hardware Store (207-824-2158), 73 Main St., Bethel. All kinds of old-fashioned hardware, along with up-to-date products and fine service.

Maine Line Products (207-824-2522; mainelineproducts.com), 23 Main St., Bethel. Made-in-Maine products and souvenirs, among which the standout is the Maine Woodsman's Weatherstick. We have one tacked to our back porch, and it consistently points up to predict fair weather and down for foul. A second store, an expanded version of this old landmark, is open in Locke

Diane Foulds

BOOKS-N-THINGS

Mills/Greenwood: even more pine furniture, toys, wind chimes, buckets, birdhouses. Balsam pillows are made in Lewiston.

Timberlake Home Store (207-824-6545 or 1-800-780-6681; stimberlake .com), 158 Mayville Rd. (Rt. 2 east), Bethel. The showroom has windows on the woodworking shop, where tours are offered and everything is hand built. People who are interested in Shaker furniture will love this place.

Ruthie's Clothing (207-824-2989), Main St., Bethel. From elegant little cocktail dresses to smooth sweaters in jewel colors, Ruthie's selection is worth investigating.

✳ Special Events

March: **Handicapped Skiing Skiathon** (third weekend). **The Annual Dumont Cup** (Sunday River Resort), started after Bethel native Simon Dumont broke the quarterpipe record in 2008.

June: **Androscoggin River Canoe/ Kayak Race**.

July: **Bethel Historical Society Fourth of July Celebration**. **Bethel Annual Art Fair** (first Saturday). **Strawberry Festival**, Locke Mills Union Church (date depends on when strawberries are ready; announced in local papers). **Annual Gem, Mineral, and Jewelry Show** (second weekend) at Telstar High School in Bethel—exhibits, demonstrations, and guided field trips to local quarries. **Mollyockett Days** (third weekend)—festivities include a road race, parade, bicycle obstacle course, fiddle contest, and fireworks, all to honor an 18th-century medicine woman who helped the first settlers.

August: **Andover Old Home Days** (first weekend). **Annual Maine State Triathlon Classic** (second weekend), Bethel, and the Saturday before, **Kid's Triathlon**. **Sudbury Canada Days** (second weekend), Bethel—children's parade, historical exhibits, old-time crafts demonstrations, bean supper, and variety show.

Third weekend of September: **Bethel Harvest Fest and Chowdah and Apple Pie Contest**.

Columbus Day weekend: **Fall Festival at Sunday River Ski Resort** includes the now world-famous wife-carrying championship—it started here—free chairlift rides, wine tasting, crafts, and much more.

day after Thanksgiving: **True Hometown Craft and Wares Fair**.

December: A series of Christmas fairs and festivals climaxes with a **Living Nativity** on the Bethel common the Sunday before Christmas. Free horse-drawn wagon rides on Saturdays. **New Year's at Bethel Historical Society**, potluck supper and candlelight open house at Mason House.

RANGELEY LAKES REGION

Rangeley Lake itself is only 9 miles long, but the Rangeley Lakes Region includes 112 lakes and ponds, among them vast sheets of water with names like Mooselookmeguntic, Cupsuptic, and Aziscohos.

The scenery is so magnificent that segments of the two roads leading into Rangeley, Rts. 4 and 17, have been designated National Scenic Byways. In summer be sure to approach the town of Rangeley via Rt. 17 and pull out at the Height o' Land. Below you, four of the six major Rangeley Lakes glisten blue-black, ringed by high mountains. Patterned only by sun and clouds, uninterrupted by any village or even a building, this green-blue sea of fir and hardwoods flows north and west to far horizons.

A spate of 1863 magazine and newspaper stories first publicized this area as "home of the largest brook trout in America," and two local women ensured its fishing fame through ensuing decades. In the 1880s Phillips native Cornelia "Fly Rod" Crosby pioneered the use of the light fly rod and artificial lure and in 1897 became the first Registered Maine Guide; in 1924 Carrie Stevens, a local milliner, fashioned a streamer fly from gray feathers and caught a 6-pound, 13-ounce brook trout at Upper Dam. Stevens took second prize in *Field & Stream's* annual competition, and the Gray Ghost remains one of the most popular fishing flies sold.

The Rangeley Lakes Historical Society is papered with photographs and filled with mementos of the 1880s through the 1930s, an era in which trainloads of fishermen and visitors arrived in Rangeley every day throughout the summer, to stay in dozens of wooden summer hotels and numerous sporting camps on islands and outlying lakes.

In the 1940s and 1950s hotels closed and burned, and in the 1980s many sporting camps were sold off as individual "condominiums," but the resort has continued to evolve as a magnificent, low-key destination.

Landlocked salmon now augment trout in both local lakes and streams, and fly-fishing equipment and guides are easy to come by. Moose-watching, kayaking, and canoeing, as well as hiking and golf, are big draws. There are more shops and restaurants, events, and entertainment here than at any time since the 1930s.

Rangeley is a town of 1,500 year-round residents, and "downtown" is a short string of single-story frame buildings along the lake. The village of Oquossoc, 7 miles west, is just a scattering of shops and restaurants on a peninsula between Rangeley and Mooselookmeguntic Lakes. The summer population zooms to 6,000,

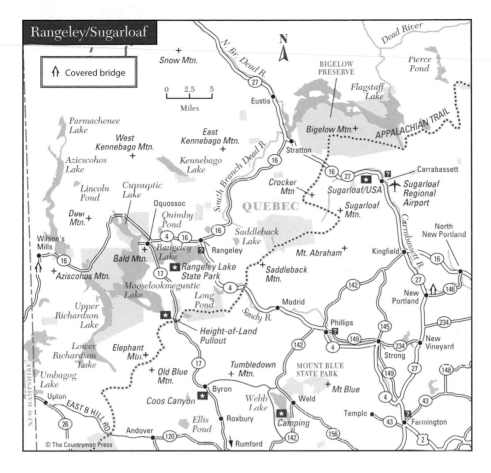

Rangeley/Sugarloaf

↑ Covered bridge

N

0   2.5   5
Miles

Dead River

BIGELOW PRESERVE

Pierce Pond

Snow Mtn. +

N. Br. Dead R.

27

Flagstaff Lake

Eustis

Parmachenee Lake

West Kennebago Mtn. +

East Kennebago Mtn. +

Bigelow Mtn. +

APPALACHIAN TRAIL

Stratton

Aziscoohos Lake

Kennebago Lake

16

16   27   ★   ❓

Carrabassett

Sugarloaf Regional Airport

Lincoln Pond

Cupsuptic Lake

Oquossoc

South Branch Dead R.

Crocker Mtn. +

Sugarloaf/USA

Sugarloaf Mtn. +

Deer Mtn. +

Quimby Pond

QUEBEC

Carrabassett R.

North New Portland

Wilson's Mills

4   16

16

Saddleback Lake

Rangeley ❓ Rangeley

Mt. Abraham +

Kingfield

16

16

Bald Mtn.

Rangeley Lake

★ Rangeley Lake State Park

Saddleback Mtn. +

142

27

146

Aziscoohos Mtn. +

Mooselookmeguntic Lake

17

Long Pond

4

New Portland

Upper Richardson Lake

★

Sandy R.

Madrid

Phillips

❓

145

234

Lower Richardson Lake

Elephant Mtn. +

17

Tumbledown Mtn. +

142   4   149

234

New Vineyard

Umbagog Lake

Old Blue Mtn. +

MOUNT BLUE STATE PARK

Strong

149   27   148

Upton

EAST B HILL RD

Coos Canyon ★

Byron

Webb Lake

Weld

Mt Blue +

4   43

NEW HAMPSHIRE

26

Andover

120

Ellis Pond

Roxbury

★ Camping

156

Temple

43   ❓   Farmington

↓ Rumford

142

2

© The Countryman Press

but both year-round homes and camps are hidden away by the water, and much of that water is itself sequestered in woodland.

Saddleback, Rangeley's 4,120-foot, 66-trail mountain, is one of New England's best ski resorts, with huge investments in trails, condominiums, and amenities in the last few years. Because the area's snow is so dependable, a separate and well-groomed cross-country system has also evolved, and both skiing and snowshoeing options in the backcountry abound.

The big news about this western neck of the Maine woods is that it's being preserved. Within the past dozen years hundreds of square miles have been protected through cooperative ventures involving state agencies, timberland owners, and the Rangeley Lakes Heritage Trust.

GUIDANCE Rangeley Lakes Region Chamber of Commerce (207-864-5364 or 1-800-MT-LAKES; rangeleymaine.com), P.O. Box 317, Rangeley 04970. Open year-round, Mon.–Sat. 10–4. The chamber maintains a walk-in information center in the village, publishes a handy *Accommodations and Services Guide, Who, What, Where & When*, and an indispensable map. The *Rangeley Hiking Trail Guide* put out by TRAC, Trails for Rangeley Area Coalition, is also sold here for $2, with maps for Angel Falls, Mountain Pond, and four more.

GETTING THERE *By car:* From points south, take the Maine Turnpike to exit 75 (Auburn), then take Rt. 4 to Rangeley. In summer the slightly longer (roughly half an hour) but more scenic route is to turn off Rt. 4 onto Rt. 108 in Livermore, follow it to Rumford, and then take Rt. 17 to Oquossoc. From the Bethel area, take Rt. 17 to Rumford. From New Hampshire's White Mountains, take Rt. 16 east.

By bus: **Northeast Charter & Tour** (1-888-593-6328; northeastchartertour.com) is a charter and tour bus operator that runs a door-to-door bus service to and from the Portland International Jetport; Boston's Logan Airport; Manchester, New Hampshire; and all of New England.

WHEN TO COME Rangeley's water is the focus of fishermen and -women in summer and fall, and its hills have good trails. Saddleback Mountain makes this a winter destination as well, as skiers are discovering the charms of a place still off the radar.

✳ To See

MUSEUMS ✪ Rangeley Lakes Region Historical Society (207-864-2333), 2472 Main St., Rangeley. Open late June–Aug., Mon.–Sat. 10–noon, or when the flag is out. This is a great little museum occupying a former bank building in the middle of town. It features photographs and local memorabilia from Rangeley's grand old hotels, sporting camps, trains, and lake steamers. Note the basement jail cell and the bird egg collection, coveted by the Smithsonian Museum.

❧ **Wilhelm Reich Museum** (207-864-3443; wilhelmreichmuseum.org), Dodge Pond Rd., off Rt. 4/16 between Rangeley and Oquossoc. Open July and Aug., Wed.–Sun. 1–5; in Sept., Sat. 1–5. $6 adults, 12 and under free. The 175-acre property, Orgonon, is worth a visit for the view alone. Wilhelm Reich (1897–1957) was a pioneer psychoanalyst with controversial theories about sexual energy. A short documentary video profiles the man and his work. The museum occupies a stone observatory that Reich helped design; it contains biographical exhibits, scientific equipment, paintings, and a library and study that remain as Reich left them. The wooded trails on the property are open daily year-round 9–5; leashed pets welcome.

❧ **Rangeley Lakes Region Logging Museum** (207-864-3939/5595), Rt. 16, 1 mile east of Rangeley Village. Open Memorial Day–Aug., weekends 11–2 or by appointment. Founded by woodsman and sculptor Rodney Richard, the museum features paintings about logging in the 1920s by local artist Alden Grant; also traditional woodcarving and logging equipment.

Rangeley Outdoor Sporting Heritage Museum (207-864-5647; rangeleyout doormuseum.org), corner of Rts. 4 and 17, Oquossoc Village. Built in 2009–10, this new museum focusing on outdoor sports has a typical sporting camp as an entry room. It features native Carrie Stevens, originator of the Gray Ghost fly; 150 of the flies that she tied are on display, including the last one she made, and flies made based on her patterns are for sale. Fish mounts and paintings by Herb Welch, 1879–1960, like his unusual grouping of seven brook trout under a glass bubble, are exhibited. White Nose Pete, a carving by Shang Wheeler, portrays a fish credited with stealing many a fisherman's flies. An 11-pound, 2-ounce, brook trout caught in 1897 in Upper Dam, near where Carrie Stevens lived, is on display as well.

Phillips Historical Society (207-639-3111), Pleasant St., P.O. Box 216, Phillips 04966. Open June–Sept., first and third Sun. 1–3, and the third week in Aug. for Old Home Days; also by appointment. The historical society is based in an 1820 house in the middle of the village. Exhibits include a significant Portland Glass collection, Fly-Rod Crosby memorabilia, as well as pictures of the town's own resort era, when it had three hotels, and of the Sandy River Rangeley Lakes Railroad.

Weld Historical Society (207-585-2542), Weld Village. Open July and Aug., Wed. and Sat. 1–3, and by appointment. The 1842 house is filled with period furniture, clothing, and photographs. The original Town House (1845) features farming, logging, and ice cutting tools. Other buildings include Dr. Proctor's 1880s office (containing his equipment), a spruce gum shop that became a library around 1900, and a reconstructed garage/workshop filled with tools, artifacts, and school and post office equipment.

SCENIC DRIVES The roads in this area offer such great scenery that sections of Rts. 4 and 17 are included in a National Scenic Byway.

Phillips/Weld/Byron/Oquossoc/Rangeley loop

Rt. 4 to Phillips and Rt. 142 to Weld. Follow Rt. 4 from Rangeley 12 miles south to **Small's Falls** and on to Phillips, once the center of the Sandy River–Rangeley Lakes "2-footer" line, now a quiet residential area. Plan to come the first or third Sun. of the month, or on foliage weekends, to ride the rails behind the steam train. Stop at the **Phillips Historical Society** and ask directions to **Daggett Rock**, a massive 50-foot-high boulder that glaciers deposited several miles from town (off Rt. 142), having knocked it off Saddleback Mountain (the nearest place that matches it geologically). It's a pleasant mile's walk and has been the local sight-to-see in Phillips for more than a century. From Rt. 4 near Phillips, it's 12 miles on Rt. 142 to **Weld**, a quiet old lake village with several good hiking options, including **Tumbledown Mountain** and **Mount Blue**. You can also swim in **Lake Webb** at **Mount Blue State Park.**

Weld to Byron. From Weld, it's 12 miles to Byron. Drive 2 miles north on Rt. 142 to the STATE BEACH sign; turn left, go 0.5 mile, and turn right on the first gravel road. This is Byron Rd., well packed. Soon you follow the Swift River (stop and pan for gold) down into **Coos Canyon**; the picnic area and waterfalls are at the junction with Rt. 17. This is said to be the first place in America where gold was panned.

Rt. 17 to Oquossoc. From the picnic area, drive north on Rt. 17 for 10 miles to the **Height o' Land** (the pullout is on the other side of the road), from which the view is a spectacular spread of lakes and mountains; the view from the **Rangeley Lake Overlook** (northbound side of the road, a couple of miles farther) offers another panorama.

From Oquossoc, it's a beautiful drive west along the lakes on Rt. 16 to Errol. Roughly 20 miles west of Rangeley, be sure to detour 0.3 mile to see the **Bennett Covered Bridge** (1898–99) spanning the Magalloway River in Wilson's Mills; follow signs to the Aziscohos Valley Camping Area.

Whether you are coming from Bethel or following the above loop, pick up Rt. 17 just beyond the **Mexico Chicken Coop Restaurant** (207-364-2710) on Rt. 2. Despite its exterior, this is a good way stop for Italian food, chicken, a huge salad bar, and fresh pastries.

✳ To Do

AIR TOURS Acadian Seaplanes (207-252-6630; acadianseaplanes.com), Rangeley. A 30-minute tour of fall foliage and the lakes was $89 a person in 2011, and "Sights on a Shoestring," which lasts 15 minutes, was $56. Moose tours, history tours, regional tours, and more are available in this Cessna 180 seaplane piloted by Keith Deschambeault, who has a commercial pilot's license. Charter flights to inns, sporting camps, and cities like Portland are also offered.

BIRDING Birders can often see Bicknell's thrushes and perhaps blackpolls, boreal chickadees, and more above 2,500 feet at the peak of Saddleback Mountain, and the base lodge has a hiking map available. Check the stand of spruce near the parking lot at Hunter Cove, cared for by the Rangeley Lakes Heritage Trust, for boreal chickadees as well, and the same organization's Boy Scout Rd., a dead-end dirt road, is home to gray jays. Bald Mountain, in between Rangeley and Mooselookmeguntic Lakes, is another good place for boreal bird species.

COOS CANYON

Christina Tree

BOAT RENTALS Check with the chamber of commerce about the 13 places in town that rent motorboats, canoes, sailboats, and kayaks. **River's Edge Sports** (207-864-5582), Rt. 4, Oquossoc, rents canoes and kayaks and offers shuttle service. **Saddleback Marina on Rangeley Lake** (207-864-3463 or 207-864-5496), Rt. 4, Oquossoc, offers the largest choice of motorboats.

BOAT TOURS *Oquossoc Lady* (207-864-2038), 2473 Main St., Rangeley. Daily one-hour cruises Memorial Day–Columbus Day, departing from Saddleback Marina in Oquossoc Village, take visitors by Naramantic Island, Rangeley Lake State Park, and more, with narration about Rangeley region history by Captain Kevin Sinnett. $25 adults, ages 10 and under $10.

CAMPING Wilderness camping is a part of what this area is about. The **Stephen Phillips Preserve** (207-864-

2003), Oquossoc, maintains 70 campsites with fireplaces, picnic tables, and toilet facilities; $16 per site per couple, $8 teenagers or extra person, $5 children. Also see **Rangeley Lake State Park** under *Green Space*. **Aziscohos Valley Camping Area** (207-486-3271), in Wilson's Mills, has 34 sites and offers easy canoe or kayak access to Magalloway River.

CANOEING AND KAYAKING Rangeley is the departure point for an 8-mile paddle to Oquossoc. On Lake Mooselookmeguntic a 12-mile paddle south to Upper Dam is popular; many people portage around the dam and paddle another 8 miles down Upper Richardson Lake and through the Narrows to South Arm. Kayaks can be rented from **River's Edge Sports** (207-864-5582), Rt. 4 in Oquossoc. They are also available from **Ecopelagicon, A Nature Store** (207-864-2771; ecopelagicon.com) in the village of Rangeley, which offers guided tours and kayaking instruction.

A section of the 700-mile **Northern Forest Canoe Trail**, which follows the ancient water route of Native Americans traveling from New York to Fort Kent, comes through Umbagog Lake, the Richardson Lakes, and Mooselookmeguntic and Rangeley Lakes before hitting a long portage to the South Branch of the Dead River. This section takes two to five days to complete. A map, produced by **Native Trails Inc.** (P.O. Box 240, Waldoboro 04572), is available for $5.95 from the Rangeley Lakes Heritage Trust (207-864-7311) and from Ecopelagicon in Rangeley.

FISHING As noted in the chapter introduction, fishing put Rangeley on the map. Both brook trout and landlocked salmon remain plentiful, and while early spring and Sept. remain the big fishing seasons, summer months now also lure many anglers with fishfinders, downriggers, rods, and reels. Rangeley has, however, always been best known as a fly-fishing mecca, and both local sporting stores, **River's Edge Sports** (207-864-5582), Rt. 4 in Oquossoc, and the **Rangeley Region Sport Shop** (207-864-5615), Main St., Rangeley, specialize in fly-tying equipment; they are also sources of advice on where to fish and with whom (a list of local guides is posted). Request a list of members of the **Rangeley Region Guides & Sportsmen's Association** (rangeleyguidesandsportsmen.org), P.O. Box 244, Rangeley 04970. The group traces its origins to 1896. The current chamber of commerce guide also lists local Registered Maine Guides as well as camps that specialize in boats, equipment, and guides. Nonresident fishing licenses, sold at sporting stores, are $11 per day, $43 for seven days.

FITNESS CENTER **Rangeley Region Physical Rehab and Wellness Pavilion** (207-864-2900; rangeleyhealth.org), Dallas Hill Rd., Rangeley. This splendid community facility offers exercise equipment, showers, and daily exercise classes including yoga.

GOLD PANNING **Coos Canyon**, on Rt. 17, 23 miles south of Oquossoc, is said to be the first place in America where gold was panned. The Swift River churns through a beautiful natural gorge, and there are picnic tables. Free gold-panning demonstrations are offered, and equipment can be rented or bought at the **Coos Canyon Rock & Gift Store** (207-364-4900).

GOLF Mingo Springs Golf Course (207-864-5021), Proctor Rd. (off Rt. 4), Rangeley. A historic (since 1925) par-71, 18-hole course with lake views; instruction, carts, and club rentals.

Evergreen Golf Club & Golf School (207-864-9055), 528 Dallas Hill Rd., Rangeley. This nine-hole course built in 2002 has spectacular views, with five tees on each hole so everyone can play.

GUIDE SERVICE Mountain Woman Guide Service (207-562-4971 or 207-357-4971; mountainwomanguideservice.com), Dixfield. Michelle Young is a registered Maine guide who takes individuals and groups on trips into the woods. One tour goes to Forest Lodge, author Louise Dickinson Rich's home on Rapid River where she wrote *We Took to the Woods*; the tour is made with the assistance of Aldro French. $120 per person for a full day. Fly-fishing, hiking on the Appalachian Trail, day hikes tailored to a person's fitness level; Young also works as an interpretive ranger at Mount Blue State Park.

See **Rangeley Outdoor Sporting Heritage Museum** or the chamber, above, to obtain advice on guide services.

HIKING The Rangeley regional map published by the chamber of commerce outlines more than a dozen well-used hiking paths, including a portion of the Appalachian Trail that passes over **Saddleback Mountain**. The most popular is the trail to the summit of **Bald Mountain** (3 miles roundtrip) with sweeping views of lakes, woods, and more mountains. Other favorites are Bemis Stream Trail up **Elephant Mountain** (six hours roundtrip) and the mile walk in to **Angels Falls**—which is roughly 4 miles off Rt. 17, and listed in the *Rangeley Hiking Trail Guide* sold at the chamber of commerce.

In Weld the tried-and-true trails are **Mount Blue** (3.25 miles) and **Tumbledown Mountain** (a particularly varied climb with a high elevation).

MOOSE-WATCHING Rt. 16 north from Rangeley to Stratton is a good bet for seeing moose at dusk, but drive with caution.

RAILROAD EXCURSION ✒ **Sandy River & Rangeley Lakes Railroad** (207-778-3621; srrl-rr.org), Phillips. Runs on the first and third Sunday of each month, June–Columbus Day; runs continuously through Phillips Old Home Days in late Aug. and Fall Foliage Days in late Sept. and early Oct., and on other special occasions (check the website). $6 adults, $1 ages

MINGO SPRINGS GOLF COURSE, RANGELEY
Nancy English

7–13, free 7 and under. From 1873 until 1935 this narrow-gauge line spawned resort and lumbering communities along its 115-mile length. Begun as seven distinct lines, it was eventually acquired by the Maine Central. Shops and a large roundhouse were built by railroad companies in Phillips. Since 1969 volunteers have been working to rebuild a part of the railroad, producing a replica of the old steam locomotive and the roundhouse, and laying 0.6 mile of track so that you can rattle along in an 1884 car just far enough to get a sense of getting around Franklin County "back when." Seven original railroad buildings remain—including Sanders Station and a freight shed. A depot houses railroad memorabilia; rolling stock now includes five boxcars, three coaches, two excursion cars, and two cabooses.

SUMMER PROGRAMS Rangeley Parks and Recreation Department Summer Programs (207-864-3326), open to everyone vacationing in town, include lessons in fly casting and tying, golf, canoeing, swimming, tennis, and much more.

SWIMMING Rangeley Lake State Park offers a beautiful, secluded grass beach and swimming area plus scattered picnic sites. Day-use fee; free under age 12. There is also a town beach with lifeguards, picnic tables, and a playground at **Lakeside Park** in the village of Rangeley. Almost all lodging places offer water access.

Mount Blue State Park also has a nice swimming area.

Coos Canyon, Rt. 17, Byron. It's terrifying to watch kids jump from the cliffs and bridge here, but there are several inviting pools among the smooth rocks and cascades.

✷ Winter Sports

CROSS-COUNTRY SKIING Rangeley Lakes Trail Center at Lower Saddleback Mountain (207-864-4309), 524 Saddleback Mountain Rd., Rangeley. More than 55 kilometers of groomed trails with a skating lane and a track for classic skiing, 4 miles from downtown Rangeley

Mount Blue State Park (207-585-2347), off Rt. 156, Weld, offers extensive cross-country skiing trails.

DOWNHILL SKIING ✍ Saddleback Mountain (207-864-5671; snow phone, 1 800-458-7502; saddlebackmaine.com), off Dallas Hill Rd., Rangeley. This is a very big downhill ski area with a fiercely loyal following, on the verge of wider popularity under a new owner making a huge investment. Saddleback itself, 4,120 feet high and now webbed with 66 trails and glades serviced by two quad chairlifts, two double chairs, and one T-bar, forms the centerpiece in a semicircle of mountains rising above a small lake. Top-to-bottom snowmaking augments more than 200 inches of annual snowfall to keep the slopes open from the end of November into

SADDLEBACK'S BASE LODGE

Christina Tree

April. Trails and slopes include glade skiing, a 2.5-mile beginner trail, and an above-tree-line snowfield in spring. The vertical drop is 2,000 feet. A 44-acre glade was cut in 2009. Intermediate runs such as Grey Ghost and Green Weaver are memorable cruising lanes. Experts will find plenty of challenge on Tightline, Wardens Worry, and the Nightmare Glades; and there's a snowboard park with a 200-foot half-pipe. Facilities include a three-story lodge with cafeteria, lounge, ski school, shop, rentals, nursery, and mountain warming hut. Expansion here was blocked for 26 years by an impasse with the National Park Service over the segment of the Appalachian Trail that passes over Saddleback, but former president Clinton's 11th-hour

Christina Tree

SKIING AT SADDLEBACK MOUNTAIN

moves to expand national park holdings cleared the way. The mountain's new owner has more trails under construction and a hotel in the future. $49 adults, $39 ages 7–18 and college students, 6 and under free. About 40 condominium units can be rented through the mountain's main telephone number, at a range of $125 to $220 a night.

SNOWMOBILING is huge in this region. The **Rangeley Snowmobile Club** (rangeleysnowmobile.com), subsidized by the town, maintains hundreds of miles of well-marked trails connecting with systems throughout Maine and Canada. Snowmobile rentals are available from **Polaris Snowmobile Rentals from River's Edge Sports** (207-864-5582).

SNOWSHOEING Marked trails abound on local conservation land; ask for more information at the Rangeley Lake Region Chamber of Commerce, 207-864-5364.

✳ Green Space

Lakeside Park, in the middle of the village of Rangeley, is a great spot with picnic tables, grills, a playground, portable toilets, and a boat launch.

❧ **Rangeley Lake State Park** (207-864-3858) covers more than 700 acres, including 117 acres on the shore. Open May 15–end of Sept. There are scattered picnic sites and barbecue grills near the swimming area, an idyllic swimming area, a boat launch, and a children's play area; $4.50 nonresident adults, $1 ages 5–12.

Mount Blue State Park (207-585-2261), off Rt. 156, Weld. Open May 30–Sept. 30, but center open till mid-Oct., and trail open through the fall. This 6,000-acre park includes Mount Blue itself, towering 3,187 feet above the valley floor, and a beachside tenting area (136 sites) on Lake Webb. The lake is 1.5 miles wide, 7 miles long, and provides good fishing for black bass, white and yellow perch, pickerel, trout, and salmon. There are boat rentals and a nature center complete with fireplace. The view from the Center Hill area looks like the opening of a Paramount picture. Despite its beauty and the outstanding hiking, this is one of the few state camping facilities ($25 for nonresidents) that rarely fill up, except on August weekends. Day-use fee $6 per person for nonresidents, $4 for Mainers, children 5–11 $1.

✍ **Small's Falls**, Rt. 4, 12 miles south of Rangeley. The Sandy River drops abruptly through a small gorge, which you can climb behind railings. A popular picnic spot. You can follow the trail to **Chandlers Mill Stream Falls**, equally spectacular.

Hunter Cove Wildlife Sanctuary, off Rt. 4/16, 2.5 miles west of Rangeley Village (across from Dodge Pond). A 95-acre Rangeley Lakes Heritage Trust preserve with color-coded trails lead-

Nancy English

SMALL'S FALLS, RANGELEY

ing to the cove (boat launch). Bring insect repellent, waterproof footwear, and a picnic (tables are near the parking lot, and benches are scattered throughout).

Rangeley Lakes Heritage Trust (207-864-7311), Rt. 4/16, Oquossoc, open weekdays 9–4:30, Sun. 9–1. Since the trust's founding in 1991, more than 12,300 acres have been preserved, including 45 miles of lake and river frontage, 15 islands, and a 2,443-foot mountain. Request the map/guide and inquire about the guided hikes and nature-study programs offered.

Hatchery Brook Preserve is easily accessible, just 0.5 mile north of town on Rt. 4 (take a left on Manor Brook Rd. and look for the trailhead on your right in another 0.25 mile). We were lucky enough to hike this easy, rewarding loop in blueberry/raspberry season Yum. There were also bunchberries and nice views of Rangeley Lake. This 50-acre Rangeley Lakes Heritage Trust property was at one time slated for a 50-lot subdivision.

THE SECLUDED BEACH AT RANGELEY LAKE STATE PARK

Nancy English

The Stephen Phillips Memorial Preserve Trust (207-864-2003) has preserved many miles of shore on Mooselookmeguntic and maintains a number of campsites (see *To Do— Camping*).

Also see *Lodging—Campgrounds*.

✳ Lodging

INNS AND LODGES

✪ ⏀ ♿ **Kawanhee Inn** (207-585-2000; maineinn.net), 12 Anne's Way, Weld 04285. Open Memorial Day–Columbus Day. This Maine lodge set atop a slope overlooking Lake Webb has a paneled lobby and dining room, moose and deer presiding over the stone fireplaces, and birch trunks standing in for columns. Four lodge rooms share a bath, eight have private bath, and all feature a Maine-lodge decor. Eight cabins (one-, two-, and three-bedroom) sit by the lake, six with kitchenette and two with full kitchen. This is one of the most beautiful old lodges around, and its restaurant (see *Dining Out*) serves excellent meals. Rooms $110–180 B&B; cabins $1,150–1,400 per week.

♿ **The Loon Lodge Inn and Restaurant** (207-864-5666; loon

THE FRONT PORCH OF THE KAWANHEE INN LOOKS OUT ON WEBB LAKE

Nancy English

Nancy English

LOON LODGE, RANGELEY

lodgeme.com), 16 Pickford Rd., P.O. Box 676, Rangeley 04970. Log exterior walls and indoor pine paneling, a large stone fireplace, and the moose-antler chandelier in **Pickford Pub** create a mountain lodge ambience. Modern amenities make it enjoyable, as in the Nordic Room, with its rocking chair ready for contemplation of Rangeley Lake and its surrounding mountains. The upstairs can be hot in summer, despite the ceiling fans. Nine rooms, two with detached bath and three that share a bathroom, include two suites for families. Two new rooms with king bed are on the ground floor, with picture windows looking at the lake, an exterior entrance, and private bath. Dinners are recommended (see *Dining Out*); guests are on their own for breakfast. $117–160.

🐾 ♿ **Country Club Inn** (207-864-3831; countryclubinnrangeley.com), Rt. 4, P.O. Box 680, Rangeley 04970. Open year-round except Apr. and Nov. This friendly retreat, set on a rise, offers the best views of Rangeley Lake of any lodging in the region. The 20 old-fashioned rooms, all with private bath, have picture windows framing water and mountains. Although set by the Mingo Springs Golf Course, only half its summer patrons even play golf; it was built by millionaire sportsmen as a private club in the late 1920s. Massive stone fireplaces face each other across a living room with knotty-pine walls, plenty of books, and puzzles. Owner-manager Margie Jamison is the second generation of her family to run the inn; her husband, Steve, is chef in the restaurant (see *Dining Out*). In winter you can cross-country ski from the door, and in summer there's an outdoor pool, also with a magnificent view. $139 B&B for two; $209 MAP. Off-season rates available.

🐾 ♿ **Bald Mountain Camps** (207-864-3671; baldmountaincamps.com), Bald Mountain Rd., P.O. Box 332, Oquossoc 04964. Open year-round. This is a surviving American Plan (all three meals) fishing resort that dates to 1897, with fresh seafood or baby back ribs for dinner; cabins can also be rented without meals. Fireplaces are in 15 cabins, all remodeled to include an efficiency or complete kitchen. Amenities include a safe sand beach; tennis courts; use of canoes, kayaks, and sailboats; and motorboat rentals. Right on Mooselookmeguntic Lake, the camp exudes the kind of hospitality found under long-term ownership of Stephen

and Fernlyn Philbrick. Fly-fishing and hiking adventures from here offered as well. $155–225 MAP adults, 125–250 without meals, in Aug.; less for children and during May and June; one-week minimum in July and Aug., but occasionally there are a few days open. Some pets accepted. Friday nights feature a lobster cookout.

♿ **Rangeley Inn and Motor Lodge** (207-864-3341 or 1-800-666-3687; rangeleyinn.com), Rt. 4, Rangeley 04970. Motor lodge open year-round, inn open in winter and June–Nov. This blue-shingled, three-story landmark, on the site of a vanished grand hotel that stood across the road overlooking the lake, is owned by Jean-Charles and Dominique Gould; the classic hotel lobby dates to 1907. More than 30 guest rooms are in the main building, 6 with (somewhat stained) claw-foot tub, some with water views, all comfortably furnished and old-fashioned, although unfortunately the TV next door may be audible. Among 15 units in the motel overlooking Haley Pond, 12 are remodeled, 2 have two-person whirlpool bath, and 4 have a woodstove. $84–154 double. Dinner Wed.–Sun. in the pub, winter and June–Nov. 1.

THE HAMMOCK OFFERS A GREAT VIEW AT BALD MOUNTAIN CAMPS

Nancy English

BED & BREAKFASTS Pleasant Street Inn Bed & Breakfast (207-864-5916; pleasantstreetinnbb.com), 104 Pleasant St., Rangeley. Rob and Jan Welch offer expertise in hiking and skiing, including quiet spots for cross-country skiing. Shuttling cars for hikers, making reservations, and pickups after a dinner are part of their services. The well-appointed B&B has beds with adjustable firmness, only one item on the checked-off list. Jan's quilts are on the beds in the five quiet rooms, each with tile-floored private bath and TV. Early risers can enjoy muffins and cereals; then a full breakfast, perhaps shirred eggs or blueberry pancakes, is served between 8 and 9. Rates $135–155, with discounts for multiple nights.

Oquossoc's Own (207-864-5584), P.O. Box 27, Oquossoc 04964. Open daily year-round. Since 1982 Joanne Koob has been sharing her comfy village home and its four guest rooms, making a full breakfast, frequently served early enough for men to get out into the woods to work. Her friendly, down-home presence makes this a home-away-from-home for many of her repeat guests. Rooms share two baths. $90 double, $60 single, no charge for ages 12 and under.

MOTELS ☀ ৬ Rangeley Saddle-back Inn (207-864-3434; rangeley saddlebackinn.com), 2303 Main St., Rangeley. On the Interconnected Trail System (ITS) beloved by snowmobilers and near Saddleback Mountain, this inn has new, comfortable beds, flat-screen TVs, and an indoor pool and Jacuzzi. There are 40 rooms, most with two queen beds; all have private bath, microwave, mini fridge, and a view of Rangeley Lake. The Sunset Grille (see *Eating Out*) serves pub fare. Rooms $85–195.

SPORTING CAMPS Geared to serious fishermen in May, June, and September, and to families in July and August, these are true destination resorts, but don't expect organized activities.

☀ ♪ Bosebuck Mountain Camps (207-670-0013; bosebuck.com), Wilson's Mills 03579. Open year-round, except Apr. Accessible by boat or a 14-mile private gravel road, the camps are sited at the remote end of Aziscohos Lake and on ITS 84. Wendy and Michael Yates bought this site in 2007, and have been sprucing up the traditional cabins. A wilderness navigation seminar is offered in June and Aug.; women's groups and artists come here, too. The lodge dining room overlooks the water, and next to it is a book-lined living room. The 12 cabins have a woodstove, electric lights, flush toilet, and shower, powered by a generator that never shuts off. Three full meals, with prime rib on Sat., are included in the rate, $140 per person per night; in July and first two weeks of Aug., $99 per person per night, with 15 percent gratuity, distributed to staff, added at checkout.

☀ ♪ Lakewood Camps (207-243-2959; lakewoodcamps.com), Middle Dam, Lower Richardson Lake, P.O. Box 1275, Rangeley 04970. Open after ice-out through Sept. Owners are Whit and Maureen Carter. Specialty fly-fishing for landlocked salmon and trout in 5 miles of the Rapid River. Twelve truly remote cabins; meals feature fresh-baked breads, cakes, and pies. Access is by boat from Andover. This is very much the same area described in Louise Dickinson Rich's *We Took to the Woods*. $160 per person (two-day minimum), double occupancy, includes three full meals; $120 children 12–16, $70 6–11, age 5 and younger free. $22 pets, 15 percent gratuity not included. No credit cards; cash or check only.

COTTAGES AND CONDOS

✏ Rangeley still has an unusual number of traditional family-geared "camps" and second homes available for rental year-round. Check with the chamber of commerce (rangeleymaine.com) for listings and local rental agents.

Clearwater Sporting Camps (207-864-5424; clearwatercampsmaine .com), Bald Mountain Rd., Oquossoc 04964. Open from ice-out through Oct. Four cottages, all different, are scattered on private waterfront ledges along Mooselookmeguntic Lake; the fronts of two of the cottages open out almost completely onto the lake. This is a very private, beautiful spot. A year-round log home is for rent as well. Michael and Tina Warren also offer boat rentals, a boat launch, swimming, and guide service, specializing in fly-fishing. Cabins $150 per day double; $950 per week. Log home $1,400. No pets.

Mooselookmeguntic House Cabin Rentals (207-864-2962; mooselook meguntacrentals.com), Haines Landing, Oquossoc 04964. Open ice-out to Columbus Day. The grand old hotel is gone, but the eight log cabins are well maintained and occupy a great site with a beach and marina. Many of the one- and two bedroom cabins are on the water and have fireplace or wood-stove. $600–800 per week.

North Camps (207-864-2247; north camps.com), P.O. Box 341, Oquossoc 04964 (write to E. B. Gibson). Open May–Oct. Twelve cottages on Rangeley Lake among birches on a spacious lawn, with fireplace or woodstove, modern bath, screened porch, and access to the beach, tennis, sailboats, fishing boats, and canoes. In July and Aug., weekly rentals preferred.

$425–775 weekly, $85 to $195 per night for two to eight people.

Hunter Cove on Rangeley Lake (207-864-3383; huntercove.com), 334 Mingo Loop, Rangeley 04970. Open year-round. Chris and Ralph Egerhei offer eight nicely equipped one- and two-bedroom lakeside cabins with loft, full kitchen, one with hot tub. $150–210 per night; $950–1,200 per week.

Saddleback Mountain (207-864-5671; snow phone, 1-866-918-2225; saddlebackmaine.com), off Dallas Hill Rd., Rangeley. Rock Pond, White Birch, Mountain Brook, and South Branch condominium units, about 40 available for rent, are located on the mountain, many with ski-in/ski-out access, and with breathtaking views of the Longfellow Mountains. Vacation packages available.

CAMPGROUNDS For reservations in the following state parks, call in-state 1-800-332-1501, out-of-state 207-624-9950.

✏ **Rangeley Lake State Park**, between Rts. 17 and 4, at the southern rim of Rangeley Lake. Some 50 camp-sites are well spaced among fir and spruce trees; facilities include a secluded beach and boat launch, picnic sites, three shower buildings, one new, with hot showers at no extra charge, and a children's play area. One group camping site has a shelter. $20 for non-residents. Some wilderness sites on Mooselookmeguntic Lake are accessible only by boat; inquire at the chamber of commerce.

Mount Blue State Park (207-585-2347), Weld. Campsites here ($20) tend to fill up later than those in better-known parks.

Coos Canyon Campground (207-364-3880; cooscanyoncabins.com), on

Rt. 17, 445 Swift River Rd., Byron, 23 miles south of Oquossoc, is only about half an hour from Rangeley, but at these sites you feel as though you're in the middle of the woods. Swimming holes and riverside camping, with kids jumping off the cliffs during the day. Any adults interested? At $16 per night, plus tax, the rates can't be beat. There's a small store and a shower house. Two fully equipped units in a log cabin are $120 per night for two adults and two children under 12. Ten RV sites, too.

✳ Where to Eat

DINING OUT Also see *Where to Eat* listings in "Sugarloaf and the Carrabassett Valley."

✪ **Kawanhee Inn** (207-585-2000; maineinn.net), 12 Anne's Way, Weld 04285. Open Memorial Day–Columbus Day. Rustic tapenade and Maine lobster Alfredo were on a 2011 menu. Dining is lovely on the screened porch in good weather, or by the fire when it's cold. Entrées $16–28.

The Loon Lodge Inn and Restaurant (207-864-5666; loonlodgeme

THE DINING ROOM AT THE COUNTRY CLUB INN, RANGELEY

Nancy English

.com), 16 Pickford Rd., Rangeley. Dining on the deck overlooking Rangeley Lake on a summer night is the way life should be. Spanish duck was one entrée on a recent dinner menu with a wonderful spicy flavor, and seafood and steaks with or without shrimp or scallops are more good choices. Dates wrapped with bacon with slices of chorizo hit a home run. Entrées $20–32.

⚘ **The Gingerbread House** (207-864-3602; gingerbreadhouserestaurant .net), Rt. 4/16, Oquossoc. Open for breakfast, lunch, and dinner year-round, fewer days in winter, closed Nov. and Apr. An ice cream parlor since the turn of the 20th century, preserved and expanded by the Kfoury family. Breakfast might be blueberry waffles, and lunch crabcakes or chicken pesto salad. For dinner, the ribs are long-braised and coated with blueberry chipotle barbecue sauce (with a goat cheese fritter to start), or meat loaf, or whatever fish is fresh, at this family-friendly place. Dinner entrées $16–29.

Country Club Inn (207-864-3831; countryclubinnrangeley.com), Rangeley. Open for breakfast daily and for dinner Wed.–Sun. in summer and fall; weekends in winter by reservation. The inn sits on a rise above Rangeley Lake, the dining room windows maximize the view, and the food is good. Chef Steve Jamison's menu changes frequently but might include veal Gruyère; roast duck with bing cherry sauce is available every night. Entrées $17–32, including a salad.

Bald Mountain Camps (207-864-3671; baldmountaincamps.com), Bald Mountain Rd., Oquossoc. Served during the summer months. Dinner by reservation is available to non-guests in this classic sporting camp dining room by the lake. The set menu varies with the night; Tuesday might be braised short ribs, Maryland fried chicken, fish cakes, or vegetarian stew.

EATING OUT The Pour House in the Rangeley Inn (207-864-3341; rangeleyinn.com), 51 Main St., Rangeley. Every town needs a pub like this, with reasonably priced pub grub such as steakburgers, chicken potpie, and good chowder. Also prime rib and baked haddock. Three courses for $23.

⚓ BMC Diner (207-864-5844), Main St. and Richardson Ave., Rangeley. Open for breakfast all day, and lunch; Sun. for breakfast only. The favorite place in town for breakfast; the veggie omelet is full of good spinach and other vegetables. Friendly service.

The Sunset Grille (207-864-2662; saddlebackmotorinn.com), 2303 Main St., Rangeley. Located next door to the Rangeley Saddleback Inn, this popular place serves hamburgers, pasta, calzones, barbecued ribs, and other good pub fare. Entrées $6.50–22.

Red Onion (207-864-5022), Main St., Rangeley. Open daily for lunch and dinner. A friendly Italian American dining place with a sunroom and biergarten; fresh-dough pizzas and daily specials. Recommended by locals—even if the menu doesn't spell Parmesan right.

Parkside & Main (207-864-3774), 2520 Main St., Rangeley. Open daily, with later hours in summer. An attractive dining room with plenty of windows and a deck overlooking the lake. Large menu with burgers, good homemade chowders, seafood, pastas, and daily specials.

The Four Seasons Café (207-864-2020; fourseasonscafe.com), Rt. 4, Oquossoc. Open for breakfast, lunch, and dinner, closed part of April. A woodstove, tables with checked green cloths, and a big menu with Mexican dishes, salads, good soups, sandwiches, and vegetarian specials all make this a good place to eat. Fresh-dough pizzas are also a specialty. Fish, lobster, clams, and scallops are served as well. Prime rib on Fri. night, house pies. Entrées $17–29. Two-for-one dinners Thu.

Moosely Bagels and Scoops Ice Cream (207-864-5955), 2588 Main St., Rangeley. Open for breakfast and lunch and ice cream Mon.–Sat. 5:30–8:30, breakfast Sun. 6:30–6:00. Call for hours off-season. Great lakeside location and good bagels, enormous, family-sized tender blueberry muffins, and an array of coffee choices. For lunch soup, salad, and a lot of vegetarian options. Fridays come in for fresh fish.

⚓ Pine Tree Frosty (207-864-5894), 2459 Main St., Rangeley. Gifford's ice cream.

Lakeside Convenience (207-864-5888), Main St., Rangeley. Great fried chicken, usually in at 9 AM and sold out by 2 PM., on weekdays only.

Scotty's Lobster Pound (207-864-2493), 17 Rumford Rd. (Rt. 17), Rangeley, in Oquossoc Village. Call

MORNING GLORY BAKESHOP, WELD

Nancy English

ahead, and give an hour's notice, to order cooked lobsters, 5 PM and 5:30 PM pickup; lobster rolls are made to order with 4 ounces of knuckle and claw lobster meat.

BAKERY Morning Glory Bake Shop (207-585-2479), 19 Church St. (Rt. 142), Weld. Behind an 1870 farmhouse is Cheryl and Frederick England's excellent bakery, good for a variety of breads, moose cookies, whoopie pies, and chewy oatmeal cookies. Open daily Memorial Day–Columbus Day.

✳ Entertainment

🎵 **Lakeside Youth Theater** (207-864-5000), Main St., Rangeley. A renovated landmark that offers first-run films; matinees on rainy days when the flag is hung out. Off-season shows on weekends.

Rangeley Friends of the Performing Arts sponsors a July–Aug. series of performances by top entertainers and musicians at local churches, lodges, and the high school. For the current schedule, check with the chamber of commerce.

BOG POND POTTERY, PHILLIPS

Nancy English

✳ Selective Shopping

Alpine Shop (207-864-3741), Main St., Rangeley. Open daily year-round. The town's premier clothing store, with name-brand sportswear and Maine gifts.

✪ **Bog Pond Pottery** (207-639-5327; robsieminski.com, dianathomasceramics .com, bogpondpotters.com), 63 Bog Pond Rd. (just off Rt. 4), Phillips. Diana Thomas and Rob Sieminski both make outstanding pottery at this farmhouse surrounded by flowers. Their raku work is fired in a wood-burning kiln for 24 hours or more. Sieminski's work is in the Philadelphia Museum of Art; with deeply textured surfaces and wood-ash glazing, it resembles stone or wood. Thomas makes graceful cups and elegantly patterned vessels that make your morning coffee drinking profound. The August studio sale is a great opportunity for making a purchase.

Books, Lines, and Thinkers (207-864-4355), Main St., Rangeley. Open year-round; hours vary depending on season. Wess Connally offers a good selection of art as well as books and music and sponsors a regular book discussion group; the next meeting's selection is featured by the cash register.

🎵 **The Mad Whittler** (207-864-5595), Main St., Rangeley. Rodney Richard sculpts animals and folk characters using a chain saw and jackknife, and his son Rodney Jr. executes his own whimsical creations with similar tools; chances are one or the other will be there working away. Look for the OPEN flag on the shop. Rodney Sr. lives in the neighboring house, so if no one is in the shop, "honk on the horn or bang on the door. Better yet, call ahead."

🎵 **Ecopelagicon, A Nature Store** (207-864-2771), 3 Pond St., Rangeley.

In the middle of town but with windows on Haley Pond. Kites, life jackets, camping stuff, and wonderful things for nature lovers, from bird and reptile guides to books on mountain trails and good maps. A line of skin products with fine scents like wild rose and balsam sits in a nook in the front of the store. Also kayak rentals, instruction, and tours (see *Canoeing and Kayaking*).

The Gallery at Stoney Batter Station (207-864-3373), Oquossoc. Open Memorial Day–mid-Oct., daily 10–4; Thu.–Sun. in winter. Art shares the space with rustic furnishings, from stick benches to birch log birdhouses. Ceramics, lamps, and much more.

✳ Special Events

All events are in Rangeley unless otherwise noted
January: **Rangeley Snodeo**—snowmobile rally and cross-country ski races.

February: **New England Pond Hockey**.

July: **Independence Day** parade and fireworks, silent auction, cookout; **Strawberry Festival**; **Old-Time Fiddlers Contest**; and **Logging Museum Festival Days**. **Heritage Day Fair** (final Saturday) in Weld Village.

August: **Sidewalk Art Show**; **Annual Blueberry Festival**; **Outdoor Sporting Heritage Days**; **Phillips Old Home Days** (third week). **Oquossoc Day**—dog show, sailing race, dinner, and more.

Third Sunday of September: **Saddleback Day Fall Festival**.

First Saturday of October: **Rangeley Lakes Logging Museum Apple Festival**.

December: **Walk to Bethlehem Pageant**, Main St.

SUGARLOAF AND
THE CARRABASSETT VALLEY

The second highest mountain in the state, Sugarloaf faces another 4,000-footer across the Carrabassett Valley—a narrow defile that accommodates a 17-mile-long town.

Carrabassett Valley is a most unusual town. In 1972, when it was created from Crockertown and Jerusalem townships, voters numbered 32. The school and post office are still down in Kingfield, south of the valley; the nearest chain supermarket, and hospital are still in Farmington, 36 miles away. There are just 781 full-time residents, but there are now more than 5,000 "beds." Instead of "uptown" and "downtown," people say "on-mountain" and "off-mountain."

On-mountain, at the top of Sugarloaf's access road, stands one of New England's largest self-contained ski villages: a handful of shops and more than a dozen restaurants, a seven-story brick hotel, and a church. A chairlift hoists skiers up to the base lodge from lower parking lots and from hundreds of condominiums clustered around the Sugarloaf Inn. More condominiums are scattered farther down the slope, all served by a chairlift. From all places you can also ski down to the Carrabassett Valley Ski Touring Center, Maine's largest cross-country trail network.

More than 800 condominiums are scattered among firs and birches. To fill them in summer, Sugarloaf has built an outstanding 18-hole golf course; maintains one of the country's top-rated golf schools; fosters a lively special-events program; promotes rafting, mountain biking, and hiking; and even seriously attempts to eliminate blackflies.

Spring through fall the focus shifts off-mountain to the backwoods hiking and fishing north of the valley. Just beyond the village of Stratton, Rt. 27 crosses a corner of Flagstaff Lake and continues through Cathedral Pines, an impressive sight and a good place to picnic. The 30,000-acre Bigelow Preserve, which embraces the lake and great swatches of this area, offers swimming, fishing, and camping. Eustis, a small outpost on the lake, caters to sportsmen and serves as a P.O. box for sporting camps squirreled away in the surrounding woodland.

Kingfield, at the southern entrance to the Carrabassett Valley, was founded in 1816. This stately town has long been a woodworking center and produced the first bobbins for America's first knitting mill; for some time it also supplied most of the country's yo-yo blanks. It is, however, best known as the onetime home of the Stanley twins, inventors of the steamer automobile and the dry-plate coating machine for modern photography. The Stanley Museum includes fascinating photos of rural Maine in the 1890s by Chansonetta, sister of the two inventors. Kingfield continues to produce wood products and also offers outstanding lodging and dining.

The Carrabassett River doesn't stop at Kingfield. Follow it south as it wanders west off Rt. 27 at New Portland, then a short way along Rt. 146, to see the striking vintage-1841 Wire Bridge. Continue on Rt. 146 and then west on Rt. 16 if you're heading for The Forks and the North Woods; to reach the coast, take Rt. 27 south through Farmington, a gracious old college town with several good restaurants and an unusual opera museum.

GUIDANCE Sugarloaf's toll-free reservations and information number for the eastern seaboard is 1-800-THE-LOAF, 843-5623; you can also call 207-237-2000, or log onto sugarloaf.com. Pick up a copy of *Maine's Western Mountains and Lakes Region*, an area guide.

GETTING THERE *By air:* **Portland International Jetport** (207-779-7301), 2½ hours away, offers connections to all points. **Rental cars** are available at the airport.

By car: From Boston it theoretically takes four hours to reach the Carrabassett Valley. Take the Maine Turnpike to exit 75 (Auburn), then Rt. 4 to Rt. 2, to Rt. 27; or take I-95 to Augusta, then Rt. 27 the rest of the way. (We swear by the latter route, but others swear by the former.)

By bus: **Northeast Charter & Tour** (1-888-593-6328; northeastchartertour.com) is a charter and tour bus operator that runs a door-to-door bus service to and from the Portland International Jetport; Boston's Logan Airport; Manchester, New Hampshire; and all of New England.

GETTING AROUND In ski season the **Valley Ski Shuttle Bus** runs from the base lodge to the Carrabassett Valley Ski Touring Center and Rt. 27 lodges.

WHEN TO COME Summer hikes and winter skiing trips work in this area, with its year-round accommodations and restaurants. Sporting camps run from spring ice-out to late fall. Whitewater rafting is at its prime in spring.

✳ To See

MUSEUMS 🐾 **Stanley Museum** (207-265-2729; stanleymuseum.org), 40 School St., Kingfield. Open June–Oct., Tue.–Sun. 1–4; Nov.–May, Tue.–Fri. 1–4. $4 adults, $3 seniors, $2 ages 11 and under. Housed in a stately wooden school donated by the Stanley family in 1903, this is a varied collection of inventions by the Stanley twins, F. O. and F. E. (it was their invention of the airbrush in the 1870s that made their fortune). Exhibits range from violins to the steam car for which the Stanleys are best known. Three Stanley Steamers (made between 1905 and 1916) are on exhibit.

Nordica Homestead Museum (207-778-2042), 116 Nordica Lane on Holley Rd. (off Rt. 4/27), north of Farmington. Open June–mid-Sept., Tue.–Sat. 10–noon and 1–5, Sun. 1–5. Appointment-only till Oct. 15. Adults $2, children $1. This 19th-century farmhouse is the unlikely repository for the costumes, jewelry, personal mementos, and exotic gifts given to the opera star Lillian Norton, who was born here (she later changed her name to Nordica).

Nowetah's American Indian Museum (207-628-4981; maine museums.org), 2 Colegrove Rd., jut off Rt. 27, New Portland. Open daily 10–5; no admission charge. Nowetah Cyr—a descendant of St. Francis Abenaki and member of the Paugussett Nation—and her husband, Tom Cyr, display Native American artifacts from the United States, Canada, and South America, with a focus on the Abenaki of Maine. More than 600 Native American Maine baskets and bark containers are displayed in one room, and quill-work baskets, arrowheads, a birch-bark canoe, and a dugout canoe are on display in another. Almost all the items in the gift shop are made by Native Americans.

Nancy English

NOWETAH'S AMERICAN INDIAN MUSEUM

Red School House Museum (207-778-6083), Farmington Fairgrounds, Farmington. Open by appointment. A schoolhouse built in 1852 and used as a school until 1958, this building was moved to the fairgrounds in 2006, where it sits near an Agricultural Museum, maple syrup house, and blacksmith forge, popular draws during Farmington Fair in mid-Sept. The schoolhouse has been filled with old school items and artifacts.

Wilton Farm & Home Museum (207-645-2091; wiltonmaine.org), Canal St., Wilton. Open July–Aug., Sat. 1–4, and during Wilton Blueberry Festival. A Civil War–era building housing items owned by the Bass family, Bass shoes, period costumes, a display on Sylvia Hardy ("the Maine Giantess"), and a large collection of Maine bottles, among other things. A working forge is sometimes in action.

NOWETAH'S AMERICAN INDIAN MUSEUM

Nancy English

HISTORIC SITES Kingfield Historical House (207-265-4032; king field-maine.gov), 45 High St., Kingfield. Open June–Sept. Wed. 10–2, Sun. 1–4, during Kingfield Days in July, and by appointment. Built in 1890, this high-Victorian house museum operated by the Kingfield Historical Society is full of period furnishings and the personal possessions of Maine's first governor, William King (where Kingfield got its name), and

Chansonetta Stanley Emmons, a photographer. Changing exhibits throughout the house, with its Scotch Firetube Steam Boiler, and country store in the barn.

Dead River Historical Society (207-246-2271), Rts. 16 and 27, Stratton. Open weekends in summer 11–3. A memorial to the "lost" towns of Flagstaff and Dead River, flooded in 1950 to create today's 22,000-acre, 24-mile Flagstaff Lake. Artifacts include carpentry and logging tools, china and glass. When the water is low foundations and cellars, including one of a round barn, rise out of Dead River.

Wire Bridge, on Wire Bridge Rd., off Rt. 146 (not far) off Rt. 27 in New Portland. Nowhere near anywhere, this amazing-looking suspension bridge across the Carrabassett River has two massive shingled stanchions. The bridge is one of Maine's 19th-century engineering feats (built in 1864–66, and renovated in 1961). There's a good swimming hole just downstream and a place to picnic across the bridge; take a right through the ball field and go 0.5 mile on the dirt road. Note the parking area and path to the river.

FOR FAMILIES ✍ **Sugarloaf Outdoor Adventure Camp** (207-237-6909), Riverside Park, Rt. 27, Carrabassett Valley. Runs weekdays July–mid-Aug. Begun as a town program and now operated by Sugarloaf. Open to visitors (reservations required); designed for ages 4–13: archery, swimming, biking, golf, climbing, camping, fly-fishing, and arts and crafts.

SCENIC DRIVES Rt. 142 from Kingfield to Phillips (11 miles) runs through farmland backed by Mount Abraham. Stop at the **Phillips Historical Society** and **Daggett Rock** and continue to **Mount Blue State Park**; return to Kingfield via New Vineyard and New Portland, stopping to see the **Wire Bridge**.

THE WIRE BRIDGE IN NEW PORTLAND

Kim Grant

Rt. 16 though North New Portland and Embden is the most scenic as well as the most direct route from Kingfield to the Upper Kennebec Valley and Moosehead Lake.

✳ To Do

BOATING See *Fishing* for rental canoes, kayaks, and motorboats.

CANOEING AND KAYAKING The **Carrabassett River** above East New Portland is a good spring paddling spot, with Class II and III whitewater. The north branch of the **Dead River** from the dam in Eustis to the landing after the Stratton bridge is another good paddle, as is the upper branch of the **Kennebago River**.

FISHING Through **Guide Adventures at Sugarloaf**, guests can take spring and summer fly-fishing lessons with Bonnie Holden, master Maine guide (1-800-THE-LOAF). The village of Stratton, north of Sugarloaf, serves as the gateway to serious fishing country. **Northland Cash Supply** (207-246-2376) is a genuine backwoods general store that also carries plenty of fishing gear: "We've got everything, clothing, souvenirs, wine, the Lottery." In Eustis, **Tim Pond Wilderness Camps** is a traditional fishing enclave. In Farmington, **Aardvark Outfitters** (207-778-3330) offers a wide selection of fly-fishing gear. Inquire about fly-fishing schools at Sugarloaf.

GOLF Sugarloaf Golf Club (207-237-2000), Sugarloaf. This spectacular 18-hole, par-72 course, designed by Robert Trent Jones Jr., is ranked among the nation's best, as is its golf school.

✐ **Junior Golf Camp** (207-237-2000), Sugarloaf (five midweek days), designed for ages 12–18, is offered several times between June and Aug.

THE 11TH HOLE AT SUGARLOAF GOLF CLUB

HIKING There are a number of 4,000-footers in the vicinity, and rewarding trails up **Mount Abraham** and **Bigelow Mountain**. The APPALACHIAN TRAIL signs are easy to spot on Rt. 27 just south of Stratton; popular treks include the two hours to **Cranberry Pond** or four-plus hours (one-way) to **Cranberry Peak**. The chamber of commerce usually stocks copies of the Maine Bureau of Parks and Lands' detailed map to trails in the 35,000-acre **Bigelow Preserve**, encompassing the several above-tree-line trails in the Bigelow Range (the trails are far older than the preserve, which dates to 1976 when a proposal to turn these mountains into "the Aspen of the East" was defeated by a public referendum).

⚲ **West Mountain Falls** on the Sugarloaf Golf Course is an easy hike to a swimming and picnic spot on the South Branch of the Carrabassett River. Begin at the Sugarloaf Clubhouse.

Poplar Stream Falls is a 51-foot cascade with a swimming hole below. Turn off Rt. 27 at the Valley Crossing and follow this road to the abandoned road marked by a snowmobile sign. Follow this road 1.5 miles.

Check in at the Sugarloaf Outdoor Center, then head up **Burnt Mountain Trail**, a 3-mile hike to the 3,600-foot summit. At the top you'll have a 360-degree view of mountains, Sugarloaf's Snowfields, and Carrabassett Valley towns. The trail follows a streambed through soft- and hardwoods.

The Maine Huts and Trails System (207-265-2400; reservations, 1-877-634-8824; mainehuts.org), 375 N. Main St., Kingfield. This vibrant organization is creating a 180-mile trail for summer hiking, fishing, swimming and paddling and winter snowshoeing and skiing; 45 miles are now open. On the route from Carrabassett Valley to Dead River, visitors can stay at the Poplar Stream Falls hut and at Flagstaff hut on Flagstaff Lake, where canoes and kayaks are available; Grand Falls hut on the Dead River is the last hut now in service. A 14.2 mile stretch separates Grand Falls from the Forks, suitable in winter only for experienced skiers. The final route will run from the Mahoosucs to Moosehead, with a total of up to 12 huts for overnight shelter. In 2012 or 2013, a fourth hut will be under construction south of Carrabasset Valley. The "huts" are large enough to accommodate somewhere between 32 to 40 guests, with use under the "leave no trace" system advised. Call the organization for maps and information about vacation packages that include meals and lodging, at the huts for hiking, canoeing, and swimming. (See *Hiking* in Upper Kennebec.) Fishing, swimming, paddling and hiking are summer activities; winter skiing is the biggest draw. Members receive better pricing, free use of canoes and kayaks, and attend the fall barbecue for free. $69–99 per night per person includes breakfast and dinner in any of the facilities. Reservations required ($100 extra if you drop in, and there may be no beds available).

In Farmington, **Flint Woods** and **Bonney Woods** (mainetrailfinder.com), with old-growth hemlock, hold good trails very close to the village. The website maine trailfinder.com shows the easy routes.

MOOSE-WATCHING Moose Cruises (207-237-4201) depart from the Sugarloaf Mountain Hotel on Mon. evening June–Sept. $20 adults, $10 children. Ride the "Moose Express" van to moose-watching spots.

MOUNTAIN BIKING The **Sugarloaf Outdoor Center** (207-237-2000), Rt. 17, is the hub of a trail system designed for cross-country skiers that also serves bikers well. The more adventurous can, of course, hit any number of abandoned logging roads. More information is available at the Carrabassett Valley Recreation Department (207-237-5566).

A 19.5-mile loop begins at Tufulio's Restaurant (see *Eating Out*). Park there, cross the Carriage Rd. bridge, and turn left onto Houston Brook Rd. This will lead you into the **Bigelow Preserve** on doubletrack logging roads. When the road forks, heading uphill with a hard right, stay instead to the left on the singletrack trail. You'll go past Stratton Brook Pond and the Appalachian Trailhead. When you reach Rt. 27, head south to Bigelow Station. Follow the Narrow Gauge Trail back to Tufulio's. This is a good trip for intermediate-level bikers.

SWIMMING *Cathedral Pines*, Rt. 27, Stratton. Just north of town, turn right into the campground and follow signs to the public beach, with changing rooms and a playground, on Flagstaff Lake. Free.

Riverside Park, Rt. 27, 0.5 mile south of Ayotte's Country Store, is among the Carrabassett River's popular swimming holes. It features a natural waterslide and a very small beach, ideal for small children. Look for a deeper swimming hole off Rt. 27, 0.5 mile south of Riverside Park on the corner of the entrance to Spring Farm.

Also see **Wire Bridge** under *Historic Sites*.

TENNIS Riverside Park, Rt. 27, Carrabassett Valley. This municipal park along the Carrabassett River also features volleyball, basketball, a playground, and bathroom facilities.

WHITEWATER RAFTING See the outfitters listed in "Upper Kennebec Valley" and reserve a ride: phone 1-800-RAFT-MEE.

Sugarloaf has entered into a partnership with Northern Outdoors (1-800-765-RAFT), providing rafting trips and packages.

✳ Winter Sports

CROSS-COUNTRY SKIING Sugarloaf Outdoor Center (207-237-6830), Rt. 27, Carrabassett Valley. Open in-season 9 AM–dusk. This is Maine's largest touring network, with 100 kilometers of trail loops, including race loops (with snowmaking) for timed runs. Rentals and instruction are available, and are free with a downhill lift ticket. The center itself includes the **Bull Moose Bakery**, which serves soups and sandwiches, and provides space to relax in front of a fire with a view of Sugarloaf.

SUGARLOAF

Titcomb Mountain Ski Touring Center (207-778-9031; titcomb mountain.com), Morrison Hill Rd. (off Rt. 2/4), West Farmington. A varied network of 16 kilometers of groomed trails and unlimited ungroomed trails, plus a lodge with snack bar, fireplace, and ski rentals. $15–25 adults, $12–20 ages 6–12, depending on day of week; under 6 free.

Also see **The Maine Huts and Trails System** under *Hiking*.

DOWNHILL SKIING/SNOW-BOARDING *Sugarloaf* (general information, 207-237-2000; snow report, ext. 6808; on-mountain reservations, 1-800-THE-LOAF; sugarloaf

.com). Sugarloaf Mountain Corporation was formed in the early 1950s by local skiers, and growth was steady but slow into the 1970s. Then a boom decade produced one of New England's largest self-contained resorts, including a base village complete with a seven-story brick hotel and a forest of condominiums. Sugarloaf has been expanding and improving snowmaking and services ever since. Snowmaking now even covers much of its alpine cap. Trails number 138, and glades add up to 55 miles. The vertical drop is a whopping 2,820 feet. The 14 lifts include two detachable quads, a triple chair, eight double chairs, a T-bar, and a surface lift. Facilities include a Perfect Turn Development Center, a Perfect Kids school, a ski shop, rentals, a base lodge, a cafeteria, a nursery (day and night), a game room, and a total of 12 bars and restaurants. The nursery is first-rate; there are children's programs for 3- to 12-year-olds; also mini mountain tickets for beginners. In 2009–10 one-day lift rates were $75 adults, $64 young adults 13–18, $51 juniors 6–12 and seniors. Also multiday, early- and late-season, and packaged rates. Lifts are free for kids 5 and under.

ICE SKATING Sugarloaf Outdoor Center (207-237-6830) maintains an Olympic-sized, lighted rink and rents skates.

SNOWMOBILING Snowmobile trails are outlined on many maps available locally; a favorite destination is **Flagstaff Lodge** (maintained as a warming hut) in the Bigelow Preserve. **Flagstaff Rentals** and **T&L Enterprises** (207-246-4276), Stratton, rent snowmobiles.

TUBING Sugarloaf offers a Tubing Park for kids with a surface lift on the trail called the Birches.

✳ Lodging

On-mountain
Sugarloaf Inn and Condominiums (207-237-2000 or 1-800-THE-LOAF; sugarloaf.com), Carrabassett Valley 04947. More than 250 ski-in, ski-out condominiums are in the rental pool. Built gradually over more than 20 years (they include the first condos in Maine), they represent a range of styles and sites; when making a reservation, you might want to ask about convenience to the base complex, the Sugarloaf Sports and Fitness Club (to which all condo guests have access), or the golf club. The 42-room Sugarloaf Inn offers attractive standard rooms and fourth-floor family spaces with lofts; there's a comfortable living room with fireplace and a solarium restaurant and bar called **The Shipyard Brew Haus**. The front desk is staffed around the clock, and the inn is handy to the health club as well as to the mountain. Packages $69–299 per person in winter, from $99 in golf season.

Sugarloaf Mountain Hotel & Conference Center (1-800-527-9879), RR 1, Box 2200, Carrabassett Valley 04947. So close to the base complex that it dwarfs the base lodge, this is a massive, seven-story, 120-room brick condominium hotel with a gabled roof and central tower. Rooms feature a small refrigerator and microwave. Request a view of the mountain or you might get stuck overlooking the less attractive back of the hotel. A pair of two-bedroom suites come with a living room and kitchen. The two palatial tower penthouses each holds three bedrooms, three baths, and a hot tub. Health club with two hot tubs (open at noon) and sauna and steam room. Midwinter $109–159 per night for a one- or two-bedroom, $224–650 for suites; less in summer; multiday discounts.

Also see **The Maine Huts and Trails System** under *Hiking*.

Off-mountain
INNS AND BED & BREAKFASTS
🐾 🦮 **The Herbert Grand Hotel** (207-265-2000 or 1-888-656-9922; herbertgrandhotel.com), 246 Main St., P.O. Box 67, Kingfield 04947. Open year-round. This three-story Beaux Arts–style hotel was billed as a "palace in the wilderness" when it opened in 1918 in the center of Kingfield. The "fumed oak" walls of the lobby have been rubbed to a high polish, the paint refreshed, and the exterior renewed; the interior underwent renewal in 2011. The sink on the dining room wall is where stagecoach customers used to clean up before dining. The 26 rooms (including 4 suites) are furnished with antiques and cable TV, AC, and private bath. $69–179, plus tax and a 3 percent gratuity. Pets are welcome for a fee.

Three Stanley Avenue (207-265-5541; stanleyavenue.com), Kingfield

THE HERBERT GRAND IN KINGFIELD
Nancy English

04947. Designed by a younger brother of the Stanley twins, now an attractive B&B with six Victorian-inspired rooms (three with private bath) next to the ornate restaurant One Stanley Avenue, also owned by Dan Davis (see *Dining Out*). Breakfast, granola and eggs or blueberry pancakes, is included in the rates, $60–80.

The Mountain Village Inn (207-265-2030; mountainvillageinn.com), 164 Main St., Kingfield. The 1850s farmhouse has been carefully updated, and the six guest rooms—all with private bath, some with whirlpool tubs and cedar shower—have antique or cottage beds and good mattresses. Call in your arrival time, and the two dogs will be kept inside. For breakfast count on organic oatmeal, organic granola, and eggs from the chickens kept in the enormous white barn. $89–119.

MOTEL 🦮 🐾 **Spillover Motel** (207-246-6571), P.O. Box 427, Stratton 04982. An attractive, two-story, 20-unit (16 nonsmoking) motel just south of Stratton Village. Spanking clean, with two double beds to a unit, cable TV, and phone. $72–92 per unit includes continental breakfast; $5 pets.

SPORTING CAMPS 🐾 🦮 **Tim Pond Wilderness Camps** (207-243-2947; in winter, 207-897-4056; timpond.com), Eustis 04936. Open May–Nov. Located on a pond where there are no other camps, and down a road with gated access, with 11 log cabins, each with a fieldstone fireplace or woodstove. The tranquility here can wash away all stress, in a rocking chair on a cabin porch or in a quiet canoe. Fly-fish, deer and moose hunt, mountain bike, hike, moose-watch, swim, or canoe on or around this clear, remote lake surrounded by 4,450 acres of woodland. $175 single per night (plus 15 percent gratuity) includes meals, cabin, boat and motor. Ten percent discount July–Aug. Pets $10. Dinner by reservation for people who want just a meal July–Sept.

Grant's Kennebago Camps (1-800-633-4815; grantscamps.com), P.O. Box 786, Rangeley. John and Carolyn Blunt run this traditional Maine sporting camp down 9 miles of private road with 18 cabins, all with woodstove, private bath, and screened porch, near the edge of Kennebago Lake and its own dock. Three meals a day are served in the lodge's knotty-pine-paneled dining room, and might be prime rib or lobster, with a brownie sundae for dessert. Five miles of trails are maintained by the owners for hiking. Fly-fishing and bird hunting. $165 a night for adults during a three-or-more-night stay, $185 a night per person for two nights or less.

COTTAGES AND CONDOS For a list of rental units ranging from classic old A-frames to classy condos, contact the **Sugarloaf Area Chamber of Commerce** (see *Guidance*).

CAMPGROUNDS ❀ ✿ **Cathedral Pines Campground** (207-246-3491; gopinescamping.com), Rt. 27, Eustis 04936. Open mid-May–Sept. Three hundred town-owned acres on Flagstaff Lake, with 115 wooded tent and RV sites set amid towering red pines. Recreation hall, beach, playground, and canoe and paddleboat rentals. Rates $20–25.

❀ ✿ **Deer Farm Camps & Campground** (207-265-4599 or 207-265-2241; deerfarmcamps.com), Tufts Pond Rd., Kingfield 04947. Open May–mid-Oct. Fifty wooded tent and RV sites near Tufts Pond (good swimming); facilities include a store, playground, and hot showers. $18 tent

sites, $22 with water and electric; hookups available. $250 per week for cabins.

✹ Where to Eat

DINING OUT One Stanley Avenue (207-265-5541; stanleyavenue.com), Kingfield. Open mid-Dec.–mid-Apr. 5–9:30, except Mon. Reservations recommended. Guests can have a drink in the Victorian parlor, then proceed to one of three intimate dining rooms. Entrées include maple and cider chicken, rabbit with raspberry sauce, and beef-and-chestnut pie, and include local produce like fiddlehead ferns. Owner-chef Dan Davis describes his methods as classic, the results as distinctly regional. $21–35 includes fresh bread, salad, vegetables, starch, coffee, and tea, but it's difficult to pass on the wines and desserts.

Hugs Italian Cuisine (207-237-2392), 3001 Town Line Rd. (Rt. 27). Open mid-July mid-Oct. Wed.–Sun. for dinner, closed through Nov.; open every night for dinner in winter. The green metal roof and board-and-batten siding keep this restaurant looking modest— but inside you'll find some great food. Past the shrine to pasta, among festoons of grapevines, you can enjoy wild mushroom ravioli with Gorgonzola, fresh tomato and spinach sauce, accompanied by great pesto bread—or chicken, veal, and seafood. All entrées can be altered, our good waiter told us.

The Double Diamond Restaurant (207-237-2222, ext. 4220), Sugarloaf Mountain Hotel, Carrabassett Valley. Lounge 7–10, dinner 4–9:30. This is the most ambitious restaurant in the Sugarloaf complex. The menu ranges from lobster (served nightly from a tank on premises) to prime rib on Thu. Entrées begin at $13–25.

Bullwinkle's (1-800-THE-LOAF), at the top of Bucksaw chair. On Sat. night (and special nights by appointment) this place converts from a daytime ski cafeteria into a charming on-mountain full-service restaurant. Reserve early, because it fills up quickly in high season. We were lucky enough to ride up in the Sno-Cat during a lovely snowstorm. Soups like lobster and corn bisque were spectacular, and the venison and lobster filled us up nicely after a day on the slopes. Two sittings per night means you can have a drink in the **Widowmaker Lounge** at the base of the mountain before or after, watching the powder collect on the runs you'll ski the next morning.

EATING OUT ((ᵥ)) **The Orange Cat Café** (207-265-2860; orangecatcafe .com), The Brick Castle, 329 Main St., Kingfield. Open 7–5 in winter, 7–3 in summer. Good coffee and homemade scones are served under a map of the world; you can also get great lunch dishes, like a jalapeño chicken salad sandwich ($6.50) or spinach, bacon, and blue cheese salad ($6.95); best hot chocolate in the valley. In summer count on ice cubes made with coffee for iced coffee—full strength and perfect.

🦞 ♪ **Longfellows Restaurant** (207-265-4394), 247 Main St., Kingfield. Open year-round for lunch from 11 and dinner, 5–9. An attractive, informal dining place in a 19th-century building decorated with photos of 19th-century Kingfield. A find for budget-conscious families, with reasonably good food and two-for-one dinners Tue. Deck overlooking Carrabassett River. Entrées $7–17.

♪ ⅚ **Tufulio's Restaurant & Bar** (207-235-2010), Rt. 27, Carrabassett (6 miles south of Sugarloaf). Open for dinner 5–9:30 daily; happy hour begins at 4. A pleasant dining room with large oak booths, specializing in pasta, pizza, seafood, steaks, and microbrews. Children's menu and game room.

♪ **The Woodsman** (207-265-2561), Rt. 27, Kingfield (north end of town). Open Mon.–Sat. for breakfast and lunch; Sun. for breakfast only. Pine-paneled, decorated with logging tools and pictures, this is a friendly barn of a place. Good for stacks of pancakes, omelets, homemade soups, and local gossip.

The Rack (207-237-2211; therackbbq .com), Sugarloaf Access Rd., Carrabassett. Barbecue and pulled pork are the focuses but there are other options, from fresh fish to pasta. Seth Wescott, co-owner of this restaurant, thrilled Maine both times he won the snowboard cross gold medal in the Winter Olympics in 2006 and 2010. Entrées $15–25. Live entertainment in winter and less often in summer.

In Farmington
Soup for You! Cafe (207-779-0799), 222 Broadway. This small restaurant offers homemade soups, salads, and sandwiches that bear the names of *Seinfeld* characters and other whimsical monikers like Don Quixote and Barking Spider. Smoothies, cappuccino, and espresso, too.

The Homestead Bakery Restaurant (207-778-6162), 186 Broadway (Rt. 43). Open Tue.–Fri. 8 AM–9 PM, Sat. 8–9, Sun.–Mon. 8–2. Dinner choices include steaks, seafood, chicken, and vegetarian options, like vegetable ravioli in vodka sauce, as well as Cajun-spiced duck diavolo. Entrées $15–24.

Thai Smile (207-778-0790), 103 Narrow Gauge Square. Opened in Oct. 2011 to the open arms of area diners, this fine Thai restaurant serves sushi and Thai specialties; a family business in Kennebunkport got the owner off to a good start. Go for the barbecued eel.

🍦 **Gifford's Famous Ice Cream** (207-778-3617), 293 Main St. (Rt. 4/27). Open seasonally at 11 or noon. Nearby Skowhegan is home base for this exceptional ice cream, made in more than 40 flavors.

✳ Selective Shopping

🖊 **Devaney, Doak & Garret Booksellers** (207-778-3454; ddgbooks.com), 193 Broadway, Farmington. Open daily. A bookstore worthy of a college town, and one with a good children's section. Comfortable seating invites lingering. Readings from local and Maine authors.

Reny's (207-778-4631; renys.com), 200 Broadway, Farmington. Filling a former silent-movie house, the statewide chain of fine discount goods has a popular store here that features a restored stage and balconies.

Twice-Sold Tales (207-778-4411), 155 Main St., Farmington. Specializing in Maine history and Maine literature, and nonfiction, but carrying mysteries and more, this eclectic collection is well organized.

Sugarwood Gallery (207-778-9105; sugarwoodgallery.com), 248 Broadway, Farmington. A cooperative gallery showing the work of local artisans, mostly woodwork, stained glass, and pottery.

Mainestone Jewelry (207-778-6560), 179 Broadway, Farmington. Ron and Cindy Gelinas craft much of the jewelry here—made from Maine-mined gems—but some is made by local craftspeople.

✳ Special Events

January: **White White World Week**—snow sculpture contest, annual Dummy Jump, and discounts at Sugarloaf.

February: **Polar Blast**, Eustis/Stratton—a snowmobile jump, cribbage tournament, and chowder/chili cook-off.

March: **St. Patrick's Day Fireworks**, Sugarloaf Mountain.

April: **Easter Festival at Sugarloaf**—costume parade, Easter egg hunt on the slopes, and sunrise service on the summit.

June: **Family Fun Days**, Eustis/Stratton—games and children's events, parade, fireworks, put on by the Flagstaff Area Business Association (207-670-0808).

Mid-July: **Kingfield Days Celebration**—four days with parade, art exhibits, potluck supper.

August: **Wilton Blueberry Festival**, Wilton.

Third week of September: **Farmington Fair**, with popular harness racing and livestock exhibits.

October: **Corn Maze and Pumpkin Patch** (sandyriverfarms.com), Rts. 2 and 27, 3 miles south of Farmington at Sandy River Farms. A 10-acre fall extravaganza with food, hayrides, and some haunting.

December: **Yellow-Nosed Vole Day**, Sugarloaf Mountain. **Chester Greenwood Day**, Farmington, honors the local inventor of the earmuff with a parade and variety show.

The Kennebec 6
Valley

AUGUSTA AND MID-MAINE,
Including the Belgrade
Lakes Region

THE UPPER KENNEBEC VALLEY AND
MOOSE RIVER VALLEY,
Including The Forks and Jackman

AUGUSTA AND MID-MAINE
Including the Belgrade Lakes Region

Augusta was selected as the nascent state's capital in 1827 because then, as now, so many travelers come this way, whether headed up or down the coast, into or out of Maine's interior. First I-95 and now the Rt. 3 connector make it all too easy, however, to bypass the city.

If time permits, approach Augusta via the Kennebec instead of the highway. Follow Rt. 201, the old river road, at least for the 6 miles from Gardiner up through Hallowell's mid-19th-century Water Street, lined with antiques and specialty shops and restaurants. However you come, don't skip the Maine State Museum, which does an excellent job of showcasing Maine's natural history and traditional industries, as well as tracing human habitation back 12,000 years.

AUGUSTA FROM FORT WESTERN

Christina Tree

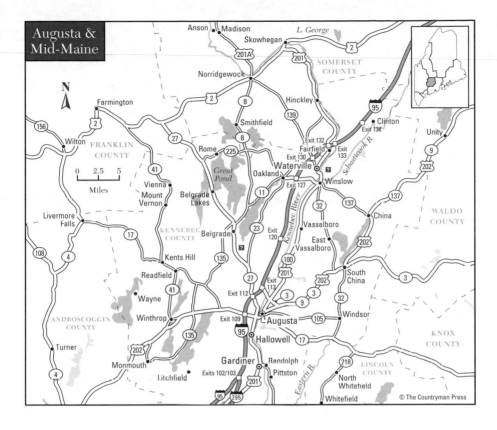

Augusta and neighboring Hallowell both mark the site of Native American villages. In 1625 the Pilgrims came here to trade "seven hundred pounds of good beaver and some other furs" with the Wabanaki for a "shallop's load of corn." They procured a grant for a strip of land 15 miles wide on either side of the Kennebec, built a storehouse, and with the proceeds of their beaver trade were soon able to pay off their London creditors. With the decline of the fur trade and rising hostilities with the Wabanaki, the tract of land was sold to four Boston merchants. It wasn't until 1754, when the British constructed Fort Western (now reconstructed), that serious settlement began.

The statehouse, designed by Charles Bulfinch and built of granite from neighboring Hallowell, was completed in 1832 (it's been expanded and largely rebuilt since). During the mid-19th century, this area boomed: Some 500 boats were built along the river between Winslow and Gardiner, and river traffic between Augusta and Boston thrived.

This Lower Kennebec Valley remains rolling, open farmland with breathtaking views from its ridge roads, spotted with spring-fed lakes. It was the site of numerous, now vanished 19th-century summer hotels and boardinghouses and still is home to many summer camps. The Belgrade Lakes Region, just north of Augusta, remains a low-key *On Golden Pond* kind of resort area with old-style family-geared "sporting camps," summer rental cottages, and widely scattered B&Bs. East of the city, the China Lakes is another old low-profile summer haven. Golf courses (former farms) are proliferating. Art lovers find their way to the stellar Colby College Museum of Art in Waterville, and the Maine International Film Festival draws cinephiles to town in July. Long-established summer theater continues to thrive in Monmouth and Skowhegan.

The latter town, sited at one of the major drops in the Kennebec River, is an obvious road-food stop on your way north up the Kennebec Valley. Stroll Skowhegan's reawakening Main Street, and find one of the walking bridges across the gorge or view the Kennebec from the gem of a small museum and research center honoring the late U.S. senator Margaret Chase Smith, "the Lady from Maine."

Those who would rather shadow the Kennebec north can follow its curve through the gracious old town of Norridgewock and on up Rt. 201A through Anson and Embden (just across a bridge from Solon), where petroglyphs are evidence of a Native American culture that dates back several thousand years.

GUIDANCE Kennebec Valley Chamber of Commerce (207-623-4559; augustamaine.) runs a website worth checking for current updates.

Mid-Maine Chamber of Commerce (207-873-3315; midmainechamber.com). Covers the Belgrade and China Lakes as well as Waterville. Their office, 50 Elm St., Waterville, is open weekdays 9–5.

Belgrade Lakes Region Business Group, Inc. (207-495-2744; belgradelakes maine.com) maintains a good website and a seasonal information booth on Rt. 27 in Belgrade.

Skowhegan Chamber of Commerce (207-474-3621; skoweganchamber.com), 23 Commercial St., is open year-round 9–5 weekdays and Sat. 10–2 in summer months. Rt. 201 snakes through downtown, right by this office.

West Gardiner Service Plaza (582-0160), I-95 exit 102 north, 102 south; I-295 exit 51; check the Maine Tourist Association desk beyond the crafts center.

GETTING THERE *By air:* **Augusta State Airport** (augustaairport.org) is served by **Cape Air** (capeair.com) to Boston. Check the website for car rentals and taxis.

By bus: **Concord Coach Lines** (1-800-639-3317; concordcoachlines.com) offers service from Portland and Boston, stopping at the new **Augusta Transportation Center** (207-622-0808, ext. 450), 9 Industrial Dr., just off I-95 exit 112 (head north on Rt. 8/27). Open 5:30 AM–7:45 PM. Taxis are available. Also long-term parking spaces (free for two weeks).

Greyhound (207-622-1601) stops at the airport in Augusta, also in Waterville.

By car: From points south, Rt. 295 is both quicker and cheaper than I-95 (the Maine Turnpike). The two merge just south of Augusta, and both access the new West Gardiner Service Plaza. Note the connector (exit 113) bypassing Augusta and facilitating access to Rt. 3 east. For Rt. 3 via downtown Augusta take exit 112; for Belgrade Lakes, exit 127; for Rt. 201 north through Hinkley and Skowhegan, exit 133.

SUGGESTED READING *A Midwife's Tale*, a Pulitzer Prize winner by Laurel Thatcher Ulrich, vividly describes life in this area 1785–1812. *Empire Falls*, a Pulitzer Prize–winning novel by Richard Russo, describes current life in a town resembling Waterville.

Hallowell (hallowell.org). Two miles south of Augusta, this "city" (pop. 2,467), with its line of brick two- and three-story buildings along the Kennebec River, looks much the way it did at the time this, not Augusta, was the region's commercial center. Shipbuilding and granite quarrying were the big industries here, along with ice. Residential streets, stepped into the slope above the shops, are worth driving to see fine houses and churches dating to every decade in the 19th century. The city's revival dates to the 1970s. A road-widening proposal threatened to level most of Water Street, but residents rallied; the anniversary of their protest, the last weekend in July, is now observed as **Old Hallowell Day**. Note the "**Museum in the Streets**" consisting of 19 archival photos and captions on buildings along Water and neighboring streets. Walk in **Vaughan Woods**, part of the city's most historic estate, dating to the 18th century. **Water Street**, now all a National Historic District, is lined with quality, individually owned shops (no chain stores) and the best restaurants around.

Gardiner (pop. 6,100). Sited at the confluence of the Kennebec River and Cobbosseecontee Stream, this old industrial (shoe, textile, and paper) town has been hovering on the verge of renaissance for more than a decade. It was home to Pulitzer Prize–winning poet **Edwin Arlington Robinson** (1869–1935), best known for his poem "Richard Cory" and collection of *Tilbury Town* poems; check earobinson.com for his life story and a Tilbury Town walking tour. The **A1 Diner** and **Renys** are a draw for travelers and locals alike, as are performances at the **Johnson Hall Performing Arts Center**.

Waterville (pop. 15,970). The thinly disguised subject of Richard Russo's novel *Empire Falls*, this old mill town is 25 miles upriver from Augusta. It's home to a major art museum and some interesting restaurants. **Colby College** (207-872-3000; colby.edu) is the pride of the city. Founded in 1813, it enrolls some 1,800 students at its 714-acre campus, with ivy-covered brick buildings, a 128-acre arboretum and bird sanctuary (with nature trails and a picnic area), and the 274-seat **Strider Theater**, offering performances throughout the year. For a self-guided tour, stop by admissions. The **Colby College Museum of Art** is extraordinary (see *To See*). Whether you reach the city from I-95 exit 127 (Rt. 137) or exit 130 (Rt. 104), access to the college is well marked, as is the way to "Downtown," literally down by the river; a large parking lot serves the shops and restaurants there along Silver and Main Sts.

The **Waterville-Winslow Two Cent Bridge** on Front St. is one of the only known toll footbridges in the country (now free). The **Redington Museum and Apothecary** (207-872-9439; redingtonmuseum.org), 64 Silver St. (open seasonally, Tue.–Sat. 10–2), houses the local historical collection.

DOWNTOWN HALLOWELL

Christina Tree

Belgrade Lakes (belgradelakesmaine
.com). There is no Belgrade Lake per
se; the towns here are Rome, Oakland,
Smithfield, and Mount Vernon as well
as Belgrade. There are seven lakes,
with Great Pond, at the center, flanked
by Long Pond to the west, Salmon
Lake (connected to) McGrath Pond
and Messalonskee Lake on the west,
North Pond to the north, and East
Pond to the northeast. **Belgrade
Lakes Village** at the center sits
astride Rt. 27 on a narrow land bridge
between Long and Grand Ponds; many
customers of **Day's Store** (the region's
epicenter; see *Selective Shopping*)
come by boat. The lakeshores are dotted but not lined with summer cottages.
There are several traditional, full-service family-geared "camps," the kind that have
since vanished from all of Maine save the North Woods. Nothing much seems to
have changed around here since the 1950s. Summer is all about swimming, boating, and fishing, and there's even a lakeside roller rink. This was, in fact, the area
that inspired Ernest Thompson's play and then movie, *On Golden Pond*. Thanks to
the **Belgrade Regional Conservation Alliance**
(belgradelakes.org), the 6,000-acre Kennebec Highlands have been preserved.
There's a trail up Blueberry Hill that families have hiked for generations.

DOWNTOWN GARDINER

Christina Tree

SKOWHEGAN INDIAN STATUE

Bill Davis

Winthrop (pop. 2,980). A proud town
with 12 lakes and many summer cottages within its boundaries, Winthrop
seems to be thriving despite closure of
the woolen mill. There are interesting
shops and restaurants.

Skowhegan (pop. 8,875). In Wabanaki
the name is said to mean "watch for
fish." This, one of the major falls in the
Kennebec River, has long been harnessed to generate power for both textile and woodworking mills. Skowhegan
is also shire town of Somerset County
and a major north–south (Rt. 201) and
east–west (Rt. 2) crossroads. Stop
downtown (there's parking behind the
Water St. shops and restaurants) to
view the gorge from one of two pedestrian bridges or from **Coburn Park** on
the eastern edge of town. If it's a hot
day, **Lake George Regional Park**
(see *Swimming*) is worth the detour.
The Kennebec doglegs west here
and Rt. 201A follows it up through

in **Solon**. Whichever way you go, be sure to stop by the riverside **Margaret Chase Smith Library Center**. This is really an outstanding small museum (see *To See*). On the way check out the **Skowhegan History House** (skowheganhisrtoryhouse.org; 66 Elm St.), open Memorial–Columbus Day, Tue.–Sat. 1–4. Skowhegan is also home to **Gifford's Ice Cream**, the **Skowhegan State Fair**, and the **Skowhegan Lakewood Theater** on Lake Wesserunsett, billed as America's Oldest Summer Theater. The prestigious **Skowhegan School of Painting and Sculpture** (skowheganart.org) holds an intensive nine-week summer residency program, squirreled away on a 300-acre campus 4 miles from town, and also opens its evening lectures to the public.

✳ To See

In Augusta

✪ ✎ ♿ **Maine State Museum** (207-287-2301; mainestatemuseum.org), housed in the State Library/Archives building in the State House Complex, marked from Sewall St., also accessible from State St. (Rt. 201/27). Open Tue.–Fri. 9–5, Sat. 10–4. Closed holidays and state government holidays. Maine's best-kept secret, this is a superb and extensive museum, just a few blocks off the interstate but badly posted. It's well worth finding, especially if there are children along. It's a great way to break a long drive. Allow an hour minimum.

The *Back to Nature* exhibit features animals such as the lynx and snowshoe rabbit, deer, moose, beaver, and birds in their convincingly detailed habitats (the trout are real) with plenty of sound effects. The *Maine Bounty* exhibits depict the way the state's natural resources have been developed through fishing, agriculture, granite quarrying, ice harvesting, shipbuilding, lumbering, and more. Exhibits include a gigantic wagon used to haul stone from quarries and the equally huge Lombard Log Hauler and 1846 narrow-gauge locomotive Lion, used to transport lumber. Archival films such as *From Stump to Ship* bring the era to life. *Made in Maine* depicts more than a dozen 19th-century industrial scenes: textile mills and shops producing shoes, guns, fishing rods, and more, again with sound effects. Don't miss the fourth floor with its *At Home in Maine* galleries depicting domestic life from the 1800s through 1960s.

MAINE STATE MUSEUM

Christina Tree

Yet another outstanding exhibit, *12,000 Years in Maine*, traces the story of human habitation in the state from the Paleo Indians up through the "ceramic period" (3,000 BC–AD 500) with genuine artifacts and reproductions of petroglyphs. It also dramatizes early European explorations and displays 19th-century Penobscot and Passamaquoddy craftsmanship, from highly decorative bent-birch boxes to birch-bark canoes. Check the website for current special exhibits and don't miss the gift store.

Directions: From I-95 exit 109 follow Western Ave. (Rt. 17/202) and turn right at the light across from the armory (posted for the capitol complex). Follow signs for the State House until you see the museum posted (a right turn onto Sewall St.), then turn into the parking lot. The museum is in the low-slung modern building that also houses the state library and archives. If you miss the first turn, continue around the rotary, take Rt. 27/201 south, then make your first right after passing the capitol. This takes you to the other side of the same parking lot.

Christina Tree

MAINE STATE MUSEUM

Tours of the State House (by reservation weekdays 9–1 through the museum). The governor's 1830 mansion, Blaine House (blainehouse.org), is open Tue.–Thu. 2–4.

Fort Western (207-626-2385; oldfortwestern.org), City Center Plaza, 16 Cony St., Augusta. Open Memorial Day–Labor Day, 1–4; Labor Day–Columbus Day, weekends only, 1–4; Nov.–Jan., first Sun. of every month, 1–3. $6 per adult, $4 ages 6–16. The original 16-room garrison house has been restored to reflect its use as a fort, trading post, and lodge from 1754 to 1810. The blockhouse and stockade are reproductions, but the main house (barracks and store) is original. The fort, a National Historic Landmark, is the oldest surviving wooden fort in New England. Costumed characters answer questions and demonstrate 18th-century domestic activities. Check the website for many special events.

In Waterville

✪ ♿ **Colby College Museum of Art** (207-859-5600; colby.edu/museum), Colby College, 5600 Mayflower Hill Dr. Open Tue.–Sat. 10–4:30, Sun. noon–4:30, Thu. until 8. Free. Closed Mon. and major holidays. If this museum were on the coast, it would be as well known as Rockland's Farnsworth. For art lovers, it's definitely worth a trip. The Alfond-Lunder Family Pavilion, planned as part of the 2007 Lunder gift and currently under construction, will provide 10,000 square feet of additional exhibition space. Select galleries are open through construction, which will be completed in 2013 to coincide with Colby's bicentennial celebration. The permanent collection numbers some 7,000 pieces of 18th-, 19th-, and 20th-century art and—particularly unusual for a teaching museum—it has the largest exhibit area of any art museum

CITY POINT, VINALHAVEN, **BY MARSDEN HARTLEY**

Colby College Museum of Art/Gift of Alex Katz Foundation

in Maine. Founded only in 1959, the museum has been amazingly lucky in not only the generosity but also the quality of its donors, most recently Peter and Paula Lunder's gift of 500 works of art, including 200 prints by James McNeill Whistler, also paintings by Edward Hopper and Georgia O'Keeffe and sculptures by Augustus Saint-Gaudens and Alexander Calder. The Lunders had previously donated a 13-gallery wing to display more of the college's own collection, with its particular strength in American contemporary art, including significant Maine-based works by Marsden Hartley, John Marin, George Bellows, and Rockwell Kent. The Paul J. Schupf Wing rotates more than 700 paintings, prints, and works on paper by Alex Katz. Major special exhibits, also frequent gallery talks, performances, and receptions throughout the year are listed on the website, along with directions. The museum sounds trickier to find than it is. It's minutes off I-95 exit 127. Head toward downtown Waterville on Rt. 127 and follow the blue COLBY signs. Turn left at the light opposite Inland Hospital on First Rangeway, and at the T turn left onto Mayflower Hill Dr. The building is beyond the main campus quad, with easy parking both in front of the building and behind the Bixler Fine Art Building.

Fort Halifax, Rt. 201 (1 mile south of the Waterville–Winslow Bridge at the junction of the Kennebec and Sebasticook Rivers). Just a blockhouse remains, but it's original, built in 1754—the oldest in the United States. There's also a park with picnic tables here.

Along Route 201 north

⚓ **L. C. Bates Museum** (207-238-4250; gwh.org), Rt. 201, Hinckley. A few miles up Rt. 201 from I-95, exit 133. Open Wed.–Sat. 10–4:30, Sun. 1–4:30; closed Sun. off-season, but look for the OPEN flag; it's frequently staffed on "closed" days. *Note:* The museum is unheated. $3 adults, $1 ages 17 and under. Across the road from the Kennebec River, one in a lineup of brick buildings that are part of the campus of the Good-Will Hinckley School (founded in 1889 for "disadvantaged chidden"), this ponderous Romanesque building houses a large and wonderfully old-fashioned collection, with stuffed wildlife, dioramas by noted American impressionist Charles D. Hubbard, and some significant Wabanaki craftsmanship, with examples ranging from several thousand years old to early-20th-century items. Allow at least an hour. The annual summer art exhibit, usually incorporating work by faculty and/or students at the nearby Skowhegan School of Painting, is a bonus. The 2,540-acre campus includes many miles of walking and biking trails, an arboretum, and a picnic area. Inquire about family-geared programs ranging from jewelry making (highlighting the museum's gem collection) to guided forest walks.

THE TRAPPER BY WINSLOW HOMER
Colby College Museum of Art/Gift of Mrs. Harold T. Pulsfer

Margaret Chase Smith Library Center (207-474-7133; mcslibrary .org), 54 Norridgewock Ave., Skowhegan (turn left at the first traffic light heading north out of town). Open year-round Mon.–Fri. 10–4. Free. Set in 15 acres above the Kennebec, this expanded version of Senator Smith's home is a major museum to an era as well as to a stateswoman who voted her conscience in the face of overwhelming opposition. She is credited with putting an end to the reign of national paranoia instigated by Senator Joseph R. McCarthy. Well worth a stop for the exhibits. This research and conference center houses over 300,000 documents relating to "the lady from Maine," as Margaret Chase Smith (1897–1995) was known during her years as a congresswoman (1940–49) and U.S. senator (1949–73). Check the website for many special events.

Also see the **South Solon Meeting House** in the Upper Kennebec Valley chapter.

Christina Tree

MARGARET CHASE SMITH LIBRARY CENTER

FOR FAMILIES ✐ **Children's Discovery Museum** (207-622-2209; childrensdiscoverymuseum.org), 171 Capitol St. (next to Harvest Time Natural Foods), Augusta. Open Tue.–Thu. 10–4, Fri. and Sat. 10–5, and Sun. 11–4; extended hours during school vacations and summer. $5.50 per child, $4.50 per adult. A newly relocated and expanded hands-on museum, with a stage for performing skits, a puppet theater, a construction area, computer games, double train tracks, a nature center, a music area, a supermarket, and more.

✐ **D.E.W. Animal Kingdom** (207-293-2837; dewanimalkingdom.com), 918 Pond Rd. (Rt. 41), West Mount Vernon. Open May–mid-Sept. daily except Mon., weekends in Apr. and through foliage 10–5. $10 ages 3–99. Julie and Bob Miner stress that this is a "farm," not a "zoo." But what began as a traditional farm with pigs and cows has evolved into the most exotic menagerie in New England: more than 200 animals contained within chain-link pens on 43 wooded acres. What's striking is the way the animals relate to Julie and Bob, who have raised most from birth. Cougars and lions nuzzle them. A female lynx offers her tail to be pulled. The tigers lumber up to be hugged. Eddie the Camel offers slurpy kisses to visitors as well. A wallaby baby peeks from its mother's pouch. Mallard and eider ducks follow you around. It's certainly a magical place. You can feed the several kinds of goats, but this isn't a petting farm—just a place to marvel at animals that are native (deer and black bear) or fairly familiar (ostrich and llamas), and also those you may have only read about—from badgers to black leopards and a white tiger, some so exotic you couldn't have imagined them.

✐ **Norlands Living History Center** (207-897-4366; norlands.org), 290 Norlands Rd., Livermore. From Rt. 4 take Rt. 108 east for 1.2 miles, then travel 1.6 miles up Norlands Rd. Open in summer months for guided tours Tue. and Thu. 11–4, also for seasonal events and school programs. Live-in programs also available. This 455-

WABANAKI CULTURAL LANDMARKS

Wabanaki heritage is particularly strong along this stretch of the Kennebec River. Your clue might be the 62-foot-high **Skowhegan Indian**, billed as "the world's largest sculptured wooden Indian." Carved by sculptor Bernard Langlais in 1969, he stands in the downtown parking lot, visible (and accessible) from Rt. 201. Finding genuine evidence of longtime Indian habitation, however, requires some sleuthing. There are two sites, one commemorating an early-18th-century Indian mission village and the second consisting of genuine Indian petroglyphs. To find the first from Skowhegan, follow Rt. 201A along the Kennebec for just a few miles to Norridgewock. If you are interested only in the petroglyphs, you can remain on Rt. 201 into Solon.

French Jesuit Sebastian Rasle established the mission in Norridgewock, insisting that Native American lands "were given them of God, to them and their children forever." Rasle and his mission were wiped out by the English in 1724. **Norridgewock Oosoola Park** features a totem pole topped by a frog (this is a good picnic spot and boat-launch site). The site of the village itself is marked by a pleasant riverside picnic area in a pine grove.

The **petroglyphs** are in Embden on an arrowhead-shaped rock that juts into the Kennebec. From Rt. 201 in Solon, turn at the sign for the Evergreens Campground and Restaurant. Cross the Kennebec and turn south on Rt. 201A. The trail to the river is just down the road; it's not marked, but it's easy to see. If you are coming from the mission village site, continue straight ahead; the road hugs the river all the way to Solon. Also see the L. C. Bates Museum in *To See*.

RECONSTRUCTION FROM PREHISTORIC ARCHAEOLOGICAL SITE, MAINE STATE MUSEUM
Maine State Museum, Augusta, Maine

acre complex includes a restored Victorian mansion, large barn, farmer's cottage, church, granite library, and one-room schoolhouse. These buildings and grounds provide the backdrop for rural late-19th-century living history experiences ranging from tours to daylong and overnight programs. Become a scholar in the one-room schoolhouse, hear the story of the Washburn family and their 11 sons and daughters, or take part in the daily chores of the 1870s.

✴ To Do

BALLOONING **Sails Aloft** (207-623-1136), based near Augusta, offers sightseeing flights in central and Midcoast Maine.

BICYCLING **The Kennebec River Rail Trail** (krrt.org) runs along the river most of the way from Augusta (most easily accessed from Capitol Park) through Hallowell to Gardiner (at the Hannaford parking lot). It's popular with bicyclists, runners, and strollers.

BOAT EXCURSIONS **Great Pond Marina** (207-495-2213; greatpondmarina .com), Belgrade Lakes Village, operates the **Mail Boat** on Great Pond. Also moorings, boat rentals (canoes, sailboards, sailboats, fishing boats), and service. **Belgrade Boat Canoe & Kayak Rental** (207-495-3421; belgradeboatrentals.com) rents small fishing boats, canoes, and kayaks; free delivery and pickup.

FISHING The **Belgrade Lakes** are a big lure for anglers. The seven ponds and lakes harbor smallmouth bass, brook, pickerel, and landlocked salmon, among many other species. The sporting camps listed under *Lodging* all offer rental boats and cater to fishermen, especially in May, June, and Sept. **Day's Store** (207-495-2205) in Belgrade Lakes Village is a source of fishing licenses and devotes an entire floor to fishing gear.

GOLF AND TENNIS **Belgrade Lakes Golf Club** (207-495-GOLF; belgrade lakesgolf.com), Belgrade, is a relatively new, highly rated 18-hole golf course, designed by renowned English golf architect Clive Clark. Just off Rt. 27 with views of both Great and Long Ponds. Fees vary with season. Restaurant open to the public.

Natanis Golf Club (207-622-3561), Webber Pond off Rt. 201, Vassalboro, offers a 36-hole course and tennis courts. **Waterville Country Club** (207-465-9861), Waterville (off I-95), 18 holes, clubhouse with restaurant, carts, and caddies. **Lakewood Golf Course** (207-474-5955; lakewoodgolfmaine.com), off Rt. 201A, Madison, 18 holes on the west side of Lake Wesserunsett.

KAYAKING AND CANOEING **Maine Wilderness Tours** (207-465-4333; mainewildernesstours.com), guided canoe and kayak trips on the Belgrade Lakes and down the Kennebec as well as fishing, moose-watching, and rafting farther afield. Also see *Boating* for rentals. Mercer Bog is a great spot for kayaking (ask locally).

ROLLER SKATING **Sunbeam Roller Rink** (207-362-4951), 830 Village Rd. (Rt. 8), Smithfield in the Belgrade Lakes, next door to Sunset Camps on the shore of North Pond. Opens seasonally; call for hours.

SPA The Senator Inn & Spa (207-622-3138), 284 Western Ave., Augusta. The three-story spa wing contains a fitness center, saltwater lap pool, aerobics and yoga studio, hot tub and steam room, and outdoor pool. A full menu of spa services is offered: hairstyling, manicure and pedicure, coloring, and a long list of skin care, massage, and other treatments for both men and women. All treatments include full use of the facilities.

SWIMMING ✿ **Peacock Beach State Park,** Richmond (just off Rt. 201, 10 miles south of Augusta). A small, beautiful sand beach on Pleasant Pond; lifeguards and picnic facilities. $3 adults, free under age 12.

On the southern edge of **Belgrade Lakes Village**, **Long Pond Public Beach** is on Lakeshore Dr. (off West Rd.), **Oakland Town Beach** on Messalonskee Lake, and **Rome Town Beach** on Great Pond (Frederick Lane off Rt. 225). The **Belgrade Community Center** (207-495-3481), 1 Center Dr. (off Rt. 27 south of the village), offers lakefront and a pool.

Lake George Regional Park (207-474-1292), Rt. 2, 8 miles east of Skowhegan. Open seasonally with two sand beaches on either side of the lake; changing rooms, restrooms, boat launch, and picnicking facilities. (Also see *Green Space.*)

Lake St. George State Park (207-589-4255), Rt. 3, Liberty. A pleasant, clean, clear lake with a sandy beach and changing facilities; a perfect break if en route from Augusta to the coast. $4 day-use fee.

✳ Green Space

Capitol Park, across from the State House Complex, is a good place for a picnic. Also located here is the Maine Vietnam Veteran's Memorial, three triangular structures with a cutout section in the shape of soldiers that visitors can walk through.

Pine Tree State Arboretum (207-621-0031), 153 Hospital St., Augusta. (At Cony Circle—the big rotary across the bridge from downtown Augusta—turn south along the river; it's a short way down on the left, across from the Augusta Mental Health Institute.) Open daily dawn to dusk. Visitors center open 8–4 weekdays. There are 224 acres, with trails through woods and fields. More than 600 trees and shrubs (including rhododendrons and lilacs as well as hostas and a rock garden). Cross-country ski trails, too.

Jamies Pond Wildlife Management Area, Meadow Hill Rd., Hallowell. These 800 acres of woodlands, managed by the Maine Department of Inland Fisheries and Wildlife, include 6 miles of trails good for walking and cross-country skiing, and a 107-acre pond. There is a small parking lot and a launch ramp.

Lake George Regional Park (207-474-1292), Rt. 2, 8 miles east of Skowhegan. This 320-acre lakeside park, site of a 19th-century mineral spring resort, then a summer camp, was acquired by the state in 1992 and is maintained by a nonprofit group for year-round use. Ten kilometers of trails for mountain biking and cross-country skiing. Inquire about an evolving museum. Nominal admission charged in summer; see *Swimming*.

Coburn Park, Water St. (Rt. 2 east) on the edge of downtown Skowhegan. This riverside park with a lily pond and formal landscaping hosts a regular concert series in July and Aug.

Kennebec Land Trust (tklt.org) has protected more than 3,200 acres of land in the Kennebec River and Lakes region with most properties open to visitors. Check the website for public programs, field trips, and the extensive list of properties, among them **Vaughan Woods** in Hallowell. In 1791 Charles Vaughan settled in the town named for his grandfather Benjamin Hallowell; in 1797 his brother Benjamin arrived and built himself a fine house here, transforming the property into an agricultural showplace. A substantial portion of this property remains in the family seven generations later, and 152 acres have been granted as a conservation easement to the Kennebec Land Trust. Vaughan Woods represents the largest acreage open to the public, and it's beautiful: webbed with footpaths through mixed forest and open fields. The best entrance is from Litchfield Rd. at the end of Middle St. Park at the stone wall and look for the path.

Belgrade Regional Conservation Alliance (207-495-6039; belgradelakes.org) publishes detailed maps to its major holdings. Check the website for details about hiking the **French Mountain**, **Mount Philip**, and the **Kennebec Highlands** trails. Pick up the Belgrade Lakes Region free map at the visitors booth or Day's Store to locate these trailheads as well **Blueberry Hill** with its great view of Long Pond. There's a state-maintained overlook. Also note the small park just north of Day's Store in Belgrade Lakes Village, a handy picnic spot.

✳ Lodging

In the Augusta area

♂ ✪ ♟ ♿ **Maple Hill Farm Bed & Breakfast Inn & Conference Center** (207-622-2708 or 1-800-622-2708; maplebb.com), 11 Inn Rd. (off the Outlet Rd.), Hallowell 04347. This pleasant hilltop farmhouse isn't far from the turnpike and downtown Augusta but has an away-from-it-all feel, set amid rolling fields. There are wooded trails, a spring-fed swimming hole, and a small abandoned quarry adjoining an 800-acre wildlife reservation. Scott Cowger, a veteran of 10 years in the state legislature, is the inn's outgoing meeter and greeter; Vincent Hannan is the skilled chef. Together they have created a special place, the first in Maine to be certified as a green lodging, with solar electricity and hot water and energy supplied by a wind turbine. There are also many small touches, like the guests' names posted on their doors and the fact that all eight tastefully furnished rooms have a phone, cable TV, DVD, CD player, clock-radio, air-conditioning, and private bath (four with whirlpool tub). As you meander up the driveway, watch for chickens (which provide the morning eggs). Goats, many llamas, and a pony are also in residence. This is, however, more of a grown-up than a family retreat, although children are welcome. You enter through the former kitchen, now an informal pub with local brews. Guests can enjoy the library with its fireplace. There is plenty of local resource material here, and Scott delights in helping guests explore the area. The Gathering Place (seating up to 135 people) and renovated Carriage House are perfect for wedding receptions and meetings (the inn is fully licensed). In winter trails are available for cross-country skiing and snowshoeing. A full breakfast with menu choices is included in $105–205 high season, $90–165 off.

The Benjamin Wales House Bed & Breakfast (1-877-323-4712; benjamin wales.com; 49 Middle St., Hallowell 04347. An imposing Federal-style, 1820 house set above its gardens with

Christina Tree

MAPLE HILL FARM, HALLOWELL

four guest rooms, a library, sitting and breakfast rooms. The four guest rooms are air-conditioned, with cable TV and private bath. There's a grand piano and a regulation pool table in the parlor. $129–149 late May–Oct., otherwise $99–139, including a full breakfast.

🐾 & **Senator Inn and Spa** (207-622-5804 or 1-877-772-2224; senatorinn .com), 284 Western Ave., Augusta 04330. A longtime gathering spot for Maine politicians, this property, with 122 guest rooms and suites, extends far back from the road and offers one of the area's best restaurants and a full-service spa featuring a glass-walled, Grecian-columned saltwater lap pool, hot tub, and fitness center (see *Dining Out* and *To Do*). Just off I-95 and minutes from downtown Augusta, this is a surprisingly quiet, friendly, and relaxing place to stay. Units include attractive suites with fireplace, writing area, jetted tub, and fridge. You'll also find an inviting little bar. $88–209, from $188 for spa suites. $9 per pet.

In the Belgrade Lakes region

🐾 🐕 & **Village Inn** (107-495-3553; villageinnducks.com), 157 Main St. (Rt. 27), Belgrade Village 04918. Bet-

ter known as a restaurant (see *Dining Out*), this middle-of-the-village, two-story '60s motel is attached to the inn, angled to face the garden rather than road. Each of the eight rooms is distinctive, decorated with care by innkeeper Susan Grover. All have cable and AC . No minimum stay. $115 for rooms, $220 for a two-room suite with deck . Rates includes a fruit, yogurt, and muffin breakfast. The inn backs on Great Pond, and Long Pond is across the road. Walk to shops and marinas.

& **Wings Hill Inn** (207-495-2400 or 1 866-495-2400; wingshillinn.com), Rt. 27 and Dry Point Dr., Belgrade Lakes 04918. Open year-round. This 200-year-old white-clapboard farmhouse rambles across a knoll, above its lawns just north of the village of Belgrade Lakes, overlooking Long Pond. The name recalls a onetime owner, U.S. Air Force general Edmund "Wings" Hill. Current innkeepers Christopher and Tracey Anderson met in culinary school, and the inn is known for fine dining (see *Dining Out*). The six guest rooms, all with private bath (one with a Jacuzzi), have been individually decorated with an eye for romance. $115–195 includes a three course breakfast and afternoon tea.

The Pressey House Lakeside Bed & Breakfast (207-465-3500; pressey house.com), 32 Belgrade Rd., Oakland 04963. Open year-round. Lorie and Lorne McMillan have divided an 1850s octagonal house with an ell and attached barn on Messalonskee Lake into five guest units, each with its own bedroom, bath, living room with TV, and kitchen. A large common room with a fireplace overlooks the water. Guests can use a canoe, paddleboat, and two kayaks, or swim off the dock. Just 2.5 miles off I-95. Open year-round. $140–235 including breakfast; less off-season.

FAMILY-GEARED SPORTING CAMPS ✇ ♿ **Bear Spring Camps** (207-397-2341; bearspringcamps.com), 60 Jamaica Point Rd., Rome 04957. Open mid-May–Sept. Ron and Peg Churchill are the fourth generation to run this very special family resort and fishing spot, set on 400 acres of woods and fields on Great Pond. It's been in Peg's family since 1910. Writer E. B. White summered here as a kid and would certainly recognize the rambling white farmhouse with all those rockers on the porch. Serious anglers come in early May for trout and pike, and in July there are still bass. The 32 cabins, each different, are strung along the shore of Great Pond, two to four bedrooms, each with a bathroom, hot and cold water, a shower, heat, an open fireplace, and a dock. There's a tennis court, a golf driving range, and a variety of lawn games. The swimming is great (the bottom is sandy). Meals are served in the farmhouse set a ways back across open lawns from the lake. The big meal is still at noon. "People get sleepy and tend to take a nap after lunch, then get going again," Peg explains. Early morning and sunset are magical. Lots of loons. Weekly rates July–Labor Day: $965–1,125 per couple includes all meals; special children's rates. Motor and pontoon boats, Kayaks and canoes available.

🐾 ✇ **Alden Camps** (207-465-7703; aldencamps.com), 3 Alden Camps Cove, Oakland 04963. Founded by A. Fred Alden in 1911 with just one rental unit, it's still in the family with 18 one- to three-bedroom log cabins with screened porch and woodstove or Franklin fireplace, scattered among the pines on the shores of East Pond. Meals are served in a wonderfully rambling old clapboard house with a big dining room, sitting area, and long porch. Activities include fishing, golf nearby, swimming, waterskiing, boating, tennis, hiking, and several playing fields. Children are welcome, and pets can be accommodated for an extra fee. $117–151 per person per day, and $702–1,068 per person per week, includes all three meals; off-season from $94 per person per day and $564 per week. Children's rates Pet fee.

✇ **Castle Island Camps** (207-495-3312; in winter, 207-293-2266; castleislandcamps.com), P.O. Box 251, Belgrade Lakes 04918. Open late April–mid-Sept. John and Rhonda Rice are the owners of this great old family compound: a dozen comfortable cottages clustered on a small island (connected by bridges) in 12-mile Long

BEAR SPRING CAMPS, BELGRADE LAKES

Christina Tree

CASTLE ISLAND CAMPS, BELGRADE LAKES

Pond. The camps have been in Rhonda's family since 1929. Geared to fishing (the pond is stocked; rental boats are available). Three daily meals are served in the cozy central lodge, where guests also gather around an open fireplace, and in a recreation room with pool tables, table tennis, and darts. $160 per couple per day, $1,100 per week, children's rates.

☀ ♂ **Whisperwood Lodge and Cottages** (207-465-3983; whisperwood lodge.com), 102 Taylor Woods Rd., Belgrade 04917. Open mid-May late Sept. Doug and Candee McCarthy host another traditional sporting camp, this one seriously fishing-focused. Tidy one- and two-bedroom cottages with screened porches overlook Salmon Lake, known for its largemouth and smallmouth bass fishing. Late May–late Aug. $60 per person (double) per day (three-day minimum), $595 per week, children's rates; less off-season. This includes three meals as well as use of kayaks, canoes, game room, swim area, firewood. Fishing licenses.

COTTAGES Many seasonal rentals are available. See Belgrade Reservation Center (belgraderental.com).

The **Pleasant Street Inn** (207-680-2515; 84pleasantstreet .com), 84 Pleasant St., Waterville 04901, within walking distance of downtown. The seven guest rooms, five with a private bath, are bright and cheery with TV, AC, and beds covered by colorful quilts. Guests have access to a common area that includes kitchen, dining room, and a living room with TV/DVD. $60–95.

♂ **Home-Nest Farm** (207-897-4125), 76 Baldwin Hill Rd., Fayette 04349. Open year-round. The main house, built in 1784, offers a panoramic view of the White Mountains. Lilac Cottage (1800) and the Red Schoolhouse (1830) are available for rent as separate units. The property has been in the Sturdevant family for seven generations. $80 for one room; house rates are $140 daily, $700 weekly for one- to three-bedroom units with kitchens; all include breakfast. Two-night minimum stay July–Oct.

♿ **A Rise and Shine Bed and Breakfast** (207-933-9876; riseand shinebb.com), 19 Moose Run Dr. (Rt. 135), Monmouth 04259. Ten miles west of Augusta, with a distant view of Lake Cobbosseecontee, this rambling house with its even larger stables was for many years a racehorse farm, part of a 2,000-acre spread belonging to the Woolworth family. Locals Tom Crocker and Lorette Comeau have replaced 76 windows, used up some 300 gallons of paint, and installed gas- or pellet-fired hearths in many of the eight guest rooms. Lorette has also painted murals on many walls. Our favorite is the Sunshine Room, the former master bedroom with a king-sized bed, hearth, and steam shower. $125–180 includes a full breakfast. Cottage $300 a night. Horses are welcome, and there's lake access.

✳ Where to Eat

DINING OUT

In Augusta/Hallowell

✪ **Slate's** (207-622-9575; slates restaurant.com), 163 Water St., Hallowell. Open Tue.–Fri. for lunch and dinner, Sat.–Sun. for brunch and dinner. Reserve if possible. First opened in 1979, renovated and reopened in 2008 after a devastating fire, this is a special place that chef-owner Wendy Larson describes as a mix of music, art, and great food. The several rooms are all brightly painted and display local art. Lunch on a crêpe for two, stuffed with fresh crabmeat, artichoke hearts, and Jarlsberg cheese ($15). Dine on seafood Alfredo (pastas are made here) or seared boneless duck breast with orange ginger glaze (dinner entrées $11.50–22). Check out the website for the names, some of them nationally known, playing in Monday-night concerts (8:15). This is also a great spot for lunch: crêpes, salads, pizzas with whole wheat crust, and chicken pie.

Hattie's Chowder House (207-621-4114; hattieslobsterstew.com), 103 Water St., Hallowell. Open daily for lunch and dinner. Spacious and pleas-ant, this is a great spot for chowders and lobster stew. Harriett Schmidtt markets her lobster stew nationally, but it was the light, nicely herbed haddock chowder that really got our attention. We pleaded with Harriett until she revealed the secret: "A little sherry." The lunch menu also includes a wide choice of salads, burgers, and club sandwiches. To all this the dinner menu adds pastas, meat, and chicken dishes as well as seafood fried, baked, and stuffed. The seafood casserole is thick with scallops, shrimp, and crab.

✐ **Cloud 9 at the Senator Inn & Spa** (207-622-0320), 284 Western Ave., Augusta. Open daily 6:30 AM–9 PM; lounge 11–11. Some of the region's best dining can be found just off I-95 in "the Senator," the capital's prime gathering spot. Cloud 9 is a large but artfully divided restaurant with a con-temporary bistro decor. Maine crab-cake is unusually light and tasty, and lobster is served up many ways. Options include country chicken pie in a puff pastry, Maine seafood stew over fresh pasta, and maple-ginger glazed salmon. Be warned: Portions are large. At lunch there's also a soup, salad, and pizza buffet. Desserts include spa options as well as the likes of tiramisu espresso and rum-flavored Italian pas-try. Entrées $9.99–26.99. Children's menu. A Sunday brunch buffet (11–2).

In the Belgrade Lakes region

Wings Hill Inn (207-495-2400), Rt. 27, Belgrade Lakes Village. Open for dinner May–Sept. (five-course prix fixe), Thu.–Sun.; Oct.–Dec., Fri. and Sat. (three-course option); seatings at 6 and 8. Reservations requested. Chef-owner Christopher Anderson and his wife, Tracey (who makes the desserts), trained at the Culinary Institute of America. Together they orchestrate seasonal five-course prix fixe menus served to a maximum of 16 diners

SLATE'S RESTAURANT, HALLOWELL

Christina Tree

seated in adjoining rooms. An evening's feast might begin with a walnut and feta pâté in a phyllo crust, moving on to curried chicken soup or gazpacho, a salad of greens or a small Caesar, and a choice of four entrées, among them excellent sea bass with chanterelles and leeks, a fantastic eggplant Parmesan, and rack of lamb. To finish, there is frozen Grand Marnier mousse or brown sugar crème brûlée. The menu changes every week. Service is friendly and fast, and tables are set off by themselves. Diners bring their own wine, served by the staff at the table (no corking fee); an 18 percent service fee is added to the $75 prix fixe bill. Inquire about three-course $27 "Bistro Nights."

❂ Village Inn (207-495-3553), Rt. 27, Belgrade Lakes. Open Easter–mid-Oct., daily 5–9 in-season, Thu.–Sun off-season. This is a large, old-fashioned dining landmark with a lake view and lot of atmosphere. Also lawn dining. Note the mural depicting the19th-century Belgrade Hotel, one of several summer inns once here. The Village Inn, dating to 1921, is the last link with that era. It's a full menu with a choice of char-grilled steaks, but the specialty is duckling, roasted for up to 12 hours and served with a choice of sauces, including brandied black cherry, Madagascar with green peppercorn, and Thai lemongrass. You might begin with oysters (from Taunton Bay) Rockefeller. Entrées $17.95–28.95. One-quarter roast duckling, $17.95. The Tavern offers casual fare by the water, music Wed., Sun. in summer.

❂ Riverside Farm Market & Café (207-465-4439; riversidefarmmarket .com), 291 Fairfield St. (Rt. 23), Oakland. Lunch Tue.–Sat., 11–3, dinner Tue.–Sat 5:30–8:30, brunch Sun. 10–2. Just off the beaten track, a handsome little restaurant with a deck, overlook-

Christina Tree

RIVERSIDE CAFÉ, OAKLAND, OVERLOOKS ITS VINEYARD

ing a vineyard that slopes to a pond. Begun as a farm stand in 1990, the complex also includes a market that sells the house-produced vintages under the label "Laissez Faire." Soups are made daily, and our veggie sandwich was a delight. Pamini, salads, wraps, daily specials. The creative dinner menu features local produce and wine pairings: a Mediterranean pasta bowl ($18) with a suggested Riesling ($18) or Valpolicalla ($20), say, or saltimbocca ($20) with a Merlot. At Sunday brunch try the crêpes.

In Waterville
Apollo's Bistro (207-872-8736), 91 Silver St. Open for dinner Thu.–Sat. 5:30–10:30. Reserve. Located on the second floor of a cupola-topped Victorian mansion—the first floor is occupied by a salon and spa under the same management—this elegant little restaurant has prided itself on using locally grown ingredients for 30 years, also on cooking them slowly and carefully. You might begin with an organic beet salad or roasted parsnip soup and dine on a homemade pasta or sea bass stuffed with carrots, orange, pine nuts, and herbs. Entrées $16–24.

The Last Unicorn (207-873-6378), 8 Silver St. Open daily 11–9, until 10 Fri. and Sat.; Sun. brunch until 2:30. Colorful and conveniently sited right off the central parking lot. There are usually 15 different dinner specials; soups, desserts, and most dressings and spreads are made here. You might dine on sautéed veal Marsala with spinach, apples, and grapes. Dinner entrées $18.95–25.95. Also a great, reasonably priced lunch option, seasonal streetside café.

EATING OUT

In Augusta
Riverfront Barbeque & Grill (207-622-8899), 300 Water St. Open daily for lunch and dinner. An offshoot of Bath's famous Beal Street Barbeque and considered to be just as good: slow-smoked chicken and ribs, daily-made soups with corn bread, chili, seafood and sausage jambalaya, and more.

Also see **Cloud 9** at the Senator Inn & Spa under *Dining Out*. It makes a reasonably priced bet for breakfast and lunch; also brick-oven pizza.

Downtown Diner (207-623-9656), 204 Water St. Open 5–2 weekdays, 6–Sat., 7–1 Sun. Mike and Kim Meserwy own this bright spot in downtown, handy to Fort Western. Serious all-day breakfasts include steak and eggs and porkers in a blanket (sausages wrapped in small, fluffy pancakes); also freshly made soups, burgers, meat loaf, and pies.

In Hallowell
✄ **Slates Bakery and Deli** (207-622-4101), 165 Water St. Open weekdays 8–6, Sat. 9–6, Sun. 10–4. $3 children's menu. Neighboring **Slate's Restaurant** (see *Dining Out*) is great for a more leisurely lunch. This combination café-bakery is all about freshly baked

breads, cakes, and pies as well as morning muffins and croissants. It's a good source of ready-made sandwiches, wraps, and burritos to take to the riverbank or Vaughan Woods. It's also a pleasant spot to eat and check email.

Liberal Cup (207-623-2739), 115 Water St. Open for lunch and dinner, Fri. and Sat. until 10. Mid-Maine's brewpub, noisy on the bar side, less so in the dining room. Half a dozen good brews (crafted here) on tap. Live music Thu.–Sat. evenings. Most menu items, including sandwiches, are served all day, along with shepherd's pie, fish-and-chips, and drunken pot roast.

Café de Bangkok (207-622-2638), 232 Water St. Just south of the village with river views, this is a highly respected local dining option. The menu includes the usual Tom Yum and miso soups, a soft-shell crispy crab salad with hot chili lime sauce on lettuce, "pad" and fried rice dishes. The chef's specials include crispy fried red snapper with ginger sauce and vegetables, and half a crispy roast duck with peanut sauce and steamed vegetables. Entrées $10–25. Lunch specials include a sushi combo.

Lucky Garden (207-622-3465), 218 Water St. A popular Chinese restaurant offering Mandarin, Szechuan, and Cantonese dishes. House specialties include General Tso's chicken, crispy shrimp, and Peking duck. Entrées $8–25. The dining room has a river view. Lunch buffet $7.95 adult, $3.95 children under 10.

In Gardiner
The A1 Diner (207-582-4804; a1diner.com), 3 Bridge St. Open Mon.–Sat. for all three meals, brunch only on Sun. (8–1). A vintage-1946 Worcester diner with plenty of Formica, blue

vinyl booths, blue and black tile, and a 14-stool, marble-topped counter. In addition to typical diner fare there are some surprises. The breakfast menu includes banana almond French toast and a wide variety of omelets. At lunch and dinner we usually go for the specials and freshly made soups, but there is always meat loaf, baked beans, and a choice of salads and veggie options. Beverages include herbal tea, imported beers and wines. The restroom is outside and in through the kitchen door.

In Waterville/Winslow

Jorgensen's Café (207-872-8711), 103 Main St., Waterville. An inviting café with at least a dozen flavored coffees, as well as tea and espresso choices. The deli serves quiche, soups, salads, and sandwiches. Coffee and tea supplies.

✪ **Barrels Community Market** (207-660-4844; barrelsmarket.com), 74 Main St., Waterville A great addition to downtown, a community-owned market and café showcasing local, sustainable produce, meats, milk, cheeses, also crafts and food products. Great salad bar and breads by Black Crow Bakery.

✪ **Selah Tea Café** (207-660-9181; selahteacafe.com), 177 Main St., Waterville Open Mon.–Sat. 7 AM–10 PM. A sunny café with soothing colors and comfortable seating, a wide choice of loose-leaf teas and coffees; you'll also find yummy caffeine-free Belgian chocolate latte, and crio bru cocoa from roasted and ground cocoa beans. A veggie breakfast sandwich as well as meaty specials. Specialty sandwiches include a vegan wrap, salads, flat-bread pizza, baked Brie, more.

The Villager Restaurant (207-872-6231), 40 W. Concourse, Waterville. An old-fashioned coffee shop with reasonably priced sandwiches (cream cheese and olive for $3.70), also lasagna, mac-and-cheese, and Italian-style potato salad plates. Most dinner items are under $10.

Lobster Trap & Steakhouse (207-872-0529), 25 Bay St. (Rt. 201), Winslow. Open daily 11–9. Just across the bridge if you follow Rt. 137 from downtown over the Kennebec. Since 1986, this is the local place to eat lobster, preferably on the deck picnic tables overlooking the river. Seafood fried, baked and stuffed. Reasonable prices.

♫ **Cancun** (207-872-7400), 14 Silver St., Waterville. A big barn of a place. Wings and salads as well as Mexican basics, $11 dinner special. There's a kids' menu, and it's a great place to come with small children.

Pad Thai Too (207-859-8900; pad thaitoo.wordpress.com), 400 Kennedy Memorial Drive (Rt. 137), Waterville. Open for lunch and dinner, Tue.–Sat.; from 4 Sun.–Mon. Loved locally for the freshness of ingredients and quality of a standard Thai restaurant menu.

Also see **The Last Unicorn** in *Dining Out*, a good lunch option.

THE A1 DINER, GARDINER

Christina Tree

In the Belgrade Lakes region

&. **The Sunset Grille** (207-495-2439),
4 West Rd., Belgrade Lakes Village.
Open year-round, Mon–Thu. 7–9,
Fri.–Sat. 7–midnight. Hopping in the
summer, casual family fare served
waterside. Sat.-evening karaoke.

Alden Camps (207-465-7703; alden
camps.com), 3 Alden Camps Cove,
Oakland. Non-guests are welcome by
reservation—and if you can't stay at
one of the local sporting camps, you
should sample the atmosphere. The
from-scratch food is generous, varied,
and good, too. Set price.

The Old Post Office Café (207-293-
4978; oldpostofficecafe.com), 366
Pond Rd., Mount Vernon village. Open
daily 7–2:30. Check the website for
dinner/music nights. A chef-owned
local gathering spot wih a screened
porch overlooking the lake.

Also see **Day's Store** under *Special
Stores*, good for pizza and sandwiches
for picnicking, and **Riverside Farm
Market & Café** under *Dining Out*.
It's a great bet for lunch. **Belgrade
Lakes Golf Club** (see *To Do*) has a
restaurant with the area's best view.

In China

✪ ✎ **The China Dine-ah** (207-445-
5700; chinadine-ah.com), 281 Lakeview Dr. (Rt. 202, 1.5 miles off Rt. 3).
Open Tue.–Sat. from 7 AM through
dinner, until 3 Sun., closed Mon.
Hugely popular with locals, this relatively new eatery has the feel of a landmark establishment. It's a big, barnlike
family restaurant with a wide choice of
seating, from booths to the big, welcoming counter. A good road-food
break for motorists heading Down
East. No surprises here but generous
portions, a good dried haddock sandwich with house-made tartar sauce
with great crabcakes, and a loaded sirloin steak and cheese. Dinner choices

range from liver and onions to prime
rib (Fri. and Sat. while it lasts). Great
prices on specials. Fully licensed.

In Skowhegan

✎ **Ken's Family Restaurant** (207-
474-3120; kensfamilyrestaurant.com),
411 Madison Ave. (Rt. 201). Open
Mon.–Thu. 10:30–8; for breakfast, too,
Fri.–Sun. Family-run (by the Dionne
family) and -geared since 1972. Children's menu. Known for seafood but
generally a good bet.

Heritage House Restaurant (207-
474-5100; townemotel.com), 182
Madison Ave. (Rt. 201). Open for
lunch (buffet Tue.–Fri.) and dinner. A
popular restaurant with a strong local
following . The large menu always
includes six fresh seafood entrées (such
as sea scallops tempura with apricot
mustard dip), medallions of beef with
brandied mushroom sauce, and Cajun
chicken breast with wine, lemon,
capers, and mushrooms. Most entrées
$15–20.

Old Mill Pub (207-474-6627), 41-R
Water St. Open Mon.–Sat. for lunch
and dinner in summer; check off-
season. It's just where you may want to
stop en route: a picturesque old mill
building set back from the main drag
with a seasonal deck overlooking a
gorge in the Kennebec, with views
downriver as well as of the dam. A
friendly bar and scattered tables; sandwiches (a good Reuben), quiche, and
specials for lunch; spinach lasagna or
stir-fried shrimp for dinner; music on
Thu. and Sat.

Empire Grill (207-374-3440), 105
Water St. Open 6 AM–8 PM, weekends
till 6. Re-created as a stage set for
Empire Falls, this is a classic '50s diner
with an eight-stool counter, good coffee and food. Specials on the day we
stopped by included kale soup.

Liam Davis
GIFFORD'S ICE CREAM, SKOWHEGAN

Gifford's Ice Cream (207-474-2257; giffordsicecream.com), Upper Madison Ave. (Rt. 201 north; look for the big plastic moose). Proudly served throughout Maine, century-old, family-owned Gifford's is made in Skowhegan, and this is its prime local outlet, a classic ice cream stand serving 50 flavors, including Lobster Tracks and Maine Birch Bark, in cones, cups, parfaits, frappes, sodas, more. Limited picnic tables out back overlook a mini golf course.

In Winthrop
🍴 **Sully's** (207-377-5663), corner of Union and Main Sts. Open Mon.–Sat. for lunch and dinner, Sun. dinner noon–7. Set back from Main St. with plenty of parking to accommodate its local following. Salads as well as burgers and sandwiches for lunch, seafood dishes, like a seafood medley that includes lobster and salad; liver and onions and an old-fashioned roast turkey dinner.

✳ Entertainment

LIVE PERFORMANCES 🍴 **Theater at Monmouth** (207-933-2952; theateratmonmouth.org), Main St., Mon-

mouth. Summer/fall season shows July–Oct. Housed in Cumston Hall, a striking turn-of-the-20th-century building designed as a combination theater, library, and town hall. A resident nonprofit company specializes in Shakespeare but also presents contemporary shows throughout the season.

🍴 **Lakewood Theater** (207-474-7176; lakewoodtheater.org), off Rt. 201, 6 miles north of Skowhegan on Lake Wesserunsett, billed as America's Oldest Summer Theater. A resident company performs Memorial Day–mid-Sept., Thu.–Sat. at 8, alternate Sun., and Wed. matinees. The Lakewood Jesters stage morning performances for children. The restaurant specializes in pretheater dinners.

Waterville Opera House (207-873-7000; operahouse.org), 93 Main St., Waterville, presents a number of shows throughout the year, including music performances and theater productions. It's also a prime venue for the 10-day Maine International Film Festival (see *Film*).

Gaslight Theater (207-626-3698; gaslighttheater.org), City Hall Auditorium, Hallowell. This community

THE EMPIRE GRILL, SKOWHEGAN
Christina Tree

theater stages productions throughout the year.

Johnson Hall Performing Arts Center (207-582-7144; johnsonhall.org), 280 Water St., Gardiner. A restored historic space where workshops, dances, and other performances occur frequently.

FILM Maine International Film Festival (207-861-8138; miff.org), 177 Maine St., Waterville. In existence for more than a decade, this weeklong, mid-July festival has evolved into a major event screening scores of films from around the world—although always including some made in Maine—and attracting noted actors, directors, and screenwriters as speakers and lecturers.

Railroad Square Cinema (207-873-4021; railroadsquarecinema.com), Main St., Waterville. From I-95 exit 130 head toward downtown; turn left between Burger King and the railroad tracks. Art and foreign films, and in mid-July home of the Maine International Film Festival.

Skowhegan Drive-in (207-474-9277), Rt. 201 south. A genuine 1950s drive-in with nightly double features "under the stars" in July and Aug.; weekends in June.

Strand Cinema (207-474-3451), Court St., Skowhegan. A 1929 jewel, recently, lovingly revamped with nightly films, reasonable prices.

✱ Selective Shopping

In Hallowell
ANTIQUES A dozen antiques stores cluster here, each with a different specialty. **Brass and Friends** (207-626-3287), 154 Water St. (look for the gargoyles atop the building), is a large trove of antique lighting fixtures. **Josiah Smith Antiques** (207-622-

4188), 101 2nd St., specializes in Asian and British ceramics and early glass. **Johnson-Marsano Antiques** (207-623-6263), 172 Water St., sells Victorian, art deco, and estate jewelry.

ANTIQUARIAN BOOKS Merrill's Bookshop (207-623-2055), 134 Water St., on the second floor because this side of Water St. still occasionally floods in spring. This is an antiquarian bookshop among antiquarian bookshops. Some 50,000 titles include many odd and unusual volumes. Particular emphasis on Americana, Maine books, history—including a large Civil War collection—and literature. There is also a room filled with books for a buck.

SPECIAL STORES Kennebec River Artisans (207-623-2345; kennebecriverartisans.com), 130 Water St. Open year-round, showcasing the work of Maine artisans and craftsmen. This is a truly special shop, good for cards, clothing, jewelry, and much, much more.

Brahms Mount (800-545-9347; brahmsmount.com), 19 Central St., Hallowell. Open Mon.–Fri. 8:30–5. The small, picturesquely weathered wooden building, a couple of blocks up from Water Street, houses authentic, clattering antique looms that producing beautiful fabrics—linen and cotton blankets and throws, scarves, pillows, and towels. Sold throughout the country at exclusive stores, they are also available next door at the company store. Check out the baby blankets! We found a stunning woven pillow for the living room couch.

Elsewhere
ANTIQUES Antiques Fairfield Antiques Mall (207-453-4100; fairfield antiquesmall.com), Rt. 201, Hinckley. Open daily 8:30–5, with three floors of

antiques under one roof, the largest group shop in central Maine. **Hilltop Antiques** (1-800-899-6987), 52 Water St., Skowhegan. Two floors (16 rooms) filled with "fresh picked merchandise."

BOOKS Barnes & Noble Booksellers (207-621-0038), the Marketplace at Augusta, directly across from the Augusta Civic Center. A full-service bookstore with music and computer software sections, as well as a café.

Apple Valley Books (207-377-3967; applevalleybooks.com), 121 Main St., Winthrop. Rita Moran and Eric Robbins run a welcoming full-service bookstore, stocking used as well as new titles.

SPECIAL STORES Renys (207-582-4012), 185 Water St., Gardiner, and at 73 Main St. in Madison. Open weekdays 9–5:30, Fri. until 8, Sat. 9–5, Sun. 10–4. Don't pass up this amazing Maine discount department store, good for quality clothing and shoes, for peanut butter, art supplies, and a range of everything in between. This is a two-story emporium that fills a good chunk of Gardiner's beautiful but otherwise sleepy Main St.

Marden's Discount Store (207-873-6112), 458 Kennedy Memorial Dr., Waterville. Maine's salvage and surplus chain with 10 stores. The Waterville outlet is well worth checking.

New Balance Outlet Store (207-474-6231; newbalance.com), 13 Walnut St. (Rt. 201, south of the bridge), Skowhegan. Open Mon.–Sat. 9–6, Sun. 11–5. Housed in a former school, this is a major outlet with a wide selection of athletic gear as well as shoes made in town.

The Green Spot (207-465-7242), 818 Kennedy Dr. (Rt. 137), Oakland. Open May–Columbus Day, daily 9–7; closed

Tue. A quarter mile or so west of I-95 look for a small yellow store on the left. Locally loved as a source of amazing daily fresh breads, organic produce, fine wines, and terrific deli items, Tanya and Brenda Athanus's small store on the way from Waterville to Oakland is well worth seeking out.

Johnny's Selected Seeds (207-861-3900; johnnyseeds.com), 955 Benton Ave., Winslow. Open Mon.–Sat. in-season, selective days off-season. A catalog seed company with more than 2,000 varieties.

Day's Store (207-495-2205; go2days .com), 180 Main St., Belgrade Lakes Village.Open daily 7 AM–8 PM, until 9 in summer: groceries, liquor, fishing licenses and gear, boots, gifts, gas, pizza, soups and sandwiches, etc. This is the true center of the Belgrade Lakes.

Maine Made & More (207-465-2274; mainemadeandmore.com), Maine St., Belgrade Lakes Village, and 93 Main St., Waterville. Sweatshirts, cards, souvenirs; the "more" is a concession to who makes those sweatshirts, T-shirts, etc., these days.

Stoney End Farm (207-397-4214), 441 Mercer Rd., Rome. A great farm stand with veggies, honey, eggs, maple syrup, strawberries, raspberries, blueberries, quilted items, and two donkeys to feed.

✳ Special Events

June–July: During its nine-week sessions the prestigious **Skowhegan School of Painting and Sculpture** (207-474-9345) sponsors a lecture series on weekday evenings that's free and open to the public.

July: Beginning the last week in June **The Whatever Family Festival** (kennebecvalley.org) climaxes July 4 and entails many events—children's performances, soapbox derby, Learn the River Day, entertainment, carnival, and more. **Maine International Film Festival** (midmonth) in Waterville (miff.org). **Old Hallowell Day** (third weekend)—parade and fireworks, crafts and games. **Pittston Fair**, Pittston.

August: **Skowhegan State Fair**, one of the oldest and biggest fairs in New England—harness racing, a midway, agricultural exhibits, big-name entertainment, tractor and oxen pulls. **China Community Days**, China. Public supper, fishing derby, scavenger hunt. In late Aug., **Father Rasle Days** (madison.com) is a weekend of festivities commemorating the 18th-century Jesuit priest and native village destroyed by the British. **Windsor Fair**, Windsor, runs the last week through Labor Day.

September: **Oosoola Fun Day**, Norridgewock (Labor Day), includes the state's oldest frog-jumping contest (up to 300 contestants) around a frog-topped totem pole; also canoe races, crafts fair, flower and pet contests, live music, barbecue. **Litchfield Fair**, Litchfield. **Common Ground Country Fair**, Unity, a celebration of rural living sponsored by the Maine Organic Farmers and Gardeners Association (mofga.org).

October **Octoberfest**, Belgrade Lakes.

THE UPPER KENNEBEC VALLEY AND MOOSE RIVER VALLEY
Including The Forks and Jackman

By rights this upper stretch of the Kennebec Valley and certainly the Moose River Valley belong in the "Maine Highlands" section of this book, but the Kennebec is a north–south corridor, linking northern woodlands with mid-Maine mills and farms. Solon, north of Skowhegan, is the divide, and Bingham, 8 miles north, has the feel of the woodland hub that it is.

The 78-mile stretch of Rt. 201 north from Solon to the Canadian border is now officially the Old Canada Road Scenic Byway, with a granite marker at its gateway on Robbins Hill. From this rise the valley rolls away north to the distant, blue peaks of Sugarloaf and the Bigelow Range. Along the way interpretive panels at scenic way stops tell the story of this magnificent but haunting valley.

The Kennebec River itself rises in Moosehead Lake and flows south, as did most 19th-century traffic along this route. More than a million French Canadian and Irish families came looking for work in New England logging camps, farms, and factories. This stretch of Rt. 201 is now also a link in the 233-mile Kennebec-Chaudiere International Corridor, stretching from Quebec City to Bath near the mouth of the river. Whatever its titles, this remains a busy, twisty, two-lane road, and traffic flows both ways far too quickly. It's also frequented by both lumber trucks and lumbering moose. Drive carefully!

Once upon a time, the river was the highway. For more than 140 years beginning in 1835, logs were floated down from the woods to the mills. Then in 1976 fishing guide Wayne Hockmeyer discovered the rush of riding the whitewater through dramatic 12-mile-long Kennebec Gorge, deep in the woods, miles northeast of Rt. 201. On that first ride Hockmeyer had to contend with logs hurtling all around him, but as luck would have it, 1976 also marked the year in which environmentalists managed to outlaw log drives on the Kennebec.

A dozen or so rafting companies presently vie for space to take advantage of up to 8,000 cubic feet of water per second released every morning from late spring through mid-October from the Harris Hydroelectric Station. In and around The Forks, a community (pop. 60) at the confluence of the Kennebec and Dead Rivers, whitewater rafting has spawned extensive lodging and dining facilities that also cater to snowmobilers, hunters, hikers, and travelers passing through—many of

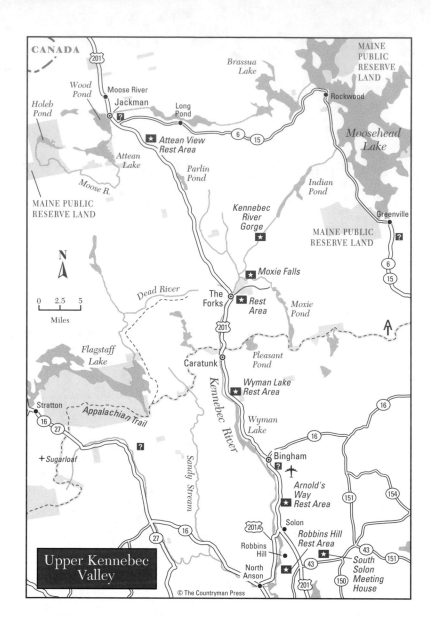

CANADA

Brassua
Lake

MAINE
PUBLIC
RESERVE
LAND

Wood
Pond

Moose River

Jackman

Rockwood

Holeb
Pond

Long
Pond

Moosehead
Lake

Attean View
Rest Area

Attean
Lake

Parlin
Pond

Indian
Pond

Greenville

Moose R.

MAINE PUBLIC
RESERVE LAND

Kennebec
River
Gorge

MAINE PUBLIC
RESERVE LAND

N

Moxie Falls

Dead River

The
Forks

Rest
Area

Moxie
Pond

0   2.5   5

Miles

Flagstaff
Lake

Caratunk

Pleasant
Pond

Wyman Lake
Rest Area

Appalachian Trail

Stratton

Kennebec River

Wyman
Lake

Sugarloaf

Sandy Stream

Bingham

Arnold's
Way
Rest Area

Solon

Robbins Hill
Rest Area

Robbins
Hill

South
Solon
Meeting
House

North
Anson

Upper Kennebec
Valley

© The Countryman Press

whom spend an extra day or two here once they discover the accessibility of this valley's waterfalls and summits, its remote ponds for fishing and kayaking, and its woods roads for bicycling.

Empty as it seemed when rafting began, this stretch of the Upper Kennebec was a 19th-century resort area of sorts. A 100-room, four-story Forks Hotel was built in 1860, and the 120-room Lake Parlin Lodge soon followed. Caratunk, The Forks, and Jackman were all railroad stops; "rusticators" came to fish, hike, and view natural wonders, like 90-foot Moxie Falls. Increasingly whitewater rafting outfitters are styling themselves "adventure companies," offering present-day rusticators a choice of rock climbing, moose safaris, bicycle and kayak rentals, and more.

Bingham (pop. 1,200), 23 miles south of the Forks, is the only sizable town in Upper Kennebec Valley. Just north of town a 155-foot-high hydro-dam walls up the river, raising it more than 120 feet and creating wide, shimmering 13-mile long Wyman Lake.

At The Forks, Rt. 201 itself forks off from the Kennebec River, heading north-west through lonely but beautiful woodland. The Parlin Pond pullout is aptly about moose. Don't fail to stop at the Attean View Rest Area south of Jackman, with its spectacular panorama and panels devoted to 19th-century migration.

Jackman and Moose River form a community (divided by a short bridge) on Big Wood Lake. In warm weather you notice that something is missing here and don't realize what it is unless you revisit in winter. It's snow. Winter is actually high sea-son. Snow softens the severity of this shrunken old border community. Named for the man who built the Canada Road from the border down to The Forks, Jackman boomed after the Canadian Pacific Railroad arrived in 1888, setting the lumbering industry into high gear.

Most of Jackman's mills have disappeared, but this former rail junction is now a major hub of Maine's snowmobiling network and 400 miles of ATV trails. With restaurants and reasonably priced camps, it's also a base for exceptional canoeing and kayaking.

To stay in Maine turn off Rt. 201 onto Rt. 15/6, a lonely 31-mile road that fol-lows the Moose River east to Moosehead Lake. Otherwise it's a roughly three-hour drive from Jackman to Quebec City.

GUIDANCE The Forks Area Chamber of Commerce (forksarea.com) has an excellent website, as does the **Jackman-Moose River Region Chamber of Commerce** (207-668-4171 or 1-888-633-5225; jackmanmaine.org); this also main-tains a Rt. 201 seasonal welcome center near the lakeside town park.

GETTING THERE *By car:* The obvious route from points south and west is I-95 to exit 133, then Rt. 201 north all the way to The Forks. The approach from the Rangeley and Sugarloaf areas, Rt. 16, is also a beautiful drive.

WHEN TO COME Whitewater raft-ing and fishing commence in April, but we prefer paddling in warmer months. June is buggy. July through mid-October are glorious, with fall bringing plenty of color. Hikers should check the "seasons" described under *Hunt-ing.* Snow usually begins in November but has been more plentiful in recent years during late February and March.

BORDER CROSSING NOTES Jack-man is 17 miles from the Canadian

DOWNTOWN BINGHAM

Liam Davis

border. For a detailed list of requirements for both U.S. and Canadian citizens, see the "Washington County" introduction.

✳ To See

Listed south to north along Route 201
Note: See the **L. C. Bates Museum** and the **Margaret Chase Smith Library Center** in the previous chapter's *To See*; both are rewarding stops along Rt. 201 south of Solon.

Old Canada Road rest areas have interpretive panels (and outhouses). Just north of the junction with Rt. 43 look for Robbins Hill. Access is over the brow of the hill (heading north); there are picnic tables, a 0.5-mile trail with interpretive panels, and the spectacular view described in the chapter intro. Twenty panels in all are scattered along Rt. 201 in pullouts and rest areas between this point and Jackman. At **Arnold's Way Rest Area**, on the Bingham town line, panels chronicle the 1775 saga of Colonel Benedict Arnold and his more than 1,000 men traveling this way in a heroic but luckless attempt to capture Quebec. The **Lake Wyman Rest Area** is a pine-shaded and carpeted lakeside spot with picnic tables; panels tell of Indian habitation and the 1932 creation of the lake. **The Forks** pullout is just below the bridge at the actual fork in the river. Panels describe 19th-century lumbering and river runs while logging trucks rumble over the bridge.

Moxie Falls is said to be the highest falls (90 feet) in New England. From The Forks rest area on Rt. 201, it's 1.8 miles down Lake Moxie Rd. to the parking area. An easy 0.6-mile trail leads to the falls. The pools below are a popular swimming hole.

More Old Canada Road rest areas: Note the pullout at **Parlin Pond**, one of the spots you are most likely to see moose, the subject of its interpretive panels. **Attean View**, the next pullout, is a must-see. The view is splendid: **Attean Lake**

ROBBINS HILL MARKS THE BEGINNING OF THE OLD CANADA ROAD SCENIC BYWAY

Christina Tree

SOUTH SOLON MEETING HOUSE

(207-643-2555 or 207-643-2721), South Solon. Turn east off Rt. 201 onto Rt. 43, then continue 1.5 miles to Meeting House Rd. and north to the crossroads at South Solon with the 1842 Greek Revival meetinghouse. Open daily year-round. The classically plain, white-clapboard exterior of this building belies its colorful interior: The walls and ceiling were almost entirely frescoed in the 1950s by artists from the nearby Skowhegan School (skowheganart.org), still one of the country's most prestigious summer arts programs. The building is maintained by the South Solon Historical Society (SSHS), a small, all-volunteer group that includes descendants of the church's original congregation. The center of a rural community from 1842 until 1900, the building was then abandoned as population shifted south to Skowhegan's mills. It was restored 35 years later as a venue for summer services. Vincent Price was among actors from the nearby Lakewood Theater (lakewood theater.org) who read scripture here. World War II interrupted this pattern, but in the 1950s a wealthy student at the Skowhegan School became enamored with the Greek Revival meetinghouse, envisioning its blank interior walls as a potential showcase for fresco artists. She funded a national competition for a series of fellowships at the school, to be awarded over the five summers needed for this project. Winners included several nationally recognized artists.

SOUTH SOLON MEETING HOUSE EXTERIOR

Christina Tree

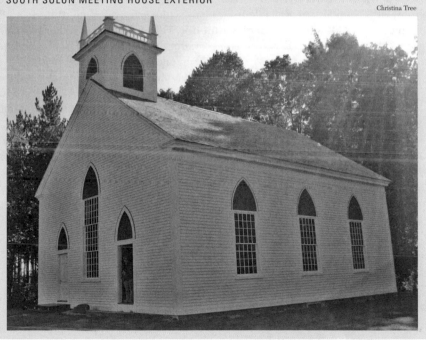

and the whole string of ponds linked by the Moose River, with the western mountains as a backdrop. There are picnic tables and restrooms. Note the trail leading to **Owls Head** (see *Hiking*).

Jackman–Moose River Historical Museum, Main St., Jackman. Open Memorial Day–late Sept., Fri. 1–4, more often when volunteers permit. Housed in a former town hall (with restrooms), this museum's displays convey a sense of the outpost area; note the prisoner-of-war camp once sited on Parlin Pond.

Northern Outdoors

MOXIE FALLS

✳ To Do

AIR TAXI Coleman Flying Service (207-668-4436) operates the Moose River Seaplane Base.

Jackman Air Tours (207-668-4461), 7 Attean Rd., Jackman. Jim Schoenmann offers scenic air tours of the entire area.

ATVS This is a mecca for people who love to ride their all-terrain vehicles, with 400 miles of trails. Bingham and Jackman are both hubs. Rentals are available from **Northern Rivers** (see *Whitewater Rafting*) in Bingham.

BIKING AND MOUNTAIN BIKING Local terrain varies from old logging roads to tote paths. Rentals are available from many whitewater rafting outfitters. A 12-mile multiuse (ATV/walking/biking) **Kennebec Valley Trail** now follows the old railbed along the river from Solon to Bingham. The 16.8-mile road from Pleasant Pond to Moxie Falls is also a favorite among bicyclists. **Maine Huts & Trails** (1-877-634-8824; mainehuts .org). At this writing the first 37 miles are completed of an evolving hiking/mountain biking/skiing trail runs from Flagstaff Lake (north of Sugarloaf) along the Dead River, each spaced one day's hike or ski from the next. See *Hiking* for details. In **Jackman** check with the chamber of commerce for details about the Sandy Bay Loop north of town.

LAKE WYMAN SCENIC BYWAY REST AREA

Christina Tree

CANOEING AND KAYAKING The **Moose River Bow Trip** is a Maine classic: A series of pristine ponds forms a 34-mile meandering route that winds back to the point of origin, eliminating the need for a shuttle. The fishing is fine, 21 remote campsites are scattered along the way, and the put-in is accessible. One major portage is required. Canoe rentals are available from a variety of local sources. Several rafting companies rent canoes and offer guided trips, but the kayaking specialists here are Registered Maine Guides Andy and Leslie McKendry at **Cry of the Loon Outdoor Adventures** (207-668-7808; cryoftheloon.net) east of Jackman, who offer a fully outfitted and guided Moose River Bow Trip as well as one- to seven-day tours throughout northwestern Maine. They also offer canoe and kayak rentals and shuttle services. Most whitewater outfitters rent kayaks and/or stable "funyaks."

FISHING is what the sporting camps (see *Lodging*) are all about. The catch includes landlocked salmon, trout, and togue. Rental boats and canoes are readily available. Camps also supply guides, and a number of them are listed on the Jackman chamber's website.

GOLF Moose River Golf Course (207-668-5331), Rt. 201, Moose River (just north of Jackman). Mid-May–mid-Oct.; club rental, putting green, nine holes.

HIKING *Note:* The **Appalachian Trail** (AT) crosses Rt. 201 in Caratunk and climbs Pleasant Pond Mountain (below).

Maine Huts & Trails (1-877-634-8824; mainehuts.org). At this writing the first three huts and first 37 miles are completed of an evolving hiking/mountain biking/skiing trail that runs from Flagstaff Lake (north of Sugarloaf) along the Dead River, each spaced one day's hike or ski from the next. The "huts" are really lodges, fully staffed during the summer, fall, and winter seasons, serving three daily meals. The **Grand Falls Hut** is 14.2 miles from the trailhead in West Forks, a long day's hike so plan an early start if you want to spend the night there. Obviously you don't have to go the whole way. The trail, which follows the Dead River into this wilderness area, is free from ATVs. Lodging is $67–99 with two meals, $39 per child; $30–35 per night in off-seasons (no meals).

Pleasant Pond Mountain in Caratunk. With an open ledge peak at 2,477 feet, the view is 360 degrees. It's a 1½-hour hike. Turn east off Rt. 201 at the Maine Forest Service Station in Caratunk and head toward Pleasant Pond on the road across from the post office and general store. At the fork (with Pleasant Pond in view), bear left. The pavement ends, the road narrows, and at 5 miles from the post office take Fire Lane 13 on the right. The trail begins on the left just beyond the AT lean-to.

Coburn Mountain is the site of the former Enchanted Mountain ski area. The gravel access road off Rt. 201 begins about 10 miles north of Berry's Store. The Forks snowmobile club maintains a trail to the summit of the mountain, along the old ski area service road. At 3,750 feet, it's the highest groomed snowmobile trail in Maine and can be hiked in summer. The 360-degree view from the open summit and its tower includes Mount Katahdin (68 miles to the northeast) and Sugarloaf Mountain (30 miles southwest).

Owls Head, Jackman. A 0.75-mile hike begins at the Attean View pullout on Rt. 201 (see *To See*) south of Jackman Village. This is one of Maine's most amazing easily accessible panoramas, stretching all the way to the Canadian border and encompassing Big Wood Lake, Slide Down Mountain, and Spencer Valley. The trail begins at the north end of the picnic area.

Moxie Falls is the area's easiest and most famous hike (see *To See*).

HUNTING Deer seasons runs from late Oct. through Nov. Moose hunting usually begins the second week in Oct. (by permit only); bears are hunted Aug.–Nov. and partridge, Oct.–Dec.

MOOSE-WATCHING The best time to see a moose is at dawn or dusk. Favorite local moose crossings include Moxie Rd. from The Forks to Moxie Pond; the Central Maine Power Company road from Moxie Pond to Indian Pond; the 25 miles north from The Forks to Jackman on Rt. 201; and the 30 miles from Jackman to Rockwood on Rt. 6/15. Drive these stretches carefully; residents all know someone who has died in a car–moose collision. Moose Safaris are offered May–Oct. by most outfitters.

✳ Winter Sports

SNOWMOBILING is huge in this region, with **The Forks** and **Jackman** serving as a hubs hundreds of miles of the Interconnecting Trail System (ITS) over mountains, rivers, and lakes and through woods with connections to the Rangeley and Moosehead areas, and to Canada (for which trail passes must be purchased). Rentals and guided trips are available from most major rafting companies.

Northern Outdoors (northernoutdoors.com) offers rentals, guided tours, and packages. Also check with the Jackman Region Chamber of Commerce (jackman maine.org) for the extensive trail network in that area.

CROSS-COUNTRY SKIING Maine Huts & Trails (1-877-634-8824; maine huts.org). In winter the trail from West Forks to Grand Falls Hut is groomed for both classic and diagonal stride. It's 14.2 miles to the hut and the trail has more than a 10 percent grade in places—a death march for novice skiers, but good ones can have a lot of fun. An early start is recommended. If you don't want to go all the way, this is still the best wilderness ski trail in the area, free from snowmobile traffic. See *Hiking* for more.

✳ Whitewater Rafting

The 12-mile run down the Kennebec River from Harris Dam begins with 4 miles of Class II and IV rapids—notably Magic Falls, though this comes early in the trip—and after that it's all fun. The slightly more challenging run on the Dead River, available less often (releases are less frequent), is also offered by most outfitters. The safety records for all outfitters are excellent, or they wouldn't be in this rigorously monitored business.

Apr.–Oct. rates include a river ride and a chance to view (and buy) slides of the day's adventures, also usually a steak and chicken barbecue. The minimum suggested age is 10 on the Upper Kennebec and 8 on the lower section, compared with 15 on the Dead River.

River trips begin between 7 and 9 and end between 3 and 4. Obviously it makes sense to spend the night before at your outfitter's base camp, hence our attempt to describe what's available.

Northern Outdoors

RAFTING THE KENNEBEC

Variables: The time of the morning put-in, whether you eat along the river or back at camp afterward, the size and nature of the group you will be rafting with, and the comfort level of the lodging. Note that some outfitters are on lakes or ponds, good for kayaking and canoeing. Some outfitters also offer additional activities: overnight camping trips, rock climbing, and more.

Note: Children, seniors, and others who want to experience smaller rapids can join the trip later in the day. Midweek trips are generally more family-geared. Weekends draw a younger, wilder crowd.

Although whitewater rafting began as a big singles sport, it's becoming more and more popular with families, who frequently combine it with a visit to Quebec City. Minimum age requirements vary, but weight is often a consideration (usually no less than 90 pounds). We identify the outfitters who cater to kids or who offer Lower Kennebec trips geared to children.

Raft Maine (1-800-723-8633; raftmaine.com) offers a good website and represents the seven local outfitters; the phone is handled on a rotating basis by each of the rafting companies.

OUTFITTERS WITH LODGING ✪ 🖉 ((ψ)) **Northern Outdoors** (207-663-4466 or 1-800-765-7238; northernoutdoors.com), Rt. 201, The Forks. Open year-round. The first and still the biggest outfitter on the Kennebec. The Forks Center is an open-timbered lodge with high ceilings, a huge hearth, comfortable seating, a cheerful dining room, along with its own **Kennebec River Pub & Brewery** (see *Where to Eat*). Amenities include a pool, private pond, volleyball, basketball, sauna, giant hot tub, and free WiFi. Accommodations range from riverside camping to lakeside cabins, from lodge rooms to "logdominiums" (condo-style units with lofts and a kitchen/dining area). Northern Outdoors also offers float trips, ATV trails, and plenty of nearby hiking. Inquire about "family camps," where children as young as 8 are welcome. In winter the lodge caters to snowmobilers with snowmobile rentals and guided tours.

✪ 🖉 **Magic Falls Rafting** (207-663-2220 or 1-800-207-7238; magicfalls.com), P.O. Box 9, West Forks 04985. This family-owned, long-established outfitter has an extensive base complex squirreled away down on the banks of the Dead River in The Forks. Dave and Donna Neddeau invested all their savings in a canoe, raft, house trailer, and two cabins back in 1989 and now offer 40 rafts, 25 inflatable kayaks, a climbing tower, recreation pavilion, and campground. They've also built **Dead River Lodge** (♿) with nicely decorated king and queen rooms, also family rooms with bunks, each with half-bath and, downstairs, a living room with big-screen TV, frequently rented by small groups or available to individual guests. There is a renovated farmhouse sleeping up to 16, too. In addition to rafting trips on the Kennebec and Dead Rivers, they offer "Out Back" camping adventures with rafting, hiking, a wildlife safari, campfire meals, and a funyak trip plus a variety of lodging packages.

Moxie Outdoor Adventures (1-800-866-6943; moxierafting.com), HC 63, Box 60, The Forks 04985. This long-established outfitter is based in a set of traditional cabins on Lake Moxie, offering camping, platform tents, and cabin lodging, a lake house (sleeping 16) specializing in two- and three-day canoe trips (including a 12-passenger "Voyageur" canoe) as well as rafting, funyaking, and floatplane rides.

✍ **Crab Apple White Water** (207-663-4491 or 1-800-553-7238; crabappleinc .com), 3 Lake Moxie Rd., The Forks 04985. A family-owned and -geared outfitter with a base camp that offers eight luxury suites (with wet bar, fridge, Jacuzzi, and deck); also four cottages accommodating four to eight people in bunk-style rooms, six motel units, and a large lodge with a restaurant right in The Forks. "Funyaks" (inflatable kayaks) and half-day float trips are also offered. Amenities include a paintball field. Rafting/lodging packages.

Windfall Outdoor Center (1-800-683-2009; raftwindfall.com), Rt. 201, Jackman. Windfall offers rafting on both the Dead and the Kennebec with lodging choices ranging from campground and RV to lakeside cabins. Geared to church and non-profit groups. Drinking is discouraged.

✍ **Adventure Bound** (1-888-606-7238; adv-bound.com), Rt. 201, a 20-acre site in Caratunk. A family- and kids-geared outfitter. Facilities include an outdoor pool, indoor climbing wall, and ice cream bar. It has its own base lodge and cabin-tent village.

Professional River Runners (1-800-325-3911; proriverrunners.com), West Forks. The specialty is overnight trips, beginning with a run down the East Outlet and campout the night before you run the Kennebec. Kids welcome.

RUSTIC RESORT

✪ ✍ **Attean Lake Lodge** (207-668-3792; atteanlodge.com), P.O. Box 475, Jackman 04945. Open Memorial Day weekend–Sept. Sited on Birch Island in 5-mile-long Attean Lake, accessed by shuttle from the end of Attean Rd., off Rt. 201. Surrounded by mountains, this is Maine's premier family-run and family-geared sporting camp. It was established in 1903 when the far

Attean Lake Lodge

VIEW FROM THE PORCH OF A CABIN AT ATTEAN LAKE RESORT

shore of the lake was a flagstop on the Canadian Pacific Railroad. The 18 traditional peeled spruce log cabins are a mix of old and new, all genuinely rustic, with light from gas and kerosene lamps, heat from Franklin stoves, but baths are full and sparkling, linens and beds, comfy. The mountain and lake views from each deck are so splendid that you want to just to sit until it all soaks in. Families with young children opt for the cabins, near the dock and sandy beach; others cluster in the pines at the end of a wooded path (be sure

North Country Adventures (1-800-348-8871; northcountryrivers.com). The former Maine Whitewater base in Bingham is on 60 acres with camping and RV sites, platform tents, and basic new log cabins, also a very basic base lodge and a private airport on the riverside grounds. Moose safaris are offered, and ATV rentals and guided trips are a specialty.

Three Rivers (1-800-786-6878; threeriversfun.com), 2265 Rt. 201, West Forks 04985. The emphasis here is on fun, with packages including food and nightlife.

✴ Other Lodging

LODGES & CABINS 🐾 𝄢 **Riverside Inn** (207-672-3215), 178 Main St. (Rt. 201), P.O. Box 65, Bingham 04920. Maine natives Scott and Vicki Stanchfield have transformed this century-old riverside lodge into an appealing place to stay with eight guest rooms (four shared baths). They've restored the hardwood floors and reopened the wood-burning fireplaces in the twin parlors. Every room has a TV, but there's also shared space; guests tend to mingle over evening cheese and crackers or, later, samosas around the fire pit while Scott strums his guitar. The backyard is fitted with croquet and horseshoes, but Scott urges guests to get out and hike to local beauty spots. He also rents kayaks and offers shuttles from Solon. $80 per room with coffee and muffins.

Inn by the River (207-663-2181; innbytheriver.com), HCR 63 Box 24, West Forks 04985. Open year-round. A contemporary lodging, built to resemble a 19th-century inn. It's across the road from the river but sits on a bluff. There are 10 nicely decorated guest

to bring flashlights!). The spacious, open-timbered lodge was completed in 1987, to replace the original lodge, which burned to the ground in 1979.

"After the fire, we talked about selling," recalls Brad Holden, the second generation of his family, to operate the camps. Although Attean had a loyal clientele, the appeal of the island resort was obviously diminished without its traditional central gathering place. It took 12 years to rebuild the lodge (designed and largely constructed by Brad himself, with big assists from wife Andrea and son Barrett). It's a beauty. Before and after meals, Brad or Andrea can usually be found behind the check-in desk with the canoe suspended above it, while guests play card and board games or check their computers in the many-windowed, comfortable corners of central lodge room. There's also a library and children's playroom. During the day visitors scatter widely, taking advantage of motorboats, canoes, kayaks, and sailboats to explore this pristine, mountain-ringed lake—spotted with 22 islands—and trails that lead to moose meccas and summit views. For serious fishermen, guides can arrange multiday trips, sleeping in backwoods cabins. One way or another guests work up an appetite for the generous breakfasts and dinner (wine and beer are available) and box lunches. July–Aug. $335 adult, $2,100 per week, Before and after, $270 per day, $1,700 per week, less for third adult and children.

rooms with private bath, some with whirlpool tub and private porch; many have river views. There's a big fireplace in the living room, plus a cozy pub. Three meals are served. Rates include breakfast. In winter this spot is popular with snowmobilers because it's on a major trail. $79–129 includes breakfast.

Hawk's Nest Lodge (207-663-2020; hawksnestlodge.com), Rt. 201, West Forks. A whitewater rafting guide for 25 years, Peter Doste settled in and built two lodges in the West Forks. Hawk's Nest is a striking three-story post, beam, and glass construct with a restaurant/lounge on the first floor and some amazing chain-saw sculptures both inside and out. The four suites are each different, from $125 for two. The River House up the road sleeps 16, available by the night, $500–640.

Lake Parlin Lodge (207-688-9060 or 1-888-668-9060; lakeparlinlodge.com), 6003 Main St., Lake Parlin 04945. The onetime community here (between the Forks and Jackman), which included the Lake Parlin House Hotel, has about disappeared. Still, it's one of the

prettiest sites around, with cabins that were a rafting company base until Joe and Liz Kruz bought the property, opening a brand-new open-timbered lodge with a restaurant in 2011. It's well positioned for snowmobiling as well as rafting, hiking, and swimming. Rooms are in the main lodge, a mini lodge with five bedrooms, and the one- and two-bedroom cabins with full kitchen, living room, and propane fireplace. Rooms from $120 (two-night minimum). Also see *Eating Out*.

In the Jackman area

🐾 **Sally Mountain Cabins** (207-668-5621 or 1-800-644-5621; sallymtcabins .com), 9 Elm St., Jackman 04945. Open year-round. Sited at the end of a quiet street, right on Big Moose Lake, these basic but cheerful housekeeping cabins with cable TV each accommodate two to five people. As many as 10 can stay in larger condo-style units across the street. $35 per person per night, $210 per person per week. Free for ages 4 and under, and for pets. Inquire about rental boats, canoes, and ice-fishing shacks.

🐾 ⚓ **Cedar Ridge Outfitters** (207-668-4169; cedarridgeoutfitters.com), 36 Attean Rd., Jackman 04945. Registered Maine Guides Hal and Debbie Blood have been steadily expanding this serious hunting operation. Sited on a quiet road are 7 two- and three-bedroom housekeeping cabins with TV, VCR, and phone. Amenities include hot tubs and a heated swimming pool; "adventure packages" include fishing, hunting, guided snowmobiling, and whitewater rafting. $42 per person per night, less for children, longer stays.

Bishop's Country Inn Motel (207-668-3231 or 1-888-991-7669; bishops motel.com), 461 Main St., Jackman 04945. This two-story motel in the middle of Jackman Village offers clean and spacious rooms and all the bells

RIVERSIDE INN, BINGHAM

Bill Davis

and whistles it takes for AAA to give it three diamonds. Reasonable rates.

✳ Where to Eat

Listings are in geographic order along Route 201, south to north
In this little-populated area the line between "eating out" and "dining out" blurs—and if you're between rafting, hunting, and snowmobiling seasons, it comes down to what's open. See *Eating Out* in Skowhegan in the previous chapter for suggestions between I-95 and the Canada Road.

In Bingham
✎ **Maplewood Family Restaurant** (207-672-3330), 418 Main St. Open Tue.–Sat. 11–9, Sun. from 8 with brunch until 1. Recently expanded to accommodate rafting groups, the large menu specializes in fresh seafood chowder, BBQ, and baby back ribs. There's a Sat.-night buffet, full bar, kids' menu, and play area. Sandwiches all day.

In The Forks
✎ **Kennebec River Pub & Brewery** (207-663-4466), Northern Outdoors, Rt. 201. Open daily year-round for all three meals. This is an inviting brew-pub with half a dozen beers ranging from light summer ale to robust stout. There's also a pine-sided, informal dining room hung with archival photos of The Forks in its big-time logging and old resort days. Good for burgers, salads, and baskets, also dinner entrées ranging from stuffed portobello mushrooms to a full rack of Class V Stout BBQ Ribs. Kids' meals all include Gifford's ice cream. Entrées $15–24.

Inn by the River (207-663-2181), Rt. 201. Open June–Aug., Jan.–March to the public for breakfast and dinner. Otherwise usually weekends, but check. Dinner entrées include steak, baked stuffed haddock, chicken

Parmesan, and roast duck with bacon, brandy, and mango chutney glaze, $16–20.

Marshall's Bar and Restaurant (207-663-4455), Rt. 201. Open seasonally for lunch and dinner. Chris Hewke has revived this century-old hotel, a prime source of pizza, fried baskets, and salads, burgers, and steak-house-style dinner entrées. Live music and "events" on weekends.

((ψ)) **Hawk's Nest** (207-663-2020; hawksnestlodge.com), Rt. 201, West Forks village. If it's open, this is the obvious place for lunch and dinner in The Forks; days and hours vary with the season. New Haven–style pizza is the specialty, also burgers, sandwiches, salads, chicken Parmesan, linguine, pub food.

✎ **Crab Apple** (1-800-553-7238), Crab Apple Acres, just off Rt. 201. Open daily for dinner Memorial Day–Labor Day; otherwise check. This outfitter's large base lodge includes both a pub and a more formal restaurant. Dinner options range from vegetable pasta Alfredo to prime rib and Yorkshire pudding. Children's menu.

✎ **Lake Parlin Lodge** (207-668-9060; lakeparlinlodge.com), Rt. 201, Lake Parlin. Open Fri.–Sat. 5–9, Sun. 8–3 in season. Call to make sure it's open. This is an attractive, new lodge with a lunch/dinner menu serving sandwiches

KENNEBEC RIVER PUB & BREWERY AT NORTHERN OUTDOORS, THE FORKS
Christina Tree

and burgers, also fried seafood and chicken, prime rib dinner specials for $21.99. Children's menu.

In Jackman

○ **Mama Bear's** (207-668-4222), Rt. 201. Open 4 AM–8 PM, from 6 AM on weekends. We always seem to stop here for lunch. It's totally pleasant with great daily specials and a menu ranging from poutine to scallops in white wine. Fully licensed.

Four Seasons Restaurant (207-668-7778), 17 Main St. Open 5 AM–9 PM. One big room, booths, good road food, blackboard specials. Fully licensed.

Schmooses (207-668-7799), 513 Main St. Open daily from 11:30. This is a classy North Woods "lounge" with a moose depicted in smoked glass, handsome fieldstone hearths, and a dance floor that comes to life with a DJ Thu.–Sat. At dinner a 10-ounce steak with king crab is $19.99.

The Bigwood Steakhouse (207-668-5572), 1 Forest St. Open from 4 PM Thu.–Sun. Meal-sized salads, pasta, and Cajun dishes, as well as BBQ ribs, but hand-cut steaks are the specialty, all served in Kim and Karen Hewke's home. ("The kids grew up and moved out. Now they can't come back.") FYI: Son Chris now owns the Marshall's in The Forks. The full menu is available as takeout.

JACKMAN TRADING POST

Christina Tree

Bill Davis

MAMA BEAR'S IN JACKMAN

✳ Selective Shopping

General stores in Solon and on up through Jackman are generally the only stores, ergo community centers. Our favorite is **Berry's in The Forks** (open 4:30 AM–7:30 PM), a source of fishing/hunting licenses and liquor, lunch, flannel jackets, rubber boots, and groceries, as well as gas. Stuffed birds and other wildlife are scattered throughout the store, most of it shot by Gordon Berry, who has been behind the counter for 40 years. Until the rafting/snowmobiling boom hit, Berry notes, he and his parents could manage the place alone; now it takes a staff of up to 10.

Jackman Trading Post (207-666-2761; moosealley.com), 281 Main St. (Rt. 201 south of the village). Open May–Thanksgiving, 8–6. A peerless selection of Far North T-shirts and souvenirs.

✳ Special Events

March: **Northeast Sled Dog Races**, Jackman—a three-day professional race.

September: **Fly-In**, Gadabout Gaddis Airport, Bingham (207-672-4100).

November: **West Forks Fish & Game Annual Hunter's Supper** (207-663-2121).

Maine Highlands 7

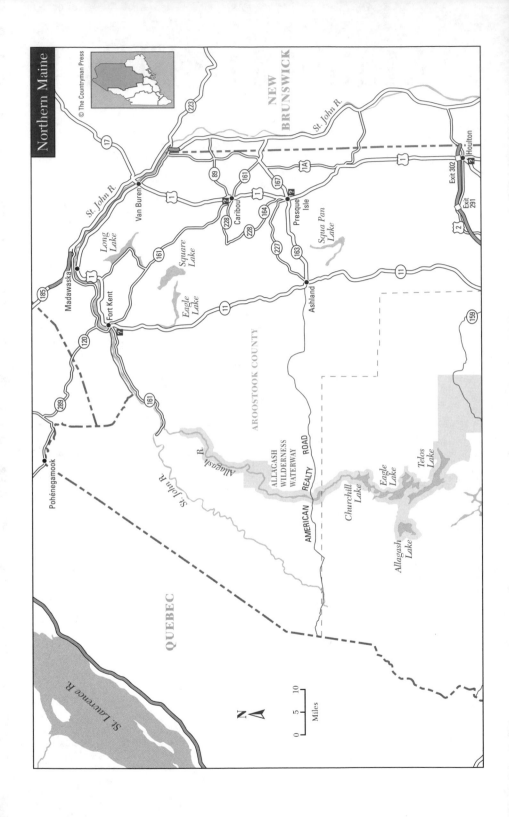

Northern Maine

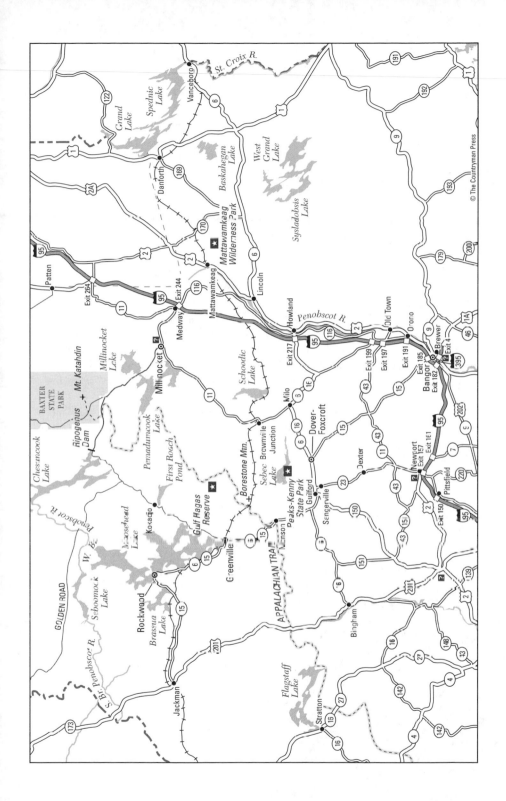

BANGOR AREA

Bangor is both the natural gateway to much of central, northern, and eastern Maine and the largest city in the region. It makes a good layover spot for those venturing into either the Baxter State Park region, the Moosehead Lake region, or the vast expanse of Aroostook County. With Brewer on the other side of the Penobscot River, and Orono, home of the main campus of the University of Maine, the Bangor metropolitan area is a vibrant commercial and cultural hub. The Bangor Mall on the north side of the city is the largest in northern Maine, and Bangor International Airport (referred to locally as BIA) is a departure point for flights to every corner of the globe.

Once the home of the National Folk Festival, Bangor began to host the American Folk Festival in 2005, celebrating the richness and variety of American culture through music, dance, traditional storytelling, and food.

Residents will tell you wistfully that the city's real glory days were in the mid-19th century, when the pine tree was arboreal gold and Bangor was the most important lumber port in the world. Back then the city was a brawling, boisterous boomtown where fortunes were quickly made and lost in timber deals and land speculation. Local lumber barons built grandiose hilltop mansions, sparing no expense. After a long winter's work in the woods, the loggers who labored for them spent their hard-earned money, roistering in the bars and brothels of the city's notorious red-light district, known as "the Devil's Half Acre," most of which was wiped out in a 1911 fire. A 21-and-older tour guided by the Bangor Museum brings the district back to (imaginary) life.

The Bangor of today has recovered some of its notoriety with the enormous Hollywood Slots Hotel & Raceway, the only slot machine gaming floor in the state. Its hours, from 8 AM to 4 AM, reveal the lure for in-state and out-of-state travelers.

SCULPTURE IN MARKET SQUARE

Kim Grant

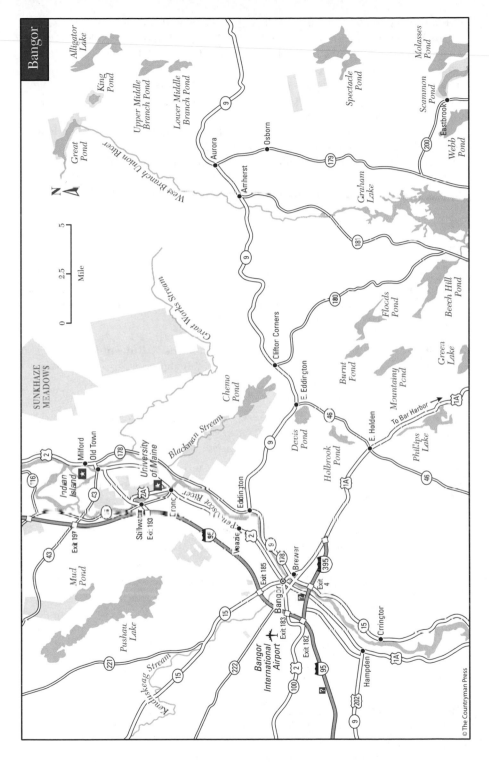

Bangor

© The Countryman Press

But walking tours of the historic districts are a good diversion, and far less risky.

The West Market Square Historic District is a mid-19th-century block of downtown shops. The Broadway area is lined with the Federal-style homes of early prominent citizens and lumber barons' mansions. Across town, West Broadway holds a number of even more ornate homes, including the turreted and thoroughly spooky-looking Victorian home of author Stephen King, with its one-of-a-kind bat-and-cobweb wrought-iron fence.

The outsized symbol of Bangor's romantic timber boom era is native son Paul Bunyan. The mythical lumberjack superhero was conceived in tall-tale-swapping sessions in the logging camps of northern Maine and the saloons of the Devil's Half Acre. When most of the tall stands of virgin pine in Maine's North Woods had been cut down, ending the boom, lumberjacks began moving west, taking Paul with them—and making him bigger and his feats more incredible with every move. Scattered across the forested northern tier of the United States, all the way to the Pacific Northwest, are villages and small towns named Bangor settled by nostalgic Maine loggers who all had a Paul Bunyan tale to tell.

Paul Bunyan is still very much a presence here: A 31-foot-high fiberglass statue of the great logger, wearing a red-and-black-checked shirt and carrying a huge ax, stands in a city park named for him—and casts a long shadow just across the street from Hollywood Slots Hotel & Raceway.

GUIDANCE Greater Bangor Convention and Visitors Bureau (207-947-5205 and 1-800-991-6673; visitbangormaine.com) operates staffed, year-round information centers at 40 Harlow St. and at Bangor International Airport, and at the Harbormaster's Office on the waterfront in the summer.

Bangor Region Chamber of Commerce (207-947-0307; bangorregion.com), Maine Ave., Bangor 04402. No visitors center during construction of the Bangor Auditorium. Contact GBCVB above with tourism inquiries.

Maine Tourism Association maintains two rest areas/information centers on I-95 in Hamden between exits 175 and 180: northbound (207-862-6628) and southbound (207-862-6638).

GETTING THERE *By air:* **Bangor International Airport** (207-992-4600; fly bangor.com) is served by Delta Air Lines, Allegiant Air, and U.S. Airways Express. **Rental cars** are available at the airport.

By bus: **Greyhound** (207-942-1700), **West Transportation** (207-546-2823), and **Cyr Bus Line** (207-827-2335 or 1-800-244-2335) offer bus daily service. Cyr Bus Line provides daily trips all the way to Fort Kent, with stops in between. **Concord Coach Lines** (207-945-5000 or 1-800-639-5150) has express trips, complete with movies and music, daily from Portland and Boston.

By car: I-95 north from Augusta and south from Millinocket; Rt. 9 from Calais; Rt. 1A from Bar Harbor.

WHEN TO COME The American Folk Festival draws a lot of folks at the end of August, but other reasons to explore—from the Penobscot Nation Museum on Indian Island to a unique home brewing shop and great restaurants downtown—suggest a visit anytime. If you come in midwinter, you can try to imagine how the lumberjacks managed in the deep woods.

✷ Villages

Hampden. Adjacent to Bangor, but offering a more rural setting. The academically excellent Hampden Academy is found here.

Orono. A college town, housing the University of Maine, but still a small town where almost everyone knows everyone else. Downtown there are some nice shops and local dining landmarks, and on campus look for a wide variety of cultural activities.

Old Town. Definitely a mill town, but also the home of the famous Old Town Canoe factory. There's a great little museum worth visiting.

Winterport. An old river town, once home of many sea captains and now a quiet little area with a historic district. Walking-tour brochure available from area businesses; check out 4Points BBQ and Parings at Winterport Winery.

✷ To See and Do

CANOEING AND KAYAKING Sunrise International (207-942-9300 or 1-888-490-9300; sunriseexpeditions.com), 4 Union Plaza, Suite 2, Bangor, is one of the state's best river expedition, guided-kayaking and -canoeing businesses. Martin Brown started Sunrise County Canoe Expeditions, a traditional Maine guiding business, in 1973, and it is now Maine's oldest river guide and outfitter service. A master Maine guide since 1970, Brown has taken his customers out west and far north, to the high Arctic and to desert canyons. But the St. Croix, St. John, and Machias Rivers, as well as other eastern and northern Maine waterways, are explored in scheduled trips every year from May to Oct. Guide author Chris Tree and one of her sons took the St. Croix trip with Brown years ago and said, "It was fabulous."

MUSEUMS Cole Land Transportation Museum (207-990-3600; colemuseum .org), 405 Perry Rd. (near junction of I-95 and I-395), Bangor. Open May 1–Nov. 11, daily 9–5. $7 adults, $5 seniors, under 19 free. A collection of 200 antique Maine vehicles going back to the 19th century: snowplows, wagons, trucks, sleds, rail equipment, and more. A World War II memorial, Korean Veterans Memorial, Vietnam Veterans Memorial, and Purple Heart Memorial are all on-site.

Hose 5 Fire Museum (207-945-3229), 247 State St., Bangor. Open by appointment. A working fire station until 1993, now a museum with firefighting artifacts from the area. Three fully restored fire engines, wooden water mains, and plenty of historical pictures on display. Free, but donations gladly accepted.

University of Maine Museums, Rt. 2A, Orono. **Hudson Museum** (207-581-1901), in the **Collins Center for**

COLE LAND TRANSPORTATION MUSEUM

Nancy English

the Arts (open Mon.–Fri. 9–4, Sat. 11–4) is an exceptional anthropological collection including a special section on Maine Native Americans and Maine history. Tour programs are offered by prior arrangement. **Page Farm Home Museum** (207-581-4100; umaine.edu/pagefarm), on the University of Maine–Orono campus. Open daily May 15–Sept. 15, 9–4; closed Sun. and Mon. off-season. Free. Historical farm implements and household items from 1865 to 1940.

University of Maine Museum of Art (207-561-3350; umma.umaine.edu), 40 Harlow St., Bangor, shows a fraction of its 4,500-work collection, which includes an extensive selection of 19th- and 20th-century European and American prints by Goya, Picasso, Homer, and Whistler, as well as modern American paintings by George Inness, John Marin, Andrew Wyeth, and others. The museum also hosts four exhibitions a year of modern and contemporary art.

Old Town Museum (207-827-7256; oldtownmuseum.com), 353 Main St., Old Town. Open early June–end of Aug., Fri.–Sun. 1–4. St. Mary's Catholic Church houses a great little museum with exhibits on the Penobscot tribe and on local logging, early area photos, an original birch-bark canoe, and well-informed guides.

Maine Forest and Logging Museum at Leonard's Mills (207-974-6278; leonardsmills.com), Leonard's Mills, off Rt. 178 in Bradley (take Rt. 9 north from Brewer; turn left onto Rt. 178 and watch for signs). Open during daylight hours. Varying admission. "Living History Days" on two weekends, one in mid-July and another in Oct., feature people in period attire with horses or oxen. Located on the site of a 1790s logging and milling community, this museum includes a covered bridge, water-powered sawmill, millpond, saw pit, barn, and trapper's line camp. Other special events include Children's Day, Woodsmen's Day, and winter sleigh rides; call to find out about the changing schedule.

HISTORIC HOMES AND SITES Bangor Museum and History Center (207-942-1900; bangormuseum.org), 159 Union St., Bangor. Open May–Mar., Tue.–Sat. 10–4. $7 adults, children and members free, but fee depends on program. The museum is located in the Thomas A. Hill House. The downstairs of the Hill House has been restored to its 19th-century grandeur with Victorian furnishings and an elegant double parlor. The exhibit *No Boundaries: Women's Roles in the Civil Way* is featured in 2012. Walking-tour maps and tours of Mount Hope Cemetery are available. The *Edgar Allan Poe et al.* exhibit in fall is highly recommended. **Mount Hope Cemetery** in Bangor is one of the nation's oldest garden cemeteries, designed by noted Maine architect Charles G. Bryant. Abraham Lincoln's first vice president, Hannibal Hamlin, is buried here.

FOR FAMILIES ♂ Maine Discovery Museum (207-262-7200; mainediscovery museum.org), 74 Main St., Bangor. The largest children's museum north of Boston, with three floors of kid-oriented displays and activities. Science and music exhibits on the third floor include a giant body to climb through and the Recollections Room, with lights that follow movement. The second floor has exhibits about world trade with a cargo ship, warehouses, and an airplane. $7.50 per person, 12 months and older.

GAMBLING Hollywood Slots Hotel & Raceway (207-561-6100 or 1-877-779-7771; hollywoodslots.com), 500 Main St., Bangor. Mon.–Thu. 8 AM–1 AM, Fri. 8 AM–

INDIAN ISLAND

In 1786 the Penobscot tribe deeded most of Maine to Massachusetts in exchange for 140 small islands in the Penobscot River. An 18th-century agreement (discovered in the 1970s) detailed that Indian Island (much of it now valuable) belonged to the tribe and brought the island a new school and a large community center, which attracts crowds to play high-stakes bingo (call 1-800-255-1293 or visit penobscotbingo.com for the schedule). Today the Indian Island Reservation, the Penobscot homeland for more than 5,000 years, and connected by bridge to Old Town, is occupied by about 500 tribal members. At 12 Downstreet St., the **Penobscot Nation Museum** (207-827-4153; penobscotnation.org) is open year-round Mon.–Thu. 9–2 and Sat. 10–4. The museum occupies the former Indian agent's office, the fifth building on the right after crossing the bridge. Museum coordinator James Neptune greets visitors, explaining that the birch table was made by the legendary Passamaquoddy craftsman Tomah Joseph (who taught Franklin Roosevelt to paddle a canoe) and that the beaded deerskin dress belonged to Indian Island's Molly Spotted Elk, a dancer, actress, and writer known around the world in the late 1930s. Most items in this authentic and informal collection—which includes a 200-year-old birch-bark canoe and some exquisite beaded works, war bonnets, war clubs, and basketry—have a human story. Several videos about the history of the Penobscot Nation can be shown upon request. The island is accessible from Rt. 2, marked from I-95 exit 197.

A FANCY BASKET BY CLARA NEPTUNE KEEZER

Hudson Museum, University of Maine–Orono

2 AM, Sat. 8 AM–2 AM, Sun. 8 AM–1 AM. You must be 21 to enter and use the slot machines. Younger people can enter the restaurant and the hotel, but no one under 21 can enter the slot machine area (except licensed employees). Revenues from Hollywood Slots, shared with the state, the city of Bangor, and other entities, have exceeded predictions: It took in almost $62 million in September 2011 (totals listed at maine.gov/dps/GambBoard/FinancialInformation.htm). Bangor, with plus or minus half a million dollars a month as its 1 percent annual share, is building a new auditorium and civic center. The business comprises 1,000 slot and video poker machines, a 152-room hotel, a 1,500-car parking garage, a lounge with live entertainment on weekends, a simulcast theater for off-track betting, a buffet, and a snack bar.

GOLF **Bangor Municipal Golf Course** (207-941-0232; bangorgc.com), Webster Ave., Bangor; 27 holes. **Penobscot Valley Country Club** (207-866-2423), Bangor Rd., Orono; 18 holes. **Hermon Meadow Golf Club** (207-848-3741; herman meadow.com), 281 Billings Rd., Hermon; 18 holes.

SWIMMING ✍ **Jenkins' Beach**. Popular beach on Green Lake for families with children. Store and snack bar.

Violette's Public Beach and Boat Landing (207-843-6876), Dedham (between Ellsworth and Bangor). $4 admission. Also on Green Lake, a popular spot for college students and young adults. Swim float with slide, boat launch, and picnic tables.

Beth Pancoe Aquatic Center (207-992-4490; bangormaine.gov), run by the Bangor Parks and Recreation Department. An outdoor Olympic-sized pool with a waterslide and a couple of fountains, this facility has a slow slope into the water, easy on the old and young, and was built with a gift from Stephen King, Bangor's best-selling novelist. Open end of June–Aug. $1 children, $2 resident adults; $2 children, $4 adults from away.

DOWNHILL AND CROSS-COUNTRY SKIING **Mt. Hermon Ski Area** (207-848-5192; skihermonmountain.com), Newburg Rd., Hermon (3 miles off I-95 from exit 173, Carmel; or off Rt. 2 from Bangor). Popular local downhill skiing area, with a chairlift and a T-bar and 20 runs (the longest is 3,500 feet); rentals available; base lodge, night skiing, snowboarding. A tubing park, with a lift, runs Wed.–Sun. ($12 tickets). Day passes for adults $25, 12 and under $20.

See also **Sunkhaze Meadows** under *Green Space*.

✳ Green Space

Sunkhaze Meadows National Wildlife Refuge, Milford. Unstaffed. Contact the Maine Coastal Islands Wildlife Refuge Milbridge office (207-546-2124) for information. Just north of Bangor, this 11,500-acre refuge includes nearly 7 miles of Sunkhaze Stream and 12 miles of tributary streams. Recreation includes canoeing, hiking, hunting, and fishing—contact refuge staff for regulations. Also excellent bird-watching and cross-country skiing.

ORONO BOG WALK

Nancy English

The *Greater Bangor Region* guidebook is available at the Greater Bangor Convention & Visitors Bureau visitors center and lists all trails for biking, walking, picnicking, running, hiking, cross-country skiing, and other outdoor activities.

✪ **The Orono Bog Walk and the Rolland F. Perry Bangor City Forest** (207-581-1697 for Jim Bird, direc-

Nancy English

ORONO BOG WALK

tor of Orono Bog Boardwalk; orono bogwalk.org), located 1.5 miles north of the intersection of Stillwater Ave. and Hogan Rd. at Bangor Mall, on Tripp Dr., Bangor. Open May–late Nov., this 1-mile looping boardwalk winds into a carpet of peat moss, and signs help you identify the fascinating vegetation that thrives in acidic dampness. The seasons bring colorful changes and wild visitors throughout the year. Guided walks are offered on Sat.; check the website for the schedule and subject matter. Another 9 miles of trails lace Bangor City Forest. Birders are on the prowl for yellow-rumped warblers, black-throated green warblers, and many others that migrate through.

✳ Lodging

Hollywood Slots Hotel and Race-way (207-561-6100; hollywoodslots
.com), 500 Main St., Bangor 04401.
With 152 rooms ready for guests who like to gamble and play the slots in the casino (and play roulette, blackjack, and three-card poker in 2012, after winning local voters' approval), this hotel is a destination for many visitors to Bangor, and 42 inch TVs, exercise room, and buffet breakfast are included. Rates run around $129–159.

🐾 **Fireside Inn and Suites** (207-942-1234; firesideinnbangor.com), 570 Main St., Bangor 04401. A 51-room hotel that is clean, comfortable, and convenient. Next door to Hollywood Slots, this place is busier than ever. All the basic conveniences, including mini fridge, microwave oven, and cable TV.
Geaghan's, the on-site restaurant with a microbrewery, serves decent food, with Irish specials. $90–150, including continental breakfast. Children under 18 stay free.

♿ **The Charles Inn** (207-992-2820; thecharlesinn.com), 20 Broad St., Ban-

gor 04401. A historic art gallery hotel on West Market Square, a vest-pocket park in the heart of downtown Bangor, is a perfect location for getting to know the city. Connie Boivin bought this hotel in 2005; 35 large rooms are simple and somewhat worn, some with solid mahogany or cherry beds. All have private bath, air-conditioning, and TV. A continental kosher or nonkosher breakfast is included. $69–109 depending on season. Count on a good cocktail at the hotel bar.

Country Inn at the Mall (207-941-0200 or 1-800-244-3961; countryinnat themall.net), 936 Stillwater Ave., Bangor 04401. Despite the name, this is essentially a 96-room motel—but brighter and better decorated than most. There's no restaurant, newsstand, or gift shop, but with the Bangor Mall (largest in northern Maine) right next door that's not an inconvenience.
$75–111 with continental breakfast.

🐾 ♿ **The Lucerne Inn** (207-843-5123 or 1-800-325-5123; lucerneinn.com), 2517 Main Rd., Holden 04429. An

Nancy English

DOWNTOWN BANGOR

1812 mansion on Rt. 1A, overlooking Phillips Lake in East Holden. Best known as a restaurant (see *Dining Out*), it also has 31 rooms with private bath (whirlpool), working fireplace, heated towel bars, phone and TV. Outdoor heated pool. $119–219 in-season includes continental breakfast. Lower rates off-season.

Howard Johnson's Hotel (207-942-5251; hojo.com), 336 Odlin Rd., Bangor. Just plain, clean rooms—starting at $72, and five minutes from the airport.

Note: Bangor also has many hotels and motels, mainly located by the mall and near the airport. Contact the Greater **Bangor Convention and Visitors Bureau** (207-947-5205 and 1-800-991-6673; visitbangormaine.com) for more information.

✴ Where to Eat

DINING OUT Thistles Restaurant (207-945-5480; thistlesrestaurant.com), 175 Exchange St., Bangor. Open for lunch Tue.–Sat. 11–2:30 and dinner 4:30–9. A fine-dining place that does many things perfectly, the Argentinean dishes in particular. Chef-owner Alejandro Rave puts together tangy chimichurri sauce for steaks and

empanadas. Spanish paella is served in paella pans, with fresh seafood and chicken. Half portions fit a smaller appetite and cost $10–15. Entrées $17–28. Sleek modern decor.

The Fiddlehead (207-942-3336), 84 Hammond St., Bangor. Open Tue.–Sun. Bouillabaisse with calamari, shrimp, scallops, haddock, and tomato and roasted red pepper rouille; pork chop with char siu and Japanese fried rice; and spinach and wild mushroom Wellington with goat cheese cream and 18-year balsamic are examples of an intriguing menu that expands the hopes of a traveler with an appetite. Laura Albin and chef Melissa Chaiken opened in August 2009 and can pour you a Maine martini, made with Allen's Coffee Brandy, the best-selling liquor in the state, and heavy cream.

Massimo's Cucina Italiana (207-945-5600; massimoscucinaitaliana.com), 96 Hammond St., Bangor. Zuppa di cozze, mussels with white wine and garlic, or spinach salad with Gorgonzola makes a wonderful introduction to dinner at Massimo's; then head right to the linguine alla carbonara or tortellacci stuffed with beef and veal. Seared rib eye or lamb chops are served as secondi. $10–25.

The Lucerne Inn (207-843-5123 or 1-800-325-5123; lucerneinn.com), 2517 Main Rd., Rt. 1A, East Holden (11 miles out of Bangor, heading toward Ellsworth). Open for dinner daily, as well as a popular Sunday brunch, at this grand old mansion with a view of Phillips Lake. Brunch specialties include Belgian waffles and chicken cordon bleu. Entrées start at $20; more than $29 for a steamed lobster or filet mignon. Baked stuffed haddock is a popular dish, as is seafood risotto.

Reverend Noble's Pub (207-942-5180) and **Ipanema Bar and Grill** (207-942-9339), 10 Broad St., Bangor. Steve Parlee owns these two businesses. The pub is on the second floor serving burgers and pub food. Ipanema offers Caribbean food like skewers of double jerk chicken or steak with coffee bourbon sauce. Live entertainment. The fun and relaxed atmosphere, good cocktails, and good food make this a find.

Luna Bar & Grill (207-990-2233; lunabarandgrill.net), 49 Park St., Bangor. Open Tue.–Sat. for dinner. Grilled burgers, seared duck with caramelized onion flan and cherry compote, filet osso buco, and miso-glazed sea bass with jasmine rice and bok choy. $9–32. Bar is open till 1 AM, with bar menu available. Large selection of single-malt Scotch, wine; Tue. is half-price martini night.

L'Aperitif Tapas Restaurant and Eurolounge (207-974-3113; laperitif .com), 193 Broad St., Bangor. Open Tue.–Sat 5–midnight. Small servings of prosciutto mac-and-cheese, hummus, pork tenderloin with blueberry as "tapas," plus entrées. Comfortable leather couches in the Eurolounge.

EATING OUT Tesoro's (207-942-6699), 114 Harlow St., Bangor.

Located across from the Bangor Public Library, this family-run restaurant serves good Italian American food— like chicken Parmesan and veal and peppers—in generous portions and is famous for its pizza. Cash only; ATM nearby.

Paddy Murphy's Irish Pub (207-945-6800; paddymurphyspub.com), 26 Main St., Bangor. Hungarian mushroom soup and hot pulled pork sandwich. Colcannon, Guinness beef stew, bangers and mash with pork sausages. Entrées $9–23.

Giacomo's (207-947-3702; giacomos-bangor.com), 1 Central St., Bangor. Open Mon.–Wed. 7–6, Thu.–Fri. till 9, Sat. 8–9, Sun. 11–3. Brett Settle has run Giacomo's since Sept. 2009. His kitchen turns out "vegetable antipasta"—focaccia stuffed with roasted red peppers, artichoke hearts, olives, and Fontina, for example. Wine and fine coffee served.

Captain Nick's (207-942-6444), 1165 Union St., Bangor. Open daily for lunch and dinner. A large, locally popular place with good seafood and steaks.

✍ **Governor's** (207-947-7704; governorsrestaurant.com), 643 Broadway in Bangor; and 963 Stillwater Ave. in Old Town (207-827-7630). Open from early breakfast to late dinner. The Stillwater restaurant is the original in a statewide chain. A large breakfast menu, but this place is popular at all meals; hamburgers, steaks, specials like shepherd's pie, fresh strawberry pie, ice cream.

🦞 **Dysart's** (207-942-4878; dysarts .com), Coldbrook Rd., Hermon (I-95, exit 180). Open 24 hours. Billed as "the biggest truck stop in Maine," but it isn't just truckers who eat here. Known for great road food, good prices, and a 1-pound burger.

Homemade bread and seafood are specialties.

Pat's Pizza (207-866-2111), 11 Mill St., Orono. A local landmark, especially popular with high school and university students and families. Now franchised throughout the state, this is the original with booths and a jukebox, back dining room, and downstairs taproom; Pat's son Bruce and his family still run the place. Pizza, sandwiches, Italian dinners.

Java Joe's Café (207-990-0500), 98 Central St., Bangor. Breakfast, lunch, and the all-important morning latte. Open Mon.–Sat. 7:30–4, with bagels, eggs, sandwiches, salads and wraps, and Thai specialties.

Sea Dog Brewing Company (207-947-8004; seadogbrewing.com), 26 Front St. Open 11:30 AM–1 AM daily. Microbrews and a long menu of seafood, burgers, and steaks. A great deck next to the Penobscot River, and the winter view is good, too.

COFFEEHOUSES AND SNACKS

✐ **The Store Ampersand** (207-866-4110), 22 Mill St., Orono. A combination health food store, coffee bar, and gift shop. Great for snacks (try the big cookies) and specialty items. Wine and cheese.

Friar's Bakehouse (207-947-3770; franciscansofbangor.com), 21 Central St., Bangor. Open Tue.–Thu. 7–3, Fri. till 6, Sat. 8–2, give or take four minutes. This bakery run by the Franciscan Brothers of Hungary, a Roman Catholic order from Brewer, makes and sells muffins, chocolate chip cookies, whoopie pies, and lots of bread. A chapel up the stairs is always open for prayer and meditation.

Bagel Central (207-947-1654; bagel centralbangor.com), 33 Central St., Bangor. Open Mon.–Thu. 6–6, Fri. 6–5:30, closed Sat., Sun. 6–2. Bagels, bialys, and spinach knish at this kosher deli. We hear the leek and potato soup is perfect in winter; avocado vegetable sandwich, great in summer. There is a line out the door every Sunday.

✳ Entertainment

✐ **Collins Center for the Arts** (207-581-1805; box office, 207-581-1755; collinscenterforthearts.org), at the University of Maine in Orono, has become the cultural center for the area. It hosts a wide variety of concerts and events, from classical to country-and-western, children's theater, and dance. Many performances are held in Hutchins Concert Hall, Maine's first concert hall.

✐ **Penobscot Theatre Company** (207-942-3333; penobscottheatre.org), 131 Main St., Bangor. This company has been putting on quality shows since 1973. Performing in the Bangor Opera House, the company presents a variety of plays during the season; *Ink*, a world premier, was a recent production. In summer the company sponsors the Northern Writes New Play Festi-

FRIAR'S BAKEHOUSE

Nancy English

Nancy English

BAGEL CENTRAL

val, dedicated to the development of new work.

The Maine Masque (207-581-1792; umaine.edu/mainemasque), Hauck Auditorium, University of Maine, Orono. Classic and contemporary plays presented Oct.–May by University of Maine theater students.

Bass Park, 100 Dutton St., Bangor. An enormous construction project under way till 2013 leaves the old **Bangor Auditorium** and **Civic Center** (207-947-5555) operational till then. The park also hosts the **Bangor State Fair**, and **Raceway** (207-561-6100) featuring harness racing Thu.–Sun., May–July; Hollywood Slots (see *Gambling*) is across the street. Band concerts in the park by the Paul Bunyan statue on Tue. in summer.

Bangor Symphony Orchestra (207-581-1755; bangorsymphony.com). The symphony began in 1895 and is still going strong, with performances at the Collins Center for the Arts Oct.–May.

✳ Selective Shopping

BOOKSTORES

In Bangor
Antique Marketplace & Café (207-941-2111; antiquemarketplacecafe

.com), 65 Main St., Bangor. Open daily. Seventy dealers sell antiques, jewelry, furniture, rugs, tin ads, and, from four book dealers, books of all kinds. **Sarah Faragher's** stock includes secondhand editions of great books, with an emphasis on Maine, history, travel, poetry, and literature, and you can also find books from **W. J. Lippincott**.

BookMarcs Book Store (207-942-3206; bookmarcs.com), 78 Harlow St. A first-rate, full-service downtown bookstore with new, used, and discounted books. Particular specialties are books about Maine and by Maine authors. Java Joe's Café is connected to the store.

✿ **The Briar Patch** (207-941-0255), 27 Central St. A large and exceptional children's bookstore, with creative toys, puzzles, and games.

Top Shelf Comics (207-947-4939; tcomics.com), 25 Central St., Bangor. All the newest comics, as well as old comics, and coins and paper money.

Elsewhere
Mr. Paperback (207-942-9191). This store at the Airport Mall has a good selection of Maine books.

ANTIQUE MARKETPLACE AND CAFÉ

Nancy English

Books-A-Million (207-990-3300), 116 Bangor Mall Blvd. at Bangor Mall. This business took over an outpost of the now-closed **Borders** chain, and is a good place to both find a book, movie, or CD, and drink coffee.

CANOES Old Town Canoe Visitors' Center and Factory Outlet Store (207-827-1530; oldtowncanoe.com), 125 Gilman Falls Ave., Old Town. Open daily Apr.–Sept.; closed Sun.–Mon. Oct.–Mar. Varieties of canoes and kayaks sold include polyethylene, wood, and Royalex. Factory-tour video shows how canoes are made. Memorabilia and museum-quality wooden canoes and a birch-bark canoe are on display, not for sale. Many accessories from parent company Johnson Outdoors as well as from Eureka Tent, Necky Kayak, and more.

SPECIAL SHOPS Winterport Boot Shop (207-989-6492), 264 State St., Twin City Plaza, Brewer. Largest selection of Red Wing work boots in the Northeast. Proper fit for sizes 4–16, all widths.

Valentine Footwear (207-907-2128; valentinefootwear.com), 115 Main St., Bangor. Opened in 2011 by the daughter of the owner of Winterport Boot Shop, Valentine Footwear was embraced with open arms. "Well-made, comfortable-yet-cute shoes" selected by a woman brought up in the business and on sale here.

Antique Marketplace & Café (207-941-2111; antiquemarketplacecafe .com), 65 Main St., Bangor. Booths display antiques (also see *Books*), and the café serves tea, coffee, sandwiches, salads, and pie.

🌿 **The Grasshopper Shop** (207-947-5989; grasshoppershop.com), Bangor International Airport. Trendy women's, children's, and infants' clothing, as well as toys, jewelry, gifts, and housewares.

One Lupine Fiber Arts (207-992-4140 and 207-299-6716; onelupine .com), 170 Park St., Bangor. Open Mon.–Sat. 11–5, Tue.–Fri. 11–6. Felting, scrollwork ornaments, and chiffon scarves in beautiful colors, as well as coats, balls, and other felt items, many made with Maine-based yarns and fibers, also available for sale. American-made fine handwork from jewelry to pottery and painting.

Central Street Farmhouse (207-992-4454; centralstreetfarmhouse .com), 30 Central St., Bangor. The spiritual center of homebrewing, with "Maine's largest selections of grain and hops." Maple syrup, feed-bag shopping bags, and fine local products for sale; upstairs is a baby boutique with onesies and cloth diapers made here.

✳ Special Events

April: **Kenduskeag Stream Canoe Race**.

All summer: Free outdoor movies, **Pickering Square**; **Cool Sounds** concerts; **Tommyknockers and More Bus Tour**, the only Stephen King Literary tour in the world.

July: **Bangor State Fair**, Bass Park—agricultural fair with harness racing.

August: **WLBZ Sidewalk Art Festival**, downtown Bangor. **American Folk Festival** (last weekend), Bangor—a celebration of American culture through song, dance, storytelling, and food. Free. **KahBang Music, Film & Art Festival**.

Weekend after Labor Day: **Bangor Car Show: Wheels on the Waterfront**—more than 300 cars.

New Year's Eve: **Downtown Countdown** in Bangor centers on a beach ball wrapped in Christmas lights that gets thrown off a tall building.

THE NORTH MAINE WOODS

Like "Down East," the "North Maine Woods" may seem a bit of a mirage, always over the next hill. Much of this land lies within the area already described in this book as the "Western Mountains and Lakes Region." However, the one particular tract of forest that tends to be equated with "the Maine Woods" is the section bordered on the north and west by Canada, the one that on highway maps shows no roads. This is the largest stretch of unpeopled woodland in the East, but wilderness it's not.

Private ownership of this sector, technically part of Maine's 10.5 million acres known as the unorganized townships, dates to the 1820s when Maine was securing independence from Massachusetts. The mother state, her coffers at their usual low, stipulated that an even division of all previously undeeded wilderness be part of the separation agreement. The woods were quickly sold by the legislature for 12¢ to 38¢ per acre.

Pine was king, and men had already been working this woodland for decades. They lived together in remote lumber camps such as the one Thoreau visited in 1846 at Chesuncook. They worked in subzero temperatures, harvesting and hauling logs on sleds to frozen rivers. They rode those logs through the roaring spring runoffs, driving them across vast lakes and sometimes hundreds of miles downstream to mills. These were lumberjacks, the stuff of children's stories and adult songs, articles, and books. They were the cowboys of the East, larger than ordinary men.

What's largely forgotten is that by the second half of the 19th century, the North Maine Woods were more accessible and popular with visitors than they are today. By 1853 *Atlantic Monthly* editor James Russell Lowell could chug toward Moosehead on a cinder-spraying train; by 1900 Bostonians could ride comfortably to Greenville in a day, while Manhattanites could bed down in a Pullman and

LUMBER TRUCKS RULE ON THE GOLDEN ROAD

Liam Davis

Christina Tree

MOUNT KATAHDIN

sleep their way to the foot of Moosehead Lake. The Bangor & Aroostook Railroad published annual glossy illustrated guidebooks to Moosehead and its environs, and detailed maps were circulated.

By 1882 the Kineo House, with 500 guest rooms and half a mile of verandas overlooking Moosehead Lake, was said to be the largest hotel in America. In Greenville, Sanders & Sons, the era's L.L. Bean, outfitted city "sports" with the clothing, firearms, and fishing gear with which to meet their guides and board steamers bound for far corners of the lake, frequently continuing on by foot and canoe to dozens of backwoods "sporting camps."

With the advent of World War I, the Depression, and the switch from rails to roads, the North Woods dimmed as a travel destination. In the 1920s the steamboat *Katahdin*, once the pride of the Moosehead fleet, was sold to a logging company as a towboat, and the Maine state legislature refused to protect woodland around Mount Katahdin, the state's highest mountain. Governor Percival Baxter bought the core of current Baxter State Park with his own money. In 1938 the Kineo House burned to the ground.

In ensuing decades the wisdom of Governor Baxter's purchase became increasingly apparent. Mount Katahdin, as the terminus of the 2,144-mile Appalachian Trail from Georgia, attracted recognition and serious hikers from throughout the world. Hunters and fishermen continued to make spring and fall trips to their fathers' haunts, and families to find their way to reasonably priced lake camps. In 1966 a 92-mile ribbon of lakes, ponds, rivers, and streams running northwest from Baxter State Park was designated the Allagash Wilderness Waterway, triggering interest among canoeists—though only a very narrow corridor was actually preserved because the state owns only 400 to 800 feet from the high-water mark. Still, it can control activities up to a mile on each side of the river.

MALE MOOSE

Maine Office of Tourism

Meanwhile the timber industry was transforming. This woodland was harvested initially for tall timber, but in the late 19th century the value of less desirable softwood increased when the process of making paper from wood fibers was rediscovered. (It seems that the method first used in AD 105 had been forgotten, and New England mills had been using rags to make paper.) By the turn of the 20th century many pulp and paper mills had moved to their softwood source. The city of Millinocket boomed into existence. The population skyrocketed from two families to 2,000 people between 1888 and 1900, and to 5,000 in 1912, around mammoth mills built by Great Northern, which also maintained far-flung farms to support more widely scattered lumber camps.

In 1900 it's said that some 30,000 men worked seasonally in the Maine woods. By 1970, however, just 6,500 loggers were working year-round; by 1988 this number fell to 3,660. On the other hand, the total wood harvest in Maine doubled between 1940 and 1970, and again by the mid-1980s. These numbers mirror technological changes, from axes to chain saws, skidders, and ultimately mammoth machines unselectively cutting thousands of trees per day, creating clear-cuts as large as 8 miles square. Today the Maine Forest Practices Act does not allow clear-cuts larger than 75 acres.

Changes in North Woods ownership in recent years have been cataclysmic. Through most of the 20th century large timber companies assumed much of the management responsibility and taxes as well as the cost of building hundreds of miles of roads (log drives ended in the 1970s) in this area. They also accommodated limited recreation, maintaining campsites and honoring long-term leases for both commercial and private camps. In recent decades, however, mergers and sales have fragmented ownership, and much of this "working forest" has been bought by firms without local ties, and not just by timber companies but by investment businesses as well. During the 1990s, 3,000 seasonal camps were built within the state's unorganized territories (not all of them in this particular area) and far more than half of that 10.5 million acres allocated to private ownership in 1827 has changed hands in the past decade. Since 1998 one-third of the land in Maine's North Woods has changed hands.

North Woods ownership continues to shift and splinter. On the one hand, the organization RESTORE: The North Woods advocates creation of a North Woods National Park. On the other, park opponents argue that a national park would destroy the traditional economy and lifestyle in the region. Maine's Bureau of Parks and Lands has quietly acquired large tracts, and major nonprofit groups such as The Nature Conservancy, The New England Forestry Foundation, The Forest Society of Maine, and the Appalachian Mountain Club have secured thousands of acres outright and over 1 million acres in easements that permit timber management. Grassroots coalition groups like the Northern Forest Alliance work quietly to maintain the balance between economic and recreational needs.

Forms of recreation have also significantly altered in recent decades, notably with the popularity of snowmobiling and whitewater rafting, thanks to the area's relatively reliable snow cover and even more reliable whitewater releases on the West Branch of the Penobscot River. Many visitors also now use all-terrain vehicles (ATVs) on woods roads. The resurgence of the moose population has sparked these animals' popularity as something to see rather than shoot. Fly-fishing, kayaking, dogsledding, hiking, and cross-country skiing all contribute to the rediscovery of the beauty of these magnificent woods, a phenomenon not to be confused with second-home development.

To date the effect of increased visitation has been limited. In the lake-studded area around Millinocket and Mount Katahdin, rafting outfitters have established bases and lodging options. On the western shore of Moosehead Lake, the family-owned Birches resort now holds 11,000 acres geared to nonmotorized use, and east of the lake the Appalachian Mountain Club (AMC) has acquired 66,500 aces and three historic, full-service sporting camps dedicated to hiking, biking, cross-country skiing, and snowshoeing. The country's oldest nonprofit outdoor recreation and conservation group, the AMC is working to maintain an extensive trail system.

North Maine Woods, a long-established nonprofit cooperative organization of landowners, still maintains hundreds of campsites and operates staffed checkpoints at entry points to industrial logging roads (visitors pay a day-use and camping fee). These roads have themselves altered the look and nature of the North Woods. Many remote sporting camps, for a century accessible only by water, and more recently by air, are now a bumpy ride from the nearest town. However, many of the sporting camps themselves haven't changed since the turn of the 20th century. They are Maine's inland windjammers, holdovers from another era and a precious endangered Maine species, threatened by competition from the region's new second-home owners as well by land sales and access.

Maine's North Woods are at a tipping point. Seattle-based Plum Creek Timber Company, the country's largest landowner, has received permission from Maine's Land Use Regulation Commission (LURC) to rezone thousands of acres around Moosehead Lake—which it had purchased at $200 per acre, when it was zoned for forestry and backcountry recreation. Given the current recession, Plum Creek's plans for house lots and resorts are on hold, but it remains the largest single land development proposal in Maine's history. Come soon.

There are four major approaches to the North Woods. The longest, most scenic route is up the Kennebec River, stopping to raft in The Forks, and along the Moose River to the village of Rockwood at the dramatic narrows of Moosehead Lake, then down along the lake to Greenville, New England's largest seaplane base.

From Rockwood or Greenville you can hop a floatplane to a sporting camp or set off up the eastern shore of Moosehead to the woodland outpost of Kokadjo and on up to the Golden Road, a 96-mile private logging road running east from Quebec through uninterrupted forest to Millinocket. As Thoreau did in the 1850s, you can canoe up magnificent Chesuncook Lake, camping or staying in the outpost of Chesuncook Village. With increased interest in rafting down the West Branch of the Penobscot River through Ripogenus Gorge and the Cribworks, this stretch of the Golden Road has become known as the West Branch Region.

The second and third routes, leading respectively to Greenville and Millinocket, both begin at the I-95 exit in Newport and head up through Southern Piscataquis County, itself an area of small villages, large lakes, and stretches of woodland that here include Gulf Hagas, Maine's most magnificent gorge.

For those who come this distance primarily to climb Mount Katahdin and camp in Baxter State Park, or to raft the West Branch of the Penobscot, the quickest route is up I-95 to Medway and in through Millinocket; it's 18 miles to the Togue Pond Gatehouse and Baxter State Park.

While I-95 has replaced the Penobscot River as the highway into the North Maine Woods, it has not displaced Bangor, sited on both the river and I-95 (25 miles east of Newport and 60 miles south of Medway) as the area's commercial hub and gateway. A recent effort promotes the two counties—Penobscot and Piscataquis, which include Moosehead Lake, Baxter State Park, Bangor, and a good portion of the North Maine Woods—as a distinct region named "the Maine Highlands."

Contrary to its potato-fields image, Aroostook County to the north is also largely wooded and includes a major portion of the Allagash Wilderness Waterway. Northern reaches of Baxter State Park and the lakes nearby are best accessed from the park's northern entrance via Patten in "The County." Both Ashland and Portage are also points of entry, and Shin Pond serves as the seaplane base for this northernmost reach of the North Maine Woods.

GUIDANCE **North Maine Woods** (207-435-6213; northmainewoods.org) publishes map/guides that show logging roads with current checkpoints, user fees, campsites, and a list of outfitters and camps licensed and insured to operate on the property. The website is excellent.

Maine Bureau of Parks and Lands (207-287-3821; parksandlands.com). The bureau publishes a map/guide identifying holdings, but what's golden here is the website. It details specific areas such as Nahmakanta Public Reserved Land—43,000 acres of backcountry hiking trails and remote campsites.

Maine Sporting Camp Association (mainesportingcamps.com) maintains an excellent website.

Maine Forest Products Council (maineforest.org) offers links to local resources. Also check the **New England Forestry Foundation** (newenglandforestry.org), the **Northern Forest Alliance** (northernforestalliance.org), and **The Nature Conservancy** (nature.org).

SUGGESTED READING *Northeastern Wilds: Journeys of Discovery in the Northern Forest*, photography and text by Stephen Gorman (Appalachian Mountain Club Books, 2002). *The Maine Woods*, by Henry David Thoreau (Penguin Nature Library). *The Maine Atlas and Gazetteer* (DeLorme, 2007) is essential for navigating this region.

MOOSEHEAD LAKE AREA

As Rt. 15 crests Indian Hill, you see for a moment what Henry David Thoreau described so well from this spot in 1858: "A suitably wild looking sheet of water, sprinkled with low islands . . . covered with shaggy spruce and other wild wood." After a sunset by the shore of Moosehead Lake you also see what he meant by: "A lake is the Earth's eye, looking into which the beholder measures the depth of his own nature."

Moosehead is Maine's largest lake—40 miles long, up to 20 miles wide, with some 400 miles of shoreline—and its surface is spotted with more than 50 islands. Greenville at its toe is the sole "organized" town (pop. 1,314 in winter, around 10,000 in summer). Rockwood, with fewer than 300 residents, is halfway up the western shore.

Moosehead's shoreline remains predominantly green, but Maine's Land Use Regulatory Commission (LURC) has approved the request by Seattle-based Plum Creek Timber Company for rezoning to permit some 975 homes plus resort units in the area. Given the current recession, not much is happening—but the green light is there.

The good news is that as timber companies have moved to divest themselves of many thousands of acres of forest in this region, state and nonprofit conservation organizations, partnering with one another and with Plum Creek and other commercial owners, have preserved 800,000 continuous acres to the east of Moosehead Lake with a mix of responsible forestry practices and recreation. The Appalachian Mountain Club (AMC), long known for its services to hikers in the White Mountains of New Hampshire, has acquired three classic old sporting camps and is partnering with a fourth to encourage educational programs and non-motorized recreation within a 63-mile-long corridor stretching from the Katahdin Iron Works north to Baxter State Park, including hundreds of lakes and ponds and many mountains, notably majestic 3,644-foot-high White Cap, the highest peak between Bigelow and Katahdin.

Greenville began as a farm town but soon discovered its best crops to be winter lumbering and summer tourists—a group that, since train service and grand hotels have vanished, now consists largely of anglers, canoeists, and whitewater rafters in spring and summer, and hunters in late fall. Thanks to snowmobilers, augmented by cross-country skiers and ice fishermen, winter is now almost equally as popular. In late September and early fall when the foliage is most brilliant and mirrored in the lake, leaf-peepers are, however, still surprisingly few.

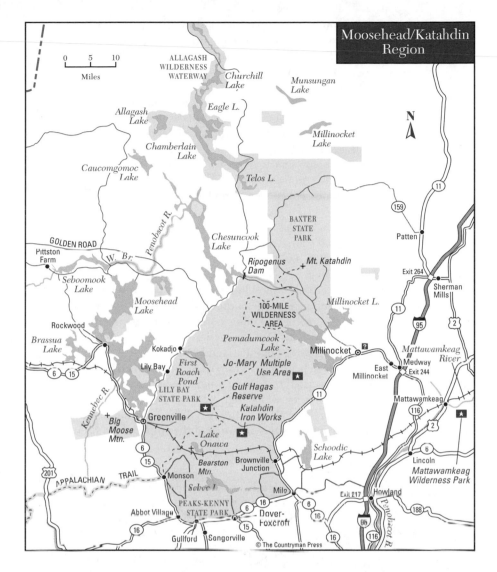

Moosehead/Katahdin Region

Unlike 1890s "sports" (the game hunters and trophy fishermen who put Moosehead Lake on the world's resort map), many current outdoors enthusiasts want to watch—not kill—wildlife and to experience "wilderness" completely but quickly; that is, by plunging through whitewater in a rubber raft, pedaling a mountain bike over woods trails, or paddling an hour or two in Thoreau's trail or in search of a moose.

Moosehead has become Maine's moose mecca. Experts debate whether the name of the lake stems from its shape or from the number of moose you can see there. During "Moosemainea," a mid-May through mid-June festival that courts Moosemaniacs with a series of special events, moose sightings average 3,500.

Immense and flanked by mountains, the lake possesses unusual beauty and offers families a wide choice of rustic, old-fashioned "camps" at reasonable prices as well as an increasing number of upscale inns and B&Bs. Greenville remains a lumbermen's depot with a salting of souvenir and offbeat shops. It's also still a major seaplane base, with flying services competing to ferry visitors to remote camps and campsites in the working woodland to the north and east.

The community of Rockwood, half an hour's drive north of Greenville on the lake's west shore, is even more of an outpost: a cluster of sporting camps and stores between the lake and the Moose River. Rockwood sits at the lake's narrows, across from its most dramatic landmark: the sheer cliff face of Mount Kineo, a place revered by Native Americans. According to local legend, the mountain is the petrified remains of a monster moose sent to earth by the Great Spirit as a punishment for sins. It was also the Native Americans' source of a flintlike stone used for arrowheads. The Mount Kineo House once stood at the foot of this outcropping. First opened as a tavern in 1847, it evolved into one of the largest hotels in America, maintaining its own farm as well as a golf course, yacht club, and stables. It's all but vanished, but the gold course remains. Most of Kineo, an islandlike peninsula, is now owned by the state, and the climb to the abrupt summit is one of the most rewarding hikes in Maine.

Most Greenville visitors explore Moosehead's eastern shore at least as far as Lily Bay State Park, and many continue to the outpost village of Kokadjo, prime moose-watching country. It's another 40 miles northeast over private roads to Chesuncook Lake and to Ripogenus Dam, from which logging roads lead north into the Allagash and east to Baxter State Park and Millinocket.

In winter this vast area is dependably snow covered and stays that way well into March, a phenomenon appreciated by snowmobilers—who have become the mainstay of the winter economy, enabling area lodging, including remote camps, to remain open. Formal trail systems, along with several sporting camps, cater to cross-country skiers. In recent years the presence of the Appalachian Mountain

MOUNT KINEO FROM ROCKWOOD LANDING

Bill Davis

Bill Davis

NORTHEAST GUIDE SERVICE, GREENVILLE

Club, offering lodge-to-lodge skiing, snowshoeing, and dogsledding as well as hiking and mountain biking, has contributed substantially to the appeal of traversing this backcountry, especially in all its frozen magnificence.

GUIDANCE Moosehead Lake Region Chamber of Commerce (207-695-2702 or 1-888-876-2778; mooseheadlake.org) is a four-season resource. The walk-in information center is at the DOT rest area, 2 miles south of town on Rt. 15, open year-round, Mon.–Sat. 10–4.

GETTING THERE *By car:* Greenville is 54 miles north of I-95 exit 157, at Newport. Follow Rt. 7 to Dexter, Rt. 23 to Sangerville (Guilford), and Rt. 15 to Greenville. The longer, more scenic route is up Rt. 201 (I-95 exit 133) through The Forks (see "Upper Kennebec Valley" for suggestions about whitewater rafting). From Rt. 201 in Jackman, take Rt. 5/15 east to Rockwood.

GETTING AROUND *By air:* **Currier's Flying Service** (207-695-2778; curriers flyingservice.com), Greenville Junction, offers day trips; scenic flights, including Mount Katahdin, Mount Kineo, and others; and service to camps. They will book camps and guides. **Jack's Air Service** (207-695-3020), May–Oct. 1, caters to Allagash canoe trips, fly-ins to housekeeping cottages, and sightseeing flights.

By car: If you plan to venture out on the area's network of private roads, be forewarned that there are periodic gate fees and you need a car with high clearance, preferably four wheel drive.

By boat: **Kineo Shuttle** (207-534-9012) has frequent in-season departures from Rockwood Landing to Kineo for hiking and golf.

WHEN TO COME Greenville's seasons begin with spring fishing, which overlaps with "Moosemainea." June can be uncomfortably buggy (blackflies). The busy season is July 4 through the mid-September annual "fly-in" of floatplanes from all over North America. Fall is beautiful but low-key until deer season begins in mid-November. With snow comes snowmobile season. March brings bright blue days and dependable snow cover; it's our favorite month for ski treks in this region.

✳ To See

Moose. Don't leave the area without seeing at least one. In this area moose are said to outnumber people three to one. "Moosemainea," sponsored by the Moosehead Lake Chamber of Commerce, is mid-May–mid-June, but chances are you can spot the lake's mascot any dawn or dusk at local hangouts like the DOT site on Rt. 15, 4.5 miles south of Indian Hill, Lazy Tom Bog in Kokadjo, or on the road from Rockwood to Pittston Farm. Best, however, to leave the driving to someone else. The **Birches Resort** (207-534-7305) in Rockwood offers moose cruises aboard pontoon boats as well as moose safaris by kayak. **Northwoods Outfitters** (207-695-3288) and **Young's Guide Service** (207-695-2661) in Greenville offer moose-watching excursions by kayak or canoe. **Northeast Guide Service** (207-695-0151) offers early-evening van tours, motorboat tours, and canoe or kayak paddles into their secret spots. **Historic Pittston Farm** (207-280-0000) north of Rockwood is deep in moose country, an added incentive for many to drive up there or to **Northern Pride Lodge** (207-695-2890) for dinner. See mooseheadlake.org for more outfitters offering moose safaris.

THE S/S *KATAHDIN* SETS OUT FROM GREENVILLE

♂ ♿ The **S/S *Katahdin*** and **Moosehead Marine Museum** (207-695-2716; katahdincruises.com), Greenville. This vintage-1914 steamboat sails Tue.–Sat., late June–Columbus Day, on a fairly complicated schedule. Three-hour cruises are the most popular ($32 adults, $28 seniors, $17 ages 11–16), and depart at 12:30 PM. Five-hour cruises on selective Wed. require a minimum of 30 people. One of 50 steamboats on the lake at its height as a resort destination, the Katahdin was the last to survive, converted to diesel in 1922 and in the 1930s modified to haul booms of logs, something we can remember her doing in 1976, the year of the nation's last log drive. This graceful 115-foot, 225-passenger boat was restored through volunteer effort and relaunched in 1985. The Louis Oakes Map Room displays regional, historical maps, and displays depict the lake's resort history from 1836.

Eveleth-Crafts-Sheridan House (207-695-2909; mooseheadhistory.org), 444 Pritham Ave., Greenville. Guided tours offered June–Sept., Wed.–Fri. 1–4. $5 adults, $2 children under 12. Home of the Moosehead Historical Society, this is a genuinely interesting 19th-century home with an 1880s kitchen and displays on the region's history, including postcards and photos picturing early hotels and steamboats; changing exhibits. The carriage house has been renovated as a lumberman's museum. There is a fine collection of Indian artifacts, also a one-room schoolhouse. The related **Center for Moosehead History**, 6 Lakeview Ave., Greenville, housed in a former Universalist church, is open Thu.–Sat. 10–4 with exhibits of Native American artifacts and an evolving local aviation museum and changing exhibits.

SCENIC DRIVES

Along the western shore
Follow Rt. 6/15 north through Greenville Junction to Rockwood and take the **shuttle to Mount Kineo** (see *Getting Around*); allow the better part of a day for exploring this dramatic spot. From Rockwood, you can stop by **The Birches**

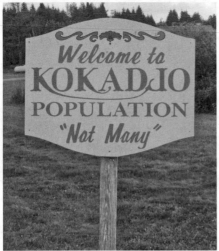

Bill Davis

KOKADJO IS 18 MILES NORTH OF GREEVILLE

Resort (see *Lodging*) for dinner or a boat excursion, and continue north for another bumpy 20 miles to **Historic Pittston Farm** (again, see *Lodging*)— once the hub of Great Northern's operations for this entire western swath of North Woods. Note that from Rockwood you can also continue on to Quebec City (via Jackman).

Along the eastern shore

Lily Bay State Park (207-695-2700), 8 miles north of Greenville, offers a sandy beach, a grassy picnicking area, and camping. It's a superlatively beautiful spot. $4.50 nonresidents, $3 residents, $1.50 all seniors day-use fee.

Kokadjo, 18 miles north of Greenville, is a 100-acre parcel of independently owned land on First Roach Pond, in the center of lumber-company-owned forest. Most of the buildings here were once part of a lumbering station and are now camps attached to the **Kokadjo Trading Post** (serving meals and renting cabins and ATVs); **Northern Pride Lodge** rents canoes and boats.

Greenville Road to the Golden Road. Continuing north, remember to pull over for lumber trucks. This is their road and it's deeply rutted in spots, improving slightly beyond the (now unstaffed) gate entering paper company land but still extremely rough for the dozen miles before you hit the Golden Road. Turn right (east). **Cushing's Landing**, at the foot of Chesuncook Lake, is worth a stop. The **woodsman's memorial** here was created from a post in the doorway of a Bangor tavern; it's decorated with tools of the trade and an iron bean pot. This is also the logical boat launch for visiting **Chesuncook Village**, one of the few surviving examples of a 19th-century North Maine Woods lumbermen's village, now on the National Register of Historic Places. In summer access is by charter aircraft from Greenville or by boat from Chesuncook Dam. In winter you can come by snowmobile. Writing about the village in 1853, Henry David Thoreau noted, "Here immigration is a tide which may ebb when it has swept away the pines." Today a church, a graveyard (relocated from the shore to a hollow in the woods when Great Northern raised the level of the lake a few years ago), the **Chesuncook Lake Lodge** (see

LILY BAY STATE PARK

Christina Tree

Lodging), and a huddle of houses are all that remain of the village.

Ripogenus Dam, just east of Chesuncook Lake, is a spot from which to view the gorge. Rafting trips on the West Branch of the Penobscot begin a mile downstream, below the power station. This is the most challenging commercial whitewater run in Maine. The river drops more than 70 feet per mile—seething and roiling through **Ripogenus Gorge**—and continues another 12 miles, with stretches of relatively calm water punctuated by steep drops. Cross Ripogenus Dam to the **Telos Road**, leading to the **Allagash Wilderness Waterway**, a 92-mile-long chain of lakes, ponds, rivers, and streams that snakes through the heart of the North Woods. The traditional

Christina Tree

CUSHING'S LANDING AT THE FOOT OF CHESUNCOOK LAKE

canoe trip through the Allagash takes 10 days, but 2- and 3-day trips can be worked out. Brook trout, togue, and lake whitefish are plentiful. For details, see *Canoeing the Allagash* in "What's Where" in the front of the book and *Canoe and Kayak Guided Trips*, below. Continue on along the Golden Road to **Baxter State Park** and Millinocket.

✳ To Do

AIRPLANE RIDES See *Getting Around*.

ATV TOURING The region is home to a 300-plus-mile trail system. **Moosehead ATV Riders** (207-695-8928), the local club, also maintain a well-marked trail system on the west side of Moosehead Lake; **Northwoods Outfitters** (207-695-3288) and **Moose Mountain Inn** (207-695-3321) rent ATVs.

BIRDING Warblers and many elusive species, including the boreal chickadee, gray jay, black-backed woodpecker, Bicknell's thrush, and white-winged crossbill, can be found in local bogs and woodland. Also see *Hiking*. The **Appalachian Mountain Club** offers birding programs at its Little Lyford Lodge and Cabins and Medawisla Wilderness Lodge and Cabins (see *Lodging*). For **Borestone Mountain Audubon Sanctuary** see *Hiking*. The beautiful old lodges here are available for rent to groups (207-781-2330).

BOAT EXCURSIONS See S/S *Katahdin* under *To See*. That's the big one.

The Black Frog (207-695-1100) in Greenville offers seasonal cocktail cruises (4–6) from its restaurant. **The Birches Resort** (207-534-7305; birches.com) offers seasonal pontoon-boat cruises around Mount Kineo from its marina in Rockwood. **Northwoods Outfitters** (1-866-223-1380; maineoutfitter.com) also offers excursions to Mount Kineo and sunset cruises.

BOAT RENTALS Beaver Cove Marina (207-695-3526), 16 Coveside Rd. (off Lily Bay Rd.). Powerboats, fishing skiffs, canoes, and kayaks.

CANOE AND KAYAKING RENTALS are available in Greenville from **Northwoods Outfitters** (1-866-223-1380; maineoutfitter.com) and **Indian Hill Trading Post** (207-695-2104); in Rockwood from **The Birches Resort** (207-534-75305; birches.com). See mooseheadlake.org for a more extensive list. Northwoods Outfitters offers shuttle service.

Note: Most sporting camps also rent canoes or kayaks, and flying services will ferry canoes into remote back-country.

Shannon LeRoy, courtesy of the AMC

KAYAKERS MEET MOOSE

CANOE AND KAYAK GUIDED TRIPS ✍ **Allagash Canoe Trips** (207-237-3077; allagashcanoetrips.com), based in Greenville, May–Oct. A family business since 1953, this is the oldest continuously running guided canoe trip service in Maine. It's now operated by third-generation guide Chip Cochrane and offers weeklong expeditions into the Allagash Wilderness Waterway, on the West Branch of the Penobscot, and on the St. John River. Also special teen trips. Sept.–May, Chip (a former member of the U.S. ski team) coaches at Carrabassett Valley Academy at Sugarloaf. **Northwoods Outfitters** (maineoutfitters.com) offers four- to seven-day Allagash and multiday guided canoe trips. Greenville-based **Northeast Guide Service** (northeastguideservice.com) offers overnight guided paddling trips.

FLY-FISHING AT MEDAWISLA NEAR MOOSEHEAD LAKE

Lori Duff, courtesy of the AMC

FISHING This region is a famed source of eastern brook trout, lake trout, blue-back trout, landlocked salmon, and smallmouth bass. Aside from its centerpiece lake (75,000 acres), the region includes 600 lakes and ponds, 30-plus miles of mainstream rivers, and more than 3,000 miles of tributaries. Rental boats and boat launches are so plentiful that they defy listing (see mooseheadlake.org).

There are two prime sources of fishing information: the state's **Inland Fisheries and Wildlife office** (207-695-3756), Greenville, and the **Maine Guide Fly Shop and Guide Service**

(207-695-2266), Main St., Greenville. At the Fly Shop, Dan Legere sells 314 different flies and a wide assortment of gear; he also works with local guides to outfit you with a boat and guide or to set up a river float trip or a fly-in expedition. The resurgence of fly-fishing as a popular sport is reflected in the variety of gear and guides available in this shop. Deep lake trolling is, however, also popular. Also see *Lodging—Sporting Camps*; all are on water and cater to fishermen.

Ice fishing usually begins in January and ends with March. Icehouse rentals are available locally. Inquire at the chamber.

GOLF Mount Kineo Golf Course (207-534-9012; in winter, 207-236-2906). A spectacularly sited nine-hole course at Kineo, accessible by frequent boat service from Rockwood; carts and club rentals; the clubhouse sells subs and snacks. Dating to the 1880s, this is one of the oldest golf courses in New England.

HIKING The not-to-be-missed hike in this area is **Mount Kineo**, described in *Green Space*.

Gulf Hagas, billed as the "Grand Canyon of Maine," is described in the Katahdin chapter. It's also accessible from Greenville via Airport Rd. When the pavement ends it's another 12.6 miles to the Hedgehog Gate ($10 for out-of-staters), where you can pick up a map. It's another 2 miles to the trailhead parking lot. In winter it's also accessible by snowshoe or ski from the AMC's Little Lyford and Gorman Chairback lodges (see *Lodging*).

𝒮 **Borestone Mountain Audubon Sanctuary** (207-781-2330, ext. 215; maine audubon.org). From Rt. 6/15 in Monson turn north onto Elliotsville Rd. Proceed 8 miles and cross the bridge over Big Wilson Falls. Bear left, uphill over railroad tracks. Park in lot on your left, across from the sanctuary gate. A good hike for families. The trail begins at 800 feet in elevation, and connected trails lead 2.5 miles to Borestone's rocky West Peak; a blazed trail continues another 0.5 mile to the East Peak (elevation 2,000 feet) for a 360-degree view.

Check local sources for details about hiking **Little and Big Spencer Mountains** and **Elephant Mountain,**

HORSEBACK RIDING Rockies Golden Acres (207-695-3229; cell, 207-280-0136), Greenville, offers 1½- to 2-hour trail rides through the woods to Sawyer Pond; mountain views.

MARINAS Big Lake Equipment Marina (207-695-4487), 25 Lakeview St., Greenville, offers slips, fuel, and supplies. **Beaver Cove Marina** (207-395-3526; beavercovemarina.com), 8 miles north of Greenville on the eastern side of the lake, offers slips, boat launch, fuel, repairs; also see *Boat Rentals*.

MOUNTAIN BIKING Rentals are available from **Northwoods Outfitters** (207-695-3288) in Greenville and from **The Birches Resort** (207-534-7305) in Rockwood, which maintains an extensive trail network on its 10,000 wooded acres.

The Appalachian Mountain Club (outdoors.org/mwi) maintains an ever-increasing network of bike/ski trails among and around its backwoods lodges and cabins.

RECREATIONAL FACILITY ✐ **Greenville Athletic Complex** at Greenville High School, Pritham Ave., Greenville. Facilities include an outdoor rink for skateboarding, roller hockey in summer, and ice hockey in winter, as well as a 0.25-mile, 8-foot-wide paved in-line skating track; also a sand volleyball court, a 0.25-mile running track, outdoor tennis courts, a basketball court, and a playground.

SWIMMING See **Lily Bay State Park** under *Scenic Drives*.

Red Cross Beach, halfway between Greenville Village and the Junction, is a good beach on the lake, with lifeguards.

WHITEWATER RAFTING AND KAYAKING Moosehead Lake is equidistant from Maine's two most popular rafting routes—**Kennebec Gorge** and **Ripogenus Gorge**. See "Upper Kennebec" and "Katahdin Region." **Northeast Guide Service** (1-888-484-3317; northeastguideservice.com), based at the Indian Trading Post Plaza, Greenville. Veteran guide Jeremy Hargreaves offers daily rafting trips mid-April–mid-Oct.; also moose tours.

✳ Winter Sports

CROSS-COUNTRY SKIING AND SNOWSHOEING Formal touring centers aside, this region's vast network of snowmobile trails and frozen lakes constitutes splendid opportunities for backcountry skiing.

Northwoods Outfitters (207-695-3288), Main St., Greenville, is a full-service retail shop, selling and renting cross-country skis and snowshoes; offering a list of trails.

Birches Ski Touring Center (207-534-7305), Rockwood, rents equipment, offers lessons, and maintains an extensive network of trails, taking advantage of an 11,000-acre forested spread across the neck between Brassua and Moosehead Lakes; you can spend the night in yurts spaced along the trail. You can also ski to Tomhegan, 10 miles up the lake, or out past the ice-fishing shanties to Kineo. Rentals and instruction; snowshoes, too.

The Appalachian Mountain Club (outdoors.org) owns **Little Lyford Lodge and Cabins** and **Medawisla Wilderness Lodge and Cabins**, both remote sporting camps, and with **West Branch Pond Camps** (see *Remote Sporting Camps*) maintains 80 miles of groomed ski trails for lodge-to-lodge cross-country tours. We did this and can vouch for the improved access the AMC has brought to one of the most splendid cross-country experiences in New England.

DOGSLEDDING **Moose Country Guiding Adventures** (207-876-4907; moosecountrysafaris.com), 191 N. Dexter Rd., Sangerville. Ed Mathew offers one- and two-hour trips in the Moosehead Lake region, with heated warming huts along the way. **Song in the Woods** (207-876-4736; songinthewoods.com), Abbot. Stephen Medera and his team of huskies offer sled rides ranging from two hours to multiday adventures. Also see **Nahmakanta Lake Camps** (207-731-8888; mainedogsledding.com) in the Katahdin chapter. Based at in Rainbow Township, halfway between Greenville and Millinocket, this is the most extensive dogsledding program around.

SNOWMOBILING is huge in this area, with 500 well-maintained miles of snowmobile trails. **Moosehead Riders Snowmobile Club** offers a 24-hour trail-condition report (207-695-4561) on the 166-mile trail circumnavigating the lake. The club also sponsors guided tours. Interconnecting Trail System (ITS) Rts. 85, 86, and 87 run directly through the area, and there are many locally groomed trails as well. The 100-mile Moosehead Trail circles the lake. Rt. 66 runs east–west from Mount Kineo to Kokadjo. Snowmobile rentals and guided tours are available from **Northwoods Outfitters** (207-695-3288) and **Moosehead Motorsports** (207-695-2020) in Greenville; in Rockwood **The Birches Resort** (1-800-825-9453) rents and offers guided tours. Northeast of the lake **Kokadjo Trading Post** (207-695-3993) offers rentals, cabins, and food at the hub of a trail system. See moose headlake.org for additional rental listings.

✳ Green Space

Mount Kineo is an islandlike peninsula with trails to the back side of the famous cliff that rises 763 feet above the water and the apron of land once occupied by the Kineo House resort. Most of the peninsula (8,000 acres) is now state-owned, and trails along its circumference and up the back of the cliff are maintained. Take the Indian Trail, which heads straight up over ledges that are a distinct green: This is one of the world's largest masses of rhyolite, a flintlike volcanic rock. The trail is shaded by red pines, oaks, and a surprising variety of hardwoods. The view down the lake from the fire tower is spectacular. The Bridle Trail is easier for the descent, and a good option on the way up for small children. A carriage trail also circles Mount Kineo, which is accessible from Rockwood by frequent water shuttle (see *Boat Excursions*). Bring a picnic.

Katahdin Iron Works Property falls between the Katahdin and Moosehead Lake areas, a 37,000-acre tract of forest maintained by the **Appalachian Mountain Club** (outdoors.org) with more than 55 miles of trails for hiking, snowshoeing, skiing, and mountain biking. Local snowmobile clubs also maintain 17.5 miles of groomed trails, including the east–west ITS route connecting Greenville and Brownville. Campsite reservations can be made through the **KI Jo-Mary Multiple Use Forest** (207-965-8135). Hunting, fishing, and trapping are allowed, but to protect the integrity of the headwaters of the West Branch and Pleasant Rivers, the surrounding area is closed to motorized traffic; 113 miles of logging roads remain open. The AMC maintains **Little Lyford Lodge and Cabins** and **Gorman Chairback Lodge and Cabins** in this area (see *Lodging*). **Moose Point Cabin** is available for rent. The AMC maintains an office in Greenville (207-695-3085). The **Appalachian Trail** traverses this area, and the **Gulf Hagas** section (detailed under *Green Space* in the Katahdin chapter) is spectacular. The **Chairback Mountain** section of the AT (16 miles east of Greenville) is also a popular hike.

WATERFALLS See **Gulf Hagas** (see *Green Space* in "Katahdin Region") and **Moxie Falls** (see *To See* in "Upper Kennebec Valley"), both accessible from the Greenville area. Check local sources for walking into **Little Wilson Falls**, a majestic 57-foot cascade in a forested setting.

✳ Lodging

INNS ○ ♂ The Blair Hill Inn (207-695-0224; blairhillinn.com), 351 Lily Bay Rd., P.O. Box 1288, Greenville 04441. Open seasonally. Overlooking Moosehead Lake from high atop Blair Hill, this is Maine's most gracious inland inn. The airy 1891 Victorian mansion is set high on Blair Hill with a sweeping lake view and Moose Mountain directly across—framed by huge old picture windows. The spectacular view can also be contemplated from comfortable wicker on the veranda, deep armchairs by the hearth in the living room, or tables in the dining room or delightful pub, which also has a fireplace. The mansion has been sensitively restored to its original grandeur—and then some—by Dan and Ruth McLaughlin. Upstairs guest rooms have all been deftly decorated and offer sitting area, a featherbed, fine linens, and flat-screen TVs, DVD, and CD player. Seven rooms overlook the lake (four have a wood-burning fireplace), and there is one two-room suite, good for families (children must be 10 or older). All baths are private and most are fairly spectacular, fitted with hand-cut soaps and terry-cloth robes, but there are no Jacuzzis. The original master bedroom has a hearth and a king-sized four-poster, but we could spend a week in Room 6, on the third floor, nestled under the eaves but with the same view and a terrific bath. From spring through fall the inn is filled with fresh flowers from its garden. $350–495 includes a multicourse breakfast, served on the sunporch. A five-course prix fixe dinner is served Thu.–Sat. (see *Dining Out*). Summer concerts are presented on the lawn.

⟁ The Lodge at Moosehead Lake (207-695-4400 or 1-800-825-6977; lodgeatmooseheadlake.com), 368 Lily Bay Rd., P.O. Box 1167, Greenville

04441. Open except April. In this handsome house above the lake, Linda and Dennis Bortis offer five guest rooms each designed around a theme. Carved four-poster beds depict each theme (moose, bear, loon, totem). All rooms have cable TV, gas fireplace, air-conditioning, and bath with Jacuzzi tub. A carriage house holds four suites, each with double Jacuzzi and private deck. The former owner's quarters are now another large and luxurious suite, comfortably accommodating two couples. Common space includes a living room and an informal downstairs pub with a pool table. A full breakfast is served in the glass-walled dining room, and dinner is served Fri.–Sun. In high season $275–680 (for the deluxe suite), from $219 off-season, includes a full breakfast.

♂ ⟁ Greenville Inn (207-695-2206 or 1-888-695-6000; greenvilleinn.com), Norris St., P.O. Box 1194, Greenville 04441. Open all year (B&B Nov.–May). A lumber baron's mansion set atop a hill with a view of Moosehead Lake. Rich wood paneling, embossed walls, working fireplaces, and leaded glass all contribute to the sense of elegance. Terry and Jeffrey Johannemann

THE GREENVILLE INN IS A LUMBER BARON'S MANSION

Bill Davis

have added air-conditioning. A master suite with a fireplace in a separate sitting room has a lake view, and there are four more attractive second-floor rooms in the mansion itself, two more spacious suites (one good for a family of six) in the Carriage House, and six cottages that sit high behind the inn, each tastefully decorated. A separate Tower Suite, painted Valentine red, has been designed for romance with an in-room, two-person Jacuzzi. Rooms $140-245, suites $275–450, cottages $240–265, buffet breakfast included; many packages. Also see *Dining Out*.

Lodging note: The above trio of inns represents by far the most elegant inn-style lodging anywhere in inland Maine and are best savored in combination with one of the area's traditional sporting camps. We suggest first heading for the woods, then luxuriating in town.

BED & BREAKFASTS Pleasant Street Inn (207-695-3400; pleasant stinn.com), 26 Pleasant St., P.O. Box 1261, Greenville 04441. An 1890s house, built proudly with a square tower and tiger oak woodwork on a quiet side street by the owner of the

JOHN WILLARD OFFERS FLOATPLANE RIDES FROM THE BIRCHES

Christina Tree

region's first big outfitter. Mary Bobletz is the innkeeper, offering six guest rooms of varying sizes and decor. A fourth-floor Tower Room, available to all, commands a view of the lake. Other common spaces include an upstairs and downstairs sitting room, a well-stocked butler's pantry, and a dining room with a fireplace, the setting for full breakfasts included in $115–165.

EASILY ACCESSIBLE SPORTING CAMPS ☉ ✖ ✿ ⚓ The Birches Resort (207-534-7305 or 1-800-825-WILD; birches.com), P.O. Box 41, Rockwood 04478. Open year-round. Since 1969 members of the Willard family have been transforming this 1930s sporting camp into a genuine all-season, many-faceted resort with more than 10,000 wooded acres. The 17 rustic cabins are spaced among birch trees along Moosehead Lake, overlooking Mount Kineo. They range from one to four bedrooms and from traditional hand-hewn log "camps" to a luxurious contemporary cabin with four bedrooms, four baths, and a hot tub. Each has at least a porch and a Franklin stove or fireplace in a sitting room, and all have a kitchen (some don't have an oven), but three meals are offered at the lodge. Inquire about "lakeside homes" and other rentals. The lodge features a cheerful open-timbered dining room (see *Dining Out*), an inviting lobby, and a living room with a hearth and a corner pub with tree stump stools. Upstairs the four guest rooms have decks overlooking the lake (shared bath); there are also "Kozy Kabins" near the lodge and several yurts scattered along wooded cross-country skiing/biking trails. Facilities include an outside hot tub and sauna near the lodge and a fitness center out by the marina. Moose cruises and guided kayak, hiking, backwoods jeep, and

A LAKESIDE CABIN AT THE BIRCHES
RESORT

biking tours are offered, along with fly-fishing, whitewater rafting, and scenic floatplane rides with innkeeper John Willard Jr., who will also shuttle guests to a secluded cove on Lake Brassau for swimming and kayaking. Sailboats, kayaks, canoes, fishing boats, and mountain bikes are available. In winter this is a major cross-country ski center, but snowmobiles are also rented and there's ice fishing within walking distance of the cabins. $85–128 double in the lodge; $100–225 per night and $1,080–1,240 per week for one- and two-bedroom "rustic" cabins; $333 per night for the luxury four-bedroom cabin sleeping eight. Cabin tents begin at $85 per first person per night, $15 per additional person; yurts begin at $80. Pets are $10 per night. Inquire about rafting, canoeing, and other packages.

☀ Wilsons on Moosehead Lake (1-800-817-2549), Greenville Junction 04442. Open year-round. Scott and Alison Snell and family have rejuvenated this classic complex just south of the East Outlet of the Kennebec River (beloved by fishermen and great for family rafting) and right on Moosehead, with 20-mile views across the

lake. Its former centerpiece, a tower-topped hotel in which President Grant once spent New Year's Day, is gone, but the area is nicely landscaped. The housekeeping cottages, one to five bedrooms, have screened porches and several have woodstoves or fireplaces. Boats, canoes, and kayak rentals, as well as guiding, are available. One-bedroom cabins $85–130 per couple, $550–795 per week.

✪ ☀ ✿ ✍ Grey Ghost Camps (207-534-7362; grayghostcamps.com), P.O. Box 35, Rockwood 02278. A dozen nicely renovated 1950s fishing camps on the Moose River, with access to Moosehead Lake. In the same family for 40 years, now ably managed by Steve and Amy Lane. One- and three-bedroom cabins, each with a full kitchen, bath, living room, TV, VCR, and CD. From $80 per night, weekly rates. Kayaks included. Boat rentals, laundry facilities, docking. Pets are $5 per day.

✿ ✍ Beaver Cove Camps (207-695-3717 or 1-800-577-3717; beavercovecamps.com), P.O. Box 1233, Greenville 04441. Open year-round. Eight miles north of Greenville on the eastern shore of Moosehead Lake are six fully equipped housekeeping cabins (four waterfront) dating to 1905, each with full kitchen and bath. Owners Dave and Marilyn Goodwin offer launching and docking facilities, canoe and kayak rentals, and wilderness guide service. $110–160 per couple per night, $660–960 per week plus $25 for each additional person; $10 per pet per night. Two-night minimum stay.

✿ Wilson Pond Camps (207-695-2860; wilsonpondcamps.com), 51 Lower Wilson Pond Rd., Greenville 04441. Open year-round. Bob and Martine Young are the owners of five modern, waterfront cottages (most with woodstove) and two cottages overlooking 7-mile-long Lower Wilson

Pond, 3.5 miles from downtown Greenville. A remote cottage called Top Secret Lodge, on Upper Wilson Pond, accepts pets. The housekeeping cottages offer one to three bedrooms, fully equipped kitchen, and screened-in porch. Boats and motors, kayak and canoe rentals are available. From $125 a day for two off-season to $900 a week for three; two-day minimum in July and Aug. $20 for linen and towels.

🐾 🐾 ♿ **Maynard's in Maine** (207-534-7703; maynardsinmaine.com), just off Rt. 6/15 over the bridge in Rockwood 04478. Open May–hunting season. "The only thing we change around here is the linen," says Gail Maynard, who helps run the sportsmen's camp founded by her husband's grandfather in 1919. Overlooking the Moose River, a short walk from Moosehead Lake, Maynard's includes 14 tidy moss-green frame buildings with dark Edwardian furniture, much of it from the grand old Mount Kineo Hotel. The lodge is filled with mounted fish, birds, and other trophies. Two meals a day are served, plus one "packed." Per person $70 with three meals, $45 in a house-keeping cabin (no meals). $20 per pet (for duration of the stay).

REMOTE FULL-SERVICE SPORTING CAMPS (requiring a four-wheel-drive or high-clearance vehicle, and in winter possibly either snowmobile or nonmotorized access; inquire about fly-in access).

🐾 🐾 **Chesuncook Lake House and Cabins** (207-745-5330; chesuncooklakehouse.com), Rt. 76, P.O. Box 656, Greenville 04441. Open year-round. At a homey, 1864 farmhouse, David and Luisa Surprenant are carrying on a long-standing tradition of hospitality with four guest rooms (shared bath) and nearby cabins. For an additional charge guests can be shuttled in by boat or snowmobile; they can also hike, fly, ski, or canoe in. With braided rugs, patterned tin walls and ceilings, comfortable furnishings, and woodstoves, not to mention running water, beds with sheets and blankets, and the enticing aromas emanating from the big Vulcan stove in the kitchen, this is a peaceful, magical spot. When we last visited it was winter and our car was parked 14 miles down a snow-covered tote road. $120–140 person per night includes three meals. Small weddings can be arranged, using Chesuncook Village Church.

🐾 **Historic Pittston Farm** (207-280-0000; pittstonfarm.com), Rockwood 04478. Overlooking Seboomook Lake, 20 rough miles north of Rockwood via dirt road, also accessible by seaplane. Great Northern Paper Company built the clapboard lodge and barns here, establishing the farm in the early 1900s as a base for woodland operations. The era of "booming" (floating logs across the lakes) ended in 1971, and the property was used seasonally by the Boy Scouts. Restored as a year-round lodge by the previous owners, it's been

OF ALL THE CLASSIC MAINE CAMPS, MAYNARDS IS *THE* CLASSIC

Bill Davis

JEN AND BOB MILLS RUN HISTORIC PITTSTON FARM

Christina Tree

further upgraded by Bob and Jen Mills, who offer 15 homey rooms with shared baths (including two large bunk rooms on the third floor) in the lodge and seven attractive, pine-paneled units with bath in the Carriage House, also seven cabins, each accommodating four to nine people. There are also two mobile home units in the woods, and an RV campground. Common space in the lodge includes a living room with TV and a baby grand; the dining room with a electric hearth and plenty of mounted game; and comfortable seat-

ing on the screened porch. The complex is powered by its own wind turbine. From $109 with all meals in the lodge, $114 per person per night for housekeeping cabins and mobile homes. Inquire about tent sites and weekly rates; check the website for many special packages.

Spencer Pond Camps (207-745-1599; spencerpond.com), 806 Spencer Pond Rd., Greenville 04441. Open May–mid-Nov. This long-established cluster of six waterfront housekeeping camps (sleeping 2–10) changed hands in 2009, but Christine Howe and Dana Black are carrying on the camps' hospitable tradition. Christine spent summers here during the period in which they were owned by her grandparents. This is an exceptionally beautiful spot, 14 miles from the closest neighbor. Fly in or drive, 34 miles north of Greenville via a logging road from Lily Bay Rd. Guests are welcome to fresh vegetables from the gardens. Along with gas and kerosene lights and hand-pumped water, each cottage is stocked with cooking utensils and dishes, is furnished with handmade quilts and rocking chairs, and has a private shower room

THE VIEW OF SPENCER MOUNTAIN FROM SPENCER POND CAMPS

Christina Tree

AMC MAINE WOODS INITIATIVE

Founded in 1876 to blaze and map trails through the White Mountains, the Boston-based **Appalachian Mountain Club** (outdoors.org; reservations, 207-358-5187) played a significant role in the creation of the White Mountain National Forest and is still best known for its lodges and high huts catering to hikers in New Hampshire's Presidential and Franconia Ranges. More recently the AMC has focused on the "100-Mile Wilderness Region" east of Moosehead

Christina Tree

LITTLE LYFORD LODGE

Lake. It currently conserves 66,500 acres, working with local partners to foster recreation and sustainable forestry. It also maintains three classic old sporting camps, Little Lyford Lodge and Cabins, Gorman Chairback Lodge and Cabins, and Medawisla Wilderness Lodge and Cabins. The nonprofit works with privately owned West Branch Pond Camps to promote guided and self-guided lodge-to-lodge cross-country skiing, guided dogsledding, and snowshoeing in winter using more than 80 miles of maintained trails as well as hiking programs at the camps ("lodges" in AMC-speak) themselves. We can vouch for the beauty of skiing from West Branch Pond Camps to Little Lyford with the AMC guides and shuttle service. The three AMC lodges are fully staffed. Open early Jan.–Mar.; early May–Oct. (Medawisla is closed in summer 2012 for reconstruction.) Towels and linens are provided at Gorman Chairback. Guests supply their own towels and linens at the other lodges. Also see *Hiking, Cross-Country Skiing,* and *Green Space.*

✪ ⚓ **Little Lyford Lodge and Cabins**, 16 miles east of Greenville on the Katahdin Iron Works logging road. Open early Jan.–late Mar. and early May–Oct. Reservations are required. Sited in a sheltered alpine valley, these camps were built in the 1870s as a logging company station on a "tote road." The nine log cabins (without plumbing or electricity) sleep from one to six. Each has a private outhouse. A bunkhouse sleeps 12. The central lodge houses the dining room and space to relax. A spiffy new bathroom/shower house is open year-round, and there's a sauna in winter. **Gulf Hagas** (see *Green Space* in "Katahdin Region") is a 7-mile roundtrip hike or ski, and five other trails begin at the camp. In winter you can ski or dogsled to the camps or hitch a snowmobile shuttle, along with your gear. Spring, summer, and fall offer fly-fishing for wild brook trout in the two

Little Lyford ponds and West Branch of the Pleasant River. From the camps it's a short walk through the woods a small pond where canoes are stashed. Paddle across and follow a short path to the larger pond. So it goes. Guests make their picnic fixings after breakfast and off they go. The camps are 2 miles off the Appalachian Trail. $119–$125 per person in the cabins, $78 in the bunkhouse, includes all meals; less for youths (ages 13–17), children (2–12), and AMC members, also for three- and five-night stays. There's a charge for the snowmobile shuttle and gear shuttle.

Gorman Chairback Lodge and Cabins, 20 miles on logging roads west of Greenville, 15 west of Rt. 11 in Brownville. Open late Dec.–late Mar. and mid-May–Oct. Sited on secluded Long Pond, some 5 miles from Little Lyford. This is another classic sporting camp, dating from 1867, There are two new deluxe private cabins with private baths and eight shore-side cabins, with woodstoves and gas lights, each sleeping up to five. A separate bunkhouse sleeping 12. Hot showers and composting toilets are in the spiffy new Leadership in Energy and Environmental Design (LEED)–registered "green" central lodge, opened in 2012. Solar panels provide power to the lodge, which also offers a wood-fired sauna in winter. There's a sandy beach, good swimming; also free use of kayaks and canoes for guests. Regular cabin $134–141, deluxe cabin with private bath $144–151. Bunkhouse $99 (year-round). Fees include linens and towels as well as three meals. Less for youths (ages 13–17), children (2–12), and AMC members, also for three- and five-night stays.

 Medawisla. The AMC offers seven fully equipped cabins with woodstove, gas lamp, and propane cookstove, sleeping 2–10 people. Cabins have their own bathroom and shower in warm-weather months; a central hot shower house is provided in winter. We love the "reading room," a spot outside overlooking a dam that once held the only road in. Boats and canoes are available. The loons on the soundtrack from the movie *On Golden Pond* were taped here. Rates, all meals included, are $119–125 per person; discounts for three- and five-night stays, also youth's, children's, and

GATHERING FOR LUNCH AT LITTLE LYFORD   Bill Davis

AMC member rates. This is a cross-country ski haven with close to 30 miles of trails; dogsledding trips can be arranged. Medawisla is pet-friendly. Call for details. Open Jan. 13–Mar. 18, Thu.–Mon.; closed Tue.–Wed. Full-service only. Medawisla is closed in summer 2012 for reconstruction.

✪ 🐾 ✐ ♿ **West Branch Pond Camps** (207-695-2561; westbranchpondcamps .com), P.O. Box 1153, Greenville 04441. A 45-minute drive, an easy 18 miles north of downtown Greenville on the Lily Bay Rd., then a 10-mile drive in. Open after ice-out through Sept., and Feb. 1–Mar. 24. Eric Stirling is the fourth generation of his family to run this classic cluster of weathered, waterside log sporting camps and lodge with a view across the lake to the majestic 3,644-foot-high bulk of White Cap Mountain. With the help of his mom, Carol, a legendary cook who herself managed the camps for decades, and his vivacious photographer wife, Mildred, Eric has opened a new chapter in the long history of these camps. The family now owns the property outright (after almost a century of leasing the land), and easements protect the surrounding woodland and White Cap itself from development. Stirling maintains 15 kilometers of trails for nonmotorized recreation. These connect with trails maintained by the AMC, and in conjunction with them, Stirling offers cross-country, snowshoeing, and dogsledding treks. All nine cabins (total capacity 36) have woodstove, electricity, and bath but the plumbing is seasonal: outhouse and washbasin in winter (honestly, it's okay). The furnishings are comfortable, with some rare "rustic" pieces. Rowboats and canoes are available. Food is hearty New England fare with a set menu—prime rib on Thursday and turkey dinner on Sunday—with fresh vegetables and greens from the organic garden June–Sept. and vegetarian fare on request. In summer meals are served in the classic old lodge dining room; in winter guests gather in the big county kitchen. It's no secret that First West Branch Pond is the area's prime moose-viewing spot. $55–100 per person per day includes three meals, firewood, and use of a canoe; $55 children 5–11.

GORMAN CHAIRBACK'S LODGE HAS BEEN REBUILT BY THE AMC

Kevin Breunig, courtesy of the AMC

(Sunshower) and outhouse. The camp library is stocked for rainy days, with many reference books for nature study. $25–55 per person per night, $15 per child over age 8. Canoe available.

Tomhegan Wilderness Resort (207-534-7712; tomhegan.com), P.O. Box 310, Rockwood 04478. Open more or less year-round. A 10-mile ride up a dirt road from Rockwood Village and then a lengthy, bumpy ride down a private road. The rewards are 1.5 miles of frontage on Moosehead Lake and a string of 1910 hand-hewn two-bedroom housekeeping cottages (one with four bedrooms) set back above lawns, along a wooden boardwalk. Guests are not to bring ATVs or pets because tame deer wander through the grounds. Boats, kayaks, and canoes are available. Cabins range $600–1,295 per week; lodge apartments begin at $110 per night. Rates are based on up to four people; after that it's $20 per child, $40 per adult.

On the way to Greenville

The Guilford Bed & Breakfast (207-876-3477; guilfordbandb.com), 24 Elm St., P.O. Box 178, Guilford 04443. Harland and Isobel Young offer warm hospitality in their gracious 1905 mansion built by the family of the local woolen mill owner. A great stop on the way to the Moosehead or Katahdin region. Four second-floor rooms (one with two queen beds) are unusually attractive, each with private bath; one delightful third-floor guest room has a stained-glass window. $125–149 for rooms with private bath, including a full breakfast.

RENTALS Private camp rentals are listed with the chamber of commerce at mooseheadlake.org. Also check listings at moosheadrentals.com.

CAMPGROUNDS & **Lily Bay State Park** (207-695-2700). Open May–Oct.

15. Nine miles north of Greenville on the east shore of Moosehead Lake, this 925-acre park contains 91 well-spaced sites, many along the shore. Two are wheelchair-accessible; facilities include a shower house, boat launch, and beach. $24 for nonresidents, $14 for Maine residents. It's advisable to reserve online at maine.gov/parks/reservations.

Seboomook Wilderness Campground (207-280-0555; seboomook wildernesscampground.us), HC 85, Box 560, Rockwood 04478. Open May–Dec. Accessed by dirt road (some 32 miles from Rockwood), in the northwest corner of the lake. Sites for RVs and tents; Adirondack shelters on the water. Photos in the camp store (where there's an ice cream parlor) document this site's days as a World War II POW camp. Nine cabins. Canoe, kayak, and boat rentals.

Maine State Forest Service (207-695-3721) maintains free (first-come, first-served) "authorized sites" (no fire permit required) and "permit sites" (permit required) scattered on both public and private land along Moosehead Lake and on several of its islands.

✳ Where to Eat

DINING OUT Blair Hill Inn (207-695-0224; blairhill.com), Lily Bay Rd., Greenville. Open to the public late June–mid-Oct., Thu.–Sat. Reservations recommended. A five-course menu with a choice of three entrées, served in the dining room or on the side porch with lake views. Guests tend to come early for a cocktail in the bar by the fire or on the porch to settle in with a drink and watch the sunset. The menu changes each weekend, taking advantage of the freshest produce available. Chef Jonathan Cox has scoured the region to find his purveyors. You might begin with crisp

DINNER AT BLAIR HILL INN

Christina Tree

peekytoe crabcake with local peaches and blackberry aioli, then savor a roasted heirloom squash and tomato soup topped with olive tapenade, then a salad of honey crisp apple, walnuts, and greens with a blue cheese vinaigrette. Poached lobster with fresh corn, baby turnips, and a homemade spinach and ricotta manicotti was one of the most delicious meals we can remember. We topped it off with a mixed berry vol-au-vent with pastry cream and white wine glaçage. $59 prix fixe.

Greenville Inn (207-695-2206 or 1-888-695-6000), Norris St., Greenville. Dinner served late June–mid-Oct., Mon.–Sat. Reservations requested. The oval-shaped dining room in this classic lumber baron's mansion is charming, with views up the lake. Chef Paul has won a following with menus that feature gluten-free dishes, including pan-roasted, miso-glazed duck breast, and roasted locally raised lamb. There's always also a vegan option. Entrées $28–38.

The Birches Resort (207-534-2242), Rockwood. Open year-round: daily in summer, check otherwise. This popular resort (see *Lodging*) has a classic rustic dining room—log sided with a massive stone hearth, a canoe turned upside down in the open rafters, and hurricane lamps on the highly polished tables. Add the view of the lake. The food is family-geared and -priced. We made them mistake of ordering the mussels steamed in wine and garlic for each of us—one order would have sufficed for three. The baby back ribs could feed two. Entrées come with salad, a veggie, and starch: $14–24. Reservations suggested. There's also an inviting pub. $13.95–21.95. Lunch soups, sandwiches, and salads.

Northern Pride Lodge (207-695-2890), Kokadjo. Open year-round. Reservations required. The dining room in this lumber baron's hunting lodge is a heated sunporch overlooking a campground on First Roach Pond. Destination dining combined with moose-watching, half an hour's drive north of downtown Greenfield. Rental canoes and kayaks are offered along with pontoon rides. Dining choices might include crispy roast duckling with a homemade orange sauce, and baked salmon with the house raspberry maple glaze. Entrées are $19.95–21.95, including sides and a choice of salad.

🍴 Maynard's Dining Room (207-534-7703), off Rt. 6/15, Rockwood. Open Mother's Day–Columbus Day for dinner 5–7:30 Fri. and Sat.; otherwise from 5:30. Dine much as your grandparents would have in the traditional old lodge dining room overlooking the Moose River. Choices vary with the night; $21.95 includes entrée, juice or soup, salad, choice of potato or veggie, bread, dessert, and beverage. BYOB. Saturday, it's baby back ribs or chicken Parmesan, and Sunday is roast turkey or baked Virginia ham. This is known as a first-rate place to dine.

Historic Pittston Farm (207-280-0000; pittstonfarm.com), Rockwood 04478. Open year-round 7 AM–7 PM. Destination dining, not because the food is gourmet but because this is a great backwoods destination, a reason to head up the 20-mile bumpy road north of Rockwood or (much better) to fly in. This classic outpost (see *Lodging*), a wilderness farm on the National Historic Register, was built in the early 1900s as a major hub of Great Northern's logging operations. Breakfast is ready by 4:30 AM during hunting season; otherwise, 7 AM. Lunch includes a make-your-own sandwich bar, fish stews, and burgers. It offers good home cooking under current ownership by Jen and Bob Mills. It's a buffet all-you-can-eat dinner 5–7 every night. BYOB.

EATING OUT

In Greenville

✪ ✐ **Rod 'n' Reel Café** (207-695-0388), downtown Greenville, across from the lake. Open year-round from 4 for dinner. Greenville on Sunday night tends to shut down tight by 8 PM, the hour we knocked on the window of this cozy-looking restaurant, which had just closed its kitchen. Karen LeClair, however, is not about to let anyone go hungry, and she fed us, at the bar, one of the best baked haddocks in memory. We've been back many times since. The menu runs from a hot dog or burger to prime rib (Fri. and Sat. only). Fully licensed. Reasonably priced, Tadpoles menu and senior discounts.

✐ **Kelly's Landing** (307-695-4438; kellysatmoosehed.com), Greenville Junction. Open daily for lunch through dinner, a big friendly dining room with a fireplace, shady, long deck by the water in summer, less crowded in summer than downtown options. Corned beef hash at breakfast, fresh soups and salad bar at lunch, big dinner menu features prime rib, nightly specials. Easy parking and docking.

The Black Frog (207-695-1100; theblackfrog.com), Pritham Ave. Open daily for lunch and dinner. Leigh Turner was a founder of The Road Kill Café in Greenville Junction not that many years ago. Ask and he will recount his brush with Wall Street, a brief period during which Road Kill Cafés proliferated around New England but then went bust. The Black Frog offers waterside dining with a menu featuring the likes of "the chicken that didn't make it across the road," "oops-soups," and burgers ranging from "cheesy weasel" to "skunk breath." Go for the specials. The thing is that what's good here is really good—and this is the best lakeside view in town, definitely the place for lunch.

Blue Loon Café (207-695-2583), 393 Pritham Ave. Open breakfast–dinner. New and no view but this pleasant, chef-owned restaurant is a big hit. Brick-oven, thin-crust pizza is the specialty at lunch; house-made salsa and pizza. Try the veal Marsala at dinner. Wine, draft beer.

✐ **Auntie M's Family Restaurant** (207-695-2238), Lily Bay Rd. Open 5 AM–closing; great breakfast, homemade soups, and specials.

Flatlander's Pub (207-695-3373), Pritham Ave. Open daily (except in winter when it's closed on Wed.) from 11 AM "'til close." Hamburgers, broasted chicken, seafood; homemade desserts.

Stress Free Moose Pub & Café (207-695-3100), 65 Pritham Ave. Lunch–10 PM weekdays, till 11 Fri.–Sat. Dining on the back deck with a lake view in summer, otherwise inside around the bar and with limited seating by the deli; coffeehouse atmosphere upstairs. Regulars swear by the chili.

Jamieson's Market/Jamo's Pizza (207-695-2201), Pritham Ave. and West St. This is a downtown source of fast, good, reasonably priced takeout ranging from breakfast sandwiches through subs, dagwoods, and wraps to pizza; also groceries, beer, wine, worms and crawlers.

Beyond Greenville

Kokadjo Trading Post (207-695-3993; kokadjo.com), Kokadjo. Open 7 AM–closing; earlier during hunting season. Fred and Marie Candeloro offer a cozy dining room with a large fieldstone fireplace and a view of First Roach Pond. Terrific fish sandwich at lunch, custom cut Black Angus steaks at dinner. Inquire about cabins.

Spring Creek Bar-B-Q (207-997-7025), Rt. 15, Monson. Open Thu.–Sat. 10–8, Sun. 8–5 (or when the

food is gone); also open Mon. seasonally. Closed Dec. and Apr. Ribs are the big specialty here, but you might want to reserve (you can call days ahead), because they run out toward the end of the day. Also good for standard road food.

✳ Selective Shopping

In Greenville

Indian Hill Trading Post (207-695-3376), Greenville. Open daily year-round, Thu. until 9. Huge—a combination sports store, supermarket, and general store, stocking everything you might need for a week or two in the woods.

Moosehead Traders (207-695-3806), Moosehead Center Mall, Rt. 15 in downtown Greenville. Open May–Oct. Unexpectedly upscale, with furs, moose-antler chandeliers, camp furnishings, and gifts. The moose is not for sale.

Joe Bolf, Woodcarver (207-695-3002; joebolf.com), 11 Minden St., across from the firehouse, Greenville. Open year-round, generally Mon.–Sat. Bolf is the area's outstanding carver of signs (WELCOME TO GREENVILLE is a sample); also chain-saw sculpture, totem poles, figures, and camp furniture.

Great Eastern Clothing Company (207-695-0770), a trendy emporium, has replaced the old landmark Indian Store in Greenville's Shaw Block.

Northwoods Outfitters (207-695-3288), selling sporting gear and wear, now occupies the space vacated by Greenville's other old commercial landmark, Sanders Store. It includes a small cyber café.

The Corner Shop (207-695-2142), corner of Main and Pritham (across from Great Eastern Clothing), Greenville; gifts, books, magazines.

THERE'S GOOD SHOPPING IN GREENVILLE
Christina Tree

JOE BOLF, CHAIN-SAW CARVER

Moosin' Around Maine (207-695-3939), Pritham Ave., downtown Greenville. Pottery, jewelry, blown glass from Maine and beyond.

See also **Maine Guide Fly Shop** under *Fishing*.

January: **Ice fishing derby**, Greenville.

February: **Snofest**, Greenville—snowmobile events, 100-mile sled dog race.

Late May–mid-June: **Moosemainea** month (mooseheadlake.org) throughout the area.

July: The **Fourth of July** is big in Greenville, with a crafts fair, food booths, music, parade, fireworks, and street dance. **Thoreau-Wabanaki Festival**. **Friday Night Concert Series** at the Gazebo.

August: **Forest Heritage Days**, Greenville—crafts fair and many forestry-related events.

Second weekend of September: **International Seaplane Fly-In Weekend**, Greenville.

Columbus Day weekend: **Moose on the Run**, a 5K race.

KATAHDIN REGION
Including Gulf Hagas,
Lower Piscataquis, and Lincoln Lakes

Mile-high Mount Katahdin rises massively from a vast green woodland sea, mirrored in nearby lakes and clearly visible from a surprising distance. Maine's highest mountain and the northern terminus of the Appalachian Trail, it's been synonymous with hiking since Henry David Thoreau described his first climb to the top in 1846.

The trails leading to the summit still represent the most popular hikes in the state, but climbers can also choose from several less-trafficked mountains within the surrounding 204,733 acres of Baxter State Park, all with views of Katahdin itself. In all the park offers hiking on 300 trail miles, as well as fishing on remote lakes and ponds.

Hiking is just one of the many ways to accomplish what's described locally as "getting out," which is what this area is all about. Fishing and hunting have long been a way of life, and in recent decades whitewater rafters have been plunging down the West Branch of the Penobscot River through Ripogenus Gorge, the ultimate rafting run in the Northeast.

Early-morning and evening moose-watching is another summer ritual. Organized excursions are offered, but there are also some well-known spots where you're likely to see moose at sunset. The winter months are predictably snowy, and there's a big commitment to maintaining snowmobile, cross-country ski, and snowshoeing systems. Dogsledding and ice fishing are also draws.

The big town here is Millinocket, a lumbering outpost with some 5,000 souls that boomed to life around the Great Northern Paper Company at the turn of the 20th century. There are major drops in the Penobscot River—110 feet in Millinocket itself, and 25 and 50 feet in East Millinocket. In recent years the mills on these sites have changed ownership repeatedly, and layoffs have cost some 600 jobs. Currently the two mills are owned by Cate Street Capital, a New Hampshire green technology investment company. The East Millinocket Mill is operating; Cate Street has expressed interest in reopening a mill in Millinocket, though no time line has been set.

Millinocket is also the name of the pristine lake east of Mount Katahdin, separated by a narrow causeway from Ambajejus Lake, which becomes Pemadumcook

Lake, flowing in turn into North Twin Lake, South Twin Lake, and Elbow Lake. Even without Katahdin, these lakes would be impressive, and with this magnificent centerpiece they can be downright magical, especially at sunset, when you sit quietly, listening to the haunting call of the loons.

Southwest of Millinocket, lower Piscataquis County is largely woodland traversed (north–south) by Rt. 11, the old road to Millinocket before the advent of I-95. This is a slice of "the real Maine," with Dover-Foxcroft (pop. circa 4,200) as its big town. The very real and relatively little-known treasures here are 13-mile-long Sebec Lake, site of Peaks-Kenny State Park, and Gulf Hagas, billed as "Maine's Grand Canyon." Southeast of Millinocket, the Lincoln Lakes region offers some 15 lakes as well as the Penobscot and Mattawamkeag Rivers.

GUIDANCE Katahdin Area Chamber of Commerce (207-723-4443; katahdin maine.com), 1029 Central St. (Rt. 11/157), Millinocket 04462. This information center is generally open weekdays. An unstaffed information kiosk is sited on Rt. 157 in Medway, just off I-95 exit 244.

The Baxter State Park Headquarters (207-723-5140; baxterstateparkauthority .com), 64 Balsam Dr., Millinocket 04462, is open Memorial Day–Columbus Day, daily 8–4; otherwise weekdays. Just off Rt. 11/57 on a service road (next to McDonald's), it offers picnic tables, restrooms, and a selection of guides to the park. This is primarily a reservation center (it's 18 miles east of the park itself), but a useful stop if you are coming from I-95 and want to check on conditions (traffic as well as weather) before proceeding. A Visitor Information Center located just before Togue Pond Gate (open Memorial Day–Labor Day) offers trip advice, up-to-date weather and trail information, and map/guides.

Southern Piscataquis County Chamber of Commerce (207-564-7533; spccc .org), 1033 South St. (Rt. 7). This log information center is open Wed.–Fri. 9–2, when volunteers are available. The website lists many rental camps and other lodging options.

GETTING THERE The most direct route is I-95 to exit 244 in Medway (73 miles northeast of Bangor), and 12 miles into Millinocket. From here, it's about 10 miles to Millinocket Lake, and from there another 8 miles to the Togue Pond entrance

VIEW OF KATAHDIN FROM TWIN PINE CAMPS

Christina Tree

to Baxter State Park. Exit I-95 in Newport and follow Rt. 11/7 north to Dover-Foxcroft for **Peaks-Kenny State Park** on up through Milo and Brownville Junction (the turnoff for **Gulf Hagas**). From the Midcoast the shortest way to this area is Rt. 220 north from Waldoboro to Newport, a beautiful drive in its own right; stop for a dip in **Lake St. George State Park** in Liberty, midway.

From the Moosehead Lake area: Millinocket is 70 miles northeast of Greenville—but getting there is an adventure. For a detailed description see *Scenic Drives* in "Moosehead Lake Area." The 18 miles to Kokadjo are paved, but the next stretch, "the Greenville Road," is badly marked and maintained. Once you hit the **Golden Road** (turn right), however, the surface improves. This legendary 96-mile logging road, owned by private companies, runs from Millinocket to Quebec. It's mostly paved along the West Branch of the Penobscot; you can cross over onto the paved Baxter State Park Rd. at Ambajejus Lake. Logging trucks, which operate on weekdays, have the right-of-way; slow down and pull to the side to permit them to pass. Your odds of spotting a moose here are high.

GETTING AROUND Katahdin Air Service Inc. (207-723-8378 or 1-866-359-6246; katahdinair.com), Millinocket. Available May–Nov. to fly in to remote camps and shuttle in canoes and campers; will drop hikers at points along the Appalachian Trail. **West Branch Aviation** (207-723-4375; katahdingateway.com/wba) in Millinocket also serves remote camps.

WHEN TO COME Spring draws fishermen; June brings moose-watching and blackflies; July and August are great for swimming, canoeing, and rafting; September and early October are best for hiking and foliage. Snowfall is dependable February into April, less so in December and January, which bring subzero temperatures. March can be magnificent, the brightest days of the year with intense blue skies above dazzling white lakes and mountains.

✷ Must See

KATAHDIN Maine's Mount Fuji, this is the region's number one year-round sight-to-see, not just to climb. Check out **Baxter State Park** in *Green Space* for suggested vantage points within the park. Don't miss a sunset! At dusk locals and visitors alike gather at nearby lakes to watch the big sky as well as big mountain change hues. If you come no nearer than the interstate, don't pass up I-95's **A. J. Allee Scenic Overlook**, some 15 miles beyond the Medway exit. Katahdin is impressive even at that distance.

Patten Lumbermen's Museum (207-528-2650; lumbermensmuseum.org), Shin Pond Rd. (Rt. 159), Patten. Open Memorial Day–June, Fri.–Sun. 10–4. July–Columbus Day, Tue.–Sun. 10–4. Nominal admission. The museum, which encompasses more than 4,000 displays housed in nine buildings, was founded in 1962 by bacteriologist Lore Rogers and log driver Caleb Scribner. Exhibits range from giant log haulers to "gum books," the lumberman's scrimshaw: intricately carved boxes in which to keep spruce gum, a popular gift for a sweetheart. There are replicas of logging camps from different periods, dioramas, machinery, and photos. This road leads to the Matagamon Gate, the northern, less trafficked corner of Baxter State Park.

Ambajejus Boom House (moreairphotos.com/boomhouse), Ambajejus Lake. Open year-round. Accessible via boat or snowmobile, or even by walking if you don't mind getting your feet wet. Riverman Chuck Harris has single-handedly restored this old boom house, former quarters for log drivers, as a museum about life during the river drives. Exhibits include tools, paintings, and photographs among the artifacts of the river-driving years. **Katahdin Scenic Cruises** at Big Moose Inn (207-723-8391) and **Maine Quest Adventures** (207-447-5011; maine questdventures.com) offer access by boat.

Katahdin Iron Works. Open mid-Apr.–Nov. Turn at the small sign on Rt. 11, 5 miles north of Brownville Junction, and go another 6 miles up the gravel road. The spot was a sacred place for Native Americans, who found yellow ocher paint here. From the 1840s until 1890, an ironworks prospered in this remote spot, spawning a village to house its 200 workers and producing 2,000 tons of raw iron annually. Guests of the **Silver Lake Hotel** (1880s–1913) here came on the same narrow-gauge railroad that carried away the iron. All that remains is a big old blast furnace and an iron kiln. The site may not be worth your effort unless you plan to continue on down the gravel road to hike in **Gulf Hagas** (see *Green Space*) or to camp.

Abbott Museum, Dexter (dexterhistoricalsociety.com). Open mid-June–Sept., daily except Sun. Stop by the information center and gift shop, with a restroom, on Rt. 7 (14 miles north of I-95 exit 157) to get directions to the this unusual local museum housed in an 1854 gristmill that's literally "down" town. It's an added reason to take a break and explore this lively main street, sited several hundred feet lower than the (literal) highway. Best known for Dexter shoes, the town of 4,000 adds another 1,000 or so summer residents along the shores of Lake Wassookeag, which is more than 400 feet above downtown. The downtown is also noteworthy for its clock tower and several tempting shops, including a big Renys (see "What's Where").

✵ To Do

AIR RIDE Katahdin Air Service, Inc. (207-723-8378; katahdinair.com), based on the Golden Road in Millinocket. Since 1946 Katahdin Air has been serving remote camps and offering fishing on remote ponds. It also offers frequent scenic flights, ranging from a 15 minute flight along the base of Mount Katahdin to a day exploring Henderson Pond and Debsconeag Lake. Inquire about fly-in fishing trips and fly-and-dine packages. **West Branch Aviation LLC** (207-723-4375), based at the Millinocket Municipal Airport (16 Medway Rd.), offers scenic flights and shuttle service using both sea- and standard planes. Aircraft rental and hangar space also available.

BOAT CRUISES Katahdin Scenic Cruises (207-723-8391) offers wildlife cruises on Millinocket Lake daily June–Oct., as does **Maine Quest Adventures** (207-447-5011; mainequestadventures.com). **New England Outdoor Center** (207-723-5438 or 1-800-766-7238; neoc.com), 30 Twin Pines Lane, Millinocket, also offers family float trips and moose cruises on Millinocket Lake.

CAMPING AND CANOEING EXPEDITIONS This area is often used as a starting point for trips on the Allagash Wilderness Waterway (see "Aroostook County") and St. John River. There is also good canoeing on the East and West

BAXTER STATE PARK

(baxterstateauthority.com). Like Acadia National Park, Baxter State Park's acreage was amassed privately and given to the public as a gift. In this case it was the gift of one individual: Percival Baxter (1876–1969). In 1921, at age 44, Baxter became one of the state's youngest governors; he was then reelected for another term. He was unsuccessful, however, in convincing the Maine legislature to protect Katahdin and surrounding lands. Instead, in 1930 he himself paid

Baxter Park Authority

PERCIVAL BAXTER AND KATAHDIN

$25,000 to buy 6,000 acres that included Maine's highest mountain. For the remainder of his life he continued to negotiate with paper companies and other landowners to increase the size of the park. Thanks to his legacy, it continued to grow even after his death and presently encompasses 209,501 acres.

While nominally a state park, it receives no state funds, and the Baxter State Park Authority operates under its own unique and complicated rules, dedicated to ensuring that this preserve "Shall forever be kept and remain in the Natural Wild State." Camping and even day-use admissions to the park are strictly limited. Rental canoes are available at several locations in the park.

There are only two entry points: Togue Pond Gate, 18 miles east of Millinocket, by far the most popular, is open 6 AM–10 PM (5 AM during busy summer months and some fall weekends; please call the park to verify), May 15–Oct. 15. Matagamon Gate, in the northeast corner of the park, is also open 6 AM–10 PM mid-May–Oct. 15. Vehicles with Maine plates are admitted free, but others pay a $14 day-use fee.

The list of rules governing the park is long and detailed. No motorcycles, motorized trail bikes, ATVs, or pets are allowed in. Bicycles can be used on maintained roads only. Snowmobiles are allowed only on the ungroomed main Tote Road in the park. The list goes on; the park goes through periodic reviews of the regulations, so pick up a current copy at headquarters or the visitors center, or check the website before heading in.

The park is open daily, but note the restricted camping periods and the special-use permits required Dec.–Mar. Vehicular access is not guaranteed once snow blocks the roads, usually after Oct. 15, the end of the camping season. Also note that a park prohibition on the collection of any park plants, animals, or artifacts is strictly enforced unless you have applied at least six months in advance and have been approved by the director.

Ever since the 1860s—when Henry David Thoreau's account of his 1846 ascent of "Ktaadn" began to circulate—the demanding trails to Maine's highest summit (5,267 feet) have been among the most popular in the state. Climbing Katahdin itself is considered a rite of passage in Maine and much of the rest of New England. The result is a steady stream of humanity up and down the Katahdin trails, while other peaks, such as 3,488-foot Doubletop, offer excellent, less crowded hiking and views of Katahdin to boot.

Day-trippers should be aware that the number of vehicles allowed at specific trailheads is finite; when the parking lots fill, people are turned away. Eighty percent of day-trippers head for lots in the southern end of the park, with access to the most popular trails—but with 42 miles of road, 46 mountain peaks, and 205 miles of trails, there's plenty of room for everyone.

It's now possible to reserve a trailhead parking space at some of the park's most popular trailheads—Roaring Brook, Abol, and Katahdin Stream; check the BSP website. There is still some room for first-come, first-served arrivals, but be aware that the number of vehicles allowed at specific trailheads is finite. When the parking lots fill, people are turned away. Eighty percent of day-trippers head for lots in the southern end of the park, with access to the most popular trails—but with 42 miles of road, 46 mountain peaks, and 205 miles of trails, there's plenty of room for everyone.

The climb to Katahdin's summit and back takes 10 hours. If you are determined to access the parking area for the Knife's Edge Trail (the legendary narrow link between Baxter and Pamola Peaks) via the Chimney Pond Trail, arrive early to give yourself the necessary time for this hike. Sleep in if you're heading to one of the less-popular trailheads; later in the day there's rarely a line.

The pamphlet *Day Use Hiking Guide*, available at the Togue Pond Visitors Center (located a short way before the Togue Pond Gate), locates and describes 32 trails. Park staff, here and at both gates, suggest appropriate trails, given conditions and the time of day. Arriving midafternoon on a July Sunday we were advised to take the Hunt Trail (a popular way to the peak) only as far as Katahdin Stream Falls.

Another popular hike is Sentinel Mountain from the Kidney Pond Trailhead. The trail traverses moderate wooded terrain until the very end, when it abruptly ascends to a series of excellent vantage points with views in several directions.

A flat alternative is the Daicey Pond Nature Trail, 1.7 miles around Daicey Pond. Doubletop Mountain offers a full day hike with several mileage options: 9.6 miles roundtrip hiking up and down from Kidney Pond Trailhead, 6.6 miles roundtrip from the Nesowadnehunk Trailhead, and 7.9 miles hiking from Kidney to Nesowadnehunk Trailhead or vice versa. South Turner Mountain Trail from Roaring Brook via Sandy Stream Pond (4 miles roundtrip) is a good wildlife-watching trail. Many hikers base themselves at Chimney Pond Campground and tackle Katahdin from there on one of several trails. A wide selection of retail maps and trail guidebooks is available at park headquarters. *Katahdin: A Guide to Baxter State Park and Katahdin*, by Stephen Clark, and *50 Hikes in the Maine Mountains*, by Cloe Chunn (Backcountry Guides), detail many of Baxter's trails.

CAMPING RESERVATIONS Camping is permitted May 15–Oct. 15 and Dec.–Apr. 1. Summer reservations for sites throughout the park are on a rolling basis. Space can be reserved four months in advance by mail or in person, and still-available sites can also be reserved 14 or fewer days in advance by phone with a credit card. Download the form at baxterstate parkauthority.com. The 10 campgrounds are widely scattered; there are no hookups, and you carry out what you carry in. Two campgrounds, Daicey Pond and Kidney Pond, offer traditional cabins with beds, gas lanterns, firewood, and tables and chairs; $55 a night for a two-bed cabin, $75 for three-bed cabins, $100 for a four-bed cabin, and $150 for a six-person cabin. Six more campgrounds, accessible by road, offer a mix of bunkhouses, lean-tos, and tent sites (in summer bunkhouses cost $11 per person per night; lean-tos and tenting sites are $30. Two other popular campgrounds, Chimney Pond and Russell Pond, require hiking in. Several individual backcountry sites are available by reservation for backpackers. Check restrictions before planning your trip. Ideally, allow three to five days at a campground like Trout Brook Farm, in the northern wilderness area of the park, or base yourself at Russell Pond (a 7- or 9-mile hike in from the road, depending on where you begin) and hike to the Grand Falls and Lookout Ledges.

Payment must accompany the reservation request. The mailing address is Baxter State Park, 64 Balsam Dr., Millinocket 04462. Enclose a stamped, self-addressed envelope for confirmation. July through mid-Aug. weekends fill quickly, but tent sites midweek and earlier or later in the season are possible. For a current update on this rolling reservation system, contact the park directly (see *Guidance*) or visit its website.

(not for beginners) Branches of the Penobscot River as well on the area's many lakes.

Katahdin Outfitters (207-723-5700 or 1-800-862-2663; katahdinoutfitters.com) in Millinocket specializes in trips up the Allagash. **New England Outdoor Center** (207-723-5438 or 1-800-766-7238; neoc.com), offers a canoe and kayak school, guided tours, and rentals. **Maine Quest Adventures** (207-447-5011) offers canoe and kayak trips; kayak and canoe rentals are available from most camps (see *Lodging*). **Peaks-Kenny State Park** (see *Green Space*) rents canoes to use on Sebec Lake.

FISHING Dolby Flowage is good for bass fishing, and the West Branch of the Penobscot River offers good salmon and trout angling. Check out the **Maine Department of Inland Fisheries and Wildlife**'s excellent website (mefish wildlife.com) for Katahdin area fishing spots and much more. **Maine Quest Adventures** (207-447-5011; mainequestadventures.com) offers customized fishing trips, from half a day to three days. **New England Outdoor Center** (207-723-5438; see *Whitewater Rafting*) offers guided fishing trips. Licenses are available at the **Millinocket municipal office** on Penobscot Ave., and at many of the area's stores, including **Lennie's Supercttc** in Medway, the **Katahdin General Store** in Millinocket, and **North Woods Trading Post** on Millinocket Lake. For a complete list of guide services, contact the **North Maine Woods office** (207-435-6213; northmainewoods.org) in Ashland and the **Katahdin Area Chamber of Commerce** (207-723-4443; katahdinmaine.com) in Millinocket.

GOLF Highlands Golf Course (207-794-2433), Town Farm Rd., Lincoln; 18 holes with full-service clubhouse, rental carts, and clubs. **Green Valley Golf Course** (207-732-3006), Rt. 2, West Enfield. Eight holes. **Hillcrest Golf Course** (207-723-8410), 59 Grove St., Millinocket. Nine holes with full-service clubhouse, rental carts, and clubs.

HIKING See **Baxter State Park** and **Gulf Hagas** under *Green Space*.

HORSEBACK RIDING & **Northern Maine Riding Adventures** (207-564-3451; mainetrailrides.com), Dover-Foxcroft. Judy and Bob Flury-Strehlke, licensed Maine guides and skilled equestrians, lead rides from their four-season facility into remote backcountry. Half-day and full-day rides, also lessons. Overnight trips (experienced riders only) offered during foliage season with stays at the AMC Gorman Chairback and Little Lyford Lodges (see the Moosehead chapter). Special-needs riders are welcome. Judy is a nationally recognized specialist in centered riding.

MOOSE-WATCHING

In and around Millinocket
Maine-ly Photos (207-723-5465; mainelyphotos.com) offers early-morning and evening van tours; money back if you don't see a moose. **Maine Quest Adventures** (207-447-5011; mainequestadventures.com) offer canoe and kayak moose-spotting paddles, also moose cruises via pontoon boat on Katahdin Lake. **New England Outdoor Center** (1-800-766-7238; neoc.com) uses boats as well as vans.

Alternatively, ask locally about likely moose-watching spots. There are a number of these within Baxter State Park; staff at the Togue Pond Gate dispense maps and direct you.

SWIMMING ✍ **Peaks-Kenny State Park** in Dover-Foxcroft is a great family beach, with lawns, playground equipment, and a roped-in swimming area. Hiking trails and camping; day-use fee.

Mattawamkeag Wilderness Park (207-736-4881 or 1-888-724-2465), off Rt. 2 in Mattawamkeag (11 miles southeast of I-95's Medway exit), offers a sand beach on the river, also picnic tables, hot showers, a recreation hall, and a playground. Nominal day-use fee.

✍ **Medway Recreation Complex** in Medway has a family beach, picnic area, volleyball, playground equipment, and a roped-in swimming area on the East Branch of the Penobscot River.

Ambajejus Lake has a public boat landing and also offers a small public beach.

Note: Swimming opportunities abound in Baxter State Park and the many lakes around Millinocket.

WHITEWATER RAFTING The West Branch of the Penobscot represents the ultimate challenge in Maine rafting, best for experienced rafters (to run the whole river you must be at least 15). Rafters are bused from their base camps to the put-in below McKay Station. The 12-mile trip begins with a 2-mile descent through Ripogenus Gorge (Class V rapids), and then drops down through the infamous Cribworks and on to Nesowadnehunk Falls. Trips run late Apr.–mid-Oct., but we suggest midsummer through early foliage season. Rates are lower midweek than on weekends.

✪ **New England Outdoor Center** (207-723-5438 or 1-800-766-7238; neoc.com). Founded by Matt Polstein in 1982, this is by far the oldest outfitter and offers the largest range of lodging options to rafters, also family float trips on the West Branch of the Penobscot and custom half-day trips to accommodate beginners. The rafting base is the **Penobscot Outdoor Center** (penobscotoutdoorcenter .com) on Pockwockamus Pond, the closest commercial campground to Baxter State Park. Facilities include the **Paddle Pub** (June–Sept., 7 AM-9 PM daily), hot tub, game room, sauna, canoes, and kayaks; lodging is at campsites, in cabin tents, and cabins. Nearby **Twin Pine Camps** on Millinocket Lake offers a range of cabins and exceptional new Guest Houses and Trailside Cabins on an extensive property with a spectacular view of Katahdin (see *Lodging*). The property includes **River Driver's Pub** (see *Dining Out*).

Three Rivers Whitewater (1-800-786-6878; threeriversfun.com) maintains a 26-acre Penobscot Outpost facility in Millinocket. Inquire about skydiving.

North Country Rivers (1-800-348-8871; ncrivers.com) is based at the Big Moose Inn, Cabins & Campground (see *Lodging*).

✷ Winter Sports

CROSS-COUNTRY SKIING AND SNOWSHOEING **Millinocket Municipal X-C Ski Area** is the name of the community's free, 40-kilometer-plus network of groomed cross-country ski trails (20 kilometers novice, 10km intermediate, and

Christina Tree

WENDE GRAY CROSS-COUNTRY SKIS ON
RAINBOW LAKE

10km expert terrain). These are divided between two distinct areas, linked by a 5-mile wooded trail. The Bait Hole Area is well marked 2.7 miles south of town on Rt. 11; the Northern Timber Cruisers Clubhouse (see *Snowmobiling*) on the Baxter State Park Rd. is the departure point for the second network. Many skiers also continue on the Baxter State Park Rd. and ski Periphery or Telos Rds. Within Baxter State Park, the road to the Hidden Springs campground is maintained for skiers. Trail maps are available at the area information kiosk on Rt. 244 in Medway, just off I-95. Local skiers take pride in the fact that they can usually ski 100 days of the year.

Note: **Nahmakanta Lake Camps** and **Katahdin Lake Wilderness Camps** cater to cross-country skiers, offering spectacular backcountry trails, and are accessible only by skis. See *Lodging*.

DOGSLED TOURS Maine Dogsledding Adventures (207-731-8888; maine dogsledding.com), Nahmakanta Lake Camps, Rainbow Township. Don and Angel Hibbs have traveled 40,000 miles by dog team, finishing in the top 10 of the 1995 Yukon Quest—a 1,000-mile race in Alaska—and first in the Labrador 400 (mile) event in Canada. They offer long dogsled runs down wooded trails and across frozen lakes with no need to slow for human traffic. Guests are permitted to drive the teams; inquire about lodging packages ranging from half a day to three days. Winter access is by dogsled or skis; see *Lodging*.

SNOWMOBILING This region offers more than 350 miles of groomed trails, and more than 10 snowmobile clubs in the area to consult. A snowmobile map available at the Katahdin Area Chamber of Commerce shows the Interconnecting Trail System (ITS) trails. **The Northern Timber Cruisers Antique Snowmobile Museum** (northern timbercruisers.com), on the Baxter State Park Rd. next to the group's clubhouse, traces the history of snowmobiling in the region. It's open winter weekends.

New England Outdoor Center (207-723-5438 or 1-800-767238; neoc

DOGSLEDDING ACROSS RAINBOW LAKE
FROM NAHMAKANTA

Christina Tree

.com) has the area's largest rental fleet at Twin Pines (see *Lodging*). They offer half-day, full-day, and overnight guided snowmobile excursions, multiday packages, and a complete shop.

✳ Green Space

Gulf Hagas Reserve is a remote part of the Appalachian Trail corridor, jointly owned and managed by the Appalachian Trail Conference and the National Park Service. It's best accessed (3.1 miles) from the Katahdin Iron Works, marked from Rt. 11 in Brownsville. At the North Maine Woods Gate ($10 nonresidents, $9 residents) you can purchase a trail map. The parking area for the trailhead is at Hay Brook. Billed as the Grand Canyon of Maine, this 2.5-mile-long gorge with walls up to 40 feet high was carved by the West Branch of the Pleasant River. At the beginning of the trail you will need to cross the river in ankle- to calf-high water. Bring water shoes for the crossing, or be prepared to take off your shoes and wade barefoot (be aware that the rocks are very slippery; find a good walking stick to help with balance). The trail threads a 35-acre stand of virgin white pines, some more than 130 feet tall, a landmark in its own right known as **The Hermitage** and preserved by The Nature Conservancy in Maine. The trail then follows the river, along the Appalachian Trail for a ways, but turns off along the rim of the canyon toward dramatic **Screw Auger Falls** and on through **The Jaws** to **Buttermilk Falls**, **Stair Fall**s, and **Billings Falls**. We started early in the day and found ourselves alone for most of the hike. The trail winds through the woods, almost always moving either up or down, with a series of small side paths. Turnouts offer great views of the falls and the gorge. The hike back is flatter, and logs cover mud in some spots. The Gulf Hagas trails are much less traveled than those at Katahdin; many visitors come only as far as the first waterfall for a swim and a picnic. Allow six to eight hours for the hike, and plan to camp at one of the waterside campsites within the **Jo-Mary Lake Campground**. In winter we have also skied in to Gulf Hagas from Little Lyford Pond Camps (see "Moosehead Lake Area"), a magnificent experience. See the *AMC Maine Woods Initiative* sidebar in the Moosehead chapter for details about Little Lyford and Gorman Chairback Lodges and Camps, both AMC facilities from which you can access Gulf Hagas.

VIEW OF GULF HAGAS FROM THE APPALACHIAN TRAIL
Courtesy of the Appalachian Mountain Club

Mattawamkeag Wilderness Park (207-736-4881 or 1-888-724-2465), Rt. 2, Mattawamkeag. This town-owned preserve offers 15 miles of hiking trails, campsites, and canoeing and swimming along the Mattawamkeag River 11 miles south of the I-95 Medway exit.

Peaks-Kenny State Park (207-564-2003), Sebec Lake Rd., Dover-Foxcroft. The centerpiece of this park is Sebec Lake (13 miles long, 3 miles wide) with its popular beach, but there are also 9 miles of hiking trails and campsites.

Also see Jo-Mary Multiple Use Forest under *Campgrounds* and Borestone Mountain Sanctuary in "Moosehead Lake Area."

Newport/Dover-Foxcroft Rail Trail. This 17-mile, multiuse trail begins in Newport, running from the north side of Rt. 7 in Newport to Fairview St. in Dover-Foxcroft, threading woods, farms, and wetlands along Sebasticook Lake, Corundel Lake, and the Sebasticook and Piscataquis Rivers.

✳ Lodging

Note: For details about motels handy to I-95, check with the Katahdin Area Chamber of Commerce (katahdinmaine.org).

All lodgings are in and around Millinocket 04462 unless otherwise noted

✪ 🐾 ✍ **Twin Pine Camps** and **Coveside Guesthouses** (1-800-766-7238; neoc.com), P.O. Box 669. The site on Millinocket Lake with its view of Katahdin is superb, and the property now offers a sampling of Matt Polstein's planned Ktaadn eco-resort. Presently there are six new "Green Built" Coveside Guest Houses set back from the lake in a wooded area. Using recycled, nontoxic, and local materials to meet LEED (Leadership in Energy and Environmental Design) certification standards, these luxurious cabins retain the traditional Maine camp overhang, albeit two stories high, supported by two entire tree trunks. Warmed with radiant heat, they have three bedrooms and two full baths, a living room with cathedral ceilings and gas fireplace, a sunroom, and a patio with a grill. Rates are currently $578 per couple per night, but there are many packages midweek and off-season, weekly rates. The **River Driver's Pub** (see *Dining Out*), which has recently relocated to this property from downtown Millinocket, now serves as a centerpiece for Twin Pines, which includes a total of 17 widely varied housekeeping cabins, most scattered under the pines, accommodating between 6 and 20 people ($211–241 per couple for smaller cabins, from $392 for those sleeping up to a dozen). All share a rec lodge with a hot tub, satellite TV, Ping-Pong, and ample outdoor space, with a swim beach. Canoes and kayaks are available for guests; kayaks and motorboats are rented. The property is a bit more than 8 miles from the Togue Pond entrance to Baxter State Park. New England Outdoor Center is the area's whitewater rafting outfitter, and also offers guided fishing and moose tours and winter snowmobiling.

♿ **5 Lakes Lodge** (207-723-5045; 5lakeslodge.com), HC 74, Box 544, South Twin Lake 04462. Open year-round. Debbie and Rick LeVasseur, both locally born and raised, have created a luxury lodge on the footprint of a dramatically sited marina on a narrow point of land on South Twin Lake,

COVESIDE GUEST HOUSES AT TWIN PINE CAMPS

Christina Tree

surrounded by water, with a superb view of Katahdin. Windows maximize lake and mountain views. The five spacious guest rooms are named for the lakes and feature log bed, gas fireplace, cathedral ceiling, and Jacuzzi. Both Debbie and Rick are active outdoorspeople who've been in the local hospitality business since the 1980s and know not only the local waters and woods but how to enjoy them to the max. They enjoy nothing more than tuning guests in and turning them on to the best that this region offers. $175–275, depending on the season, includes a full breakfast. Inquire about a rental cottage. Free use of kayaks and canoes.

✪ **Big Moose Inn, Cabins & Campground** (207-723-8391; big moose cabins.com), P.O. Box 98. Open June–Oct. This classic 1830s cedar-shake inn has been run by Laurie Boynton-Cormier's family since 1977. The restaurant is named for her mother, Fredericka (see *Dining Out*). We love the old-fashioned lobby with the moose above the hearth. There are

Christina Tree

THE MOOSE AT BIG MOOSE INN

THE LIVING ROOM AT 5 LAKES LODGE

Liam Davis

eight clean and comfortable, antiques-furnished guest rooms with double or twin beds sharing three baths, and six suites with private bath. There are also 14 cabins—including 4 large enough for groups, and several right on the lake—as well as 35 tent sites and six lean-tos. Sited between Millinocket and Ambajejus Lakes with access to swimming, this is the nearest full-service facility to Baxter State Park, 8 miles from the Togue Pond entrance and 8 miles from Millinocket. $53–56 per person for inn rooms and $149 per couple for the suites; $49 per person for cabins; $10 per person per campsite; $13 for lean-tos. Canoe and kayaks available. A general store is part of this complex. Breakfast is available to guests. This is also the base for **North Country Rivers** (see *Whitewater Rafting*) and **Katahdin Scenic Cruises** (see *Air Rides*).

The Young House Bed & Breakfast (207-723-5452; theyounghousebandb .com), 193 Central St. Former Floridians Micki and Fred Schumacher have rehabbed a handsome old home within walking distance of downtown shops and restaurants. They offer five cozy rooms, each with queen bed and private bath. $90 per night includes a full breakfast.

☙ **Shin Pond Village** (207-528-2900; shinpond.com), 1489 Shin Pond Rd., Mount Chase 04765. Ten miles down Rt. 159 from Patten. Open year-round. Craig and Terry Hill run this recreational facility, which offers campsites, housekeeping cottages, and housekeeping "guest suites." The north entrance to Baxter State Park isn't far. Cottages accommodate three to eight people and have full bath, linens, towels, and cookware. Canoe and kayak rentals in summer; snowmobile rentals in winter. Cottages are $119 per couple, $749 per week; guest suites $94 per couple, $399 per week, more for more people.

Mountain Glory Farm (1-800-219-7950; mountaingloryfarm.com), 199 Happy Corner Rd., Patten 04765. Open year-round. Christina Shipps has a knack for finding Maine's most beautiful places, and sharing them. A while back she turned the old Captain's Quarters in Stonington into the outstanding Inn on the Harbor, more recently she fell under the spell of the Katahdin area, buying this 1980s farmhouse with its view of the mile-high mountain. There are two tastefully renovated apartments, one with two bedrooms and the other with the view of Katahdin from its sitting room. Not far from the North Gate of Baxter State Park. $103–110 per night, $630–665 per week.

Brewster Inn (207-924-3130; brewster inn.com), 37 Zion's Hill Rd., Dexter 04930. Open year-round. Dexter is a proud old Maine town, and this is its proudest house, built in the 1930s for Governor (later Senator) Ralph Owen Brewster by noted architect John Calvin Stevens. Brits Mark and Judith Stephens offer nine guest rooms and two suites. $69–149.

REMOTE SPORTING CAMPS

Note: Also see *Remote Sporting Camps* in the preceding and following chapters.

♿ **Bradford Camps** (207-746-7777; bradfordcamps.com), P.O. Box 729, Ashland 04732. Open following ice-out through Nov. Sited at the Aroostook River's headwaters, Munsungan Lake, almost 60 miles from the nearest town but easily accessible by commercial floatplane from Bangor, Millinocket, and other points. This is a century-old, classic sporting camp with an unusually tidy lodge set amid well-tended lawns. Eight hand-hewn log, lakeside cabins all have full private bath. Depending on the season, this is all about fly-fishing (landlocked salmon and brook trout) and hunting, but you can also enjoy canoeing and kayaking, swimming, and fly-out day trips, including whitewater rafting. $148 per person per night includes meals; kids and weekly rates; packages. Guides, boats, and fly-out trips are extra. Family rates in July and Aug. Inquire about two remote outpost cabins. Your hosts are Karen and Igor Sikorsky—and yes, Igor is the son of the pioneer aviator best known for developing the helicopter.

☙ ☙ **Frost Pond Camps** (radiophone, 207-695-2821; frostpondcamps.com), HC 76, Box 620 Ripogenus Dam, Greenville 04441. Open year-round. Off the Golden Road (35 miles from Millinocket, 45 miles from Greenville), across Ripogenus Dam, and 3 miles up along Chesuncook Lake and then down to Frost Pond. Gene Thompson and Maureen Raynes, both Registered

Master Maine Guides, are the owners of these seven traditional housekeeping cottages (five on the waterfront) and 10 campsites on the shore of Frost Pond. Cabins have gas lights, refrigerator, and stove and are heated by woodstove in spring, fall, and winter. One has plumbing; each of the others has a clean pit toilet. A great base for exploring the wilderness. $98–118 per couple per cabin (one to three people). Minimum two-night stay. Rental boats, canoes, and kayaks.

Katahdin Lake Wilderness Camps (207-837-1599; katahdinlakewilderness camps.com), P.O. Box 314, Millinocket 04462. Privately owned but on land owned by and accessed through Baxter State Park, these legendary 1880s camps offer the view of Mount Katahdin depicted by artists from Frederick Church to Marsden Hartley

NAHMAKANTA LAKE CAMPS CATER TO DOGSLEDDERS, SKIERS, AND SNOWSHOERS

Christina Tree

and James Fitzgerald. Spring through fall you can fly in, or hike the 3.3-mile trail from Roaring Brook Rd. in the park. Dec.–Mar. the camps welcome those hardy souls who ski the 16 miles in from the Abol Bridge Store (gear is transported by snowmobile). Ten log cabins (one to eight people per cabin) and a main lodge (with a library and dining room) are built on a bluff overlooking the lake. All have a woodstove and propane lights; some are fitted out for housekeeping. Facilities include a spring, outhouses, a beach, dock, and canoes. The view of Mount Katahdin continues to lure artists, and the 717-acre lake yields native brook trout May–Sept. No access for snowmobilers. The camps are currently owned by Charles FitzGerald and managed by Holly and Bryce Hamilton. $125–130 per adult, $50 per child per day includes linens and towels, breakfast, dinner, and a trail lunch. The housekeeping rate (BYO sleeping bags, towels, and food) is $30 per adult, $15 per child. Winter rates are slightly higher. No credit cards.

☙ **Nahmakanta Lake Camps** (207-731-8888 or 1-877-731-8888; nahmakanta.com), P.O. Box 544, Millinocket 04462. Open year-round. Founded in 1872, this is a remote set of nine recently renovated lakefront cabins (accommodating two to eight people) with picture windows, screened porch, woodstove, gas lights, and fridge, plus six newly constructed shower houses with hot water and flush toilets behind the cabins. Guests can choose from housekeeping at $80 per person per day, $110 MAP (breakfast and dinner), or $140 per person with all meals (packed lunch); special children's rates. All plans include use of rowboats and canoes; guide service, and dogsled tours in winter, are the house specialties. Nahmakanta is within walking distance of the

Appalachian Trail. In summer access is via road, but in winter you need to ski in—which, may the record reflect, we have done (10 miles).

☃ ✦ **Bowlin Camps** (207-528-2022; bowlincamps.com), P.O. Box 251, Patten 04765. Open year-round, a classic Maine sporting camp with 10 classic, rustic cabins with electric and gas light, wood heat, one dating to 1895, three with private bath and cooking facilities—but three meals are served in the central lodge. Not far from the Northern Gate of Baxter State Park, the camps are nicely sited on the East Branch of the Penobscot River with trails to ponds and waterfalls, and rental canoes for an easy paddle (shuttle service offered). Families are welcome in July, Aug.; otherwise this is a serious fishing and hunting base, equally popular with snowmobilers. There are cross-country trails. From $35 per person per night, $595 per week.

☃ ☀ ✦ **Nugent's and McNally's Camps** (207-944-5991; nugent-mcnallycamps .com), HCR 76, Box 632, Greenville 04441. Among the most famous and remote sporting camps, 50 miles north of Millinocket between Baxter State Park and Allagash Mountain. It's best reached via floatplane; otherwise, it's a 4-mile boat or snowmobile ride up Chamberlain Lake, also a beautiful ski. The housekeeping cabins have the traditional front overhang and outhouses; they sleep 2 to 20. All have gas lights, fridge, cookstoves, and woodstoves for heat. Boats are available. AP, MAP, or housekeeping plans available. $33–100 per person. BYO sleeping bags and towels.

Also see **Libby Sporting Camps** in the Aroostook chapter.

CAMPGROUNDS ☃ ✦ Katahdin Shadows Campground & Cabins

(207-746-9349 or 1-800-794-5267; katahdinshadows.com), Rt. 157, Medway 04460. David and Theresa Violette own this full-service, family-geared four-season campground with a central lodge, swimming pool, dock, weekend hayrides, a big playground, athletic fields, a "community kitchen," tent and hookup sites, hutniks, and well-designed cabins with kitchen facilities. Pets are welcome. Tent sites $23–32, cabins $26, larger cabins with kitchenettes up to $101. Rates are based on two people; $5 per extra person, free under age 18. Weekly rates. Special events.

KI Jo-Mary Multiple Use Forest (207-965-8135). Open May–Oct. A 200,000-plus-acre tract of commercial forest stretching almost from Greenville on the west to the Katahdin Iron Works on the east, and north to Millinocket. There are 150 miles of privately maintained roads (logging trucks have right-of-way) and widely scattered campsites. Seasonal checkpoints charge day-use and camping fees. Good fishing, hunting, and plenty of solitude. The **Jo-Mary Lake Campground** (207-723-8117), open mid-May–Oct. 1, offers 60 campsites, flush toilets, and hot showers, and is handy to Gulf Hagas.

Peaks-Kenny State Park (207-564-2003), Rt. 153, 6 miles from Dover-Foxcroft. Open mid-May–Sept. with 56 campsites on Sebec Lake. Reservations are a must; for details see *Camping* in "What's Where."

Mattawamkeag Wilderness Park (207-746-4881; mwpark.com), Mattawamkeag (off Rt. 2; half an hour's drive from the I-95 Medway exit). A town-run park with 50 campsites for RVs and tents, 11 Adirondack shelters, bathrooms, hot showers, a small store, a recreation building, picnic facilities, 15 miles of hiking trails, 60 miles of canoeing on the Mattawamkeag River with patches of whitewater, and bass, salmon, and trout fishing.

Allagash Gateway Campsite and Camps (207-723-9215; allagash gateway.com), P.O. Box 396, Millinocket 04462. Open May–Nov.; winter rentals by reservation. Location, location! Off the Golden Road, 28 miles west of Millinocket, sited on Ripogenus Lake. Longtime owners Bill and Jan Reeves offer housekeeping cabins, RV and primitive sites, hot showers, a marina, canoe rentals, and shuttle service to the upper West Branch of the Penobscot.

Abol Bridge Campground and Store (207-447-5803; abolcampground .com), 18.5 Golden Road, Millinocket 04462. Open May 1–Thanksgiving. The sore is also open Jan.–Mar., selling homemade takeout as well as groceries and fuel. Tent and trailer sites on the West Branch of the Penobscot River at Abol Stream.

The **Department of Conservation** (parksandlands.com) Northern Region Office in Ashland (207-435-7963) can also supply information and pamphlet guides to campsites in the Penobscot River Corridor and other nearby holdings. This is wilderness camping geared to experienced outdoorsmen.

Also see **Baxter State Park** in *Green Space* and both the Penobscot Outdoor Center (penobscotoutdoorcenter .com) and the Rice Farm Campground (neoc.com), described in *Whitewater Rafting*.

✳ Where to Eat

All entries are in Millinocket unless otherwise noted
DINING OUT

✐ & **Chanterelle's at the River Driver's Pub** (207-723-5523.neoc.com),

Black Cat Rd. off State Park Rd, 8 miles east of Millinocket (turn at the 35 MPH sign). Nicely sited, facing down through Twin Pine Camps to Katahdin Lake with a great view of its namesake mountain. With a solid reputation from its previous location, this new facility (opened in Sept. 2011) should be a winner. It's good for all three meals in-season with a choice between the family-geared pub (burgers, mac-and-cheese) and the more formal Chanterelle's, named for the tastiest of wild mushrooms, theoretically growing outside the door. The dinner menu might feature pork osso buco and pan-seared scallops. Entrées $19–26.

& **Fredericka's at Big Moose Inn** (207-723-8391), Millinocket Lake, 8 miles west of Millinocket on Baxter State Park Rd. Open for dinner Wed.–Sat., June–early Oct.; also Sun. July–Aug. Hot breakfast is served Sat.–Sun. in-season to B&B guests. Dinner reservations suggested. Accessible by boat, and the most convenient dining to Baxter State Park and to lakeside lodging on the lakes east of Millinocket. Laurie Cormier tells us that the restaurant is named for her mother and that everything is made from scratch, including the risotto and gnocchi. It's a pleasant dining room, but we prefer the sunporch. The menu ranges from chicken to flat-iron steak to duck in a fennel blueberry reduction. Entrées $18–22. The **Loose Moose Bar and Grill** (open Thu.–Sat), with good pub grub and live music, is usually jammed.

EATING OUT ☉ (ᵖ) **Appalachian Trail Café** (207-723-6720), 210 Penobscot Ave., Millinocket. Open 5 AM–8 PM daily, year-round. A beloved landmark, good burgers, omelets, doughnuts (try the pumpkin), pies, home cooking, and reasonable prices.

The walls and back counter are filled with AT photos and memorabilia, and there's a computer for checking email. Owners Paul and Jamie Renaud literally walked into town after completing the 2,175-mile trek from Georgia. They were puzzled by the café's name, given its lack of any obvious link to the trail. They didn't mean to buy it, but it came with the Appalachian Trail Lodge down the street, which they did buy. They kept the cooks, just rehabbed the kitchen and redecorated the café.

✻ **Pelletier Loggers Family Restaurant Bar and Grill** (207-723-6100; americanloggers.com), 57 Penobscot Ave., Millinocket. Open year-round 5 AM–9 PM or later for breakfast, lunch, and dinner. The logging truck jutting from its facade gets your attention, and inside it just gets better. Seems that the Discovery Channel's *American Loggers* reality show features the Pelletier family, local loggers who spent $1 million transforming the former Downtown Restaurant and Laundromat into a spacious pine-paneled lounge and grill with a large stone fireplace and decor that includes moose and deer heads, a chain saw and truck grille, and waiters wearing Pelletier logging uniforms. The menu is large and so are the portions. Try the "clear cut" salad.

✻ **Scootic Inn Restaurant** (207-723-4566), 70 Penobscot Ave. Open for lunch and dinner Mon.–Sat. from 11, Sun. at 3. George and Bea Simon are third-generation owners. Menu choices include fresh dough pizza, calzones, pasta entrées, seafood, and smoked baby back ribs. Children's menu.

Orvieto Market & Deli (207-723-8399), 67 Prospect St. Joel and Debra Dicentes's market offers homemade tomato sauce, pastas, stuffed breads,

and other makings for dinner at rental camps; also take-out sandwiches and panini.

ROAD FOOD ✻ **Elaine's Basket Café** (207-943-2705), 24 W. Main St., Milo. Open daily for breakfast and lunch. Pleasant atmosphere, good food, good service, standout doughnuts and pies.

✪ **Coburn Family Restaurant** (207-943-5140), 66 Park St. Milo. Open 6 AM–7 PM. A cheery, friendly diner, good for franks and beans or a lobster roll. Daily specials.

The Nor'easter Restaurant (207-564-2122), 44 North St., Dover-Foxcroft. Open daily lunch–dinner. A good bet for fried seafood, pizza, and "broasted" chicken with fries and slaw. Children's menu.

In **Newport** road-food and fuel sources cluster around the I-95 exit. Check out **Anglers** (207-368-3374; anglersseafoodrestaurant.com), 542 Elm St. (Rt. 7/100 near the jct. of 2), one in a small chain of Maine restaurants featuring fresh fish, great onion rings.

PELLETIER LOGGERS FAMILY RESTAURANT, MILLINOCKET

Christina Tree

✳ Entertainment

Center Theatre for the Performing Arts (207-564-8943; centertheatre .org), 20 E. Main St., Dover-Foxcroft. A vintage movie theater that's been restored as a venue for live performance and film. Check the website for current listings.

The Junction General Store and Entertainment Park (207-965-8876; thejunctiongeneral.com), 197 Davis St. (Rt. 11). Billed as "Maine's largest entertainment & Music Park," featuring drive-in movies, frequent big-name bands and performers, a store, and camping.

✳ Selective Shopping

In Millinocket

✪ **North Light Gallery** (207-723-4414; artnorthlight.com), 356 Penobscot Ave. Open year-round, Mon.–Sat. 10–6. Marsha Donahue has worked in Maine's leading coastal galleries and is well acquainted with the state's leading artists. This gallery showcases some two dozen artists and sculptors as well as well as her own work, all focusing on interior Maine. It includes her own exceptional paintings, also crafted items, prints, and many other reasons to stop by.

Katahdin General Store (207-723-4123), 160 Bates St., is a source of hunting and fishing licenses, gas, live bait, groceries, cold beer, camping permits, and the largest selection of camping and sporting gear in the area. Also check out the **Hungry Moose**

Sandwich Shop & Deli, good for daily-made sandwiches and soups.

Memories of Maine Gallery (207-723-4834; memoriesofmaine.com), 80 Penobscot Ave., features art and photography by Jean McLean; also sells jewelry, antiques, and gifts by Maine crafters, as well as customized laser framing.

North Woods Trading Post (207-723-4326), Baxter State Park Rd. Open May–Oct., 8–7. This is an oasis for campers and hikers, the nearest store to Baxter State Park, selling fishing licenses, basic groceries, snacks, books, and pizza.

✳ Special Events

February: **Winterfest** in Millinocket—snowmobile parade, antique snowmobile display, bonfire, cross-country ski events, and poker run.

July: **4th of July Festival**, Millinocket—parade, music, vendors, fireworks. It's a big deal for people in this area. Many come home for the 4th of July, and there is usually two to three days' worth of activities. **Summerfest**, East Millinocket, features a weekend full of activities and a fireworks display.

August: **Katahdin Area Wooden Canoe Festival** in Medway showcases the wooden canoe with demonstrations, a canoe race, and more.

September: **Trails End Festival** honoring through-hikers on the AT.

October: **Fly-in and car show** at Millinocket Airport.

AROOSTOOK COUNTY

Aroostook is Maine's least populated county but the largest in area, almost as large as all of Massachusetts. Within the state it's usually referred to simply as The County. The name *Aroostook* comes from a Native American word meaning "beautiful river," but the beauty is spread across the landscape. The luminosity of its sky—broader seeming than elsewhere in New England—is The County's most striking characteristic. Bounded by Canada on two sides and the North Maine Woods on the third, Aroostook is so far off traditional tourist routes—it actually gets more visitors in winter than it does in summer—that many New England maps omit it entirely. Maine pundits are fond of noting that Portland is as far from Fort Kent, the northern terminus of Rt. 1, as it is from New York City.

Although admittedly rural, Aroostook has long suffered from the popular misconception that all it has to offer are views of potato fields. In fact, The County is rich in cultural traditions, friendly faces, and has an interesting ethnic heritage that includes a Swedish colony and a string of French-speaking Acadian settlements. Small but fascinating historical museums are scattered from the southern part of The County to its northern tip at the top of the state.

Acadians trace their lineage to French settlers who came to farm and fish in what is now Nova Scotia in the early 1600s and who, in 1755, were forcibly deported by an English governor. This "Grand Dérangement," which dispersed a population of some 10,000 Acadians, brutally divided families (a tale told by Longfellow in "Evangeline"). Many were returned to France, only to make their way back to a warmer New World in Louisiana, and many were resettled in New Brunswick, from which they were once more dislodged after the American Revolution when the British government gave their land to loyalists from the former colonies.

In a meadow overlooking the St. John River behind Madawaska's Tante Blanche Museum (named for an 18th-century local Acadian folk heroine), a large marble cross and an outsized wooden sculpture of a voyageur in his canoe mark the spot on which several hundred of these displaced Acadians landed in 1785. They settled both sides of the St. John River, an area known as Mattawaska ("land of the porcupine"). Not until 1842 did the river—still Rivière St-Jean to Acadians—become the formal boundary dividing Canada and Maine.

The 1842 Webster-Ashburton Treaty settled the Aroostook War, a footnote in American history recalled in the 1830s wooden blockhouses at Fort Kent and Fort Fairfield. Until relatively recently this bloodless conflict between the United States

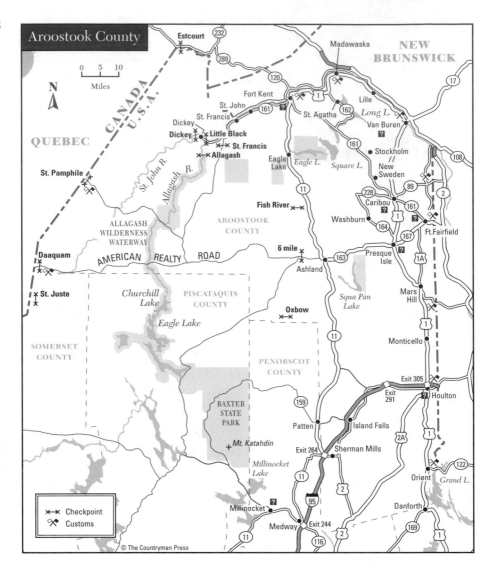

Aroostook County

© The Countryman Press

and Canada was the area's chief historic claim, but the valley's distinctive Acadian heritage is gaining increasing recognition.

In 1976 Acadian Village, a seasonal living history museum, was created in Van Buren. Now consisting of 16 buildings, many historic and most moved to the Rt. 1 site from around the St. John Valley, it's the scene of many special events. But the Acadian heritage is also visible in the very shape of St. John Valley towns, where wooden houses are strung out along roads that stretch like arms from the cathedral-sized Catholic churches always at their heart.

Despite intense pressure to assimilate from both civil and ecclesiastical authorities—at one time children could be punished for speaking French anywhere on public school grounds, and parochial schools also discouraged the language— Acadians have stubbornly preserved their traditions and distinctive "Valley

French," a blend of old Acadian and Quebec dialects. Today bilingual signage is common in the valley, schools offer French immersion programs, Catholic churches have Masses in both French and English, and there is a bicultural studies program at the Fort Kent campus of the University of Maine, which also has an extensive collection of Acadian historical materials.

In 2014 the St. John River Valley with Quebec and New Brunswick on the Canadian side will host the World Acadian Congress. Telling the story of Acadia will involve sporting events, family reunions (perhaps as many as 120), and an array of events. Quebec City and Louisiana will have to wait for their turn until 2019. Maine is contributing $1 million to the event; past events have drawn 50,000 visitors. You may want to make a reservation early.

Swedes, who settled in and around New Sweden after the Civil War, are a far smaller and more assimilated community than the Acadians but have preserved some colorful Old World traditions. Best known of these is a Midsommar Festival that attracts Swedish Americans and other visitors from around the country. The Swedes also made an enduring recreational contribution to The County: They are credited with introducing cross-country skiing. At New Sweden Museum you can learn about one of the most interesting immigration stories in American history.

The County cannot be easily categorized topographically. Within the boundaries there are three distinct regions, each with a unique feel and appearance. The Upper St. John Valley, at the top of The County, is a broad ribbon of river land backed by woodland to the west and by a high, open plateau to the east; it has its own distinctly Acadian look, language, and cuisine. Central Aroostook—the rolling farmland around Fort Fairfield, Presque Isle, and Caribou—is generally equated with the entire county. It, too, has its appeal, especially around Washburn and New Sweden, sites of two of New England's more interesting museums. In recent years, Fort Fairfield and Easton have welcomed a community of Amish, who have become farmers and brought horse-drawn wagons to the long winding roads of The County. Houlton, the northern terminus of I-95 and the county seat, is in southern Aroostook, a mix of farmland, lonely woods, and lakes; another community of Amish are settled in Smyrna, running a fine general store.

Four million of Aroostook's 5 million acres are wooded, forestland that includes most of the Allagash Wilderness Waterway and more than 1,000 lakes. Many visitors actually enter The

SORTING POTATOES DURING HARVEST IN BRIDGEWATER

County in canoes, paddling down the Allagash River, which flows north and empties into the St. John River at Allagash, a minuscule hamlet that's become widely known as Mattagash to readers of novels (*The Funeral Makers*, *Once Upon a Time on the Banks*, and *The Weight of Winter*) by native Cathie Pelletier. Local residents will tell you that the names of Pelletier's characters have been changed only as slightly as that of her town, and that the interplay between Catholics and Protestants (descendants of Acadian and Scottish settlers, respectively) chronicled in her books remains very real.

Aroostook County produces about 850,000 tons of potatoes a year on 56,000 acres. Family farms, the staple of The County's landscape, are still going strong, and schoolkids get out in the third week of September to help with the potato harvest. The potato industry has stabilized over 10 years, says Tim Hobbs, director of development on the Maine Potato Board, who adds that the seed potato facility at the Porter Seed Farm, growing mini tubers, allows Maine to be in control of the plant's true life cycle.

Other crops, notably organic wheat, broccoli, canola, soybeans, and oats, diversify the agriculture.

Ask locally for directions to the best places to walk, ski, and fish; feast on fiddleheads, ployes (buckwheat crêpes), and poutine (fries with cheese and gravy). B&Bs are small (often just two or three rooms), with a more personal feel than most downstate.

Winter brings predictable snowfall and is the big draw. Most visitors come in this season to snowmobile (The County has 2,200 miles of maintained snowmobile trails), snowshoe, or dogsled. (Dogsled races are held annually.) The Maine Winter Sports Center, a nonprofit organization that encourages traditional snow sports, recently opened state-of-the-art facilities in Fort Kent and Presque Isle for biathlon and cross-country training, both with free groomed public trail systems.

Winter driving is considered less daunting here than elsewhere in Maine because, thanks to the region's consistently low temperatures, the snow is drier and less icy. Summer temperatures also tend to be cooler, and in early July the potato fields are a spread of pink and white blossoms. Fall colors, which usually peak in the last weeks of September at the end of potato harvest, include reddening barley fields as well as maples.

The conventional loop tour around The County is I-95 to its terminus at Houlton, then Rt. 1 north to "America's First Mile" in Fort Kent and back down Rt. 11. We suggest doing it in reverse—the views from the highway are more scenic going clockwise.

Canada's proximity means that residents of The County are as likely to travel across the border to dine or shop as to venture into other parts of the state. An international bridge over the St. John River links the downtowns of Madawaska and Edmundston, New Brunswick, for instance, making them in effect one mini metropolis. So we also include a few Canadian recommendations within this chapter—but remember, a passport is now necessary for reentry into the United States.

GUIDANCE Aroostook County Tourism (1-888-216-2463; visitaroostook.com), Caribou, can send you a regional guide with places to stay and eat; it also lists activities and guide services.

Otherwise, The County is divided into three distinct regions. For details about northern Aroostook (the Upper St. John Valley), contact the **Greater Fort Kent**

Area Chamber of Commerce (207-834-5354; fortkentchamber.com), P.O. Box 430, Fort Kent 04743; and the **Greater Madawaska Area Chamber of Commerce** (207-728-7000; greatermadawaskachamber.com), 363 Main St., Madawaska 04756. A walk-in information center at the Fort Kent Blockhouse, staffed by Boy Scouts, is open seasonally. For central Aroostook, contact the **Central Aroostook Chamber of Commerce** (207-764-6561; centralaroostookchamber.org), P.O. Box 672, Presque Isle 04769; and **Caribou Area Chamber of Commerce** (207-498-6156; cariboumaine.net), 393 Main St., Caribou 04736. For southern Aroostook, see the **Greater Houlton Chamber of Commerce** (207-532-4216; houlton chamber.com), 109-B Main St., Houlton 04730.

The big walk-in **Information Center** in The County, operated by the town of Houlton, is just off I-95 at the intersection of Rt. 1 in Houlton (207-532-6346).

Note: The North Maine Woods information office on Rt. 1 in Ashland is described under *Guidance* in "The North Maine Woods."

GETTING THERE *By car:* Our preferred route is to take I-95 to Benedicta or Sherman Mills, then Rt. 11 up through Patten, Ashland, and Eagle Lake to Fort Kent, from which you can explore west to Allagash and east along the Upper St. John Valley to St. Agatha and/or Van Buren. Stop at the New Sweden Museum, for a meal in Caribou, and for a final overnight in the Houlton area. An alternative route through The County, especially if you are beginning Down East, is to follow Rt. 1 through rolling hills and past scenic lakes (Grand Lake is breathtaking from the top of one hill), through tiny town centers, to Houlton. From here, continue through Presque Isle and Caribou to Van Buren, then follow Rt. 1 along the St. John River to Fort Kent. Return on Rt. 11 to Sherman Mills, where you can pick up I-95 south.

By plane: Regularly scheduled service to **Presque Isle/Northern Maine Regional Airport** is limited to U.S. Airways Express (1-800-428-4322).

By bus: **Cyr Bus Line** (207-827-2335 or 1-800-244-2335) operates daily between Fort Kent and Bangor.

WHEN TO COME Snowmobilers and cross-country skiers flock here in the deep of winter to pursue their sports, but the long summer days appeal to many of us. The roads stretch out for miles, inviting the bicycle trips that are a natural for the area, and the lakes and museums along the Acadian region's northern stretch are open and ready for visitors when the weather warms up, when the sporting camps do much of their business. Hunters will want to arrange a visit in fall.

✹ To See

MUSEUMS A brochure detailing The County's historical museums and attractions is available from most area chambers of commerce. Following are those we found of particular interest (in order of suggested routing). Because most of these museums are entirely run by volunteers, and there are many miles between them, always call before visiting to be sure they are open.

See "Katahdin Region" for details about the **Lumbermen's Museum** in Patten.

Fort Kent Historical Society Museum (207-834-5354), Main and Market Sts., Fort Kent. Open June–Labor Day, Tue.–Fri. noon–4, by appointment off-season.

The former Bangor & Aroostook Railroad depot is filled with local memorabilia and exhibits on the economic and social history of the area, focusing on lumbering and agriculture.

Fort Kent Blockhouse Museum, off Rt. 1, Fort Kent. Open Memorial Day–Labor Day, 9–7:30, a Maine state park maintained by the state Bureau of Parks and Lands and the local Boy Scout troop. This symbol of the northern terminus of Rt. 1 is a convincingly ancient, if much-restored, two-story 1830s blockhouse with its original foundation and walls. Documents and mementos from the Aroostook Bloodless War are exhibited inside. Be sure to wander down to the Fish River behind the blockhouse, a pleasant walk to picnic and tenting sites.

Madawaska Historic Center and Acadian Cross Shrine (207-728-3606), Rt. 1, Madawaska. The complex includes the **Tante Blanche Acadia Museum** (local memorabilia) open June–mid-Sept., Wed.–Sun. 11–4, but check for changing hours. If you follow the dirt road behind the museum to the river, you'll see the 18th-century **Albert Homestead**, plus the Voyageur statue and stone cross described in the introduction to this chapter.

Acadian Village & Levasseur-Dube Art Museum (207-868-5042; connect maine.com/acadianvillage), Rt. 1, Van Buren. Open mid-June–mid-Sept., daily noon–5. The 17 buildings include a school and store, a barbershop, a train station, old homesteads with period furnishings, a jail, and a reconstructed 18th-century log church. $6 adults, $3 children.

St. Agathe Historical Society Museum (207-543-6911), 534 Main St., St. Agathe. Open late June–early Sept., Tue.–Sun. 1–4. The oldest house in this unusually pleasant village on Long Lake, the Pelletier-Marquis home dates just to 1854; it's filled with a sense of the town's unusually rich ethnic and social history. Enter through **The Preservation Center**, behind the museum, which holds religious, domestic, and military artifacts, along with an extensive photo collection.

Musée Culturel du Mont-Carmel (207-895-3339), Rt. 1, Lille. Open by chance or appointment. A wooden 1909 church, this beautiful structure has been painstakingly restored by the Association culturelle et historique du Mont-Carmel. Musicians perform under its now solid roof. Two gilded archangels blowing trumpets stand at the top of this landmark's two towers. An exhibition space down the street, Gallerie Lille-sur-St. Jean, 1022 Main St., a former general store, holds art and history exhibits.

♪ New Sweden Historical Society Museum (in-season, 207-316-7306; off-season, 207-896-5240), just east of Rt. 161, New Sweden. Open late May–Labor Day, Mon.–Fri. noon–4, weekends 1–4. Entering the community's reconstructed Kapitoleum (meetinghouse), you are faced with the imposing bust of William Widgery Thomas, the Portland man sent by

MUSÉE CULTUREL DU MONT-CARMEL
Nancy English

President Lincoln to Sweden in 1863 to halt the sale of iron to the Confederacy. Thomas quickly learned Swedish, married two countesses (the second after her sister, Thomas's first wife, died), and eventually devoted his sizable energies to establishing a colony of Swedish farmers in Maine. In 1870 the House of Representatives authorized the project, granting 100 acres of woodland to each Swedish family. A pink granite memorial in a pine grove behind the museum complex commemorates the arrival and hardships of those who settled here between 1870 and 1875. Despite the severe climate and thin soil (Thomas had been struck by the similarities between Sweden and northern Maine), New Sweden prospered, with 1,400 immigrants in 1895 and 689 buildings, including 3 churches, 7 general stores, and 2 railroad stations. New Sweden's annual festivals draw thousands of local descendants. The museum remains a cultural touchstone for Swedes living throughout the Northeast, and the town continues to attract visitors from Sweden, even an occasional immigrant. Also check out nearby Thomas Park, with a picnic area, the monument and cemetery behind the museum, and the other historic buildings in New Sweden, including the Larsson Ostlund Log Home, Lars Noak Blacksmith and Woodworking Shop, and the one-room Schoolhouse.

The Salmon Brook Historical Society (207-455-4339), Rt. 164, Washburn. Open July 4–Labor Day, Wed. 8–11 and Sat. 1–4; tours by appointment. The pleasant 1852 **Benjamin C. Wilder Farmstead** (13 rooms of 1850–1900 period furnishings) and the **Aroostook Agricultural Museum** (potato-harvesting tools and trivia housed in the neighboring barn) offer a sense of life and potato farming in the late 19th century. Washburn's Taterstate Frozen Foods claims to have invented the frozen french fry.

✒ **Nylander Museum** (207-493-4209; nylandermuseum.org), 657 Main St., Caribou. May–Oct., Mon.–Sat. 12:30–4:30; Nov.–Apr., Wed. 9–5, or by appointment. A small but intriguing museum displaying permanent collections of fossils, minerals and rocks, shells and other marine life, butterflies and moths, birds, and early human artifacts, most collected by Swedish-born Olof Nylander; also a medicinal herb garden in the back, with traditional Native American plants.

Caribou Historical Center (207-498-2556), Rt. 1, Caribou. Open June–Aug., Wed.–Sat. 11–5. A log building filled with local memorabilia from the mid-19th century to the 1930s, including antiques, historical papers, photographs, home furnishings, and tools. Also a replica of an 1860s one-room school with a bell in the cupola.

Vera Estey House and the Presque Isle Historical Society (207-762-1151; pihistory.org), 16 3rd St., Presque Isle. Open by appointment. Many original furnishings, with period additions. The Presque Isle Firehouse is also under restoration, and includes the original area jail. Kim Smith, historical society treasurer, gives guided walking tours of historic Presque Isle while wearing a copy of an 1890s walking dress. Free.

Northern Maine Museum of Science (207-768-9482; umpi.maine.edu/info /nmms/museum.htm), Folsom Hall, University of Maine–Presque Isle. Open daily. Interesting exhibits, including an herbarium (library of plant species), a coral-reef environment, an extensive display of plant and shell specimens collected by Leroy Norton (a well-known local amateur naturalist), topographic maps, and Aroostook potato varieties, among much more.

The Presque Isle Air Museum (207-764-2542), 650 Airport Dr., Presque Isle. Open during normal airport hours. The Presque Isle Historical Society has created this museum as a testament to the rich history of air travel in Presque Isle. During World War II, Presque Isle became the departure point for planes and equipment going overseas. An army airfield was created, and more planes left PIAAF bound for Europe than from any other U.S. base. In the early 1960s the missile wing was deactivated and the base was closed.

Aroostook County Historical and Art Museum (207-532-2519), 109 Main St., Houlton. Open Memorial Day–Labor Day, Tue.–Sat. 1–4 and by appointment. Same building as the Houlton Area Chamber of Commerce. A large, well-organized collection of local memorabilia.

Oakfield Railroad Museum (207-757-8575), Station St., Oakfield. Open Memorial Day–Labor Day, Sat., Sun., and holidays 1–4. This 1910 Bangor & Aroostook Railroad station is one of three remaining wood-framed railroad stations between Searsport and Fort Kent. Exhibits include photographs from the early days of the railroad, vintage signs and advertising pieces, maps, newspapers, a rail motor car, and a C-66 caboose.

Southern Aroostook Agricultural Museum (207-538-9300; oldplow.org), 1664 Rt. 1, Littletown. A. E. Mooers Milk and Cream cart got around on a sled, as you learn in this museum dedicated to the history of local farming. The Potato House has a fine display of beautiful potato bags created by farms, and the Farm House is dedicated to domestic life. Public suppers ($8 per person in 2011) are held through summer and fall.

CHURCHES As noted in the introduction to this chapter, tall, elaborate, French Canadian–style Catholic churches form the heart of most Upper St. John Valley villages: **St. Thomas Aquinas** in Madawaska, **St. Louis** in Fort Kent (with distinctive open filigree steeples and a fine carillon), **St. David's** in the village of St. David, and **St. Luce** in Frenchville. When the twin-spired wooden church dominating the village of Lille was decommissioned, it was donated by the bishop of Portland to the Association culterelle et historique du Mont-Carmel, which converted it into **Musée culturel du Mont-Carmel** (see above), an Acadian cultural center and a setting for concerts and workshops.

OTHER ATTRACTIONS ✪ ✑ ⴲ **A. E. Howell Wildlife Conservation Center and Spruce Acres Refuge** (207-532-6880; spruceacresrefuge.org), 101 Lycette Rd. (off Rt. 1), Amity 04471-5114 (14 miles south of Houlton). Open May–mid-Oct., and weather permitting till Nov. 15, Mon.–Sat. 10–3; $10 adults 15 and older, AARP $2 discount, children 14 and under free. Art Howell Jr., one of the best-known and -respected of more than 90 wild animal rehabilitators in the state, specializes in rehabilitating black bears, moose, deer, wolves, and bald eagles that have been wounded, to return them to the wild if possible. The center has 64 acres of woods with a picnic area and a pond stocked with fish for members; also a camping area. No dogs are allowed. Handicapped-accessible. "Moose Man of Baxter Park" Bill Silliker's photographs have been donated to raise funds to benefit wildlife; prints, murals, books are for sale here.

Aroostook National Wildlife Refuge (207-328-4634; friendsofaroostooknwr .org), Limestone. Covering 5,252 acres with 6.5 miles of trails for hiking and cross-country skiing, this refuge was created when the Loring Air Force Base in Limestone was decommissioned. Upland sandpipers nest here in summer; boreal birds can be seen. Mink frogs love these wetlands.

The World's Largest Scale Model of the Solar System. Kevin McCartney, a professor at the University of Maine at Presque Isle and director of the Northern Maine Museum of Science, headed the construction by many different schools and organizations of this solar system. The scale model, both in diameter of planets and in distance between planets, is 1:93,000,000. Jupiter, the largest planet, is 5 feet in diameter. Pluto, just an inch in diameter, is located at the Maine Tourism Association's Information Center in Houlton. Dwarf planets more than 90 miles from the "sun" are new additions in Topsfield. An informational brochure details where the planets are along Rt. 1 from Houlton to Presque Isle, and facts about the solar system.

ART Reed Art Gallery (207-768-9611), 181 Main St., University of Maine at Presque Isle. Open year-round. About six exhibitions a year are presented here of work from Maine and New Brunswick artists.

SCENIC DRIVES Flat Mountain. The single most memorable landscape that we found in all Aroostook is easily accessible if you know where to turn. The high plateau is well named Flat Mountain and is just above but invisible from Rt. 1 east of Fort Kent. Ask locally about the road through the back settlements from Frenchville to St. Agatha, a lake resort with several good restaurants.

Watson Settlement Covered Bridge. Follow Main St. through Houlton's Market Square Historic District (a *Walking Tour Guide* to this area is available from the chamber of commerce) until it turns into Military St. (dating to the Aroostook War). Turn north on Foxcroft Rd.; in 2 miles note your first view of Mars Hill Mountain (the area's only mountain, at 1,660 feet). The mountain's ownership was disputed in the Aroostook War; it is now a ski area. At roughly 3.5 miles, note the road on your left descending to a small iron bridge across the Meduxnekeag River; the covered bridge, built in 1902, is midway down this hill. The road rejoins Rt. 1 10 minutes north of Houlton.

✳ To Do

BIKING Mojo (207-760-9500; mojooutdoorsports.com), 719 Main St., Presque Isle. Clinics, women's programs, and mountain and road group rides. Paddling and river tubing, too. Winter brings group skiing.

Also see **Nordic Heritage Center** in *Winter Sports*.

CANOEING Allagash Wilderness Waterway. This is considered *the* canoe trip in Maine, and after a three-day expedition we have to agree. The whole trip, 92 miles of lake and river canoeing, takes far longer than three days. We put in at Round Pond and paddled the shorter 32-mile trip to Allagash Village. Though it's possible to shuttle your own vehicles, leaving one at the beginning and one at the end, we recommend using a transportation service, which will bring you, your gear, and your canoes into your put-in spot and retrieve you at takeout. This simplifies the parking issue; also, you won't have to go back into the woods to retrieve your car at the end of the trip, and the transportation companies are experienced in negotiating the bumpy dirt roads that can lead to blown tires and rocks thrown at the windshield. **Norman L'Italien** (207-398-3187), P.O. Box 67, St. Francis 04774, was well informed, helpful, and friendly. After we checked in at the gate (road-use fee of $8 per person for non-Maine-residents per day, $5 for residents; overnight camping fee $5 per person per night for non-Maine-residents, $4 for residents), his driver dropped us off at the bridge just above Round Pond and told us to call when we were off the river. Norman also operates **Pelletier's Campground** (207-398-3187) in St. Francis, a good spot to stay the night before your departure. Keep in mind that the trip to the area from Sherman Mills, where you leave I-95, is at least three hours; head up the night before your trip. Plan to arrive in daylight if you need to set up tents. The **Maine Bureau of Parks and Lands** (207-941-4014) manages the wilderness waterway and is a source of general information as well as a map and a list of outfitters.

Paddling and floating with the current, sunlight twinkling off the water, you'll feel you're truly in a wilderness paradise. Even when the sun hid behind the clouds, the river wasn't the least bit gloomy or less beautiful. We were there on Labor Day weekend, and the weather and bugs cooperated quite nicely—but come prepared for both rain and pests. Blackflies, mosquitoes, and no-see-ums can be brutal, so bring plenty of bug repellent, maybe even protective netting. On our trip, however, bugs were not a problem, and we slept out underneath the stars two of the three nights. Remember that there are no stores around the next corner; if you leave it at home, you do without. Pack light, but bring enough spare clothing so that if some gets wet, you'll still be comfortable. Pack in waterproof backpacks, or seal items in plastic bags to prevent soaking should your canoe tip. Bring extra garbage bags to wrap around sleeping bags and pillows. Don't forget a camera and extra film or disks. **Allagash Falls** is particularly nice, and the portage around the waterfall is an easy 0.5-mile hike. The trail and picnic area are well maintained. This is actually a good place to cook a solid meal, using up your heaviest supplies before carrying your stuff around the falls. The trip after the falls to Allagash is just one more overnight, and if you plan remaining meals accordingly, you can lighten your load around the portage.

Campsites on the waterway are clean and comfortable, with plenty of space for a group to spread out. Sites are available on a first-come, first-served basis, so the earlier in the day you begin paddling, the better choice you have. During our visit the river was far from crowded, even on a holiday weekend. We saw fewer than 15 people outside our group on our three-day journey. The rangers keep track of who is on the river, so there's no need to be nervous that you will be too isolated should something happen. If you're not an experienced canoeist, don't worry: A three-day trip is easily manageable without putting too much strain on infrequently used muscles. Paddling the whole waterway takes 7 to 10 days, though it's best to be flexible in case wind or rain delays your trip.

If you aren't comfortable venturing out on your own, several area guides can take you down the river. Following are a few suggestions. Contact **North Maine Woods** (see *Guidance* in "The North Maine Woods") for other options.

Allagash Guide Service (207-398-3418; allagashguideservice.com), 928 Allagash Rd., Allagash. Kelley Lizotte and Sean Lizotte, a Registered Maine Guide, rent paddles and canoes and also offer transport and car pickup. Guided trips here and on the St. John River.

Allagash Canoe Trips (207-237-3077; allagashcanoetrips.com). This outfitting company was founded in 1953. Chip Cochrane and other guides lead trips, providing all equipment and meals.

FARM TOUR ✂ **Knot-II-Bragg Farm** (207-455-8386; knotiibragg.com), 469 New Dunn Town Rd., Wade 04786. Open by appointment June–Oct., Tue.–Sat. 10–4. $6.50 adults, $5 children. Natalia Bragg, a practicing herbalist and in the sixth generation of women to practice herbal craft in her family, talks about the history and herbal lore of the area. Her company makes Old Log Driver's products, which include natural painkillers; all products are for sale, as is handmade soap and twig furniture. Ask for a copy of the tourist guide to Washburn that she put together, detailing all businesses in the northern Maine community. Monthly classes in traditional herbal healing.

FISHING The catch here is so rich and varied that it's recognized throughout the country. Salmon grow to unusual size, and trout are also large and numerous. The 80-mile Fish River chain of rivers and lakes (Eagle, Long, and Square Lakes) is legendary in fishing circles. Fish strike longer in the season than they do farther south, and fall fishing begins earlier. Contact the Maine Department of Inland Fisheries and Wildlife in Ashland (207-435-3231; in-state, 1-800-353-6334).

GOLF The County's topography lends itself to golf, and the sport is so popular that most towns maintain at least a nine-hole course. The most famous course, with 18 holes, is **Aroostook Valley Country Club**, Fort Fairfield (207-476-8083; avcc.ca); its tees are split between Canada and Maine. The 18-hole **Va-Jo-Wa Golf Course** (207-463-2128) in Island Falls and the **Presque Isle Country Club** (207-764-0439) are also considered above par. **Houlton Community Golf Club** (207-532-2662) is on offer in the south. **Caribou Country Club** (207-493-3933; caribougolf .com), Rt. 161, Caribou, is a nine-hole course designed by Geoffrey Cornish. **Mars Hill Country Club** (207-425-4802; golfmhcc.com), 75 Country Club Rd., Mars Hill, has 18 holes.

HIKING See the **Debouille Management Unit** and **Aroostook State Park** under *Green Space.*

Fish River Falls. Ask locally for directions to the trail that leads from the former Fort Kent airport down along the river, an unusually beautiful footway through pines. Note the swimming holes below the falls. **The Dyke in Fort Kent** is also worth finding: a 0.5-mile walk along the Fish River. The trail up **Mount Carmel** (views up and down the river valley) begins on Rt. 1 at the state rest area near the Madawaska–Grand Isle town line.

KAYAKING Perception of Aroostook (207-764-5506; perceptionofaroostook .com), Presque Isle. Kayak rentals and river trips with guide Leo Freeman. The business offers shuttles for day trips on the Aroostook River; a lunch at Rum Rapids (see *Lodging*) is featured on one trip.

❄ Winter Sports

CROSS-COUNTRY SKIING The same reliable snow that serves snowmobilers allows residents to take advantage of hundreds of miles of trails maintained exclusively for cross-country skiing by local towns and clubs. Any town office or chamber of commerce will steer you to local trails.

Maine Winter Sports Center (207-328-0991; mainewsc.org). The organization, funded by the Libra Foundation, has developed a network of community trails for use by schoolchildren and local residents, and hosted the World Cup Biathlon in 2004, combining rifle marksmanship with cross-county skiing. MWSC has built two Nordic events facilities, used for training high school skiers and Olympic hopefuls. **10th Mountain Division Center** (207-834-6203) in Fort Kent includes a biathlon range, links to recreational ski trails, and a handsome lodge. A similar facility, the **Nordic Heritage Center** (207-328-0991) in Presque Isle, focuses on cross-country skiing. Mountain bike races have also been hosted in recent years.

DOWNHILL SKIING Big Rock (207-425-6711 or 1-866-529-2695; bigrockmaine .com), 37 Graves Rd., Mars Hill. A downhill and cross-country facility owned by Maine Winter Sports Center, this place focuses on getting everyone involved, with adult weekday tickets at $25, weekend at $30, seniors and juniors $25, and over 75 and under 5 free. **Lonesome Pine Trails** (207-834-5202; lonesomepinetrails.org) in Fort Kent and **Quoggy Jo** (207-764-3248) in Presque Isle are two more places to downhill ski.

SNOWMOBILING is the single biggest reason that visitors come to The County. It's the easiest way to see some of the more remote sporting camps and wilderness areas, since riding over well-maintained trails is often smoother than bumping down logging roads in summer. Trails lead from one end of The County to the other and are far too numerous for us to detail here. Call any Aroostook County chamber of commerce for a *Trail Map to Northern Maine* detailing 2,200 miles of trails maintained by The County's 40-plus snowmobile clubs and including locations of clubhouses, warming huts, and service areas. On the back of the map are ads for several companies that cater to snowmobilers, from rentals and service to lodging and dining.

❋ Green Space

Debouille Management Unit, including Debouille Mountain and several ponds, is a 23,461-acre preserve managed jointly by the state and North Maine Woods (charging gate and camping fees; see *Guidance* in "North Maine Woods"), accessible by gated logging roads from St. Francis and Portage. Campsites are clustered around ponds (good for trout) and near hiking trails leading to the distinctive summit of Debouille Mountain. For details, contact the Bureau of Public Lands in Presque Isle (207-764-2033).

Aroostook State Park (207-768-8341; fws.gov/northeast/Aroostook), marked from Rt. 1, 4 miles south of Presque Isle. Open May 15–Oct. 15. A 600-acre park with swimming and picnicking at Echo Lake; also 30 campsites (June 15–Labor Day only) at 1,213-foot Quaggy Joe Mountain—which offers hiking trails with views from the north peak across a sea of woodland to Mount Katahdin. In the small

Maxie Anderson Memorial Park next door, a tin replica of the *Double Eagle II* commemorates the 1978 liftoff of the first hot-air balloon to successfully cross the Atlantic.

Aroostook National Wildlife Refuge (207-328-4634), Loring Commerce Center, formerly Loring Air Force Base), 97 Refuge Rd., Limestone. At 5,252 acres, this former airfield's grasslands welcome migrating birds; 6.5 miles of trails allow visitors glimpses of the birds—including the American black duck—along with 10 ponds and many streams and brooks. (The refuge is 8 miles from Caribou.) Buildings have been demolished to clear the area for wildlife, and wetlands are under restoration. The visitors center has limited summer hours listed at the website (friendsofaroostooknwr.org).

Aroostook Valley Trail and **Bangor and Aroostook Trail** (207-493-4224). A 75-mile recreational trail system connecting Caribou, Woodland, New Sweden, Washburn, Perham, Stockholm, and Van Buren. Many bogs, marshes, wetlands, and streams lie along these trails, which are owned by the Maine Bureau of Parks and Lands. There are several parking lots and rest areas on the trails as well. Good for biking, walking, cross-country skiing, and snowmobiling.

Also see **Fish River Falls** under *Hiking* and the **Allagash Wilderness Waterway** under *Canoeing*.

✷ Lodging

HOTELS ♿ **Presque Isle Hampton Inn** (207-760-9292; presqueisle .hamptoninn.com), 768 Main St., Presque Isle. New in fall 2009, this 93-room facility is an upgrade from other local accommodations, offering non-smoking and smoking bedrooms with one king or two queen beds and one suite. All rooms have air-conditioning, cable TV with movies, and granite countertop in the bathroom. Indoor heated pool, fitness center, and a hot breakfast included in the rates. From about $115.

The Northeastland Hotel (207-768-5321 or 1-800-244-5321; northeastland hotel.com), 436 Main St., Presque Isle 04769. Built in 1934 in the heart of downtown, this 51-room, three-story hotel remains a favorite with business and pleasure travelers. Guest rooms are unusually large, sparely furnished, and spotless, equipped with a full, mirrored closet. The **Sidewalk Café** serves all three meals and has a liquor license. Double rooms (two queen beds) are $97–110.

🐾 **Presque Isle Inn and Convention Center** (207-764-3321 or 1-800-533-3971; presqueisleinn.com), 116 Main St. (Rt. 1), Presque Isle 04769. With 151 guest rooms and suites as well as meeting and banquet space, this is the largest facility of its kind in The County, popular with snowmobilers in winter, when rates are higher. Amenities include an Italian restaurant, bar and lounge, heated indoor pool, and full fitness center. $98.

🐾 **Caribou Inn and Convention Center** (207-498-3733 or 1-800-235-0466; caribouinn.com), junction of Rts. 1 and 164, Caribou 04736. This is a sprawling 73-room motor inn with an indoor pool, hot tub and fitness center, and the full-service **Greenhouse Restaurant**. Rooms are large, suites have kitchenettes, and it fills a need. This is snowmobiler central, the guests mostly male. $96 and up.

☃ **Northern Door Inn** ("La Porte du Nord") (207-834-3133; northerndoor inn.com), 356 W. Main St., Fort Kent 04743. A pleasant and comfortable 43-unit property located directly across from the international bridge to Canada and drawing guests (including many snowmobilers in winter) from both sides of the border. $76–88 for a double includes continental breakfast, with doughnuts.

BED & BREAKFASTS ❧ **Old Iron Inn** (207-492-4766; oldironinn.com), 155 High St., Caribou 04736. Kate and Kevin McCartney offer three rooms, all with private bath, furnished with attractive antiques and old irons, from tiny little irons for pressing ruffles to big ones; a band of trivets to set them on ring the living room wall. Furnished apartments and a furnished two-bedroom guest cottage are available for longer stays. The hosts are up to date on everything going on in The County; Kate can recommend ski places, musical events, and fine restaurants. $79, $89 in summer, includes a good breakfast. After opening her establishment in 1992, Kate McCartney celebrated her inn's 20th anniversary in 2012.

OLD IRON INN

Nancy English

☃ **Four Seasons Inn of Soldier Pond** (207-834-4722; fourseasonsinn ofsoldierpond.com), 13 Church St., Wallagrass. Five miles from Fort Kent, this inn has six guest rooms, each with private bath. Three rooms have double Jacuzzi and one, a single Jacuzzi bath. "Candles & Bubbles" is painted a deep burgundy and has double marble sinks. This inn is on the snowmobile trail. Breakfast is made to order, with eggs and Belgian waffles always available. $109–199.

SPORTING CAMPS Gardner's Sporting Camps (207-398-3168), 858 Allagash Rd., Allagash 04774. Open May–Dec. Five tidy camps along a ridge overlooking the confluence of the St. John and Allagash Rivers across the road from Roy and Maude Gardner's welcoming old farmhouse. B&B and hiking, hunting, camping, and fishing guide service also offered. $30–35 per person per night; $175 per week.

✪ ☃ **Libby Sporting Camps** (207-435-8274; libbycamps.com), P.O. Box 810, Ashland 04732. Open ice-out through Nov. One of the area's original sporting camps, which has been Libby-owned and -operated since 1890. The peeled spruce cabins overlook 6-mile-long northern Millinocket Lake and are lighted with propane; handmade quilts cover the beds. In the day guides can take you to 40 lakes and ponds for fishing—3- to 4-pound trout have been caught recently—orchid hunting, a night at one of 10 outpost cabins, or just exploring. In between, Ellen Libby and daughter-in-law Jessica serve great meals in the lodge, with homemade bread. Matt Libby can tell you where the taxidermy bobcat, lynx, and golden eagle, to name a few in the lodge, arrived from. There is a seaplane based at the camps, available at a fee for day and overnight trips. $175 per person ($200 single) per night includes all meals, boats, motor, kayaks, sailboat, and canoes. Pets welcome, $10 fee. Named the 2009 *Yankee* magazine best nature vacation.

Red River Sporting Camps (207-435-6207; redrivercamps.com), 26 miles from Portage. Open late May–early Oct. Cabins sit next to Island Pond at this remote camp with a reputation for good cooking, run by Joe and Jen Brophy-Price. Two small cabins and three larger, with one that holds as many as eight people, are $120 per person American Plan, with housekeeping services, linens, towels, and use of boats, canoes, and more. $60 per person for three housekeeping cabins includes bed linens, wood-burning stove, and gas lamps; the private island cabin includes a porch swing.

MOTEL 🐾 𝒮 ♿ **Brookside Inn** (207-757-8456), 2277 Rt. 2, Smyrna Mills 04780. Just north of exit 291 off I-95, this is a plain place with nine units; the basics are all here, including air-conditioning. You'll also be next door to a wonderful, inexpensive restaurant, the Brookside, that does all the home cooking everybody else used to do (see *Eating Out*). Rates $60 single, $70 double.

Long Lake Motor Inn (207-543-5006), Rt. 162, St. Agatha 04772. Ken and Arlene Lerman pride themselves on the cleanliness and friendliness of this motel overlooking Long Lake. There is a lounge, and continental breakfast is included in $64 for a standard room, double occupancy. The suite ($80) has a whirlpool.

✳ Where to Eat

South to north
DINING OUT Horn of Plenty (207-532-2260), 382 North St., Houlton. The extraordinary Horn of Plenty features international dishes made by owner-chef William Roderick, a Johnson & Wales graduate. The Texas-coffee-rubbed steak and seafood tettrazini—scallops, shrimp, and crabmeat in sherry cream sauce on linguine—are likely on the menu, because they are so very popular. Entrées $7–19.

The Courtyard Café (207-532-0787; thecourtyardcafe.biz), 61 Main St., Houlton. Lunch Mon.–Fri. and dinner Tue.–Sat. Sandwiches, daily specials, coffee, and homemade crisps and pies. The "Forget-Me-Not" is a roast beef sandwich made with herb and garlic cream cheese ($7.75).

The Vault Restaurant (207-532-2222), 64 Main St., Houlton. Open Tue.–Sat. 5–10. Reservations recommended. Escargots to start and veal, steak, and seafood Alfredo for a main dish at this well-recommended and popular place for a good dinner, offering some seats inside a bank vault. Ralph and Miriam Zuriak are the owners.

Canterbury Royale Gourmet Dining Rooms (207-472-4910), 182 Sam Everett Rd., Fort Fairfield. Reserve one of these two elegant rooms with hand-carved paneling for a special private dinner, with entrées you choose in advance of your visit. Seven courses might include quail stuffed with basil ricotta, served with cherry brandy reduction, or spicy shrimp and haddock with a grilled T-bone. An average of $50 includes all courses. $22 weekend chef's choice brunch, too.

Boondock's Grille (207-472-6074), 294 Main St., Fort Fairfield. "Good, honest home cooking with a woodsy decor," according to Kate McCartney of the Old Iron Inn. Opened in 2009 by Steve and Vicki Adams, this restaurant has a following for Vicki's cheesecakes; meat loaf and fish chowder, pizza and burgers are mainstays. Entrées $7–22.

Café Sorpreso (207-764-1854; cafe sorpreso.com), 415 Main St., Presque Isle. Sophisticated dining with Oktoberfest, A Night in Provence, and other culinary events, this café serves steak, rack of lamb, seafood crêpes, and spinach lasagna from its changing menu. Entrées $14–30, with several vegetarian dishes.

Karl's German Cuisine (506-473-6252; lakeside-lodge.com), Grand Falls, New Brunswick, Canada. Open mid-Apr.–Nov., closed Mon. A reservation is advisable at Karl's, where you will find every kind of schnitzel, homemade spaetzle, sauerbraten, and other German specialties. End with Black Forest torte or Bavarian cheese cream torte. Entrées start at $11.

York's (506-273-2847), Perth Andover, New Brunswick, Canada. Open seasonally (spring–early fall), Tue.–Sun. for lunch and dinner. A large, popular dining room overlooking the St. John River. Home cooking, from steak to lobster and duck. Huge portions are wheeled out in a trolley.

Napoli's (207-492-1102), 6 Center St., Caribou. A friendly Italian restaurant with good spaghetti and sausage, Napoli's is a welcome spot for pizza and generous, fresh salads. The small Greek salad was plenty large, the Chianti on special was tart and fruity, and the marinara sang with flavor. Entrées $7–16.

& **Long Lake Sporting Club** (207-543-7584 or 1-800-431-7584; longlake sportingclub.com), Rt. 162, Sinclair. Open daily year-round. Sit down in the lounge with a drink, order, and then go to your table when your meal is ready. Specialties include appetizer platters (wings, mozzarella sticks, ribs, and shrimp), steaks, seafood, jumbo lobsters (3½-pound hard-shells), and barbecued ribs. Huge portions. Right on

Long Lake with terrific views. Entrées $15–30.

✪ **Eureka Hall** (207-896-3196), Stockholm. Call ahead to check hours. A charming airy room serving with steak, seafood, local organic produce, and homemade breads and desserts. Sunday breakfast in winter features the fabulous homemade Danishes of owner Suzy Anderson, which you can sometimes buy next door at Anderson's store.

& **Lakeview Restaurant** (207-543-6331; lakeviewrestaurant.biz), Lakeview Dr., St. Agatha. Open daily for lunch and dinner; breakfast weekends only except during winter, when it's daily. Set on a hilltop with a view across the lake and valley. Steak, seafood, and barbecued baby back ribs are the specialties. Entrées $11–22.

EATING OUT ✔ & **Brookside Restaurant** (207-757-8456), 2277 Rt. 2, Smyrna Mills (at exit 291 off I-95). Old-fashioned the right way, with homemade pies, great meat loaf, and lobster rolls. The fried clams are rated

EUREKA HALL'S HOMEMADE DANISHES

Nancy English

high. And so reasonable. Carmel and Carl Watson are the owners.

Elm Tree Diner (207-532-3777), 146 Bangor Rd., Houlton. Now in a rebuilt building risen from the ashes of the original business, Elm Tree Diner has been thriving since 1947. The Swiss cheese mushroom burger was recommended by the owner of York's Books (see *Selective Shopping*). Diner owner Gary Dwyer likes the homemade bread and muffins for breakfast. On weekends the popular roast turkey or pork can come with turnip or squash. Entrées $7–13.

◢ **The Crow's Nest** (207-540-1800; thecrowsnest.com), 150 Maysville St., Presque Isle. Sandwiches, salads, steaks, seafood, and more.

The Irish Setter Pub (207-764-5400), 710 Main St., Presque Isle. Pub fare and good beer.

Cindy's Sub Shop (207-498-6021), 264 Sweden St., Caribou. Open daily 7:30 AM–9 PM, 9–7 on Sun., closed on Sun. between Christmas and Easter. Turkey and bacon sub, great lobster rolls, homemade soups like chicken stew and fish chowder. Homemade pies, "Swirl Delight" squares, and whoopie pies, too.

Frederick's Southside Restaurant (207-498-3404), 507 Main St., Caribou. Open for lunch and dinner, closed Mon. Big portions and reasonable prices.

Doris's Café (207-834-6262), Fort Kent Mills. Open for breakfast and lunch; everything prepared from scratch. What's for breakfast? "Anything you'd like, ma'am," the friendly owner said.

ICE CREAM Burger Boy (207-498-2329), 234 Sweden St., Caribou. Yes, there are burgers, but ice cream is the draw, with Gifford's hard ice cream

Nancy English
CABBAGES SOLD ON THE HONOR SYSTEM JUST OUTSIDE CARIBOU

and Garelick Farms soft serve. Open March 24–Labor Day. **Houlton Farms Dairy** in the Aroostook Centre Mall, Presque Isle, is open year-round, and serves up ice cream in the summer around the county.

✳ Entertainment
MUSIC Caribou Performing Arts Center (207-493-4278; caribouschools .org/PAC), Caribou High School, 308 Sweden St. A full calendar of concerts, dance, ballet, and performances.

✳ Selective Shopping
Bradbury Barrel Co. (207-429-8141 or 1-800-332-6021; bradburybarrel .com), 479 Main Rd., Bridgewater. Showroom of white cedar barrels— which used to be the way potatoes traveled around the country—as well as other wood products. Mail-order catalog.

Works of Heart (207-492-0860; maineworksofheart.com), 1 Water St., Caribou, sells locally made items like forged railroad stakes transformed into a coat hook rack, pottery, wood carvings, blueberry jam, and more.

Deep in the Woods Gift Shop (207-435-6171; deepinthewoodsgiftshop .com), 685 Oxbow Rd., Oxbow, sells locally made baskets, handmade bowls of black cherrywood, crocheted doilies, candles, and much more, including Christmas trees—there are 15,000 outside the shop door.

Bouchard Family Farm (207-834-3237; ployes.com), 3 Strip Rd. (at Rt. 161), Fort Kent. Stop by the family kitchen and buy a bag of ploye mix. Ployes are crêpelike pancakes made with buckwheat flour (no eggs, no milk, no sugar, no oil, no cholesterol, no fat—*c'est magnifique*).

✎ **Goughan Farms** (207-496-1731), Rt. 161, Fort Fairfield. Open weekdays 10–5, Sun. noon–5. Pick-your-own strawberries; also a farm stand and animal barn. Every fall a corn maze covers 6 acres; $6.50 per person to walk the maze includes an ice cream, made here, and highly recommended. Berries grown here are made into purees to flavor the ice cream. Hayrides on request.

Wilderness Variety Store (207-528-2626), Shin Pond. Catering to sportsmen and snowmobilers, this store sells hunting licenses and is a tagging station as well as a general store.

GALLERIES Visions (207-532-9119), 66 Main St., Houlton. A retail shop that shows the work of Aroostook County residents, Visions represents more than 45 artists and craftsmen, from photographers to print makers to painters. The store also sells music and books.

Rainbarrow Studio (207-538-9416; rainbarrowstudio.blogspot.com), 1783 Rt. 1, Littleton. Frank Sullivan has a studio and gallery in an old potato house. His eloquent, graceful work in oil and pastels, contemporary landscapes of barns, potato fields, and Aroostook County, is on display.

Morning Star Art & Framing (207-764-1810), 422 Main St., Presque Isle. Exhibiting the work of many artists

and craftsmen in Aroostook, with American Indian baskets, jewelry, and wood bowls.

Marsh Hawk Meadow Gallery (207-476-8481; marshhawkmeadowgallery.com), 28 Marsh Hawk Meadow, Fort Fairfield. Photographs of nature, sailing, seascapes, and of Europe and South America. Focused on the unique and diverse aspects of Maine. Prints $15–40.

BOOKSTORES Volumes Book Store (207-532-7727), 75 Bangor St., Houlton. Volumes boasts the largest selection of used books in The County, some 100,000 of them, and carries new books along with Maine souvenirs and gifts. If you can't find what you're looking for, proprietor Gerry Berthelette can lay his hands on it almost instantly.

York's Books (207-532-3354), 19 Market Square, Houlton. All-new book selection, cards, and chocolates.

Mr. Paperback (207-492-2080), 30 Skyway Dr., Caribou. Great selection of books, both hard- and soft covers.

Box of Books (207-493-3244), 678 Fort Fairfield Rd., Caribou. Colleen Harmon runs a casual used-book store; buy one, trade one for one, or take a box, fill it up from the unalphabetized but loosely organized piles; the books are likely to be inexpensive.

✱ Special Events

February: **Mardi Gras** in Fort Kent—the five days before Ash Wednesday bring a parade, ice sculptures, kids' day, Franco-American music, and exhibitions. **Long Lake Ice Fishing Derby** (207-534-7805), St. Agatha. **Moose Stomper Weekend** (207-532-4216), Houlton.

Early March: The **Can Am Sled Dog Race**—Triple Crown 60- and 250-mile races, starting and ending at Fort Kent.

June: **Acadian Festival** in Madawaska—parade, traditional Acadian supper, and talent revue. **Midsommar** (weekend nearest June 21) is celebrated at Thomas Park in New Sweden and at the New Sweden Historical Society Museum with Swedish music, dancing, and food. **Aroostook State Park Birding Festival**, Presque Isle.

July: **Maine Potato Blossom Festival**, Fort Fairfield—a week of activities including mashed-potato wrestling, Potato Blossom Queen pageant, parade, entertainment, dancing, industry dinner, and fireworks.

End of July/beginning of August: **Historical Pavilion**, Northern Maine Fair, Presque Isle, in the Forum Building Tue.–Thu. during fair week. Historical societies put on a show with individual displays, like "freeze-modeling" in antique costumes that

won the 2007 "Best Living History Display," by Kim Smith and students from Presque Isle.

August: **Northern Maine Fair**, Presque Isle. With good food, rides, animals, a music festival, and an agricultural museum with a lumberjack roundup, this fair won the award for best agricultural exhibit hall in 2010. **Potato Feast Days** in Houlton—arts and crafts, potato-barrel-rolling contest, potato games, carnival, and more. **Ployes Festival and Muskie Fishing Derby** (1-800-733-3563; second weekend), Fort Kent—a celebration of the beloved buckwheat crêpe and other traditional Acadian dishes. **Crown of Maine Balloon Festival** (207-764-6561; crownofmaineballoonfest.org), Presque Isle.

First Saturday in December: **Holiday Light Parade**, Presque Isle.

INDEX